Genesis

BAKER COMMENTARY *on the* OLD TESTAMENT

PENTATEUCH

Bill T. Arnold, Editor

Volumes now available

Genesis, John Goldingay

Genesis

John Goldingay

Baker Academic
a division of Baker Publishing Group
Grand Rapids, Michigan

Published by Baker Academic
a division of Baker Publishing Group
PO Box 6287, Grand Rapids, MI 49516-6287
www.bakeracademic.com

Printed in the United States of America

Library of Congress Cataloging-in-Publication Data
Names: Goldingay, John, author.
Title: Genesis / John Goldingay.
Description: Grand Rapids, Michigan : Baker Academic, a division of Baker Publishing Group, 2020. | Series: Baker commentary on the Old Testament. Pentateuch | Includes bibliographical references and index. | Summary: "A highly regarded Old Testament scholar offers a substantive yet useful commentary on the book of Genesis"—Provided by publisher.
Identifiers: LCCN 2019052671 | ISBN 9780801035722 (cloth)
Subjects: LCSH: Bible. Genesis—Commentaries.
Classification: LCC BS1235.53 .G64 2020 | DDC 222/.1107—dc23
LC record available at https://lccn.loc.gov/2019052671

Unless otherwise indicated, all Scripture quotations are the author's translation.

Baker Publishing Group publications use paper produced from sustainable forestry practices and post-consumer waste whenever possible.

23 24 25 26 27 28 8 7 6 5 4 3 2

Contents

Series Preface

If the ancient books we call the "Old Testament" were studied simply as witnesses to a bygone era, they would still merit continued scrutiny and analysis. Were they merely works of great antiquity, reflecting the thoughts, actions, and worldviews of writers from a faraway world, they would still garner great interest. They would arouse our curiosity about the history, society, and culture of that long-ago period of human civilization. And if these ancient volumes were also of high literary quality—as the books of the Old Testament certainly are—an entirely separate field of investigation would no doubt be needed to understand and appreciate those qualities and rhetorical properties.

Of course, today we have such texts from ancient Babylonia, such as the Enuma Elish, the Gilgamesh Epic, and others, as well as similarly soaring belles lettres from Egypt, Syria-Palestine, Greece, and Rome. Surely Israelite literature is among the greatest ever produced—with its tales of homeless ancestors trekking across ancient lands while following the deity's call to be a blessing to all the world, a covenant-making deity in love with a people of little political significance, and divinely ordained kings and prophets rising and falling with the fortunes of the nation. If such were all that the books of the Old Testament offered, we would certainly continue to acknowledge their great worth. And for many readers, this is all that the Old Testament books represent.

However, this is not the whole story. The truth is that these books are considered by millions of readers through the centuries as much more—as the Word of God. We mean by this that the books of the Old Testament have a divine origin, they are divinely inspired, and somehow they say what God intended for them to say. Of course, there are as many different ways of explaining what this means and of understanding inspiration as there are believers in the truthfulness of these books. But in general, Christians turn to these writings as trustworthy and authoritative expressions of God's will.

Fascination with the books of the Old Testament has not diminished for two thousand years. It is safe to say with some degree of confidence that these books will continue to command our attention. As long as there are believers in the Jewish and Christian traditions of faith, there will be a need for fresh readings and attractively presented commentaries to aid in the interpretation of these ancient documents.

The Pentateuch is the fountainhead from which the Bible's "Torah" (its teaching) flows. From this source—Genesis, Exodus, Leviticus, Numbers, and Deuteronomy—we are given to understand the very nature of God, creation, humankind, sin, salvation, atonement, sacrifice, holiness, and righteousness. All these themes find rootage and are in fact defined in the pages of the Pentateuch. Today's believers want and need reliable resources for reading these important texts.

The Baker Commentary on the Old Testament (BCOT): Pentateuch series represents one attempt to address this need in the church. The volumes in the series are critically informed and respect the integrity of the original discourse as well as the theological dimensions of the text. That is, the commentaries consider not merely what God originally said through the authors of the Torah but also what God is saying today through these ancient books.

The need for a commentary series on the Pentateuch that is both critically engaged and sensitive to the theological contributions of the text is especially pressing given that the relationship between law and gospel has been a perennial problem for the church. Moreover, advances have been made in the past twenty years on the relationship between law and narrative in the Pentateuch, on the way the various legal corpora of the Pentateuch relate to each other diachronically, and on the Pentateuch's contribution to theological studies more generally. These factors have not yet found expression in the type of comprehensive textual treatment possible only in a detailed commentary. Fortunately, a growing number of scholars are engaging in a critical investigation of the text, especially in methodologies that arise naturally and appropriately from the biblical documents themselves and can be combined with sensitivity to the theological contours of the text.

Each commentary in this series not only highlights the distinctive features unique to each biblical book but also reflects the unique approach of the one commenting on it. Each volume provides a fresh translation of the Hebrew text along with section-by-section comments. Each contributor carefully attends to (1) the meaning and significance of the ancient discourse and, where appropriate, (2) its reception in Jewish and Christian tradition, (3) the text's relation and contribution to the canon of Scripture as a whole, and (4) the text's implications for our contemporary setting. In this way, these commentaries not only lay bare the perspectives of the ancient human authors but also bring their voices into dialogue with other words that God has spoken—and is speaking—through Scripture and tradition, doing so in a way that dignifies the relevance of the Pentateuch as a contemporary word from God rather than merely an ancient, dusty book from antiquity. It is our hope that these BCOT: Pentateuch volumes will enable us all to hear this word from God afresh for the benefit of the church universal.

Bill T. Arnold
Paul S. Amos Professor of Old Testament Interpretation
Asbury Theological Seminary

Author's Preface

I wrote this commentary in the following way.

1. I first made a translation, utilizing an earlier version of the translation in *The First Testament: A New Translation*[1] but then reworking it as I wrote the commentary (all biblical translations are my own unless otherwise stated).
2. I wrote what I could by way of commentary on the basis of what I had in my head and my imagination, with the aid of lexica, concordances, grammars, and *Biblia Hebraica Quinta* (Tal, *Genesis*), without referring to other secondary works except when I was stuck.
3. I read a selection of works on Genesis, including the following:
   a. Early Jewish interpretation such as the Septuagint, Aquila, Symmachus (if its author was Jewish), the Genesis Apocryphon, Jubilees, Philo, the New Testament, and the Targums.
   b. Early Christian interpretation such as Theodotion and the Vulgate and African, Asian, and European writers such as Ephrem, Chrysostom, Didymus, Jerome, Origen, and Augustine.
   c. Medieval Jewish interpretation such as Genesis Rabbah, Ibn Ezra, Rashi, and Qimchi.
   d. Reformation interpretation such as Calvin, Luther, and Willet.
   e. Nineteenth-century interpretation such as Keil and Delitzsch, Dillmann, Skinner, Driver, and Gunkel (to stretch a point: Gunkel's commentary was published in 1901).
   f. Twentieth-century interpretation such as Barth, Zimmerli, Speiser, von Rad, Westermann, Wenham, Seebass, Sarna, Fretheim, Hamilton, and Brueggemann.

1. See also Goldingay and Wright, *Bible for Everyone*.

g. Twenty-first-century interpretation: Post-critical, critical, pre-critical; African, Asian, American, and European.

On the basis of this reading, I modified and expanded my initial draft and asked my wife, Kathleen Scott Goldingay, to read it (comments derived from her observations are acknowledged as KSG). I have not made a point of indicating whether I share my understanding with most scholars or with recent scholars, partly because being the majority or being recent is not necessarily an indication of being right. I have indicated some points at which my view is idiosyncratic, though being idiosyncratic is not necessarily an indication of being wrong.

Two general idiosyncrasies you will notice are the following. The Jewish name for the collection of Jewish writings that begin with Genesis is the Torah, the Prophets, and the Writings. The New Testament name for them is the Scriptures. Two or three centuries after Jesus's day, Christians started calling them the Old Testament. I think it's rather a misleading name; it suggests they are antiquated and out of date. So I usually refer to them as the First Testament.

The other general idiosyncrasy arises from the fact that many familiar versions of First Testament names (e.g., Eve, Cain, Abel, Egypt) are some distance from the Hebrew form or totally different from it (Ḥavvah, Qayin, Hebel, Miṣrayim). These changes result from transliteration over the centuries into Greek, then Latin, then English, and from replacing Israelite names by modern ones. In my translation I have used a more literal transliteration of the consonants in names, though I have ignored aleph and ayin when they come at the beginning or end of names (e.g., Adam), and I have not tried to represent the subtleties of Hebrew vowels (hence, e.g., Adam not *ʾādām*). In the commentary itself, I have used the familiar form of familiar names.

There is nothing more beautiful in Holy Scripture than Genesis as a whole. (Luther, *Genesis 31–37*, 313)

Certain interpreters weary themselves in the fabrication of subtleties; but it is our business . . . to cultivate sobriety. . . . There are also some things, concerning which . . . I shall not be ashamed to acknowledge my ignorance, because I do not choose to wander in uncertain speculations. (Calvin, *Genesis*, 2:412–13)

One of the false gods of theologians, philosophers, and other academics is called method. . . . The tyranny of methodolatry hinders new discoveries. . . . The god Method is in fact a subordinate deity, serving Higher Powers . . . social and cultural institutions . . . patriarchy. (Daly, *Beyond God the Father*, 11)

If anyone wishes to hear and understand these words literally he ought to gather with the Jews rather than with the Christians. (Origen, *Homilies on Genesis*, 121)

The reason God granted those generations [in Gen. 5] such long lives may have been to enable them to study . . . over a long period of time. . . . A lifetime of 70 years as we know it today is simply not long enough to accumulate this type of knowledge. (Qimchi, *Genesis*, on Gen. 5:4)

Whoever, then, thinks that he understands the Holy Scriptures, or any part of them, but puts such an interpretation upon them as does not tend to build up this twofold love of God and our neighbor, does not yet understand them as he ought. If, on the other hand, a man draws a meaning from them that may be used for the building up of love, even though he does not happen upon the precise meaning which the author whom he reads intended to express in that place, his error is not pernicious, and he is wholly clear from the charge of deception. (Augustine, *Christian Doctrine* 1.36.40)

To read with intelligent charity. (A. Jacobs, *Theology of Reading*, 1)

Love is productive of knowledge. (A. Jacobs, *Theology of Reading*, 46, summarizing Nussbaum)

The initial trait of charitable hermeneutics is *attentiveness*. (A. Jacobs, *Theology of Reading*, 52, summarizing Bakhtin)

It is this commitment to faithfulness that we must bring to our lives as readers if we would govern our reading by the law of love. (A. Jacobs, *Theology of Reading*, 64)

Genuine love of others is *kenotic*. . . . [It] requires an emptying out of one's own self and a consequent refilling of the emptied consciousness with attention to the Other. (A. Jacobs, *Theology of Reading*, 104)

The Lord God will grant me retirement in His own time. (Luther, *Genesis 38–44*, 54)

Abbreviations

Bibliographic and General

[ ]	Chapter and verse numbers as they appear in printed Hebrew Bibles are enclosed in square brackets when they differ from the English
AASOR	Annual of the American Schools of Oriental Research
AB	Anchor Bible
ACCS	Ancient Christian Commentary on Scripture
AcT	*Acta Theologica*
AJPS	*Asian Journal of Pentecostal Studies*
ANET	J. B. Pritchard, ed. *Ancient Near Eastern Texts Relating to the Old Testament*. 3rd ed. Princeton: Princeton University Press, 1969
Aq	Aquila's Greek translation, as documented in Field, *Origenis Hexaplorum quae supersunt*
ASOR	American Schools of Oriental Research
AsJT	*Asia Journal of Theology*
ASV	American Standard Version
AUSS	*Andrews University Seminary Studies*
BAR	*Biblical Archaeology Review*
BASOR	*Bulletin of the American Schools of Oriental Research*
BBR	*Bulletin for Biblical Research*
BBRSup	Bulletin for Biblical Research Supplements
BCE	before the Common Era
BCOT	Baker Commentary on the Old Testament
BDB	F. Brown, S. R. Driver, and C. A. Briggs, eds. *A Hebrew and English Lexicon of the Old Testament*. Corrected ed. Oxford: Clarendon, 1962
BeO	*Bibbia e Oriente*
BETL	Bibliotheca Ephemeridum Theologicarum Lovaniensium
BH	Biblical Hebrew
BibInt	*Biblical Interpretation*
BibInt	Biblical Interpretation Series

BN	*Biblische Notizen*
BRev	*Bible Review*
BSac	*Bibliotheca Sacra*
BT	*The Bible Translator*
BZABR	Beihefte zur Zeitschrift für die altorientalische und biblische Rechtsgeschichte
BZAW	Beihefte zur Zeitschrift für die alttestamentliche Wissenschaft
CBET	Contributions to Biblical Exegesis and Theology
CBQ	*Catholic Biblical Quarterly*
CC	Continental Commentary
CD	*Church Dogmatics*. By K. Barth. 14 vols. Edinburgh: T&T Clark, 1936–69
CE	Common Era
cent.	century
CTJ	*Calvin Theological Journal*
CurBR	*Currents in Biblical Research*
CurBS	*Currents in Research: Biblical Studies*
CurTM	*Currents in Theology and Mission*
DCH	*The Dictionary of Classical Hebrew*. Edited by D. J. A. Clines et al. 8 vols. Vols. 1–5, Sheffield, UK: Sheffield Academic. Vols. 6–8, Sheffield, UK: Sheffield Phoenix, 1993–2011
DDD	*Dictionary of Deities and Demons in the Bible*. Edited by K. van der Toorn, B. Becking, and P. W. van der Horst. Rev. ed. Grand Rapids: Eerdmans, 1999
DG	J. C. L. Gibson. *Davidson's Introductory Hebrew Grammar—Syntax*. Edinburgh: T&T Clark, 1994
DJD	Discoveries in the Judaean Desert
DSS	F. García Martínez and E. J. C. Tigchelaar, eds. *The Dead Sea Scrolls*. Repr., Leiden: Brill, 2000
DTT	M. Jastrow. *A Dictionary of the Targumim, the Talmud Babli and Yerushalmi, and the Midrashic Literature*. New York: Choreb, 1926
e.g.	*exempli gratia*, for example
esp.	especially
ETL	*Ephemerides Theologicae Lovanienses*
EuroJTh	*European Journal of Theology*
EvQ	*Evangelical Quarterly*
FAT	Forschungen zum Alten Testament
FOTL	Forms of the Old Testament Literature
Gk.	Greek
GKC	*Gesenius' Hebrew Grammar*. Edited by E. Kautzsch. Translated by A. E. Cowley. 2nd ed. Repr., Oxford: Oxford University Press, 1966
GOTR	*Greek Orthodox Theological Review*
HALOT	*The Hebrew and Aramaic Lexicon of the Old Testament*. By L. Koehler et al. Translated by M. E. J. Richardson. Leiden: Brill, 2001
hapax	hapax legomenenon, a word occurring in the Bible only once
Hb.	Hebrew
HBT	*Horizons in Biblical Theology*

HS	*Hebrew Studies*
HTR	*Harvard Theological Review*
HUCA	*Hebrew Union College Annual*
IBHS	*An Introduction to Biblical Hebrew Syntax*. By Bruce K. Waltke and M. O'Connor. Winona Lake, IN: Eisenbrauns, 1990
Int	*Interpretation*
IOQS	International Organization for Qumran Studies
ISBL	Indiana Studies in Biblical Literature
JAAR	*Journal of the American Academy of Religion*
JAB	*Journal of the Aramaic Bible*
JANER	*Journal of Ancient Near Eastern Religions*
JANESCU	*Journal of the Ancient Near Eastern Society of Columbia University*
JAOS	*Journal of the American Oriental Society*
JATS	*Journal of the Adventist Theological Society*
JBL	*Journal of Biblical Literature*
JBQ	*Jewish Bible Quarterly*
JEH	*Journal of Ecclesiastical History*
JESOT	*Journal for the Evangelical Study of the Old Testament*
JETS	*Journal of the Evangelical Theological Society*
JFSR	*Journal of Feminist Studies in Religion*
JJS	*Journal of Jewish Studies*
JM	P. Joüon. *A Grammar of Biblical Hebrew*. Translated and revised by T. Muraoka. Rome: Pontifical Biblical Institute, 1991
JNES	*Journal of Near Eastern Studies*
JPT	*Journal of Pentecostal Theology*
JR	*Journal of Religion*
JRE	*Journal of Religious Ethics*
JSem	*Journal for Semitics*
JSJSup	Supplements to the Journal for the Study of Judaism
JSNTSup	Journal for the Study of the New Testament Supplement Series
JSOT	*Journal for the Study of the Old Testament*
JSOTSup	Journal for the Study of the Old Testament Supplement Series
JSS	*Journal of Semitic Studies*
JTI	*Journal of Theological Interpretation*
JTS	*Journal of Theological Studies*
JTSA	*Journal of Theology for Southern Africa*
K	The Kethib, the "written" consonantal Masoretic Text
KCC	Kidner Classic Commentaries
KD	*Kerygma und Dogma*
KJV	King James Version
KSG	contribution from Kathleen Scott Goldingay
LHBOTS	Library of Hebrew Bible/Old Testament Studies
lit.	literally
LTQ	*Lexington Theological Quarterly*
LXX	Septuagint, as printed in A. Rahlfs, ed., *Septuaginta*. 9th ed. Repr., Stuttgart: Württembergische Bibelanstalt, 1971
MS(S)	manuscript(s)

MT — Masoretic Text, as printed in Tal, *Genesis*
MT^{L} — Leningrad Codex of the Masoretic Text
NEB — New English Bible
NETS — *A New English Translation of the Septuagint*. Edited by A. Pietersma and B. G. Wright. New York: Oxford University Press, 2007
NIV — New International Version (2011)
NJPS — *The Tanakh: The Holy Scriptures: The New JPS Translation according to the Traditional Hebrew Text*. 2nd ed. Philadelphia: Jewish Publication Society, 1999
NPNF^{2} — *A Select Library of Nicene and Post-Nicene Fathers of the Christian Church*. 2nd series. Edited by Philip Schaff and Henry Wace. 14 vols. New York: Christian Literature, 1890–1900. Repr., Grand Rapids: Eerdmans, 1988
NRSV — New Revised Standard Version
NT — New Testament
OT — Old Testament
OTE — *Old Testament Essays*
OTP — *Old Testament Pseudepigrapha*. Edited by J. H. Charlesworth. 2 vols. Garden City, NY: Doubleday, 1983–85
OtSt — Oudtestamentische Studiën
PL — Patrologia Latina. Edited by J.-P. Migne. 217 vols. Paris, 1844–55
PRSt — *Perspectives in Religious Studies*
Q — Qumran manuscripts (e.g., 4QGen^{h} denotes Genesis manuscript "h" from Qumran Cave 4)
RB — *Revue biblique*
ResQ — *Restoration Quarterly*
RevExp — *Review and Expositor*
RevScRel — *Revue des sciences religieuses*
RSR — *Recherches de science religieuse*
SBL — Society of Biblical Literature
ScEs — *Science et Esprit*
Sem — *Semitica*
SemeiaSt — Semeia Studies
SJ — Studia Judaica
SJOT — *Scandinavian Journal of the Old Testament*
SP — Samaritan Pentateuch, as noted in Tal, *Genesis*
STDJ — Studies on the Texts of the Desert of Judah
s.v. — *sub verbo*, under the word
Sym — Symmachus's Greek translation, as documented in Field, *Origenis Hexaplorum quae supersunt*
SymS — Symposium Series
TBN — Themes in Biblical Narrative
TDOT — *Theological Dictionary of the Old Testament*. Edited by G. J. Botterweck and H. Ringgren. Translated by J. T. Willis et al. 15 vols. Grand Rapids: Eerdmans, 1974–2006
Tg(s) — Targum(s)
TGl — *Theologie und Glaube*

Th	Theodotion's Greek translation, as documented in Field, *Origenis Hexaplorum quae supersunt*
ThTo	*Theology Today*
TOTC	Tyndale Old Testament Commentaries
TTH	*A Treatise on the Use of the Tenses in Hebrew and Some Other Syntactical Questions*. By S. R. Driver. 3rd ed. Oxford: Oxford University Press, 1892
TynBul	*Tyndale Bulletin*
TZ	*Theologische Zeitschrift*
Vg	Vulgate, as printed in R. Weber, ed. *Biblia sacra iuxta vulgatam versionem*. 3rd ed. Stuttgart: Deutsche Bibelanstalt, 1983
VT	*Vetus Testamentum*
VTSup	Supplements to Vetus Testamentum
WBC	Word Biblical Commentary
WTJ	*Westminster Theological Journal*
WUNT	Wissenschaftliche Untersuchungen zum Neuen Testament
WW	*Word and World*
ZAW	*Zeitschrift für die alttestamentliche Wissenschaft*

First (Old) Testament / Hebrew Bible

Gen.	Genesis	Song	Song of Songs
Exod.	Exodus	Isa.	Isaiah
Lev.	Leviticus	Jer.	Jeremiah
Num.	Numbers	Lam.	Lamentations
Deut.	Deuteronomy	Ezek.	Ezekiel
Josh.	Joshua	Dan.	Daniel
Judg.	Judges	Hosea	Hosea
Ruth	Ruth	Joel	Joel
1–2 Sam.	1–2 Samuel	Amos	Amos
1–2 Kings	1–2 Kings	Obad.	Obadiah
1–2 Chron.	1–2 Chronicles	Jon.	Jonah
Ezra	Ezra	Mic.	Micah
Neh.	Nehemiah	Nah.	Nahum
Esther	Esther	Hab.	Habakkuk
Job	Job	Zeph.	Zephaniah
Ps(s).	Psalm(s)	Hag.	Haggai
Prov.	Proverbs	Zech.	Zechariah
Eccles.	Ecclesiastes	Mal.	Malachi

New Testament

Matt.	Matthew	Acts	Acts
Mark	Mark	Rom.	Romans
Luke	Luke	1–2 Cor.	1–2 Corinthians
John	John	Gal.	Galatians

Eph.	Ephesians	Heb.	Hebrews
Phil.	Philippians	James	James
Col.	Colossians	1–2 Pet.	1–2 Peter
1–2 Thess.	1–2 Thessalonians	1–3 John	1–3 John
1–2 Tim.	1–2 Timothy	Jude	Jude
Titus	Titus	Rev.	Revelation
Philem.	Philemon		

Old Testament Apocrypha / Deuterocanonical Books

1–2 Esd.	1–2 Esdras	Sir.	Sirach
Jdt.	Judith	Wis.	Wisdom (of Solomon)
1–4 Macc.	1–4 Maccabees		

Other Jewish and Christian Writings

Ant.	Josephus, *Jewish Antiquities*
b.	Babylonian Talmud
Ber.	Berakhot
B. Metz.	Bava Metzi'a
1 En.	1 Enoch
Gen. Rab.	Genesis Rabbah (Neusner translation)
Hag.	Hagigah
Jub.	Jubilees (Wintermute translation, *OTP* 2:35–142)
Meg.	Megillah
1QapGen	Genesis Apocryphon (*DSS* 1:28–49)
Sanh.	Sanhedrin
Shabb.	Shabbat
Shev.	Shevi'it
Tg. Neof.	Targum Neofiti
Tg. Onq.	Targum Onqelos
Tg. Ps.-J.	Targum Pseudo-Jonathan
y.	Jerusalem Talmud

Introduction

> The sacred laws having been written in five books, the first is called and inscribed Genesis, deriving its title from the origin (*genesis*) of the world, which it contains at the beginning; although there are ten thousand other matters also introduced which refer to peace and to war, or to fertility and barrenness, or to hunger and plenty, or to the terrible destructions which have taken place on earth by the agency of fire and water; or, on the contrary, to the birth and rapid propagation of animals and plants in accordance with the admirable arrangement of the atmosphere, and the seasons of the year, and of men, some of whom lived in accordance with virtue, while others were associated with wickedness. (Philo, *On Abraham* 1.1)

Genesis tells many stories about God's relationship with individuals and about their relationships with one another—about husbands and wives, parents and children, and birth and death; about leaders, political relationships, conflict, and negotiation; about migration and famine; about work and worship and prayer. These stories appear in Genesis as a whole in the context of a larger-scale story about the origin of the world as the audience knows it and about the audience's ancestors. In turn, the framework of Genesis as a whole and its context in the Scriptures depict Genesis as an account of the opening stages in God's working out his purpose in the world. In the Christian Scriptures, it then pairs with Revelation. These two scrolls form a frame around the biblical story, telling how the world began and how it will end, with the Scriptures in between relating what happens in the interim.

Within the First Testament, Genesis is the first in a sequence of scrolls extending to the end of 2 Kings. The sequence tells the story of Yahweh and Israel from its beginning to Yahweh's destruction of the Ephraimite state in 722 BCE and of the Judahite state in 587 BCE. Genesis introduces the sequence by relating two aspects of Israel's prehistory. Its immediate prehistory is Yahweh's summons of Israel's ancestors from Mesopotamia and his dealings with them until they find themselves in Egypt, where the real history of "Israel" begins. Its further and ultimate prehistory is Yahweh's summoning into being the creation as a whole and his dealings with the world as a whole. Making Genesis the introduction to Israel's story suggests that one can understand Israel only against this double background and that one can understand creation and those ancestors only in light of where their stories lead.

Thus Genesis both is and is not a self-contained scroll; it is both complete and incomplete. It resembles the first series in a long-running television drama. It ends in Gen. 50 with some resolution of a number of the issues that the drama has raised, and in particular with some resolution of the family strife that dominates the last third of the book.[1] It is thus a distinct scroll; Exodus is then another. Genesis tells a story that has some coherence as it relates the normative way Israel came to understand the sequence of events before it escaped from Egypt to travel to Canaan. But Genesis thus also leads into Exodus. It ends with a recognition that its story needs to continue if Yahweh's aim in calling the world into being and summoning Abraham and Sarah is to find fulfillment. It is incomplete in the sense that it focuses on God's intention to bless the world and to bless Abraham, and to fulfill the former intention through the latter, and this aim has not been fulfilled by the end of Genesis. A key aspect of God's blessing of Abraham's family and a means whereby God is to bless the nations is the family's coming into possession of the country of Canaan, yet at the end of Genesis they are living as a migrant community in Egypt. In itself this incompleteness would not make the scroll incomplete. But the Genesis story continues in the next scroll within the First Testament, and so does the story in the next scroll, as continues to happen with each scroll that follows (Exodus, Leviticus, Numbers . . .), onward to 2 Kings. Even then, God's intention has not been fulfilled, but there is no doubt that 2 Kings marks the end of the sequence that began in Genesis, because over the page in the Torah and the Prophets is Isaiah, and over the page in the First Testament in its Greek and English order is . . . Adam again.

The Narrative and the Genealogies

For the most part, Genesis is a narrative, a report of a series of connected events; it is not poetry, nor is it a record of someone telling other people what they should think or do, nor is it prayer or praise. It is dominated by past tense verbs (someone did this or that), not by future tense verbs (this is what is going to happen) or imperatives (this is what you should do) or appeals (please do this). It tells a story.

1. Thus D. L. Petersen ("Genesis of Genesis," 28) calls it "a book in its own right."

The narrative as a whole works largely by offering a chain of individual stories averaging maybe 400–500 words in Hebrew (rather more in English), most of which can stand alone to a fair degree, and most of which count as a chapter in a printed Bible. The stories also belong to sequences (e.g., stories about Abraham and Sarah), some tighter, some looser, so that something of their significance emerges from their place in their sequence as well as their place in Genesis as a whole. In this respect they again resemble the episodes in a television series.

A key role in the organizing and signposting of these sequences is played by accounts of people's "lines of descent," or genealogies, lists of ancestors and descendants—the Hebrew word is *tôlədôt*, from the verb meaning "father" or "give birth." Such lines of descent in the Scriptures fulfill several functions. They may offer insight on characters by relating their background; they may provide validation for the status of characters; they may establish relationships between Israel and other peoples; they may suggest continuity within a people over the centuries; they may indicate links between peoples or periods that are otherwise widely separate; they may help establish chronology.[2] We should not overemphasize the distinction in significance between stories and genealogies. "The genealogical form operates as a mode of storytelling."[3]

Genesis describes these lists as "lines of descent" frequently within 1:1–11:26 (see 2:4a; 5:1; 6:9; 10:1, 32; 11:10). The description usually leads into what follows, but it may summarize what precedes (see 2:4a; 10:32). The expression features more sparingly in 11:27–50:36 (see 11:27; 25:12, 13, 19; 36:1, 9; 37:2). The lists play a key role in giving structure to the scroll, in providing a framework for the sequences of stories, and in marking key transitions in the scroll and thus in its narrative.[4] "Genesis is a book whose plot is genealogy."[5] The lines of descent signal the stages in the story of the world and of the three generations of Israel's ancestors.[6] Utilizing the clues they offer, I treat Genesis as dividing into four parts:[7]

Part One: The lines of descent of the heavens and the earth, through Noah (1:1–11:26)

Part Two: The lines of descent of Terah, through Abraham and Sarah (11.27–25.11)

Part Three: The lines of descent of Isaac and Rebekah, through Jacob (25:12–35:29)

Part Four: The lines of descent of Jacob, through Joseph (36:1–50:26)

2. See Y. Levin, "Understanding Biblical Genealogies."

3. Mbuvi, *Belonging in Genesis*, 43.

4. See Hieke, *Die Genealogien der Genesis*; Thomas, *These Are the Generations*.

5. Steinberg, "Genealogical Framework," 41.

6. See further Carr, "*Biblos Geneseōs* Revisited."

7. Luther (*Genesis 6–14*, 236, 245) describes Adam to Noah as the church's first age, Noah to Abraham as the second age, and Abraham as beginning the third age.

The four parts give expression to four key truths about God. In Part One God is especially disciplinary, though also merciful. He chastens Adam and Eve, and Cain, and in due course the entire world, and then he chastens the nations as a whole after the building of the Babel tower. In Part Two he is especially promissory, though also demanding. He makes promises to Abraham and Sarah that seem more than unlikely of fulfillment, but he starts fulfilling them. In Part Three he is accommodating, though also persistent. In being involved with Isaac and Rebekah, he continues to work via their faith and their stupidity and those of their son. In Part Four God is proactive, though also interactive. He implements a plan to ensure the future of Jacob's family by harnessing tensions within the family and inspiring solutions to a crisis that threatens the life of Egypt.

Story and History

Genesis tells a story. But there are many kinds of story. One way of categorizing them is to divide them into fact and fiction, into historical narrative and works of the imagination. Factual stories tell of things that happened; fictional stories tell of things that did not happen. Both categories are of some help in understanding Genesis but are misleading if assumed to tell the whole truth. On one hand, Genesis tells about things that God historically did—he created the world, did so in a purposeful way, made it a good place, put humanity in charge of it, set about putting it right when it went wrong, made promises to Israel's ancestors and set about seeing that they were fulfilled, and so on. On the other hand, Genesis tells its story in a way that uses techniques characterizing works of the imagination: it talks about a tree that conveys knowledge and about sphinxes and a swordlike flame guarding a garden, it uses numbers symbolically, it tells the audience what people in the story are thinking, and it organizes its individual stories into arrangements such as palistrophes.

A major preoccupation in recent Western study of Genesis has been the relationship of its narrative to historical events in the world and in the Middle East. How can we understand that relationship? In a Western context, believers and secular people may assume that Genesis deserves to be taken seriously only if it tells a factual story. Believers may then focus on defending its factuality; secular people may dismiss it in the conviction that it is not factual. Both sides are misled by modern Western assumptions. Two analogies may help an understanding of the nature of Genesis.[8]

From the Middle East itself, we do not have examples of long prose works that compare with Genesis. But from First Testament times we do have examples from elsewhere in the Mediterranean world, notably the Greek histories

8. On the issues raised here, see further Goldingay, *Israel's Gospel*, 859–83.

of Herodotus (who was born in Turkey) and Thucydides (who was born in Greece). Both lived in the same century as Ezra and Nehemiah. Both are concerned with events of their own people's recent history but want to help people understand these events by seeing them against their historical background. So both include copious factual material. Yet these authors also include stories that they value as traditional stories and not as factual accounts. They include speeches by participants in the events that are the product of their own imagination. And they include evaluative judgments on the right and wrong, the good sense and bad sense, in what happened. They thus have a broad view of what telling their people's story means. It means passing on their people's traditions, using their imagination, and making their comments, as well as passing on facts.

The modern Western world suggests another parallel. I have drawn an analogy between Genesis to Kings and a TV series. Most such TV series are fiction, though they may take place in factual places and be based on factual situations. Other series and many movies tell the story of factual events but use imagination in doing so. There is a multi-year TV series about the reign of Queen Elizabeth II, called *The Crown*. It follows the history of events in Britain through the period in question, which are matters of public record—events such as the Suez crisis in 1957. It also incorporates reflection by different characters on the British constitution and accounts of conversations between the queen and other people. It thus combines factual data with the fruits of the author's active imagination and reflection.

One of the trickiest tasks in interpretation is determining whether an author was seeking to write history or fiction. Whereas some readers of Genesis have seen it as simply history, others as pure fiction, it looks more like something in between, like the Greek histories or like movies "based on fact" that use imagination to bring out the significance of events. In Genesis, the Holy Spirit inspired an author or authors to use their imagination to tell their factually based story. And while interpreters have worked hard in seeking to establish how far it is factual and how far traditional and how far imaginative, their work has not led to agreed results. In this commentary I have therefore not given much attention to this question, since I believe that the text of Genesis is what the Holy Spirit and the human author want us to study.

Interpreters have used a number of terms to describe what kind of story-based-on-fact Genesis might be or might include. There are several such terms used to describe traditional stories:

saga: a long story about a community and/or its heroes that has been handed down orally over the centuries. Behind Gen. 12–35, one can see saga material.

legend: a story about an impressive and important individual that again may have been handed down over time. Genesis 22:1–19 is an example.

explanation: a story that explains the origin of something to answer the questions of people living later. Genesis 23 is an example.

The word *myth* has also been applied to Genesis, and it can be used in a positive way, but it tends to suggest a story about a fantasy world; Gen. 6:1–4 has been seen as an example.[9]

Understanding Stories

While one can see saga and legend behind Genesis, the stories are more than transcripts of such traditional stories. Genesis makes use of folk material, but it is not folk literature. While folk literature is designed to engage, to entertain, and to amuse, underneath much humor lies a serious meaning;[10] in Genesis, folk material passed down in the life of the Israelite clans has been turned into more reflective, literary, and sophisticated stories.

There are then other terms to describe such stories:

short story: one composed by an author who sets up a question and tells of a sequence of events that may initially complicate the question but eventually resolve it. Genesis 24 is an example.

novelette: a longer story composed by an author, possibly with a more complex plot, and focusing on an individual. The Joseph story in Genesis is an example.

report or *chronicle*: a narrative that gives a sequential account of events without providing a plot to the sequence or a tension that needs to be resolved. Genesis 29:31–30:24 is an example.

Since many of the stories in Genesis appear to be composed in a reflective and sophisticated way, approaches to interpretation that focus on plot and theme aid their understanding (compared with modern short stories, character is less important than plot and theme in Genesis). An interpreter may therefore ask:

- What is the question, problem, or issue that the story starts from?
- What is its answer to the question, its solution of the problem, or its resolution of the issue?
- How does it get from question/problem/issue to answer/solution/resolution?
- Are there obstacles that need to be overcome on the way?
- Does the telling of the story incidentally allow other insights to emerge?
- Does the story leave issues unresolved?

9. Coats, *Genesis*, 318–19. See further the introductory comments on Gen. 1.
10. Bascom, "Four Functions of Folklore," 290.

- Does it incorporate surprising features that hold readers' attention to the end?
- What is the author's viewpoint?
- Who is the story's implied audience, the people it seems designed to speak to?
- Who is the main character in the story?
- Who are the other characters, and what role do they have?
- How do the events in the story affect them or change them?

One can ask these questions about Genesis as a whole: what is the backstory to Yahweh's bringing the Israelites out of Egypt and taking them to the country of Canaan? Its answer is clear: Yahweh had made promises to Israel's ancestors that he needed to keep. In turn, that answer prompts another question: why did Yahweh make those promises? The answer is apparent: the ancestors related to the project that Yahweh set in motion in creating the world in the first place.

Such formulations provide some of the background to the fact that human characters are not as central to the stories in Genesis as they are to modern stories. The main character in Genesis is God, as is the case elsewhere in the First Testament.

Genesis also shares additional features with other books in the First Testament.

- It sometimes organizes stories as palistrophes (chiasms), units in which the second half mirrors the first half. The Jacob story is the great example in Genesis.
- It often incorporates two related or parallel stories. There are two creation stories, two accounts of God making a covenant with Abraham, and in the Joseph story dreams come in pairs.
- It makes much use of irony, which (for instance) suggests the way things work out differently from the way people expect.
- It often reports events in a way that first gives a general account and then goes back to relate more detail. Thus it commonly prefers a dramatic order to a chronological order.
- It makes use of paronomasia, the way words may point to reality; it thus presupposes the revelatory potential of words, especially of names (e.g., Eve, Cain).

The Origin of Genesis

Genesis gives no indication of its authorship and no direct indication of when it was written. Jewish and Christian tradition came to describe it as

"The First Book of Moses" and thus as the introduction to Exodus through Deuteronomy, but that description parallels the description of the Psalms as David's and of Proverbs, Ecclesiastes, and the Song of Songs as Solomon's. These are not statements about authorship. As one of the five Moses scrolls, Genesis has particular authority for the Jewish and Christian communities, but the authority came first and the description as Mosaic expresses its having authority, rather than vice versa.

The relationship between Genesis and Exodus through 2 Kings suggests that it came into being in the form that we have it after Judah's fall to the Babylonians in 587, and occasional notes in the scroll fit with an origin in this period. For instance, not only does 12:6 postdate the time when the Canaanites were in Canaan (and therefore come from well after Moses's day); 11:31 also has Abraham and Sarah setting out from "Ur of the Chaldeans," but the Chaldeans became the rulers of Babylonia only with the arrival of Nabopolassar in 626. Yet such notes are few, and it seems implausible to think of Genesis being created from scratch in the Babylonian period; it must have issued from the compilation and reworking of materials that had accumulated over centuries. The story of Ezra bringing the Torah scroll from Babylon to Jerusalem in 458 (see Ezra 7) may mark the point when the Torah as we know it had come into being, during the Persian period.[11]

Since the late nineteenth century, it has been common for commentaries on Genesis to give considerable attention to tracing the origin of the material before it reached its final form, and on the basis of such study to tracing the history of the events to which Genesis refers and the history of the development of Israelite religious beliefs. Such study of the origin of the material is potentially significant for an understanding of the text. For much of the twentieth century, there was a broad scholarly consensus about this process of development, accumulation, compilation, and reworking, but this consensus existed more because scholars needed to have some working hypothesis than because it was based on evidence. Several scholars in the late twentieth and early twenty-first centuries declared that the consensus view resembled the emperor who had no clothes and suggested that the Persian period played a much more creative role in the development of the Pentateuch. Indeed, "Abraham's wanderings in Palestine and Egypt are nothing in comparison to the virtual travels he has experienced at the hands of the scholarly community." It has been so exegetically; even more obviously, "chronologically, the dating of the patriarchs along a timeline from 2000 BCE to the post-exilic period went into free fall, occurring within a short period of forty years."[12] Yet even if "it is widely agreed that the Persian period is the most likely historical setting for

11. For a reformulated version of this critical position, see Hendel, "Historical Context." A useful introduction to the traditional JEDP theory focusing on Genesis is Kawashima, "Sources and Redaction."

12. Noort, "Abraham and the Nations," 4.

the final editing of Genesis," such a conclusion may not aid the interpretation of the scroll in that "the implications of this consensus are disputed": for instance, it can be read as ethnocentric or as resisting ethnocentricity.[13] And even if there is currently a scholarly consensus on the origin of Genesis, there is no reason to think that the latest scholarly views on the question will have said the last word. Tracing the origin of the Pentateuch is an instance of "problems in biblical studies which are so complex that they seem never to find an agreed resolution, yet which are so fascinating that scholars never give up the quest."[14]

I have not usually referred to the latest critical views on the origin of different passages in Genesis, not least because they will not be the latest critical conclusions by the time you read this commentary. One cannot base an understanding of Genesis on knowing the date of its stories or on seeing it as the expression of the ideology of a particular group or period in Israel's history. I seek to understand it as it stands against the broad context of the life of Israel, as a repository of Israel's collective memory or a reflective reworking of that memory that so commended itself to the community that the community held on to it when it let other memories fall away. Just as we know virtually nothing about how Genesis came into existence, we know virtually nothing about the process whereby it came to be part of the Scriptures. We do know that the Torah and the Prophets were part of the Scriptures by the time of Ben Sira.

The First Testament, the New Testament, and modern critical study do suggest several contexts against which to read Genesis, and as exercises in imagination I have sometimes noted how a story might impact an audience in particular periods. These exercises presuppose that most people came to know the stories by listening to them being read from the scroll or retold on the basis of the scroll. It is so in the Western world: people's knowledge comes from hearing Genesis read in church if they are lucky, or from what preachers or Sunday school teachers tell them. It was also thus in the ancient world; hardly any Israelites would have possessed a copy of the scroll and read it in the way intellectuals read books.

The Text and Language of Genesis

The traditional starting point for identifying the Hebrew text of Genesis, as of other parts of the First Testament, is the "Masoretic Text" (MT), the version codified by Jewish scholars about 1000 CE, and the translation in this commentary follows the version of that text printed in the standard scholarly edition, *Biblia Hebraica Quinta*, edited by Abraham Tal. We have fragmentary copies of manuscripts of Genesis from Qumran that are a thousand years older than

13. Brett, "Abraham's 'Heretical' Imperative," 168.

14. Nicholson, *Pentateuch in the Twentieth Century*, v. Cf. Vervenne, "Genesis 1,1–2,4," 36.

the MT and many manuscripts belonging to the Masoretic tradition from later in the medieval period. From later in the medieval period we also have copies of the Samaritan Pentateuch, with the text in Samaritan script as preserved among the Samaritans and thus in a separate tradition from the Masoretic. From the time between the Qumran scrolls and the Masoretic Text, we have manuscripts of the Pentateuch translated into Greek (the Septuagint), Latin (the Vulgate), and Syriac (the Peshiṭta). From these translations one can try to infer the Hebrew text they were based on and thus gain access to another tradition of the Hebrew text.

There are countless small differences between these versions of the text, and it is likely that one or other of these different versions are sometimes closer to the text of Genesis as it might have been known (say) in Jerusalem in 300 BCE than the MT is. In addition, biblical scholars have made countless suggestions for changing the MT to what they believe is an earlier version of the text. In some cases it is easy to see how the other traditions and these suggestions are tidying the form of the text in the MT, which was originally a bit untidy. And generally I am inclined to think that any attempt of mine to establish a more authentic text would likely be mistaken as often as it was right, so that the end result would be on average no more authentic than the MT. So I have nearly always worked with the MT.

Hebrew syntax is simple, and sentences commonly unfold in a simple way: "The upper ocean came onto the earth for forty days, and the water increased, and it lifted the chest, and it rose up from on the earth, and the water grew strong, and it increased greatly on the earth, and the chest moved on the face of the water" (6:17–18: to illustrate the point, I have made the translation quite literal). Further, Hebrew sentences usually follow an order different from regular English order, with the verb coming first. Thus translating word for word, "Came the upper ocean onto the earth for forty days, and increased the water, and it lifted the chest, and it rose up from on the earth, and grew strong the water and increased greatly on the earth, and moved the chest on the face of the water" (following the word order in English introduces some ambiguity into the sentences, but it does not usually do so in Hebrew). Yet further, Hebrew is an inflected language, which means that "it lifted" is one word, as is "it rose up" and "it increased."

Working within the framework of those basic conventions, Genesis can introduce subtlety into the way it communicates. For instance,

If the "and" between clauses is missing, it indicates that the sentences do not relate in the regular way; possibly the first clause leads into the second.

If the subject or the object or some other expression comes before the verb, it has emphasis.[15] However, in a noun clause, context and other

15. See Bandstra, "Word Order and Emphasis."

considerations must determine which is subject and which is predicate,[16] and emphasis is thus harder to spot.

If a pronoun ("it" in the above examples) is expressed, which is unnecessary to the sense because it is contained within the verb, it has emphasis.

In the translation, while I have often omitted the "ands" to make things flow, I have sought to bring out these points. Two other frequent conventions in Genesis (commented on in the footnotes) are the following:

Hebrew makes less use of adverbs than English; it uses repetition instead. So instead of saying, "You will definitely die," it says, "Dying you will die" ("dying" is a gerund not a participle).

To signify a statement that is also an act (a "performative act"), such as "I hereby give," Hebrew uses a qatal (perfect) verb, which would usually mean "I have given." I translate such verbs with the English present tense: "I am giving."

16. See Redford, *Study*, 34–35.

Part One

The Lines of Descent of the Heavens and the Earth

(1:1–11:26)

Within Genesis as a whole as the backstory to Yahweh's involvement with Israel, the immediate backstory to that narrative is the promises Yahweh made to Israel's ancestors, which include the idea that all earth's families are to seek the blessing that came to these ancestors (e.g., 12:3). The further backstory to Gen. 11:27–50:26 is God's dealings with the world as a whole. These dealings are the subject of Gen. 1:1–11:26. It relates how God's purpose to bless the world goes back to the very beginning, before which there can hardly be a backstory. The question it considers is clear: why did God settle on one particular family as a means of blessing the entire world? The answer is that God had tried blessing the entire world, and it hadn't worked. Indeed, God had tried it twice, and neither time did it work.

In Gen. 1:1–11:26 the story from creation to Abraham is a story in two acts in which Adam and his sons and then Noah and his sons play key roles. The account of the people's lines of descent (notably 5:1–32 and 11:10–26) contributes to the shaping of the story. Interwoven with the lines of descent, the stories bring a focus on key moments, especially in the times of Adam and Noah. But lines of descent and stories interweave in a complicated rather than a straightforward way. While there are the regular "lines of descent," this expression is also used to introduce the Noah story at 6:9; to introduce 10:1–32, which includes the Nimrod story; and most surprisingly at 2:4a to close off 1:1–2:3. Further, 4:17–18 is surely a line of descent, but it is not labeled as such. In substance, then, the chapters can be outlined as follows.

Lines of descent	Story
1:1–2:4a	2:4b–4:16
4:17–18	4:19–26
5:1–32	6:1–9:29
10:1–7	10:8–12
10:13–32	11:1–9
11:10–26	

The non-straightforward nature of this sequencing makes it unsurprising that there are various ways of understanding the structure of 1:1–11:26.[17]

Since Gen. 1:1–11:26 is the backstory to Gen. 11:27–50:26 and Genesis as a whole is the backstory to the great narrative extending from Exodus through 2 Kings, it seems logically necessary that Genesis in some sense relates events that happened. God did create the world as a good place, humanity chose not to do as God said, and the situation became one that could not be rectified. At the same time, the opening chapters of Genesis portray the world in a way that recurs in the closing chapters of Revelation (e.g., with sacramental trees and a snake that talks) and that does not correspond to our experience. I infer that Genesis often tells its historical story symbolically. Further, Genesis shows an acquaintance with other Middle Eastern stories about the world's origins and about a great deluge, though it sets the message of its story over against them rather than simply following them. I infer that the authors of Genesis took up traditional materials that they knew from their cultural context and truths that they knew about God from God's dealings with Israel, and they used these imaginatively to compose a historical parable that told the real truth about the way God had dealt with the world from the beginning.

17. See Richelle, "La structure littéraire de l'Histoire Primitive."

1
How God Created the World

(1:1–2:4a)

Overview

God created the heavens and the earth. But the initial question set up by the opening verses of Gen. 1 concerns how God will get to the creation of the heavens and the earth from a situation in which the earth is an empty void and darkness is over the face of the Deep (1:1–2). The answer to that question comes by means of an eight-stage process: four stages set the scene, and four fill in the scene. God makes this process the agenda for a week's work—so he fits two stages into days three and six (1:3–31). Some of the holding power of a story comes from its dealing with problems or obstacles or diversions that threaten or delay the move from question to resolution (as happens in stories such as 2:4b–25 or 11:27–13:4). Here, the account of the first three days (which only put in place the framework for creation) sets up the suspense, and the account of the second three days resolves it. The way the story unfolds also makes it possible to repeat and thus emphasize some themes, such as God's systematic way of working, God's authority and power, and the goodness of what God brings into being. God is effectively the one character in the story, and by the end we have learned a lot about him. A question it might seem implicitly to raise is how the story fits with what the audience knows about the world and about humanity that does not seem to be "good." It implicitly then answers that question by saying, "There was nothing bad about it when God made it."

A surprise feature to keep people watching through the credits is God's stopping work for day seven and making the seventh day of the week sacred. That closing note opens up the possibility that there was another question the story answered. Why does Israel observe the Sabbath? The answer is that Israel is thereby following the pattern of God's work in creation. The storyteller's viewpoint is that of a teacher who wants to encourage people to keep the Sabbath, who through the use of sanctified imagination "knows" all about the process of creation and about God's thinking and speaking on those days when no human beings were present, and who could thus teach authoritatively about it.

Translation

1:1 At the beginning of God's creating[1]
the heavens and the earth,
2When the earth[2] was[3] an empty void,
with darkness over the face of the deep,
And God's wind[4] quivering[5]
over the face of the water,

1. The LXX and Vg have the more sonorous, impressive, and theologically suggestive "In the beginning God created" (cf. Brayford, *Genesis*, 205–7) while Tg. Onq. has "in former times God created"; cf. Qimchi, *Genesis*, on the verse; Reno, *Genesis*, 29–39; J. Lim, "Explication of an Exegetical Enigma." While *bərēʾšît* might possibly be understood as absolute, "in the beginning," one would expect *bārēʾšît*. The form *rēʾšît* is usually construct and refers to the beginning of something, here suggesting "at the beginning of [when] God created" (for the construction cf. Isa. 29:1; Hosea 1:2; JM 129p; DG 13; cf. Ibn Ezra, *Genesis*, 22; Holmstedt, "Restrictive Syntax of Genesis i 1"). Oswald ("Das Erstlingswerk Gottes") argues for "As the beginning"; cf. L'Hour, "*Réʾshît* et *beréʾshît* encore et toujours"; and for a survey of possible interpretations of the phrase, see Moskala, "Interpretation of *Bereʾšît*." On the LXX interpretation, one wonders, "The beginning of what?" (as Augustine reports the Manichees asking: see *Two Books on Genesis*, 49). On either translation God was creating against the background of the empty void that already exists or that he makes exist, with no implication that somebody else must have brought the empty void into being before God transformed it. For the argument that *bārāʾ* means "separate," see van Wolde, "Why the Verb *brʾ* Does Not Mean 'to Create'"; Wardlaw, "Meaning of *brʾ* in Genesis 1:1–2:3"; van Wolde, "Separation and Creation in Genesis."

2. The noun precedes the verb, suggesting that this is a circumstantial clause (a similar circumstantial clause begins Gen. 3), which works against the idea that v. 2 is the main clause following on v. 1.

3. Scofield (*Scofield Reference Bible*, 3) sees v. 1 as referring to the original creation, which underwent cataclysmic change because of an act of divine judgment likely related to the fall of angels (v. 2); v. 3 then begins an account of God's renewing creation. For earlier expositions of this view (and for a recent advocacy of the view that one can calculate the date of creation from Genesis, namely ca. 4200 BCE), see J. Tanner, "Old Testament Chronology."

4. Vg has *spiritus* (spirit, breath, or breeze) while the LXX has *pneuma* (spirit, breath, or wind). The link with the water suggests wind or breeze (cf. Tg. Onq.), and 8:1 supports this inference. The same link suggests that it is "God's wind" rather than "a godlike/supernatural/mighty wind" (and see next note). For the translation "spirit of God" see, e.g., Freedman, "*rwḥ ʾlhym*."

5. The verb *rāḥap* comes elsewhere only in Deut. 32:11 (a bird flapping or fluttering) and Jer. 23:9 (bones trembling). "Brooding" (Jerome, *Hebrew Questions on Genesis*, 30; see further

[3]God said,[6] "Light!"[7]
and light came into being.
[4]God saw that the light was good;[8]
and God made a distinction between the light and the darkness.
[5]God called the light "day";
the darkness he called "night."
There was evening and there was morning,
day one.

[6]God said,

"A dome[9] in the middle of the water,
so it will be making water distinct from water!"
[7]God made the dome and made a distinction
between the water that was under the dome
and the water that was above the dome.
So it came to be;
[8]God called the dome "heavens."
There was evening and there was morning,
a second day.

[9]God said:

"The water under the heavens is to gather
into one place,[10]
So the dry land may appear!"—
so it came to be.
[10]God called the dry land "earth,"
and the gathering of water he called "seas,"
and God saw that it was good.

Hayward's notes, 102–4) seems to depend on Syriac usage (see Basil, "On the Hexaemeron," 31; also BDB). Whatever the verb's precise meaning, it also works against the translation "a mighty wind": it suggests something calmer or calming.

6. The waw apodosis follows on from the extraposed expression occupying vv. 1–2; cf. Isa. 48:4, where also a prepositional phrase is continued by circumstantial clauses (cf. GKC 111h, 143d).

7. Literally, "There is to be light." The standard English translation, "Let there be light," necessitated by the lack of a third-person imperative in English, is misleading because it makes God seem to be addressing someone and urging them to give permission or to stop hindering something.

8. Literally, "saw the light, that it was good"; on the word order, see JM 158d. *DCH* translates "how good," but the idea that *kî* can be an adverb seems questionable. At 18:20 *HALOT* takes *kî* as an emphatic particle, attractively inviting here the translation "indeed good," but the expression *rā'â kî* (saw that) is too common to infer this usage on one or two occasions.

9. Again, literally, "There is to be a dome."

10. For *māqôm* 4QGen[hl] has *mqwh* (gathering place; cf. LXX), perhaps assimilating to v. 10 (Tal, *Genesis*, 5, 78*).

11God said:

"The earth is to grow vegetation,
plant generating seed,
Fruit tree[11] producing fruit by its species,
with its seed in it, on the earth!"—
so it came to be.
12The earth put out vegetation,
plant generating seed by its species,
And tree producing fruit with its seed in it by its species,
and God saw that it was good.
13There was evening and there was morning,
a third day.

14God said,

"Lights[12] in the dome of the heavens
to make a distinction between day and night!
They will be as signs for[13] set times[14]
and days and years.
15They will be as lights in the heavens' dome,
to give light on the earth";
so it came to be.
16God made
the two big lights,
The bigger light to rule the day,
the smaller light to rule the night,
and the stars.
17God put them in the heavens' dome,
to give light on the earth,
18To rule over the day and over the night,
to make a distinction between light and darkness;
and God saw that it was good.
19There was evening and there was morning,
a fourth day.

20God said,

"The water is to teem
with living creatures.

11. SP, LXX, Vg, and Tg. Ps.-J. have "and fruit trees," as in v. 12, which strictly implies that both plant and fruit tree are subsets of *deše'* (vegetation), the word for grass or hay. The MT's asyndetic reading (with Tg. Onq. and Tg. Neof.) probably implies three objects for the verb (grass, plant, fruit tree), which is more apposite since "fruit tree" is not really appropriate as a subset of *deše'*.

12. Again, literally, "There are to be lights."

13. Literally, "signs and."

14. The traditional English translation as "seasons" is misleading; *mô'ēd* refers not to an agricultural season or to seasons such as summer and winter but to a specific time that is fixed by God—that is, the time for a festival (see, e.g., Rudolph, "Festivals in Genesis 1:14").

Birds are to fly over the earth,
over the face of the heavens' dome!"
21God created the big sea monsters
and every living creature that moves,
with which the water teems, by their species,
And every winged bird by its species;
and God saw that it was good.
22God blessed them:
"Be fruitful, be numerous.
Fill the water in the seas;
birds are to be numerous on the earth."
23There was evening and there was morning,
a fifth day.

24God said,

"The earth is to put out
the living creature by its species—
Animal, moving thing,
and the living thing of the earth, by its species!"—
so it came to be.
25God made
the living thing of the earth by its species,
animal by its species,
And everything that moves on the ground by its
species;
and God saw that it was good.

26God said,

"Let us make humanity in our image, as our likeness,
so they can hold sway over the fish in the sea,
Over the birds in the heavens,
over the animals,
Over all the earth,
and over all the things that move on the earth."
27So God created humanity in his image;
he created it in the image of God;
he created them male and female.
28God blessed them,
and said to them,
"Be fruitful, be numerous,
fill the earth and subjugate it.
Hold sway over the fish in the sea,
over the birds in the heavens,
and over every living thing that moves on the
earth."

29God said,

"Here, I am giving you[15]
all the plants that generate seed,
Which are on the face of all the earth,
and every tree with fruit that generates seed.[16]
These will be food for you,
30for every living thing of the earth,
For all the birds in the heavens,
and for all the things that move on the earth,
Which have living breath in them,
all the green plants as food";
so it came to be.

31God saw all that he had made:
and there—it was very good.
And there was evening and there was morning,
the sixth day.

2:1So the heavens were finished,
and the earth, and all their army.[17]
2On the seventh[18] day God finished[19]
his work that he had been doing.
So on the seventh day he stopped[20]
from all his work that he had been doing.
3God blessed the seventh day
and made it sacred.
Because on it God stopped
from his entire work of creation that he had been doing.[21]

4aThese[22] are the lines of descent of the heavens and the earth
when they were created.[23]

15. The declarative/performative qatal suggests a speech act, "I hereby give."

16. God omits the *deše'*, which makes sense if it refers to grass or hay, which human beings do not eat.

17. For *ṣābā'*, the regular word for an army, the LXX has *kosmos*, which lacks the Hebrew's martial implications and rather suggests "the finely tuned magnificence of the created universe" (Brayford, *Genesis*, 225); the Vg has *ornatus*, a standard translation of *kosmos* but a word that can also mean (military) equipment.

18. The SP and LXX deal with the oddity of God finishing the work on the seventh day by changing seventh to sixth. Krüger ("Schöpfung und Sabbat") argues that the LXX and SP have the original reading. Contrast Tov, "Searching for the 'Original' Bible."

19. NIV "by the seventh day God had finished" makes good sense as an alternative solution to the problem recognized by the LXX and SP (see previous note), but both the preposition and the verb tense are the same in v. 2b.

20. Cf. LXX; and Driver, *Genesis*, 18. "Rested" (Vg) overinterprets *šābat*.

21. Literally, "from his entire work which he had created, in making."

22. "'These' are the things mentioned above" (Rashi, *Br'šyt*, 19).

23. The MT treats the whole of v. 4 as one sentence (so also the LXX) and as an introduction to 2:5–3:24. More often the formula in v. 4a is a complete sentence, and it makes sense to treat just v. 4b as the introduction to what follows (see the comment on 2:4a).

Interpretation

The medieval chapter divisions in printed Hebrew and English Bibles separate the six days of creation from the day when God "stopped," which thus becomes 2:1–3. In the MT,[24] the seventh day belongs with the first six: the text actually has a chapter or unit marker (a *petuḥah*) after the account of each of the seven days of the week whose story is told in Gen. 1:1–2:3, so that Genesis begins with seven short "chapters" (the MT's next unit stretches from 2:4 to 3:21). One might even argue that "the key to understanding the intrinsic nature of the Genesis cosmology is in an element that is often neglected, the seventh day."[25] I thus treat the account of all seven days as the first section of Genesis (and I will refer to it loosely as "Gen. 1"). But I will treat the section as 1:1–2:4a, for reasons explained in the comment on 2:4a.

In form or genre, there is nothing to compare Gen. 1 with.[26] It is written in what one might call poetic prose or prosaic poetry. Its Hebrew has some classic marks of prose style, such as waw-consecutives, relative particles, and object markers. It also has some classic marks of verse: it makes little use of the definite article; much of it can be laid out in lines of about six words in which the second half complements the first half; it manifests much restatement within these lines—repetition involving variation rather than exact replication ("parallelism"); and it describes things in a figurative way, using images and figures of speech.[27] It is "poetic historiography."[28]

Corresponding to these two indicators of the kind of passage it is, listeners might bring to it expectations pointing in more than one direction. Genesis 1 is the beginning of the long narrative extending from Genesis to 2 Kings, which might make them ask how far it resembles the prose ending of that narrative, in 2 Kings 25. Listeners might also ask how far it resembles poetic descriptions of creation such as Yahweh's own account in Job 38–39 and/or Jeremiah's account in Jer. 10:12–13 and/or Ms. Wisdom's account in Prov. 8:22–31.[29]

As the beginning of that long narrative extending from Genesis to 2 Kings, in its prosaic aspect Gen. 1 speaks of something that happened in history.

24. More specifically, in the MT^{L}; the other MT manuscripts lack the division markers in Gen. 1–2 (Tal, *Genesis*, 11*).

25. Walton, "Creation in Genesis 1:1–2:3," 58.

26. Cf. Seebass, *Genesis*, 1:62.

27. See further de la Lama, "Reiteraciones"; Polak, "Poetic Style and Parallelism"; R. Robinson, "Poetry of Creation."

28. Diepstra and Laughery, "Interpreting Science and Scripture," 10–11; they attribute this phrase to P. Ricoeur but do not give a reference. But Fouts ("Selected Lexical and Grammatical Studies," 88–89) questions the idea that Gen. 1 is poetry at all. For recent discussions about how literally historical Gen. 1 is and how figurative, see Charles, *Reading Genesis 1–2*.

29. Though Landes ("Creation Tradition in Proverbs") stresses the poetic features in Prov. 8 over against the prosaic nature of Gen. 1.

But in its poetic aspect it speaks in the manner of those other accounts: it communicates dramatically and in symbols and images. While the authors of the story might well have worked out that the sun was the source of light in the world,[30] this awareness need not have held them back from painting a theologically suggestive picture in which God, the source of all light, first creates light, then creates the sun. The audience might notice artificial aspects to the six-day sequence (there seems to be not much to do on day one and rather a lot to do on days three and six) and/or might intuitively realize that the chapter was not portraying God doing a literal week's work and then having a day off. As is the case in Jeremiah, Job, or Proverbs, God inspires a picture of creation that involves imagery and metaphor in order to communicate the truth about creation, rather than inspiring a literal account that nobody would have understood (at least, I don't understand *A Brief History of Time*,[31] and nor—I have heard it said—do most of the nine million people who bought the book). Thus a theologian such as Chrysostom classically emphasizes the considerateness (*synkatabasis*) of the way God speaks in the Scriptures, starting where people are in order to communicate his truth.[32] The ease with which Western readers assume that Gen. 1 is simply a prosaic narrative like 2 Kings 25 makes it advantageous to lay it out as verse and thereby draw attention to its poetic aspect. Realistically, it describes creation as an event that happened but is not accessible to us. We cannot investigate it by historical method. It is not unhistorical or timeless. But it is "'non-historical' history."[33]

Like those other accounts of creation, then, Gen. 1 speaks of God's making the world in a way designed to communicate and to bring a message home to people in their context. One way it does so is by taking up motifs from familiar creation stories and tweaking them to give a more reliable portrait of the significance of the real God's act of creation. It is common to refer to Gen. 1 as a myth and even more common to refer to those other creation stories as myths, but the word *myth* is used in so many different ways that it deserves to appear on the list of proscribed terms along with eschatology and apocalyptic. Genesis 1 and other peoples' creation stories are imaginative poetic accounts of how the world came to be. From none of them can we derive information on what the video camera would have caught if it had been there. From all of them we may derive some true information about the nature and purpose of the world and the nature of God. Yet another reason for hesitating to describe Gen. 1 as myth is that it stands at the beginning of a narrative that as a whole tells a story in some sense historical, as is not the case with other Middle Eastern accounts of creation.[34]

30. See the comment on 1:3.

31. Hawking, *Brief History of Time*.

32. See, e.g., Chrysostom, *Homilies on Genesis 1–17*, 42–45.

33. Barth, *CD* 3.1:79.

34. Cf. M. Smith, "Is Genesis 1 a Creation Myth?"

The narrator of the story in 2 Kings 25 may have witnessed the events described there, or may (like Luke, according to the introduction to his Gospel) have talked to people who witnessed the events or may have listened to the story that had been passed on for a generation or so. The author of Gen. 1 did not witness the events that are described and has not been able to talk to people who witnessed them or listen to a story passed down by people who did so (with the possible exception of 1:27–30). He or she is either more like the author of Job or Proverbs, who imagines what creation would have been like, or like Jeremiah, whom God told about the manner of his creation.[35] It makes no difference whether one thinks in terms of divinely inspired human imagination or humanly mediated divine revelation, because either way Gen. 1 offers a trustworthy figurative account of God's historical act of creation.

The narrator introduces God's words and reports on God's action and provides the account's "narrative thread," which calms or tempers what would otherwise be the "overpowering" nature of God's own relentless commanding words with their "controlled energy and force."[36] The six "chapters" in Gen. 1 contain similar elements and have a similar structure, but each one is individualized; the First Testament commonly thus employs repetition with variation rather than engaging in exact repetition.[37] The elements are these:

1. God speaks a word of command.
2. The command is obeyed and/or God does what the command speaks of.
3. Thus "so it came to be."
4. God looks at what has come into being and declares that it is good.
5. God names the thing he has brought into being.
6. The day comes to an end.

The variants are:

Day 1 has no "so it came to be."

Day 2 has no "and God saw that it was good."[38]

Day 3 has two words of command and two fulfillments.

35. Cf. Keil and Delitzsch, *Pentateuch*, 44–45. Wiseman (*Creation Revealed*) interprets the six days of Gen. 1 as the period during which God gave such a revelation to Moses.

36. Fishbane, *Text and Texture*, 7, 8.

37. LXX makes the repetition more consistent (see Tov, "Harmonizing Character of the Septuagint"), unless the LXX is following a more consistent Hebrew original (see, e.g., Hendel, *Text of Genesis 1–11*, 16–39; Johann Cook, "Septuagint of Genesis"; Brown, *Structure, Role, and Ideology*). Bouteneff (*Beginnings*, 185–90) sets the LXX and NRSV texts alongside each other.

38. Thus one hardly needs a special explanation for the omission of this phrase in vv. 6–8 (see Ramantswana, "Day Two of Creation").

Day 4 has no naming.

Day 5 has no "so it came to be" and no naming.

Day 6 has three words from God and the declaration "very good," but no naming.

Day 7 has no naming or declaration about goodness or about "evening and morning."

Only days 1 through 3 incorporate the setting up of a distinction or naming; only days 4 through 6 include creating or blessing. The seven days' work is structured as follows:

Day 1	light	**Day 4**	lights in the sky
Day 2	waters separated	**Day 5**	waters filled
Day 3	land appears land produces growth	**Day 6**	land produces creatures humanity to rule over them
	Day 7 all is finished		

Thus the first three days lay the foundations for the second three days, which fill them out, with days 3 and 6 each requiring two sets of actions. Perhaps the author of Genesis knew a story that told of eight acts of creation but fits them into six days so that they can form part of one week's work.[39]

Genesis 1 covers matters that Gen. 2–3 will also cover, and one could see it as in effect offering an anticipatory interpretation or anticipatory midrash on Gen. 2–3. One aspect of the nature of midrash is to take up questions raised by the scriptural text and puzzling aspects of it and then to offer some clarification of them. Since the end of the nineteenth century, the usual scholarly view of Gen. 1–3 is that the more folktale-like Gen. 2–3 story is older than Gen. 1, which has seemed more sophisticated, and understanding Gen. 1 as a midrash on Gen. 2–3 does illumine Gen. 1. Paradoxically, indeed, seeing it as offering an explanation of Gen. 2–3 helps clarify otherwise puzzling features of Gen. 1 itself. But the order of the chapters in Genesis invites us to work the logic the other way around: that is, Gen. 2–3 will clarify puzzling questions raised by Gen. 1. Indeed, given that the basis for dating different parts of Genesis is shaky, one might see Gen. 2–3 as a supplement to Gen. 1. The opening chapter left the origin of evil unexplained and would leave people with a puzzling account of the world. Genesis 2–3 answers the question it raises and/or raises questions about the earlier story.[40]

39. See, e.g., Krüger, "Genesis 1:1–2:3 and the Development of the Pentateuch."

40. So Otto, "Die Paradieserzählung Genesis 2–3"; Otto, "Die Urmenschen im Paradies"; cf. Waschke, "Zum Verhältnis von Ruhe und Arbeit"; Davies, "Making It"; more narrowly regarding the image of God, MacDonald, "Text in Search of Context." Phillips ("Creation")

Whether or not Gen. 1 is the Bible's first creation story, it is certainly not the world's first creation story. We have in fragmentary form a number of older creation stories, of which the fullest are When on High (Enuma Elish) and Atrahasis ("Exceedingly-wise," the name of its hero). When on High[41] tells the story of the origin of the gods themselves, who were made from some earlier, already-existent entities. Conflict among these beings eventually issues in the triumph of one of the younger gods, Marduk, through whose initiative humanity is then created. More important, in the dynamic of the story, Marduk establishes Babylon as his sacred city, with its temple as the proper place to offer sacrifice. The First Testament story ultimately wants to affirm that actually *the* God is Yahweh, and *the* sacred city is Jerusalem. Indeed, the story of the creation of the world has been seen to picture it as a kind of sanctuary,[42] though if such themes are present in Gen. 1, they are under the surface; there is not even a city in Gen. 1. Israel does not appear in the creation story; the First Testament has Israel "arriving late to its own story."[43] Atrahasis[44] tells of the creation of humanity to relieve the gods from their labor on the farm and elsewhere, but the growing human population disturbs the gods, so they first attempt population control but eventually decide to bring a devastating flood. A rogue god informs Atrahasis, who constructs a boat for himself and some animals in which they survive. Atrahasis then offers sacrifice, around which the hungry gods swarm like flies. The overlaps in Gen. 1 with other Middle Eastern creation accounts open up the possibility that the people whom the storyteller hoped would listen to the story are acquainted with these other accounts and for a variety of reasons might be tempted to take them seriously. Genesis 1 seeks to get them to commit themselves to the truth of this version. Genesis 1 is formulating the *real* story, which pictures deity, creation, and humanity in a markedly different way.[45]

1:1–3. "With no introduction and little fanfare, the text announces with utmost simplicity that it was God—and God *alone*—who created the cosmos."[46] The way in which "*God*, the personal Lord, stands here at the beginning" contrasts with all other accounts of creation.[47] And "God comes on stage with a complete absence of preliminaries. Who is God? What is God? Where

then argues that Acts 1–7 mediates between the P and the J understanding. See also Goldingay, "Postmodernizing Eve and Adam."

41. See, e.g., Hays, *Hidden Riches*, 41–59; *ANET* 60–72; Hurowitz, "Genesis of Genesis"; Keel and Schroer, *Creation: Biblical Theologies*.

42. See, e.g., Walton, "Creation in Genesis 1:1–2:3"; Walton, *Lost World*; Walton, *Genesis 1*.

43. Mbuvi, *Belonging in Genesis*, 1.

44. See Lambert and Millard, *Atra-ḫasīs*; Matthews and Benjamin, *Old Testament Parallels*, 16–27.

45. See, e.g., Fieger, "Die Erschaffung der Schöpfung"; Sparks, "*Enūma Elish*."

46. Arnold, *Genesis*, 36.

47. Zimmerli, *1. Mose 1–11*, 36.

does he hail from? How does he differ from other deities?"[48] This chapter will answer those questions.

As is commonly the case with First Testament books, the opening expression in Genesis, "In the beginning" (*bərēʾšît*), provides the Genesis scroll with its title in Hebrew. More literally, Gen. 1 begins "in the beginning of [when] God created the heavens and the earth"; Gen. 2:4b will likewise begin "in the day of God's making the heavens and the earth." When on High similarly begins, "When the heavens above did not exist, and earth beneath had not come into being."[49] Unlike When on High, however, Genesis would not have imagined (or rather, would not at all agree) that God came into being from some already-existing matter. But like When on High, Gen. 1 is a story about the creation of the world; the creation of humanity is subordinate to the broader story (in Gen. 2–3 the creation of humanity is more central; it thus compares more with Atrahasis).

The complexity of the opening sentence that occupies vv. 1–3 also anticipates the complexity of the corresponding opening sentence constituting 2:4b–7. In Gen. 1 too it will become clear that "the heavens and the earth" does not denote the entire cosmos—the world's upper reservoir lies above the heavens and its lower water lies below the earth. The heavens and the earth denote the world within whose boundaries humanity lives. Nor does "the heavens" suggest heaven in the sense of God's dwelling. It is thus advantageous to translate *šāmayim* literally as "heavens" rather than as "heaven."[50]

In a context such as Gen. 1, the English word "create" may by definition seem to refer to God's bringing everything into existence way back at the beginning. But we also speak of "continuous creation," of God's continuing to bring things into existence; creation is not just a once-for-all past event (cf. Ps. 104:30). And we speak of God (and us) as being creative in envisaging and shaping new possibilities where there might have seemed to be none (cf. Ps. 51:10 [51:12]). We also speak of creativity in more trivial connections, so that creation talk is subjected to "inflation."[51] In an analogous way, the Hebrew word translated "create" (*bārāʾ*) has broader meanings. It can suggest any action that can only be predicated of God and action that is novel, extraordinary, and effortless.[52] The Prophets use the verb most often, especially in referring to something that God is going to do in restoring his people's fortunes (e.g., Isa. 41:20; 45:7–8; 48:7; 65:17–18). Creation denotes a sovereign act whereby God transforms disorder, jumble, and disarray into form, harmony, and peace; thus the First Testament uses this verb only with God as the subject.

48. Sternberg, *Poetics of Biblical Narrative*, 322.

49. Hays, *Hidden Riches*, 41.

50. Although *šāmayim* and *mayim* (water) look dual, they are plural (see GKC 88d; JM 91f).

51. Zimmerli, *1. Mose 1–11*, 38.

52. Cf. Skinner, *Genesis*, 15.

At the original creation, God so acted on a vast scale in bringing into being "the heavens and the earth." He created the world in which people live and also the vast panoply of the sky in which they can see sun and moon and planets. He turned a miscellany of raw materials into a magnificent cosmos. One aspect of the good news in Gen. 1 is that God's acting at the beginning implies that he could do it again. This significant aspect of creation links with the text's speaking of God and not of Yahweh (as Gen. 2 will). Writer and audience know that "God" means Yahweh (as Tg. Onq. makes explicit), but the word *God* points to his being the deity with all power and all authority to act as creator once again.

The beginning with which Genesis opens is not the absolute beginning of everything in the material cosmos. Genesis is not starting from the moment when nothing apart from God existed. Further, it says nothing about the origin of other supernatural beings. One way this creation story differs from those of other ancient peoples is "its lack of interest in the realm of heaven." It deals "solely with what lies beneath the celestial realm."[53] It starts from the existence of the earth, but from a situation in which the earth is only an empty void. Its words continue to anticipate 2:4b, which will follow its opening clause about the making of the earth and the heavens with the elaboration "when no bush of the open country was in the earth yet, and no plant of the open country was growing yet." Both beginnings picture a situation with potential, but a situation that requires action if it is to become actual. Genesis would also not have imagined (or rather, would not at all agree) that the world was created from some already-existing matter that God had not brought into being (as When on High says) or that the world was created out of God (as the Memphite Theology says: see the comment on v. 3). But it does not concern itself with the ultimate origin of the raw material of creation.

"Empty void" (v. 2) is *tōhû wābōhû*, a hendiadys and an onomatopoeic expression that doesn't exactly mean anything but rather conveys an impression of wha-wha-wha. BDB comments that the primary meaning of *tōhû* is "difficult to seize." The Tg appropriately has "desolate and empty." The expression suggests the presence and the reality of something that in English (as in the LXX and Vg) is most easily characterized by negatives: it is shapeless and formless, like a trackless waste, or like outer space (cf. Job 12:24; 26:7). Translations sometimes use the word *chaos* in rendering *tōhû wābōhû*, which is both suggestive and misleading. It is misleading in that When on High tells of conflict among the gods that issued in the violence and chaos out of which humanity was created;[54] there is no such backstory in Genesis and no chaos before creation, just unformed raw material.[55] This aspect of

53. Sarna, *Genesis*, 3.

54. See, e.g., Hays, *Hidden Riches*, 41–73.

55. See Ouro, "Earth of Genesis 1:2"; Tsumura, *Creation and Destruction*, 9–35, and further, 36–76.

Gen. 1 makes the chapter rather calm and undramatic compared with When on High, with its account of the conflict between Marduk and Tiamat. "The ancient Babylonian myth (or foundational story) that strongly resembles Gen. 1 has one great dissimilarity from it: in that myth, creation begins with a murder."[56]

The word *chaos* is nevertheless suggestive in that the only other two occurrences of *tōhû wābōhû* (Isa. 34:11; Jer. 4:23) describe the results of an act of destruction by God, in response to the wrongdoing of Edom and of Israel. If one reads those passages in light of Gen. 1, in the order in which they come in the Scriptures, they make the frightening point that those acts of destruction reverse God's work of creation, and "chaos" is not an inappropriate word in connection with these prophetic threats.[57] Conversely, however, when people read Gen. 1 after experiencing an act of destruction (Jeremiah is referring to the coming destruction of Jerusalem), this creation story becomes massively encouraging. It declares that things began with God acting to give substance, shape, and order to *tōhû wābōhû*, which suggests that *tōhû wābōhû* need not be the end of the nations' story or of Israel's story.[58] "According to this phrase the situation in which the earth finds itself is the very opposite of promising. It is quite hopeless."[59] But the decades after the destruction of Jerusalem are the time when the verb "create" comes into its own in Isa. 40–55.

Similar resonances attach to the parallel picture of darkness over the face of the deep. Darkness is another image to describe the results of Yahweh's act of destruction (e.g., Isa. 9:2 [1]; 47:5; Amos 5:18, 20). And "the deep" suggests the powerful, dynamic, energetic forces embodied in the might of the ocean or in the subterranean waters that burst out in waterfalls and springs. They needn't be threatening (cf. Deut. 8:7; 33:13), but they can be if you are in the wrong place at the wrong time (cf. Gen. 7:11; 8:2). "This is a frightening image: desolation below and desolation above."[60]

Then there is "God's wind quivering over the face of" those waters. If v. 2b as a whole were parallel to v. 2a, then "God's wind" might need to be a negative image, but "quivering" (*rāḥap*) does not point to a threatening action. "God's wind" rather suggests another ironic and provocative comparison to When on High, because there Marduk let loose a wind at Tiamat that she swallowed so that it blew her up and made her easy to kill. While there is no direct link between Tiamat's name and the word for deep, *təhôm*, some people listening to the Genesis story might spot the similarity between the word and the name. Here, God's breath or wind is hovering in a positive fashion over the surface of the water, perhaps so as to calm any negative energy (contrast

56. R. Adler in Eskenazi and Weiss, *Torah*, 29.
57. See, e.g., van Ruiten, "Back to Chaos."
58. Cf. Peery, "Genesis 1:1–2:3."
59. Barth, *CD* 3.1:104.
60. Luzzatto, *Genesis*, on Gen. 1:2.

Dan. 7:2). It is "a merciful wind" (Tg. Ps.-J., Tg. Neof.). "Creation means the irruption and revelation of the divine compassion."[61] The description of the wind thus quivering over the face of the water also anticipates a question that might be raised by 2:5–6. If (a) God had not sent rain, but (b) there was a stream coming up from the earth, who or what made the stream come up? Here is the answer.

Against that background we get the description of God's first creative act (v. 3). Light is the opposite of darkness, metaphorically as well as literally (again, cf. Isa. 9:2 [1]; 45:7). Genesis does not say that God "created" light; perhaps rather he willed it to emanate from himself.[62] His generating light means his setting a limit to darkness: "darkness is no longer boundless but is given its place in the rhythm of time."[63] As a body does not come alive until God breathes in his life, so the raw material of creation does not come alight until God bids light come into it.

In this first act God goes about creation by issuing a directive (cf. Ps. 33:6; John 1:1–5). He is like a king or general who speaks, and things happen.[64] Yet his words are not exactly a command; they are not addressed to anyone. They work more like magic. God speaks, and something happens in a way that need not involve anyone doing anything. Simply by speaking, "God calls into being things that did not exist" (Rom. 4:17).[65] The same motif appears in an Egyptian account of creation that seems to have been composed sometime between the period of Moses and that of Isaiah, the Memphite Theology.[66] Whereas God could have simply willed light into being, he speaks it into being as a performative act and thereby brings language itself into being.[67]

People in the ancient world were quite aware that talk of light and of day and night really presupposes the existence of sun and moon and stars. They knew that the sun was the source of light in the world.[68] But there can be light on earth on a cloudy day when the sun is not shining, and this fact can act as a reminder that the sun is not the ultimate source of light. God wraps himself in light as if it is his clothing (Ps. 104:2). "The light born from God is the very Wisdom of God, but the light made by God is something mutable."[69] In God's light we see light (Ps. 36:9 [10]).[70] And there can be evening and morning on

61. Barth, *CD* 3.1:111.

62. Cf. M. Smith, "Light in Genesis 1:3."

63. Noort, "Creation of Light in Genesis 1:1–5," 20.

64. See Barth, *CD* 3.1:110–18.

65. Cf. Luther, *Genesis 1–5*, 21.

66. Cf. Hays, *Hidden Riches*, 66. See further Atwell, "Egyptian Source for Genesis 1."

67. Yovel, "Creation of Language," 214–16.

68. The Manichees certainly knew: see Augustine, *Two Books on Genesis*, 68–69. See further the quotations in Louth, *Genesis 1–11*, 6–19.

69. Augustine, *Literal Interpretation of Genesis*, 158.

70. Reno, *Genesis*, 46.

the first day even before sun and moon have been created because these are God's days, not earthly days.[71]

1:4–5. In the First Testament the word for "good" (*ṭôb*) has a similar range of meanings to the English word. It can suggest something that feels good or that looks good or that is morally good; we should not try to tighten the word's meaning.[72] Targum Neof. often uses the words "beautiful and proper." Anticipating the questions that will arise in Gen. 2–3 over whether the creation actually is good, or when it becomes good, or whether it includes bad things (2:9, 18; cf. 6:5), and thus over where the badness in creation comes from, Gen. 1 declares that the badness does not come from creation itself. God checked it out and made sure. Henceforth in Gen. 1 "this repeated refrain" that God says that it was good "punctuates Gen. 1 like an exclamation point."[73]

One might have expected that light would simply replace darkness, but it does not. Here, at least, Genesis is speaking not of metaphorical light and darkness, which signify blessing and trouble (darkness being the negative backcloth to light, as it was in v. 2). It is speaking of material light and darkness, which are part of the rhythm of daily life for the human world and the animal world (Ps. 104:19–23). So light is good, but darkness is not simply bad—it makes sleep natural (Tg. Ps.-J. has night being made for creatures to rest). In this connection Genesis introduces the key verb "make a distinction," or "separate" (*bādal* hiphil), which comes five times in this chapter and six times in Lev. 10–11 and 20. In Leviticus it refers to Israel's making a distinction between the sacred and the ordinary and between the taboo and the clean, which includes a separation between things that can be eaten and things that cannot; that separation is related to the distinction between Israel and other peoples. Genesis 1 establishes that the making of distinctions is not just an Israelite peculiarity. It fits the pattern of creation. "The concept of separation is one of the most important aspects of the account of creation."[74]

God names the light and the darkness, a sign of his lordship over them. Whereas it might be obvious that the day belongs to God, the night does, too (Ps. 74:16).[75] And then the first day of creation is over.[76] It might seem a short day's work, but it was foundational. The working day comes to an end with the evening, which then looks forward to the next day. We may infer that "no darkness has the power to prevent the light from being called and actually being day again—true day. . . . Day was constituted by an act of God. But

71. Cf. Skillen, "Seven Days of Creation," 120.

72. Cf. Gericke, "Philosophical Clarification." See also Klopfenstein, "'Und siehe, es war sehr gut!'"

73. Reno, *Genesis*, 49.

74. Harland, *Value of Human Life*, 100.

75. Cf. Barth, *CD* 3.1:129.

76. On the history of the question whether these are 24-hour days (as I assume), see Hilbrands, "Die Länge der Schöpfungstage."

now we can say further that it was constituted by an act of God which when it is performed is resumed and continued by God."[77] Speaking of "evening and morning" might imply the assumption that the day starts in the evening, but it doesn't require it, and the evidence elsewhere is ambiguous.[78]

1:6–8. The background to God's second act is the presence of water—on earth's surface, underneath it and springing up, and in the sky, from which it falls from time to time. The second day's mode of creation corresponds to the first's. God speaks out what needs to happen, it happens, Genesis refers to the significance of God's action in connection with the making of a distinction, God names what he has made, then the day comes to an end. The "dome" is the sky, which has the appearance of a solid vault when one looks up from earth. It will hold back the upper water except when God allows it to come through (cf. 7:11–12; 2 Kings 7:2; Ps. 104:13). It will thus make a distinction between the two bodies of water. Here God "makes" the dome rather than simply summoning it into existence. Whereas Josephus (*Ant.* 1.1.1) sees God as here making rain and dew possible, Genesis sees God as stopping water from being overwhelming. "The creation of the firmament, with its comprehensive opposition of form to formlessness, of the possibility of life to the necessity of death, aims at a peaceful and meaningful existence of the creature before and with its Creator."[79]

Once again, we should not be wooden in interpreting the Genesis poetry as it portrays the dome.[80] The Israelites had noticed that rain came from clouds (Job 36:27–28; Jer. 10:13). And once again, Genesis's account of the dome contrasts with the account in When on High, where Marduk makes the dome by splitting Tiamat like a shellfish, using the top half as the dome, and setting guards to make sure that Tiamat's water does not escape.

1:9–13. The presupposition of vv. 6–8 is that water still covers the earth. God needs to undertake another act of separation (though the word does not come), between the water and the dry land that is allowed to emerge from the water. Once again God creates by speaking the distinction into being, names and thus asserts authority, and sees that it (the earth or the general result?) is good.

On this day that declaration is not the end of the story. There is a further act to follow, or rather a further self-fulfilling command to utter—again things happen just because God speaks. The command mandates that the things that grow have within themselves the capacity to reproduce. God will not need to be involved in continuous creation. Growing things will have the power to produce a seed-bearing crop. And they will reproduce their own like. One

77. Barth, *CD* 3.1:133.

78. See Stroes, "Does the Day Begin in the Evening or Morning?"

79. Barth, *CD* 3.1:135.

80. Indeed, Younker and Davidson ("Myth of the Solid Heavenly Dome") argue against the idea that the *rāqîaʿ* is described as something solid and metal-like.

can know that figs will produce figs and grapes will produce grapes. It need not have been so. The word for "species" (*mîn*) restates that point yet also draws attention to the wondrous variety and comprehensiveness of what God creates.[81] Further, God has here provided for humanity's needs before even creating the first human beings.[82]

1:14–19. Having put in place the framework for the cosmos's life over the first three days of the week, God goes back to the beginning to add the contents to the framework. "The Genesis account of God's seven days . . . has an architectural quality. . . . Day builds on day. The picture of God's creative work shows something like the construction of a seven-story dwelling in which each level adds to and depends on the ones that came before it."[83]

Once again God speaks a third-person command (vv. 14–15). It refers to sources of light in the sky, like the electric lights set into a ceiling. The point of the lamps is not merely to give light on the earth; v. 3 has taken care of that need. The lamps relate again to the making of distinctions. They are "signs." Whereas the introduction of light made a distinction between light and darkness, putting the lamps in the sky will make a distinction between day and night in the sense that they will make it possible to determine when day ends and night begins, and when night ends and day begins. It will therefore be clear when the evening offering and morning offering are to be made. The two lamps will contribute to the structuring of people's relationship with God. They will do so in a broader calendrical way by providing information on the beginning and ending of the Sabbath, on the beginning of each new month with its special offerings, and on the time for Pesaḥ, Flat Bread, Shavuot, New Year, Atonement Day, Sukkot, and in due course Hanukkah and Purim. Further, outside Gen. 1 the word for these lights (*mā'ôr*) mainly occurs to designate the sanctuary lamps (e.g., Exod. 35:8, 14, 28), which hints at the idea that the structure of the created world anticipates the structure of the sanctuary and/or that the sanctuary mirrors the created world. The creation story invites Judahites living after the destruction of the Jerusalem sanctuary to see themselves as still living in a sanctuary.

Once again (vv. 16–19) the declaration that something is to happen is accompanied by a declaration that God made it happen, as in vv. 7–8. While God thus makes the sun and the moon, they are not named, unlike day, night, heavens, earth, and seas. Alongside this odd fact is the offhand determination of a further object of God's making, "and the stars." Even for people who do not know what a vast panoply the stars comprise, this comment might seem to understate their impressiveness. Therein may lie the point. For many people in Israel's context, sun, moon, and stars signified deities standing

81. See Neville, "Differentiation in Genesis 1."

82. Barth, *CD* 3.1:152.

83. Skillen, "Seven Days of Creation," 123–24.

behind these entities, which were the means of the gods' determining events on earth. Genesis puts them in their place as mere lampposts in the sky.[84] They rule, but they rule on behalf of the real God and in a way that helps people structure their relationship with God.[85]

1:20–23. God returns to the consideration of the dome and the water, the subject in vv. 6–8. First are the creatures of the sea. If God created them, there is no doubt that he rules over the deep of which v. 2 spoke. The term for the living beings (*nepeš ḥayyâ*) in the water will be applied to the first human being (2:7), but here it specifically applies to the "big sea monsters." For the first time since v. 1, Genesis speaks of God's "creating"; *bārāʾ* again asserts the sovereignty and power of God's act in relation to such impressive and frightening creatures as well as the other creatures of the water. And Genesis again implies an acerbic comment on other Middle Eastern creation stories. While a sea monster (*tannîn*) might be just a crocodile, it can also be the embodiment of dynamic power asserted against order in the world and against God (Isa. 27:1; 51:9). It is another designation for Leviathan or for Sea itself. Genesis makes no direct reference to such beings and here reduces them to mere impressive water creatures whom God in his dynamic sovereignty brought into being (cf. Ps. 104:26). There is nothing to be frightened of here.[86]

Beneath the dome there are to be the birds, distinguished by their species. That word again draws attention to the variety of the creation that God brings into being, but it has a further implication. Species (*mîn*) is another term that links with Leviticus. It comes seven times in this chapter in connection with the animate creation, and seven more times in a similar connection in 6:20; 7:14. It comes nine times in Lev. 11, and five more times in a similar connection in Deut. 14:13–18; Ezek. 47:10. "The creation narrative sets the stage for . . . the dietary law of Leviticus 11."[87] It supports and undergirds Israel's commitment to the instructions about food in the Torah. Creating the differences in species makes it possible for people to work out which creatures may be eaten and which may not.

"Move" (*rāmaś*) is another unusual word common to Gen. 1–9 (ten times) and Leviticus (three times; four times in the rest of the First Testament). In close association, "teem" (*šāraṣ*) recurs in Gen. 1–9 (five times) and Lev. 11 (five times); the related noun *šereṣ* also recurs in both contexts. All these entities that God created are good, notwithstanding that eating some will be forbidden to Israel and that some can seem to stand for those powers that assert themselves against order and against God.

84. Cf. Zimmerli, *1. Mose 1–11*, 61–62.

85. But Gertz ("Antibabylonische Polemik?") critiques the idea that Genesis engages in anti-Babylonian polemic here.

86. Cf. Vogels, "'And God Created.'"

87. Firmage, "Genesis 1 and the Priestly Agenda," 114.

God not only created the water creatures and the birds; God blessed them (*bārak*) (vv. 22–23). The implication of blessing is spelled out in the parallelism of the line and in the verbs that follow. God blesses by telling creatures that they can be fruitful. The Scriptures speak of blessing more or less exclusively in connection with animate creatures, upon whom it conveys the capacity to be fruitful. The imperatives and the jussive that follow the act of blessing are the kind of commands that really constitute promises.[88] God's personal relationship with the animate world expresses itself in the fact that he speaks to it, as he will later speak to humanity; the reality of that relationship is reflected in the First Testament's assumption that nature is capable of responding to God in worship.

1:24–25. Day six in turn pairs with day three, though the precise nature of the pairing will not be explicit until vv. 29–30. As the earth brought out or sent out vegetation, so it is to bring out or send out animals. As the water was to teem with living creatures, so is the land. "Animal" (*bəhēmâ*) commonly denotes cattle; "moving thing" suggests things that crawl as opposed to creatures with legs (this verb described water creatures in v. 21); "living things" perhaps then denotes animals of the wild. If one wonders how the earth was to fulfill the commission to bring out these creatures, then Genesis sidesteps the question by declaring that God made them. There is no blessing or commission to increase; perhaps Gen. 1 is hastening on to what follows.

1:26–28. The chapter now abandons something of its "terse rigidity" and becomes more poetic.[89]

> Now all things were already arrived at their own end: "the heaven and the earth," as Moses says, "were finished," and all things that lie between them, and the particular things were adorned with their appropriate beauty; the heaven with the rays of the stars, the sea and air with the living creatures that swim and fly, and the earth with all varieties of plants and animals, to all which, empowered by the Divine will, it gave birth together; the earth was full, too, of her produce, bringing forth fruits at the same time with flowers; the meadows were full of all that grows therein, and all the mountain ridges, and summits, and every hill-side, and slope, and hollow, were crowned with young grass, and with the varied produce of the trees, just risen from the ground, yet shot up at once into their perfect beauty; and all the beasts that had come into life at God's command were rejoicing, we may suppose, and skipping about, running to and fro in the thickets in herds according to their kind, while every sheltered and shady spot was ringing with the chants of the song-birds. And at sea, we may suppose, the sight to be seen was of the like kind, as it had just settled to quiet and calm in the gathering together of its depths, where havens and harbours spontaneously hollowed out on the coasts made the sea reconciled with the land; and the gentle motion of the waves vied in beauty with the meadows, rippling

88. See GKC 110c; *IBHS* 34.4c.
89. Skinner, *Genesis*, 30.

> delicately with light and harmless breezes that skimmed the surface; and all the wealth of creation by land and sea was ready, and none was there to share it.[90]

Against this background, there is a second declaration that "God said," introducing another commission, as happened on day three. But whereas the seven preceding occurrences of "God said" introduced commissions in the jussive, this eighth occurrence introduces a cohortative. God speaks not about what other entities must do but about what he must do. He could easily have said, "Earth is to bring out human beings"; the move to a cohortative suggests a more direct involvement on God's part with this act of creation.

Strikingly, the act is not initially described as "creation" but simply as "making." But the novelty of this act of making is further underlined by God's saying not "I am going to make" but "We are going to make." While the God who speaks is the trinitarian God, engaged in this act of making as Father, Son, and Spirit, and he might have had a smile on his face in inspiring Genesis to use this plural form, the author of Genesis and the people listening to the creation story did not know this fact about God's creating humanity, so this insight was not the one God wanted to convey to them in inspiring the report of his words in this form.[91] God might be associating himself with other supernatural beings (see, e.g., b. Sanh. 38b); but neither here nor in other passages where the plural recurs (e.g., 3:22; 11:7; Isa. 6:8) is there reference to such beings in the context (the seraphs in Isa. 6 are not beings who would have this kind of role), and one wonders about the idea of humanity being made in the image of other supernatural beings. The form of the words might reflect the plural of majesty whereby a king or queen says, "We have decided," meaning "I have decided." The plural then underlines the authority of the one who speaks; it draws attention to the difference and the boundary between God and humanity even while making a point about humanity being made like God.[92] Or the plural might suggest self-deliberation,[93] which was appropriate (Gen. Rab. 8.1–4 suggests) in light of the way things are going to go wrong with humanity.

Human beings are to be made in God's image (*bəṣelem*) and as God's likeness (*kidmûtēnû*). Outside Genesis, the first noun generally refers to a statue, usually one that represents a deity (e.g., Num. 33:52; Ezek. 7:20), though

90. Gregory of Nyssa, *On the Making of Man* 1.5 (*NPNF*[2] 5:389–90).

91. Cf. Calvin against Luther, *Genesis 1–5*, 57–59, though "darkly," Luther notes, so that only after Jesus came can the point be clear; and cf. Barth, *CD* 3.1:191–92. Cf. also Augustine, *Literal Meaning of Genesis*, 1:95 (Augustine also finds Father, Word, and Spirit in Gen. 1:1–3: *Literal Meaning of Genesis*, 1:23–26). Chrysostom (*Homilies on Genesis 1–17*, 109) thinks only of the Father and the Son. Johnson ("Genesis 1:26–28") reflects on the fruitfulness of thinking about the image of God and God as Trinity. Keiser ("Divine Plural") argues for a reference to some form of plurality in the Godhead.

92. See Eslinger, "Enigmatic Plurals."

93. So GKC 124g.

in a notable exception it denotes the statue of a king in Nebuchadnezzar's dream (Dan. 2; and cf. Dan. 3). Some Mesopotamian texts refer to the king as made in the god's image and thus as ruling with his authority; Gen. 1 says that humanity does so.[94] Whereas "image" usually has negative connotations, "likeness" refers more neutrally to a thing that resembles something else (Ezek. 1 and 10 have most of the occurrences). The first word, then, suggests that human beings will physically represent God in a living and lively way that contrasts with a "regular" divine image.[95] The second word suggests that they will be godlike in the way they do so. Along with the extra nuance attaching to the extra noun is the extra nuance attaching to the second preposition. The two prepositions recur in 5:3 with their nouns switched, so we should not make too much of the distinction between them. But the *k* does underline that humanity will be the very likeness of God. Humanity's nature "blurs . . . the otherwise sharp distinction between creator and creation."[96] We already know from Gen. 1 that God's characteristics include the capacity to create, speak authoritatively, see, think, make distinctions, name, make, put in place, bless, and command. The idol images used by other peoples in their worship have mouths, eyes, ears, noses, hands, and feet, but they cannot speak, see, hear, smell, act, or walk, and their devotees end up like them (Pss. 115:4–8; 135:15–18). The real God can do those things, and human beings have the body parts that enable them to be the physical representations and representatives of that God. "Valid manifestation of divine presence is not found in consecrated wood, stone, or metal. Rather, humankind is the locus of divine presence."[97]

Genesis 2 will describe human beings and animals as similar to each other in their origin. They are made by the same process, from the same stuff, and both end up as "living beings." Genesis 1 anticipates questions about whether or how they are different. The deliberation involved in making human beings marks a difference in the process of making them and in the result: they are declared to be more like God than like the other animate beings. Further, in Gen. 3 the snake suggests that God doesn't want humanity to be like God, and God in due course notes that through their disobedience they have become like God in a negative sense, in their recognition of good and bad that issues from their asserting their own authority. Genesis 1 makes clear that there is a sense in which God intends them to be like him.[98]

The rest of v. 26 spells out the implications of being godlike or provides the rationale for it; the verse also indicates the sense in which human beings have authority in the world. They are made to hold sway over or control the animate

94. See, e.g., J. Miller, "In the 'Image' and 'Likeness' of God," 294–95; Schellenberg, "Humankind as the 'Image of God'"; but esp. Middleton, *Liberating Image*.

95. See McDowell, *Image of God*.

96. McBride, "Divine Protocol," 16–17.

97. Herring, "'Transubstantiated' Humanity," 494.

98. See further Sawyer, "Image of God."

creation on God's behalf. As in When on High and in Gen. 2, humanity is created to work on God's behalf. "Hold sway" (*rādâ*) suggests a rule that is enforced, as when Israel's enemies rule over Israel (Lev. 26:17) and when Israel eventually reverses that rule (Isa. 14:2). This control need not be harsh (cf. Lev. 25:43, 46, 53), but it is one imposed on subjects who may not welcome it. In the immediate term, humanity will express this authority by naming the animals (Gen. 2:19–20), for which action God's present words provide the rationale. In contrast, Gen. 3 will trace the beginning of the human tragedy to Adam and Eve's yielding to a suggestion from one of the creatures that God made. Genesis 1 anticipates the possibility of such resistance to God's will from the animate world and presupposes that humanity is to exercise authority over it. God begins with the fish, as he began with the sea creatures in vv. 20–23, though their being explicitly the object of humanity's sway anticipates a question that might arise in 2:19–20, where the human being names (and thus implicitly has authority over) only land animals and birds.

So God "created" humanity (v. 27). While translations normally lay out Gen. 1 as prose, they may treat v. 27 as a poetic line (e.g., NRSV). It then is an exceptional instance. Whereas poetic lines in Hebrew generally comprise two cola, here there are three, with "created" coming in each one, which further adds to the significance of what happens on this day. In the unexpected third colon Genesis adds that God created them "male and female." In Gen. 2 the creation of Eve from a part of Adam might raise the question whether there was femaleness in Adam that could be recycled in this way. It could seem that God had made *ʾādām* male and female—which is what 1:28 suggests.[99] Another question that may be raised by Gen. 3 is whether the man or the woman was responsible for humanity's disobedience. And what of the declaration in Gen. 3 that henceforth a man will rule over his woman? The NT can talk in terms of Adam's responsibility for that first act of disobedience (Rom. 5:12, 14) and in terms of Eve's responsibility (1 Tim. 2:14). Genesis 1 invites people listening to the story to see male and female both together as made in God's image and as both together designed to rule over the world, not to rule one over the other. Does it also invite people to infer that God is both male and female?[100]

The blessing of fruitfulness follows (v. 28), suggesting another aspect of the significance of humanity's being made male and female. Only as male and female can they be fruitful.[101] Again Gen. 1 links with what will follow in Gen. 2, where Eve is created in order to make it possible for humanity to look after God's orchard; her being female and able to bear children is at least an aspect of the way she fulfills that role. The commission to be numerous

99. Cf. Ephrem, *Genesis*, 94–95; and see de Moor, "Duality in God and Man"; contrast Noort, "Creation of Man and Woman," 4–10.

100. So Gudbergsen, "God Consists of Both."

101. Cf. Niskanen, "Poetics of Adam."

and to fill the earth corresponds to the commission to the rest of the animate world, while the distinctive charge to hold sway over that world also follows. But God now speaks of subjugating it (*kābaš*), an even more forceful word, used of Israel's conquest of Canaan and of the enforced servitude of people within Israel (e.g., Num. 32:22, 29; Jer. 34:11, 16). The commission again anticipates the failure of Gen. 3, where the man and the woman do not subjugate the snake. And the absence of a declaration that God saw humanity as good might anticipate the events of Gen. 3,[102] though the "very good" of v. 31 will follow in a moment.

1:29–30. Yet one more "God said" further emphasizes the work of the sixth day. God's words are the most remarkable ones in the chapter in what they don't say. God gives what grows to the animate world as its food but does not invite members of the animate world to eat one another. This note in Gen. 1 again anticipatorily spells out the implications of Gen. 2, where Adam is sent into God's orchard to serve it and look after it and is invited to eat from all the trees, but only to name the animals. The fact that Gen. 1 does not think about the "problem" that some animals are apparently built to be carnivorous may point to another insight about the chapter as a whole: this account of the creation focuses on portraying a world that is structured and ordered. Everything has its place and its proper lifestyle. Perhaps it was okay for lions to be carnivorous.

1:31. At the end of the last working day of the week, the day that has occupied so much space in the chapter, God stands back once more, as he has at the end of each day, and now looks with satisfaction at the week's work. The creation of the world is complete. It looks really good. God is like a craftsman who knows what he is making and is not surprised at what emerges from his work yet who stands back when he has finished and is pleased with what he sees; the individual parts of something may be impressive, but the whole will be even more so.[103] Although the following chapters will raise questions about the goodness of creation, Gen. 1 anticipates them and declares that it is very good.

2:1–3. So God has completed the work of creating the cosmos and its army. The latter term applies directly to the "heavenly host," the sun, the moon, and the stars. They are the forces that Yahweh controls and makes use of in governing the earth and to whom Israel will be tempted to bow down as if they were gods (Deut. 4:19; 17:3). The creation story has anticipatorily reminded Israel that these entities are part of created reality.

Genesis speaks loosely of God finishing his work on the seventh day (v. 2)—strictly, he had finished it on the sixth, though Gen. Rab. 10.9 suggests

102. Cf. Augustine, *Literal Meaning of Genesis*, 1:101; more recently Ramantswana, "Humanity Not Pronounced Good."

103. Cf. Augustine, *Two Books on Genesis*, 59–60, 80.

that on the seventh day God created tranquility, pleasure, well-being, and peace. But he now stops (*šābat*). Whereas When on High emphasizes that creating humanity makes it possible for the gods to rest, Genesis does not refer to God's resting. The seventh day is simply God's stopping day. If the reference to *tōhû wābōhû* and to the deep indicated a problem that Gen. 1 needed to solve, then stopping because the work is done announces that the problem is indeed resolved. The phrase "God finished his work" near the beginning of Genesis also anticipates the note that "Moses finished the work" on the sanctuary, near the end of Exodus (40:33).

If blessing (Gen. 2:3) suggests making fruitful,[104] blessing the seventh day has suggestive implications, hinting that God "ordained that happy consequences attach to its celebration."[105] Genesis Rabbah 12 comments that God blessed it with special lights, special food, special offerings, and Torah study. How unbiblical is any legalistic understanding of the Sabbath, which for the Jewish people is a joy![106] But given that the First Testament normally speaks of blessing only animate things, Genesis might be expecting its hearers to compare the theme of blessing God.[107] The verb will then suggest praising. This understanding could link with the declaration that God made this day sacred. While the first six days of the week are ordinary, and humanity can use them as it wishes, the seventh day is special. God claims it; it belongs to him. People are not to trespass on it. When "the distinguished word *qadosh* [holy] is used for the first time, . . . it is applied to time," to a day.[108] Whereas When on High ends with the making of a temple, Gen. 1 ends with the sanctifying of a day. Genesis makes no statement about the Sabbath being made for humanity. "It is an ordinance of the kosmos like any other part of the creative operations."[109]

"The seven-day pattern of Gen. 1:1–2:3 transforms something as simple as the weekly calendar . . . into a constant reminder of God's creative sovereignty. *Every week* of human history becomes a mnemonic stroll through creation itself."[110] The "time-consciousness" of the First Testament begins here, as does the in-time activity of God. Yet for human beings, time begins with a day of rest, not a day of work (so it was a happy innovation when the church made the first day of the week a holiday).[111] The organization of time by seven-day weeks is another distinctive aspect of Israelite life, and Gen. 1 buttresses it by tracing it back to creation. But it does not use the noun

104. See the comment on 1:22.
105. Dillmann, *Genesis*, 1:91.
106. Zimmerli, *1. Mose 1–11*, 105.
107. Cf. Calvin, *Genesis*, 1:107.
108. Heschel, *Sabbath*, 9; cf. Skillen, "Seven Days of Creation," 133.
109. Skinner, *Genesis*, 35.
110. Arnold, *Genesis*, 49–50, emphasis original.
111. Barth, *CD* 3.2:457, 458.

šabbāt or have God telling anyone about its sacredness or speak of any human obligation regarding it.[112] Such revelation will come only in Exod. 16, in the First Testament's only clear reference to Gen. 1 (i.e., Exod. 20:11),[113] and in Exod. 23:12. Exodus will then also speak of God resting on the seventh day and of animals having the chance to do so. And there it will emerge that this divine rest is one in which human beings and animals share rather than one that human work makes possible.[114]

Sabbath stopping becomes one of the ways Israel as God's special people mirrors God and models what it means to be truly human.[115] As an exordium to the Torah, Gen. 1 presupposes that "the law corresponds to the world and the world to the law," so that a person who lives in accordance with the law thus lives as a "citizen of the world," living in harmony with it.[116] And the point about human beings stopping for one day in seven may be implicit in Genesis. Given that Gen. 2 will record Yahweh's shaping of a man to serve and keep the earth, Gen. 2:3 anticipatorily implies that people are to work only for six days.[117] Writings from the Babylonian and Persian periods imply that Judah's failure to observe the Sabbath was one reason for Yahweh's bringing about the fall of Jerusalem and the exile (see, e.g., Jer. 17; Ezek. 20), and for people reading this creation story in these periods, omitting mention of the human obligation regarding the Sabbath might be an encouragement. The Sabbath is not just something to make people feel guilty.

There is no "evening and morning" at the end of the seventh day. Perhaps "the Sabbath of God has no evening,"[118] and the seventh day continues although God continues to be at work; God and we live during the seventh day (cf. John 5:17). But other features of the first six days also fail to appear here, such as the naming and the comment on its being good. God's stopping on the seventh day does not rule out God's starting again on the eighth day (which John 5:17 would also fit).

Hebrews 4:4 creatively relates the talk of God's stopping in Gen. 2:2 to the First Testament's talk of Israel's stopping in connection with Israel's arrival in Canaan in Ps. 95 (cf. e.g., Deut. 12:9; Josh. 21:44 [21:42]) and to the stopping associated with the salvation that is opened up to us through Jesus. Although the MT talks about "rest" (*mənûḥâ*) in connection with Israel's arrival in Canaan, the LXX assimilates its language to that of Gen. 2 and thus

112. Jubilees 2.17–33 makes up extensively for this omission.

113. See Hoffman, "First Creation Story."

114. Cf. Wallace, "Rest for the Earth?," 53–54.

115. But contrast the argument of Cole, "Sabbath and Genesis 2:1–3."

116. Philo, *On the Creation of the World* 1.3.

117. Cf. Arnold, "Genesis as Holiness Preamble," 334–36. Hart ("Genesis 1:1–2:3 as a Prologue," 316) notes that "work" in Gen. 2:1–3 is *məlā'kâ*, the ordinary word for human work.

118. Keil and Delitzsch, *Pentateuch*, 69; cf. Augustine, *Confessions* 35 [50–51]—though these authors have reservations about the idea.

talks about Israel "stopping" (*katapauō*), not about rest, and Heb. 3:7–4:11 follows. But Ps. 95 indicates that being in the promised land doesn't mean that people have yet entered God's stopping. "There remains a sabbathing for the people of God." Coming to trust in Jesus opens up the possibility of entering into God's seventh-day stopping in the new Jerusalem. Paradoxically, entering into that stopping involves a lot of effort (Heb. 4:11).[119]

2:4a. The MT takes 2:4a as the beginning of a new unit; similar formulations in passages such as 5:1; 6:9 introduce what follows. But this understanding does not work for 2:4a, since what follows is not an account of the origins of the heavens and the earth.[120] Genesis 2:4a is a footnote to 1:1–2:3,[121] as the expression in 10:32 is a footnote to what precedes. In its reference to creation and to the heavens and the earth, it corresponds to and pairs with 1:1. The distinctiveness of its location matches the distinctiveness of the meaning of the term "lines of descent" (*tôlədôt*) on this first occurrence. The traditional translation "generations" reflects the expression's etymology (noted in the introduction to this commentary) and its usage elsewhere. But Gen. 1 is not a "genealogy"; the expression refers metaphorically to the process whereby the cosmos came into being. Given the innovative nature of this metaphorical use of the expression, it would have made a puzzling opening for the first verse of Genesis, but in light of Gen. 1 as a whole, it can be understood, and it can anticipatorily make a link between the process whereby the world came into being and the process whereby humanity comes into being from Adam to Noah and from Noah to Abraham.

Implications

Creation

The world had a beginning. It has not always existed.[122] And the world came into being because God acted; it did not just happen. "There are those who look at nature and do not consider God, as if all things do not happen in God. But these are greatly in error."[123] The world came into being because God created, God said, God saw, God made a distinction, God called, God

119. Skillen ("Seven Days of Creation," 112) takes Heb. 4 as a "signpost" for reading the significance of Gen. 1 within the context of the Scriptures as a whole.

120. See, e.g., Seebass, *Genesis*, 1:62. "Heavens and earth" can hardly be a subjective genitive (Hamilton, *Genesis 1–17*, 151); they do not generate the garden and its human beings. Stordalen ("Genesis 2,4") argues for the forward-looking understanding here, and Derouchie ("The Blessing-Commission") has more recently argued that all these headings are introductions rather than conclusions. Gertz ("Formation of the Primeval History," 114–18) calls it a "redactional bridge" between 1:1–2:3 and 2:4b–3:24.

121. Cf. Chrysostom, *Homilies on Genesis 1–17*, 157–59.

122. Cf. Ambrose of Milan, *Hexameron, Paradise, and Cain and Abel*, 7–8.

123. Oecolampadius, *Genesis*, 74–75.

made, God put, God blessed, God finished, God made sacred, God stopped. In Gen. 1 God is

> the mighty Creator who takes on the role of the great actor in time and narrative. On this register, the cosmic revelatory drama of God speaking, acting, and proclaiming is to be considered as *sculpting in time*. . . . While there is a revealed dimension of transhistoricity to God's being Creator, God's profound kinship with time, displayed in narrative, life, and the cosmos, provokes a hermeneutical trajectory that subverts any exclusively atemporal or salvific agenda in Genesis.[124]

God's speaking and acting were an expression of his thoughtfulness and insight. The expression "At the beginning" makes Gen. Rab. 1.1 think of Ms. Wisdom's being "the beginning" in Prov. 8:22 and then of the fact that Ms. Wisdom was (on one understanding of the puzzling word *ʾāmôn*) a craftworker (Prov. 8:30). Further, Wisdom can be identified with Torah, which suggests the inference that Yahweh created the world on the basis of consultation with the Torah—which (Prov. 8:22 also indicates) God had created before going on to create the world. To put it more historically, "Genesis 1 sets forth both implicitly and explicitly the rationale on which the Torah's religion will be founded, or by which the Torah's religion will make sense."[125]

God's bringing the world into being was careful and organized. It resembled the work of someone who knows he has a week's work to do, thinks through what he needs to do, makes a plan, and implements it. Then "God views his work and is satisfied with it; this means that God loves his work and therefore wills to preserve it."[126] Genesis makes the first of the Scriptures' characteristic comments about God's real-time engagement with the world. While God knew that he was commissioning something good, there is a difference between knowing ahead of time and looking at it in such a way as to see that it is good. It is an aspect of God's intrinsic temporality. Genesis is not worried about implying that God was not perfect before he has the experience of seeing something that he had not seen before because it did not exist before.

God had several ways of bringing things into being. He spoke in third-person commands that worked as if by magic or that worked like the speech of a king or a commander in chief, so that things happened by the authority of his word. He made things like a builder. He created things like an emperor who causes things to happen by his sovereign power. He blessed things and thereby gave them the power to increase. He commissioned them to do so.[127]

124. Diepstra and Laughery, "Sculpting in Time," 300, emphasis original; their title phrase comes from Tarkovsky, *Sculpting in Time*.

125. Greenstein, "Presenting Genesis 1," 4; Greenstein goes on to be deconstructive later in the paper.

126. Bonhoeffer, *Creation and Fall; Temptation*, 25.

127. Cf. Watson (*Text, Church and World*, 140–45), though Watson prefers to speak in terms of three models, which facilitates the making of a link with trinitarian thinking (313);

In bringing the world into being, God speaks in the third person ("such and such is to happen") in a way that distances him from the world, in the second person ("be fruitful") in a way that implies a personal relationship with the world, and in the first person ("let us make") in a way that implies personal involvement in what happens. Transcendence and immanence are thus both aspects of God's relationship with the world.[128]

It came into being through the action of the one God. The process was deliberate, thoughtful, and smooth. It involved "the complete and effortless control of God over his creation,"[129] without struggle, conflict, or effort. Thus the significance of Gen. 1 is "to render God, as it were, visible to us in all his works. . . . The Lord, that he may invite us to the knowledge of himself, places the fabric of heaven and earth before our eyes, rendering himself, in a certain manner, manifest in them."[130] Its portrayal of God is in its way just as anthropomorphic as that of Gen. 2–3.[131] Further, to say that "God saw; God evaluated; God named; God separated," and so on, is to indicate that "the creating God is not only the acting God, but also the reacting God, the God who responds to that which has been created."[132]

Genesis 1 does not say why God created the world. He just decided to. It was simply his will. You cannot get behind that fact.[133] And whereas other peoples told stories about what God or the gods were doing before creation, Genesis does not. "Was He in a state of rest or not? Augustine relates in his *Confessions* that someone had answered to this effect: 'God was making hell ready for those who pried into meddlesome questions.'"[134] It also tells us nothing about the creation of angels or about their fall.[135] It tells us nothing about the empirical process whereby the world came into being. Its poetic nature (even if it is poetic prose rather than actual verse) means that we cannot make inferences of this kind from it. Its account rules out nontheistic evolution; it does not support creationism or theistic evolution, but it would allow them; it most obviously supports intelligent design.[136] Yet the intent of the Torah is

while Fretheim (*God and the World*, 34–48) has nine modes of creation from Gen. 1–2 and seven images of God the creator.

128. See, e.g., Möller, "Images of God."

129. Childs, *Myth and Reality in the Old Testament*, 33.

130. Calvin, *Genesis*, 1:58–59; cf. J. Thompson, *Genesis 1–11*, 8–9.

131. See Knafl, *Forming God*, 53–71.

132. Welker, "What Is Creation?," 61.

133. Cf. Augustine, *Two Books on Genesis*, 51–52.

134. Luther, *Genesis 1–5*, 10 (referring to Augustine, *Confessions* 11.12).

135. Cf. Luther, *Genesis 1–5*, 22–23. Jubilees 2.2 makes up for the first omission, apparently taking off from the assumption that *ʾĕlōhîm* in 1:2 refers to such beings (van Ruiten, *Primaeval History Interpreted*, 25). Augustine (*City of God* 12.9) thinks they must be included in the "light" of Day 1.

136. On these issues, see, e.g., K. Miller, *Perspectives on an Evolving Creation*; Barton and Wilkinson, *Reading Genesis after Darwin*; Rose, *Evolution-Creation Struggle*.

not to inform about the natural sciences but to keep human beings straight on the way of making right decisions and to establish in their mind a trust in his oneness and providence.[137]

The world came into being through God's setting to work on a situation that was desolate and empty and transforming it into something that had form and beauty, order and structure, life and fruitfulness. Genesis 1 is not talking about *creatio ex nihilo*, creation out of nothing; theology's use of that Latin expression puts us on the track of its context in ideas that became important much later.[138] Genesis does not say that God created the raw material for creation, though other passages in the First Testament clearly show its assumption that God did so. Genesis's interest lies elsewhere. One result is that we learn in Gen. 1 of God's craftsmanship.[139] We do not lose theologically by declining to read *creatio ex nihilo* into Genesis (because that doctrine is true anyway); we gain.[140]

"The God of the Christian confession . . . is Elohim, the God of Israel." And "the Lord of this sphere [of Israel's history] is God the Creator; and it is only as such that He is the Lord of the sphere of the world." For him to be the creator means his doing something—namely, creating; and his creative action happens not out of time and history but in time and history.[141] Thus, while "the Church of Christ bears witness to the end of all things" and "lives from the end," Gen. 1 shows that the Scriptures have things to say about creation and about the beginning; it is not the case that only from Christ can we know what the beginning is or that "the Scriptures need to be read and proclaimed wholly from the viewpoint of the end."[142] The order of the Scriptures indicates that they have nothing to say about Christ outside the context of what we know from the beginning. Only by starting from the beginning can we know who Christ is. Thus John 1:1–5 is in part an exposition of Gen. 1, using the account of creation to illumine who Jesus is;[143] likewise, Col. 1:15 and 2 Cor. 4:4 describe Jesus as the image of God (cf. also Phil. 2:6). Such passages parallel the later finding of the Trinity in Gen. 1 in that they do not help us understand Gen. 1 itself, though by a feedback process they have implications for our broader understanding of creation and of humanity. Jews and Christians naturally read Gen. 1 in light of their own faith, so that in Judaism the Torah became the agent of creation and in Christian faith

137. Luzzatto, *Genesis*, on Gen. 1:1.

138. See, e.g., Konkel ("'Und siehe, es war sehr gut,'" 596–97), who sees the idea as coming first in the Vg (it is not even in 2 Macc. 7:28; Rom. 4:17; or Heb. 11:3). Cf. Barth, *CD* 3.2:152–55.

139. Chrysostom, *Homilies on Genesis 1–17*, 36.

140. Against Reno, *Genesis*, 39–46.

141. Barth, *CD* 3.1:12, 14, 15.

142. Against Bonhoeffer, *Creation and Fall; Temptation*, 9, 10, with which compare Moltmann, *God in Creation*, 55.

143. See, e.g., Menken, "Genesis in John's Gospel and 1 John," 88–90.

Jesus became the agent of creation.[144] But we lose out if we do not consider what Gen. 1 in its own right has to say about creator and creation. And while God is the God of the covenant, "creation occurs 'in the beginning,' whereas covenant belongs in the middle."[145]

The Image of God

Genesis 1:26–27 "are perhaps the verses of the Old Testament most commented on by the Fathers," and the doctrine of humanity's creation in God's image is "the foundation of patristic anthropology."[146] In modern times, too, "scarcely any verse in the whole of the Old Testament has retained such interest," though "this interest has been confined almost exclusively to the area of church doctrine."[147] God's image has then been located (for instance) in humanity's intellect, spiritual nature, ethical nature, freedom, memory, will, self-consciousness, relational nature, and capacity to rule. As is the case with *creatio ex nihilo*, it is telling that theology commonly uses the Latin expression *imago Dei* in connection with this discussion. The terms and the content of the discussion come from Western thinking rather than from Gen. 1. The First Testament as a whole does attribute all the above characteristics to humanity, but Gen. 1:26–27 provide no basis for associating "the image of God" with them except perhaps the capacity to rule.[148] The monumental doctrinal edifice is not unscriptural, but when represented as based on these verses, it falls over.[149] Or perhaps we should turn this argument on its head and acknowledge that "language of 'the image of God' is a relatively underdetermined place-holder for something that can only be more clearly defined by seeing how the canonical narrative develops, beyond Genesis, and indeed beyond the OT."[150]

Being in the image of God means that humanity rules over the earth. Why and in what sense does humanity need to do so? Genesis 2–3 provides some immediate answers. Looking beyond Gen. 2–3 may suggest that humanity will need to constrain the animals in order to have living space for itself.[151] Israelites might fear that the animal world could overwhelm the human world; this

144. See P. Alexander, "In the Beginning."

145. Cf. Watson, *Text and Truth*, 230, 232. Watson goes on (237–39) to read the Jesus story in light of the seven days of creation (rather than simply vice versa).

146. Louth, *Genesis 1–11*, 27.

147. Westermann, *Genesis 1–11*, 148; cf. Sexton's positive comments on the work of Stanley Grenz in his "*Imago Dei* Once Again." On the diverse interpretations of the image of God, see, e.g., Jónsson, *Image of God*; Towner, "Clones of God"; Simango, "Imago Dei."

148. Cf. Middleton, *Liberating Image*.

149. Cf. Gunkel, *Genesis*, 114.

150. So Briggs, "Humans in the Image of God," 112. MacDonald ("*Imago Dei* and Election") sympathetically reviews Barth's use of the expression.

151. Cf. Wöhrle, "Dominium terrae."

commission in Genesis promises that it will not.[152] It perhaps also presupposes an awareness of conflict characterizing the animate world (cf. Isa. 11:6–9)[153] and envisions humanity driving it into harmony. "A central function of government in the Hebrew conception is to check oppression": thus "the authority of the human governors exists, among other things, to repress violence among the animals"—perhaps peacefully taming them.[154] The goodness of creation evidently does not exclude its requiring control, but the godlike nature of humanity's rule will express itself in being liberating rather than harsh.

Humanity's exercise of authority over the animal world does not indicate that it is superior to it.[155] My boss exercises authority over me but he seems not to see himself as superior to me. Indeed, authority combines with subordination; humanity serves the garden (Gen. 2:15), but serving the soil requires the exercise of violent force upon it. One significant aspect of the commission may lie not in the intention that humanity will *hold sway* (as opposed to caring for or living in harmony with or being threatened by) but in the intention that *humanity* (as opposed to kings) will hold sway.[156] And holding sway is the work of a shepherd-king.[157] The commission to rule does not encourage exploitation; humanity is not given the right to eat animals.[158] The vision of harmony in Gen. 1:26–30 links with this apparent expectation that the diet of human beings and animals will be vegetarian.[159] Perhaps the audience was expected to be no more literalist in its understanding of this aspect of the Genesis parable than it was of other aspects. But killing for food involves violence, so not eating each other coheres with a vision for harmony. The harmony linked to the beginning in Gen. 1 becomes a promise for the end in Isa. 11,[160] though even at the beginning it was a commission rather than an actuality. Genesis portrays creation as completed and does not think in terms of continuous creation or of human beings as co-creators with God or of creation as unfinished project, yet the outworking of God's creation project involves humanity as creatures made in God's image.

Man and woman together are made in God's image. One implication of v. 27 (in association with 2:24) is that God's creation intention was that one man and one woman should marry and should then be together for life, but God does not simply leave people to their own devices when they do not live

152. Cf. Rüterswörden, *Dominum Terrae*, 130.

153. Cf. Mincato, "A Questão Do 'Subjugai a Terra' em *Gn* 1,28," 376.

154. Houston, "Sex or Violence," 144. Cf. Bauckham, "Humans, Animals, and the Environment," 179–83.

155. Cf. Nwaoru, "Genesis 1,28."

156. See, e.g., Brett, *Genesis*, 28.

157. Cf. Pentiuc, "Holding Sway."

158. Keel and Schroer, *Creation*, 146.

159. Cf. McLaughlin, "Meatless Dominion."

160. Cf. Gunkel, *Genesis*, 115.

up to the creation vision (see Deut. 24:1–4; Mark 10:6; Matt. 19:4).[161] Jesus's collocating Gen. 1–2 and Deut. 24 in connection with a question about divorce suggests an approach to the ethical and theological issues raised by polygamy, same-sex marriage, and transgender issues. Of course, Jesus is seeking to expound the significance of Genesis in connection with a question raised in his context, and his comments should not be regarded as holding readers back from studying Genesis in its own right.[162]

Paul's declaration that man as opposed to woman is God's image and glory (1 Cor. 11:7) also depends on the collocation of Gen. 1:26–27 with Gen. 2, where the woman is created second. On the other hand, in 1 Cor. 11 his accepting the assumption that women as well as men prophesy and pray in worship fits the declaration in Gen. 1 that all humanity, male and female, embodies God's image and is commissioned to rule the earth. In Gen. 1–2 there are no hierarchies of authority within humanity.[163] Paul's declaration in Gal. 3:28, which uses the expression "male and female" as it comes in Gen. 1:27 LXX, further suggests that through Jesus, God reasserts a correspondence between male and female in terms of relationship to God, a correspondence going back to creation. And his inclusion in Gal. 3:28 of Jew and Gentile and of slave and free suggests further implications of the declaration that all humanity is made in God's image.[164]

Being in God's image and being male and female leads into a commission to be fruitful. One implication of Gen. 1:27–28 is that "the spiritual significance of sexual union in scripture does not simply encourage romanticized images of intimacy, nor does it draw upon Dionysian images of orgiastic ecstasy." Its significance lies in its capacity to generate new life. It "gives birth to a future."[165] Further, James 3:9 derives an ethical principle from humanity's being in God's image. "Man has been depicted by the Lord God, his artist. He is fortunate in having a craftsman and a painter of distinction. He should not erase that painting"[166]—in himself or in someone else. An implication is that human disobedience did not destroy God's image in humanity, though it did tarnish it. The image of God cleaned up through Jesus then has two principal parts: wisdom and holiness (cf. Col. 3:10; Eph. 4:24).[167] "Let us always, therefore, contemplate that image of God that we can be transformed to his likeness."[168]

161. See, e.g., Ahearne-Kroll, "Genesis in Mark's Gospel," 30–34; Browne, "Genesis in Matthew's Gospel," 44–46; and their references.

162. Cf. Wénin, "'Une chair unique' ou 'une seule chair'?"

163. Cf. Middleton, "Liberating Image."

164. But Gen. 17 may also be in the background of Gal. 3:28; see the discussion of "Circumcision" at the end of the comments on Gen. 17 below.

165. Reno, *Genesis*, 56.

166. Ambrose, *Hexameron, Paradise, and Cain and Abel*, 259.

167. Perkins, "Exposition of the Creed," 1:151; cf. J. Thompson, *Genesis 1–11*, 43.

168. Origen, *Homilies on Genesis*, 66.

Humanity's spoiling of the world in modern times has been blamed on the alleged anthropocentrism of Gen. 1. One consideration that makes this charge implausible is that it apparently took two or three millennia for the creation story to have this effect, which suggests that other ideological factors were at work in the spoiling.[169] Indeed, one might reverse the accusation: "the order of the cosmos portrayed in Genesis has been unprecedentedly disrupted by modern humanity's scientific-technological project of unlimited domination of the whole world."[170]

Genesis makes clear that humanity is not the center of creation. The world was not created for humanity; if anything, humanity was created for the world. This insight is one of the pointers to the significance of Gen. 1 for ecological concerns.[171] Conversely, some of humanity's achievements in modern times, such as the conquest of diseases and the decrease in infant mortality, might be seen as ways that humanity is subduing the earth. But again, the fact that millennia have passed suggests that other ideological factors are at work. "It happens through divine power that the waters do not pass over us. . . . For what is our entire life on earth but a passage through the Red Sea, where on both sides the sea stood like high walls? Because it is very certain that the sea is far higher than the earth, God, up to the present time, commands the waters to remain in suspense and restrains them by His Word lest they burst upon us as they burst forth in the deluge."[172] But if it is human action that has issued in the melting of the polar icecaps, we might be unwise to assume that God's original constraining of the water of the oceans so as to let the land emerge means he will always protect the land mass.

169. See further Goldingay, *Israel's Gospel*, 114–15. For a nuanced study, see Harrison, "Subduing the Earth"; and for the history of the text's interpretation, see Jeremy Cohen, *"Be Fertile and Increase."*

170. Bauckham, "Humans, Animals, and the Environment," 185.

171. See, e.g., Okyere, "Bible, Ecology and Sustainable Development"; and more generally for Gen. 1–11, see van Wolde, "Facing the Earth."

172. Luther, *Genesis 1–5*, 35.

2
How God Made the Garden and Its Servants

(2:4b–25)

Overview

The MT has no unit break at the end of Gen. 2; the text runs on into chapter 3. It is thus for convenience that I separate 2:4b–25 from 3:1–24; they form the two acts of one drama.[1] The first act does have its own arc of completeness arising from its focus on Yahweh's creation of a garden. The initial question it raises is like the one raised by the beginning of Gen. 1: the phraseology is similar. There's nothing growing on the earth, partly because there's no one to till the soil in which things could grow. So how will God succeed in making earth and heavens (v. 4b) when there is nothing growing (v. 5–6)? The initial answer appears: by planting a garden or orchard and shaping a human being to look after it (vv. 7–9), providing a good water supply for the earth as a whole (vv. 10–14), and giving the human being permissions and instructions (vv. 15–17). But that's where problems arise on the way: the human being can't fulfill the commission on his own (v. 18), and animals won't meet the need (vv. 19–20). So God shapes another human being to share the task with the first one (vv. 21–25). The opening act of the drama could then look complete on its own, and two lines of verse mark its climax at 2:23. But the chapter leaves unexplained the two trees that it mentions, so we wonder about them. Further,

1. Cf. Gibson, *Genesis*, 1:98–99. Bauks ("Text- and Reception-Historical Reflections") argues that they were originally separate units for which 2:25 was shaped as a bridge. Scotchmer ("Lessons from Paradise") understands Gen. 2–3 as a palistrophe.

the implied audience for the story is people who are involved in farming and marriage and who don't live in this garden, and the story doesn't make clear how it fits in with some things they know about the world and about life as it really is. So perhaps they are waiting for the other shoe to drop, and it will drop in Gen. 3.

Translation

4bAt the time of[2] Yahweh God's making earth and heavens,[3] **5**and when no bush of the open country was in the earth yet,[4] and no plant of the open country was growing yet (because Yahweh God had not made it rain on the earth), and there was no human being to serve[5] the ground, **6**though a stream[6] was going up from the earth and watering the entire face of the ground, **7**Yahweh God shaped the human being with dirt[7] from the ground and blew into its nostrils living breath, and the human being became a living person. **8**Yahweh God planted[8] a garden[9] in Lush,[10] on the east,[11] and put there the human being that he had shaped. **9**Yahweh

2. Literally, "on the day of," but the expression can be used in a looser way.

3. The MT treats v. 4 as one sentence, but more often the formula in v. 4a is itself a complete sentence, and v. 4b makes sense as the introduction to what follows (see the translation note to 2:4a).

4. The finite verb clauses in v. 5 continue the infinitival clause in v. 4b, instancing the yiqtol's capacity to signify past continuous tense in clauses that are marked as circumstantial by the noun preceding the verb.

5. The LXX and Vg have "work," but *ʿābad* is the regular word for "serve."

6. *ʾĒd* comes otherwise only in Job 36:27, where the context suggests cloud or mist; cf. the Tg and Ibn Ezra (*Genesis*, 52) here and Rogland, "Interpreting *ʾd* in Genesis 2.5–6." But the LXX, Vg, and Aq assume reference to a spring or stream, which better fits the present context, where the *ʾēd* is going up. See Tsumura, *Creation and Destruction*, 85–106.

7. Here *ʿāpār* suggests dry earth rather than dust; the Vg has *limus*, which means dirt or mud. Augustine (*Two Books on Genesis*, 102–4) presupposes "mud."

8. The Vg has "however the LORD God had planted" and the NIV "now the LORD God had planted," but the regular word order (verb preceding subject) does not suggest a circumstantial clause, and the waw-consecutive does not suggest a pluperfect translation. The same objection applies in connection with v. 18.

9. A *paradeisos* in the LXX (cf. the Vg), which is ultimately a Persian word meaning "garden." It comes to have the connotation of paradise, though that development may issue from the LXX's use of the word (cf. Brayford, *Genesis*, 228) rather than because the LXX overtranslates. Westermann (*Genesis 1–11*, 208–10) notes the various ways of describing the place called *ʿēden* in the First Testament.

10. Following vv. 4b–6, it would make sense if *ʿēden* denoted the "steppe," in the midst of which Yahweh God plants a fertile garden, but the idea that *ʿēden* could mean "steppe" seems fallacious; cf. B. Kedar-Kopfstein, *TDOT* 10:487, s.v. *ʿēden*. Elsewhere, words related to *ʿēden* mean luxurious or delightful (see BDB).

11. *Qedem* means "before" and thus "east" because it is "before" people who orient themselves facing the sun; Rashi (*Brʾšyt*, 23) takes the expression to denote east of Eden. *Qedem*

God made to grow up from the ground every tree that is desirable to look
at and good for food, with the life-tree in the middle of the garden, and
the good-and-bad-knowledge tree.
10There was a river going out of Lush to water the garden, and from
there it would divide and become four headwaters. **11**The name of the
first was Pišon; it was the one going around the entire Ḥavilah region,
where the gold is. **12**(The gold of that region is good; ruby[12] and emerald[13]
stone are there.) **13**The name of the second river was Giḥon; it was the
one going around the entire Kuš region. **14**The name of the third river was
Ḥiddeqel; it was the one going east of Aššur.[14] The fourth river was the
Perat.
15So Yahweh God got the human being and set him down in Lush
Garden to serve it and keep it. **16**Yahweh God ordered the human being:
"From every tree in the garden you may definitely eat,[15] **17**but from the
good-and-bad-knowledge tree you will not[16] eat, because at the time[17]
you eat from it, you will definitely die." **18**But Yahweh God said, "It's not
good for the human being to be on his own. I'll make him help equivalent
to him."[18]
19Yahweh God shaped from the ground every creature of the open
country and every bird of the heavens and brought them to the human
being to see what he would call it. Whatever the human being called a
living being, it became its name. **20**So the human being gave names to
all the animals, to the birds of the heavens, and to all the creatures of

---

can also mean before you in time; which opens up the possibility of understanding *miqqedem* to refer to God's having created the garden "long ago" (as in, e.g., Mic. 5:2 [5:1]), as would be implied on the assumption that Gen. 1 and 2 tell chronologically sequential rather than parallel stories (see the Tg, Aq, Sym, Th).

12. *Bədōlaḥ* comes only here and in Num. 11:7. The Vg renders *bdellium*, a resin used in making perfume, but this translation looks like a guess based on the similarity of the words. The context suggests a word for a gem; the LXX has a word for charcoal, which might suggest a dark red stone such as ruby.

13. *Śōham* recurs elsewhere in lists of gems (e.g., Ezek 28:13). The LXX has a "green" stone, which suggests emerald. Targums Onq. and Ps.-J. have beryl, of which emerald is a subset. Targum Neof. has pearl. The Vg has onyx.

14. The town rather than the country, to judge from the description of the river as east of Aššur.

15. Here and in v. 17 God uses the idiom that combines an infinitive and its cognate finite verb to indicate emphasis.

16. The negative is *lōʾ* and not *ʾal*, as in the Decalogue.

17. Strictly "on the day," but see the footnote on v. 4b, where the same expression occurs.

18. The expression *kənegdô* appears only here, though *k* is a common preposition and *neged* a fairly common word meaning "in front of." So the expression means literally "according to what is in front of him," in other words "corresponding to him" (cf. BDB), as his counterpart; cf. the Vg *simile*. But one needs to be careful of someone who is one's equal in this way and is over against one: "Should he not be worthy, then she is opposite him to fight" (Rashi, *Brʾšyt*, 27).

the open country. But for a human being[19] he didn't find[20] help equivalent to him.

21So Yahweh God made a coma fall on the human being so he slept, got one of his ribs,[21] and closed up its place with flesh. **22**Yahweh God built[22] the rib that he'd got from the human being into a woman and brought her to the human being. **23**The human being said:

> This one, finally,[23] is bone from my bones,
> flesh from my flesh!
> This one will be called woman,
> because from a man[24] this one was got.

24That's why a man abandons his father and his mother and attaches himself to his woman and they become one flesh.

25The two of them were naked, the man and his woman,[25] but they felt no shame.[26]

19. Previously *ʾādām* has had the article (except in v. 5, where the context indicates indefinite meaning). Here it lacks the article, and it could be translated Adam. Indeed, the Tg has Adam from v. 7, the LXX from v. 16, and the Vg from v. 19, even where *ʾādām* has the article. They thus treat *hāʾādām* as if it were a noun that has become a proper noun, as is sometimes said to be so with *habbaʿal* and *haśśāṭān* (see *IBHS* 13.6a). But the only clear example of this usage is *hāʾĕlōhîm*, which is a special case. More likely *hāʾādām* means "the human being/man," and here *ʾādām* is indefinite.

20. The LXX, Vg, Tg. Onq., and Tg. Ps.-J. take as impersonal active and translate "there was not found," perhaps to safeguard against the idea that Yahweh God now discovered something. Targum Neof. rather implies that the human being did the (not) finding, which works grammatically (since *hāʾādām* is the antecedent) and makes good sense.

21. Only here does *ṣelaʿ* apparently mean "rib"; usually it denotes the "side" of something. Thus God might have taken the man's whole "side." The LXX, Vg could have either meaning; Tg. Ps.-J. specifies that the word refers to the thirteenth rib on the right side.

22. The metaphor is apposite in that *ṣēlaʿ* is most commonly an architectural term for the side of a building (Sarna, *Genesis*, 22).

23. *Happaʿam* (lit., "the stroke/beat") suggests something that happens at last, after delay or disappointment (cf. 9:34, 35; 30:20; 46:30; Judg. 15:3; 16:18).

24. *ʾIššâ* was taken from *ʾîš*; the audience would be aware that adding an *-â* ending is a way one forms a feminine noun, though in this case the nouns are probably not etymologically related (cf. Speiser, *Genesis*, 18; and cf. BDB). Whereas *ʾādām* denotes a human being as opposed to an animal, *ʾîš* denotes an individual person as opposed to a group. While Tg. Ps.-J., Tg. Neof., Sym, and Th have "from a man," like the MT, LXX and SP have "from her man," which introduces a more explicit reference to marriage; Tg. Onq. *bʿlh* (her master) makes the point even clearer. See Dafni, "*ʾšh ky mʾiš*."

25. Or "his wife"; *ʾîš* and *ʾiššâ* are also the usual Hebrew words for husband and wife. Hebrew has the more technical words *baʿal* and *bəʿûlâ*, which mean "master/owner" and "owned," but the First Testament rarely uses them with this meaning.

26. Verse 25 would make good sense as the introduction to Gen. 3 (so NJPS), but its waw-consecutive form (followed by a circumstantial clause opening up a different subject, in 3:1) makes it look more like a continuation from what precedes. Seebass (*Genesis*, 1:115) sees it as "linking" 2:18–24 and 3:1–21.

Interpretation

Genesis 2–3 mostly tells its story in more straightforward prose than Gen. 1,[27] and it speaks of many familiar human realities: the land's need of watering and working, the lovely appearance and taste of the fruit from many trees, the rivers that can play a key role in irrigation, the richness of gold and precious gems, the corporate nature of the work of farming, the mutual recognition of a man and a woman, and their abandonment of parental obligations for this new commitment. The story tells of the origin of such familiar realities but paradoxically does so by making more sustained use of figures of speech: God shaping a human body like a potter shaping clay, God breathing into the body, God planting a garden, the four rivers, the good-and-bad-knowledge tree, the life-tree, the naming of the animals, God putting the man into a coma, God building a woman from a part of the man.

The portrayal of events and of the dynamics of life thus does not correspond to the portrayal of God's acts in the rest of the Scriptures beyond Gen. 2–3, or in regular human experience. It does compare in some ways with the portrayal in Revelation. Does the story indicate that God simply acted in different ways at the beginning of the world's story and that he will again act in different ways at the end? Rather, I take its nonrealistic form to suggest that (like Gen. 1) it is not a historiographic story. On the one hand, its integral relationship with the succeeding chapters in the unfolding First Testament story (and with Revelation) suggests that it does refer to things that happened at some time; it is not simply a parable of how things always are for human beings. But on the other hand, neither is it simply a straightforward account of what the video camera might have caught. It is a parabolic account of something that happened, like Nathan's parable in 2 Sam. 12:1–4. Second Samuel 11–12 offers a literal account of David's actions, followed by that parabolic account. Both relate events; the first does so literally, the second figuratively.[28] The nonrealistic nature of the portrayal in Gen. 2–3 suggests that it provides a figurative rather than a literal account of how God made the garden and its servants and how they went wrong. It is still a historical account in that it describes not how God always creates and how human beings always go wrong, but how God created at the beginning and how human beings went wrong at the beginning in a way that had fateful consequences for all humanity.

The story works as follows:

How God shaped a man (2:4b–7)

How God planted a garden (2:8–9)

A sidebar on the rivers watering the garden (2:10–14)

27. But Wyatt ("Royal Garden") lays it out as verse.

28. I owe this analogy to Kidner, *Genesis*, 66.

How God provided for the man, yet acknowledged a further need (2:15–18)
A sidebar on how God brought the animals for the man to name (2:19–20)
How God created the woman and brought her to the man (2:21–25)

Like Gen. 1, the chapter incorporates a number of motifs paralleling motifs in other Middle Eastern creation stories that speak of human beings made from clay, of humanity being created to work, of gardens, of life-giving plants, and of forbidden fruit: see, for example, the Sumerian Eridu Genesis,[29] the Akkadian Atrahasis story[30] (both speak of creation and of a flood), the Akkadian Gilgamesh story,[31] and the story of Adapa,[32] as well as When on High. Some of these parallels suggest acquaintance with such stories and/or reflect the culture shared by Israel and other Middle Eastern peoples. But Gen. 2–3 gives less indication than Gen. 1 of being designed to challenge the perspective of other Middle Eastern stories; it focuses on narrating its own story, which in its own right tells the true tale of God bringing humanity into being.[33] Comparing the stories within the framework of the kind of intertextuality that does not presuppose a direct relationship between stories may nevertheless help us perceive aspects of Gen. 2 in its own right. In Genesis, then, the first human being is created from dirt and from the breath of a living God, not from clay and the flesh and blood of a dead god. The garden is one whose fruit humanity is encouraged to enjoy. Humanity will work there; in this sense it is not a paradise. But there is no suggestion that humanity's work will inevitably be toilsome or that it was designed to relieve God from work or that it relates to worshiping God or feeding God. Woman and man are made separately to work together. Genesis 3 will relate how humanity ignores God's instructions rather than heeding them and pays a terrible, ongoing price for doing so, but Genesis focuses less on the quest for immortality or the loss of immortality than some other Middle Eastern stories and focuses more on God's forming man and woman as partners in the work of his garden.[34]

The verses about the four rivers (vv. 10–14) can be removed without disturbing the flow of the chapter—indeed, it makes the passage more even; and there is some unevenness about the references to the life-tree and the good-and-bad-knowledge tree. But there is no scholarly consensus on the way the chapters may have developed, and investigation into possibly earlier versions of the stories does not seem to make a significant contribution to understanding the chapters as we have them.

29. See Jacobsen, *Harps That Once*.
30. See Lambert and Millard, *Atraḫasis*.
31. See *ANET* 72–99 (esp. tablets I–II) with Speiser's comments, *Genesis*, 26–27.
32. See *ANET* 101–3.
33. See, e.g., Wenham, *Genesis 1–15*, 52–53.
34. Cf. Keel and Schroer, *Creation*, 117–22.

2:4b–7. The story begins in a way paralleling Gen. 1, with a background general reference to the process that will follow (v. 4b; cf. 1:1), then a more specific description of the unformed state of things before God acts (vv. 5–6; cf. 1:2), then God's first concrete act (v. 7; cf. 1:3). Whereas Gen. 1 was concerned with "the cosmic plan of creation," Gen. 2 is interested in the human being "as a cultivator of his environment and as a moral agent." And whereas Gen. 1 had a vertical perspective and had God as the constant subject of verbs denoting action and speech, in Gen. 2 the world and humanity are the subject of many of the verbs. In Gen. 1 God doesn't play dice with the universe; in Gen. 2 he does.[35]

Thus Gen. 2 moves (v. 4b) from talking about the beginning and about the heavens and the earth and about creating (1:1; 2:4a) to talking about the day or time and about earth and heavens and about making.[36] In this creation story "we are dealing in some sense with a history of creation from inside," as is suggested by the reversing of the order of the words to "the earth and the heavens."[37] Genesis now speaks of "Yahweh God." The MT and Tg camouflage the name Yahweh by providing it with the vowels of the word for "the Lord," to encourage readers to use that term instead, and other translations of Genesis replace it by the word for Lord in their languages, which obscures the point Genesis makes. The double title comes nineteen times in Gen. 2–3, almost half the occurrences in the entire First Testament; most of the others are in Chronicles. It combines the regular Hebrew term for God that appeared throughout the preceding chapter, *ʾĕlōhîm*, with the name of God, Yahweh, which will appear eleven times in the following chapter. If Gen. 2–3 itself had simply used the same Yahweh, one can imagine that people listening to the story might have wondered whether he was a different deity from the "God" of Gen. 1—especially if they knew that other peoples had creation stories that involved a number of gods. The double expression thus fulfills a midrashic function like that featured at many points within Gen. 1 by anticipating and answering that possible question about whether Yahweh is the God who created the whole heavens and earth of whom we have just read, or a different deity. It might also be no coincidence that Chronicles and Gen. 2–3 have this double expression in common. During the Second Temple period, Jews became less inclined to use the name Yahweh and more inclined to use the word "God" (as the book of Daniel, among others, shows), perhaps partly because the name might obscure the fact that the God of Israel was the God of the heavens and the earth, and in Chronicles the double expression safeguards the fact that Yahweh is the God of the heavens and the earth and the fact that the God of the heavens and the earth is Yahweh. In Gen.

35. Alter, *Art of Biblical Narrative*, 141, 142, 144 (referring to a saying of A. Einstein, for which see, e.g., Hermanns, *Einstein and the Poet*, 58).

36. Cf. M. Smith, *Priestly Vision*, 131–33.

37. Barth, *CD* 3.1:233, 235.

2–3, too, the double expression can both confirm that the creator who acts in Gen. 2–3 is the God of the heavens and the earth and confirm that the God of the heavens and the earth is Yahweh the God of Israel. The God of creation is the God of Israel; the God of Israel is the God of creation. The God who has a purpose for the whole cosmos is the God who entered into a relationship with Israel; the God who entered into a relationship with Israel is the God who has a purpose for the whole cosmos. "As *Elohim* is a name of power and justice, given unto God in the creation: so now *Iehovah* a name of mercy, is attributed unto God, the whole worke being finished, because therein his mercy appeared: or rather now after God had made his worke full and complete, he is also set forth in his full and complete titles."[38]

The garden story begins (2:5–6) by taking us back to the situation presupposed by 1:2, though it expresses things differently. Whereas Gen. 1 stood back and portrayed the big picture of the heavens and the earth, Gen. 2 stands close up and speaks not of the face of the deep (1:2) but of the face of the ground.[39] It imagines what it would have been like to position oneself on the earth, in open country (that is, land that has not been cultivated, which is all the land there is), when God has not yet furnished it with plants, people, and animals. "Bushes" (*śîaḥ*) are wilderness or desert shrubs (21:15) that are not human food unless someone is desperate (Job 30:4, 7) but would be a reasonable resource for goats and some other animals of the wild; the term might cover pasturage in general. "Plants" (*ʿēśeb*) could denote pasturage but also grains, the staple for human beings in the Middle East (see esp. Ps. 104:14);[40] in 1:29–30 the word covered both animal and human food. Genesis 2 describes the kind of land that could support animals and human beings. But there is nothing growing at the moment, because it hasn't rained yet, and anyway there are no farmers to channel the water or to manage the growth of anything that does sprout and to look after it; in the absence of such tending, the land will simply continue as open country. There is the potential for such growth, because a stream comes up from the earth's underground water resources, and it would be possible for a gardener to harness this resource and irrigate plants. What is needed is an *ʾādām* to serve the *ʾădāmâ*. The first significance in the word *ʾādām* lies here. The earth needs an earthling to exercise responsibility for it, to identify with it in a way appropriate to the similarity in their designations. The "divine mandate of the first account ('fill the earth and subdue it' 1:28) is unpacked in the purpose clause of the second ('to till it and keep it,' 2:15)."[41] Humanity's relationship to the ground is one of service—service of God and service of the ground, for whose sake humanity was created. "The

38. Willet, *Hexapla in Genesin & Exodum*, 21.
39. Cf. M. Smith, *Priestly Vision*, 133.
40. Cf. Cairus, "Grain and Rain."
41. Arnold, *Genesis*, 4.

purpose of human beings . . . is grounded (pardon the pun) in Earth."[42] Need drives Gen. 2 as it does not drive Gen. 1.[43] Thus "a graphic sense of 'earthiness'" pervades Gen. 2–3; these chapters were written "by someone for whom creation was not an abstraction."[44]

So Yahweh God "forms" a laborer (v. 7). The verb (*yāṣar*) is different from "make" and "create." It suggests the shaping of something by a potter or another craftsperson (e.g., Isa. 29:16; 30:14; 41:25; 44:9, 10, 12; 45:9). To judge from other references in the First Testament, "dirt" suggests frailty, fragility, and flimsiness (e.g., Job 10:9; 34:15).[45] It also suggests that the body was dark, not white![46] As well as being made for the sake of the *ʾădāmâ*, the *ʾādām* is made *from* the *ʾădāmâ*. In serving it, he serves not something alien but something to which he is materially related. Yahweh God then turns the body into a living person by breathing life into it. The expression *nišmat ḥayyâ* (living breath, breath of life, life-giving breath) comes only here, though 7:22 has "the breath of the spirit of life," and that passage indicates that this breath is possessed by the rest of the animate creation as well as by humanity. Likewise, the term for a living person, *nepeš ḥayyâ*, is the one used to describe the sea creatures, animals, and birds in 1:20 and 2:19. Breath, obviously enough, is the difference between an inanimate body and a live person; Gen. 2 uses this fact in picturing how the first person came into being. God will not need to breathe into each person who comes into existence (he doesn't even need to breathe into the first woman). One might think in terms of God's giving procreative power to humanity that conveys the capacity to generate a living person and not just a lifeless body (cf. Isa. 42:5), though Elihu notes that God can take back his breath or his spirit (*rûaḥ*; Job 34:14; cf. 32:8; 33:4; Ps. 104:29). And Yahweh does breathe into lifeless bodies again in Ezek. 37, "the most powerful commentary on Gen. 2⁷."[47] Genesis does not mention blood in connection with the making of the live human being, notwithstanding the Israelite awareness that blood is life (cf. Gen. 9:4–6), perhaps because the involvement of divine blood in creation is integral to other Middle Eastern creation stories;[48] conversely, these other Middle Eastern stories do not speak in terms of something like *nišmat ḥayyâ* being breathed into humanity,[49] nor does Genesis think of a human person as body plus soul, or body plus soul plus spirit.[50]

42. Swenson, "Earth Tells the Lessons of Cain," 33.
43. Reno, *Genesis*, 67.
44. Newsom, "Common Ground," 63.
45. Cf. Soden, "From the Dust."
46. Cf. De La Torre, *Genesis*, 42.
47. Barth, *CD* 3.1:249.
48. So Anthonioz, "Le sang est la vie."
49. See Noort, "'Was ist der Mensch?'"
50. So Josephus, *Ant.* 1.1.2.

2:8–9. Meanwhile the potter himself becomes a gardener.[51] Yahweh God's planting a garden or orchard is again the small-scale, local equivalent of the large-scale, cosmic action in Gen. 1:3–13, though making the orchard follows on shaping the human being, in the reverse of the order in Gen. 1. Both orders make the same point: there is an intrinsic relationship between the creation of humanity and the creation of the fruitful world, with humanity being created to look after the fruitful world. The orchard is located in Lush: I follow the Vg in translating the name *ʿēden* rather than transliterating the word on the assumption that Eden is simply a name (so the LXX). Even if one transliterates, the word's associations are significant, as is the case with the names Adam and Eve. Eden-things are delightful, even luxurious (2 Sam. 1:24; Ps. 36:8 [36:9]; Jer. 51:34; related words appear in Gen. 49:20; Neh. 9:25; Isa. 47:8; Lam. 4:5). Here the implication is that God's orchard is in a fertile, fruitful region. Perhaps it is fertile through being well watered in the way v. 6 describes, though v. 6 implies that at the moment it is by no means lush, so the name may be anticipatory. In terms of literal geography, the land's location to the east of author and audience suggests Mesopotamia, where two great rivers irrigate the land.[52] Yet the east, where the sun rises, is a symbolic place, the in-between space on the borders of earth and heaven, the place where Gilgamesh needs to go in his quest for immortality.[53] There is something to be said for facing east in prayer: we are seeking our ancient home.[54]

In this verdant or potentially verdant region, Yahweh God makes fruit trees grow (v. 9): the garden is indeed an orchard.[55] The trees are attractive to look at as well as bearing fruit that is good to eat. The garden recalls parks like that of the Assyrian king Sargon II, with its almond, quince, and plum trees.[56] Yahweh God puts there two further trees. The phrase tree of life/life-tree/living tree/life-giving tree parallels the phrase breath of life/life-breath/living breath/life-giving breath. But whereas the phrase "breath of life" comes only here, "tree of life" recurs as a metaphor in Prov. 3:18; 11:30; 13:12; 15:4: paying attention to insight, living faithfully, experiencing the fulfillment of your hopes, and having someone speak words of comfort when they are needed—all these are life-giving realities. Proverbs' metaphor becomes a theological symbol in Genesis. The tree of life has a broader background in Middle Eastern symbolism,[57] which is one factor in its being a "most salient, and problematic,

51. Cf. Hartley, *Genesis 1–17*, 161.

52. Görg ("Beobachtungen") suggests the recently discovered tell of the anciently flourishing kingdom of Qatna in Syria.

53. See Woods, "At the Edge of the World"; van Dyk, "In Search of Eden."

54. Basil the Great, "De Spiritu Sancto" (*NPNF*[2] 8:42); cf. Louth, *Genesis 1–11*, 54.

55. On the implications of the term *gan* (garden, orchard), see Meyers, "Food and the First Family," 146–51.

56. Van der Kooij, "Story of Paradise," 9–10.

57. Cf. Bauks, "Sacred Trees."

motif."[58] Apparently the fact that God has infused the human being with his breath does not mean he will simply live forever. Humanity was not created immortal.[59] The human being will need to eat the fruit of this sacramental tree in order to live on (cf. 3:22). The story again presupposes the empirical realities of human life. People do live for quite a while, but eventually they stop breathing and die. Here God's idea is that they can eat of the life-tree and thus be able to evade this dynamic. But at this point Genesis does not tell us anything more about the life-tree than that it is there in the middle of the garden. The information about the life-tree is a note addressed to the audience of the story. Genesis will not refer to it again until 3:22–24; the note here is a bit of background for the audience to keep in mind and to recall when we come to that point in the narrative.

Proverbs also refers to knowledge much more often than any other book in the First Testament (e.g., 1:4, 7, 22, 29), with the frequent implication that *da'at* covers acknowledgment or recognition in the way one lives, in living in light of the facts, as well as denoting intellectual understanding. And good and bad is a recurring antithesis in Proverbs (e.g., 11:27; 13:21; 14:22; 15:15; 17:20; 31:12).[60] A more telling reference to good and bad is the "remarkable inversion" of Genesis in 1 Kings 3:9: as king, Solomon needs to be able to discern between good and bad (see also Deut. 1:39).[61] While good and bad can be a moral antithesis, in Proverbs as in 1 Kings it commonly suggests an antithesis between what is wise and brings a good result and what it stupid and brings trouble.[62] The good-and-bad-knowledge tree, then, is a sacramental aid to making good decisions and avoiding bad decisions, a means of acquiring insight for life (cf. 3:6). It is food that enables people to grow up morally and pragmatically.

2:10–14. The paragraph about the river spells out the implications of v. 6, though it speaks in different terms.

Somewhere in Lush (v. 10) a river emerged from the ground in the manner of the Jordan in northern Israel, where it bursts out fully formed from the foothills of Hermon. It first irrigated the garden and then split into four rivers flowing into the rest of the world.

Pishon (vv. 11–12) appears only here. Havilah appears in contexts that suggest Egypt and Arabia (10:7, 29; 25:18; 1 Sam. 15:7), which might imply that Pishon refers to the Persian Gulf and/or the Red Sea, an area traditionally associated with gold and precious stones.

58. Lanfer, *Remembering Eden*, 33. Lanfer proceeds to survey the extensive reference to the tree of life beyond the Hebrew Bible itself.

59. On this question, see Schmid, "Loss of Immortality?"

60. See Forti, "Polarity of Wisdom"; Guillaume, "Demise of Lady Wisdom."

61. Cf. Barth, *CD* 2.1:433.

62. Even if "good and bad" may occasionally mean "everything" (2 Sam. 14:17 compared with 14:20), that understanding hardly fits this context (see Gen. 3:22; Kidner, *Genesis*, 63).

Gihon (v. 13) is the stream arising on the east side of Jerusalem and providing the city with its water, but Kush denotes Sudan, which suggests that Gihon would have to denote the Nile. Possibly the use of the apparent names Pishon and Gihon trades on their etymologies as "Springer" and "Burster" (there would not be much difference between the two).

Ḥiddeqel and Perat (v. 14) are the Tigris and the Euphrates, the two great Mesopotamian rivers. One way or another, then, the four rivers cover the world around Israel. "Suddenly we find ourselves in our historical and geographical world. . . . This strangely profound section strives without doubt to sketch the real geographical world."[63] It is a real place, even if we cannot locate it.[64]

2:15–18. After the excursus in vv. 10–14, Genesis returns to the main sequence of events to relate the fulfillment of the project initiated in vv. 4b–9: Yahweh God's aim is to have someone to serve the ground (v. 5), and he is setting him in a place with plentiful provision (v. 9).

Yahweh God now makes explicit (v. 15) that the human being will serve the garden by looking after it. The garden is not merely a place to enjoy, but a place to work. Supplementing the idea of "serving" (*ʿābad*) with the reference to "keeping" (*šāmar*) is slightly puzzling: will the garden need protection? The verb's appearing will turn out to be ironic in light of 3:24 and 4:9. In the broader context of the Torah, serving and keeping the sanctuary will be the responsibility of priests (e.g., Num. 3:7–8), and this commission to the man is one of several hints that might invite readers of Genesis to see the sanctuary as a kind of reestablishment of Lush Garden and to see the human beings as having a priestly role in the garden as itself a kind of sanctuary.[65] To go into the sanctuary, then, is to reenter Lush Garden, an especially welcome notion when life outside the sanctuary was discouraging. But in the immediate context, serving and keeping may suggest the awareness that there are two aspects to life on the farm—cultivating plants and caring for animals (cf. *šāmar* in 30:31).[66] The "work" will surely be a joy. We may have seen men "cultivating the land with such pleasure that it is a severe punishment for them to be called away from it to something else," even now when enjoyment of this work has been marred by humanity's disobedience. The audience is invited to think of it as it was designed, "when the gifts of

63. Von Rad, *Genesis*, 77. On the possible identities of the places, see further Jericke, *Die Ortsangaben im Buch Genesis*, 25–37.

64. Barth, *CD* 3.1:253.

65. Cf. Wenham, *Genesis 1–15*, 67; Stordalen, "Heaven on Earth—or Not?"; Hudson, "From Chaos to Cosmos"; Stager, "Jerusalem as Eden"; R. Hendel, "Other Edens"; Schachter, "Garden of Eden"; Walton, *Lost World of Adam and Eve*. Jubilees 3 assumes that the garden was a sanctuary (see van Ruiten, *Primaeval History Reinterpreted*, 85–89). In critique, see, e.g., Gordon, "Evensong in Eden," 18–21.

66. Meyers ("Food and the First Family," 148–49) suggests rather that keeping is what people will need to do to the fruit trees, which do not need working (cf. Neh. 2:8).

God's creation came forth in a joyful and abundant harvest with the help of man's effort. . . . What more impressive and wonderful spectacle than this?"[67]

The human being may eat the fruit from any of the orchard's trees (v. 16). It is the other side of his relationship with the garden; the provision parallels the gift of food in 1:29–30. Perhaps the life-tree is included, but nothing is said about it; perhaps the assumption is that the human being will not need to eat from it until death threatens.

The note about the good-and-bad-knowledge tree (v. 17) is also background to Gen. 3, but Yahweh God does explain something of its importance. This tree looks good, but it is lethally poisonous.[68] Over against the life-tree, "the tree of knowledge is the tree of death."[69] Yahweh God's words in v. 16 about the trees in general involved his "commanding," though they were more permissive or promissory than compulsory, like the imperatives in 1:22. The verb "command" might suggest that the emphasis in vv. 16–17 lies on the prohibition in v. 17. The prohibition is strange in light of the recognition in the First Testament elsewhere that knowing good and bad, and being able to determine the difference between them, is a key skill for life. It resembles God's later strange command that Abraham should sacrifice Isaac, even if it seems less scandalous. That command will explicitly be a test; this command implicitly is a test. It gives humanity the opportunity of obedience.[70] Perhaps passing the test would open up the possibility of eating from this tree.[71] One way or another, "the question of the prohibition is haunting."[72] The goodness of creation (Gen. 1) is not compromised by the presence of test or danger or threat or constraint. "One might wish for a garden without such dangerous trees. But that is not given to us."[73]

"At the time you eat from it" is more literally "on the day you eat of it" (cf. the LXX), though the human being will not actually die on the day he eats of it. The Vg has "whenever" (whereas the Vg was notably precise when the same time expression came in v. 4), perhaps inferring that we should not be too literal in understanding Yahweh God's words. Actually, they will not die "on the day" or "at the time" or "whenever." Adam will live for over eight hundred more years (5:3–5). Jubilees 4.29–30 neatly appeals to the fact that a thousand years are in God's sight just like a day (Ps. 90:4).[74] Symmachus has "You will become mortal" and Tg. Ps.-J. similarly has "You will become liable

67. Augustine, *Literal Meaning of Genesis*, 2:44–45.
68. Cf. Gunkel, *Genesis*, 10.
69. Bonhoeffer, *Creation and Fall; Temptation*, 59.
70. Cf. Tonstad, "Message of the Trees"; Wénin, "Le précepte d'Adonaï Dieu."
71. Cf. Mettinger, *Eden Narrative*.
72. M. Jacobs, *Gender, Power, and Persuasion*, 30.
73. Brueggemann, *Genesis*, 45.
74. Cf. Ron, "Book of Jubilees," 148–49.

to die" (i.e., liable to the death penalty). Given that humanity was not created immortal (otherwise the tree of life would have been unnecessary), the threat is not of mortality but of losing the possibility of enjoying and serving the garden on an ongoing basis rather than only for one's threescore years and ten; implicitly, it might thus be a threat of expulsion from the garden, where the life-tree was.[75] But perhaps Yahweh God does mean that the man will die "on the day" or "at the time" but will turn out to be more lenient than he threatens.[76] He is, after all, sovereign in relation to his own word: he can even change his curse into a blessing.[77] Arguably, there will be nothing surprising about the human disobedience (at least, for people who know ancient Near Eastern stories or know the story of Israel or know themselves). The surprise lies in the fact that death does not follow.[78] Yet there is also something surprising about a holy book that begins with a command that is immediately disobeyed and a God who fails to carry out a threat.[79]

The goodness of creation is compromised (v. 18) by the fact that the human being whom God has created is "on his own" (*ləbaddô*). Other passages where this expression occurs (e.g., 30:40; Exod. 12:16; Deut. 8:3) make clear that Yahweh God is not referring to the man's being lonely but to his being single-handed. By himself he cannot fulfill the task of serving the ground and looking after the garden. One would have thought that "the human is formed to be autonomous and functional. The completed being, however, reveals a deficit."[80] Only after creating one human being does Yahweh God articulate the awareness that making only one and putting him in the garden on his own will not work; Yahweh God's relationship with his world is interactive. The human being will need the appropriate help (*ʿēzer*). A king has a staff who are his help (Ezek. 12:14), who are thus subordinate to him. But usually "help" denotes someone strong and powerful who can help by getting one out of a mess; the term nearly always refers to Yahweh (e.g., Exod. 18:4; Deut. 33:7, 26, 29; and ten times in Psalms). Here, "equivalent to him" suggests a counterpart, something in between a subordinate and a superior. Wherein lies the help? Another human being would help the man serve and care for the garden.[81] If the first man just needed physical help on the farm,

75. Cf. Sarna, *Genesis*, 21.

76. See, e.g., the discussions in Gordon ("Ethics of Eden") and in J. Lim ("Did the Scholar[s] Get It Right?") with references to the earlier argument between Barr ("Is God a Liar?") and Moberly ("Did the Interpreters Get It Right?"). Yahweh's not imposing death on the first human couple is one of the ways in which Gen. 2–3 prefigures the story of Israel's disobedience at Sinai in Exod. 32 (Joosten, "Que s'est-il passé au jardin d'Eden?").

77. Zimmerli, *1. Mose 1–11*, 178.

78. Cf. Yamada, "What Does Manzanar Have to Do with Eden?," 111.

79. Dershowitz, *Genesis of Justice*, 30–31.

80. M. Jacobs, *Gender, Power, and Persuasion*, 35.

81. Cf. Ephrem, *Genesis*, 104. DeClaissé-Walford ("Genesis 2") suggests a much broader understanding.

however, then another man would do fine. The First Testament does hint at the idea that a man works out in the fields, while a woman works at home cooking, making clothes, and so on. Both roles are vital; neither is more important or superior to the other.[82] But one man and one woman won't be enough in the long term; there is another kind of help that the man will need.[83]

2:19–20. Whereas Gen. 1 implies that God plans his actions and systematically implements his plans, Gen. 2 portrays him acting more serendipitously and in a way that interacts with what human beings do. At first it might seem as if Yahweh God wonders if one of the animals would serve as a help to the man, as if his creative work involves experimenting[84] or as if he is playing the jokester or trickster.[85] But Genesis rather describes his action as designed to establish what the man will call the animals. Thus vv. 19–20 form another sidebar that raises suspense as we wonder what God will do about the issue raised in v. 18.[86] As is the case with its unexplained reference to the life-tree, Genesis leaves us for a moment with the recognition that the man needs help and then goes off in a different direction.

Yahweh God shapes the animals from the ground (v. 19), as he had so shaped the human being. Again, there is a superficial clash between the order of events in Gen. 2 and that in Gen. 1, where the animals are created first, but the story's point is the same. By inviting the human being to name the creatures, Yahweh God puts them under his authority; Gen. 2 once again reexpresses the point in Gen. 1. Genesis perhaps implies something about humanity's relationship with the animal world similar to its point about the garden. While naming the animals implies some authority in relation to them, naming may also imply a recognition of their individual nature and a degree of intimacy with them; they are not total strangers to humanity. Animals are vital helps in working the land, and their shared origin in being shaped from the ground, along with being "living beings" like the human being who has been inbreathed by God, might also have given plausibility to the idea that animals might suffice as help to the man. The verse thus continues to raise suspense, though perhaps it is significant that it refers to the animals of the wild and the birds, not to cattle.

Cattle likely do then feature as the object of the actual naming (v. 20): "animals" (*bəhēmâ*) often denotes livestock (e.g., 34:23; 36:6; 47:18). But the result of Yahweh God's involving the man in naming the animals is that the

82. See Meyers, "Gender Roles"; Meyers, *Discovering Eve*.

83. So, e.g., Augustine, *Literal Meaning of Genesis*, 2:73–75; Luther, *Genesis 1–5*, 115–19. But contrast Efthimiadis-Keith, "Genesis 2:18–25."

84. Zimmerli, *1. Mose 1–11*, 138; cf. Seebass, *Genesis*, 1:117.

85. Cf. Wurst, "'Beloved, Come Back to Me,'" 91.

86. Cf. Coats, *Genesis*, 53.

man himself recognizes that none of them will do as a help in the sense of a help equivalent to him.[87]

2:21–24. Yahweh God does not now do the obvious thing, which is to create another human being. His alternative procedure certifies the fact of oneness in the nature of man and woman (and of all who will be born from them)[88] and also explains the sense of oneness that human beings may have with one another over against animals and the particular sense that a man and a woman may have in relation to each other, as if they have found their other half. It undergirds that sense.

God acts (vv. 21–23) first as an anesthetist and surgeon and then as a builder or reconstructive surgeon. Then "God himself, like the father of the bride, leads the woman to the man."[89] And the man recognizes the woman as his own flesh and blood, as English puts it (cf. the similar phrases in 29:14; Judg. 9:2; 2 Sam. 5:1; 19:12–13 [19:13–14]). He does not name the woman in the way he names the animals (he will actually name her in 3:20). His declaration that she will be called woman is more a declaration of recognition and of her actual equivalence than an exercise of authority. It is neatly symbolized by the similarity of the words for man and woman, *ʾîš* and *ʾiššâ*.

The story of the woman's origin explains another odd fact about human life (v. 24). Genesis is not here laying down rules for marriage as an institution, though it presupposes marriage as an institution.[90] It is describing what happens rather than what should happen, though the latter follows.[91] Now marriage means a woman leaving her father and mother to join her husband. Occasionally it may mean moving a long way (see Gen. 24), but more often it simply means moving across the street. Both man and woman might go out from their parents to a little house of their own or to share with another couple within the extended family. Yet a man does not leave his parents in the sense that his wife leaves hers; the new couple forms a subset within the broader family to which he belongs. Nevertheless, the man does abandon (*ʿāzab*) his family. It is a strong verb (see, e.g., Ruth 1:16; 2:11; 1 Kings 19:20; Jer. 14:5; 49:11; and frequently in connection with Israel abandoning Yahweh). Abandoning means giving up one obligation and taking on another. Likewise, a man attaches himself to his wife in a way that replaces his attachment to his parents. Often "attach oneself" (*dābaq*; see, e.g., Ruth 1:14; 2 Sam. 20:2) also refers to relationships with Yahweh, as does "abandon."[92] It does not refer to

87. Whitekettle ("Oxen Can Plow") argues that it is humanlike intelligence that even the domestic animals lack but that the woman will have.

88. Cf. Ambrose, *Hexameron, Paradise, and Cain and Abel*, 327.

89. Von Rad, *Genesis*, 82; cf. Luther, *Genesis 1–5*, 134.

90. See the nuanced discussion in Batto, "Institution of Marriage."

91. For variants on this alternative, see Krueger, "Etiology or Obligation."

92. Warner ("'Therefore a Man Leaves His Father'") suggests that 2:24 explains the instinct to marry someone of another ethnic group.

the physical sexual union. And while the expression "one flesh" comes only here in the First Testament, other references to flesh (*bāśār*; e.g., Gen. 37:27; Neh. 5:5) do not suggest a reference to sex but to forming one family unit that replaces the one into which one was born. It is a strange phenomenon. After all, the man was born from his parents and he has formed one community with them through his life so far. But the origin of woman in being constructed out of man explains why this transfer of loyalty is natural. Whereas the man and the woman have been one flesh with their respective parents, now they become one flesh with each other. They become one new family unit, as if they have been born that way, because in a sense they had been, the man declares when he calls her "bones from my bones" and "flesh from my flesh" (cf. Gen. 29:14; Judg. 9:2; 2 Sam. 5:1; 19:12–13 [19:13–14]).

2:25. Possibly the assumption that v. 24 refers to sex (which is explicit in the Tg) has been encouraged by the reference to nakedness and shame in v. 25. But that reference also has other connotations.[93] Only occasionally does nakedness or shame have sexual associations. Being naked (*ʿārûm*) usually implies being poor and resourceless and therefore humiliated (e.g., Job 1:21; 22:6; 24:7, 10; Amos 2:16; Mic. 1:8). And shame may indicate that you thought you had resources but your resources turned out not to be trustworthy (Job 6:20). A particular reason for shame, then, is that you should have been trusting in God (e.g., Pss. 22:5 [22:6]; 25:2, 3, 20) but you failed to do so and put your trust elsewhere (e.g., Ezra 8:22; Jer. 2:36), and your stupidity is now exposed. Or in general, wrongdoing makes you ashamed (Ezra 9:6; Jer. 31:19). Such references to shame bring out the second of the two main connotations of shame itself. It is a term from relationships with other people, specifically the group to which one belongs and whose acceptance one needs. It is also a term for one's relationship with oneself; one needs a sense of self-acceptance. The first couple have nothing, but they don't feel shamed by the fact. They can trust in God. Humanity is designed to live in trust and dependence on God and not to feel there is anything wrong with that dependence or any reason to be ashamed of it. In contrast, "the essence of shame" lies in "discomfort at the complete exposure of one's creatureliness."[94]

Implications

Body and Soul, Man and Woman, Obligation and Freedom

Western thinking has commonly seen humanity as comprising a body and a soul that is semi-independent of the body. In Genesis, God formed a human being from the same stuff as the rest of the material world and breathed breath

93. See Magonet, "Themes of Genesis 2–3."
94. Biddle, "Genesis 3," 362; cf. also Snoeberger, "Nakedness and Coverings."

into him. It is the combination of person and breath that makes what the KJV calls "a living soul." This analysis applies to animals as well as human beings. The distinctiveness of humanity lies in the nature of the person rather than in its breath. So at the beginning the first human being did not comprise a body and a soul that was separate from the body. God did not shape a body out of matter and shape a soul out of something else. God shaped a person that combined what we might call a body and what we might call a personality or soul, but these two are aspects of the one person. There is no body without a personality/soul and no personality/soul without a body. Before God breathed in his breath, the whole person (body and personality/soul) was not yet alive; when the person stops breathing, the whole person (body and personality/soul) ceases to be alive. Once God has breathed in his breath, God relates to the living person as a whole (body and personality/soul); there is no relating to a person's personality/soul except as expressed in a body, and no relating to a body except as expressive of a personality/soul. And this whole person (body and personality/soul) was destined to experience eternal life; it is not conceivable how the body could experience eternal life separate from the personality/soul or how the personality/soul could experience eternal life without the body.

In its account of the origin of woman, Genesis confronts some common assumptions. The woman's creation as a help to the man does not imply that she is secondary in importance; together, both of them are secondary in importance to God's garden. It does not imply that she is subordinate to him; he does not have authority over her. She is not created to be a companion or soul-friend but a coworker. Man and woman are not so different that there is no possibility of mutual understanding between them; they have a common origin. Their origin explains the way a man and a woman set up a new home semi-independent of their parents, with a mutual commitment that rules out their parents continuing to have authority over them. Their becoming one flesh denotes not merely their sexual union but also their becoming a new proto-family, an insight that coheres with Paul's scandalized comment that sex with a prostitute means a man becomes one flesh with her (1 Cor. 6:16); it is not merely a physical union. It also coheres with his analogy between a man abandoning his parents to become one with his wife and believers in Jesus becoming part of his body, part of a new community in the church (Eph. 5:31). Paul is also inspired to draw some inferences from the order of the creation of the man and the woman (1 Cor. 11:2–16; 1 Tim. 2:8–15) that do not emerge from Genesis itself but were appropriate in the context that they address; Gen. 6:1–4 will show why it would be wise for the women not to tempt the angels.[95]

"The creature does not exist casually. It does not merely exist, but exists meaningfully. In its existence it realises a purpose and plan and order."[96] Hu-

95. See, e.g., Peerbolte, "Man, Woman, and the Angels."
96. Barth, *CD* 3.1:231.

manity was created to serve and look after the garden. "The meaning of human life is to be found in tilling the acres, and not so much in dwelling in a luxury garden."[97] If readers might be tempted to think that the verb *ʿābad* had lost the connotation of "serve" and simply meant "work" or "till," which would suggest an activity designed simply for the benefit of the workers, to enable them to profit from the soil, the pairing of the verb *ʿābad* with the verb *šāmar* ("keep/look after/care for/protect") would safeguard against that temptation. The work of the gardener was designed to enable the ground to find its own fulfillment in being productive—even though this productivity would also benefit the servants. So the relationship of human beings and garden involved a mutual symbiosis. Humanity was given no freedom to rape the earth.

Human beings are created with massive free will regarding how they live, but Genesis thinks about free will within a different framework from the one that has preoccupied modernity (and often antiquity, actually).[98]

> Who could adequately admire the generosity of the common Lord of all? With what great kindness he regales the creature who has not yet anything to show for himself? I mean, he did not confine to half the garden the enjoyment he permitted, nor bid him abstain from most things and retain the enjoyment of the remainder. Instead, he wanted him to partake of everything in the garden and ordered him to abstain from the one tree only, showing through these things he had no other purpose in his actions than that he should be able to recognize the one responsible for such acts of kindness.[99]

Humanity is free in most connections but limited in one connection. Yet the constraint on that freedom is not one that humanity is forced to accept. Within the framework of modernity's understanding of free will, "human beings have been given freedom enough to destroy themselves."[100] The good-and-bad-knowledge tree was the free-will tree. To put it another way, God is in the permission business. Even the command to hold back from the one tree is a kind of permission, to hold back from something bad and hold to God's own will. It is the permission or freedom to be faithful to God that is restored through Jesus's dying for us and through the gift of the Holy Spirit. But the man and the woman prefer to give themselves another kind of permission and freedom, a permission to renounce the grace of God. Their use of their free will tricks them into servitude.[101]

97. Becking, "Signs from the Garden," 26.

98. See Visotzky, "Will and Grace."

99. Chrysostom, *Homilies on Genesis 1–17*, 187–88; cf. Willet, *Hexapla in Genesin & Exodum*, 26.

100. Fretheim, "Genesis," 356.

101. Barth, *CD* 2.2:593–94.

3

How Things Went Wrong

(3:1–24)

Overview

In the second act of the story told in Gen. 2:4b–3:24, there is a main question or problem: how did the man and the woman end up outside the garden that they were created to serve? The answer is that one of God's creatures asserts itself, and they yield to it instead of asserting authority over it.[1] They eat from the forbidden tree and lose the right to eat from the other tree. And God declares consequences that will naturally follow and consequences that he will cause to follow. The end of the story makes explicit for the listeners where it was going from the beginning. In this chapter there are no logistical problems to be solved on the way, as there were in Gen. 2, which reflects how Gen. 3 is not a complete story but simply the second half of Gen. 2:4b–3:24 in which everything goes downhill. The MT takes the edge off the story's toughness by locating the end of the unit after 3:21 (with only a paragraph break, a setumah, at 3:24). The story thus ends with grace and mercy. But the motifs of vv. 22–24 (good-and-bad-knowledge, life-tree, garden) are motifs from 2:4b–3:21 and themes that need closing off, so 2:4b–3:24 has to be allowed its solemn ending. It will be 4:25–26 that eventually closes the story of beginnings on a more hopeful note.

Translation

> [1]Now the snake was shrewder than any creature of the open country that Yahweh God had made. It said to the woman, "God really said,[2] 'You will

1. Cf. Keil and Delitzsch, *Pentateuch*, 93–94.

2. The LXX and Vg take the double conjunction *ʾap kî* to mean "Why?" English versions generally have something like "Did God really say?" But there is no philological basis for

not eat from any tree in the garden?!'" **2**The woman said to the snake,
"We may eat from the fruit of the trees in the garden, **3**but from the fruit
of the tree that's in the middle of the garden, God said, 'You will not eat
from it and you will not touch it, so that you don't die.'" **4**The snake said
to the woman, "You will not 'definitely die.'"[3] **5**Rather, he knows,[4] God
does, that at the time you eat from it, your eyes will open,[5] and you'll
become like God,[6] knowing good and bad."

6The woman saw that the tree was good to eat and that it was an ob-
ject of longing to the eyes, and the tree was desirable for conveying wis-
dom.[7] So she got some of its fruit and ate, and also gave some to her
man with her,[8] and he ate. **7**The eyes of the two of them opened and they
knew that they were naked, so they sewed fig leaves together and made
themselves loincloths.

8They heard the sound of Yahweh God walking about[9] in the garden
toward[10] the breezy time of the day,[11] so the man and his woman hid
from the face of Yahweh God among the trees in the garden. **9**Yahweh
God called to the man and said to him, "Where are you?"[12] **10**He said,
"I heard the sound of you in the garden, and I was afraid because I was
naked, so I hid." **11**He said, "Who told you that you were naked? Have
you eaten from the tree that I ordered you not to eat from?" **12**The man

---

understanding the expression interrogatively; 4QGen[k] prefixes it with the interrogative *h* to produce this understanding. Speiser (*Genesis*, 21, 23) renders "even though," comparing the use of *gam kî*, but this leaves a harsh ellipsis at the end of the verse. I follow Tyndale, who has "Ah syr [surely] that God hath said," which one could indeed then see as implicitly interrogative.

3. The snake picks up Yahweh God's use of the idiom that involves combining an infinitive and cognate finite verb (see the translation note to 2:16). When this idiom is negatived, the word order would usually be "Definitely you will not die." Here the snake puts the negative first. But the translation "You will not definitely die" would sound more equivocal than the snake surely intends. More likely the snake puts the negative first "to concentrate the emphasis on the neg[ative] part[icle] rather than on the verbal idea" (Skinner, *Genesis*, 74–75) and thus to negative the words as Yahweh God uttered them.

4. The participle coming first indicates some emphasis (*TTH* 135.4).

5. The waw-consecutive follows on the infinitival expression, "at the time of your eating from it." The LXX, Vg translate the verb as passive "will be opened," but the form is niphal, not pual. Niphal commonly functions as an intransitive equivalent to qal.

6. The Tg assumes that the snake means "like gods"—i.e., lower supernatural beings. Cf. Soggin, "'You Will Be like God.'"

7. "Desirable to look at" (LXX, cf. Vg) seems an undertranslation of *śākal* hiphil in the context.

8. The Vg omits "with her," which encourages readers to excuse the man of any responsibility for what is happening (see Parker, "Blaming Eve Alone").

9. The hitpael of *hālak* suggests he was not merely walking (see *IBHS* 26.1.2).

10. For this use of *l*, see BDB 516–17.

11. Literally, "the wind of the day." For alternative understandings, see Niehaus, "In the Wind of the Storm"; Grundke, "Tempest in a Teapot?"; Stuart, "'Cool of the Day.'"

12. Targums Neof. and Ps.-J. have substantial additions to exclude the idea that Yahweh God does not know where the man and the woman are.

said, "The woman you put with me—she gave to me[13] from the tree, and I ate." **13**Yahweh God said to the woman, "What is this that you've done?" The woman said, "The snake—it deceived me,[14] and I ate."

14Yahweh God said to the snake, "Because you've done this:

> You're cursed, more than[15] every animal,
> and more than every creature of the open country.
> On your stomach you'll go and dirt you'll eat,
> all the days of your life.
> **15**Enmity I will set in place
> between you and the woman,
> And between your offspring
> and her offspring.
> He'll strike[16] you on the head,
> you'll strike him on the heel."

16To the woman he said,

> "I will make very great[17] your pain in connection with pregnancy;[18]
> in painfulness you will give birth to children.[19]
> Toward your man will be your desire,
> but he—he will rule over you."

17To Adam he said, "Because you listened to the voice of your woman and ate from the tree that I ordered you, 'You will not eat from it':

> The ground is cursed because of you;[20]
> in pain you will eat from it
> all the days of your life.

13. "Gave" and "put" are both forms of *nātan*; "the repeated verb" conveys the way the man "passes the buck" both to the woman and to God (Alter, *Genesis*, 13).

14. Aq "led me on/induced me" is a more accurate description than the verb the woman uses.

15. The LXX has "away from," a more usual meaning for *min*, but "cursed away from" is harsh in Hebrew as in English, and the sequence of references to a curse (3:14, 17; 4:11) makes better sense on the assumption that *min* means "above" (cf. the Vg's "among").

16. The verb *šûp* comes only in this verse and in Job 9:17; Ps. 139:11. In postbiblical Hebrew it means smooth/polish/rub, which doesn't fit (though cf. Aq). But BH also has a verb *šā'ap*, of which *šûp* looks like a by-form; or rather, BH has two verbs *šā'ap*, one meaning crush, the other pant after (cf. the LXX). Possibly the first occurrence here is the first verb, and the latter one the second (cf. the Vg, which has "crush" and "lie in wait"). The Vg's "she will crush" encouraged the application of the colon to Mary, but the pronoun is the masculine *hû'* (cf. LXX): thus Vermigli (*In Primum Librum Mosis*, on the verse) notes that the Latin should read *ipsum* not *ipsa*.

17. While the verb *rābâ* (hiphil) could signify "make greater/increase," an intensifying of something that already exists (cf. e.g., NRSV), in the context it more likely denotes "make great" starting from scratch (cf. NIV).

18. Literally, "your pain and your pregnancy." Novick ("Pain and Production in Eden") derives *'iṣṣābôn* from *'āṣab* II and renders, "I will greatly lengthen your forming/gestation."

19. "Apposition . . . enhances the similarity between two clauses" (DG 147a).

20. The LXX, Vg, have "in your work," implying *b'bwdk* for *b'bwrk*.

18Thorn and thistle it will grow for you,
 but you will eat the plants of the open country.
19By the sweat of your face
 you will eat bread,
Until you go back to the ground,
 because you were gotten from it.
Because you were dirt,
 and you will go back to dirt."

20The man named his woman Ḥavvah, because she became the mother of every living person.[21] 21And Yahweh God made for Adam and his woman leather[22] coats, and clothed them.

22But Yahweh God said, "Here, the man has become like one of us in knowing good and bad.[23] So now, so that he can't put out his hand and also get from the life-tree and eat, and live through the ages. . . ."[24] 23So Yahweh God sent him off from Lush Garden to serve the ground from which he was made. 24Yahweh God drove the man out and made the sphinxes dwell[25] on the east of Lush Garden, with a swordlike flame whirling, to keep the way to the life-tree.

Interpretation

Although Gen. 2 may have seemed complete enough in some ways, listeners will have known that it left many ends untied. Why don't we now live in that lush garden? How did tending the ground turn out to be so hard? Whatever happened to the good-and-bad-knowledge tree? What was the life-tree about, and how did humanity apparently lose access to it? What happened to human authority over the animal creation? Why did the relationship between a man and a woman become fraught, even though the one was created from the other? Why did relationships between married couples and their parents become fraught? How did we come to be ashamed of our naked dependence on God and to hide from God? This complex story offers insight on those questions, without exactly answering them all.

21. *Ḥay*. Whereas some words with which the text links names are similar in spelling but are etymologically unrelated, in this case the name and the word, while spelled differently, are etymologically related (see BDB).

22. A homonym of the root of the word for leather, *ʿwr*, also generates words referring to blindness, which is apposite for people who have just gained a sad form of sight (cf. Schneider and Seelenfreund, "Kotnot Or").

23. Targum Onq. has "become unique, from it [the tree] knowing good and bad" (see Luc, "Like One of Us?"); Tg. Ps.-J. and Tg. Neof. are similar.

24. Literally, "to the age."

25. For *wayyaškēn* Tg. Neof. and Tg. Ps.-J. may imply the interesting reading *wayyiškōn*, suggesting that Yahweh now settled east of the garden; see R. Eichler, "When God Abandoned the Garden of Eden."

The chapter thus continues to describe familiar human realities—temptation that issues from the created world, the ease of yielding to it, the ease of mistrusting God's goodwill,[26] the shame of wrongdoing, the inclination to hide from God, the inclination to blame, the enmity between snake and human beings, the pain of parenthood, the tension built into marriage, the toughness of agriculture, the impossibility of evading death. And for the most part it describes them in regular prose, like most of Gen. 2, but its horrifying denouement in Yahweh God's words in vv. 14–19 manifests rhythm and some parallelism. In coming to a climax with some verse, it again parallels Gen. 2, though it does so in a grievous way, not least because it reverses the man's earlier joyful poetic exclamation (contrast 3:16 with 2:23).

Genesis 3 also continues to portray events in a way that contrasts with the portrayal of God's acts in the rest of the Scriptures and in regular human experience: it speaks of a talking snake, of a tree that opened eyes, of God out for an evening walk in his garden, of God asking questions as if he doesn't know the answers, of a banishing from God's garden, and of sphinxes and a flaming sword. Genesis continues to narrate a historical parable. It tells of a once-for-all occasion at the beginning of human history, when humanity chose to disobey God and thereby ruined things for all humanity, but it tells this historical story in a figurative way (see further the introductory comments on 2:4b–25 above).

Genesis 3 has a further feature. Although it responds to most of the questions raised in Gen. 2, it also raises questions that it does not answer: it declines to tie up its own loose ends. Indeed, in this chapter "a sea of questions arises."[27] For how long were the couple happy and untempted in the garden? Why does the snake want to use its shrewdness in the way it does? Why did Yahweh God let it operate the way it does? Why does it approach the woman rather than the man? How does the woman know the answer to its question since she was not there when Yahweh God issued his prohibition? Why does she add "touch" to Yahweh God's injunction—did it come from the man or is it her idea? Is she properly playing it safe or improperly adding to Yahweh God's word? Is she confused about which tree they are not to eat from, given that it was the life-tree that was directly described as "in the middle of the garden" (though the phrase may also have applied to the good-and-bad-knowledge tree)? What is the man doing while the snake is having its conversation with the woman? Why is the man silent? Does the snake tell the truth when it contradicts God about their not dying and when it says they will become like God/gods through eating of the forbidden tree? Is the woman correct when she says that the snake deceived her? Why does Yahweh God call to the man rather than the woman? When Yahweh God asks his questions, does he know

26. Krüger ("Sündenfall?," 95) sees a failure of trust as the original sin in Gen. 3.
27. Luther, *Genesis 1–5*, 144.

the answers to them? What is the significance of Yahweh God's imposing pain on the man and the woman and not implementing the threat that when they eat from the tree they will die? It is possible to suggest plausible answers to some of these questions, but their overall effect is to leave as much mystery as the mystery about human experience from which Gen. 2–3 begins.

The story unfolds as follows:

A conversation between the snake and the woman, and the consequences (3:1–7)

A conversation between Yahweh God and the couple (3:8–13)

Yahweh God's declarations issuing from the conversation (3:14–19)

A series of actions that follow—naming, clothing, banishing, guarding (3:20–24)

3:1–7. It's easy enough to see that snakes are shrewd (*ʿārûm*); they don't look spectacularly threatening like lions, but they can lie in wait and get people, with fatal results. In itself, shrewdness is not a negative quality (e.g., Prov. 14:8, 15, 18); it denotes the capacity to make sensible decisions that will work out well and to get people to do what you want them to do. It is not incompatible with honesty and submission to Yahweh (cf. the context of comments on shrewdness in Prov. 1:4; 8:5, 12). But it is a more ambiguous word than *ḥākām*, the word usually translated "wise," and in this context it has the advantage that it makes for a paronomasia with the word for naked in the previous verse (*ʿărûmîm*, in the plural).[28] The snake is a bare(faced) liar,[29] a trickster.[30] Its being *ʿārûm* will bring an end to the couple's feeling comfortable about being *ʿărûmîm*. Other creatures that Yahweh God made are more obviously dangerous. But the snake is clever and devious in a way that the other creatures are not—though that may not be saying much.[31] Its shrewdness finds expression in attributing negative motivations to Yahweh God. Does it also lie in approaching the woman? She was not there when Yahweh God gave the man the instructions about the trees, which the snake is going to twist in more than one way.

Yet if you were seeking a symbol for shrewdness, would it be the snake that first came to mind? In Prov. 30:24–28 it is the ant, the hyrax, the locust, and the lizard that epitomize wisdom or cleverness. Conversely, if you were thinking about the snake and what it might symbolize, would it be shrewdness that first came to mind? Elsewhere it is the snake's frightening capacity to bite and poison and kill (e.g., Exod. 4:3; Num. 21:6–9; Pss. 58:4 [5]; 140:3

28. Cf. Ron, "Wordplay."
29. Dennison, "Eschatological Reversal."
30. Ollenburger, "Creation and Peace," 152.
31. Cf. Ephrem, *Genesis*, 107.

[4]; Isa. 14:29). But the First Testament also hints that Israel recognized a link between a snake and the traditional religion of the land (see 2 Kings 18:1–4); a number of snake figurines have shown up in archaeological sites in Israel.[32] The snake can be a symbol of fertility and a symbol of healing. One or two passages suggest a link between a snake and a supernatural power of evil that is resistant to God (Job 26:13; Isa. 27:1; cf. Rev. 12:9; 20:2); even if there was no conflict with such forces at the background of creation, creation did issue in conflict.[33] Another paronomasia links the snake (*nāḥāš*) with divination (*naḥaš*).[34] Outside the Scriptures, in the Gilgamesh story (tablet XI)[35] a snake steals the plant that could have restored Gilgamesh's youth, and in modern economic thinking the snake might suggest the "potential, predatory capabilities of humans" as these are "captured by the abstraction 'economic man.'"[36] These different possibilities are bewildering. Perhaps the extensive symbolic and mythic background to the snake outside Gen. 3 draws attention to the "demythologizing" that takes place here, where the snake is simply one of the creatures that Yahweh God made.[37]

The story evidently doesn't expect the woman to be fazed by a snake that talks (Gen. 3:2–3), any more than Balaam was fazed by a donkey that talked (Num. 22:21–35).[38] And evidently the snake can assume that the woman knows about Yahweh God issuing a prohibition in connection with the trees and knows it applies to her as well as to the man. But we have noted that the question of how she was supposed to know (had the man told her, or had Yahweh God?) is only one of the questions raised by her conversation with the snake, along with whether she is confused about which tree is which, and whence comes the additional requirement that they are not to touch the tree in question.[39] Leaving much unclear points out the story's tragic as well as willful aspects and invites restraint in our passing judgment on the woman and the man. Everything was so clear, except that it wasn't.

Further (vv. 4–5), it is significant that the woman doesn't quote Yahweh God's actual words, "You will definitely die," whereas the snake does quote those words, in order to deny them, and also takes up Yahweh God's reference to "the time you eat from it." Genesis doesn't say that the snake "tempts" the woman. Indeed, if "tempt" means "try to get someone to do the wrong thing," Hebrew does not have a word meaning "tempt": while *nāsâ* and the related

32. See, e.g., Wurst, "'Beloved, Come Back to Me,'" 95–96.

33. Cf. Ramantswana, "Conflicts at Creation."

34. D. Smith, "Divining Snake."

35. See *ANET* 96.

36. So Wagner-Tsukamoto, "Paradise Story," 163.

37. Sarna, *Genesis*, 24.

38. Howard ("Animal Speech") compares these two stories.

39. Genesis Rabbah 19.3 notes that the woman's addition goes against Prov. 30:6 (cf. Rashi, *Brʾšyt*, 31). Further, as she adds on, the snake takes away; between them they contravene both warnings in Deut. 4:2 (de Villiers, "Sin, Suffering, Sagacity," 8).

noun *massâ* can be translated "tempt," they then refer to humanity testing God or God testing humanity. The snake does not "tempt" the woman in the sense of suggesting something she might do (contrast Satan's "tempting" of Jesus). Nor does it tell a lie when it declares that eating from the good-and-bad-knowledge tree will give them a godlike capacity and cause their eyes to open; here the opening of eyes refers to the capacity to see things that are otherwise invisible (cf. Num. 22:31; 2 Kings 6:17). But the snake does deceive the woman, by implicitly questioning God's motives for his prohibition and by contradicting what he had said about the further consequences of eating from the tree (thus 1 Tim. 2:14 rightly refers to Eve's being "deceived"). But the snake leaves the woman to work out what to do in response to its contradiction and its slur. And therein lies its shrewdness. The snake's speech is an invitation into absurdity, it is the original piece of "bad theology," and it is also "the establishment of ethics."[40] Its beguiling involves questioning the meaning of a command that was quite clear. It is typical that our resistance to God's command works in this way.[41] Hermeneutics is a wonderful art. One might thus think that the temptation should have been rather easy to resist; it might seem a temptation that had been reduced in force in the way that Yahweh later placed constraints around the testing of Job (and cf. 1 Cor. 10:13).[42] But the snake turns out to be more powerful than God.[43]

In a sense, the woman's logic (v. 6) can hardly be faulted. There is nothing wrong with things being good to eat and good to look at or good for conveying wisdom; that last description of the tree fits the idea that good-and-bad-knowledge signifies the capacity to decide between what is good and bad morally and its effects. The verb "convey wisdom" (*śākal*) occurs almost exclusively in the hiphil, both with the hiphil's more common causative meaning ("make wise") and with the rarer declarative meaning ("show wisdom"); the latter meaning spills over into the idea of being successful through the exercise of wisdom (see, e.g., Prov. 1:3; 16:20, 22; 21:11, 12, 16). It is a fine way of paraphrasing the idea of good-and-bad-knowledge. The trouble is that the snake "has already made a deadly attack on the artlessness of obedience,"[44] for "very dangerous is the temptation, when it is suggested to us, that God is not to be obeyed, except so far as the reason of his command is apparent."[45] The next puzzle is aroused by the fact that apparently the man has been there "with her" through her conversation with the snake. It was already implied when the snake addressed the woman but used the plural when it said "you." "It's not good for the woman to be alone" any more than for the man to be

40. Barth, *CD* 4.1:411, 420, 449.
41. Barth, *CD* 2.2:670.
42. So Vermigli, *In Primum Librum Mosis*, on 4:1 (cf. J. Thompson, *Genesis 1–11*, 116).
43. M. Jacobs, *Gender, Power, and Persuasion*, 57–58.
44. Von Rad, *Genesis*, 85.
45. Calvin, *Genesis*, 1:147–48.

alone, but effectively she is alone; she needed help, too, and she didn't get it.[46] How does the man come simply to accede to the woman's suggestion? "He simply fell into line."[47] She doesn't need to tempt or deceive or beguile him.[48] "Great was the man's indifference, too."[49] So the man and the woman continue to stand together "as one flesh."[50] Both of them eat, and both of them have the experience that follows. Genesis does not fault either more than the other.

Through the eating, their eyes open (v. 7a), though what they see falls short of the snake's promise. They see something visible that they have missed or whose significance they have missed, rather than something that is invisible and life transforming in a positive way. They become self-conscious and thus self-centered.[51] Yahweh God will later comment that they now do know good and bad, though the idea that knowing they are naked constitutes this knowledge seems not to fit. More likely it was the act of eating the fruit that constituted and thus conveyed the knowledge. In effect, God had told them what counted as good and bad, but in eating from the tree they have made up their own minds about the question and thus asserted their knowledge. They had been challenged to trust God for that knowledge, and they declined to do so.

They now stand exposed before Yahweh God (v. 7b) and so try to do something about it. There would be some poetic appropriateness if the fig tree had been the good-and-bad-knowledge tree from which they ate, so that it is from this same tree that they now devise their makeshift covering (cf. b. Sanh. 70b).[52] The fig tree does produce the largest leaves of the common fruit trees in Israel,[53] though grapevine leaves are almost as big. But maybe more plausible is the inference that making clothes from fig leaves was a pathetic project for people who were hoping to become wise.[54]

3:8–13. "After this transgression, the reader is prepared for swift and terrible annihilation of the human couple." Instead, they hear the sound of Yahweh God walking about in the garden, and subsequently they hear his voice

46. Olson, "Untying the Knot?," 78.

47. Westermann, *Genesis 1–11*, 250. Genesis Rabbah 19.3, 5 speculates that the man and the woman had made love, and he was now sleeping it off, and that the woman shared the fruit with the man because she knew she was going to die and didn't want him to live on and marry someone else.

48. Cf. Oecolampadius, *Genesis*, 166–67.

49. Chrysostom, *Homilies on Genesis 1–17*, 215.

50. Cf. Fretheim, "Genesis," 361.

51. Cf. Newsom, "Common Ground," 69.

52. The idea that it was an apple may derive from the fact that the Latin for apple is *malum*, which in the Vg is also the word for a bad thing in 2:9, 17; 3:5, 22. I have argued elsewhere that it was the apricot: see Goldingay, *After Eating the Apricot*, 45.

53. Cf. Qimchi, *Genesis*, on the verse.

54. Cf. Lambden, "From Fig Leaves to Fingernails," 76.

calling to them.[55] "The anthropomorphism of the scene is again enormous."[56] Given that Genesis gives no hint about how much time has elapsed between Yahweh God's bringing the woman to the man and the events just described, we do not know whether the couple has had a time of bliss with each other and with God.[57] And we do not know whether Yahweh God is in the habit of taking a walk in the garden as the cool of late afternoon arrives and whether he is looking to meet with the man and the woman, though the verb "walk about" implies that he isn't simply out looking for them. All we know is that God goes for a walk on this occasion, and the man and the woman know they need to hide. Far from gaining wisdom, they have gained stupidity, shown by thinking that they can hide from God.[58] Perhaps Genesis implies that it is the sound of the breeze that suggests the presence of Yahweh God—in which case their fear of it anticipates Lev. 26:36.[59] But the sound (*qôl*) of someone walking suggests the sound of footsteps (cf. 1 Kings 14:6). Yahweh God's making his footsteps audible could be a gesture of grace, an invitation to come and talk.[60]

Perhaps God's calling out to the man (v. 9), like a father or mother looking for one of their children, implies that the man is in some way responsible for the couple. If so, the man's remarkable incompetence during the event described in vv. 1–7 gives him further reason for hiding. And Yahweh God might call out "Where are you" because he doesn't know or because he wants to give the man the chance to emerge voluntarily. "The words 'Where are you?' are words of the Law," though they are also spoken "affectionately."[61] Yahweh God wants to "engage in conversation with him so that he not be too bewildered to repent."[62] Declarations about the all-knowing God (e.g., 1 Sam. 2:3; 1 John 3:2) are like commentaries on the "dark and menacing text" of Gen. 3:8–9, where the man and the woman think they can hide from God but find that they cannot. There is a strange comfort in the fact that God does not let us fall out of his knowledge and his thoughts even when we are wayward.[63]

Nor do we know whether the man has spotted the illogic (v. 10) in still describing himself as naked even though they have covered themselves up a bit. At least he perceives something: he perceives that he has reason to be afraid of Yahweh God. The reason for his fear is not really that he is naked. If anything, it is because he is not naked, and his covering himself has issued from his ignoring the one limitation Yahweh God has placed on him.

55. Arnold, *Genesis*, 66.

56. Seebass, *Genesis*, 1:122.

57. Jubilees 3.17 provides the answer: seven years. See further the discussion in Calvin, *Genesis*, 1:156–57.

58. Cf. Luther, *Genesis 1–5*, 172.

59. So Luther, *Genesis 1–5*, 169–71.

60. Cf. Ephrem, *Genesis*, 115.

61. Luther, *Genesis 1–5*, 173, 186.

62. Rashi, *Brʾšyt*, 34, comparing Gen. 4:7; Num. 22:9.

63. Barth, *CD* 2.1:554.

Again, we do not know whether Yahweh God's further request for information (v. 11) indicates that he doesn't know the answer to his question or is again trying to draw the man out, but it's beginning to look more like the former, which fits with other passages in the Scriptures that portray Yahweh as not knowing things (Gen. 22 is a significant example). Presumably, God could choose to know the answers to his questions, but holding back from knowing could make for a more genuine relationship with human beings. The alternative "does he not know or is he trying to bring us out" then becomes false.

Before answering the question, the man makes his excuses (v. 12), which involve a denial of the responsibility that Yahweh God has implied and a preemptive attempt to transfer blame to the woman and to Yahweh God himself. It is quite a lot to achieve in nine words. Only in the last single word of his reply, "and I ate," does the man answer the question. It anticipates David's two-word (in Hebrew) response to Nathan, "I have done wrong in relation to Yahweh" (2 Sam. 12:13). Both responses constitute admissions of wrongdoing but not admissions that constitute repentance, to judge from the way the man is more focused on his excuses,[64] and the way David will continue as an unchanged man, and the way we are not told that either of the wrongdoers finds forgiveness, though they do find mercy.[65]

So Yahweh God turns to the woman (v. 13) and addresses to her a question that looks more clearly rhetorical yet meets with a similar response: first deny responsibility, then push the blame somewhere else (though she does hold back from pointing out that it was Yahweh God who made the snake so clever), then end up the same as the man did.

3:14–19. Yahweh reverses the order of his responses in light of the answers he has received: first the snake, then the woman, then the man. A transition to poetry marks the gravity of Yahweh God's words; "the curses . . . are the narrator's main concern."[66] At each point Yahweh God declares that life is now going to be the way the people listening to the story experience it, in relation to the animate world, in relation to being a woman, and in relation to being a man. The negative aspects to life that Yahweh God will describe are not the way things were meant to be, but they are the way they now will be. Yahweh speaks both of how things will be, without indicating how they will come about (vv. 14, 16b, 17–19), and of how he himself will take action to make things happen (vv. 15, 16a). There is a natural process involved by which the creatures' actions produce their fruit and also a divine intention involved by which Yahweh's personal will is put into effect.

64. Cf. Ephrem's comments (*Genesis*, 114–15) on the couple's declining to repent.

65. Some translations have Yahweh "forgiving" David, but the word is not one of the usual words for "forgive"; it means something like the enigmatic "Yahweh has made your wrongdoing pass on."

66. Gunkel, *Genesis*, 20.

The snake (v. 14) is given no opportunity to make his excuses ("Well, you created me this way, and wasn't it a good idea for me to test their commitment, as you will agree to the testing of Job's?"). The snake alone "is summarily sentenced without interrogation—a token of God's withering disdain"; the snake is impotent and insignificant.[67] First, Yahweh God introduces the word "curse," the terrible antithesis to the word "blessing" (1:22, 28; 2:3) that will rival it through Gen. 1–12 and beyond. It is not exactly the opposite of blessing. It does not merely mean "make fruitless" as "bless" means "make fruitful." Its negative implications are broader. The snake will just crawl and eat dirt. The one who was *ʿārûm* (shrewd) becomes the one who is *ʾārûr* (cursed).[68] In effect, indeed, "more shrewd than any creature of the open country" gives way to "more cursed than any creature of the open country" (cf. Gen. Rab. 19.2). There need be no implication that the rest of the animal world is cursed; the snake is cursed in a way that other animals are not. And there need be no implication that Genesis assumes that until this moment snakes had legs and did not seem to eat dirt, nor that it thinks they literally eat dirt. The comment resembles some of the "therefores" relating to names, which imply "so it's appropriate that it's called. . ." (e.g., 19:22; 25:30; 31:48; 33:17). To put it another way, originally there was nothing wrong with the snake's manner of movement, but now its slither is "ignominious" and the sign of being cursed.[69]

Further, the snake will appropriately live in ongoing enmity with humanity (v. 15). Yahweh God starts with the woman herself, then moves to her offspring—in other words, to all humanity. The enmity will express itself in a logical way. On one hand, the woman's offspring will strike at the head of the snake, and on the other, the snake will strike at the heel of the offspring. And "neither wishes to wound, but to kill."[70] Irenaeus saw Yahweh God's reference to the woman's offspring's hitting the snake on the head as fulfilled in Jesus's victory over Satan,[71] and later v. 15 came to be described as the Protevangelium, the first gospel preaching.[72] But there is no indication in Genesis that Yahweh God's words are a promise of victory; they are rather a warning of an ongoing conflict. Targums Neof. and Ps.-J. rather gloss the warning with a promise and a threat: on one hand, people who keep the Torah will win the victory over the snake; on the other, people who do not do so will be struck down by it. While v. 15 speaks literally about humanity's relationship with snakes, it is also suggestive metaphorically. The woman has opened the

67. Sarna, *Genesis*, 24.

68. Fretheim, "Genesis," 363.

69. Willet, *Hexapla in Genesin & Exodum*, 28.

70. Gunkel, *Genesis*, 20.

71. See Irenaeus, *Against Heresies* 5.21.1.

72. The *Oxford English Dictionary* attributes this description to the seventeenth-century English writer Peter Heylin.

doors to a dark power: now the doors will always be open, and humanity is daily to be exposed to attack by that power.[73]

Yahweh God goes on to address the woman (v. 16a). In his words to her and to the man, the word "pain" as a consequence of human wrongdoing enters the reality of humanity's story.[74] One reason for the woman's creation as a help to the man was that she would be able to have children. But her experience of motherhood will be affected by her action. As Yahweh God had spoken of causing enmity between the snake and the woman and her offspring, so he is going to take deliberate action in this other connection: "I will make . . ." It is hardly conceivable that giving birth could ever have been painless,[75] and it wouldn't be difficult for an Israelite to realize this. Perhaps the stress in Yahweh God's words lies on how great the pain is going to be, or perhaps the reference to this pain parallels the reference to the snake crawling: the pain will now have the meaning Yahweh here attaches to it. But Yahweh actually refers to the pain of conception or pregnancy, not the pain of giving birth (though the parallel colon does refer to giving birth).[76] Perhaps the pain of pregnancy will be the pain of motherhood in a broader sense, "the pain of rearing children,"[77] pain such as that involved in having one son kill another son (Gen. 4).[78] Either way, the pain becoming great (*rābâ* hiphil) contrasts grievously with the intention that the offspring of the man and woman should be great in numbers (*rābâ* qal, 1:28).[79]

The woman's relationship with her husband will also be spoiled (v. 16b)—or more spoiled than it is already. What is the desire to which Yahweh refers? After enduring the pain of childbirth, Gen. Rab. comments, a woman might say she will never have sex again, but actually, she will want to.[80] Like the English word "desire," Hebrew *təšûqâ* can refer to something improper or something proper: see 4:7 and Song 7:11, the only two other occurrences. Her husband's ruling could then point to the other side of the sexual consequences of a spoiled situation, the husband imposing himself on his wife. Or it could point to a patriarchal attitude that will run through life as a whole, which will mean the man and the woman losing the equality in the relationship that issued from their being created in God's image and from her being a help to him. "'To love and to cherish' becomes 'To desire and to dominate.'"[81] But

73. Frey, *Buch der Anfänge*, 50 (cf. von Rad, *Genesis*, 90).

74. Cf. Bergey, "Pathologie et guérison spirituelle."

75. Cf. Augustine's comments in *Two Books on Genesis*, 123–24.

76. See van Ruiten, "Eve's Pain in Childbearing?"

77. Rashi's comment (*Br'šyt*, 37) on the first of the references to pain.

78. Meyers (*Discovering Eve*, 95–121; *Rediscovering Eve*, 88–102) rather refers it to the hard work of life on the farm, which will involve her working as much as her husband.

79. Cf. Ouro, "Linguistic and Thematic Parallels," 50–51.

80. In classic midrashic fashion, the comment in Gen. Rab. 20.7 clarifies the relationship between the statement in the first half of the verse and the statement in the second.

81. Kidner, *Genesis*, 71.

other rabbinic comments suggest that we should not think only of sexual desire when Yahweh refers to the woman's desire or longing or inclination to (re)turn to her man from whom she came (*təšûqâ* is not far from *təšûbâ*).[82]

Finally (vv. 17–19), and at greatest length, Yahweh God addresses the man, who is now named for the first time (in the MT; in the LXX and Vg he has been "Adam" since 2:19). Once again there is a curse, now a curse on the ground. Yahweh God "determined that his anger should, like a deluge, overflow all parts of the earth," even though it will still be true that the earth is full of God's mercy or commitment (*ḥesed*; Ps. 33:5).[83] Once again the curse will not mean making fruitless but that farming will no longer be the unalloyed joy that it might have been. It will be unpleasant and painfully hard work. As the woman's helping will become painful, so will the man's. He was created to be a gardener, but he will become just a peasant. Fortunately, the First Testament does not elsewhere express such a gloomy view of the farmer's lot,[84] as it does not express such a gloomy view of motherhood. God's bark is worse than his bite.

The curse will work itself out (v. 18) in the man's having to cope with opposition as he works in order to eat from the land. He will not be enjoying the fruit trees in the orchard. He will be outside the garden in the open country, where he started life back in 2:4b–7 before Yahweh God planted the garden and put him there to look after it. He will eat the plants that he grows there, fighting against the natural instinct of the land to produce thorn and thistle.

Working in the garden would surely have involved some sweat (v. 19), as motherhood would surely have involved some pain, so the point in this further set of couplets likely lies especially in the second and third of them. The need to sweat in order to eat will continue all through a man's life until it comes to its pointless end. There will be a certain relief and a certain appropriateness about that end. The statement about being dirt and going back to dirt looks like an independent saying; variants (esp. of the second colon) appear elsewhere (Job 10:9; Ps. 90:3; Eccles. 3:20), and it is also used in the "ashing" at an Ash Wednesday service, "From dust you came, and to dust you will return."

3:20–21. What about "at the time you eat from it, you will definitely die," and what about the life-tree? Before we get something like an answer to those questions, a delay raises the tension,[85] though its two footnotes also take the edge off the grievousness of what has been said and of what will follow. The first footnote involves the man exercising authority in naming his wife. Neither men nor women were perhaps as troubled by that assumption of authority as many men and women are in the modern West, and anyway the stress lies

82. See Lohr, "Sexual Desire?"
83. Calvin, *Genesis*, 1:173.
84. Cf. Skinner, *Genesis*, 83, 84.
85. Cf. Coats, *Genesis*, 56.

on the name the man gives the woman. It is a name that speaks of life, notwithstanding her having been the one who opened the way to death. Eve is not the mother of anything yet; this first footnote is the narrator's comment made in light of later events.

The second footnote (v. 21) relates the act of graciousness by which Yahweh God provides Adam and his woman with better clothes than the ones they have devised. So the Torah almost begins with God personally providing clothes for Adam and Eve, and it ends with Yahweh personally burying Moses.[86] Perhaps this provision, too, presupposes life outside the garden. And/or perhaps it indicates that (like good-and-bad-knowledge) the desire for clothing was not so inappropriate; clothing is a mark of honor. The point is that they need to let God provide it.[87]

3:22–24. But then there is the further, final punishment, which rounds off the story by taking us back to the creation of the garden and the life-tree and the good-and-bad-knowledge tree.

Yahweh God's words (v. 22) presuppose something implied by chapter 2, that the man and the woman were not created inherently immortal but would need to eat of the life-tree in order to live on. It is in some way something like a means of resurrection, though without the necessity to die. Yahweh God here implies that they have not yet eaten from the life-tree, and Gen. 2 may not imply that they even know about it (they wouldn't need it yet).

Further (vv. 23–24), with some irony, whereas the man was to serve and keep the garden (2:15), now serving and keeping are separated. Expulsion from the garden does not mean ceasing to serve the ground, but the man will now be serving the land outside the garden instead of serving the garden. And instead of being involved in keeping or guarding it, the way to the garden needs to be kept or guarded from him. Sphinxes (*kərubîm*) are beings that combine features of animals and of birds and perhaps of human beings. They are not "cherubic"; they are "terrible fighters."[88] They appear in various connections in the First Testament. Most commonly, crafted sphinxes stand over the covenant chest in the wilderness sanctuary and in the temple. They perhaps implicitly guard it, though they more explicitly function as support for Yahweh's throne (cf. Ezek. 10). Equivalent figures (*kuribu*) stood outside Mesopotamian temples.[89] In turn, the sword may suggest the flashing blades of a scythed chariot wheel.[90] Sphinxes and a flaming sword bring the grievous story to a close. Since the garden is to the east from the perspective of the

86. Cf. Qimchi, *Genesis*, on the verse; he attributes the comment to Simlai, the third-century sage.

87. Cf. Wilder, "Illumination and Investiture."

88. Ellul, *Meaning of the City*, 4.

89. Sarna, *Genesis*, 375.

90. So Lichtenstein, "Fearsome Sword of Genesis 3:24." Winitzer ("Etana in Eden") notes a similar motif in the Etana story from Babylon (*ANET* 114–18 [116a]).

listeners (2:8), the implication of 3:24 is that the first couple settles somewhere even farther east and farther away from Canaan.

Implications

Fall, Original Sin?

The study of Gen. 3 provides examples of at least three forms of theological interpretation of the Scriptures. The first is the articulation of the theological statements that are on the surface of the text. The second is the articulation of theological statements that one might say are implicit in the text. The third is the use of the text to make theological statements that are extrinsic to the text but are true to the Scriptures more generally. In suggesting such interpretations to the story's author, one might expect him or her to say "Yes, the first one is something I meant, the second one isn't something I meant but I can see that it brings out implications in what I said, but in the third one you are using my words to say something different from anything I meant." The third is sometimes termed the fuller sense, but it seems more appropriate to keep that description for the second; the third is more like allegory. The interpretation of v. 15 as the Protevangelium is an example of the third (see the comments on 3:15).

The key overt theological statement in Gen. 3 is that God has banished humanity from his garden and barred the way to it, and in so doing he barred the way to the tree of life. In keeping with that action, the rest of the First Testament does not concern itself with eternal life; it accepts the fact that we die and go to be with our family. Within the Scriptures as a whole, the circle is completed only in their last pages, where the life-tree reappears in the new Jerusalem and access to it is promised to people who have washed their robes (Rev. 22:2, 14, 19; cf. also 2:7). It is Jesus's execution that makes this cleansing possible. People who identify with Jesus have some experience of the life of the new Jerusalem even now, but they await the true fulfillment of God's creation purpose that will come when they have been physically raised to new life and are thus in a position to walk the streets of the city. But Genesis has no such vision of an ultimate fulfillment of God's purpose (it has no "eschatology").[91] God has put his creation project on hold. Meanwhile, it is partly true that "the meaning of life is that it stops" (anon.).

The beguiling that led to this terrible result came from a creature that God had made and that was present in the garden. It did not come from a supernatural being. Paul, too, notes that it came from a snake (2 Cor. 11:3). Revelation 12:9 and 20:2 do describe Satan as "the snake," which invites us to see Satan as a deceiver with the characteristics of this snake in Genesis. It may

91. Cf. Schüle, "'Und siehe, es war sehr gut,'" 21.

also invite the inference that Satan was behind the snake. And this inference fits the way Isa. 27:1 uses the word "snake" to denote the First Testament's equivalent to Satan, Leviathan (cf. Job 26:13).[92] But the theological insight expressed in Genesis itself remains significant: the beguiling came from within creation. "No *diabolia ex machina* are set in motion" to explain humanity's perverted use of its freedom.[93] Perhaps God commissioned the snake to find out whether humanity would do as he said, as God commissioned Satan to find out whether Jesus would do so (Matt. 4:1).

Second Esdras 7:118 describes what happened in the garden as the "fall" of the first human beings, and this metaphor has found its way into Christian theology, but it compromises the theological significance of Gen. 3. First, to speak of the first human beings as falling portrays them as having an exalted position before they fell. Genesis 3 does not give that impression. They were not created morally good or evil, or spiritually mature. They were like children who needed to grow to maturity by coping with the challenges and experiences that came to them. In the second century CE, Irenaeus emphasizes this insight, and his understanding has been seen as antithetical to that of Augustine and as pointing toward the idea that the fall was a fall upward, a move toward maturity as humanity takes responsibility for its own moral judgments.[94] But Irenaeus's own treatment of Gen. 3 does not make the move from "the first man and woman were not yet mature" to "therefore making their own decision about the good-and-bad-knowledge tree was a step toward maturity"; he follows Genesis itself in seeing Adam as being "disobedient to God" through yielding to the blandishments of the snake, so that "when they were put out of Paradise, Adam and his wife Eve fell into many troubles of anxious grief, going about with sorrow and toil and lamentation in this world."[95] A second disadvantage of the "fall" image is its implication that they were the victims of what happened. Genesis 3 implies that they jumped, not that they fell. The occasion was a rebellion, not a fall, though Gen. 3 has no specific word to describe the couple's act of disobedience.

Given the disadvantages of the word *fall*, it is fortuitous that the Torah, the Prophets, the Writings, and the NT do not use the word *fall* for this event, though in the absence of another convenient term it has proved useful to summarize Paul's point about the origin of human wrongdoing in Rom. 5:12–21. Here Paul brings out theological implications of Gen. 3 that lie beneath its surface. Sin came into the world through one human being, and death came in as a consequence (cf. 1 Cor. 15:21–22, 45–49). While Gen. 3 does not portray

92. See further Reno, *Genesis*, 77–89.

93. Bonhoeffer, *Creation and Fall; Temptation*, 70–71.

94. See, e.g., Hick, *Evil and the God of Love*; more recently, Bechtel, "Rethinking the Interpretation"; Ladoceur, "Evolution and Genesis 2–3"; Lang, "Three Philosophers in Paradise."

95. Irenaeus, *The Proof of the Apostolic Preaching* 16–17 (cf., e.g., *Heresies* 5.23); and see Hamilton, *Genesis 1–17*, 211.

humanity as created immortal, it does imply that humanity could have made the move from limited life to lasting life by eating from the life-tree and that by its disobedience it forfeited that possibility, so that this disobedience did mean that death came in. And the influence of the first human beings on their descendants means that death has come to all humanity, as Rom. 5:12 says.

At Rom. 5:12, the Vg has all humanity sinning "in Adam," and this translation encouraged the development of the doctrine of original sin, which (in the formulation of the Anglican Thirty-Nine Articles of Religion) "standeth not in the following of Adam, . . . but it is the fault and corruption of the Nature of every man, that naturally is engendered of the offspring of Adam; whereby man is very far gone from original righteousness, and is of his own nature inclined to evil, so that the flesh lusteth always contrary to the Spirit; and therefore in every person born into this world, it deserveth God's wrath and damnation." While Genesis does not suggest that all subsequent humanity is implicated in Adam's own sin and therefore shares in his guilt, its account of the human story as it unfolds after Gen. 3 does suggest a certain inevitability about human sinfulness, which Christian theological reflection makes more explicit: "It took the work of the last Adam to bring home to us our full downfall in the first Adam."[96] We might put it in sociological rather than psychological terms: Adam and Eve's rebellion did not change individual human makeup, but it did fatally change the environment in which all human beings would now be born.[97]

There is little subsequent reference to Gen. 3 in the First Testament, especially compared with the importance of the chapter in Paul and in subsequent Christian theology.[98] The book with which it most resonates is Ecclesiastes. Like Ecclesiastes, Gen. 3 honors the ambiguity of humanity's position in the world. As created by God and living in God's world, human beings are both responsible for the things that they do and are also victims of the things that happen to them. If the readers of Gen. 3 are like the man and the woman in the story who long for "reason without pathos,"[99] for understanding without vulnerability, for an escape from anxiety that does not involve trust, they will be disappointed. Like Ecclesiastes (and like Job 38–41), Gen. 3 sees humanity as challenged to live by trust in God where we cannot understand, to be satisfied with partial insights into our lives, and to give up aspirations to finding our own way to wisdom.

96. Kidner, *Genesis*, 67.

97. There is a set of discussions of these issues in Cavanaugh and J. Smith (*Evolution and the Fall*) and another set from a slightly more conservative perspective than mine in Madueme and Reeves, *Adam, the Fall, and Original Sin*.

98. On the equivalent contrast between the church fathers and the rabbis, see Reuling, "The Christian and the Rabbinic Adam."

99. Gunkel, *Genesis*, 31, but in Brueggemann's translation of "Vernunft ohne Pathos," *Genesis*, 54.

Genesis 3 offers various possible ways of conceptualizing the nature of the original sin. It may be the wish to make up one's own mind, to exercise free will, to exercise choice. It may be pride. It may be ambition, the longing to be like God or to be God. It may be desire (but Gen. 3 is not very interested in sex and does not suggest a link between sin and sex). None of these characteristics are wrong in themselves, but they are all capable of going wrong. Genesis 3 itself does not explain human wrongdoing; it remains a mystery. It redirects the question about sin's origin in order to focus rather on its nature, as "the conscious disobedience of man to the will of God."[100] The speech of the snake, "like all bad theology—of which this speech is the original—is itself only an interpretation of human existence which does not explicitly express but only implies a call to disobedience."[101] We may trace the process whereby the man and the woman came to do what they did, yet such tracing does not explain the action; "a chasm opens," and "it becomes really inconceivable how the evil could have been committed."[102]

Nor does Gen. 3 explain the origin of evil in the broader sense. It does presuppose that God created a good world (the point that Gen. 1 makes explicit), but it also presupposes that God's good created world had puzzling features, pressures, and temptations. In connection with evil in the world, its message indeed compares with that of Job 38–41, which challenges Job to accept that he will not understand everything (not least what has happened to him), to come to terms with the fact that the world does not revolve around him, and to live with the evidence and thus the conviction that God is not doing too bad a job of running the world. The narrator of Gen. 3 does not imply access to much of God's will and intentions and so does not imply that people listening to the story should grasp them.[103] "Many readers assume that the biblical author had fairly complete resolution on theological matters." But Gen. 3 does not give this impression regarding the question of how to resolve the conflict between the presence of evil in the world and God's reign over it. It does not resolve the "conundrum"; it "merely expresses it."[104]

Paul can see Adam as the one responsible for the coming of sin and death into the world (Rom. 5:14; 1 Cor. 15:22); yet in the context of a series of warnings about womanhood Sir. 25:24 reminds its readers that the beginning of sin came from a woman, and because of her we all die. Likewise Paul elsewhere bases a requirement that women should learn in submission on the fact that the man was formed first, not the woman, and that it was the woman who was deceived and became a sinner, not the man (1 Tim. 2:14: it is a common critical view that Paul himself didn't write 1 Timothy, but this

100. Childs, *Myth and Reality in the Old Testament*, 49.
101. Barth, *CD* 4.1:421.
102. Bonhoeffer, *Creation and Fall; Temptation*, 82.
103. Cf. Stordalen, "God of the Eden Narrative."
104. Diepstra and Laughery, "Exploring the Possible Worlds of Genesis 2–3," 316.

possibility doesn't affect the question of the theological interrelationship of the passages). Romans, 1 Corinthians, and 1 Timothy are all using Gen. 3 through the inspiration of the Holy Spirit to illumine and support their points, though in none of the passages do the points issue from Gen. 3 itself. It is evenhanded in its attribution of blame to the man and the woman: the woman sins by her words, the man by his silence.[105] Paul's further comment that women need to stay in submission to their husbands, not least if they are to be preserved through childbirth (1 Tim. 2:15), may reflect Gen. 3:16 LXX, which speaks of the woman having "recourse" to her man.[106] First John 2:16 issues a warning to the faithful that sees an ongoing significance in Gen. 3:6, a warning about the desires of our physical nature ("good to eat"), about desires that arise from what we see ("an object of longing to the eyes"), and about pretentiousness ("desirable for conveying wisdom"); compare also the three temptations in Matt. 4:1–11; Luke 4:1–13.[107] The implication is that Gen. 3 does describe the ongoing dynamics of human decision making as well as describing something that happened once for all.

105. See, e.g., Sharon, "Doom of Paradise."

106. Cf. W. Loader, "Genesis 3:16–19 LXX in Reception"; and more broadly, Aageson, "Genesis in the Deutero-Pauline Epistles," 118–22.

107. Reno, *Genesis*, 90.

4
How Things Got Worse

(4:1–26)

Overview

The question or the problem that would make the audience listen attentively when the storyteller had reached the end of Gen. 3 is apparent: what will happen to the first human couple and their destiny to fill the earth? The answer comes in Gen. 4: (a) they have a son who worships God; (b) they have another son who also worships God, and God likes his worship more, so his brother kills him and starts a line that continues accordingly; (c) they have a third son so that things can start again. One might treat Gen. 2:4b–4:26 as a three-act drama; Gen. 3 came to such a discouraging end, and for a while Gen. 4 portrays things as getting worse, but it closes with a note of hope. Yet Gen. 4 has its own coherence as a story. The account of the birth of the two sons, their work, and their worship (vv. 1–4a) raises the audience's anticipation: maybe things outside the garden will not be so hopeless. If the audience simply entertains that hope, it has missed hints that catastrophe may again be on the way, and this possibility now looms (vv. 4b–7). The audience waits to see how Cain will react, but disaster indeed ensues (v. 8). So what will happen now? The dynamics of the answer (vv. 9–16) overlap with those in 3:8–24. The dynamics of what follows (vv. 17–18) in turn reprise the beginning of 4:1–4a, while the dynamics of the next scene (vv. 19–24) reprise those of 4:4b–8. We therefore expect another confrontation like God's confrontation with Adam and Eve and with Cain, but instead the sequence breaks off, and vv. 25–26 close the story with grace and mercy and thanksgiving and worship. The Hollywood ending enables the audience to go home and sleep and dream.

Translation

1Now[1] the man slept with his woman, Ḥavvah, she got pregnant, and
she gave birth to Qayin and said, "I've generated[2] someone with
Yahweh"![3] **2**She went on to give birth to his brother, Hebel.[4] Hebel be-
came one who pastured sheep, while[5] Qayin became one who served
the ground.

3After some time, Qayin brought some of the fruit of the ground as
an offering for Yahweh, **4**while Hebel, too, brought some of the firstborn
of his flock, some[6] of the fat parts. Yahweh recognized Hebel and his
offering, **5**but Qayin and his offering Yahweh did not recognize. It really
enraged Qayin and his face glowered.[7] **6**Yahweh said to Qayin,

> Why has it enraged you,
>   why has your face glowered?
> **7**If you do what's good, there'll be a lifting up,[8] won't there,
>   but if you don't do what's good,

1. The clause opens with the subject, signaling a new stage in the narrative (cf. Bandstra, "Word Order and Emphasis," 120).

2. The LXX, Vg have "acquired," the much more common meaning of *qānâ*, but "generated" better fits the present context (following on Gen. 2–3), fits the use of the preposition *ʾet*, and fits the description of her offspring as *ʾîš* (see E. Lipiński on *qānâ*, *TDOT* 13:58–63). Bokovoy ("Did Eve Acquire, Create, or Procreate?") translates "procreated."

3. The expression is strange in Hebrew as in English—more so because *ʾîš* (someone), the word for an individual, usually denotes a grown man, though she will eventually have "generated" him when he is grown up.

4. The name first appears here in a position where it has the pausal form *hābel*, which thus becomes Abel in the LXX and Vg. See the translation note on v. 18 on the spelling of Lemek.

5. The clause opens with the subject, signaling the contrast with the preceding clause; so also in v. 4. Placing the object first in v. 5a has a similar effect.

6. Taking the waw as explanatory, with GKC 154a.

7. Literally, "fell"; but the English expression "his face fell" came to mean "he was sad," whereas the context here indicates that the expression means to scowl or sulk (cf. Luther, *Genesis 1–5*, 261). In the qal the Hebrew expression comes only here, but the hiphil in Jer. 3:12 has this meaning (Job 29:24 is more obscure) (the English phrase comes in Mark 10:22 in some translations, but it is not a literal translation of the verb *stygnazō* there). See Marsden, "Cain's Face, and Other Problems."

8. The LXX takes the rare noun *śəʾēt* from *nāśāʾ* (in form it might alternatively be an infinitive construct) to denote the raising of the sacrifice, but this would be an unparalleled usage. The Tg, Sym take it to denote forgiving, which is a plausible meaning for a word derived from *nāśāʾ*, with its common implication of carrying wrongdoing, but the context has not indicated that Qayin's offering involved wrongdoing that required forgiveness, and while his anger might now require forgiveness, making this link entails some connecting of dots; further, there are no other instances of the noun meaning forgiveness. The Vg has "receiving," to which the same applies. Following on the previous line, Yahweh might be referring to Qayin's lifting his face instead of lowering it in a scowl (cf. Ibn Ezra, *Genesis*, 82). In Gen. 49:3; Job 13:11; 31:23; Ps. 62:4 [62:5]; and Hab. 1:7, the noun means exaltation or honoring (cf. Sipilä and van der Spuy, "'To Lift Up'").

At the entrance wrongdoing[9] is something lying,[10]
and toward you is its desire,[11]
but you—you're to rule over it."[12]

8Qayin told Hebel his brother.[13] And while they were in the open coun-
try, Qayin set upon Hebel his brother and killed him.
9Yahweh said to Qayin, "Where's Hebel, your brother?" He said, "I
don't know—am I the one who keeps guard over my brother?" **10**He
said, "What have you done? The sound of[14] your brother's spilt blood[15]
is crying out to me from the ground. **11**There, you are cursed, more
than[16] the ground that has opened its mouth to receive your brother's
spilt blood from your hand. **12**When you serve the ground, it is no more
to give its energy to you. A drifter, a vagrant, you will be on the
earth."

9. Morales ("Crouching Demon, Hidden Lamb") suggests "sin offering" for *ḥaṭṭā't*, but would Yahweh suggest that a sin offering avails for deliberate wrongdoing?

10. Whereas "wrongdoing," the subject of the clause, is feminine, this participle is masculine, and masculine continues in the next two cola; apparently the participle takes the place of a noun for "animal" (GKC 132 note 2). It "is frequently and plausibly identified with Akk[adian] *rābiṣu*, denoting various officials and also demons, especially those that guard entrances to buildings" (Wenham, *Genesis 1–15*, 106). Indeed, Loiseau ("Gen. 4,7") notes that *ḥaṭṭā't* is suspiciously similar to an Akkadian word for a watcher, a word that can apply to a demon. Perhaps *rōbēṣ* should read *tirbōṣ* (haplography), "wrongdoing lies in wait" (e.g., Hendel, *Text of Genesis 1–11*, 46). Crouch ("*ḥṭ't* as Interpolative Gloss") takes *ḥaṭṭā't* as an addition clarifying the negative implications of *rōbēṣ*.

11. The LXX implies "his [Hebel's] desire" and in the next colon "rule over him," which suggests a closer parallel with the comment about the brothers' parents in 3:17, but this understanding depends on the LXX's lack of the masculine antecedent "something lying," to which the MT's suffixes refer back.

12. Whereas the yiqtol *timšōl* has its expected simple future meaning in 37:8 (cf. 3:16), a yiqtol can denote "you must/may/can" (Exod. 20:9 is a good example), and this understanding fits the context (cf. *TTH* 39a). The move from "thou shalt" in the KJV to "do thou" in the ASV gives John Steinbeck cause for reflection in *East of Eden*, 219; cf. Schöpflin, "Genesis 4,7."

13. Literally, "said to Hebel his brother." The absolute use of *'āmar* is almost unique, but cf. Exod. 19:25; 2 Chron. 32:24 (Skinner, *Genesis*, 107); 2 Sam. 21:2; 2 Chron. 1:2 (Reis, "What Cain Said," 109; she translates "spoke against"). LXX adds "Let's go out into the open country" (cf. the Vg; see Brayford, *Genesis*, 252), which makes for a smoother reading; the Hebrew equivalent to the extra words could have been lost through a scribe's eye jumping from one occurrence of "the open country" to the next. See further Scarlata, *Outside of Eden*, 111–30. Lohr ("Righteous Abel, Wicked Cain," 490) sees the addition of these words as one of the indications that the LXX deliberately paints a negative portrait of Cain and thereby "explains" Yahweh's acceptance of Abel and not of Cain.

14. GKC 146b understands *qôl* as an exclamation ("Hark!"), but the MT's conjunctive accent suggests taking it as construct (cf. LXX, Vg, Tg).

15. The plural of the word for "blood" denotes shed blood.

16. See the footnote to 3:14.

13Qayin said to Yahweh, "My waywardness[17] is too big to carry.[18]
14Here, you've driven me away today from the face of the ground, and from your face I'm to conceal myself, and I'm to be a drifter, a vagrant on the earth—and anyone who finds me may kill me." **15**But Yahweh said to him, "Therefore,[19] anyone who kills Qayin, sevenfold[20] it's to be redressed." So Yahweh set a mark for Qayin in order that no one who found him would strike him down. **16**Then Qayin went out from being before Yahweh's face and lived in in the country of Drifting, east of Lush.

17Qayin slept with his woman, she got pregnant, and she gave birth to Ḥanok. He was building a town, and he named the town after his son Ḥanok. **18**To Ḥanok was born Irad. Irad fathered[21] Mehuyaʾel, Mehiyaʾel[22] fathered Metusaʾel, and Metusaʾel fathered Lemek.[23] **19**Lemek got himself two women; the name of one was Adah, the name of the second Ṣillah. **20**Adah gave birth to Yabal; he was the ancestor of everyone who lives with a tent and livestock.[24] **21**His brother's name was Yubal; he was the ancestor of everyone who plays guitar or pipe. **22**Ṣillah, she too gave birth, to Tubal Qayin,[25] forger, every craftsman in copper and iron.[26] Tubal-qayin's sister was Naʿamah.

23Lemek said to his women,

> Adah and Ṣillah, listen to my voice;
> as Lemek's women, give ear to my word.

17. I assume (with *HALOT* rather than BDB and *DCH*) that there is one root verb *ʿāwâ*, from which the noun *ʿāwōn* ultimately derives, though Hebrew speakers might not be aware of that link. The conventional English translation of *ʿāwōn* is the rather colorless "iniquity." It follows the Vg's less colorless *iniquitas*, whose etymological meaning is "unevenness," which is not far from the possible resonances of *ʿāwōn*, with its link to *ʿāwâ*. Etymologically, then, *ʿāwōn* implies bending or twisting, and it could suggest those connotations. The LXX here as often elsewhere has "my punishment" in the sense of the penalty for my waywardness, but this seems to be an unnecessary complication. Contrast the Tg.

18. The LXX, Vg, Tg. Onq. have "forgive."

19. For *lākēn*, the LXX, Vg imply *lōʾ kēn*, "Not so!" Aq has "therefore."

20. The Tg takes the word to denote seven generations (cf. vv. 17–24).

21. The subject commonly precedes the verb in such lists, which fits the fact that the subject provides the new information and thus has emphasis (see the translation note to 22:1).

22. The MT has preserved two forms of this name next to one another.

23. The quasi-circumstantial word order in v. 18 has the effect of hurrying the reader on to Lemek's action in v. 19 and to what follows. On its first occurrence Lemek's name is pointed Lāmek because it is in pause, and via the LXX and Vg (for whom the way of reading the word would already be familiar) this pointing generates the misspelling of the name in English—as happened with Hebel.

24. Adverbial accusative (Seebass, *Genesis*, 1:166).

25. A possible explanation of the double name is that both words mean "smith" and that the second explains the first and/or distinguishes this Tubal from the Tubal in, e.g., 10:2, where it is implicitly also the name of a people (cf. *HALOT*). The LXX omits Qayin, perhaps suspicious of the repetition.

26. The description of Tubal-qayin is difficult to construe, and neither the LXX, Vg, or Tg nor scholarly suggestions offer a clear lead toward emending the text.

Because I've killed someone for wounding me,
a young man for injuring me.
24If for Qayin it's redressed sevenfold,
for Lemek seventy-sevenfold.

25Once more Adam slept with his woman, and she gave birth to a son.
She named him Šet, because "God has set in place for me another off-
spring in place of Hebel, because Qayin killed him." 26To Šet, too, a son
was born, and he named him Enoš.

At that time a beginning was made[27] to calling out with the name Yahweh.[28]

Interpretation

"At last we have passed over that expanse of text on which all expositors have toiled exceedingly. . . . The chapters that follow are less subject to debate."[29] Luther makes this comment before starting his exposition of Gen. 4, on which he then goes on to spend as much time as he spent on Gen. 3 and more time than he spent on Gen. 1 or Gen. 2.[30] Christian tradition sets Gen. 1–3 sharply off from Gen. 4 and succeeding chapters, but Genesis itself does not do so. The story of Adam and Eve's children and what goes wrong with them follows straight on from the story of the parents and what went wrong with them. Once again the story raises familiar human issues: sex, pregnancy, the birth of children, the roles of different children, sibling rivalry, the making of offerings, God blessing one person and not another, the multiplying of sexual relationships, conflict and violence in the community.[31] But Adam and Eve's children stand at the center of the chapter. There is one son, and then another son, and readers wonder how they will relate. The answer is discouraging, indeed "frightening,"[32] and there is not too much improvement in the story of their grandchildren and great-grandchildren and so on. But at least the chapter closes on a note of hope, as if all is not lost: it goes back to its starting point and introduces another son.

In this way and in its overall dynamic, Gen. 4 parallels Gen. 3, but it sees things playing out within the family and outside the garden. Once again someone gives in to a bad idea, Yahweh asks more than one (possibly rhetorical)

27. The LXX, Vg, and Tg have an active verb, of which Enoš would then be the subject; on the MT's more allusive expression, see Gordon, "Who 'Began to Call on the Name of the Lord'?"

28. The construct is epexegetical, not possessive ("the name of Yahweh"; cf. GKC 128k).

29. Luther, *Genesis 1–5*, 237.

30. In *Genesis 1–11*, Westermann spends 104 pages on Gen. 1:1–2:4a, 101 pages on Gen. 2:4b–3:24, and 66 pages on Gen. 4. The chapter does raise several tricky questions: cf. Chung, "Conflicting Readings."

31. Cf. Angélico, "Agonia, Cristianismo e Saudade."

32. Seebass, *Genesis*, 1:164.

question,[33] a guilty party is evasive or self-defensive, there is talk of a tension between desiring and ruling over, there is a curse, there is some expression of mercy by Yahweh, but once again there is a driving out to land east of Lush. Accompanying its concern with a sibling relationship rather than a marriage relationship is its portrayal of the development of human life—the growth of the family, the first offerings to Yahweh, the building of a town, the beginnings of culture and technology, and the first calling out with Yahweh's name. Genesis 4 portrays people's lives in a more true-to-life way than Gen. 3; there is no talking snake or Yahweh going for an afternoon walk or whirling, flaming sword. There is a remarkably conversational relationship between Yahweh and Cain. But whereas Adam and Eve simply must leave the garden and Yahweh stays involved with them, Cain must leave the face or presence of Yahweh. There will be no more conversations between God and human beings until the Abraham story (Gen. 15).[34] On the other hand, the story ends with the birth of another child and with him having a child and thus with the promise of an alternative to Cain's line, and with people beginning to call out with Yahweh's name.

If "the most prominent anthropological theme in the Old Testament is that of violence,"[35] then it is appropriate that the story of Cain killing Abel features early in the account of life outside the garden. The first scene relates the background and the deed itself, "the beginning of a murder."[36] The second relates Yahweh's response. The third tells of the subsequent life of Cain and his family.[37] The fourth speaks of how Adam and Eve start again.

- Cain kills Abel (4:1–8)
  - Eve gives birth to Cain and Abel (vv. 1–2a)
  - Cain and Abel have different occupations (v. 2b)
  - Cain and Abel bring different offerings, and Yahweh reacts differently (vv. 3–5a)
  - Cain gets angry (v. 5b)
  - Yahweh issues a challenge (vv. 6–7)
  - Cain kills Abel (v. 8)
- Yahweh banishes Cain (4:9–16)
  - Yahweh confronts Cain (v. 9)
  - Yahweh issues a sentence (vv. 10–12)

33. Questions play a key role in Gen. 4: see Craig, "Questions outside Eden."

34. T. Thompson ("Genesis 4") traces further the way Gen. 4 takes on themes from Gen. 3.

35. E. Peels, "World's First Murder," 19; cf. Schwager, *Must There Be Scapegoats?*

36. Angelats, "Elements per a una lectura de Gn 4,1–16," 15.

37. On the Mesopotamian background to Genesis's account of the development of civilization, see Lowery, *Toward a Poetics of Genesis 1–11*, 122–227.

Cain protests (vv. 13–14)
Yahweh alleviates the sentence (vv. 15–16)
Cain starts a family (4:17–24)
Cain initiates a family line and builds a town (vv. 17–18)
Lamech starts two families (v. 19)
They have different occupations (vv. 20–22)
Lamech speaks of vengeance (vv. 23–24)
Adam and Eve start again (4:25–26)
Eve gives birth to Seth (vv. 25–26a)
People begin to call on Yahweh (v. 26b)

4:1–2. "Slept with" is literally "knew," both being euphemisms for "had sex with." Hebrew uses the verb "know" even in connection with casual sex, so there is no suggestion that sex is a deep way of "knowing." On the other hand, using this verb (which recurs in v. 9) conveys some irony because the theme of knowing is significant in Gen. 2–3.[38] It is not explicit that Adam and Eve had never had sex in Eden, though it may be implied. But the importance lies in where the sex led. Eve starts to live up to her name and starts being a help to Adam by giving birth to Cain. The name (more precisely Qayin) comes from the root *qyn*, which means "to forge"; the Kenites/Qenites/Qinites (e.g., 15:19) are perhaps so called because they were metalworkers.[39] The name is thus etymologically unrelated to *qānâ*, meaning "acquire," or in this context meaning "have" (in the sense of "have a baby"), or "generate," but the name points to a suggestive link.[40] Eve had Cain with Adam, but what strikes her is that she had him with Yahweh. Having a baby does involve a man, a woman, and God, but modern Western talk of a couple being pregnant needs not to imperil the significance of the fact that it is actually the woman who is pregnant, and modern ways of making pregnancy and safe birth possible do not imperil the fact that a woman has a baby with God. The birth is a hopeful event, and Eve's comment is a hopeful statement. The couple's disobedience (initiated by Eve) has not broken their relationship with Yahweh. Yahweh is involved in Eve's life outside the garden, and Eve is not hiding from Yahweh anymore. Whether or not giving birth is more painful than it might have been (3:16), it is dangerous, and Eve's successfully giving birth is another indication that she has done so "with Yahweh." In a

38. Cf. Rudman, "A Little Knowledge Is a Dangerous Thing."

39. The story has been thought to reflect Israel's awareness of them; but if it does at all, it is not interested in this question; it is the two brothers who interest Genesis (cf. Zimmerli, *1. Mose 1–11*, 229–30).

40. Josephus (*Ant.* 1.2.1–2) implies that Cain lives up to his name by being continually interested in acquiring things.

moment her sons will also give expression to their relationship with Yahweh. Verse 1 perhaps implies that it was Eve who named Cain, as she will name Seth (v. 25); either mother or father can be the name giver in the First Testament (in v. 26 Seth names Enosh). More explicitly, in her exclamation about the meaning of Cain's name, she speaks as the archetypal "joyful mother of children" (Ps. 113:9).[41]

Neither Eve nor the narrator comments on her second son's name (v. 2a). Maybe it's insignificant; not every name has implications. But the names of Eve and Cain were explicitly significant, as will be the name of the third son (v. 25). Adam's name was implicitly significant, too, given the recurrence of the word *ʾādām* with the meaning "man" and of the word for the "ground," *ʾădāmâ*, from which and for which he was made. And Abel (more precisely Hebel) means "breath," not breath in the sense of the means of life but breath in the sense of something insubstantial and evanescent, like an idol, or (in Ecclesiastes) like all human endeavor in its ultimate emptiness and fruitlessness. Does the name that contrasts with Cain's indicate that he doesn't mean as much to Eve as Cain did? The firstborn is commonly the son who counts most.[42] It will transpire that Eve's second son is easily blown away. Presumably it was not what they had in mind in naming the boy, and as a name *hebel* could have another meaning (herdsman is the most attractive of the possibilities),[43] or it could simply be a name. The explicit point that Gen. 4 keeps repeating about Abel is not the meaning of his name but the relationship he has with Cain: he is Cain's brother, the brother of his murderer (vv. 2, 8a, 8b, 9a, 9b, 10, 11); compare the way the book of Ruth keeps identifying Ruth as "a/the Moabite." Maybe they were even twins—there's no second reference to sex and pregnancy before the report of his birth and naming.

Keeping flocks and working the soil (v. 2b) are two key human occupations. For the average Israelite family, there are two key tasks outside the home: looking after the animals and tending the ground. The two brothers take one task each. It would be nice then to picture them as being a help to each other, as a man and his wife are designed to be, but actually in Genesis "brothers are naturally rivals."[44] Only the second of the occupations was directly mentioned in Gen. 1–3 as the task for which humanity was created, which perhaps suggests it was the more important. Even girls can look after sheep (see, e.g., Exod. 2:16), so it might naturally be the task that falls to the younger brother.[45] Admittedly, keeping the sheep would be a key aspect of people who were made in God's image holding sway over the animals (1:26–28), and "keeping" has been in other ways an important motif in Genesis already (2:15; 3:24). But

41. Cf. Westermann, *Genesis 1–11*, 289.
42. Cf. De La Torre, *Genesis*, 93–94.
43. Cf. Sarna, *Genesis*, 32; for other possibilities, see BDB and K. Seybold, *TDOT* 3:313.
44. Cf. Westermann, *Genesis 1–11*, 286.
45. Cf. Meyers, "Food and the First Family," 151–52.

the elder brother gets the task that Yahweh explicitly commissioned, while his little brother gets the secondary task. In v. 2b Abel comes first and Cain second; perhaps Genesis is just letting the order fluctuate for the sake of variety: Cain-Abel, then Abel-Cain, then Cain-Abel again in v. 3.

4:3–5. Genesis introduces the making of offerings (as it introduced God in chapter 1) in a way that presupposes that the listeners know enough about them to make sense of what it says—as of course they do. Genesis assumes that worship needs no explanation. As a lead-in to his comment about God having made us for himself so that our hearts are restless until they find their rest in him, Augustine declares that God stirs human beings to take pleasure in praising him.[46] And any people except Westerners and other urbanized people know that it is a natural human thing to bring presents to God, as natural as bringing a present to a human being, though such offerings to a human being can indicate insecurity in the relationship (the other "offerings" in Genesis are Jacob's offering to Esau and his sons' offering to Joseph in Gen. 32–33 and 43). Gifts from the fruit of the ground will be an integral part of the offerings for which Yahweh in due course issues regulations in Deut. 26:1–11 (see also Lev. 2, though those regulations relate to grain offerings in particular). Cain and Abel's making offerings on their own initiative suggests that in subsequently issuing instructions for these offerings, Yahweh is adopting that human instinct and harnessing it to the relationship between Israel and himself, as he does with the institution of kingship, the building of the temple, and (one might infer) the institution of priesthood. The reference to the fruit of the ground is neat, given the significance of fruit in Gen. 1:11–12, 29 (positively) and 3:1–6 (more equivocally), and given the significance of those later instructions in Deut. 26:1–11 about bringing the first of the *fruits* of the ground to the place Yahweh chooses, in an acknowledgment that Yahweh has fulfilled his promises and given his people the land.

It would also be natural for Abel to bring an offering of what issues from his work (v. 4), but here the problems start. Abel's offering also corresponds to regulations that will feature later in the Torah (see Lev. 1, but especially Deut. 12). While there is no doubt that Cain's offering is a proper one, Deut. 26:1–11 will talk about the *firstfruits* of the ground, and Cain's offering does not correspond to that expectation.[47] In contrast, Abel brings some of the firstborn of his flock, as Deut. 12 will say. He brings specifically some of the fat parts, on which Lev. 3 will lay great emphasis: the offerer and Yahweh share the sacrificial meal, but Yahweh gets the juiciest parts of the animal. And here Yahweh "recognizes" Abel and his offering. The verb (*šāʿâ*) is unusual. It is used only here of a positive regard by God; occasionally it applies to human recognition of or regard for God (e.g., Isa. 17:7–8; 31:1). Presumably

46. Augustine, *Confessions* 1.1; cf. Reno, *Genesis*, 97.
47. Though Tg. Ps.-J. makes it do so; cf. Shepherd, "Translating and Supplementing," 126.

it indicates that Yahweh accepts the offering, perhaps that he likes its smell (cf. Gen. 8:21), though Genesis notes first that Yahweh accepts the person.[48] Perhaps he gives some sign of this acceptance like the one in Lev. 9:24 or Judg. 6:20–21. But we are reduced to guesswork on that question. "As a reader, one has more questions of the text than the narrator is interested in."[49]

Whatever was the sign of recognition, Yahweh did not give it to Cain (v. 5). We might have wondered if we should blame the victim by asking whether Abel had been trying to do better than his brother: "You bring some ordinary offerings from your work, I'll bring some extraordinary ones from mine, and we all know that meat is better than vegetables." Or we might have suspected that there was some other difference in their attitude, one that worked in Abel's favor rather than against him (cf. Heb. 11:4). Or we might have seen the difference as the first instance of a pattern that will recur whereby Yahweh favors the second son rather than the first, against the social norm. Or we might have wondered whether sacrifices that involve shedding of blood are more pleasing to Yahweh.[50] Or we might have seen the difference in Yahweh's response as pointing to another mystery like the mysteries in Gen. 2–3 and the mystery for Job about the way Yahweh treats him; we cannot always know why God acts the way he does. The subsequent stories about God's "mysterious choice to elevate one brother to prominence" suggest that God's attentiveness to Abel's sacrifice and not Cain's is not driven by what they do.[51] But actually Genesis has drawn attention to the differences between the quality of the brothers' offerings, "some of the firstborn of his flock, some of the fat parts," over against "some of the fruit of the ground." This difference makes it not surprising that there is the difference in Yahweh's response. "It is not the distinction between the two professions that leads to deadly conflict, . . . but the offering to God which two brothers make of their produce."[52] So Cain gets angry and goes into a huff—an understandable reaction to rejection.

4:6–7. "Although Cain's sacrifice is ignored by God, his anger is not."[53] There is enough rhythm, parallelism, and figurative speech to imply that Yahweh's words of confrontation take poetic form, like the words in 3:14–19.

First (v. 6), Yahweh asks a double rhetorical question. Its implication is that instead of getting into a huff, Cain ought to have thought about what has just happened and about why Yahweh might have appreciated Abel's gift in a way he did not appreciate Cain's.

48. Cf. Calvin, *Genesis*, 1:194.

49. Seebass, *Genesis*, 1:152.

50. On early discussion of this question between Jews and Christians, see Yayward, "What Did Cain Do Wrong?"

51. Kaminsky, *Yet I Loved Jacob*, 23.

52. Wittenberg, "Alienation and 'Emancipation' from the Earth," 107. Contrast J. Allen, "Mixed Economies of Cain and Abel."

53. Schlimm, *From Fratricide to Forgiveness*, 137.

In making the point (v. 7a), Yahweh implies that Cain has thus not done something "good." That root recurs, as the verb whose related adjective has come fifteen times in chapters 1–3. Cain's giving has not corresponded to the goodness of what God made and has not suggested that Cain has inherited the ability to recognize the difference between good and bad. His doing something that didn't really count as good doesn't imply that he had done something wrong. It did mean he didn't get an enthusiastic response from Yahweh. It is through having this experience that he is in danger of wrongdoing. The kind of testing experience that came to his mother (and will come to Abraham and to Job) is now coming to him.[54] "Wrongdoing" is *ḥaṭṭā'āt*, conventionally translated "sin"; it suggests failing to meet God's standards, more because one doesn't try than because one tries and falls short. With some irony, the word does not occur in Gen. 2–3, which is regularly and plausibly seen as the story of how sin entered the world.[55] In Yahweh's own way of speaking, the moment when someone has offered something to him and then has found that Yahweh's response is negative is the moment when sin threatens. Wrongdoing lies there relaxed, like a sheep or lion having a nice rest (the best-known occurrence of the verb is Ps. 23:2). The entrance it is keeping an eye on is presumably that of Cain's tent (cf. 18:1), or metaphorically that of Cain's life. There's no suggestion that it's crouching while waiting to pounce. It's quite comfortable and laid back. It knows it won't need to do anything very shrewd to catch this victim.

It does have its eye on Cain (v. 7b). "Desire" is the word Yahweh has used to describe the woman's feelings toward her man (3:16).[56] Whatever the moral significance of that desire, there is no doubt that this desire is threatening. It will aim to issue in a consuming of its object. As in that earlier verse, "ruling" is set over against "desire." Like Eve in relation to Adam is the animal's desire in relation to Cain. So what kind of creature lies at the entrance to the tent and might pounce? The link with Gen. 2–3 makes one wonder whether it is again a snake.[57] Cain's parents had been told to exercise authority over the animal creation; instead they gave in to its blandishments. Cain is told that he needs to rule over the wrongdoing that lies at the door and is waiting to catch him in the same way. Targums Ps.-J. and Neof. underline the freedom Yahweh gives Cain to master wrongdoing, and Erasmus refers to these verses in his defense of the notion of free will.[58] Luther responds that the exhortation that Cain should master wrongdoing does not mean that he can.[59] While Erasmus has the better of the exegetical argument, Luther

54. Cf. Pfoh, "Genesis 4 Revisited."
55. Cf. Abraham, "Feminist Hermeneutics."
56. Hendel ("Leitwort Style") lists many such links of words within Gen. 1–11.
57. Cf. Scarlata, *Outside of Eden*, 80–81; Gordon, "'Couch' or 'Crouch'?"
58. Erasmus, "Discussion of Freewill," in *Collected Works*, 76:33.
59. Luther, *Genesis 1–5*, 269.

has the better of the theological one. But the two theologians are operating with different notions of free will, and both are seeking to push the implications of the text in a more logical way than is possible. Much of this verse is allusive and ambiguous, and we need to leave it that way. As is the case with Gen. 3, this story works by raising more questions than it answers.[60]

4:8. Cain has nothing to say back to Yahweh. Perhaps he was not listening. He believes that actions speak louder than words. He turns his plowshare into a sword.[61] "Unable to kill God, Cain kills God's favorite."[62] The account of the horrific slaying is terse, short, and to the point.

> O Cain, what are you doing? Don't you know to whom you're talking? Don't you understand that this conversation is taking place with your brother? Don't you realize that he was born of the same mother as you?[63]

For Cain, such considerations are overwhelmed by the need to bury his burden of shame and of the necessity to face every day the brother whom Yahweh prefers (KSG). The open country is where you do something that no one can see (Deut. 22:25–27). Thus "the first man who was really naturally born into this real world is a murderer."[64] There is something Gothic about Cain.[65]

4:9. Yahweh responds with a question like the one he addressed to Adam (3:9), which might again imply that he is holding back from knowing the answer or simply giving Cain the chance to own up to what he has done—the effect is the same. Cain's response begins with a lie. Then he asks his own rhetorical question, which implies his assumption that Yahweh doesn't know the answer, and he incorporates another occurrence of the verb "keep" (cf. 2:15; 3:24). Does Cain mean that Yahweh is the person who ought to know the answer to his own question? After all, Yahweh is supposed to be the keeper of his people (e.g., Pss. 121:3, 4, 5; 145:20).[66] Indeed, Cain thereby raises a troubling question, for Yahweh has not been keeping Abel, or (for that matter) keeping Cain by keeping him from falling to temptation. And/or is Cain also making a snide observation about his own occupation and about his brother's occupation, about which Yahweh might seem to be enthusiastic? Abel pastured sheep, about which Yahweh had said nothing. Cain kept the ground, a project about which Yahweh was enthusiastic. Is Cain supposed to keep his brother as well?

60. Cf. Gertz, "Variations autour du récit de Caïn et Abel."
61. Cf. Kahl, "Fratricide and Ecocide," 63.
62. Schlimm, *From Fratricide to Forgiveness*, 139.
63. Chrysostom, *Homilies on Genesis 18–45*, 22.
64. Noort, "Genesis 4:1–16," 105; cf. Zimmerli, *1. Mose 1–11*, 230.
65. See Ng, "Death and the Double."
66. See Vogels, "'Guardian of My Brother, Me?'"

4:10–12. Yet another rhetorical question follows. Yahweh does know what has happened, but not merely through his general omniscience. "Cry out" is almost a technical word for the cry of the needy or the oppressed, addressed to human beings with power, or to God (e.g., Pss. 34:17 [34:18]; 77:1 [77:2]). It transpires that the scream of people who are treated wrongly is not silenced when they are killed. While they themselves may cry out before it happens, their blood continues to scream afterward. It does so because it falls onto the ground and lies there as a stain that cannot be missed. A slaying cannot simply be ignored as if it did not matter. It puts the world out of kilter. Shed blood cries out for redress. It does not cry out without there being someone listening. "Abel was dead to Cain, but not to God."[67]

A curse therefore follows (v. 11). In his parents' story the snake has been cursed and the ground has been cursed, but now the wrongdoer himself is cursed, with a combination of or a cross between those two curses. As God spoke performatively in bringing the world into being, so he continues to speak performatively.[68] Cain receives a curse like the snake's, a "more than" curse. This "more than" compares Cain to the ground that was the object of the curse uttered to his father. This curse appropriately and necessarily banishes him from the ground because of the scream that arises from it. There is no way that Cain can now be tending the ground and expecting it to produce its fruit. He has served the ground and brought the fruit of the ground, but now he has alienated the ground.[69] At the same time and in a strange fashion, the curse respects Cain in a way that ignoring his action or easily forgiving it would not. Rather than simply sending him off in shame with no means of making good for what he has done, it treats him as a responsible human being and even invites him to repent. Nor does Yahweh give him the escape of death. Perhaps Yahweh will rather have him go on with life and be the means of creating the town and carving out a new future for humanity and even thus making some redress for his wrongdoing and working off his shame (KSG).

The result (v. 12) is that whereas he had been the one who took up Yahweh's commission to his parents to serve the ground, who had brought his not-good-enough offering from it to Yahweh, and who had shed his brother's blood, he will find that the ground will no longer yield its fruitfulness to him. Energy (*kōaḥ*) is not something that only personal beings possess. The world of nature has life and a voice and a will. It is personal and alive.[70] The ground has a mouth, and Abel's blood has a voice. The world of nature can praise, protest, and cooperate with humanity or resist it. The notion of the

67. J. Thompson (*Genesis 1–11*, 200), paraphrasing Erasmus's comment (*Collected Works*, 44:245) on Heb. 11:4.

68. See Vermeulen, "Verbal Creation," 305–6.

69. Cf. Gunkel, *Genesis*, 45.

70. Cf. Wittenberg, "Alienation and 'Emancipation' from the Earth," 108–10; cf. Jørstad, "Ground That Opened Its Mouth."

ground having energy thus continues the personification involved in the talk of Abel's blood crying out. The created world is alive and can behave with the determination of a human being. Hence Cain's life as a farmer is finished. He can only be a vagabond and a wanderer. They are two similar participles (*nāʿ* and *nād*) to make essentially the same point. The words do not suggest honor or have positive connotations, like words such as nomad or Bedouin. They rather indicate that Cain is to be a homeless hobo. Cain becomes "without God, . . . without home, . . . without food."[71]

4:13–14. "Under the weight of this curse Cain goes to pieces."[72] The conversation continues as Cain issues his own protest. As was the case with his parents, there is no expression of penitence but only regret at the consequences of his action for him.

He introduces another of the First Testament's key expressions for sin (v. 13), "waywardness" (*ʿāwōn*). Yahweh had warned him that he was in danger of "wrongdoing"; he himself recognizes that he has already acted deviantly. Yahweh has made clear that he must carry responsibility for his deviant behavior. But the burden is too heavy. "In truth there is not misery greater than to be deserted and despised by God; for the anarchy of fools is cruel and very intolerable; but to be despised by the great King, and to fall down as an abject person cast down from the government of the Supreme Power is an indescribable affliction."[73] But Cain has not recognized that fact. Nor is he referring to the psychological burden of his waywardness, as is often the connotation of the English expression "the burden of sin." It might be better if he did mean that he felt this burden. He is referring to the objective consequences of his waywardness that Yahweh has just pronounced. It is perhaps a surprising complaint. Abel's shed blood was surely crying out for the shedding of Cain's blood, and one might have expected that murder would carry the death penalty. It does not, but Cain is not recognizing his luck or the divine mercy.

Rather, he goes on (v. 14) to expand on the negative implications of Yahweh's pronouncement. He protests about God, about himself, and about other people, as one does in a psalm.[74] Yahweh has driven his father out of Lush to serve the ground outside (3:23–24); Yahweh is driving him out from the face of that ground. Cain speaks as if it has already happened, in accordance with the way Hebrew can speak of a future event as if it has already taken place, especially when Yahweh has decided it, and it's therefore certain to happen (it is the way prophecies sometimes speak). There are two faces that humanity was designed to serve and to live in fellowship with: the face of the ground and the face of Yahweh. Cain will no longer be able to look either in the face. Both will be hostile. The ground will refuse to yield its energy. And although

71. Frey, *Buch der Anfänge*, 78–79; cf. E. Peels, "World's First Murder," 28.

72. Von Rad, *Genesis*, 103.

73. Philo, *Questions and Answers on Genesis* 1.73.

74. Cf. Westermann, *Genesis 1–11*, 309.

his parents had understandably but futilely hidden from Yahweh's face after eating from the tree, Cain had not tried to hide after killing Abel, but now he knows he will have to conceal himself from Yahweh's face. The hostility of that face is not merely a matter of an attitude or a look. The expression on a person's face can issue either in blessing or in trouble (e.g., 16:6, 8; 31:2, 5; and famously, Num. 6:25). Cain knows how the look on the face will be and whose look it will be. His position anticipates that of the manager in Jesus's parable who is to be thrown out of his job and worries about not being strong enough to dig and being ashamed to beg (Luke 16:3). But further, a homeless hobo who belongs to no place and no community has no security. Indeed, some obligation rests on the community to take redress on a murderer. Another reason why Cain will have to leave the tilled land is that as a murderer he is an outcast. "In some ways it is a fate worse than death."[75]

(So far, we would have assumed that the only human beings who exist are Adam, Eve, Cain, and Abel, but the story is evidently at ease with the implication that there are many more people around. Perhaps Cain's potential executioners are yet-unmentioned siblings [cf. 5:4]—after all, Eve is the mother of all. But the chapters are historical parables, and in a parable one does not press the details.)

4:15–16. As happened with Adam and Eve, Yahweh mercifully tempers his retribution: "The curse is not the final and only word of God about the brother-murderer."[76] Although Yahweh might have said, "Tough, that's what you'll deserve in return for murdering Abel," instead he declares that redress will be exacted on Cain's own murderer. "God does not let go of the unreconciled one."[77] Evidently it is impossible to second-guess what Yahweh will do. It's also difficult to see what sevenfold redress would constitute. Presumably it doesn't mean seven of the potential murderer's family being killed. More likely it is a figure of speech, like "an eye for an eye and a tooth for a tooth." Verse 24 supports this possibility: it means frighteningly full redress. What the mark on Cain constituted, we also do not know.[78] Targum Ps.-J. takes the "mark" to be one of the letters from God's name, which would mean that attacking Cain would be attacking God (cf. James 3:9). "The riddle of his future existence" is that "because of his murder, he is cursed by separation from God," and yet he is also "incomprehensibly guarded and supported by God's protection"[79] (according to Jub. 4.31–32, it doesn't save him from being killed through his house collapsing on him eventually).

The place where he makes his home (v. 16) is appropriately called Drifting (*nôd*; "The Land of Nod" came to suggest sleep in British English). East of

75. Hamilton, *Genesis 1–17*, 232.
76. Zimmerli, *1. Mose 1–11*, 233.
77. Brueggemann, *Genesis*, 63.
78. Moberly ("Mark of Cain") argues that it is the threat in v. 15a itself.
79. Von Rad, *Genesis*, 103.

Lush is where the sphinxes and flaming sword were (3:24); the reference to the location draws attention to the garden's inaccessibility to him.[80]

4:17–18. Genesis does not concern itself with the identity of Cain's potential executioners; it also does not ask where his wife came from (at v. 1, Tg. Ps.-J. has Eve giving birth to a twin sister as well as Cain, and Jub. 4.1–9 identifies his wife as his sister Avan). Genesis is interested rather in the fact that Cain and his wife repeat his parents' story (see v. 1). Their son's name implies "Dedication" (compare the name of the Hanukkah festival, the occasion of the temple's rededication after the defilement by Antiochus Epiphanes). Presumably Cain was seeking to deal with the implications of being banished from the ground when he set about building a town, presumably the world's first. The listeners will be familiar with the way towns become a refuge for people who have no land.[81] Town life thus has at best an ambiguous beginning.

The story hastens through four more generations (v. 18) in order to reach the next figure on which it will focus. Genesis will manifest a pattern whereby it covers briefly the son whose line is not the one in which Yahweh is especially at work before coming to a more expansive treatment of the son on whose line the future depends (Japhet and Ham before Shem, Ishmael before Isaac, Esau before Jacob: Gen. 10; 25; 36). This pattern finds its first iteration in 4:17–26. Yet Cain's line gets more extensive treatment than this pattern would make one expect; it has some significance in its own right. This fact is noteworthy when set over against Cain's being a murderer, whereas figures such as Ishmael and Esau were not such wrongdoers.

4:19–22. Lamech causes the story to pause for a moment: he is the initiator of another familiar reality, polygamous marriage. In the First Testament and elsewhere, there are two main reasons for having more than one wife: status and a first wife's inability to have children. For Lamech the second consideration seems irrelevant (vv. 20–22), but the first may apply (cf. vv. 23–24). Genesis makes no negative judgment on Lamech's polygamy, though his being the man who wreaks personal vengeance, for which he boasts in vv. 23–24, may point in that direction.

The story continues to provide the listeners with the background to realities they know (v. 20). While any family would need to look after its animals (cf. v. 2), one might divide lifestyles more broadly between the settled farmer and the more nomadic shepherd or cattleman. While Cain was condemned to the life of a wanderer, the positive spin to put on that designation is to call it the lifestyle of a shepherd or cowboy. A shepherd must keep on the move in the marginal land between cultivable country and desert, looking for provision for sheep and cattle and living in a tent rather than a house in a village. Such is the life of Lamech's first son.

80. Cf. Ellul, *Meaning of the City*, 4.

81. Luciani, "Gn 4,17 (la première ville) et ses commentaires."

Another category of people that one finds in a town (v. 21) is those who are involved in arts and crafts, and such is Yabal's brother Yubal. It is appropriate for him to bear a name derived from those three consonants, since a *yôbēl* is a horn (the word lies behind the term "Jubilee," a festival heralded by the blowing of a horn). The instruments mentioned, however, are guitar (*kinnôr*), standing for stringed instruments in general, and pipe, standing for all instruments that one blows.

Yabal's and Yubal's half brother (v. 22) is the ancestor of another group of craftworkers from the town. Tubal is another name that suggests the same root as Yabal and Yubal. The mention of his sister perhaps makes for balance in the mention of the two offspring of Adah and Sillah. Copper (with the alloy bronze, which *nəḥōšet* also covers) and iron were the two most significant metals worked in the ancient world. The second half of Tubal's name may have nothing to do with the Cain earlier in the chapter, given that related languages have words resembling *qayin* that mean metalworker (see BDB)—or rather, it may designate Tubal in light of the etymological meaning of that name.

4:23–24. Lamech's chief claim to fame, or infamy, issues from composing the first human verse; previous verse in Genesis has been God's. Lamech's verse is neater. It comprises three lines with parallelism, 4-4, 4-2, and 3-3. As "Lamech's women" are the same people as "Adah and Sillah," so "a young man" can be the same person as "a man," but the second word heightens and gives precision to the first, and "seventy-sevenfold" heightens "sevenfold." Tellingly, each of the first four cola closes with the first-person sufformative, or suffix, "my . . . my . . . me . . . me," though "its disciplined form only accentuates the barbarity of the message."[82] One boasts to one's womenfolk, and Lamech does so. What might be the background to the poem? Who had wounded Lamech, and who had he killed? Or is this poem simply a boast about the kind of man he claims to be?—"No one had better mess with me!"[83] In that case, we need not assume that the young man is the same as the man.[84] Either way, the point is that things are getting worse and worse in Genesis. In Gen. 3 there is disobedience. In 4:1–16 there is murder. In 4:17–24 there is the threat of murder upon murder. The human inclination to take disproportionate redress underlies the need for the limitation to equivalence that the Torah will later require (see Exod. 21:23–25, where the words for "wound" and "injury" recur). Recording the poem brings to a climax the story's hints at the ambiguity involved in the development of human culture. If we may assume that Lamech has used a weapon to strike down his victim and that he would have sung or chanted his poem, then the story speaks of the origin of music, technology, and poetry but illustrates them from the life of Lamech as

82. Wenham, *Genesis 1–15*, 114.
83. Cf. Calvin, *Genesis*, 1:219–21.
84. Cf. Hamilton, *Genesis 1–17*, 241.

their first horrifying exploiter. There is even an ambiguity in the significance of his speaking thus to his women, given that his words could be read as a confession—but the words are addressed to them rather than to God (KSG).

4:25–26. The poem's "negative pole" thus perhaps "outweighs the positive signs of culture's progress."[85] "Even though humanity advances culturally and technologically, things are not at all the way they should be between humans and their Creator."[86] Fortunately the unit will not end (in the MT or in printed Bibles) until a more unequivocally positive note has been sounded.[87]

We have forgotten about Adam and Eve (v. 25), and obviously the story has moved on far beyond their day, but now it moves back to the aftermath of Cain's killing of Abel. Seth's name (more precisely, Šet) recalls the verb *šît*, which we can fortuitously render "set in place." But Eve's words about setting offspring in place also recall 3:15, with hopeful irony, while her renewed mention of Abel and Cain recalls Yahweh's words about the pain of motherhood in 3:16. In the very act of naming she is "erecting a monument, as it were, to her other son."[88] Genesis deals briefly with the line on whom the future does not depend before dealing at greater length with the line on whom it does depend, and it sometimes tells its story in a dramatic sequence rather than in chronological order. In light of this pattern, we need not have assumed that Seth was born after Abel's murder rather than while the two older boys were young. But as 4:25 makes clear, in this case he actually was born later.

Whereas Eve named Seth, Seth names Enosh (v. 26), an ordinary word for "man," like *ʾādām*. In effect, Eve herself has expressed the conviction that God has initiated an alternative line to that of Cain, one that will take the place of a line that would have descended from Abel. Her statement of faith is even more spectacular than the one with which the chapter began (given what has happened in between). The evidence for the truth of her conviction is that at this time (that is, way back in the time of Adam, Eve, Seth, and Enosh, the very first human generations), people start calling out with Yahweh's name, as will Abraham (12:8; 13:4; 21:33) and Isaac (26:25). Like the making of offerings, such calling out most often suggests praise and thus proclamation (e.g., Pss. 80:19 [80:18]; 105:1; 116:13, 17). When people worship, it is in words as well as by means of offerings. The addition of the expression "with Yahweh's name" underlines how this praise is vocal and not merely in the heart, which is what makes it by its nature also proclamation; the very nature of worship is also to be witness. Calling out with Yahweh's name in prayer (e.g., Ps. 116:4; Isa. 64:7 [64:6]) can accompany offerings; it also is vocal and links with proclamation.

85. Coats, *Genesis*, 68.

86. Lowery, *Toward a Poetics of Genesis 1–11*, 240.

87. Though not in the Tg, which gives a negative slant to the calling in v. 26: it suggests lax or illicit worship (cf. e.g., Qimchi, *Genesis*, on the verse); nor in Zimmerli, *1. Mose 1–11*, 243, which treats the sections as 4:1–24 and 4:25–5:32.

88. Chrysostom, *Homilies on Genesis 18–45*, 45.

People are appealing to the real God as he will reveal himself to Israel. They are not calling on some other deity who can't really do anything as they make offerings to such a deity (cf. 1 Kings 18:24–26). Praise, proclamation, and prayer make an appeal to the real God of whom humanity knew from creation. Humanity did not need to evolve through various other ("primitive"?) forms of religion and worship; God had made himself known to them from the beginning. The reference to calling out with *Yahweh's* name is especially bold and significant. Exodus 3 and 6 will relate how Yahweh first reveals his name to Moses. Here in the time before Moses, people would not have been literally calling with Yahweh's name. But the author of Gen. 4 knows that it is Yahweh whom people have acknowledged in this earlier time, even if they do not literally call him by that name. After all, it is Yahweh who created the world and Yahweh who makes promises to Abraham. So the stress in v. 26b lies on the fact that people are starting to praise, proclaim, and make requests of the real God.[89] Genesis 4 thus finally juxtaposes "radical sin . . . , high culture . . . , and confessional religion . . . in an uneasy combination."[90]

Implications

Though Dead, They Still Speak

Genesis 4 has stimulated a particularly extensive history of interpretation.[91] Hebrews 11:4–5 sees Abel as a model of relating to God on the basis of trust, which is a plausible inference from Gen. 4, though not a point it makes. The point that Genesis makes is that trust is not just a matter of an attitude of heart. It involves bringing the produce of one's work as an offering to God and offering him the best. One is then to expect that God will respond to one's offering—perhaps with recognition, perhaps not. Genesis 4 itself ensures that the point Heb. 11 goes on to make is true, that "even death does not mute Abel's voice."[92] Even if "innocent blood has no voice . . . discernible by human ears, . . . it has one that reaches God, as the cry of a wicked deed demanding vengeance."[93] Thus "Abel's death meant, in many ways, a new life for him."[94] But innocent blood can speak in two ways. The martyrs' blood cries out for redress, and God promises it (cf. Rev. 6:10–11). At the same time, as Heb. 12:24 also notes, the blood of Jesus makes a different appeal, and God responds to that appeal too.[95]

89. See Bakon, "And He Called."
90. Brueggemann, *Genesis*, 67.
91. See esp. Byron, *Cain and Abel*.
92. Hamilton, *Genesis 1–17*, 246.
93. Keil and Delitzsch, *Pentateuch*, 113.
94. Byron, *Cain and Abel*, 204.
95. See Hilhorst, "Abel's Speaking."

Cain, too, still speaks. In contrast to Abel, Cain gives an example of which believers are to be wary (Jude 11). While Adam was expelled from God's garden for his disobedience, Cain was put under a curse and expelled from God's presence for his fratricide, though the exegetical tradition has been harder on Cain than God himself was.[96] The "fall" in this story is much worse than the "fall" in Gen. 3. "What is so shocking about the whole event is that a man like him, who does his work and presents his offering to God, is capable of this"; it is what God's unequal treatment of two brothers can lead to (see Luke 15:11–32).[97] Yet to Cain, God is pastor, judge, and protector.[98] And even if it is possible to see a basis in Abel's action for God's responding to him, we can see nothing in Cain that provides a basis for God's responding to him. It is just an act of grace.[99] "Cain murders—and walks."[100] His murderous act is but the beginning of a horrific and grievous history of members of the people of God shedding each other's blood (Matt. 23:35). Only one step back from that shedding of blood is the hatred that members of the people of God have harbored toward one another (1 John 3:11–15).[101] Luke 15 also recognizes that the elder brother may find it hard to live with his younger sibling; he is a Cain-like figure.[102] But Ps. 133 promises that brothers can live together.

Lamech, too, still speaks. The development of civilization, music, technology, and poetry is part of the earliest history of humanity, in all the ambiguity of that history, reflected in the varying exegeses of 4:17–24.[103] One must do justice to both sides of the ambiguity. On the other hand, priesthood is not part of that earliest history. Nor is kingship, as it is in (for instance) the Sumerian King List, a list of kings on a stone tablet from Sumer in Iraq, various versions of which date from the third, second, and first millennia BCE. According to the king list, "kingship was lowered from heaven."[104] Yet the development of kingship in Israel will relate to facing the implications of the negative side to the development of civilization and technology.

And Seth still speaks. Genesis 1 does not imply that being made in God's image signifies that humanity has a spiritual nature that enables it to relate to God. But the Gen. 2–4 stories do indicate that humanity has that capacity, and the end of Gen. 4 makes the point most explicitly. Alongside the making of offerings that are the best of the fruit of one's work, another key aspect of relating to God in worship is a verbal, out-loud calling with God's name

96. Byron, *Cain and Abel*, e.g., 93, 207–12.
97. Westermann, *Genesis 1–11*, 302.
98. See H. Peels, "In het teken van Kaïn," 187.
99. Cf. Barth, *CD* 2.2:341, 355.
100. Dershowitz, *Genesis of Justice*, 48.
101. See, e.g., Menken, "Genesis in John's Gospel and 1 John," 95–97.
102. Brueggemann, *Genesis*, 61–62.
103. On which see Paul, "Genesis 4:17–24."
104. *ANET* 265. See further Jacobsen, *Sumerian King List*.

in praise, proclamation, and prayer, made in light of God's revelation of who he is. There are people who focus on what they can achieve by science, technology, culture, self-analysis, development of gifts, and action to put things right according to their light, and others who focus on calling upon God (KSG).

5
From Adam to Noah

(5:1–6:8)

Overview

The resumptive opening of Gen. 5 takes us back to the beginning of the Genesis story in the manner of the resumptive opening to an episode in a television series; the narrative arc of Gen. 1–4 (creation, waywardness, disaster, encouragement) will recur over Gen. 5–8. The narrative arc of this introduction to the deluge story leads the listeners along before kicking them in the teeth. The record of Adam's line of descent in Gen. 5 builds on the hopefulness of the end of Gen. 4, but it has to be realistic about the fact that each of the people who are mentioned died (except the mysterious Enoch); they did not have access to the life-tree. So the listeners might again be waiting for the other shoe to drop. Even if they are waiting, the beginning of Gen. 6 has a devastating impact. A question lies behind Gen. 5:1–6:8: why does the deluge need to happen? The answer is perplexing. Like Gen. 3, the section raises questions as well as resolving them. Genesis 5 is ambiguous in its implications, the story in 6:1–2 mystifies, the declaration of intent in 6:3 is a puzzle, and the footnote in 6:4 is enigmatic. In some respects the conclusion in 6:5–8 is only too clear, but not so clear is how it follows from what precedes, and it raises questions of its own. Yahweh regrets? Yahweh will wipe out? And why will he favor Noah? The author of Gen. 5:1–6:8 has some supernatural knowledge (for instance, about some things that God is thinking) but does not know everything. As was the case in Gen. 3, the effect is to recognize the tragic and mysterious aspect to human experience as well as the willful and intelligible aspect, and by facing it to help us to live with it.

Translation

5:1 This is the document with Adam's[1] lines of descent.

At the time of[2] God's creating humanity, it was in the likeness of God that he made it. **2**Male and female he created them, and he blessed them and named them "humanity" at the time of their being created.

- **3**Adam lived 130 years, fathered someone[3] in his likeness, as his image, and named him Šet. **4**Adam's time[4] after fathering Šet came to 800 years, and he fathered sons and daughters. **5**So the entire time that Adam lived came to 930 years. Then he died.[5]
- **6**Šet lived 105 years, and fathered Enoš. **7**Šet lived 807 years after fathering Enoš, and fathered sons and daughters. **8**So Šet's entire time came to 912 years. Then he died.
- **9**Enoš lived 90 years, and fathered Qenan. **10**Enoš lived 815 years after fathering Qenan, and fathered sons and daughters. **11**So Enoš's entire time came to 905 years. Then he died.
- **12**Qenan lived 70 years, and fathered Mahalalʾel. **13**Qenan lived 840 years after fathering Mahalalʾel, and fathered sons and daughters. **14**So Qenan's entire time came to 910 years. Then he died.
- **15**Mahalalʾel lived 65 years, and fathered Yered. **16**Mahalalʾel lived 830 years after fathering Yered, and fathered sons and daughters. **17**So Mahalalʾel's entire time came to 895 years. Then he died.
- **18**Yered lived 162 years, and fathered Ḥanok.[6] **19**Yered lived 800 years after fathering Ḥanok, and fathered sons and daughters. **20**So Yered's entire time came to 962 years. Then he died.
- **21**Ḥanok lived 65 years, and fathered Metušelaḥ. **22**Ḥanok walked about with God[7] 300 years after fathering Metušelaḥ, and fa-

1. Through vv. 1–3 *ʾādām* is anarthrous and thus could refer either to Adam or to humanity; the LXX has humanity here but Adam in vv. 1b–2. But following on 4:25, here *ʾādām* likely denotes Adam, while vv. 1b–2 in resuming 1:27–28 must be referring to humanity.

2. More literally, "on the day of," and again in v. 2; see the footnote to 2:4b.

3. The MT has no word for "someone"; in other words, the verb has no object. Hutzli ("Procreation of Seth by Adam") suggests the inference that Seth is portrayed as asexual to safeguard the asexuality of the God in whose image he was procreated.

4. More literally, "days"—contrast the singular in vv. 1–2 to denote a punctiliar time.

5. Targum Neof. takes the edge off this tough-minded conclusion to each paragraph by paraphrasing, "He was gathered from the midst of the world"; compare the formula in a passage such as 25:8.

6. The form "Enoch" follows the LXX transliteration.

7. As in 3:8, the hitpael of *hālak* suggests that he was not merely walking (see *IBHS* 26.1.2). The LXX has him "pleasing" God (cf. Heb. 11:5), which more appropriately is its translation of the different expression "walk about before me" in 17:1. The Tg similarly has Hanok "walking in awe" of Yahweh or "serving in truth" before Yahweh. "Walked about with God" rather suggests friendship.

thered sons and daughters. **23**So Ḥanok's entire time came to[8]
365 years. **24**Ḥanok walked about with God, and then he was no
more, because God took him.

- **25**Metušelaḥ lived 187 years, and fathered Lemek. **26**Metušelaḥ
lived 782 years after fathering Lemek, and fathered sons and
daughters. **27**So Metušelaḥ's entire time came to 969 years.
Then he died.
- **28**Lemek lived 182 years, fathered a son, **29**and named him Noaḥ,
saying: "This man: he'll relieve us[9] from our work,[10] from the pain
of our hands, from the ground that Yahweh cursed." **30**Lemek
lived 595 years after fathering Noaḥ, and fathered sons and
daughters. **31**So Lemek's entire time came to 777 years. Then he
died.
- **32**Noaḥ lived 500 years, and Noaḥ fathered Šem, Ḥam, and
Yepet.[11]

6:1 But when humanity started to be numerous on the face of the
ground and daughters were born to them, **2**the divine beings[12] saw that
the human daughters were good[13] and got women for themselves, any
one that they chose. **3**Yahweh said, "My spirit will not govern[14] over hu-
manity through the ages, in that indeed[15] it is flesh. Its time will be 120

8. The verb is oddly singular; on the other occurrences in vv. 5, 8, 11, 14, 17, 20, 27, and 31 it is plural, and the LXX and Vg assimilate this occurrence to that usage.

9. For *yənaḥămēnû*, the LXX has "give us respite," implying a form of the verb *nûaḥ*; see the comment.

10. *Maʿăśēnû* spelled thus looks like the singular form of the noun (cf. the LXX); contrast the plural spelling at Isa. 26:12. But the Vg takes this as a defective spelling of the plural. See the discussion in Tal, *Genesis*, 91*.

11. In the MT's *yāpet* (cf. the LXX's *Iaphet*, also the Vg, and thus English Japhet), the *ā* vowel comes from the name's pausal vocalization (cf. 4:2 and the note).

12. Different editions of the LXX, the other Greek translations, and the Tgs translate *bənê-hāʾĕlōhîm* in varying ways, reflecting how controversial the phrase came to be: see Tal, *Genesis*, 91–92*; Brayford, *Genesis*, 260; Aberbach and Grossfeld, *Targum Onkelos to Genesis*, 50–51; P. Alexander, "Targumim and Early Exegesis."

13. The LXX renders *kalos* rather than *agathos*, which might imply that they looked good; yet it used the same adjective in Gen. 1. The Vg used *bonus* in Gen. 1 but here uses *pulcher*, which makes more explicit that they looked good. Targum Ps.-J. expands on the point with reference to their makeup and their exposure of themselves.

14. *Yādôn* looks like a form from an otherwise unknown verb *dûn* (BDB) or *dānan* (Hendel, "Nephilim Were on the Earth," 15; cf. *HALOT*). I take it as an irregular yiqtol from *dîn* (BDB), which would mean "rule, exercise authority" (Zech. 3:7) or possibly "contend" (Eccles. 6:10); cf. Sym's *krinei*; also more paraphrastically Tg. Ps.-J., Tg. Neof. The LXX, Vg, Tg. Onq. have "abide, dwell," which might imply *yādôr* (cf. 4Q252, part of 4QCommentary on Genesis; also Ps. 84:11, something of an Aramaism) but is "perhaps nothing more than a plausible guess" (Skinner, *Genesis*, 143). Rashi comments, "There are many aggadic comments on *lōʾ yādôn*" (*Brʾšyt*, 61).

15. *Bəšaggam*: the preposition *bə* followed by the particle *š* followed by the adverb *gam*; cf. the LXX, Vg. Some MSS have *bəšaggām*, which would mean "because of their going astray" (see BDB under *šāgag*).

years."[16] [4]Now the Fallen[17] were on the earth at that time and also afterward, when the divine beings were sleeping with[18] the human daughters and they were giving birth for them. Those were the strong men that were of old, famous men.

[5]Yahweh saw that humanity's bad state on the earth was great. The entire shaping of its heart's[19] intentions was simply bad, all day. [6]Yahweh regretted[20] that he had made humanity on the earth. It pained his heart. [7]Yahweh said, "I will wipe out the humanity that I created from the face of the ground, from humanity to animals to moving things to birds in the heavens, because I regret that I made them." [8]But Noaḥ—he found favor in Yahweh's eyes.[21]

Interpretation

If a "document" about Adam's line of descent begins here (5:1), where does it end? The medieval chapter division makes a break after the birth of Noah's sons (5:32). But while the MT has a number of paragraph and unit breaks through Gen. 5, it has no break after 5:32; it has a unit break after 6:4, another after 6:8, another after 9:17, and another after 9:29. This last has a good claim to be designated the end of the "document," because 9:28–29 completes the formulaic description of Noah that begins in 5:32; a new heading then follows in 10:1, "The lines of descent of Noah's sons, Shem, Ham, and Japhet." Those data suggest taking 5:1–9:29 as a section of the book. Admittedly, the original "document" might have gone straight from 5:32 to 9:28–29, with the intervening material later inserted into it in the process whereby Genesis itself came into being. Further, 6:9 already provides a resumptive heading to introduce what follows as "Noah's lines of descent," which rather invites readers to see these words as the opening of a section; it is the beginning of the second synagogue parashah (lection) in Genesis, following on 1:1–6:8 and running on to 11:32. We will accept this invitation and treat 5:1–6:8 as a section.

16. The Tgs make explicit that the 120 years are time for humanity to turn back.

17. Rashi (*Brʾšyt*, 61) notes that *hannəpilîm* were so called because they "fell" and caused the world's "downfall." Although Tg. Onq. here replaces *hannəpilîm* with "the strong men" as in v. 4, which might imply a desire to safeguard against speculative interpretations of the idea of fallen angels, in v. 4 it makes explicit reference to angels that fell (Aberbach and Grossfeld, *Targum Onkelos to Genesis*, 53). The LXX, Vg have "giants" (cf. the context of Num. 13:33).

18. Literally, "coming (in)to."

19. One would usually render *lēb* as "mind" in such a context, but it suggests "heart" in v. 6.

20. The Vg *paenituit* issues in the English translation "repented," which now gives a misleading impression, whereas like the Hebrew verb, the Latin verb means "be sorry, regret."

21. GKC 142b takes the word order with the subject first to indicate that the clause provides background information and that the verb should be rendered in the pluperfect. But it is simpler to take the word order as indicating that the clause offers a contrast with what precedes (DG 142c).

Genesis 5 is the first example of the Scriptures summarizing a lengthy period of time and history by means of a genealogical list. The lists take various forms. Genesis 10 will comprise simply names without ages, as will the lists in 1 Chron. 1–9; Matt. 1:1–17; Luke 3:23–38. But Gen. 10 and 1 Chron. 1–9 do incorporate some anecdotes or other expansions, as does Gen. 5 in its accounts of Enoch and Lamech. The lists in 1 Chron. 1:1–4 and Luke 3:36–38 correspond closely to Gen. 5. Genealogies are a brisk and efficient way of communicating the passage of time and the development of a story, a little like the speeded-up summaries of "previously on" that sometimes open episodes of a television series. But whatever their precise form, they carry messages, as does a separate genealogical list such as the one that closes the story of Ruth or the lists incorporated in Ezra-Nehemiah.

"Genealogies evoke the forward thrust of time. They are emblems of the future." The new genesis in Gen. 5 "evokes the possibility of a new future," notwithstanding what has preceded.[22] It offers "a construction of reality alternative to the one presented in Gen. 4"[23] and shows how God's creation purpose is being fulfilled. Humanity is experiencing God's blessing and is filling the earth. The ages that people live show that humanity is flourishing. But the list also shows that "death reigned from Adam until Moses" (Rom. 5:14), and thus incidentally until Noah. There is a more specific point about the figures relating how long people lived. Almost everyone lives for more than nine hundred years (in one case for almost nine hundred years) but for less than a thousand years. The exceptions are Enoch, who disappears after 365 years, and Lamech, who lives 777 years. Those two specific figures look significant. One is the number of days in a solar year. The other recalls the wide-ranging significance of seven as the number of days in the week (see 2:2–3) and as a feature of the earlier Lamech story (see 4:23–24). The other figures have in common that each falls a little short of a millennium: it could have seemed that each ancestor might live for a thousand years, might live forever, but not one does. Instead, each of their stories ends with the solemn footnote, "then he died . . . then he died . . . then he died. . . ."

The list in Matthew is schematized so as to comprise three fourteen-generation sections; comparison with the First Testament lists that it uses reveals how it constructs the fourteen-generation scheme by being selective in who it includes and omits. Genesis 5 similarly uses traditional material to generate a list that makes points about the passing of time from Adam to Noah. When Matthew says "Thus all the generations from Abraham to David were fourteen, and from David to the transportation to Babylon fourteen, and from the transportation to Babylon to the Anointed fourteen," it is not making a literal statement about history, and neither is Gen. 5 when it says that,

22. Reno, *Genesis*, 111.
23. Brett, *Genesis*, 39.

for example, someone fathered children at the age of 130 and subsequently lived on for a further 800 years. Author and listeners may have accepted the figures at their face value (as readers of Matt. 1 may take its fourteens literally), and our judgment that the figures are not making a literal statement issues from a Western framework. Yet author and listeners might have noticed some questions that the numbers raise: for instance, Noah apparently outlived Nahor, and Shem outlived Abraham. Indeed, the Hebrew text raises fewer difficulties than the Septuagint, according to whose figures Methusalaḥ did not die until after the flood.[24]

> Perhaps only a scholar studying the written Genesis scroll would be aware of the questions raised by various of the numbers. Hearing the scroll read would more likely invoke awe, the mystery of life and death, and the connectivity of the actions of the generations one to another. It also allows a stretching of the imagination to lengths of time such as hint at the lengthy time frame of the universe, which we convey by speaking of in terms of light years. Further, as modern readers we are inclined to think that our individual actions are all-important, but Gen. 5 reminds us of the importance of the long-term world story and draws attention to the birthing of children as a most important factor in this story, because it is the means through which life continues. (KSG)

In addition, the material on the long-living ancestors again compares and contrasts with the Sumerian King List.[25] The classic version of the King List says that between the lowering of kingship from heaven and the flood, eight Sumerian kings reigned for 241,200 years. The Sumerian kings after the flood then reigned for periods more like the lifetimes in Gen. 5 (twenty-three kings ruled for 24,510 years). Genesis 5 implies an awareness of such traditions (not necessarily this particular one) that spoke of the long lives of people in early times. There are eight figures between Adam and Noah, as there are eight early Sumerian kings. But Gen. 5 tells of ordinary people, not kings; these ordinary people descend from one another, whereas the kings of the different towns do not; it is their lifetimes and their families that are in focus, not their reigns; and the lifetimes associated with them are modest compared with those of the kings. Genesis 5 might thus have an effect on its readers parallel to the effect of Gen. 1 in light of a comparison and contrast with When on High. It might provoke the thought "You know those silly Sumerian statistics? Well, here are some less outlandish ones."

Genesis 5 also has points of comparison with Gen. 1; traditional source criticism sees Gen. 5 as the original continuation of Gen. 1.[26] Even less than

24. See Jerome, *Hebrew Questions on Genesis*, 35–36 (with Hayward's notes, 128). Josephus (*Ant.* 1.3.9) suggests that people lived longer in those days because they ate more sensibly.

25. See the comments under the heading "Though Dead, They Still Speak" at the end of the commentary on Gen. 4.

26. See, e.g., Gunkel, *Genesis*, 102–38; von Rad, *Genesis*, 43–71.

Gen. 1 is Gen. 5 a story with a plot or a question that it resolves, though it becomes part of a story with a plot and a question through its association with 6:1–8. In itself it is an account of a sequence of people, with no development. Its names overlap with the ones in Gen. 4: Seth and Enosh reappear at the beginning of the list, Enoch in the middle, and Lamech at the end. Qenan, Mahalal'el, Yered, and Methuselah are new names, though all are similar to names in Gen. 4: Qenan to Qayin, Mahalal'el to Mehuya'el, Yered to Irad, Methuselah to Metusa'el. The overlaps and similarities suggest that the two lists derive from different versions of the same list or set of stories. Genesis has used one version of the list to provide a picture of Cain's line and another version of the list to provide a picture of Seth's line. Elements in Gen. 5 that manifest characteristics associated with the Yahwist strand in Genesis (see the comments on vv. 1 and 29) indicate that the interweaving of sources in Genesis has been accompanied by some redaction.

Its points of connection with Gen. 4 further clarify the nature of Gen. 5 as a bridge between the Adam story and the Noah story. Whereas things happen in Gen. 4, nothing really happens in Gen. 5; the Genesis narrative marks time. In Gen. 5, in contrast with Gen. 4, there is neither positive nor negative development. The two accounts of events from Adam to Lamech complement each other as the two accounts of creation in Gen. 1 and Gen. 2–3 complement each other, though they appear in an abb′b′ order. Genesis 2–3 and 4 give a dynamic account of creation and of events from the creation to the eve of the flood; there is development both positive and negative. Genesis 1 and 5 give a steady-state version. In human history, one generation follows another without there being progress or development, or for that matter deterioration.[27] There is birth and growing up and procreating and living on—and dying. It is possible for individuals to stand out within this line. They may have a relationship with God that evokes wonder, though what happens to them may be a mystery. They may have hopes for their children that are fulfilled. They may be responsible for discoveries that make the tough side to human life more bearable. And Jesus eventually appears at the end of this line that begins with Adam (Luke 3:23–38), but nothing about this line as Gen. 5 documents it would make one expect Jesus to come at the end. Yet he does, and one needs to understand this line in order to understand Jesus.

With the exceptions of Enoch and Lamech, the ancestors' ages are 912, 905, 895, 962, and 969 years, averaging 929 years. In the SP the numbers for Yered, Methuselah, and Lamech are shorter, while in the LXX most of the fathers have their first son later but the total ages are mostly the same as the MT.[28] We do not know what lies behind the numbers. Some differences in the LXX and SP recensions may be designed to avoid the impression that some of the

27. Cf. Westermann, *Genesis 1–11*, 347.

28. For the details, see Skinner, *Genesis*, 134; Wenham, *Genesis 1–15*, 131.

figures lived on through the deluge.[29] And/or they may play a role in the devising of a timeline from creation to the exodus, the building of the temple, the fall of Jerusalem in 587, and the fall of Jerusalem in 70 CE, in which case the period from creation to the exodus is 2,666 years, or two-thirds of four millennia.[30] For readers unacquainted with this chronological framework, they simply underline the impression of concrete reality that belongs to the list.

While 6:1–8 carries straight on from 5:32 in the MT without a paragraph or unit break, in form as well as in message it makes for a contrast. Indeed, it makes for a double contrast, because the MT's unit break after 6:4 marks a sharp shift in form and message between vv. 1–4 and 5–8. Whereas Gen. 4 tells a discouraging story that ends with a glimmer of light, Gen. 5:1–6:8 tells a story that is more encouraging but ends with darkness.

Genesis 6:1–8 continues to describe a world that is both like and unlike the world the audience would know. It is like that world in that it begins from the reality of sexual disorder and the levying of sexual expectations by powerful males on females for whom resistance may be impossible. The general issue was raised in 3:16, will recur in Genesis, and will be presupposed by rules in the Torah that seek to constrain it and to protect women's rights. This world is unlike the audience's world in that the powerful figures are an alien class or classes, beings one does not meet nowadays. Yahweh's own assessment of the state of the world is that things are uniformly bad. That assessment puts into question the entire validity or success of the creation project. While comparison would again be possible with the bad state that might characterize the audience's world, the bad state of things in its day is surely nothing compared with the state things have reached according to 6:5–7.

The account in 6:1–4 works in a jerky fashion that has no parallel earlier or later in Genesis, which enhances the disturbing effect of what it describes. Grammatically, vv. 1–2 are coherent enough, and v. 3 follows smoothly with a waw-consecutive, but in content v. 3 involves a jump. Verse 4 begins as a circumstantial clause whose relationship to v. 3 in content, with its reference to the "Fallen," is unstated, though it is semi-clarified by the amplification in the middle of the verse. Verse 4 closes with another circumstantial clause whose relationship in content with what precedes is unstated: are the strong and famous men the offspring or the sons of the divine beings or the Fallen—or what? It is impossible to resolve all these questions with certainty; the passage expresses itself with an allusiveness, ambiguity, and murkiness that is intrinsic to its message about the dark strangeness of the events or situations that it describes. The author may be adapting an older traditional story with a background outside mainstream First Testament thinking,[31] but the mere

29. Cf. Tov, "Genealogical Lists in Genesis"; Hendel, *Text of Genesis 1–11*, 61–80.

30. Cf. von Rad, *Genesis*, 67. For a critique of such theories, see Hendel, "Hasmonean Edition of MT Genesis?"

31. For possibilities, see J. Day, *Creation to Babel*, 93–97.

fact that the passage is jerky, unique, and parallel to works outside the First Testament does not constitute strong evidence of this point. Many later Jewish and non-Jewish works have the same features.

A further lurch is then involved in the move from vv. 1–4 to vv. 5–8, though a lurch of a different kind from the internal jerkiness within vv. 1–4. In contrast to what has preceded in 5:1–6:4, in vv. 5–8 there comes a coherent theological judgment on the state of the world in the time to which it refers, expressed in connected and coherent regular prose sentences. In its talk of "humanity" and "creation" and "pain" and "the face of the ground," it picks up familiar motifs, and in that context its talk of things being "bad" resonates with the earlier importance of the word "good," especially in Gen. 1. At the same time, it introduces a range of new motifs: its talk of the mind's intentions, of Yahweh's regret, and of favor or grace. Here the narrator speaks freely and innovatively in reflecting on the implications of the story, making something like a statement from systematic theology.[32] Yet its summary description of the bad state of things is surprising, following on chapters 1–5 and even on 6:1–4; we have had little hint that things are as bad as it says. But its closing reference to Noah makes a link with chapter 5, while 6:9 suggests the opening of a new section.

5:1–2. Genesis 5 begins, however, in a way overlapping with 2:4a. The expression "lines of descent" (*tôlədôt*) appeared there in the retrospective footnote to 1:1–2:3, and one might see v. 1a here as a retrospective footnote to Gen. 4. But the formulation of v. 1a as a whole, with its reference to a "document" (unique in Genesis), differs from that in 2:4a. And what follows in Gen. 5 looks more like Adam's line of descent than Gen. 4 does. This reference is forward-looking and introductory, "as though making a fresh start and wanting to sooth Adam and Eve's grief which the murderer had presumed to inflict upon them with the death of his brother by raising his hand against Abel."[33]

"At the time of God's creating human beings" (v. 1b) then parallels "at the time of Yahweh God's making earth and heavens," the opening words in 2:4b–3:24, though "creating" is more a Gen. 1 word, and every subsequent expression in 5:1b–2 (humanity, likeness, make, male and female, create, bless, name) picks up from Gen. 1. So vv. 1b–2 as a whole forms a resumptive introduction to Gen. 5. Among the nuanced formulations are the defining of *ʾādām* as both male and female[34] and God's own naming of humanity, which perhaps reasserts his authority at the beginning of the account of humanity itself going about procreation.[35]

5:3–5. The description of Adam's fathering with its talk of image and likeness further recalls Gen. 1, while also taking its language further and providing

32. Cf. von Rad, *Genesis*, 113.
33. Chrysostom, *Homilies on Genesis 18–45*, 53.
34. Cf. Didymus, *Genesis*, 136.
35. So Sarna, *Genesis*, 41.

a midrashic answer to one or two other questions that might be raised by Gen. 2–4. In Eve, Adam could recognize someone who was like him, because she was made from a part of him. Subsequent human beings do not come into being in that way. How far is Seth like Adam? Adam fathers Seth as someone who is indeed "in his likeness, as his image." The prepositions and the nouns are the same as those in 1:26, but there they were paired in the opposite way, and the suffixes referred to God. The variation in the order of the nouns puts the emphasis on Seth's likeness to his father in character and follows it up with an assertion that he also shares his father's physical nature. The account of these lines of descent follows on the stories of Cain and of Lamech, who did not behave in a particularly godlike fashion, or even a particularly Adam-like fashion. Against this background, Tg. Ps.-J. notes, Gen. 5 affirms that Seth was indeed his father's son and resembled him. God passes on his image by creating; Adam passes on his image by procreating. Understanding the latter may then contribute to an understanding of the former.[36]

Does Seth share in God's image and likeness? Is he totally like God, as Adam was when created? Or is he nothing like God, because Adam has lost God's image and likeness?[37] The broader context of the Scriptures suggests that human beings are still made in God's image, but that this image is somewhat tainted, so that the answer would lie in between these two alternatives. Seth is in both images, "which gives him an unfortunate bipolarity" shared by subsequent humanity.[38] Such an inference fits the formulation in its distinctiveness and also fits its context.[39] Genesis 2–4 has made clear that humanity has failed to fulfill the role for which it was created as embodying God's image. If one considers Gen. 1 and 5 (as the P narrative) separately from Gen. 2–4, reading Gen. 5 in light of Gen. 1 makes more striking and significant the contrast between "in our image, as our likeness" and "in his likeness, as his image." Humanity is one: made in God's image and likeness and made in the image and likeness of one generation after another.

In other respects, the account of Adam lays down the formula that will run through the chapter. Humanity's creation as male and female (notwithstanding the formula's referring only to fathering) and its blessing are indeed beginning to work themselves out. The description of Adam and his descendants fathering sons and daughters illustrates that process and also opens up the possibility of a midrashic answer to the question "Who would be the people who were a threat to Cain and from whom Cain found a wife?" But Adam's story ends with "the first obituary in human history," a moment anticipated since 2:17.[40]

36. Cf. Ortlund, "Image of Adam, Son of God."
37. Cf. Luther, *Genesis 1–5*, 339–40.
38. Arnold, *Genesis*, 86.
39. Cf. Simango, "Meaning of the *Imago Dei*."
40. Arnold, *Genesis*, 87.

5:6–20. The accounts of Seth, Enosh, Qenan, Mahalal'el, and Yered unfold in a consistent way, without variation in the formula: when *x* had lived *y* years, he fathered *z*; *x* lived for *aaa* years after fathering *z* and fathered sons and daughters, so the entire time of *x* came to *bbb* years, then he died. A human life is one characterized by life, procreating the next generation, living on, and dying.

5:21–24. Only Enoch and Noah (6:9) walked about with God. Walking about *in front of* God (17:1) suggests transparency and implies conformity to expectations, but "walking about *with* God" suggests ongoing companionship of life; it can refer to keeping ordinary human company (1 Sam. 25:15). It suggests close friendship. Whereas Yahweh has walked about in the garden, and Adam and Eve have wanted to avoid him, Enoch wanted to walk about with God, and he enjoyed doing so for three hundred years after fathering his first son. He lived a complete life of 365 years, then disappeared. The story hints at a link between his walking about with God and God's taking him, though it does not explain the link. The account of his disappearance is a cross between the accounts of Moses's dying (Deut. 34) and of Elijah's being taken by Yahweh into the heavens (2 Kings 2). Like Moses, Enoch disappears, though Deut. 34 speaks explicitly of Moses's dying. Like Elijah, Enoch is taken by God, but there is no account of the way it happened. As the manner of Moses's and Elijah's departure made it possible for them to appear with Jesus, the manner of Enoch's disappearance makes it possible to infer that he has been taken to be with God (the references to God's "getting" in Pss. 49:15 [49:16]; 73:24 have been understood to refer to such a taking, but the contexts suggest that they refer to rescue from death and restoration to honor).[41] Such a destiny would qualify Enoch to reveal things about affairs in the heavens. He thus becomes the inspiration of the vast Enoch literature from Second Temple times, to which Jude 14–15 refers. Admittedly, "he was no more" could simply be a euphemism for dying (e.g., Gen. 42:13, 32; Job 7:8, 21; Pss. 37:10, 36; 39:13 [39:14]; 104:35; Jer. 31:15), and "taking" him could likewise denote bringing about his death (cf. Ezek. 24:16; Gen. Rab. 25.1). Targum Onq. asserts that indeed Yahweh "got" Enoch in that he "caused him to die," to safeguard against people attending to the Enoch material with its speculative-looking pseudo-visions.[42] In contrast, Tg. Ps.-J. makes explicit that he ascended into the firmament and was given the name Metatron, the name of an archangel and heavenly scribe.

Hebrews 11:5–6 follows the LXX in its translation of Gen. 5:24 and thus makes explicit that Enoch did not die and that God "transferred" him to a different place. It makes a different point from Gen. 5:24 in commenting that Enoch pleased God rather than that he lived in fellowship with God; he

41. On these passages, see Goldingay, *Psalms 42–89*.
42. See Aberbach and Grossfeld, *Targum Onkelos to Genesis*, 48–49; cf. Rashi, *Br'šyt*, 57.

"channeled all his love and desire into fulfilling the will of God."[43] The context of Heb. 11 as a whole, however, makes the point that even people such as Enoch "did not receive what was promised" because they will only reach the fullness of God's purpose for them when they do so in "our" company on resurrection day and in the new Jerusalem. Enoch still awaits the resurrection: "Christ's flesh therefore must make a way into heaven before any man's flesh beside can enter."[44] If Enoch was taken into the heavens, it is not a hint at the resurrection that will come to all God's people. It is simply something extraordinary that God did for this friend of his.

5:25–32. The accounts of Methuselah and Lamech follow the formula, but the paragraph on Lamech has two further features. He lived for 777 years, and he fathered Noah. He makes a link between his son's name and the significance he will have, though as often happens, the link is indirect and in this case seems also whimsical. Lamech could easily have connected Noah's name with the verb *nûaḥ*, which means "rest," which would have fit what Lamech goes on to say; one could think of Noah making rest available to humanity. Instead, Lamech speaks of Noah bringing relief or comfort, using the piel (transitive) verb *niḥam*.[45] The usage introduces further whimsy, since this verb will shortly recur in the niphal (reflexive) in 6:6–7 with a rather different meaning, and since forms of *nûaḥ* actually will appear in 8:4, 9, 21.[46] Lamech himself says that Noah will bring humanity relief from the consequences of Yahweh's curse on the ground, which turned farming into painful work. How will he do so? With yet further whimsy, Jerome thinks in terms of people resting in death because of the flood.[47] Ephrem thinks of his making an offering,[48] which will bring God rest (*nîḥōaḥ*, from the root that underlies Noah's name; 8:21; cf. Gen. Rab. 25.2). More down-to-earth is the suggestion that Noah will bring humanity relief through discovering how to make wine (9:20): at the end of a backbreaking day's work, a man can relax with a glass of wine and God's curse on the ground is thereby alleviated, perhaps even lifted.[49] Jeremiah 16:7 makes the link between sorrow (*naḥămô*) on one hand and wine on the other as a means of relief or comfort (*tanḥûmîm*; cf. also Prov. 31:6–7 for this idea, though the word "relief" or "comfort" does not appear there).

Genesis 5 finally begins the formulaic account of Noah and his sons (v. 32). The story of the flood will now interrupt it, pending its completion in 9:28–29, as a vast further instance of the way particularities can do so (cf. vv. 21–24,

43. Qimchi, *Genesis*, on the verse.

44. Willet, *Hexapla in Genesin & Exodum*, 57.

45. Cf. the agonizing in Gen. Rab. 25.2.

46. Retrospectively, Gen. Rab. 33.3 sees these passages as the real reason for Noah's being called by that name.

47. Jerome, *Hebrew Questions on Genesis*, 36.

48. Ephrem, *Genesis*, 134.

49. Cf. Hamilton, *Genesis 1–17*, 259.

28–31). The other variation from the formula at this point is the mention of three sons, which trailers their subsequent importance in 9:18–10:32.

6:1–2. Humanity is starting to fulfill its commission to be plentiful (1:28), as Gen. 5 has suggested. It has not been driven away from the face of the ground, as Cain feared would happen to him (4:14). Genesis 4 focused on sons, but Gen. 5 kept referring to daughters, and these verses pick up that reference. But the chapter begins with a waw-consecutive, and the sentences that follow suggest that the waw implies "but," not merely "and."

"The divine beings" (v. 2) are more literally "the sons of divine beings," *bənê-hāʾĕlōhîm*. The phrase comes otherwise only in Job 1:6 and 2:1 (*bənê-ʾĕlōhîm* without the article appears again in Job 38:7). *Bənê ʾēlîm* appears in Pss. 29:1; 89:6 [7] and *bənê ʿelyôn* in Ps. 82:6. Qumran documents include similar references;[50] particularly significant is the 4QDeut^{j} reading at Deut. 32:8 (*bny ʾlhym*) and the 4QDeut^{q} reading at Deut. 32:43 (*kl ʾlhym*; see translations such as NRSV, and NIV margin).[51] The equivalent singular expression in Aramaic, *bar-ʾĕlāhîn*, comes in Dan. 3:25. In all these passages these figures are supernatural beings who are subordinate to Yahweh and thus not divine in the same sense that Yahweh is. They are elsewhere referred to simply as *ʾĕlōhîm*, "gods" (e.g., Ps. 8:5 [8:6]). Indeed, the compound expression compares with expressions such as "sons of the prophets" (e.g., 2 Kings 2:3), which denotes members of a prophetic community. So the Genesis phrase might be translated "beings who belong to the class 'gods,'"[52] and "sons of the gods" need not carry implications regarding their parentage; hence the translation "divine beings."

English can distinguish between God with an uppercase G, a term that applies to only one being and is in effect a name, and gods with a lowercase g, which can apply to other supernatural beings. This distinction corresponds to one the First Testament makes, though Hebrew does not have a typographical way of showing this. While such "divine beings" are not deities in the same sense as Yahweh, the one real deity, they are supernatural beings, and they are not very different from the figures referred to elsewhere as the heavenly army (e.g., 1 Kings 22:19; 2 Kings 17:16) or as Yahweh's aides (*malʾākîm*; e.g., Gen. 28:12) or as the leaders of the nations (*śārîm*; Dan. 10) or in Greek as messengers (*angeloi*). Such is the assumption about the figures in Gen. 6 in early Jewish works such as 1 En. 6–11, and it is likely thus presupposed by 1 Pet. 3:19–20; 2 Pet. 2:4–6, and Jude 6.[53]

The *bənê-hāʾĕlōhîm*, then, are supernatural beings who gaze at the daughters of humanity, presumably the women referred to in v. 1, and like what

50. See *DCH* 2:206–7.

51. See Ulrich, *Qumran Cave 4.IX*, 90, 141; and the discussion in, e.g., Tigay, *Deuteronomy*, 513–18.

52. So GKC 128v; DG 35; JM 129j.

53. Cf. Kidner, *Genesis*, 84.

they see. "The sense of [vv. 1–2] is perfectly clear."[54] Only after NT times did alternative understandings of *bənê-hāʾĕlōhîm* arise. The king can be called the son of God (e.g., Ps. 2); hence comes the idea that the sons of God might be kings. Israel can be called the son of God (e.g., Exod. 4:22) and the children of the living God (*bənê ʾēl-ḥay*; Hosea 1:10 [2:1]); hence comes the idea that the sons of God might be the line of the elect that began with Seth. Judges can perhaps be called *ʾĕlōhîm* (e.g., Exod. 21:6), hence the idea that the *bənê-hāʾĕlōhîm* might be judges. Such alternative understandings that avoid the scandalous connotations of the interpretation assumed in NT times gained traction in Christian and Jewish circles; Gen. Rab. 26.5 reports a curse on anyone who says they are actually sons of God.[55]

The divine beings saw that the human daughters were good (*ṭôb*); with grievous irony, it is the expression used of God's seeing in 1:4, 10, 12, 18, 21, 25. While looking good hardly excludes being physically attractive, it is hardly the main point, any more than in Gen. 1. If Genesis had wanted to focus on the women's physical attractiveness, it could have used a word such as *yāpeh*, which Abraham uses of Sarah in this connection (e.g., 12:11, 14). And the following verses will suggest that the point about their attractiveness lies elsewhere. It made the divine beings "get some of the women for themselves." "Get" a woman is the regular expression for marrying a wife. The verb (*lāqaḥ*) need not have forceful connotations; it can mean "receive" or "accept." Nor need it exclude a woman's having a say in the matter, as is clear from stories such as those of Isaac and Rebekah (Gen. 24). Families are also involved in the making of marriages (Gen. 28–29; 34). But the expression in v. 2 does indicate where the initiative lies. The point is underlined by the further expression "any one that they chose."[56]

6:3–4. The further waw-consecutive indicates that v. 3 follows straight on from vv. 1–2, but the jerkiness of these verses means that any interpretation involves connecting dots. The next time someone will get a woman it will be Pharaoh (12:15, 19), and it causes a reaction; so it will be when David does so (2 Sam. 11–12).[57] Here the reaction comes from Yahweh, as it does in David's case. What follows thus implies that the divine beings' activity raises some questions.

Many Middle Eastern stories tell of gods and goddesses engaging in sex, having sex with human beings, and having children with them, and tell about the birth of giants.[58] The questions the story raises would thus not be merely

54. Skinner, *Genesis*, 141. But Fockner ("Reopening the Discussion") questions this consensus.

55. See further, e.g., Newman, "Ancient Exegesis of Genesis 6:2, 4"; Oberhänsli-Widmer, *Bilder vom Bösen*, 93–124.

56. In this "crossing of divinely ordained boundaries," it seems hard to suggest that "human beings may be viewed as prime movers" (so Routledge, "'My Spirit,'" 246).

57. Cf. Westermann, *Genesis 1–11*, 366–67.

58. See, e.g., Westermann, *Genesis 1–11*, 379–81.

logistical. But Jesus's comment about angels not marrying (Mark 12:25) coheres with a comment in b. Hag. 16a: demons propagate like human beings, as they eat and drink and die like human beings, whereas none of these things apply to angels.[59] Once again Genesis parallels other Middle Eastern stories but differs from them. Genesis itself may provide a hint of why Yahweh might object to supernatural beings marrying human beings: God declares in Gen. 1 that different creatures are to reproduce by their species. The story's location as a lead-in to the account of the flood coheres with the idea that the supernatural beings were ignoring constraints put upon them. Their action also worryingly recalls the way the first woman "saw" that the fruit was "good" and therefore "got" some (3:6).[60]

The question of whether humanity should continue permanently (*ləʿōlām*) recalls 3:22. The rest of Genesis does not suggest that 120 years is a cap to be placed on a human lifetime, nor does the 120-year figure feature elsewhere in the First Testament as such a limit, though Deut. 34:7 might allude to it.[61] More likely it is a cap to be placed on how long Yahweh intends to allow human life on earth to continue. The LXX makes the point explicit by translating "abide among *these* people"[62] (cf. Tg. Ps.-J., Tg. Neof.; 1 Pet. 3:20 carries the same implication). Human life will continue for just three more generations,[63] in keeping with the principle to be articulated in passages such as Exod. 20:5. Beyond that time, Yahweh will not carry on exercising his beneficent authority and constraint over humanity in the way he has been doing. The significance of the references to Yahweh's spirit (*rûaḥ*) and to flesh (*bāśār*) will be clarified by 6:17; 7:15, 21–22. Speaking of Yahweh's spirit is the same as speaking of Yahweh's breath (*nəšāmâ*, 2:7); Gen. 7:22 will speak of "the breath of the spirit of life." Both terms can apply both to human beings and to animals (for *rûaḥ* in this latter connection, cf. Ps. 104:29–30). Yahweh is declaring that he does not intend to continue ruling over or within humanity by means of his breath in the way humanity needs—and without that breath, humanity is merely flesh, the same as animals; it has no life.

What is unexplained is that the activity by the supernatural beings issues in action against humanity; the question will be extended in v. 7, when Yahweh declares the intention to wipe out the rest of the animate creation because of the state of humanity. Perhaps it is simply that the created world as a whole (of which the divine beings are part) are bound up in the bundle of life together; they stand or fall together. But Genesis does not make the point explicit.

59. This comment coheres with an observation by Barth (*CD* 3.3:531–32) that the beings cannot be fallen angels because the notion of fallen angels is incoherent.

60. Cf. Wenham, *Genesis 1–15*, 141.

61. See Schmid, "Genesis in the Pentateuch," 38–40; Bührer ("Göttersöhne und Menschentöchter") sees the allusion in the reverse direction.

62. Cf. van Ruiten, "Nomadic Angels," 263.

63. Cf. Sarna, *Genesis*, 46.

Jerkiness now comes to dominate (v. 4). A circumstantial clause followed by appended temporal phrases ("now the Fallen were on the earth at that time and also afterward") leads into a double relative clause in the yiqtol/wəqatal with past imperfect/frequentative reference ("when the divine beings were having sex with the daughters of human beings and they were giving birth for them"). Finally, there is a noun clause ("those were the strong men that were of old, famous men"). The interrelationship of the three clauses is tricky to determine, as is the question of how many groups of people the verse denotes when it refers to the Fallen, the divine beings, and the strong men/famous men. The verse seems to be going out of its way to avoid saying that either the Fallen or the strong/famous men are the offspring of the unions. The immediate antecedent of "those" is the divine beings, though one might more naturally assume that the strong/famous men are the Fallen.

The Fallen (*nəpilîm*) appear only here and in Num. 13:33, in the report of Israelite spies who have gone to reconnoiter Canaan. Failing to convince the assembly that the task ahead of Israel is too demanding, the spies amplify their report by testifying to the threatening size of the Canaanites, among whom the Fallen number; they do not actually say that the Fallen themselves are exceptionally big, and anyway the story implies that their report cannot necessarily be trusted. In that passage, however, the LXX assumes it can be and translates *nəpilîm* by the word *gigantes* (giants), while the Vg translates it *monstra* (monsters); here in Gen. 6:4 both translations use the word *gigantes*. Understanding the Fallen to be people of huge size invites the inference that they were the monstrous offspring of the unions reported in vv. 1–2, though this is the inference Genesis seems to forestall. "Fallen" rather points toward seeing them as the kind of supernatural beings that will later be termed "fallen angels." That understanding could invite the inference that "the Fallen" is another designation of the divine beings themselves whose activity vv. 1–2 reported, and it might just be possible to construe v. 4a that way ("Now the Fallen were on the earth at that time and also afterward, the divine beings who were having sex . . ."). But then there is the further reference to some renowned "strong men" (*gibbôrîm*), a term soon to be applied to Noah's great-grandson Nimrod (10:8–9), but here more naturally applied to the Fallen. So the most plausible way of construing the verse is to infer that the three terms refer to two groups, the Fallen who are also the renowned strong men, and the supernatural beings. And we do not know anything about the Fallen/renowned strong men except what those terms convey.

The parenthesis "and also afterward" could refer to the awareness that the Fallen (and the renowned/strong men) were not confined to those pre-Flood days (though people listening to this story might have noticed that these Fallen must have fallen in the deluge, unless one of them rode on the roof of the ark).[64] But the context suggests that the "afterward" is rather a reference to the 120 years between Yahweh's making his decision and implementing it. In turn that possibility links with the one extra note in this verse whose reference is clear: after Yahweh made his declaration, not only did the sons of the divine beings continue to have sex with the daughters of human beings (declining to observe that boundary between themselves and the women God had created); the latter were giving birth to their offspring.

People listening to this story have to accept that the verse, which has the nature of a postscript,[65] declines to make the links we would like to have between the supernatural figures, the Fallen, the renowned/strong men, and the unions between the supernatural figures and the human girls, and between all these and Yahweh's decision reported in v. 3. No matter how long we ponder the verses, the lines between the dots remain missing. The verses invite people to see that they are looking back on strange days, days like the ones when a tree could enable you to transcend death and when Yahweh would go for a walk and when a snake talked and when Yahweh put a mark on a murderer, days whose characteristics somehow explained how Yahweh came to a decision to flood the earth. Further, as with the talking snake, the audience is expected to imagine the stories it hears, but perhaps not necessarily to infer that things simply happened the way the stories describe.

Elsewhere, not least in 1 Enoch, the activity of supernatural figures is the origin of sin in the world. Genesis does not make that link. Genesis 3 attributed the origin of sin to human disobedience, and 6:5–6 will go on to do the same.[66]

6:5–6. Once again there is a leap from one verse to the next, but the leap is accompanied by verbal links. Humanity had started to become *great* in numbers, and the supernatural figures had seen that the human women were *good*, but Yahweh sees that the *bad* state of humanity is *great*. The occurrence of *rōb* (great) regarding numbers leads into the sadly contrasting occurrence of *rabbâ* (regarding the bad state of humanity), and the occurrence of *ṭōbōt* (good) leads into the occurrence of *rā'â* (bad); the latter again also sadly recalls the recurrent "he saw that it was good" of Gen. 1. Humanity is in a grievous and tragic state. The next sentence also makes clear that the moral connotations of *ra'* (morally bad as well as experientially bad) apply, too. The point could hardly be made more forcefully than it is made in v. 5b. The word "shaping" (*yēṣer*) also carries some sadness, because it is related to the term for Yahweh's shaping (*yāṣar*) the first human being (2:7–8). How misshapen things have become. Likewise, the "intentions" of the mind need not have been by definition bad; the next occurrences of the word will relate to plans for building the wilderness sanctuary (Exod. 31:4; 35:32–35). But

64. Cf. Moberly, "How Should One Read?," 12. Targum Ps.-J. (on 14:13) says one did so ride.

65. Seebass, *Genesis*, 1:190.

66. Cf. Davies, "And Enoch Was Not."

here the intentions actually are bad, bad, bad. In retrospect, it transpires that the divine beings' judgment on the human daughters was mistaken.[67] Genesis 6:5–8 is not a statement about how things always are with humanity but a statement about how things were in Noah's time (see further 8:21). It does make a horrifying statement about how they were at that point. Perhaps people in the audience need to ask themselves whether things are similar in their time, or in their nation, or in their community. The story's description of things as bad also invites them to hold together the idea of things being ugly and things being wicked. They are in a state that is the opposite of the way they were created as "good."

So Yahweh regrets his entire project (v. 6). The story of creation has been a disappointment. The verb (*niḥam* niphal) makes for an ironic and sad link with 5:29, or it underlines the need that Lamech's hope should find fulfillment. The verb plays a key role in the Scriptures' description of Yahweh's relationship with the world, in connection with the past ("regret" is then the idea) or in connection with the future ("relent" is then the idea). While it is sometimes used of human beings (e.g., Judg. 21:6, 15), Yahweh is the subject of the vast majority of its occurrences, not least at key points in the stories of Noah, Moses, and David.[68] It forcefully expresses the flexibility of God's relationship with events in the world. "Genesis 6:6 then is testimony to the personal relationship between God and man."[69] His experiencing regret shows that Yahweh lives in time and tries things out to see if they will work, and when they do not work, he takes action to try something different or to remedy the situation. While Yahweh transcends time and exists yesterday, today, and forever, his eternal existence does not preclude his being involved with the world and with humanity in a time sequence. While Genesis may presuppose that Yahweh has the capacity to be all-knowing and may presuppose that he has used that capacity and has foreseen how humanity's action in the world would turn out, the point it makes is that nevertheless Yahweh responds to these events emotionally and conatively within time, in the flow of events. Genesis Rabbah 27.6 notes that regretting need not imply that he was surprised. You can know something is going to happen, yet still be saddened by it when it does. Thus God experiences frustration and disappointment. He is now sorry he made humanity. The pain that the woman would feel (*ʿeṣeb*; 3:16) and the pain that the man would feel (*ʿiṣṣābôn*; 3:16–17; cf. 5:29) are the pain that Yahweh now feels (*ʿāṣab* hitpael).

While we have assumed that Yahweh's declarations in 3:14–19 implied anger, this pain is the first emotion that has been explicitly ascribed to Yahweh in Genesis, and in the deluge story God expresses sorrow and regret, but

67. Cf. Kaminski, "Beautiful Women?"
68. Cf. Sonnet, "God's Repentance."
69. Harland, *Value of Human Life*, 83.

not anger. "The response of the divine heart" in its pain is set alongside "the basic character of the human heart" in its bad intentions.[70] At this moment Yahweh's pain is the opposite of his joy at his works elsewhere (Ps. 104:31).[71] The Scriptures do not provide a basis for taking Yahweh's pain or regret as any more of an anthropomorphism than other statements about Yahweh such as that he loves or is compassionate. As humanity's nature and experience include operating in time and knowing a before and an after, so it is an aspect of the nature of the God in whose image humanity is made. "The image of God in the flood story is perhaps best described as a grieving and pained parent, distressed over what has happened to the human race."[72] Further, in the aftermath of the deluge God will go on to place constraints around his options for the future. In Gen. 6–9 as in Gen. 1–2 we have set before us in the opening pages of the Scriptures an understanding of God that is presumably meant to guide our understanding of the Scriptures that follow and that clashes with assumptions about God that Christians commonly take for granted.[73] God walks with humanity through history and experiences its joys and its vicissitudes, its achievements and its frustrations. His being God provides the reassurance that no frustration or miscarriage confounds him, as the deluge story shows and as the Jesus story will show. His being God means he will always find a way through. He will never be defeated.

God's disappointment with creation anticipates the disappointment he will have with his people. He never says he regrets choosing them (rather surprisingly, given the strength of some of his statements about them), but on the other occasions in the First Testament when he is said to be caused pain, the cause will be his people (Ps. 78:40; Isa. 63:10). God will have such high hopes for Israel, but Israel will decline to live up to them.

> I myself had said,
> "How gladly I'll put you among my children
> And give you a desirable country,
> the most splendid domain of the nations."
> I said you'd call me "Father,"
> and not turn back from following me.
> Actually, as a woman breaks faith with her lover,
> so you broke faith with me,
> Israel's household. (Jer. 3:19–20)

It has already been like that with creation. "The essential fracture between creator and creation is the premise and agenda of the flood narrative" that

70. Fretheim, "Genesis," 389.
71. Cf. Ibn Ezra, *Genesis*, 97.
72. Fretheim, "Self-Limiting God," 186.
73. Fretheim, "Self-Limiting God," 186.

will follow.[74] But the fact that God looks in the face the disappointing nature of creation but responds with a commitment to persevering with it is then an encouragement with regard to his maintaining commitment to his people.

6:7–8. So Yahweh resolves to wipe out everything on earth. His regret is with humanity, not with creation in its entirety. God had created humanity to look after the earth, and it has been a spectacular failure. Yet he has decided to wipe out the rest of the animate creation along with humanity. In some way it is implicated in the bad state of humanity. Yahweh does not explain why it follows that he will wipe out the animate creation along with humanity. Perhaps the assumption is that the animal world needs humanity to look after it and exercise authority over it. Or perhaps the extent of the divine action underlines the horrific nature of the human wickedness.[75] Or perhaps it illustrates how there is a kind of overflow of the results of human wrongdoing, as when David's census brings trouble on the whole land.[76] For good or ill, the destiny and fate of creation is tied up with that of humanity (cf. Rom. 8:21).[77]

But Noah "found favor in Yahweh's eyes" (v. 8). The term "favor" or "grace" (*ḥēn*) occurs in Genesis only in this compound expression "found favor in the eyes of," usually of human relationships. It commonly indicates a favor that is not earned; it just happens (e.g., 18:3; 19:19; 30:27; 39:21; 47:25, 29; 50:4), though it can refer to favor that one seeks to earn (32:5 [32:6]; 33:8, 10, 15; 34:11; 39:4). The lack of any attempt on Noah's part to find favor with Yahweh suggests that here Yahweh himself is the source of it. Noah did not "win favor" with God; he found it. Maybe he wasn't even looking for it.[78] He found favor "not because he was righteous, but so that he might be righteous."[79] The basis for his being exempt from drowning, along with his family and the representatives of the rest of creation, is not his deserving it but God's purpose. He is just lucky. But he has to respond.

Implications

On Ignoring the Great Divide

Genesis 6:1–4 issues the reminder that "the great cleavage is not between heaven and earth. It is, rather, between God on the one hand and the powers of both heaven and earth on the other. All of both 'heaven and earth' stand

74. Brueggemann, *Genesis*, 74.

75. Cf. Calvin, *Genesis*, 1:250.

76. Cf. Willet, *Hexapla in Genesin & Exodum*, 63.

77. Cf. Chrysostom, *Homilies on Genesis 18–45*, 80–81.

78. The NEB has he "won favour," as does Didymus (*Genesis*, 151), who declares that he both sought and found.

79. Pellikan, *Commentaria Bibliorum*, 1:10r, as quoted in J. Thompson, *Genesis 1–11*, 244.

over against God and are responsive to him"[80]—or at least responsible to him. Although the form of the stories in Gen. 1–11 does not invite us to hypothesize a one-to-one relationship between story and history, it does invite us to assume the presence of some factual reference in the historical parable (the word *myth* has been used to describe vv. 1–4, but it is a word of vague meaning that is worth avoiding).[81] Here its implication would be that while humanity is responsible in key ways for wrongdoing in the world, we are also the (cooperative) victims of rebellion on the part of supernatural forces. It is as well that Jesus came to defeat them.

Genesis 6:1–4 leaves its listeners to work out the implications of its extraordinary story rather than telling them what those implications are. The audience might see humanity as implicated in the event that is related, and might do so in several ways. People might put themselves into the position of the fathers and families of the women who were taken in marriage. How did they come to allow this to happen? Are they repeating the unthinking submission of the first man to the suggestion of the snake? They might put themselves in the position of the women themselves. How did they come to accept these marriages? Are they repeating the unthinking submission of the first woman? They might identify with the supernatural figures themselves. Are they seeking to transgress the limits that God set for humanity, raising themselves above their station like the king of Babel in Isa. 14?[82] In its effect this approach is then not so different from the implications of seeing the *bənê-hā'ĕlōhîm* as human leaders. In raising these questions, Gen. 6:1–4 compares with Deuteronomy in its assumptions about the link between disobedience to Yahweh and trouble that follows. But the audience might face these questions in an awed and sympathetic fashion (esp. in considering the experience of the women), not a judgmental one.

The other way an audience might work out the story's implications relates to the other aspect of Gen. 2–3. While the garden story offers a partial explanation of the way things are for humanity in the world, its explanation is only partial, and it leaves questions unanswered. Here the story raises questions such as these: Why did the supernatural figures intervene in the way they did? Why did God respond to the action of these beings by setting a limit to *human* life? Why does God destroy all life on earth because of the bad dealings and situation of humanity? How do vv. 5–7 follow from vv. 1–4 and from 1:1–6:4 as a whole? How did Noah find favor with God? Like Gen. 2–3, the opening of Gen. 6 owns the mystery and the unanswered questions about our position in the world and about God's actions. It thus compares with Ecclesiastes and Job.

80. Brueggemann, *Genesis*, 72.

81. See the introduction to this commentary and the introduction to 1:1–2:4a above.

82. Cf. Westermann, *Genesis 1–11*, 382.

The references in 2 Pet. 2:4 and Jude 6 to the events related in Gen. 6:1–4 suggest overlapping considerations, though the two epistles base themselves on the elaborated versions of the story in 1 Enoch. The 2 Peter reference starts as if to warn its readers to learn from the fate of the angels who get sent to hell, but before coming to its warning it reminds its readers that God is able to rescue the godly from trial. Jude reminds its readers of the mercy of Jesus, which is able to bring them to eternal life; urges them to be merciful to people who doubt and to save others by snatching them from the fire; and closes by recalling that God is able to keep them from stumbling and present them before his glorious presence. (In 1 En. 12–13 itself, the Lookouts urge Enoch to go and preach to the disobedient angels, and they ask him to pray for them.)

6
The Deluge from Above and Below

(6:9–8:22)

Overview

The question for this next section emerges from what precedes. If God is going to wipe out life on the earth, is that the end of the creation project? The audience knows that it wasn't, otherwise it wouldn't be there listening. But how is God going to reboot the creation project? Evidently Noah is part of the answer to that question, but how? And what will be the status of this rebooted creation? When things go wrong again, will God wipe out its inhabitants again? How secure is humanity in the world?

Although it would have been easy enough for God to destroy everything and start again, God does not do so. The new creation will be a relaunching of the old creation, as Eve was constructed from Adam rather than made from scratch. Noah is the means of continuity between the old and the new and also the means of saving representatives of the entire creation. And at the end of the story God says, "Never again." Maintaining the continuity tells the audience that it is one with the original creation and with God's purpose for it. Saying "never again" enables the audience to feel secure in the world.

Translation

6:9 These are Noaḥ's lines of descent.

Now Noaḥ, a faithful man, was a person of integrity among his
generations—Noaḥ walked about with God.[1] **10**Noaḥ fathered three sons,

1. On the expression "walk about with," see the footnote to 5:22. Here the clause is asyndetically related to the previous one, and "with God" precedes the verb, suggesting that it is subordinate to the preceding clause.

Šem, Ḥam, and Yepet. 11But the earth had become devastated before God; the earth was full of violence.

12God saw the earth: and there, it had become devastated, because all flesh had devastated its way on the earth. 13So God said to Noaḥ, "The end[2] of all flesh has come before me, because the earth is full of violence through them. Here, I'm going to devastate[3] them, with the earth.

14Make for yourself a chest[4] of sealed wood.[5] With compartments[6] you're to make[7] the chest, and cover it inside and outside with pitch. 15This is how you're to make it: the length of the chest three hundred cubits, its width fifty cubits, and its height thirty cubits. 16You're to make a gable[8] for the chest, to finish it to a cubit upward,[9] and to put the entrance of the chest in its side. You're to make it with bottom, second, and third levels. 17And I: here, I'm going to bring the upper ocean as water onto the earth, to devastate all flesh in which there is living breath from under the heavens. Everything on the earth will breathe its last. 18But I will implement[10] my pact with you.

You're to come into the chest, you, your sons, your wife, and your sons' wives with you. 19And of every living thing, of all flesh, you're to bring two of each into the chest to keep alive with you. They are to be a male and a female. 20Of bird by its species, of animal by its species, and of everything that moves on the ground by its species, two of each are to come to you, to keep them alive. 21And you: get yourself some of all

2. The LXX has *kairos*, perhaps "the critical moment" (cf. Origen, *Homilies on Genesis*, 72), which would also be true.

3. Three times (cf. 6:17; 7:4) Yahweh uses a participle as we do in English if we say "I'm coming" when we have not yet begun to move (JM 121e; *IBHS* 37.6f; GKC 116p); he is about to act, and you had better believe it.

4. *Tēbâ*, an Egyptian word borrowed simply to designate this extraordinary construction and otherwise used to refer only to the coffer in which Moses's mother floats him on the Nile.

5. English versions take *gōper* to denote an otherwise unknown kind of wood, "gopher," but in postbiblical Hebrew *gāpar* refers to making something watertight by the use of bitumen (*DTT*, 263); cf. the BH word for bitumen, *goprît* and the word *kōper*, which comes later in the verse. Thus Jerome (*Hebrew Questions on Genesis*, 37 [PL 23:949]) translates *bituminata*; cf. also Aq.

6. Literally, "nests"; repointing *qinnîm* to *qānîm* produces the meaning "reeds" (see J. Day, *Creation to Babel*, 113–22).

7. Yahweh speaks in the imperative at the beginning and near the end of his words to Noah in vv. 14–21 but speaks in the yiqtol in between, which perhaps makes his words a stronger declaration of what Noah *will* definitely do.

8. The word *ṣōhar* comes only here; the Vg has "window" (perhaps linking with *ṣohŏrayim*, midday), but the context suggests a word denoting a roof.

9. Possibly this difficult phrase indicates that the chest is to have a pitched roof with the center a cubit higher than the walls (cf. Gen. Rab. 31.11).

10. Not "confirm" (Wenham, *Genesis 1–15*, 149, 175); *qûm* hiphil denotes establishing something, not reinforcing it, and there has been no mention of an existent pact to be confirmed. In a looser sense one could say that God had been living in a covenantal relationship with humanity and/or with Noaḥ, but Genesis has not spoken in these terms.

food that's eaten and gather it for yourself. It will be food for you and for them."

22Noaḥ acted in accordance with all that God ordered him. So he
did.

7:1 So Yahweh said to Noaḥ, "Go into the chest, you and your entire household, because I've seen that you're a person who is faithful before me in this generation. **2**Of every pure animal get yourself seven of each, a male and its mate, and of an animal that's not pure, two, a male and its mate, **3**also of the bird in the heavens seven of each, a male and a female, to keep offspring alive on the face of the entire earth. **4**Because in seven more days I'm going to make it rain on the earth for forty days and forty nights and wipe out everything that had been established that I made, from on the face of the ground."

5Noaḥ acted in accordance with all that God ordered him.

6Now Noaḥ was a man of six hundred years when the upper ocean came as water onto the earth. **7**Noaḥ came into the chest, he, his sons, his wife, and his sons' wives with him, in the face of the water of the upper ocean. **8**Of the pure animal, of the animal that's not pure, of the bird, and everything that moves on the ground, **9**two of each came to Noaḥ into the chest, a male and a female, as God ordered Noaḥ.

10After the seven days, the water of the upper ocean came onto the earth. **11**In the six-hundredth year[11] of Noaḥ's life, in the second month, on the seventeenth day of the month, on this day all the springs in the great deep broke out and the apertures in the heavens opened. **12**The downpour[12] came on the earth forty days and forty nights. **13**On this very day Noaḥ came into the chest, he, Šem, Ḥam, and Yepet, Noaḥ's sons, and Noaḥ's wife, and his sons' three wives, **14**they and every living thing by its species, every animal by its species, everything that moves on the earth by its species, and everything that flies by its species, every bird, every winged thing. **15**They came to Noaḥ into the chest, two each of all flesh in which was living breath. **16**So the ones who came, a male and a female from all flesh, came as God ordered him. And Yahweh shut him in.

17The upper ocean came onto the earth for forty days, and the water increased and lifted the chest, and it rose up from on the earth. **18**The water grew strong and increased greatly on the earth, and the chest moved on the face of the water. **19**When the water grew very, very strong on the earth, all the lofty mountains under the entire heavens were covered. **20**As the water grew strong fifteen cubits higher, the mountains were covered. **21**All flesh moving on the earth breathed its last, by way of bird, of animal, of living thing, of everything that teems on the earth, and

11. Literally, "in the year of six-hundred, the year": with compound numbers "year" can be repeated (cf. GKC 134o).

12. *Gešem* is sometimes translated "shower," which gives the wrong impression. See 1 Kings 18:41; Ps. 68:9 [68:10]; Ezek. 13:11, 13; 38:22.

all humanity. **22**Everything that had living spirit, breath,[13] in its nostrils, everything that was on the dry land, died. **23**It wiped out everything that had been established on the face of the ground, from human being to animal to moving thing to bird in the heavens. They were wiped out from the earth. Only Noaḥ and those with him in the chest remained. **24**The water grew strong on the earth for one hundred and fifty days.

8:1 But God was mindful of Noaḥ and every living thing and every animal that was with him in the chest.

So God made a wind pass over the earth and the water abated. **2**The springs in the deep and the apertures in the heavens were blocked up, the downpour from the heavens held back, **3**and the water gradually withdrew from on the earth. The water decreased at the end of one hundred and fifty days, **4**and the chest came to rest in the seventh month, on the seventeenth day of the month, on the Ararat[14] mountains. **5**As the water gradually decreased[15] until the tenth month, in the tenth, on the first of the month, the tops of the mountains appeared.

6At the end of forty days, Noaḥ opened a window in the chest that he had made **7**and sent out a raven.[16] It continued to go out and come back[17] until the water dried up from on the earth. **8**He sent out a pigeon from being with him to see if the water had diminished from on the face of the ground, **9**but the pigeon didn't find a place to alight for the sole of its foot and it came back to him to the chest, because there was water on the face of the entire earth. So he put out his hand, got it, and brought it to him into the chest. **10**He waited again seven more days and once more sent out the pigeon from the chest. **11**The pigeon came to him at evening time, and there, in its mouth a plucked-off olive leaf. So Noaḥ knew that the water had diminished from on the earth. **12**He waited again seven more days and sent out the pigeon, and it didn't come back to him again.

13So in the six hundred and first year, in the first, on the first of the month, the water dried from on the earth. Noaḥ removed the chest's cover and saw: there, the face of the ground was dry. **14**In the second month, on the twenty-seventh day of the month, the earth was dried out.

15God spoke to Noaḥ: **16**"Get out of the chest, you, your wife, your sons, and your sons' wives with you. **17**Every living thing that's with you from all flesh, by way of bird, of animal, and of everything that moves on

13. Literally, "the breath of the spirit of life," a combination of "breath of life/living breath" (cf. 2:7) and "spirit of life/living spirit" (cf. 7:15).

14. Sym, Aq, Th have "Armenian."

15. On this unique verbal usage (*hāyâ* followed by two infinitive absolutes), see Gzella, "Zum periphrastischen Infinitiv."

16. Literally, "the raven"; see GKC 126r.

17. The idiomatic expression begins with a finite verb followed by its infinitive absolute, "it went out in going out," i.e., "it went out repeatedly," then adds a second infinitive absolute from a different root so that in effect there is an ellipsis of the related second finite verb. See *IBHS* 135.3c; JM 123m; GKC 113s; DG 101c.

the earth: get them out[18] with you, so they may teem on the earth and
be fruitful and be numerous on the earth."
18So Noaḥ got out, he, his sons, his wife, and his sons' wives with
him. **19**Every living thing, everything that moves, and every bird, every-
thing that moves on the earth got out of the chest by their families.
20Noaḥ built an altar for Yahweh, got some of every pure animal and
of every pure bird, and offered up burnt offerings on the altar, **21**and Yah-
weh smelled the restful smell. Yahweh said in his heart,[19] "I won't yet
again diminish the ground on account of humanity because[20] the shaping
of the human heart is bad from its youth. I won't yet again strike down
every living thing, as I did.

> **22**All earth's days yet,[21]
>   seedtime and harvest, cold and heat,
> Summer and winter, day and night—
>   they will not stop."

Interpretation

The heading at 6:9 marks a new beginning following on 5:1, and a new synagogue lection begins here. But the backdrop to the plot and drama of the story that will now unfold is the summary statement in 6:5–8. That statement made clear that Yahweh has to take some action, but it also set up a tension between Yahweh's intentions and his attitude to Noah—or it did not indicate the relationship between the intention and the attitude. Against that backdrop, the section unfolds as follows.

6:9–13 restates that background, in reverse order: Noah's standing before God, the devastating and devastated situation of the earth, and God's consequent intention. It constitutes the "exposition," the statement of background information, for what follows.[22] In the Overview to this section we noted questions it answers from an a posteriori perspective. The exposition points to questions that need answering on the basis of what has preceded. How can God show proper disapproval of earth's violence, recognize Noah's distinctive faithfulness, and lay the

18. Qal *hayṣēʾ* is an "irregular" form (GKC 69v), almost as if the verb were an initial *y* verb (see GKC 70).

19. Literally, "to his heart."

20. NIV has "even though," but the regular meaning of *kî* when linking statements is "because"; it is doubtful whether it ever means "although." See Harland, *Value of Human Life*, 119–21, and my comments below, though Moberly ("On Interpreting the Mind of God," 57) concludes that "the exegetical issue eludes clear resolution."

21. The "yet" picks up from the repeated use in v. 21, though the MT here spells *ʿōd* rather than *ʿôd*.

22. Cf. Coats, *Genesis*, 73.

foundations for relaunching the creation plan? The rest of the section answers these questions.

6:14–21 begins to provide the answers by relating God's commission to Noah to build a huge chest in which Noah's family and representatives of all earth's species can be kept safe.

6:22 ends this first stage in the story by reassuring us that Noah did as God told him.

7:1–4 describes Yahweh's commission to Noah to get the survival party into the chest.

7:5 ends the second stage by again reassuring us that Noah did as God told him.

7:6–16a relates how they all got into the chest, with some raising of suspense as we continue to await the coming of the deluge announced back in 6:13.

7:16b ends the third stage with Yahweh making sure that the survival party is secure.

7:17–24 describes the deluge with its catastrophic consequences, from which only Noah and his party are exempt.

8:1a ends the fourth stage by affirming that God was mindful of Noah and also forms a bridge to the fifth stage in the story; it constitutes the turning point in the story, ending the first act and heralding the second act.

8:1b–5 relates how God took action to make the flood diminish.

8:6–14 describes how Noah established that the flood had gone.

8:15–17 relates how God told Noah to get his family out of the chest so that the creation project can be resumed.

8:18–19 brings to an end the long fifth stage by describing how Noah did as he was told in bringing his family out of the chest, with the animate creation following.

8:20–22 corresponds to the opening subsection 6:9–13 (and thus also recalls 6:5–8). Noah expresses his faithfulness by making an offering, and Yahweh declares that he will never again strike down or destroy the earth because of its bad dealings. Thus Yahweh has shown proper disapproval of earth's violence, recognized Noah's distinctive faithfulness, and laid the foundations for relaunching the creation plan.

Genesis combines chronological patterning with relating the story in that linear fashion. The pattern is palistrophic in its references to the years of Noah's life and to periods of 7, 40, and 150 days. Genesis 8:1 is again shown to be the center point of the palistrophe.[23]

23. B. W. Anderson, "From Analysis to Synthesis," 38; cf. Wenham, *Genesis 1–15*, 156. For critique, see Pleins, *When the Great Abyss Opened*, 24–25.

7 days' notice from God of a 40-day deluge; it's year 600 in Noah's life (7:4, 6)
  after 7 days the deluge starts, on the 17th day of the 2nd month of year 600 in Noah's life (7:10–11)
    for 40 days and nights the deluge continues (7:12, 17)
      for 150 days the water grows deeper (7:24)
      after 150 days the water decreases, until the 10th of the 10th month; on the 17th of the 7th the chest stops (8:3–5)
    after 40 days Noah sends out a raven then a pigeon (8:6–9)
  after 7 days he sends out the pigeon again (8:10–11)
after 7 days he sends out the pigeon again; it's the 1st day in the 1st month and then the 27th day of the 2nd month of year 601 in Noah's life (8:12–14)

The math apparently presupposes that the first 40 days are part of the 150 days that the deluge continues, and that 150 days is a way of saying 5 lunar months.[24] The pattern combines an interest in broad chronology (the flood lasts a year) with neatness of arrangement (the 7-7-40-150-150-40-7-7 scheme) in a way that compares with Gen. 5 and again with Matt. 1:1–17. As Matthew will omit some figures from his genealogy so that his 14-14-14 pattern works, Genesis implicitly wraps its first period of 40 days into its first period of 150 days so as to combine its palistrophic scheme with its picture of the flood lasting a year. Further, by distinguishing two stages in the earth's drying out, it pictures the flood lasting both a lunar year and a solar year.[25]

The form of a palistrophe can point toward something simply going somewhere and back again and thus getting nowhere, but a palistrophe may work more like parallelism in the sense that the second or return half may not merely repeat the first but may take matters forward. This instance does combine the form of a palistrophe with the form of a story that sets up a question or problem and then sets about resolving it.

Further, combined with the linear plot and the palistrophic structure is a pattern whereby God acts, God gives Noah orders, and Noah obeys.

God looks (6:12)
  God tells Noah to build a giant chest (6:13–21)
    Noah does as God says (6:22)
  God tells Noah to get everyone into the chest (7:1–4)
    Noah does as God says and the deluge happens (7:5–16a)
God shuts Noah in and the deluge continues (7:16b–24)

24. On the flood chronology, see further, e.g., Kidner, *Genesis*, 98–99; Sarna, *Genesis*, 376; Wenham, *Genesis 1–15*, 179–81; and their references.

25. Cf., e.g., Ephrem, *Genesis*, 141.

God is mindful and the waters abate (8:1–14)
God tells Noah to get everyone out of the chest (8:15–17)
Noah does as God says and offers him a sacrifice (8:18–20)
God smells and speaks to himself (8:21–22)

The interweaving of the statements is significant, and so is the impossibility of interrelating them as neatly as cause and effect. It is not because Noah is obedient that God is mindful; God just is. It is not because God told Noah to build an altar and offer a sacrifice that Noah does so; Noah just does. The relationship between God and Noah or Noah and God is not programmed and predictable but independent and free.

Within these frameworks, Genesis says little about the logistics of the monumental task of building the chest, collecting the animals, controlling them, and feeding them, not to say coping with their defecation. It is not that people in the ancient world didn't notice these matters,[26] as Western readers do. It's just that Genesis's interest lies elsewhere. Its own further emphases include the following:

1. God's act in bringing devastation on the earth corresponds to the way humanity has brought devastation on the earth.
2. The act of devastation involves an undoing of the act of creation. Whereas the sky dome had held back the upper water from the earth, this upper ocean is now let loose on the earth again, and the water under the earth is also allowed to contribute to the flooding.
3. The animals and birds are important in the story, which is not simply about the survival of Noah and his family but also about the relaunching of God's creation project. The birds play a role in establishing that the flood has ceased.

Although 6:9–13 restates 6:5–8, it speaks of "God," whereas 6:5–8 spoke of "Yahweh." In traditional source-critical terms, then, vv. 5–8 are J's introduction to the story of the deluge, while vv. 9–13 are P's introduction. Thus far Genesis has combined P and J in large chunks (roughly, Gen. 1 and 5 are P and Gen. 2 though 4 are J); here it interweaves them more delicately. Possibly the intricate nature of both versions of the story requires this treatment; simply setting them one after the other would be harder. Or possibly we should infer that P is adapting and supplementing the J story rather than there being two separate complete stories that a later author interwove. Either way, we can broadly infer how some sequences of verses came from J and others from P, following clues such as their terms for God and their way of numbering the animals (P just talks of pairs of each species, J talks in terms of one pair of

26. See, e.g., Augustine's comments, *City of God* 15.17; cf. Louth, *Genesis 1–11*, 133.

impure animals and seven pairs of pure animals). But two versions of the stories cannot be divided into separate, continuous versions with no remainder; if there were two complete versions, Genesis has done some abbreviating and smoothing in the course of combining them. Thus (for instance) Genesis contains no J account of Yahweh's commission to Noah to build the chest and of Noah doing so; as incorporated in Genesis, the J account goes straight from God's decision (6:5–8) to his commission to Noah to go into the chest (7:1–5).[27] Possibly the inclusion in Genesis of P's creation story as it stood facilitated the retaining of its poetic character, while the interweaving and reworking of the two versions of the flood story sacrificed it.

6:9–10. Against the background of what has preceded, the idea that Noah will have lines of descent is quite a statement of hope. Yet whereas the heading at 5:1 covered the whole of Adam's line from Adam to Noah, the heading at 6:9 really covers only Noah's story; his sons will acquire a new heading at 10:1. Noah is characterized in three ways. First, he is faithful (*ṣaddîq*). It is the first occurrence of a key First Testament word, and Noah is the only person in the First Testament who is ever so described.[28] It is commonly translated "righteous," but this term does not convey the important relational implications of the word. To be *ṣaddîq* is to live in the right way with God and with one's family and community. Second, he is a person of integrity (*tāmîm*). The common translation of this further key First Testament word is "blameless," which is again misleading. The word does not denote the absence of something (so that it might imply being sinless) but the presence of something. Applied to a sacrificial animal, it denotes one that is whole; applied to a person, it denotes someone who is wholly committed in relationship with God and with other people. Thus there is not very much difference between faithfulness and integrity, as Ps. 15 suggests in expounding the way both qualities find expression in a person's life. Putting the two words alongside each other is not to say two separate things but to underline the qualities indicated by both. Given what we have read in vv. 5–7, we can see that in his faithfulness and integrity, Noah would indeed be a man whose life contrasted with the lives of his contemporaries—indeed with those of any generation.[29]

The third expression, he "walked about with God," is the phrase used to describe Enoch. While the word order in vv. 5–9 suggests that Noah was

27. For varying understandings of the process whereby Genesis came to interweave J and P, and for observations on how the sources might have been read in their own right, see, e.g., Skinner, *Genesis*, 147–69; Westermann, *Genesis 1–11*, 384–458; Coats, *Genesis*, 73–82; Wenham, *Genesis 1–15*, 167–69. Hays (*Hidden Riches*, 82–85) lays out the text, distinguishing between the two versions and also editorial additions. Rendsburg ("Biblical Flood Story") sees the biblical story as more broadly following Gilgamesh and using Israelite material to modify it.

28. Cf. Harland, *Value of Human Life*, 45. "God loved this man for his righteousness [*dikaiosynē*]" (Josephus, *Ant.* 1.3.2).

29. See the discussion in Jeffrey M. Cohen, "*Be-Dorotav*."

the man he was because he found favor with Yahweh rather than that his faithfulness and integrity were what won him Yahweh's favor, the order of the expressions within v. 9 (to complement this point) suggests that it was because Noah was faithful and a man of integrity that he was able to walk about with God in the way that friends do.[30] Given that vv. 5–8 are J's introduction to the deluge story, J stresses God's favor; given that vv. 9–10 are P's introduction, P emphasizes Noah's commitment and responsibility; and in combination Genesis affirms both. Noah's being a man of faithfulness and integrity followed from finding favor with God and from being able to walk about in God's company. There would have been no faithfulness and integrity without God, but there would have been no faithfulness and integrity without Noah. That God can say "I've seen that you're a person who is faithful before me in this generation" is "a wonderful testimony and worthy of trust: what could be better than when the Creator himself, he who brings everything into being, delivers such a verdict on the just man?"[31] He is indeed a man who "by his trust condemned the world" and became an heir of the destiny that belongs to God's people through that trust (Heb. 11:7). But if you are condemned by Noah, he cannot save you; you would have to identify with him (Ezek. 14:12–20).

6:11–13. Two key terms describing the earth complement the three terms describing Noah. The earth has become devastated (*šāḥat* niphal; vv. 11, 12), devastated "before God": the significance of the second expression in this context emerges when one compares and contrasts with the reappearance of the phrase in v. 13 and in 7:1. The point is made vividly as the narrator's "there" invites us to imagine God looking at the scene. While Noah's faithfulness is there before God's eyes (7:1), that statement contrasts with the devastation of the earth that is before his eyes (perhaps with the implication that it is flagrant),[32] and with the "end" that is before the eyes of his imagination, according to v. 13. Perhaps there is an implication that both the devastation and the end are before him in court; the phrase recurs in Exod. 22:9; Lam. 1:22; Esther 9:11. The devastation results from the fact that humanity has devastated its way (*šāḥat* hiphil; 6:12). In response, God is going to devastate humanity (*šāḥat* piel and hiphil; 6:13, 17; 9:11, 13). Verse 19 uses the word "flesh" in a way that includes the rest of the animate world, making that reference explicit; v. 12 includes no pointer to this broader reference. Humanity is the "flesh" that has devastated the earth, and God's devastating will put the seal on its devastating. "Destruction is thereby intrinsically related to corruption, violence leads in to violence."[33]

30. Cf. Didymus, *Genesis*, 153 (though he is working with the LXX, which has "pleasing to God" for "walked about with God").

31. Chrysostom, *Homilies on Genesis 18–45*, 115.

32. So Ibn Ezra, *Genesis*, 99.

33. Fretheim, "God of the Flood Story," 30.

Humanity has devastated the earth by filling it with violence or violation (*ḥāmās*; 6:11, 13). It is the first use of the verb "fill" since 1:22–23, 28.[34] God had commissioned human beings to fill the earth, and they had filled it all right, but not as commissioned. Fortuitously (or perhaps it is more than chance) English has the two similar words "violence" and "violation" to match the Hebrew noun *ḥāmās*, with the related verb *ḥāmas*, which have both meanings. The verb refers to violating God's teaching (e.g., Zeph. 3:4) or violating people (e.g., Jer. 22:3). The double use of the Hebrew word suggests that it points to the kind of violation that involves violence to people and the kind of violence that involves violation of the law. *Ḥāmās* refers to violation of God's rules and violation to people as an expression of such lawlessness. The violence to which it refers always constitutes violation, which is what makes it wrong; the focus of the word does not lie on the violation of the person. The First Testament does assume that the violation of a person is wrong, but this assumption is not the one that underlies its use of the word *ḥāmās*. This word rather draws attention to the fact that unwarranted violation of a person is a violation of principles that God has laid down. It is, indeed, an act of violation against God insofar as humanity is made in God's image (James 3:9).

God's response (v. 13) is to speak to Noah. He apparently speaks directly with Noah about his intentions, which puts Noah into the same category as Adam, Abraham, and Moses.[35] God sums up the point about violence and devastation and underlines it by repeating the words (devastated, full of violence, devastated, devastated, full of violence, devastate) and by now taking them on his own lips. He also takes up and reverses phrases from Gen. 1, where he "said" things about creation and then "saw" that creation was good. Here he "sees" and then "says" things about devastation.[36] And he adds the further key term, "the end" (*qēṣ*). Like its English equivalent, the Hebrew term is just an ordinary, nonthreatening word (e.g., 8:6; 41:1), but in some circumstances it can become a terrifying one. Amos once declared that the end was coming upon Ephraim (Amos 8:2), and his words made an impression on Ezekiel (Ezek. 7:1–6). Here in Genesis "the end" is a shorthand alternative for the talk of devastation that runs through vv. 11–13. Targum Neof. suggestively paraphrases, "The outcry of all flesh has come up before me." Humanity has brought the life of the earth to an end, this fact has come to God's notice, and God intends to validate that action. Perhaps the logic of v. 13 also follows and nuances that of v. 7. Human beings were supposed to hold sway over the earth and subjugate it (1:26, 28), but instead they have joined it in its violence.[37] The talk of *ḥāmās* in vv. 11 and 13 recalls the violent action of Cain and Lamech and possibly that of the supernatural beings; in addition, the first man and

34. Cf. Alter, *Genesis*, 28.
35. Cf. Stanton, "Asking Questions."
36. Cf. Gardner, "Ecojustice," 118; Hendel, "Poetics of Myth in Genesis," 162–63.
37. Cf. Gardner, "Ecojustice," 128.

woman, and again the divine beings, were involved in violating God's instructions and the boundaries God had laid down. Indeed, "Gen. 3–6 catalogues a crescendo of undifferentiated violence propagating uncontrollably."[38] And therefore humanity will be devastated "with the earth." God has imagined what it would be like to commit the final act of devastation and bring earth's life to an end, looked the possibility in the eye, and determined to do it. Genesis moves from creation to apocalypse.[39] In English we might then speak of God himself undertaking a final act of violence. Hebrew would not speak in terms of God doing *ḥāmās*, because *ḥāmās* is by definition wrong; it is "virtually a technical term for the oppression of the weak by the strong."[40] But the Scriptures are quite willing to describe God acting violently in the sense in which we use the word in English, where violence (e.g., on the part of law enforcement) can be a proper response to wrongdoing.

A further comparison and contrast with Amos is that Yahweh's first announcements to Amos of devastation for Ephraim (Amos 7:1–6) meet with protests from the prophet, which Yahweh heeds, though Yahweh's subsequent announcements (Amos 7:7–9; 8:1–3) meet with no such protests. Neither does this announcement to Noah. On the other hand, rhetorically one aspect of the significance of Amos 7–8 is that people who hear Amos describing his visions, perhaps during a festival at Beth El, or who hear his scroll read out would be wise to respond by turning from their waywardness so that Yahweh might relent (even if he has not said he would do so) and/or by recognizing that Yahweh has acted properly in letting them experience catastrophe, so that this experience was not without meaning. The same would be true of the deluge story. It was designed to be heard where necessary by people who might need to turn from their waywardness and thus avert such a catastrophe coming to them or who might need to turn from their waywardness because it has fallen upon them. From the declaration that devastation is coming "emerges the loving kindness and goodness of God in foretelling what was to come, his purpose being to suppress the evil through fear of what was expected," as happened in the case of the Ninevites.[41]

6:14–18a. What now follows manifests a charming illogic but also a jaw-dropping horror; the reading of the story deserves a long pause to give God's words a chance to sink in (KSG). God's devastating indictment about devastation could have seemed to allow for no exceptions, but actually God has not abandoned his creation project. In this connection Noah is to construct

38. Walker, "Noah and the Season of Violence," 379. Walker is reading the Noah story in light of R. Girard's work on violence: see, e.g., J. Williams, *Girard Reader*.

39. Cf. Kirk-Duggan, "Characterizations, Comedy, and Catastrophe," 231.

40. Walker, "Noah and the Season of Violence," 380.

41. Didymus, *Genesis*, 159. Targum Ps.-J. sees this significance in the seven-day wait of 7:4; Chrysostom sees it in the difference between the first forty days and the time that follows (*Homilies on Genesis 18–45*, 132).

a gigantic container (a cubit is about half a yard), though it will be rather smaller than Utnapishtim's—rectangular rather than cuboid, and having three rather than seven levels.[42] Its purpose is dramatically held back until the specification is complete, though its shape might remind readers of the Jerusalem sanctuary, as Utnapishtim's container might remind people of temple structures that they knew.[43] It will need to have rooms, and it will need to be sealed with pitch, because it is to be a floating refuge from Yahweh's coming act of devastation whereby earth is to be overwhelmed by the "upper ocean" (*mabbûl*). The term is another that comes only in these chapters and in Ps. 29:10. The Psalms reference puts us on the track of its meaning. It denotes the ocean that sits above the sky, the reservoir of water held back by God's original act of creation. It will engulf the earth and kill everything.

Yet God will set up a pact (*bərît*) with Noah (v. 18a). It is the first occurrence of another key First Testament word, whose implications will be spelled out in chapter 9 (see the comments there). God's speaking of what he *will* do suggests that he is referring not to the undertaking to preserve Noah and his family from the act of devastation but to that undertaking that will follow afterward. Genesis is here summarizing where the story is going and the ultimate nature of God's intention. The declaration that he intends to set up this pact will make it a little easier to cope with his intention in the shorter term to destabilize everything (see further 7:4, 23) and a little easier for Noah to illustrate how "we derive alacrity from hope."[44] The declaration also means that the chest can be "the matrix of a new creation";[45] one might then take it as a symbol of the city of God on its pilgrimage in history,[46] with baptism as the door to this chest (1 Pet. 3:21), though one might be wise to be wary of generating a detailed allegory out of such an approach. Such allegories, "if not actually scholarly, are nevertheless harmless, inasmuch as they contain no error; and one may use them—except in debates—for the sake of embellishment,"[47] even though there may be in them "scarcely anything solid."[48]

6:18b–22. Noah's family will then get into the chest. A family includes the women whom the parents' sons have married as well as the parents and the sons themselves, but Mr. and Ms. Noah's daughters now belong to other families. To Western readers, at least, their abandonment will seem harsh;

42. See "Flood Stories" at the end of this chapter for Utnapishtim's account along with other Middle Eastern flood stories.

43. Cf. Lanckau, "Gottliche Reue und menschlicher Trost," 126; Holloway, "What Ship Goes There."

44. Calvin, *Genesis*, 1:269.

45. Sarna, *Genesis*, 50.

46. Augustine, *City of God* 15.26; cf. Louth, *Genesis 1–11*, 131.

47. Luther, *Lectures on Genesis 6–14*, 68.

48. Calvin, *Genesis*, 1:257.

that feeling reflects a different way of looking at family, but it also presupposes a different focus in God's action. The point about the chest is not to save specific individuals; it relates to God's purpose for his world. The same applies to the saving of examples of each of the species. The listing of the categories of creatures "by their species" takes up the account of creation (1:21–25). Whereas God could have simply started again by creating new human beings and new animals, he chooses not to. At this point in the story, the instruction about taking food likely implies things that grow, in keeping with Gen. 1, but 7:1–5 may supplement that idea.

Noah does as he is told (v. 22). The MT's paragraph break and the medieval chapter division neatly draw attention to this note.

7:1–5. The reference to Yahweh signals that Genesis moves to following the J version of the story when it tells of the command to get into the chest, and it also nuances the instruction about the animals. In using the name Yahweh, J safeguards the point that it was Yahweh who was involved with Noah, even though Noah did not himself know the name. Genesis again notes that Yahweh is involved with him because Noah is faithful. The declaration explains both the reason why Yahweh preserves Noah and his family and the reason why Noah and his family make a reliable basis for Yahweh's rebooting his creation project.[49]

J nuances Yahweh's instructions about the animate creation (vv. 2–3) in distinguishing between pure and impure creatures—ones that can be offered to Yahweh in sacrifice and ones that cannot. The Sinai revelation will be the explicit locus of detailed instructions regarding this area of life, as it will be regarding other areas, and P's omission of reference to this distinction between pure and impure fits the way Leviticus will provide these instructions. P does not project such instructions backward in time, just as it does not project the use of Yahweh's name into an earlier time. But in principle there will be nothing very novel about the distinction that will eventually be expounded in Leviticus; most societies make such a distinction in some way. J can naturally portray a faithful person like Noah as encouraged to work with it and portray Yahweh as presupposing the distinction. While part of the point about having the animals in the chest is to keep them alive, J may also assume that part of the point is for Noah and his family to have something to eat. So Yahweh instructs Noah to take on board plenty of the animals that can be eaten, but just token examples of the ones that cannot, to keep those species alive. Among the latter, what about ones that die through natural causes before they have a chance to procreate? We must not be literalist in understanding the story.

The declaration that everything set in place by Yahweh is going to be wiped out (v. 4) would be even more frightening if Yahweh had not said that

49. Cf. Westermann, *Genesis 1–11*, 426–27.

he intended to set in place a more secure base for the future (6:18; both times forms from *qûm*).

Once again, Noah does as he is told (v. 5).

7:6–16. The story spells out Noah's obedience and relates how things worked out as God said. Even the animals do as God said, without apparently being told; they submit to the authority that God gave humanity at the beginning.[50] The story form of the account of the deluge enables Genesis to make subtle theological points in a way that will be taken further when Exodus speaks of God declaring the intention to stiffen Pharaoh's resolve, then of Pharaoh's resolve being stiff and of Pharaoh stiffening his resolve, and only subsequently of God actually stiffening Pharaoh's resolve. In this case the theological subtlety concerns the sovereignty of God, of nature, and of Noah. Genesis speaks of God's decisions, but mostly of nature's actions. God declares the intention to destroy, but nature wreaks the destruction. God's activity is confined to shutting the door in the chest and then being mindful and sending a wind over the earth, though once again nature effects its own withdrawal. And Genesis speaks of God's decisions and nature's actions, but also of Noah's cooperation, without which the story would collapse—or rather, God would have to rework his plan.

The account of the deluge (vv. 11–12) describes the engulfing of the earth in terms that recall Gen. 1; God is indeed reversing his work of creation. He had then established the dome to hold back the water in the heavens, while evidently allowing for some apertures through which rain could fall; now he lets the apertures be wide open. What falls is more than rain (*māṭār*; cf. v. 4); it is an overwhelming downpour (*gešem*, v. 12). Further, in Gen. 1 the background of God's activity was the presence of darkness over the face of the subterranean deep, and God also made sure that the land was secure from encroaching water; now he also lets the subterranean deep bubble up uncontrollably. The deluge is "a catastrophe involving the entire cosmos. When the heavenly ocean breaks forth upon the earth below, and the primeval sea beneath the earth, which is restrained by God, now freed from its bonds, gushes up through yawning chasms onto the earth, then there is a destruction of the entire cosmic system."[51] Giving the date of the deluge indicates "the absolute concreteness and reality of God's activity."[52]

"This very day" (vv. 13–16a) is a day when God does something particularly significant in fulfillment of his word or when human beings do something particularly significant in response to his word (17:23, 26; Exod. 12:17, 41, 51). "A fullness of detail and a studied solemnity" then characterize the account of "the entrance of the obedient, pious man into the place of salvation

50. Cf. Calvin, *Genesis*, 1:269.
51. Von Rad, *Genesis*, 124.
52. Von Rad, *Genesis*, 123.

or preservation," while "the participation of every species of animal in this solemn procession reflects the same attitude that we have seen in Gen. 1: all living beings belong together and the blessing holds for all."[53] The verse-by-verse repetitions in the children's song that relate how "the animals went in two by two" in their procession pick up the repetitions in the account: they "came . . . came . . . came . . . came," with the coup de grâce following at the end of the repetitions: "as God ordered him." The listing of the categories of each creature "by its species" takes up the account of creation again (Gen. 1:21–25).

And Yahweh shut Noah in (v. 16b). No doubt literally Noah shut the door—as Utnapishtim does in the Mesopotamian Gilgamesh story that tells of a great flood (tablet XI)—but metaphorically Yahweh did, ensuring that the water would not be able to gain access to the chest. Perhaps God also wanted to keep other people out.[54]

7:17–24. There follows the detailed account of the process of the deluge and its effects. Initially Genesis simply describes the awe-inspiring nature of the flood. Even an audience that knows only about the mountains in its region and not about the Himalayas could be stunned at the picture the account paints. Perhaps it would momentarily forget what the deluge was designed to accomplish. And the repeated verb "increased" might remind it of the occurrences of the same verb in the imperative in the creation story, in a quite different connection (1:22, 28, there translated "be numerous"). But the breathtaking effect of the picture then gives way to horror (vv. 21–23). Everything "breathed its last," expired (*gûaʿ*), in keeping with God's word (6:17). To put it in stark, everyday words, everything "died." It no longer had in its nostrils the breath of life, the breath that makes the difference between life and death; again the process of creation is reversed (2:7). The event "wiped out" everything, obliterated it (*māḥâ*), in keeping with God's word (6:7; 7:4). Using the transitive form of this verb without an explicit subject and then using the passive verb draws indirect attention to the unnamed agent of the elimination. Its horror is both underlined and qualified by the subsequent verb "remained" (*šāʾar*) in 7:23. With its related nouns, the verb recurs in Israel's later story in portrayals of the cataclysmic nature of the disasters Yahweh threatens and brings to Israel, which allow only leftovers or remains or a remnant to survive—but at least they allow something to survive, which can be the nucleus of a new future.

8:1–5. "But God was mindful of Noah" (*zākar*). The medieval chapter division neatly draws attention to this turning point in the story. Yet another key verb appears. It is conventionally translated "remember," but the Hebrew word has connotations beyond those of that English verb. It can apply to the

53. Westermann, *Genesis 1–11*, 436.
54. So Ephrem, *Genesis*, 141.

future, not just the past; it can signify a deliberate act, not just an accidental one; and it can point not just to a mental event but to an action one takes on the basis of what one applies one's mind to. The chest could be the matrix of a new creation only because God was mindful or remembered. That statement "must not be weakened as though it were a figure of speech meaning that God acted as if He had forgotten."[55] The statement takes its place along with the declarations that God regretted and felt pain as markers of God's living in linear time with the world, not only in eternity. God has memory; but distinctive to God is the capacity to control his memory. And further, although human beings may do nothing on the basis of what they remember, for God forgetting and remembering are actions. God has been putting Noah out of mind as far as action is concerned and now sets his mind on him and thus initiates action. Genesis now abandons the reticence it showed when it did not refer to God's action while describing the bringing of the deluge in 7:10–24: God makes a wind pass over the earth, so that the water abates. If the deluge means the undoing of creation, God is now beginning a new act of creation. Floods of water have not quenched love (Song 8:7).[56] Once more a wind passes over the earth (Tgs. Ps.-J. and Neof. again call it "a merciful wind"), and once more the water comes under control (cf. 1:2), and it is God who makes it do so. The springs below the earth close, as do the apertures in the dome above. The rain therefore stops, and gradually the water returns to the place that God allocated to it at the beginning (1:6–10), in a way that corresponds to the gradual way in which it had grown to overwhelm the earth.

Thus the chest comes to rest (*nûaḥ*, the verb from which Noah's name comes; vv. 4–5). Ararat, an area rather than a single mountain, also appears in 2 Kings 19:37; Isa. 37:38; Jer. 51:27, without any great indication of its location, though somewhere in Assyria would make sense, and thus somewhere in eastern Turkey, Armenia, or northern Iran. The name compares with that of the kingdom of Urartu in Armenia. The mountains' appearing further suggests that creation is returning (cf. 1:9).[57]

8:6–12. The account of the birds (one of the detailed points of contact with the Utnapishtim account) extends the suspense of the story. With the landing of the chest, we might have thought that Noah was home and dry; but it is a while before he is. The vignette about the birds "subtly lets us witness the waiting and hoping of those enclosed in the ark."[58] It's said that sailors used to rely on birds to tell them whether they were near land.[59] The experiments with the birds establish whether it's safe to think of disembarking. The vignette underlines the way the destinies of humanity and of the rest of the animate

55. Luther, *Genesis 6–14*, 104.
56. Didymus, *Genesis*, 176.
57. Cf. Alter, *Genesis*, 34.
58. Von Rad, *Genesis*, 117.
59. Cf. Skinner, *Genesis*, 156.

creation are interwoven. Noah has made it possible for the animate creation to survive; the animate creation makes it possible for him to know he really has survived. Noah sends out a raven and a pigeon, as happens in Utnapishtim's story, though there the pigeon goes first and the raven last, with a swallow in between. Genesis Rabbah 33.5 nicely hints that the reason for sending a raven would be that it is good at finding food for a servant of God (1 Kings 17:6), though the raven is also a scavenger and an impure bird (Lev. 11:15); it would thus find acceptable food before a pigeon did.[60] Pigeons are pure birds that commonly feature in connection with sacrifice (e.g., Lev. 1:14; Luke 2:24). The olive branch was already a symbol of peace in the ancient world,[61] but the pigeon might have brought the olive branch so that it could start building a nest,[62] though in this context the point may be that the olive is one of the most basic requirements for life in Israel. Josephus nicely has the pigeon covered in mud as well as carrying the olive branch.[63] As the narrative's "there" had invited the audience to look at the world's moral devastation through God's eyes (6:12), now its "there" (8:11) invites it to watch through Noah's eyes as the pigeon returns with good news (there will be another "there" in 8:13).

8:13–19. The deluge has lasted a year, whether one works by a lunar or by a solar calendar. The command that God then issues is the kind that gives permission and an invitation. "The loving Lord's goodness" expresses itself in the way "he brought the good man out of the ark, freeing him from life there and releasing him from that strange and distressing prison, and bestowed on him the reward for his endurance in the words, 'Increase and multiply.'"[64] But it is also a command to play that part. Noah, his family, and the animate beings can leave the chest to begin to take their part in the renewal of the creation project (cf. 1:20–28). "The whole of creation recovers its proper order, both the soil reawakening to productivity as well as everything else that had been created."[65]

8:20–22. The first thing Noah does is worship God. He's like someone released from prison who therefore wants to give public testimony to what God has done for him (so Gen. Rab. 34.1).

Thus (v. 20) "Noah, having left the ark, does not proceed to build a tower or a house, or to plow the fields, but to build an altar."[66] Cain and Abel made offerings to God, and we might assume that their offerings involved an altar,

60. Moberly ("Why Did Noah Send Out a Raven?") suggests that Noah is "symbolically replicating" God's action (8:1).

61. Cf. Skinner, *Genesis*, 156.

62. Cf. Keiter, "Noah and the Dove."

63. Josephus, *Ant.* 1.3.5.

64. Chrysostom, *Homilies on Genesis 18–45*, 162.

65. Chrysostom, *Homilies on Genesis 18–45*, 156.

66. J. Brenz, *Opera 1: Commentarii in Genesis* . . . (Tübingen: Gruppenbach, 1576), 105, as quoted in J. Thompson, *Genesis 1–11*, 282.

but here Genesis explicitly mentions Noah's building an altar. Conversely, accounts of subsequent altar building (12:7–8; 13:18; 22:9; 26:25; 33:20; 35:1–7; the last reference is the only occasion when God commissions the construction) do not always refer to the offering of sacrifices—the building of the altar is significant in its own right. It means proclaiming Yahweh's name over an area; it signifies that this area belongs to Yahweh. And it means recognizing this place as a place where Yahweh has acted. Both significances could apply in Gen. 8. But here, Genesis talks about both altar and sacrifice. It notes the practical reason why one builds an altar. It is hardly the moment for an expiatory sacrifice;[67] Christian readers need to keep recalling that expiation or propitiation is not the most common significance of sacrifice. A thank offering would have seemed quite appropriate, the kind of sacrifice that involves a fellowship meal between Yahweh and the offerers. Noah actually offers a whole offering, the kind of sacrifice that involves giving the entire animal to Yahweh, the kind of sacrifice that Gen. 22 will require, a sign of total personal commitment. Such a sacrifice might well accompany a prayer that God will never flood the earth again.[68]

God likes the smell of Noah's offerings (v. 21a). As God regrets and remembers, so the God of the Scriptures, like the gods of other Middle Eastern peoples, is not only not a timeless being; he is also not a spiritual being whose nature is quite other than that of the beings he created. He created beings in his image, and he is like them. As well as having the full range of emotions such as love, hate, joy, pleasure, and anger, God has the full range of capacities such as seeing, hearing, feeling—and smelling. Indeed b. Ber. 43b asks, "Whence do we learn that a blessing should be said over sweet odours?" And it answers, "Because it says, Let every soul [*nəšāmâ*, breath] praise the Lord [Ps. 150:6]. What is that which gives enjoyment to the soul and not to the body?—You must say that this is fragrant smell." Smell is spiritual.[69] The difference between Yahweh and other so-called gods is that his eyes, ears, and nose work, as theirs do not (see the comment on 1:26–28). It would be a shame to view it as merely a dead metaphor. The idea of sacrifice having a smell that Yahweh likes (or does not like) occurs later as well as earlier in First Testament times and in the NT (e.g., Exod. 29:18; Lev. 1:9; Isa. 1:13; Ezek. 6:13; Eph. 5:2). For Genesis and its audience, what might be significant is the relatively *non*-anthropomorphic nature of the expression, if people were familiar with the Mesopotamian picture of the gods clustering like flies in their hunger.[70] And Yahweh finds the smell of the sacrifice restful (*nîḥōaḥ*), another word derived from the same root as Noah's name (cf. v. 4). It would

67. Against, e.g., Gunkel, *Genesis*, 66; cf. 1QapGen 10.13; and Jub. 6.1–2, with van Ruiten's comments, *Primaeval History Reinterpreted*, 224–26.

68. So Josephus, *Ant.* 1.3.7.

69. Cf. Marwil, "Soothing Savor," 170.

70. Cf. Kidner, *Genesis*, 93.

be a nice counter to the "stench of ungodliness"[71] and the stench of death all over the earth.

In what sense do the offerings and the smell generate the decision never again to bring such catastrophe on the earth? The backdrop to the story of the deluge was a cataclysmically gloomy assessment of humanity's moral state. But Noah has proved to be an exception to that assessment, and the offering he has brought has confirmed that all is not totally lost. It is possible to start over. Yahweh had tried cursing the snake and the ground and one of the human beings, and it had gotten no one anywhere. He will not devastate the ground again. "Diminish" (*qālal* piel) has implications similar to "curse" (*ʾārar*) in Gen. 3 and 4, but "curse" refers to the process whereby something terrible happens through someone, whose words have power, speaking words that are bound to find fulfillment, whereas "diminish" refers to the results of that process. It suggests turning an object or a person into something slight and of no account, making it shrink to nothing, or counting it as nothing (cf. 1 Sam. 18:23; Job 40:4; Isa. 49:6). It is the opposite of blessing, which implies making something fruitful and enabling growth. Here, "diminish" rather than "curse" picks up from 8:8, 11: the water has diminished and abated from the land; Yahweh will not again let the ground diminish by letting the water overwhelm it. He will not again strike down (*nākâ* hiphil) everything living. Whereas Yahweh does not get involved in willful violence or *ḥāmās*, he does get involved in proper violence, for which *nākâ* hiphil is the nearest that Hebrew has to a technical term. But whereas proper violence may work as punishment or chastisement, Yahweh also recognizes that in itself it does not take him toward the achievement of his creation purpose. Yahweh is not referring to an abrogation of the curse in 3:17–19 (which the audience's experience would have told them had not been abrogated) but to a promise never again to bring a disaster like the deluge. Thus "the real significance of the Flood as God's judgement" lies in "God's pledge that such a judgement will not happen again."[72]

The reason (v. 21b) relates to the human waywardness described in devastating fashion in 6:5–6; the mention of the divine heart and the human heart takes up the reference there. "The same condition, which in the prologue is the basis for God's judgment, in the epilogue reveals God's grace and providence. The contrast between God's punishing anger and his supporting grace, which pervades the whole Bible, is here presented quite untheologically, even almost inappropriately. It seems almost like indulgence, an adjustment by God toward man's sinfulness."[73] While humanity's youth may be the youth of each individual, in the context it is more likely the youth of humanity that Gen. 1–6

71. Luther, *Genesis 6–14*, 117.
72. Bauckham, *Bible in Politics*, 134.
73. Von Rad, *Genesis*, 119; the first sentence is in italics in the original.

has related. But what is the nature of the "because" relating to its waywardness? The obvious understanding is that Yahweh acknowledges that cursing the ground gets no one anywhere because of the extent and depth of human waywardness. Instead of cursing the ground because of that waywardness, he will need to live with it and/or do something else about it. The sinfulness of the human heart is first the reason for divine judgment and then the reason for holding back from judgment.[74] This understanding implies a profound insight, but it is rather subtle. More likely the because clause explicates the phrase "on account of humanity." The bad state of the human heart will not make Yahweh diminish the ground again. The implication of the two possible understandings is not very different. Humanity will continue to exist on account of God's mercy, not on account of its deserving. Noah's sacrifice has encouraged Yahweh to make that commitment. Genesis "has a dim view of the human heart"; it raises a question about whether human beings can transcend the calculated self-interest that inevitably leads to death.[75] The judgment that "the shaping of the human heart is bad from its youth" is less severe than the judgment that "the entire shaping of its heart's intentions was simply bad, all day" (6:5).[76] Yet this more general but more moderate judgment gives no basis for optimism about human moral progress, and the world has seen no progress since Noah's day. Humanity continues to be inclined to devastate the earth and to be inclined to violation and violence. "There will be wars and rumors of wars" (Matt. 24:6). In setting the world going again, God has looked in the face the fact that the human heart is in a bad shape and has promised that he will put up with it rather than destroy the world. These verses "belong indisputably to the weightiest in the whole Bible."[77]

Yahweh spells out his commitment in a series of poetic cola (v. 22). Because English puts subjects before verbs, the sentence looks ordinary, but in Hebrew it is unusual because verbs usually come first. It opens with a noun phrase picking up from v. 21 with its "yet," and it closes with a verbal expression for which we thus need to wait for an unaccustomed time. The phrases in between pair aba′b′: seedtime/harvest is reexpressed as summer/winter, and cold/heat is reexpressed as day/night. Internally, the phrases work abb′a′: seedtime/harvest then summer/winter; cold/heat then day/night.[78] So the audience is invited to think about the ordering of time on the large scale (the seasons of

74. Cf. Barth, *CD* 2.1:103.

75. Brueggemann, *Genesis*, 82.

76. Cf. Sarna, *Genesis*, 59.

77. Seebass, *Genesis*, 1:220.

78. Only at the end does the nature of the pairing become clear to a reader in the northern hemisphere, where "cold/heat" sounds as if it should pair with "seedtime/harvest" and "summer/winter." It seems as if the first three phrases refer to the seasons and that the fourth phrase stands on its own, but in the Middle East the temperature difference between day and night is often more noticeable.

the year) and on the small scale (within each twenty-four-hour period), and it is eventually reassured that this ordering will not break down. The crucial sequence of sowing as the rainy season comes and harvest in the summer will continue. Day/night takes us back to Gen. 1, as does the promise that they will not "stop" just because Yahweh has "stopped" creating (2:1–3). At the beginning, God established the rhythm of day and night with some implication of permanency, but human rebellion meant the forgoing of such certainty. Now God makes that rhythm the object of a promise.[79] Back in Gen. 1, God gave the animate creation and the things that grow from the ground the power to procreate. Now he extends the promise to an assurance that the broader creation will not act in such a way as to frustrate their capacity. The First Testament knows that Yahweh acts linearly and acts in history. It knows that Yahweh also acts cyclically and acts in the round of nature.[80]

For Isa. 54:9 this promise becomes a model for the commitment that God will make to Zion. Set alongside God's disappointment with his people, which parallels his disappointment with created humanity,[81] will be a divine oath not to act in wrath against his people, which will parallel the divine renunciation of the idea of cursing the earth again. The experienced security of God's earth is a guarantee of the security of God's people. Admittedly, thereby "God's unfailing promises make room for more violence."[82]

Implications

Flood Stories

There are many Middle Eastern deluge stories, in origin dating from before Moses's day. As is the case with the creation stories, Genesis shares aspects of its theology and message with them and has concrete motifs in common with them, while other aspects of its theology and message are different, as is its detailed story. Once again, Genesis may be consciously telling a story that contrasts with Middle Eastern equivalents.[83] At one level the reason for the existence of many such stories is that there were a number of floods in the Tigris-Euphrates plain, and even storytellers who have not personally experienced a flood would be able to imagine one. But the phenomenon also needs to be compared with the existence of flood stories in other parts of the world and with the many Western stories of intergalactic battle and alien invasion. Such stories become the screen on which perennial human issues

79. Cf. Barth, *CD* 1.2:48.

80. Cf. Westermann, *Genesis 1–11*, 458.

81. See the comment on 6:5–6.

82. Fretheim, "Violence," 124.

83. See, e.g., Wenham, *Genesis 1–15*, 159–66; Hays, *Hidden Riches*, 75–95; Noort, "Stories of the Great Flood"; Pfost, "Literary Analysis."

can be projected. Western movies project questions into the future and ask whether there will be a future. Middle Eastern stories project them into the past and ask about the security of the created world. They speak "of the threat to human existence and at the same time of its permanence."[84]

The most famous Middle Eastern deluge story is the one told by Utnapishtim to Gilgamesh, the king of Uruk. Like the Genesis story, it forms part of a much larger work, in this case a poem telling of Gilgamesh's quest for eternal life after the death of his friend Enkidu. Utnapishtim relates how the gods decide to flood the town of Shuruppak on the Euphrates. A flood there that has left archaeological indications may have been part of the background to the story's development.[85] In a way that Utnapishtim can overhear, one of the gods speaks about the need to construct a boat and take examples of all species on it. Utnapishtim gives an account of the making of the boat and its launching, then of the frightening nature of the storm that comes. The boat survives the storm, the water abates, and Utnapishtim sends out a pigeon, a swallow, and a raven to see if they find a place to land. In due course he offers a sacrifice, though this action provokes argument among the gods about who has enabled Utnapishtim to escape the flood. He is rewarded with the gift of eternal life, though this does no good to Gilgamesh.

The other deluge narrative that is most comparable with Genesis is the older story of Atrahasis, which lies behind the flood story element in the Gilgamesh narrative. It also has a broader plot, which more closely parallels that of Genesis: the gods create the world, then determine to destroy it because of the behavior of human beings, who disturb the gods by their noisy rebelliousness. In both Gilgamesh and Atrahasis, the flood is the action of last resort, after the gods have tried other chastisements.

As is the case with the creation story and its relationship with stories such as When on High, the deluge story thus manifests points of detail that are hardly coincidental, along with a different total perspective.[86] In Genesis the question of human immortality is not a theme; there is only one God to be involved, so he combines the roles taken by different Mesopotamian gods; he brings about the deluge because of human wrongdoing, not just because human beings are a nuisance.[87] The Genesis story is rather prosaic and down to earth compared with the Mesopotamian epics.[88] On the other hand, while Gen. 6–8 cannot be laid out as poetry in the manner of Gen. 1, it closes with some poetic lines and may include one or two others (NJPS finds a poetic couplet in 7:11b). Its inclusion of a number of rare expressions—such as the

84. Westermann, *Genesis 1–11*, 395.

85. Cf. Sarna, *Genesis*, 48.

86. But Grünwaldt ("Wenn Gott nur einer ist") suggests that we have something to learn from the way Genesis learns from other understandings of the deluge in its context.

87. Cf. Lanckau, "Gottliche Reue und menschlicher Trost."

88. Cf. Gunkel, *Genesis*, 72–73.

words for chest, sealed, pitch, compartments, gable, ocean, and what had been established (6:14, 16, 17; 7:4, 23), and the difficult phrases "finish it to a cubit upward" and "breath of the spirit of life" (6:16; 7:22)—may reflect a poetic background. The same possibility applies to some of the repetitions of words, which parallels that in Gen. 1.[89]

Although many Western readers might have preferred that this story not be in the Scriptures, one reason why it is here may be that "a story of a flood is in some way a given in the world of ancient Israel," so that the question becomes what is characteristic and distinctive of this particular flood story.[90] The perspective of Genesis again contrasts with that of Middle Eastern equivalents. In Gilgamesh Tablet XI, the god Enlil determines to destroy humanity because of the noise people make, but Ea, the god who created humanity, commissions Atrahasis to build a boat so that humanity can survive the flood. In Genesis the reason for devastating the world is that humanity has already devastated it by its violence, but the fact that Yahweh alone is God means that he is both the one who devastates and the one who enables humanity to survive. The person through whom God makes it possible is not an impressive human hero like Utnapishtim but just a good man who does what God says.[91] The broader Genesis story of the deluge is concerned not with the destiny of an individual, such as Gilgamesh, but with the destiny of the world as a whole; ensuring the survival of one man and his family is integral to the divine intention in bringing about the catastrophe, rather than something that might or might not have come about, depending on differences among the gods.

89. Cf. Sarna, *Genesis*, 49.
90. Moberly, "On Interpreting the Mind of God," 63.
91. Cf. Wenham, *Genesis 1–15*, 165–66.

7

The Blessing, the Pact, and the Fall

(9:1–29)

Overview

Genesis 9 comprises two codas to the Noah story, though speaking in terms of two codas might imply an underestimate of the chapter's importance. If anything, the account of the aftermath of the deluge brings the Noah story to a double climax rather than an anticlimax. As usual, in considering both parts of the chapter, we can ask what problem or question they raise, perhaps a problem or question for the audience of Genesis.

The first coda (vv. 1–17) is an extended midrash on 8:20–22. Those verses might raise a question: "Really? How do those words relate to all the things we have heard in 6:9–8:19?" Genesis is not merely speaking of "distant primeval things" but also answering a question about the present, because it is speaking about "our world age."[1] The opening part of the response to that question makes explicit that God really is setting creation going again. He is doing so in full recognition of the truth about the violation that led to the deluge, and he is incorporating some commands that issue from that truth. To that, one might again respond, "Really?" Thus the latter part of the response to that question turns the promise from 8:20–22 into a pact with a sign, which God will therefore not be able to avoid keeping. The first coda, then, constitutes a rounding off of the deluge story as God lays down the "new world-order"[2] for the new world.

In retrospect, the second coda (vv. 18–29) illustrates why humanity needs such a commitment from God. This second coda is a little story with a question

1. Von Rad, *Genesis*, 127.
2. Skinner, *Genesis*, 169.

and an answer, though it parallels other Genesis stories in raising as many questions as it answers. Its own question is apparent: why do the Canaanites end up as servants to the Israelites? And the answer is that they pay a price for something their father did, as is often the case in human experience.

Translation

1God blessed Noah and his sons and said to them, "Be fruitful, be
numerous, fill the earth. **2**Awe toward you and dread toward you[3] will
be upon every living thing on the earth, upon every bird in the sky, with
everything that moves on the ground, and with all the fish in the sea;
they're given into your hand. **3**Everything that moves, that's living, will be
yours as food. Like the green plants, I am giving[4] you everything. **4**How-
ever, flesh with its life, its blood, you will not eat.
5And, however,

Your blood, belonging to your lives, I will require;
  from the hand of every living thing I will require it.
From the hand of a human being,[5]
  from the hand of an individual for his brother,
  I will require the life of a human being.
6One who pours out the blood of a human being,
  through a human being[6] his blood will pour out.
Because it was in God's image
  that he made a human being.[7]
7But you: be fruitful, be numerous,
  teem on the earth, be numerous[8] on it."

8Then God said to Noah and to his sons with him: **9**"And I: here, I'm
going to implement my pact with you, with your offspring after you, **10**and
with every living being that's with you: bird, animal, and every living thing
on the earth with you, of all that came out of the chest, for every living
thing on the earth. **11**I will implement my pact with you, and all flesh will

3. A hendiadys: cf. Speiser's "dread fear" (*Genesis*, 58).

4. The declarative/performative qatal suggests a speech act, "I hereby give"; another comes in v. 13.

5. *Hā'ādam* with the article through vv. 5–6.

6. The Vg omits *bā'ādām*. Targum Neof. takes it to mean "by a human being," and Tg. Onq. and Tg. Ps.-J. expand it to denote by a human court, to safeguard against private vengeance (cf. Aberbach and Grossfeld, *Targum Onkelos*, 65). But the LXX has "for his blood," which suggests translating the MT "for a human being" (cf. Brayford, *Genesis*, 272–73); and see the comment.

7. The LXX and Vg tidy up the text to eliminate the move to a third-person reference to God in v. 6b, but such moves are common in the First Testament (cf. v. 16), partly reflecting the fact that a human being is here speaking for God, so that either "I" or "he" is appropriate.

8. For the MT's repeated *rəbû*, the LXX implies *rədû*, "hold sway," conforming to 1:28.

not be cut off again by the water of the upper ocean. The upper ocean will not again become something to devastate the earth."

12And God said, "This is the sign of the pact that I'm going to set between me and you and every living creature that's with you, to agelong generations. **13**My bow I am setting[9] in the mist. It will be a sign of the pact between me and the earth. **14**When I spread mist on the earth and the bow appears in the mist, **15**I will be mindful of my pact that's between me and you and every living creature among all flesh, and the water will not again become an upper-ocean outburst to devastate all flesh. **16**The bow will be in the mist and I will see it, being mindful of the agelong pact between God and every living creature among all flesh that's on the earth." **17**So God said to Noah, "This will be the sign of the pact that I am implementing between me and all flesh that's on the earth."

18Noah's sons who came out of the chest were Šem, Ḥam, and Yepet, while Ḥam was the father of Kenaʿan. **19**These three were Noah's sons, and from them the entire earth dispersed.[10]

20Noah was the first, as the man of the ground, who planted a vineyard.[11] **21**He drank some of the wine and got drunk, and he exposed himself inside his tent. **22**Ḥam, Kenaʿan's father, saw his father's naked body and told his two brothers outside. **23**Šem and Yepet took a cover, put it on both their shoulders, walked backward, and covered up their father's naked body, with their faces turned backward, so they didn't see their father's naked body.

24Noah woke up from his wine and came to know what his youngest son had done to him. **25**He said,

> Cursed be Kenaʿan:
> he is to be the lowest servant[12] to his brothers.
>
> **26**And he said,
> Blessed be Yahweh, the God of Šem:
>   may Kenaʿan be a servant to them.[13]

9. The declarative/performative qatal again suggests a speech act: "I hereby set"; cf. v. 17.

10. *Nāpəṣâ* from *nāpaṣ*, a by-form of *pûṣ*.

11. Literally, "was the first, . . . and he planted." Hardly "was the first tiller of the soil, and he planted," nor need the LXX imply this understanding (against *NETS*); see the discussion in Brayford, *Genesis*, 275–76. But understood this way, the words would presumably be designating Noah as the first person to take up farming after the deluge. For the absolute use of *ḥālal* hiphil followed by waw-consecutive, cf. Ezra 3:8; the more regular construction comes in Gen. 10:8.

12. Literally, "the servant of servants," For the translation "servant" for *ʿebed*, cf. Common English Bible. "Slave" (NRSV, NIV) is misleading; *ʿebed* does not usually denote someone who is the property of another, and the people of Gibeon (see the comment on 9:24–27) became servants, not slaves. LXX *pais oiketēs*; Vg *servus* could mean either slave or servant. Midrash Tanḥuma B takes the phrase to denote a permanent servant as opposed to one who would be freed after a period of years (see Lev. 25:46; Aberbach and Grossfeld, *Targum Onkelos to Genesis*, 68–69; also Tg. Neof.).

13. The LXX, Vg take *lāmô* as meaning "to him" (Vg translates similarly in v. 27); on this possibility, see GKC 103f, note 3). But the usual plural understanding fits, following up the collective singular *šēm* (and *yepet*).

[27]May God open up[14] Yepet,
may he[15] dwell in the tents of Šem,[16]
and may Kenaʿan be a servant to them.

[28]Noah lived after the upper-ocean outburst for 350 years. [29]So Noah's entire time came to 950 years. Then he died.

Interpretation

Given that Gen. 9 comprises a further address by God elaborating on 8:21–22 and a further story about Noah, separating it off from what precedes is slightly arbitrary and done for convenience, though the chapter division does mark the move from J material to P material: that is, 9:1–17 is P's vast equivalent to or midrash on 8:22–23. MT has a unit break after 9:17 and another after 9:29; the summary statement in 9:28–29 is actually the completion of the summary statement about Noah begun in 5:32.[17] So 9:1–29, which is marked as a unit by the medieval chapter division, may reasonably be treated as a third unit within 5:1–9:29. Genesis 10:1 then has a heading for the new line of descent, the line of Noah's sons.

The chapter works as follows:

9:1–7: God renews the creation blessing and commission[18] but adds a new feature and also a new requirement. Verses 1 and 7 form a frame around the subsection, which the MT closes with a paragraph marker.

9:8–17: God speaks of implementing a pact with Noah and his sons, a bow in the clouds being a sign of its permanent nature. Verses 8 and 17 form a frame around the subsection, which the MT closes with a unit marker.

9:18–19: A summary footnote to vv. 1–17.

9:20–27: A story about Noah and his sons and grandson.

9:28–29: The final completion of Noah's story, which the MT closes with a unit marker.

14. *Yapt* makes for paronomasia with *yepet*. *HALOT* and *DCH* assume that there are two verbs *pātâ*; BDB assumes that there is a verb *yapat*, of which this is the only clear instance, but with some derived words suggesting simple or open-minded and a denominative verb derived from the latter; *DTT* assumes that there is one verb with both sorts of meaning.

15. That is, God; cf. Tg. Onq.; Gen. Rab. 36.8; Ephrem, *Genesis*, 146. "May he [Yepet]" is less likely; it is not obvious what Yepet's living in Šem's tents would mean, and it is natural to take the subject of this colon to be the same as the subject of the previous colon.

16. "Tents of Šem" (*ʾāhŏlê šēm*) makes for another paronomasia, with "God of Šem" (*ʾĕlōhê šēm*).

17. See the introduction to 5:1–6:8 above.

18. See Mulzac, "Genesis 9:1–7."

The story in vv. 18–27 is laconic and puzzling. Like Gen. 2–3 and 4, it raises many questions that it does not answer. Was Noah the first vinedresser? Was he truly the first person to discover the effects of letting grapes ferment? Was he at fault for getting drunk? Was he at fault for exposing himself? In what sense was it his tent? Where was Ms. Noah? How did Ham happen to see him unclothed? Is "saw his father's naked body" a literal statement or a euphemism? If it is a literal statement, what was so wrong with Ham's reaction? Why is Ham called Noah's youngest son? Why does Noah declare a curse on Canaan rather than on Ham? Was Noah's reaction appropriate? Why does Noah bless the God of Shem rather than Shem himself? What is the meaning of the prayer that God may open up Japhet? Who does Noah envisage as dwelling in the tents of Shem?

The story itself clarifies only some of these questions, and we must accept its opacity over others. As is again the case with the stories in Gen. 2–4, this opacity is part of its nature. In telling a story that raises more questions than it answers, it again invites us to live with the fact that not all questions have answers that we can see (cf. Job). At the same time, we can look for clues that enable us to fill in the gaps in the story with some conviction.

The clue to one key aspect of its focus lies in the unexpected reference to Canaan in the opening verse, which leads into four more references to Canaan in the story, more than to Noah, Shem, Ham, or Japhet. Canaan is not part of the bigger narrative yet. His birth will feature only in passing in 10:6, while 10:15–19 will list his descendants. Genesis 11–13 will then refer to the Canaanites' presence in the country that bears their name, a presence that complicates Yahweh's promise of the country to Abraham and Sarah, and the rest of Genesis will often refer to Canaan; one of its implicit questions will continue to be how Canaan can become the domain of Abraham and Sarah's descendants.

But many people listening to this story know about Canaan as part of the broader story of what God has been doing with them. The Canaanites are part of their own lives as Shem, Ham, and Japhet are not. Outside the genealogies in Chronicles, the names of Noah's sons appear only in the occasional description of Egypt as the country of Ham (cf. Pss. 78:51; 105:23, 27; 106:22), though another link is that Canaan was long an underling of Egypt. While some First Testament passages can speak as if the Israelites under Joshua eliminated the Canaanites, other passages make clear that actually "the Israelites lived among the Canaanites" and intermarried with them (Judg. 3:5; see further Ps. 106:34–39). David's ill-fated census had to include the towns of the Hivvites and Canaanites (2 Sam. 24:7), and at least until Solomon's day Canaanites still lived in the big town of Gezer, not far from Jerusalem (1 Kings 9:16). The question of how to think of the Canaanites could have been a live issue in the listeners' day, and this story provides them with some allusive hints.

The tale it tells means that the second climax to Noah's story all but undoes the new world order proclaimed by the first climax. Realism confronts what could be utopianism.[19] Thus the chapter as a whole parallels Gen. 1–4, with P again leading the way and J then subverting it. Or perhaps one may put the matter the other way around: the unconditional promise of a new world order implies that the world can live with the mess to which the unsavory subsequent story testifies and that God's blessing (v. 1) will not be frustrated by Noah's curse (v. 25). And as the close of Gen. 1–4 tells of people calling out with the name Yahweh, the close of Gen. 9 tells of Noah blessing Yahweh.

9:1–4. Whereas the good news in 8:21–22 concerned the way God spoke to himself (though the existence of the report implies that he shared his thinking), the good news in P's account concerns the way he speaks to Noah and his sons.

The further initial excitement in God's words (v. 1) is that they report his renewing the blessing on humanity and the commission that P reported in Gen. 1. God exactly repeats his opening words in 1:28 except for the change in the object, as "Noah and his sons" replaces "them." Blessing is again spelled out in terms of numerical fruitfulness; God wants the earth filled. God is committed to humanity's having a new beginning. Amusingly, in 1:28 "them" referred to male and female humanity; here the women are left out, which would make it hard to fulfill the commission. The reason for the difference is that 1:28 looked forward to 2:18–25 (on which it incorporated an anticipatory midrash), whereas 9:1 looks forward to 9:18–27. This commission to fill the earth contrasts with the aftermath of the flood in Atrahasis, where the gods are concerned to limit human fecundity in the conviction that it caused the problems that made the flood necessary.[20] It also reasserts the desirability of this filling, which contrasts with the other filling of 6:11, 13.

God goes on (v. 2), as he did in 1:28, to speak of humanity's position in relation to the rest of the animate world. He speaks of the creatures in slightly different terms, but the differences do not seem significant, and initially the nature of their relationship to humanity might not seem very different. Earlier he spoke of humanity as subjugating and holding sway; humanity's turning proper subjugation into improper violence might lie behind God's omitting subjugation from this commission.[21] Here he speaks of the creatures showing awe and dread. There is nothing wrong with awe and dread (*môrāʾ*, *ḥat*); they are attitudes that God's people are supposed to take toward God. The two related verbs come together in Mal. 2:5. But while the first word very often has these positive connotations, the connotations of the second are more usually negative, which hints that God's point here may be more sinister.

19. Gertz, "Hams Sündenfall," 95.

20. See Römer, "La création des hommes et leur multiplication."

21. Cf. Gardner, "Ecojustice," 128.

That possibility finds support in the way related words come together in (e.g.) Deut. 11:25. God's declaration that the animate world is given into humanity's hand or power is also not encouraging for it (see, e.g., 14:20; 16:6). Yet another negative hint is the way God does not repeat the original creation blessing on the animate world.

God's point is indeed more sinister (v. 3). "Although Noah is in some sense a new Adam . . . , the world is no new Eden."[22] The two most general expressions from v. 2 (things that move, that are living), which were also the last summary expressions in 1:28, recur with what one might see as good news for Noah and his sons but bad news for the animate world. Notwithstanding the promise in v. 2, lions and tigers are not obviously scared of human beings, though one ought not to worry too much about that fact, especially in light of God's promise that now follows.[23] At the beginning God said "I am giving you . . . the green plants as food" (1:29–30), and 1QapGen 11 has God only repeating the permission to eat things that grow from the ground.[24] But in v. 3 God now takes up the same expression to apply it to everything in the animate world that is alive. He does not say that the dietary extension also applies to the animate beings themselves. Nor does he explain the dietary extension, though perhaps it links with the commission to humanity to maintain control of the animate world, on one hand, and with the actual growth in violence in the world, on the other.

There is a qualification on the permission (v. 4). The pattern of generous provision and a single prohibition recurs from 2:16–17.[25] Human beings may not eat flesh with its life, its *nepeš*. An animate being may be described as being a *nepeš*, a life or living creature or soul (1:24; 2:7), or as having a *nepeš*, a life or soul (1:20, 21). The word's connotations are unlike those of the English word "soul" if we think of a human being as combined of two elements, body and soul, of which the second is semi-independent of the first and is the locus of the real person.[26] The connotations of *nepeš* are more like those of the word *soul* if one thinks in terms of soul music or of a person who is soulful. But because *nepeš* often suggests *life*, it links closely with blood. When a human being or another creature loses a lot of blood, it loses its life, which indicates that there is a sense in which the life is in the blood (Lev. 17:11). Human beings may not eat the life and therefore may not eat the blood. The ban God pronounces is a straight prohibition, with no qualification or sanction, like the prohibitions in the Decalogue, and it uses the strong negative *lōʾ* as they do, rather than the more regular *ʾal*. Like them,

22. Fretheim, "Genesis," 398.

23. Cf. Calvin, *Genesis*, 1:290–91.

24. See *DSS* 1:34–35; cf. Falk, "Divergence from Genesis," 200–202; and more broadly Shemesh, "Vegetarian Ideology."

25. Hamilton, *Genesis 1–17*, 314.

26. See the section on body and soul at the end of the comments on Gen. 2.

again, it does not specify exactly what it applies to. Does it cover not eating an animal that is still half alive, as predatory animals themselves may, and/or not tearing a limb off a living animal, and/or not draining the blood from an animal you have killed, and/or not eating an animal that has died of natural causes from which you could not drain the blood (this consideration might underlie the specific permission in v. 3 to eat creatures that are alive)?[27] Once more, Genesis does not give reasons for this limitation; perhaps they seemed obvious. Perhaps there is a link with the description of the first human being as becoming a living being through God breathing into him. The life and thus the blood issues from God, so that eating the blood would be consuming something that belongs to God and must be allowed to return to him. People are indeed therefore to let the blood drain from an animal before eating it. As Gen. 1 did not say anything about the "problem" that some animals are built to be carnivorous, here God says nothing about giving permission to such animals to become themselves (as we might think of it). His concern is with the regulating and ordering of human life and with how the regulating and ordering of life looks from the angle of humanity. It is humanity that he addresses here. As he implies in speaking to Job (Job 38–39), how he relates to the animals is between him and them.

9:5–7. There remains something more serious about the blood of a human being. Whereas people may shed an animal's blood and drain it in preparing to eat the animal's flesh, neither human beings nor animals may shed human blood at all. The seriousness of the matter is expressed by the rhythmic nature of the declarations, with their repetitions and parallelism. In the first bicolon, both cola end with the same verb. In v. 5 three cola begin "from the hand of." Then its final colon includes a third occurrence of the verb, so that the verse as a whole incorporates three occurrences of the verb and three of the prepositional phrase. In turn, v. 6 is a perfect abcc′b′a′ bicolon.

"Require" (*dāraš*) (v. 5) is a serious and threatening word. More generally the verb means "go to see" or "search for," with "the element of movement as a presupposition for the process."[28] The verb's everyday usage includes the idea of investigation into wrongdoing (Ezra 10:16), but where God becomes the subject, it acquires more menacing connotations. The correlative verb to such "seeking" is "finding." God is not merely investigating; he knows what has happened (cf. 42:22?). He is taking action on the basis of what he knows (cf. Ps. 10). Thus one of the verb's nuances (as here) is "taking redress." The objects of this action are not merely human beings but also animals, since the pact will apply to animals as well as human beings (v. 10); rules in the Torah such as Exod. 21:28–32 presuppose this principle. Perhaps the implication is that the unevenness or disorder caused by the taking of a life is leveled or

27. Cf. Wenham, *Genesis 1–15*, 192.

28. S. Wagner, *TDOT* 3:294, s.v. *dāraš*.

rectified by the taking of another life. With the taking of life by a human being, there is the further consideration that, as human beings, killer and victim were brothers; the declaration also carries an irony after Gen. 4. Perhaps its point includes a warning not to take Yahweh's sparing of Cain as a precedent.

"Pour" (*šāpak*) (v. 6) underlines the violence of the action that brings death; pouring is what someone does to water—or anger (Pss. 22:14 [22:15]; 79:6). Once again God speaks categorically, not in the negative second-person form that characterizes the Decalogue, but in the positive third-person form of 4:15. In a further contrast with the Decalogue, where murder is but one of the wrongs that Yahweh proscribes, "here in Gen. 9 murder is something utterly on its own; nothing can be compared with it."[29] "Through" a human being (*bə*) is an unusual expression. It might imply that a human being is the agent of the redress of which v. 5 spoke, and the logic of v. 6b would then be that the executioner's being made in God's image means sharing in responsibility for getting and keeping the world under control (1:26–28),[30] sharing in God's openness to exercising violence.[31] This expectation would further nuance the reference to brothers in the previous verse; it is the family's task to see that the leveling happens. But the use of the preposition parallels its appearance in the expression "a life *for* a life" (Deut. 19:21; cf. 2 Sam. 3:27; 14:7),[32] and more likely the line rather declares that one death will lead to another, without clarifying the question of who is responsible for ensuring the leveling that v. 5 points to. It may thus be simply a warning or prediction of how violence will beget violence.[33] Beginning with 17:14, many pronouncements and rules in the Torah and elsewhere declare that a person will be "cut off," and these declarations are warnings that God will take the required action. Here the reminder that the victim of murder is someone made in God's image suggests that it is God who will be taking action in response to the attack on himself.

At last (v. 7), God turns back from all the solemn talk about killing and returns to the commission or promise with which vv. 1–7 began, closing the bracket opened in v. 1. First he repeats the identical two words with which he began in v. 1, then as a variant on "fill the earth" he adds "teem on the earth"—which was earlier used just of sea creatures (1:20) and then of the nonhuman creation as a whole (7:21; 8:17). And as a final underscoring, he repeats "be numerous."

9:8–11. "Chances were that the good man was still beside himself and his mind still prey to fear; and it was likely that if some light shower should happen to fall, he would be bound to become distraught and quite upset at

29. Westermann, *Genesis 1–11*, 468.
30. Cf. Ephrem, *Genesis*, 145.
31. Cf. S. Wilson, "Blood Vengeance."
32. Cf. Sarna, *Genesis*, 357.
33. Cf. Coats, *Genesis*, 78.

the thought of such a deluge overwhelming the world once again."[34] Perhaps God might indeed need to allow that Noah and his sons could wonder how secure is the fulfillment of the promises implied by the commissions in v. 1; they didn't work out very well the first time.[35] God has said that he will not devastate the world again (8:21–22). How conditional is that promise?

God undergirds it with a "pact" (*bərît*) (v. 9), the pact to which he has referred in 6:18. He introduces it with the special phrase "And I: here, I am going to . . . ," leading into a participle, which he has used leading into a more sinister participle in 6:17 (and cf. 6:13; 7:4); as there, the participle refers to something God is about to do. Further, this "and I" corresponds to the "and you" in v. 7 and implies a relationship between the commission in vv. 1–7 and the promises that now follow. English translations conventionally speak of a "covenant," but that English word has a significance of its own. The Hebrew word is both broader and narrower. It covers the ground suggested by the English words "treaty," "contract," and "pact," as well as "covenant." But it need not suggest mutuality in the way that "covenant" does,[36] and thus it also overlaps with the English word "pledge." Here God is indeed making a pact *with* Noah and his sons and *with* their offspring, but it is a one-sided pact, a pledge or self-obligation or solemn promise. As much is implied by his declaration that *he* will implement it; a mutual pact would require a shared act of implementation. The one-sided nature of the pact will be more explicit in vv. 12–17, where also the essential nature of a pact as opposed to a bare promise will be reflected in the provision of a supportive sign relating to it. The beneficiaries of the pact are not only Noah and his sons but also their offspring (*zeraʿ*). It is the first occurrence (with this connotation) of another word that will be of ongoing importance in Genesis (e.g., 12:7; 13:15–16; 15:18; 17:7–10). God's commitment looks way beyond the present generation, points to his long-term involvement with people, and signals the way he will work through families. Again it is whimsical that God mentions only the men, not the women who will need to have a role in this connection. The collocation of pact and offspring will recur in Gen. 17, though one should not assimilate the two pacts. "Something happens between God and Abraham in Gen. 17. Abraham responds in word and action. But nothing happens between God and Noah" as this pact is being made. "There is an address by God to Noah, and no reaction at all on Noah's part."[37]

The one-sided nature of the pact is further reflected (v. 10) in the fact that humanity is not its only beneficiary. God is also making it *with* the rest of the animate world, which is "with" Noah and his sons. At creation, humanity was brought into being for the sake of the animate world, to keep it under

34. Chrysostom, *Homilies on Genesis 18–45*, 185.
35. Cf. Rashi, *Brʾšyt,* 93.
36. See Eynde, "Missing Link."
37. Westermann, *Genesis 1–11*, 471.

control. During the deluge, God's mindfulness applied not only to Noah but to every living thing.[38] As creation is rebooted, the animate world gains its security from God's commitment to humanity. God reverts to the familiar talk of every living being—spelled out as bird, animal, and every living thing—and then as all that came out of the chest, every living thing on the earth. God is firmly and inescapably tying his hands. There is no wiggle room here.

To make the commitment even more inescapable (v. 11), God repeats the promise about the pact. Specifically, there will be no more pouring out of the upper ocean to cut off all flesh or devastate the earth. God again seals off his escape routes as he takes up expressions from 6:9–8:22: "all flesh" (seven times), "water of the upper ocean" (twice, and three other occurrences of "upper ocean"), "devastate" (twice with this meaning, and three other occurrences). The link between human devastation and divine devastation is broken.[39]

9:12–17. Talk in terms of a pact as opposed to a mere promise makes one expect the provision of a sign; it is this provision that constitutes the difference. But before specifying the sign, God ties his hands yet further. The pact applies not only to the present generation and to its offspring and to every living creature, as vv. 9–10 said, but also to "agelong generations," to "the generations of *ʿôlām*." A word such as "eternal" might be misleading, but the term is the furthest-reaching expression that Hebrew has. Whereas the situation in the world that God created remains affected by the waywardness of humanity, this word of God to humanity after the deluge makes for something better than God said at creation or in his words that renewed the creation commission in vv. 1–11.[40] Further and in a more literalistic fashion, God speaks of putting the sign "between me and between you and between every living creature," repeating the word "between" before "you" and before "every" in accordance with the way Hebrew works. Like the repeated "with," the repeated "between" underlines the paradoxically reciprocal nature of this one-sided pact.[41] At the same time, the unusual expression "setting" the pact, which prepares the way for the coming reference to "setting" the bow in the mist, involves the use of the verb *nātan*, whose regular meaning is "give." It thus hints at and underscores the gracious nature of the pact.

A sign (v. 13) need not have an intrinsic relationship to what it connotes; examples are Hezekiah's sign (2 Kings 20:8–11) and the convention that green signifies "go" and red "stop," or that a dot on a line of type signifies the end of a sentence. But the Scriptures' signs that relate to pacts (and some other signs) commonly have an intrinsic relationship to what they signify, as is the case with circumcision (see Gen. 17)[42] and with baptism (which connotes

38. Cf. Chalmers, "Importance of the Noahic Covenant," 213.
39. Cf. Olley, "Mixed Blessings for Animals," 138.
40. Zimmerli, *1. Mose 1–11*, 351.
41. Westermann, *Genesis 1–11*, 473.
42. See the comment.

both death and cleansing). So it is with this sign. The word "bow" occurs over seventy times in the First Testament, and everywhere but here and in Ezek. 1:28 it denotes the bow as a literal weapon of war. As a sign, it has the same significance. Once more, Genesis reworks a motif from other Middle Eastern stories. In When on High 6.82–91, for instance, Marduk takes the bow with which he has defeated Tiamat and sets it up in the sky as a constellation of stars.[43] Here God gives a more immediately encouraging significance to the weapon. He is laying aside the weapon with which he might attack the earth.[44] God's covenant extends not only beyond Noah to the animate world but also beyond animate creatures to the earth itself—the earth that had become devastated and was then due for devastation (6:12–13). Genesis might or might not assume that the rainbow itself was already familiar;[45] on the former assumption, the pronouncement about the rainbow takes a known reality and gives it a new meaning, as the later rule about circumcision will take a known practice and give it a new meaning. But Genesis would be more interested in making that contrast with When on High than in the history of meteorology.

From now on (vv. 14–15), when Yahweh makes mist or cloud cover the earth and when a rainbow also appears, it will have a message for him and for humanity. The word for mist or cloud (*ʿānān*) is not a regular word for a raincloud but one that usually denotes the mist or cloud that both draws attention to and shields people from the awe-inspiring presence of God (e.g., Exod. 13:21–22; 24:15–16). Counterintuitively, the appearance of the (rain) bow will act not as an encouragement to God to make war against the world, maybe by shooting fiery lightning arrows as God can (Ps. 78:48), but as a discouragement to him because it will remind him of his pact. He is like the king of a superpower who has made a pact with an underling within his empire and has foregone the freedom to use his firepower against this underling. Such a pact presupposes a mutual commitment, and such a king is not bound by the pact if the underling rebels. But God's pact is one-sided; he has surrendered that freedom even while facing the fact that the underling will rebel. When he sees the bow, it will make him "mindful" of that pact, as he has been "mindful" of Noah (8:1).[46] "The gospel of this God is that he remembers." And "his remembering . . . asserts that God is not preoccupied with himself but with his covenant partner, creation."[47]

In case they are still not convinced (vv. 16–17), God says it again, and then again. He speaks in a way that offers the most encouraging security to humanity. "The Holy Spirit is prolix, but not without purpose."[48]

43. Cf. Sarna, *Genesis*, 63; for the text, see Hays, *Hidden Riches*, 56.
44. Van Wolde, "One Bow or Another?"; see also Kissling, "Rainbow in Genesis 9:12–17."
45. The latter is Luther's view (*Genesis 6–14*, 149); Calvin (*Genesis* 2:299) calls it "frivolous."
46. See the comment.
47. Brueggemann, *Genesis*, 85.
48. Luther, *Genesis 6–14*, 143.

God's promise that he will not devastate the world again (except in connection with the creation of new heavens and a new earth)[49] might or might not indicate that God will stop humanity from doing so. But anyway, the interim security of the world is not a guarantee of its ultimate security. Further, Isa. 24 may be plausibly taken to imply that God reserves the right to devastate the world again for disregarding the "agelong pact." The mistakenness of people who scoff at this idea will thus be exposed (2 Pet. 3:6–7). In this sense "the days of 'the man'" will resemble "the days of Noah" (Luke 17:26–27). As the spiritual puts it,

> God gave Noah the rainbow sign,
> No more water but fire next time,
> Better get a home in that rock.[50]

God's spelling out his promises here follows on his spelling out his commission in vv. 1–7, with the implication that there is a link between them.[51] The categories of conditional and unconditional do not help an understanding of the dynamic and personal nature of the covenantal relationship between God and people, any more than they help in understanding covenantal relationships such as marriage. But equally, entering into such relationships does not carry with it the assumption that one can do as one pleases, as Paul notes in Rom. 6. Relationships are two-sided.

9:18–19. The note about Noah's sons closes off the deluge story, introduces the last Noah story that will immediately follow by referring to Canaan, and previews the account of the dispersion of humanity that will come later (see 10:18; 11:1–9). It is important to the security of the world as a whole that this dispersion issues from Noah's sons, to whose offspring God made the promises associated with the pact.

9:20–23. Like the story of the original creation, the story of the rebooting of creation begins with a human being tending the ground. Noah is fulfilling the original creation purpose.[52] But the story then adds a new note. Maybe the idea of cultivating a vineyard is new, in which case Noah repeats the dynamic of Gen. 4 with its account of the development of technology. Yet the audience might assume that both the garden and the ground outside the garden grew grapes along with olives (cf. 8:11), figs (3:7), and other produce with which everyone was familiar; that there were vineyards before the deluge; and maybe that there was wine. In that case, Noah is simply the first person after the deluge to farm and to cultivate vines. The subsequent reference

49. Indeed, Kreider ("Flood Is as Bad as It Gets") questions whether he will do so then.
50. Cf. Towner, "Genesis 9:8–17," 168.
51. Cf. Mason, "Another Flood?," though he does talk in terms of conditional and unconditional.
52. Cf. Brueggemann, *Genesis*, 89.

to Noah in his tent suggests a Bedouin lifestyle, which can combine with a little agriculture and viticulture. Either way, the vineyard would be an image with much resonance for the audience,[53] which itself was Yahweh's vineyard (e.g., Isa. 5:1–7; Jer. 12:10). Vineyards, like olive orchards, were an important aspect of Israel's economy. Wine was an important element in its worship (e.g., Lev. 23:13; 1 Chron. 9:29) and an important joy of everyday life (Ps. 104:15; Eccles. 9:7).

But maybe (v. 21) no one has discovered what happens when grapes are left to ferment,[54] and the First Testament does pay much attention to the trouble that drinking wine can cause. Whether or not Noah's viticulture is a new achievement, creation is plagued by another disaster, a kind of fall, as happened in Gen. 1–4. Once more the trouble issues from within creation, though the story does not explicitly attribute any responsibility to the element within creation through which the trouble comes, nor to the human being to whom and through whom it comes. Maybe it's just one of those things. The overlap of motifs with Gen. 1–4 continues in the account of Noah's exposing himself, which would not have been a problem back at the beginning (2:25). Maybe it wouldn't be a problem now if Ms. Noah had been around.[55]

Indeed, maybe it wouldn't be a problem now if not for Ham's action (v. 22). After all, Noah was in his tent; he wasn't exposing himself in public. An Ugaritic story relates how a dutiful son "takes [his father] by the hand when he's drunk, carries him when he's sated with wine";[56] Ham is not a dutiful son. Genesis reminds us that Ham is Canaan's father and that this story links with events in the listeners' day. It is not just something quirky and shameful that happened back then in the story of humanity's ancestors. While the word for "naked body" (*'erwâ*) comes from a verb meaning "be bare" in quite a neutral sense, and the noun has a morally neutral sense in its other occurrence in Genesis (42:9, 12), in the vast majority of occurrences in the First Testament it refers to someone's genitals ("private parts" is a near English equivalent), and it appears elsewhere in combination with the verbs "expose" (cf. v. 21) or "see" (cf. esp. Lev. 18; 20; Ezek. 16). And references to such seeing or exposing are linked with a view of the Canaanites (Lev. 18:3) and of the customs of the people God intends to drive out of the land so that Israel may possess it (Lev. 20:22–24), and with the slur that Jerusalem's origin and birth were from the country of the Canaanites (Ezek. 16:1–3). Further, in such passages "exposing the naked body" of someone or "seeing" it is a kind of metonymy or synecdoche and euphemism for having sex with them. The implication would thus be that Ham sexually assaulted his father—or

53. Cf. Fretheim, "Genesis," 403.

54. So, e.g., Qimchi, *Genesis*, on v. 20.

55. Cf. Musculus, *In Mosis Genesim plenissimi commentarii*, 249; cf. J. Thompson, *Genesis 1–11*, 306.

56. From Aqhat A, *ANET* 150.

his mother.[57] And in passages such as Lev. 18 and 20, "the prohibitions of sexual violation and indignity embody a rejection of Canaanite ways of life and values."[58]

The response of the other two brothers (v. 23) raises questions about that implication, in that the description of their action seems designed to suggest that seeing their father's naked body simply means seeing their father's naked body, which many cultures would regard as imperiling proper regard between children and parents and proper family order. So the story is ambiguous over the nature of Ham's act. Indeed, the slow and careful way in which Genesis describes the brothers' slow and careful action seems designed to draw attention away from Ham's act. It draws a veil of ambiguity over it (appositely) and rather draws attention to the brothers' act of propriety.[59] But either way, something has happened that involves a compromising of the relationship between father and son and parallels the fracturing of the relationship between brothers in Gen. 4. And it is something that anticipates or embodies the compromising of proper sexual relationships within the family, which the audience would associate with Canaan. Perhaps, then, the ambiguity over what Ham has done functions to associate the mere looking (which Ham has done) with the improper actions (which Lev. 18 and 20 prohibit).[60]

9:24–27. The account of the outrage and the act of piety leads into the account of the curse (v. 24–25) and the blessing (vv. 26–27).[61]

We come to Noah's first words in the Scriptures (v. 24): "He built a ship, gathered a crew, weathered a storm, offered a sacrifice, and lived righteously, but the text never mentions any words that he spoke. A more taciturn man would be difficult to find. Now he finally speaks, though some will doubt whether this is the most auspicious way to enter the world conversationally."[62] It is a converse of the possible implication that Noah's silence (which contrasts with the volubility of the heroes in the other flood narratives) makes the point that it is God's activity that counts, not that of human beings. All Noah has to do is act as God says.[63] If it is Ham who is described as Noah's youngest son, the usual order—Shem, Ham, and Japhet—is not in order of age. But more likely "youngest son" somehow refers to Canaan. The account of Noah's reaction once more reworks the balance over understanding what specifically either Ham or Canaan have done to Noah. Does he know what has happened because he hears people talking about his exposing himself?[64]

57. See, e.g., Bergsma and Hahn, "Noah's Nakedness."
58. Brueggemann, *Genesis*, 91.
59. Cf. Wenham, *Genesis 1–15*, 200.
60. See further Embry, "'Naked Narrative.'"
61. Westermann, *Genesis 1–11*, 483.
62. Hamilton, *Genesis 1–17*, 324.
63. So Pfost, "Literary Analysis," 12.
64. Targum Ps.-J. explains that he discovered the event through a dream.

Noah's response (v. 25a) suggests something worse than seeing, but again his reaction may simply mean that Noah is pictured as cursing the practices Leviticus proscribes. Blessing and cursing involve a declaration that something good or bad should and will happen to someone, a declaration made by someone whose words have power to bring about what they announce by a dynamic that cannot further be analyzed but simply reflects the power that resides in that person. While God especially has such power (cf. 1:22, 28; 3:14, 17; 4:11), some human beings can also have it (e.g., 49:7; Josh. 6:26; 9:23). So a blessing or a curse is more powerful than a prayer, though there is likely an assumption that neither a blessing nor a curse can "work" unless God complies with it (cf. the sequence in Ruth 1:19–20, and other occurrences of the expression "blessed to/for/regarding/by [*le*] Yahweh" as in Gen. 14:19; 24:31; Judg. 17:2). It is Ham's son rather than Ham himself whom Noah curses. Yahweh himself will often declare that he attends to the waywardness of parents in connection with their children (e.g., Exod. 20:5), and Noah presupposes that reality about the way things work out in human lives. On this occasion, the action of Noah's son will be matched by the fate of Ham's son. Cursing a person's son is a most powerful way of cursing the person. It means cursing the future of his line. And Jub. 7.13 has Ham as displeased as modern readers at the treatment of Canaan. But for people listening to the story, the object of the curse is the ancestor of the people of Canaan whom they know, who are the epitome of abhorrent sexual practices. "For the Hebrews, Canaan is the most natural historical embodiment of Ham."[65]

Further (v. 25b), one of the few objects of a human curse in the First Testament is the people of Gibeon, who are Hivvites and are thus "sons" of Canaan (10:17; Josh. 9); they are a subset of Canaanites. They deceive Joshua into exempting them from the slaughter of other Canaanites, but Joshua feels free to turn them into permanent servants, with responsibility for the arduous tasks of getting wood and water for the community and specifically for the sanctuary. For the audience of Genesis, the story in Joshua and this story explain why the Gibeonites have that position. While Genesis leaves people to work out whether Noah's curse is an appropriate response to his son's act, that broader context suggests no questioning of it. It is not unusual in many cultures to assume that there should be ranking among brothers for the sake of order in the family when the father is gone and to assume that the oldest brother in a family should have authority in the family—hence the incongruity of the idea that the older should serve the younger (25:23; cf. 27:29, 40). While the point here might thus be that Canaan will be put into a particularly lowly servitude, in the context of Gen. 1–11 Noah's curse more likely links with the awareness that human wrongdoing not only disrupts harmony between humanity and the animate world, between men and women (Gen. 3), and

65. Dillmann, *Genesis*, 1:307.

between brothers (Gen. 4); it also disrupts relationship between fathers and sons and brings an end to the ideal egalitarian relationship between brothers, and it does so in a way that brings abject or permanent servitude. "Sinne maketh the brother borne of the same parent a servant."[66] It's surprising that Genesis doesn't note a link between the name *Kənaʿan* and the verb *kānaʿ*, which means "bow down." Noah's own point is a broader or more concrete one. Canaan is to be a servant to Ham's brothers, who are the ancestors of two much wider groups than merely the Israelites (see 10:1–31). But there is no historical context with which we can connect this idea. And there is no basis for linking Canaan's being a servant to the enslavement of black people in the Americas.[67] The theory of race is "constructed on" rather than "constructed from" Genesis.[68]

The descendants of Shem (v. 26) are listed in 10:21–31. Yahweh is understood to be the God of all of them (cf. 4:26). The prayer that Yahweh be blessed implies an ellipsis; it presupposes that Yahweh will bless Shem and that Yahweh will therefore be blessed in the sense of praised.[69] Noah recognizes the work of God's grace in his son as the source of his decency and offers praise to God rather than congratulating his son or himself.[70] The prayer thus also adds to the unpredictable nature of Noah's words (is he still under the influence?); as well as cursing not Ham but Ham's son, he blesses not Shem but his God.[71] There is nothing straightforward about this story. But this unexpected blessing does mean that near its end the miserable story includes praise of Yahweh, like Gen. 4. The experience of humanity in the everyday world is one in which people of integrity, who have been the recipients of God's grace, can make mistakes for which it is hard to see whether they should be held responsible. They can be betrayed by their children or grandchildren, who then in turn pay a terrible price for their waywardness. Family and specifically sexual relationships can be the context in which this waywardness is expressed. The challenge to further people of integrity is to seek to restore seemliness, and as they do so they may find God dwelling in their midst and opening them up in a way that generates the praise of God.

The prayer that God should open up Japhet (v. 27) might refer to giving land to his descendants, who will be listed in 10:2–5, but the context may rather suggest opening him up so that he responds to Yahweh.[72] Either way,

66. Willet, *Hexapla in Genesin & Exodum*, 91, following Chrysostom.

67. See, e.g., Aaron, "Early Rabbinic Exegesis"; Robertson, "Current Critical Questions"; and esp. Haynes, *Noah's Curse*; and more broadly Knust, "Who's Afraid of Canaan's Curse?"

68. Mbuvi, *Belonging in Genesis*, 71.

69. Cf. Gunkel, *Genesis*, 81.

70. Musculus, *In Mosis Genesim plenissimi commentarii*, 255; cf. J. Thompson, *Genesis 1–11*, 316.

71. Hamilton, *Genesis 1–17*, 325.

72. Cf. Luther, *Genesis 6–14*, 182–84.

the prayer offers a contrast when it speaks of God dwelling in Shem's tents and reaffirms the idea that Canaan will be a servant to the two brothers. Genesis 10:6–20 will suggest that there is no such curse on Canaan for quite a while: "Ham's offspring took possession of the most beautiful places and luxuries in the whole world."[73] Perhaps we are to infer that the waywardness of the Amorites was not yet full (15:16). Looking back from the circumstances of the audience of Genesis, people can see that Noah's curse did eventually work. But looking forward from the circumstances in which it is uttered, the future is open.

9:28–29. At last we come to the end of the formulaic description of Noah's life in accordance with the pattern of Gen. 5, the description that began in 5:32 and has been interrupted by 6:1–9:27. We thus come to the end of a unit both in the MT and according to the medieval division. "Then he died." No immortality for him, like that of Utnapishtim.

Implications

Blood

Humanity does not live in the age of Adam and Eve or in Lush Garden, but we do live in the age of the renewed creation commission. And if the animate world feels awe and dread toward humanity, "it is surely obvious that the possession of such power confers upon man a very definite responsibility towards non-human life."[74] Thus "this blessing which gives this authority over the beasts to man must not be taken lightly." And that gift and the revelation of how to cultivate wine "are reliable and excellent proofs that God no longer hates man but is kindly disposed toward him." God has been able to turn from his "strange work" of acting in wrath to his more natural compassion.[75]

Perhaps God's allowing for animate creatures to eat one another is a concession to creation's self-centeredness, in keeping with the principle Jesus enunciates in Matt. 19:3–9. It would then not be surprising if many people who want to embody God's delivering them from self-centeredness give up eating other creatures, in keeping with the possibility Jesus points to in Matt. 19:10–12. To put Jesus's approach in different terms, here as elsewhere in Genesis "overt ideologies of human dominance, male dominance or primogeniture are allowed to stand, but alternative perspectives are juxtaposed in such a way as to undermine the dominant ideology."[76]

If all the rules in the Torah express love for God or love for neighbor (Matt. 22:40), then refraining from eating blood most obviously belongs in the first

73. Selnecker, *In Genesin*, 355; cf. J. Thompson, *Genesis 1–11*, 324.

74. Barth, *CD* 3.4:251.

75. Luther, *Genesis 6–14*, 133, 134.

76. Brett, *Genesis*, 44 (the clauses are italicized in the original).

category. It is a way of showing respect for God, to whom life belongs. But in addition, "the killing of animals carries within it the danger of blood-lust (Num. 23:24; Deut. 32:42; Jer. 46:10), of killing for the sake of killing, of blood-thirstiness." Killing animals can easily be brutal and barbaric. This consideration links with what follows. "One's conduct toward other people is not to be separated from one's conduct toward animals."[77] Or perhaps, if the life of animals becomes cheap, so does all life.[78] The ban on eating the blood of an animal was unique to Israel; it was one of those observances that marked Israel out.[79] It was then carried over into Christian faith (Acts 15:29) and into Islam.

God's requiring the blood of an animate being that sheds human blood overlaps with but does not exactly correspond to regulations for capital punishment. First, it applies to all animate beings, not just human beings. But second, it does see the killing of one human person by another as particularly reprobate, because human beings are, after all, members of the same family. It does not clearly indicate that members of the family have responsibility for the redress.[80] It does make clear the more fundamental point that God ensures this redress one way or another. The Torah's provision for due inquiry and for asylum towns presupposes that the family has responsibility for taking God's redress but seeks to make sure that no one is executed when they are innocent of murderous intent, and much of the proper concern about execution in the United States has this background. But further, even if God does here require human beings to take action to ensure redress for murder, "one cannot simply transfer v. 6 to the statute book unless one is prepared to include vv. 4 and 5a with it."[81]

The prohibition on eating an animal's blood and on killing another human being are two of the "Noachian commands"; other Noachian commands ban idolatry/denial of God, blasphemy, incest/adultery, and robbery, and require the setting up of courts of law.[82] The term "Noachian commands" does not imply the belief that they came from the revelation to Noah but that Gentiles who keep these commands that are binding on all humanity are true sons and daughters of Noah and are acceptable to God. The decisions of the Jerusalem Council (Acts 15:29) reflect the way of thinking expressed in the Noachian commands.

77. Westermann, *Genesis 1–11*, 465.
78. Cf. Willet, *Hexapla in Genesin & Exodum*, 87, following Chrysostom.
79. Cf. Marin i Tourné, "'Demanaré comptes de la vostra sang,'" 41–49.
80. For discussion, see, e.g., Verster, "Respek vir die lewe en die doodstraf."
81. Kidner, *Genesis*, 101.
82. See, e.g., b. Sanh. 56a.

8
The Nations and the Narrowing

(10:1–11:26)

Overview

Genesis 10:1–11:26 finally turns to the question of how its narrative about God's relationship with the created world and with humanity as a whole relates to the focus on Terah's family that will now follow. Typically, it answers that question by means of an interweaving of lines of descent and stories. The first line of descent and the first story (10:1–32) relates the way the descendants of Noah spread through the world, but the order in which it records these descendants puts Noah's sons in reverse order (Japhet, then Ham, then Shem), because it is from Shem that Terah's line will be born. The second story (11:1–9) confirms Yahweh's involvement in ensuring that people spread over the world rather than sticking in one place, but the second line of descent (11:10–26) confirms the focus on Shem's line. So God is interested in the whole world, but the line that leads to Terah is especially significant.

To put it another way, the question underlying 10:1–11:26 is this: "How does the story of Noah become the story of humanity, and the story of humanity become the story of Abraham's family?" And the answer is that it happens

- by a natural process in which Noah's descendants grow to fill the world as we know it,
- by the achievements of a hero like Nimrod at the heart of the civilized world,
- by God's compelling the world's peoples to spread over the world, and
- by a natural process in which Shem's descendants propagate until Abraham's family comes into being.

The section leaves unresolved the relationship between these two themes, God's involvement with the whole world and God's particular involvement with some of Shem's descendants. The unresolved question means the audience must listen to what will follow in the section that begins with 11:27.

Translation

10:1 So these are the lines of descent of Noah's sons, Šem, Ḥam, and Yepet. Sons were born to them after the upper ocean event.

2The sons of Yepet: Gomer, Magog, Maday, Yavan, Tubal, Mešek, and Tiras.
3The sons of Gomer: Aškenaz, Ripat, and Togarmah.
4The sons of Yavan: Elišah, Taršiš, Kittites, and Dodanites.[1]

5From these, the nations on far shores[2] parted into their countries, each with its language, by their kin groups, in their nations.

6The sons of Ḥam: Kuš, Miṣrayim, Puṭ, and Kenaʿan.
7The sons of Kuš: Seba, Ḥavilah, Sabtah, Raʿmah, and Sabteka.
The sons of Raʿmah: Šeba and Dedan.

8Kuš fathered[3] Nimrod, who was the first to become[4] a strongman on the earth. **9**He became a strongman as a hunter[5] before Yahweh; that's why it's said,

Like Nimrod, a strongman as a hunter
before Yahweh.

10The beginning[6] of his realm was Babel, Erek, Akkad, and Kalneh, in the country of Šinʿar. **11**From that country he went out to Aššur[7] and built Nineveh and the town

1. For *dōdānîm*, the LXX implies *rōdānîm* (cf. 1 Chron. 1:7). Reference to Rhodes would fit the context, and in Hebrew the letters for *r* and *d* look similar.

2. The LXX, Vg have "island nations," but "islands" is too narrow for *ʾiyyîm*, which denotes places one reaches by sea.

3. In vv. 8–26 the subject precedes the verb *yālad*, which fits the fact that the subject provides the new information in a genealogy and in this sense has emphasis (see the footnote to 22:1).

4. The verb *ḥālal* recurs from 9:20, here followed by an infinitive, the more regular construction.

5. Literally, "a strongman of hunting."

6. In isolation *rēʾšît* might refer to the "core" of his kingdom, but vv. 11–12 describe its expansion, so "beginning" is more likely.

7. The Hebrew has no preposition "to," so one could translate "Aššur went out" (cf. Tg. Onq., Tg. Neof.), but the introduction of Aššur is then abrupt, and he will be introduced in v. 22 as a descendant of Šem. The preposition is omitted after *yāṣāʾ* in 27:3 and after other verbs of "going" in 24:27; 26:23 (see GKC 118f; and cf. Tg. Ps.-J.). Micah 5:6 [5:5] suggests the assumption that Nimrod went to Aššur.

squares,[8] Kalah, **12**and Resen between Nineveh and
Kalah: that's the big town.

13Miṣrayim fathered Ludites, Anamites, Lehabites, Naptuḥites,
14Patrusites, Kasluḥites (from whom the Pelištites went out),
and Kaptorites.
15Kenaʿan fathered Ṣidon his firstborn, Ḥet, **16**the Yebusites, the
Amorites, the Girgašites, **17**the Hivvites, the Arqites, the Sin-
ites, **18**the Arvadites, the Ṣemarites, and the Ḥamatites.
Later, the Kenaʿanite kin groups dispersed **19**and the
Kenaʿanite border reached from Ṣidon until you come
to Gerar, near Azzah, until you come to Sedom, Amorah,
Admah, and Ṣeboyim, near Laša.

20These are the descendants of Ḥam by their kin groups, by their lan-
guages, in their countries, in their nations.

21There[9] were also born to Šem, the ancestor of all the descen-
dants of Eber, the brother of Yepet (the oldest)[10]—**22**the de-
scendants of Šem: Elam, Aššur, Arpakšad, Lud, and Aram.
23The descendants of Aram: Uṣ, Ḥul, Geter, and Maš.
24Arpakšad fathered Šelaḥ, Šelaḥ fathered Eber.
25Two sons were born to Eber: the name of the first was
Peleg, because in his time the earth divided, and the
name of the second was Yoqṭan.
26Yoqṭan fathered Almodad, Šelep, Ḥaṣarmavet, Yeraḥ,
27Hadoram, Uzal, Diqlah, **28**Obal, Abimaʾel, Šeba, **29**Opir,
Havilah, and Yobab. All these were descendants of
Yoqṭan. **30**The places where they lived went from Meša
until you come to Separ, the eastern highland.
31These are the descendants of Šem by their kin groups, by
their languages, in their countries, by their nations.

32These are the kin groups of Noah's sons by their lines of descent
according to their nations. From these the nations parted in the earth
after the upper ocean outburst.

11:1 Now the entire earth was of one language and common[11] words.
2As people moved on in[12] the east, they found a valley in the region of

8. Cf. the Vg for this understanding of *rəḥōbōt ʿîr*, with Hamilton's comments (*Genesis 1–17*, 340); the LXX takes it as the name of an otherwise unknown city.

9. There is no word for "sons"; the construction breaks down.

10. The LXX assumes that "the oldest" describes Yepet, but the order of the brothers when they are listed is always Šem, Ḥam, Yepet (9:24 raises special problems: see the comment). More likely, "the eldest" describes Šem. Perhaps the LXX was misled by the order of the genealogies in this chapter, but on any theory these genealogies do not come in order of age.

11. Literally, "one."

12. The LXX, Vg have "from," the natural understanding of *min*, but this meaning does not always apply in such expressions (cf. 2:8; 3:24; 12:8; 13:11), and it makes poor sense here. Targum Onq. has *b* in place of *min*.

Šinʿar and lived there. **3**They said, one to his neighbor, "Come on, let's
make bricks and bake them thoroughly"; so they had brick in place of
stone, and tar in place of cement. **4**They said, "Come on, let's build
ourselves a town and a tower with its top in the heavens, and make a
name for ourselves, so we don't disperse over the face of the entire
earth."

5Yahweh went down to see the town and the tower that the human be-
ings had made. **6**Yahweh said, "Here, one people with one language for
all of them, and this is the first thing they do. So now, nothing that they
may scheme to do is closed off from them. **7**Come on, let's go down and
make a babble[13] of their language there, so one person won't be able to
hear his neighbor's language."

8So Yahweh dispersed them from there over the face of the en-
tire earth, and they left off from building the town. **9**That's why people
named[14] it Babel, because there Yahweh made a babble of the language
of the entire earth, and from there Yahweh dispersed them over the face
of the entire earth.

10These are Šem's lines of descent.

> Šem was a man of 100 years and fathered Arpakšad, two
> years after the upper ocean outburst.[15] **11**After fathering
> Arpakšad, Šem lived 500 years and fathered sons and
> daughters.
>
> **12**When Arpakšad had lived 35 years, he fathered Šelaḥ.
> **13**After fathering Šelaḥ, Arpakšad lived 403 years and fa-
> thered sons and daughters.[16]
>
> **14**When Šelaḥ had lived 30 years, he fathered Eber. **15**After
> fathering Eber, Šelaḥ lived 403 years and fathered sons
> and daughters.
>
> **16**Eber lived 34 years and fathered Peleg. **17**After father-
> ing Peleg, Eber lived 430 years and fathered sons and
> daughters.
>
> **18**Peleg lived 30 years and fathered Reʿu. **19**After father-
> ing Reʿu, Peleg lived 209 years and fathered sons and
> daughters.
>
> **20**Reʿu lived 32 years and fathered Śerug. **21**After father-
> ing Śerug, Reʿu lived 207 years and fathered sons and
> daughters.

13. *Nābəlâ*, suggestively similar to the word for moral stupidity, *nābēlâ* (Wenham, *Genesis 1–15*, 235).

14. Literally, "one named" (GKC 144d).

15. Genesis 5:32 combined with 7:6 suggest that Šem would be 102 when Arpakšad was born; perhaps we should take the 500 and 100 in these texts as approximate.

16. In vv. 7–26, the numbers vary between the MT, SP, and LXX; the Vg corresponds to the MT except in v. 13. The MT's numbers mean that, e.g., Šem is still alive in the time of Jacob; perhaps the SP and LXX reflect recensions that had therefore modified the numbers (cf. the comment on the numbers in Gen. 5).

22Śerug lived 30 years and fathered Naḥor. 23After fathering Naḥor, Śerug lived 200 years and fathered sons and daughters.
24Naḥor lived 29 years and fathered Teraḥ. 25After fathering Teraḥ, Naḥor lived 119 years and fathered sons and daughters.
26Teraḥ lived 70 years and fathered Abram, Naḥor, and Haran.

Interpretation

In the MT 10:1–32 is one unit, 11:1–9 is another, and 11:10–12:9 is the next; paragraph breaks come after 10:14; 10:20; and 11:32, as well as after each of the entries in 11:10–26, while the synagogue lection that began at 6:9 ends at 11:32. But at 10:1 and at 11:27 there are headings referring to "lines of descent," and such headings indicate significant transitions in the story at 2:4a; 5:1; and 6:9. They will do so again at 25:12 and 19, marking the transition to the story of Ishmael and Isaac. Luther thus sees Genesis's "third book" as beginning at 11:27.[17] I treat 10:1–11:26 as one unit bridging the Noah story and the Abraham story by tracing lines of descent and telling stories, in a way analogous to 5:1–6:8. It gives four parallel accounts of this process.

Genesis 10:1–7, 13–32 is a genealogy explaining how the nations around Israel came to "part in the earth" (10:32).
- The introduction to the account of Noah's sons (10:1)
- Japhet's descendants (10:2–5)
  - Peoples descended from Japhet (10:2–4)
  - A concluding note about these nations spreading (10:5)
- Ham's descendants (10:6–20)
  - Peoples descended from Ham (10:6–7)
    - A story about Nimrod, one of Ham's descendants (10:8–12)
  - Peoples that Ham's sons fathered (10:13–18a)
    - A note about the spread of the Kenaʿanite kin groups (10:18b–19)
  - A conclusion to the list of the peoples descended from Ham (10:20)
- Shem's descendants (10:21–31)
  - Peoples descended from Shem (10:21–23)
  - Peoples that Shem's sons fathered (10:24–29)
    - A note about where Yoqṭan's descendants settled (10:30)

17. Luther, *Genesis 6–14*, 236. Calvin (*Genesis*, 1:338, 341) calls the division at 12:1 "absurd," though he locates the new beginning of a section at 11:31.

A conclusion to the list of the peoples descended from Shem (10:31)

The conclusion to the account of Noah's sons (10:32)

Genesis 10:8–12 is a story incorporated into that genealogy, explaining how Mesopotamia in particular came to grow:

The man Nimrod was (10:8–9)

The things he did (10:10–12)

Genesis 11:1–9 is a second story, explaining how the nations came to "be dispersed over the face of the entire earth" (11:9):

What people were (11:1)

What people did (11:2–4)

What Yahweh did (11:5–8)

What Yahweh thereby effected (11:9)

Genesis 11:10–26 is a second genealogy, providing the background to the way the focus of Genesis will now narrow down. It resumes Shem's genealogy, expanding on 10:21–31 but focusing on the line of Shem's third son. The transition from the first genealogy to a second parallels that between Gen. 4 and Gen. 5, and the form of this genealogy corresponds to the form of Gen. 5; both come from P.

10:1, 32. Verses 1 and 32 form an introduction and conclusion to Gen. 10. As happened in chapter 5, "time is restarted."[18] The first lines of descent are thus those of Noah's three sons, who themselves fathered peoples all over the world, portrayed from the perspective of Israelites surveying the world around them. Formally the list speaks of them having individual children, but the children are the names of peoples. Shem, Ham, and Japhet are the only individuals in the main list (Nimrod is the one other individual who appears in Gen. 10). Indeed, the list closes by speaking of the people in the list as descendants, nations, and kin groups. The account presupposes thinking that parallels the description of George Washington as father of the United States or of Gandhi as the father of India. The list "gives a first impression of system and lack of system wonderfully interwoven."[19] It combines materials from P and J. The background may sometimes suggest the Judahite monarchy, sometimes the neo-Babylonian period (notably, the parallels with Ezekiel). Genesis 5 and Gen. 11 are simple, "linear" genealogies; while Gen. 10 is a more complex, "segmented" genealogy as it deals with all three of Noah's sons and their descendants in such a way as to undergird an understanding of

18. Reno, *Genesis*, 130.

19. Westermann, *Genesis 1–11*, 498.

the interrelationships of the descendants—in this case the peoples descended from them.

The genealogy of Shem, Ham, and Japhet includes seventy-one names. By omitting from the count Nimrod or the Philistines (who appear in a periphrasis), the number can be reduced to seventy, a number that signals comprehensiveness (e.g., 46:27); later, at least, it suggests the number of nations in the world.[20] The genealogy offers a comprehensive picture of the world as it developed from Noah's day onward, a verbal "map" of the known world organized around Noah's three sons. It thus pictures how the world has a fundamental unity.[21] At the same time, its portrayal can be related to the ancient world's great spheres of imperial power.[22] The chapter combines a comprehensive framework with detailed vignettes, snapshots, and data of the kind that were available from stories people told and from knowledge that people had through Judah's trading relations.[23] It says nothing of God being directly involved in the growth that it relates; the development comes about by the natural power that God has bestowed upon or infused into humanity. Yet the chapter presupposes that this development thus issues from God's blessing, and it gives concrete expression to the history of that blessing. It is not a mere generalization but an account "tracing the lines from the sons of Noah across the whole map of the world" as known within its purview.[24]

Each of the three groups of Noah's descendants is characterized in terms of countries, languages, kin groups, and nations. A country is an entity that has a land, has a common language, is ethnically related, and has a political form. The chapter thus understands the nations' interrelationships geographically, linguistically, familially and thus ethnically (though not racially in the sense of skin color), and politically (Canaan belongs with Ham in this connection). In an understated way it also understands the world of nations salvation-historically (Shem comes last). "If we consider the dramatic excitement of history during the centuries when the table of nations was formed, we must be astonished at the political dispassionateness of this document," compared with the prophecies about the nations in Isaiah, Jeremiah, and Ezekiel from approximately the same period.[25] Although the lists presuppose an Israelite audience, Israel is not even mentioned.

10:2–5. Noah's sons come in reverse order, in accordance with the recurrent practice in Genesis of moving from the less relevant to the more relevant. Japhet's descendants cover a band of territory north of Israel, from Armenia

20. See the comment on 11:8–9; also Luke 10.
21. Brueggemann, *Genesis*, 91.
22. So Hieke, "Die Völkertafel," 32.
23. Cf. Westermann, *Genesis 1–11*, 502–3.
24. Cf. Westermann, *Genesis 1–11*, 529.
25. Von Rad, *Genesis*, 140.

through Turkey to Ionia.[26] Gomer (cf. Ezek. 38:6) may be the Cimmerians, a people associated with Assyria and eastern Turkey. Magog (cf. Ezek. 38:2; 39:6) is otherwise unknown, but the context of the other names suggests somewhere in Turkey. Maday is Media. Yavan (Ionia) is on the western coast of Turkey. Tubal and Meshek (e.g., Ezek. 38:2–3) are in eastern Turkey. Tiras may be the Tursha mentioned in an Egyptian text as an invading people from across the Mediterranean. As a group, then, one may plausibly locate all these peoples in Turkey and the area of Asia to its east. The same applies to the "sons" of Gomer: Ashkenaz (cf. Jer. 51:27) may be the Scythians; Ripat is otherwise unknown; Togarmah (cf. Ezek. 27:14; 38:6) may be Tegarama in eastern Turkey.

Elishah (Ezek. 27:7; Gen. 10:4) is a Mediterranean island, perhaps Cyprus or Crete. Josephus[27] identifies Tarshish as Tarsus, but Tarshish is a place name that recurs in the First Testament and generally suggests somewhere further away. It is traditionally identified with Tartessus in Spain;[28] the LXX transliterates here but at other passages (e.g., Isa. 23:1) thinks of Carthage. The Kittites (e.g., Ezek. 27:6) are the people of Kition, a town on Cyprus. Dodona is in northwestern Greece, but it is a significant location as the oldest Greek oracle sanctuary. Perhaps, then, v. 4 interweaves two nearby places and two far-off ones. And perhaps this Greek reference links with parallels between the list in Gen. 10 and Greek genealogical lists.[29]

These places (v. 5) are thus a cross-section of locations in Turkey and the country to the west and east, from which people spread out into the rest of that area. Many would be locations known through Jerusalem's trading relations. The description of them as nations on far shores suggests particular reference to the island and coastal peoples of v. 4.

10:6–7. Ham's descendants, listed in vv. 7–20, cover a wide tract of territory south of Judah, from the Arabian Gulf across North Africa, but also including Canaan itself. Kush is the southern part of Egypt and the northern part of Sudan (*sudan* is an Arabic word for black people). Miṣrayim is Egypt itself ("Egypt" comes from the name of an Egyptian ruler or a sanctuary; "Miṣrayim" is closer to the modern Arabic name). Puṭ is Libya (*libuē* is its Greek name, though the LXX and Vg simply transliterate here). Canaan denotes the area from Egypt to Lebanon; it appears with Egypt in the list, perhaps since it has been commonly under Egyptian control. So this list works roughly from south to north.

It fits that the "sons" and "grandsons" of Kush (v. 7) are places in North Africa and Arabia. They are mixed up, but for Judah they would have in common their being Judah's trading partners to its south. For Ḥavilah, compare

26. Concerning the peoples in vv. 2–4, see further, e.g., *HALOT*.
27. Josephus, *Ant.* 1.6.1; cf. Tg. Ps.-J.
28. See J. Day, "Where Was Tarshish?"
29. On which see Darshan, "Biblical Account."

2:11; 25:18; for Sheba, see, for example, 1 Kings 10; Ezek. 27:22. Possibly Sheba is in Arabia and Seba in North Africa.[30]

10:8–12. These verses in the genealogical list make a formal interlude of the kind that appears in such lists in 1 Chronicles (e.g., 4:8–10). Suddenly we are reading about an individual instead of the embodiment of a people. It's a reminder that the role played by individuals of energy and drive is decisive to the development of peoples and nations and empires. It's surprising to see a descendant of Kush finding his way to Mesopotamia and making his mark there, and Nimrod does not feature in the list of Kush's descendants in v. 7. His story is appended to it, raising the question of whether it relates to someone or somewhere else of the same name. And there are such, the Kuššu or Kassites, who ruled Babylonia between the sixteenth and twelfth centuries,[31] and the earlier important Sumerian town of Kish near Babylon.[32] But outside Gen. 10 and the description of Assyria as "Nimrod's country" in Mic. 5:6 [5:5], we have no references to anyone of this name or to anyone with the list of achievements that are here credited to Nimrod. He is a figure like Cain or Noah, whose story can concretely and engagingly embody the impressive development of human achievement—in his case, the progress of the great states of the Middle East. Thus his story strikes a different note from the rest of the chapter, which describes a process of the natural growth of peoples. His story relates the complementary role played in the development of nations and empires by a man of drive and initiative.

As someone who has gained a reputation as a strongman (v. 8), Nimrod belongs to the same category as Gideon (ironically?), Jephthah, David, and Alexander (Judg. 6:12; 11:1; 1 Sam. 9:1; Dan. 11:1), among many others. Perhaps he is simply the first such in the story of history after the deluge (as Noah is the first farmer), or perhaps he is an entirely new kind of political and military strongman. If he comes from the Kush mentioned in v. 6, then the world's first strongman is a black man.[33]

Specifically, he is a strongman as a hunter (v. 9); perhaps he is thus fulfilling the post-deluge commission to let the animate world be in dreadful awe of humanity. That promise thus applies not only to domestic animals but also to the wild animals that human beings eat—such as deer, gazelle, and antelope. It would also apply to wild animals that are a threat to human communities, for whose security a king bears responsibility; kings are sometimes described as hunters.[34] While Nimrod thus gains a reputation as a formidable and heroic fighter, what is most remarkable about him is that he is a strongman "before

30. On the other names, see, e.g., *HALOT*. See further Montgomery, *Arabia and the Bible*, 37–53.

31. See Driver, *Genesis*, 120.

32. See Y. Levin, "Nimrod the Mighty."

33. Cf. Oduyọye, *Sons of God*, 27.

34. See, e.g., Westermann, *Genesis 1–11*, 516; Strawn, "Comparative Approaches," 132–34.

Yahweh." The earth has been "devastated before God"; Noah is "faithful before me," God says (6:11; 7:1). When God looks at the earth, he sees devastation; when he looks at Noah, he sees faithfulness.[35] When he looks at Nimrod, he sees a strongman and a hunter. The precise phrase "before Yahweh" comes five more times in Genesis (18:22; 19:13, 27; 24:52; 27:7), each time referring to prayer. The pattern continues in succeeding books. It is a metaphor deriving from the way people physically appear before the image of their deity. Prayer and worship involve standing "before Yahweh" (lit., "to the face of Yahweh") in a true though more figurative sense, given that Yahweh properly has no image. Worshipers are really in Yahweh's presence, and Yahweh's face really turns toward them. Apparently Nimrod becomes a byword for his three characteristics as a strongman, a hunter, and someone who stands before Yahweh. So the astonishing picture of his achievements parallels not so much the picture of Cain as the picture of Noah. Nimrod is a strongman "before Yahweh" as Noah is someone who walks about with God (6:9). The description also anticipates the commission to Abraham to walk about "before me," with transparency and integrity. It lacks even the qualifications of Noah's achievements that issue from the close of his story. Nimrod is God's hero and a hero for God, "created by him, receiving from him God's blessing."[36] We should not infer anything from the fact that his name recalls the verb *mārad* (rebel); "do not attempt to ascertain the meaning of any names encountered in the Bible if Scripture itself does not explain them."[37]

Yet more remarkable in the description of Nimrod as king (v. 10) is the description of the beginning of his kingdom or realm as Babel, Erek, Akkad, and Kalneh, in southern Mesopotamia. Babel, after all, was one of the oldest and most important cities there; Erek or Uruk was one of the earliest Sumerian cities; Akkad was the seat of Sargon I and his dynasty; Shinar is a familiar First Testament term for Babylonia in general. Kalneh is otherwise unknown, but it is presumably also in Babylonia.[38]

The astonishing portrait of Nimrod continues (vv. 11–12) in the account of his venturing out from Shinar to northern Mesopotamia, into the area of the kingdom of Assyria. Asshur itself, Nineveh, and Kalah were key and impressive cities on the River Tigris; each was a capital of Assyria at different times, and their names would be familiar to many readers of Genesis. The literal historical reality is that the original Babylonian Empire indeed

35. Cf. Driver, *Genesis*, 120.

36. Chrysostom, *Homilies on Genesis 18–45*, 218. Knohl ("Nimrod, Son of Cush," 50) notes the similarity of the Genesis phrase to an equivalent Mesopotamian expression.

37. Ibn Ezra, *Genesis*, 132; he recognizes that "before Yahweh" implies worship. Contrast, e.g., Tg. Ps.-J.; Tg. Neof. (which calls Nimrod "a strongman in sin"); and recently Hom, "Mighty Hunter before YHWH"; Petrovich, "Identifying Nimrod."

38. On the location of these places, see Jericke, *Die Ortsangaben im Buch Genesis*, 42–54.

predated and influenced the Assyrian Empire.[39] Nineveh's town squares were apparently undeveloped areas of the city. Resen is apparently the abbreviated form of a name equivalent to Hebrew *rōʾš ʿayin* (source of a spring; *HALOT*); while the name occurs in Assyrian texts, we do not know of a Resen between Nineveh and Kalah.[40] The closing reference to the big town would apply less appropriately to Resen than to Nineveh or to Kalah, which was earlier more important than Nineveh (the modern name of Kalah is Nimrud).

10:13–20. After the Nimrod story, Genesis reverts to the record of Ham's descendants. It moves on from Kush to Egypt and thus back to Africa. The Ludites, Anamites, Lehabites, Naptuhites, and Patrusites are apparently all Egyptian or North African peoples (see, e.g., *HALOT*), though we have hard evidence only for the last as the people of Pathros, between Lower Egypt and Kush. More intriguing are the Kasluhites and Kaphtorites because of the mention of the Pelishtites, the Philistines, who are elsewhere linked with Kaphtor (Jer. 47:7; Amos 9:7). The Kaphtorites are the Cretans; we do not know who the Kasluhites were.

Ham's next son is Canaan (vv. 15–19), of whom we heard much in 9:18–27. Many of the peoples and places that follow will become familiar in the First Testament story. Sidon (which can cover Tyre, subsequently more important) marks Canaan's far northern border, in the area that continued to be Canaanite or Phoenician when one would no longer use the term Canaan for the area farther south that was thoroughly Israelite. Ḥet is the eponymous ancestor of the Hittites (see, e.g., Gen. 23), probably to be distinguished from the Ḫatti who once ruled a great empire centered on Turkey.

The Jebusites (v. 16) are the people who lived in Jerusalem. The Amorites lived in the Mamre area (cf. 14:13), likewise to be distinguished from the broader Amurru of Mesopotamia, though the term is also used (like Canaanites) to denote the pre-Israelite inhabitants of Syria-Palestine in general. The Girgashites are unknown except for references in the lists of pre-Israelite peoples, though their name is intriguingly similar to that of the Gergesenes/Gerasenes/Gadarenes of Matt. 8:28; Mark 5:1; Luke 8:26, 37.[41]

The Hivvites (vv. 17–18a) are also unknown outside the lists of pre-Israelite peoples, but they are sometimes associated with northern Canaan (e.g., Josh. 11:3), and the following peoples belong to the north, to the Phoenician towns of Arqa, Siannu in Phoenicia, Arvad, and Ṣumur (see, e.g., *HALOT*), and to the inland northern town of Hamat, which sometimes marks Israel's northern border (e.g., Num. 34:8).

39. Hendel ("Genesis 1–11 and Its Mesopotamian Problem," 30) sees Genesis as appropriating a piece of Mesopotamian history and claiming its hero as "before Yahweh."

40. Unless you go a rather indirect way, as Hurowitz ("In Search of Resen") suggests in arguing for the identification of Resen with Dur-Sharrukin. See also van der Kooij, "City of Babel"; Fenton, "Nimrod's Cities."

41. Hamilton, *Genesis 1–17*, 341.

The subsequent dispersal or spread of the Canaanites (vv. 18b–19) might presuppose that they originally belonged in the highland and in the north but spread southwest into the coastal areas. But the reason for the author and the audience to be interested in these links, and the means by which they might have known about them, would again be trading relations between Jerusalem and the Canaanite/Phoenician towns. Gerar (Gen. 20:1; 26:1) was evidently near Azzah (Gaza), while Sodom, Gomorrah, Admah, and Seboyim were at the south end of the Dead Sea—as apparently was Lasha, which Jerome identifies as Callirhoe on the eastern side.[42]

The summary note about the Hamites (v. 20) confirms that Genesis is not simply talking about a family genealogy but is surveying the development of kin groups and language groups in different countries and nations.

10:21–31. The descendants of Shem come last, even though he is Japhet's older brother, because Shem's line leads into what follows in 11:10–26, where Eber will also feature, and thus leads into the Abraham story that comes next. The descendants of Shem cover the territory east and southeast of Israel.

Elam (vv. 22–24) was a great power even farther east than Babylonia, the other side of the Persian Gulf. Asshur was to the north of Babylonia, but Arpakšad seems in some way to stand for Babylonia itself. Lud is presumably to be distinguished from the home of the earlier Ludites in v. 13; the context suggests a people among those east and north of Canaan, which puts the Lydians in western Turkey quite a distance away. Aram as a state is approximately equivalent to modern Syria (that modern name is derived from "Assyria"), but the Arameans also spread into Mesopotamia, and the descendants of Aram presumably live in that broad area. We will come across Shelaḥ (whose location is unknown) along with Eber in 11:10–26.

Before we get there (vv. 25–30), Genesis speaks of Eber's descendants. The earth's dividing (*pālag*) might be the rift between peoples that 11:1–9 will relate; *pālag* appears in such a connection in Ps. 55:9 [55:10] (cf. the equivalent Aramaic word in Dan. 2:41). And we will hear more of Peleg in 11:10–26. Meanwhile, Genesis provides the information about Yoqṭan's line—once again, it thus deals first with the line that matters less in terms of the story it will go on to tell. Some of the names have definite links with South Arabia, the southernmost part of the Arabian peninsula, centered on modern Yemen. For instance, Shelep is the name of a district or tribe in Yemen, and Ḥaṣarmavet is Hadramaut, an area of Yemen. It seems a fair guess that the rest of the names also relate to places in this area. The only one that is well known in the First Testament is Ophir, a source of good gold (e.g., Job 28:16). As with the list of Phoenician/Canaanite towns in vv. 18–19, the reason for the author and the audience to be interested in these links and the means by which they might have known about them would be Judah's trading relations with them.

42. Jerome, *Hebrew Questions on Genesis*, 42; cf. Gen. Rab. 37.6; Tg. Ps.-J.; Tg. Neof.

The account of Shem's descendants and of Noah's descendants is now complete (vv. 31–32). It is an account of how the nations have parted (*pārad*; cf. v. 4, and later 13:9, 11, 14; 25:23) or "divided" (v. 25). This motif announced an important theme in the story that follows.

11:1–9. This narrative from J complements the lines of descent in a way parallel to 10:8–12. The lines of descent make a theological statement in one way; the story makes it in another. The question with which it concerns itself is this: how and why did peoples who all had a common origin end up speaking different languages and unable to communicate? Indeed, it suggests approaches to several questions. Not untypically within Gen. 1–11, it provides "multiple aetiologies: not only for human beings having many different languages, but also for the dispersal of humanity throughout the earth, and for the origin of the place name Babel."[43] There are two aspects to its answer to the questions: these results came about because of some action that people took and because of some responsive action that Yahweh took. Whereas Gen. 10 described the spreading of the nations through the earth positively and as a natural process, no reference to God being needed, 11:1–9 sees it as involving human waywardness on one hand and divine intervention on the other.[44] Genesis 10 saw plurality of locations and languages as an outworking of God's blessings. Genesis 11 sees it (in effect) as a result of God's curse, yet paradoxically this curse implies a kind of blessing. As is the case with 2:18–25—a story that can stand on its own and answers a question raised within it and articulated at the end of it—Gen. 10 has come to be part of a bigger story in 10:1–11:26. Genesis 10:1–11:26 is itself part of a yet bigger story in 1:1–11:26, which, as part of Genesis, is in turn part of the story extending from Genesis to Kings. The story as a whole does not have equivalents elsewhere in the Middle East, like the creation and flood narratives, though there are parallels there and in other parts of the world to its individual motifs of the dispersion of peoples, the building of a tower, and the division into different languages.[45] Maybe the story is "a deliberate expression of ideas that are in antipodal opposition to some cherished notions of ancient Mesopotamia."[46]

43. Day, *Creation to Babel*, 181.

44. Cf. Tadiello, "La dispersione occasione positiva di crescita."

45. See the comment on 11:3; and see, e.g., Wenham, *Genesis 1–15*, 236–37. He also notes the prominence of assonance in the story and suggests a detailed palistrophic understanding of it on the basis of parallels between the two halves (*Genesis 1–15*, 235; cf. Fokkelman, *Narrative Art in Genesis*, 11–45), though v. 6 does not fit into the outline (cf. Harland, "Vertical or Horizontal," 519–20). Baden ("Tower of Babel") discusses more broadly the interrelationship of such literary approaches and of historical criticism.

46. Sarna, *Genesis*, 81. Uehlinger (*Weltreich und "eine Rede"*) sees it as originally a polemic against a world power of the day that has as its background an unfinished building project of Sargon II. Reimer ("Tower of Babel") rather finds its background in the fall of the Uruk Empire. Penley ("Historical Reading") sees it in the collapse of the Sumerian civilization. Sherman (*Babel's Tower Translated*) surveys the history of the story's interpretation.

So the story goes back (v. 1) behind the account of the lines of descent, to a time when it can picture the entire earth as having one language (contrast 10:5, 20, 31). It is a little speculative to infer that everyone's original language was Hebrew.[47] But it is God's promise that towns in Egypt will come to speak the language of Canaan (Isa. 19:18).[48]

The talk of people moving on or traveling in the east (v. 2) reminds one of 2:8, though more immediately this story is about things moving on after the deluge, and "east" may rather be the audience's position; what is happening takes place east of Canaan. Specifically, the people are in Shinar, Babylonia (see 10:10). The valley (*beqaʿ*) is thus something more like a plain than a canyon (cf. Deut. 34:3; Ezek. 37:1–2; and the Beqaʿ in Lebanon), even if it ultimately has mountainous sides. The talk of "finding" (*māṣāʾ*) a valley rather implies that they were looking for one; they did not just "chance upon" this place (*qārâ*). Apparently they have had enough of dispersing through the earth. Perhaps we should picture them as moving by wagon train through mountains and at last discovering a vale where settlement was more practical. A location that would later be as notable as that of Shinar and Babel would surely be an impressive place to settle. So they have settled there, which doesn't seem unreasonable. (An incidental advantage of locating the story in Babylonia will emerge in v. 9.)

The proposal that follows (v. 3) is a more evidently different matter. They all speak the same language, so they can discuss a plan. The account of the plan recalls some lines in When on High that describe gods making bricks for a lofty temple where Marduk's image was to be put. It is a sacral act.[49] In Genesis, the making of the bricks is a human act and it is, well, just the making of bricks. Further, the account hints at an irony. In Judah, nature provides stone for building; these builders make mudbrick to build with. The character of the bonding material is not so clear, but the word for "tar" (*ḥōmer*) is the word for the coating Moses's mother will give to the casket in which she puts him (Exod. 2:3), and it contrasts with the cement that the Israelites will use in connection with Pharaoh's building projects (Exod. 1:14). So maybe Genesis is noting another human technological innovation, but maybe it is scoffing at the makeshift nature of the work it describes. Indeed, the story as a whole can be read as a satire on a Mesopotamian account of a building project.[50]

The further description of the project also suggests scoffing (v. 4). The people are building a town and a tower that reaches to the sky. Mudbrick is all very well for ordinary people's houses (an Israelite might think), but surely not for a town, even less for a tower (cf. Isa. 9:10 [9:9])—still less one of

47. See, e.g., Rashi, *Brʾšyt*, 105; Tg. Ps.-J.; and Mozeson, "Could Pre-Hebrew Be the *Safa Ahat*?"

48. Calvin, *Genesis*, 1:331.

49. Westermann, *Genesis 1–11*, 545–46; cf. *ANET* 68–69; Hays, *Hidden Riches*, 55–56.

50. See Giorgetti, "'Mock Building Account.'"

these dimensions, even if the people speak hyperbolically, as when we speak of skyscrapers (cf. Deut. 1:28).[51] The story may presuppose the existence of the ziggurats in Mesopotamian cities, towers that reach into the sky to symbolize and facilitate contact between humanity and God, like the towers and spires of churches and cathedrals.[52] Genesis is more specific about two further significances of the building project. The builders want to make a name for themselves. The idea of making a name could suggest gaining power.[53] But there's no suggestion of imperial pretension or tyrannical coercion; it's a community formulating a plan that people agree on.[54] And in the context the further implication is that they feel threatened by other peoples. As was the case in Gen. 4, one would not have guessed that there were other peoples around who might be a threat, but in this story there are. A tower (*migdāl*) is a defensive structure; it is somewhere to hide (e.g., Judg. 9:46–53).[55] So a practical usefulness attaches to a tower. But in addition, the building of town and tower may impress these other peoples with the achievements of the builders and dissuade them from discounting the builders more generally. Yet further, building a town (and one with security) means they can settle down more definitively in this welcoming valley. Again the logic parallels the logic in Gen. 4; Cain, the man sentenced to being a wanderer, set about building a town. Whereas dispersing over the whole earth seems fine in 9:19, here it is something to be resisted. But a focus on building high may be counterproductive (Isa. 2:10–18). The aim is not the same as the one described in Isa. 14, or at least it is more complex; the expression does not suggest an assault on heaven, as becomes explicit in Jub. 10.18–19.[56] The people's motivation is not so much ambition as lethargy mixed with fatigue and fear.

Yahweh comes down to look (v. 5). God can be actively involved in the world, but his actual home is in the heavens (Ps. 115:3; Isa. 66:1). From that perspective, what seems humanly impressive may look pathetic. One expects a deity to show up for the dedication of a building and for its blessing; Yahweh shows up for a different reason and with different results.[57] There is no description of the actual building; Genesis leaps on to the action by Yahweh that presupposes at least their beginning to carry out the plan, though v. 8 will make clear that not all the work is done. The effect of moving straight

51. Cf. Willet, *Hexapla in Genesin & Exodum*, 107, 108.

52. See further Anthonioz, *Babel la tête dans le ciel*; she relates the story to the destruction of the Jerusalem temple.

53. Cf. Bornapé, "El motive de un 'nombre' en la historia de la Torre de Babel."

54. Cf. Sherman, *Babel's Tower Translated*, 27.

55. Which argues against a link with the ziggurat (Uehlinger, *Weltreich und "eine Rede,"* 231–36; cf. Marlowe ("Sin of Shinar"), who stresses the aggressive as well as the defensive nature of the builders' project.

56. Cf. Ron, "Book of Jubilees and the Midrash Part 3." On this traditional understanding, see further Hiebert, "Babel: Babble or Blueprint?"

57. Giorgetti, "'Mock Building Account,'" 13–19.

from their plan to Yahweh's descent is to set their aim and Yahweh's action in tension and in contrast. They want to reach to the heavens (though it does not say to God). God comes down from his abode (though it does not say from the heavens). Far from invading God's abode, they got nowhere near it. Indeed, Yahweh needs to make quite a journey even to see it. "The one who sits in the heavens laughs" (Ps. 2:4).[58] But as is often the case, Yahweh does not rely on what he can know from a distance by divine omniscience or on what his aides report. His interest in the world makes him check things out (cf. 18:21). He is like a parent sitting downstairs and letting the children get on with things in their rooms upstairs until the parent thinks things sound too quiet or too noisy and determines to investigate. One could say that Yahweh's coming to investigate is an act of grace.[59] But there is no "Where are you?" or "Where is your brother?" or "What are you doing?" Indeed, it is "ominous" that Yahweh and the human beings do not stand in dialogue in this story.[60]

One question behind this story (v. 6) is why humanity speaks so many languages, and the answer now begins to appear. Yahweh is not very bothered about the tower, which reaches nowhere important. But Yahweh asks, "Who knows where these peoples' action will lead?" Genesis does not give examples of where it might lead (was the building of the tower an ancient equivalent to globalization?).[61] But the question suggests some overlap with the idea of humanity's eating from the good-and-bad-knowledge tree and where it might lead (3:22). The challenge that comes to Job is to recognize that Yahweh is the one for whom no scheme is closed off (42:2; the verb *bāṣar* in the niphal comes only in these two passages).[62] If there is no scheme closed off to them, they have become like God. The fall in relationships with God (Gen. 3) and with one's brother (Gen. 4) and with one's parents (Gen. 9) becomes the fall of nations.

Yahweh apparently returns home to deliberate (v. 7). He does not behave instinctively; he does not go in for gut reactions. There is often a delay between his saying he will punish and his doing so. But whereas the "let us" of 1:26 issued in the making of humanity, this "let us" issues in its unmaking. Their "come on" (v. 3) meets its counterpart in his "come on." First, he goes down to look; then he goes down to act by causing trouble (as in Exod. 3:8, though there the Israelites will be beneficiaries). The proposed action is very mild. Yahweh does not determine simply to demolish the tower and destroy the town. Anyway, the people might then simply decide to build another.

Yahweh does take action (vv. 8–9). While Genesis may presuppose that returning to the heavens means returning to the heavenly court for some

58. Cf. von Rad, *Genesis*, 147.
59. Cf. Barth, *CD* 3.4:316.
60. Fretheim, "Genesis," 411.
61. Cf. Ojo, "Is Globalization a Re-enactment?"
62. Cf. Westermann, *Genesis 1–11*, 551.

deliberation on what to do, his "let us" does not seem to imply that a heavenly crowd is going to take action. It is Yahweh who acts. Targum Ps.-J. does neatly have him consulting with "the seventy angels that stand before him," who will be the beings in charge of each of the nations and who then go and implement the judgment—appositely, since each has the language of his people and the characters of its writing in his hand. Given that Yahweh doesn't seem very worried about the town and tower in themselves, the aim and result of his action is to make it practically impossible for the people to live together. Perhaps there is an implication that their wanting to settle down in one place implies resistance to God's desire that they should fill the earth. More explicitly, Yahweh doesn't want them to be able to work together, because it's likely to issue in devising means of security that don't depend on him. The advantage of locating the story in Babel is that the town's name recalls the Hebrew word *bālal*, which means "mix." It would do no harm if people were also aware of the possibility that the etymological meaning of Babel is actually "God's Gate," or that this phrase expresses another popular etymology,[63] and/or that the Akkadian verb *abālu* means something like "disperse."[64]

11:10–26. As the genealogy in Gen. 5 led into the account of Lamech's hopes for Noah, this genealogy leads into a more detailed account of Teraḥ's family line. It is an "in-between text."[65] Whereas any development toward the story of Israel's ancestors was understated in Gen. 10, here it becomes more overt. And as in Gen. 10, this unit describes developments from Shem's time to Abraham's time as a natural process (indeed, the same will be true of the family's departure from Ur). There is nothing divinely orchestrated about the emergence of Shem's line (the other theological side to the account will come in 12:1), but in it God's blessing is being worked out on the way to the line of Abraham.[66] If Abraham's ancestors served other gods (Josh. 24:2), it was from the effectiveness of God's blessing that they lived and grew, even though they didn't realize it.[67]

The accounts of Shem, Arpakšad, Shelaḥ, Eber, Peleg, Reʿu, Serug, and Nahor unfold in a consistent way without any variation in the formula. When *x* had lived *y* years, he fathered *z*; *x* lived for *aaa* years after fathering *z*, and he fathered sons and daughters. The elements in the formula thus correspond to those in 5:6–20, but the formula does not go on to total the years of the person's lifetime or add the note about him dying. Maybe this difference links with the fact that the ages of the figures in this list are much nearer the ages the audience would be familiar with from its own experience. The people from Adam and Eve to Noah lived in a different world or a different age, but

63. Cf. Gunkel, *Genesis*, 97.
64. See Grossman, "Double Etymology"; see also the translation note to 11:7.
65. Seebass, *Genesis*, 1:288.
66. See Kaminski, *From Noah to Israel*.
67. Westermann, *Genesis 1–11*, 566.

the people from Noah to Abraham lived in something closer to the regular world. The move from monumentally long lives to just slightly impossible lives parallels the move in the Sumerian King List to reigns before the flood of lengths such as 28,800 years and 36,000 years to reigns after the flood in the hundreds of years, when third-millennium kings become people mentioned in inscriptions.[68]

The names of Shem, Arpakšad, Shelaḥ, Eber, and Peleg recur from 10:21–25. That earlier list implied that Arpakšad was not Shem's firstborn; this list ignores his older brothers because it focuses on the line that will lead to Abraham. The earlier list had then included the descendants of Yoqṭan, Peleg's brother, but had set aside Peleg's descendants Reʿu, Serug, and Nahor, who therefore feature here. The account of Nahor's son Teraḥ then deviates from the formula by providing the names of three sons, because of their significance in the detail that will follow. And the account of Teraḥ stops with the formula unfinished, as happened in 5:32, and for a parallel reason; it will be completed in a distinctive fashion in 11:32. Perhaps it is significant that both accounts end with three sons.

From Adam to Noah ten generations passed, the last entry being incomplete. From Shem to Teraḥ nine generations pass, the last entry again being incomplete. Someone who counts the numbers will be looking for another entry, which the LXX provides by incorporating another Qenan (cf. 5:12) between Arpakšad and Šelaḥ (cf. Jub. 8.1–4), and which the MT will eventually provide in the person of Abraham.

Implications

Peoples, Nations, and Languages

Only after the deluge and after God's giving of his covenant (Gen. 9:1–17) does Genesis talk about peoples and nations. They have no place in Gen. 1–9. Is the implication that they are not part of God's creation design? It is in the context of this covenanted but flawed new creation that they emerge.[69] Is God chiefly interested in his people or in those other peoples? Genesis 10–11 is part of the story that leads to a focus on Israel's ancestors in Gen. 12–50. Yet God's blessing is being worked out among other peoples. Even Canaan grows and spreads like other descendants of Noah.[70] Genesis 10–11 manifests a wide-ranging interest in the world as a whole, an interest that is strictly unnecessary to a focus on Israel. It presupposes that Israel appropriately asks about the significance of other peoples, and it implies God's missional concern

68. *ANET* 265. See further Jacobsen, *Sumerian King List*. Josephus (*Ant*. 1.3.4) describes the figures in Gen. 5 as rulers.

69. Cf. Barth, *CD* 3.4:310–14.

70. See Habel, "Canaan, Land of Promise."

for the nations.[71] "There is a tension between the universal sovereignty (and *providence*) of God, who cares for and *presides* over all nations (10:1–32) and the *election* of God, who focuses on this distinctive people (11:10–29)." Thus "(a) creation can and must be understood historically, and (b) Israel can and must be understood cosmically."[72] And Jesus can and must be understood both as the descendant of Teraḥ's line (Matt. 1:1–17) and as the descendant of the line that goes behind Teraḥ to the figures whose names appear earlier in Gen. 11 (Luke 3:23–38).

In a useful formulation, Gen. 10:5, 20, and 31 speak of Noah's descendants as identifiable by countries, languages, kin groups, and nations. A people is an entity that generally has a country, a land. It has a common language. It is ethnically related. And it has a political form. All four contribute to its identity and to its sense of identity.

A people's land is a source for providing needed food, and its having borders provides security. If talk of nations was a latecomer in Gen. 1–11, so was talk of lands. But it will become central, though in a paradoxical way, from the end of Gen. 11 onward.[73]

A people's common language makes communication possible. At the end of the history of the world's origins, the Bible opens up the problem of language.[74] Further, while the Babel story refers only to linguistic diversity, language is an aspect of culture,[75] and the story's ambivalence about language points to an ambivalence about culture that parallels Gen. 4's ambivalences. Although at a superficial level humanity had one language, arguably earlier chapters in Genesis have been all about noncommunication. The imposition of diversity in language is a positive step toward the fulfillment of Yahweh's purpose for the world, which embraces diversity. In this sense "the Babel story is not a narrative about the end of communication, but about its beginning."[76] And this story evokes a "great homesickness."[77] Judahites under the domination of Assyria, Babylon, or Persia are aware that the exercise of imperial power over them requires linguistic communication. For peoples subordinate to the imperial power, Yahweh's facilitating the development of multiple languages is thus a blessing, not a curse. "Gen. 11:1–9 problematizes the unity of language, from the point of view of human hubris or excess, as an instrument of oppression,"[78] though the story's affirmation of diversity could also be

71. See Ballenger, "Missiological Thoughts."

72. Brueggemann, *Genesis*, 94, 95, emphasis original.

73. See the comments on 12:7a.

74. Seebass, *Genesis*, 1:286.

75. Cf. Hiebert, "Tower of Babel"; cf. Strong, "Shattering the Image of God."

76. Moyaert, "'Babelish' World," 217. She is particularly concerned to undermine the gloomy implications of the cultural-linguistic theory of religion.

77. Barth, *CD* 3.4:318.

78. Croatto, "Reading of the Story," 222. Cf. (also from Latin American perspective) Míguez-Bonino, "Genesis 11:1–9."

harnessed to a system such as apartheid.[79] The background to imposing disunity is God's desire for people to spread through the world and not be too united. Or rather, God wants there to be a unity that facilitates scattering, not a unity that resists scattering, thus the kind of unity that Pentecost issued in (sometimes) and that the new Jerusalem will finally embody.[80] Where there is resistance to God's purpose in Gen. 11, "God does not make use of battering rams to break down walls"; he merely confuses people's languages. "This is truly an astonishing method of conquering cities and of demolishing walls, but it is the surest and easiest of all." Whereas the mixing up of people's languages might seem a slight punishment, in reality it is "a terrible one," "issuing in disunity and hatred." For this reason Pentecost was "a great blessing and an outstanding miracle": God "tears down the wall" between us (Eph. 2:14).[81]

A people's ethnic or familial nature or self-understanding undergirds its mutual commitment by encouraging people to see it as the family writ large. In tension with that reality, Gen. 10 reminds Israel that the peoples among whom God's blessing is worked out are one in their relationship to Noah. God "made from one all the ethnic groups among human beings to dwell on the face of all the earth, establishing the bounds of the set times and the boundaries of where they dwelt" (Acts 17:26). Their shared relationship to Noah means they are one family. Ignoring the genealogies in Genesis has the effect of "blunting the ethical impact of its depiction of all humanity as members of a single family."[82] The family embraces mighty empires—Assyria, Babylon, Media, and Greece—that will be Israel's overlords and oppressors and also its deliverers and benefactors. It embraces peoples with whom Israel will have trading relationships as equals and peoples on whom Israel itself will make war.

A people's political structure enables a group much larger than a family to make decisions. Here is a portrait of nations developing through God's blessing and individuals such as Nimrod encouraging the development of infrastructure; alongside that is the portrait of nations feeling the need to build towers for protection, thus expressing their fear and their assumption that they must take responsibility for their survival. But "if Yahweh doesn't build a house, in vain the builders have labored on it" (Ps. 127:1).[83] And finding that you have made a name for yourself as an incidental result of doing something significant (e.g., 2 Sam. 8:13; Isa. 63:12) is one thing; trying to make a name

79. See General Synod of the Dutch Reformed Church, *Human Relations*, 13–21. See further Rathbone, "Unity and Scattering."

80. Cf. Hock, "From Babel to the New Jerusalem."

81. Luther, *Genesis 6–14*, 225, 214–15.

82. Mbuvi, *Belonging in Genesis*, 106.

83. Cf. Chrysostom, *Homilies on Genesis 18–45*, 223.

for yourself by doing something significant is another,[84] like professors writing books because otherwise they won't be given tenure.

As with Yahweh's action against Adam and Eve, against Cain, and against humanity in the deluge, Yahweh's action against Babel is tempered by an insistence on continuing to persevere with his purpose through humanity, to protect, and to be merciful. Is it still so?[85] While the Abraham and Sarah story will provide a more explicit positive answer, the fact that dispersal has previously been a positive rather than a negative idea (9:19; 10:18) hints that the negative act has a positive aim.

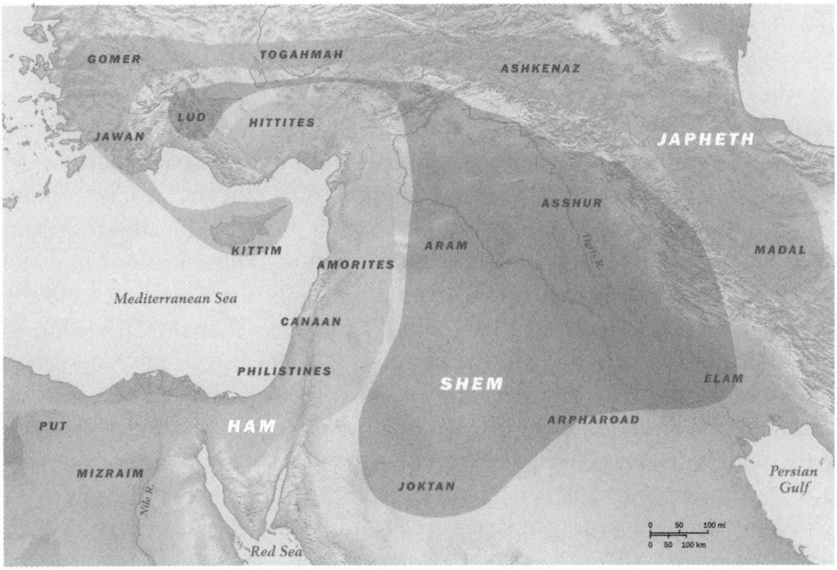

Genesis 10 Nations

84. Cf. Lacocque, "Whatever Happened?," 33–34.
85. Cf. von Rad, *Genesis*, 149.

Part Two

Terah's Lines of Descent through Abraham

(11:27–25:11)

"Thus far, the creation project has turned out quite against the dreams of the creator," but "the one who calls the worlds into being now makes a second call."[1] Once again he reboots the project. With 11:27 "an epochal juncture in the history of humankind has been reached."[2] But "God is no longer engaging in damage control, as he was in the first eleven chapters of the Torah."[3]

In this connection, Part Two of Genesis focuses on Yahweh's dealings with Abraham and Sarah. The story of creation and of things unraveling was a "primordial" and "universal" story, and one would have expected the story of God's putting things right to have the same characteristics. But not for the last time, God changes his way of effecting his purpose. "God's plan is universal *in scope*" but now "not universal in method or means."[4] It's now effected through particular people in a particular place. The transition from 1:1–11:26 to what follows marks a transition from God's act of creation to God's entering into a covenant relationship with a particular people; the

1. Brueggemann, *Genesis*, 96, 105.
2. Sarna, *Genesis*, 86–87.
3. Levenson, *Inheriting Abraham*, 20.
4. Reno, *Genesis*, 137, 138, emphasis original.

linking of these two stories in one scroll marks the "indissoluble" nature of the connection between the two.[5] No creation without covenant; no covenant without creation.

Genesis 11:27–50:26 then divides into a three-part drama, the story of three generations of a family: Abraham and Sarah (11:27–25:11), Isaac and Rebekah (25:12–35:29), and Jacob and his sons (36:1–50:26). A heading announcing "lines of descent" that are to follow introduces each part. Within 11:27–25:11, the opening unit tells of the background and of how things begin. What follows constitutes a series of stories concerning how Yahweh's purpose is repeatedly imperiled but is safeguarded and partially fulfilled. Genesis 11:27–25:11 relates the story of a God who makes outrageous demands, issues extraordinary promises, and intervenes to see that his purpose is fulfilled. People such as Abraham and Sarah sometimes trust God, and sometimes their trust fails: there are two stories about passing off one's wife as a sister (with another to follow in Gen. 26) and three stories about quarrels over land (with another to follow in Gen. 26). Genesis 11:27–12:8 and 12:9–13:4 form an opening pair of units that lay out two sides to Yahweh (he commands and promises) and two sides to Abraham (he obeys and trusts, and his faith and commitment waver), which the subsequent stories then further illustrate. The first five units lead into one another:

Terah moves, Yahweh issues a summons and promises, Abraham obeys (11:27–12:8)
Yahweh's promises aren't working out, Abraham panics (12:9–13:4)
Yahweh's promises aren't working out, Abraham makes a sacrifice to Lot (13:5–18)
The sacrifice has repercussions that require another commitment (14:1–24)
Yahweh gives a reassurance about offspring and a pact relating to the land (15:1–21)

That last unit marks a transition to the middle units,[6] which center on the promise of offspring:

A false start, with conflict and resolution (16:1–16)
A pact relating to the promise, with a sign (17:1–27)
A reiteration of the promise, with a contrasting story about Abraham's nephew (18:1–19:38)
Another endangering of the potential mother of the offspring (20:1–18)

5. Barth, *CD* 3.1:62; and for what follows, see the continuation of the chapter in Barth on "Creation, History and Creation History."

6. Cf. Seebass, *Genesis*, 2.1:1

The birth of a son to Sarah, with conflicts and resolutions (21:1–34)
The testing of Abraham regarding Isaac (22:1–19)

The third section takes the story to a close:

A family report, Sarah's death, and the acquiring of a family burial place (22:20–23:20)
The acquisition of a wife for Isaac (24:1–67)
Abraham's preparation for dying and his death (25:1–11)

Compared with the succeeding two parts of the drama, 11:27–25:11 comprises a series of stories that in themselves are relatively self-contained, though part of their significance emerges from their place in the sequence to which they belong.

9

The Background, the Summons, and the Promises

(11:27–12:8)

Overview

The initial question that 11:27–12:8 answers is this: "How did Abraham and Sarah come to be in Canaan?" The story offers three sorts of answers.

- It happened because Terah decided to move his family from Ur.
- It happened because Yahweh bade Abraham go to Canaan.
- It happened because Abraham did as Yahweh said.

With his bidding to Abraham, Yahweh associates a series of promises.

- He will live in the country to which Yahweh directs him.
- He will be blessed and thus fruitful and will thus become a big nation.
- He will experience Yahweh's protection.
- He will become a standard and means whereby other nations will seek blessing.

But there are obstacles and complications on the way.

- Sarah can't have children.
- Terah gets diverted from continuing to Canaan and eventually dies in Harran.

- Abraham's brother dies, so Abraham must take his nephew Lot with him.
- The Canaanites occupy the country.

We have not seen the last of some of these obstacles and complications.

Translation

11:27 So[1] these are Teraḥ's lines of descent.
Teraḥ fathered Abram,[2] Naḥor, and Haran, and Haran fathered Lot.
28Haran died in the presence of[3] Teraḥ his father in the country that was
his homeland, Ur[4] of the Kaśdites.[5] **29**Abram and Naḥor got themselves
wives; the name of Abram's wife was Śaray and the name of Naḥor's wife
was Milkah bat Haran, the father of Milkah and of Yiskah. **30**But Śaray
was infertile;[6] she had no child.[7]
31Teraḥ took Abram his son, Lot ben Haran his grandson, and Śaray his
daughter-in-law, Abram's wife,[8] and they left Ur of the Kaśdites together[9]
to go to the country of Kenaʿan, but they came as far as Ḥarran[10] and
lived there. **32**Teraḥ's time came to 205[11] years, and Teraḥ died in Ḥarran.
12:1 But Yahweh said[12] to Abram:

> Take yourself[13] from your country,
> from your homeland, and from your father's household,

1. The waw prefix indicates that the section carries straight on from 11:10–26.
2. On Abra[ha]m and Saray/Sarah's names, see the comment on 17:5, 15.
3. *ʿAl-pənê* hardly means simply "before" (Vg); cf. Dillmann, *Genesis*, 1:406. Retief ("When Interpretation Traditions Speak Too Loud") argues for "in the face of (in confrontation with)."
4. A homonym means flame or fire, not least an idolmaker's fire or a persecutor's fire (e.g., Isa. 31:9; 44:16; 47:14; 50:11), which encourages the development of a midrash about Abraham being threatened by fire at the hand of the Chaldeans and about Haran the idolmaker ending up in a fiery furnace (see, e.g., Jub. 12; Tg. Ps.-J.; Rashi, *Brʾšyt*, 112).
5. For *kaśdîm* the LXX has *chaldaiōn*, the Vg *chaldaeorum*—hence English "Chaldeans." The (older) Babylonian form has *š*, the Assyrian form *l* (see *HALOT*).
6. If *ʿăqārâ* could simply mean childless, without the implication of infertile (so Sarna, *Genesis*, 87), it would preserve suspense for the unfolding of the story, but the suggestion seems doubtful (see, e.g., H.-J. Fabry on the word, *TDOT* 11:322).
7. As in 3:16, apposition enhances the similarity/opposition between clauses (DG 147ab).
8. The SP and some LXX manuscripts add Nahor to this verse (the SP also adds Milkah) in light of Nahor and Milkah's being there later (see Gen. 24; 29:4–5).
9. Literally, "with them."
10. In the MT *ḥārān* (contrast the LXX's *charran*) because the MT usually avoids doubling *r* and lengthens the preceding vowel to compensate (cf. GKC 22s); transliterating as Ḥarran makes clearer the difference from the name of Terah's son Haran (which begins with *he* not *ḥet*).
11. The SP has 145, which solves a chronological problem (see the comments on 12:1–3 below). Acts 7:4 might presuppose the SP's reading or might simply be referring to the order of events in the MT narrative (cf. the reference to Exod. 3 in Mark 12:26).
12. KJV "had said"; cf. the previous footnote and the comment, and the discussion in *TTH* 76.
13. Literally, "go for yourself."

To the country that I will enable you to see,
 2so I may[14] make you into a big nation.
I will bless you and I intend to make your name big[15]
 and you are to become[16] a blessing.
3I intend to bless the people who bless you,
 but the person who diminishes you[17] I will curse.[18]
All the kin groups on the earth
 will gain blessing[19] by you.

4Abram went as Yahweh spoke to him, and Lot went with him. Abram was a man of seventy-five years when he left Ḥarran.

5So Abram took Śaray his wife, Lot his brother's son, all the property that they had acquired, and all the people that they had produced[20] in Ḥarran, and left to go to the country of Kenaʿan. They came to the country of Kenaʿan, **6**and Abram passed through the country[21] as far as the site at Šekem, as far as Teacher's Oak.[22] Now the Kenaʿanites were then in the country. **7**But Yahweh appeared to Abram and said, "To your offspring

14. Cf. DG 94, remark 8, though "and thus I will" (consequence rather than purpose) is also possible (cf. JM 116b); but "and I will" (LXX, Vg) undertranslates.

15. The verb is cohortative; so also is the first verb in v. 3.

16. More literally, "so be a blessing!"—that is, the verb is imperative, which suggests purpose when following on a cohortative (cf. *TTH* 65; DG 86d), but also the kind of imperative that conveys a promise—as well as the kind of promise that conveys an imperative (see Biden, "Morpho-Syntax of Genesis 12:1–3").

17. The LXX, Vg, SP have plural for this participle, assimilating to the first.

18. Whereas the cohortative verbs translated "intend to" suggest deliberate will, the ordinary yiqtol for this final verb suggests something less intrinsic to Yahweh's purpose (see P. Miller, "Syntax and Theology"). The other first-person verbs in vv. 1–2 have suffixes, which means that they cannot take cohortative form, though one might see them as having that significance de facto; this last verb is the only one where Yahweh could have used the cohortative and does not.

19. The niphal verb could have passive, reflexive, or middle connotations. For passive, cf. *DCH*; Grüneberg, *Abraham, Blessing and the Nations*. But Genesis could have used pual to convey this meaning (e.g., Num. 22:6; 2 Sam. 7:29; Pss. 112:2; 128:4). For reflexive, cf. BDB, *HALOT*; Rashi, *Brʾšyt*, 117; Noort, "Abraham and the Nations," 18–30. But hitpael in 22:18; 26:4 has reflexive meaning, and it seems less likely that niphal here simply means the same thing. More likely it has middle connotations. In substance, the translation makes little difference; in one way or another, the nations will be blessed through Abraham.

20. In good evangelical fashion, Tg. Onq., Tg. Neof. takes this phrase to refer to the souls they had converted.

21. The LXX adds "in its length," making more explicit that Abraham is behaving as if entering into legal possession of the country (Ska, "Gen. 12,6"); cf. 13:17 and the comment.

22. Or *ʾēlôn* might mean terebinth. Genesis 35:4 refers to an *ʾēlâ* near Shechem; cf. also Josh. 24:26; Judg. 9:6, 37 for similar words. Linking the right word to the right tree is difficult. Both are leafy and have wide-spreading branches, but they are quite different, though there are many varieties of oak. The terebinth also has red berries and grows pistachio nuts. The Vg and Tg have "plain" for "oak," perhaps by associating the reference to the Teacher's Oak with the reference to Oak Vale in Judg. 7:1 and thus guarding against any idea that Abraham was involved in wrongful worship (Aberbach and Grossfeld, *Targum Onkelos*, 79–80; and see more generally Hutzli, "Interventions"). Targum Neof. also has "Vision" for "Teacher," implying a

I will give this country," and he built an altar there for Yahweh, who had appeared to him. 8He went on from there to the mountain country on the east of Bet-el, and spread his tent, Bet-el on the west, Haʿay on the east. He built an altar there for Yahweh and called out with the name Yahweh.

Interpretation

The MT's unit runs from 11:10 to 12:9, while the new synagogue lection begins at 12:1 and continues to 17:27. One can see why the devisers of the synagogue lectionary and of the medieval chapter divisions were attracted to the resonant declaration in 12:1. But in the introduction to this commentary, we have noted how a heading such as "these are Terah's lines of descent" (11:27) looks like the introduction to one of the major parts of Genesis as a whole. In this case, the opening scenes in Part Two concern Yahweh's dealings with Terah's son Abraham and his wife Sarah; and a narrative arc does come to completion with 12:8 as Abraham arrives in Canaan, builds altars there, names Yahweh's name there, and spreads his tent there in a way that implies more than an overnight stay while on the way to somewhere else. "Within the book of Genesis, no section is more significant than 11:27–12:9."[23] (I would say 11:27–12:8.) It is quite a statement.[24]

While the account of Terah's lines of descent continues from 11:26, it thus opens with a new heading and then reprises information from v. 26b before segueing in vv. 27b–30 into more information on the family. Such material might appear in an account of someone's lines of descent, especially a segmented genealogy such as 10:1–32, but it provides much more detail than appeared in the linear genealogy in 11:10–26, detail significant as background to what will follow. In v. 31 it immediately leads into an account of Terah's moving his family from Ur. Only with v. 32 do we get the genealogical information that would bring Terah's details to a close, but not in the same form as vv. 10–26: it gives the total number of his years instead of the number of years he lived after the birth of his sons; then the account closes with a note about his dying. It thus resembles the pattern in Gen. 5, but its point here is that Terah died in Harran and did not accompany Abraham to Canaan.

The switch in the synagogue lection at 12:1 reflects the transition from the lines of descent and story in 11:27–32, whose framework comes from P, to the story beginning in 12:1, whose framework comes from J. Combining passages from the two earlier versions generates some uncertainty about the order and

---

link with *rāʾâ* rather than *yārâ*—and not inappropriately in view of Yahweh's appearing to Abraham (*rāʾâ*) in v. 7.

23. Wenham, *Genesis 1–15*, 281.

24. Campbell ("Refusing God's Blessing") sees the passage as facing both ways and as a turning point.

interrelationship of events. Genesis 12 begins with a waw-consecutive, which one way or another links it closely with 11:27–32, though how to understand the waw-consecutive (specifically, whether it denotes an event consecutive on events in the previous verses) is a different matter. The importance of Yahweh's words once again receives emphasis through their being expressed in lines that can be scanned as poetic bicola and that manifest some parallelism. They begin with a command, but they quickly segue into a series of promises. And they begin with an act of separation from the rest of the world and a promise for Abraham that sets him over against the world, but they segue into a promise indicating that Abraham's blessing has significance for other peoples. The move repeats itself in heightened fashion as Yahweh speaks of blessing and tough-minded protection but also of all the world's kin groups seeking the kind of blessing Abraham will enjoy.

The unit as a whole takes up themes and motifs from Part One of Genesis, from its beginning with creation and then through the Noah story to its end: lines of descent, blessing and curse, land and increase, fathering and getting wives, altars and calling in Yahweh's name, gaining a name.[25] At work here is the same God with the same purpose. In addition, the unit introduces people and places that will be significant as the chapters unfold: Abraham and the childless Sarah; Nahor and Milkah back in the homeland near Harran; Lot, for whom Abraham has responsibility; the promise about becoming a big nation and having a big name and becoming a blessing; Yahweh's protection from anyone who tries to cut them down; the promise to give Abraham's offspring the country, notwithstanding the Canaanites' presence there; and the places Shechem and Beth El. In other words, though we can analyze the section in terms of the way it answers the question "How did Abraham and Sarah come to be in Canaan?" in some respects the questions the unit answers are not within the section itself but beyond it. The unit is indeed an introduction to Part Two of Genesis as a whole. The unit also illustrates how different parties take initiatives from time to time in this story. To oversimplify slightly:

Terah takes an initiative (11:27–32)
Yahweh takes an initiative (12.1–8)
Abraham takes initiatives (12:9–14:24)
Yahweh takes an initiative (15:1–21)
Sarah takes an initiative (16:1–16)
Yahweh takes initiatives (17:1–19:38)
Abraham takes an initiative (20:1–18)
Yahweh takes initiatives (21:1–22:19)
Abraham takes initiatives (22:20–25:11)

25. On the relationship with 11:1–9, see esp. Awabdy, "Babel."

11:27–30. In v. 27, after the initial reprise of material from the encouraging genealogy in vv. 10–26, with its lack of reference to anyone dying, the account of Terah's lines of descent gives way to something more mixed: one of Terah's sons dies (v. 28). Parents are not supposed to have to bury their children, but in a traditional society they must often do so; while the family is in Ur, Terah has had this experience. It might be tempting to attribute Haran's death to his serving other gods,[26] but he was hardly the only one (see Josh. 24:2), so more likely Genesis takes his death as just one of those things. The geographical context is "Ur of the Kasdites" (Chaldeans), presumably the Ur in Lower Mesopotamia, near the Persian Gulf, one of the great cities in Babylonia; some of these cities were listed in 10:10. But there was also more than one city called something like Ur in Upper Mesopotamia, nearer Harran, and such a reference might make more sense.[27] Although the Chaldeans were not in Mesopotamia until some centuries after Abraham's day and were not the rulers of Ur until about the time Babylon became the great imperial power (hence the references in 2 Kings 24–25), they would have been there when people listened to the story in a later time, and the term identifies the city for them.

Before they leave Ur, Terah's surviving sons marry (v. 29). Sarah's parents are not identified; the later effect will be to bring a surprise when Abraham calls Sarah his sister (12:13; 20:12)—if it is true. Nor does Genesis give us any more information about Iskah. Nor are we told of the interesting meaning of Sarah's name (queen/princess; see *DCH*), which forms an interesting pair with Milkah (queen). Nor therefore does Genesis note that "Sarah" looks like the name of the wife of the moon-god Sin while "Milkah" looks like a title of Ishtar, the queen of heaven, daughter of Sin; the moon-god was a significant figure in the religion of Ur and of Harran.[28] We will hear nothing more of Iskah, but we will hear more of Milkah in Gen. 24. The "main characteristics" attributed to Sarah are these: "no family, married, barren, beautiful, and old."[29]

The further family sadness is that Abraham's wife cannot have children (v. 30); the double statement of the point underscores it. It is not just sadness for Abraham and Sarah. It is also a worry for Terah: one son dead, another who will not have children; does this family have a viable future? The lack of a heading referring to Abraham's "lines of descent" adds to the suspense in this connection. The Hebrew word for "child" comes from the same root (*yālad*) as the words for lines of descent, for fathered, and for homeland in Gen. 11:27–28. Sarah cannot play her part in what is signified by those words. As well as being key to the future of this family, her playing this part is key

26. See the translation note.
27. See Hamilton, *Genesis 1–17*, 363–65.
28. See Westermann, *Genesis 12–36*, 138; Sarna, *Genesis*, 87.
29. T. Schneider, *Mothers of Promise*, 25.

(we are about to discover) to the fulfillment of God's purpose.[30] Sarah's inability to have children is therefore an important aspect of the background to the story of Abraham and Sarah that will follow. Part One of Genesis has referred to no one's infertility; having children has not seemed to be a problem. In Parts Two and Three it becomes a problem. Yahweh chooses to work through someone who has no potential for achieving the thing he wishes to achieve. The Babylonian conquest of Judah put Zion into the same position, and Yahweh reformulated his promise to it in that context (Isa. 54). The situation when the people of God has no capacity to generate a future is the situation to which God's promise speaks.

11:31–32. So it is Terah who sets the family going on a move to Canaan. The connection of Ur with the Chaldeans hints at more than a geographical point about Ur, perhaps a religious point and/or a political one. Is Terah implicitly taking leave of Babylonian religion and taking leave of the empire? In the former connection, moving to Canaan will hardly be an improvement; and the account of Abraham's family that will follow (with their cattle and sheep and tents) suggests that members of Terah's family are not themselves urban people: they do not live in Ur itself. So Terah's making this move is difficult to interpret. Is sadness about Haran[31] and worry about Abraham part of the background? There is no hint that they migrate because God tells them to do so, and in general the opening chapters of Genesis have been unfolding because people do the natural thing. Why is Canaan their intended destination? And why then do they go to Harran, 500–600 miles northwest of Ur, just north of the present-day border between Iraq and Turkey? There is no need to go that far north to get to Canaan.[32] Is the implication that only the narrator knows that they are on their way to Canaan? Perhaps they are like Bedouin, simply on the move because that is their lifestyle. Anyway, people listening to the story will know something of what is presupposed by the laconic account of their journey, though later hints in Genesis implicitly expand on the summary (e.g., 12:5; 13:5–18). They surely take everything they have and everything they need for their travels—flocks and other livestock, tents, grain supplies, skins of olive oil, tools, looms, ovens, gold and silver for bartering. They perhaps travel at about ten miles per day (wagon trains across the United States in the nineteenth century traveled at ten to twenty miles per day), stopping early each evening to set up camp and cook. If they went directly from Ur to Harran, the journey would have taken two months.

With what sense of sadness and failure does Terah eventually die in Harran (v. 32)? The opening paragraphs of the story of Abraham and Sarah do not

30. Arnold, *Genesis*, 128.
31. Cf. Josephus, *Ant.* 1.6.5.
32. Cf. Sarna, *Genesis*, 88.

look like the beginning of anything. It is not a story of how human willfulness spoils things but of how circumstances spoil things.

12:1–3. The waw-consecutive naturally suggests that Yahweh's bidding to Abraham follows on the death of Terah. But if Terah is 70 when Abraham is born and lives until he is 205 (11:26, 32) and Abraham is 75 now (12:4), then Terah is not dead yet. In one sense, the fact that 11:31–32 came from P and 12:1–9 from J could explain the disjunction, though it does not explain how the two passages interrelate in Genesis itself. Here, it seems that 12:1 is backtracking.[33] Genesis 11:27–12:8 then incorporates one of those occasions when Genesis abandons chronological order to tie off one section of the story before focusing on where the story has taken a new turn in the meanwhile. Terah and his decision-making is the past. He's dead even though he is still alive.[34] What Yahweh now says to Abraham is the future. Abraham now needs to be the decision maker. Thus "human agency plays a real role" in the restoring of humanity, yet human initiative plays less; Abraham's action is "responsive, not originative."[35] And in order to fulfill God's commission, Abraham doesn't need to do anything except go and let God fulfill his promises (he is not responsible for furthering God's kingdom or bringing it in or extending it or working for it). Meanwhile, the rest of the family remains ensconced in Harran, as their subsequent location in this area will presuppose. Ur was once their "homeland" (11:28), but Harran is now (24:4, 7), and in Harran Yahweh speaks to Abraham and sets him on the move. We can then only guess at the relationship between Terah's decision to take his family to Canaan and Yahweh's bidding Abraham to go there (but see 15:7). And although we know about Abraham from 11:27–31, we don't know anything of his character or of any reason why Yahweh should have settled on him.[36] God's "choosing" or "election" of Abraham (though Genesis does not use this word) does not imply, for example, ethnic superiority, as Deut. 9:4–6 will make explicit. And paradoxically, his apparently being the eldest son might seem to disqualify him, whereas the "conspiracy of nature and circumstance" seems to favor Lot (Nahor has been left behind in Ur, Sarai is infertile, and Lot's father is dead).[37]

But Yahweh tells Abraham what he is now to do. It's conventional to refer to the "call" of Abraham; the expression comes in Isa. 51:2 and Heb. 11:8, though not here. If it is a call, it is a peremptory one, like Paul's call to be an apostle (Rom. 1:1; 1 Cor. 1:1), which involved blinding him and throwing him off his horse. God's call is more a summons. It means God is telling someone what to do, like a master tells his servant. It's not an invitation. It

33. Cf. Ibn Ezra, *Genesis*, 147–48; he notes that the Scriptures often put things in a nonchronological order. Jubilees 12.28–31 has Abraham going with Terah's blessing.

34. Cf. Rashi's comments, *Br'šyt*, 114.

35. Reno, *Genesis*, 143.

36. Cf. Luther, *Genesis 6–14*, 247–48; Luther indeed assumes that Abraham was an idolater.

37. Levenson, *Death and Resurrection*, 83.

may involve hating father and the rest of one's family (Luke 14:26).[38] This "Yahweh said" resembles the one that tells Cain to master wrongdoing or tells Noah to get into his container ship. It's irrational and demanding, like Yahweh's original command to Adam and Eve. Yahweh is not suggesting that Abraham think about a possible relocation or a possible vocation. He's giving him an order. And it's devastating in its negativity. Yahweh piles up the sacrifice he is demanding: your country, but not just your country, your homeland; not just your homeland but your family.[39] The words' overlapping reference adds to their impact. They recall the comment that a man abandons his father and mother (2:24). Yahweh's commission is thus demanding. Home is safe and protected. Leaving home means abandoning that security.[40] But precisely because Abraham's name is to be turned into a name of blessing for all earth's kin groups, he must leave his own country, his homeland, and his father's household.[41]

The only information he gets about where he is going (vv. 1b–2) is that it is a country that Yahweh will enable him to see in due course. Oh, thanks! It's another hint that while the narrator knows that the family is on their way to Canaan (11:31), no one else does—not when they leave Ur and not when they leave Harran. Abraham leaves, not knowing where he is going (Heb. 11:8). People listening to the story who collude with the narrator, too, live in suspense for a verse or three about where the journey will take him.[42]

God gives Abraham no inducements in terms of a land flowing with milk and honey.[43] But Abraham goes with promises from Yahweh. The first is that he will become a big nation. It's surprising that God thus uses the word *gôy* rather than the word *ʿam*, "people." It was the latter word that came in 11:6; one might have expected the terms to come the other way around.[44] Genesis implies some ambivalence about what might be called the polity of a people.[45] Abraham's offspring is not a nation, but it is to become one. The other nations are kin groups, like Abraham. The promise about becoming a people or a nation is implausible, especially for a man whose wife cannot have children. Whether it would be implausible for people listening to the story would depend on when they lived. In Moses's day Abraham's descendants have become a nation, a substantial people that one can think of as a political entity (e.g., Exod. 1:7; 19:6). In David's or Solomon's day, or in Omri's day, this record of Yahweh's words would invite people to rejoice in what Yahweh has done

38. Cf. Didymus, *Genesis*, 183.
39. Cf. Dillmann, *Genesis*, 2:9.
40. Gunkel, *Genesis*, 163.
41. Cf. Barth, *CD* 2.2:355.
42. Cf. Calvin, *Genesis*, 1:344.
43. Cf. Qimchi, *Genesis*, on the verse.
44. Cf. Mbuvi, *Belonging in Genesis*, 101.
45. Cf. Petersen, "Polities in Genesis 12–36."

in fulfilling his promise. Throughout Judah's history and into the exile (see Isa. 51:2) and during the Second Temple period, it would raise the question of whether it was a promise Yahweh was really going to fulfill for them. The same question would arise regarding the idea of having a big name.

Yahweh underscores the implausibility of his promise when he goes on to make explicit that he will bless Abraham, because "blessing" itself means numerical fruitfulness. To judge from the repetitions, blessing is the key word in the promise in vv. 2–3. "Yahweh showers Abraham with blessings."[46] This promise takes up God's action in 1:28 and 9:1. The extent of the promise's fulfillment (Yahweh implies) means that other people will be astonished. The tower builders in Gen. 11 wanted to make a name for themselves but succeeded only in a way they didn't intend. Yahweh himself will do it for the person who is not seeking it. It will thus mean that Abraham becomes a blessing, which means being the kind of person whose name is used in prayers for blessing: "May God bless you as he blessed *x*" (cf. Prov. 10:7; Zech. 8:13). Abraham will become the gold standard of blessings. "His blessings and his fame will be so great that they will spill over to benefit those around him."[47]

Yahweh goes on (v. 3) to restate the point, further tweaking the significance of the word "blessing." There is a kind of blessing that only God can do—the kind that God promised in the first reference to blessing in v. 2. There is also a derived or derivative version of that blessing that some people can do, which is the opposite of the cursing that Noah did in 9:25, the kind of blessing that Melchizedek or Aaron or Balaam will do (Gen. 14:19; Num. 6:23; 22–23). Such people declare that someone will be blessed by God, and it happens. There will be people who for one reason or another bless Abraham in this sense; and Yahweh will bless them. On the other hand, there will be an occasional individual who diminishes Abraham, who declares that he is going to become nothing (it's the word Yahweh used in 8:21). Yahweh will protect Abraham from the diminishing that this person desires. One might expect Yahweh to say that he will diminish that person, but he actually says he will curse that person (as Noah did). "Yahweh does not command Abraham to go out in order to bring about curse, although that may happen in the process."[48] The point about the curse is to effect that protection. A blunter version of the promise will come from a foreigner's lips, at the other end of the story in the Torah, when the Israelites are about to arrive in Canaan (Num. 24:9). But here, Yahweh further restates the promise about Abraham becoming a blessing and restates it in ultra-high-definition rainbow colors. All the kin groups of the earth will gain blessing by Abraham. They will not merely pray for blessing like Abraham's; they will receive it because of him. Genesis is

46. Gunkel, *Genesis*, 164.
47. Qimchi, *Genesis*, on the verse.
48. P. Miller, "Syntax and Theology in Genesis xii 3a," 474.

not specific about how it will happen, though it will occasionally tell stories that one might see as examples—the story of Joseph in Egypt is the fullest one. Paul will see the promise fulfilled in even more rainbow colors (Gal. 3:8). What is clear here is that God's "choosing" or "election" of Abraham is not designed ultimately to exclude other peoples but to include them. Belonging to the non-elect does not imply belonging to the anti-elect.[49]

"It is no small honour to be 'Abraham's seed.'"[50] Fortunately for Gentiles, one need not be physically descended from Abraham in order to be his son or daughter; one "natural" son of Abraham affirms that you can be adopted into his family on the basis of trusting in God as Abraham did (Rom. 4:16; Gal. 3:7–9). After Jesus's execution and resurrection, God promises that the Jewish people will now see all the nations finding blessing through them and along with them, as he has said to Abraham (Acts 3:25–26).[51] And it happens. People who trust in Jesus and thus belong to him do count as the offspring of Abraham and are among the heirs of his promise, whatever their race or social position or gender. In the giving of the Spirit, the blessing of Abraham comes to them, the blessing destined for all nations (Gal. 3:8, 14, 28–29). Unfortunately, they must then take seriously John the Baptizer's warning not to think that they are okay because they are Abraham's children (Matt. 3:9).

12:4. Yahweh says "go"; Abraham goes. "Whom . . . would these words not have disturbed? He reveals to him neither the place nor the country." But instead of asking, Abraham just goes.[52] The two occurrences of the verb "go" bookend vv. 1–4. The motif of obedience corresponds to this motif in the Noah story (cf. 6:22; 7:5). Including Lot in the company apparently does not conflict with the idea of doing as Yahweh has said; as Abraham's nephew, he counts as a member of Abraham's own household.[53] The laconic summary again does not convey the magnitude of the venture. It means another 400–500 miles of travel on perhaps a more demanding (and a more dangerous) journey, which involves climbing some mountain ridges and descending into some valleys. Toward the end, simply the descent from the Golan Heights into the depths of the Jordan Valley and up the other side of that valley into Canaan proper at the point now called the Bridge of Jacob's Daughter—if we imagine them taking that route—would be a nightmare as well as an excitement. Given that the ages in the Abraham story have moved closer to the ages that would fit the listeners' experience and that Abraham will be 175 when he dies (25:7), one could perhaps think of him as thirty-five or forty in literal terms at this point.

49. See MacDonald, "Did God Choose the Patriarchs?," 257, following Kaminsky, *Yet Jacob I Loved*.

50. Barth, *CD* 3.2:214.

51. On the both-and of Jews and Gentiles in Acts 3, see Mallen, "Genesis in Luke-Acts," 70–74.

52. Chrysostom, *Homilies on Genesis 18–45*, 244.

53. But see Vaughn, "'And Lot Went with Him.'"

12:5–8. A resumptive summary introduces the more detailed account of the more significant latter stages of the journey. It makes explicit that they indeed took everything they possessed. They have apparently done well in Harran. While they are not permitted to stay there, they are not required to leave anything behind, though the need to take Lot and his flocks and herds and tents will cause complications later (13:5–7). The other people Abraham takes are presumably his and Lot's staff, people such as herdsmen (13:7) with their families. It's quite an entourage, this wagon train. Only now is there reference to Canaan as their destination. The audience is invited to imagine them as having little clue where they are going until this point, a little like the original North American pioneers making the journey westward.

The narrative hastens on (v. 6a), bypassing unnamed the great city of Hazor, which overlooks the unnamed Lake Kinneret and guards this main route, and crossing unnamed the Jezreel valley. The pioneers climb into the Samarian highlands to Shechem, between the two mountains where Joshua will proclaim Yahweh's blessings and curses when he has enabled the Israelites to win their first key victories in Canaan (Josh. 8:30–35; cf. Deut. 11:29; 27:12). For the audience it would be the first major place of significance that the wagon train would reach. "Site" (*māqôm*) is the ordinary word for a place but also the word for a place of worship, and this connotation will apply in the expression "place at Shechem." At Tel Balata on the edge of the modern city of Nablus, the location of ancient Shechem, archaeologist George Ernest Wright reerected a "standing stone" that he inferred would have been there when Abraham arrived.[54] People who stand on the site are looking at something that Abraham would have looked at. What Abraham also saw was a great oak or terebinth that evidently had some religious significance. It was a Teacher's Oak, perhaps one under which a teacher would sit, as Deborah did (Judg. 4:5). One way or another, great trees were places where God met with people and places that thus became sacred (cf. Gen. 13:18; 14:13; 18:1; 35:8), though none of Genesis's references to trees specifically connect them with religious rites.[55]

The Canaanites being then in the country (v. 6b) means it was their sanctuary and their sacred tree. Like the reference to Ur, the assumption that Canaanites are now gone from this area implies a time after the Israelites' have gained complete control of Canaan. What we know from Genesis so far about the Canaanites is that on one hand they are under God's curse (9:25) and are due to be the servants of Shem (9:26–27), but on the other hand they have spread and flourished in the same way as other peoples (10:15–19). While in due course Yahweh will commission the Israelites to implement the curse, and some of the Canaanites will end up as their servants, in Genesis

54. See Wright, *Shechem*.
55. Cf. Bar, "Abraham's Trees."

that idea is on hold and relationships between Abraham's family and the Canaanites are friendly.

Yahweh appears to Abraham (12:7a) at this Canaanite sanctuary and near this tree. "And appeared" (*wayyērā̂*) comes from the verb meaning "see" (*rā'â*) and both are quite like the words for "teacher" (*môreh*) from the verb "teach" (*yārâ*). Against the background of the reality noted by v. 6b, then, Yahweh does not merely speak; he appears.[56] While he may have appeared to Abraham in a dream, as he does to Jacob (28:10–17), many references to his "appearing" involve only words (e.g., 17:1), and certainly the significance of the revelation is the promise Yahweh gives. Yahweh's appearing in Genesis is less spectacular than his appearing subsequently in the First Testament, and it is subordinate to his speaking.[57] In this context, then, the implication of the move from "said" (v. 1) to "appeared" (v. 7) is to highlight the further promise that follows. Yahweh is going to give this country to Abraham's eventual offspring. There is some inevitability about the need to give Abraham's descendants a country if they are to be a nation, let alone a big nation. "Offspring and land must go together; one without the other is useless and dangerous. How do you work land without children to fill it and care for it? How do you feed children without land? One without the other leads to war raids, poverty, starvation, and slavery" (KSG). And territory is even more integral to the notion of nationhood than to being a people. But why this country? The First Testament never answers that question, though it may hint at two reasons. One is its geographical location between the great empires of the Middle East (see Isa. 19:23–25). The other is that Yahweh is particularly disgusted with the Canaanites, or at least will be in due course, and Abraham's descendants will be the means of putting them down; Gen. 15:16 will explain why he cannot morally give the country to Abraham at the moment.

Having now a promise and a location (v. 7b), Abraham gets away with erecting his own altar in this Canaanite sanctuary. Constructing an altar is a proper response to Yahweh appearing. There's no reference to offering sacrifice on this altar, as is the case with most of the altars in Genesis (12:8; 13:18; 26:25; 33:20; 35:1–7; also Exod. 17:15). The appearing marks this location as a place where God has broken through from the heavens to the earth. It deserves preserving for that reason, and it deserves marking in light of the possibility that it has become a portal; God might break through here again.

Beth El and Ai (Ha'ay, "The Ruin"; v. 8) would come next—they precede Shechem in Josh. 7–8, when Joshua is coming in the opposite direction. This leg of Abraham's journey would take only a day or two. When Shechem becomes the first capital of northern Israel (Ephraim), Beth El will be its nearest sanctuary for festivals (1 Kings 12:25–32). If 28:19 indicates that Jacob actually

56. Cf. Chrysostom, *Homilies on Genesis 18–45*, 256–59.

57. Brown, "Manifest Diversity," 3–6.

gave the place its name, then Genesis here uses it in anticipation of that naming. "Spreading tents" suggests that the entourage settles here for a while, as the context suggests when the phrase recurs in 26:25; 35:21 (though not 33:19). There's no reference to Yahweh appearing or speaking here, but there is reference to Abraham worshiping. He names Yahweh here (metaphorically speaking—he didn't literally use the name, which hasn't been revealed yet). And he builds another altar. Archaeological investigation suggests that there was already a shrine here, so the scenario compares with that at Shechem. The collocation of building an altar and calling out with the name Yahweh points to another significance of altar building: worship of heart and voice is never enough. Building altars means that body as well as spirit is involved, partly so that other people can see the worship.[58] Both the proclaiming and the altar building would be an act of witness.[59] Naming Yahweh and building an altar also express the fact that Yahweh is present in this country and claims it, though the promise about blessing implies that this claim need not be exclusivist. Spreading tents, building an altar, and calling out with the name Yahweh[60] bring the story to a neat interim close.

58. Calvin, *Genesis*, 1:353–54.
59. Cf. Riecker, "Ein theologischer Ansatz."
60. On this expression, see the footnote and comment on 4:26.

10
The Imperiling of Sarah

(12:9–13:4)

Overview

While there is more of the country for Abraham to name Yahweh's name over, the opening words of 12:10 indicate the question on which this new section focuses. What is Abraham to do if life is not working out in the country Yahweh has promised?

- Move somewhere else?
- Be economical with the truth to save his skin even if it puts Sarah at risk?
- Hope to do well as a result of his economy?
- Bring trouble on the people who treat him well, and earn their rebuke?
- Go back home with his tail between his legs but with his profit?
- Get back to calling in Yahweh's name?

"Abram no sooner receives the promise than he has to leave it behind"[1]—or at least he chooses to do so. Has he forgotten the promise? Or has God? But eventually he gets back to Canaan with Sarah and Lot and all his possessions, and moves about through the southland (the Negev) to the last place where he had built an altar, and calls in Yahweh's name there, recovering the dynamic of 12:1–8.

"There have never been any theologians or other readers whom the passage before us would not have offended."[2] It is the kind of story where someone

1. Fretheim, "Genesis," 430.
2. Luther, *Genesis 6–14*, 288.

takes an action whose consequences they do not foresee, and another action whose consequences they do not foresee, so that they end up in a mess that would have made them not start down this road if they had known where it led. But in this instance of that dynamic, Yahweh intervenes and things work out all right for everyone, though that aspect of it offends theologians and other readers, too.

Translation

12:9 Abram moved on, gradually moving on[3] to the southland,[4] **10**but there was a famine[5] in the region,[6] and Abram went down to Miṣrayim to reside as an alien there, because the famine was severe in the region. **11**As he was near arriving in Miṣrayim, he said to Śaray his wife, "Here, please: I know[7] that you're a woman who's attractive in appearance. **12**When the Miṣrites see you and say, 'She's his wife,' they may kill me and let you live.[8] **13**Please say that you're my sister, in order that things may be good for me because of you and I myself may live, thanks to you." **14**So when Abram came to Miṣrayim, the Miṣrites saw that the woman was very attractive, **15**Parʿoh's officials[9] saw her and praised her to Parʿoh, and the woman was taken into Parʿoh's household.**16**And for Abram things were good because of her; he had flock, herd, donkeys, servants, maidservants, female donkeys, and camels.

17But Yahweh brought major afflictions on Parʿoh and his household on account of Śaray, Abram's wife. **18**Parʿoh called for Abram and said, "What is this that you've done to me? Why didn't you tell me that she was your wife? **19**Why is it that you said, 'She's my sister,' so I got her for myself as a wife? Now, here's your wife, get her and go." **20**Parʿoh gave men orders concerning him and sent him off, with his wife and all that he had. **13:1**So Abram went up from Miṣrayim, he and his wife and all that he had, and Lot with him, to the southland.

3. More literally but idiomatically, "moved on, in going and in moving on."

4. For *hannegbâ* the Vg, Aq, Sym, Tg have "to the south," suggesting simply a direction of travel, but the same expression means "to the southland" in 13:1; simple *negbâ* is the expression for "southward" in 13:14. Etymologically *negeb* suggests dry land, and the LXX has "the wilderness" each time. See Aberbach and Grossfeld, *Targum Onkelos*, 80–81.

5. More literally, "hunger."

6. *ʾEreṣ* is the ordinary word for a country, but it can refer to a narrower area (e.g., 13:6–7; 20:1; 22:2) or a broader one (e.g., 2:11–14) as well as to the earth as a whole (e.g., 10:32; 14:9, 22).

7. In other contexts Abraham's qatal verb could imply that he had "come to know," raising the question whether he had not noticed before (see, e.g., Gen. Rab. 40.4); but *yādaʿ* is commonly a quasi-stative (JM 112a).

8. The abb′a′ order ("kill me and you let-live") underlines the contrast between "me" and "you" and their respective fates.

9. In Egyptian, "Pharaoh" originally meant "great house," so the phrase is comparable to "White House officials."

2Now Abram was a very substantial man in livestock, in silver, and in
gold. 3In his movings on, he went from the southland as far as Bet-el,
as far as the site where his tent had been formerly, between Bet-el and
Haʿay, 4the site of the altar that he had made there at first. There Abram
called out with the name Yahweh.

Interpretation

In the MT the stories of the Egyptian escapade and of the subsequent parting from Lot form one unit, but they look like two separate stories dealing with interestingly opposite questions—the problem of scarcity and the problem of abundance. Both stories also link with the sections on either side, in 12:1–8 and 14:1–24. The medieval chapter division in English and Hebrew Bibles separates the scarcity story and the abundance story, but it does so rather early; 13:1 links backward, taking Abraham's family and the narrative back to where it started in 12:9. One could then see the narrative arc as ending at 13:1, yet 13:2–4 continues to relate to that arc in the sense that it takes Abraham and the audience back to where we were in 12:8. And one clue to the story's interpretation is a set of comparisons and contrasts with 12:1–8:

Genesis 12:1–8	Genesis 12:9–13:4
Yahweh tells Abraham to go (12:1)	Abraham continues to go (12:9)
Yahweh makes promises (12:2–3)	Yahweh is silent (12:10a)*
Abraham goes as Yahweh said (12:4)	Abraham goes (12:10b)
The Canaanites are there (12:6)	The Egyptians are there (12:10–13)
Yahweh appears and speaks (12:7)	Yahweh is silent but brings afflictions (12:14–17)
Abraham builds altars (12:7, 8)	Abraham builds nothing (12:18–20)
Abraham calls in Yahweh's name (12:8)	Abraham returns and calls in Yahweh's name (13:1–4)

*See Pickering, "Divine Silence."

If 12:1–8 is programmatic for Abraham's story, so is 12:9–13:4.[10]

The story starts from how God's promises may not find fulfillment in the way one might reasonably expect, from how people sometimes cope with that experience, and from how God sometimes deals with the consequences of their actions for the sake of his wider purpose. Abraham starts off by trying to do the responsible and right thing but gets himself into a mess, from which Yahweh rescues him without rebuking him. Genesis Rabbah 40.1 comments that Ps. 33:18–19 "refers to Abraham":

10. Cf. von Rad, *Genesis*, 164.

> Yahweh's eye is on people who revere him,
>   on people who wait for his commitment,
> To rescue them from death,
>   to keep them alive when food is gone. (Ps. 33:18–19)

It's not obvious that at this moment he is one who "reveres" or "waits"; the story does not aim to provide readers with either a good or a bad example of faithfulness. It's about God's faithfulness to his purpose, even when his people are unfaithful. It's less an account of a trial of Abraham's faith than an indication of how the God who gave Abraham his promises "now also watches over him and his wife, to the extent even of rescuing him from dangers which he has brought on himself."[11] Thus "may God be true, but every human being a liar" (Rom. 3:4, quoting Ps. 116:11).

As commonly happens in a story, the movement from question to answer is complicated. Further, the narrative often does not comment on what people are thinking. Two pieces of speech dominate the story, one by Abraham, one by Pharaoh, and both look for a response, but neither gets a response in words, only in action. One must see what can be inferred from their actions, which may show what the people are thinking. The questions and the responses and their possible implications then appear:

Question: What is Abraham to do about the food shortage?
Response: Take everyone to Egypt.
Implication: There was nothing wrong with this action.

Question: Unexpected problem: What's he to do about the danger there?
Response: Say Sarah is his sister.
Implication: Sarah agrees.

Question: Unexpected problem: What's he to do about Sarah being put in the harem?
Response: Collect the money.
Implication: He can congratulate himself and thank God.

Question: Unexpected problem: What's he to do about Pharaoh's rebuke?
Response: Take the money and run.
Implication: He needs to get back to the way things were.

The lack of overt response to the words of Abraham and Pharaoh means that their words stand with force in their own right, inviting a response from

11. Dillmann, *Genesis*, 2:17.

the audience: What do you think of what Abraham says? What would you say if you were Sarah? What do you think of what Pharaoh says? What would you say if you were Abraham?

The story anticipates the later story of Abraham's descendants' stay in Egypt. Again a shortage of food will drive people to go there. Again they will be resident aliens there rather than citizens (cf. 15:13). Again they will bring affliction on Pharaoh and his household. Again Pharaoh will send them off and they will go up from Egypt enriched. If Israelites in Egypt knew this story, it could encourage them to see that their ancestors have been this way before and Yahweh has made things work out. For a later audience that colludes with the storyteller in listening through the story in Exodus as if they don't know the outcome, this earlier story makes the same promise to them.

12:9–10. Abraham and his company do not settle for long near Beth El. In v. 8 "spreading tents" suggested stopping for a while, while "moved on, gradually moving on" implies setting up the encampment at a series of different places. It might suggest that they are simply moving around as nomadic shepherds do. But they need to enter into symbolic if discreet possession of Canaan as a whole. It's another thirty miles from Beth El to Mamre, where Abraham will settle in Gen. 13, and another thirty to Beer Sheba in the Negev, where he will settle later. Beer Sheba will mark the traditional southernmost boundary of the country in Israelite times, but there is neither biblical nor archaeological indication of there being a town at Beer Sheba in Abraham's day. And neither Mamre nor Beer Sheba is mentioned, as Dan has not been mentioned when they arrive in Canaan, and as Jerusalem is unmentioned as they make the journey south.

But now there is a different reason not to settle (v. 10a). Food shortage is a recurring issue in the First Testament (e.g., 26:1; 42:5; 43:1; Ruth 1:1). The mountain country where Shechem, Beth El, and Mamre are located (which is also the main area where Abraham's descendants will eventually settle and is thus where many people in the audience live) is marginal land. The area roughly corresponds to the "West Bank" or the Palestinian territory. Water rights are still an issue here. The east side of the mountain ridge gets minimal rain and supports only shepherding; in First Testament times much of the west side was forest, and even the area where one might grow some wheat does not get rain consistently enough for people to be sure of a crop every year. In order to call this a land flowing with milk and sweetness, one would need to include the plains. Even so, it is sometimes reasonable to see a poor harvest as something extraordinary that might happen as God's chastisement for the people's waywardness (e.g., 2 Sam. 21; 1 Kings 8:35–37). And the further south Abraham goes, the drier the land becomes. Yet food shortage fits ill with the promises Yahweh has made to Abraham.

So what is Abraham to do? Is Yahweh testing him?[12] The temptation to act on the basis of not trusting comes after a great act of trust.[13] But Genesis makes no comment on what God is doing in letting the shortage strike Abraham nor on whether Abraham is doing the right thing. Looking back from 1 Kings 8:35–37, one can think that he might have talked to Yahweh about it. Yet there is no reference to calling in Yahweh's name between 12:8 and 13:4.

The repetition of reference to the food shortage (v. 10b) implies that they have tried to cope with it for a while, but eventually the situation becomes impossible. In good times the Canaanites might be prepared to barter grain with Abraham, but perhaps not in tough times. So Abraham's family and staff have nothing to eat. What is Abraham to do? Ironically, before Yahweh summons Abraham to Canaan and makes his promises, Abraham was living in a region where water was not so much of an issue because of the presence of the two great Mesopotamian rivers. The Nile likewise made Egypt's position less vulnerable than Canaan's (the Egyptians viewed rain as a second-best substitute for the Nile). It made Egypt a natural direction to look during a food shortage, as it will be in the Joseph story. One "goes down" from mountainous Canaan to Egypt and "goes up" from Egypt to Canaan. A letter from an Egyptian border official in about Moses's time refers to Bedouin-type Edomites seeking entry to Egypt "to keep them alive and to keep their cattle alive."[14] To speak of "residing as an alien" (*gûr*, with the noun *gēr*) in Egypt presupposes the position of people who live in a country that is not their own, who are not citizens. It is the position of Abraham's people in Canaan (23:4; 35:27; more generally Exod. 6:4) but also in the various other places where they go (e.g., Gen. 21:23; 26:3).

12:11–16. Perhaps Abraham has not thought through how things will work out. If in real terms Abraham is the equivalent of thirty to forty, Sarah might be thirty to thirty-five and maybe looks better than the average woman of that age because she has not gone through a half dozen pregnancies or more.[15]

Is there any reason for Abraham's fear of the Egyptians (v. 12)? Similar words about killing and letting live recur in Exod. 1:16, 22, so maybe Abraham is being realistic[16]—at least to a later audience it might seem so. Yet 1QapGen 19 has the danger revealed to Abraham in a dream,[17] which excuses Abraham from responsibility for deceit,[18] makes Sarah cry, and has Pharaoh indeed minded to kill Abraham. But in Genesis itself, Pharaoh's later protest in vv.

12. So Rashi, *Br'šyt*, 120.
13. Cf. Brueggemann, *Genesis*, 126.
14. See *ANET* 259.
15. Cf. Calvin, *Genesis*, 1:361.
16. Cf. van Dijk-Hemmes, *Double Voice of Her Desire*, 140.
17. *DSS* 1:38–43.
18. Cf. van Ruiten, "Book of Jubilees and the Genesis Apocryphon," 564.

18–19 hardly supports Abraham's fear.[19] What is its basis? Is Abraham simply fearful of the Other? It's said that men are ambivalent about their wives' attractiveness and sexuality. It makes a man feel good to have other men fancy his wife, but it also feels a bit dangerous.[20] If Abraham feels this ambivalence, it will turn out that he is justified, though his action perhaps implies that he doesn't take into account God's promise in v. 3. He evidently cannot assume patriarchal authority over Sarah (it's not the last story indicating that); he has to be polite and respectful to win her cooperation. He needs to say "please" more than once.[21]

Abraham's scheme (v. 13) involves being economical with the truth in either the narrower or the looser sense. "Sister" can suggest "sweetheart" (e.g., Song 4:9–10),[22] and later Abraham will claim that Sarah is his (half) sister and she will confirm it (20:1–18), so maybe he is revealing only one of the relevant facts. But we don't know if they are both lying on that later occasion. Genesis never tells us her parents' identity. And Genesis may look at Abraham (or Abraham might look at himself) the same way Exodus looks at the midwives in Exod. 2:15–22: one does not owe truthfulness to people who are using their power in an untruthful way. But does he not recognize that his scheme for protecting himself imperils Sarah? It will transpire that things go very well for Abraham. But in the first instance, by "things being good," Abraham simply means that he won't get killed (the same parallelism comes in Jer. 38:20).[23] Perhaps he doesn't imagine simply surrendering Sarah to some other man but being able as her brother to fend off suitors.[24] Sarah apparently agrees; her "silent acquiescence . . . contrasts markedly with the enterprising initiatives of the women who birthed the Exodus narrative, those shrewd quick-thinking midwives, and its celebrator, the daringly outspoken Miriam."[25] She is "faced with a Sophie's Choice" and "she did what she had to do. If sleeping with the enemy would save Abraham and get them through the famine, so be it."[26]

Events confirm Abraham's assessment of his wife's attractiveness and its results (vv. 14–15).[27] If Abraham isn't very patriarchal, Sarah needs to deal with the patriarchal state of the world in general and of politics in particular. Perhaps Abraham had not worked out that it would be Pharaoh's staff who took a fancy to Sarah on their master's behalf. An important person like a

19. Cf. De La Torre, *Genesis*, 150.
20. See Exum, "Who's Afraid of 'The Endangered Ancestress'?"
21. Cf. Davidson, "Genesis Matriarchs Engage Feminism," 170.
22. Cf. Sarna, *Genesis*, 95.
23. Cf. Sarna, *Genesis*, 95, and the footnote to v. 12b.
24. Cf. Wenham, *Genesis 1–15*, 288.
25. McKinlay, "Who's/Whose Sarah?," 141.
26. Visotzky, *Genesis of Ethics*, 31.
27. 1QapGen 20 expatiates at some length on the assessment by Pharaoh's staff.

pharaoh keeps a harem as a mark of his status, and Sarah must join it. Maybe she never actually meets Pharaoh, perhaps because she will need a six-month beauty treatment like Esther,[28] though at least moving into Pharaoh's household will give her the chance to develop a distaste for Egyptian idolatry, garlic, and onions.[29] A poem attributed to Ephrem imagines Sarah's own opinions on this entire episode.[30] But the story does not look at things from her viewpoint, and neither does Abraham or Pharaoh.[31] It does indicate an ambiguity about both the men she is involved with, in the way they treat her. And "the confrontation between Abram and Pharaoh does not end with the defeat of the wicked and the triumph of the upright. The central protagonists remain morally ambiguous."[32]

Abraham profits from the scheme (v. 16). He is treated as his sister's guardian and receives the kinds of wedding gifts that a wealthy man can give. "Flocks" includes sheep and goats; "herds" includes oxen, bulls, and cows; (male) donkeys carry things; female donkeys carry people; camels carry both. Camels appear several times in Genesis, but there is little other evidence for them in Canaan until after Moses's day, so they may be another result of the story being told in terms that work for later listeners. Either way, they are a marker of distinctive prosperity.

12:17–13:1. What are Abraham and Sarah thinking? And what actually happens in the harem? We don't discover the answers to these questions, but we have some indication of what Yahweh is thinking. It won't be the last time in Genesis that Yahweh is absent during trouble but then intervenes.[33] He is not prepared to surrender Sarah, as Abraham is. Sarah is integral to the plan Yahweh has formulated, which he has announced in 12:2. Genesis draws attention to the real point about Sarah's relationship to Abraham. She is his wife, whether or not she is his sister. "Afflictions" is nicely the term that accompanies reference to food shortage in 1 Kings 8:35–37, with a hint that Abraham has brought trouble on the Egyptians in order to try to resolve the trouble he is in, though the bulk of occurrences of the term come in Lev. 13–14 to describe the skin ailment commonly termed leprosy. It wouldn't be surprising if these afflictions are venereal disease, which would inhibit sexual activity and thus protect Sarah.[34] But more scarily for an Egyptian, the next time the Torah refers to an "affliction," it is the death of Egypt's firstborn (Exod. 11:1). And like that trouble, this trouble comes because God acts, not

28. Cf. Jerome, *Hebrew Questions on Genesis*, 44.
29. So Ephrem, *Genesis*, 149.
30. See Brock, "Creating Women's Voices."
31. Cf. van Dijk-Hemmes, *Double Voice*, 136–45.
32. B. Eichler, "On Reading Genesis 12:10–20," 27.
33. M. Jacobs, *Gender, Power, and Persuasion*, 87.
34. Cf. Ibn Ezra, *Genesis*, 156; and at length, 1QapGen 20, which also reassures the reader that Pharaoh did not approach Sarah or have sex with her (so also Tg. Ps.-J.).

because wrongdoing "naturally" has its outworking. As usual, adversity for a leader means adversity for his household, as blessing for a leader means blessing for his household. Yahweh is evidently not troubled about the "unfairness" involved in his treatment of Pharaoh and the Egyptians. There are bigger issues at stake. And presumably the afflictions disappear once the Egyptians have sent away Abraham and Sarah.

We do discover what Pharaoh is thinking (vv. 18–19). While Gen. 12 has not previously referred to the call of Abraham, it now does, but it is Pharaoh who does the calling. We don't discover how Pharaoh learns the fuller truth about Sarah's status (contrast 20:1–3). We do see Pharaoh doing the right thing, which is also the thing that is in his interest. "The Egyptian emerges rather saintly, but Abram, the one in whom the Egyptians and other nations are to be blessed, appears rather sinister."[35] Indeed, he brings curse rather than blessing.

So Pharaoh sends Abraham off (12:20–13:1), as Yahweh God sent off Adam and Eve from his garden (3:23). They return to the southland,[36] to where things started to go wrong, and to where the story can get back on track. Genesis draws attention to the combined presence of Abraham and his possessions and Sarah and Lot, as in 12:5.

13:2–4. Abraham's livestock include the ones given him by Pharaoh as a wedding gift for Sarah. Perhaps the same applies to the silver and gold,[37] if the anticipation of the exodus holds further: see Exod. 11:2, just after the reference to affliction (also 3:22; 12:35; also Gen. 20:16; and the description of wedding gifts in 24:53). Getting back to the southland, he resumes his Bedouin-like "moving on" but retraces his footsteps back to where he was in 12:8, back to the altar he had set up there, and back to doing his own calling, with Yahweh's name,[38] as he had earlier called out there. Yes, the story is back on track.

35. Hamilton, *Genesis 1–17*, 385.

36. After teaching Babylonian arithmetic and astronomy to the Egyptians, Josephus says (*Ant.* 1.8.2).

37. So 1QapGen adds silver and gold in 12:16.

38. On this expression, see the footnote and the comment on 4:26.

11
The Scarcity of Land

(13:5–18)

Overview

In a sense, the problem in this next story is the problem of abundance: both Abraham and Lot have many flocks and herds and people. But in another sense, it is again the problem of scarcity: there are not enough resources to fulfill the existing needs. What is Abraham to do when the resultant twofold problem issues in conflict within the extended family? The answer is, split, and be generous: let Lot choose the land he wants, and Abraham will go elsewhere. That generosity solves the problem of conflict. But Abraham's action again has unforeseen consequences. One is that Lot chooses to go and live near the wicked city of Sodom. Another is that he has left Abraham without a possible heir.[1] But yet another is a renewed and more explicit promise by Yahweh to Abraham.

Translation

5Now Lot, who went with Abram, also had flock and herd and tents, **6**and
the region couldn't support them living as one, because their property
was great. So they couldn't live as one, **7**and there was argument be-
tween the herdsmen of Abram's livestock and the herdsmen of Lot's
livestock; the Kenaʿanite (the Perizzite)[2] was then living in the region.
8So Abram said to Lot, "Please, there mustn't be arguing between me
and you and between my herdsmen and your herdsmen, because we're

1. Cf. Helyer, "Separation of Abraham and Lot."
2. The *w* is explanatory (see the footnote to 4:4).

men who are brothers.[3] **9**The entire country is before you, isn't it? Part
from me, please: if you go north, I'll go south, but if you go south, I'll
go north."[4] **10**Lot lifted his eyes and looked at the entire Yarden area,
that it was well-watered, all of it, before Yahweh devastated Sedom and
Amorah—like Yahweh's garden, like the country of Miṣrayim, as you
come to Ṣoʿar; **11**and Lot chose for himself the entire Yarden area.

So Lot moved on east,[5] and they parted, each from his brother.
12Whereas Abram lived in the country of Kenaʿan, Lot lived in the towns
in the area and put up his tents near Sedom. **13**Now the people of
Sedom were bad, wrongdoers in relation to Yahweh, greatly.

14But Yahweh said[6] to Abram after Lot parted from him, "Lift your
eyes, please, and look, from the site where you are, to the north, to the
south, to the east, and to the west,[7] **15**because the entire country that
you're looking at—I will give it to you and to your offspring, through the
ages.[8] **16**I will make your offspring like the earth's dirt, so if a person
could count the earth's dirt, your offspring will also be counted. **17**Set off,
walk about in the country, through its length and its width, because I will
give it to you."

18Abram moved his tents and came and lived by the Mamre Oaks,[9]
which were at Hebron, and built an altar for Yahweh there.

Interpretation

Like 12:10–13:4, this narrative takes off from 12:1–9. Yahweh's promise of blessing is finding fulfillment, but once again Abraham faces a situation in which Yahweh's promise about the land is not working out. In the course of the story, Yahweh reaffirms that promise, and Abraham again spreads his tents by some impressive trees and again builds an altar, this time near Mamre, which he must have passed as he moved to the southland (12:9), but it was not mentioned.

The story also parallels 12:10–13:4 in that it tells of a problem that Abraham must face; this time the specific carryover from 12:1–9 is not Sarah but Lot. It once again recounts how Abraham proposes a risky solution to the problem

3. Literally, "men, brothers": in the apposition, the second noun more closely defines the first (GKC 131b). "Brothers" has the broad sense of "relatives": so also in, e.g., Gen. 14; 16; 24; 31.

4. Literally, left, right, right, left, because Hebrew thinking often orients by imagining one is standing looking east.

5. Literally, "from the front": see previous note, and the footnote to 2:8 (also 3:24; 11:2; 12:8).

6. The word order with the subject coming before the verb is unusual and draws attention to the newness of this subsection.

7. Here Yahweh uses a different way of referring to directions—toward Mount Zaphon, toward the Negev, in front of you, and toward the [Mediterranean] sea.

8. Literally, "to the age."

9. Targum Onq. has "Mamre Plains," Tg. Neof. "Vision Plain," Tg. Ps.-J. "Mamre Vison" (see the footnote to 12:6; also Maher, *Targum Pseudo-Jonathan: Genesis*, 55).

that arises. Once again Abraham acts without consulting Yahweh, though there would hardly be any suggestion that he acted wrongly. Once again his solution, while risky for Abraham, is also (perhaps less obviously) risky for the one to whom he proposes it; the narrator eventually draws attention to the risk. Once again, Yahweh intervenes on Abraham's behalf. Once again the story closes with Abraham moving and reaching out to Yahweh.

The story also prepares the way for the next chapter (see 14:12) and for Gen. 18–19. It breaks into five paragraphs:

The problem (13:5–7)

Abraham proposes a solution (13:8–9)

Lot accepts the proposal, but the narrator draws attention to a snag (13:10–13)

Yahweh renews and expands on his promise to Abraham (13:14–17)

Abraham moves to live near Mamre (13:18)

Genesis tells us little about the quarrel itself (Tgs. Neof. and Ps.-J. make up for this lack), which puts the focus on Abraham's solution, Lot's decision, and Yahweh's promise that follows.

It's great when brothers and sisters, aunts and uncles, can live as one (Ps. 133), but it's not always possible. When there's a problem, the answer may be to give up trying and to part amicably, which may work out fine (Acts 15:36–40) but may not. In the preceding story, Abraham perhaps tried to do the responsible but risky thing and got himself into a mess, out of which Yahweh rescued him without rebuking him. In this story, Abraham tries to do the responsible but risky thing and thereby gives Lot the chance to get himself into a mess, out of which Yahweh will rescue him, and Abraham finds Yahweh reaffirming his commitment to him. Because of the way things work out, however, does Abraham too easily let Lot go down to Sodom? The story "depicts the tragedy associated with separation from the family of Abram."[10]

13:5–7. Both branches of Nahor's family have increased their livestock and tents (i.e., the families that live in them),[11] and within this extended family, the relationship between Abraham and Lot is a little ambiguous. Abraham is Lot's uncle and guardian, but Lot is evidently also the head of his own household and entourage, no doubt partly inherited from his father, Haran. "As long as Abraham and Lot were not too rich, their shepherds were able to get along easily"; but flourishing brings its problems (a story set in Europe would then decide things by means of a duel).[12] The Beth El area where the two companies are living is too confined for them. Towns such as Beth El are

10. Coats, *Genesis*, 118. See further Rickett, "Rethinking."

11. Skinner, *Genesis*, 251.

12. Gunkel, *Genesis*, 173.

Canaanite settlements, in the broad sense of the word "Canaanite" as denoting the pre-Israelite inhabitants of the land in general. Perizzite is a more specific term. It usually comes only in strings of descriptions of those pre-Israelite inhabitants (e.g., 15:20), and it is similar to a word for villagers (*pərāzîm*, peraz-ites). But the three times when it occurs outside of those strings of terms all suggest a geographical link with the Beth El-Shechem area (see 34:30; Josh. 17:15; Judg. 1:4–5).[13] The term thus fits here as a more specific description of the Canaanites who live in this region. Such settled peoples (as opposed to groups that focused more on shepherding) controlled the areas around their towns and pastured their own flocks there. The area further away from their towns to the east led down the mountain slopes of wilderness land, with less grass and less water (that's why the towns were not there). One can see how Abraham and Lot could have a problem.

13:8–9. So Abraham proposes a solution for the problem over grazing. Lot is as much an heir to Yahweh's promise about the land as Abraham is. He can go north to the Shiloh, Shechem, or Samaria region, in which case Abraham will go south down the mountain ridge to Mamre or Beer Sheba, or it can be the other way around. Lot can choose. Twice Abraham says "please," as he did to Sarah. Does it indicate that Abraham is a wimp who doesn't like conflict (Gen. 16 will support that idea), or is he just being polite? Is he being generous, or does he simply need to solve a problem? Is his offer an expression of his trust in God's promise? There is no more indication of that possibility than there is of his having a failure of trust in 12:10. In this story, Yahweh's affirmation of his promise follows on his suggestion to Lot rather than being the basis of it.

13:10–13. Perhaps, then, "with typical ancient Near Eastern obsequiousness, Abram defers to his nephew to decide which portion of the land to take," which should lead to Lot deferring to Abraham (cf. the courteous negotiation in Gen. 23). But "shockingly, he agrees to make the selection himself" and promptly chooses the Jordan Valley, "leaving the dry and rocky hill country to his uncle."[14] Lot does not look either north or south but east. Beth El is near a crossroads on the ridge; one road wends its way down into the Jordan Valley and another wends its way toward the Mediterranean, as it does today (nowadays Jerusalem is the best-known crossroads, but this change issued from Jerusalem's own development as Israel's capital). In the wilderness to the east shepherds would have less competition, but what strikes Lot is that getting to the bottom of the precipitous mountain slopes (the land falls 4000 feet in ten or fifteen miles) means reaching country watered by springs and by the Jordan itself. It is the southernmost, wide, flat-bottomed vale through which the Jordan runs as it reaches the Dead Sea. Taking "the Jordan area" to

13. Cf. Driver, *Genesis*, 152.

14. Arnold, *Genesis*, 140.

denote this vale makes geographical sense. It would be odd to think that the term included the Dead Sea itself (cf. Deut. 34:3). With regard to the Dead Sea area, the narrator might imply a contrast between the landscape at this time and in the narrator's and audience's day, when things are rather arid, though even in the audience's day there were the fabulous oases at Ein Feshka and Ein Gedi ("the best place in the world and . . . a remnant of Paradise")[15] as there are now, and there are freshwater springs southeast of the Dead Sea. But maybe Sodom, Gomorrah, and Zoʿar were north of the Dead Sea (there is no consensus on their location), and the area around Jericho which people come to when they go down that road from Beth El is an oasis, then and now. One can follow Lot's gaze as he sees and realizes how fantastic the landscape is.[16] It is so well watered, which is one of the first things any settler must think about, especially a shepherd. It reminds one of Egypt, which was such a contrast with the Negev. As Egypt has the Nile as its water supply, this land has the Jordan and the springs. Indeed, it's like Yahweh's garden! That expression did not come in Gen. 2–3, but those chapters were talking about something you could call Yahweh's garden. And whether or not this comparison is Lot's perspective, it is that of the narrator and the audience, especially if they read Genesis sequentially. In speaking of devastation (13:10), the narrator is reminding the audience of the deluge story, as well as anticipating Gen. 18–19 with its references to Sodom and Gomorrah. The area around Zoʿar also gets mention as favored because it is going to be significant later (see 19:22).

Logically enough, then, Lot elects to move down into the Jordan Valley (vv. 11–12). If Sodom is farther south, his moving there presumably implies that in those days it is just as hospitable as Jericho. But is he thereby moving out of the promised land? And doesn't he know what sort of people live there (v. 13)? The description of them recalls the description of the entire world before the deluge and thus provides a further anticipation of the story that will follow in Gen. 18–19. How strange that this Paradise-like land should be inhabited by such bad people![17] Targum Onq. specifies that their wrongdoing involves their use of money and of their bodies, which fits the description in Gen. 18, with its pointing to the cry of the oppressed and to sexual waywardness (Tg. Neof. has sexual sin, murder, and idolatry, which matches the regular Jewish definition of basic sins, and Tg. Ps.-J. combines both expansions).[18] It will turn out that "his 'seeing' and his knowing are too limited."[19] Lot is "one of

15. Luther, *Genesis 6–14*, 368 (one wonders how he knew, but perhaps it is just an inference from the reference to Yahweh's garden).

16. Cf. Westermann, *Genesis 12–36*, 177.

17. Luther, *Genesis 6–14*, 345.

18. Cf. McNamara, *Targum Neofiti: Genesis*, 49; Maher, *Targum Pseudo-Jonathan: Genesis*, 54; also Willet, *Hexapla in Genesin & Exodum*, 128–29.

19. Fretheim, *Abraham*, 67.

those people destined repeatedly to make bad choices."[20] He has and he raises "boundary issues."[21]

13:14–17. As is often the case, the narrative does not make the link with this next paragraph explicit. It leaves the listeners to think about possible links. Is Yahweh responding with generosity to Abraham's generosity? Is he responding to Abraham's risk-taking? Is he responding to Lot's taking what looks like superb land? Is he simply reaffirming the promise in a way that relates to his own purpose? Or is he implying that Lot has just forfeited any share in the land promised to Abraham?[22] His formulation of the promise is markedly different from that in 12:1–3, where Yahweh makes no commitment regarding land (that comes only in 12:7). Here his words follow on what proceeds. Lot has lifted his eyes and looked; now Yahweh invites Abraham to lift his eyes and look (this expression comes only here in Gen. 1–17). Yahweh speaks politely ("please") as Abraham did to Sarah and to Lot (only four times does God say "please," each time when asking someone to believe or do something outrageous—cf. 15:5; 22:2; Exod. 11:2).[23] Yahweh refers to the "site" where Abraham is; that word comes in Gen. 1–17 only in connection with the places where Abraham worships, at Shechem and at Beth El. As Abraham had pointed out that the entire country was before Lot (there is no better place to look in all four directions than the mountain ridge near Beth El),[24] so Yahweh draws Abraham's attention to the entire country before him. Abraham invited Lot to think about north and south, up and down the mountain range, and Lot looked east; Yahweh invites Abraham to look north, south, east, and west. As was the case with Abraham's words to Lot, so Yahweh's words engage with listeners' knowledge or imagination. In speaking of the points of the compass, his words picture mountains, valley, and sea (the word for "west" is "sea," and the word for "north" is "Zaphon," the great mountain to the far north). Abraham draws Lot's attention to the entire country because he is prepared to give it to Lot; Yahweh draws Abraham's attention to it because he is prepared to give it to Abraham and to his offspring as a permanent possession (*ʿad ʿôlām*), to last as long as his pact with Noah. Yahweh is matching Abraham's generosity but vastly exceeding it. One can imagine this promise causing some puzzlement and heartache for (say) the much-reduced Ephraimite state on the eve of its actual demise in 722, or the

20. Blenkinsopp, *Abraham*, 51. But Gen. 13 leaves this point understated, and in some readings his character gets worse as time goes by (see Rickett, "Creating an Unrighteous Outsider"), while in some he becomes more righteous; cf. Lundbom, "Parataxis."

21. Sabo, "Blurred Boundaries," 433.

22. Cf. Qimchi, *Genesis*, on the verse.

23. Hamilton, *Genesis 1–17*, 394.

24. In 1QapGen 21.8–12 God tells Abraham to go to Ramat Hazor, north of Beth El, from which he has the best view in all four directions, and it is from here that God issues his promise.

much-reduced Judahite state later, or the little Babylonian and then Persian province in the sixth or fifth century. But it might also inspire hope for them.

Yahweh promises the land to Abraham's "offspring" (v. 15). In Gal. 3:16 Paul takes up the fact that the word is singular (Hb. *zeraʿ*; Gk. *sperma*), which fits the fact that *the* offspring of Abraham is the one person Jesus. The Hebrew word (*zeraʿ*) is collective; it is used just once to refer to seeds for sowing (1 Sam. 8:15), though in everyday life that usage was surely common. The Greek word is also commonly collective, though the plural reference to seeds for sowing is more common in the NT. But no one would think that the singular word in Hebrew or in Greek would denote one offspring as opposed to many. Like much of the NT's use of the Scriptures, Paul is starting from something he knows (one descendant of Abraham was key to the fulfillment of God's promises) and working back to identify something that must have been in the back of God's mind in making this promise and in inspiring this particular Scripture.

Many offspring will be needed to occupy this land, and they will be given, too (v. 16). It's more common for dirt to be a discouraging image (cf. 18:27), but it can be encouraging (28:14; Num. 23:10). This commitment, too, would inspire puzzlement and heartache and hope. There's some irony about this promise when size has been the problem that gave rise to the quarrel.[25] Perhaps we should put the logic the other way around. Don't worry about not having enough land because there are too many people. There will be much land, and therefore there can be many people.

So Abraham, too, is to set off (v. 17) and move around the country some more, both length and width. It is not merely so that he can exercise his own imagination, like Moses viewing the promised land. It is by walking across a tract of land that one takes possession of it.[26]

13:18. The step Abraham takes as a consequence is tiny. It's really his offspring who will cash Yahweh's check. Abraham simply moves again southward, halfway to Beer Sheba, and settles for a while at Mamre, which is then identified with the later Hebron. The Mamre Oaks are two or three miles north of Hebron itself, according to which tradition you follow. Mamre appears only in Genesis; in Genesis Hebron appears only to explain the location of Mamre to a later generation.

25. Westermann, *Genesis 12–36*, 172.
26. Cf. Gen. Rab. 41.10; Gitay, "Promise."

12
The Empire Strikes Back

(14:1–24)

Overview

Genesis 10–13 first told of developments in the audience's entire world, following on humanity's new start after the deluge, and then segued into a focus on Abraham's family. Genesis 14 returns for a moment to that broader world, because Abraham is drawn into an involvement outside the family. The story's question then arises: what will happen when the empire strikes back?

"The empire" is a coalition of kings. As is the case in Gen. 10–11, not all their kingdoms can be identified, though they include two that appeared there, Shinar (which was the starting point of Nimrod's empire) and Elam (cf. 10:10, 22; 11:2). But the phrase "the empire strikes back" sometimes refers to the subjects of an empire asserting themselves against the imperial power, and in Gen. 14 both references apply. Five city-states in the Dead Sea area have lived under the yoke of imperial authority for over a decade but then rebel (strike back 1). The imperial coalition engages in a wide-ranging and successful campaign to reassert its authority (strike back 2). But it makes the mistake of including among its captives from Sodom someone from Abraham's family, which leads to Abraham pursuing the coalition force and defeating it (strike back 3). On his return, Abraham is acknowledged by the priest-king of Salem (to whom he pays a tithe of his plunder) and by the king of Sodom (to whom he insists on returning the rest, less expenses).

Translation

1In the time of Amrapel king of Šinʿar, Aryok king of Ellasar,[1]
Kedorlaʿomer king of Elam, and Tidʿal king of nations, **2**they[2] did battle
with Bera king of Sedom, Birša king of Amorah, Šinʾab king of Admah,
Šemʾeber king of Ṣeboyim, and the king of Bela (i.e., Ṣoʿar). **3**All these[3]
joined together in the Siddim Vale (i.e., the Salt Sea). **4**For twelve years
they had served Kedorlaʿomer, but the thirteenth year, they
rebelled.

5In the fourteenth year, Kedorlaʿomer and the kings who were with
him came and struck down the Repaʾites at Ašterot Qarnayim, the
Zuzites at Ham, the Emim at Qiryatayim Plain, **6**and the Horites in their
highland, Seʿir as far as Paʾran Oak, which is near the wilderness. **7**They
went back and came to Decision Spring (i.e., Qadeš), and struck down
the entire area[4] of the Amaleqites, and also the Amorites who were living
in Ḥaṣaṣon Tamar.

8Then the king of Sedom, the king of Amorah, the king of Admah, the
king of Ṣeboyim, and the king of Bela (i.e., Ṣoʿar) went out, and lined
up with them for battle in the Siddim Vale: **9**Kedorlaʿomer king of Elam,
Tidal king of nations, Amrapel king of Šinʿar, and Aryok king of Ellasar,
four kings against the five. **10**Now the Siddim Vale was pit after pit[5] of
bitumen; the kings of Sedom and Amorah fled and fell into them,[6] while
the rest fled to the highland. **11**They[7] got all the property of Sedom and
Amorah and all their food, and went.

12So they got Lot and his property, the son of Abram's brother, and
went; he was living in Sedom. **13**Someone who escaped came and told
Abram the Ibrite. He was dwelling by the Oaks of Mamre the Amorite,
brother of Eškol and brother of Aner; these were holders of a pact with
Abram.

14So Abram heard that his brother had been taken captive, and he un-
leashed[8] his trained men (people born in his household),[9] 318 of them,
and went in pursuit as far as Dan. **15**He and his servants split up against
them by night, struck them down, and pursued them as far as Ḥobah,
which is north of Dammeseq. **16**He took back all the property, and took

1. Sym, the Vg have Pontus; 1QapGen similarly has Cappadocia.

2. The syntax in vv. 1–2 breaks down; "they" denotes all four kings, as, e.g., the Vg makes clear.

3. That is, the kings in v. 2.

4. MT *śədēh*; the LXX implies *śārê*, "officers."

5. Literally, "pits, pits."

6. For *nāpal* denoting a voluntary "fall," see, e.g., 17:3; 24:64; 33:4; in Jer. 38:19 it means flee to/take refuge (Hamilton, *Genesis 1–17*, 403).

7. That is, the four kings in v. 9.

8. *Wayyāreq* is hiphil from *rûq* or *rîq*, which would mean more literally "emptied out" but can refer to drawing a sword; here it would involve metonymy (Tal, *Genesis*, 114*). The SP has *wayyādeq* (implying the easy confusion of *d* and *r* in Hebrew) from a hypothesized *dûq*, meaning "number" or "muster" (cf. the LXX, Vg; *HALOT*, *DCH*).

9. The phrase in brackets explains the rare expression *ḥănîkāyw* (Gunkel, *Genesis*, 277).

back both his brother Lot and his property, and also the women and the
company.
17The king of Sedom went out to meet him after he got back from
striking down Kedorlaʿomer and the kings that were with him, in the
Šaveh Vale[10] (i.e., the King's Vale), **18**and Melki-ṣedeq king of Śalem
brought out bread and wine (he was priest[11] of El Elyon) **19**and blessed
him:

> Blessed be Abram by El Elyon,
> generator of heavens and earth,
> **20**And El Elyon be blessed,
> who has unshielded[12] your attackers into your hand.

He gave him a tenth of everything.
21The king of Sedom said to Abram, "Give me the people but take
the property for yourself." **22**But Abram said to the king of Sedom, "I am
raising my hand to Yahweh,[13] El Elyon, generator of heavens and earth:
23'From a thread to a boot strap,[14] if I get anything of yours. . . .'[15] So you
will not say, 'I'm the one who made Abram wealthy.' **24**Nothing for me,[16]
only what the boys have eaten, and the share of the men who went with
me, Aner, Eškol, and Mamre—they may get their share."

Interpretation

Only in this chapter does the Abraham narrative refer to events and nations in the international context. In theory it might enable one to relate the Genesis narrative to a more specific context in the time before Moses, but actually we know virtually nothing about the individuals or the peoples involved in the story. It is "a world of its own."[17] Presumably the audience suffers from the same ignorance. The narrator either has some historical information that we cannot control, or created the narrative out of an inspired imagination to make the history-like story.

10. Etymologically, Šaveh itself means "plain" (see BDB), so this double expression anticipates the English phrase "Beqa Valley" ("Valley Valley").

11. Targums Onq. and Ps.-J. speak of Melchizedek "ministering" rather than as being a priest, to avoid the questions that issue from his not being an Aaronide and to sidestep the Christian idea that Jesus was a priest in succession to Melchizedek (cf. Aberbach and Grossfeld, *Targum Onkelos*, 89–91; Maher, *Targum Pseudo-Jonathan: Genesis*, 58).

12. *Māgan* piel, a denominative from *māgēn* (shield), apparently piel privative (see GKC 52h; *IBHS* 24.4cd).

13. The declarative/performative qatal verb suggests a speech act, "I hereby raise." The LXX, 1QapGen omit Yahweh; SP has "God."

14. See Morschauser, "Campaigning."

15. As commonly happens, the rest of the oath is left to speak for itself.

16. The rare *bilʿădê*, perhaps etymologically "not to" (see BDB 116).

17. Köhler, *Theologie des Alten Testaments*, 39; cf. von Rad, *Genesis*, 170.

It is a long time before we discover how the chapter relates to Abraham. It will turn out that the first half tells the audience the background to that question, and it is a thrilling story in its own right. We first enjoy reading about a rebellion on the part of the city-states down in the Jordan Valley against their overlords from the far north and east, about an expedition on the part of the latter to put the city-states in their place, and about a battle that ends with the kings of Sodom and Gomorrah hiding in bitumen pits and with the eastern kings taking much plunder. Woo hoo! This entertaining story could be complete in its own right, but as the introduction to what follows it functions dramatically as a long raising of suspense. Its links with Gen. 10 and specifically with the Nimrod story (as king of Shinar, Amrapel has been identified with Nimrod)[18] suggest that it reaffirms Yahweh's involvement with developments in the affairs of the nations.[19]

The element in the story that brings it into connection with the Abraham narrative (vv. 12–16), and specifically with Gen. 13, is that the overlords also take Lot. Serves him right, because he is now not merely encamped near Sodom but living in Sodom! As happened in Gen. 12–13, however, Abraham sees this crisis as requiring action. He pursues the four kings with his citizen's army, defeats them, and rescues Lot and the rest of the plunder. The story thus portrays Abraham as more dynamic than he was in Gen. 12–13—indeed, as the kind of figure we read about in Judges.[20] His triumphant return would make another satisfactory ending to the story, though one might have expected Abraham to call on Yahweh's name if not to build an altar down in Sodom (cf. 12:7, 8; 13:4, 18).

We do get something equivalent to such a conclusion (vv. 17–24), though it takes a distinctive form. When Abraham returns for his victory parade, the greeting party includes not only the king of Sodom (who has had a shower in the Dead Sea, though it hasn't stopped him from smelling of bitumen) but also the king of Salem. Presumably the scene is therefore on the mountain ridge where Melchizedek lives and where Abraham is on his way home to Mamre. As a priest, Melchizedek can bless Abraham and bless the God who has given Abraham the victory. He thus brings a first fulfillment of the promise in 12:2–3 that there will be people who bless Abraham—indeed, fulfillment of the promise that his name will be great and that people will find blessing through him. Abraham therefore gives him, as God's representative, a tithe of the plunder from the battle, though not without nuancing Melchizedek's description of the deity. The king of Sodom invites him to keep the rest of the plunder; the king has been seen as surly,[21] which would make him an embodiment of the person who "diminishes" Abraham in 12:2–3, but he can as easily

18. E.g., Rashi, *Br'šyt*, 129.
19. Cf. Fretheim, *Abraham*, 70.
20. Cf. Westermann, *Genesis 12–36*.
21. See, e.g., Wenham, *Genesis 1–15*, 315–18.

be seen as also positively recognizing Abraham[22] and thus as another positive fulfillment of that promise. But Abraham declines, not wanting to be in hock to the king of Sodom. One can imagine that the story spoke to the trickiness and necessary subtlety of relationships with neighbors and their religion and theology in Israel. In addition, the audience knows that the Davidic king is the successor of Melchizedek (Ps. 110:4, the only other First Testament reference to him).[23] Abraham is "bowing before the one who is holding the place for the future anointed one."[24] So one can imagine insights the story might offer in different contexts in Israel's history, but as usual, the story gives no concrete indication of the context in which it was composed or told.[25]

14:1–3. Two of the first four kings come from places we know, Shinar (i.e., Babylonia; cf. 10:10) and Elam (cf. 10:22), to its east. We do not know where Ellasar was, nor who were the "nations" of which Tidal was king. And we have no references to any kings called Amrapel, Aryok, or Kedorla'omer, though Tidal may be equivalent to Tudḫaliaš, the name of four Hittite kings.[26] That link pairs with the tradition locating Ellasar in Turkey,[27] and together the four kings might then represent a wide swath of powers from Turkey through Iraq to Iran, much like the accounts in Gen. 10. What is clear is that they represent an impressive coalition from the great imperial centers to the north and east. Genesis Rabbah 42.2 comments on how encounters with four kingdoms form a bracket around Israel's history (cf. Dan. 2 and 7).

Their victims (vv. 2–3) are much smaller fry, the kings of little city-states down in the Jordan Valley. We know of Sodom, Gomorrah, and Zo'ar from Gen. 13, and Admah and Seboyim from 10:19. All five were presumably located around the Dead Sea (cf. v. 3), but we do not know their precise location. The kings' names do not occur elsewhere, though it may be no coincidence that Bera sounds like a bad guy (*ra'*) and Birsha sounds like a faithless guy (*reša'*). Nor do we know where Siddim Vale was, only that it was in the area of the Dead Sea (which is its Arabic name; "Salt Sea" is the regular Hebrew name).[28] And we have no basis for dating any battle that may have involved these nine kings.

22. So, e.g., Luther, *Genesis 6–14*, 394–95.

23. Mathews (*Melchizedek's Alternative Priestly Order*) suggests several less-specific intertextual links.

24. Von Rad, *Genesis*, 175–76.

25. Westermann (*Genesis 12–36*, 188–90) surveys the "three main questions" that "have dominated the whole course of the study of Gen. 14"—the questions of historicity, of a document as the basis of the chapter, and of the chapter's unity and composition—and comes to less agnostic conclusions than mine, as does Wenham (*Genesis 1–15*, 318–20) in his discussion of the story's historical value.

26. So, e.g., Sarna, *Genesis*, 103.

27. See the translation note above.

28. See Tal, *Genesis*, 110–12*, for the versions' treatment of the names (and 112–16* for later names in the chapter).

14:4–7. Genesis now backtracks to give us the battle's context. As subjects of Kedorlaʿomer, the five city-states' value may have lain in the area's mineral resources.

By the next year (vv. 5–6) Kedorlaʿomer has persuaded the other kings to ally with him to put the city-states in their place. The kings take their time getting to the Jordan Valley. Perhaps these other peoples have joined in the rebellion, though if so, one might expect Genesis to say so. Perhaps, then, the kings make their expedition worthwhile by taking over these other places, or perhaps they engage in preemptive strikes to prevent these other peoples from coming to the five kings' support. Anyway, they first make their battling way north to south through the highland east of the Jordan and thus above the location of the five towns. Although we cannot identify the four kings, their route is broadly identifiable as following the "King's Highway" (Num. 20:17), the main road east of the Jordan for traders and armies. Ashterot Qarnayim is in the Golan, there is a town called Ham not far away, and Seʿir is farther south. Paʾran extends much further down into Sinai, but at its northern end Paʾran Oak (*ʾêl paʾran*) makes one think of Elat,[29] and the kings might be concerned to assert authority over this further significant point on the trade routes. Presumably Qiryatayim Plain is on the same north-south line and might well link with the Qiryatayim in Num. 32:37. The peoples they defeated there, the Repaʾites, Zuzites/Zamzummites, Emites, and Horites, also appear in Deut. 2:10–12, 20–23 as pre-Israelite inhabitants of that area east of the Jordan.

From their farthest point south, the four kings then proceed northwest (v. 7) to Qadesh, the key town in northern Sinai, a center for the Amaleqites (cf. Num. 13:29); the name Decision Spring suggests that it is the location for a powwow.[30] From Qadesh they swerve back northeast and down into the Jordan Valley to Ḥaṣaṣon Tamar, whose inhabitants are simply designated by the all-purpose term "Amorites." The place's name suggests something to do with gravel and something to do with a palm, an odd combination, though it fits a location near the Dead Sea. Ḥaṣaṣon Tamar is identified with Ein Gedi in 2 Chron. 20:2 (cf. Tg. Onq. here), which makes geographical sense insofar as lower Ein Gedi is on the Dead Sea, though the descent from upper Ein Gedi is perilous.

14:8–11. The city-state kings perhaps realize that Kedorlaʿomer and company have put down their neighbors and potential allies on all sides, and they must face up to the four kings on their own. The story leaps over their inevitable defeat to the aftermath. With a smirk on his face the narrator reports how two of the kings jump into bitumen pits to avoid being caught and killed, while the others run for the hills (which the easterners have already captured).

29. Cf. BDB 18b.
30. Cf. Rashi, *Brʾšyt*, 132.

Meanwhile, Kedorlaʿomer makes off with the plunder, which helps make the whole venture worthwhile, and with the food that feeds the army.

14:12–13. In itself the story could end there, but it doesn't. And following on 13:12–13 it might raise the question of what happens to Lot. Taking captives is another practice that makes war worthwhile, but the mention of Lot alone reflects the particular interest of the story.

In 13:18 one would have thought that Mamre (v. 13), up on the mountain ridge to the west, was simply a place name, but here it is the name of a person; Mamre's two brothers also have names that are also names of places. The three are "holders/lords of Abraham's pact": that is, Abraham has entered into a mutual alliance with them that, among other things, commits them not to attack each other and to watch each other's backs. In this context, Abraham is called an Ibrite, a "Hebrew." The LXX translates the word "emigrant" or "transient,"[31] which fits its similarity to the Akkadian term *ḫabiru* (with variants), denoting people who are outsiders in relation to the society in question and of questionable social status; it's a term like "gypsies." And within the First Testament, it often has this connotation. But in this context, Abraham's being an Ibrite, a descendant of Eber, is set over against Mamre's being an Amorite, a descendant of Ham (see Gen. 10); so it is more likely an ethnic term.[32]

14:14–16. Like the account of the five kings' defeat, the account of Abraham's expedition is told briskly, leaving us to fill in the gaps. It apparently doesn't need saying that the people with whom Abraham has a pact will join him in the venture. The narrative also reads as if we know that Abraham's company is much larger than we might have guessed even from the information that Abraham's family and Lot's family cannot all fit in the land around Beth El. A fighting force of 318 implies that the total number of clan members was in four figures, but further significance to the number 318 may emerge at 15:2. Abraham's company comprises men who were born and raised in his household as servants, who are therefore unquestionably loyal to him; they are not mercenaries or people whom he captured or bought. They are people he has trained or brought up: "Train a youth in connection with his way, and when he is old he will not depart from it" (Prov. 22:6). After the four kings have made their triumphant departure from the Dead Sea area by going straight up the Jordan Valley, Abraham catches up with them at what will eventually be the northern border of Israel itself, the natural border between Canaan and Syria. Dan will be its name after the Danites move there in the Judges period. One does wonder what the kings are doing so far north if they are on their way to Damascus, Babylonia, and Elam, though

31. See Brayford, *Genesis*, 294.
32. Cf. Arnold, *Genesis*, 147.

it would be a less circuitous route on the way to Turkey; perhaps they have other conquests in mind.[33]

Abraham and his makeshift army divide into several companies (v. 15), come upon the four kings by night with the advantage of surprise, and turn their orderly march homeward into a flight, for those who are lucky enough not to get struck down. "The victors become the victims."[34] Whereas Damascus would be on the way home for them (Abraham has presumably not been there since his journey summarized in Gen. 12), we don't know how far beyond Damascus Hobah is.

So Abraham is able to take back Lot and his people (v. 16) and also to take back to the five city-states the property plundered from them and the people who had been captured, including the women whose future life as captives would hardly bear thinking about.[35]

14:17–20. Once again, the story could end there, but it doesn't. It might raise the question of what happened to all that stuff. Did Abraham just keep it, the same way he kept his (arguably ill-gotten) gains from Pharaoh? The king of Sodom (the story is interested simply in him because of the link with Lot) might be asking himself that question. Is he asking it when he comes out and climbs the mountain ridge to meet the returning victor? The Shaveh Vale is mentioned only here in the First Testament, but the King's Vale with which the narrator identifies it appears in 2 Sam. 18:18 as the location of Absalom's Pillar, which was presumably near Jerusalem, and 1QapGen 22.14 plausibly locates it at Bet-hakkerem.

The appearance of the king of Shalem (v. 18) is then a surprise,[36] but the location at least provides the geographical logic for it, if Shalem is a name for Jerusalem (*yərûšālayim*) (cf. Ps. 76:2). Elsewhere in the First Testament, however, Jerusalem is the home of the Yebusites (until David captures it), and its name is Yebus (2 Chron. 3:1 also identifies Moriah in Gen. 22 with Jerusalem). The name Malki-ṣedeq means Faithfulness-is-my-king or My-king-is-faithfulness, faithfulness being a name or attribute of the deity whom Melchizedek serves. The name compares with that of Adonizedek (My-lord-is-faithfulness) and of Zedekiah (Yahu-is-my-faithfulness). Genesis goes on to call Melchizedek's deity "God On High" (*ʾēl ʿelyôn*), implicitly a designation for Yahweh in Ps. 78:35; the simple "On High" is such a designation elsewhere (e.g., Ps. 73:11). But *ʾēl* is also the Canaanites' designation for the supreme deity, and "God On High" is a way of describing the most senior deity in the traditional religion of Canaan. Melchizedek is not only king but also priest

33. Cf. Keil and Delitzsch, *Pentateuch*, 206.

34. Coats, *Genesis*, 119.

35. Cf. Luther, *Genesis 6–14*, 377.

36. Removing the account of his appearance (vv. 18–20) makes the chapter smoother. Granerød (*Abraham and Melchizedek*) has argued most systemically for its secondary nature; contrast Tatu, "Making Sense of Melchizedek."

(as presumably was the king of Sodom, though he brings no gifts or greeting). Bread and water would be welcome refreshment; bread and wine would make the event special.[37]

In his capacity as priest as well as king, Melchizedek pronounces blessings (v. 19a). The First Testament generally suggests the principle of the separation of powers between the world of worship and the world of economics and politics. There are kings or governors and there are priests, not to say prophets. Melchizedek is both king and priest, which is risky but is working okay at that moment. The Davidic king inherits his position (Ps. 110), which is risky and sometimes does not work well. Elsewhere in Genesis, pronouncing blessings is the privilege and responsibility of the family and in particular of the father of the family (e.g., 24:60; 28:1; 31:55 [32:1]; 49:28); it is an aspect of the quasi-priestly role of the father, who also leads the family in worship. Priestly blessing comes in when there are priests (Num. 6:23–27). Other (settled) peoples, however, already have priests who lead worship and bless people. They are the channels through whom people reach out to God and God reaches out to people. They ensure that there is real contact and communication between people and God and between God and people. They also protect people from the inherently overwhelming aspect of contact with God and from the accidentally overwhelming aspect of that contact when there is something about you beyond your regular humanness that clashes too much with who God is.

Melchizedek blesses Abraham by praying that God may bless him (v. 19b), presumably because of the action he has undertaken in rescuing the women and the rest of the company and the property of the five kings (who are also Melchizedek's allies?). He blesses Abraham in the name of God On High, who is "generator [*qōnēh*] of heavens and earth"—a description that naturally goes with his being "God On High." The usual First Testament expression is "maker of heavens and earth" (Ps. 115:15; 121:2; 124:8; 134:3; 146:6). In Hebrew *qōnēh* would most often suggest an acquirer or owner (e.g., Isa. 1:3; 24:2; the Vg has "owner" in v. 22). But among the Canaanites the word refers to God as the creator (the LXX and Vg have "who created").[38]

Melchizedek goes on (v. 20) to bless God. There was reason to bless Abraham—he took the decisive action that rescued the women and the company. There was also reason to bless God: he gave Abraham the victory. He had "unshielded" Abraham's victims—made it impossible for them to defend themselves; the rare verb comes from the common word for a shield (*māgēn*). One might have expected the verb to mean "shield," but it is closer to meaning "unshield" here and in Hosea 11:8 (the other occurrence is Prov. 4:9). The

37. Elgavish ("Encounter of Abram and Melchizedek") sees them as suggesting a covenant-making ceremony in which Melchizedek is recognizing Abraham. Josephus (*Ant.* 1.10.2) calls it simply a feast.

38. Cf. Westermann, *Genesis 12–36*, 205, and his references; see also the footnote to 4:1.

significance of using this word will become clearer in 15:2. While the story did not refer to God giving Abraham the victory, Melchizedek knows where such victories come from. Presumably it is Abraham who gives Melchizedek a tenth of everything—in other words, he gives him a tithe (Hebrew has the one word, *ma'ăśēr*, but English separated out the two meanings). Although the notion of tithing is well known in the First Testament (e.g., 28:22; Deut. 14:22; 26:12; Neh. 10:37–38 [10:38–39]), there is no exact parallel for this one-time tithe; Num. 31:25–41 and 1 Sam. 8:15, 17 are partial parallels.[39] By giving one day a week to God and doing nothing on that day, in recognition that the whole week is a gift from God, a person frees up the other six days; likewise, by giving one possession in ten to God and doing nothing with it, in recognition that everything is a gift from God, a person frees up the other nine-tenths.

In the Qumran scroll 11QMelchizedek (11Q13), Melchizedek has become a supernatural being with a role in the final judgment.[40] Hebrews 5–7 sees Jesus as having inherited Melchizedek's position as priest in a way that is quite logical if he is the heir of David and the Messiah. It wouldn't be surprising if the readers of Hebrews knew ideas like the ones that appear in 11QMelchizedek (Heb. 1 suggests they were interested in angels) and if Hebrews was offering them a preferable way of thinking about Melchizedek in relation to Jesus, but Hebrews contains no direct pointers to this possibility. It is more interested in the possibility that emerges from the Melchizedek story of establishing the Messiah's (and thus Jesus's) position as a priest even though he is not from the clan of Levi. Indeed, being a priest like Melchizedek is better than being a Levitical priest (see esp. Heb. 7)! But in an odd way, the strangely isolated position and person of Melchizedek suggests links with the unique position and person of Jesus. So Hebrews says, "Let Gen. 14 help you understand something of the significance of Jesus."[41] Melchizedek does manage to combine power in politics and power in worship. He is the giver of blessing to people and to God. He brings not merely bread and water but bread and wine, not merely the staple that we need but something extra that we don't need. Subsequent to NT times, Melchizedek's bread and wine had to make Christians think of the Eucharist.[42]

14:21–24. So what's to happen to the other nine-tenths? The king of Sodom has an answer that expresses his gratitude.

Abraham doesn't like his answer (v. 22). His reasoning is implicit in his preamble. When someone says something solemnly or swears that something is true, they raise their hand toward God, as they do when they pray (e.g., Deut. 32:40). They are drawing God's attention to what they are saying and inviting God to take action if they are lying or if they don't mean what they

39. Cf. Sarna, *Genesis*, 110.

40. See *DSS* 2:1206–9; and, e.g., Reiss, "Melchizedek Traditions."

41. See, e.g., Docherty, "Genesis in Hebrews," 133–37.

42. Jerome, *Hebrew Questions on Genesis*, 47.

say or if they fail to do what they say. And the God to whom Abraham thus appeals is God On High, generator of heavens and earth, God as Melchizedek spoke of him. Here as elsewhere, Genesis assumes the validity of the religion of other peoples.[43] Yet Abraham prefaces that description of God with the name Yahweh. Like other references to Yahweh in Genesis, putting the name "Yahweh" on Abraham's lips is technically an anachronism. Yahweh has not yet invited his people to call him by that name. But it is indeed Yahweh who has been acting in enabling Abraham to rescue Lot, so the anachronism is a technicality. The affirmation of substance in the words put on Abraham's lips is that, while Abraham can properly recognize that Melchizedek serves the real God, in order to have a fuller picture of the real God one needs to see this God as the one involved in the story of Abraham and his descendants who live in the context of God's promise to them.

The substance of Abraham's solemn declaration to the king (v. 23) is that he doesn't want the plunder. Melchizedek's blessing of God and Abraham's giving Melchizedek a tithe have recognized that God made Abraham's victory possible. Accepting the plunder would let the king of Sodom be the one who makes Abraham rich. Actually, it is God who does so. Abraham rejects zero-sum thinking.[44] And we know that there is reason to be wary when you are eating with the king of a place like Sodom, whose proposal provokes a more negative reaction than the one Abraham has to Pharaoh.

There is that other reason for taking plunder (v. 24). Going on military expeditions is a costly business, and the plunder offsets expenses. Abraham's staff had to take their supplies, so they should put in their expense claims. And Abraham's three allies (and no doubt their staff) should have their share.

Implications

Big Powers and Little Powers

How do the people of God relate to the world scene? They should not forget that the life of the nations continues to develop within the broad context of God's blessing, though they should also keep in mind that big powers enjoy being big powers and extending their empires, because they like power and because they can thus enrich themselves. Conversely, little powers don't much like being under the control of big powers, because it tends to cost them in taxes and because they also like being in control of their own destiny. But they may need to choose their moment to assert their independence. In the context of the history of Ephraim and Judah, it could suggest the moral that the underlings of an empire need to think twice before rebelling against the empire.

43. See Cohn, "Negotiating with the Natives."
44. Brichto, *Names of God*, 196–97.

The people of God sometimes find themselves caught up in the assertive actions of big powers and the resistance of little powers. Does Abraham then set an example?[45] One might compare him with Moses when he strikes down an Egyptian who is beating an Israelite.[46] But the people of God or other entities then need not merely to choose their moment wisely but also to take into account the obligations placed upon them by their relationships within the people of God as a whole. Making war is more likely to be the morally right course if we are acting in faithfulness to the people of God or to other people who are the victims of wrongful treatment. And we may not refuse to act just because it was their own fault that the victims got into a mess. On the other hand, if we succeed, liberators do not enrich themselves through their exploits, especially at the expense of those they liberate. Abraham anticipates the stance of Gideon.[47] Declining the plunder from the expedition suggests that he is prepared to be in the world but he will not be sucked into being of it.

Successfully doing the right thing in a political or military context may require both our commitment and God's involvement. Genesis 14 itself does not refer to God's involvement. The rescue comes about because Abraham acts. But "Melchizedek confesses their God as both creator and redeemer . . . in a way that Abraham had not. . . . Melchizedek is represented as Abraham's teacher regarding the activity of their common deity."[48] Whereas Lot the insider becomes an outsider, Melchizedek the outsider speaks like an insider. While insiders can become a threat or a problem, outsiders can become a blessing.[49] Melchizedek recognizes that God is both "generator of heavens and earth" and one who "has delivered your attackers into your hand." The LXX, Vg have "who created heavens and earth," but Melchizedek's formula uses a participle, which is more open to pointing to God's ongoing activity. The five psalm references to Yahweh's being maker of heavens and earth, noted above, have parallel implications. They associate Yahweh's being maker of heavens and earth either with Yahweh blessing us or with Yahweh helping us.[50] Genesis and Psalms see God's activity as creator as not just relating to the past; it also has implications in the present.

45. In the context of the Peasants' Revolt, Luther (*Genesis 6–14*, 375) insists not. Granerød (*Abraham and Melchizedek*) relates Gen. 14 to the Judahite community in the Persian (or Greek) period, which it urges to stand up for itself.

46. Calvin, *Genesis*, 1:383.

47. Cf. Westermann, *Genesis 12–36*, 202.

48. Fretheim, *Abraham*, 11.

49. Cf. Fretheim, *Abraham*, 68–69.

50. Cf. Brueggemann, *Genesis*, 137.

13
"But Lord Yahweh . . ."

(15:1–21)

Overview

Whereas the main focus in Gen. 12–14 has been the land that Abraham's offspring will possess, Gen. 15–22 will focus more on the offspring themselves. Genesis 15 marks the shift; "offspring" is a key word (see vv. 3, 5, 13, 18).[1] Verses 1–6 begin from the possessions that Yahweh promises Abraham; Abraham's concern is to whom he will pass them. Yahweh affirms that he will have offspring, and Abraham responds with a commitment of trust. Verses 7–21 reassert Yahweh's promise of the land and ends with his demonstration of commitment, which includes his actual conveying of the gift of the land to Abraham's nonexistent offspring. In both connections, Gen. 15 "is most centrally concerned with delay."[2]

Translation

1Subsequently, Yahweh's word came[3] to Abram in a vision:

Don't be afraid, Abram.
I will be your shield,
and your wages will be very big.[4]

1. Cf. Seebass, *Genesis*, 2.1:69.

2. Lipton, *Revisions of the Night*, 217.

3. Literally, "was" or "happened" or "became."

4. Literally, "[will be] a much-making exceedingly"; the infinitive absolute functions as a gerund (GKC 131q). Here 1QapGen 22 introduces the promises with a note on how much Yahweh has enriched Abraham in the ten years since he left Harran.

2But Abram said, "Lord[5] Yahweh, what will you give me, when I'm
going to depart childless, and the heir[6] to my household is Dammešeq,
Eliʿezer?" **3**So Abram said, "There, you haven't given me offspring. And
there, someone from my household will come into possession from me."[7]
4But there, Yahweh's word came to him: "This man won't come into pos-
session from you. No, only someone who comes from your insides—he'll
come into possession from you." **5**He took him outside and said, "Look at
the heavens, please, and count the stars, if you can count them." He said
to him, "That's what your offspring will be like." **6**And in that he trusted in
Yahweh,[8] he deemed it[9] as faithfulness on his part.

7He said to him, "I am Yahweh who[10] got you out from Ur of the
Kaśdites to give you this country as a possession." **8**But he said, "Lord
Yahweh, how may I know that I will come into possession of it?" **9**He said
to him, "Get me a three-year-old heifer,[11] a three-year-old goat, a three-
year-old ram, a pigeon, and a baby bird." **10**He got him all these, cut them
in half, and put one half opposite its neighbor, but he didn't cut the bird
in half. **11**The screecher came down on the carcasses, but Abram drove
them away. **12**As the sun was about to go, a coma fell on Abram, and
there, a great dark dread was falling on him.

13He said to Abram, "You can know for sure[12] that your offspring
will be resident aliens in a country not theirs, and they will serve them

5. *ʾĂdōnāy* may be the word for lord in the plural with a first-person suffix (thus "my lord"; cf. BDB, *HALOT*, *DCH*) or the word for lord with an archaic intensive plural sufformative (hence "great lord"; cf. the LXX, Vg); see O. Eissfeldt's discussion of *ʾādôn* in *TDOT* 1:59–72.

6. *Ben-mešek*: the second word comes only here, and the meaning has to be guessed from the context. For some solutions to the mystery of v. 2b, see, e.g., Hamilton, *Genesis*, 420–22; Seebass, "Gen. 15 2b."

7. In this context *yāraš* denotes inheriting, but in itself the verb simply refers to secure ownership, not possession through inheriting. See the recurrence of the verb and related noun in vv. 7–8.

8. The verb is simple waw plus qatal. GKC 112ss takes it as suggesting continuance; but the following waw-consecutive is then difficult. DG 84c suggests that it sums up what has gone before: "so he trusted." *TTH* 133 calls it an isolated irregularity (cf. JM 119z).

9. The LXX and Vg have passive verbs "it was deemed," implying that the third-person singular is impersonal. The clause then refers to a deeming about Abraham rather than by Abraham (cf. the niphal verb in Ps. 106:31; and the niphal verbs in passages such as Lev. 7:18). But there are no pointers to this impersonal understanding. While Yahweh is the subject of the qatal in Ps. 32:2, and Qimchi assumes that understanding here (*Genesis*, on the verse), the construction as a whole here is different. Klein ("Who Counted Righteousness to Whom?") discusses the question from a Jewish angle. Luther sees the idea that Abraham is the subject as satanic (*Genesis 15–20*, 21). Seebass (*Genesis*, 2.1:63) renders "He [Yahweh] planned" an act of *ṣədāqâ*, whose implications are not so different from Abraham's seeing Yahweh's promise as an act of *ṣədāqâ*, though it is open to an eschatological rereading (see Hwang, "Eschatology in Genesis 15:6"). See further the comment.

10. Or "I Yahweh am the one who" (cf. Seebass, *Genesis*, 2.1:72). Having no equivalent to a noun clause, English cannot represent the Hebrew expression in its openness.

11. Literally, "a heifer that is made three." Targum Onq. takes *məšullešet* each time to mean "threefold."

12. The infinitive precedes the finite verb for emphasis: literally, "with knowing you may know."

and they will humble them,[13] for 400 years. **14**But the nation that they serve I'm indeed going to judge. After this they will get out with much property.

> **15**And you: you will go to your forebears with things being well;
> you'll be buried in a good old age.
> **16**In the fourth generation they will come back here,
> because the Amorite's waywardness is not complete
> heretofore.

17The sun went and there was deep darkness, and there, a smoking oven, a blazing torch, that passed between those pieces. **18**On that day Yahweh solemnized a pact with Abram, saying, "To your offspring I am giving[14] this country, from the Miṣrayim river[15] to the big river (the River Perat): **19**the Qenite, the Qenizzite, the Qadmonite, **20**the Hittite, the Perizzite, the Rephaʾites, **21**the Amorite, the Kenaʿanite, the Girgašite,[16] and the Yebusite."

Interpretation

At the end of Gen. 14 the MT has only a paragraph break, not a unit break; indeed, it treats Gen. 14–17 as one unit. And the opening of Gen. 15 does link back to Gen. 14, with which Gen. 15 has a series of verbal links (see the comments on vv. 1–2, 14–18). But Gen. 15 moves from a primary focus on the promise of land to include more focus on the promise of offspring, and the medieval chapter division generates a plausible understanding of the unit it devises. The dominant features of the two unequal parts of the chapter are a double dialogue. Twice Yahweh reaffirms his promises to Abraham, twice Abraham voices unease, and twice Yahweh responds with more reaffirmation.[17] A key question underlies the dialogue: what are the nature and basis of a relationship with Yahweh? Following the two sequences of dialogue, there comes the twofold answer. The relationship is one of trust that Yahweh himself is faithful in the relationships and the commitments he enters into, a belief based on the pact he has made and has given evidence of.

> Yahweh identifies himself and makes promises (partly in a poetic line) (15:1)
> Abraham responds with a "but" (15:2–3)

13. The MT puts the mid-verse marker at this point, indicating plausibly that the 400 years covers the whole stay, not just the time of humbling.

14. The declarative/performative qatal suggests a speech act, "I hereby give"; contrast the yiqtol in 12:7 (Seebass, *Genesis*, 2.1:77).

15. For the MT's *nahar*, Tg. Onq. has the more usual *naḥal*, "wadi."

16. The SP, LXX add the Hivvite (cf. 10:17), whom one would indeed expect in the list (e.g., Exod. 3:8, 17; 13:5).

17. Cf. Sarna, *Genesis*, 111–12.

Yahweh makes promises and gives him something extraordinary to look at (15:4–5)
The narrator reports Abraham's trust in Yahweh (15:6)
Yahweh identifies himself and makes promises (15:7)
Abraham responds with a "but" (15:8)
Yahweh makes promises and gives him something extraordinary to look at (partly in two poetic lines; 15:9–17)
The narrator reports Yahweh's making of a pact with Abraham (15:18–21)

There is not so much action in this story; the chapter is closer to being simply a dialogue.[18] The questioning in v. 8 that might seem strange after v. 6, the self-announcement by Yahweh in v. 7 despite his having presented himself in v. 2, and the impression in vv. 12–17 that evening is falling, whereas it was already dark in v. 5[19]—all reflect the rhetorical rather than linear unfolding of chapter 15. The chapter looks at the same question twice and comprises two complementary reflections on it.[20]

15:1–2. The opening words (lit., "after these things") do not usually imply any logical connection between two events (e.g., 40:1), though they can invite the audience to wonder whether there is a connection (e.g., 22:1). Here a link will soon become clear. Genesis 13:5–18 relates how a defining or crossroads moment in Abraham's story leads into a promise from Yahweh. That sequence now recurs. The sequence also overlaps with 12:1–8, where a word from Yahweh set the series of events going: Abraham went on the challenging journey that Yahweh commissioned, and then Yahweh appeared to him. It contrasts with the sequence that followed in 12:9–13:4, where there was another defining moment and a decisive response by Abraham followed by a divine response that came in actions rather than in words or visions. The word for vision here (*maḥăzeh*) otherwise appears in the Torah only in Num. 24:4, 16, at the other end of the story in Genesis to Numbers, when Yahweh renews the promise of blessing for Israel at the end of its wilderness journey (Ezek. 13:7 is its sole other occurrence in the First Testament). Although Genesis makes other references to Yahweh "appearing" (*rāʾâ* niphal; e.g., 17:1; 18:1), the Torah does not use the verb *ḥāzâ*, and in Hebrew as in English, words for "vision" hint at something more out-of-the-ordinary than words for "appearing" (that is, while *ḥāzâ* can be used for ordinary seeing, *rāʾâ* is the more usual word in that connection). And something out-of-the-ordinary is indeed to follow. On the

18. Coats, *Genesis*, 125.

19. Gunkel, *Genesis*, 176, 182. Ha (*Genesis 15*, 30–33) surveys consequent source-critical and redactional approaches to the chapter, though his major thesis is that Gen. 15 is a kind of "theological compendium" to the pentateuchal history as a whole. Fidler ("Genesis xv") suggests that vv. 7–18 backtrack on vv. 1–6.

20. See Brichto, *Names of God*, 203–12.

other hand, a "vision" may suggest something inside Abraham's head (though real), whereas "appearing" may suggest something externalized (cf. 18:1). In general, talk of visions and of that other kind of appearing/seeing fits what prophets speak of, which coheres with the fact that here there is a "word" to follow, and then something to see—something amazing but "natural" in v. 5 and something extraordinary and fantastic in vv. 9–17. Further, elsewhere the expression "Yahweh's word came to . . ." introduces Yahweh's words to a prophet (e.g., 1 Sam. 15:10; 1 Kings 17:2; Jer. 1:4; Ezek. 1:2), so that it provides a neat anticipation of the later description of Abraham as a prophet (20:7).[21] One way or another, "this is not 'just another' divine word."[22]

The exhortation "Don't be afraid" (v. 1b) comes in two sorts of connection in the First Testament. It comes in connection with Yahweh's appearing, an experience to which fear is an appropriate reaction because of the danger of being in the high-voltage presence of God (e.g., Exod. 20:20 [20:17]). More often it appears in contexts where there is a more down-to-earth reason for being afraid (e.g., 21:17; 26:24; 35:17; 43:23; 46:3; 50:19, 21). Here, what follows suggests this more usual significance. In other Middle Eastern texts, it comes in messages of encouragement to a king (cf. Isa. 7:4; 37:6), but in the First Testament, at least, the usage is more general. Isaiah 41:10–13 addresses Israel as "Abraham's offspring" and urges Israel, "Don't be afraid" (Gen. Rab. 44.3). Melchizedek has pointed out that God "unshielded" Abraham's opponents (14:20), and God now declares that the reason for not being afraid is that God is and will be Abraham's "shield." The second and third cola of Yahweh's words are noun clauses (lit., "I your shield, and your wages very big"). The declaration about being a shield will apply in the present and the future (cf., e.g., Pss. 18:2, 30 [18:3, 31]; 28:7; 33:20), though the declaration about the wages is more future oriented. In substance though not in words, that declaration about wages also links back with 14:17–24. Abraham declined to profit from his venture. He could have simply assumed that Yahweh was giving him the plunder to keep, as he gave him the victory, but he didn't. Yet arguably, refusing to take plunder is not a practical way to live in the world and to commit yourself to doing what needs to be done or should be done. Abraham has a huge retinue to provide for. Yahweh affirms his assumption and promises that he will not only survive but also thrive. He will be rewarded. God promises to make sure that his people get their wages. Jesus promises that people who for his sake have abandoned family and land (that is, their means of support) will receive them a hundredfold in the present age. The significance of these promises is their implausibility. If they obviously corresponded to experience, they would hardly be needed. The faithful in Israel

21. Cf. Tg. Neof.'s observation that this is "a word of prophecy." In source-critical terms, it is thus one of the indications that this story comes in part from the Elohistic material about Abraham.

22. Fretheim, "Genesis," 444.

and the faithful followers of Jesus are challenged to live by them even when they don't seem to come true. They are challenged not to be afraid (which is said to be the most common command in the Scriptures). The shielding promise is rather important too.

Abraham seems to be able to accept Yahweh's promise (v. 2a); his worry lies elsewhere. Here comes the transition to the theme of offspring. Abraham's question is clear: to whom will he be able to pass on this reward? In the Middle East it may have been possible to adopt someone to inherit one's estate and look after one's affairs and obligations, and Abraham assumes that he needs to do so, but he doesn't like it. "Wages make a future possible, but a childless person has no future."[23] Here for the first time we get words from Abraham that address God—and they are questions that respond to God's promises.[24] Here for the first time Yahweh is "Lord." In Genesis this form of address comes only in chapters 15 and 18–20 (the combined address "Lord Yahweh" recurs in v. 8 and comes only here in Genesis–Numbers). It regularly suggests both deference and boldness. One might say "Lord" when recognizing that Yahweh is the sovereign God yet be speaking in a way that could imply effrontery. What's the point in talking about wages when a person has no one to pass on the wealth to? The fact that Sarah cannot have children has been sitting uneasily at the side of the narrative since 11:30, but now Abraham puts it on the table. There is again some ambiguity in the portrayal of Abraham, though one could still say, "The sign that strengthens faith is not given to the unbeliever or to the doubter, but to the believer."[25] And his relationship with God suggests that deference and forthrightness go together in speaking to God (cf. Mark 14:35–36). One can be forthright if one is also prepared to submit to God as Lord; one can submit to God as Lord if one can also be forthright. "The Lord sometimes concedes to his children, that they may freely express any objection which comes into their mind."[26] The prayer relationship is a relationship with a Father, and in that relationship children are able to be plainspoken in the context of deference and to be deferent in the context of a freedom to be plainspoken. Trust and questioning interweave.

The meaning of Abraham's further comment about Eliezer (v. 2b) is perplexing, but again one significance of the words is that they make links back with 14:14–24 through the references to Abraham's household and to Damascus. Another possible link is that Eliezer's name translates numerically into the figure 318 (cf. 14:15; see, e.g., Gen. Rab. 44.9). The name recurs in the First Testament, but this Eliezer appears only here. It is odd that there is no mention of Lot, the nephew who came from Harran as a member of

23. Zimmerli, *1. Mose 12–25*, 50.
24. Cf. Fretheim, *Abraham*, 35.
25. Gunkel, *Genesis*, 180; cf. Luther, *Genesis 15–20*, 29–30.
26. Calvin, *Genesis*, 1:413.

Abraham's household; maybe Abraham simply takes for granted that Lot has eliminated himself from consideration.[27]

15:3–6. Fortunately, Abraham goes on to express his point more straightforwardly, though also more confrontationally. Notwithstanding the "Lord Yahweh" salutation, he is indeed quite confident about being forthright in what he says to God. Yahweh has been talking about giving him his wages, but there is a more important giving that Abraham is concerned about, and Yahweh has not given the one thing Abraham really wants. The person from his household who will look after things for him after he dies will be someone who belongs to his wider entourage, but his own offspring will not be the one who becomes the owner of all that he possesses.

The straight talking pays off (v. 4), and the promise from 12:2–3, 7; 13:15–16 becomes more explicit. Yahweh sets "your insides" against "my household,"[28] leaving himself very little wiggle room. The promise compares with God's later promise to David (2 Sam. 7:12) and thus anticipatorily implies that it belongs to Abraham's offspring as a whole, not just to the king.[29] Yet Jesus doesn't reiterate and generalize this promise as he reiterates and generalizes the one about wages, even though sadness at not being able to pass on the family business is not confined to traditional societies but is quite cross-cultural, like sadness about never having had children. He does reiterate the promise of fruitfulness (e.g., Mark 4). There are other forms of fecundity, of "capacity to touch hearts and to give life."[30]

Unnecessarily and unprompted, Yahweh goes on to make the promise more spectacular (v. 5). Yahweh again says "please" in connection with making an outrageous undertaking, as he did in connection with the promise of land and people in 13:14–17. He again invites Abraham to look—not this time at the land but at the night sky; visions commonly come at night (unless this bidding gains force from it being daytime!).[31] The simile he suggests is again ridiculous (count the dirt, count the stars?).

Abraham's immediate reaction is therefore significant (v. 6). Another key verb makes its first appearance, "trust" (*'āman* hiphil). The First Testament speaks often of *not* trusting (e.g., Deut. 1:32; 9:23; 2 Kings 17:14; Ps. 78:22), which highlights the remarkable nature of Abraham's reaction. Although the verb can suggest mental assent to some words, it more characteristically denotes that one is placing one's entire reliance on someone else, entrusting oneself to this person. The syntax suggests that this trust is not something that Abraham now shows for the first time but an attitude that has already characterized him, as one can see (e.g., in 12:1–8). So the comment makes

27. Cf. Heard, *Dynamics of Diselection*, 26–27.
28. Westermann, *Genesis 12–36*, 221.
29. Cf. Römer, "Abraham's Righteousness and Sacrifice," 12.
30. Vanier, *Man and Woman*, 141.
31. So Noegel, "Crux and a Taunt."

something explicit that has been only implicit. The logic and the grammar then suggest that the one who does the trusting is also the one who does the deeming. As an expression of his trust, Abraham concludes that he can believe that Yahweh will be faithful to him and to his promise. Yahweh will show *ṣədāqâ*; he will do the right thing by Abraham. Genesis 6:9 has commented on Noah's *ṣədāqâ* as someone who lived in the right way in his relationship with God and with the other people in his family and community. In this respect Noah was God-like. Actually, Yahweh is the original one who lives rightly in his relationship with people. An aspect of Abraham's trust is that he is prepared to see Yahweh as having that characteristic and to expect that it will be expressed in his faithfulness to his promise. "The only difference between us and Abraham is this, that Abraham believed the promises."[32]

The LXX translates v. 6 as "It was reckoned to him as *dikaiosynē*"; the agent of the deeming is then Yahweh.[33] When the LXX's translation is reflected in Rom. 4:3, 22; Gal. 3:6; James 2:23, this assumption applies. God is counting Abraham as someone who is *dikaios*. There were believers in Jesus who insisted that observances such as circumcision and other requirements from the Torah must be added to trust in Jesus if people are to count as *dikaioi*. Paul appeals to Abraham's story to show that it cannot be so; Yahweh treated Abraham as *dikaios* on the basis of his trust in his promise. With the irony that often obtains in connection with NT references to the First Testament, Paul's quotation takes these particular scriptural words in a way that is not inherent to them, but his point is a good First Testament one. The Genesis reference to Abraham's trust is a comment on the stance he has taken toward Yahweh in response to his promise and commission from the beginning, and (Paul accurately notes) the requirement of circumcision has not been made yet. James can make an opposite point on the basis of this same comment on Abraham's trust, with the same irony. Perhaps James needs to deal with people who think that all you have to do is believe and thus that there is no need for observances such as baptism or for sacrificial generosity to needy believers. And he can note that the later requirement of circumcision is a fulfillment of the requirement of trust—a filling out of this expectation.[34]

For readers over the past thousand years or so, there is a further double complication about understanding Gen. 15:6 and the NT's references to it. For Genesis, the question at issue is *ṣədāqâ*—Yahweh's *ṣədāqâ* (in MT) and/or Abraham's *ṣədāqâ* (in the LXX and the NT). But the LXX has translated *ṣədāqâ* with the word *dikaiosynē*, which is then routinely translated into English as "righteousness." And Paul and James have added the word *dikaiōsis*, which becomes "justification." Since the medieval period, in particular, Chris-

32. Luther, *Genesis 21–25*, 16.

33. See further the translation note.

34. See further D. Allen, "Genesis in James, 1 and 2 Peter and Jude," 148–53.

tian theology has then commonly understood the NT to be picturing the relationship between God and his people in quasi-legal terms. This understanding contrasts with that in Genesis and in Paul or James. Someone who is *ṣaddîq* is someone who is in a right relationship with God and with other people—someone who does the right thing by God and by other people. And God's *ṣədāqâ* or *dikaiosynē* is that faithfulness whereby God does the right thing in relation to Abraham and his offspring and thus stays in right relationship with them. The MT's implication is that the calling of the people of God is to follow Abraham by trusting in that *ṣədāqâ*. The LXX's point and Paul's point is that as they do so, God looks on them as people who are *ṣaddîqîm*; they are right with him. And James's point is that this trust will also find expression in doing the right thing.

15:7–12. For the first time in the First Testament, Yahweh declares "I [am] Yahweh." In a polytheistic context such a self-introduction might be necessary to indicate who speaks. Here this kind of self-introduction reminds the addressees that they must take the speaker seriously. But in this instance, as in some others, the significance and force of the self-introduction is increased by the description that follows: compare 28:13, but also and especially Exod. 20:2, where Yahweh uses the same verb as here ("got you out from") with regard to getting Israel out of Egypt, that "household of serfs" (cf. v. 13 here). Yahweh goes on to reaffirm the other promise, about the land, picking up 11:28, 31; 12:1. It is the first time Genesis has said that Yahweh got Abraham out from Ur (making explicit something implicit in 12:1?), and the formulation would remind the audience of another way in which his dealings with Abraham anticipated his dealings with Israel in getting them out of Egypt. Yahweh goes on to pick up Abraham's "possession" language, not in connection with who will inherit from Abraham, but with regard to the secure tenure that Yahweh will give Abraham.

Once again, Abraham addresses God as Lord Yahweh (v. 8) and signals to him and to the audience that he is about to say something submissive but bold. If we read the chapter linearly, the implication is that his trusting Yahweh regarding offspring does not carry over into immediately trusting Yahweh regarding the land. Please, can he have some grounds for believing Yahweh's promise?

Yes, he can (vv. 9–10). Whereas one might have expected Yahweh to decline or to issue a rebuke, we may again compare Abraham and Moses in how Yahweh deals with them: Moses gets away with questioning Yahweh three times before being scolded for the fourth (see Exod. 3–4). Although Yahweh's giving a sign fits his action on other occasions, there would be no basis for predicting how Yahweh will go about convincing Abraham on this occasion. He is first to assemble nine animals and two birds, which would be an expensive collection and gives another pointer to the size of Abraham's "household." We don't know why the rite involves these particular creatures; they would all count as clean, but they don't correspond to lists of creatures for sacrifice, and Abraham does not treat them in the manner of a sacrifice—there will be no spattering of blood or offering or burning[35] (in Jub. 14 Abraham builds an altar, pours out their blood on it, and offers them up). Though sometimes the First Testament likes to relate how Yahweh gives instructions that are then fulfilled, here the narrator skips the instructions to move briskly on to what Abraham does. Perhaps the reason the birds were not cut in half (cf. Lev. 1:17) was that they were so small; they were perhaps laid opposite each other.

Not surprisingly, scavenger birds think they have found their dinner (v. 11). The birds recall the half-bird, half-human "snatchers" ("harpies") of Greek and Roman mythology.[36] In the context of Genesis, they recall the fearsome sphinxes of Gen. 3:24, if they combined birds' wings with animal and/or human features. Later references to the screechers (Isa. 18:6; 46:11; Jer. 12:9; Ezek. 39:4) suggest that they might make the audience think of peoples who would attack Abraham's offspring and Yahweh's purpose for them (cf. Tg. Neof., Tg. Ps.-J.), and vv. 12–20 may support that understanding. Although the report had proceeded with haste in omitting the instructions for what Abraham was to do, the account of the scavengers adds to the suspense as we continue to wait for the response to Abraham's question and for the event that has been heralded, though it also anticipates the promise if the scavengers suggest the peoples who will be referred to and named in vv. 13, 16, and 19–21.

A moment comes (v. 12) when Abraham would be incapable of driving them away because he was overcome by a coma and by darkness. The description of the great dark dread prepares the audience for the fact that Yahweh is about to appear, and the narrative's "there" invites us to watch the scene (the dynamic will recur in v. 17).

15:13–16. You want to "know"? You will definitely know. The chapter continues to raise suspense by holding back the description of Yahweh's appearing while it first repeats the promise recalled by v. 7. As is commonly the case, in doing so Yahweh elaborates the promise yet also raises suspense further by portraying "the dark stretch of history which is to be experienced by Abraham's descendants before the promise is fulfilled."[37] The audience knows the identity of the unnamed country where Abraham's offspring will be resident as aliens (*gēr*). Maybe Abraham himself could work it out because he has been that way before (12:10). At this time he is a resident alien in a country that is not his (23:4; 35:27). But this other residency will be different: whereas in Canaan there is no central government that can oppress aliens, so that they just have to stay on the right side of the people in a particular area (e.g., 20:1; 21:23, 34), in Egypt there is a central government, and they

35. Cf. Keil and Delitzsch, *Pentateuch*, 213–14.
36. Driver, *Genesis*, 177.
37. Von Rad, *Genesis*, 182.

will find themselves in the position of state serfs. It will humble them (*ʿānâ* piel)—treat them as people with no rights, and worse (see Exod. 1:11–12). Their 400-year stay there is approximately equivalent to the 430 years of Exod. 12:40–41. If the audience wonders why it took so long for Israel to gain possession of Canaan, Genesis is providing an answer. And if it is wondering about Yahweh's fulfillment of promises that apply to it, Yahweh's words imply pointers toward an answer.

One aspect of the answer is that the years through which Israel's ancestors are stuck in Egypt will not last forever (v. 14). The job of a judge is to see that deliverance comes to people who are treated as if they have no rights (e.g., Jer. 5:28; 22:16), and Yahweh will act as judge (*dîn*) so that Abraham's offspring do get out of the country where they have no rights. The First Testament would mostly use the verb *šāpaṭ* in speaking of such judgment (e.g., 16:5; 18:25), but here Yahweh uses the verb *dîn* in its participial form *dān*, which generates a link with the reference to Dan (also *dān*) in 14:14. There follows another link with what has preceded. The people will come out with much "property"—the not-very-common word that recurred in the previous chapter (14:11, 12, 16, 21; see also 12:5; 13:6). More explicitly than happened in v. 1, Yahweh brings out into the open the question whether Abraham (and his offspring) can survive by living in the unworldly way that Abraham adopted in refusing to keep Sodom's property. They will do more than survive. Their being resident aliens at best, state serfs and people with no rights at worst, will not mean that they have lost forever the relative prosperity that the family knew when they came from Harran and when they settled near Beth El and near Mamre after Abraham's own Egyptian adventure.

Yahweh sums up his promise in two bicola (vv. 15–16). The first relates to Abraham himself. He will not see these events that are centuries away, but he can relax and know that they are going to come about. In the parallel cola, first Yahweh speaks not neutrally or solemnly about Abraham "departing" (as Abraham did in v. 2) or about his "dying," but positively or encouragingly about his joining his ancestors. It's a slightly audacious way to speak of death, because while Abraham and Sarah's descendants will join them in the tomb that Abraham will acquire in Mamre (Gen. 23), Abraham and Sarah will not join their ancestors who were buried hundreds of miles away. Perhaps the assumption is that in Sheol they will join them. However, the stress lies on the expression that follows. Abraham will pass away *bəšālôm*: not merely "in peace" but with things going well for the rest of his life until the end, which they pretty much do (cf. the promise to Hezekiah, Isa. 39:8). The word *šālôm* makes a link with the reference to Melchizedek as king of *šālēm* in 14:18. Abraham will come to the grave in a good old age (175, which one might see as equivalent to 80 or 90 in our terms), like a shock of grain going up to the threshing floor at its season (Job 5:26).[38] Genesis 25:7–10 relates the fulfillment of the promise when Abraham is buried by his two oldest sons and joins Sarah.

It is not quite so clear that the companion summary promise about Abraham's offspring (v. 16) is a poetic line; it scans as 4–5 in the MT, and the cola are complementary, but they show parallelism only in the closing word in each. But I will give it the benefit of the doubt, and taking it as poetic may provide support for understanding four generations as a figurative expression for four lifetimes and thus four centuries (cf. v. 13)—though alternatively the four generations might stretch from Levi to Moses (via Kohat and Amram).[39] The second colon notes that Yahweh's fulfillment of his promises to Abraham has to work along with Yahweh being fair in his treatment of the people in country at the moment; in this context "Amorites" is a general term for the pre-Israelite inhabitants of the land, as "Canaanites" often is. But the allusion to them as Amorite takes up the references to the Amorite in 14:7 and 13. Yahweh cannot simply throw out the current inhabitants of the country in favor of Abraham's offspring whom he wishes to favor, even for the sake of his own purpose for the world as a whole. The Amorites must and will have lots of time to turn from their waywardness before Yahweh will be able to say, "That's it." In a parallelism between the two lines of Yahweh's promise, the allusion to Amorite waywardness being "complete" (*šālēm*) pairs with the allusion to "things being well" for Abraham (*šālôm*), as well as linking with the reference to the town of *šālēm* in 14:18. Leviticus 18:24–28 will specify (in the context of Lev. 18 as a whole) that the waywardness of the country's pre-Israelite inhabitants[40] may lie in the way they conduct their marital, familial, and sexual lives, which defile the country and will make it vomit them out, as it will do to Abraham's descendants if they live the same way.

15:17–21. To Abraham's question "How may I know?" Yahweh's response so far has again been simply to restate the promise in ultra-high-definition rainbow colors, thereby simply raising suspense. As it gets dark there comes the sign for which vv. 9–12 made the preparations. The preparations presuppose that the making of a commitment between two parties can involve the tearing apart of an animal, which implies an enacted prayer: if I do not keep my commitment to this pact, may I be torn apart like this animal (see Jer. 34:18–19). Middle Eastern treaties refer to such rites and prayers.[41] In an eighth-century inscription from Sefire near Aleppo, for instance, Matti'el the king of Arpad declares, "[As] this calf is cut up, thus Matti'el and his nobles will be cut up."[42] Here the smoking oven, which can also be described as a blazing

38. Von Rad, *Genesis*, 182.

39. So, e.g., Ibn Ezra, *Genesis*, 175.

40. On "waywardness," see also on 4:13.

41. See, e.g., Hamilton, *Genesis 1–17*, 430–32.

42. See *ANET* 660. Another treaty imposed on the king of Arpad is more specifically gruesome (see *ANET* 532–33).

torch, represents Yahweh himself, though Genesis does not quite say that Yahweh *is* the oven or the torch. It might convey to Abraham the message "Keep well away, this is dangerous." While the description might make the audience think of the fire pillar and cloud pillar at the exodus or the fiery and cloudy appearing of Yahweh at Sinai, the wording is distinctive to this passage. "All this is mystifying and is surely meant to be so."[43] But Yahweh is submitting himself to a familiar human ceremony. His passing between the parts of the animals is his enacted prayer that he may be torn apart like them if he does not keep his promise. "It is an extraordinary summit in the narrative,"[44] the most profound self-humbling of God in the First Testament.[45] No wonder Abraham trusted in Yahweh and deemed it as faithfulness on his part.

Thus (the narrator comments) Yahweh "solemnized a pact with Abraham" (v. 18). Abraham has a pact with Mamre, Eshkol, and Aner (14:13); Yahweh now offers him a different one. Literally, Yahweh "cut" the pact; one can see why this is a regular expression for the formal making of a "pact" or covenant.[46] Like Yahweh's pact with Noah, it is made "with" Abraham, despite the fact that Abraham is not required to do anything to make the pact work. Saying that Yahweh solemnized a pact *for* Abraham would be more logical; only Yahweh walked between the pieces of the creatures and enacted the self-curse. Yahweh goes on to summarize once more both aspects of the promise as he speaks of giving the *country* to Abraham's *offspring*. They are two aspects of one commitment. The reprise again adds yet more high definition. First, the outward bounds of the land will extend hyperbolically from the Nile to the Euphrates.[47] The expression "the Egyptian River" comes only here; the usual word for the Nile is *hayyəʾōr* (cf. 41:1–2), but its eastern branch is apparently *haššîḥôr*, which can be seen as the edge of the promised land (Josh. 13:3; 1 Chron. 13:5). In the terms of literal geography, the southern boundary will be the Egyptian Wadi (that is, Wadi El-Arish, just south of the modern border between Gaza and Egypt), as in passages such as Num. 34:5; Josh. 15:4; 1 Kings 8:65. Although the First Testament never pictures Egypt as an actual part of the short-lived Israelite empire, it does so picture land as far as the Euphrates—that is, including Syria (see 1 Kings 4:21–25 [5:1–5]; 1 Chron. 18:3; cf. Deut. 1:7; Josh. 1:4). But perhaps the expression in v. 17 denotes the land between that of Mesopotamia and that of Egypt.

Internally (vv. 18–21), it will mean taking over the land of ten peoples; the list is the first and most comprehensive of the many such lists in the First Testament. The Qenites lived south of Judah and were the group to whom Moses's father-in-law belonged (Judg. 1:16); the Qenizzites lived in southern

43. Alter, *Genesis*, 66.
44. Arnold, *Genesis*, 159.
45. Cf. C. Levin, "Jahwe und Abraham im Dialog," 257.
46. On this word, see 9:8–11 and the comment.
47. Cf. Dillmann, *Genesis*, 2:66.

Judah, to judge from Num. 32:12; the Qadmonites appear only here, but their name suggests that they are easterners. Genesis has already mentioned the Hittites (10:15), Perizzites (13:7), Repa'ites (14:5), Amorites (10:16), Canaanites (9:18), Girgashites (10:16), and Yebusites (10:16). These peoples represented nowhere near all the peoples of the area from Egypt to the Euphrates; 1 Kings 4:21–25 [5:1–5] implies a distinction between that larger area that Solomon ruled and the smaller area within it (which had once been the territory of these peoples), where the Israelites themselves actually lived.

Implications

The Promise of Land

God makes an agelong pact with Abraham's offspring that they will enjoy his blessing, that they will be fruitful, that he will be God for them, and that they will possess the land of Canaan. The First Testament assumes throughout that these promises hold, even though they are often belied by events. The promise to give the land of Canaan to Abraham's offspring first surfaced in 12:7, became a promise in perpetuity in 13:15, in 15:18–20 explicitly comes to designate the land currently occupied by ten peoples, but also in 15:16 has a significant rider attached to it. Though God can do what he likes with the world (see Amos 9:7; Rom. 9:17–18), he also recognizes a commitment to act in a fair way with people. In this connection Gen. 15:16 is "one of the pivotal sayings of the Old Testament."[48] God does not commission Israel to charge into Canaan just because he wants to throw the Canaanites out. Nor does Israel simply make up the idea that God has commissioned them to charge into Canaan—or if they do, they recognize that their action needs a moral rationale, and if the rationale is phony, their argument collapses.

In Gen. 15:16 God also recognizes a commitment to act in a long-tempered way. Genesis 15 offers one clue to the reasons why God's promises do not find fulfillment, at least for a long time. God effects his purpose not unilaterally but in interaction with nations and individuals, modifying or rescheduling his intentions in light of how human beings act. Second Peter 3 sees this commitment as lying behind the delay in Jesus's appearing.

The comment about waywardness in 15:16 would raise tricky questions for Israel itself. Was the promise of the land to Abraham's offspring implicitly conditional, so that Abraham's descendants could be deemed to have forfeited it by their waywardness? They do get thrown out of the land in 722 and 587 on such a basis. Yet they come back to at least part of the land.

Further, Abraham's offspring were destined to become a big people, and they did so; then through Jesus they became an exponentially bigger people.

48. Kidner, *Genesis*, 125.

And this new version of Abraham's people is not a nation and does not have a land. So what has happened to the promise to give his people the land, and to do so "permanently" (*ʿad-ʿôlām*)? Did God change his mind without telling anyone? Do we read too much into the "permanently"? Can we qualify it without qualifying the idea that Yahweh is God and that he enfolds his people "permanently" (Pss. 90:2; 103:17; 125:2)? But Isa. 32:14, 17 has an interesting "permanently" followed by a limiting "until," which perhaps hints that Yahweh can or would qualify or change his "permanently" only in order to put something better in its place. Did he do so through Jesus?

Through Jesus, God more than fulfills the promise of blessing by means of the gift of the Holy Spirit and more than fulfils the promise of fruitfulness through the giving of the Holy Spirit to the Gentiles. He threatens that the Jewish people may be cast off, but it seems to be a casting off only of the generation that declines to recognize Jesus. God's commitment to the Jewish people still stands. That fact would imply that his promise regarding the land of Canaan still stands, because a relationship to the land is integral to the being of Israel. The NT does not give any indication that this promise concerning the land no longer applies, in the way that it indicates that rules about circumcision and about cleanness and taboo no longer apply. Jesus confirms God's commitment to the Jewish people rather than terminating it, and the land is an aspect of that commitment. Thus the Jewish people's freedom since the late nineteenth century to return to the land has seemed to many Jewish and Christian people to be a process whereby God has been faithful to this promise. This view need not imply affirmation of the policies of the State of Israel. Nor need it imply sidestepping the implications of Gen. 15:16.

The NT hardly implies that the gift of Jesus and of the Holy Spirit replaces the gift of the land. The notion of Israel as a distinctive people does not disappear, and that notion is hard to make sense of without its having the notion of a land attached. A group needs land in order really to be a people and live. As long as there is still an Israel that is a definable people, God's permanent promise of the land is surely part of God's continuing commitment to it—though that consideration no more overrides questions about the rights of other people who have some claim on this land than was the case in Abraham's day. Further, for the wider Israel, which includes Gentiles who believe in Jesus, this land where Jesus lived, died, and rose could never lose its importance—as the phenomenon of pilgrimage suggests.

14

"But Saray . . ."

(16:1–16)

Overview

For some chapters now, Genesis will focus more resolutely on the question of offspring for Abraham and Sarah. In Gen. 16 we see the plot:

1. a. Whereas Gen. 15 raised Abraham's question about having offspring ("What will Yahweh do?"), Gen. 16 raises Sarah's question: "What are we to do?"
   b. And she provides an answer: "Let's see if Hagar can have a baby."
2. a. The trouble is that Hagar's pregnancy divides the two women and leads to Hagar's running away.
   b. But Yahweh's envoy finds her and sends her back with a promise regarding her son, and this promising leads to Hagar's naming God.
3. a. The eventual outcome of Sarah's proposal is thus "Yes, Hagar can have a baby," and the problem is thus solved.
   b. Except that the solution will turn out not to be God's solution (see Gen. 17).

The story thus involves Sarah, Abraham, Hagar, Yahweh's envoy, Yahweh himself, and Ishmael, and it unfolds in six scenes, dominated by conversation.

1. Sarah and Abraham: the marriage relationship (16:1–4a)
2. Sarah and Hagar: the friction (16:4b–6)
3. Hagar and the envoy: the finding (16:7–9)
4. Hagar and the envoy: the promise (16:10–12)

5. Hagar and Yahweh: the naming (16:13–14)
6. Hagar and Ishmael: the birthing (16:15–16)

Translation

1Now Śaray, Abram's wife, had not given birth for him, but she had a Miṣrite maidservant; her name was Hagar. **2**Śaray said to Abram, "Here, please: Yahweh has held me back from giving birth. Sleep with[1] my maidservant, please; maybe I can build myself up[2] through her." Abram listened to Śaray's voice, **3**and Śaray, Abram's wife, got Hagar the Miṣrite, her maidservant (at the end of ten years of Abram's living in the country of Kenaʿan), and gave her to Abram her husband as a wife for him. **4a**He slept with Hagar and she got pregnant.

4bShe saw that she was pregnant, and her mistress became diminished in her eyes. **5**Śaray said to Abram, "The violation done to me is because of you. I myself put my maidservant in your arms, she's seen that she's pregnant, and I've become diminished in her eyes. Yahweh decide between me and you!" **6**Abram said to Śaray, "Here, your maidservant is in your hand. Do to her what's good in your eyes." So Śaray humbled her, and she took flight from her.

7But Yahweh's envoy found her near a certain water spring[3] in the wilderness, near the spring on the Šur road. **8**He said, "Hagar, maidservant of Śaray, where have you come from[4] and where are you going?" She said, "From Śaray, my mistress—I'm taking flight." **9**Yahweh's envoy said to her, "Go back to your mistress. Let yourself be humbled[5] under her hand."

10But Yahweh's envoy said to her:

> "I will make your offspring really numerous,
> it won't be able to be counted up because of the number."

11And Yahweh's envoy said to her:

> "There, you're pregnant
> and you're going to give birth[6] to a son.
> You're to name him Yišmaʿeʾl,
> because Yahweh has listened to your humbling.[7]

1. Literally, "come to"; so also in v. 4.
2. *ʾIbbāneh* from *bānâ*. The verb form also hints at the word for son (*ben*); cf. the LXX's "so that you may father a child."
3. Literally, "near the water spring"; see GKC 126r.
4. Most SP MSS have *ʾwy* ("Oh [where]") instead of the interrogative *ʾy*, which makes the envoy more compassionate (Tal, *Genesis*, 118*).
5. Targum Onq. has "Let yourself be made to serve," which is less scandalous.
6. On the participle's form, see GKC 94f; but JM 89j sees it rather as a cross between participle and qatal.
7. Targum Onq. has "accepted your prayer," a rather different point.

[12]And he—he'll be humanity's wild donkey,[8]
his hand against everyone,
Everyone's hand against him,
and he'll dwell in the face of all his brothers.

[13]She named[9] Yahweh who spoke to her, "You are El roʾi,"[10] because (she said), "Is it really here that I would have looked for[11] the one who was looking at me?"[12] [14]That's why people named the well "Ḥay Roʾi Well."[13] There, it's between Qadeš and Bered.

[15]So Hagar gave birth to a son for Abram, and Abram named his son, to whom Hagar gave birth, Yišmaʿeʾl. [16]Abram was a man of eighty-six years when Hagar gave birth to Yišmaʿeʾl for Abram.

Interpretation

In the MT, Gen. 16 is a paragraph within Gen. 14–17, like Gen. 15. Following on Gen. 15, one would expect Gen. 16 to be a story about Abraham, and there are references to Abraham in the frame around the chapter and on the way along. The story's question would then be whether Abraham is really going to have a son (cf. v. 1a), and if so, how. And its answer is yes (vv. 15–16), but by a route that

a. is surprising (vv. 1b–4a),
b. brings family conflict and suffering (vv. 4b–6),
c. necessitates a divine intervention to get things back on the rails (vv. 7–9),
d. heralds a promising yet surprising future for the boy (vv. 10–12), and
e. issues in a revelation for his mother (vv. 13–14).

Whereas vv. 10–11 would make one think that Ishmael will indeed be the fulfillment of Yahweh's promise to Abraham, v. 12 subverts that idea,[14] and

8. Cf. the Tg. But GKC 128kl suggests "a wild donkey of a human being" (cf. Prov. 15:20). *HALOT* notes the suggestion that *pereʾ* means "zebra."

9. The Tg has "she called on."

10. *Rŏʾî*, a noun (see BDB 909a). The LXX and Vg imply *rōʾî*, a participle with first-person suffix, as in v. 13b.

11. Hagar's words are elliptical, but for the use of *ʾaḥărê* (usually "after") cf. 2 Kings 14:19 (Booij, "Hagar's Words"; see further Koenen, "Wer sieht wen?"). The Vg implies *ʾăḥōrê* "[seen] the back of" (cf. Exod. 33:23).

12. While *rōʾî* could be the pausal form of the noun *rŏʾî* that came earlier in the verse, it makes better sense taken as a participle with first-person suffix (cf. BDB 909a; see also Tal, *Genesis*, 119*).

13. "The well of the living one, the one looking at me." I take the name as a noun clause, like names such as Melchizedek: it then means, "The living one looks at me" or "The one who looks at me lives." Cf. Skinner, *Genesis*, 288.

14. Cf. Dillmann, *Genesis*, 2:68.

Gen. 17 will deconstruct this story's significance. This son is not the right one. "The dominant narrative tension throughout the story of Abraham" continues to be "one of delay."[15]

While one can thus read Gen. 16 as Abraham's story, he actually is marginal to it. Its opening makes one anticipate a story about Sarah, and at first she controls the plot. The story's problem is that Sarah cannot give Abraham a son (v. 1a). Its question is whether Sarah can solve the problem, and initially it seems that she can (vv. 1–4a). But Hagar's pregnancy complicates Sarah's position, and she tries to regain control, but her action complicates things some more (vv. 4b–6); the pattern is like the one in 12:9–20. Sarah then disappears from the story as agent or potential mother; the references to her in the third person (vv. 8, 9) underscore the point. While Hagar is instructed to go back and submit to her, we are not told whether she does so. And when the baby is born, Sarah is nowhere to be seen.

Sarah and Hagar are mistress and maidservant, wealthy and poor, Israelite and Egyptian, infertile and pregnant—both of them Abraham's wives, two women who thus have come to look down on each other. Genesis 16 is a story about the suffering of two women and the conflict between them, conflict in which Abraham has only a supporting (?) role. But the most prominent person in the story is Hagar. One could then say that the question underlying the story is this: how did an Egyptian servant girl come to be the mother of Abraham's firstborn (vv. 15–16)? The short answer appears: because her mistress could not conceive (vv. 1–4a). And the story could have gone straight from vv. 1–4a to vv. 15–16. Indeed, Jub. 14.21–24 makes it do so:

> And Abram rejoiced, and he told all of these things to Sarai his wife. And he believed that he would have seed, but she did not give birth. And Sarai advised Abram, her husband, and she said to him: "Go into Hagar, my Egyptian maid. It may be that I will build seed for you from her." And Abram heard his wife Sarai's word and he said, "Do (it)." And Sarai took Hagar, her Egyptian maid, and she gave her to Abram, her husband, so that she might be a wife. And he went into her. And she conceived and bore a son and he called him Ishmael, in the fifth year of this week. And that year was the eighty-sixth year in the life of Abram.

In Gen. 16 itself, the route from conception to birth is complicated:

a. Hagar's pregnancy issues in problems between her and Sarah (vv. 4b),
b. Sarah falls into oppressing Hagar, so Hagar runs away (vv. 5–6), but
c. Yahweh's envoy sends her back (vv. 7–9).

15. Reno, *Genesis*, 163.

Again, the story could have gone straight from there to the birth (from v. 9 to vv. 15–16). But the envoy's meeting with Hagar delays the denouement of the story further:

a. He makes promises to her about the number of her descendants (v. 10),
b. He provides a significant name for her son (v. 11),
c. He outlines her son's destiny (v. 12), and
d. She makes her response to God (vv. 13–14).

Although the chapter explains the identity of the Ishmaelites and the name of a well, there is thus so much more to it than this explanatory function requires. And while the story is set in the context of the wider narrative that relates how Yahweh's promise works out, Gen. 16 itself makes no reference to that theme as its context.[16] While it does take further the motif of the promise of a son, Gen. 16 is the first of a number of stories in Genesis of women who assert responsibility for their own destiny[17] and stories about family conflict—conflict between brothers and between wives. It contains no direct clues to a historical or social context beyond the realities of contexts in which such issues are important to people. It is the first of two stories about conflict between Sarah, Abraham, and Hagar; traditionally, Gen. 21 is seen as an Elohistic version, Gen. 16 as a conflation of J and P versions.

16:1–4a. Genesis 15 began with the anxiety, resentment, grief, disillusion, and sense of failure on the part of a man when he and his wife have not been able to have children. Genesis 16 begins with the grief, resentment, anxiety, disillusion, and sense of failure on the part of a woman. For women even more than for men, these are cross-cultural realities. Only a woman experiences menstruation, conception, pregnancy, birthing, nursing, weaning, and menopause, and these realities are integral to womanhood (to womanhood in general; different women feel differently about them). Most specifically, Sarah has not given birth to children "for him." She feels she has failed as a wife. (Neither party is concerned about the fulfillment of Yahweh's broader promise and purpose.) It's hard to know what to do in circumstances such as not being able to have a baby. It would be nice to think that Sarah prayed about her experience, like Hannah (1 Sam. 1). The Scriptures do urge people to pray and protest to God about such experiences, and they sometimes relate spectacular answers from God. But they also imply recognition that other such prayers are met with silence, and they relate with sympathy the way people do what they must do in tough circumstances. The audience should not be too hard on Sarah, or on Abraham if he doesn't know what to do at any point in this story.

16. Cf. Coats, *Genesis*, 130.
17. Cf. Seebass, *Genesis*, 2.1:94–95.

Sarah has an Egyptian maidservant, Hagar (v. 1b). We immediately thus discover three significant facts about her. She is an Egyptian, which suggests that she is part of Abraham and Sarah's family as a result of the Egyptian escapade related in 12:9–13:4. Thus 1QapGen 20.31–32 relates how Pharaoh gave her to Sarah. Like the servant girl in 2 Kings 5, she is a long way from home, though not an impossibly long way. She will set off for home in this story, but Yahweh will not let her get there; it is better to be a foreigner in this family through which Yahweh is at work than to be at home in Egypt (cf. Heb. 11:24–26), though it would be hard to believe it, and as far as we know she has no way of realizing it at the moment. Her position means that she is neither one thing nor the other. She is an Egyptian, but she is in Canaan. She is part of Abraham's family, but she is a foreigner. Paul's connecting Hagar with Mount Sinai "in Arabia" (Gal. 4:25) may link with references to "the Hagrites" in the First Testament (e.g., Ps. 83:6 [83:7]).[18] A second fact about her is that she is a maidservant or servant girl, the female equivalent to a servant. In her relationship to Sarah, she is a young female equivalent to the senior male servant who will play a key role in Gen. 24. That male servant belongs to Abraham and works for him in his capacity as master of the household; Hagar belongs to Sarah and works for her in her capacity as mistress of the household. The stories in Gen. 24 and 2 Kings 5 show that a servant's position need not be unpleasant or unrewarding, and it is misleading to think of such servants as "slaves" in the Euro-American sense, but the Hagar story will go on to show that their position can be vulnerable to the whim of their master or mistress. In that culture, you might be born as a servant because your parents were servants. You or your family might hit hard times and no longer be able to survive independently; thus you might need to enter service, and you might then be bought by a different master. You might be captured in war. We don't know how Hagar originally came to be a servant. We know that there are other maidservants in the household (12:16); Hagar is Sarah's personal assistant. The third fact about her is that we know her name. We don't know the name of the servant in Gen. 24 or the servant girl in 2 Kings 5, but Genesis gives us the names of all three servant girls it mentions (the others are Zilpah and Bilhah), though in each case it may be because of their sons' significance. Recording her name does contribute to Hagar's becoming a real person in the story. It also makes for a contrast with Abraham and Sarah's never using her name. To them she is simply "my/your maidservant." To Yahweh she is an individual and the object of his care, not just the vessel of Abraham and Sarah's child and the means of achieving Yahweh's purpose (KSG).

Sarah herself has a theology or spirituality (v. 2a). Genesis 11:30 described her as infertile and as having no children; the latter is an empirical fact, while the former is a plausible inference about her physical nature (only now does

18. Cf. Zimmerli, *1. Mose 12–25*, 62.

it become clear that the problem is not Abraham's). Her own observation more than a decade later, according to v. 3, is that she is childless because Yahweh has held her back from conceiving. The verb (*ʿāṣar*) is used several times in this connection; in another recurrent use it refers to Yahweh stopping up the sky so no rain falls. The First Testament doesn't suggest that every time a woman cannot have children it means Yahweh has closed her womb any more than that every time the rain fails it means Yahweh has stopped up the sky (though perhaps at one level that would be true). Often it's just one of those things. The First Testament does assume that Yahweh sometimes deliberately takes this action; ironically, Abraham and Sarah will shortly cause it to happen to some other women (20:18). But it's as hard to move from the general ("Yahweh sometimes closes wombs") to the particular ("Yahweh has closed my womb") as it is impossible to move from the particular ("Yahweh has opened my womb") to the general ("Yahweh always opens wombs"). This narrative does not comment on whether Sarah is right. Further, as well as having a theology, Sarah has a strategy, as do many would-be parents. In Western culture the strategy may involve in vitro fertilization or surrogacy. Sarah's proposal involves a form of surrogacy known in traditional societies where an infertile woman arranges or agrees for her husband to have sex with another woman whose child then counts as the infertile woman's child.[19] The act is thus not adultery; it does not involve illicit sex on the part of a married person. It is more an aspect of or a variant on polygamy, and in this case, v. 3 relates that Sarah does give Hagar to Abraham as a second wife. Maybe Sarah will then be able to "build herself up" through Hagar (cf. 30:3). Sarah will become a house(hold), whereas at the moment she and Abraham are simply a couple. Maybe she is concerned to have someone to pass on her dowry.[20] Maybe she also knows that mothers who adopt sometimes mysteriously then become pregnant when they couldn't before. There's no suggestion that she is operating on the basis of a "works-righteousness."[21] There's nothing wrong in principle with taking such an initiative; Rachel and Leah do so.[22] And there's nothing to raise questions about whether it's a "good-faith offer."[23]

Abraham agrees (v. 2b). Why not? It is an acceptable procedure in the culture. Abraham takes decisive action in 13:5–18 and in 14:1–24, and Yahweh becomes involved in the events. But here "no mighty patriarch is Abram, but rather the silent, acquiescent, and minor figure in a drama between two

19. See, e.g., Hamilton, *Genesis 1–17*, 444–45; Speiser, *Genesis*, 119–21. In Kenya, Shisanya ("Reflection," 147) says, when a man is sterile, close relatives similarly sire on his behalf, though secretly. Mbuwayesango ("Childlessness") gives a similar account of practice in Zimbabwe.

20. See Drey, "Role of Hagar," 186–89.

21. Against Reno, *Genesis*, 164.

22. Cf. Kaminsky, *Yet I Loved Jacob*, 32–33.

23. Visotzky, *Genesis of Ethics*, 43.

women."[24] And maybe it's worrying to the audience that the sequence of the woman making a suggestion and the man agreeing to it without thinking too much has an unfortunate precedent ("You listened to the voice of your wife," 3:17). Further, Abraham's taking decisive action in 12:9–13:4 had ambiguous results. And one wonders whether with hindsight, Abraham might later have concluded that consulting Yahweh about Sarah's suggestion would have been a good idea. "How we are to assess Sarai's attempt to circumvent her sterility is shrouded in ambiguity."[25]

Anyway, Sarah arranges and concludes a marriage (v. 3), giving her servant girl (who is likely a teenager) to a man who is old enough to be her father or grandfather. There is some irony about Sarah repeating the treatment she received at her husband's hands in Egypt.[26] But nothing happens that would necessarily seem odd to any of the parties. To judge from regulations in the Torah that are designed to restrain abuse, a man might well marry one of his household's servant girls or a servant girl who has been captured in war (see Exod. 21:2–11; Deut. 21:10–14). The girl might or might not have a choice, as Rebekah did about marrying Isaac, sight unseen (Gen. 24). We learn nothing about Hagar having any say in what happens. But a servant girl might regard such a marriage as a great step up in the world in terms of status and economic security. There is further irony about the language Genesis uses. Normally a man "gets" a wife or his parents "get" one for him (e.g., 4:19; 11:29; 12:19; 20:2; 21:21; 24:4; 25:1, 20; 28:2; 34:4). Here a wife gets another wife for her husband. And while there is something sad about a wife having to make this arrangement, the son of a polygamous marriage once told me that his mother was only too pleased to have a hand in choosing one of her friends to be his father's second wife. Hagar would presumably be a "secondary wife," as 25:6 implies (and see 22:24),[27] but Genesis here uses the ordinary word (*ʾiššâ*) for a woman or a wife, which it used for Sarah. The unnecessary repetition of this word to describe Sarah at the beginning of the verse (after all, we know that Sarah is Abraham's wife) and then its appearance as the last word in the verse does underline the incongruity of what happens for Western readers. But ten years have passed, so can Sarah be blamed? (This verse provided Jewish thinking with an argument to allow a man to divorce his wife after ten years if she has not been able to have children; see, e.g., Gen. Rab. 45.2.)

The strategy works (v. 4a). What does Abraham think? What are Abraham's fantasies about sex with a nubile, dark-skinned girl? The story is not concerned with such questions, and it implies that Abraham would not be concerned. It's a marital act, but it's a transaction. The important consideration is what follows when they all discover that Hagar is pregnant.

24. Trible, *Texts of Terror*, 11.
25. Levenson, *Death and Resurrection of the Beloved Son*, 90.
26. De La Torre, *Genesis*, 173.
27. See the comment there.

16:4b–6. Not surprisingly, the pregnancy changes the dynamics in the relationship of Sarah and Hagar. "Rather than solving the problem, . . . this plan soon resulted in the first '[rivalrous] love triangle' in the Bible."[28] It seems likely to change the women's relationships with Abraham too, but Genesis gives no hints in this direction, and it does seem to imply that for Abraham the sexual relationship is simply a transaction. One can understand Genesis to be commenting in v. 4b that Sarah becomes diminished in her own eyes;[29] it is not surprising if Hagar's pregnancy has that effect. But in Sarah's view—v. 5 will tell us—she has become diminished in Hagar's eyes. Hagar is now "a woman with attitude."[30] She is guilty of "reckless eyeballing."[31] Again, it is not surprising if this young foreign servant is rather proud of the fact that she can get pregnant when her mistress can't, that Yahweh has favored her as he has not favored Sarah. "In conceiving a child for her mistress, Hagar has seen a new reality that challenges the power structure."[32] In this entourage, Sarah has the power, but Hagar has the functioning womb, and she threatens to outrank her; Sarah becomes a nobody.[33] But unbeknownst to Hagar, that effect of getting pregnant is scary. "The person who diminishes you I will curse," Yahweh has promised Abraham (12:3). Hagar might have heard stories about servant girls in her position who became uppity and thought that they might replace the first wife (a development that Hammurabi's Law Code §§145–46 regulates against; cf. also Prov. 30:21–23).[34]

Once again, Sarah has a theology or spirituality (v. 5). She feels violated by Hagar. This feeling might seem like an overreaction (see the use of the word *ḥāmās* in 6:11, 13 and the comment), but it is apparently a real reaction, and the word "violation" may suggest a fear of the development Hammurabi presupposes. Anyhow, it's Abraham's fault; one might see these words, too, as hard to justify, given that it was her idea, not his. Now she wants Yahweh to decide who's responsible and who therefore needs to do something about it. It is in principle an appropriate stance, and she is clear what Yahweh's judgment will be, like David in 1 Sam. 24:12, 15 [24:13, 16].[35] Yahweh, after all, is supposed to be one who "cares for the weak and oppressed who cannot help themselves."[36] Implicitly, Sarah is also suggesting that Abraham, as head of the household, needs to accept some responsibility for the actions of his new wife rather than leaving God to sort it out. "Why does the Holy

28. Stancil, "Genesis 16:1–16; 21:8–21," 394.
29. Cf. Heard, *Dynamics of Diselection*, 65–66.
30. Rulon-Miller, "Hagar," 60.
31. See Splawn, "Reckless Eyeballing."
32. Trible, *Texts of Terror*, 13.
33. Mbuvi, *Belonging in Genesis*, 116, 126.
34. See *ANET* 172; Hays, *Hidden Riches*, 126.
35. Cf. Wenham, *Genesis 16–50*, 8.
36. Gunkel, *Genesis*, 185.

Spirit mention these quarrels? . . . Was there nothing more important or more profitable to record?" But it is useful to us that the Scriptures speak of such realities.[37]

Perhaps Abraham accepts responsibility (v. 6), though he "may well have sighed privately over his temperamental wife (Prov. 25:24; 27:15; Sir. 25:16ff.; 26:6–7)."[38] Either he then subcontracts responsibility to Sarah and gives her the power to decide what should be done, or he assumes that Hagar's being his (secondary) wife doesn't change her status as Sarah's maidservant, and Sarah is in charge of her maidservants. Encouraging Sarah to do what is good in her eyes might again follow unwise precedents (see 3:6; 6:2). The action it encourages is not merely a restoration of or insistence on Hagar's maidservant status. It also encourages Sarah to put her down. The hand to which Abraham surrenders Hagar is "a hard hand, which humbles the hated rival."[39] Is Sarah powerless to control her own rage over her infertility and the humiliation it has brought her?[40] While her action corresponds to the rule in Hammurabi about putting the maidservant in her place, "humble" (*ʿānâ* piel) was ironically the word that described Hagar's compatriots' coming treatment of Sarah's offspring (15:13). Sarah indeed treats Hagar as more like a slave than a servant (again, cf. Deut. 21:14). It's not surprising that Hagar takes flight (*bāraḥ*); again it's a word that will apply to the Israelites escaping from Egypt (Exod. 14:5). Hard masters always take the risk of servants fleeing (cf. Deut. 23:15–16 [23:16–17]). Even if you're pregnant, "better all the dangers of the desert path than humiliation in Sarah's tent."[41] As Abraham has not worried too much about his unborn child in telling Sarah she can do as she wishes with Hagar, so Sarah has not worried too much about him in the way she has treated her, and so Hagar runs away with Abraham's child in her womb.[42] She also thereby "denies Sarai's claim of Hagar's child as hers, heir to Abram."[43] Hagar takes responsibility for herself and her future and her baby.[44]

16:7–9. Thus far, it's been a very human story, sadly familiar, with its first scene ending in disaster for all concerned: "Hagar has lost her home, Sarai her maid, and Abram his second wife and newborn child."[45] Perhaps no one escapes it without some discredit,[46] though the story's ambiguities make it inappropriate to focus on allocating blame.[47] Now something supernatural

37. Luther, *Genesis 15–20*, 53–54.
38. Gunkel, *Genesis*, 185.
39. Zimmerli, *1. Mose 12–25*, 63.
40. Cf. M. Jacobs, *Gender, Power, and Persuasion*, 139–40.
41. Gunkel, *Genesis*, 185.
42. Cf. Fretheim, *Abraham*, 96.
43. De La Torre, *Genesis*, 175.
44. Cf. Masenya, "Bosadi (Womanhood) Reading," 282.
45. Wenham, *Genesis 16–50*, 9.
46. Cf. Willet, *Hexapla in Genesin & Exodum*, 155.
47. Cf. Mbuvi, *Belonging in Genesis*, 127.

occurs, as happens in a number of these stories (see 12:1 within 11:27–12:8; 12:17 within 12:9–13:4; 13:14–17 within 13:5–18).

It's the first appearance of an envoy from Yahweh (v. 7). Such an envoy (*mal'āk*) is like a presidential aide sent to investigate some question or to implement a presidential decision. The LXX's translation *angelos*, suggesting a messenger, is misleading, as is English "angel"; the Hebrew word is related to *məlā'kâ*, which is simply "work." This envoy is out on the job looking for Hagar on Yahweh's behalf. "Hagar was not running away in order to find God, but an 'angel of Yahweh' found her running."[48] To Hagar, this must just seem like an ordinary man (cf. 18:2 in association with 19:1). Being found in the wilderness by a man or by Yahweh's envoy might or might not be good news; it will turn out to be a mixture. Presumably Yahweh sent this aide, but Genesis has no explanation for the sending. God does not usually send an aide after a runaway slave, though Abraham might do so. But Hagar has become no ordinary runaway: she is carrying Abraham's child. Shur is a wilderness area on the inland route from Canaan to Egypt (cf. 20:1; 25:18; Exod. 15:22–23). The road to or through Shur would be a natural place to look for Hagar as she tries to go back home to Egypt. She will have been walking for a week. Has she stopped by the spring just to get a drink and a rest, or to stay overnight, or to hitch a ride, or to see if some kinder master will take her into his entourage? Is she giving up her impossible trek, or is she nearly home?

The envoy is the first person to address Hagar (v. 8), and he addresses her by name. His questions are the natural ones to ask of a fellow traveler. For Yahweh's envoy, they are questions to which (one would think) he already knows the answers, as is the case with Yahweh in Gen. 3–4. After all, he knows her name and he knows where to find her. But at least part of what is going on is that Hagar needs to articulate the answers to herself and to him and to the people listening to her story. However, she replies only to the first of the envoy's questions; while we assume that she is on her way home to Egypt, she does not talk about that. Even revealing what she does reveal might be dangerous; there could be a reward for returning a runaway servant.

In fact, the envoy moves in this direction (v. 9). Indeed, his response might seem extraordinarily hard, and the instruction to walk a week back again is not its toughest aspect. "It is the most pointed counter-example to the misleading over-generalization . . . that the biblical God is on the side of the impoverished and the oppressed."[49] Why does he make this requirement of her? Because Hagar is the maidservant and Sarah is the mistress. Hagar is to return to her mistress, not to her husband. But behind that fact is Sarah's being the wife of the man whose baby Hagar is carrying. Yes, Hagar has been drawn into that family through which Yahweh is at work, and she cannot be

48. Arnold, *Genesis*, 164.

49. Levenson, *Death and Resurrection of the Beloved Son*, 93.

allowed out of it, even if it means humbling, suffering, and harsh treatment. In the long run, it will be in her best interests too. Indeed, perhaps the envoy is concerned with her interests even in the short run. She is a pregnant woman out in the desert, perhaps with still some distance to go before she reaches her former home. Perhaps he's not simply being tough but is rescuing her. Her story illustrates how "God is intimately involved with those who suffer, but often not in a cataclysmic way."[50]

16:10–12. That understanding fits with the further things he has to say. If Sarah has become diminished in Hagar's eyes, Hagar has laid herself open to Yahweh's curse (Gen. 12:1–3), but instead the envoy blesses her in a way that fits the promise to Abraham in those verses. "To accompany Hagar on her return, God showers her with promises."[51] Putting the words of blessing in poetic lines underlines their importance and authority. Again, as often happens, the aide speaks as if he is Yahweh. He is passing along Yahweh's own words (see v. 13). Indeed, it is the envoy's key function—he actually is a messenger. "God is present not in the messenger, but in the message."[52]

The first poetic line (v. 10) is full of resonances. Genesis has spoken before about Yahweh determining to "make very numerous," to "make very great": he said it at 3:16, that other occasion when a man listened too easily to his wife. Yahweh then went on to speak about the pain of the woman's pregnancy. Here he promises to make very great the woman's offspring—great in the sense of numerous, as the parallel colon indicates; 25:12–18 will relate the fulfillment of the promise. This promise about offspring does pick up Yahweh's promise to the man whose child she will bear. It especially recalls 15:5 with its reference to the impossibility of counting up how many there are. The promise will be repeated for him and for Isaac and for Jacob; Hagar is the only woman to whom it is given. The necessity for her to return to Abraham and Sarah is implicit. Her offspring needs to be born in that context.

For the third time in three verses (v. 11a), Genesis notes that it is Yahweh's envoy who speaks the words that will follow. The repetition underscores that they are to be taken seriously, whether they are a hard bidding or an encouraging promise. The bidding should be seen in light of the promise and the promise in light of the bidding, as was the case in Yahweh's first words to Abraham (12:1–3). These words by the envoy constitute the first occurrence of a formulation that will recur in the Scriptures, though each occurrence has a distinctive significance in its context.[53] Such announcements of a son's birth to women who are not expecting to have one may include the appearing of an envoy and a greeting, an announcement of a coming pregnancy and of the birth of a son, the specifying of the boy's name and an explanation of

50. B. Tanner, "My Sister Sarah," 67–68.
51. Fretheim, *Abraham*, 105.
52. Westermann, *Genesis 12–36*, 244.
53. See, e.g., Westermann, *Genesis 12–36*, 245–46.

it, and a declaration about what will become of him (see Judg. 13:3–5; Isa. 7:14–16; Luke 1:18–22).

Here the follow-up promise (v. 11b) indeed first adds the child's sex and then determines his name. If Hagar is tempted to think it is a tough requirement that she should go back to submit to Sarah's ill treatment, then the explanation might take the edge off the sense that Yahweh is treating her as hard as Sarah did and is not paying much attention to Hagar herself. Actually, Yahweh has been listening to Sarah's treatment of her, and Hagar is to name her son accordingly. The name "Ishmael" recurs elsewhere (e.g., 2 Kings 25:23, 25; 1 Chron. 8:38); in regular usage it would likely express his parents' prayer for their child, "May God listen." Here it constitutes an affirmation. Ishmael is the first person to be named before being born.[54] Genesis does not tell us that Sarah prayed in light of her conviction that Yahweh had closed her womb or that Hagar prayed in the midst of her suffering. It does tell us that God has been listening to the harshness of what Sarah has said and done to Hagar. Sarah has declared the hope that Yahweh will decide between herself and Abraham; he has decided between her and Hagar. As happens in other passages (not least 14:18–23), Genesis combines the reference to El in Ishmael's name (compare the name Israel) with a reference to Yahweh, whom the envoy does represent but whose name someone living in Abraham's day would not use.

Then there is the child's destiny (v. 12). Half Egyptian, half Abrahamic, his mother a maidservant and a secondary wife, what chance does he have? But Ishmael will not be someone you can mess with. He'll be like the wild donkeys of the wilderness that you can't tame (cf. Job 39:5–8). "He will be free among men. . . . No stranger will rule over him."[55] If people want to be in conflict with him, he will give as good as he gets. Like the story about Noah, Ham, and Canaan in Gen. 9, for the audience this declaration about Ishmael may explain why the Ishmaelites are the people they are. The Ishmaelites feature in Mesopotamian inscriptions from Israelite times, and they are traditionally understood to be the ancestors of the Arabs. But there are few references to them in the First Testament and no indications of poor relationships with Israel (indeed, see, e.g., 1 Chron. 2:17; 27:30). They are strange, yet they are family.[56] The envoy's characterization of Ishmael as aggressive and determined may suggest that he will be a true son of his father, as Abraham was portrayed in Gen. 14.

16:13–14. Hagar's response adds a naming of God to the narrative's naming of her. "Hagar is a theologian,"[57] the Scriptures' first theologian, and the only person in the First Testament who gives God a name. The context of this

54. Cf. Willet, *Hexapla in Genesin & Exodum*, 155.

55. Ibn Ezra, *Genesis*, 180. The words are thus not inherently pejorative; cf. Heard, "Road to Paran," 277–79.

56. Cf. Noort, "Created in the Image of the Son," 35.

57. Cf. Trible, *Texts of Terror*, 18. See further Egger, *"Hagar, woher kommst du?"*

declaration indicates the nature of theology as a response to a recognition that God has spoken to you; Hagar has recognized it. The form of the declaration, "You are . . . ," also marks Hagar as someone who addresses God in praise (cf. Ps. 77:14 [77:15]).[58] She knows that theology is doxology. It is paradoxical for Genesis to say that Hagar is giving a name to Yahweh, since she does not know that Yahweh is the name of the God she is naming. She gives him a name that incorporates the term for God in Ishmael's name and that thus also parallels the one Melchizedek used. He called God *ʾēl ʿelyôn*; Hagar calls God *ʾēl rŏʾî*. He is "God of seeing/sight," which nicely covers both "God who sees" and "God whom I see." He had spoken of hearing—hearing her ill treatment at the hands of Sarah, the truth expressed in Ishmael's name. She speaks of his seeing—seeing her on the run. She knows that seeing Yahweh's envoy is more or less the same as seeing God, though without the danger. He has seen her; she has seen him. The movement between talk by the envoy and by Yahweh himself will recur in 31:11–14.

The well also gains its name from what has happened there (v. 14)—or at least, the name reminds people of this story. Again, some of the people listening to the story would know the well. At that well God has made himself known as "The one who sees me lives" or "The one who lives sees me," as he has made himself known at Jerusalem as God On High. So they will call on God by that name at this well. Its location near Qadesh (cf. 14:7) is on the way from Mamre to Shur, though we don't know where Bered is.

16:15–16. The story seems to assume that Hagar does as the envoy says, but it doesn't say so, and specifically it doesn't say that she returns to Sarah. If anything, she returns to Abraham. She has her son, and Abraham names him in accordance with what the envoy said to her and the fact that she has borne his child. While one might have liked the story to end with Hagar's naming the child (mothers and/or fathers can name children in the First Testament), Abraham's naming him confirms his recognition and acceptance of the child and the child's clear place at the center of the family. On the other hand, Sarah's not naming him and the omission of any reference to her at the close of the story—though she has been the one who set going the process whereby he was born—implies that her hope has not been realized that through him she might build herself up.[59] It is Abraham who gets built up (he is maybe forty-five or fifty in our terms), and so does Hagar. Thus the story doesn't resolve the tension from which it started; it drops the tension for new motifs,[60] as sometimes happens in family conflicts. In other respects the story comes to a happy end, with God's promise fulfilled and no rebuke from God.

58. Cf. Westermann, *Genesis 12–36*, 247.
59. Cf. Hamilton, *Genesis 1–17*, 458.
60. Coats, *Genesis*, 131.

Implications

Hagar and Ishmael

Genesis 12–22 can be plausibly read concentrically:[61]

the call; blessing promised (12a)
  Abraham in a foreign land; wife-sister motif (12b)
    Lot in danger; Sodom (13–14)
      covenant (15)
        Hagar and Ishmael (16)
      covenant (17)
    Lot in danger; Sodom (18–19)
  Abraham in a foreign land; wife-sister motif (20)
        Hagar and Ishmael (21)
the call; blessing confirmed (22)

It is then a feature of the palistrophe that Hagar and Ishmael come at its center and disturb it again before it comes to an end.[62] The story illustrates how "God has not exclusively committed himself to Abraham-Sarah. God's concern is not confined to the elect line. There is passion and concern for the troubled ones who stand outside that line."[63] Yahweh listens to the humbling of Hagar as he will listen to the humbling of the Israelites in Egypt. Yahweh sees her and makes himself known to her as the one who is looking after her, as he will see the Israelites' suffering under the Egyptians. He lets Hagar see him in the Sinai desert as he will let Moses see him in the Sinai desert. He is involved in the destiny of the Ishmaelites as he is involved in the destiny of the Israelites, even though they have different places in the working out of his purpose. And humanity's wild donkeys, with their fierceness and aggressiveness, are among the people made in his image. The question is only what they do with their fierceness and aggressiveness.

"In the messenger's greeting Hagar has met God in action, reaching the earth and beholding the human in her distress."[64] Abraham and Sarah may have acted in accordance with Middle Eastern law and custom, but God implicitly critiques it.[65] Luke 1 then reaches back to the Hagar story when it "narrates a similar meeting with a messenger of God, which evokes the same reaction: 'For he has regarded the low estate of his handmaiden.'" Further, God's

61. Cf. Magonet, *Bible Lives*, 25; Crotty ("Near Sacrifice of Isaac," 194) neatly adds the genealogies in 11:10–32 and 25:18 to the structure, though the plausibility of this addition depends on seeing 23:1–24:67 as later additions.

62. Cf. Goldingay, "Place of Ishmael."

63. Brueggemann, *Genesis*, 153. Cf. Simopoulos, "Who Was Hagar?" Contrast Okoye, "Sarah and Hagar."

64. Westermann, *Genesis 12–36*, 250.

65. Cf. Angel, "Sarah's Treatment of Hagar."

self-revelation here through his messenger suggests a way of understanding his self-revelation through Jesus. The person of the messenger of Yahweh, both divine and human, suggests a biblical (rather than Greek) starting point for thinking about the incarnation.[66]

But in a Western and postcolonial context it is important to note that Hagar is an African woman.[67] And "for more than a hundred years Hagar—the African slave of the Hebrew woman Sarah—has appeared in the deposits of African-American culture. Sculptors, writers, poets, scholars, preachers and just plain folks have passed along the biblical figure Hagar to generation after generation of black folks."[68] Women who experience "slavery, poverty, ethnicity, sexual and economic exploitation, surrogacy, rape, domestic violence, homelessness, motherhood, single-parenting and radical encounters with God"[69] have been able to find themselves in Hagar's story. The encounter with God is God's encounter with her, and she is someone whom the story treats "with special honors."[70] In scholarly writing over recent decades, her story has become a dominant theme in the study of Gen. 12–50.[71]

Appreciative and troubled readings of Hagar's story overlap with appreciative and troubled readings of Paul's Letter to Philemon. Paul's sending Onesimus back to Philemon follows the example of the envoy in the Hagar story, though Onesimus is a slave in the Roman sense and not merely a servant in the Middle Eastern sense. One would prefer both the servant and the slave to be freed, but both the envoy and the apostle combine realism with theological considerations. The envoy is perhaps being realistic about a pregnant woman trekking through the desert and is taking account of whose baby she is carrying (not Sarah's!). The apostle is perhaps being realistic about the integral place of slavery in the life of the Roman Empire and is taking account of the revolution that Jesus has nevertheless brought to the relationship of masters and slaves. "God liberates and God does not always liberate the oppressed. God speaks comforting words to the survival and quality-of-life struggle of many families."[72] God "does not always liberate the oppressed as they would like, but . . . hears and responds to the cry of the desperate." Thus "God is at work in both liberation and survival," and we need a theology of support and care and a theology of survival.[73]

66. Westermann, *Genesis 12–36*, 250.

67. See Adamo and Eghwubare, "African Wife of Abraham."

68. D. Williams, *Sisters in the Wilderness*, 2.

69. Cf. D. Williams, *Sisters in the Wilderness*, 4 (see further 15–33); also De La Torre, *Genesis*, 171; Trible, *Texts of Terror*, 9–35; Sherwood, "Hagar and Ishmael"; Andrews, "Genesis 16:1–16." Durant ("It's Complicated") reflects on the task of interpreting the text when one does not belong to the margins.

70. T. Schneider, *Mothers of Promise*, 103.

71. For Africa itself, see Shisanya ("Reflection"); for Iraq, see Sherwood ("Hagar and Ishmael," 302).

72. D. Williams, *Sisters in the Wilderness*, 199.

73. Sakenfeld, *Just Wives?*, 7, 21–22.

15
The Pact and Its Sign

(17:1–27)

Overview

Like Gen. 15, this chapter reports Yahweh's intention to make a pact with Abraham (the word "pact" comes thirteen times, more than any other chapter in the Scriptures) to give him many descendants and to give him the land of Canaan as his possession. Whereas Gen. 15 speaks most of the land but also of the descendants, Gen. 17 speaks most of the descendants but also of the land. In Gen. 15 Yahweh solemnizes the pact on his part by a visible ritual; in Gen. 17 Abraham implements the pact on his part by a visible sign. In Gen. 17 God

- declares that the pact will be permanent and heightens other aspects of the promises,
- gives Abraham and Sarah new names,
- requires the men in the family to practice circumcision,
- insists that the main promise will be fulfilled through a son that Sarah will yet bear, and
- adds a promise for Ishmael and emphasizes the inclusion of the rest of the household.

Genesis 17 has been seen as the high point or "watershed" of the Abraham story.[1] One might then see it as answering a question: what is the fundamental

1. Wenham, *Genesis 16–50*, 16. But the discussion of "Hagar and Ismael" above notes that the concentric structure of Gen. 12–22 works against that suggestion.

nature of God's pact or covenant with Abraham and thus with Israel? The answer is that it involves

- God's agelong promise that Abraham's offspring will be a numerous people, that they will possess the land of Canaan, and that he will be God for them; and
- their practice of circumcision, their living transparently in integrity before him, and their recognizing their membership of a larger family.

Translation

1Abram was a man of ninety-nine years. Yahweh appeared to Abram and said to him, "I am El Šadday. Walk about before me and be a person of integrity; **2**and I will make[2] my pact between me and you, and make you very, very numerous." **3**Abram fell on his face.

God spoke with him: **4**"I myself—here is my pact with you. You will become the ancestor of a horde of nations. **5**You will no longer be named Abram: your name will be Abraham, because I am making you[3] the "ancestor of a horde" of nations. **6**I will enable you to be very, very fruitful and make you into nations. From you kings will go out. **7**I will implement my pact between me and you and your offspring after you, through their generations, as an agelong pact, to be God for you and for your offspring after you. **8**I will give to you, and to your offspring after you, the country where you are residing as aliens, the entire country of Kenaʿan, as an agelong holding, and I will be God for them."

9And God said to Abraham, "But you: my pact you're to keep, you and your offspring after you, through their generations. **10**This is my pact that you people are[4] to keep, between me and you and your offspring after you: every male being circumcised on your part.[5] **11**You're to be circumcised in the flesh of your foreskin.[6] It will be a sign of a pact between me and you. **12**As a child of eight days, every male is to be circumcised on your part, through your generations. One born in the household or acquired for silver from any foreigner, who doesn't belong to your offspring: **13**he is definitely to be circumcised,[7] one born in your household

2. A cohortative follows on the imperative: you bind yourself to acting, and I then bind myself to acting (cf. *IBHS* 34.6).

3. The performative/declaratory qatal suggests a speech act, "I hereby make you" (cf. Seebass, *Genesis*, 2.1:97), followed by waw-consecutives; the sequence recurs in vv. 16 and 20.

4. The MT moves to plural "you" at this point; the LXX has singular here but plural later in the verse.

5. For *lākem* the LXX, Vg have "[every male] of you," but the word order suggests something more like *lə* of agency as in 14:17; 31:15 (cf. BDB 514a; Althann, "*mwl*").

6. On the form of the verb and the construction, see GKC 67dd, 121d.

7. The infinitive precedes the finite verb for emphasis: literally, "with circumcising he is to be circumcised."

or acquired for silver. My pact in your flesh will be an agelong pact. **14**A foreskinned male, who is not circumcised in the flesh of his foreskin:[8] that person will be cut off from his people. He has contravened[9] my pact."

15And God said to Abraham: "Śaray, your wife: you're not to name her Śaray, because her name will be Śarah. **16**I will bless her. I am indeed giving you a son from her. I will bless her and she will become nations; there will be kings of peoples from her."[10] **17**Abraham fell on his face, laughed,[11] and said to himself, "To a man of a hundred years will a child be born, or will Śarah—will a woman of ninety years give birth?"[12]

18Abraham said to God, "If only Yišmaʿeʾl might live before you." **19**God said, "Well: Śarah your wife, she's going to give birth to a son for you, and you're to name him Yiṣḥaq. I will implement my pact with him as an agelong pact for his offspring after him. **20**As for Yišmaʿeʾl: I've listened. There, I am blessing him. I will enable him to be fruitful and very, very numerous. Twelve leaders he will father, and I will make him a big nation. **21**But my pact I will implement with Yiṣḥaq, to whom Śarah will give birth for you at this set time next year." **22**So he finished speaking with him. And God withdrew[13] from Abraham.

23So Abraham got Yišmaʿeʾl his son and all those born in his household and all those acquired with his silver, every male among the people in Abraham's household, and circumcised the flesh of their foreskin, on that very day, as God had spoken with him. **24**Abraham was a man of ninety-nine years when he was circumcised (the flesh of his foreskin),[14] **25**while Yišmaʿeʾl his son was a boy of thirteen years when he was circumcised in the flesh of his foreskin. **26**On this very day Abraham was circumcised, he and Yišmaʿeʾl his son, **27**and all the men in his household, born in the household and acquired with silver from a foreigner—they were circumcised with him.

8. The LXX adds "on the eighth day," which Thiessen ("Text of Genesis 17:14") suggests is the older reading.

9. The LXX's "scattered," the Vg's "made invalid," and English versions' "broken" overtranslate. *Pārar* hiphil is the opposite of *šāmar* (v. 9), not the opposite of *qûm* hiphil (cf. Skinner, *Genesis*, 293).

10. More literally, "She will be nations; kings of peoples from her will be"—complementary clauses that work by parataxis in abb′a′ order. In v. 16b some LXX MSS, Vg have "bless him . . . he will become . . . from him" (cf. Tal, *Genesis*, 120*).

11. Jubilees 15.17 and the Tgs have "rejoiced" or "wondered."

12. The double question is formulated in an odd way, highlighting the expression of incredulity (GKC 150g).

13. The LXX and Vg translate *wayyaʿal* more literally, "went up," but the verb can refer, e.g., to enemies withdrawing (as in 1 Kings 15:19), and it does not imply God going up into the heavens—God did not come down from there (v. 1). God usually "appears" rather than "comes down."

14. The *ʾet* that appears in vv. 11, 14, 25 does not appear here (the SP supplies it).

Interpretation

Even more than Gen. 15, and in contrast to Gen. 16, for the most part Gen. 17 is not much of a narrative,[15] until the end, nor even a dialogue,[16] but a piece of theological teaching,[17] laying down a rule.

God appears and speaks; Abraham falls on his face (17:1–3a)
God speaks to Abraham, making promises ("I myself . . .") (17:3b–8)
God speaks to Abraham, issuing requirements ("but you . . .") (17:9–14)
God speaks to Abraham about Sarah, making promises ("Śaray, your wife . . .") (17:15–16)
Abraham falls on his face and speaks to himself (17:17)
Abraham speaks to God (17:18)
God responds (17:19–21)
God finishes speaking and disappears (17:22)
Abraham does as God said (17:23–26)

For the third time in Genesis, Yahweh takes an initiative in speaking to Abraham.

- In 12:1–8 Yahweh promises him increase and a land (in 12:9–14:24 Yahweh reasserts his promises, in response to an initiative by Abraham).
- In 15:1–21 Yahweh promises him increase and land and undergirds the promise by making a pact.
- In 16:1–16 Yahweh reasserts his promises in response to an initiative by Sarah.
- In 17:1–27 Yahweh promises him increase and land, undergirds the promise by making a pact, and four times repeats that the promises are permanent.

After this systematic account, there is no more to be said.[18]

The stress on permanence in Gen. 17 suggests that one question behind the chapter is whether there is a time limit to God's promises.[19] The declaration that there is no time limit would be important to the listeners in contexts when it might seem that the two promises no longer apply. The eighth and seventh centuries would be such a context, when Ephraim was cut down and then

15. Cf., e.g., Westermann, *Genesis 12–36*, 254.
16. Cf. Coats, *Genesis*, 136.
17. Cf. Gunkel, *Genesis*, 263.
18. Wenham (*Genesis 16–50*, 16–17) further details the development in the promises.
19. Cf. the discussion of "The Promise of Land" at the end of the comments on Gen. 15 above.

overrun by Assyria. The Babylonian period would be such a context, especially for Judahites in exile. And the Persian period would be such a context, when Judah is a tiny remnant in land and population.

The stress on God's initiative in making promises is accompanied by the laying down of a condition that is not hard to fulfill and that we have no record of the people failing to fulfill, unlike (say) Sabbath observance, at least until the second century (see, e.g., 1 Macc. 1:15, 48, 60–61).[20] To the people of God the chapter therefore says, "You're circumcised, aren't you? So you qualify to see God's promise fulfilled. And here is the promise!" The audience knows that Yahweh has fulfilled his crazy promise about Sarah having a baby, at which Abraham laughs; the reminder would be an encouragement to believe the impossible in their day (cf. Isa. 51:1–2).[21]

The focus on Ishmael in Gen. 17 may suggest another question underlying the chapter, as well as underlying Gen. 16. Genesis 17 leaves Ishmael in an ambiguous position. He is circumcised like everyone else, yet the covenant belongs to Isaac. The Israelites know the Ishmaelites, know they are related to Israel, know they are not their enemies, know (apparently) that Ishmael is Abraham's first son. So what is the status of Ishmael's line?

As an account of God making a covenant, Gen. 17 is traditionally seen as P's equivalent to Gen. 15. It generally speaks of "God" rather than of "Yahweh" (the occurrence of this name in v. 1 would be a result of the process whereby the sources were combined), and it manifests P's characteristic liking for figures. As the P creation story provided the rationale for observing the Sabbath and the P Noah story provided the validation for the rule about abstaining from blood, the P Abraham story here explains the origin of circumcision.[22] Genesis 18 will again tell of God promising that Sarah will have a baby in her old age. So Gen. 17 is the P version of Gen. 18 as well as the P version of Gen. 15.

17:1–3a. Thirteen years have passed since the birth of Ishmael; he is about to become a man. Abraham has reason to be living a relaxed life as he goes about his business of looking after sheep, confident in the fulfillment of God's promise through Ishmael (and maybe there is no reason for Sarah and Hagar not to be relaxed about it too, but we will hear nothing of them until chapters 18–21). Abraham is about to become a hundred years old, and there is no doubt that he and Sarah are people of maturity.[23] But it is an appropriate age for something climactic to happen to him.[24]

20. And see the extensive expansion of Gen. 17 in Jub. 15 (see, e.g., Segal, *Book of Jubilees*, 229–45; van Ruiten, *Abraham in the Book of Jubilees*, 137–67).

21. Cf. van Dijk-Hemmes, *Double Voice of Her Desire*, 46.

22. But it's also been suggested that the original P version of the story lacked the rule about circumcision in vv. 9–14: see Seebass, *Genesis*, 2.1:111–12.

23. Origen, *Homilies on Genesis*, 92.

24. Cf. Speiser, *Genesis*, 126.

And Yahweh appears to him (v. 1b) as he did in 12:7 when he first made the promise of land; he had meanwhile spoken to him in a vision, in 15:1. Either way (appearance or vision), the point about the manifestation is the message that follows. The manifestation gives force and authenticity to the message. The message is not just something Abraham imagines. By his self-introduction Yahweh points up the momentousness of the message that is coming, as he did in 15:7. In keeping with recurrent practice in Genesis, while the narrator identifies him as Yahweh, it has him speaking of himself in a way appropriate to the period before the revelation of this name in Exodus. He declares, "I am El Shadday." The name compares with El Elyon and El Roʿi, the names used by Melchizedek and Hagar. This name comes four more times in Gen. 12–50 and then in Exod. 6:3 (also Ezek. 10:5). The term *Shadday* on its own occurs occasionally elsewhere, especially in Job, where it is again appropriate on the lips of people outside the sphere of the revelation of the name *Yahweh*. If we ignore the anachronistic use of the name Yahweh, in Gen. 1–11 God is simply God; in Gen. 12–50 he is characteristically El Shadday; it is with his appearing to Moses in Exodus that he becomes Yahweh. Whereas Genesis explicitly interprets El Roʿi, and the second element in El Elyon surely has the same meaning as it has in ordinary usage, the meaning of Shadday is not obvious, and neither Genesis nor the rest of the First Testament explains it. The nearest we get to an explanation is the link with the verb *šādad* in Isa. 13:6, which would suggest the meaning "Devastator." Possibly the Vg's translation "omnipotent" is a watered-down version of an assumed link with *šādad*. But generally it's simply a name, used outside contexts where the name Yahweh is appropriate. Here, the LXX has simply "your God," which corresponds to the expression's suggestion of God's nearness to his people.[25]

God's subsequent words in v. 1b follow the pattern of 12:1–3: first a command, then a promise. The command picks up the verb used of Enoch and Noah (5:22, 24; 6:9), though God speaks of walking about "before me," not "with me." He may not be excluding Abraham's walking with him as his friend, as Enoch and Noah did (cf. 2 Chron. 20:7; Isa. 41:8). But the imperative makes a difference. Elsewhere "Stand before me" suggests service (e.g., 41:46 and cf. the Tg here), like the English expression "Wait on me," whereas "Walk about before me" implies transparency.[26] It suggests "Live as if you were always in my presence. Who would not be ashamed to sin, even a little, in the presence of some great man, much less God?"[27] God's expectations regarding Abraham's walking about, his living of his life, are spelled out as involving a life of integrity; this term too applies descriptively to Noah (6:9). That's what the walk needs to look like.

25. Cf. Seebass, *Genesis*, 2.1:100. But also see further the comments on 49:25a.

26. Cf. Driver, *Genesis*, 185.

27. Andrew of Saint Victor, *Exposition on Genesis*, as quoted in Schroeder, *Genesis*, 144.

The promise that the prescription introduces (v. 2) is the establishing of a pact between the two parties, "a solemn, binding assurance which can correspond to an oath, and whose content can be the same as a promise."[28] God speaks neither of implementing this pact (P's usual expression: see v. 7) nor of cutting it (J's expression in Gen. 15) but of making it or setting it or putting it, using the verb *nātan*, which would more commonly suggest giving it, as in 9:12 (the only other occurrences of the phrase are Num. 25:12 and Sir. 44:22). The verb underlines further the generous and gracious nature of God's action (cf. vv. 5, 6, 8, 16, 20 for more "giving"). The pact will be a "covenant of love,"[29] a "covenant of grace abounding."[30] While it is a pact "with you," later "between me and you" (cf. 9:12), it's really "my pact."[31] Yahweh is giving notice that this moment is an occasion when he is revising the terms of the pact between him and Abraham—in Abraham's favor. God thus assumes the freedom, from time to time, to rework the terms of his pact with his people, like any great king. Sinai will be the great example. In a sense there is one pact between God and his people through the Scriptures,[32] but in another sense there are many. Each time he revises the terms of the pact, God gives his people the chance to reaffirm their commitment to it—or better, he requires them to reaffirm their commitment to it. How does God's expectation that his people should walk with integrity before him relate to his promises? The pact is being made now, when there is hardly time for the fulfillment of that requirement. In this sense the requirement of walking in integrity is not a condition of the making of the pact. Yet one should not be too rationalistic in asking such questions. The implication for the listeners is that there is always a link between the way we walk and the way God fulfills his promises. The promises demand that we walk aright, even when the promises come first.

Abraham's reaction (v. 3a) matches the fact that God has "appeared," but it is an extreme such reaction. He will fall on his face again in v. 17, but the phrase will not then recur until Lev. 9:24.

17:3b–8. God's words rework his earlier promises. Abraham will become not merely a big nation (12:2; cf. also 13:16; 15:5; 16:10) but the ancestor of a horde of nations. Although Genesis may go on to imply fulfillment of this promise in the existence of peoples such as the Ishmaelites, Edomites, Midianites, and Amaleqites—who will feature in Genesis[33]—"nations" in Gen. 10 means much more, and so may "nations" here.[34] The promise about nations never recurs in the form of a reference to a "horde"; putting it that

28. Westermann, *Genesis 12–36*, 259. See further the comments on 9:9.
29. Rashi, *Brʾšyt*, 161.
30. Blenkinsopp, *Abraham*, 104.
31. Gunkel, *Genesis*, 263.
32. Cf. Niehaus, "God's Covenant with Abraham."
33. Cf. Sarna, *Genesis*, 124.
34. Cf. von Rad, *Genesis*, 194–95.

way leads into the change of name that follows. A horde is a *hāmôn*, and *ʾabrām* is now to become *ʾabrāhām* (v. 5). Names are often important in the Scriptures, as they are in Western culture, where a change of name (e.g., in marriage) is often significant. Names are not just labels. Etymologically, we are not sure of the origin of the names *ʾabrām* or *ʾabrāhām*,[35] and part of the point lies in the change itself. Naming gives expression to the fact that God is lord over Abraham[36] (cf. the name changes in 2 Kings 23:34; 24:17, which have no significance beyond an assertion of imperial sovereignty). This naming does also suggest God's doing something new for Abraham, an act of new creation.[37] And it gives new expression to his promise and intention through the paronomasia with the word for a horde; "the name focuses not on his personal relationship with God but on his relationship to the nations. The name looks outward."[38]

God's promise of extraordinary fruitfulness (v. 6) draws attention to further implications of God's undertakings in this chapter. Making numerous and fruitful are motifs in Gen. 1 and again in Gen. 8–9, while we have noted that talk of "nations" recurs in Gen. 10. God sets humanity going with the intention that it should be fruitful and numerous, God resets humanity going with the same intention, and the growth of nations is a realization of that intention. Now Abraham is brought into connection with this objective. God's intention in creation is to be realized in him and his offspring. There were no kings in Gen. 10, but there are plenty in Gen. 14, so God's additional reference to kings nuances the point further.[39]

God's further reformulating of the pact (v. 7) involves making it permanent or agelong, like the Noah pact with the world as a whole (9:12, 16), which makes for another way in which God's dealings with Abraham implement his purpose for all humanity. God also encapsulates the pact's implications in terms of "being God for you and for your offspring." Elsewhere, "I will be God for you and you will be a people for me" (e.g., Jer. 31:33; Ezek. 37:27) expresses the two-sided nature of this pact; here the other side of the relationship has been implied in v. 1 and will follow in vv. 9–14, and even on its own, the idea of being your God implies "so you had better treat me as such" (cf. Lev. 11:45; 22:33). But in v. 7 God speaks only of being God for them, in keeping with the promissory nature of vv. 4–7 (cf. Exod. 29:45, when God comes to dwell in the wilderness sanctuary).[40]

The further spelling out of God's commitment (v. 8) relates to the gift of the land, which is also to be permanent or agelong. God thus reconfirms the

35. See, e.g., *HALOT*.
36. Cf. Coats, *Genesis*, 134.
37. Zimmerli, *1. Mose 12–25*, 70.
38. Fretheim, "Genesis," 459.
39. See Diffey, "Royal Promise in Genesis."
40. Cf. Skinner, *Genesis*, 293.

promise in 13:15, adding the word "holding" (*ʾăḥuzzâ*). This term most often refers to the parcel of land that a family "holds" and of which it is (in theory) the secure and permanent possessor, though "owner" is not quite the word, since the land still belongs to God. Here God uses this word of the nation's secure possession of Canaan, a possession that is theologically though not epistemologically prior to the possession of parcels of land by families.

17:9–14. Written into the pact there is indeed an obligation that Abraham must fulfill, as there was not in Gen. 9 or in Gen. 15. Verses 10–14 resemble the form of collections of rules in Exodus or Leviticus and may have a similar origin.[41]

The obligation is the circumcising of the males within the community (v. 10). Circumcision *is* the pact; by synecdoche,[42] that is, it is the sign of the pact. It denotes cutting off the skin that extends forward beyond the end of the penis. Its removal as a ceremonial and/or religious act is known among many peoples; it is also commonly claimed to be medically beneficial. God is taking a practice known in many cultures and giving it a new significance in connection with the pact between himself and his people, as he does with (e.g.) sacrifice and cleansing rituals. Whereas "you" was singular in v. 9, now it is plural; the obligation rests on the community as a whole, on the mothers and grandmothers as well as the fathers and grandfathers (cf. Exod. 4:24–26!). Although it is administered only to the males, Israel did not draw the inference that the pact did not apply to females. "Was Sarah part of the covenant?" Her role in childbearing is not ancillary but essential to the covenant.[43] (There is no evidence of female circumcision as a religious practice in the ancient world, nor of its being medically beneficial.)

So circumcision will function as the sign of the pact (v. 11). "Circumcision was God's brand."[44] The rainbow was to be put in place by God as a sign for him but also secondarily as a sign for human beings. Circumcision was to be undertaken by human beings as a sign for them but also secondarily as a sign for God. God does not identify how it works as a sign, but if we ask whether it is a sign with an intrinsic relationship to what it signifies, like the rainbow, then the context of the sign is suggestive. The pact puts most emphasis on fruitfulness,[45] but it also incorporates the gift of the country of Canaan. Circumcision could symbolize the consecration of the men's means of being fruitful and of their means of countering the sexual waywardness of which the Canaanites were believed to be guilty.[46]

41. Cf. Sarna, *Genesis*, 125.
42. Hamilton, *Genesis 1–17*, 470.
43. R. H. Sohn in Eskenazi and Weiss, *Torah*, 80.
44. Kidner, *Genesis*, 129.
45. See Eilberg-Schwartz, *Savage in Judaism*, 141–76, for this emphasis on the significance of circumcision.
46. See the comments on 15:16.

It is babies who are to be circumcised (vv. 12–13). Cultures vary over whether there is a particular age for the ceremony; God lays down one. The eighth-day rule means that it comes at the end of a mother's initial seven-day taboo period following birth (Lev. 12:1–3). The requirement of circumcision applies as much to people in the family who do not belong to Abraham's own offspring as to those who do. In Israel, at least, some servants (most servants?) would be fellow Israelites (e.g., Deut. 15:12–18), but some would not be, and to make sure that no gray areas remain, Genesis mentions two categories of foreign servants—people born of foreigners within the family (Ishmael would have counted if his father had been another Egyptian) and foreigners who come into the family from outside. In both cases they count as members of the family and are therefore circumcised. They are beneficiaries of the pact that God has made, and they are under obligation to it.

What if someone neglects to be circumcised (v. 14)? Presumably God is talking about an adult who for some reason was not circumcised as a baby[47] (cf. Exod. 4:24–26), though wondering about this question is maybe again too prosaic; the point about the verse is to underscore further the integral link between circumcision and God's pact. Someone who declines circumcision forfeits his place in his people. Maybe his relatives are expected to throw him out or maybe the verse is a warning that God will do so (again, see Exod. 4:24–26; also Lev. 20:3–6). "Be cut or be cut off."[48] The ambiguity over the cutting off again suggests that the point is not the sanction but the need to avoid ever incurring it.

17:15–17. Further revelations follow. Abraham is not the only person to have a new name. As with Abraham, it is the actual move from Śāray to Śārāh that is significant, rather than a meaning attaching to the names; likely both mean "queen," but Genesis does not refer to the fact. Giving Sarai a new name also points to her being within this new pact, even if she does not receive the physical sign of it.

The promise of blessing follows (v. 16), another note taken up from 1:28 and 12:2. It is not surprising to find it spelled out in terms of the gift of a son—yet it is surprising, because we thought that the question of a son for Abraham and Sarah had been resolved in Gen. 16. The nations and kings of which vv. 5–6 speak are to be directly her descendants, not merely indirectly so.

Pardonably, to Abraham (v. 17) the idea that Sarah might yet have a baby seems simply implausible. They have been trying for all these years, and she is ninety (forty-five or fifty in our terms?). Again Abraham falls on his face in awe, as in v. 3. The gravity of that bodily response might suggest that his laugh, the first laugh in the Scriptures, is not a laugh of derision but a laugh of wonder, like Sarah's laugh in Gen. 21, when the boy is born. His questions,

47. Cf. Ibn Ezra, *Genesis*, 186.
48. Hamilton, *Genesis 1–17*, 473.

then, express amazement, not doubt. They are not so different from the questions in Gen. 15. Yet perhaps here is a difference when "laughter and the internal dialogue have displaced groveling as a response to divine presence."[49]

17:18–22. What about Ishmael? Unlike a Western reader, Abraham does not ask the reasons for God's action. He just says, "If only . . ." (*lû*). "If only" usually applies to the past; this "if only" is the only one in the Scriptures addressed to God and relating to the future. It is a kind of prayer, then, and Abraham knows how to pray; he will do so quite productively in Gen. 18. "Living before you" suggests enjoying life someplace where "you" are looking and smiling and providing. In v. 1 God said, "Walk about before me"; Abraham asks that something of this kind apply to Ishmael.

God reacts to Abraham's plea (v. 19) first with a restatement of the intention he announced in v. 16. He does not tell Abraham why he proposes to operate in the way he does. Perhaps we are to infer that he has never accepted Sarah's way of seeking to make sure that his promise finds fulfillment and that he insists on using his own way, even though Gen. 12–14 has told us stories of where he was prepared to work via human initiatives, but he does not say. Instead, he both expands on what he said before and indicates further that his mind is made up by telling Abraham what his son's name is to be. Actually, it seems that Abraham has suggested the boy's name for him. "Laughed" in v. 17 was *yiṣḥāq*; exactly that word will be the boy's name. In itself (without the waw-consecutive) its implication would be "May he laugh." The name does not make explicit the identity of the "he" (like the name Ishmael, "God listens"), and it could designate the boy as one who laughs (compare the explanation of the name Jacob), but in origin it would likely refer to God (like the name Joseph). The name speaks of God's smiling on Isaac, of "the laugh, the promise and the miracle that made his birth possible."[50] That smile is expressed in his making a pact *with* Isaac and *for* his offspring.[51]

It's not that God is not listening to Abraham (v. 20); there follows some response to his plea. Again, God works with the significance of a name. God says, "As for 'God listens,' I've listened."[52] He is not merely referring back to the listening in 16:11. He has now listened to Abraham, and new promises for Ishmael issue as a result. Ishmael too is to be the beneficiary of a promise about blessing and fruitfulness and abundant numerousness. God makes the promise the more certain by speaking as if it has already happened, because he has said it, and therefore in effect it has indeed happened. While the people listening to the story know that Isaac will generate twelve leaders among his

49. Sabbath, "Sacred Tropes," 359.

50. Kidner, *Genesis*, 130.

51. See the comments on 15:18 on "with" and "for"; and *DCH* 266b on the possible implications of the "for."

52. Cf. Alter, *Genesis*, 75.

grandchildren, here God promises that Ishmael will do so too, a generation earlier in the story (25:12–18). He will be a big nation, as God promised Abraham (cf. 12:2). God's choosing one does not mean rejecting the other.[53]

But God goes on to reaffirm that the reworked pact that he has been talking about (v. 21) will indeed belong to Isaac. Maybe Abraham will eventually get it. In restating his intention once more, God again leaves himself with little wiggle room. Sarah will conceive in three months' time. Isaac will be born at this "set time" (*môʿēd*) next year. How neat if it turns out that the appearance and the birth both happen at a "set time" such as firstfruits (Jub. 15 expands on this possibility)!

With that, God is done (v. 22). He goes. It was a real appearing; it's a real departure.

17:23–27. So Abraham sets about his macabre task; Genesis "reports it in detail (still without becoming graphic),"[54] just to assure us that Abraham did as he was told, like Noah. Since there are presumably at least 318 grown men alone, one would like to think he had some help, and/or it was hardly a task accomplished in one day (and see 34:24–25). But the phrase "on that very day" (e.g., 7:13; Exod. 12:17; Deut. 32:48; Josh. 5:11) draws attention to the importance of this epoch-making moment. Abraham is doing his part in putting into effect this new version of God's pact with him. If there is any doubt about the significance of his laughter in v. 17, there is no doubt about his obedience.[55] Apparently Ishmael is one of the people who benefit from and are responsible to the pact, even though it will be made with Isaac. There is some tension between the latter declaration and Genesis's noting three times that Ishmael was among those circumcised. Ishmael is thus not "specifically excluded from the covenant line."[56] The tension can be resolved by assuming that vv. 15–22 are "clumsy additions" by someone who was a bit stupid.[57] But in the text as we have it, the implication is that even as circumcision becomes *the* marker of God's pact with Israel, it is not exclusive. Its application to Ishmael might remind the audience that Abraham is to be the ancestor of nations.[58] Though Western readers may be concerned that the servants are having an unpleasant operation imposed on them,[59] for Genesis the repeated reference to servants carries the implication that they are not to be left out. Circumcision is a democratic rite. It "allows for a genuine openness to the outsider."[60]

53. Cf. Barth, *CD* 2.2:355.
54. Von Rad, *Genesis*, 198.
55. Cf. Brayford, *Genesis*, 310.
56. Against Fretheim, *Abraham*, 45.
57. Cf., e.g., Grünwaldt, *Exil und Identität*, 9–70; the description is Brett's (*Genesis*, 63–64).
58. Cf. Hamilton, *Genesis 1–17*, 480.
59. Cf. De La Torre, *Genesis*, 180.
60. Cf. Fretheim, "Genesis," 459, 460.

There seems no reason to question the Arab peoples' tradition that their ancestry goes back to Ishmael. They are thus the beneficiaries of God's promise regarding Ishmael.

Implications

Circumcision

When Abraham and his offspring are required to be circumcised as an expression of their commitment to God and his pact with them, it "does not make the covenant bilateral,"[61] even though the sign does become integral to the covenant. The status of circumcision is similar to that of baptism. When baptism becomes a sign of belonging to Jesus as God again expresses his freedom to rework the terms of his pact and cancels the circumcision requirement, baptism becomes an obligation tied up with God's welcoming people into the Jesus family, though not exactly a condition of it.

Some Jews who came to trust in Jesus believed that both Jews and Gentile believers in Jesus were required to be circumcised (e.g., Acts 15:1). In that situation, at least, this insistence compromised the principle that the gospel issues from God's grace.[62] Circumcision was not part of the relationship between God and Abraham at the beginning, and it need not continue to be part of the relationship between God and Abraham's offspring. Abraham received the seal of circumcision after his relationship with God was established on the basis of his trust in God's promise (Rom. 4:9–11). Paul opposes the idea that people who come to believe in Jesus need to be circumcised. "Neither Circumcision under the Law, nor Baptisme under the Gospell, [is] absolutely necessary."[63] Yet both are required by the covenant.

The snag with abandoning circumcision lies in losing what the sign symbolized. In general terms, it reflects God expecting that a commitment from his people should be expressed in what they do with their bodies and not merely in what they do with their inner beings. When people come to identify with Jesus's dying for them, they still share in disavowing the fleshly body as he did when he was circumcised (Col. 2:11). But "the future of the covenant in Christ is a future in the body" (e.g., Rom. 6:19; Gal. 6:17).[64] As long as people do not require circumcision as a condition of belonging to the people of God, then there is a case for continuing to observe the rite (cf. Acts 16:3; Gal. 2:3). And specifically, people's commitment needs to express itself in their sex lives. For a man, circumcision points to the disciplining of the means of sexual expression. Perhaps it was appropriate that "the promulgator of the

61. Fretheim, *Abraham*, 43.
62. See the comments on 15:6.
63. Willet, *Hexapla in Genesin & Exodum*, 166.
64. Reno, *Genesis*, 178.

eternal law requires the mark of carnal circumcision only in males, because in the sexual relationship the man is more impetuous than the woman,"[65] though in the modern West women may feel less constrained in their sexual relationships than was traditionally so.[66]

It was always the case that "circumcision functions in the flesh but not according to the flesh"[67]—that is, it was never limited to people who belong to the offspring of Abraham, nor to masters as opposed to servants, as Gen. 17 makes explicit. Circumcision would be a mark of distinctiveness for the community—a concrete, intentional, and costly sign, and one that embraced both "born" and "bought."[68] It went along with a new name. Both suggested a new and climactic stage in the differentiation of Abraham from his environment.[69]

Baptism corresponds to circumcision, then, in being open to all peoples and to both servants and masters. It may or may not contrast with circumcision according to whether or not it works by families (Reformed theology argues that it does). It does contrast with circumcision in being open to both sexes, thus avoiding the odd fact that the Abrahamic and Mosaic covenant was open to both sexes though the covenant sign was not. The Galatians, at least (see Gal. 3:28), perhaps saw a wider contrast: baptism makes no distinction on the basis of ethnicity, class, or gender.[70]

With circumcision and with baptism, it is no use for someone to accept the sign without also manifesting the reality it signifies, the integrity of walking before God with which Gen. 17 begins. Genesis presupposes the expectation that the First Testament will later make explicit, that Israel needs to have its mind as well as its body circumcised (e.g., Deut. 10:16). It would be odd to think of an inner circumcision if there is no outer circumcision; it would be odd to think of an outer circumcision if there was no inner circumcision. The parallel with baptism continues to hold. It would be odd to think of an inner cleansing and dying if there was no outward sign of dying and of cleansing; it would also be odd to think of an outward baptism if there was no dying and cleansing of the whole person. Baptism can also be an empty ritual. It can take on a life of its own that has no relation to its being a sign of God's commitment to us and ours to God. The need to avoid this possibility is one of the ways circumcision helps us understand baptism (Col. 2.11–13).[71]

65. Ambrose, *On Abraham* 2.11.78–79 as quoted in Sheridan, *Genesis 12–50*, 55. Cf. Philo, *Questions and Answers on Genesis* 3.47.

66. See Goldingay, "Significance of Circumcision."

67. Reno, *Genesis*, 179.

68. Brueggemann, "Genesis 17:1–22," 56.

69. Cf. Fleischman, "On the Significance of a Name Change."

70. See Martin, "Covenant of Circumcision."

71. Ironically, given Paul's polemic elsewhere (Brueggemann, *Genesis*, 155–56).

16
The Three Visitors

(18:1–19:38)

Overview

Genesis 13:10–13 prepared us for an account of a catastrophe in Sodom, and it raised the question how this catastrophe would affect Lot, while Gen. 17 told of God's promise concerning a son for Sarah but didn't indicate how Sarah would come to know about it. Genesis 18–19 fills in these two gaps. First there is another appearance to Abraham that incorporates the announcement to Sarah and a chance for her to laugh. In due course there is an account of the disaster that comes to Sodom and the rescue of Lot and his family. Within this main story is an account of a dialogue between Yahweh and Abraham about the propriety of bringing catastrophe. And appended to the main story is a postscript about Lot and his daughters. The chapters give no indication that the events in these chapters followed on the events in Gen. 17, and it makes more sense to see this account as parallel to Gen. 17.[1] The repetition of the story about the giving of the promise underlines its importance.[2]

The chapter implies another underlying question: was Yahweh fair to Sodom? And the answer might be as follows:

a. Yahweh's primary commitment is to Abraham and Sarah, whether or not they deserve it.
b. Tied up with that commitment is Yahweh's intention that Abraham should be the means whereby blessing comes to the world.

1. Calvin (*Genesis*, 1:468) considers this possibility, though he then "prefers" to see these events as subsequent to the previous revelation.

2. Cf. Luther, *Genesis 15–20*, 177.

c. Abraham's dialogue presses Yahweh on when he would be merciful to a town such as Sodom.
d. The envoys' mission is designed to check whether it is fair to bring disaster—and it surely does so.
e. The postscript shows what happens to some people who are too close to Sodom.

Translation

18:1 So Yahweh appeared to him[3] by the Mamre Oaks, when he was sitting at the tent entrance as the day grew hot.

2He lifted his eyes and saw, and there, three men were standing near him. He saw them and ran to meet them from the tent entrance, bowed to the ground, **3**and said, "My lords,[4] please, if I've found favor in your eyes, don't pass by your servant, please. **4**May a little water please be brought? Bathe your feet. Rest under the tree. **5**I'll get a bit of bread. Sustain your heart, you can pass on afterward, because of the fact that you've passed near your servant." They said, "Yes, you may do as you've spoken."

6Abraham hurried to the tent to Sarah and said, "Hurry, three measures[5] of fine flour (meal), knead it, make loaves." **7**Out to the herd Abraham ran, got a nice, tender calf, and gave it to the boy,[6] and he hurried to prepare it. **8**He got yogurt and milk and the calf that he'd prepared and set it before them, and while he stood near them under the tree, they ate.

9They said to him, "Where's Sarah your wife?" He said, "There, in the tent." **10**He said, "I will definitely come back to you at the time when there is life,[7] and there, Sarah your wife will have a son." Sarah was listening at the tent entrance; it was behind him. **11**Now Abraham and Sarah were old,

3. Not naming Abraham at the beginning of the chapter suggests continuity with what precedes and fits with the idea that 18:1–15 is another account of the same incident as Gen. 17 (see the comment).

4. *ʾĂdōnāy* is the form for addressing "the Lord" (cf. vv. 27, 30, 31, 32), and "you" in the rest of v. 3 is singular; the spelling reminds the audience that Abraham is addressing "the Lord." But vv. 1–15 as a whole give the impression that Abraham does not yet know that this is the Lord, and a switch between plural and singular recurs through the section. In 19:2 Lot uses *ʾădōnay* as the form of address to the two "men" (the LXX, Vg, Tg switch there from "Lord" to "lords"). When *ʾădōnāy* recurs in 19:18, it is in pause, which might explain the pointing; it could be understood as "Lord" or "lords." The short spelling (*ō* not *ô*) in all three verses is the usual form in references to God rather than to human lords. But conversely, Judg. 13:8 has the long spelling *ʾădônāy* in address to Yahweh.

5. We don't know the size of a "measure" (*səʾâ*).

6. Or perhaps "a boy" (cf. GKC 126r). Otherwise, it might almost make one think of Ishmael (cf. Qimchi's comment, *Genesis*, on the verse).

7. Taking *ḥayyâ* as the noun meaning "life" (cf. the Vg, Tg. Onq., Tg. Ps.-J.?); it might alternatively be a feminine adjective (thus "the time [when she is] alive/pregnant/recovering

going on in years; the way women menstruate had left off from happening
for Sarah. **12**So Sarah laughed inside, saying, "After I'm withered, there
will have been[8] lushness[9] for me, with my lord[10] old!"
13Yahweh said to Abraham, "Why is it that Sarah laughed, saying,
'Will I really give birth, in that[11] I'm old?' **14**Is a thing too extraordinary for
Yahweh? At this set time I will come back to you, at the time when there
is life, and Sarah will have a son." **15**Sarah lied, saying, "I didn't laugh,"
because she was afraid. He said, "No, you did laugh."
16From there the men set off, and they looked down at Sedom, with
Abraham going with them to send them off.
17But Yahweh[12]—he said, "Am I going to hide from Abraham what
I'm going to do, **18**when Abraham is indeed to become a big, numer-
ous nation, and all the nations on the earth are to gain blessing[13] by
him?—**19**because I've acknowledged him in order that[14] he may order his
children and his household after him, and they will keep Yahweh's way by
practicing faithfulness in the exercise of authority, in order that Yahweh
may bring about for Abraham what he's spoken concerning him."
20So Yahweh said, "The outcry against Sedom and Amorah,[15] because
it's big, and their wrongdoing, because it's very grave:[16] **21**I must go down
and see whether they have brought about complete ruin,[17] in keeping with
the outcry against it[18] that has come to me. If not, I must acknowledge it."

[after giving birth]"): see, e.g., Sarna, *Genesis*, 130; *DTT* 451–52). The LXX lets the allusive expression be a vaguer reference to "next year."

8. The verb is qatal. See GKC 106n.

9. The Vg translates the hapax *ʿednâ* as "pleasure," but etymological considerations rather suggest something like abundance and a link with *ʿēden* (see the comment on 2:8) and thus hint that Sarah is asking whether there could be any possibility of recapturing Eden (cf. A. Davis, "Eden Revisited").

10. It is unusual for Sarah to refer to her husband as "lord" instead of the more common expression *ʾîšî*, literally, "my man" (e.g., 29:32).

11. On *w* clauses in Genesis followed by a pronoun or noun preceding the verb, with such an implication, see W. Osborne, "Anteriority and Justification."

12. The placing of the subject before the verb indicates that a new theme is being introduced here.

13. On the translation, see the footnote to 12:3.

14. The LXX, Vg "I know that" disregards the suffix "him" and the *ləmaʿan*; more likely *yādaʿ* has its idiomatic meaning.

15. Van Wolde ("Outcry, Knowledge, and Judgment") argues for the more obvious translation "the outcry *of* Sodom and Gomorrah," but it is hard to make sense of that, especially in 19:13. Commentators such as Driver (*Genesis*, 196) and Seebass (*Genesis*, 2.1:117) thus argue for "the outcry *about* Sodom and Gomorrah."

16. Putting the subjects before the "because" gives them focus (Bandstra, "Word Order and Emphasis," 121).

17. For the expression *ʿāśâ kālâ* see, e.g., Jer. 4:27; 5:10, though it usually refers to God's bringing about such destruction (cf. the Tg here). The LXX, Vg imply that here alone it means "acted totally."

18. See the footnote to v. 20, which has *zəʿāqâ*, while v. 21 has *ṣəʿāqâ*, but there seems to be no significance in the alternation.

22The men turned their face from there and went to Sedom, while Abraham was still standing before Yahweh.[19] **23**Abraham came up and said, "Will you really sweep away the faithful person with the faithless person? **24**Maybe there are fifty faithful people within the town. Will you really sweep it away and not bear with[20] the place for the sake of the fifty faithful people within it? **25**A desecration for you,[21] to do a thing like this, putting to death the faithful with the faithless, so the faithful and the faithless are the same. A desecration for you! Isn't the one who exercises authority over the entire earth to exercise authority?"[22] **26**Yahweh said, "If I find in Sedom fifty faithful people within the town, I will bear with the entire place on account of them."

27Abraham averred:[23] "There, please: I've resolved to speak to my Lord, when I'm dirt and ash.[24] **28**Maybe the fifty faithful will be five short. Will you devastate the entire town because of five?" He said, "I won't devastate it if I find there forty-five."

29He spoke yet again to him: "Maybe forty will be found there?" He said, "I won't act, on account of the forty." **30**He said, "May it please not enrage my Lord, and I will speak. Maybe thirty will be found there." He said, "I won't act if I find there thirty." **31**He said, "There, please: I've resolved to speak with my Lord. Maybe twenty will be found there." He said, "I won't devastate it on account of the twenty." **32**He said, "May it please not enrage my Lord, and I will speak one last time. Maybe ten will be found there." He said, "I won't devastate it on account of the ten."

33Yahweh went when he had finished speaking to Abraham, and Abraham went back to his place.

19:1 The two envoys came to Sedom in the evening, and Lot was sitting at the gateway of Sedom. Lot saw them and got up to meet them. He bowed low, his face to the ground. **2**He said, "Here, my lords, please do turn aside to your servant's house so you can stay the night and bathe

19. According to a note in Gen. Rab. 49.7, the text originally read "Yahweh stood before Abraham"; scribes then thought this daring reading could not be right and emended it, and it is one of the eighteen such "corrections of the scribes" in the First Testament (see McCarthy, *Tiqqune Sopherim*). "Regardless of the original word order—Abraham standing before Yahweh or vice versa—the narrator's voice here creates a slight pause in the action, as though Abraham were pondering whether or not to speak up" (Arnold, *Genesis*, 182).

20. *Nāśā'* with an object such as waywardness can in effect mean "forgive," but here the verb is followed by *lə* (the two usages come together in Num. 14:18–19). Targum Onq. and the LXX have "let go," Vg "spare" here.

21. "In no way" (LXX) or "far be it from you" (Vg) undertranslates *ḥālilâ* (see BDB).

22. English versions have something like "Isn't the one who exercises authority . . . to act justly?" but this translation obscures Abraham's use of the verb *šāpaṭ* and then the related noun *mišpāṭ*. "The Heb. is more pointed and forcible than the English: 'shall not the *judge* of all the earth do *judgement*?'—do what the title which He bears implies" (Driver, *Genesis*, 197, emphasis original).

23. *ʿĀnâ* usually means "respond," but in some passages there is nothing to "respond" to, and the verb can carry the connotation of aver or testify in a formal sense.

24. A hendiadys inspired by paronomasia (*ʿāpār wāʾēper*).

your feet. Then you can start early and go on your way." They said, "No, because we can stay the night in the square." **3**But he pressed them hard, so they turned aside to him and came into his house. He made a banquet for them and baked flat bread, and they ate.

4Before they could go to bed, the townspeople, the Sedomites, surrounded the house, from young right to old, the entire people, from every part. **5**They called to Lot and said to him, "Where are the men who came to you tonight? Bring them out so we can sleep with them."[25] **6**Lot went out to them at the entrance, though he shut the door behind him. **7**He said, "My brothers, don't act badly, please. **8**So, please: I have two daughters who haven't slept with a man. Let me bring them out to you, and you can do to them whatever is good in your eyes. Only don't do anything to these men, because of the fact that they've come under the shelter of my roof-beam."

9But they said, "Come up here."[26] They said, 'The man came to reside as an alien, and he's actually exercising authority.[27] Now we'll act badly with you, worse than with them." They pressed hard against the man (against Lot) and came up to break the door. **10**But the men put out their hand and got Lot to come to them, into the house, and they shut the door. **11**As for the people who were at the entrance of the house, they struck them down with a daze, from young right to old, so they became weary of trying to find the entrance.

12The men said to Lot, "Who else do you have here—son-in-law, your sons, your daughters, anyone who belongs to you in the town? Take them out of the place. **13**Because we're going to devastate this place, because the outcry before Yahweh against them[28] has become so big that Yahweh has sent us to devastate it." **14**So Lot went out and spoke to his sons-in-law, who had gotten[29] his daughters, and said "Set off, get out of this place, because Yahweh is going to devastate the town." But in the eyes of his sons-in-law he was like someone making people laugh.

15As dawn came, the envoys pressed Lot, saying, "Set off, get your wife and your two daughters who are to be found here, so you're not swept away because of the town's waywardness." **16**He delayed, so the men took firm hold of his hand, his wife's hand, and his two daughters' hand, by Yahweh's pity on him, got him out, and set him down outside the town.

17When they had gotten them outside, one said, "Escape for your life, don't gaze behind you, don't halt anywhere in the area around. Escape to

25. On the verb, see the comment on 4:1. But Pirson ("Does Lot Know about *Yadaʿ*?"), for instance, thinks that *yādaʿ* is at least ambiguous here and does not clearly refer to sex, as it does in v. 8 as well as 4:1. Cf. Doyle, "Sin of Sodom"; R. Bailey, "Why Do Readers Believe Lot?"

26. The LXX and Vg have "Get away over there," but the use of the verb *nāgaš* is then odd, and it has its regular meaning later in the verse (see Heard, "What Does the Mob Want?").

27. The infinitive precedes the finite verb for emphasis: literally, "with judging he's judging."

28. See the footnote to 18:20.

29. Cf. the LXX, Tg. Ps.-J. for the past translation of the participle; contrast the Vg.

the highland, so you're not swept away." **18**Lot said to them, "No, please,
my lords![30] **19**There, please: your servant has found favor in your eyes,
and you've acted in such big commitment with me in preserving my life.
But I—I can't flee to the highland so that the bad event doesn't attach
itself to me and I die. **20**Here, please—this town's near for fleeing to, and
it's small. I can flee there, it's small, so my life can be preserved." **21**He
said to him, "Here, I'm accepting you[31] in this thing too, in not overthrow-
ing the town that you spoke of. **22**Hurry up and escape there, because I
can't do anything till you come there." (That's why people named[32] the
town Ṣoʿar.)

23As the sun came out on the earth and Lot arrived at Ṣoʿar, **24**Yahweh
rained on Sedom and Amorah burning sulfur from Yahweh, from the heav-
ens. **25**He overthrew these towns and the entire area around and all the
people living in the towns and what grew in the ground.

26But his wife gazed behind him and became a salt pilaster.

27Abraham started early in the morning for the place where he had
stood before Yahweh **28**and looked out over the face of Sedom and Amo-
rah and over the entire face of the land in the area. He saw, and there,
vapor from the land went up like the vapor from a kiln.

29So it was that when God devastated the towns of the area, God was
mindful of Abraham and sent Lot out from the middle of the overthrow,
when he overthrew the towns in which Lot lived.

30Lot went up from Ṣoʿar and lived in the highland, his two daughters
with him, because he was afraid to live in Ṣoʿar. He lived in a certain
cave,[33] he and his two daughters. **31**The firstborn said to the younger
one, "Our father is old and there's no one in the world[34] to be with us[35] in
the way of the entire world. **32**Come on, let's get our father to drink wine
so we can sleep with him and get offspring alive through our father." **33**So
they got their father to drink wine that night, and the firstborn went in
and slept with her father. He didn't know when she lay down or when she
got up. **34**Next day the firstborn said to the younger one, "There, I slept
with my father last night. Let's get him to drink wine tonight as well, and
you come and sleep with him, so we can get offspring alive through our
father." **35**So they got their father to drink wine that night as well, and
the younger one got up and slept with him. He didn't know when she lay
down or when she got up.

36So Lot's two daughters got pregnant through their father. **37**The
firstborn gave birth to a son and named him Moʾab. He's the ancestor of

30. See the footnote to 18:3.

31. Literally, "I have lifted your face"; the declarative/performative qatal suggests a speech act, "I hereby accept."

32. The verb is singular, "one named."

33. Literally, "the cave" (see GKC 126r).

34. In isolation, one might translate *bāʾāreṣ* as "in the region" (cf. v. 28), but *hāʾāreṣ* later in the sentence must mean "world."

35. Literally, "to come on us."

Mo'ab until today. 38The younger one also gave birth to a son and named
him Ben-ammi. He's the ancestor of the Ammonites until today.

Interpretation

Genesis 18:1–19:38 is a long and complex unit relating a sequence of events mostly taking place over almost twenty-four hours.[36] In the MT it forms one paragraph within the unit running from 18:1–21:21; one may guess that the medieval division into two chapters is made for convenience. It outlines as follows:

Introduction (18:1a)

- Lunchtime: three humanlike figures appear at Abraham's encampment, he shows them hospitality, and they promise that Sarah will have a son (18:1b–15)
- The "men" start to set off for Sodom (18:16)
  - Yahweh reflects on the action they are about to undertake and tells Abraham about it (18:17–21)
- The "men" (or two of them) go to Sodom (18:22)
  - Abraham challenges Yahweh about the action (18:23–38)
  - Yahweh withdraws from Abraham (18:39)
- Evening: the two men, now termed "envoys," meet Lot in Sodom and urge him to leave before a catastrophe arrives (19:1–14)
- Dawn: they hurry Lot out of Sodom (19:15–22)
- Sunrise: Lot reaches Zo'ar and the catastrophe duly arrives (19:23–26)
- That same morning: Abraham looks out at what has happened (19:27–28)

Closing summary (19:29)

Coda about Lot and his daughters (19:30–38)

While the unit thus tells a complete story taking place over a day (except for the coda), it is not entirely self-contained:

1. It fills out the trailer in 13:10–13.
2. Its opening refers to Abraham simply as "him" (18:1), and 18:1–15 suggests seeing it as another version of the giving of a promise about Sarah having a baby, which was one of the themes in Gen. 17 (there is

36. Cf. Letellier, *Day in Mamre*.

no suggestion in Gen. 18 that God has already given the promise and that this is a repetition).

3. Whereas the announcement to Hagar about her son (Gen. 16) leads into the account of his being born, the fulfillment does not follow here—it has to wait until Gen. 21.
4. The exchange about Sarah's laughter (18:13–15) ends in a dramatic way, but also not in a way that suggests closure—which will also come in Gen. 21.

In Gen. 8–9 Yahweh promised never again to bring a deluge. Genesis 18–19 implies that he may well bring other smaller-scale catastrophes. The story thus raises the question "How can we speak of divine judgment in the world?"[37] The Scriptures suggest at least one answer: by valuing the reassurance that the agents of persecution and oppression in the world will meet their judgment (e.g., 2 Pet. 2:6–8). While the chapters incidentally provide some explanation for the apparently devastated state of Sodom and give an account of the origins of the Ammonites and Moabites, they also offer a warning to Israel about what happens to an Israelite town if it behaves like Sodom and Gomorrah (cf. Isa. 1:9–10; Ezek. 16; Amos 4:11). The people of God must see themselves as Sodom and as thus in danger of Sodom's fate. Jesus in effect makes the same point (Matt. 10:15; 11:20–24). So the story drives the church to respond to it "by making sure we speak of it as a warning to the church as the object of God's judgment."[38]

In the first episode (18:1–16), visitors arrive at Abraham's encampment, he makes a feast for them, and they announce that Sarah will have a baby. This first episode in the unit makes sense in itself, though like the unit as a whole, it is only semi-complete. It presupposes that we know who "he" is, and at the end it does not tell us why the "men" are going to Sodom—or exactly how the story links with 13:10–13. In addition, the point of the account of the feast is not clear. Is it simply a raising of suspense for 18:9–15?[39] The feast does not relate closely to the bringing of the promise to Sarah and to the tension caused by her laugh. Further, there is some unclarity about how many visitors there are and about their identity. While one might ask whether this unclarity indicates that more than one version of the story has been combined, it may rather be a sign of sophistication in storytelling, an indication of awareness that some subtlety is required in talking about visits by God and by his envoys who appear in human form and about the way the recipients of these visits understand what is going on.

37. Fretheim, *Abraham*, 74.
38. Fretheim, *Abraham*, 74.
39. Cf. Coats, *Genesis*, 142.

In 18:17–33, the second episode, Yahweh speaks (to himself?) about the need to tell Abraham what is going on (vv. 17–19) and speaks (to Abraham?) about what he intends. As (two of) the visitors go off to Sodom, Abraham engages Yahweh in a dialogue about whether he will sweep the town away if there are some faithful people there. Dramatically, the divine speeches and the dialogue bridge the time when the visitors are on their way to Sodom. They also provide the theological background to what will happen there. The language of Yahweh's statements and of the dialogue is more conceptual, and the talk about faithfulness and the exercise of authority matches the language of the prophets, the Psalms, and the wisdom books. It constitutes an anticipatory reflection on the events related in Gen. 19 rather than having anything to do with 18:1–15.[40] If the statements and the dialogue raise more sophisticated questions than the stories do, they are not thereby shown to be a later reflection on the story. Theological simplicity and sophistication coexist in the United States in the twenty-first century, and there is no reason to suppose that they did not coexist in Judah. Similar issues to the ones raised in 18:17–33 are raised in different periods, in Hosea, Jeremiah, Ezekiel, and Job. So 18:17–33 might be a reflection on an earlier story that occupies the bulk of Gen. 18–19, and while the story as a whole is traditionally assumed to come from J, 18:17–33 is often seen as a later addition to the main story line.[41] But there is no strong evidence in this direction.

In the third episode (19:1–29) the visitors arrive at Sodom, and Lot makes a feast for them. The comparison and contrast with Abraham's feast now explain the significance of similar features in the first episode in the story. The three visitors have two tasks: "one is to promise a beginning. . . . The other is to effect an ending."[42] The story as a whole is more about Sodom and Lot than about Abraham, and the feast in the first scene is a backdrop to this one. After Lot's banquet, things go wrong in a way that answers the questions raised by 18:20–21 and by the dialogue: it is clear that the entire community is involved in faithlessness. There is no suggestion that Lot and his family count as "faithful."[43] Lot starts that way, but subsequent events raise questions about the designation. The reasons for his rescue are Yahweh's pity (19:16), the envoys' grace and commitment (v. 19), and Yahweh's mindfulness of Abraham (v. 29). Lot's dealings with the Sodomites make his person stand in contrast with Abraham. Abraham is a hero; Lot is a buffoon and a failure,[44] "not so much the antithesis of Abraham as a pale and failed imitation."[45] His sons-in-law laugh in a different way from Sarah. The visitors bring a message

40. Cf. e.g., Zimmerli, *1. Mose 12–25*, 81–82.

41. See further, e.g., Lyons, *Canon and Exegesis*, 137–50.

42. Brueggemann, *Genesis*, 162 (most words of both sentences are in italics).

43. Cf. Coats, *Genesis*, 141.

44. Coats, *Genesis*, 144.

45. Reno, *Genesis*, 186; cf. Origen's contrast, *Homilies on Genesis*, 103–4.

to Lot as they brought one to Abraham, a message that does not get heeded by Lot's wife, as their earlier message received an equivocal response from Abraham's wife. Their message takes up the terms "outcry" and "devastation" from Yahweh's speeches and the dialogue. The talk of devastation also recalls the deluge story, with which, indeed, Gen. 19 compares and contrasts.[46] Both stories tell of an overwhelming catastrophe that constitutes punishment for human waywardness, though one is universal and the other local, and the characters of Noah and Lot contrast. Verse 29 closes off 18:1–19:29 in terms that recall the deluge story.

The coda (19:30–38) relates how Lot's life falls further apart: he abandons Zoʿar, he takes refuge in a cave, and his daughters rape him in order to open up a future for themselves. The coda makes for a snide comparison with Noah in his drunkenness and the consequences. It also contrasts the future of Lot's line with the future of Abraham's line, of which Gen. 18 spoke.

18:1. Genesis again reports how Yahweh appears to Abraham (cf. 12:7; 17:1)—for the last time, in so many words. Abraham is not named, which enhances the continuity from Gen. 17. The scene is the place where Abraham settled at 13:8 and where he has presumably been living ever since. Thus the story also picks up from when he and Lot parted and Lot went to live near Sodom, that town of wrongdoers that was destined for eventual devastation. Abraham has perhaps been out in the early morning checking that his staff are properly about their jobs with the sheep and cattle, and later in the afternoon he may be out and about again, but in the middle of the day everyone would relax. On the other hand, Tg. Neof. and Tg. Ps.-J. have the story picking up from 17:23–27 in picturing Abraham as recovering from circumcising himself, and Rashi thus sees God as engaged in visiting the sick.[47]

18:2–8. The declaration that Yahweh appears to Abraham is odd since it is not immediately followed by a message from Yahweh (contrast 12:7; 17:1).[48] The arrival of three travelers at "the hottest (and drowsiest) time of the day"[49] is surprising. One might expect them to be resting—though the heat does not usually get oppressive along the mountain ridge where Mamre sits. They seem to appear suddenly, a little startlingly, as supernatural figures do.[50] But "appeared" is an odd word because Yahweh is concealed. He is "in disguise."[51] The chapter tells the story from the narrator's perspective in v. 1 and then tells it from Abraham's perspective. Although the narrator has told us that Yahweh is appearing to Abraham, Yahweh does not make it obvious to him.

46. Cf. Seebass, *Genesis*, 2.1:139.
47. Rashi, *Brʾšyt*, 172.
48. Cf. Sarna, *Genesis*, 128.
49. Skinner, *Genesis*, 299.
50. Cf. Gunkel, *Genesis*, 192.
51. Brayford, *Genesis*, 310.

There is no "I am Yahweh" or "I am El Shadday" or "I am your shield." All Abraham sees is three "men": the narrative's "there" invites us to watch their arrival with him. He is about to show hospitality to angels without knowing it (Heb. 13:2).[52] Why are there three of them, Tg. Neof. and Tg. Ps.-J. ask? The answer: one to give the message about Sarah having a baby, one to rescue Lot, one to bring the disaster on Sodom (b. B. Metz. 86 identifies them as Michael, Raphael, and Gabriel).[53] It fits much of the presentation if they are Yahweh and two envoys.[54] But through the two chapters there is no absolute consistency or consistent development in the presentation (God and/or men and/or angels?), which gives a true impression of the ambiguity inherent in the experience and the event. Abraham's initial look is the casual glance of someone half asleep, but it soon has him wide awake; the old man leaps to his feet, then bows to the ground. The three figures are not giving the impression that they are just passing and are on their way (contrast Luke 24:28). They have deliberately stopped, and they are hanging about waiting, like Abraham's servant at the well (Gen. 24:13).

Abraham knows his duty in the circumstances (vv. 3–5). There are no truck stops along this mountain crest. While travelers would not expect free food from settlements they passed, they might expect to be given water and to be able to barter for food. Abraham's words to them may be conventional, but the verses that follow show that they are not just words (though one does wonder if he treats every passerby this way, or whether there is evidently something special about these three).[55]

Even to a non-Western reader the account that follows (vv. 6–8) will surely seem amusing. The impression one gets is not of the patriarch of a large clan but of a man and his wife with their single "boy." It is of course the man's job to fire up the grill and the woman's to care for the other things. So the ninety-nine-year-old is scurrying here and running there and hurrying his eighty-nine-year-old wife to begin making a vast amount of bread, while he himself is hastening to kill, prepare, and roast a calf (which, I am advised, would take some eight hours), along with the appropriate side dishes. Perhaps one is rather to imagine him butchering some steaks and grilling or boiling them before he presents them to his guests, though the word order in v. 7a already implies that his action will take more than a few minutes, as will Sarah's.[56] He leaves the guests to eat, standing a little space away like a server; the host would give the guests the best and stand back himself. It is just as well that the three "men" were not simply passersby but rather people who had come especially to see Sarah and Abraham: eating

52. Cf. Hamilton, *Genesis 18–50*, 9.
53. Cf. Zimmerli, *1. Mose 12–25*, 79.
54. E.g., Keil and Delitzsch, *Pentateuch*, 228.
55. Cf. Calvin, *Genesis*, 1:469.
56. Cf. Abela, "Inversion."

meat would not be an everyday event, and Abraham's hospitality is the most over-the-top version imaginable. The hospitality theme will turn out to be important in the story as a whole, as will its over-the-top nature. It would surely be hard to know when to kill the fatted calf so as to make a banquet for three passersby, as it is difficult to know whether to give to everyone who asks (Luke 6:30). But "if we are deceived now and then, well and good."[57] Another consideration in the telling of the story is that the feast fits some of the regulations for sacrifice; Abraham "is behaving more wisely than he realized."[58]

18:9–12. The audience might be wondering why the narrator said that Yahweh is appearing. What is the point of the appearance? The visitors now come to their business. They know Abraham's wife's name. Is it the kind of knowledge that puts Abraham on the track of their being more than three passing strangers? Are they prophets?[59] Why then do they ask about her whereabouts? Do they want to make sure she is within earshot? The head of a family like Abraham sits outside his tent as the front of the family in its relating to the outside world. A woman like Sarah sits inside, relating to that world and keeping out of the meeting of men.

The transition to "I" (v. 10) marks an explicit beginning of the process whereby it becomes clear to Abraham that they are not simply three coequal men. One of them is senior to the others, speaks of himself over against them, and makes an extraordinary declaration. But he doesn't speak in terms of making something happen (namely, causing Sarah to have a baby) and thus indicate that he is God; his speech could again be that of a prophet. He speaks of coming back "when there is life," which v. 14 will confirm is the same as the "set time" of 17:21, and thus sounds like the time when Sarah will give birth; he does not speak of coming to cause her to conceive as she will need to do in a few weeks' time if the baby is to be born in a year's time (actually, there will be no reference to his coming back in either connection: is one to think of him as the one who makes the birth happen behind the scenes?). These words suggest that we view the giving of this promise as an alternative version of the one in Gen. 17. Here as there, the promise is given to Abraham, but here Sarah is within earshot, only just inside the tent.

The statement that Sarah was in or beyond menopause (vv. 11–12) might seem to be an understatement, but we have noted that in our terms we might see her as middle aged. Whereas Abraham laughed earlier (17:12), here Sarah laughs. "Humour is the opposite of all self-admiration and self-praise,"[60] and the laugh might be her expression of wonder (cf. Tg. Neof., Tg. Ps.-J.; also Heb. 11:11), though she becomes embarrassed about it. She describes

57. Luther, *Genesis 15–20*, 183.
58. Wenham, *Genesis 16–50*, 47.
59. Cf. the discussion in Ibn Ezra, *Genesis*, 192–94.
60. Barth, *CD* 3.4:666.

herself as if she is a worn-out garment or someone who is all wrinkly (e.g., Lam. 3:4). Age has done its ravaging on her body, on the outside and in the shriveling of her womb. Her exclamation is in effect a question expressing astonishment at the idea that she is going to be fertile, with her husband surely being past it, too.

18:13–15. We remain unclear how far Abraham understands what is going on; the narrator tells us that Yahweh is speaking, but he refers to himself in the third person, so it may not be clear to Abraham. Although Sarah had only laughed inside, the "man" has prophetic insight; he knows about her laugh. Yahweh may imply that Sarah's laugh was a laugh of unbelief rather than of amazement, but it won't make any difference. Yahweh's action is not dependent on Sarah's faith, partly because he's not acting for her and Abraham's sake anyway.

In a sense she would not even be entitled to a laugh of amazement (v. 14). Describing something as "extraordinary" need not imply that it is miraculous in the sense of requiring God's action (see, e.g., 2 Sam. 1:26), but more often than not things that are "extraordinary" are God's acts (e.g., Ps. 29:7). So by definition the answer to the question is "No." "Israel stands before God's word of promise but characteristically finds that word beyond reason and belief. . . . If the question of the Lord is answered, 'Yes, some things are too hard, impossible for God,' then God is not yet confessed as God. We have not yet conceded radical freedom to God." But fortunately "the resolve of God to open a future by a new heir does not depend on the readiness of Abraham and Sarah to accept it. God keeps his own counsel and will work his own will."[61]

Sarah feels rebuked (v. 15). Evidently she, at least, has no idea who she is talking with. But she has only laughed inside, so it isn't a big lie. And this exchange, with the two further references to laughing, reminds the audience of the name of the child who will be born and of the more unequivocal laughter that will come to Sarah then (21:6). And/or it leaves the audience with a sense that we haven't yet reached the end of the discussion of laughter that comes to a halt here.[62]

18:16–19. The visitors have completed the first stage of their mission. They are now off to stage two. From a point not far from Mamre, it is possible to look down toward the Dead Sea and the site of Sodom, as Abraham and Lot looked down back in 13:5–18.

But as Abraham is sending them off (v. 17), Yahweh reflects to himself, or speaks to the other two, whom he customarily consults as members of the divine council (Jer. 23:18).[63] Either way, they will eventually proceed on their own (see v. 22, and 19:1). The principle behind Yahweh's question finds further

61. Brueggemann, *Genesis*, 158, 159, 160.
62. Cf. Fretheim, *Abraham*, 116.
63. Cf. Wenham, *Genesis 16–50*, 50.

expression in Amos 3:7, but the rationale and the reference there are different. He reveals to prophets the action he intends to take, so that they can tell people about it. Here he plans to tell Abraham about the investigation that he is about to undertake (vv. 20–21 imply he has not made up his mind about the action he intends in light of what he discovers).[64] Targum Neof. has him reflecting that Abraham is, after all, his friend (cf. Isa. 41:8).

The rationale for telling Abraham about the investigation (v. 18) is also different, though Yahweh's logic is expressed allusively. The rationale lies in his promise to Abraham, which he summarizes in words that virtually repeat 12:3 ("numerous" is an addition, and 12:3 had "kin groups" rather than "nations"). Nations are to find blessing through Abraham, and to that end, Abraham needs to know the principles upon which Yahweh works with nations.

To that same end (v. 19) it is necessary that his household should be an embodiment of the priorities that Yahweh expects of humanity as a whole. Yahweh has "known" Abraham in the sense of taking notice of and paying regard to him. In effect he has chosen him. The same verb comes in this connection in Amos 3:2, but the use of the unusual verb links with the theme of Yahweh making a pact with Abraham (Gen. 15 and 17). In the political world, two parties can talk about "acknowledging" one another in connection with the mutual recognition involved in a pact; in the religious world, Yahweh "acknowledges" his people and they "acknowledge" him.[65] One object of singling out Abraham in that way is that he should give orders to his offspring and his "household"—here we revert to the picture of Abraham as the head of a sizeable group, though not of course yet of a vast number of children. Yahweh adds reference to generations to come. He's not just going to make a difference in his lifetime. The difference he is to make is that following Yahweh's instructions will mean that his household will "keep Yahweh's way." That phrase can mean the unique way Yahweh acts, or the way Yahweh acts that people are to imitate, or the way Yahweh expects people to act—the latter two could be the same thing. Here it will denote one or the other of them and in effect it will have the same meaning as living one's life before Yahweh (17:1) with transparency and integrity. Yahweh goes on to define that way of life as doing *ṣədāqâ ûmišpāṭ*, the classic hendiadys that runs through the Psalms and the Prophets. We know about *ṣədāqâ* from 15:6 and of the root *šāpaṭ* from 16:5. In combination the two words suggest a commitment to faithful relationships before God and in the community that find expression in the way one makes decisions. It is everything that the Torah, the Prophets, and the Psalms will expect by way of a life lived Yahweh's way. This is a monumental expectation that Yahweh has of Abraham, that he should not only walk before him with integrity but

64. Cf. MacDonald, "Listening to Abraham."
65. See Huffmon, "Treaty Background."

should also ensure that his entourage walks that way. Abraham must put his effort into this task if he expects Yahweh to fulfill his promises about him. Because Abraham is so important to the fulfillment of Yahweh's purpose for the world, Abraham needs to understand the principles on which Yahweh is working. Yahweh's hopes are only partially fulfilled in Genesis.[66]

18:20–21. If Yahweh is not speaking out loud in vv. 17–19, it seems likely that the new introduction "so Yahweh said" indicates that he is doing so now, since Abraham's words will shortly presuppose that Abraham somehow knows Yahweh's intentions. The references to an outcry (*zəʿāqâ*/*ṣəʿāqâ*) cohere with the reference to *ṣədāqâ ûmišpāṭ* in v. 19. The classic pointer to the link is Isa. 5:7. When there is an outcry on the part of people who are being robbed of their land or who have to watch people indulging themselves when they lack enough to eat or who are deprived of their rights when the elders are supposed to be resolving disputes in a fair way at the town gate, then the community has failed to exercise its responsibility for *ṣədāqâ ûmišpāṭ*. Targum Ps.-J. gives the reason for the outcry regarding Sodom and Gomorrah: "They oppress the poor and decree that whoever gives a morsel of bread to the needy will be burned by fire." Yahweh has heard tell that within Sodom and Gomorrah and/or in its relationships with the people who live around the towns, there is huge wrongdoing of this kind. The blood of people who have been robbed of their lives one way or another has been crying out (Gen. 4:10), and Yahweh has heard it. While Gen. 19 will focus on sexual waywardness in Sodom (cf. Jude 7),[67] elsewhere the First Testament sees Sodom as an embodiment of this broader social and moral failure (e.g., Isa. 1:10–31; Ezek. 16).

But Yahweh does not act on the basis of hearsay (v. 21). He will go down and take a look, as he did at the Babel tower (11:5).

18:22–26. Abraham and the three visitors have apparently been standing at the beginning of the descent to the Dead Sea. Two of the three now set off. The short way to Sodom would again be via Ein Gedi (though see the comment on 14:7); the more civilized way for ordinary human beings would be via Arad and Nahal Zohar or via Beer Sheba and the Scorpions' Ascent, south of the Dead Sea. Meanwhile Abraham is still standing in front of Yahweh in the position of a servant (e.g., 41:46), the position he has been occupying since the three visitors arrived. But it seems that he now knows who the third visitor is, from vv. 20–21. And the nature of his servanthood is about to change. It will become more that of a prophet, who may ask his Lord quite confrontational questions—again like Amos.[68]

Thus Abraham comes up (*nāgaš*) to Yahweh (v. 23). The verb can denote a priest or Levite approaching God or approaching the altar or the sanctuary

66. Cf. Warner, "Keeping the Way of Yhwh."
67. On the importance of that theme in Gen. 19, see Peterson, "Sin of Sodom Revisited."
68. Gunkel, *Genesis*, 203.

(e.g., Exod. 19:22; Num. 4:19; 8:19). It's a solemn thing to do. But Abraham doesn't fall down as he did in 17:1. He shows a kind of confidence and boldness in this coming up to God. There is even more boldness about his question, as there was about his question and wish in 17:17–18. As was the case there, it's not formally a prayer, though it likely implies one. For the audience it's a dialogue from which they might learn both to think and to pray. The faithless (*rāšāʿ*) is the opposite of the faithful, though less obviously so than is suggested by the antithetical relationship of those two words in English. The faithless ignore obligations to human beings or to God. They do what they like. They ignore the needs of people who have a claim on them. If a town is nearly full of such people, but there are some faithful people there, would Yahweh really sweep away the faithful with the faithless who deserve it? Abraham is not asking a question that relates to Lot in particular or praying for Lot. He's asking a question about a town, praying for Sodom.[69] He speaks about "a faithful person" and "a faithless person." They are types: he is not thinking of there being one individual of either type.[70]

After all, it may seem unlikely that a town is 100 percent faithless people (vv. 24–25). If Yahweh treated the faithful and the faithless in the same way, God would be dishonoring himself. He would not be being God. He would be behaving like (say) an Israelite offering one of his children to another deity (Lev. 18:21; 20:3). It's an extraordinarily strong declaration. Abraham has no compunction about pointing out to God things that are obvious. It seems necessary to do so, just in case Yahweh is not taking them into account as much as he might. Yahweh has been talking about Abraham's obligation to exercise authority over his household in a faithful way. Abraham turns this talk back on God. It's God's job to exercise authority. Is this action what he would call exercising authority? The question will also drive Abraham's audience to think about what they mean by fairness and how they think of God and to see that God would rather acquit some guilty than condemn some innocent.[71] Like Amos, again (e.g., Amos 7:1–9), Abraham does not ask Yahweh just to save the fifty. Perhaps he simply recognizes that life is not like that. By their nature, events like the fall of Samaria or of Jerusalem overwhelm the entire town. What about the destruction of Sodom?

Yahweh accepts the argument (v. 26). He has not declared the intention to destroy Sodom, only to investigate it—but with the implication that action will then be necessary. There is no indication that he had not thought of the possibility Abraham raises or that he needs persuading.

69. Cf. Keil and Delitzsch, *Pentateuch*, 230; contrast Tg. Ps.-J.
70. Contrast the discussion in Lyons, *Canon and Exegesis*, 186–97.
71. Dershowitz, *Genesis of Justice*, 86.

18:27–28. Abraham is thus emboldened to press him further, though to speak of bargaining or bartering is misleading.[72] He recognizes that as a human being he is shaped from dirt (2:7); in addition, being in the dirt suggests being lowly (1 Sam. 2:8; 1 Kings 16:2). Ash appears with dirt in Job 30:19; 42:6. It is usually a sign of mourning, perhaps because being covered in ash suggests being grimy and disheveled through proximity to or contact with the fire on which people cooked and relied for warmth, and then because they deliberately smear it on themselves to enhance the impression of unkemptness. The link between ash and mourning may also suggest mortality, a likely implication of being made from dirt (Gen. 3:19). So Abraham is saying, "I'm just a mortal human being before the Lord." But it doesn't stop him from asking his question. Cunningly, he takes up the verb "devastate" (*šāḥat*), which Yahweh had used of the deluge (e.g., 6:13), an action he had promised not to repeat (9:11, 15).[73] Did Yahweh mean it? Again Yahweh accepts the argument.

18:29–32. Abraham presses on, now astutely adding the verb "enrage," which featured in Yahweh's rebuke of Cain (4:5–6). Yahweh keeps agreeing. Eventually they come down to ten, which perhaps implies one family. If the audience were to ask "What if there are less than ten?" the story that follows in 19:1–29 may give the answer, if Lot and his family can be counted as among the "faithful."[74] But ten is also the minimum number for a Jewish prayer meeting (cf. b. Meg. 23b, which could usefully have claimed this passage among its prooftexts),[75] and Tg. Ps.-J. takes that fact as the clue to Abraham's numbers. They had started from fifty, as indicating a minyan in each of the five towns, with the eventual implication that even a prayer meeting in one town could have forestalled the calamity.[76]

18:33. The conversation is one that Yahweh wanted to initiate (vv. 17–21). Abraham stands in the manner of someone serving Yahweh while he is confronting Yahweh, but Yahweh waits there for him to do so. He serves Yahweh by asking his questions for the sake of the people hearing this story. And when Yahweh is done with the service that Abraham has provided, Yahweh goes, as he did in 17:22, and Abraham returns to his tent. The sidebar to episode one in this story is over. By his prayer and his questions, Abraham has fulfilled the vocation to which v. 18 refers. He has been a blessing.[77]

72. See MacDonald, "Listening to Abraham," 30–35; Bridge ("Audacious Request") considers the passage as illustrating "politeness theory."

73. The verb there was piel rather than hiphil, but it was hiphil in 6:13, and the piel will recur here in 19:13, 29.

74. Cf. Wenham, *Genesis 16–50*, 53. For other possible answers, Lyons, *Canon and Exegesis*, 211–14.

75. Cf. Ibn Ezra, *Genesis*, 200.

76. See further Blenkinsopp, "Judge of All the Earth," 9–10.

77. Cf. Lipton, "Limits of Intercession."

19:1–3. So episode two can commence. While Yahweh and Abraham have been having their dialogue, the other two visitors have reached Sodom. As Abraham now knows that one visitor was Yahweh in human form, so it is now explicit that the other two are envoys,[78] though there is no indication that Lot realizes it. Like the three when they arrived at Mamre, they seem just like human beings. As we are apparently invited to suspend disbelief about how long it would have taken to make the lunch that Abraham commissioned and organized in 18:6–8, so it is with regard to the journey to Sodom (it would have taken human beings several days in real time). Lot might not be the only Sodom resident sitting in the gate plaza at the end of the day's work, as the cool of the evening arrives; many men of the town gather there. Since it is now dinnertime, the visitors' arrival forms the same test of hospitality as the three brought to Abraham, and Lot passes the test. Sitting near the Sodom gateway like Abraham sitting at the tent entrance, he hastens to meet and greet the visitors when he sees them and bows down before them like Abraham. While he doesn't run as Abraham did, he does bow even lower than Abraham, face to the ground.

"Sirs," he begins (v. 2), like Abraham.[79] His invitation again includes the chance to bathe the muck off their feet and in due course to be on their way, but otherwise it is the invitation appropriate to the evening rather than to lunchtime—not a sandwich and some water but somewhere to stay for the night and the chance to make an early start in the morning. It is not impossible to shelter in the town square (it would feel safer than in the open country), though it is not ideal: see Judg. 19, which makes for horrifying comparison and contrast with Gen. 19. The envoys politely refuse (as they did not in 18:3–5); it is the appropriate response, though one does not expect the refusal to be accepted.

Lot duly coerces them (v. 3). Like Abraham with his fatted calf, he goes beyond the call of duty. Indeed, he emulates Abraham with his banquet and his flat bread, which they would hardly need after that gargantuan lunch. What a worthy nephew of Abraham Lot is![80]

19:4–5. Then things fall apart. Perhaps the men of the town, in particular, are indeed in the square when the visitors arrive and Lot invites them in, though the story does not say so. But when the story now refers to the *ʾănāšîm* of the town, the *ʾănāšîm* of Sodom, there is no particular reason to think that they are just the men. While there are passages that use phrases such as *hāʾănāšîm ʿal-hannāšîm* (Exod. 35:22) to refer to men and women respectively, expressions such as *ʾanšê hāʾāreṣ*, the people of the country (Lev. 18:11), denote the community as a whole. Here the emphatic terminology

78. See the comment on 16:7.

79. But see the footnote to 18:3.

80. On Abraham and Lot as hosts, see Peleg, "Was Lot a Good Host?"; Safren, "Hospitality Compared"; and MacDonald, "Hospitality and Hostility."

("the entire people, from every part") suggests that the whole community is there, not just the men.[81] It indicates that there are not going to be ten people here to make Yahweh spare the town if the question arises, as it is about to. "The text focuses on communal responsibility, on what happens when sin and its effects become systemic, that is, so pervasive that an entire community is caught up in them."[82]

The town proposes something like gang rape (v. 5). Given that the visitors are (apparently) men, the proposal might imply homosexual rape, but it might just as likely imply that it will be women who will have sex with them,[83] which would also make for a link with vv. 30–38. Although Western readers are inclined to think of sex as related to love and commitment or to sensual pleasure (or both), the phenomenon of rape generally presupposes that it relates to power and humiliation or shaming.[84] Here, at least, it is a response to fear.[85] The whole town is afraid of these strangers.

19:6–8. The reason Lot shuts the door behind him is to protect the envoys. If vv. 4–5 seem hard to believe, what follows is more so. Commendably, Lot wants to keep the Sodomites, his "brothers," from doing something bad. Genesis picks up the word "bad" that came in 6:5; 8:21; Lot is in the process of proving that Yahweh's assessment of Sodom still applies (cf. also 13:13).

Lot thinks he might be able to protect the envoys by offering the Sodomites his daughters (v. 8). But what is the point of the offer? Though it has been suggested that Lot is fulfilling the expectations of Israelite hospitality by offering them for sex,[86] commentators do not provide evidence for this interpretation beyond a reference to Judg. 19, which is hardly narrated as a positive expression of Israelite values. Admittedly, an offer of sex with his virgin daughters might interest the men in the crowd. But is Lot then serious, or is he trying to jolt the community to its senses? Can the Sodomites tell the difference between what is bad and what is good in their own eyes? The word for "sleeping with" again more literally means "knowing." Have they profited at all from their ultimate parents' eating from the *good*-and-*bad-knowledge* tree? But anyway, Lot does not invite the crowd to sleep with his daughters, and it's not obvious why this would satisfy their reasons

81. Cf. Doyle, "'Knock, Knock," 446. On the possibility that heterosexual wishes lie behind the passage, see also Vandermeersch, "Sodomites." Toensing ("Women of Sodom and Gomorrah") considers various aspects of the role and position of women in Gen. 19, but not this one.

82. Cf. Fretheim, *Abraham*, 89.

83. As far as we know, it was Philo (*On Abraham* 27.137) who first identified the sin of Sodom as homosexuality, specifically homosexual rape (cf. De La Torre, *Genesis*, 194). See also Nissinen, *Homoeroticism*, 45–49, 93–97.

84. See, e.g., Hendel, Kronfeld, and Pardes, "Gender and Sexuality," 84; Bechtel, "Boundary Issues"; Waters, "Reading Sodom."

85. Cf. Bechtel, "Feminist Reading."

86. So, e.g., Gunkel, *Genesis*, 207.

for wanting to "know" the strangers. Maybe Lot is rather offering them as hostages.[87]

19:9–11. Although Lot had been sitting in the gateway like the citizens of Sodom, the actual citizens now put him in his place. Though he thinks they are his "brothers," they remind him of his actual status as a resident alien whose green card can be withdrawn at any moment.[88] First, they tell him to get away from the door that he has shut. Then, unbeknownst to themselves, they pay him a compliment. The audience knows Yahweh's expectation that Abraham should exercise authority in accordance with faithfulness; in connection with Yahweh's intentions for Sodom, the audience also knows that Abraham has been challenging Yahweh about the proper exercise of authority. Lot has been faithful in his exercise of hospitality to the two "men" (2 Pet. 2:7–8 describes him as *dikaios*, the Greek word equivalent to *ṣaddîq*), and now ironically the Sodomites "accuse" him of daring to behave as if *mišpāṭ* in Sodom is his business. "Up to this point in the Genesis story, Lot has enjoyed a measure of peace and stability alongside the Sodomites, as long as he did not challenge the social hierarchy. Now that he seeks to defend two strangers, whose social status is even lower than his own, he is to suffer the same aggression that the visitors have attracted."[89] Like good postmodern people, the Sodomites suggest that "Lot should not presume to force his social values on them."[90] If he resists their doing something that he says is bad, they will show him what bad dealing feels like.[91]

In the events that follow (vv. 10–11), the two "men" protect Lot, shut the door again, and show that they are more than ordinary men by terminating for a while the Sodomites' capacity to fulfill their aims. Again Genesis notes that the whole community is involved, "from young right to old."

19:12–14. The story jumps forward: it would be logical to have the intention that comes as v. 13 preceding the exhortation to action that comes in v. 12. But the action is what is required, so it comes first. The envoys again show a mixture of prophetic knowledge and ignorance. The answer to the question in v. 12 is two daughters and two virtual sons-in-law, and/or one or more actual sons-in-law; in the latter case there are more daughters to take into account. In addition, there is a wife, who is taken for granted. The fact that they total rather less than the ten at which Abraham stopped in his quizzing of Yahweh might link with that stopping point. They need to get out rather than thinking that Yahweh may hold back from acting against the town.

87. See Morschauser, "'Hospitality,'" 474–82; it is one aspect of a broader reconfiguring of 19:1–9 as a juridical event.

88. On the significance of the resident alien motif in Gen. 19, see Fields, *Sodom and Gomorrah*, 27–53.

89. Brett, *Genesis*, 67–68.

90. Brayford, *Genesis*, 319.

91. Van Wolde ("Outcry") thus locates Sodom's outcry (18:20) in this protest.

Lot's family needs to escape because Yahweh is going to act (v. 13). Perhaps the townspeople's behavior and their refusal to respond to Lot are the last straw. More precisely, the two "men" are going to act on Yahweh's behalf: it is part of what envoys are for. They explicitly pick up the talk of outcry and devastation from Yahweh's words and from the dialogue in 18:20–32; the reference to family members implicitly takes up the reference to the possibility of there being ten faithful people in Sodom.

The "sons-in-law" (v. 14) might have been young men in the position of Mary's almost-husband Joseph—"virtual sons-in-law" in that they are legally yoked to Lot's daughters but the marriage has not yet taken place. However, the reference in v. 15 to daughters in Lot's house implies that other daughters are no longer there and suggests that the sons-in-law are the husbands of Lot's older daughters. Lot goes to talk to the husbands as the heads of the households where his older daughters now live. Laughter again features in the story, but with unfortunate implications.

19:15–26. Lot is dithering.[92] It's another expression of his ambivalent relationship with Sodom, which has attracted him because of its positive qualities. In some ways he is a faithful man, though dim-witted pragmatically as well as morally—a Jekyll and Hyde character.[93] Fortunately for him the envoys roll their eyes, have pity on him, and strong-arm him and his family out of the town so that they don't get "swept away" (the verb picked up from 18:23, 24). The envoys don't intend then to transport them to safety. Lot needs to take responsibility for himself (the "you" in v. 17 is singular) and presumably for his family.

There is still little prospect of his doing so (vv. 18–20). Lot has indeed experienced grace and commitment (*ḥēn* and *ḥesed*). The former nicely puts him in the same category as Noah (6:8) and also Abraham (18:3). He then has the distinction of being the first person in the Scriptures to talk about *ḥesed*, which denotes the kind of commitment that anticipates faithfulness and is itself thus an expression of grace and also the kind of commitment that keeps going when its recipient has behaved in a way that forfeits any right to expect faithfulness. By definition, grace and commitment are undeserved, but by definition they then look for a response. Lot doesn't understand that implication. He would just like more of them. Apparently he thinks he won't be able to get to the mountains in time to escape the effects of the catastrophe and illogically thinks he could be safe in a nearby town that won't be affected by the disaster, like people who ignore instructions to evacuate when a hurricane is forecast and instead take refuge in their attic.

Again the envoy (or is it Yahweh, who has now arrived?) rolls his eyes (vv. 21–22), and Lot finds that sometimes God grants unreasonable requests for

92. Cf. Lyons, *Canon and Exegesis*, 243.

93. Turner, "Lot as Jekyll and Hyde."

more grace and commitment.[94] Indeed, the envoy or Yahweh says he can't take action until Lot gets his act together.[95] It would be unfitting for him as God. His statement is the converse of Abraham's challenges about exercising authority in the way proper to the God of all the earth and about what desecrates Yahweh (18:25). There is nothing outside God that binds God; but God is bound by who he is. *Ṣāʿîr* means "small" (it comes four times in vv. 30–38 to describe Lot's younger daughter as opposed to his elder daughter). *Ṣoʿar* is Little-ton.

Apparently Lot and company get themselves to Zoʿar (vv. 23–25) between first light and sunup, which is hardly more than half an hour or so (Tg. Ps.-J. gives them three hours for the journey). We don't know exactly where any of the towns are, so we don't know the distance, but the story is again talking dramatic time rather than real time, though it is now doing so in connection with the travel time required by human beings as well as by supernatural visitors. Lot and family thus arrive at the moment when Yahweh devastates Sodom, Gomorrah, and the surrounding area, along with everything that grows, and presumably with those substantial flocks and herds belonging to Lot (and to other Sodomites). An earthquake in the Dead Sea region could doubtless release asphalt and sulfur into the sky that could then fall "from the heavens," but Genesis says only that the disaster is one that Yahweh directly brings about. And "burning sulfur" is a conventional image for horrific means of destruction (Deut. 29:23 [29:22]; Ps. 11:6; Isa. 30:23; 34:9; Ezek. 38:22).[96]

Apparently his wife looks back behind Lot (v. 26), who has pushed his family out ahead of him. Although Yahweh directly rains down the burning sulfur, he does not personally strike down Lot's wife. Her simply feeling compelled to look back is easy to imagine, a natural human instinct. She is not a wicked person like some other people in Genesis whom one could mention. Targum Neof. explains that she is a Sodomite herself who thus looks back to see what will happen to her family. Another midrash gives her the name Irit or Idit and explains that she looked back because she had left behind those two other daughters (who were already married to those two sons-in-law). Deuteronomy 29:23 [22] perhaps implies that everyone in Sodom was turned into salt pilasters,[97] which would include the two daughters, whose fate a mother might have willed to share. Thus "she was turned into salt either because God couldn't forgive her this desire . . . or because He could."[98] Was it a catatonic reaction to the trauma of what she was going through?[99] To be literalistic,

94. See Dishi, "Saving Zoar"; Tonson, "Mercy without Covenant."

95. Cf. Cyril of Alexandria, as quoted in Petit, *La chaîne sur la Genèse*, 3:156; cf. Sheridan, *Genesis 12–50*, 78.

96. Cf. Westermann, *Genesis 12–36*, 306.

97. Cf. Qimchi on the passage.

98. Goldstein, "Looking Back," 41; cf. Cheon ("Filling the Gap"), who reads the story in light of a Korean legend.

99. So Luger, "Flood."

maybe the reference to her looking implies she delays and is overwhelmed by the burning sulfur that is overwhelming everyone and then became encrusted with salt.[100] It's possible to imagine her as one of the salt formations around the southern part of the Dead Sea. Indeed, Wis. 10:7 refers to it, and Josephus (*Ant.* 1.11.4) says he has seen it. When Pompeii was destroyed, "a volcanic gas settled over the city, asphyxiating many of the citizens while they slept. The city was then covered with heavy deposits of volcanic ash up to a depth of about twenty feet in which human and animal life was entombed. . . . The chemical content of the ash . . . apparently turned human bodies into some chemical substance that was sufficiently hard to allow the surrounding ash to retain a perfect cast of the bodies."[101] Even if we sympathize with Lot's wife, we need to see her fate as a warning (Luke 17:26–32). But it's all right, says Tg. Neof.: she is there only until resurrection day.

19:27–29. Meanwhile, Abraham gets going early that same morning. The verb (*šākam* hiphil) commonly signifies a serious commitment to doing something, something you therefore get up early to do (it described Lot's expectations about the envoys' early departure in v. 2). Abraham knows from Yahweh's revelation that the catastrophe is imminent. He returns to the point where he sent off the envoys, where he then had his dialogue with Yahweh, and from where he could see the devastation. The narrator's "there" again draws us into looking at the scene though his eyes. Now "Abraham looks down on the scene of the disaster—and is silent."[102] Genesis does not tell us whether he knows that Lot has been saved, though the audience knows.[103]

In what sense has God been mindful of Abraham (v. 29)? Abraham's dialogue with Yahweh has not saved Sodom, though it has expressed his bold and passionate concern for the town, and as far as one can tell, it was not out of a concern to save only Lot. This reference to God's mindfulness links back more directly not to Gen. 18 but to the deluge story (see 8:1). The further occurrence of the verb "devastate" (cf. 18:28, 31, 32; 19:13, 14) also makes the link (cf. 6:13, 17; 9:11, 15). Indeed, the talk of "God" rather than "Yahweh" (as in 8:1, but in this verse alone in 18:1–19:38) underscores it.[104] God has been mindful of Abraham as he was mindful of Noah, though the direct beneficiary of the mindfulness is Abraham's nephew Lot and his family instead of Noah and his family. God has been mindful of a commitment to Abraham and thus to his family.

19:30–38. Lot continues to dither. Is he afraid that the inhabitants of Zoʿar will turn out the same as the inhabitants of Sodom or that there might be another disaster? Is he failing to have faith in the envoys' word? Or is he being

100. So Keil and Delitzsch, *Pentateuch*, 236.
101. Hamilton, *Genesis 18–50*, 48, summarizing Boyd, *Tells*, 85–87.
102. Westermann, *Genesis 12–36*, 308.
103. Cf. Lyons, *Canon and Exegesis*, 249.
104. Cf. Wenham, *Genesis 16–50*, 45, though in source-critical terms it points to P.

wiser than he was when he went to live near Sodom in the first place? Does he note the irony in the difference between how well he was doing back then (13:5–6) and how pathetic are his circumstances now? The only other cave in Genesis will be the one where his aunt and uncle are buried; elsewhere in the Scriptures caves are just places where desperate people hide. Lot and his daughters are such people. His action implies that there is no hope.

His daughters refuse to give up on hope (vv. 31–35), though the action they then take raises eyebrows. The story that follows again recalls Noah; Lot too has unpleasant experiences from the interaction of drink and sex with his offspring, for which he can hardly be held totally responsible, though in its brief summary of Gen. 18–19, Jub. 16.1–9 does have room to condemn what happens as an unprecedented sin, and specifically to condemn Lot for what happens. "At the beginning of the chapter he was willing to let the virginity of his daughters be forcibly defiled, without even informing them, in order to save lives. Now, in order to 'maintain life,' his daughters have lost their virginity by forcing themselves upon him without his knowledge."[105] Thus their seduction of their own father "can be considered poetic justice—a fitting fate for someone willing to bargain away his daughters' sexuality."[106] But maybe "Lot, incapacitated by drunkenness and sleep, did not remember that he had lost his wife, but he thought she was present."[107] Having been set on the way by God's promise through being part of the family of his uncle Abraham (Gen. 12), he first turned aside from this association (Gen. 13), then needed rescuing by him (Gen. 14): has he now "finally slipped completely from God's hand"? But Genesis recounts the story with sympathy for a man who was not so much wicked as foolish.[108]

Compared with their father, his daughters are clear thinking, purposeful, and resourceful (whence did they get the wine?), even if equally misguided. "The narrator presents both sisters as acting out of desperation, indicating that neither should be judged too harshly."[109] Their position somewhat resembles Sarah's in Gen. 16 or Rachel's in Gen. 30 or Tamar's in Gen. 38. Desperate circumstances require desperate measures. Their father will not live forever (though he is presumably quite a bit younger than his uncle Abraham), and they are going to be on their own. They make a moral choice, "opting for the family's survival over

105. Sarna, *Genesis*, 140.

106. Brett, *Genesis*, 68.

107. Andrew of Saint Victor, *Exposition on Genesis*, as quoted in Schroeder, *Genesis*, 151; contrast Jerome's incredulity (*Hebrew Questions on Genesis*, 52) at the idea of a man having sex without realizing it (see further Hayward's comments, 171–72). Ephrem (*Genesis*, 163–64) has an imaginative midrash on how the two women deceived their father so as to get him drunk and then deceived him about the source of their pregnancy.

108. Von Rad, *Genesis*, 219.

109. Grossman, "'Associative Meanings,'" 57. Grossman thinks that the narrator is more sympathetic to the younger daughter. Cf. also Hunt, "Two Daughters."

its honor."[110] In what sense are there no potential partners to have sex with them in the way the world regularly does? Are they thinking of the world within their reach? Is the comment another observation on the people who live in places like Zoʿar? Do they suspect that the catastrophe has overwhelmed the entire human world?[111] They have seen their hometown destroyed, the destruction has embraced their elder sisters and their husbands (or their own prospective husbands), they have seen their mother die, and their father has withdrawn from life, like Jonah sleeping in the depths of the boat. Perhaps "the incest of these women [might] be purer than the chastity of many women."[112]

In light of where the story ends (vv. 36–38), it might bring a smirk to the audience's faces. "You know those Moabites and Ammonites [who did not appear in Gen. 10)]? Let me tell you where they came from!" While the audience might well find their scheme obnoxious, it is also a way that Abraham becomes the "father" of many nations.[113] And Yahweh will give land to both these nations that descend from Lot and will protect them from the Israelites (Deut. 2:9, 19).[114] "Verses 30–38 hardly offer themselves as a kerygma"; they are folk material.[115] But the Scriptures make every excuse for the two women and for Lot. So given that we are sinners, we should resist the temptation to condemn them.[116] And shall we not marvel that these daughters of a mother who understandably gave in to her hopelessness, "these intrepid women, were able to survive, to live on, to become the mothers of great nations?"[117]

Implications

Three Persons, One God?

From time to time God "appears" in the world in human form. So far in Genesis, God has appeared in order to give extra force to commitments and promises he makes to Abraham (12:7; 17:1; and the "vision" in 15:1), and this consideration may also be implicit in Gen. 18. God's appearing is then a gracious and merciful act for the sake of people. But the explicit reason for

110. Hendel, Kronfeld, and Pardes, "Gender and Sexuality," 88.

111. Ephrem (*Genesis*, 162) has them assuming that the catastrophe was as devastating as the deluge in the time of Noah (cf. Wickes, "Ephrem's Interpretation of Genesis," 52).

112. Origen, *Homilies on Genesis*, 117.

113. Brett, *Genesis*, 69.

114. Cf. Lyons, "Eternal Liminality of Lot," 13. Carmichael ("Legal and Ethical Reflections") makes links with Lev. 18:7 and Deut. 23:2–6, but the former speaks of sons and mothers and the latter provides a rationale different from a link with Gen. 19. Fields (*Sodom and Gomorrah*, 147–52) rather links the story with enmity between Israel and Moab/Ammon. On the ambiguity of the First Testament's attitude to Moab and Ammon, see also Noort, "Abraham and the Nations," 14–17.

115. Seebass, *Genesis*, 2.1:157.

116. Chrysostom, *Homilies on Genesis 18–45*, 464–65.

117. Visotzky, *Genesis of Ethics*, 85.

God's appearing in Gen. 18 is to check out the situation in the world (18:21), as God did in 11:7 (without reference to "appearing"). Here he visits the world for his own sake—or for humanity's sake in the sense that he comes to ensure that he treats humanity in a fair way. Even if he might know what is happening because he can see from his position in the heavens or because he can send his envoys, he comes in person to check things out. He does not rely on remote knowledge; he becomes involved.[118]

As Luther sees it, one advantage of the Gen. 18 account of his appearing is its "unique evidence concerning the Trinity," though Luther knows that Jewish scholars laugh at this understanding.[119] Ibn Ezra indeed notes that some people say, "God is three men: He is one and He is three and they are inseparable," but he observes that this idea does not fit the way the passage talks in terms of God, and then of three angels, one of whom brings the message to Sarah while the other two go off to destroy Sodom and to save Lot.[120] Augustine also argues from the alternating references to the persons that the three are angels (as Heb. 13:2 implies), even though God was in all three and was working through them in a remarkable way.[121] Luther in the end grants that, historically understood, the passage does not refer to the Trinity but that an exposition along these lines may nevertheless be edifying. It adorns rather than proves.[122]

Such approaches to understanding the three visitors are instructive in the way they do not provide satisfying answers. They point us in a different direction for the significance of how they are portrayed. How does God so appear in the world in human form? In one sense it is quite an easy thing; he made humanity in his image, so appearing in human form is not so complicated. The appearing of God as an *ʾîš* again suggests a biblical rather than a Greek starting point for understanding Jesus's incarnation.[123]

Yet the story suggests complications by portraying changes over how many visitors there are at different points; the audience may wonder whether they are the same sort of beings, whether all three "represent" God, or whether one represents God and the other two are envoys, who also, however, in some sense "represent" God.[124] Although some movement in the portrayal issues from switching between telling the story from the perspective of the narrator (who knows more than Abraham does) and telling it from the perspective

118. See further Carlson's comments ("Open God," 191–92) on Yahweh as the subject of the verb *yādaʿ* in Gen. 18–19.

119. Luther, *Genesis 15–20*, 177, 190. Reno (*Genesis*, 183) supports the trinitarian understanding.

120. Ibn Ezra, *Genesis*, 189–90.

121. Augustine, *City of God* 16.29. See more broadly Doerfler, "Entertaining the Trinity Unawares"; cf. Willet, *Hexapla in Genesin & Exodum*, 169.

122. Luther, *Genesis 15–20*, 194–95.

123. Cf. Hamori, "Divine Embodiment."

124. On ways of handling such questions, see Lyons, *Canon and Exegesis*, 151–61.

of the participants, this dynamic does not explain everything. Some of the ambiguity reflects the narrator's own lack of clarity (narrators in the First Testament may know more than the characters in their stories, but they are not omniscient), which reflects the inherent mystery of the reality the narrative describes. The elusiveness recurs when God is incarnate in Jesus and when the church finds it hard to conceptualize insights about the nature of God and about the person of Jesus, which it must do as much by means of paradox and by negative statements as by clarity and by positive statements. Finding the Trinity in the First Testament obscures more than it clarifies. It hinders our hearing what God was and is saying through this story.

Intercession and Theodicy

Although Abraham's dialogue with God has traditionally been taken as a model of intercession,[125] Western interests have inspired interpreters to locate the importance of the dialogue in its significance for theodicy;[126] Westermann calls it a theological discussion.[127] Von Rad gives the impression of being caught between these alternative understandings, but in the end his indecision is creative. The conversation between Abraham and God happens, he notes, "in view of the sinful city lying at a distance in the valley, the city which had no idea either of its judge or of its intercessor." But "Abraham is not especially concerned with saving Lot, not even with saving Sodom." The dialogue is a means of discussing a theological question. Further, Sodom does not stand for a town outside the covenant people. "Sodom is here for Israel the pattern of a human community toward which Yahweh's eyes turn in judgment." A question is posed: "What determines God's judgment on Sodom, the wickedness of the many or the innocence of the few?" But, von Rad also comments, "The narrator would scarcely feel himself badly misunderstood if we were to read this text from the viewpoint of intercession and its power."[128] As intercession, it compares with Amos 7. "It's a forceful and impulsive prayer, as if Abraham wanted to compel God to forgive."[129] The story encourages the audience to think, but in light of the thinking that it encourages, it also drives it to be faithful, because a small number of faithful may make all the difference. The story also drives the audience to pray, to advocate with God.[130] "What gives Abraham the 'right' to argue with God and question his intentions?" The

125. See, e.g., Tg; Chrysostom, *Homilies on Genesis 18–45*, 426–29; Calvin, *Genesis*, 1:487–89.

126. See Brueggemann, *Genesis*, 167–76.

127. Westermann, *Genesis 12–36*, 291; cf. Ben Zvi, "Dialogue"; T. Miller, "Relationships."

128. Von Rad, *Genesis*, 207, 208, 209.

129. Luther, *Genesis 15–20*, 235.

130. Cf. Fretheim, *Abraham*, 85–86.

answer must be the covenantal relationship between God and Israel, which puts obligations on God as well as on Abraham.[131]

The First Testament may indeed be interested in the question of theodicy, or at least it offers materials that facilitate reflection on the question. Will Yahweh be bound to destroy Sodom if he finds that the rumor about its waywardness is broadly true? Yahweh agrees that he is not bound by any such system.[132] On the other hand, neither is he bound to operate in the way Gen. 18 describes. "God does not here bind himself by a perpetual rule" but "speaks thus, in order to make it better known, that he does not, on light grounds, proceed to the destruction of a city."[133] While Yahweh here declares that he will spare a town if there are ten faithful people there, in Jer. 5:1 he says he will do so if there is one truthful person there. On the other hand, in Ezek. 14:12–23 Yahweh declares that he would not withhold judgment even if one famously faithful person (such as Noah) were there.[134] And he brings judgment on Jerusalem despite the presence of people such as Jeremiah and Ezekiel, though for them it's not the end of the story. Further, if there is a tension between 18:23–33 and 19:1–28, and if (for instance) 18:23–33 is a critique of the assumptions underlying 19:1–28,[135] then Genesis invites us to work with the tension rather than letting either passage override or silence the other. In Amos 7–9, too, both perspectives appear. The question of the waywardness and the punishment of communities is too complicated for there to be one answer. Each time the question arises, God thinks about it afresh and decides how to weigh the different considerations at that time. And this reality is one reason why prayer makes a difference as we urge God to weigh the considerations in a different way from the one he may be inclined to take.

Jeremiah 31:29–30 and Ezek. 18 can also be brought into the framework of this discussion, but their concern is different. Their issue is whether Yahweh punishes one generation for the wrongdoing of an earlier generation.[136] The issue in Job is different again: "He finishes off the person of integrity and the faithless person" (Job 9:22).

131. So Dershowitz, *Genesis of Justice*, 71–72.

132. Cf. Fretheim, *Abraham*, 81.

133. Calvin, *Genesis*, 1:488–89.

134. See further Lipton, "Limits of Intercession"; Blenkinsopp, "Abraham and the Righteous of Sodom."

135. So Brueggemann, *Genesis*, 162–76; though Ben Zvi ("Dialogue," 45) and Bolin ("Role of Exchange") seem to imply that the critique works in the opposite direction.

136. See also the comments of MacDonald, "Listening to Abraham," 38–39.

17
Abraham and Abimelek, Part One

(20:1–18)

Overview

Genesis 20 tells a story like the one in 12:9–13:4. Abraham goes to live in a certain ruler's territory as a resident alien, he's afraid that the people there will kill him in order to take hold of Sarah, and he therefore asks her to say she is his sister. The king does get hold of Sarah, but God intervenes and causes sickness in the ruler's household. The ruler discovers the cause, challenges Abraham, and gives Sarah back. Abraham ends up vastly enriched by the adventure.

This second story differs from the first in taking place in Gerar rather than Egypt, and the ruler is a person of noteworthy integrity. God appears to him and informs him that Abraham is a prophet who can plead for him, Abraham explains that Sarah really is his (half) sister, and the ruler invites him to stay in his realm rather than leave immediately.

Knowledge of the first story helps to make sense of the second story, while conversely the second story helps to clarify questions raised by the first.

Translation

1Abraham moved on from there to the southland[1] region and lived between Qadeš and Šur, and resided as an alien in Gerar.[2] **2**Abraham said

1. See the footnote to 12:9.
2. Appositely, given the similarity of the name to the verb *gûr*.

of[3] Śarah his wife, "She's my sister."[4] Abimelek king of Gerar sent and got Śarah, **3**but God came to Abimelek in a dream by night and said to him, "Here, you're a dead man[5] because of the woman that you got. She belongs to someone."[6]

4Now Abimelek had not approached her.[7] He said, "Lord, a nation, yes, a faithful one—would you kill it? **5**That man said to me, 'She's my sister,' didn't he? And she herself also said, 'He's my brother.' It was with integrity in my heart and with freedom from guilt in the palms of my hands[8] that I did this." **6**God said to him in the dream, "I myself both know that you did this with integrity in your heart and have also held you back from doing wrong in relation to me. That's why I didn't permit you to touch her. **7**So now give the man's wife back, because he's a prophet, and he can plead for you. Save your life. But if you don't give her back, acknowledge that you will definitely die,[9] you and everything that's yours."

8Abimelek started early in the morning, called for all his servants, and spoke all these things in their ears. The men were in great awe.[10] **9**Abimelek called for Abraham and said to him, "What have you done to us? How did I do wrong in relation to you, that you've brought a big wrong on me and on my entire kingdom? You've done deeds with me that shouldn't be done."

10So Abimelek said to Abraham, "What did you see that you did this thing?" **11**Abraham said, "Because I said, 'There's just no awe for God in this place, and they'll kill me on account of my wife.' **12**And also, she truly is my sister, my father's daughter, admittedly not my mother's daughter. So she became my wife, **13**and when God made me wander[11] from my father's household, I said to her, 'This is the commitment with which you're to act toward me. In[12] the entire region[13] to which we come: say about me, "He's my brother."'"

3. The use of *ʾel* with this sense is unusual (Tal, *Genesis*, 126*).

4. LXX adds an explanation based on 26:7.

5. Less colloquially, "You are going to die."

6. Literally, "she is owned by an owner," using the verb *bāʿal* and the noun *baʿal*, the more legal term for a husband (e.g., Exod. 21:3; Deut. 22:22; cf. Sarah's use of the noun *ʾādōn* in 18:12).

7. For the verb referring to sex, see, e.g., Deut. 22:14; Isa. 8:3.

8. Literally, "in my palms/fists."

9. As in 2:17, God uses the idiom that combines an infinitive and its cognate finite verb to indicate emphasis; the idiom recurs with another verb in v. 18.

10. Although "were very frightened" would follow from the threat in v. 7, and Abimelek is surely making clear that he intends to take the appropriate action, reference to a positive awe leads with irony into v. 11.

11. To Abimelek the plural verb would suggest "gods" (cf. Alter, *Genesis*, 95), but see 31:53 (Laban); 35:7 (Jacob); cf. GKC 145i. The verb itself is also scandalous; the Tgs turn the nations into the subject. See the discussion in Schmutzer, "Did the Gods Cause Abraham's Wandering?"

12. The preposition *ʾel* is slightly odd (though see BDB 40b); in the context, perhaps its use was influenced by the idea of motion toward.

13. For this meaning of *māqôm*, see Exod. 3:8; 23:20. The LXX has "every place" for *kol-hammāqôm*, but the article would make that meaning unique (as GKC 127e notes).

14Abimelek got flock and herd, servants and maidservants, and gave
them to Abraham, and gave his wife Śarah back to him. **15**Abimelek said,
"Here, my country is before you. Live wherever is good in your eyes."
16To Śarah he said, "Here, I'm giving[14] your brother a thousand pieces of
silver. Here, it will be cover over the eyes for you and for everyone who is
with you and with everyone, and you'll be vindicated."[15]
17Abraham pleaded with God and God healed Abimelek and his wife
and his handmaids, and they gave birth **18**(because Yahweh had totally
held back every womb belonging to Abimelek's household on account of
Śarah, Abraham's wife).

Interpretation

Genesis 20 is an intriguingly told tale, a "refined" narrative, artfully composed, its tension heightened through withholding information that the audience needs in order to understand it and giving some of this information only later.[16] The audience might wonder why Abraham said that Sarah was his sister; its guess would be confirmed or disconfirmed or its uncertainty resolved by vv. 10–13. It might wonder how God held Abimelek back from touching Sarah and why he needed Abraham's prayers; vv. 17–18 would confirm or disconfirm its guesses or resolve its uncertainty. It might wonder why Abraham moved from Mamre to the Negev; v. 13 might make it infer that such movements were part of Abraham's anticipatorily entering into possession of more and more of the promised land. Further, as it listens to the story, knowing or not knowing the story in 12:1–13:4 would make a difference.[17] Why did Abraham move from the Negev to Gerar? People who knew the earlier story might infer that there was a famine in the Negev. Why was Abimelek interested in Sarah? People might infer that it was her political value as a member of Abraham's family, but if they knew the earlier story, they might infer that it was her attractiveness. She is eighty-nine, but in "real" terms that's more like fifty, and fifty-year old women can be attractive; they can also be worldly wise and efficient (see Prov. 31), and she could be a potential management asset (KSG). Why is God so concerned to protect Sarah? People who know the broader story of Abraham and Sarah will know that she is due to be the mother of the child through whom God intends to fulfill his promise of blessing.

14. The declarative/performative qatal suggests a speech act, "I hereby give."

15. *Wəʾēt kōl wənōkāḥat* is widely regarded as unintelligible (e.g., Tal, *Genesis*, 128*), though the general sense is clear. I take *ʾēt* as the preposition rather than the sign of the object. *Nōkāḥat* is a feminine niphal participle whose subject is Sarah, though the participle has no antecedent; adding a shewa at the end turns it into second-person qatal (cf. BDB).

16. Gunkel, *Genesis*, 219.

17. Cf. Van Seters's comments, *Abraham in History and Tradition*, 171–75; and Rashkow, "Intertextuality."

While some elements in the first story could thus provide background to the second, some elements in the second story answer questions raised by the first. Did Sarah go along with Abraham's plan? Was she prepared even to sacrifice her own sexual integrity? Sometimes women have been prepared to do so in such a situation (KSG). Maybe she said what she was supposed to say. Did Pharaoh have sex with her? Maybe the afflictions that came upon him and his household stopped him. How would someone like Pharaoh have known that it was his taking Sarah that explained the afflictions among his household? Maybe a dream is the answer. Maybe a ruler who acts in that way is nevertheless a person of integrity. Was Abraham as much of a rogue as he seems to have been in relation to Pharaoh and Sarah? Yes, and more, though he has some pathetic excuses. Did the event ruin Sarah's reputation? Maybe Pharaoh compensated her in a way that would make her innocence clear. What happened to the household after Pharaoh had released Sarah? Maybe Abraham prayed for him and for them, and the story ended happily for everyone.

This last feature puts us on the track of its possible broader point, which connects with its place in the Abraham and Sarah narrative as a whole. Yahweh's initial directive and promise to Abraham related to land, increase, and blessing—experienced and mediated. Genesis 12:9–13:4 relates an event that imperiled the entire project. Genesis 20 reopens the questions raised there, particularly the question whether Abraham can have a wholesome relationship with other nations and whether God cares about them. Here Abraham again imperils that possibility, but God reaches out to Abimelek. God is caught between Abraham, to whom he is committed though he is a rogue, and Abimelek, who is a person of integrity and faithfulness but whom Abraham has led into unwitting wrongdoing. God takes action against Abimelek to stop him from going further into wrongdoing and also gets Abimelek to put things right. He uses Abraham as a means of restoring Abimelek from the mess Abraham has gotten Abimelek into and as a means of his household being blessed. And he uses Abimelek as a means of blessing Abraham. The chapter thus conveys a mixed message in relation to God's promise to Abraham. Will he possess the land? Verse 13 suggests a glimmer of a reassurance. Will he have offspring? God has shown himself able to open Gerar's wombs, but not Sarah's yet. Will Abraham be a blessing? Not so much, but at least he can be the means of reversing a curse.

The second story never comments on the fact that the event is apparently a repeat of an earlier one (unless v. 13 implies it). Nor does it ask why Abraham makes the same mistake twice. Though it might seem "astonishing"[18] and implausible that the same sort of thing should recur, it seems not much less plausible that it should have happened once. The more significant question

18. Wenham, *Genesis 16–50*, 75.

is why the Scriptures include a second, similar story. Why do we need to read such a story twice? Presumably the second story is told and included in the Scriptures because it raises issues that are important enough to discuss twice and because it discusses them in a way that also allows insights to emerge that did not emerge from the first version. Whereas the first story, with its reference to Sarah's attractiveness, suggests implications regarding a husband's attitude about his wife's sexuality, the absence of this reference in the second story and the anthropological background suggests implications regarding the way a husband may seek to use his wife in connection with politics or business or church. Women are often pawns, not least in the context of migration. Genesis 20 is more reflective than 12:9–13:4. Dialogue between God and Abimelek and between Abimelek and Abraham is more prominent than action. There is comparison and contrast between the dialogues: both involve accusation that cannot be contested and then defense that asks for extenuating circumstances to be taken into account, but in Abraham's case the extenuating circumstances do not remove his guilt.[19] Key elements in the action appear only in parentheses near the end.

The MT makes Gen. 20 a second paragraph within 18:1–21:21, following on 18:1–19:38. In traditional pentateuchal criticism, it belongs to the Elohistic version of Abraham's story, in which it is the equivalent of 12:9–13:4 in the Yahwistic version. The obvious marker is the use of the word *ʾĕlōhîm* for God (though the closing parenthetical remark refers to Yahweh), but dreams are also characteristic of the Elohistic version.[20]

The setting of Gen. 20 in the context of the surrounding chapters raises another question, about the geographical references in these chapters. The data are as follows:

Abraham moves to live in the Negev (20:1a)

He goes as a temporary resident to Gerar (20:1b)

After her expulsion from the family, Hagar wanders in the Beer Sheba wilderness (21:14)

Abraham and the king of Gerar make a pact at Beer Sheba (21:22–31)

The king returns to Philistine territory (21:32)

Abraham is a long-time temporary resident in Philistine territory (21:33)

Abraham lives in Beer Sheba (22:19)

Among the implications of these data, and the questions they raise, are the following.

19. See Westermann, *Genesis 12–36*, 318–19, 324.

20. For alternative critical theories, see, e.g., Lipton, *Revisions of the Night*, 35–62.

a. The Negev in general and the Beer Sheba region in particular was home for Abraham through the period covered by these stories, which assumption raises no difficulties.
b. The Philistines are present in Abraham's day and control the Beer Sheba region. But most biblical references to the Philistines and all nonbiblical references come from the period after the Israelites are in Canaan, nor are the Philistines associated with an area as far southeast as Beer Sheba.
c. While 10:18–19 refers to a place called Gerar near Gaza, forty or fifty miles north of Qadesh and Shur in what was subsequently Philistine territory, it describes it as Canaanite territory; and Abimelek looks like a Canaanite name, not a Philistine one, like Melchizedek, though it is also the name of Gideon's son (Judg. 8:31).
d. Jubilees 16.10 has Abraham living "between Qadesh and Shur in the mountains of Gerar"—a different Gerar.[21]

I infer that the Gerar to which Gen. 20–22 refers is this southern Gerar in the Negev, and that the inhabitants of the area are called Philistines because it was Philistines who controlled the region around the northern Gerar when the story was being told in the time between Moses and David, though the area would have been counted broadly as Canaan. But the audience might be bemused at the idea of Abraham getting involved with "Canaanites" in the way he does with "Philistines."

20:1–3. The unusual introduction to the chapter, with its account of Abraham's move, marks it as background to Gen. 20–21. It also portrays the relocation as a kind of reprise of movements in 12:9–10 and 16:7, 14; both links imply some irony. There need be no particular reason for Abraham to move from Mamre to the Negev; tent-dwelling shepherd groups do move around. The area around Mamre gets more rainfall and therefore grows more grass, but for the same reason there might be more competition for pasture in that region (cf. 13:5–7, especially the reference to the other peoples living in the area). But maybe "from there" suggests getting away from the scene of the events in Gen. 18–19 and specifically from Lot (so Gen. Rab. 50.1–4); or perhaps (more positively) Abraham is continuing the process of fulfilling God's command to settle in all the parts of Canaan.[22] Specifically, he is staying temporarily in Gerar as a resident alien, as Lot had been in Sodom and as he had been in Egypt. Like the towns in the Dead Sea area that feature in Gen. 14, a place such as Gerar would be a nominally independent city-state that had a king whom one might think of as more like a mayor but that was subject to Egyptian control of its foreign policy and to Egyptian taxation.

21. See, e.g., Hanna and Norris, *Patriarchs*, 71–81; and cf. Gunkel, *Genesis*, 218–19.
22. So Qimchi, *Genesis*, on the verse.

In Gerar a question about Sarah arises (v. 2), as it did in 12:10–20. Perhaps we are to infer that Sarah would be just as good looking in the eyes of Abimelek twenty years after the Egyptian escapade, when she was a mere seventy;[23] it would be a wise view for a husband to take. But the convention that leaders use their womenfolk as diplomatic currency or that they value them as management assets makes this assumption unnecessary. The convention might mean that Abimelek has quite a harem even if only one wife (v. 17). His saying that he "got" Sarah might imply that he married her (cf. the use of the verb in 19:14), but to make this point it is common to add "as wife" (25:1, 20; 28:2, 6, 9), as Pharaoh did (12:19), and Sarah is here invariably described as Abraham's wife.[24]

The first distinctive theme in this version of the story (v. 3) is God's appearing to Abimelek in a dream; such appearing will recur in the stories of Jacob and Laban and extensively in the Joseph story (Gen. 28; 31; 37–42). The two methods of discipline that God employs in relation to Abimelek are dreams and afflictions.[25] Sometimes God acts to stop a person from doing something that would be objectively wrong; God warned Cain but didn't stop him and (as far as we know) didn't warn the people of Sodom. God can also appear and give revelations in dreams to individuals outside the chosen people as well as to members of his chosen people (see also, e.g., Daniel). While the First Testament can dismiss dreams or issue warnings about them (e.g., Jer. 23:25–32; Eccles. 5:3, 7 [5:2, 6]), as it can about prophecies and visions, in principle it doesn't regard them as questionable in value or as inferior to other ways God communicates or people gain insight. A deity's communicating with a king in a dream is also a familiar Middle Eastern notion. The king would be unwise to trust every dream, but he will be able to test this one by confronting Abraham with its contents. The story thus complements the earlier one in that 12:12 went straight to the afflictions Abraham brought about and never indicated how Pharaoh knew their cause, while this version jumps to the latter question and refers to the afflictions only later. God speaks to Abimelek not to declare a judge's judgment but to warn him about the danger he is in.[26] Although the Torah will make death the penalty for adultery, we know of no occasions when the penalty was exacted, and it is often a mistake to interpret the Torah as laying down laws for applying in the court, though in any case the Torah's rules have not yet been laid down. But further, the danger about adultery lies at least as much from the cuckolded husband as from the law (cf. Prov. 6:34–35): "She belongs to someone" (v. 3).

20:4–7. Western readers would have thought that "getting" a woman as a wife or a member of one's harem would mean having sex with her at the first

23. So, e.g., Willet, *Hexapla in Genesin & Exodum*, 187.
24. Cf. M. Jacobs, *Gender, Power, and Persuasion*, 91.
25. Qimchi, *Genesis*, on v. 3.
26. Cf. Seebass, *Genesis*, 2.1:164–65.

opportunity. But if a woman is prized as much as a sign of prestige or a means of making diplomatic alliances or a management resource as for reasons to do with sex, she is more like an item of clothing or jewelry in a Western context, which a purchaser may not feel the need to wear immediately (or maybe she would need an extensive beauty treatment like Esther, especially after spending a few decades in the desert).[27] Abimelek addresses God as "Lord" in the same way as Abraham did in Gen. 18 (and Moses in Exod. 4–5; 34:9). His reference to killing a nation perhaps presupposes the afflictions of which we will hear in due course, which are not confined to the king (see vv. 17–18): if the royal household is never going to have any more babies, it does imperil the nation. God himself is the prospective executioner, which makes even clearer that v. 3 was not speaking simply of capital punishment for adultery. Perhaps the implicit point is that God will go to any lengths to protect Sarah because of her destiny to bear the child in whom God's promise is due for fulfillment within a matter of months, and Abimelek's action unwittingly puts it in jeopardy.[28] But there's no explicit reference to this consideration, and it's the king's moral position that is in focus.[29] His own words presuppose that a nation can be faithful. The word resonates with 18:23–32 and hints that Gerar is no Sodom. So the question it suggests is this: "Will God destroy the people of Gerar as he did the people of Sodom? Is Gerar next?"[30]—even if the trouble issues from their being in the wrong place at the wrong time rather than being as deserving as Sodom? (KSG).

To underline his point (v. 5), Abimelek adds a claim to integrity, which is ironically the quality God expects of Abraham (17:1), and a claim to have the same qualities as Noah possessed (6:9). Is there a comedic, parodic aspect to the portrait?[31] "My hands are clean," moreover, he adds. The word (*nāqîn*) denotes being free of liability and thus exempt from punishment or obligation (Abraham will apply the related verb to his servant's freedom from liability if he does his duty in seeking out a wife for Isaac). Faithfulness is thus spelled out in both positive and negative terms, in the presence of inner integrity and in the absence of wrongful outward action. So it's possible for a ruler and a nation to be characterized by faithfulness and integrity. Faithfulness is a matter of the inner person and its intentions and desires. It's also a matter of outward action with the hands and other parts of the body. But even if a person acts in ignorance and/or through being misled by someone else, their actions can be objectively wrong and can incur guilt. The narrative has not told us that Sarah has confirmed Abraham's statement about their relationship, as it has not told us about the afflictions in the royal household. It focuses on

27. KSG; and cf. the comment on 12:14–15.
28. Cf. Kidner, *Genesis*, 139.
29. Cf. von Rad, *Genesis*, 225.
30. Arnold, *Genesis*, 190; he then translates *gam* as "also."
31. So Novick, "'Almost, at Times, the Fool.'"

certain features of the story, sometimes simply leaving the audience to fill in the gaps, sometimes filling them in later.

God confirms Abimelek's claim (v. 6), apparently restating his words about clean hands with more general words about wrongdoing; God knows Abimelek is nothing like Sodom (13:13; 18:20). All Canaanites should not be tarred with the same brush.[32] Again the audience needs to fill in the gaps (or will be able to do so later) by working out that the afflictions are the means whereby God holds him back. He did so for Sarah's sake, for Abraham's sake, for Abimelek's sake, and for the sake of marital propriety, but also for his own sake. Abimelek's wrongdoing would be committed "against me" both for moral-type reasons (cf. 39:9) and because Sarah has that special place in his purpose.

But Abimelek must take action (v. 7), as Cain needed to but did not. God's warning is also the one he issued to Eve (2:17), of which she took little notice. Here, both the fact of v. 3 and the fact of v. 6 must be taken into account. The fact of v. 6 can only win over the fact of v. 3 if Abimelek takes the necessary action. Even though he has not had sex with Sarah, and even though it is not his fault that he has taken a married woman into his harem, he is still a dead man unless he puts things right. God makes two other striking points. One is that Abimelek's actions will indeed have further consequences not just for himself but also for the rest of his household, perhaps for his realm as a whole. Rulers are either a blessing or a curse to their people. The other is that Abraham has a role to play in putting things right. He doesn't need to repent, though that might do no harm, and it is just as well that he doesn't need to do that, because he doesn't. Rather, while God could presumably put things right without Abraham being involved, he intends to involve Abraham in a way that might be seen as a form of repentance—not repentance in the form of sorrow but repentance in the sense of a change of direction. Instead of walking in a way that brings Abimelek trouble, he is to walk in a way that restores things for Abimelek. Abraham will be able to do so because he is a prophet, which means being a member of God's cabinet who can speak up there on Abimelek's behalf. We have had hints that Abraham is a quasi-prophetic figure (15:1–2; 18:17–21, 22–33); here his status is explicit.[33] Technically it is another anachronism; the point of the designation is that Abraham can fulfill a key aspect of what belonged to the role of a prophet in the audience's day. And a prophet can pray for people outside the chosen people as well as for insiders. "Pleading" (*pālal* hitpael) in this context means intercession, asking God to do something for someone else (cf. 1 Sam. 12:19, 23 about Samuel as a prophet), though in other contexts it can mean asking God to do something for oneself (e.g., 1 Sam. 1; 1 Kings 8). While this word

32. See Holmgren, "Looking Back."

33. See further Branch, "Genesis 20"; Todd, "Patriarch and Prophet."

and related words usually denote prayer, they sometimes refer to the making of judicial decisions. So the English word "plead," which likewise has courtroom connotations, conveys the implications of a prophet's being a member of the divine cabinet where decisions are made and therefore being able to issue a plea there on someone's behalf.

20:8–13. Abraham got going early to check out what happened to Sodom (19:27); in a nice inversion, Abimelek gets going briskly the morning after his dream and tells his staff about it, and they respond in the appropriate fashion.

Then (vv. 9–10) he confronts Abraham about his wrongdoing in words similar to Pharaoh's (12:18). He speaks in elegantly poetic fashion, in the circumstances (done-wrong-wrong-doings-done-done). While the audience knows that Abimelek's wrongdoing would imperil God's purpose to have Sarah bear Isaac, Abimelek himself is concerned about the "great sin" of adultery as one form of sexual outrage that is "not done," in Israel (Gen. 34:7; 2 Sam. 13:12) or anywhere else.[34] He doesn't call it a *nəbālâ*, an act of villainy (Gen. 34:7; cf. *nābāl* in 2 Sam. 13:13), but he could have.[35] The redundant renewed introduction to his further question in v. 10 points to Abraham's inability to reply to this rebuke, as in 12:18–19.[36] Abimelek thus begins by restating the second of his questions in v. 9.

Abraham's initial response (vv. 11–12) has already been anticipatorily proved wrong by everything that we have heard in vv. 3–8, while his fear parallels his fear in 12:11–12. His response then explains how he was being economical with the truth there and here. Further irony issues from this admission's following on 19:30–38. Is he as bad as Lot? While the rules in the Torah will not mention sex between a father and a daughter, they will explicitly forbid marrying your half sister (Lev. 18:9, 11; 20:17), though 2 Sam. 13:13 implies that such rules may have been more theory than practice.

Abraham's description of being made to wander from Terah's household (v. 13) sounds like an attempt to make excuses and blame God for the deception into which he was driven (for the verb, cf. 21:14; also Ps. 107:4). Yet his reference to the "commitment" (*ḥesed*) he needed from Sarah does convey something of the magnitude of what he asked of her. There is again more than one irony in the way Abraham here picks up this word, which Lot has introduced to the Scriptures (19:19).[37] Abraham now tells us that he has asked Sarah to show this commitment recurrently, from 12:11–12 onward, which makes one ask whether the two occasions we know about are the only two. It fits with the way "many nomadic peoples . . . use their women as a means of establishing relations with the sedentary population"; the stranger establishes a relationship with the people among whom he comes by offering his sister

34. See, e.g., Van Seters, *Abraham*, 76.
35. Cf. Seebass, *Genesis*, 2.1:166–67.
36. Cf. Skinner, *Genesis*, 318.
37. See the comment there.

or daughter to them, but if he has to offer his wife, he has to present her as his sister.[38] The yet further irony is that *ḥesed* has an Aramaic homonym denoting something as shameful or disgraceful, and its single occurrence in the First Testament comes in one of the rules forbidding marriage to a half sister (Lev. 20:17).[39] It's as if Abraham is acknowledging that he told Sarah to undertake something shameful and disgraceful, if she is indeed his half sister.

20:14–16. The sequence of events again overlaps with the one in 12:9–13:4. There Pharaoh showered gifts on Abraham to win the hand of his "sister"; here Abimelek showers the same gifts on Abraham, minus donkeys and camels. Abraham is the one who is in the wrong; Abimelek is the one who makes amends.

Further (v. 15), whereas Pharaoh had revoked Abraham's residence permit, Abimelek continues to demonstrate what a faithful man he is by encouraging Abraham to stay and to live in Gerar, and not merely to be a resident alien.

His additional gift of a huge amount of silver, the equivalent of cash (v. 16), extends the implicit correspondence with the earlier story: see 13:2. The thousand silver pieces compare with the twenty for which Joseph's brothers sold him (37:28), the fifteen that Hosea paid for his wife (Hosea 3:2), the ten sheqels per year that Micah paid his Levite (Judg. 17), and the four hundred sheqels that Abraham is about to pay for a burial cave (Gen. 23).[40] The gift constitutes a public compensation either for taking Sarah into his harem when she was already married or for dismissing her from it in a way possibly suggesting that she was somehow at fault or unsatisfactory. It means that people will no longer look down on Sarah and her staff. The expression "covering over the eyes" involves catachresis. One would usually speak of covering wrongdoing or shame so that the eyes cannot see it (e.g., Ps. 32:1; Prov. 12:16), or of shame covering someone (e.g., Obad. 10; Mic. 7:10). Abimelek will cover the implicit shame he has brought on Sarah; no one will be able to see it.[41] He still calls Abraham his brother, which perhaps also contributes to the avoidance of any sense that shame attaches to Sarah.

20:17–18. The story closes with the intercession that has been in prospect but has not happened, and with the explanation of why it is needed, which has been presupposed but not made explicit. God has spoken of action then prayer, which is the sequence here. It is when Abimelek has put things right that Abraham can pray for his healing. So the innocent Abimelek must get the guilty Abraham to pray for him. "How complicated are the theological ideas that the narrative thus suggests!"[42] What do you do if you lead someone

38. Pitt-Rivers, *Fate of Shechem*, 159.

39. See Hepner, "Abraham's Incestuous Marriage," 148.

40. See the comment on 23:15 for further comparisons.

41. Kotzé ("Interpretation of *kswt ʿynym*") rather suggests that the covering protects from the evil eye.

42. Von Rad, *Genesis*, 223.

into a moral mess? Remember that God cares about him and be prepared to pray for him. Abraham's prayer is the first explicit intercessory prayer in the Scriptures, if we discount 18:23–32. "When our father, Abraham, prayed in this way, the knot was untied" and people could pray for one another (Gen. Rab. 52.13). Intercession thus makes a difference. God sometimes acts in response to intercession and does things that he would otherwise not do. Yet in this case, at least, it is God who commissions the intercession, which makes for an overlap with 18:23–32. Intercession is an aspect of the way he involves his people in working out his purpose in the world, or a way of letting them be a means of bringing blessing in the world.

In due course Jesus will come, and the blessing will come more systematically to the Gentile world.

> At that time, therefore, both the house of Abimelech and his handmaids whom the Lord healed, will bear sons of the Church. For this is the time in which "the barren" will bear, and in which "many are the children of the desolate, more than of her who has a husband." For the Lord opened the womb of the barren and made it fruitful, so that she bears a nation "all at once." But also the saints cry out and say: "Lord, from fear of you we have conceived in the womb and given birth; we have produced the spirits of your salvation on the earth." Whence also Paul likewise says, "My little children, of whom I am in labor again, until Christ be formed in you."[43]

At least there's no doubt about Isaac's paternity (v. 18).

43. Origen, *Homilies on Genesis*, 125, referring to Gal. 4:27; Isa. 54:1; 66:8; 26:18; Gal. 4:19.

18

Abraham and His Son, Part One

(21:1–21)

Overview

At last Sarah becomes pregnant and has her son, though this raises the question of the relative status of Abraham's two sons. In a sense we know the answer to the question (17:19–21). How will the divine intention be worked out? Sarah unwittingly opens up a possibility. But her action also necessitates God's further intervention to save the life of Abraham's firstborn. The way is also now open for Ishmael to grow toward the destiny God has announced for him but to do so in a way that distances him definitively from the life of Abraham's family and leaves Isaac without rival as the means of God fulfilling his promises regarding Abraham's line.

Translation

> **1**But Yahweh—he[1] attended to Śarah as he had said. Yahweh acted for
> Śarah as he had spoken, **2**and Śarah became pregnant and gave birth
> to a son for Abraham in his old age, at the set time of which God had
> spoken to him. **3**Abraham named his son, who had been born to him,
> to whom Śarah had given birth for him, Yiṣḥaq. **4**Abraham circumcised
> Yiṣḥaq his son as a child of eight days, as God had ordered him, **5**Abra-
> ham being a man of a hundred years when his son Yiṣḥaq was born to
> him. **6**Śarah said,

1. The subject comes before the verb, suggesting some emphasis, and/or a contrast over against 19:30–38 (Seebass, *Genesis*, 2.1:174), and/or the resumption of the theme of Yahweh's promise from Gen. 17–18 (Arnold, *Genesis*, 194).

God has made laughter for me,
since everyone who hears will laugh about me.[2]

7And she said,

Who would have pronounced[3] to Abraham,
"Śarah has nursed children"?—
but I've given birth to a son for his old age.

8The child grew and was weaned. Abraham made a big banquet on the
day that Yiṣḥaq was weaned, **9**but Śarah saw the son of Hagar the Miṣrite,
to whom she gave birth for Abraham, making people laugh.[4] **10**She said to
Abraham, "Drive out this handmaid[5] and her son, because this handmaid's
son is not to come into possession with my son, with Yiṣḥaq."

11The thing was very bad in Abraham's eyes, on account of his son.
12But God said to Abraham, "It isn't to be bad in your eyes about the
boy or about your handmaid. Everything that Śarah says to you, listen to
her voice, because it's through Yiṣḥaq that offspring will be named for
you. **13**But the son of the handmaid: I will make him into a nation, too,
because he's your offspring."

14Abraham started early in the morning, got bread and a skin of water,
and gave them to Hagar (he put them on her shoulder),[6] and the child,[7] and
sent her away. She went and wandered about in the Beʾer Šeba wilderness,
15but the water from the skin came to an end. She thrust the child under
one of the bushes **16**and went and sat herself down at a distance, going a
bowshot away,[8] because (she said), "I will not watch[9] the child die."

2. The LXX, Vg have "laugh with me."

3. The rare verb *mālal* (piel), an Aramaism, could remind the audience of the verb for "circumcise" (*mûl*; v. 4), which indeed seems to have a by-form *mālal*.

4. One Jewish tradition infers that this "playing about" could have involved idolatry (cf. Exod. 32:6), while Gen. 39:14 might imply sexual abuse or molesting, and 2 Sam. 2:14 could suggest that Ishmael was shooting at Isaac but claiming he was only playing (see Gen. Rab. 53.11); see further Blenkinsopp, *Abraham*, 92–95; Zucker, "What Sarah Saw." But there seems insufficient reason to interpret the playing in a negative way (see Sonek, *Truth, Beauty, and Goodness*, 43–47). The range of actions to which *měśaḥēq* might refer is less important to the narrator than the word itself (cf. Heard, *Dynamics of Diselection*, 84).

5. In 16:1 she was a *šipḥâ*, here an *ʾāmâ*; compare "maidservant" and "handmaid" in English. Both words are also applied to Bilhah (30:3–4). Scholars who think one of the words suggests a higher status than the other (e.g., Westermann, *Genesis 12–36*, 237–38) are not agreed on which is which (cf. Hamilton, *Genesis 18–50*, 80); see further M. Jacobs, *Gender, Power, and Persuasion*, 143–44; Yoo, "Hagar the Egyptian." More likely they are synonyms (see, e.g., Alter, *Genesis*, 67).

6. On the asyndetic clause, see *TTH* 163.

7. That is, he also gave Ishmael to Hagar, not that he put the teenager on her shoulder along with the bread and the skin of water. The odd word order compares with 22:3 and in each passage adds emphasis to the son; see Lyke, "Where Does 'the Boy' Belong?" (though I do not follow other aspects of his reading of the verse).

8. Literally, "going away [hiphil infinitive absolute] like shooters of a bow."

9. While the form of the verb *ʾerʾeh* is ambiguous, the use of the negative *ʿal* establishes that it is cohortative, not yiqtol, and a cohortative following *ʿal* would naturally denote a wish,

So she sat down at a distance and lifted up her voice and cried.[10]
17But God listened to the boy's voice, and God's envoy called to Hagar from the heavens and said to her, "What's with you, Hagar? Don't be afraid, because God has listened to the voice of the boy where he is.
18Get up, lift up the boy, take strong hold of him with your hand,[11] because I'm going to make him into a big nation."
19God opened her eyes, and she saw a well of water. She went and filled the skin with water and got the boy to drink.

20God was with the boy. He grew up and lived in the wilderness and became a bowman (an archer).[12]
21He lived in the Pa'ran Wilderness. His mother got him a wife from the country of Miṣrayim.

Interpretation

In the MT, 21:1–21 comprises the last of the three paragraphs making up 18:1–21:21. It starts by bringing the narrative back to the point it reached at the end of 13:1–17:27, the previous unit in the MT. The material in between in Gen. 18–20 has comprised a pair of diversions that have raised suspense; there have been so many threats to the derailing of the story.

Even if it does not derail, when will Abraham and Sarah see the fulfillment of the promise God gave in Gen. 17? At last it comes. The account of Isaac's birth in 21:1–7 relates the event in terms that appeared in the promises and instructions in Gen. 17–20, thus emphasizing that Yahweh has done as he said and that Abraham did as he was told. Indeed, it tells us nothing beyond what Gen. 17–20 foreshadowed.[13] The account of this event, of such importance in the context of the wider narrative, might thus seem "peculiarly understated."[14] Western readers would expect something much more concrete as well as celebratory. Yet the understated nature of the account matches the accounts of other births, beginning with 4:1–2a, 25–26. Accounts of births focus on the bare facts, though they may add some other piece of information, such as the child's name, with a comment on its significance. Here the expansion of the bare account works by recycling language from the preceding chapters, which thereby highlights how the event is indeed a fulfillment.

But what will now happen to Hagar and Ishmael? In what follows (vv. 8–21), the account

---

"May I not watch," rather than determination not to watch (see GKC 106bc; *IBHS* 34.5.1). But the logic of the verse and of her action suggest determination. Maybe she is confused.

10. The LXX has "The child lifted up his voice [and] cried," providing a better lead in to v. 17.

11. More literally, "Make your hand strong upon him"; not "take his hand" (Vg).

12. While both words are hapaxes, the first root (*rābâ*) is rare and the second more common, so the second word might explain the first.

13. Cf. Van Seters's study of Gen. 18 and 21 in *Abraham in History and Tradition*, 202–8.

14. Brueggemann, *Genesis*, 180. Contrast Jub. 16.10–19 and its expansive treatment.

tells of a great celebration (21:8),
sets up a problem (21:9–10),
makes it worse (21:11),
makes it even worse (21:12),
promises a solution to the question How will we get there? (21:13),
relates how Abraham takes action (21:14a),
describes how things get even worse (21:14b–16a),
relates the turning point (21:16b–17),
prescribes a short-term solution and repeats the long-term promise (21:18),
works out the short-term solution (21:19), and
relates the necessary beginnings to fulfillment of the long-term promise (21:20–21).

Through the drama, the narrative points to the range of feelings stirred up by the existence of Ishmael. For Sarah, resentment dissolves her laughter. For Abraham, there are grief and reluctance. For Hagar, there is the agonizing pain of a mother who thinks she is about to watch her child die (but eventually has the relief and joy of seeing him thrive). For Paul in Gal. 4, there is a new way of picturing the relationship of Jews who believe in Jesus and Jews who don't. For the modern reader, there is the scandal of the way Hagar is treated. For God, there is the need to square the circle of commitment to Isaac and to Ishmael, to Sarah and to Hagar. For Ishmael himself, there is laughter and then rejection by his father, but eventually the achieving of manhood, though among the human characters in the story, Ishmael is the one whose point of view is most unstated. He is mainly a foil for Isaac; vv. 1–21 are centrally a story about Isaac, about how Ishmael definitively leaves the stage and surrenders it to Isaac. It is a story about the elder son being "unfairly" replaced by the younger. It thus compares with the later story of Esau's loss of the blessing to Jacob (Gen. 27).

In recounting what happens to Hagar and Ishmael, this story gives even less indication that something of the kind has happened before than Gen. 20 does in its account of Abraham's passing off his wife as his sister. Traditional source criticism sees most of vv. 8–21 as the equivalent in the Elohistic Abraham story to the J version in Gen. 16. There is no unanimity over the source background to 21:1–7; its nature, as constructed from material in earlier chapters, implies that the author of Genesis devised it to provide the necessary account of Isaac's birth.

21:1–7. The formulaic account of Isaac's birth does not undermine its decisive importance—rather the opposite.

The event happens "as he had said . . . as he had spoken" (v. 1). The story of Isaac's birth begins with an emphasis on the one who brought it about.

If God had not made it happen, it would not have happened; and if it had not happened, God's promise would just have been something in the spiritual realm, without purchase in the ordinary world. To take seriously "the promissory nature of faith . . . requires a break with our prosaic world-view which does not believe in active, world-changing words from God" and that is inclined "to romanticize the promise and remove it from the arena of historical reality," in which God nevertheless does take action through people whom the world regards as good as dead (Heb. 11:11–12).[15] The lack of any reference to Abraham and Sarah having sex (contrast 4:1, 25; 16:4) underscores the point. And the verb "attended to" (*pāqad*, traditionally translated "visit") emphasizes Yahweh's special involvement in taking action to do as he has said—especially when it looks as if he is never going to do so—for his people (cf. 50:24, where again God as the subject precedes the verb) or for an individual (cf. 1 Sam. 2:21, in a similar connection to the one here). The verb's significance overlaps with that of the verb "be mindful of" (*zākar*; e.g., 8:1; 19:29), which the Tg uses here.

So Sarah gets pregnant (v. 2)—the verb was used four times of Hagar in Gen. 16, but it's never been used of Sarah before. And Sarah gives birth—the verb was used three times of Hagar, but only with a negative of Sarah (16:1) or with a question mark (17:17). The pregnancy and birth happen in Abraham's "old age," whose reality makes the idea seem so implausible (18:11–12). Genesis 18–19 and Gen. 20 have said that Sarah would have her baby next year. When will next year come? At last it comes, at the "set time" of which God spoke (cf. 17:21).

Abraham is able to follow God's instructions (vv. 3–5) in naming Isaac as God directed (17:19) and in doing what Gen. 17 says about circumcising him. In Gen. 17 Abraham protests that God's promise will mean that they are going to have a baby when he is a hundred years old and Sarah ninety, and the narrative confirms that Abraham is a hundred years old, though it politely refrains from confirming Sarah's age.

Sarah now gives her account of her response to the event (v. 6), like Eve (4:1, 25), and like Hagar when she got pregnant (16:9–13). The account contrasts with the way Abraham voices no emotional outburst.[16] Is he remembering that it will be several years before he can assume that Isaac will survive toward adulthood? But fathers may have less to say than mothers when children are born. First, Sarah tweaks earlier references to "laughing" (*ṣāḥaq*), making links with the name God has provided for Isaac; most of the First Testament occurrences of this root come in Gen. 17–21. Although the idea of Sarah having a baby made both Abraham and Sarah laugh in a way that could suggest joyful wonder but could equally signify disillusioned skepticism (a negative or

15. Brueggemann, *Genesis*, 180–81.
16. Cf. Hamilton, *Genesis 18–50*, 74.

positive disbelief), now Sarah speaks of an unequivocally happy laughter. It is a laughter that everyone will share ("will laugh" is *yiṣḥāq*, the actual form of Isaac's name), because (the narrator hints) it is significant for everyone through its relationship to God's purpose to bring blessing to everyone. So Sarah is able to laugh again and/or to laugh in a new way, compared with her laughing in Gen. 18, and she is able to imagine other people joining in her laughter. If there had been any cynical laughter on the part of Abraham or Sarah when God gave them his promise, "it has not been held against them; it has been turned into genuine joy at this new life made possible by God. God has brought an end to cynicism and despair of the future; joyful hope fills the scene."[17]

Sarah continues with a reference to nursing (v. 7), the only reference in Genesis to a mother nursing (and also something of a miracle for Sarah at her age), which leads into what follows. Far from being "pointless,"[18] her comment not only says something new over against what has preceded but in doing so also leads into what follows in vv. 8–21.

21:8–10. What will now happen to Hagar and Ishmael, Abraham's eldest son and heir presumptive?[19] "Isaac, though the son of promise, will also cause problems, tearing this family apart."[20]

The narrative moves on (v. 8) from the mention of Sarah's nursing to the account of her weaning and to a crisis at the weaning party.[21] In traditional societies mothers nurse children for longer than is customary in the West; in 2 Macc. 7:27 a mother refers to having nursed her son for three years. We don't know whether families regularly had a weaning party (though cf. 1 Sam. 1:21–24), but one might imagine Abraham's banquet as his son's third-birthday party. In a traditional society many children died in infancy, so such an occasion might constitute an implicit celebration that a child has survived these dangerous early years and has a good prospect of growing to adulthood. The party is somewhat a rite of passage.[22] And for a mother, it will be an emotional occasion.[23]

It's not quite explicit that the party is the context of what follows (v. 9), but family parties often cause crises and bring out latent issues. Ishmael (though he's not named), now a teenager (17:25), is making people laugh (at baby Isaac?) or is laughing uproariously; the verb is the one associated with Isaac's name, but now used in the piel. It's as if Ishmael is pretending to be

17. Fretheim, "Genesis," 486.
18. So Gunkel, *Genesis*, 225.
19. Blenkinsopp, *Abraham*, 85.
20. Fretheim, "Genesis," 486.
21. Cf. Seebass, *Genesis*, 2.1:175–76.
22. Westermann, *Genesis 12–36*, 338.
23. Cf. T. Schneider, *Mothers of Promise*, 34.

Isaac, the boy whose name links him with laughter, as if he's still threatening to take the place that belongs to Isaac.

Sarah is therefore "furious" (v. 10).[24] She "finds herself battling the situation she created. . . . Sarah's use for Hagar expires once Sarah's son survives, and Hagar becomes a liability to Sarah's status."[25] There's only one solution she can think of. It's the action she unwittingly (?) brought about when Hagar was pregnant (16:6). The trouble is, Yahweh then sent Hagar back. Now Sarah wants Abraham definitively to throw the two of them out, as God threw out Adam and Cain in 3:24; 4:14 (the verb is again *gāraš* piel, which in the qal means "divorce"). Once more she does not use the names of either of them: in effect Hagar is "that woman" and Ishmael is "that boy." Ironically, they have become diminished in her eyes (see 16:4).[26] She will utter the name of Isaac, but not that of Ishmael. His laughter has drawn attention to the fact that he might take what Sarah sees as Isaac's rightful place as Abraham's heir. Are we to imagine Sarah as remembering the events of a decade previously, when she arranged for Hagar to have a baby on her behalf, or as deliberately forgetting them? She makes no reference to them. But Ishmael is Abraham's legitimate first son whom Hagar bore "for Abram" (16:16). Yet a master can always "free" a servant, who then loses their share of the property.[27] Ishmael is a threat to Isaac; and "only if they die in the desert will that threat be eliminated."[28]

21:11–13. For something to be bad in your eyes means that you hate it, you are offended by it (cf. 28:8), though it may also imply that you think it is morally wrong (cf. 38:10; 48:17). While both connotations would be appropriate for Abraham as he thinks about throwing Ishmael out, the description here of Ishmael as "his son" (Isaac is "his son" in vv. 3, 4, 5)[29] suggests that his anguish is in focus. While Hagar was center stage in Gen. 16, her son becomes center stage in Gen. 21.[30]

God's response to Abraham (v. 12) may also carry both connotations. Abraham's fatherly attachment to Ishmael is proper; God is also concerned about Hagar, whom v. 11 doesn't mention.[31] Abraham is still maybe thinking that Ishmael as his firstborn should be the one through whom God's promise is fulfilled (cf. 17:18). "But then again this is the Bible, where the firstborn usually fare poorly."[32] God has determined that Isaac is the one

24. Cf. Noort, "Created in the Image," 42.
25. M. Jacobs, *Gender, Power, and Persuasion*, 150, 152.
26. Cf. Heard, *Dynamics of Diselection*, 86.
27. Cf. Sarna, *Genesis*, 146–47.
28. Tamez, "Woman," 13.
29. Cf. Fretheim, *Abraham*, 100.
30. Cf. Noort, "Created in the Image," 34.
31. Cf. Fretheim, *Abraham*, 100.
32. De La Torre, *Genesis*, 212.

through whom fulfillment will come, through whom Abraham's offspring will be "named": his genealogical line is the one that will count. Hagar and her son are discounted.[33] There is still no suggestion that Sarah and Abraham should not have taken the action that they did. Maybe God appreciates the opportunity to give expression to that important principle that you don't come first just because you're born first (cf. Cain and Abel, Esau and Jacob, Manasseh and Ephraim). But God has simply made up his mind, as Paul notes in Rom. 9:7. One might think that there is no need to go along with Sarah's extreme plan for getting Hagar and Ishmael out of the picture, but maybe the tension will never go away otherwise. Even for God, Hagar is now Abraham's "handmaid," not his "wife" (16:3). "The reader has not suspected that God would be on Sarah's side, but rather on Abraham's. But . . . God pursues his great historical purposes in, with, and under all headstrong acts of men."[34] He goes along with the dubious human plans in which the conflict issues. He does not insist on working via ideal plans and pure intentions but accepts the necessity to work through unsavory plans and questionable decisions.

But God is still pledged to fulfilling his promise regarding Ishmael (v. 13). When he chose Isaac's line, not Ishmael's, it was not because Isaac (or Sarah) deserved it, nor because Ishmael (or Hagar) did not; it was an aspect of God's fulfilling his purpose that all nations may be blessed. And in this connection "Genesis depicts God both drawing lines and blurring them."[35] Further, in vv. 12–13 "we meet theologians who know how to detect the ways of God in the midst of the tortuous ways of human beings."[36] Isaac is the elected son, but Ishmael is still the treasured son.[37] Both matter to God. "It is no unfeeling Deity who seconds Sarah's bidding to Abraham." He is "a powerful and long lived participant in the lives of succeeding generations, who at this point . . . relieves Abraham of responsibility for a decision. He himself will take over now, as guardian and guarantor of the future."[38] Will that promise really come about? The question remains as a "narrative gap" until 25:12–18 relates its answer.[39]

21:14–16a. Once again, Abraham indicates his commitment to the task by starting early in the morning (cf. 19:27; 20:8). Although in Gen. 16 he told Sarah that she could take action (and she took tough action), this time he takes action. "Sent away" (*šālaḥ* piel) is another term that can mean divorce

33. See Trible, *Texts of Terror*, 21–22.

34. Von Rad, *Genesis*, 228: in those pre-gender-inclusive language days, "men" would mean "human beings."

35. Mbuvi, *Belonging in Genesis*, 136.

36. Schwantes, "'Do Not Extend Your Hand,'" 109.

37. Brueggemann, *Genesis*, 183.

38. Brichto, *Names of God*, 219–20.

39. Sonek, *Truth, Beauty, and Goodness*, 217–18.

(cf. Deut. 24:1–4; Tg. Ps.-J. adds that Abraham gave Hagar a divorce certificate). Abraham gives Hagar provisions, though of a basic kind. It's hard to tell whether he is being caring or whether his provision is meager and mean. If they are in the southern Gerar, they are in or not far from the area that one could call the Beer Sheba wilderness (cf. Jub. 16.11; and Gen. 21:22–34). So Hagar wanders, as God had made Abraham wander (20:13), and seems not to know where she is going.

In such wilderness, when your water is finished (v. 15), you are finished, and so is your child. Hagar dumps Ishmael unceremoniously under a bush. The verb (*šālak* hiphil) is the one used for throwing Joseph into a pit (37:20, 22, 24; the LXX's verb *riptō* occurs in a similar connection in Matt. 15:30),[40] as well as recalling the one used to describe Abraham's throwing her out: "her homophonic actions mirror Abraham's."[41] She is leaving him there to die. Paradoxically, she makes a point of leaving him with some shade, seeking to make his passing a little less uncomfortable than it would be if he were lying in direct sunlight.

The pain expressed in that act finds further expression (v. 16a) in her inability to watch him die, like Etta Place refusing to stay with Butch Cassidy and Sundance and watch them die. Yet the tension in the mother's feelings means that she cannot simply abandon him. Genesis Rabbah 53.4 says a bowshot is half a mile.[42]

21:16b–19. Back in 16:1–2 Sarah's voice spoke out to Abraham, he listened, and it worked against Hagar. In 21:10–12 Sarah's voice spoke out to Abraham, and God told him to listen. Now Hagar raises her voice as Abel's blood raised its voice (4:10), and she cries; her tears are the first tears in the Scriptures. The birth that brought laughter to Sarah has brought only tears to Hagar.[43] "Hagar's was a cry without hope,"[44] and the story does not indicate that her cry was addressed to anyone.[45]

But apparently the boy cries, too, and God listens to his voice (v. 17)—which one may guess is fine with Hagar. Even if his mother, who can do nothing, cannot bear to listen, God, who can do something, listens. Hagar is not where the boy is; God listens where the boy is. God lives up to Ishmael's name (though the name is still not used in this chapter). Once again, God's envoy calls to Hagar, this time from the heavens, perhaps because God commissions the envoy there immediately upon hearing the cry. The envoy does use Hagar's name and asks her what the problem is, which needn't have been a rhetorical question and might rather have been one

40. Cf. Keil and Delitzsch, *Pentateuch*, 245.
41. A. Cohen, "Hagar and Ishmael," 252.
42. See further Chan ("'Distance of a Bowshot'"), who allows for a similar figure.
43. Levenson, *Death and Resurrection*, 106.
44. Kidner, *Genesis*, 141.
45. Cf. J. E. Cook, "Mothers and Wives," 6.

that gives Hagar the chance to speak (cf. 16:8), though on this occasion the envoy goes straight on with the exhortation/invitation given to Abraham in 15:1 (and cf. 26:24).

But Hagar needs to take action (v. 18). Twice we have been told that she sat down; the envoy tells her to get up. She has put the boy down; the envoy tells her to lift him up and grasp hold of him to help him start walking again. The envoy switches to speaking God's actual words and thus adds further force to what he says, to reaffirm God's commitment to keeping the promise that he gave to Abraham, which the envoy now gives to Hagar herself in rather different terms. "The child, parched with thirst and given up even by its own mother, will become 'a great people.'"[46]

And God opens her eyes (v. 19). In Gen. 16 the envoy found Hagar by a spring with a well. Here it's not explicit whether she is again by a well or whether God specially provides one to which he then opens her eyes. Either way, she sees something different from what she was afraid of seeing (v. 16). She and her son have turned a corner.

21:20–21. Another key scriptural phrase appears for the first time: God was with Ishmael. Subsequently, it will apply to Isaac, Jacob, and Joseph (26:3, 28; 28:18; 31:3, 5; 39:2, 3, 21, 23). In all these cases (and in subsequent stories) the First Testament does not mean that the person to whom it applies has a subjective feeling that God is with them, nor that God makes them feel supported. It means that objectively God is active in their lives and circumstances and that God makes things happen. Thus when the Scriptures say God "is with" someone, the Tg often says God "is at someone's assistance,"[47] especially when the person has the chips stacked against them. In Ishmael's case it means the boy who has been thrown out will become a successful hunter like Nimrod. The description uses different terms from the ones in the promise of 16:12, but the implications are similar.

The Paran Wilderness (v. 21) stretches down well into Sinai. It would not be surprising that Hagar looked to her home country for a wife for Ishmael. But it means that "the boy's severance from the chosen lineage is complete."[48] The end of Gen. 21 is not reconciliation and harmony but separate flourishing.[49] The way the story finishes means that Hagar and Ishmael will both be free from Egyptian oppressors and from Hebrew discrimination.[50] "Was it better when Hagar and Ishmael lived with Abraham, Sarah and later Isaac; or was it better when they were sent away?"[51]

46. Von Rad, *Genesis*, 228.
47. Maher, *Targum Pseudo-Jonathan: Genesis*, 91.
48. Levenson, *Death and Resurrection*, 109.
49. Or perhaps the story can be read as incorporating people of the Ishmaelites' lifestyle into Judah; so Horn, "Genesis 21:8–21."
50. Tamez, "Woman Who Complicated the History of Salvation," 17.
51. Sherwood, "Hagar and Ishmael," 302.

Implications

Reading Contextually

In Gal. 4 Paul draws a different point from the contrast between Hagar and Sarah than the one in Gen. 21. Paradoxically, boldly, and with Pauline chutzpah, Hagar stands for the Sinai covenant, servitude, and the earthly Jerusalem; Sarah stands for the Jerusalem above, which Paul associates with freedom and with Jesus.[52] These things are *allēgoroumena*, he says; they are figurative or can be taken figuratively. Either he means the story was designed as an allegory or illustration of the way God brings about the world's salvation, or he simply means that he intends to use the story that way. To ask which is correct might involve pressing on Paul a distinction he wasn't making. All he knows is that the Holy Spirit is inspiring him to use the story in this way. The message that the Holy Spirit wanted to bring to the original audience of the story is different from the one Paul wants to give on the basis of the account, but the Spirit was involved in both. We do not need to outlaw Paul's exposition on the basis of a more historical understanding; nor must we rule out a more historical understanding on the basis of Paul's exposition.

> Though Saint Paul, having the instinct of Gods Spirit, doth allegorize the history of Sarah and Hagar: it is therefore no warrant to every expositer and interpreter to make allegories of Scripture. . . : 1. Saint Pauls rare using of allegories, ought to teach such, that they also should be verie sparing. 2. Unlesse they could say of themselves, as Paul did, I think I have the spirit of God, 1 Cor. 7.4. They cannot challenge the like liberty in expounding of scripture, as S. Paul did: therefore it may be said unto them, as Christ said to his disciples you know not, what spirit you are of. Luk. 9.55. 3. Peter to this purpose useth a good reason; It only belongeth to God, which inspired the Scriptures, perfectly to know all things, that were to come, and not only to know them, but to dispose & direct them, as it pleaseth him, wherefore he only can appoint that things formerly done . . . should beare a true and certaine type and figure of things afterward to bee done. Man therefore that cannot dispose of things to come, is not to make types and figures, according to his owne device.[53]

A reading of Gen. 21 that starts from a post-NT context finds different significance in it. Targum Ps.-J. gives the names of Ishmael's first and second wives, Adisha (apparently a variant on Ayisha) and Fatima: they are the names

52. The ninth-century monk Rabanus Maurus ("Commentariorum in Genesim Libri Quattuor" [PL 107:439–670, esp. 544–45]) boldly but plausibly hints that one could reverse Paul's allegory: Sarah stands for the Jewish people, Hagar for the Gentiles. See J. Thompson, *Reading the Bible with the Dead*, 21; Thompson surveys interpretation of the Hagar story through church history; see also J. Thompson, "Hagar, Victim or Villain?"

53. Willet, *Hexapla in Genesin & Exodum*, 197.

of a wife and daughter of Mohammed.[54] And a millennium or more later, "the world is filled with . . . descendants of Ishmael. Nearly one billion Muslims, 85 percent of whom live outside the Middle East, call Abraham father, too. . . . They are the descendants of God's promise to Ishmael, which remains a contemporary theological reality. How is the other half of Abraham's family going to relate to these brothers and sisters?"[55] A reading of Ishmael that starts from a nineteenth-century context in the United States can take him as a heroic outcast and renegade figure, as he is for Melville.[56] A reading of Gen. 21 that starts from a twenty-first-century context finds yet another significance in it. Like Gen. 16, this chapter invites us to have our eyes open to women in our world who live with oppression derived from slavery, class, poverty, ethnicity, sexual and economic exploitation, homelessness, and the challenges of single parenting.[57] Hagar's story draws us into empathizing with women in this position and into crying out to God, to bosses, to men, and to people of the dominant group on their behalf.

54. Cf. García Martínez, "Hagar in Targum Pseudo-Jonathan," 263.

55. Fretheim, "Genesis," 490.

56. See Pardes, "Modern Literature."

57. Cf. D. Williams, *Sisters in the Wilderness*, 4 and also further 15–33; Trible, *Texts of Terror*, 9–35; Tamez, "Woman Who Complicated the History of Salvation."

19
Abraham and Abimelek, Part Two

(21:22–34)

Overview

There is again conflict and reconciliation between Abraham and Abimelek. At the background of a suggestion by Abimelek that he and Abraham should make a pact is a complaint by Abraham about the rights to a well at Beer Sheba. The resolution of the complaint opens up the possibility of peaceful ongoing life and worship on the part of Abraham's people at Beer Sheba.

Translation

> **22**At that time Abimelek and Pikol, his army officer, said to Abraham: "God be with you[1] in everything that you do. **23**But now, swear to me here by God: if you deal falsely with me or with my offspring or with my posterity. . . .[2] You're to act with me and with the country in which you've resided as an alien in accordance with the commitment with which I've acted with you." **24**Abraham said, "I myself[3] will swear."

1. The Vg has "God is with you" (cf., e.g., Zech. 8:23); the MT and LXX have no verb and are thus ambiguous. The Hebrew corresponds to, e.g., Ruth 2:4, where it is a greeting, and so it is here. Contrast 26:28, where Abimelek and Pikol are looking back over what has happened in the meantime and the verb *hāyâ* appears.

2. The rest of the oath is left to speak for itself (cf. 14:23).

3. The pronoun is expressed, underlining the speaker's commitment to the solemn promise (GKC 135a).

25Abraham had reproved[4] Abimelek concerning a well[5] of water that
Abimelek's servants had seized. 26Abimelek said, "I don't know who did
this thing. You yourself didn't tell me; I hadn't heard of it till today."
27So Abraham took flock and herd and gave them to Abimelek, and
the two of them solemnized a pact. 28Abraham put seven ewes from the
flock on their own. 29Abimelek said to Abraham, "What are these seven
ewes here that you've put on their own?" 30He said, "The seven ewes,
you are to get from my hand so it will be a witness for me that I dug this
well." 31That's why that site was called Beʾer Šeba, because the two of
them swore there. 32So they solemnized a pact at Beʾer Šeba, and Abi-
melek and Pikol, his army officer, set off and went back to the Pelištites'
country. 33He planted a tamarisk[6] at Beʾer Šeba and called out there with
the name Yahweh, Agelong God.
34Abraham resided as an alien in the Pelištites' country for a long
time.

Interpretation

Verses 22–34 form a unit in the MT; they belong together over against what precedes and what follows. One effect of placing the material here is to provide some breathing space between the drama of Isaac's birth and its aftermath and the even higher drama of the offering of Isaac.[7] The verses focus on the relationship between Abraham and Abimelek, but they read jerkily and manifest some repetition and overlap. Verses 22–24 relate how a formal agreement comes about on Abimelek's initiative (which one might be inclined to link with unfinished business from Gen. 20), while vv. 25–26 make a new start and focus on a grievance that Abraham brings to Abimelek. The passage then goes on to talk about two groups of sheep (vv. 27 and 28–30) and implies two explanations of the name of Beer Sheba as "Well of Seven" and "Well

4. By regular syntax *wəhôkiaḥ* should be past imperfect in meaning (GKC 112rr sees it as frequentative), but this understanding makes poor sense in the context—vv. 25b–26 seem to refer to one event. *TTH* 133 sees the verb as another example of "isolated irregularities" like 15:6 (see the note); cf. Hoffmann, "Die Afformativkonjugation mit präfigiertem waw." DG 84b suggests that such an instance "identifies an event as going on at roughly the same time as a previous event." More specifically, this instance indicates that the reproof did not happen after the previous event (*wayyiqtol* would then have been appropriate).

5. The LXX "wells" assimilates to 26:15, 18 (Seebass, *Genesis*, 2.1:188), as the LXX imports Ahuzzat from 26:26.

6. The LXX and Vg take *ʾešel* to denote a field or grove (cf. Aq); Tg. Ps.-J. and Tg. Neof. "orchard"; Sym and Tg. Onq. "plant"; 1 Chron. 10:12 (paralleling 1 Sam. 31:13) a tree. Some of the variants perhaps aim to avoid giving any impression of wrongful nature-type worship (see the footnote to 12:6); cf. Dillmann, *Genesis*, 2:138. Umbarger ("Abraham's Tamarisk," 199) argues that the tamarisk had positive "purifying, sanctifying properties."

7. Cf. Wenham, *Genesis 16–50*, 90.

of an Oath." One can in fact divide it into two smoother stories that might then have been interwoven:

Abimelek seeks an agreement (21:22–24)	Abraham seeks some resolution (21:25–26)
the agreement (21:27)	the resolution (21:28–30)
the naming (21:31)	the naming (21:32a)
Abimelek goes home (21:32b)	Abraham settles in Beer Sheba (21:33)

If the section does combine two stories, it wouldn't be surprising if the material comes from more than one source, but there is no consensus on how to relate it to the sources that are commonly thought to appear elsewhere in Genesis ("we are on a scholarly merry-go-round").[8] Although the two stories might then relate to different events, their interweaving rather invites us to see the passage as bringing together stories that provide two different angles on one event, as happens a number of times in Genesis. The passage then works as follows.

a. Abimelek's greeting, "God be with you," forms an appropriate opening to the passage, not least because of the link it makes with the preceding declaration that God was with Ishmael (though in v. 20 "with" was *ʾet*, in v. 22 it is *ʿim*).
b. Verses 22–24: also in accordance with occasional practice in Genesis and with Western news reports, Genesis first provides a summary version of the event, on which it will go on to give more detail.
c. Verses 25–26: the backstory explains the need for the pact as seen from Abraham's angle; the verses also make a link with 21:14–19 through the theme of the well.
d. Verses 27–32a: the making of the pact spells out Abraham's "Yes" in v. 24 and includes a clarifying of the well's status. The provision of the animals relates first to the pact in general (v. 27) and then to Abraham's claim to the well (vv. 28–30).
e. Verses 32b–34: this clarifying opens up the possibility of peaceful and settled life for a while for Abraham, with new reason for worship.

21:22–24. The reference to Abimelek, who begins what he has to say to Abraham with a polite greeting, indicates that the section picks up from Gen. 20, though "that time" sounds like a reference to the period covered by Isaac's birth and by Hagar and Ishmael's ejection. The involvement of Pikol in the negotiations that are to follow suggests that there has been some conflict between Abraham's people and Abimelek's people; vv. 25–26 indicate the cause of the conflict. In the Abraham stories we sometimes get

8. Westermann, *Genesis 12–36*, 346.

the impression of a small group of little significance in numbers and power, sometimes the impression of a group that is substantial in size and capacity. Here both impressions are mixed. Abraham is someone significant enough for Abimelek to want to make a pact with, but he is described as someone who has been a resident alien in Abimelek's territory and is still a resident alien at the end of the story. Conversely, if we think of Gerar as the later town near Gaza, it is more impressive than if we assume it is a settlement in the Negev.

Some formalizing of the relationship between Abimelek and Abraham (v. 23) might have generally seemed to be a good idea, notwithstanding Abimelek's generosity and equability (20:15), but we will shortly discover that a specific incident has exposed the need of such formalizing. Abimelek is looking for Abraham to accept an obligation to reciprocate the commitment that Abimelek has shown to him, which Gen. 20 has plentifully illustrated in telling how he handled Abraham's dishonesty and then invited Abraham to live where he liked in the territory—though Abimelek here speaks of him residing as an alien as opposed to living there. He is asking for an oath that Abraham will not deal falsely with him—which might be a snide reference to Abraham's deceptiveness or might rather be proposing a more general honest and mutually committed relationship. A traditional way to make an oath was to say "If I do *x*, then may *y* happen to me," with the second clause commonly left to the imagination (cf. 14:23).[9]

Abraham agrees to Abimelek's proposition (v. 24). In isolation, his response may seem terse,[10] though vv. 27–28 will flesh it out.

21:25–26. What follows provides background to Abimelek's request. A particular incident has suggested the need to formalize the relationship. Abraham has complained that Abimelek's servants have seized a well. It would be a serious matter. Access to water is a key issue for shepherds; if there is no water, then sheep die—as do human beings; vv. 15–19 made the point clear just now. Although the allusion to the well makes a link with vv. 15–19, the indication of some conflict implied by vv. 25–26 would explain Pikol's involvement in these negotiations. Further, Abraham's complaint raises from his side the question whether Abimelek's commitment is as unequivocal as he implies in v. 22.[11]

21:27–32. So it might have been Abraham's complaint that provoked the negotiation, but the broader consideration of a pact means that Abraham makes an offer to Abimelek, perhaps as the price of an agreement between the two parties that Abimelek will withdraw from the area where the well is and thus from the Beer Sheba area.

9. See, e.g., DG 156.
10. Wenham, *Genesis 16–50*, 92.
11. Cf. von Rad, *Genesis*, 232.

In some way the gift of the seven ewes (vv. 28–30) and Abimelek's acceptance of it confirms Abraham's ownership of the well. Perhaps it implies "I will act as if the well belongs to you, and I will buy it from you."

The pact involving seven ewes gives double significance to the name Beer Sheba (v. 31). On one hand, *šeba*ʿ is the number seven; on the other, "swear" is *šāba*ʿ. Thus Beer Sheba's name now becomes doubly appropriate: the well is both the "Seven Well" and the "Oath Well." When Genesis links meaningful names with places, there is commonly no implication that the name comes into being only at this moment; it's more that an existent name gains new significance (11:9 is a great example). So the mention of the Beer Sheba wilderness in v. 14 need not imply that this name came into use only later. Though there is a spectacular well at the archaeological site at Beer Sheba, both the site and the well date from the Israelite period; that well is not the one to which Genesis refers. But there are other wells in the area,[12] and presumably this story refers to one of these other wells. The solemnizing of a pact at Beer Sheba also makes it something of a sacred place if it was not one already, and thus v. 31 likely refers to it as a worship place, a "site" (*māqôm*) and not merely a "place" in the general sense. The audience might be expected to make that assumption, given that Beer Sheba was later known as a sanctuary (e.g., Amos 5:5). Abraham's action in v. 33 will confirm it.

The condition that Abimelek accepts (v. 32) is that his forces and staff (and his flock and herd) withdraw from the Beer Sheba area and leave it to Abraham. The agreement is a kind of repeat of the arrangement between Abraham and Lot.

21:33–34. The story reaches its high point:[13] Abraham has secured the future of his company's flock and secured his position in a nonaggression pact with the king. The event is a further mark of Abraham's entering into possession of the land of promise, even though he still lives there as a resident alien.[14] The tamarisk (which otherwise appears only in 1 Sam. 22:6; 31:13) is a tall evergreen or deciduous tree that grows in rather dry areas, which would explain Abraham's planting of this species in the Beer Sheba area. Previously he has settled near existent trees (12:6; 13:18; 14:13; 18:1); for the first time he plants one rather than building an altar (12:7, 8; 13:18), and he calls there with the name Yahweh (cf. 12:8, 13:4).[15] But he has a new name for Yahweh (the name he would not actually know). He praises the one who is "Agelong God," God Forever. The title *ʾēl ʿôlām* compares with *ʾēl ʿelyôn*, *ʾēl rŏʾî*, and *ʾēl šadday* (14:18; 16:13; 17:1), names that follow the pattern of Canaanite names for the top god—yet for Abraham, the only God. The LXX and Vg have "eternal God." The phrase could imply a recognition that this God has

12. See G. Robinson, "Wells of Beersheba" (with photographs); cf. Driver, *Genesis*, 216.
13. Seebass, *Genesis*, 2.1:189.
14. Cf. Fretheim, "Genesis," 491, 492.
15. On this expression, see the footnote and the comment on 4:26.

been God from of old (cf. *mē'ôlām* in 6:4 and the description of the one who has been alive so long in Dan. 7:9),[16] but *'ôlām* characteristically focuses on the future (e.g., 3:22; 6:3; 9:12, 16; 13:18; 17:7, 8, 13, 19); the title designates God as one who will always be God. A prayer for the beginning of the day, ultimately going back at least to a prayer book compiled in Paris in the eighth century (the Gelasian Sacramentary), asks "the all-powerful Father, the eternal God" to preserve us by his mighty power so that we may not fall into sin nor be overcome by adversity and that in all we do God may direct us to the fulfilling of his purpose. Particular experiences of God as making things work out buttress our conviction that the one who is eternal in the sense of being God forever will continue to fulfill his purpose.

The concluding note (v. 34) closes off Gen. 20–21 rather than relating to 21:22–33 in particular.[17] In a broad sense, the entire Negev area is the territory of the "Philistines"—that is, the Canaanite groups who lived in that region. But it looks as if Abraham has a secure position in the Beer Sheba region.

16. Cf. Zimmerli, *1. Mose 12–25*, 108.
17. Cf. Coats, *Genesis*, 156.

20

Abraham and His Son, Part Two

(22:1–19)

Overview

The Abraham story is working toward its end. Only Sarah's death and then the finding of a wife for Isaac before Abraham dies are to follow. But "nothing prepares the audience for this dramatic turn of events in Gen. 22."[1] Whereas God had in effect tested Abraham by requiring him to yield to Sarah's need to remove Ishmael from the picture of their life and future as a family, now God explicitly tests Abraham by requiring him to remove Isaac from the picture. As happened with Ishmael, after Abraham has proved himself, God relents of requiring Abraham to make the ultimate sacrifice of his son.

I follow the MT, which makes 22:1–19 a unit and links 22:20–24 with the story of Sarah's death and the finding of a wife for Isaac, which follow.

Translation

1Subsequently,[2] God tested Abraham.[3] He said to him, "Abraham!"
He said, "I'm here."[4] **2**He said, "Please get your son, your only

1. Ska, "Genesis 22," 266.

2. Literally, "It happened, after these things." Chrysostom (*Homilies on Genesis 46–67*, 14–15) assumes that these events followed on the events in 21:1–21, but if anything this expression avoids any implication of this kind and suggests a chronologically indeterminate sequence (see 22:20; 39:7; 40:1; 48:1).

3. While the word order is that of a circumstantial clause (cf. Dillmann, *Genesis*, 2:141), a number of instances of this order following a *wayəhî* clause look more like main clauses (e.g., 7:10; 41:1; cf. *TTH* 78). Placing the subject before the verb often does imply emphasis and/or the introduction of something "new or unexpected" (Bandstra, "Word Order and Emphasis," 116), and this consideration combined with Genesis's use of *hā'ĕlōhîm* rather than simple *'ĕlōhîm* suggests some emphasis on the fact that—yes, it was God, *the* God, who set this sequence of events going; cf. von Rad, *Genesis*, 233; Hamilton, *Genesis 18–50*, 100.

4. Or, to be more idiomatic, "Yes?"; cf. the comments of Speiser, *Genesis*, 162.

one,[5] the one you love, Yiṣḥaq, take yourself to the Epiphany region,[6]
and offer him up as a burnt offering there, on one of the mountains
that I will say to you."
3So Abraham started early in the morning, saddled his donkey, and
got two of his boys with him, and Yiṣḥaq his son. He cut the wood for
the burnt offering, set off, and went to the site that God said to him. **4**On
the third day, Abraham lifted his eyes and saw the site from a distance.
5Abraham said to his boys, "You stay here with the donkey, while I and
the boy go over there and bow low[7] and come back to you."
6Abraham got the wood for the burnt offering and put it on Yiṣḥaq
his son, and got in his own hand the fire and the cleaver,[8] and the two
of them walked together. **7**Yiṣḥaq said to Abraham his father, "Father!"
He said, "I'm here, son." He said, "Here are the fire and the wood,
but where's the sheep for the burnt offering?" **8**Abraham said, "God
is the one who will see for himself to the sheep for the burnt offer-
ing, son." The two of them walked together **9**and came to the site that
God had said to him. There Abraham built the altar, laid out the wood,
bound Yiṣḥaq his son, and placed him on the altar on top of the wood.
10Abraham put out his hand and got the cleaver to slaughter his
son.
11But Yahweh's envoy called to him from the heavens and said, "Abra-
ham, Abraham!" He said, "I'm here." **12**He said, "Don't put out your hand
to the boy, don't do anything to him, because now I acknowledge that you

5. LXX *agapēton*, "beloved," anticipating the verb that follows, implies *yədîdəkā* for the numerically inaccurate *yəḥîdəkā*.

6. Since Tyndale, English translations have transliterated *mōriyyâ*, as the Vg does at 2 Chron. 3:1 (Tg. Neof. has "Moriyyah Mountain" here), but this innovation seems implausible. The article on *hammōriyyâ* works against the assumption that the term is a name, as does the lack of reference anywhere else to "the Moriyyah region." "Moriah" was never in common use as a name (cf. Dillmann, *Genesis*, 2:142). The translation "epiphany" (for which see Luther's comment on v. 14 in *Genesis 21–25*, 139) assumes a link with the key role of the verb *rāʾâ* in the chapter (cf. the Vg; Sym; and SP's *hmwrʾh*, "the region of the vision," which for the SP also opens up the possibility of a connection with Shechem: see 12:6); this link also appears in 2 Chron 3:1. Aq has "light," deriving the word from *ʾôr*. Targum Onq. has "service" in the sense of worship, reading back from v. 14, where its expansive rendering makes the connection with the temple more explicit and where it is clearer that the Tg has understood the forms from *rāʾâ* there as forms from *yārēʾ*. Genesis Rabbah 55.7 notes that *mōriyyâ* can be linked with *tôrâ*, among other possibilities. The LXX has "to the high country," linking *mōriyyâ* with the root *rûm*. At 2 Chron. 3:1 the LXX has "the mountain of Amoria," the mountain of the Amorites, which hints at another possible way of reading the text here (cf. the Syriac translation).

7. *Šāḥâ* hitpalel (or *ḥāwâ* eshtaphel: see *HALOT*, 1457) denotes a physical bowing down (though it doubtless implies an inner bowing down); cf. the LXX's *proskyneō* as in 18:2; 19:1. Vg *adoro* suggests "speaking," but *adoro* then comes to denote "adore/reverence," and the Hebrew verb comes to be translated "worship."

8. *Maʾăkelet* comes only here, in a similar context in Judg. 19:29, and in Prov. 30:14, which all suggest more than an ordinary knife; it looks like a word from *ʾākal*, which might suggest it is a butcher's knife.

live in awe of God,[9] and you haven't held back your son, your only son,
from me."
13Abraham lifted his eyes and looked: there, behind,[10] a ram had
caught itself[11] in a thicket by its horns. Abraham went and got the ram
and offered it up as a burnt offering in place of his son. **14**Abraham
named that site "Yahweh Yirʾeh," so it's said today, "On Yahweh's moun-
tain it's seen to."[12]
15Yahweh's envoy called to Abraham a second time from the heavens
16and said, "By myself I am swearing[13] (Yahweh's declaration) that since
you've done this thing and not held back your son, your only one, **17**I will
really bless you and make your offspring really numerous,[14] like the stars
in the heavens and like the sand that's on the seashore; your offspring
will take possession of their opponents' gateway. **18**All the nations on the
earth will bless themselves[15] by your offspring, on account of the fact
that you listened to my voice."
19Abraham went back to his boys, and they set off and went together
to Beʿer Šeba. Abraham lived at Beʿer Šeba.

Interpretation

The broad outline of this story corresponds to that of Gen. 21:1–21 (it also overlaps with the other Hagar-Ishmael story in Gen. 16). God again gives Abraham instructions regarding his son, instructions that imply the son's death. Abraham again gets up early to set the process going. A supernatural envoy again calls from the heavens at the last minute to stop the boy from dying. The boy's parent again sees something they had not seen before.[16]

Verse 1a sets up the questions that the story will deal with (what was the test, how did Abraham do, what was the result?), vv. 1b–14 provide the answers, and vv. 15–19 form a coda and conclusion. Analyzing the main story can begin from the three occasions when Abraham is addressed and answers

9. Not "fear of God," which gives the wrong impression: see the comment.

10. For *ʾaḥar*, SP, LXX have *ʾeḥad* "one," which would mean simply "a" (with the easy misreading of *r* for *d*), giving a more straightforward sense.

11. Reading qatal *neʾĕḥaz* rather than participle *neʾĕḥāz* (see Tal, *Genesis*, 131*).

12. The LXX's "on the mountain the Lord was seen" implies *bāhār* for the MT's *bəhar*, though one could render the MT itself "on Yahweh's mountain he [Yahweh] is seen," or "on Yahweh's mountain one appears" (cf. Exod. 23:17; see Driver, *Genesis*, 220). Targum Onq. thus expands the verse to refer to the worship that people will offer on this mountain (understood as Zion) in the future (see Scheetz, "Canon-Conscious Interpretation"). The Vg has "on the mountain the Lord will see," implying a repetition of *yirʾeh* instead of *yērāʾeh*.

13. The performative/declarative qatal suggests a speech act, "I hereby swear."

14. Twice God prefixes the finite verb with its infinitive, for emphasis.

15. See the footnote to 12:3.

16. Jeremias ("Gen. 20–22 als theologisches Programm") also draws parallels with the preceding story in Gen. 20.

hinnēnî, "I'm here!" Each exchange signals a tense new development in the narrative;[17] each response includes a key statement by Abraham.

invocation (1b)	invocation (7a)	invocation (11a)
answer (1b)	answer (7a)	answer (11b)
speech (2)	speech (7b)	speech (12)
response/action (3–6)	response/action (8–10)	response/action (13–14)

Another way of analyzing the section begins from the three key references to Isaac as "your son, your only one," in vv. 1, 12, and 16. The first commissions the offering; the second stops the offering from becoming a literal sacrifice; the third rewards the offering.

On the basis of the dominant reference to "God" as opposed to "Yahweh," traditional source criticism sees the story as part of the Elohistic Abraham narrative (indeed as "the literary masterpiece of the Elohistic collection")[18] and sees vv. 15–19 as a later addition to the story.

22:1. The time reference is vague, but Isaac is now big enough to have a load of wood on his back, so we should imagine him as at least a teenager like Ishmael in the previous chapter. He is called both a *yeled* and a *naʿar*, words that were used of Ishmael there (and see the comment on 21:9); *naʿar* is also the term for the two "boys" who are Abraham's servants in vv. 5, 12, for the fighters in 14:24, and for Shechem when he has sex with Dinah in 34:19.[19] The story is also not explicit about where Abraham and Isaac are. Genesis 21:33–34 would imply that they are in Beer Sheba, but the "long time" might have come to an end by now, and v. 19 does not speak of them *returning* to Beer Sheba. "The most we know about the location of Abraham" is that "he stands before a word" in the sense that "he is addressed. . . . Addressed by the purposes of heaven or the pathos of earth, he is a man ready to be addressed."[20] For that matter, the story is vague about where God is and about whether he comes to Abraham in a dream (as v. 3 might imply). Nor does it say whether God's testing has some background in a heavenly consultation, as is the case in Job. Jubilees 17–18 reads Gen. 22 in light of Job and traces back the idea of testing Abraham to Prince Animosity (*maśṭēmâ*, cf. Hosea 9:7–8; the verb *śāṭam* is suspiciously similar to *śāṭān*—it comes in Job 16:9; 30:21). The testing then vindicates God's faith in Abraham and shames Prince

17. Wenham, *Genesis 16–50*, 104.

18. Skinner, *Genesis*, 328.

19. The LXX has Isaac as a "little boy" (cf. Brayford, *Genesis*, 330). Targum Ps.-J. works out that he is thirty-seven by subtracting three years of Torah study (see the comment on v. 19) from his age when he marries Rebekah (25:20; see Maher, *Targum Pseudo-Jonathan: Genesis*, 81). Josephus (*Ant.* 1.13.2) says he was twenty-five (cf. Willet, *Hexapla in Genesin & Exodum*, 199). Ibn Ezra (*Genesis*, 225) suggests he was more likely thirteen, which seems the best guess.

20. Brueggemann, *Genesis*, 187, 188.

Animosity. In Genesis, the vagueness of the chronology and geography makes for an appropriate framework within which to hear a story that seems to happen in a strange world.

The notion of God testing people recurs in the Scriptures (e.g., Exod. 15:25; 16:4; Deut. 8:2, 16; 33:8; Judg. 2:22; 3:1; 1 Thess. 2:4; James 1:2–5; see also 2:21).[21] Only here does Genesis itself explicitly refer to God testing people, and it is almost the only place where the First Testament has God testing an individual,[22] though it could have used the expression for God's dealings with Adam and Eve and with Joseph. Arguably, God has already tested Abraham a lot, and not just in Gen. 21: "with his land, and with famine. And . . . with the wealth of kings. And . . . with his wife, when she was taken (from him), and with circumcision. And . . . with Ishmael and with Hagar, his maidservant, when he sent them away" (Jub. 17.17); this test is the tenth, according to Tg. Neof. (in Jub. 18.8 Sarah's death brings the tenth). Testing people may help them to grow, but stretching people is a different notion from testing them. God's test is designed to uncover what is in people's hearts (Deut. 8:2) and to do so by seeing "whether someone will obey God's command or not."[23] The aim of a test is for someone to discover something—perhaps the one who does the testing, perhaps the one who is tested, perhaps other people. According to Augustine, the test was designed "to prove his pious obedience, and so make it known to the world, not to God,"[24] and the people hearing the story do discover something about Abraham, as do Abraham himself and Isaac. But Gen. 22 speaks explicitly of what God will discover (cf. v. 12). Yet a better way to put it is to say that God is concerned to establish something or be sure of something—God is not starting without any assumptions about Abraham one way or the other. God tests the faithful, not the faithless (Ps. 11:5); testing is a kind of compliment (cf. Gen. Rab. 55.2–3). God does not test people in a way that might break them (1 Cor. 10:13), though it would still be a good idea to pray not to be led into testing (Matt. 6:13; 26:41).[25] The test begins with God summoning Abraham like a master summoning a servant and with Abraham responding as a servant should. Apparently God, as usual, makes it easy for Abraham to be sure that God is speaking to him, which is just as well in light of what follows. "There is a great emphasis in the word, 'said,' because God indeed made trial of Abraham's faith . . . by drawing him into a contest with his [God's] own word."[26] While the audience knows that what will happen is a test, however, Abraham doesn't (like Job).[27] "The audience

21. See further Moberly, *Bible, Theology, and Faith*, 97–107.

22. Seebass (*Genesis*, 2.1:203) notes 2 Chron. 32:31 and discusses other possible exceptions.

23. Gunkel, *Genesis*, 233.

24. Augustine, *City of God* 16.32.

25. Cf. Mays ("Now I Know"), who brings together Gen. 22 and Matt. 26:36–56.

26. Calvin, *Genesis*, 1:562.

27. Cf. Zimmerli, *1. Mose 12–25*, 110–11.

knows from the beginning that the threat to Isaac is not the subject,"[28] though this fact doesn't mean it knows that God will not let Abraham go through with the deed.[29] All Abraham knows is that it is a summons and a command. As God has some assumptions about Abraham, however, so Abraham has some assumptions about God. He knows God is trustworthy, if mysterious in some of the things he asks, and he knows that God has made promises to him, and he knows that God has squared a circle before, not least in 21:1–21. It is within this framework that he hears God speak.

22:2. So the master summons, though he does so politely, as masters often do (cf. 24:2). Indeed, perhaps his "please" gives Abraham the chance to decline with impunity.[30] "Get your son" would not initially sound threatening; in the next verse Abraham will also "get" two of his other "boys" to accompany him and Isaac. But God's bidding builds up to a climax that bodes ill: your son, your only one, whom you love, Isaac. "Your son?"—yes. "Your only one?"—in literal terms, it is an odd description. As well as having a literal reference (cf. Judg. 11:34; Jer. 6:26; Amos 8:10), it carries sensitive metaphorical overtones (cf. Pss. 22:20 [21]; 25:16). Is it also a tough description on God's part? The non-peremptory command, with its "please," hints that God recognizes the horrifying nature of his command. Yet as far as God is concerned, Ishmael does not count, and in a sense it should also be so for Abraham. Indeed, it already is so, because Ishmael is gone in literal terms; he disappeared some while ago—forever, as far as Abraham knows (but see 25:9). Likewise, "whom you love"? It's the first reference to love in the Scriptures, and one thinks about where it is leading. And finally, "Isaac"—in case there is any doubt about the identity of the one we are talking about.

Get him, says God, and "take yourself": it's the command that Yahweh issued in order to set Abraham on the way to Canaan (12:6); these two verses are the only places where the phrase occurs. This expression too suggests something demanding (where might God want him to go now?) but not something horrifying. On that occasion too God had accumulated epithets of deepening poignancy: "from your country, from your homeland, from your father's household" (cf. Gen. Rab. 55.7). Now "Abraham is being asked more than to kill his son. He is being asked to give up the promised future for God's sake, in the same way he already gave up the past when he left country and family for a land he had yet to see."[31] Yet perhaps the comparison is incomplete. After all, a sacrifice centrally involves not so much giving something up as consecrating something to God.[32] But in his address to Abraham "God is clearly contradicting Himself," when he follows up his promise in 21:12

28. Coats, *Genesis*, 158.
29. Cf. Levenson, *Death and Resurrection*, 126.
30. Cf. Heard, *Dynamics of Diselection*, 94.
31. De La Torre, *Genesis*, 215.
32. See Eberhart, "Term 'Sacrifice.'"

with his command here in v. 2. "God, who formerly seemed to be his best friend, now appears to have become an enemy and a tyrant."[33] He seems not merely "to assail the paternal love of Abraham" but "to trample upon His own benevolence."[34] But Abraham's obeying "shows that he trusts God will find a way into the future. . . . Whatever conflict there may be, it is up to God to resolve it, and God is up to it."[35] The same consideration answers the question, what would have happened if Abraham had said "No"?

The word "epiphany" (*mōriyyâ*) otherwise occurs in the First Testament only in 2 Chron. 3:1 (though spelled *môriyyâ*). There, "Epiphany Mountain" is one way of describing where the temple was built, along with the place's identification as the threshing floor of Ornan the Jebusite. That passage does not make a link with Abraham, while v. 2 here (with its different spelling) does not make a link between "the Epiphany region" and Jerusalem or Salem (Gen. 14) or the Jebusites (10:16; 15:21)—nor does 1 Kings include such a reference. So within the First Testament the evidence is thin for identifying the geographical location of the place where Abraham is to go as the place where the temple is later built (not surprisingly, Samaritan tradition identifies the place with Mount Gerizim).[36] Yet it may implicitly link the two in their significance (see further v. 14, where Jub. 18.13 adds "it is Mount Zion"): the Jerusalem temple is the place where Yahweh sees to the need for sacrifice. But otherwise, we do not know where the Epiphany region was. Nor do we know why it should be the place to make an offering. God will tell Abraham exactly where to go to make the sacrifice, but the narrator will not tell us. The name is more significant than the location. It recalls the verb *rā'â* (see), which recurs in the chapter: it's the place that Abraham sees and where he sees the ram, and where God sees to things (vv. 4, 8, 13, 14). Its name is also similar to that of the Moreh Oak (12:6–7), making for another link with that long-ago bidding to move to Canaan. While that name likely suggests "Teacher's Oak," it could also remind people of this verb:[37] it too was a place where Yahweh let himself be seen (the verb came twice in 12:7) and where Abraham built his first altar, as he builds his last here.

Preceding sacrifices in Genesis were all offered on human initiative. Here for the first time God gives instructions for a sacrifice. It would be another reason for making a link between the building of the Jerusalem temple and this event. For the idea of a whole offering, see 8:20 (the only other reference in Genesis). One can hardly imagine a more sacrificial offering than to offer one's own child in this way; it is thus a monumental sign of devotion.

33. Luther, *Genesis 21–25*, 92, 94; on Luther's exposition, see further Buck, "God as Tempter."

34. Calvin, *Genesis*, 1:565.

35. Fretheim, "Genesis," 497.

36. Cf. Tal, *Genesis*, 130–31*; Kalimi, "Land of Moriah."

37. Targum Neof. has "Vision" for "Teacher" there. The LXX has "high" for both *môreh* and *mōriyyâ*.

The idea that one owes one's firstborn son to God will become familiar, but God will accept a substitute and then give him back (Exod. 22:29 [28]; 34:20). In one sense the audience might be shocked at the command, not least because the Torah forbade human sacrifice; in another sense it might not be shocked. Israel's ancestors often did not live by the Torah's rules, which had not yet been laid down. And the audience would have known of the practice of human sacrifice among other peoples in their cultural context (e.g., 2 Kings 3:27) as well as within Israel, despite what the Torah said (e.g., 2 Kings 21:6; Ps. 107:34–38; Jer. 7:31). Not that it was necessarily a regular practice;[38] and the description of the event as a test implies "no suggestion that the command to sacrifice the boy accords with established human custom."[39]

22:3–5. "What do you say to these things, Abraham? What kind of thoughts are stirring in your heart?" But Abraham "does not deliberate, he does not reconsider, he does not take counsel with any man, but immediately he sets out on the journey."[40] "The very fact that the patriarch, who lived before the age of grace and before the Law, reached such a degree of virtue of himself from the knowledge innate in his nature is sufficient to deprive us of any excuse";[41] it also makes us question the premise of that statement. Abraham lives in the age of grace. But indeed, there is no querying here as there was in Gen. 15 and 17. Nor is there any of the other kind of questioning that appeared in Gen. 18. While Genesis also says nothing directly of Abraham's feelings regarding Yahweh's bidding, First Testament narrative often hints at feelings by describing actions. Here "every sentence vibrates with restrained emotion, which shows how fully the author realises the tragic horror of the situation."[42] Every sentence is profound or subtle or enigmatic (*hintergründig*).[43] The very detailing of Abraham's actions may suggest his desire to postpone what is due to happen, to slow down what he has to do.[44]

But he makes an early start (v. 3), as he did when bidden to send off Hagar and Ishmael (21:14), again indicating an unequivocal commitment to doing as the master said. Saddling his own donkey (rather than having his boys do it) conveys the same point. He responds to the command to take himself to the Epiphany region with the same "unquestioning obedience and steadfast

38. Staubli ("Is There an Iconographic Pattern?") argues that the Canaanites were also used to the idea of redeeming their children rather than sacrificing them. On the view that Gen. 22 explains why Israelites are not to sacrifice children, see Levenson, *Death and Resurrection*.

39. E. Davis, "Self-Consciousness," 32.

40. Origen, *Homilies on Genesis*, 137, 139.

41. Chrysostom, *Homilies on Genesis 18–45*, 418. See the critique of Willet, *Hexapla in Genesin & Exodum*, 174.

42. Skinner, *Genesis*, 328.

43. Zimmerli, *1. Mose 12–25*, 113, summarizing Auerbach (*Mimesis*), which has the expression "fraught with background" (12).

44. So J. Jacobs, "Willing Obedience," 552–55.

loyalty" that he showed to the command to take himself to Canaan.[45] Instead of describing his feelings (which Western readers would think essential), Genesis goes into detail about the practicalities of the action (like a movie rather than a novel). It's not explicit why he needs to take two of his boys with him, though maybe a man of importance just would (Tg. Ps.-J. nicely specifies that they are Eliezer and Ishmael). Nor is it clear why he needs to take the wood with him, though this action may relate to the fact that he doesn't know exactly where he's going; it would be especially odd to take all that wood into Judah (where there was plenty of wood) and/or all the way to Jerusalem. But his own cutting of the wood is another marker of his commitment to the task. The context suggests that "site" (*māqôm*) again denotes a worship place (cf. 12:6; 13:3–4; 21:31). The journey is described "after the manner of a pilgrimage to a hilltop shrine."[46] It would be easier to discern the right "place" if he is to go to a worship site, but his not knowing where he is going parallels 12:1–5.

The third day (v. 4) need not imply that they were traveling for three full days (see, e.g., Luke 24:21). It might imply one day when Abraham hears Yahweh speak, one day when he makes preparations and sets off, and one day when he makes the offering. A literal three days is hardly enough time to get from Beer Sheba to Jerusalem (though enough time to get from Mamre to Jerusalem). But the expression may be comparable to "a couple of days" or "two or three days" in English (cf. Hosea 6:2), or to the "third day" or the "three days" mentioned elsewhere (e.g., Gen. 31:22; 40:20; 42:17–18; Exod. 3:18; 15:22).[47] The three days might be three days of testing as they are three days to think. Deliberately lifting his eyes is yet another marker of his commitment to doing what God said, of his "comment-less obedience."[48]

The mystery of the story increases (v. 5). Why does he leave the boys behind? Does he think they will stop him from killing Isaac?[49] Or might it seem quite natural for him to want to pray with his son on his own?[50] What does he mean when he says that he and Isaac will come back to them? Is he prevaricating? Is he thinking that he will kill Isaac and God will resuscitate him (cf. Heb. 11:17–19)? What would be the basis for that conviction? Is he second-guessing God, speaking on the basis of a hunch that God can hardly make him go through with the killing?[51] Is he implying the conviction that "once again, a seemingly impossible situation would not be beyond God's ability to resolve satisfactorily"? Insofar as he is, the event constitutes a testing

45. Sarna, *Genesis*, 150.
46. Blenkinsopp, *Abraham*, 146.
47. Genesis Rabbah 56.1 has a long list of things that happened "on the third day."
48. Seebass, *Genesis*, 2.1:201.
49. Ephrem (*Genesis*, 168) suggests the same reason for his not telling Sarah.
50. Cf. von Rad, *Genesis*, 235.
51. Cf. Brams's study (*Biblical Games*, 36–45) in light of game theory.

of God's faithfulness, even of God's wisdom in entrusting Isaac (as the one on whom his purpose depends) to Abraham.[52] Is Abraham perhaps "firmly convinced that He who said to him, *through Isaac shall your descendants be named*, was not lying"?[53] Or does he not know what he means?[54] Is it one of those things that come out of your mouth without you quite having planned it? For the audience, however, Abraham's statement "foreshadows the good news of the story's climax"[55] and functions as a reassurance that everything will turn out okay.

22:6–10. To the horror of the audience, Abraham calmly (as far as one can tell) puts on his son's back the wood for the fire on which his dismembered corpse will be burned (why is Abraham not taking the donkey that has presumably carried the wood so far?). "It is like one who carries his own cross on his shoulder" (Gen. Rab. 56.3). Abraham carries the fire (that is, the flint) with which he will light the fire under the offering, and the cleaver with which he will kill his son and cut him into pieces, as one does with a burnt offering. Does he carry them to make sure that the wood doesn't catch fire too soon and to make sure that the cleaver doesn't injure Isaac? The two walk together, itself an ironic or poignant or horrifying statement in light of what will follow.

"God produces . . . a new instrument of torture"[56] (vv. 7–8a) as Isaac asks an obvious question. Can he really not put two and two together? What about his pointed omission of reference to the cleaver? And what does Abraham mean by his "classic" answer?[57] Does he again not know what he means? Is it another of those things that come out of your mouth without you quite having planned it? Is he indirectly challenging God, who (he implies) is responsible for whatever happens (KSG)? Or does Abraham "know" that it must be a test and that somehow God will not expect him to go through with the killing? The vocative "my father" and "my son" (to translate more literally) further deepens the enormity and pathos of the scene (ten times Gen. 22 says "your/his/my son"). But for the audience, Abraham's statement again foreshadows the good news of the story's climax and thus functions as a reassurance that everything will turn out okay.

The disquieting narrative continues (vv. 8b–9). The "trusting departure" had not settled the issue of the test. "The question becomes: Will Abraham stay with the journey?"[58] Again Genesis pictures father and son walking together. It seems that both are committed to it. Neither really knows what the journey is about, but both are operating on the basis of trust and obedience.

52. Fretheim, *Abraham*, 133, 134.
53. Ephrem, *Genesis*, 168–69, with his emphasis.
54. Rashi (*Br'šyt*, 233) comments that he was prophesying.
55. Coats, *Genesis*, 160.
56. Calvin, *Genesis*, 1:568.
57. Seebass *Genesis*, 2.1:209.
58. Fretheim, "Genesis," 496.

They have found reason to trust God, and that trust provides them with reason to obey God. "In effect, Isaac trusts that his father's trust is well-placed. Abraham's trust in God has become Isaac's trust: God will provide."[59] Although the "place" was likely already a worship site, for one reason or another (such as the fact that other people worshiped other so-called gods there) Abraham builds his own altar, as he did at Shechem and near Beth El (12:7–8). The altar would be constructed of stone or mudbrick, so that a fire could be built on it. Normally the offerer first kills the creature to be offered, then puts its carcass on the fire so that it goes up in smoke to God. Abraham "goes about his task . . . with the speechless concentration of a sleepwalker, as if thus to hold off by every possible means the fate that he has no hope of averting."[60] He makes the fire first, then ties Isaac up. The verb is *ʿāqad*: hence the Jewish name for this event is the *Aqedah*, "the binding." One tied an animal's legs together before killing it.[61] Might Isaac be twisting and trying to escape, or might Abraham imagine him trying to do so? If Isaac is big enough the carry the firewood, he is big enough to resist his centenarian father.[62] Or does Isaac recognize what is going on and accept it? The tying up then simply means that Abraham acts in conformity to the rite of a burnt offering.[63] The hints in the chapter that Isaac is complicit in what is happening provide a basis for Jewish interpretation's focus on Isaac's willingness to be sacrificed, like that of Jephthah's daughter (KSG). Isaac's willingness became an inspiration in the context of the threat of martyrdom,[64] even if the story is mainly about the testing of Abraham rather than the offering or binding of Isaac.[65] The point is similarly more explicit in the Qur'an's equivalent story about Ishmael: "He said, 'O my father, do what you are commanded to do. You will find me, God willing, patient.' They both submitted" (37:102–3).[66]

The moment of great sacrifice for father and son, the kairos,[67] is about to arrive (v. 10).

22:11–12. The nature of a test is that it doesn't go on forever; it's a time-limited exercise with a particular aim in view. So the audience needn't be surprised that God doesn't intend Abraham to go through with what he asks.

59. Fretheim, *Abraham*, 131.

60. Speiser, *Genesis*, 165.

61. See references in *DTT* 1104–5. The LXX has "bound him hand and foot" (cf. Brayford, *Genesis*, 331).

62. Hamilton, *Genesis 18–50*, 110.

63. So Luther, *Genesis 21–25*, 114.

64. See, e.g., Chilton, "Genesis in Aramaic"; Kundert, *Die Opferung/Bindung Isaaks*. In a sense, then, Isaac was also being tested; though in addition Abraham was martyring his own future (Kalimi, "'Go, I Beg You'").

65. Arnold, *Genesis*, 202.

66. As quoted in Palmquist and Rudisill, "Three Perspectives," 470–71.

67. Seebass, *Genesis*, 2.1:209.

At the last possible moment God intervenes (v. 11). "With what unconcern the Divine Majesty toys with death and all the power of death" as Isaac is about to die and Abraham "dies seven times over."[68] The divine envoy calls to Abraham from the heavens; the clause is virtually the same as the one in 21:17. The words were audible and therefore compelling, and Abraham was not fooling himself that God had changed his mind.[69] Further, speaking from the heavens rather than making the journey to earth (cf. 28:12) perhaps suggests urgency. "If God had blinked, the boy would have died there. . . . In the teeth of life we seem to die, but God says no—in the teeth of death we live. If He butchers us, He makes us live."[70] So in the midst of life we are in death, and in the midst of death we are in life.[71] Also paralleling 21:17, the envoy goes on to speak with God's own "I."[72] Thus God calls, "Abraham," as he did in v. 1, this time repeating the name, with a further implication of urgency; he really needs to get Abraham's attention. And Abraham replies in the same way as he did in v. 1 and in v. 7, more coolly.

He is not to lay hands on Isaac after all (v. 12). A burnt offering involves laying one's hand on the animal to be sacrificed, but in a different sense; we use the same verb in English, but Hebrew does not (the verb in Lev. 1:4, *sāmak*, means "rest your hand"). God can terminate the test because he now "knows" something that he did not know before. In some sense God knew it beforehand, given that God's being extends through all time. Yet "the philosophers teach that there are two kinds of knowledge, knowledge of events prior to their occurrence, and knowledge of what is presently in existence."[73] To know what is going to happen is different from knowing it when it has happened. Thus there is in some sense a "before" and "after" for God, a time sequence. Luther appeals to Augustine's distinction between morning knowledge and evening knowledge,[74] though he takes it in a different direction;[75] Augustine himself thought that here God must mean, "Now I have made to be known."[76] But arguably Yahweh's declaration "Now I know" taken in its regular meaning is the "pivot" of the chapter, the "climax" toward which it moves and from which the rest of it flows.[77] Further, the common connotation of "acknowledge" carries over in the meaning of the verb (*yādaʿ*) here (cf. 18:19, 21; 20:7). Yahweh acknowledges that Abraham really does live in awe of God in the

68. Luther, *Genesis 21–25*, 115.
69. Cf. Calvin, *Genesis*, 1:570.
70. Attributed to Luther by J. Osborne, *Luther*, act 3, scene 2, p. 111.
71. Luther, *Genesis 21–25*, 116.
72. Further on the parallels between Gen. 21 and Gen. 22, see D. Lim, "Study of the Repetition."
73. Ibn Ezra, *Genesis*, 222.
74. E.g., *City of God* 11.7.
75. Luther, *Genesis 21–25*, 133.
76. *City of God* 16.32.
77. Mays, "Now I Know," 183.

sense that he is willing to do whatever God tells him to do. He could as easily have said that Abraham loves him.[78] "This fear is love."[79] "God and Abraham are now bound together in both being willing to sacrifice their sons" (KSG).

22:13–14. Abraham lifts his eyes, as he did in v. 4, with the same attentiveness, but presumably with a different kind of expectancy. Once again, the narrative's "there" invites us to look at the scene with Abraham. Like Hagar in 21:19, he sees something that might or might not have been there before. Either way, it is again God's provision, fulfilling the prescription that Abraham made in vv. 7–8 (the word for "sheep" there is a general term that can cover other bovids, and a ram is a subset of that category). Apparently Abraham does not need instruction about what to do with it.

Yahweh has seen to things (v. 14), and Abraham can therefore say "Yahweh sees," *yhwh yir'eh*. In effect it is the same experience as Hagar's (16:13–14).[80] There continues to be no direct account of Abraham's feelings (or God's), such as joy or relief. Here his reaction is conveyed through the report of his recollecting the conviction he expressed in v. 8: "God will see to" the sheep for an offering. It has been proved true. God has passed the test. So it becomes a conviction in the "today" of narrator and listeners that "Yahweh will see to it." As they themselves apparently expressed it, "on Yahweh's mountain it is seen to," it is provided. "Yahweh's mountain" is Sinai in Num. 10:33 and apparently Mount Zion in Isa. 30:29; Ps. 24:3. More broadly, but etymologically, the declaration that God provides and the belief in a doctrine of providence presuppose that God sees. Jerome notes that whenever Jews are in distress and need God's help, they say "The Lord will be seen on the mountain," that is, "just as He had pity on Abraham, He will also have pity on us"; and the sounding of the ram's horn is a reminder of the ram that was provided.[81] "God not only saw to his own sacrifice, rather he still 'sees' in the present and future."[82] To say that God sees us and sees to things for us is a statement of faith often belied by experience but based on the fact that God has seen us and seen to us in spectacular ways. "The theodicy evoked by Abraham's ascent of Mount Moriah is personal, not metaphysical. The binding of Isaac evokes the fear that sacrifice simply ends in renunciation and loss,"[83] but it does not.

22:15–18. The envoy again speaks and again does so as if it is Yahweh himself speaking. This time he is swearing an oath, the kind of promise one makes only after serious reflection and with solemnity and an awareness that it is not the oath taker and the recipient alone who are listening. In effect, Yahweh swore oaths in Gen. 15 and 17, though those chapters did not use this

78. Cf. Levenson, *Inheriting Abraham*, 80.
79. Qimchi, *Genesis*, writing on the verse in Hebrew: *hyr'h hz't hi' 'hbh*.
80. Cf. Nielsen, "To See."
81. Jerome, *Hebrew Questions on Genesis*, 56.
82. Childs, *Biblical Theology*, 334.
83. Reno, *Genesis*, 199.

language. Only human beings have explicitly sworn oaths so far in Genesis (21:22–32). Now Yahweh does so. Perhaps the implication is that this was indeed "the last trial" (cf. Gen. Rab. 56.11). The Torah will often refer back to Yahweh's oath taking (24:7; 50:24; Exod. 13:5, 11; 32:13; 33:1, and many times in Deuteronomy). Yahweh swears "by himself" (cf. Exod. 32:13; Isa. 45:13; and cf. Heb. 6:13–18). Human beings swear by someone or something other than themselves, which acts as a guarantor of their oath, asking God, in particular, to note the oath and to act against them in case of default. Yahweh is saying, "It is as if I will punish myself if I fail to do as I say"; or more realistically and profoundly, "If I do not keep My promises, I shall no longer be He who I am."[84] As if it were not enough, he adds the phrase "Yahweh's declaration," with which the audience will be familiar through the frequency with which it appears on the lips of prophets. It is a way of saying "This really is Yahweh speaking and therefore it really is going to happen" (Num. 14:28 is the only other occurrence in the Torah). Yahweh speaks thus on the basis of Abraham's willingness to give him the most important thing he has, the one whom Yahweh himself has designated as the key to the fulfillment of Yahweh's own promises. Yahweh's command had imperiled these promises; Abraham's obedience has opened the way to their fulfillment, and even their enhancement. "You have not spared the son you so longed for. . . . So take back your son."[85]

The content of the oath (vv. 17–18) is a variant on the promises Yahweh gave on that first occasion when he said "Take yourself . . . " to a place that I will enable you to "see" (12:1), and on other occasions since.

> I will bless you and I intend to make your name big,
> and you are to become a blessing.
> I intend to bless the people who bless you,
> but the person who diminishes you I will curse.
> All the kin groups on the earth
> will gain blessing by you. (12:2–3)

> Look at the heavens, please, and count the stars, if you can count them. . . . That's what your offspring will be like. (15:5)

> I am Yahweh who got you out from Ur of the Kaśdites to give you this country as a possession. (15:7)

> I will make your offspring really numerous,
> and they won't be able to be counted up because of the number. (16:10)

84. Luther, *Genesis 21–25*, 143.
85. Chrysostom, *Homilies on Genesis 46–67*, 21.

> Abraham is indeed to become a big, numerous nation, and all the nations on the earth are to gain blessing by him. (18:18)

"I will bless you" becomes "I will really bless you." The image of the sand on the seashore complements the image of the stars in the sky. The reference to possession becomes the promise that Abraham's offspring will take possession of their opponents' gateway. The talk of victory over people who are hostile to them corresponds to the promise that Yahweh will curse anyone who diminishes them. Whereas the gateway was literal in 19:1, here it has become a metaphor: the gateway stands for the town to which the gateway leads. And "gain blessing" becomes "bless themselves," which suggests the idea of praying to be blessed as Abraham is blessed. Apparently there is no conflict between Abraham's offspring taking possession of their attackers' towns and all the nations of the earth finding blessing through these offspring: nations will choose whether they open themselves to blessing or cursing. There are further parallels with the promises regarding Ishmael in Gen. 17. And it is all because Abraham heeded without question the imperious demand in vv. 1–2 (v. 18b).

22:19. The test is over (v. 19). Presumably Isaac returned too, unless he went off to study Torah (cf. Tg. Ps.-J.) or to get counseling for post-traumatic stress disorder or to think about the marriage for which he is now ready (cf. Gen. 24) because he has faced his own death.[86] But this story is about Abraham,[87] and the omission of reference to Isaac perhaps reflects Abraham's really having given up Isaac.[88] Everyone just goes home and life continues; Abraham, Isaac, and Sarah lived happily ever after, Josephus more or less says (*Ant.* 1.13.4). Except that Sarah has not been mentioned, and Abraham returns to Beer Sheba, whereas Sarah dies in Hebron. "Thus the text reads as though husband and wife were never reunited in life."[89] As there was no direct indication of Abraham's feelings about the original command, so there is no indication of his feelings about the deliverance, nor any indication of Isaac's feelings, still less any indication of Sarah's, which became another focus of Jewish reflection.[90] Such considerations are not the story's point. "The question whether Isaac will be sacrificed" was less important than the question "whether Abraham will stand up to the test."[91] The point is that

86. Levenson, *Death and Resurrection*, 142, alluding to White, "Initiation Legend."

87. Cf. Levenson's comments, *Inheriting Abraham*, 85–87. The absence of reference to Isaac is the starting point of Spiegel's *The Last Trial.*

88. Cf. Kuruvilla, "*Akedah*," 505; Leder, "Bound to the Altar," 290.

89. Trible, "Genesis 22," 190.

90. See, e.g., Kalimi, "'Go, I Beg You,'" 26–27; and cf. the poems attributed to Ephrem noted by Brock, "Creating Women's Voices." Romanska ("Sarah's Gift") reflects on the absence of Sarah from a feminist angle and in light of Derrida's *Gift of Death.*

91. Wenham, *Genesis 16–50*, 103.

Yahweh issues a command, that Abraham obeys it, and that Yahweh declares his commitment to fulfilling his promises.

Implications

Reason, Trust, Submission

"In the earliest stages of commentary on, or allusion to, the Abraham story, it was not experienced as particularly prominent or problematic."[92] Calvin, for instance, gives the chapter similar space to the chapters that precede.[93] In contrast, its omission from the *Revised Common Lectionary* perhaps reflects the extent to which in a modern Western context it seems "disturbing."[94]

In the eighteenth century, Immanuel Kant comments on its unreasonableness in *Religion within the Boundaries of Mere Reason* and defends his view in a paper arguing that the philosophy faculty in the university should be free to question the teachings of the theology faculty. "If God should really speak to a human being, the latter could still never *know* that it was God speaking. It is quite impossible for a human being to apprehend the infinite by his senses. . . . But in some cases the human being can be sure that the voice he hears is *not* God's; for if the voice commands him to do something contrary to the moral law . . . , he must consider it an illusion."[95] Genesis 22 would be an example.

The distinctiveness of Kant's work emerges from the title of *Religion within the Boundaries of Mere Reason*. Given that constraint, Kant could not work with the way the story belongs in the context of a relationship of trust between God and Abraham. And one cannot abstract the word from the one who spoke it.[96] As God begins the story with some assumptions about Abraham, so Abraham has some assumptions about God. He knows that God is trustworthy, albeit mysterious in some of the things he asks, and he knows God has made promises to him, and he knows that God has squared a circle before, not least in Gen. 21. It is in this framework that he hears God speak. The more the story of Israel continues—into the story of the exodus, the people's arrival and flourishing in Canaan, the building of the temple, the restoration of the people and rebuilding of the temple after the exile, and the deliverance from Antiochus—the more they would listen to this story in the context of their relationship with a God whom they can trust. The trustworthiness of this God is newly embodied when God gives up his own son for his people and

92. Blenkinsopp, *Abraham*, 140.

93. Calvin, *Genesis*, 1:557–74.

94. Cf. Fretheim, *Abraham*, 200.

95. I. Kant, "Conflict of the Faculties," 283, emphasis original. In "Three Perspectives" Palmquist and Rudisill provide many references to the expansive literature on Kant and Abraham.

96. Cf. Westermann, *Genesis 12–36*, 356–57.

for the world, actually doing what he did not in the end require of Abraham (Mark 1:11; Rom. 8:31–32).[97]

In the nineteenth century, Søren Kierkegaard retold the Gen. 22 story several times in ways that begin by bringing it to life but go on to make it a different story.[98] In his first version Isaac pleads with Abraham for his life, and Abraham urges him to recognize that he himself is really an idolater. "Do you think it is God's command? No, it is my desire." Then Abraham thanks God that Isaac believes him to be a monster rather than that he should lose faith in God. In another version he asks God for forgiveness that he was willing to sacrifice his son. In another version Isaac sees what his father is prepared to do and "loses the faith." Yet another version marvels at Abraham's having kept the faith all those years of living with God's implausible promise but then experiencing God apparently mocking him by fulfilling the promise and subsequently requiring him to slay Isaac. "But Abraham had faith and did not doubt; he believed the preposterous." Otherwise he would have offered himself to God instead of his son. But "he did not pray for himself" as he had for Sodom and Gomorrah. Many a father has despaired of the future through losing a child; Abraham was bidden to take his own child's life, and he readily agreed. "There were countless generations who knew the story of Abraham by heart . . . , but how many did it render sleepless?" One can understand Hegel, but not Abraham, and the Abraham story presupposes "a teleological suspension of the ethical." Kierkegaard speaks of God testing Abraham's faith, his trust in him. Yet there is no reference to faith or trust in Gen. 22. It's obedience that's the issue. Arguably, Abraham passed the faith test back in Gen. 15. In the twentieth century, Jacques Derrida entered into conversation with Kierkegaard in *The Gift of Death*. Like Kierkegaard, he is concerned with the question whether there is such a thing as a selfless, disinterested act; paradoxically, Abraham's willingness to offer his son's life (as opposed to his own) is such an act, because he is sacrificing his future. But it is a challenge unique to him. It cannot be turned into an ethical generalization. It's a command, not a law.[99]

In the twentieth century, child abuse provided another focus for concern about Gen. 22.[100] "What kind of God would command the sacrifice of a child?"[101] Here one difficulty arises from the assumption that Isaac was a child, whereas we have seen that he seems to have been at least a teenager and not someone

97. See, e.g., Rindge, "Reconfiguring."

98. De Silentio [Kierkegaard's pseudonym], *Fear and Trembling*.

99. LaCocque ("About the 'Aqedah,'" 191) responding to L. Kant, "Some Restorative Thoughts"; see also L. Kant, "Arguing with God." Kant suggests that Abraham misunderstood God and failed to argue when he should have done so.

100. See, e.g., Fretheim, "God, Abraham, and the Abuse of Isaac"; Fretheim, "'God Was with the Boy,'" 14–23.

101. Fretheim, *Abraham*, 119.

capable of being physically overwhelmed by his centenarian father.[102] But anyway, Isaac is no ordinary child, and Abraham's testing is a "patriarchal temptation" that is "non-repeatable within the Bible."[103] Genesis 22 becomes a problem when taken out of context. Yet historically, Gen. 22 has not led to a rash of child sacrifice, as Deut. 7 has not led to a rash of genocide. The picture of Isaac as a young man fits the story's retelling in the context of the First World War (Wilfred Owen, "The Parable of the Old Man and the Young") and the Vietnam War (Leonard Cohen, "Story of Isaac"). These writers treat the story as an asset rather than a liability in connection with concern about abuse. After all, Abraham was lowly or submissive enough to give up the idea of killing Isaac, unlike the people who sent off their nations' offspring to their death in those wars.

When God says that Abraham has passed the test, he does not refer to his having shown faith or trust but to his having shown that he was in awe of God.[104] Awe of God does not mean a sense of being overwhelmed in one's inner being by the awesome mystery of the supernatural God—or it does not mean simply that. It means being submissive to God. It means "moral restraint out of respect for God."[105] And it means Abraham not loving Isaac more than he loves God (in the sense of being committed to God). Abraham was prepared to sacrifice his son, his future, his eternity. But the story then provokes the question "Are you never prepared—ever—to do so? . . . Abraham's readiness was in response to the God who is Ultimate Reality, who calls us into being and gives meaning to our existence. When and where, to the call of what authority, in loyalty to what cause, in the name of what values, is it your wont to sacrifice your children—and yourself?"[106] "Through the aqedah, Abraham surrenders his beloved son to the God who made his miraculous conception possible," though then "the divine father exercises his prerogative to decline the offering he demanded."[107] Thus, "Abraham loved Isaac his son, the text says, but he placed the love of God before love of the flesh. . . . Unless you shall be obedient to all the commands, even the more difficult ones, unless you shall offer sacrifice and show that you place neither father nor mother nor sons before God, you will not know that you fear God nor will it be said of you: 'Now I know that you fear God.'"[108]

102. A. Miller's treatment of Isaac (*Untouched Key*, 137–45) in her book on childhood trauma tellingly starts from paintings of the scene rather than from the story in Genesis.

103. Childs, *Biblical Theology*, 334.

104. Cf. Kuruvilla, "*Akedah*," 498.

105. Moberly, *Bible, Theology, and Faith*, 92.

106. Brichto, *Names of God*, 289–90.

107. Levenson, *Death and Resurrection*, 141–42.

108. Origen, *Homilies on Genesis*, 143.

21
Birth and Death

(22:20–23:20)

Overview

"With the sacrifice of Isaac the test of Abraham's faith was now complete, and the purpose of his divine calling answered: the history of his life, therefore, now hastens to its termination."[1] First there is some news of his wider extended family that (among other things) alerts us to the existence of a young woman called Rebekah, who will become important in Gen. 24. Then there is news of Sarah's death, which leads into Abraham's acquisition of a final resting place for her and for himself and for Isaac, Rebekah, Leah, and Jacob.

Translation

22:20 Subsequently,[2] it was told to Abraham: "There, Milkah has given birth to children for your brother Nahor, too: **21**Uṣ his firstborn, Buz his brother, Qemuʾel the father of Aram, **22**Kesed, Hazo, Pildaš, Yidlap, and Betuʾel; **23**and Betuʾel has fathered Ribqah." To these eight Milkah gave birth for Nahor, Abraham's brother. **24**His secondary wife, her name was Reʾumah, also gave birth to Tebah, Gaham, Tahaš, and Ma'akah.

23:1 Sarah's lifetime was 127 years (the years of Sarah's life). **2**Sarah died at Arba Township (i.e., Hebron) in the country of Kenaʿan. Abraham came to lament for Sarah and cry for her. **3**Then Abraham set off from

1. Keil and Delitzsch, *Pentateuch*, 253.
2. See the footnote to 22:1.

being in the presence of his dead and spoke to the Ḥetites:[3] **4**"I'm a resident alien, a settler, living with you. Give me a burial holding with you, so I may bury my dead away from my presence." **5**The Ḥetites answered Abraham, saying to him,[4] **6**"Listen to us, sir. You're an almighty leader[5] among us. Bury your dead in the choicest of our burial places. None of us would withhold his burial place from you for burying your dead."

7Abraham got up and bowed low to the people of the country, to the Ḥetites, **8**and spoke with them: "If it's your desire that I should bury my dead away from my presence, listen to me and meet with Epron ben Ṣohar for me, **9**so he may give me the Double Cave[6] that is his and that is at the edge of his field. For the full silver may he give it to me among you as a burial holding." **10**Epron was sitting among the Ḥetites.

Epron the Ḥittite[7] answered Abraham in the ears of the Ḥetites, of all who came to the town gateway: **11**"No, sir, listen to me. The field—I am giving[8] it to you, and the cave that's in it. I am giving it to you, before the eyes of the members of my people I am giving it to you. Bury your dead." **12**Abraham bowed low before the people of the country **13**and spoke with Epron in the ears of the people of the country: "But if you yourself would please listen to me: I am giving you the silver for the field. Get it from me, so I may bury my dead there." **14**Epron answered Abraham, **15**"Sir, listen to me: land worth 400 sheqels—between me and you, what's that? Your dead: bury her." **16**Abraham listened to Epron.

So Abraham weighed out to Epron the silver that he had spoken of in the ears of the Ḥetites, 400 sheqels of silver, as current for the merchants.[9] **17**And Epron's field that is at Double, which is close to Mamre (the field and the cave that was in it and all the trees that were in the field, which were in all its border around), passed[10] **18**to Abraham as his acquisition before the eyes of the Ḥetites, of all who had come to the town gateway.

19After this Abraham buried his wife Sarah in the cave in the field at Double, close to Mamre (i.e., Hebron) in the country of Canaan. **20**So the

3. Literally, "the sons of Ḥēt"; only in speaking of Ephron himself in v. 10b does Genesis use the word *Ḥittî*.

4. For *lô* (which is almost unparalleled after *lēʾmōr*), SP and LXX imply *lōʾ*, "No!" which leads well into the next verse (cf. v. 11, though there, ironically, the LXX seems to lack the *lōʾ*) (cf. Tal, *Genesis*, 134*).

5. Literally, "a leader of God" or "God's leader" (cf. the usage in 30:8). An Israelite audience might take it more literally: cf. Abraham as God's friend (Isa. 41:8) (von Rad, *Genesis*, 243). The LXX has "king."

6. I follow the LXX, Vg, Tg in translating the name rather than transliterating it as Makpelah, which is supported by the fact that it has the article.

7. The resumptive naming of Ephron suggests the beginning of a new paragraph, following the circumstantial clause in v. 10a. The same applies within v. 16.

8. Ephron anticipatorily uses the declarative/performative qatal three times, suggesting a speech act, and Abraham follows in v. 13.

9. Hurowitz ("*kæsæp ʿober lassoḇer*") suggests background for this expression.

10. The verb *qûm*, literally, "arose"; so also in v. 20.

field and the cave that was in it passed to Abraham as a burial holding, from the Ḥetites.

Interpretation

The MT makes 22:20–24 and 23:1–20 the first two paragraphs of the three that comprise a unit, 22:20–24:67; for convenience I deal here with these first two together. The account of Nahor's offspring with its "Milkah, too" follows on from the account in Gen. 21 of Sarah's having her baby. It also prepares the way for the story about finding a wife for Isaac, which will be required if the reformulated promises in 22:15–18 are to find fulfillment; the wife will turn out to be Milkah's daughter.

The story in Gen. 23 starts from a question Abraham must face. When Sarah dies, it is an occasion of grief for Abraham, and he needs to express his grief (vv. 1–2). But the main question in Gen. 23 is different from the one that Western readers might assume. "It is remarkable that Moses, who relates the death of Sarah in a single word, uses so many in describing her burial."[11] The question that preoccupies Abraham is clear: where can Sarah be buried? Although many members of his clan must have died over the decades since his move to Canaan, Genesis raises the question at this point, in connection with Sarah, because of her importance to the plot of the bigger First Testament story and thus her importance to the audience. What has happened to their great original mother? Actually, they know the answer—they know her burial place near Hebron. How does she come to be buried there? The route from the question Abraham needs to face to the resolution, the audience thus knows, must inevitably be tricky. Abraham does not possess land in Canaan or, therefore, possess a proper burial place that could be a secure final resting place for Sarah. Somehow he must acquire one from the local people. What will the Hittites' attitude to him be? He knows a spot that would be appropriate. Will its owner be prepared to sell? How much will he ask?

According to traditional source criticism, Gen. 22:20–24 comes from the J version of Abraham's story and Gen. 23 from the P version.

22:20–24. Meanwhile back in Harran. . . . Although Abraham was commissioned to leave this family (see 11:27–29), it is still his family. Milkah and Nahor's son Betu'el and his granddaughter Rebekah will have continuing importance for him (see 24:15); there is also a neat link between the name of Nahor's grandson Aram and the town where the family lives (24:10). Though one might imagine the main list deriving from a report brought to Abraham, that one significant reference to a grandson suggests that the list is not simply a verbatim account of such a report, and the note about one of his sons and

11. Calvin, *Genesis*, 1:575.

his daughter (v. 23a) confirms that point. More likely the information about members of the family would derive from the expedition back to Aram Two-Rivers related in Gen. 24. Here, it trailers that story, though the interposition of the story of Sarah's death holds us in suspense for a while.

Maybe it is significant that there are twelve names, as in 17:20; 25:13–16; 35:22–26,[12] though those passages note the number twelve, and their lists are more straightforward. Outside Gen. 24, the names that are known from elsewhere are the names of towns or peoples—as are Nahor and Aram. They link with various parts of Arabia and Mesopotamia. Uṣ as a place name comes in, for example, 10:23; Jer. 25:20; Lam. 4:21; and Job 1:1. Buz appears in Jer. 25:23 and in Job 32:2, 6. The parallels with Job and his testing are noteworthy in the context of 22:1–19, with its account of a test (cf. Gen. Rab. 57). Someone called Keśed would be the ancestor of the Kaśdites: see 11:28. Maʿakah comes in Josh. 12:5. The passage is thus a throwback to the lists in Gen. 10–11, where names refer both to individuals and to places or peoples.

A secondary wife (*pîlegeš*) is not a concubine in the sense of a mistress or a woman with whom a man lives without being legally married to her, but a woman who is a legal wife but of a lower status and with fewer rights than a "primary wife"—for instance, her children have no inheritance rights (see 25:1–6).

23:1–2. The Abraham narrative continues to work its way toward its conclusion. Jewish interpretation was struck by the absence of Sarah from Gen. 22 and by this transition to the account of her death, and it filled in the gaps imaginatively: when Sarah heard that Isaac was going to be sacrificed, she died of shock.[13] As Genesis tells the story, another thirty-seven years have passed since Sarah gave birth to Isaac at the age of ninety, which implies up to a decade since the event in Gen. 22.

Sarah's dying in Hebron (v. 2) raises the question whether she was living in the clan settlement at Mamre while Abraham and Isaac and other members of their staff were shepherding in the Beer Sheba area. Women, after all, could have full lives and responsibilities of their own; marriage was a partnership (see Prov. 31:10–31). It would explain the sense in which Abraham "came" to mourn Sarah.[14] The alternative inference is that sometime between the events in Gen. 22 and Gen. 23 the entire settlement has moved (cf. Jub. 19.1). Arba Township (or Four Township)[15] is another pre-Israelite name for Hebron (for Arba, see Josh. 14:15; 15:13); it would be the name the Hittites would use. Genesis remarks that Sarah thus dies "in Canaan"; the comment is "unnecessary"

12. Cf. Rashi, *Brʾšyt*, 239.
13. Cf. Rashi, *Brʾšyt*, 242.
14. Rashi, *Brʾšyt*, 241.
15. Targum Neof. calls it "the town of the four ancestors," Adam, Abraham, Isaac, and Jacob; Gen. Rab. 58.4 suggests further identifications.

as a purely geographical note,[16] but it does indicate that she died in the promised land. She is the first person to be mourned in the First Testament, which befits her importance; Jacob is the only other person in Genesis to be mourned (50:10), and the account of that mourning shows what a significant public event it was.[17] By implication, Abraham's mourning was more personal to him, though it would still be outwardly expressed and thus public (see Ezekiel's account of mourning for his wife in Ezek. 24:16–17; further 2 Sam. 1:11–12; 3:31; Jer. 4:8; 16:5–7; 49:3; Joel 1:13; Mic. 1:8). Lamenting suggests the use of words, which are accompanied by tears. The reference to mourning here may imply that "Abraham fulfilled all righteousness in relation to Sarah so that now only the burial itself remains,"[18] but "lament and cry" constitute a most brief account of this mourning. "It is not the actual theme of Gen. 23."[19] While the mention of mourning is striking after the many references to death without reference to mourning in Gen. 1–22, the mention turns out to be just background to the focus on a burial place.

23:3–6. Shepherding peoples might not have fixed burial grounds, but Abraham wants one. What happens to the family's bodies matters. It matters on the assumption that death is the end; it also matters when you know that their bodies are to be raised to new life. Abraham was unconcerned about a place to sleep when he and Sarah and Isaac didn't need one; now things have changed.[20] His concern compares with the later desire of Jacob and Joseph, a wish to be buried in Canaan, the land Yahweh promised to give Abraham and his family.

For practical reasons, Abraham will need to act quickly to make burial arrangements (v. 3). Thus without undue delay he goes to talk to the Hittite men at the Hebron gateway; it need not imply that proper mourning is over. The Hittites are apparently a subgroup of Canaanites (cf. v. 2; and 10:15), the particular group that lives in the Hebron area, as the Jebusites live in the Jerusalem area. They appear most often in lists of peoples living in Canaan before Israel was there (e.g., Exod. 3:8, 17; 13:5). A great Hittite empire spread through eastern Turkey and northern Syria in the second millennium, but it did not extend this far south; these Hittites are either a subgroup of that empire who have somehow moved into Canaan, or a different group with a similar name. Abraham's friendly negotiation with them stands in some contrast with the promise that his descendants are going to take over their land (15:20).[21]

16. Wenham, *Genesis 16–50*, 126.

17. Jacob ironically and mistakenly mourns Joseph in 37:34–35, though the language there is different (*'ābal* rather than *sāpad*).

18. Gunkel, *Genesis*, 270.

19. Zimmerli, *1. Mose 12–25*, 120.

20. Cf. Luther, *Genesis 21–25*, 189–92, 198.

21. And cf. 22:17, just before (Brett, *Genesis*, 79).

Abraham of course is only a "resident alien" or "settler" in Canaan (v. 4). He combines two terms derived from verbs that have become familiar in Genesis (e.g., 19:9; 20:1; 21:23, 34; and 13:12, 18; 16:3; 19:29; 20:15). A "resident alien" (*gēr*; cf. 15:13) is someone who does not belong by right in a place; a "settler" (*tûšāb*) is someone who is nevertheless staying there semi-permanently. Added to the first noun, the second term would form the basis of Abraham's plea. For the audience, Abraham's asking for a "holding" (*ʾăḥuzzâ*) would be a significant request. God has already promised the country of Canaan to Israel as its holding (17:8), and within this holding each family later had its own holding (e.g., Lev. 25). It is within this prospective holding that Abraham and his audience know about (but the Hittites don't) that Abraham asks for somewhere to bury Sarah. He implies that the Hittites will share the assumption that corpses are taboo and that thus people cannot be buried next to living quarters. In asking that the Hittites may "give" him some land, he speaks euphemistically; he means "give it for money."

The Hittites are able to exploit the indirectness of Abraham's request (vv. 5–6). He has set in motion a set of "hard-nosed" but polite negotiations,[22] a "dance."[23] The Hittites are thus effusive, with a traditional society's gracious and generous courtesy. Their reply presupposes that they indeed have burial places separate from their settlement, for the same reason as Abraham wants one separate from his encampment. Even if he is legally a resident alien or settler, they are prepared to speak of him as a leader (*nāśîʾ*; cf. 17:20; 25:6) in that he is the head of his clan. They are thus treating him as someone of equal status to themselves (cf. the description of Shechem in 34:2). Yet their effusiveness conceals something by way of refusal, almost a "Not on your life."[24] Abraham has perhaps given too much away in drawing attention to his being a resident alien or settler. He wants a burial holding; but even as the head of a clan, how could a resident alien come to possess an actual holding? They agree only that he can have a place in one of their places. It is unlikely that they mean he can bury Sarah in one of their family tombs;[25] a family tomb is a family tomb. Perhaps they mean he can have the use of one of the caves in the area where they have their tombs, without any implication that he owns it. Might they assume that he will take her bones with him when he moves on (KSG; cf. 50:25)?

23:7–10a. Abraham is not put off and knows how to deal with the situation. So far, he and the Hittites have been sitting. Now Abraham gets up as the preliminary to bowing low (the verb that came in 22:5) to signify deference. Genesis now speaks of the Hittites as "the people of the country"; v. 10 will refer to "all who came to the town gateway," and v. 11 to "the members [*bənê*]

22. Blenkinsopp, *Abraham*, 178.
23. De La Torre, *Genesis*, 224.
24. Cf. Skinner, *Genesis*, 337.
25. Cf. Dillmann, *Genesis*, 2:154.

of my people." All these terms will refer to the citizenry of Arba Township as a whole, in the sense that "citizenry" would have had before the twentieth century in the United States—that is, it will refer to as many of the adult men as care or happen to be gathered at the town gateway. To this extent the government of Arba Township is democratic (Genesis makes no reference to a king), though not elected, and it is these people who have power to make decisions on matters concerning the community as a whole, such as questions about land.[26]

In reality Abraham knows exactly what he wants (v. 8). He has a specific piece of Hittite land in mind, not too far away from his settlement at Mamre (see v. 17). But he needs the leaders to meet (*pāgaʿ*) with Ephron for him, in the sense of mediating between them, to supervise his negotiation with Ephron. The names of Ephron and his father are Semitic (cf. 46:10; Josh. 15:9), which supports the idea that these Hittites are not connected with the Hittites to the far north.

A cave (v. 9) is the preferred location for a burial. While people could be buried in graves dug into the earth in the Western fashion, this was a second-class provision, unnecessary in a mountainous area where there are many caves. The ideal thing was a location where the entire family could be together in death as they were together in life. It was easy to adapt a cave to this end. Apparently Abraham has spotted one that would be okay, on the edge of a plot of land that Ephron farmed, and he offers to pay the market value. His mention of the price at the beginning of v. 9b (between occurrences of the polite verb "give"!) makes clear that he is talking about acquiring ownership of the cave, not just finding a spot for Sarah in a burial place he doesn't own. His reference to the edge of the plot emphasizes that he is not seeking to take over a huge tract of Hittite land. To Israelites, his coming into full possession of just a little bit of land in Canaan would nevertheless be important. Yet they might be brought up short by the idea of buying land. In Israel, in theory it was impossible to buy and sell land because it belonged to God and to the family, though Israelites had ways of getting around this rule.[27] The audience would understand the Hittites' reluctance to sell land and might even see it as something of a miracle that Abraham succeeded in buying some.

Ephron's ears prick as he sits among the men (v. 10a). As far as we know, this is the first he has heard of Abraham's plan.

23:10b–16aα. Whatever hesitations the Hittite assembly might have had, for one reason or another Ephron is prepared not to be held back by them. He speaks in the hearing of the citizenry (now differently described) because they do have the right to object to the conducting of such a transaction.

His reply (v. 11) works with conventions of negotiation in the culture, though it is difficult for us to know exactly what these conventions were.[28]

26. See S. Russell, "Abraham's Purchase."
27. Cf. De La Torre, *Genesis*, 224–26.
28. See MacDonald, "Driving a Hard Bargain."

Initially he may operate with an upside-down version of the way merchants may quote a price much higher than the one they are prepared to accept. Ephron says he is prepared simply to give Abraham the cave, and not only the cave but the field it's in. Perhaps Abraham had understated his request, and both sides knew that he would need more than the cave, or Ephron may be signaling that he will only sell the cave along with the field, or that he intends no more to give over full ownership of the land than the other Hittite leaders are prepared to do—he simply means he is giving Abraham burial space. If he makes a gift, he can then reclaim it.[29]

Abraham replies courteously but firmly (vv. 12–13) that he will of course give Ephron the value of the field. Paying for it will establish his permanent ownership. It will also mean he is no more in debt to the Hittites than he wanted to be to the Sodomites (14:22–23).[30] Metaphorically, perhaps literally, he is holding out the silver in his hand—money not having been invented, silver is the medium of exchange. He has come with his checkbook. Ephron must simply decide how much silver to take, what check to ask Abraham to write.

Ephron discreetly names his price (vv. 14–16aα). Perhaps he names an exorbitant amount, in the manner of a merchant, thinking it may put Abraham off or expecting Abraham to offer him rather less than he asks. David bought Araunah's threshing floor for fifty sheqels, Omri bought enough land to build a whole town for two talents or 6000 sheqels, and Jeremiah paid seventeen sheqels for a field (2 Sam. 24:24; 1 Kings 16:24; Jer. 32:9).[31] If so, Ephron's ploy fails. Abraham pays the asking price. Perhaps he has been careful with the thousand pieces of silver from Abimelek (20:16).

23:16aβ–18. The plaza at the town gateway is also the market, so weights would readily be available for Abraham to measure out the silver in accordance with the sheqel weight that the merchants used (the audience would likely assume a sheqel that weighed about four ounces). Evidently the town has more than one system of weights and measures, rather in the way that a liter or a gallon has different significance within different Western cultures, and as banks set the value of a currency differently according to whether someone is buying or selling. In Israel, the sanctuary sheqel was different from the market sheqel (see, e.g., Exod. 30).

So the field becomes Abraham's legal property (v. 18). The polite language of "giving" gives way to talk of "acquisition" (*miqneh*) from the verb that commonly suggests purchase.[32] The Hittite assembly has been there to witness the transaction, so there can be no dispute over it.

23:19–20. The question raised by vv. 1–2 (what is Abraham to do about burying Sarah?) is solved. The two verses comprise a double conclusion to

29. Cf. Sarna, *Genesis*, 157.
30. So Hamilton, *Genesis 18–50*, 129.
31. Hamilton, *Genesis 18–50*, 135.
32. Cf. Alter, *Genesis*, 112.

vv. 1–18. “Sarah’s burial in the promised land plants her in the future of the covenant.”[33] And “God’s word to Abraham that he would possess the land was fulfilled.”[34] Accepting the validity of the local peoples’ religion didn’t undermine the importance of gaining possession of land in Canaan.[35] Yet whereas God’s activity was prominent in 22:1–19 and will be prominent in the testimony of Abraham’s servant in Gen. 24, God is unmentioned in 22:20–23:20 except in the figure of speech in 23:6. “In the life of the people of God, so-called non-theological factors frequently play a role of a theological kind.”[36]

33. Reno, *Genesis*, 211.
34. Ibn Ezra, *Genesis*, 232.
35. See Cohn, “Negotiating (with) the Natives.”
36. Seebass, *Genesis*, 2.2:235.

22
A Wife for Isaac

(24:1–67)

Overview

More years have passed, Abraham is getting old, and Isaac needs a wife if Yahweh's promises to Abraham are to find fulfillment. Alongside the question of somewhere for the ancestors to rest in peace is the question of someone for Isaac to marry, so that he may indeed become the ancestor of many nations. And in consequence of Sarah's death, there is need of someone to take her place as matriarch of the family. So how did Abraham find a wife for Isaac? How did Rebekah, whom we know to have been born as a member of the extended family that Abraham had left behind (22:20–24), come to be Isaac's wife and Sarah's successor? The answer is that Abraham commissions his senior servant to go and find the right wife, and the servant experiences Yahweh's extraordinary providence in doing so. The story relates how this happens and how the question is resolved by answering a series of subquestions. Where should the matchmaker look (vv. 1–4)? What if the girl won't agree to the marriage (vv. 5–9)? How will the servant recognize the right girl (vv. 10–14)? When he thinks he has found her, what family does she belong to, and can he gain an entrée to it (vv. 22–28)? Will her family be willing for her to go to marry Abraham's son (vv. 29–53a)? Will she be willing to go (vv. 53b–61a)? When all the questions have been satisfactorily answered, the story can hasten to its happy conclusion (vv. 61b–67).

Translation

> [1]Abraham was a senior, going on in years, and Yahweh had blessed Abraham in every way. [2]Abraham said to his senior servant in his household,

who ruled over everything that he had, "Please put your hand under
my thigh, **3**and I'll get you to swear by Yahweh the God of the heavens
and the God of the earth that you won't get a wife for my son from the
daughters of the Kenaʿanites among whom I'm living, **4**because it's to my
country, to my homeland, that you're to go and get a wife for my son, for
Yiṣḥaq."

5The servant said to him, "Maybe the woman won't be willing to fol-
low me to this country. Should I actually get your son to go back[1] to the
country that you left?" **6**Abraham said to him, "Take care that you don't
get my son to go back there. **7**Yahweh, the God of the heavens, who
took me from my father's household and from the country that was my
homeland and spoke to me and swore to me: 'To your offspring I will give
this country'—he will send his envoy before you, and you will get a wife
for my son from there. **8**If the woman's not willing to follow you, you'll be
free from this oath to me. Only my son—don't take him back there." **9**The
servant put his hand under the thigh of Abraham his lord and swore to
him concerning this thing.

10The servant took ten camels from his lord's camels and went, with
all the good things belonging to his lord in his possession. He set off
and went to Aram Two-Rivers, to Nahor's town. **11**He got the camels to
kneel outside the town at the water well, at evening time, at the time
when the women who draw water go out. **12**He said, "Yahweh, God of my
lord Abraham, please make it happen for me today. Act with commitment
to my lord Abraham. **13**Here, I'm standing near the water spring, and the
daughters of the townspeople are going out to draw water. **14**May the
girl to whom I say 'Please tip your pitcher so I can drink,' and she says
'Drink, and I'll also water your camels'—may it be her that you've de-
cided on for your servant, for Yiṣḥaq. By this I will acknowledge that you
have acted with commitment to my lord."

15Before he'd finished speaking, there was Ribqah, who had been
born to Betuʾel ben Milkah, wife of Nahor, Abraham's brother, coming
out with her pitcher on her shoulder. **16**The girl was very good looking, a
young woman that no one had slept with.[2] She went down to the spring,
filled her pitcher, and went up. **17**The servant ran to meet her and said,
"Please let me drink down a little water from your pitcher." **18**She said,
"Drink, sir," and hurried and lowered her pitcher onto her hand and let
him drink. **19**She finished letting him drink and said, "I'll draw water for
your camels as well, till they've finished drinking." **20**She hurried and
emptied her pitcher into the trough, ran back to the well to draw, and
drew for all his camels **21**while the man was looking at her, staying quiet,
to know whether or not Yahweh had made his journey successful.

22When the camels had finished drinking, the man got a gold ring (its
weight a half sheqel) and two gold bracelets for her hands (their weight

1. The infinitive precedes the finite verb for emphasis: more literally, "taking back should I take back?"

2. Literally, "had known" (see the comment on 4:2).

ten sheqels). 23 He said, "Whose daughter are you? Please tell me, is there room at your father's house for us to stay the night?" 24 She said to him, "I'm the daughter of Betu'el ben Milkah, to whom she gave birth for Nahor." 25 And she said to him, "There's plenty of both straw and fodder with us, and also a place to stay the night." 26 The man bent his head, bowed low to Yahweh, 27 and said, "Yahweh, the God of my lord Abraham, be blessed, who hasn't abandoned his commitment and his truthfulness with my lord. I myself—Yahweh has led me on the way to the house of my lord's brothers!"[3] 28 The girl ran and told her mother's household all these actual things.

29 Now Ribqah[4] had a brother; his name was Laban. Laban ran out to the spring to the man. 30 When he saw the ring, and the bracelets on his sister's hands, and heard the words of his sister Ribqah, "This is how the man spoke to me," he came to the man. There he was, standing near the camels, near the spring. 31 He said, "Come in, you who are blessed by Yahweh. Why do you stand outside when I've cleared the house and a place for the camels?" 32 So the man came into the house. He unharnessed[5] the camels and gave straw and fodder to the camels and water to wash his feet and the feet of the men who were with him. 33 Something to eat was set[6] before him, but he said, "I won't eat until I've spoken my words." So he said, "Speak."

34 He said, "I am Abraham's servant. 35 In that Yahweh has greatly blessed my lord, he's become big. He's given him flock and herd, silver and gold, servants and maidservants, camels and donkeys. 36 Sarah, my lord's wife, gave birth to a son for my lord in her[7] old age, and he's given him everything that he has. 37 My lord got me to swear, saying 'You will not get a wife for my son from the daughters of the Kena'anites among whom I'm living in their country. 38 No, you're to go to my father's household, to my kin group, and get a wife for my son.'

39 "I said to my lord, 'Maybe the woman won't follow me.' 40 He said to me, 'Yahweh, before whom I've walked about—he will send his envoy with you and he will make your journey successful. You will get a wife for my son from my kin group. 41 Then you will be free from my imprecation when you come to my kin group, if they don't give her to you. You'll be free from my imprecation.'

3. The LXX, Tg have "brother," assimilating to v. 48.

4. The repeat of Rebekah's name suggests that a new paragraph begins here.

5. One would initially take the servant to be the subject of "unharnessed" and "gave," but it was not he who gave the water. One might then take the subject of these two verbs as impersonal, "someone." But the subject of the subsequent "he said" must be Laban, and it is simplest to take Laban as also the subject of "unharnessed" and "gave," which fits with his demonstrativeness in word and action in vv. 29–31. The LXX and SP have "they said" for the final verb, an easier reading.

6. The ketib implies qal passive *wayyîśem* (cf. 50:26; GKC 53u; 73f); the qere has hophal *wayyûśam* (Tal, *Genesis*, 138*).

7. The LXX and SP have "his."

42"So I came today to the spring and said, 'Yahweh, God of my lord
Abraham: if you could please be one who makes my journey that I'm
going on successful! 43Here, I'm standing by the water spring. May the
young lady who goes out to draw and to whom I say, "Please let me drink
a little water from your pitcher," 44and she says to me, "Drink, and I'll
also draw for your camels," may she be the woman that Yahweh has de-
cided on for my lord's son.'

45"I—before I'd finished speaking in my mind, there was Ribqah going
out with her pitcher on her shoulder. She went down to the spring and
drew. I said to her, 'Please give me a drink.' 46She hurried and lowered
her pitcher from on her shoulder and said, 'Drink, and I'll water your
camels as well.' So I drank, and she watered the camels as well. 47I
asked her, 'Whose daughter are you?' and she said, 'The daughter of
Betu'el ben Nahor, to whom Milkah gave birth for him.' I put the ring
on her nose and the bracelets on her hands, 48and I bent my head and
bowed low to Yahweh and blessed Yahweh the God of my lord Abraham,
who had led me on a true way to get the daughter of my lord's brother[8]
for his son.

49"So now: if you're going to act with commitment and truthfulness to
my lord, tell me. And if not, tell me, so I may turn my face to the right or
to the left."

50Laban and Betu'el answered,[9] "It's from Yahweh that the thing has
issued. We can't speak to you bad or good. 51Here is Ribqah before
you. Take her and go, so she can be a wife for your lord's son, as Yah-
weh has said." 52When Abraham's servant heard their words, he bowed
low to the ground before Yahweh. 53The servant brought out objects of
silver and objects of gold, and clothes, and gave them to Ribqah, and
he gave choice things[10] to her brother and to her mother. 54They ate
and drank, he and the men who were with him, and stayed the
night.

They got up in the morning, and he said, "Send me off to my lord."
55Her brother and her mother said, "The girl should stay with us for some
days—say ten.[11] Afterward, she can go." 56He said to them, "Don't make
me delay, in that Yahweh has made my journey successful. Send me
off so I can go to my lord." 57They said, "Let's call the girl and ask for
her bidding." 58They called Ribqah and said to her, "Will you go with this
man?" She said, "I'll go." 59So they sent Ribqah their sister off, with her
nanny and Abraham's servant and his men. 60They blessed Ribqah and
said to her, "Our sister, may you become thousands of myriads, and may

8. In the broad sense of "relative."

9. Literally, "Answered [singular] Laban and Betu'el, and said [plural]." For singular verb followed by plural subject, cf. v. 55; v. 61 is even closer since it has a singular verb followed by a plural verb.

10. Bar ("What Did the Servant Give?") suggests that *migdānōt* are specifically fruit.

11. Literally, "for days or ten." The expression is unclear. Targum Onq., for instance, has "a year, or [at least] ten months."

your offspring take possession of the gateway of people who are hostile to them." **61**Ribqah got up, she and her girls, and they mounted their camels and followed the man.

So the servant got Ribqah and went. **62**Now Yiṣḥaq had come from where you come to the Ḥay Roʾi Well;[12] he was living in the southland region. **63**Yiṣḥaq had gone out to think[13] in the open country, as evening turned its face. He lifted his eyes and saw: there, camels coming.

64Ribqah lifted her eyes and saw Yiṣḥaq and jumped down[14] from on the camel. **65**She said to the servant, "Who's that man walking in the open country about to meet us?" The servant said, "That's my lord." So she got her veil and covered herself. **66**The servant told Yiṣḥaq all the things that he'd done, **67**and Yiṣḥaq brought her into the tent (Sarah his mother's).[15] He got Ribqah and she became his wife, and he loved her, and Yiṣḥaq found consolation after his mother.

Interpretation

Genesis 24 tells its story at great length. It is the longest short story in Genesis, longer than the creation narrative or the account of God's making a covenant with Abraham,[16] and Gen. Rab. 60.8 notes the extraordinary phenomenon of its length, considering its lack of great significance for halakah. It has been described as a novella,[17] a short novel, though in regular English usage a novella is much longer, and that term better fits the Joseph story—which Gen. 24 does resemble in the way it portrays human actions and God's involvement with them.[18] Its length underscores the importance of finding a wife for Isaac in connection with the fulfillment of Yahweh's promises and purpose: see v. 7. Yet the story does not focus on that aspect of its significance, and in this sense it rather parallels accounts of how Jacob and Moses acquired wives. It contrasts with these narratives in telling its story with much repetition, which is one aspect of the way dialogue again dominates it. Repetition

12. "The Masoretic vocalization doesn't make much sense" (Tal, *Genesis*, 139*); the expression is tortuous. The words *bāʾ mibbôʾ bəʾēr* look as if they may reflect some dittography, but neither the versions nor modern scholarship suggests a consensus on what might have been a more original text.

13. I follow the LXX, Vg, and Tg in linking the hapax *śûaḥ* with *śîaḥ* I, which can mean talk or reflect, esp. reflect out loud (see *HALOT*, 1319–20). Other possibilities are that he was out for a walk (cf. v. 65; see *HALOT*, 1312) or that he was gardening (cf. *śîaḥ* II; see Ron, "Isaac's Personality").

14. On the use of *nāpal*, see the footnote to 14:10.

15. "Into the tent" (*hāʾōhĕlāh*) has the article (and then *-āh* indicating destination), so it is not construct; the genitive is periphrastic (see GKC 127f, which takes the bracketed phrase as a gloss).

16. Cf. Hamilton, *Genesis 18–50*, 138.

17. E.g., Gunkel, *Genesis*, 246.

18. Cf., e.g., Zimmerli, *1. Mose 12–25*, 127.

is one of the marks of folk narrative,[19] but it is also a feature of literary art.[20] Here, the repetition adds to its suspense and also ultimately underscores the involvement of Yahweh's providence in the process whereby the quest is successful. To put it in the terms of the etymology of the word "providence" and in the terms used in Gen. 22, the story relates how Yahweh "sees to it."[21] Another rhetorical feature characteristic of Genesis is its use of backtracking, describing an action and then going into reverse to describe what led to the action (see vv. 29b and 30, v. 67aα, and the rest of v. 67). It has many points of contact with the stories on either side, so it is hardly of independent origin, though in a nice contrast to later stories in which Rebekah and Laban are great schemers, here they are the objects of God's maneuvering.[22] In the terms of traditional source criticism, it comes from the J narrative about Abraham.

Though it is the only detailed scriptural account of the arranging of a marriage, Luther argues strongly that it does not aim to give instruction on how people in general should find a wife.[23] Yet it fits an emphasis in both Testaments that the people of God should marry within the "family" (see, e.g., Ezra 9:1–2; 2 Cor. 6:14–18). As Gen. 14 accepts the validity of the religion of other peoples but Gen. 23 presupposes that Israel's ancestors gain possession of land in Canaan, Gen. 24 presupposes the necessity in this connection for members of Abraham's family to marry within his wider family.[24] The issue raised by Gen. 24 is not merely ethnic or cultural identity.[25] In the First Testament there is no objection to a Moabite such as Ruth who commits herself to Yahweh and to Israel, and no objection to an Israelite such as Boaz marrying her.

Genesis 24 is also the only detailed account of an "ordinary" person's personal relationship with God, and while it appears in Genesis because of its significance in connection with the fulfillment of God's purpose, it represents in story form an understanding of that relationship that corresponds with teaching in Proverbs. In some respects it thus likely represents a vision of how one might expect that relationship to work. In the manner of Proverbs, it combines a stress on God's involvement guiding and granting success, on commitment and faithfulness on God's part and on that of human beings, on trust and on prosperity.

19. Olrik, "Epic Laws," 132–34.

20. See Alter, *Art of Biblical Narrative*, 88–113; Sternberg, *Poetics of Biblical Narrative*, 365–440.

21. See Barth, *CD* 3.3:3–4; Barth goes on to note (35) that this providence is, however, operating in connection with God pursuing his covenantal purpose.

22. See Wenham, *Genesis 16–50*, 137, 138.

23. Luther, *Genesis 21–25*, 218–99: Luther is especially concerned about clandestine betrothals and betrothal without parental approval.

24. See Cohn, "Negotiating (with) the Natives."

25. Contrast De La Torre, *Genesis*, 227–28.

24:1–4. According to the figures in Genesis, Isaac is nearly forty (25:20), Abraham is nearly 140 (17:17; 21:5), and it is two or three years after Sarah's death at 127. In our terms we might imagine Abraham as in his sixties and Isaac as in his late teens; if we think of Isaac as a little older, it might link with the possibility that Abraham is still at Mamre while Isaac is in the Negev (v. 62) and is thus absent from this scene. There is no suggestion that Abraham is near death (contrast the near-death scenes in 47:29–32; 50:24–25), and actually he still has thirty-five years to live (25:7); being senior and going on in years need not imply being about to die, as this commentator hopes (Abraham has already been described in these terms in 18:11). But in Genesis "the provision of a wife for Isaac is his last significant act before his death,"[26] as might be the case for this volume by this commentator. In the First Testament, some men arrange their own marriages (e.g., 26:34–35; 38:6), some involve their parents (e.g., 34:4; Judg. 14:1–7), and sometimes the parents take the initiative (e.g., Gen. 21:21; 38:6). The most conspicuous difference from betrothal scenes such as Gen. 29 and Exod. 2 is that the prospective groom is missing.[27] It's typical that Isaac should be acted upon rather than acting (cf. Gen. 22!).[28] But Abraham's action is not simply an instance of the pattern whereby parents take the initiative. In this story it's not going to be Abraham or Isaac who decides on the right girl for Isaac: it will be Yahweh who ensures that the quest comes out right. The recipient of Yahweh's commission and promises is taking action that relates to the fulfillment of these promises. Although in vv. 35–36 his servant will describe how Yahweh has blessed Abraham in every way, the main theme of the talk about blessing in the Abraham story (e.g., 12:1–2) conveys a promise that has not yet been fulfilled, and this chapter relates to that other blessing theme.

Once again we get the impression that Abraham is head of quite a clan (v. 2a). He doesn't abandon the settlement and the clan to undertake this long mission, and although Isaac will later send Jacob himself to find a wife, that action relates to Jacob's having endangered his own life. Abraham's commissioning a member of his staff to find a wife for his son parallels the action of Middle Eastern rulers.[29] Abraham would need someone efficient and trustworthy as his head of staff. The man is not an indentured, short-term servant of the kind that the rules in the Torah will seek to protect, but a permanent member of Abraham's household—like Hagar, though that analogy indicates the vulnerability of someone in this position. The portrait of masters and servants in nineteenth-century English novels may help to convey an impression of the relationship. He is servant and Abraham is master, but

26. Blenkinsopp, *Abraham*, 186.

27. Cf. Teugels, *Bible and Midrash*, 55.

28. Cf. Alter, *Art of Biblical Narrative*, 53; Alter notes that in this story and elsewhere Isaac contrasts with the hustling and bustling Rebekah.

29. Cf. Sasson, "Servant's Tale," 243–48.

it is a relationship of great trust on Abraham's part. If we were to think of Gen. 24 as a story about a slave, it is "the most beautiful slave narrative in the Old Testament."[30] We do not discover the head of staff's name, though it has been tempting to identify him with the Eliezer of 15:2;[31] the point about him is not his identity but the role he fulfills for Abraham. Even Isaac's name does not feature in the main body of the story except in the servant's prayer, and we are never told how the servant knows Rebekah's name, which he nevertheless uses in v. 45, while the name of her nanny does not appear in this chapter, only in 35:8. "The central interest of this narrative does not lie in concrete geographical references and personal names."[32] Only incidentally do we in due course discover that the servant takes other people with him on his mission (see v. 32).

The formal procedure that Abraham invokes (v. 2b) symbolizes the trust and vulnerability involved in the commission Abraham is about to give his servant. The action implies grasping Abraham's genitals, the source of his procreative activity (cf. 46:26; and for swearing an oath in this way, 47:29). Abraham is making himself vulnerable to his servant, and his servant is being admitted to the utter privacy of his master's body, so that in effect he is taking an oath on his master's body and on his capacity for life, the capacity he had exercised in fathering Isaac (if the practice implied a link with circumcision and the covenant,[33] one would expect a more explicit reference to such a link).

Swearing in God's name (v. 3a) requires a correlative form of vulnerability on the servant's part and makes possible Abraham's entrusting this key task to him. In agreeing to undertake the task, the servant is asking for Yahweh to act against him if he fails to do as he promises. On one hand Abraham speaks of Yahweh—anachronistically, as usual, but the name signifies that he is referring to the real God as Israel will know him and to God as the one who is involved in a special way with him in order to fulfill a purpose through his offspring. He also speaks of this God as the God of the whole cosmos, using terms reminiscent of Melchizedek's words, which Abraham also took up—there too he prefaced them with the name *Yahweh* (14:19, 22). Like the creation story and the Melchizedek story, Gen. 24 presupposes that Yahweh is the only God who really deserves to be called God.[34] The good news for the servant is that Yahweh as the God of the heavens and the earth holds sway in Mesopotamia as much as in Canaan. The phrase "the God of the heavens and the God of the earth" comes only here (24:3), though Ezra 5:11 has "God of the heavens and of the earth" in Aramaic.

30. Zimmerli, *1. Mose 12–25*, 129.
31. So, e.g., Tg. Ps.-J.; contrast Dillmann, *Genesis*, 2:160.
32. Zimmerli, *1. Mose 12–25*, 129.
33. So, e.g., Tg. Ps.-J.
34. Cf. Arnold, *Genesis*, 218.

Abraham's description of the partner he seeks for Isaac (vv. 3b–4) implies the principle of endogamy; one marries someone from one's own ethnic group. Anglo Americans mostly marry Anglo Americans; African Americans mostly marry African Americans. Problem one in getting Isaac a wife, then, is that she needs to come from his extended family, which is a long distance away. But the mention of the Canaanites implies a more specific point. For the audience the chief problem with Canaanites is their offensive practices, such as the sacrifice of children, though also the broader danger that through assimilation Israel would die out as a distinctive entity belonging to Yahweh and committed to a distinctive vocation from Yahweh. Though the stories of people such as Melchizedek suggest that Abraham's clan had less reason to be hesitant about the inhabitants of Canaan than the Israelites later had, for such listeners there was indeed reason to be wary about marrying Canaanites. Abraham's attitude would match the one widely taken in the First Testament. Admittedly, Genesis does not make this point,[35] and if Abraham is wishing to avoid religious compromise arising from Isaac's marriage, people living back in Harran might not seem much like an improvement over Canaanites. They surely served other deities; Yahweh had not been involved with them. But the ease with which not only the servant speaks of Yahweh before them (vv. 35, 40, 42, 44, 48, and 56) but they also speak of Yahweh to him (vv. 31, 50, and 51) suggests that the story's perspective is that Abraham need not worry about religious contamination from a wife with that background. Nor need he worry that he is moving outside the family within which Yahweh is at work, fulfilling his purpose to bring blessing to his family and to the world.

24:5–9. The servant points out problem two. While no one raises the question whether Isaac should have a say over who he marries, his potential bride will have a say. What if she won't play ball? It's not that she won't fancy Isaac, whom she will not see initially, but that she won't fancy leaving Mesopotamia for Canaan. Maybe Isaac therefore must go back to live in Mesopotamia? Which is more important, to marry within the extended family or to stay in Canaan?

There's no doubt about the answer to that question (vv. 6–7). Abraham states a third principle for identifying a marriage partner: as well as endogamy and avoidance of the Canaanites, there is the importance of living in light of Yahweh's promise of the land. Isaac is to be unique among Israel's ancestors for having Yahweh designate his wife, for praying for his wife to have a baby—and for never leaving the promised land.[36] Yahweh brought Abraham to Canaan with the intention that his offspring should possess this country. Abraham picks up the terms "father's household" and "homeland" from 12:1, but in using them he underlines the fact that endogamy itself is not enough.

35. Cf. Cohn, "Negotiating (with) the Natives."
36. Cf. Sasson, "Servant's Tale," 242.

The person Isaac marries must also be someone who identifies with this project of Yahweh's. Yahweh did not literally swear an oath to give the country to Abraham's offspring (Yahweh's only actual oath came in 22:15–18), but he did promise it, and for Yahweh there is no difference. When Yahweh speaks, an oath only buttresses the confidence of the recipient of the promise. Abraham knows that God made that promise, and he apparently also knows that Isaac needs to marry someone from back home (notwithstanding her mention in 22:20–24, no one seems to know about Rebekah at this stage in this story,[37] though that mention enables the audience to put two and two together). And Abraham has enough experience of Yahweh getting involved with him and his family to be able to extrapolate how Yahweh will ensure that the two aspects of his intention find fulfillment (see 16:7–12; 22:11–18). It is still quite a statement of trust. "In complete and perfect faith" he affirms that "those heavenly spirits and princes are engaged in this seemingly insignificant, carnal, and foolish work."[38] So the readers know who the servant will find, though not how he will find her; Abraham doesn't know who he will find, but he knows how he will find her.[39] The gloss on the name Yahweh that Abraham uses here, "the God of the heavens," has nearly all its parallels in Ezra, Nehemiah, and Daniel (e.g., Ezra 7:21, 23; Neh. 1:4–5; Dan. 2:18–19); it is perhaps a sign that the story gives Aramaic coloring to its story set in Aram.[40] Thus God is once again the guarantee that the servant's mission to this faraway land can be successful. He is not active only in this land.

Abraham recognizes that God does not usually compel people to fulfill his purpose (vv. 8–9). Yet Abraham has taken his initiative, and he is confident that God's leading will respond.[41] Rebekah will make her decision. The servant will have done his part.

24:10–14. One might have assumed that Abraham was sending off the servant on his own, but it is not so. Arranging a marriage requires gifts to seal or deepen the relationship between the two families, comparable to the gift-giving and celebratory meal at a Western wedding. When someone wants to take a girl a long distance away, and when the head of the household is someone as prosperous as Abraham, substantial gifts are needed, though "all the good things" is a hyperbole; it perhaps implies "examples of all the good things." Both the camels and their cargo demonstrate Abraham's wealth and prosperity to another family from whom he is seeking a wife for his son. In due course the camels will transport the women whom the servant brings home (cf. v. 61) and perhaps in the meantime the men who accompany the servant (v. 32), but they also carry the gifts for the prospective bride's family.

37. Cf. Sternberg, *Poetics of Biblical Narrative*, 133.
38. Luther, *Genesis 21–25*, 253.
39. Cf. Sternberg, *Poetics of Biblical Narrative*, 136.
40. See Rendsburg, "Some False Leads."
41. Cf. Fretheim, "Genesis," 510.

The brisk summary of the servant's journey doesn't make clear to Western readers that the distance is several hundred miles, so the journey would take several weeks (from the "today" of v. 42, Gen. Rab. 59.11 infers that God miraculously caused it to take only one day to get there, and at v. 61 Tg. Ps.-J. similarly has it taking only one day to get back). Aram of the Two Rivers is a Hebrew expression equivalent to the Greek name Mesopotamia, but it refers in particular to the northwestern part of Mesopotamia, equivalent to northern Syria and northern Iraq. The two rivers are not the Euphrates and the Tigris but the Euphrates and its tributary the Khabur.[42] Though there is a town called Nahor, it is more natural to assume that "Nahor's town" is Harran (cf. 27:43) and that the servant knows to go there. But problem three now arises: Will he be able to find the right girl?

He happens to arrive in the evening (v. 11). The camels have perhaps not drunk since they left home. While their need for water thus suggests one reason for stopping at the well and kneeling so as to be able to drink, another is that (like the town gateway) the well is a place to meet people as the cool of evening arrives and thus a place for the servant to discover if he can locate Abraham's extended family. Drawing water is usually the task of young women (cf. 1 Sam. 9:11), but in 29:1–8 male shepherds (from Harran) are just hanging about near a well, killing time.

It is a strategic moment for the servant to pray (v. 12). "Looking for a bride is a difficult matter—doubly difficult if one is supposed to choose a bride for another, but superhumanly difficult if the servant is seeking her for his young master."[43] The servant addresses Yahweh in yet a further way, as Abraham's God. It is the first occurrence of such a description (cf. 26:24; 28:13; 31:42, 53; also Ps. 47:9). Expanded to incorporate reference to Isaac and Jacob, it will link the ancestors' story with the exodus (Exod. 3:6, 15, 16; 4:5; later, 1 Kings 18:36; 1 Chron. 29:18; 30:6). Its implication is that Yahweh relates to the clan head in a way that also benefits the clan itself. The servant can himself address this God, so the idea is not that Abraham is like a priest through whom an ordinary person has to go to communicate with God. Rather, he can make Yahweh's being Abraham's God the basis for a prayer that God may do what Abraham needs. Abraham, after all, is his master, and his mission is undertaken for Abraham, in connection with the fulfillment of God's promise to him. The action he seeks will be an expression of Yahweh's commitment (*ḥesed*);[44] it is the first reference to Yahweh's commitment in Genesis. For his own sake Yahweh needs to act as the servant says, because of the kind of person Yahweh is. The prayer involves a creative linguistic usage. He asks for God to "make something happen," a

42. Cf. BDB 74b. But *naharayim* may be only a quasi-dual (cf. GKC 88c), equivalent to *Naḥrima* in the Amarna Letters (cf. Wenham, *Genesis 16–50*, 143).

43. Gunkel, *Genesis*, 251.

44. See the comment on 19:19.

paradoxical request since talk of things "happening" points away from the idea of causation.

The servant's own confidence in God finds further expression in the prayer's bold specificity (vv. 13–14). It is unparalleled elsewhere in the Scriptures. While prayers by Gideon, Elijah, and Isaiah are near counterparts, they don't relate directly to a task or to something that another person will need to do. Jonathan's ploy in 1 Sam. 14, which relies on Yahweh's making things work out, requires the Philistines to react in the right way, but it doesn't involve a prayer. The notion that Yahweh has decided on a specific bride for Isaac is a new feature in the story, which adds tension to the servant's task. The servant adds further motivation for Yahweh's answering the prayer. As well as being an *expression* of Yahweh's commitment, it will also be *evidence* of this commitment. It will lead to Yahweh's commitment being known and to his being acknowledged as this kind of God. Further, it will mean that the camels function in the story not only as markers of Abraham's wealth but also as a test of a prospective bride's worthiness to share in it.[45]

24:15–21. Whereas in folktales the right person often emerges only after a couple of false starts (cf. 1 Sam. 16; 1 Esd. 3–4), and in Josephus (*Ant.* 1.16.2) other girls refuse the servant, in this story she emerges immediately.[46] The speed with which an answer comes indicates the wonderful nature of Yahweh's answer and the evidence of his commitment to Abraham. The story provides a concrete embodiment of Isa. 65:24 (Gen. Rab. 60.4 also compares Num. 16:31 and 2 Chron. 7:1). It was an outrageous prayer, but God was okay with it. The family description of Rebekah harks back to 22:20–24, though the servant still does not yet know these facts about her. But what he can see fits the ideal requirements. The servant could perhaps tell from her dress that she was not married. The spring was evidently down some steps, and the servant watches her go down and come back up with her pitcher in brisk, businesslike fashion. It is not the last indication that Rebekah is not someone who messes around.[47]

The servant's request (vv. 17–20) soon establishes that she has the character to go with her looks and marital status. His own running indicates his urgent desire to see if his prayer is finding its answer and his journey thus meeting with success. His prayer has not asked that the first girl who shows up will be the right one, but that the first girl who agrees to give him a drink and also offers on her own initiative to water the camels will be the right one. Giving someone a little water would be a small thing. Drawing for the camels would be a huge undertaking; if they have not drunk for weeks, their capacity would be gargantuan. Initially she offers only a drink for him, which raises

45. Cf. Sternberg, *Poetics of Biblical Narrative*, 137.
46. Cf. Sternberg, *Poetics of Biblical Narrative*, 137.
47. On the characterization of Rebekah, see Gillmayr-Bucher, "Woman."

suspense—maybe she's not the right girl. But then, unprompted, she comes through with her special offer.

"While Rebekah is doing this back-breaking work" (v. 21), the servant is "gazing at her wondering."[48] The girl didn't respond in words in quite the way he prescribed, but she acted in the way prescribed. "Rebekah is a woman of deeds rather than of words. . . . In this she is a counterbalance of the servant who hardly ever stops talking."[49] As she acted, "he sipped the water and stared at her, asking 'whether the Lord had prospered his journey or not'" (Gen. Rab. 60.6). The answer to the question is unfolding before his eyes as she waters the camels. But problem four now arises: what family does she belong to, and will they welcome him?

24:22–28. The gifts show recognition of the generous and monumental nature of the task she has undertaken; they might or might not imply something more. They are lavish, but they are nothing compared with the rest of what the camels are carrying.

The gifts also prepare the way (vv. 23–25) for further questions. To Rebekah, the first question would come across not just as inquisitiveness (what right does he have to ask?) but as the lead-in to the second question. One might imagine that there would be an inn in Harran, but the servant is working with the assumption that traditional peoples accept an obligation to show hospitality to wayfarers if they can (cf. 19:1–2).[50] The replies to the questions first let the servant in on the secret that the audience knows from 22:20–24 and then establish that the servant and his entourage have found their hospitality.

So his prayer has been answered (v. 26). While lifting the head is a common posture for praise and prayer, bowing the head is an alternative (e.g., Exod. 4:31; 12:27; 34:8). Like bowing the knee, it is a sign of obeisance, to a human being or to God. As well as bowing his head, the servant bows his whole body. It is a sign that the whole person is submitting and doing obeisance, to a human being or to God—a sign to God, a sign to other people, and a sign to oneself.

The God of Abraham indeed deserves praise (v. 27). To declare out loud that God is blessed is likewise a way of acknowledging something to him, saying something in oneself, and glorifying him before other people with one's words; the use of words gives it more specific content. To commitment the servant adds truthfulness (*ʾĕmet*), another word appearing for the first time in Genesis; it adds force to "commitment." The two words commonly appear together and reinforce each other as a hendiadys, truthful commitment or committed truthfulness (e.g., 47:29; Exod. 34:6; Pss. 25:10; 57:3, 10 [57:4, 11]; 61:7 [61:8]). While *ḥesed* denotes "an act which one is not obligated to

48. T. Schneider, *Mothers of Promise*, 52.

49. Teugels, *Bible and Midrash*, 95.

50. Penchansky ("Staying the Night") notes the comparison and contrast between the use of this verb (*lîn*) in Gen. 24 and Gen. 19.

perform," *ʾĕmet* denotes keeping the promise to act in *ḥesed*.[51] Yahweh has expressed that committed truthfulness to Abraham by leading his servant to the house where Abraham's family lives.

Rebekah too runs to tell the family (v. 28). Explicitly it's her mother's household (cf. Ruth 1:8; Song 3:4; 8:2), as opposed to her father's (e.g., Gen. 38:11; Num. 30:16). It's natural for a girl to go and talk to her mother about what has just happened: "A woman feels at home only in the house of her mother" (Gen. Rab. 60.7).[52] Her father does appear in v. 50, but only secondarily to her brother Laban, and it's Laban who comes out to meet the servant in v. 29. For practical purposes he seems to be head of the family. Such "fratriarchy" is known from other traditional societies, though it may be that Bethuel is old and leadership in the family has thus passed to Laban.

24:29–33. Laban runs, too, but here Genesis relates events in nonchronological order, for dramatic effect. First Laban sees Rebekah's adornments and hears everything from her. Next he makes room for the servant, his companions, and the camels. Then he runs out. The servant has been standing by the well all this time; Laban thus hastens to invite him to the house. The affirmation "blessed by Yahweh" is a good description of his master (see vv. 1 and 35), of which the camels and their cargo (v. 10) as well as the gifts to Rebekah give plentiful evidence; apparently the servant is treated as sharing in that glory. Like anyone else in Genesis, Laban would not actually use the name *Yahweh*, but the narrative treats him as a true adherent of the God of Abraham. There's no suggestion of a negative characterization of Laban, such as will appear in Gen. 31.[53]

In the house's courtyard or outbuildings (vv. 32–33) there are surely stalls for donkeys, camels, and other animals, and in the house the practicalities of hospitality are to be observed. The servant allows the practicalities that benefit the camels and his companions, and washing his feet might be a considerate gesture. But a meal can take a while, and he has things he must say.

24:34–49. He introduces himself in terms of his relationship with his family, like Rebekah (v. 24),[54] but the narrative still doesn't tell us his name. "Blessing" is something that is "great" by definition; only here does the expression "greatly blessed" occur. The itemizing of the blessing indicates that the ten camels with their loads, and the gifts he has made to Rebekah, are only the tip of the iceberg; the servant makes the important point that Rebekah's prospective but unwitting suitor is the designated heir to all this wealth (though Genesis itself will not say so until 25:5). For economy, there would be no need to include what the servant said, which repeats what we already know, but repeating it underscores its significance, and the servant

51. Ibn Ezra, *Genesis*, 239.

52. But what of Gen. 29:12? Genesis Rabbah asks and then answers that her mother was dead.

53. See Teugels, *Bible and Midrash*, 114–18.

54. Cf. Hamilton, *Genesis 18–50*, 150.

varies the account slightly, though at some points tellingly.[55] Rebekah is now a young lady (*ʿalmâ*) rather than a young woman (*bətûlâ*)[56]—elsewhere the story usually describes her as a girl (*naʿărâ*). The words "father's household" and "kin group" now appear; the servant is appealing to a family relationship. It's the family rather than the girl that must agree to the match. There's no mention of the need to avoid taking Isaac back to Harran. Yahweh is the one before whom Abraham has walked about (cf. 17:1). The oath becomes an imprecation (that is, the curse that constitutes the sanction attached to the oath), and the servant reverses his questioning Rebekah about her family and his giving her the gifts. He says that he blesses Yahweh as the one who has led him on a true way. One effect of his story might be to apply a little religious blackmail to Rebekah's family.[57]

After giving his account of what has happened, the servant poses his question (v. 49), problem five in the story. The long retelling of what we already know also functions to raise suspense. When will we discover whether the family will agree to let Rebekah go and marry Isaac? The servant speaks now of their commitment and truthfulness (the "you" is plural). If it is not forthcoming, he will need to look elsewhere.

24:50–54a. The family can recognize Yahweh's involvement as readily as the servant can. Laban is prominent in the response, as he was in the practicalities of vv. 29–33, where Bethuel was not even mentioned (cf. the involvement of Dinah's brothers in Gen. 34 and of Tamar's brother in 2 Sam. 13).[58] Brother and father are the authoritative figures in the family (but more brother than father) and can speak for it, but they recognize that they really have no option. In light of what the servant has told them, they can say nothing ("bad or good" is a merism for "anything"). "Here is Rebekah before you" expresses the family's agreement to the marriage proposal made to it, perhaps in a conventional formula.

Once more the servant has reason to bow before Yahweh (vv. 52–53), even lower than he did in v. 26. He gives the betrothal gifts to the bride; these are apparently different and more substantial gifts than the ones he gave her when he met her and when she acted so thoughtfully. Her receiving them signifies her acceptance of the marriage proposal. The servant also gives gifts to Rebekah's brother and mother, who is also thus again mentioned though never named. Genesis 34:12 will also speak of these two forms of gift, using the technical terms for them as this passage does not.[59]

The men (v. 54a) then celebrate.

55. See van Wolde, "Telling and Retelling"; Teugels, *Bible and Midrash*, 69–90.

56. It's hard to make a distinction between these two Hebrew words (cf. Hamilton, *Genesis 18–50*, 146–47); neither specifically denotes a virgin.

57. Cf. Sternberg, *Poetics of Biblical Narrative*, 148: he calls it moral blackmail.

58. Cf. Keil and Delitzsch, *Pentateuch*, 260.

59. See further the comment on 34:12.

24:54b–61a. It might seem inappropriately hasty to want to leave so soon, but it would be natural for the servant to want to get back with his good news (and his find) as quickly as possible.

In due course Rebekah gets her say (vv. 57–58). Her accepting the betrothal gifts has indicated that she is prepared to go to marry Isaac. Problem six is whether she is prepared to go now. Yet her declaration "I'll go" also takes up the verb Yahweh used in setting Abraham on his move from Harran to Canaan (12:1, 4); she is making her commitment to join in the project Yahweh set going in commissioning Abraham.[60] Dramatically, until this point the story thus holds back giving her opportunity for acquiescence in words. "From here [it is derived] that a woman may not be given in marriage unless it is with her consent."[61]

Likewise, the blessing that leads into her departure (vv. 59–61a) has some parallels with Yahweh's original blessing of Abraham and with the restatement of that blessing in 22:17: it recognizes that Rebekah may be subject to attack and prays for her to do more than survive. Unwittingly, she has made a commitment like Abraham, and they pray that she will be blessed like Abraham.

24:61b–67. Again the story jumps quickly over a journey that takes several weeks. After the opening resumptive sentence, the focus and point of view move to Isaac. We look through his eyes at the approach of a camel train; we know better than he does that he is about to meet his mail-order bride.[62] The geography continues to be equivocal. Has Abraham been based near Beer Sheba ever since 22:19 (with Sarah living her last days, dying, and being buried in the family settlement in the Hebron area in Gen. 23)? Or did Abraham move to the family settlement in the Hebron area sometime after 22:19 so that Isaac alone is based near Beer Sheba? Either way, it's odd that Sarah's tent is in the Negev. Ironically, Isaac is in the vicinity of the well where Yahweh first met with Hagar (16:14) but where 25:11 suggests he has settled. He is apparently not out with the sheep; by evening he would have brought them home after watering them at the well. It wouldn't be surprising if he were then out walking and thinking and praying about his father's servant's mission or about the loss of his mother.[63] The way the story speaks of the servant's relating to God would fit with its implying such an assumption about Isaac (who will appear as someone who prays in 25:21). It also fits with the First Testament's assumption that dawn and dusk are the times for worship, sacrifice, and prayer. Whatever he is doing, the narrative's "there" draws us into looking through his eyes as the caravan approaches.

Meanwhile the point of view returns to Rebekah (v. 64). As Isaac lifts his eyes and sees, so she lifts her eyes and sees, and now we watch the approach of

60. Cf. Sarna, *Genesis*, 161.
61. Rashi, *Br'šyt*, 262.
62. De La Torre, *Genesis*, 231.
63. Cf. Vall, "What Was Isaac Doing?"

the meeting through her eyes. Alighting from the camel before she meets Isaac would be the polite thing to do. Jumping off the camel, when she is dressed as she would be, is quite an achievement (cf. and contrast 1 Sam. 25:23); the expression is another way of conveying the commitment and energy with which people act in this story.

Again the sentences follow a dramatic order (v. 65): presumably she has asked her question, received her answer, and put on her veil before making her jump. The servant describes Isaac as "my lord," and the close of the story makes no reference to Abraham, who was the servant's lord at the beginning and has been the servant's lord all the way through the story, but it would be overly dramatic (or underdramatic) to infer that Abraham has died by now without our being told. Apart from the consideration that the next chapter implies that he has many more years to live, the statement in v. 67 would be odd if Abraham is also dead. If Abraham is the servant's lord, then so is his son; either Abraham is at Hebron but Isaac is farther south, or Abraham is at Beer Sheba and Isaac is elsewhere in the Negev. Dramatically, the point is that Abraham sets the story going, both because it is his promise and because he is the father with responsibility for his son's marriage, but Isaac closes the story, because the broader narrative is in the midst of transferring its focus to him. Abraham and Sarah are the past, Isaac and Rebekah are the future, and the servant (whose role is more important than his name) mediates the move from one generation to the next.[64] There is no indication that Israelite women generally wore veils. In the First Testament's only other use of this word for veil (38:12–19), it functions to disguise the wearer. But the wearing of a veil at a marriage is implied in the also puckish story about Jacob's marriage (29:21–25); so Rebekah acts like the prospective bride that she is.[65]

The focus moves to the interaction between the servant and Isaac (v. 66). For some reason the story does not provide us with a third detailed but varying account of everything that happened as the servant fulfilled his mission. Nor is there is any conversation or even meeting between Isaac and Rebekah. Western readers might think that problem seven now will be whether they will like each other when they meet, and will the marriage therefore happen. That question barely surfaces.

Instead (v. 67) the story jumps forward to its happy ending, related from Isaac's angle. In effect, Rebekah and her family have already provided their answer to that question, sight unseen. Insofar as Isaac has any wiggle room in light of the action his father took and the action his servant took, this final verse provides his upbeat, positive answer to the question. The close of the story again works dramatically, not chronologically. Eventually Isaac gets Rebekah to take over Sarah's tent, which establishes her as matriarch of

64. Cf. Sarna (*Genesis*, 161), who notes that symbolically v. 34 is the chapter's middle verse.
65. Cf. Sarna, *Genesis*, 170.

the family in Sarah's place. On the way to that end, Isaac claims her and she becomes his wife; in other words, they get married, presumably with a great wedding celebration. And he loves her. Love naturally follows rather than precedes marriage when the marriage is arranged. It is the first man-woman love in Genesis. Isaac becomes someone who loves as well as someone who is loved (22:2).[66] And finally, with Rebekah in his mother's tent, he finds consolation (had he been especially close to Sarah because he had lived with her while Abraham was away shepherding elsewhere?). It's not the same as the abandoning of mother and father in 2:24, though it recalls it.

Implications

Seeking the Fulfillment of God's Purpose

As it's tricky to move from an "is" to an "ought," so it's tricky to move from a narrative to a generalization, from "Abraham/his servant acted thus" to "one should act thus," or from "God acted thus" to "God acts thus." In considering some implications of Gen. 24, for the most part I therefore retain its narrative form. It's impossible to know whether we may expect God to act as he did in this story, but a story may open up possibilities.

Abraham cannot bring about the fulfillment of the purpose that God has initiated or the promises that God has made. But there is a step he can take to open up the possibility of that fulfillment (vv. 1–4). While sometimes God instructs his people about action they should take (Gen. 12:1), sometimes they properly take initiatives in light of past instructions that establish the framework within which they are to act. There have been occasions when Abraham took an initiative that arguably did not meet that criterion, and things have gone wrong. There have been occasions when Abraham took action that had an ambiguous relationship with God's past instructions, and things have gone right. And there have been occasions when Abraham took an initiative that had an ambiguous relationship with God's past instructions, and things have gone wrong. The stories offer no surefire formula for actions that fit into God's purpose and will lead to blessing rather than trouble.

Abraham's response to his servant's initial worry recognizes this aspect of the dynamic of relationships with God. On one hand, he promises that God's envoy will guide his servant. The story gives us no basis for this reassurance except a general trust in God to facilitate Abraham's action that is designed to ensure that he does live in the context of God's instructions. Abraham does not say that God has promised that the envoy will accompany his servant, and the story does not suggest that the envoy does so in the interventionist and unmistakable way that envoys have previously operated in the Abraham

66. Cf. Brayford, *Genesis*, 342.

story. This envoy will be behind the scenes, acting via coincidences and via the process of human decision making. Abraham thus recognizes the tension and the ambiguity involved in God's acting in this way. God may be able to manipulate coincidences, but he doesn't manipulate human decision making in the sense of forcing people to do things against their will. So he may guide the servant to the ideal girl, but she may say "No."

The servant, too, takes initiatives and then asks God to work with them, as opposed to asking God for guidance regarding what he is to do and then himself working with that guidance. His prayer presupposes God's capacity to "make things happen," even though it is practically an incoherent idea. "Time and chance happen to all," whether or not they are quick, strong, smart, discerning, or knowledgeable (Eccles. 9:11). "Making something happen" (*qārâ* hiphil) is thus close to being an oxymoron. Of the other two occasions when the First Testament uses the expression, once it is something that does not require human cooperation (Num. 35:11), and once it's when Isaac's son is lying to him (Gen. 27:20). But the servant backs up his implausible prayer with an appeal to God's commitment (*ḥesed*) to Abraham and thus to the fact that he addresses Abraham's God. The servant's prayer makes clear that he himself has a direct personal relationship with God. But the basis for his appeal is the link between this particular prayer and the purpose God is pursuing though Abraham. The petition "make this happen for me" is framed on both sides with this fact. Only superficially is he praying for himself; he is praying for Abraham's sake and for Isaac's sake and even more for God's own sake. Sometimes God makes things happen in a way that defies regular explanation. Sometimes God does work through coincidences and human decision making.

God answers the prayer and "makes it happen," with just a little slippage, illustrating two aspects of the significance of prayer, both of which raise systematically irresolvable questions. First, the Scriptures imply two considerations about prayer itself that are in irresolvable tension. God encompasses all time, and all time is open to God; what is the unexperienced future to human beings is accessible to God. But prayer can make God do things he would not otherwise do and abandon things he would do—make him have a change of mind, as the Scriptures put it. Genesis 24 illustrates the genius of narrative theology in that it does not seek to explain how the two considerations fit together, but it does tell a story that illustrates their interweaving. The servant prays; God answers his prayer, which thus has made a difference; but the answer comes before he even finishes praying, which reflects how all time is open to God.

Second, the Scriptures imply two considerations about the relationship between God making things happen and human beings making things happen, which are also in irresolvable tension. The servant asked for God to bring it about that a certain girl should come to the well and by her words identify herself as God's choice for Isaac, and God did so—which shows that he can bring it about that people do as he decides without their realizing that they are fulfilling this role. Yet Rebekah had set out for the well before the servant even began to pray, let alone before he finished praying, and she did so (to infer something from the story's silence) just because she decided to, in keeping with her daily routine, rather than because she sensed a divine prompting. The slippage features in her not quite behaving as the servant prescribed, though it is near enough for the servant eventually to be satisfied and for the readers and God to be satisfied.

Neither Abraham in his words to the servant nor the servant in his words to God had said anything about Isaac's bride coming from Abraham's immediate extended family, though the servant will momentarily speak in those terms. God's answer to the servant's prayer goes far beyond what the narrator has said that he asked. The answer prompts the servant to praise. Such praise is not merely a matter of the heart. It is expressed in a bodily posture involving the intercessor's prostrating his whole body before the one who has so startlingly granted his request. And it is expressed in words spoken out loud, as is necessary if they are to give glory to the God who has acted and thus to draw other people into their recognition of him. Perhaps the implication is that Rebekah, receiving the servant's gifts and hearing his words of praise, knows the destiny that has been laid in front of her and accepts it.

Even if so, the servant recognizes that the implementing of God's will also requires the family's agreement. It, too, might say "No." Whether or not the servant's words and actions have already convinced Rebekah, the report of the entire sequence of events convinces her family. As people look back over a story that they have been told, they can say "It was a series of coincidences," but they also can say "It's from God. We can't resist its implications." And when Rebekah arrives in the Negev, it would only fit the assumptions and implications of the rest of the story if Isaac is out walking and meditating and praying (as v. 63 may imply).

23

Conclusions to Abraham's Story

(25:1–11)

Overview

Abraham's story closes with an account of his third marriage and its offspring (vv. 1–4), of his establishing the position of Isaac as his primary heir (vv. 5–6), and of his own death and burial (vv. 7–11).

Translation

> **1**Abraham again got a wife; her name was Qeturah. **2**For him she gave
> birth to Zimran, Yoqšan, Medan, Midyan, Yišbaq, and Šuah. **3**Yoqšan fa-
> thered[1] Šeba and Dedan, while Dedan's descendants were the Aššurites,
> the Letušites, and the Leʾummites, **4**and Midyan's descendants were
> Epah, Eper, Hanok, Abida, and Eldaʿah. All these were Qeturah's
> descendants.
>
> **5**Abraham gave all that he had to Yiṣḥaq, **6**but to the sons of Abra-
> ham's secondary wives Abraham gave gifts while he was still alive and
> sent them off away from Yiṣḥaq his son eastward, to the east country.
>
> **7**This is the span[2] of the years in the life that Abraham lived: 175
> years. **8**So Abraham breathed out and died,[3] at a good age, old and full,[4]
> and joined his kin. **9**Yiṣḥaq and Yišmaʿeʾl his sons buried him in the

1. On the word order, see the footnote to 4:18.
2. Literally, "These are the days."
3. The subject follows the second verb, suggesting that "expired and died" is a kind of hendiadys (cf. v. 17, also 35:29—however, there the subject comes in between the two verbs), though *IBHS* (32.3b; 39.2.5) uses the term "hendiadys" only to refer to verbs linked with conjunctive waw.
4. The SP, LXX, Vg have "full of days," assimilating to passages such as 35:29.

Double Cave in the field of Epron ben Ṣohar the Ḥetite, which is close to Mamre, 10the field that Abraham acquired from the Ḥetites. There Abraham and his wife Śarah were buried. 11After Abraham's death, God blessed Yiṣḥaq his son. Yiṣḥaq lived near the Ḥay Roʾi Well.

Interpretation

The offering of Isaac (Gen. 22), the death of Sarah, and the finding of a wife for Isaac have been taking Abraham's story toward its close, which now comes with the account of his making his will, his death and burial, and God's blessing of Isaac (vv. 5–11). The closure of his story is first delayed by the surprising account of his undertaking another marriage (vv. 1–4), which provides background to the report of his disbursement of his assets (vv. 5–6). It also gives the audience more information on the ancestors of peoples whom Israel knows and is related to—whether or not it realizes it is so related. The individual parts of the unit (vv. 1–4, 5–6, 7–11—possibly with further subdivisions) seem to be independent of one another. The MT sees the unit as one paragraph. There is no scholarly consensus on the possible background of the material (e.g., in J or P or the work of later editors).

25:1–6. The note about Abraham's taking another wife might raise two questions: When? Why? Although he might have married Qeturah after Sarah died, his fathering six more sons (let alone daughters?) in his great old age, having managed only two in the previous 137 years, might seem less likely than his having married Qeturah sometime earlier. The account of the marriage then comes here because this section is finishing off the Genesis account of Abraham's story. If he married Qeturah much earlier, the answer to the why question might be that an important person like Abraham would naturally mark his status by having more than one wife, especially given Sarah's infertility and his divorce of Hagar. One would indeed then expect him to have more than the two sons he otherwise had, one by Hagar, one by Sarah. If he married Qeturah after Sarah's death, the answer to the why would more likely be that he needed a wife to run the household, preferably someone young and energetic (see Prov. 31:10–31), rather than that the "decrepit" old man was also "lascivious,"[5] though one doesn't then like to think about the dynamics of Qeturah's relationship with Rebekah.

Either way, Abraham's children, grandchildren, and great grandchildren (vv. 2–4) are the fulfillment of the promise that he would become the ancestor of many nations (17:4–6). The lists also function in a way parallel to the

5. Cf. Luther, *Genesis 21–25*, 300, 301, quoting from Jerome, *Hebrew Questions on Genesis*, 59. The assumption that a man marries chiefly for sex evidently antedates the modern period; Jerome and Luther refer to a traditional way to solve the "problem," by seeing Qeturah as another name for Hagar (see, e.g., Rashi, *Brʾšyt*, 266).

ones in Gen. 10: they indicate that the family of Abraham as Israel's ancestor belongs, by a bond of relationship, to the greater whole comprising the peoples that live in Israel's world. These peoples "form a penumbra around the social spheres headed by Ishmael and Isaac."[6] Israel's world is not to be defined merely by the relationships of enmity with some people such as Midian and his descendants. "Human and family bonds have deeper roots than political divisions." Our later context reminds us that in Abraham, this statement also applies to the relationships of Jews, Christians, and Muslims.[7] Some of the names are elsewhere the names of individual peoples or places (e.g., Sheba and Dedan), others are plural and are thus the names of groups (e.g., Ashshurites, Letushites), while yet others might be individuals or places or peoples. The descendants include the ancestors of peoples who are thereby indicated to be the Israelites' relatives but with whom Israel was involved in trading relationships, not least in spices, which fits the fact that their mother's name suggests she was a spice girl (etymologically, "Qeturah" would mean "Spiced"). We know nothing else about most of the people who might be descended from these figures, but such links as we have suggest peoples to the east and southeast of Canaan, in northern and southern Arabia, which fits with the reference in v. 6 to Abraham sending them off eastward.[8] The Medanites feature in 37:36. The Midianites appear more frequently. They produce a wife for Moses (Exod. 2–3), who thus marries within the family of Abraham.[9] Later they appear in an unfriendly connection (e.g., Num. 31; Judg. 6). In the meantime, they appear in a neutral one: "within one generation the Midianites grow so that they fill a caravan of merchants"[10]—as for that matter do the Ishmaelites and Medanites (Gen. 37:25, 28, 36). Among the grandchildren, the order of lists in 1 Chron. 1 suggests that the Dedanites lived in Syria. Sheba has featured with different genealogies in Gen. 10:7, 28; the link with Dedan suggests that this Sheba stands for a northern branch of that group. The Ashshurites are apparently a group in Arabia (cf. BDB), a different group from people belonging to the well-known Ashshur, the Assyrians (10:22), for whom the First Testament uses the gentilic noun "Ashshur" or the expression "sons of Ashshur" and not the term Ashshurites.

But Isaac is the son of Abraham who really counts (v. 5). Deuteronomy 21:15–17 may suggest that an average Israelite cannot operate in Abraham's way; it might be another example of how his special position in the working out of God's purpose (and his antedating the instructions associated with Sinai) means that his actions are exceptional and may not provide example or warrant for everyone (see Gen. 22 and Gen. 24).

6. Brett, *Genesis*, 83.
7. Westermann, *Genesis 12–36*, 400.
8. See Montgomery, *Arabia and the Bible*, 37–53.
9. Cf. Origen, *Homilies on Genesis*, 172.
10. De La Torre, *Genesis*, 233.

But it now emerges that Qeturah is implicitly one of Abraham's secondary wives (v. 6), like Hagar, whereas in v. 1 she is simply called a wife; the point is explicit in 1 Chron. 1:32. It seems to follow from being secondary wives that one's offspring do not have inheritance rights (see on Gen. 22:24). What they receive is up to their father's discretion. Like someone in the West, Abraham is expected to decide on what happens to his estate before he dies, though presumably he does not actually transfer everything to Isaac before he dies.[11] But perhaps a man might commonly implement some bequests before he dies, which could reduce family conflict after his death.[12] Sending off Hagar's and Qeturah's sons continues the process of peoples spreading through the world that was described in Gen. 10. It does not mean that they "like Ishmael, are ultimately rejected by God" or are "shipped eastward, away from God's promise."[13] Ishmael certainly lives in the context of God's promise,[14] and it is not an adventurous inference to think that other descendants of Abraham do so as well—or at least live there in the same sense as all other peoples. And Midian, Ephah, and Sheba, along with Ishmael's two oldest sons Nebayot and Qedar (v. 13), reappear in Isa. 60:6–7, proclaiming Yahweh's praise and bringing the fruit of the spice trade to the worship of Jerusalem. Jubilees 20 has Abraham preaching a substantial farewell sermon to them with encouragements and exhortations (he goes on to preach an even more substantial one to Isaac). "These sons were sent away that there might be a true home, in the end, to return to."[15]

25:7–11. Genesis gives a full description of Abraham's dying. Observably, death means stopping breathing, expiring, breathing out for the last time and not breathing in again. Whenever the Torah uses this verb, it refers to "an easy, painless kind of death not preceded by lengthy illness."[16] In Abraham's case, after these 175 years (let us think in our terms of 95), he died at a good age. He is old and full. He has lived as long as one can imagine or hope. And it is enough. It is time to join his people or his kin, the members of the family who have passed on. He is not "in bondage to the desire of life."[17] Literally and physically, Abraham joins Sarah; while he will indeed be joining his other relatives in Sheol, they have been buried elsewhere, not in the family tomb, and Genesis is using the regular terminology in a loose, metaphorical sense,[18] as if he were in the position of people who do join their family in the family tomb. As far as the living are concerned, metaphorically and

11. Cf. Speiser, *Genesis*, 187.
12. Cf. Calvin, *Genesis*, 2:35.
13. So De La Torre, *Genesis*, 234.
14. Cf. Kaminsky's comments, *Yet I Loved Jacob*, 34.
15. Kidner, *Genesis*, 150.
16. Qimchi, *Genesis*, on the verse.
17. Calvin, *Genesis*, 2:37.
18. Cf. Ibn Ezra, *Genesis*, 246.

theologically speaking, "they belong to the ancestors who have gone before and whose memory is preserved."[19] The expression "his kin" uses the plural of the word for a people (*ʿam*), which invites the audience to reflect on the fact that Abraham is actually joining "his people" and not merely his immediate kin; "his people" are the covenant people in 17:14. Typically for Genesis, if you have lived a full life, there is no sense of there being a problem about dying and about this joining. Living means enjoying the company of one set of family members; death means moving to enjoy the company of an earlier set in relaxed fashion. And if Yahweh is the God of Abraham (Jesus argues), he is not God of the dead but of the living (Mark 12:26–27), so Abraham's life is by no means over.[20]

Neatly, Isaac and Ishmael come together to bury their father (vv. 9–10). "In this scene, fulfillment of the covenant promise is momentarily foreshadowed."[21] Although there is some sense in which Ishmael has been sent away years previously, he has evidently not been sent away too definitively (any more than Qeturah's sons), though in any case, a special significance attaches to him. The bareness of the comment about Isaac and Ishmael might make one wonder what kind of collaboration this burying involved; funerals can be occasions for reopening wounds, and Genesis does not relate a reconciliation between the brothers like the one between Jacob and Esau or Joseph and his brothers.[22] But then, Isaac and Ishmael had never had a fight. Their problem was their parents.

For a moment Genesis then returns to focus on Isaac (v. 11), in case we think that Ishmael has the same status as his brother. Yet paradoxically, Isaac is still based near the well associated with Hagar and thus with his older brother (cf. 24:62). The Abraham story closes with God's blessing of Isaac, which indicates that the history of the blessing is not coming to an end: "This history has future and hope."[23]

19. Westermann, *Genesis 12–36*, 397.
20. Cf. Origen, *Homilies on Genesis*, 172–73.
21. Reno, *Genesis*, 216.
22. Cf. Mbuvi, *Belonging in Genesis*, 144; Kozlova, "Abraham's Burial."
23. Zimmerli, *1. Mose 12–25*, 139.

Part Three

Isaac's Lines of Descent, Focusing on Jacob

(25:12–35:29)

While Part Two of Genesis was formally the story of "Terah's lines of descent," it was substantially the story of Terah's son and daughter-in-law, Abraham and Sarah. Part Three is formally the story of "Isaac's lines of descent," but it is substantially the story of Isaac and Rebekah's two sons, especially the younger of the two. The entire story of Genesis revolves around God's working through the generations; especially in Parts Two, Three, and Four, God is working through a promise that has progeny at its center.

But there is a difference in the way the three parts unfold. Even more than Part One, Part Two comprised a series of separate units that make sense on their own, though they gain extra significance through their relationship to the larger whole of which they have become part. Part Three is dominated by a long, continuous narrative in 26:34–33:20, most of whose elements make less sense out of their individual context. This continuous narrative transports Jacob from Canaan to Harran and back again, and it reflects the shape of this plot by taking the form of a palistrophe.[1] On either side of this tightly woven central narrative, there are some shorter units that could stand on their own and are less closely integrated with the central narrative. But in the context

1. As far as I know, Fishbane ("Composition and Structure") first made this observation; cf. his *Text and Texture*, 40–62.

of Part Three as a whole, they relate closely in substance to the central narrative, providing it with a framework and with introductions and conclusions.

The following is then an outline of Part Three:

Preamble: Ishmael's lines of descent (25:12–18)
Introduction: The birth of Esau and Jacob (25:19–34)
Prelude: Conflict between Isaac and Abimelek (26:1–33)

Scene 1: Jacob flees from Esau (26:34–28:9)
Scene 2: God's envoys appear to Jacob (28:10–22)
Scene 3: Jacob arrives in Harran (29:1–14)
Scene 4: Laban pulls one over on Jacob (29:15–30)
Scene 5: Jacob's wives have children (29:31–30:24)
Scene 6: Jacob pulls one over on Laban (30:25–31:2)
Scene 7: Jacob leaves Harran (31:3–54)
Scene 8: God's envoys appear to Jacob (31:55–32:32)
Scene 9: Jacob reunites with Esau (33:1–20)

Postlude: Conflict between Jacob and Shechem (34:1–31)
Conclusion: Jacob returns home; Esau and Jacob bury Isaac (35:1–26)

Though there was lots of movement in the series of relatively short stories in Part Two, the motif of flight and return forms the "arc of tension"[2] in Part Three's more coherent sequence of episodes within one story. Throughout, it is also a narrative about conflict within the family—between brothers, between relatives, between wives. Part Two was especially concerned with the vertical relationship between one generation and the next within the family as the promise is passed on and with the problematic nature of that vertical relationship. Here Part Three is especially concerned with the horizontal relationship between members of the same generation within the family and with the problematic nature of that relationship. Accounts of God's appearing and speaking interweave with the accounts of human conflict: "*human extremity* and *divine intrusion* are correlated with each other."[3]

Overlaps between some of the sections, jumpiness in the opening and closing sections, and different ways of speaking (e.g., different ways of referring to God) suggest that Part Three again brings together materials with an earlier history. I assume that a key feature of that history was the existence of at least a Yahwist and a Priestly version of the Isaac/Rebekah/Esau/Jacob story, though it may be that one version has simply been amplified by material with another perspective. Either way, an author has then worked creatively

2. Cf. Westermann, *Genesis 12–36*, 407.

3. Brueggemann, *Genesis*, 210, with his emphasis.

to produce the version that we have, and continuing scholarly disagreement over analyzing the material's origin and development again suggests that we cannot establish this earlier history, or the date of the material, or the extent to which it relates historical events, though we can imagine what it would signify to an Israelite audience. The significance would vary in different periods, though in Part Three particular implications attach to the fact that the implied audience of Genesis is the entity that the First Testament commonly refers to as "Israel." In poetic parallelism the First Testament often also refers to Israel as Jacob (e.g., Ps. 14:7; Isa. 40:27; Jer. 30:10), and Part Three of Genesis focuses on the Jacob who is renamed Israel. Perhaps the people Jacob-Israel was expected to find itself in the person of Jacob-Israel and thus to read his story with "self-critical realism."[4]

4. Fretheim, "Genesis," 516.

24
Ishmael's Lines of Descent

(25:12–18)

Overview

The preamble to the story of Isaac's family line is a brief account of Ishmael's family line, an "in-between text"[1] that in isolation one might see as a postscript to the Abraham story. The data about Ishmael's descendants add to the information in 25:1–11, and this link could provide a rationale for connecting 25:12–18 with those verses as the MT does, with only a paragraph break between vv. 1–11 and 12–18. Reading the account of Ishmael and his descendants in connection with what precedes makes Ishmael the person who concludes the Abraham story.[2] But vv. 12–18 also relate to what follows in closing off Ishmael's story before opening Isaac's.[3]

Translation

> **12**These are the lines of descent of Yišmaʿeʾl, Abraham's son, to whom
> Hagar the Miṣrite, Śarah's maidservant, gave birth for Abraham. **13**These
> are the names of Yišmaʿeʾl's sons, by their names according to their
> lines of descent. Yišmaʿeʾl's firstborn, Nebayot; and Qedar, Adbeʾel,
> Mibsam, **14**Mišma, Dumah, Maśśa, **15**Hadad, Tema, Yetur, Napiš, and
> Qedemah. **16**These are Yišmaʿeʾl's sons and these are their names, by
> their villages and by their enclosures, twelve leaders for their peoples.

1. Seebass, *Genesis*, 2.2:260.
2. Cf. Brueggemann, *Genesis*, 203.
3. Thus Zimmerli, for instance, covers 11:27–25:11 in the second volume of his commentary, *1. Mose 12–25* (he did not complete the commentary on 25:12–50:26).

[17]These are the years of Yišmaʿeʾl's life: 137 years. So he breathed out and died, and joined his kin.[4] [18]They dwelt[5] from Hawilah as far as Šur, which is close to Miṣrayim, as you come to Aššur; on the face of all his brothers he fell.[6]

Interpretation

25:12–18. In keeping with the pattern elsewhere in Genesis, 25:12–18 gives a brief account of the line on which it will not concentrate before turning to the line on which it will focus.

Ishmael's descendants (vv. 13–16), like other figures in the lines of descent in Genesis, include ancestors of peoples the Israelites know and with whom they are involved in trading relationships, who are shown to be their relatives. As is the case with many of those other figures, we know nothing else about most of the peoples who are implicitly seen as descended from these figures. The links that we do have suggest that they are peoples to the east and south of Canaan, in northern and southern Arabia; Jer. 2:10 perhaps locates Nebayot and Qedar in the far east, as Cyprus is in the far west. The twelve leaders (v. 16) invite comparison with the twelve sons of Jacob.

Jumping forward some while (v. 17), Genesis then reports the passing of Ishmael himself, in terms overlapping the ones used of Abraham, though without the reference to a good age, old and full (he lived, after all, a mere 137 years) or to his burial.

Then (v. 18), the section returns to Ishmael's offspring. Here they are associated with the area to the south and even southwest, the region with which the story connects Hagar, though the Ashshur referred to here is presumably the Arabian group mentioned in v. 3. For Shur, see 16:7, and for Havilah, see 10:7. Here it is most explicit that the story of Abraham's descendants who are born from Ishmael implies the fulfillment of Yahweh's promise to Hagar (see 16:10–12) and not just to Sarah, to Ishmael and not just to Isaac (as in due course to Edom and not just to Israel; KSG). "Ishmael was a great theologian who carefully unfolded the force and the grandeur of the promises."[7]

4. On this expression, see the comment on 25:8.

5. The LXX, Vg have "he dwelt," an easier reading.

6. For *nāpal*, the Vg has "he died," which is a common enough meaning but does not fit here. The LXX and Tg repeat the translation "dwelt" from 16:12, but the verb does not have this meaning anywhere else, even in Judg. 7:12 (cf. Rashi, *Brʾšyt*, 271). "Fall" can mean "attack," and "on the face of" could link with a verb for attack (Nah. 2:1 [2]). See *DCH* 6:720–21.

7. Luther, *Genesis 21–25*, 327.

25

Twin Sons and the Position of Firstborn

(25:19–34)

Overview

The introduction to Isaac's own story immediately establishes its major theme, the relationship between Isaac and Rebekah's twin sons. This relationship will hinge on the fact that Esau is the firstborn and therefore should have the major responsibilities and privileges in the family, while Jacob is marginally the younger and resents it, and he is the one through whom Yahweh will fulfill his promises to their grandfather and father. The introduction reports two incidents relating to this dynamic, from the twins' birth and their manhood.

Translation

19These are the lines of descent of Yiṣḥaq, Abraham's son.
Abraham fathered Yiṣḥaq, **20**and Yiṣḥaq was a man of forty years
when he got for himself as wife Ribqah daughter of Betuʾel the Aramite
of Paddan Aram, sister of Laban the Aramite.
21Yiṣḥaq entreated Yahweh on behalf of his wife, because she was
infertile. Yahweh let himself be entreated by him,[1] and Ribqah his wife
got pregnant. **22**The children pressed on one another[2] inside her, and she

1. The "tolerative niphal," when you let something happen to you, followed by *l* of the implicit agent (GKC 51c, 121f).

2. The LXX's "jump" apparently takes the verb as from *rûṣ* rather than *rāṣaṣ*; contrast the Vg.

said, "If this is how it is, why is it that I . . . ?"[3] She went to inquire of Yahweh, **23**and Yahweh said to her,

> Two nations are in your womb,
> two peoples will divide from your body.
> One people will be stronger than the other people,
> and the greater one will serve the younger one.[4]

24Her time became full for giving birth, and there, twins were in her
womb. **25**The first went out tanned, all of him, like a garment of hair. So
they named him Esaw. **26**After that, his brother went out, his hand grasping Esaw's heel. He was named[5] Yaʿaqob. Yiṣḥaq was a man of sixty years at their birthing.

27The boys grew up and Esaw became a man who knew about hunting, a man of the open country, while Jacob was a resolute[6] man, living
with tents.[7] **28**Yiṣḥaq loved Esaw because there was game in his mouth,[8] while Ribqah loved Yaʿaqob.[9]

29Yaʿaqob cooked stew.[10] Esaw came in from the open country; he
was tired. **30**Esaw said to Yaʿaqob, "Please let me guzzle some of the red stuff, this red stuff, because I'm tired" (that's why they named him
Edom). **31**Yaʿaqob said, "Sell your position as firstborn[11] today,[12] to me."
32Esaw said, "Here, I'm about to die. What use is a position as firstborn
to me?" **33**Yaʿaqob said, "Swear to me today." So he swore to him and
sold his position as firstborn to Yaʿaqob. **34**Yaʿaqob gave Esaw bread and lentil stew, and he ate and drank and got up and went. So Esaw despised the position as firstborn.

3. Rebekah's sentence breaks off. The *zeh* strengthens the *lāmmâ* (cf. 3:13; 12:18; 18:13).

4. Formally the colon is ambiguous and could mean that the younger will serve the greater/older; but that point would hardly need making. On the ambiguity, see J. Anderson, *Jacob*, 59–67.

5. The verb is active singular (contrast v. 25), more literally, "one named him."

6. *Tām* most often describes a person as having integrity (e.g., Job 1:1); cf. *tāmîm* (Gen. 6:9; 17:1) and the noun *tōm* (20:5, 6). With this meaning the description would carry heavy irony in the Jacob story, or it might anticipatorily invite readers to soften their judgment on him when he seems to act dishonorably (see Zakovitch, "Inner-Biblical Interpretation," 108). Yet a man of integrity is a man who is resolute in a particular way, and the broader meaning of resolute makes sense when applied to Jacob. The LXX, Vg have "simple," a meaning not far from "innocent" in the sense attaching to *tōm* in, e.g., 2 Sam. 15:11, while *DCH* suggests "safe" for *tāmîm* in 2 Sam. 22:33.

7. The LXX has him living "at home," which he was, but the phrase more likely relates to his occupation (cf. 4:20).

8. Presumably Isaac's mouth (cf. the LXX, Vg); compare the English expression "he had a taste for game."

9. While *ʾāhēb* meant "love" when used of Isaac in 24:67, it will mean "like" in 27:4, 9, 14.

10. Literally, he "stewed stew"; *zîd*/*zûd* more commonly refer to someone metaphorically "seething" or "being in a stew," and the expression may hint that Jacob was in a stew about Esau.

11. Cf. the LXX, Vg: not "your birthright," for which the expression is *mišpaṭ bəkôrâ* (Deut. 21:17); the same applies to the reference in Greek in Heb. 12:16.

12. I.e., "right now."

Interpretation

Genesis 25:19–32:3 is one unit in the MT (though two synagogue lections), with 25:19–34 the first section relating how Esau had the position of firstborn but surrendered it to Jacob. Jacob will thus come to be key to the future of Isaac and Rebekah's family and thereby of Abraham and Sarah's family and thereby of Yahweh's promise—but that consequence is not explicit at this point. The section outlines as follows:

Heading (25:19a)
How Isaac came to marry Rebekah: a resumptive summary of Isaac's story so far (25:19b–20)
How Rebekah got pregnant (25:21–23)
How she gave birth to two sons, Esau then Jacob (25:24–26)
How they differed (25:27–28)
How Esau gave up the position of firstborn (25:29–34)

The section compares and contrasts with 11:27–12:8 as the introduction to Part Two. It has the same kind of heading and the same kind of resumptive summary that lead into a story introducing the theme of the part as a whole and incorporating a declaration from Yahweh about how the future is going to work out for the central figures in the story. Indeed, "in these sixteen verses, we have their future lives in a nutshell."[13] Admittedly the singular word "story" gives a misleading impression even of vv. 21–34, which comprises an episodic series of snapshots strung together.[14] Although the accounts of the pregnancy and birth and of the transfer of the position as firstborn are stories that could have existed on their own as self-contained units, the linking account of the different ways Esau and Jacob grew up could hardly stand alone. It looks like a passage designed to connect those two little stories, its information derived from the chapters that will follow.[15] The section is puckish and scandalous in what it says about both Jacob and Esau. The boys are fighting in the womb? Jacob is grabbing Esau's heel? "Esau" means hairy (no it doesn't; everyone would know) and "Jacob" means grabber (no it doesn't; everyone would know)?[16] Either Isaac or Esau has game in his mouth? Father and mother (who were initially impressive and touching in their prayer and inquiring) are divided in who they like or love? Jacob is seething? Esau wants to guzzle like an animal? Jacob wants to buy the position of firstborn? Esau doesn't care about it, says he is dying, and lets him buy it with some stew?

13. Wenham, *Genesis 16–50*, 172.
14. Cf. Fretheim, "Genesis," 520.
15. Cf. Coats, *Genesis*, 186.
16. Cf. von Rad, *Genesis*, 260.

25:19–20. The heading corresponds in significance to the ones at 11:27 and 37:2 and in form to others that have recurred at less significant points such as 25:12. It makes clear that we are not really going to be reading Isaac's story but the story of his descendants. As happened in 11:27–30, the heading leads into a summary of material from preceding chapters, specifically Gen. 21–24, though Aram Two-Rivers (24:10) becomes Paddan Aram, which may mean Aram Garden or Aram Road; the Vg not inappropriately speaks of it as "Syrian Mesopotamia" (see 28:2). In the ensuing story Paddan Aram and Harran will function as alternative titles for the place where Laban lives. Possibly they go back to two different versions of the Jacob story, from circles where one or other of the titles was used.[17]

25:21–23. The chapters' focus on Isaac's progeny rather than Isaac himself receives expression as they simply presuppose the story of his own birth, growing up, and marriage (about which we know from Gen. 21–24) and leap straight forward to the birth of Isaac and Rebekah's offspring. Yahweh's insistence on prosecuting his purpose through Isaac, not Ishmael, and the clarity with which Yahweh indicates that Rebekah is the right wife for Isaac, the sparkling account of her, and specifically her family's blessing of her (24:60) have not prepared us for the news that she can't get pregnant. But Isaac and Rebekah's troublesome and sad situation as an ordinary couple, as well as their plight as the bearers of God's promise, parallels that of Isaac's parents and of other couples in Genesis and elsewhere in the First Testament. At one level it reflects the realities of life in a traditional society where nutrition may be poor, medical problems common, and resources for healing nonexistent. Yet the sadness of being unable to have children is a real-enough reality in Western society, and once more it could seem to raise questions about the true humanity or adulthood of a man and a woman.[18] Theologically, it reflects how nothing can be taken for granted even when God has apparently made all the preparations for a straightforward implementing of his intentions. "Nothing seems less accordant with reason, than that the propagation of the Church should be so small and slow"; but God is just not in a hurry, and the increase that will eventually follow thereby testifies more forcibly to its origin as in God's power and grace.[19]

This little paragraph opens (v. 21) not with the problem but with Isaac's response to it. Once again, Genesis achieves a dramatic effect by working in a nonchronological order. Isaac's action stands out as it makes for a contrast with that of his parents: when Sarah was long infertile, Abraham did nothing and Sarah eventually looked for a surrogate.[20] It also makes for a contrast with stories where it is the childless woman who prays (30:1, 22; 1 Sam. 1); here it

17. See further the introductory comment on 28:10–22.

18. Cf. V. Lieber in Eskenazi and Weiss, *Torah*, 152–53.

19. Calvin, *Genesis*, 2:40–41.

20. Cf. Rashi, *Br'šyt*, 279.

is Isaac, not Rebekah, who prays.[21] Compared with those other stories, the account of the prayer is "shockingly brief" and lacks the usual sense of frustration and grief and years of waiting,[22] or in Sarah's case the long suspense as we read through chapter after chapter and story after story following on the information about her inability to conceive, which was followed by the promise given to Abraham.[23] "Entreat" (*ʿātar*) is a First Testament technical term for intercession or supplication—that is, for soliciting something (perhaps slightly outlandish) for oneself or for someone else. It most commonly denotes Moses praying for Pharaoh (e.g., Exod. 8:8–9, 28–30 [8:4–5, 24–26]; 9:28; 10:17–18). There and here, the occurrences come in pairs: someone entreats Yahweh (qal or hiphil), then Yahweh lets himself be entreated (niphal); as we put it, he answers the prayer in the affirmative. Here, the verse proceeds with a simple sequential logic: Isaac prays because Rebekah is infertile; Yahweh answers; Rebekah gets pregnant. The reuse of the verb makes clear that Isaac's prayer makes all the difference. God does something he would not otherwise have done. Yet maybe God "so looked forward to the prayers of the patriarchs that he quasi provoked them into praying for the gift of children."[24] Presumably Isaac and Rebekah make love (cf. 16:4), but Genesis leaves that bit out (cf. 21:2), which puts the emphasis on Yahweh's making things happen. Apparently it's the only time Rebekah gets pregnant, and she is Isaac's only wife, which all makes for contrast with his father, his half brother, and his sons, though not with his mother. Rebekah is now the "complete woman" among the matriarchs: she alone has no shadow figure.[25]

Again the story leaps forward (v. 22a), though this time only a few months. "At breathtaking pace, this text moves through barrenness, answered prayer, conception, and troubled pregnancy."[26] Not surprisingly, having two babies grow inside you is more painful than having one. "Isaac's problem is getting Rebekah pregnant. Rebekah's problem is being pregnant."[27] It could make you wish you were not pregnant at all (why didn't I stop Isaac from praying?).[28] You could think the twins are fighting over who would get out first (the verb is a violent one, elsewhere denoting crushing or breaking; Tg. Ps.-J. compares the babies to men doing battle), though it will turn out that only one of them would be interested in such a question. As the information about Sarah's infertility and Yahweh's promise to Abraham set up the arc of tension for their story, the information about this conflict between Jacob and Esau sets up the

21. Cf. Brayford, *Genesis*, 343.
22. Mbuvi, *Belonging in Genesis*, 111–12.
23. Cf. Fokkelman, *Narrative Art in Genesis*, 87.
24. Qimchi, *Genesis*, on v. 20.
25. Engar, "Old Testament Women," 144; cf. Adelman, *Female Ruse*, 11–37.
26. Arnold, *Genesis*, 232.
27. Hamilton, *Genesis 18–50*, 176.
28. Cf. Luther, *Genesis 21–25*, 354.

arc of tension for their story. Brothers living as one is good, indeed lovely (Ps. 133:1), but these brothers are beginning the way they will go on. Though the narrator knows this fact and knows that Rebekah's pain comes from having conceived twins, it's not explicit that Rebekah has worked out the latter fact. She may only know about the pain. Her cry is pardonably incoherent, reflecting her agony and her fear; pregnancy is a dangerous business. But "why" is a cry that people utter in all sorts of situations; Rebekah will ask the question again in 27:45. And "why" is commonly more a rhetorical question than a prayer addressed to someone.

But like Isaac, Rebekah also knows how to pray (v. 22b), in the sense that she knows how to ask Yahweh about things. Through this little paragraph the focus lies on the way Isaac and Rebekah are relating to God. As is the case in the Hagar story, Genesis assumes the reality of the relationship between God and a woman as well as God and a man. Further, this story is the first account of someone "inquiring" of Yahweh (*dāraš*). As Hagar is the Bible's first person to make a theological statement, Rebekah is the first to ask a theological question. To do so, she "went" somewhere, perhaps to the worship site at Beer Sheba or the nearby Ḥay Ro'i Well where God had appeared to Hagar and spoken to her (16:7–14). But Genesis says nothing about how she does it when she arrives there. In Israel, if you have a question open to a yes/no answer, you can resort to the Urim and Tummim in the possession of a priest (e.g., 1 Sam. 22:10) in order to inquire of Yahweh. If you have a more open question and you need a message from Yahweh, you can resort to a prophet (e.g., 2 Kings 3:11). In the context of Saul's abandonment by Yahweh, 1 Sam. 28:6–7 mentions dreams and a medium. Gideon seems to have simply talked to Yahweh where he was (Judg. 6:36–40). It thus would not be necessary for Rebekah to consult a person in order to inquire of God; she can simply talk to him.[29]

Genesis relates matter-of-factly that she gets a response (v. 23a), as happened with Isaac's entreaty. Again it does not tell us who the response came through, and if anything it implies that God spoke to her directly as he did to Hagar and as he will to Jacob. Of course God answers when a person asks a question! Perhaps Rebekah gets a straight answer to a straight question because of the importance of this birth; and perhaps in general people get straight answers to straight questions when their questions relate to God's purpose. But the revelation that comes to Rebekah need not have indicated that she was going to have twins; it might have indicated only that she would have a baby whose own offspring would eventually became two peoples. This

29. Hamilton (*Genesis 18–50*, 176–77) notes the lack of reference to methods of divination or to mediators such as prophets; see further E. Fleming's study of "independent divination" ("'She Went to Inquire'"). Targum Neof. has Rebekah going to Shem's Study House (seek is *dāraš* and "study" is *midraš*), and Ephrem (*Genesis*, 171) has her consulting Melchizedek, whom Jewish tradition identified with Shem.

understanding would fit the link between this declaration and the motif of women such as Sarah and Hagar becoming the mothers of many nations; it did not mean that they themselves had more than one baby. Either way, the revelation from Yahweh concerns the significance of Rebekah's offspring. Ultimately, she will give birth to two peoples (the audience knows they will be Israel and Edom, as Abraham's sons became the ancestors of the Israelites and the Ishmaelites). The explanation comes in metrical lines, as Yahweh's words often do. They are not just ordinary, prosaic words. They comprise two lines that are internally parallel, with the second line also parallel to the first. As regularly happens with parallelism, within each line the second colon goes beyond the opening one. So the first line declares that there will be two nations/peoples, and what is more, they will divide.

The second line (v. 23b) goes beyond the first in speaking of the nations'/peoples' inequality, and within this line the second colon goes beyond the opening one in speaking of the greater serving the lesser or younger. Thus throughout the two lines Yahweh's words work toward a climax in the last colon. It is a scandalous climax. It's maybe not surprising that one people should be stronger than the other people. It's more shocking that the greater should serve the younger, which turns upside down the way things regularly work. Yahweh does not say he will make it happen, only that it will happen. In the event, in the short term Esau will be greater, but a reversal will come about through Jacob's action, and then another reversal (see Gen. 33:1–15). Subsequently within Genesis, Edom will become a growing nation with kings, but in the much longer term (and within Genesis–2 Kings) a reversal will come about through David's action in defeating the Edomites. It will turn out that Yahweh has accepted or been committed to Jacob and has repudiated or rejected Esau (Mal. 1:2), though Genesis does not make explicit that he himself did so before they were born, as Paul infers (Rom. 9:10–13).[30] Much of the message's significance will emerge only in light of events, as often happens with prophecies; Rebekah "must have returned from the prophet little the wiser."[31] The declaration is not a promise. Nor does it relate to the theme of God's promise to Israel's ancestors. And in this respect the declaration and the entire unit advertise something about the nature of Part Three, which makes little reference to that theme even though its context in Genesis and in the Torah gives it significance in that connection.

25:24–26. A woman waits, and she knows that the time for giving birth is approximately fixed and will reach its goal. She may suspect that she is going to have twins, but she will not be sure until the birth; but it turns out, yes, "there," twins really were in her womb. As is often the case, the "there" (traditionally, "behold") draws us into the story and "makes us share the

30. And cf. De La Torre's critique (*Genesis*, 245–47) of this way of thinking.

31. Wenham, *Genesis 16–50*, 176.

surprise which the parents experience when their offspring is born"[32] (for other examples of "there" pulling us into the story, see, e.g., 1:31; 6:12; 8:13; 15:4, 17; 22:13; 24:15, 30, 63). In light of what will follow, it is worth noting that both Esau and Jacob are an answer to prayer.

The comment on the first baby (v. 25) is complicated—it implies links that it does not make explicit. He comes out tanned, as if he is already a man of the open country (see v. 27); the only other person so described is David (1 Sam. 16:12; 17:42). The word (*ʾadmônî*) also anticipates the fact that he will be the ancestor of Edom—though v. 30 will make a different link between the name Edom and something brownish-red. Perhaps the Edomites were notoriously tanned, not to say hairy.[33] The reference to hair also anticipates both the fact that Esau will be a man who has a lot of hair (27:22), with the implication of being a bit wild, and the fact that he will live in the country of Seʿir (hair is *śēʿār*), which will be Edom's region (32:3). Further, the sound of that word for hair also overlaps with the name Esau itself (*ʿēśāw*). We don't know this name's actual etymology, and perhaps neither did the narrator, which might be why we get the sequence of convoluted comments on the name when something needs to be said to balance the more straightforward comment on Jacob's name that will follow.[34]

Because that comment on the second baby (v. 26) is simpler, it too will give people something to think about later—not least Esau (27:36; Hosea 12:3 [4]; cf. also Jer. 9:4 [9:3]). The name compares with other Middle Eastern names that link with a verb meaning "protect," and etymologically it would mean "May he [God] protect,"[35] but Genesis takes the name in a different direction in having Jacob (*yaʿăqōb*) grasp Esau's heel (*ʿāqēb*). Only at the end of the pregnancy/birth story do we learn that in Genesis's counting, twenty years have passed since Isaac and Rebekah married (in our terms we could think of Isaac as marrying at twenty with Rebekah being a teenager, and of Isaac as now thirty and Rebekah not much younger).

25:27–28. The story leaps forward another twenty years, in our way of counting. Like Cain and Abel, the boys grow up with different instincts, which their being twins would make more surprising unless the comment about Esau's appearance means they were not identical. The revelation about their dividing already begins to find fulfillment.[36] Further, both shepherding and farming were recognized occupations in settled Israel, but being a hunter over against being a shepherd or farmer was not; the First Testament makes virtually no references to game except in lists of animals you may or may not eat. Here Esau recalls Nimrod the great hunter (10:9). He is the kind of

32. Fokkelman, *Narrative Art in Genesis*, 90.
33. Cf. Gunkel, *Genesis*, 290.
34. Cf. Westermann, *Genesis 12–36*, 414.
35. See *HALOT*.
36. Cf. Gunkel, *Genesis*, 290.

man who brings home deer or antelope or gazelle such as will feed the family for quite a long time. Jacob has the more regular role of the shepherd, who stays with tents or lives in tents (cf. 4:20), looking after the sheep and cattle.[37] Esau's being a hunter will be significant in Gen. 27; Jacob's being resolute in his pursuit of Esau's primacy will soon receive further expression.

It's perhaps not surprising that Isaac likes Esau (v. 28), who brings home the barbecue that costs nothing (unlike the calf his grandfather sacrificed for his visitors). Does Rebekah like Jacob because he is the stay-at-home boy or because she knows he is the one who will win out? Jubilees 19 has Abraham (who is still alive on a literal interpretation of the Genesis chronology) encouraging Rebekah in this love because he knows that the future lies with Jacob. Genesis apparently doesn't know the reason for Rebekah's preference; that information provides background to Gen. 27. Whatever the reason, one will not be surprised if the parental attitudes issue in favoritism and in trouble. "Parents are carried with blind affection."[38]

25:29–34. If food wins father's favor, however, Jacob can play at that game.[39] For breakfast and lunch the average family might be quite happy to have some bread with olive oil for dipping, and perhaps some vegetable stew for dinner. Jacob's being more of a homebody perhaps also makes it not surprising that he cooks, and Esau's having been out hunting makes it not surprising that he is starving when he gets home.

The stew with its rich color (v. 30) might suggest to Esau that Jacob cooked up some meat left over from one of Esau's previous hunting expeditions. Reference to its red color (*ʾādōm*) makes for a more evident link with the name Edom, the country where he eventually lives (32:3), which perhaps actually got its name from the reddish-brown color of its soil or rock.

Jacob's response to Esau's request (v. 31) comes out of left field, though it fits the comment about the manner of his birth in v. 26, and even the comment about the conflict in Rebekah's womb. From the beginning Jacob has wanted to be first, and he will do anything to overtake his brother. Being the firstborn (*bəkôr*: it was the term for the firstborn animal that Abel sacrificed in 4:4) is more a matter of status than of rights. The only First Testament reference to the firstborn having "rights" comes in Deut. 21:15–17, and it relates rather theoretically to an odd marginal situation. In general, "the law of the firstborn is nothing but an expression of the exceedingly high esteem in which the first child was held. . . . The first is the best."[40] Reuben as Jacob's own firstborn is Jacob's vigor, the firstfruit of his energy (49:3). Israel is Yahweh's firstborn (Exod. 4:22)—the one to whom he is supremely attached. One might compare the way a man in the United States may give his firstborn son the same name

37. Cf. Ibn Ezra, *Genesis*, 251.
38. Willet, *Hexapla in Genesin & Exodum*, 242.
39. Cf. Alter, *Genesis*, 128.
40. M. Tsevat on *bəkôr*, *TDOT* 2:122.

as himself, and he may pass it on to the firstborn of the next generation, and so on (John Goldingay, John Goldingay Jr., John Goldingay III—though as far as I know there are no such people). It is that status that Jacob covets.

Status doesn't matter much to Esau (v. 32). He's more concerned with the fact that he's starving. He'll be dead soon, he jokes: what use will the position of firstborn be?

It means everything to Jacob (v. 33), who insists that Esau give him the status of firstborn in return for a helping of stew. Naturally, the transfer needs to be confirmed by an oath that will call down divine judgment on Esau if someday he tries to reclaim that position.

So Esau gets his stew (v. 34). Maybe it's a disappointment because it turns out to be lentil based (which could also give it a reddish-brown color), though lentils are a staple in the Middle East, not least for stew.[41] Maybe Esau has been cheated.[42] But he eats and drinks, then gets up and goes. It's a very matter-of-fact event. But the narrator's last comment recognizes it as a shocking event. Even if no rights attach to being the firstborn, the honor is huge, and in this case, as the listeners know, we are talking about being the one in whom Yahweh's promise to Abraham will be fulfilled. Esau has shrugged his shoulders and surrendered it, as Yahweh knew he would (see v. 23).

Implications

Jacob I Loved

Esau's indifference and Jacob's obsession are keys to the way the future will work out in Part Three of Genesis. There isn't much to be said for either of the young men. "If Jacob is ruthless here, Esau is feckless."[43] Thus "it's hard to know who's the bigger jerk, Esau or Jacob,"[44] which makes even clearer that God's working via one and not the other flows not from their deserving but from God's sovereignty and grace.[45] "The first will be last and the last first" (Matt. 19:30).[46] So "why Jacob instead of Esau?" Morally, there's not much to choose between them. If God were to choose someone who deserved to be chosen, he would choose nobody.[47] In commenting on God's choice of Jacob rather than Esau in Rom. 9:10–18, Paul judiciously quotes Exod. 33:19, though he slants it in an amusingly different direction from the one that obtains in Exodus. There it magnifies God's mercy (applied to this story, the mercy to

41. See Driver, *Genesis*, 254.
42. Weiss ("Ethics of Price Gouging") has studied the ethical aspects of this story.
43. Kidner, *Genesis*, 152.
44. Visotzky, *Genesis of Ethics*, 132.
45. Cf. Calvin, *Genesis*, 2:51–52.
46. Cf. Brueggemann, *Genesis*, 216.
47. Reno, *Genesis*, 218.

Jacob), whereas for Paul it magnifies God's sovereignty (God has the power not to show mercy to Esau).

Paul incorporates words from Gen. 25:23 ("the older one will serve the younger one") in his argument in Rom. 9, which gives his theological account of the puzzling fact that the bulk of God's chosen people have not come to trust in Jesus and thus become right with God. It reflects a consistent pattern in God's working out his purpose. God had a "purpose based on a choice" (Rom. 9:11), which took effect through his insistence on Isaac rather than Ishmael (Gen. 21:12; cf. Rom. 9:7–9). The ultimate aim of this purpose based on God's choice was inclusive, not exclusive: it was to bring in a huge number of Gentiles and also the entirety of Israel (Rom. 11:25–26). But in the meantime, it excluded in order ultimately to include. At this point, the older serving the younger constitutes the next stage in putting this purpose into effect.

> Rebecca being pregnant through one man, Isaac our ancestor (because they hadn't yet been born nor done anything good or bad), so that God's purpose based on a choice would continue not on the basis of deeds but on the basis of the one who called, it was said to her: *The older will serve the younger.* As it is written, *Jacob I loved, but Esau I hated.* (Rom. 9:10–13)

At the Reformation, theological commentary on Gen. 25:19–34 focused on the theme of divine election (earlier commentators such as Ephrem, Chrysostom, Origen, and Andrew of Saint Victor do not put the focus there). Calvin focuses on the contrast between the choice of one national group over against another in Genesis, and the choice of a particular group within the larger nation in Romans.[48] Luther notes that Paul treats this passage "in a rather sublime manner . . . by establishing a twofold birth, namely of the flesh and of the promise."[49] Willet emphasizes that election is based on grace, not works, and that the passage works against the views of the Pelagians.[50]

This Genesis story is part of a long narrative that indeed describes how God operates by choosing particular groups for reasons that have nothing to do with their worth. But Gen. 25:19–34 does not make that point. It tells us two things about God and his relationship with the world and with what happens in the world. The first is that God lets himself be entreated by Isaac; the birth of children to Isaac and Rebekah results from this prayer. Possibly God has decided to act in this way ahead of time; but Genesis does not say so. It says his action is a reaction to Isaac's prayer. The second is that he tells Rebekah something about the destiny of the children she would bear. Possibly God intends to make things work out this way—to divide the boys and make

48. Calvin, *Genesis*, 2:45–48.
49. Luther, *Genesis 21–25*, 366–67.
50. *Hexapla in Genesin & Exodum*, 242.

one stronger than the other and make one serve the other—but he doesn't say so. He says only that he knows things will work out this way.

In the story that follows, Jacob makes stew, Esau insists on having some, Jacob insists on his surrendering the status of firstborn, Esau despises it. Possibly Yahweh intends these things to happen and inspires them, but Genesis does not say so. It says only that human beings make some decisions and act. The broader Genesis narrative gives no basis for inferring that Yahweh intended these things to happen or inspired them. It tells us that Yahweh "acknowledges" Abraham and stipulates that Isaac should be the one through whom his purpose is put into effect. It makes no such statement about Jacob and Esau. Malachi 1:2–3 makes such a statement, and Paul lets Malachi interpret Genesis. Paul is inspired by God, and his interpretation is inspired, but it doesn't override what the Holy Spirit inspired within Gen. 25:19–34 itself, which speaks of human beings making decisions (to pray, to reach, to cook, to barter), of God knowing what will happen, and of his working their actions into the carpet he is weaving.

Yahweh also tells Israel that he indeed has acknowledged Israel alone out of all the earth's families, but that this acknowledging means he will attend to them because of their waywardness (Amos 3:2), and he reminds them that his bringing Israel up from Egypt was no different from his getting the Philistines up from Kaphtor or the Syrians from Qir (Amos 9:7). Grace is the way you get into a relationship with God, but obedience is required if you are to stay in it.[51] Paul's argument in Rom. 9–11 is not so different. If God didn't spare the branches of the Israelite vine when they failed to respond to him, neither will he spare Gentiles who have been grafted into the vine and then turn back from Jesus.

51. I adapt the formulation of E. Sanders; see, e.g., *Paul and Palestinian Judaism*.

26
Isaac and Abimelek

(26:1–33)

Overview

Genesis backtracks to recount how Isaac and Rebekah go through some experiences similar to those of Abraham and Sarah but how God reaffirms his promises and brings about some fulfillment of them. The distinctive focus of the section in this connection is the conflict they experience with their neighbors over water supply and the way Isaac's people find water. The narrative is distinctive in being just about Isaac and Rebekah. It shows how Isaac's life "is not that of a wanderer like Abraham's; Hebron, Beer-sheba, Beer-lahai-roi, and Gerar—all in the south of Palestine, being the places at which he is exclusively found. He lived, in fact, on the borderland of the two peoples (Edom and Israel), who afterwards boasted their descent from him."[1]

Translation

> **1**There was a famine in the region, apart from the first famine that happened in Abraham's time, and Yiṣḥaq went to Abimelek,[2] king of the Pelištites, to Gerar.
>
> **2**Yahweh appeared to him and said, "Don't go down to Miṣrayim.
> Dwell in the region that I'm telling you about. **3**Reside as an alien[3] in this

1. Gregory and Evert, "Book of Genesis Unfolded"; cf. Driver, *Genesis*, 255.
2. The MT[L] has *ʾăbîmmelek*, perhaps to distinguish him from the earlier *ʾăbîmelek* (see Wenham, *Genesis 16–50*, 183).
3. *Gûr* generates paronomasia with the name Gerar—an appropriate place to be a *gēr*.

region, and I will be with you and bless you,[4] because[5] to you and to your offspring I will give all these regions and implement the oath that I swore to Abraham your father. **4**I will make your offspring as numerous as the stars in the heavens, and I will give your offspring all these regions, and all the nations on earth will bless themselves by your offspring, **5**on account of the fact that Abraham listened to my voice and kept my charge, my orders, my decrees, and my instructions."

6So Yiṣḥaq lived in Gerar. **7**The people in the place asked about his wife, and he said "She's my sister" because he was afraid to say "my wife"[6] in case "the people in the place kill me because of Ribqah, because she's good looking." **8**But when he'd been there some time, Abimelek king of the Pelištites looked out through the window and saw: there was Yiṣḥaq playing around with Ribqah his wife. **9**Abimelek called for Yiṣḥaq and said, "Here, really she's your wife! How did you come to say 'She's my sister'?" Yiṣḥaq said to him, "Because I said, 'So I don't die because of her.'" **10**Abimelek said, "What is this that you've done to us? Almost, someone from the people could have slept with your wife and brought liability upon us." **11**Abimelek ordered the entire people: "Anyone who touches this man or his wife will absolutely be put to death."[7]

12Yiṣḥaq sowed in that region, and that year reaped a hundredfold.[8] Yahweh blessed him, **13**and the man got big. He went on doing so, until he got very big indeed. **14**He had livestock, flock and herd, and a large body of servants, and the Pelištites were jealous of him. **15**All the wells that his father's servants had dug in the time of Abraham his father, the Pelištites stopped up and filled with dirt.

16Abimelek said to Yiṣḥaq, "Go away from us, because you're much too numerous for us." **17**So Yiṣḥaq went from there, camped in Wadi Gerar, and lived there. **18**Yiṣḥaq again dug the water wells that they[9] had dug in the time of Abraham his father and that the Pelištites had stopped up after Abraham's death. He named them by the same names as his father had named them. **19**And Yiṣḥaq's servants dug in the wadi and found there a well of spring water.[10] **20**But the Gerar shepherds got into an argument with Yiṣḥaq's shepherds, saying "The water's ours." He named the well Ēśeq because they quarreled with him. **21**They dug another well and got into an argument over it, too, and he named it Śiṭnah. **22**He went on from there and dug another well, and they didn't argue over

4. Simple waw plus yiqtol, practically signifying "so I may be with you and bless you."

5. "Because" in effect introduces a citation of the promise to Abraham, not just a separate reason (Seebass, *Genesis*, 2.2:280).

6. The SP has *ʾištî hî*, "she is my wife" (cf. the LXX), which makes for a smoother reading.

7. Abimelek uses the idiom that combines an infinitive and its cognate finite verb to indicate emphasis, but in contrast to passages such as 2:17 and 20:7, the finite verb is hophal; see the comment. He uses the same idiom in v. 28.

8. For the hapax *šəʿārîm* LXX has *śəʿārîm*, "barley."

9. The SP and Vg make explicit that "they" refers to "the servants of his father Abraham."

10. Literally, "living water," i.e., running water.

it, so he named it Reḥobot and said, "Now Yahweh has made it wide for us and we'll be fruitful in the region."

23From there he went up[11] to Beʾer Šeba. **24**Yahweh appeared to him
that night and said, "I am the God of Abraham your father. Don't be afraid, because I am with you, and I will bless you and make your offspring numerous on account of Abraham my servant." **25**He built an altar
there and called in Yahweh's name and spread his tents there. Yiṣḥaq's servants excavated a well there.

26Meanwhile Abimelek[12] went to him from Gerar with Aḥuzzat his
aide and Pikol his army officer. **27**Yiṣḥaq said to them, "Why have you
come to me, when you were hostile to me and you sent me off from being with you?" **28**They said, "We've seen clearly that Yahweh is with
you, so we said, 'There should please be an imprecation[13] between us,' between us and you, so we may solemnize a pact with you.[14] **29**If
you act badly with us . . . ![15]—as we haven't touched you and as we've done only good with you and sent you off in peace. You're now someone blessed by Yahweh." **30**So Yiṣḥaq made a banquet for them, and
they ate and drank. **31**They started early in the morning and swore,
each to the other. And Yiṣḥaq sent them off, and they went in peace from being with him. **32**That day Yiṣḥaq's servants came and told him
about the matter of the well that they'd dug and said to him, "We've found water." **33**So he called it Šibʿah. That's why the name of the town
is Beʾer Šeba until this day.

Interpretation

Whereas the medieval chapter division associates the note about Esau in vv. 34–35 with vv. 1–33, the MT recognizes that 26:1–33 is a complete section, about Isaac, Rebekah, and Abimelek.[16] It comprises a reprise of a sequence of episodes in Abraham's story with their associated promises, though the Isaac version has features that give it its individual character. Its concrete focus lies on wells; wells are a crucial feature of the work and life of a shepherding people, especially in the Negev. The section thus tells of tension between the chief of a local people and his staff on one hand, and Isaac and his staff on the other, tension over the adequacy of water resources in the area to support both groups and over the rights to different wells. The tension leads to some sabotaging of wells but also to some discovery of new wells.

11. Perhaps in the sense of "up-country," given that Beer Sheba is not at a higher elevation.
12. The subject precedes the verb, marking a new subject and paragraph.
13. See the comment on 24:41.
14. The waw plus cohortative suggests a purpose clause (GKC 108d).
15. Abimelek leaves the rest of the terms of the oath unstated.
16. See Nicol, "Narrative Structure." He sees the unit as illustrating the interrelationship of promise, threat, and partial fulfillment that runs through much of Gen. 12–50.

This distinctive story is then set in a context that systematically aligns it with the Abraham chapters in a variety of ways. There is a famine in the region that makes Isaac move to Gerar, to Abimelek's area, from a location elsewhere in the Negev (cf. 12:9; 20:1). The background to this move is Yahweh's appearing to Isaac to tell him not to go down to Egypt because of the famine but to continue dwelling/residing as an alien in the region (compare and contrast 12:10; 14:13; 20:1; 21:23–24). Yahweh will be with him there, will bless him, and will give all these regions to him and his offspring (cf. 12:2; 17:8; 21:22). Because Abraham listened to Yahweh's voice and kept his charge, decrees, and instructions, Yahweh will thus implement the oath he swore to Abraham. He will make his offspring as numerous as the stars in the heavens, so that all the nations on the earth will bless themselves by his offspring (cf. 22:16–18). On his arrival in Gerar, Isaac tells people that his wife is his sister because he is afraid they will kill him since she is good looking (cf. 12:11–13; 20:1–13), though the exposure of his ploy comes about in a fashion that distinguishes it from the occasions in the Abraham story.

While another distinctive note is Isaac's sowing in that region and reaping abundantly, the further description of his prospering in terms of Yahweh's blessing him, and his getting to be a big man with flocks and herds and servants, follows the description of Abraham by his servant (cf. 24:35). In the midst of the consequent disputes over the wells, Yahweh's further promise of blessing and of numerous offspring comes "on account of Abraham my servant" (cf. 22:17) and leads into his building an altar, calling in Yahweh's name, and spreading his tents (cf. 12:7–8). In the context of Abimelek's hostility (cf. 24:60), there follows a conciliatory visit from Abimelek and his senior staff that issues in the solemnizing of a pact and eventually in the naming of Beer Sheba (cf. 21:22–32). Yahweh thus relates to Isaac in the way he had related to Abraham, and Isaac's story shows itself to be in continuity with Abraham's.

The section as a whole breaks into two parts: vv. 1–11 concern the move to Gerar, while vv. 12–33 concern subsequent events, with a focus on the key question of wells. Like some previous stories, the chapter involves some internal backtracking. Key to understanding the sequence of both parts is the way each begins with a summary and then goes back to give a more detailed account—again like some previous stories.

The famine and Isaac's move (26:1)

Yahweh's instructions in connection with the famine (26:2–5)

Consequences of the move (26:6–11)

Isaac's flourishing, the jealousy, and the problem over water (26:12–15)

The departure from Gerar and the discovery of water (26:16–19)

The arguments and the discovery of more water (26:20–22)

The move to Beer Sheba and the discovery of more water (26:23–25)
The visit, the pact, and the discovery of more water (26:26–33)

The two main parts of the chapter proceed by setting up questions and problems and showing how they are resolved or where they lead, though each time the resolution or result leads into the next question or problem:

Question: There's a famine: what will Isaac do? (26:1)
Response: Yahweh tells him what to do and promises to bless him (26:2–5)
Result: He lives in Gerar (26:6)

Question: What will he do about Rebekah? (26:7a)
Response: Say she's his sister (26:7b)
Result: He gets into trouble with Abimelek (26:8–11)

Question: What will Abimelek do? (26:9–10)
Response: Set up a law to protect Isaac and Rebekah (26:11)

Question: When Isaac flourishes, what will the Philistines do? (26:12–14a)
Response: Get jealous, stop up his wells, ask him to leave (26:14b–16)
Result: Isaac leaves (26:17)

Question: When they dig more wells, what will happen? (26:18–19)
Response: The Gerar shepherds will dispute them (26:20–21)
Result: They dig yet more, and Yahweh promises to bless Isaac (26:22–25)

Question: What does Abimelek want now? (26:26–27)
Response: A pact, because he sees that Yahweh is with Isaac (26:28–29)
Result: They make a pact, and Isaac finds more water (26:30–33)

The chapter has a noteworthy relationship with the chapters on either side. In its backtracking, the absence of Esau and Jacob from this story suggests that chronologically it belongs in the earlier years of Isaac and Rebekah's marriage and before the boys' birth, between 25:20 and 25:21.[17] In the other direction, if "one wonders what the editors are seeking to achieve" in incorporating a third story about someone trying to pass off his wife as his sister,[18] then a possible answer is that it makes for a dramatic pause between the first announcement of the conflict between Esau and Jacob in 25:18–24 and the

17. See further Nicol, "Chronology of Genesis."
18. Brett, *Genesis*, 86.

development of this theme in Gen. 27–33, analogous to the role of Gen. 38 in the Joseph story.[19] The second part of the section then shows how Yahweh affirms and maintains a commitment to Isaac in his own right, a theme that would not appear if the narrative proceeded straight from Gen. 25 to Gen. 27. In other words, the chapter establishes that Yahweh really is "the God of Isaac" (28:13).[20]

In traditional source-critical terms, the section belongs to J. Comparison of the three wife-sister stories has generated several possible views of the tradition history of their relationship.[21]

26:1. The chapter begins with a summary to introduce vv. 1–11. Genesis distinguishes this famine from the earlier one but reports it in similar terms. Isaac is presumably still living somewhere in the Negev; the last two concrete references have located him in the Ḥay Ro'i Well area (24:62; 25:11). He moves to Gerar—presumably again the southern Gerar, which was also in the Negev.[22] Yet this move would likely not solve the problem of the famine; if there was a famine in Isaac's region, it would affect Gerar too.[23] Maybe Isaac would not know how things were in Gerar until he got there (when there is a famine, one must do something), and/or maybe we should think of his going to the Gerar area as simply an aspect of the way shepherding peoples move around. Given that Abraham's own dealings with Abimelek and Pikol (who appears later in this chapter) took place before Isaac was born, one might ask whether the incorporation of their names, and of the reference to Gerar itself, is a way of making the story more concrete rather than a piece of historical information, and a way of enhancing the parallel with the Abraham story, unless the earlier Abimelek and Pikol named their sons after themselves. In any context, it's hard to imagine a sense in which Abimelek is king of (all) the Philistines; he will be "the Philistine king" in the sense of being chief or sheikh of the local people in this area.

26:2–5. The narrator now gives the background to v. 1b, explaining how it was that Isaac didn't follow the example set by Abraham in connection with the first famine by going to Egypt, though he did follow his example in moving to Gerar; indeed, perhaps Isaac was on the way to Egypt when the revelation came (so Jub. 24.8). Just as Isaac was not to leave the country to find a wife, he is not to leave the country to find food. He is to "dwell" there.

He is to do so (vv. 3–4) even though he will continue to be one who only "resides" as an alien in a land that is not his own; Yahweh sustains him in this connection by reaffirming to him the promises he made to Abraham.[24] He

19. Cf. Wenham, *Genesis 16–50*, 186.
20. Cf. Westermann, *Genesis 12–36*, 424.
21. See, e.g., Coats, *Genesis*, 191; Van Seters, *Abraham*, 167–91; Boase, "Life in the Shadows."
22. See the comment on 20:1.
23. Cf. Van Seters, *Abraham*, 177.
24. Cf. Calvin, *Genesis*, 2:59–60.

adds that he will be with him: it is the "I will be with you" with its practical implications[25] that enables Yahweh to tell Isaac not to go to Egypt.[26] Genesis finds it easier to shrug its shoulders about what happens between the patriarch and the foreign people than to shrug its shoulders about leaving the area that Yahweh intends to give to him and his offspring. The point is not an aversion to Egypt in particular but an aversion to leaving the promised land, which evidently includes both the Ḥay Roʾi Well and Gerar. They are within the regions that Yahweh intends to give to Isaac's offspring. The plural "regions" parallels Yahweh's promise and oath in 15:18–21, which refers to the territory of a whole series of peoples, though that territory may not stretch this far south into the Negev.[27] The plural reappears later to refer to wider Israel as a whole (1 Chron. 13:2). Yahweh thus comprehensively restates and perhaps extends his promises to Isaac's father.

Yahweh does so on the basis of Abraham's responsiveness to Yahweh (v. 5): Abraham listened to Yahweh's voice (22:18). Verses 1–5 then conclude with their most eyebrow-raising words that expand on that commendation. If Abraham kept Yahweh's charge, orders, and decrees, he did what Moses will expect of Israel (Deut. 11:1) and what David will expect of Solomon (1 Kings 2:3) (cf. also Josh. 22:3; Mal. 3:14). Using the terms that apply to the later revelation implies that the latter "does not emerge as a new reality; it stands in basic continuity with earlier articulations of God's will," which actually go back behind Abraham to creation.[28] But Genesis itself does not otherwise refer to a charge, orders, decrees, or instructions. In speaking thus of Abraham's total obedience, Yahweh indulges in a magnificent hyperbole to inspire the audience (and not least its leaders) to emulate him. In the context of Genesis, Yahweh's affirmation may have in mind the way Abraham did as Yahweh specifically "said" at various points (not least 22:3). Yahweh might have seen Abraham's having his clan circumcised as an instance of "keeping his charge." Yahweh there spoke of "keeping" his pact (17:9–10), and "charge" (*mišmeret*, 26:5) comes from the same root as that verb. In the same connection Genesis spoke of Abraham circumcising Isaac as God "ordered" (21:4). It would thus not be a stretch to see the requirement of circumcision as a decree or an instruction, though Ibn Ezra adds that by leaving Harran and by offering Isaac, Abraham does as Yahweh said.[29] Qimchi adds reference to the Noachian commandments;[30] Jub. 21 had already looked behind Noah to Enoch as the source of instructions that Abraham obeyed.[31]

25. See the comment on 21:20.
26. Cf. Chrysostom, *Homilies on Genesis 46–67*, 59.
27. Cf. Sarna, *Genesis*, 183.
28. Fretheim, "Genesis," 529.
29. Ibn Ezra, *Genesis*, 255.
30. Qimchi, *Genesis*, on v. 5.
31. See further Greengus, "Anachronism."

The logic of 26:2–5 works as follows:

> you are to do as I say, and then
> I will bless you
> because I intend to give you this region
> because I promised it to Abraham
> so I will make you numerous and give you these regions
> on account of the fact that Abraham did as I said.

The concentric shape of Yahweh's statement points to the fact that logic is actually the wrong word. The verses do not work linearly. Like the account of circumcision in Gen. 17 (see comments there), they magnificently expound the impossibility of seeing the relationship between God and people (or relationships between human beings) in a rationalistically logical way. Isaac's obedience is a logical condition but not a quasi-legal condition of his receiving Yahweh's blessing; it is a logical condition in the sense that in its absence his life would fall apart. Yahweh intends to bless him because he intends to give him the land on the basis that he had promised it to Abraham. Yet Yahweh's intention also reflects the fact that Abraham did as Yahweh said. Abraham's obedience too was not a quasi-legal condition of ensuring that Yahweh would fulfill his promises, but it was a logical condition. Yahweh is thus logically dependent on the obedience of Abraham and Isaac if he is to fulfill his intentions, though no doubt he would find other ways of fulfilling his intentions if that obedience was not forthcoming. The dynamic relationship between God's intention and Isaac's responsibility overlaps with the narrative account of the dynamic relationship between God's intention to make Pharaoh stubborn and Pharaoh's self-willed stubbornness in Exod. 4–14.[32]

26:6–11. After vv. 2–5 have given the background to v. 1, Genesis goes on to give the foreground. It now speaks of Isaac "living" in Gerar, as Abimelek had invited his father to do (20:15). Isaac's description of Rebekah offers further comparison and contrast with Abraham in Gerar (20:1–18). Like his father, Isaac could say he is merely being economical with the truth, since Rebekah came from his extended family. His exposure comes in a different way from his father's. To explain how Isaac is caught following his father's unwise example, and recalling earlier occurrences of the verb *ṣaḥaq*, which lies behind Isaac's name, the narrator imagines Abimelek from his sheikhly tent able to see inside Isaac's tent, or seeing Isaac and Rebekah out in the open somewhere, and mines further the potential of that verb with its capacity to refer to amusement in various senses (cf. 17:17; 18:12–15; 19:14; 21:6, 9). Here the problem is that Isaac is Isaac-ing with Rebekah: the euphemism implies

32. See Goldingay, *Israel's Gospel*, 349–57.

that they are having fun or amusing themselves in a way that suggests that they are more lovers than siblings.

Isaac has taken a risk (v. 10). As was the case in 20:1–18, Abimelek is concerned about the adultery that could have resulted from Isaac's giving the Gerarites the impression that Rebekah was "available" (does Genesis presuppose that she was privy to the pretext, as Abraham says Sarah was?). It would have brought "liability" on Gerar. Genesis introduces another technical term from later in the Torah, *ʾāšām*; the related adjective *ʾāšēm* will come in 42:21, but otherwise words from this root are characteristic of Leviticus. The term refers to the objective liability that attaches to us when we do something that is objectively wrong. It works not with the notion of a conscious decision to do something that one knows is wrong but with the fact that we have put the world out of kilter by wrongdoing, regardless of whether we knew what we were doing. Ignorance of a law does not deliver us from liability for breaking it. Adultery has significance whether or not the man who commits adultery knows he is doing so, and it has implications not only for the individual who becomes involved with Rebekah (cf. 12:17; 20:17–18). Targums Onq. and Ps.-J. take the "someone" to refer specifically to someone such as the king himself, as in the other wife-sister stories, which would be a more usual way for a community to be affected by the right or wrong action of an individual.

Abimelek further expresses his honor (v. 11) by taking action to ensure that Isaac's fear of the Gerarites is not realized. As happens in all three wife-sister narratives "and climactically in this third one, one moral hero emerges: Abimelek."[33] The word "touching" is nicely ambiguous; it would have different implications with respect to Isaac than to Rebekah. The formula "will absolutely be put to death" marks Abimelek's words as a legal prescription (e.g., Exod. 21:12–17).

26:12–15. There is a second, possibly more understandable potential for conflict between Abimelek's people and Isaac's people; again the dynamics parallel those of the Abraham story (see 21:22–32).

Perhaps Isaac's ability to sow seed (v. 12a), which might be wheat, results from his freedom to "live" in Gerar. There is no need to assume that he sowed in vast quantities. Although Genesis refers only occasionally to the ancestors growing things (30:14; 37:7), it is a normal if subordinate aspect of the life of a shepherding people; references to bread and lentils in Genesis have implied as much. The term "a hundredfold" (cf. the Vg) comes only here; it might imply that a handful of seed produces a hundred handfuls of seed, or a hundred measures, or a hundred times Isaac's estimate (Tg, Aq). Whichever is the right understanding, Isaac might have been happy with a tenfold crop; it is evidently a spectacular yield one way or another, and it makes for a spectacular contrast with the famine conditions referred to in v. 1.

33. Brichto, *Names of God*, 274.

Genesis goes on (vv. 12b–13) to describe Isaac's flourishing in general terms to make clear that Yahweh is treating him the same as he treated Abraham. Yahweh has fulfilled his promise that things will work out okay without Isaac's leaving the regions that are the object of Yahweh's promise—indeed, things have worked out more than okay. In anticipation, Isaac experiences the truth of Ps. 37.[34] God's relationship with Isaac in the tough experiences through which he takes him covers the down-to-earth and the "spiritual."[35] If God is involved only in the earthly, it might be tempting to think of this involvement as really just a matter of Isaac's interpreting things that could be matters of chance. If God is involved only in the speaking within Isaac's spirit, it might be tempting to think of this involvement as a figment of Isaac's imagination. And the correspondence between God's dealings with Isaac and with his father also reinforces the assumption that the same one God is involved with both of them (KSG).

The Philistines' jealousy in reaction to Isaac's all-around flourishing (vv. 14–15) is another new note in Genesis. The previous Abimelek story involved wells, one of which Abraham swore he dug near Beer Sheba (21:30). Here the wells are key to Isaac's success in growing a crop as well as in sustaining his livestock. Filling in the wells might not seem a very logical expression of spite, but it was "a practice frequently resorted to in desert warfare" (2 Kings 3:25),[36] and here it was presumably calculated to induce unwanted aliens to move off somewhere else, after which the Gerarites could re-dig the wells.

26:16–19. Once again Genesis follows up the summary statement in vv. 12–15 with a fuller account, detailing the conflict that issued from Isaac's flourishing. Stopping up the wells was perhaps an unofficial Philistine action; v. 29 implies as much (cf. 21:26). If so, it is now complemented by some official action. Isaac's herders re-dig the blocked-up wells and also find another well.

26:20–25. Camping in Wadi Gerar would not mean moving far from Gerar itself, and it is not surprising that more conflict follows. The conflict is reflected in the names of the wells, as the audience might be able to see: Eseq apparently means quarrel (though noun and verb come only here); Sitnah means opposition (the name is related to the word for an opponent, *śāṭān*). The good news is that the next well can be given a name that means "wide places"; there is a town in the Negev called Ruhaibeh that might be Isaac's Rehobot.[37]

Otherwise (vv. 24–25), the verses again reaffirm that Yahweh deals with and speaks to Isaac as he did to Abraham, "on account of Abraham" and as "the God of Abraham your father." It is the first occurrence of a title for

34. Cf. Brueggemann, *Genesis*, 223.
35. Cf. Luther, *Genesis 26–30*, 3–15.
36. Skinner, *Genesis*, 366.
37. See BDB 932b; but see the comments in E. Robinson and E. Smith, *Biblical Researches*, 1:196–98.

God of a kind that then recurs throughout Genesis and comes occasionally in Exodus as a transition is made to a more consistent use of the name Yahweh (e.g., Gen. 28:13; 31:5, 29, 42, 53; 43:23; 46:1, 3; 50:17; Exod. 3:6). The title reflects God's having made a distinctive commitment to Abraham in issuing his promises to Abraham, involving him in the fulfillment of an intention to bless his offspring and bless the nations. He renews the commitment to Isaac and to Jacob, so that eventually he becomes "the God of your/our/their fathers" (e.g., Exod. 3:13; Deut. 12:1; 1 Chron. 29:18). The implication of the title is not that God enters into a personal relationship with Abraham that is distinctive of and confined to him, but that he enters into a commitment to Abraham, a commitment of which his wider family are also beneficiaries. In this passage the converse of Yahweh's being Abraham's God is Abraham's being Yahweh's servant. Yahweh's appearing to him and making this commitment to him gives Isaac reason to build an altar at Beer Sheba, as Abraham did not.

26:26–33. Yet again the pattern follows that in 21:26–32. As Abraham had complained about Abimelek's staff taking over a well, so Isaac complains about Abimelek's withdrawing his green card. Abimelek wants to smooth things over, and he has come to see Isaac for this reason. With him and Pikol (who appeared in Gen. 21) he brings Ahuzzat his "aide," etymologically his "friend," presumably an adviser.

The new note in Abimelek's thinking (v. 28) reflects the emphasis of the chapter as a whole. Abimelek and Pikol greeted Abraham with the blessing "God be with you" (21:22). In v. 3 Yahweh promised to be with Isaac, and they have now seen the fulfillment of that promise, which means that God has protected him and blessed him (again, cf. 21:20, and see the comment there). It is therefore wise for them to be on good terms with Isaac, as they were with Abraham as a result of that earlier meeting.

As commonly happens and as he did to Abraham (21:23), Abimelek leaves the sanctions attached to the oath unstated (v. 29); God can be trusted to see that consequences follow. Abimelek's claim about his own stance in relation to Isaac puts a positive spin on this stance. Even if Abimelek knows nothing about the stopping up of the wells, Isaac can point out that Abimelek has invited him to leave the area, which looks like an expression of hostility. But Abimelek speaks of taking this action "in peace," and he indeed made sure that nobody "touched" Isaac (see v. 11).

A state banquet follows (vv. 30–31), as it surely must (cf. 31:54); eating together expresses and seals relationships. The next day everyone arises early because there is serious formal business that they are committed to concluding, and Isaac sends them off in the peace with which Abimelek claims to have sent off Isaac. The peaceful relationship is now guaranteed by the pact making, though the agreement may be more a nonaggression pact than a peaceful relationship in a fuller sense.

There is more good news (vv. 32–33). Possibly this well is the one whose initial "excavating" was described in v. 25 (hence the use of a different verb there).[38] The good news is that in the course of the excavation, they have found an actual spring. The section as a whole underscores how there is hardly anything more important than water supplies; it "spans a movement from *famine* (v. 1) to *water*."[39] Because of its water resources, there is nowhere more important in the region than Beer Sheba, in whose area yet another well is now found (see 21:31 and the comment). So the place gets a third basis for its name from now on—or rather, this third significance will so attach when there is eventually a town there (which was not the case in this ancestors' day). The name Beer Sheba will be appropriate because Isaac and Abimelek swore their oath here (*šāba*ʿ); in the context, the implication is that *šibʿâ* means "oath."

38. Cf. Speiser, *Genesis*, 201.
39. Brueggemann, *Genesis*, 225, emphasis original.

27
Why Jacob Must Move to Harran

(26:34–28:9)

Overview

There now begins the long palistrophic account of Jacob's move to Harran, his stay there, and his eventual return. This narrative dominates the story of Isaac and his family, but it focuses especially on Jacob and his relationships with Esau and with the wider extended family. It opens (26:34–35) by recounting how Esau marries two Hittite women, which leads in due course to Rebekah's urging that Jacob should marry a woman from back in Paddan Aram (27:46–28:9). The intervening story (27:1–45) relates how Rebekah arranges for Jacob to cheat Esau of the blessing that belongs to the elder son. That action explains why Jacob needs to flee from Esau's wrath and thus why Isaac does not simply send someone to get a bride for Jacob, as Abraham had done for Isaac himself.

Translation

26:34 Esaw was a man of forty years; he got as wife Yehudit[1] daughter of Beʾeri the Hittite, and Basemat daughter of Elon the Hittite,[2] **35**and they became a source of bitterness[3] in spirit to Yiṣḥaq and Ribqah.

27:1 Yiṣḥaq was old and his eyes had become too dim to see. He called Esaw his older son and said to him, "Son!" He said to him, "I'm

1. Ironically, *yəhûdît* elsewhere means Yehudite, or Jewish, and generates the name Judith.
2. The SP, LXX have Hivvite.
3. *Mōrâ* could carry the overtones of "an expression of rebellion" (from *mārâ* rather than *mārar*); cf. the Tg.

here." **2**He said, "Here, please: I'm old; I don't know the day of my death. **3**So now, pick up your equipment, please, your quiver[4] and your bow, and go out to the open country and hunt game for me. **4**Make me a dish the way I like and bring it to me so I can eat,[5] and I will give you my personal blessing[6] before I die." **5**Ribqah was listening when Yiṣḥaq was speaking to Esaw his son.

So Esaw went into the open country to hunt game to bring,[7] **6**and Ribqah said to Yaʿaqob her son: "Here, I heard your father speaking to Esaw your brother, saying **7**'Bring me game and make me a dish so I can eat, and I will bless you before Yahweh before I die.' **8**So now, son, listen to my voice, to what I'm ordering you. **9**Go to the flock, please, and get me two choice kid goats from there so I can make them into a dish for your father, the way he likes, **10**and you can bring it to your father so he can eat, so he may bless you before he dies."

11Yaʿaqob said to Ribqah his mother, "Here, my brother Esaw is a hairy man and I'm a smooth-skinned man. **12**Maybe my father will feel me and in his eyes I will be like someone being scornful,[8] and I will bring on myself diminishing,[9] not blessing." **13**His mother said to him, "Your diminishing be on me, son. Just listen to what I say. Go and get them for me." **14**So he went and got them and brought them to his mother, and his mother made a dish the way his father liked. **15**And Ribqah got herself the clothes of Esaw her older son, the best ones, which were with her in the house, and she placed them on Yaʿaqob her younger son. **16**The skin of the kid goats she placed on his hands and on the smooth part of his neck, **17**and she put the dish and the bread that she had made into the hand of Yaʿaqob her son.

18So he came[10] to his father and said, "Father!" He said, "I'm here—who are you, son?" **19**Yaʿaqob said to his father, "I'm Esaw your firstborn. I've done as you spoke to me. Please get up, sit and eat some of my game so you may give me your personal blessing." **20**Yiṣḥaq said to his son, "How is it that you were so quick in finding it, son?" He said, "Because Yahweh your God made it happen for me." **21**Yiṣḥaq said to Yaʿaqob, "Please come up so I can feel you, son, whether you're really Esaw my son or not." **22**Yaʿaqob came up to Yiṣḥaq his father, and he felt him and said, "The voice is Yaʿaqob's voice, but the hands are Esaw's

4. The meaning of this hapax is a matter of guesswork (see Tal, *Genesis*, 144–45*).

5. The cohortative marks the clause as purpose or result (GKC 108d); the idiom recurs in v. 25.

6. Literally, "and my *nepeš* will bless you"; simple waw plus yiqtol practically signifies "so my *nepeš* may . . . ," as in 26:3.

7. The LXX suggests *lə'ābîw*, "for his father," instead of *ləhābî'*, an easier reading since that verb usually has an object.

8. *Tāʿaʿ*, "scorn," carries the overtones of *tāʿâ*, "go astray," and thus "mislead," if they are not variants of the same word (so, e.g., Ibn Ezra, *Genesis*, 261; cf. Gen. Rab. 65.15).

9. As with the verb *qālal*, so with the related noun, "one does better to keep the word 'curse' for the root *'rr*; so *qll* rather means "reduce" (Seebass, *Genesis*, 2.2:296; see the comment on 8:21). It suggests shrinking as opposed to increasing.

10. The LXX, Vg "brought" implies *wayyābē'* for *wayyābō'*, assimilating to vv. 10, 14, 25.

hands." **23**He didn't recognize him because his hands were like the hands of Esaw his brother, hairy. So he blessed him.

24He said, "You're really my son Esaw?"[11] He said, "I am." **25**He said, "Bring it up to me so I can eat some of my son's game, in order that I can give you my personal blessing." He brought it up to him and he ate, and he brought him wine and he drank. **26**His father Yiṣḥaq said to him, "Please come up and kiss me, son." **27**He came up and kissed him. He smelled his clothes, and he blessed him: "See:[12] my son's smell is like the smell of the open country that Yahweh has blessed.

> **28**God give you from the dew of the heavens
> and the manifold richness[13] of the earth,
> yes, a large quantity of grain and new wine.
> **29**Peoples are to serve you,
> nations to bow low to you.
> Be[14] lord to your brothers;[15]
> may your mother's sons bow low to you.
> Those who curse you—may he be cursed;
> those who bless you—may he be blessed.[16]

30As Yiṣḥaq finished blessing Yaʿaqob, and scarcely had Yaʿaqob gone right out[17] from the presence of Yiṣḥaq his father, when Esaw his brother came from his hunting. **31**He too made a dish and brought it to his father and said to his father, "May my father get up and eat some of his son's game, in order that you may give me your personal blessing." **32**Yiṣḥaq his father said to him, "Who are you?" He said, "I'm your son, your first-born, Esaw." **33**Yiṣḥaq trembled, trembled with much force,[18] and said, "Then who was that who was hunting game and brought it to me, and I

11. The SP prefaces the verb with interrogative *h* to make explicit that the sentence is a question, as in v. 21.

12. The rare (singular) imperative alternative for *hinnēh* has no literal addressee.

13. *Mišmannê* is likely a plural construct from the noun *mišmān* (*DCH*), with the preposition *min* understood from the parallel colon. This seems preferable to reading it as a misspelling of *miššəmannê* (*min* plus the plural construct of a hapax noun *šāmān*; BDB, *HALOT*) or as an abbreviation of *mimmišmanê* (Qimchi, *Genesis*, on the verse). The plural of amplification is then explained by the succeeding colon.

14. While *hĕyēh* is the only imperative in the blessing, and there are no morphologically unambiguous jussives, the use of this imperative coheres with the context in suggesting that the rest of vv. 28–29 is more like an empowerment and commission than a prediction.

15. The LXX implies singular *ləʾaḥîkā* for the MT's *ləʾaḥeykā*, assimilating to 25:23.

16. The LXX, Vg, Tg. Neof. resolve the move from plural to singular in each colon in v. 29b (distributive singular, suggesting each one: GKC 145l) by making everything singular. Targum Onq. does so by making everything plural.

17. Genesis uses the idiom that combines an infinitive and its cognate finite verb to indicate emphasis.

18. The narrative uses an idiom that combines a verb, its related noun, an adjective, and an adverbial expression: Isaac "trembled a big trembling very much." It uses this idiom again in v. 34: "He cried a great and bitter cry, very much."

ate of it all before you came, and I blessed him? Yes, he will come to be
blessed."
34When Esaw heard his father's words, he cried out with a very loud
and bitter cry. He said to his father, "Bless me, me as well, father!"
35He said, "Your brother came with guile[19] and got your blessing." **36**He
said, "They named him 'Yaʿaqob,' didn't they? He's grabbed me by the
heel, indeed[20] twice. He got my position as firstborn, and there, he's got
my blessing now." But he said, "Haven't you saved a blessing for me?"
37Yiṣḥaq answered Esaw, "There: lord in relation to you I've made him, all
his brothers I've given him as servants, and with grain and new wine I've
sustained him. For you, then, what can I do, son?" **38**Esaw said to his fa-
ther, "Do you have one blessing, father? Bless me, me as well, father!"[21]
Esaw lifted up his voice and cried. **39**Yiṣḥaq his father answered him:
there,

> While the places where you live will be away from the manifold
> richness of the earth[22]
> and away from the dew of the heavens above,
> **40**And you will live by your sword,
> and serve your brother,
> As you wander[23]
> You will break his yoke from your neck.

41Esaw was hostile to Yaʿaqob because of the blessing with which his
father had blessed him. Esaw said to himself, "The time for grieving over
my father will arrive, and I will kill Yaʿaqob my brother." **42**Ribqah was told
the words of Esaw her older son,[24] and she sent and called for Yaʿaqob
her younger son, and said to him, "Here, Esaw your brother is going to
console himself by killing you. **43**Now, son, listen to my voice. Set off,
take flight, take yourself[25] to Ḥarran to Laban my brother **44**and stay with

19. The Tg has "with smartness," implying approval of Jacob and disapproval of Esau (so also in v. 36). Sym nicely has "by means of an ambush," Aq "by laying hands [on you]."

20. On the use of *zeh*, see the footnote to 31:38.

21. The LXX adds, "Isaac was silent," Aaron's reaction to his sons' death in Lev. 10:3.

22. The line compares and contrasts with v. 28b. The word order with the adverbial phrase preceding the verb now suggests a concessive clause (likewise in v. 40a). The preposition *min* again must be understood before *mišmannê*, now being back-projected from the second colon into the first (a recognized practice in Hebrew poetry; the link with v. 28 makes it easy enough). But the *min* now changes its meaning from partitive to locative in a way that underlines the grievousness of the loss Esau is to experience (as the MT repeats *min*, the LXX repeats *apo*, and Chrysostom [*Homilies on Genesis 46–67*, 89] assumes that it keeps the partitive meaning, though Vg changes from *de* to *in*).

23. The exact meaning of *tārîd* is debated, but the approximate meaning seems clear (see Hamilton, *Genesis 18–50*, 225); the Tg in effect makes the phrase refer to Israel's wandering from the Torah, which will justify Israel's losing the mastery over Edom.

24. As in English, the phrase "the words of Esaw her older son" is treated as if the object of an active verb "they told" (see GKC 121a).

25. "Take yourself" represents *ləkā*, literally meaning simply "for yourself"; cf. 28:2.

him for a short time until your brother's wrath turns away, **45**until your brother's anger with you turns away and he puts out of mind what you've done to him, then I'll send and get you from there. Why should I be bereaved of the two of you together[26] in one day?"

46And Ribqah said to Yiṣḥaq, "I'm dismayed about my life because of the Ḥetite women. If Yaʿaqob gets a wife from among the Ḥetite women like these, from the women of this country, what good will life be for me?" **28:1**So Yiṣḥaq called for Yaʿaqob, blessed him, and ordered him, "You will not[27] get a wife from among the Kenaʿanite women. **2**Set off, take yourself to Paddan Aram to the house of Betuʾel, your mother's father, and get yourself a wife from there from among the daughters of Laban, your mother's brother. **3**May El Šadday himself[28] bless you and enable you to be fruitful and numerous, so you become a congregation[29] of peoples.[30] **4**May he give you Abraham's blessing, you and your offspring with you, so you take possession of the country where you're residing as aliens, which God gave Abraham." **5**So Yiṣḥaq sent Yaʿaqob off, and he went to Paddan Aram to Laban ben Betuʾel, the Aramite, the brother of Ribqah, the mother of Yaʿaqob and Esaw.

6Esaw saw that his father Yiṣḥaq had blessed Yaʿaqob and sent him off to Paddan Aram to get himself a wife from there, and in blessing him had ordered him,[31] "You will not get a wife from among the Kenaʿanite women," **7**and Yaʿaqob had listened to his father and mother and gone to Paddan Aram. **8**Esaw saw that the Kenaʿanite women were bad in the eyes of Yiṣḥaq his father. **9**So Esaw went to Yišmaʿeʾl and got for himself as wife Mahalat daughter of Yišmaʿeʾl Abraham's son, sister of Nebayot, as an addition to his wives.

Interpretation

The MT makes 26:34–35 and then 27:1–28:9 two paragraphs within its larger unit, which extends from 25:18 to 32:3 and thus stretches to cover the whole of Jacob's time in Paddan Aram/Harran. But 26:34–35 seems brief to stand on its own, unconnected to the material on either side: thus the medieval chapter division makes it an unrelated footnote to the story of Isaac and Abimelek. In addition, 27:46 does not follow straight on from 27:1–45 but does lead straight into 28:1–9, so that the medieval chapter division that separates 28:1–9 from

26. For this connotation of *gam*, see GKC 154a, note 1(c).

27. As in the Decalogue, the negative is *lōʾ*, not *ʾal*, thus suggesting a particularly categorical prohibition.

28. The name of God comes before the verb, as it regularly does, suggesting emphasis.

29. *Qāhāl*: not merely "hordes" (Vg); the LXX *synagōgas* (assemblies) has nicely suggestive connotations.

30. For *ʿammîm* Tg. Onq. has *šbṭyn* (clans), which makes the expression refer to Israel rather than to the nations (Tg. Ps.-J. has a longer paraphrase).

31. See *IBHS* 32.3d for this understanding of the weqatal verb.

27:46 is also odd. It is when we get toward the end of 26:34–28:9 that we discover how 26:34–35 relates to what follows: it provides the background to Rebekah's action in 27:46–28:9. So 26:34–28:9 forms one interwoven unit,[32] the whole explaining why Jacob moved to Paddan Aram/Harran.

Genesis 26:34–35 and 27:46–28:9 on one hand and Gen. 27:1–45 on the other are complementary accounts of the background to Jacob's move. It wouldn't be surprising if these two accounts had earlier existed as separate self-contained units.[33] In the terms of traditional source criticism, 27:34–35 and 27:46–28:9 were part of the Priestly version of the Genesis story, 27:1–45 was part of the Jahwist version or issues from a combination of J and E. Genesis 27:1–45 was then inserted into its new framework (even though the narrative would read more smoothly if it were not there) because its insertion provides the answer to a question raised within 26:34–35 and 27:46–28:9: why didn't Isaac simply send for a bride from Paddan Aram, as his father had done for him? So the two interwoven stories provide different explanations for Jacob's move. It would be quite possible for both to be factual—that is, some time after the act of deception in 27:1–45 Rebekah provides Isaac with this alternative rationale for the move, and Isaac gives Jacob a different blessing from that in 27:1–45, one that relates more specifically to the Abrahamic blessing. But in the drama of Genesis, the two accounts tell different yet complementary stories, each with its own message.

On one hand, then, 26:34–35 and 27:46–28:9 show the listeners that Isaac and Rebekah make sure that Jacob follows the principle that Abraham applied to Isaac in ensuring that he got his wife from the extended family and not from among the Canaanites (24:3). Part of its message is therefore that Israelite listeners to Genesis should ensure that their children do the same. It recounts how Isaac passes on the Abrahamic blessing to Jacob, and it locates Esau and his family on the edge of the Abrahamic family (not outside it, but not at the center of it), like Ishmael. And on the other hand, 27:1–45 takes forward the wider story begun in 25:18–34. It "intensifies" that earlier story, which retrospectively becomes a prelude to this one.[34] Thus 27:1–45 picks up the implications of the revelation to Rebekah, the naming of Jacob, the description of the physical difference between the boys and their different personalities as hunter and shepherd, and the note about their parents' different feelings about them. It also takes up the theme of Yahweh's blessing, though not in terms of the Abrahamic blessing. In its own fashion it prepares the way for the account of Jacob's journey to Harran, for his stay there, and for his eventual return when Esau has mellowed. Reading from the end of 27:1–45, we can see how the plot of the story works and recognize the question it answers:

32. Cf. Seebass, *Genesis*, 2.2:296–97.

33. Westermann (*Genesis 12–36*, 444–49) treats them separately.

34. Blum, "Jacob Tradition," 189.

Question: Why does Jacob decide to move to Harran?
Answer: Because Rebekah urges him to.

Question: Why does Rebekah urge him to?
Answer: Because she hears that Esau is going to kill him.

Question: Why is Esau going to kill him?
Answer: Because Jacob defrauded him of his blessing.

Question: How does Jacob defraud him?
Answer: By pretending to be Esau.

Question: What is this blessing?
Answer: That he will enjoy abundance of provision.

Question: How does he pretend to be Esau?
Answer: By dressing as Esau and cooking like Esau.

Question: How does he come to do so?
Answer: Rebekah suggests it.

Question: How does Rebekah know Isaac's intention to bless Esau in this way?
Answer: She heard Isaac say so.

Question: Why do Isaac and Rebekah act in this way?
Answer: Because Rebekah is fond of Jacob, whereas Isaac is fond of Esau.

In keeping with a convention of folk narrative,[35] each scene in 27:1–45 involves only two of the story's four characters. Jacob and Esau never appear together, and neither do Isaac and Rebekah, which symbolizes the frictions within the family.[36] It's ironic that the one monogamous marriage in Gen. 12–50 is so dysfunctional![37] Even here, "stability does not appear to be a feature of typical family life" in Genesis.[38] While 27:1–45 can be seen as a complete story, it cries for continuance. It makes us want to know what happens next. "It does not develop a proper ending" such as resolves the tension it opens up.[39] Even

35. See Olrik, "Epic Laws," 134–35.
36. Fretheim, "Genesis," 534.
37. Cf. De La Torre, *Genesis*, 249.
38. Steinberg, "World of the Family," 285.
39. Coats, *Genesis*, 201.

when 26:34–28:9 comes to an end, it still does not come to a conclusion. What will happen to Jacob (and to Esau and to their relationship)? "The story is 'open to the front'; even by its ending it shows that it is only part of a larger whole.[40]

Why did Israel tell the story and hold on to it? Why did it gain entry into the Scriptures? What is its significance for Jewish and Christian readers?

1. It is entertaining.
2. It articulates for Israelites who they are and who the Edomites are. It confirms or explains for Israelites their being the objects of Yahweh's special blessing and the Edomites not being so. It explains Israel's sovereignty over Edom in some periods but discourages Israel from taking that sovereignty for granted, and/or explains the loss of that sovereignty. More ironically, it makes Israelites reflect on the deceptive character of their eponymous ancestor, and on the Edomites' reputation for being smart (e.g., Jer. 49:7).[41] It relates an event that plays a key role in determining how the future will turn out for Jacob's descendants.
3. It functions theologically to confirm the special place of Israel in God's purpose, which God is willing to ensure if necessary by devious means. Isaac's blessing of Jacob is God's way of putting "the grace of election" into effect.[42]
4. It provides allegories of theological truth. For Philo, Jacob is a picture of contemplation or wisdom, Esau of folly.[43] For Augustine, "The blessing of Jacob is . . . a proclamation of Christ to all nations. . . . The world like a field is filled with the odor of Christ's name: His is the blessing of the dew of heaven, that is, of the showers of divine words; and of the fruitfulness of the earth, that is, of the gathering together of the peoples: His is the plenty of grain and wine, that is, the multitude that gathers bread and wine in the sacrament of His body and blood."[44]
5. It provides positive or negative models of behavior, of a bad example of deception or a good example of shrewdness. Ironically, great expositors who stress the grace and freedom of God exert great effort to show that the people who count (Rebekah, Jacob) deserve to do so.[45]
6. It simply describes how things sometimes work out in the human story. Blessing is gained through deception! It is the way life is.[46]

40. Fokkelman, *Narrative Art in Genesis*, 105 (referring to 27:1–28:5).
41. Cf. Gunkel, *Genesis*, 308.
42. Calvin, *Genesis*, 2:82.
43. So Philo, e.g., *On Drunkenness* 2.9–10; 31.120.
44. Augustine, *City of God* 16.37.
45. See Luther, *Genesis 26–30*, 99–179; Calvin, *Genesis*, 2:81–103.
46. Cf. Brueggemann, *Genesis*, 229.

26:34–35. The information about Esau's marriages (but see further 28:9; 36:2–3) forms significant background to 27:46–28:9. The Hittites are the people of that name who appear in Gen. 23 and who live in Hebron, which 35:27–29 still associates with Isaac, Esau, and Jacob. Esau's marrying Hittite women contrasts with the instructions his grandfather gave regarding Esau's father (24:3–4), which Esau's brother will also follow, though perhaps "Esau married the one woman in the world who was suitable for him, namely, a Hittite woman."[47] Presumably it is their Hittite and thus broadly Canaanite ethnicity that offends Isaac and Rebekah; 27:46–28:9 will pick up the point.

27:1–5a. The description of Isaac underscores the narrowness of Genesis's focus on him. We have moved from incidents fairly early in his life, the early years of his and Rebekah's marriage, to a scene when he is an old man and can talk about his own death. There need be no implication that the author knew fewer stories about Isaac. The wider narrative's dramatic or rhetorical or theological priorities make for a focus on Jacob and Esau rather than on various aspects of Isaac's life.

Isaac is old and poor sighted (vv. 1–2) and aware that the time has come when he must pass on to the next generation the responsibility for the family's future. The head of a family needs to take such responsibility for determining what will happen in the family after his death (in our terms, by making a will) in order to discourage family strife after his death—though Isaac succeeds only in encouraging such strife. The story compares with the death-bed scenes of Jacob, Joseph, Joshua, Moses, and David (Gen. 48–49; 50:24–25; Deut. 31–33; Josh. 23–24; 1 Kings 2:1–9) as well as the testamentary literature from the late Second Temple period. But it is not entirely typical of such scenes. First, the description of Isaac in his old age must be somewhat formulaic. In Genesis's chronology, Isaac was sixty when Esau and Jacob were born (25:26), and Esau was forty when he married (26:34), so Isaac is at least a centenarian. But before his eventual death Jacob will have spent about twenty years in Paddan Aram and enough time back in Canaan for his children to grow to adulthood; and Isaac will live until he's 180 (35:28).[48] The language in 27:1–2 thus compares with the earlier description of Abraham and Sarah as very old (18:11) when they have seventy-five and thirty-seven years to live, respectively. "To paraphrase Mark Twain, the account of Isaac's fast-approaching demise is greatly exaggerated."[49] In our terms and more literally, we can imagine Isaac as a middle-aged man. But he is, of course, right that he doesn't know when he may die and that the passing on needs to be done earlier rather than later. The motif of failing eyesight in association with old age recurs in Jacob's own story (48:10). Its frequency as a feature of advancing age is implied in the

47. Neusner, *Genesis Rabbah*, 2:380.

48. On Luther's (*Genesis 26–30*, 99) calculation, Isaac is now 137; cf. the comments in Driver, *Genesis*, 162.

49. Hamilton, *Genesis 18–50*, 389.

comment that Moses did not suffer from it (Deut. 34:7). In this story, it plays a necessary role as a plot device, but in the Isaac story as a whole it parallels the focus on wells and the mention of sowing in the previous chapter in being a motif unique to Isaac in Genesis. It thus reflects either authorial creativity or historical reality. In addition, it anticipates the comment on Eli (1 Sam. 3:2), whose failing physical eyesight is a symbol of his failing inner insight, and Isaac seems shortsighted in this way too: he doesn't see the trouble he and Rebekah are about to cause (KSG). The quasi-testamentary scene has a second atypical aspect. Such occasions properly involve the whole family. This scene involves only one son. As his father, Abraham assumed that the future should lie with his first son, Ishmael, so Jacob assumes that the future lies with his first son, Esau. But whereas God took action to direct Abraham to focus on his second son, in this story the fulfillment of Yahweh's revelation (25:23), which Genesis has not told us Isaac knows about, will come through a human initiative of which he will also be unaware or half aware.

There are several backgrounds to Isaac's specific plan for exercising his responsibility (vv. 3–4): his treating Esau as the family's firstborn, his fondness for Esau over against Jacob, his fondness for game, and Esau's being gifted as a hunter. Is Isaac to be critiqued in this connection?[50] Isaac is going to put his whole being into this blessing. Like the making of a pact with Abimelek, the conveying of his blessing is not merely a political or commercial transaction but a personal one, so it is naturally to be set in the context of a meal, though this makes the exclusion of the rest of the family even odder. Apparently both boys have learned to cook.[51] While the listeners know that Esau has forfeited the position of firstborn and has presumably therefore forfeited the blessing that belongs to the firstborn, the narrative also has not made explicit whether Isaac knows this fact (he is in his dotage and still favors Esau).

Rebekah hears of the plan (v. 5a). Perhaps one is to picture them living in a group of tents that are close to one another so that people can hear other members of the family saying things without trying and must put in some effort to keep anything secret. But it perhaps does not occur to Isaac to keep his intention a secret, even if he knows that Rebekah favors Jacob rather than Esau.

27:5b–17. So Esau sets off; the family is apparently still based near Beer Sheba, to judge from 28:10. And Rebekah formulates her own plan regarding "her son" (v. 6), which contrasts with Isaac's plan for "his son" (v. 5a). Although Isaac has not mentioned Yahweh but simply assumes the authority to transmit the blessing, Rebekah adds the expression "before Yahweh." What does she mean? To imply a recognition that transmitting the blessing depends on Yahweh, one expects a phrase such as the one Melchizedek used

50. Cf. Sylva, "Blessing of a Wounded Patriarch."

51. Cf. Brayford, *Genesis*, 349.

(14:19). "Before Yahweh" rather suggests speaking with Yahweh's awareness, and thus really meaning what one says. Either way, her words are a chilling addition to Isaac's.

There is no "please" in her bidding to Jacob (vv. 8–10), as there was in Isaac's to Esau. She speaks with urgency, simply telling Jacob what to do. Only here does the participle "ordering" come with a feminine subject.[52] No, Rebekah is not a woman you can mess with. And although we know Jacob can cook (25:29), she is going to do the cooking to make sure it comes out to Isaac's liking. She is the one person we know to be aware of the declaration in 25:23, and she is going to see that it comes true. "Divine will concerning the inheritance of God's promise made to Abraham and then to Isaac comes to fruition through trickery."[53]

The background to Jacob's objection (vv. 11–17) lies in the original description of the boys when they were born (see 25:25–27). Whereas Esau is hairy, Jacob is smooth-skinned. The word (*ḥālāq*) comes to mean metaphorically smooth and slippery and thus deceptive in speech (e.g., Prov. 26:28), which is what Jacob will be. But Jacob fears giving Isaac the impression that he is not taking seriously the fact that the blessing will happen "before Yahweh." The rare verb for scorning (*tāʿaʿ*) suggests scornfulness in relation to God (cf. 2 Chron. 36:16)[54] and not merely a mocking of Isaac, though the reference to Isaac's eyes suggests another irony in that they are Isaac's weak point. Jacob is not concerned about the wrongness of being scornful, only about its consequences. But Rebekah (who knows what is destined) has an answer: "It becomes quite clear from Jacob's timorous objection that the mother had really thought of everything"[55] (actually, she has not: see vv. 42–45). Really, the story is not about Jacob cheating Esau. It's about Rebekah cheating Esau.[56] Her conviction that goat skin will do to give the impression of hairy arms, alongside the conviction that goat meat will do as well as game, implies some further assumptions about Isaac's dotage.[57] And if there is a problem, she will take the rap. "This really is a mother's love, readily accepting everything for her child's sake."[58]

27:18–23. Isaac's question is understandable. He has no reason to be expecting Jacob, and it's surely too soon for Esau to have completed his task. With irony, Jacob claims as Esau to be the firstborn, perhaps implying that

52. Cf. Wenham, *Genesis 16–50*, 207.

53. De La Torre, *Genesis*, 254, though the Rebekah story as a whole does not suggest that she fits the picture of the powerless person who functions as a trickster (see M. Jacobs, *Gender, Power, and Persuasion*, 110).

54. Cf. Gunkel, *Genesis*, 303.

55. Von Rad, *Genesis*, 272.

56. Westermann, *Genesis 12–36*, 438.

57. So Brayford, *Genesis*, 350–51.

58. Chrysostom, *Homilies on Genesis 46–67*, 82.

Isaac indeed doesn't know about the event related in 25:29–34, or maybe that he would not have taken the boys' transaction too seriously. He urges the apparently bedridden old man to get up and then chillingly associates Yahweh with the success he claims in having been able to fulfill Isaac's instructions so quickly. Chillingly, too, he uses the verb "make happen" (*qārâ* hiphil) which Abraham's servant used without irony in connection with finding a bride for Isaac himself (24:12). It is the first time Yahweh has been described as "your [Isaac's] God," and the expression will recur in Genesis only at 43:23, again with some irony. There and subsequently on the lips of Pharaoh it denotes Yahweh as "your God" as opposed to "my God." It does signify that Yahweh is "the God of Isaac" as well as "the God of Abraham" (26:24), though not yet "the God of Jacob" (see 28:21).

27:24–29. After the summary statement "so he blessed him" in v. 23b, the narrative again backtracks to give us more detail on the process whereby Isaac came to bless Jacob. It looks as if Isaac can smell a rat, but he lets himself be deceived. Maybe Isaac is the trickster.[59] He starts from the memory evoked by Esau's clothes. Their smell reminds him of the way Yahweh blesses the open country by making it rich with the animals of the wild.

Perhaps surprisingly, his actual blessing (v. 28) then relates first to the life of a farmer rather than to that of a hunter or shepherd, though it will be appropriate to the people who trace their descent back to Isaac and who also lie behind the later part of the blessing; many of them will be farmers. The opening verb applies to all three cola, then "the heavens" and "the earth" form a pair in the parallelism of the first two cola, as do "dew" (from above) and "richness" (from below). Dew will be both literal (dew is especially important in areas like the Negev, and elsewhere in the dry season when there is little rain)[60] and synecdoche (it stands for all the moisture that comes from the heavens). The reference to "richness" raises the question of what the richness consists in, and the line's unexpected third colon gives the answer. This third colon also implies another synecdoche (for which, cf. Deut. 33:28; Hosea 7:14):[61] grain stands for crops in general (but wheat is most important), and new wine makes one think of the fruit of trees and vines (of which the grapes that generate wine would again be most important).

The blessing goes on to widen further (v. 29), in three ways. The first two cola balance serving (a practical action) and bowing low (a symbolic action); they refer in a distinctive way to the subservience of nations and peoples to Abraham's line and thus to the Abrahamic blessing, though they do not speak

59. So Bledstein, "Binder"; and see further M. Jacobs, *Gender, Power, and Persuasion*, 111–18. Zucker ("Deceiver Deceived") argues that there is collusion between Isaac and Rebekah, who are deceiving Jacob.

60. Cf. Sarna, *Genesis*, 192–93.

61. Other passages add oil; cf. Tg. Neof. here, also Jub. 26.23, 31.

of it in those terms. In 25:23 the nations and peoples were the descendants of Esau and Jacob (the unusual word for "peoples," *ləummîm*, comes in Genesis only in these two passages, and that verse also referred to one people "serving" the other). But Isaac's blessing envisages a wider group of nations and peoples. The middle two cola offer hints as to who they are. The verbs take up the earlier ones ("be lord" restates "are to serve"; "bow low" is a simple repetition), which retrospectively suggests that the peoples and nations are Esau's (but actually Jacob's!) brother's and mother's sons—that is, peoples such as the Ishmaelites, Ammonites, Moabites, and Arameans, and the descendants of Qeturah (cf. Tg. Neof., Tg. Ps.-J.). The significance of the third pair of cola overlaps with that of the first two pairs. There will be occasions when such peoples, the neighbors of Isaac's descendants, will wish evil for them; Isaac's declaration promises that their wish will be reversed. On the other hand, when they bless them, Isaac's declaration promises that the blessing will rebound in a positive way on them too. The participles naturally replace the cohortatives of 12:3, where Yahweh speaks; they reappear (though in reverse order) in Balaam's blessing in Num. 24:9.

27:30–33. The drama of the story continues as Esau immediately arrives, just too late to stop the fraudulent act. Reacting with horror, Isaac asks a question that needs no answer, and Esau cries out bitterly. One might think that this performative act of blessing would turn out to be "unhappy" (to use the technical terminology of the concept of "performative action").[62] But Isaac and Esau (and Jacob and Rebekah?) presuppose that a blessing once given has inevitable effect. Their assumption anticipates the assumption of Jephthah and his daughter that someone who has made a pledge to Yahweh can't come back to Yahweh and say, "We made a mistake" (Judg. 11). Saul will think the same way, though his men will apparently conclude that Yahweh is more flexible than this assumption implies (1 Sam. 14:41–45). The story arouses our sympathy for two people who are "beside the point. . . . The blessing will work in spite of human character . . . and whether we are attracted to or repelled by the object of the blessing."[63]

27:34–40. In expressing his grief and anger, Isaac indulges in a double paronomasia, in connection with Jacob's name (see 25:26 and the comment) and in speaking of the position as firstborn and of blessing (*bəkōrâ*/*bərākâ*).[64] Yes, Jacob has lived up to his name, though life will get its own back on him when Laban treats him with the same guile (29:25). Is there any room for a blessing for Esau? Does Isaac have only one blessing to give?

Isaac finds three more lines of verse for him (vv. 39–40), though they are thin on good news. Indeed, they are more like a "modified curse"[65] or an

62. See Han, "Role of 'an Audience'"; and the additional comment on "Blessing" below.

63. Brueggemann, *Genesis*, 235.

64. Sarna, *Genesis*, 194.

65. Keil and Delitzsch, *Pentateuch*, 277.

"anti-blessing."[66] No, he will not enjoy what Jacob enjoys (Edom's territory, much of it at least, will not be a land flowing with milk and honey).[67] Isaac has unwittingly initiated the fulfillment of Yahweh's declaration to Rebekah about the two boys (25:23). Ironically, Jacob also will be the victim of a parallel unwitting fulfillment of Joseph's dreams through the actions of Joseph's brothers, which are designed to frustrate them. And Esau will discover that he must fight for his life instead of finding that peoples bow down to serve him. He will be the servant rather than the served. Joshua and David will eventually defeat the Edomites, though the Edomites will not stay subservient to the Israelites (see, e.g., 1 Kings 11:14; 2 Kings 8:20–22).

27:41–45. Esau's ongoing reaction is not surprising, though his determination to kill his brother (cf. Cain, 4:5–8; Absalom, 2 Sam. 13) might be more than Jacob and Rebekah anticipated. Jacob "has achieved nothing by his deception. His father's blessing is of no help in the face of his brother's hate; blessing can thrive only in a community at peace (Gen. 37–50)."[68] From here on, "the great rule of Jacob's life—and a profound expression of its existential realism—is that he gets everything he aspired to have but not in the way he imagined and at a great cost to himself."[69] He will sum up the span of his years as "bad" (47:9). And in the meantime, if Esau kills Jacob, Esau will need to flee like Cain or Absalom or be liable to execution (cf. Tg. Ps.-J.). Rebekah hears of it; Esau's having said it to himself does not exclude his saying it out loud. So the ever-decisive Rebekah makes a plan and "communicates her counterplan to her son Jacob with the same authority as she did her previous plan."[70] She is right that Esau's wrath will subside, though "some time" is much longer than she imagines.

27:46–28:5. There was no conversation between Isaac and Rebekah in 27:1–45, and the story records no reaction on Isaac's part to Jacob's fraud or to Rebekah's action. Now Rebekah speaks to Isaac, but on a different basis.

The allusion to the Hittite women (27:46) picks up the information in 26:34–35, including the reference to their becoming a source of bitterness of spirit to Isaac and Rebekah, but restates that reaction in terms of dismay or disgust. The term invites the inference that the problem is not that as Hittites, and thus in the broad sense Canaanites, Esau's wives are simply foreigners and that Rebekah, as a more recent immigrant, feels this foreignness even more strongly than Esau or Jacob or Isaac. The word for dismay or disgust (*qûṣ*) is rare, and on one significant occurrence it describes Yahweh's attitude to Canaanite religious practices (Lev. 20:23). This suggests that Rebekah feels

66. Fokkelman, *Narrative Art in Genesis*, 104.

67. Though Driver (*Genesis*, 260) gives a positive portrayal of Edom's territory in support of the view that *min* keeps its partitive meaning, so that Isaac's first line is positive, not negative.

68. Westermann, *Genesis 12–36*, 443.

69. Alter, "Literature," 24.

70. Westermann, *Genesis 12–36*, 443.

a religious revulsion, which the story's listeners are encouraged to share. The story undergirds the principle that Israelite parents should not facilitate their children marrying Canaanites, the principle that led to Rebekah's being sought out to marry Isaac! As in Gen. 24, the issue is the achievement of God's purpose through his people and thus their religious identity, not merely their ethnic or cultural identity.[71]

Isaac can take a hint (28:1–2), or—to put it another way—he knows how to be manipulated, how to be obsequious.[72] With "godly shrewdness"[73] Rebekah has not suggested what Isaac needs to do; she has allowed Isaac to fill in the gaps, creating the illusion that Isaac has the agency.[74] The medieval chapter division collaborates with her. Isaac's initiative then corresponds to the one Abraham took (24:1–2), except that Isaac sends Jacob himself—which fits the circumstances as we read 27:46–28:9 after 27:1–45. While the narrative does not indicate that Isaac himself makes this link, the result of placing 27:1–45 between 26:34–35 and 27:46–28:9 is anticipatorily to explain the issue raised by 28:1–2: we know from 27:46 why Rebekah wants to make sure that Jacob doesn't marry a Canaanite wife, but 27:1–45 explains why he needs to go and find one for himself rather than having Isaac take the same action as his father. So whereas Abraham's servant was sent off to Aram Two-Rivers (24:10), Jacob himself is sent off to Paddan Aram (cf. 25:20).

Isaac's blessing of Jacob (28:3–5) is different in form from the unequivocal declaration in 27:1–45; this blessing is a third-person prayer. It is also different in content. It begins by referring to Shadday as the one who must bring about the blessing, which initiates a link with the blessing in Gen. 17. It asks for Jacob to experience a fulfillment of the Abrahamic blessing of which that chapter speaks, using the words "be fruitful" and "be numerous" and talking about "peoples" (pl.) and about "the country where you are residing" and about God "giving" this country to Abraham (17:1, 2, 6, 8, 16, 20). These verses make explicit for the first time that the Abrahamic blessing belongs to Jacob rather than Esau.[75] In addition, Jacob makes Genesis's first reference to a "congregation" (*qāhāl*; cf. 35:11; 48:4, in contexts where the other terms will also recur, each time in connection with Jacob). The multitude that will issue from Abraham and Sarah's line (17:4–6, 16) will not be merely a horde of nations (17:4–5) but a community gathered in Yahweh's name (e.g., Exod. 12:6; Lev. 16:17; Ps. 22:22, 25 [22:23, 26]). The talk of taking possession of the country (*yāraš*) also recalls the earlier story of covenant making with Abraham (15:7). While he must be thrilled at the

71. Cf. Brueggemann, *Genesis*, 238–40; contrast De La Torre, *Genesis*, 261–62. See further the introductory "Interpretation" comments on Gen. 24.

72. Josephus, *Ant.* 1.19.1; though according to Jub. 27.6–7, Rebekah is manipulated by Jacob.

73. Luther, *Genesis 26–30*, 179.

74. Brett, *Genesis*, 89.

75. Augustine, *City of God* 16.38.

prospect of getting out of the family situation in Beer Sheba, he is being sent off on a venture with its own insecurity (KSG). The blessing should surely make him more enthusiastic about it.[76]

28:6–9. The unit closes with Esau's wives, as it began with them. These verses also thus close off the story of Jacob and Esau until 32:3, which will be the next time Esau is mentioned. A marriage between Ishmael's family and Esau has a certain appropriateness. Esau, like Ishmael, was the older brother whom God passed over in favor of the younger brother. Although the Edomites and Ishmaelites do appear elsewhere together in a list of peoples allied against Israel (Ps. 83:6), both have their own place within God's blessing, even if they are not the means of God's bringing his blessing to the world. While 25:13 mentioned Nebayot, his sister Mahalat appears only here, though the names of Esau's wives are confusing.[77]

Implications

Blessing

"Bless" and "blessing" are the key words in 26:34–28:9; they come twenty-eight times. In Genesis so far, more often than not the agent of blessing has been God: see especially 1:22, 28; 9:1; 12:2–3. In the Scriptures as a whole, God's blessing conveys fullness of life in all its aspects.

The idea that a human being can convey blessing also recurs through the Scriptures (e.g., Num. 6:23–27; 22:6, 12; 1 Sam. 2:20; 1 Kings 8:14, 55, 56; Job 29:13; Luke 2:34; 6:28; Rom. 12:14; 1 Cor. 4:12; 1 Pet. 3:9). Within Genesis, the agent of blessing is a human being on three instructive occasions so far, and now on a fourth. In 12:3 Yahweh envisages people blessing Abraham. In 14:18–20 Melchizedek blesses Abraham. In 24:60 Rebekah's family blesses Rebekah. Now in 27:28–29 and 28:1–4 Isaac blesses Jacob.

Each passage implies that the people giving the blessing have power thereby to make a difference in the lives of the people they bless. Uttering a blessing works in a way that compares with procedures in Western culture such as bequeathing, marrying, ordaining, divorcing, unfrocking, and declaring war. When I bequeath property to someone, this action changes their position and/or changes who they are. When as a minister I marry someone by saying "I declare that you are man and wife," I change who they are. When a man and a woman say "I will" to each other in the marriage service, they themselves change who they are. When a bishop says "I ordain you" to someone, the bishop changes that person from lay to clergy. When a president declares war against another nation, the words turn the home people into the other nation's

76. Chrysostom, *Homilies on Genesis 46–67*, 99.

77. See the comments on 26:34–35 and 36:2–3.

enemies (KSG). In each case the procedure involves formal solemnity and/or celebration with a shared meal. Expressed philosophically, these actions involve performative language, language that does more than communicate something; it does something. In each case, the procedure depends on the position of the person taking the action. I can bequeath only what I own; only as a bishop could I ordain. If I do not have the relevant position, my action cannot work. The background to Gen. 27 is Isaac's position as head of the family (and in particular of the Abrahamic family), which gives him the authority to bestow blessing on the members of the family, and specifically on his sons. This bestowal is like the bequeathing of property. Isaac is treating Jacob as the senior son and in view of his own imminent death is bestowing on him the blessing that goes with that position (it carries responsibilities too, but that's another story).

The wider background to the Genesis passages, to the other scriptural passages, and to some Western practices is (to connect some dots) the assumption that human beings have a capacity to convey blessing and diminishment to other human beings by virtue of God's having made them in his image and given them a commission to rule the earth. This dynamic works via interrelationships written into humanity. Priests have power to bless (14:18–20), families have power to bless (24:60), and ordinary people also have power to bless (12:3).

There need be no assumption that the head of the family or the priest or the bishop or the ordinary person exercises their power in the right way. Balaam recognizes that he is morally and religiously obliged to bless the right people, but he is not compelled to do so (see Num. 22–24). Genesis 27 indicates how the dynamic of blessing works out in this particular family, but it doesn't necessarily indicate how it is always supposed to work out. Yet if someone makes a mistake in the course of their action, it may not annul the action's effectiveness; in connection with Gen. 27, Andrew of Saint Victor notes that if a bishop ordains someone and is deceived about whom he is ordaining, "the one who received the ordination fraudulently would still be ordained."[78] Rebekah and Jacob deceived Isaac and cheated Esau, but neither Isaac nor Esau asked whether Isaac might go back to God and ask God to withdraw the blessing (see v. 33). And God lets the underdog gain blessing through deceit.[79] People have the power to bless only because God gives it to them, and in a sense it remains God's power. The dynamic works because God lets or makes it work. The blessing in Gen. 28:1–4 and some blessings elsewhere make this point especially clear when they are expressed in the form of a wish that God must make happen. God remains the ultimate source of the blessing,

78. *Exposition on Genesis*, as quoted in Schroeder, *Genesis*, 154; an equivalent point could be made about the Lord's Supper and about baptism (cf. Willet, *Hexapla in Genesin & Exodum*, 256).

79. See the discussion of this story in Ekblad, *Reading the Bible*, 76–89.

even though he has delegated some of the power of blessing (cf. the logic in Num. 6:24–26). Even Isaac's blessing in Gen. 27 "was akin to a prayer, and God accepted his prayer";[80] Josephus makes it a prayer (*Ant.* 1.18.6). It was by faith that Isaac blessed Jacob and Esau (Heb. 11:20).

The same framework applies to cursing or diminishing, which denotes the withdrawing of full life in some way. God is also the agent of such cursing or diminishing (3:14, 17; 4:11; 12:3), but human beings can exercise this capacity (9:25; 12:3; Luke 6:28; Rom. 12:14; James 3:9–10). God has the power to overrule the exercise of that power, though he may not too often intervene unasked to do so, because he would then imperil the entire arrangement. He does not micromanage. But God is perhaps more inclined to overrule curses than blessings, as 12:3 may imply (see the comment there), as he is more inclined to change his mind about fulfilling threats than about fulfilling promises.

80. Ibn Ezra, *Genesis*, 270.

28

The Stairway to Heaven

(28:10–22)

Overview

In scene 2 of the drama of Jacob's journey to Harran, Yahweh appears to Jacob in a dream while he is on the way. Yahweh's envoys are walking up and down a stairway between the heavens and the earth. Yahweh himself makes promises to Jacob that amount to affirming for him the promises to Abraham and Isaac and also looking after him when he goes to Harran. Jacob commits himself to Yahweh and sets up a pillar at the place he renames Beth El.

Translation

> **10**So Yaʿaqob left Beʾer Šeba and went to Ḥarran. **11**But he came upon[1] a certain site[2] and stayed the night there because the sun had gone. He took some[3] of the rocks from the site and put them at his head place[4]

1. Targums Neof. and Ps.-J. neatly take *pāgaʿ* to have the rarer meaning "entreat" as in 23:8, and thus "pray at," which Jacob does end up doing (see further the comment), but one would need to take the first clause in v. 11 as part of the anticipatory summary of the section.

2. Literally, "the site" (see GKC 126r).

3. Not "one of" (English versions), which would require a word for "one" (e.g., 2:21; 3:22); cf. Tg. Ps.-J.; Rashi, *Brʾšyt*, 313.

4. Accusative of place (Skinner, *Genesis*, 376; cf. the LXX), in the terms of European grammar; not "under" his head (Vg), as a pillow (for which a stone would not be very comfortable): *məraʾăšōt* suggests that it is more in the position of a headboard (cf. 1 Sam. 19:13, 16; 26:7, 11, 16; 1 Kings 19:6).

and lay down in that site. **12**And he had a dream. There—a ramp[5] stood on the earth with its top reaching to the heavens, and there—God's envoys going up and down by means of it,[6] **13**and there—Yahweh standing by it.[7] He said, "I am Yahweh, the God of Abraham your ancestor and the God of Isaac. The earth that you're lying on, I will give to you and to your offspring. **14**Your offspring will be like the earth's dirt. You'll explode to the west, to the east, to the north, and to the south. All the kin groups on the land will gain blessing through you and through your offspring. **15**There, I am with you: I will keep you wherever you go and bring you back to this piece of land,[8] because I won't abandon you until[9] I've done what I've spoken to you of."

16Yaʿaqob woke up from his sleep and said, "Yahweh is definitely here in this site, whereas I myself didn't acknowledge it," **17**and he was in awe.[10] He said, "How awe-inspiring[11] is this site! This is nothing other than the house of God, and this is [nothing other than] the gateway into the heavens!"[12] **18**Yaʿaqob started early in the morning, got the rock[13] that he had put at his head place, put it up as a standing stone, and poured oil on the top of it. **19**He named the site Bet-ʾel—Luz was the town's name at first, however. **20**And Yaʿaqob made a pledge: "If God will be with me, and will keep me on this journey that I'm going on, and will

5. The LXX and Vg have words that denote a ladder or staircase. Oblath ("'To Sleep'") suggests that it was something like a gate structure.

6. Genesis Rabbah 68.12; 69.3 assume "on him" and explain that they were over him, protecting him. This understanding of *bô* facilitates John 1:51 (cf. Menken, "Genesis in John's Gospel and 1 John," 85–88). But the repeated *hinnēh* (there) indicates that the story is being told as through Jacob's own eyes (cf. van Wolde, "Cognitive Linguistics," 138–39).

7. *Niṣṣāb ʿal* means "standing by him" in 18:2; 45:1, and "standing over him" would be appropriate, but it is not the regular connotation of *niṣṣāb ʿal*; by the reasoning given in the previous footnote, more likely Yahweh is "standing by it" (cf. 24:13, 43). The LXX and Vg have Yahweh leaning on the ladder, a nice image. Standing "over it" in the sense of "on top of it" stretches the preposition and distances Yahweh from the proximity suggested by what follows.

8. *ʾEreṣ* (earth) and *ʾădāmâ* (land), which overlap in meaning like their English equivalents, are used in an idiosyncratic way in vv. 12–15; in v. 14 Yahweh is taking up the phraseology of 12:3, where *ʾădāmâ* means the land in the world as a whole, but in v. 15 *ʾădāmâ* has a more defined meaning.

9. *ʿAd* does not imply that once Yahweh has finished, he will abandon Jacob (see GKC 164f).

10. I follow the SP's punctuation in attaching this verb to the previous sentence (Tal, *Genesis*, 148*). He was not "afraid" (see the comment on 9:2); Yahweh's words in vv. 13–15 would not invite fear.

11. See the preceding footnote.

12. Literally, "the gateway of the heavens." This expression, like "the house of God," is a construct phrase, and constructs are almost invariably definite. Constructs preceding names can be exceptions, and that preceding phrase might thus properly be rendered "a house of God," but that possibility would not apply to the second phrase. Nevertheless, the phrases do not designate the place as the one-and-only house of God or heavenly gateway, and in effect they do suggest "a house of God" and "a gateway into the heavens."

13. That is, one of the rocks referred to in v. 11; again cf. GKC 126r.

give me bread to eat and clothes to wear, **21**and I will come back[14] to
my father's household with things being well, and Yahweh will be God
for me,[15] **22**then this rock that I've put up as a standing stone—it will
be God's house, and everything that you give me—I will conscientiously
pass on a tenth[16] to you."

Interpretation

Genesis again backtracks in order to go forward—that is, although 28:5 briefly closed off the story that began at 26:34 by relating how Jacob went to the land where the family once came from, v. 10 now repeats that information before telling us about something that happened on the journey. The MT's section extends all the way from 28:10 to 32:1 [32:2], the entirety of Jacob's time in Aram, which is framed by the two similar events in 28:10–22 and 32:1–2 [32:2–3].[17] Its reference to Harran as opposed to Paddan Aram suggests that it more directly relates to 27:1–45—that is, in traditional source-critical terms it continues the Yahwist story, or it combines elements from J and E.[18] While the story comprises scene 2 in the account of the time Jacob spends away from Canaan, one aspect of its significance is to explain why Beth El has its unusual name and why people make pledges and bring tithes there (see Amos 4:4): it gives an account of the founding of the Beth El sanctuary.[19]

> Question: How did Beth El come to be a sanctuary?
> Answer: Jacob set up a standing stone there.
>
> Question: Why a standing stone?
> Answer: Because it was a stone near which he slept.

14. In vv. 21–22 the LXX's "and he will bring me back" assimilates to the form of the rest of Yahweh's statement (cf. v. 15).

15. Literally, "Yahweh will be for God for me." Verses 20b–22 comprise a sequence of yiqtol and weqatal clauses, with no syntactical indication where the if-clause gives way to the then-clause, and the LXX preserves the ambiguity of the Hebrew (on which cf. also Peleg, *Going Up*, 141–55). But whereas the Vg locates the transition before the last of the clauses in v. 21 ("then Yahweh will be God for me"), the MT's versification rightly assumes that the if-clause rather extends right through v. 21, with the transition from the if-clause to the then-clause signaled by the switch in v. 21 to clauses in which the subjects precede the verbs, which are thus yiqtol rather than weqatal. Cf. Tg. Neof.; Rashi, *Brʾšyt*, 320.

16. Literally, "tenthing I will tenth," the idiom that couples the infinitive of a verb and a finite form for emphasis.

17. Cf. Westermann, *Genesis 12–36*, 452.

18. "Modern scholars are in full agreement concerning this source analysis" (Gunkel, *Genesis*, 309). Gunkel could not know that the phrase "modern scholars agree" would become the kiss of death.

19. Cf. Coats, *Genesis*, 207.

Question: Why was he sleeping there?
Answer: It was where he happened to be when night fell.

Question: How did Beth El come to have its unusual name?
Answer: Jacob named it.

Question: Why did he give it this name?
Answer: Because Yahweh appeared in a dream and spoke to him there.

Question: How did Yahweh appear?
Answer: By a ramp on which his envoys moved up and down.

Question: What did Yahweh say?
Answer: He made promises, to which pledging and tithing was Jacob's response.

Typically, the story combines some exposition of the way Yahweh was effecting his purpose in the sequence of Israel's ancestors, some indication of the way Yahweh was meeting with the specifics of this particular person's situation, and some information about a place that was important to Israelites. "When worshipers entered the sacred site of Bethel, they saw the standing stone and the place where Jacob slept, dreamt, and vowed. Through the material landscape, invested with sacred memory, the experience of Jacob at Bethel . . . became part of the Israelite experience and practice of worship."[20]

28:10–11. We are presumably to assume that Isaac and his family have been settled in the Beer Sheba region since the last reference to Beer Sheba (or to any concrete place) in 26:23, 33. Once again, Genesis summarizes where the story is going, on a journey of several hundred miles, which would take him several weeks, before telling us about something that happened on the way.[21]

In fact, Jacob is hardly beginning his journey (v. 11), though he must have stopped for a night already on the way from Beer Sheba to Beth El. His route would involve traveling up onto the Judahite mountain crest and going back through territory that was familiar to the family, past his grandparents' home at Mamre, and on to the area of his grandfather's stop on his first journey in the opposite direction and of Yahweh's making a spectacular promise concerning the land (12:8–9; 13:14–17), a key crossroads where the north-south route meets an east-west route from the coastal plain to the Jordan Valley.[22] By

20. Hendel, "Cultural Memory," 35–36. Peleg (*Going Up*) suggests that it also symbolized the Israelites' journey out of the land—which will correspond to Jacob's—so they can be sure that their return will correspond too.

21. Cf. Ibn Ezra, *Genesis*, 275.

22. See further the comment on 13:10–13.

naming the place in due course as Beth El, the story will invite the inference that Jacob stops for the night where Abraham had called out with Yahweh's name (12:8), but Jacob seems ignorant of any such associations, and the narrative does not directly make the link. In any case, it is a big coincidence that Jacob sets up a memorial column so close to where his grandfather set up an altar. While the statement that he "came upon it" might mean he stumbled across it by accident, this verb more often denotes a deliberate meeting, as it will in 32:1 [32:2], though Jacob is not making a point of sleeping in a sanctuary in the hope of receiving a revelation. Nothing we have read of Jacob thus far would make us envisage that he would do so. Even if it is simply a "place" to Jacob, the narrative, by its threefold repetition of the word "place/site" (*māqôm*) expects the listeners to recognize that it is more. The word will recur three more times and with even clearer implications in vv. 16–19 and might be seen as the keyword in the story, pointing to its "central theme."[23] Jacob's reference in v. 17 to this place/site being the house of God suggests that there might be something like a house there, but a building need form only part of a sanctuary site; consider the temple mount in Jerusalem or the traditional English church surrounded by a "churchyard." So one could imagine Jacob bedding down in the sanctuary yard, which might be a safer location to spend the night than some places, and safer than seeking a bed with the local people (see Gen. 19; Judg. 19).[24] When he puts some rocks around his head, however, they are perhaps designed to be a kind of protective arc to make him less exposed to animals—or maybe they would be something to throw at such attackers (KSG). But the narrative doesn't make that point clear because its interest in the rocks lies in what Jacob will do with one of them in v. 18.

28:12–15. Jacob is the first ancestor explicitly said to have a significant dream, though Yahweh's appearances to Abraham and Isaac (12:7; 15:1–20; 17:1–22; 26:2–5, 24) may implicitly have taken place in dreams. But so far Abimelek (oddly?) is the one person in Genesis explicitly reported to have God speak to him in a dream (20:3, 6). There are many more dreams to follow in Genesis. In Israel and elsewhere, dreams were a familiar means whereby God spoke to people. Genesis recounts the dream in the vivid fashion that often obtains in accounts of dreams ("there . . . there . . . there . . ."), inviting the audience to use its imagination and share the dream (cf. 37:7, 9) by putting itself alongside Jacob and seeing the scene through his eyes as it unfolds.[25]

The presupposition of the dream (v. 12) is that the relationship between the physical earth and the physical heavens provides a way of picturing the relationship between the human realm and the realm where God is—not implying that if one literally flew high enough one would come to that realm.

23. So Peleg, *Going Up*, 54.
24. Cf. Josephus, *Ant.* 19.1.1.
25. Cf. Fokkelman, *Narrative Art in Genesis*, 51.

The heavenly realm is the location of Yahweh and his administration, as the high point of a town is the location of the earthly king and his administration. Divine aides thus scuttle between earth and the heavens; Genesis refers to their ascent before their descent. They are bringing information from earth to the heavens, as the smoke from Israel's daily sacrifices rises to God[26] and thus as the prayers of the faithful reach the heavens.[27] They also journey to earth to investigate what is happening there and to implement God's purposes there (cf. Gen. 18–19; Zech. 1:8–17). The word for ramp (*sullâ*) comes only here, though related words denote a mound or highway or causeway. The ramp is needed because the "angels" do not have wings: that idea comes from confusion with hybrid creatures of the kind that appear in passages such as Ezek. 1.[28] If one is to picture the ramp as a stairway, it would need to be wide to accommodate the two-way traffic that Jacob sees. When Jesus takes up the idea of the ramp or stairway in John 1:51, it illumines and is illumined by Jacob's dream. Both presuppose that the heavens and the earth are not just two separate places. In John, Jesus is a link between the two; believers in him live in the heavens as well as on the earth (Eph. 1:3; 2:6). In Christian spirituality the image of Jacob's ladder has suggested the movement of the human spirit toward God,[29] most famously in the work of John Climacus, "John of the Ladder," who lived in the sixth–seventh centuries CE.[30] This understanding also finds expression in the slave spiritual "We Are Climbing Jacob's Ladder," which could hint at a reaching and striving toward both an inward and an outward freedom through Jesus. The contrasting distinctive implication of Jacob's dream is that God's envoys are moving between earth and heaven independently of any such human movement, in a way that may be both occasional and ongoing though generally invisible to humanity.

Yahweh's standing by the ramp (v. 13) corresponds (but in a dream) to Yahweh's standing by Abraham in 18:2. It is his appearing and speaking that counts, more than the ramp and the envoys; as soon as they appear, they disappear, like Moses's burning bush, having fulfilled their function as attention-getter.[31] Yahweh's self-introduction combines his self-introduction to Abraham in 15:7, "I am Yahweh," and that to Isaac in 26:24, "I am the God of Abraham your father." To the latter Yahweh can now add "and the God of Isaac" without the shivery irony that attaches to the idea that Yahweh is Isaac's God in 27:20. The implication with such phrases is regularly not that Yahweh is "his God but not your God"; it is that Yahweh is "his God

26. So Qimchi, *Genesis*, on the verse.
27. Rashi, *Br'šyt*, 319; cf. Tg. Neof., Tg. Ps.-J.
28. Gunkel, *Genesis*, 310.
29. Cf. Reno, *Genesis*, 233.
30. Climacus wrote *Ladder of Divine Ascent*.
31. Fokkelman, *Narrative Art in Genesis*, 54.

and therefore your God." In effect the promise that follows makes that point, and in effect Yahweh affirms his answer to the prayer/wish that Isaac uttered in v. 4. Like Isaac in vv. 1–4, Yahweh makes no comment on Jacob's act of deception. The beginning of the promise in v. 13b localizes it in a way parallel to 13:4–17, also set at Beth El. Yahweh is talking about this stretch of earth on which Jacob is lying.

In v. 14 Yahweh goes on to apply to Jacob the version of that promise in 13:14–15 with its comparison with dirt and its talk of the four points of the compass, though the vivid picture of Jacob's offspring "exploding" or "breaking out" in all these directions is new (Isa. 54:2 takes it up). God is going to "force his way" into the entire world.[32] In the context, the dirt of the earth refers to the dirt that surrounds Jacob in Beth El. The promise about blessing exactly repeats the promise in 12:3, except that the clauses come in the more regular order with the verb first, and the promise adds "and through your offspring," as in 13:14–15. The addition is especially significant for Jacob as a man on a quest for the bride through whom the promise of offspring will need to be fulfilled. The word "offspring" comes three times in vv. 13–14 as it did in 13:15–16 and in 22:17–18 (even more occurrences in the promises in 17:7–10; 26:3–4). And the promise that people will gain blessing through Jacob recalibrates the point about blessing as Jacob has understood it: in Jacob's life, it has been something to be obtained for oneself.[33]

"I am with you" (v. 15) in turn applies to Jacob the commitment made to his father in 26:24. In both these passages the reminder comes in the form of a noun clause; it differs in form from the earlier promise to Isaac, "I will be with you" (26:3), though the implications are similar. "I am with you" is now "a promise for the road."[34] The declaration is spelled out in the two further undertakings that relate to Jacob's specific situation. "I will keep you" is a new promise for Jacob in his vulnerable position, and "I will bring you back" and "not abandon you" are further nuances on the promise that he uniquely needs. The last phrase presumably refers to protecting him and keeping him safe. While Yahweh's words do not make any explicit connection with the vision in v. 12, we might connect the dots and infer that the envoys are the agents through whom these promises will find fulfillment. An interest in horizontal movement complements the focus on vertical movement.[35]

28:16–19. Like Pharaoh and Solomon waking up and realizing that they have had a momentous dream (41:7; 1 Kings 3:15), Jacob wakes up and realizes what an important thing has just happened; dreams are a significant means of God giving a revelation of great consequence (cf. Matt. 1:20; 2:12, 13, 19, 22; Acts 2:17). A dream may issue from and relate to the dreamer's

32. Luther, *Genesis 25–30*, 226.
33. Cf. Hamilton, *Genesis 18–50*, 242.
34. Westermann, *Genesis 12–36*, 456.
35. Peleg, *Going Up*, 65.

inner questioning at a time of fear or anxiety, but it may also signify God's response to the need of the moment. If Jacob realizes that it is a local sanctuary where he has stopped for the night, he hasn't assumed that it has anything to do with Yahweh (anything to do with "the God of Abraham and the God of Isaac" or with "the God Shadday," he would actually say). Yet it evidently is a place where Yahweh can be present and active. How could Jacob have known (cf. the "now I know/acknowledge" of 22:12; Exod. 18:11; 1 Kings 17:24)? While God is present everywhere, he is present in different places in different ways: working, saving, refreshing, punishing, reproving, forbearing.[36] "When Jacob had gone to sleep, he thought he was sleeping in a place that was very remote from God"; actually he has been sleeping in God's house, reclining before heaven's gate.[37] Jacob has not left Yahweh's realm. It is not that he meets Yahweh here; rather, Yahweh meets him. "Jacob's expectations of encountering Yahweh somewhere between Beer-sheba and Harran were about as great as Saul's expectations of meeting the Christ somewhere between Jerusalem and Damascus."[38] But he has proved that Ps. 121 is true (Gen. Rab. 68.2); Pss. 23 and 91, also.[39]

Awe (v. 17) suggests an emotion but also a submission of the will. It was the response of Abimelek's servants to the report of his dream; it's not a surprising or unreasonable response to a revelation from Yahweh whose form is unprecedented and whose content speaks so weightily yet also so encouragingly. But Jacob's pair of inferences are remarkable. The first is the only reference to a house of God before Sinai, and even there (Exod. 23:19; 34:26) the references are prospective: they relate to a house of Yahweh that will eventually come into being. Yet evidently "Yahweh was present, that is, at home, in this place."[40] A sanctuary such as that at Beth El or at Jerusalem is "God's house" by virtue of being an earthly embodiment of God's dwelling in the heavens. Heaven is not merely or not at all a place separate from earth but a fourth dimension closely related to earth. Yet it is not particularly logical to infer from God's appearing and speaking that the place is a house of God, a place where God lives. It is not the first place where Yahweh has appeared and spoken, and the others have not been so designated. But places where God has appeared and spoken, such as Beer Sheba, had no buildings in the time of Israel's ancestors, whereas places such as Shechem and Beth El were long-established towns with sanctuaries.[41] So one might more easily imagine Jacob talking in terms of a house of God if he is in the shadow of a building at the

36. Willet, *Hexapla in Genesin & Exodum*, 260, quoting from Bernard of Clairvaux, sermon 6 on "The Dedication of the Church."

37. Ephrem, *Genesis*, 174.

38. Hamilton, *Genesis 18–50*, 238.

39. Cf. Brueggemann, *Genesis*, 245–48.

40. Gunkel, *Genesis*, 311.

41. See James Kelso, *Excavation of Bethel.*

Beth El sanctuary. If "house of God" does not link closely with the content of the dream, then "gateway into the heavens" does so link. The dream has indicated that this site is a portal, a place where earth and heaven are open to one another. If Jacob is recognizing that Yahweh has appeared to him in a Canaanite sanctuary with such significance, this recognition might link with his calling it "house of God" rather than "house of Yahweh," which would be suggested by vv. 13 and 16 and is the more common First Testament phrase. The phrase "gateway into the heavens" appears only here, but the idea that certain places are portals spells out the implications of other passages that tell of God's appearing, such as at Shechem (e.g., 12:7–8), though in that passage Genesis speaks of God as appearing at Shechem but not at Beth El—only of Abraham's building his altar at Beth El. The image of God's house and of a ramp between earth and the heavens complement each other, for Genesis and for Jesus, even while they formally clash. The image of God's home affirms the reality of God's presence; the image of a ramp affirms the distinction between God's realm and the human realm.

Once again, the description of Jacob leaving early in the morning (v. 18) suggests a commitment to a task that is thus undertaken without delay. Now we see the point about the earlier reference to rocks, one of which Jacob sets up as a *maṣṣēbâ*. It need not have been gigantic; Jacob can maneuver it since he is no wimp (29:10; 32:25). Although one might expect him to build an altar, like his father and grandfather and like Jacob himself later (e.g., 12:7–8; 26:25; 35:1), here the "standing stone" commemorates the ramp that "stood" there and the God who "stood" there (all three words come from the root *nāṣab*). In general, setting up such a stone marks a place as significant; something has happened here (cf. 35:14, 20), and this stone at his head when he had his dream is appropriate as a marker of that revelation. It memorializes the ramp and affirms that it is not just a passing phenomenon in a dream but a permanent reality.[42] While pouring oil on it anticipates the anointing of everything in the wilderness sanctuary to make it sacred (Exod. 40:9), Genesis does not call this pouring an anointing (contrast Gen. 31:13 and comment there). The Torah later outlaws standing stones (e.g., Lev. 26:1), which are tainted because of their association with the traditional religion of the country. But Jacob's standing stone antedates such problems.

Jacob's naming the place Beth El, "house of El" (v. 19), links with and in a sense issues from his recognizing this place as a house of God (*bêt ʾĕlōhîm*, his expression in vv. 17 and 22).[43] But the name Beth El implies that the expression refers to God as the local people would speak of him, as Melchizedek spoke of *ʾēl ʿelyôn*; Jacob's recognition then has similar theological implications to the perspective on Melchizedek in 14:18–20. Jacob is consciously or

42. Cf. Fokkelman, *Narrative Art in Genesis*, 66–67.

43. On Beth El and Luz, see the additional comment at the end of the comments on Gen. 35.

unconsciously confirming the place's existent name rather than devising a new one (as in 19:22; 26:33); indeed, he will again name this place Beth El in 35:15. At the same time, he is seeing new significance in it or attaching new significance to it in affirming that Yahweh is the one who has appeared here and who can thus be identified with El (see the references to Yahweh in vv. 16 and 21; and again cf. 14:22).

28:20–22. It logically follows that Jacob responds to Yahweh's commitment with his pledge or promise, though Jacob is the only person who makes a pledge or promise (a *neder*) in Genesis.

What kind of "if" does Jacob utter (v. 20b)? Since Yahweh has taken the initiative in his act of commitment, one should hardly call Jacob's commitment conditional; contrast the "if" clauses in Num. 21:2; Judg. 11:30–31; 1 Sam. 1:11; 2 Sam. 15:8, where the human beings take the initiative. Rather, the "if" has the connotation of "given that," though it might still imply a somewhat contractual understanding of Yahweh's relationship with him. Jacob begins near the end of where Yahweh ended, with the final commitments that Yahweh made. He takes up the promise of a presence that will issue in keeping him, and he nuances it with a reference to food and clothes—quite a basic hope.

He then nuances the promise about coming back (v. 21) with a reference to his family and to *šālôm*. In the context of v. 20 one might take *šālôm* to denote safety on his journey (cf. the LXX), while in the broader context one might take it to refer to peace between him and Esau. In the event, however, he will have done quite well by the time he comes back home, and v. 22b also suggests this connotation of *šālôm* here (cf. the Vg, and 29:6). The final aspect of God's commitment that Jacob takes up is the promise that he will be God for Jacob. In v. 13 Yahweh has spoken of himself as Abraham and Isaac's God; as Jacob leaves home and thus leaves the ambit where Yahweh keeps watch over Isaac's family, his promises to Jacob imply that he will now become Jacob's God, too, in fulfillment of his father's blessing and prayer. The promise corresponds to God's declaration that he will be God for Abraham and his offspring (17:7, 8; cf. Exod. 6:7; Lev. 26:12; Jer. 7:23; Ezek. 36:28).

Jacob's response (v. 22) is twofold. It first involves a synecdoche or metonymy:[44] the standing stone and its environs will be God's house, a place that warrants an attitude of reverence and awe and also of confidence that God can meet with people here. His second declaration again recalls Gen. 14, where Abraham gives Melchizedek a tenth of what he gained through his venture to liberate Lot. Here "the text is intriguingly silent on who is to receive the tithe and what is to be done with it."[45] But the logic of the passage is that Yahweh is somehow the recipient of the tithes. Tithes function in a way similar

44. Cf. Calvin, *Genesis*, 2:123.
45. Sarna, *Genesis*, 201.

to Sabbaths and firstfruits: one gives a tenth to God as an acknowledgment that the whole really belongs to him, and God is then willing for one to treat the rest as one's own. "There is a 'must' for God in this text"; there is also a "must" for Jacob.[46] Here at the close of the pledge Jacob directly addresses Yahweh, as Yahweh has directly addressed him.

46. Fretheim, "Genesis," 543.

29

Jacob Finds His Extended Family

(29:1–14)

Overview

In scene 3 of the account of Jacob's flight to Harran, Jacob continues his journey there, reaches a well near the town, meets Rachel, and goes to stay with Laban's family.

Translation

1Yaʿaqob set off[1] and went to the country of the Easterners.[2] **2**He looked, and there—a well in the open country, and there—three herds of sheep lying there by it, because people used to water the herds from that well. The rock on the well's mouth was big;[3] **3**all the herds would gather there, and people would roll the rock off the well's mouth and water the sheep and put the rock back in its place on the well's mouth.

4Yaʿaqob said to them, "Brothers, where are you from?" They said, "We're from Ḥarran." **5**He said to them, "Do you know Laban ben Nahor?" They said, "We know him." **6**He said to them, "Are things well with him?" They said, "They're well. There—Raḥel his daughter is coming with the sheep." **7**He said, "Here, the day is still long.[4] It's not time for the livestock to gather. Water the sheep and go pasture them." **8**They said, "We can't, till all the herds gather and people roll the rock from on the well's mouth and we water the sheep."

1. Literally, "lifted up his feet" (see the comment).
2. The Vg takes this phrase to mean simply "the country to the east."
3. The SP has anarthrous *ʾeben*, implying "a big stone was on the well's mouth."
4. Literally, "big."

[9]While he was still speaking with them, Raḥel came with the sheep that belonged to her father, because she was a shepherd. [10]When Yaʿaqob saw Raḥel the daughter of Laban, his mother's brother, and the flock of Laban, his mother's brother, Yaʿaqob came up, rolled the rock from on the well's mouth, and watered the flock of Laban his mother's brother; [11]and Yaʿaqob kissed Raḥel and lifted his voice and cried. [12]Yaʿaqob told Raḥel that he was her father's brother[5] and that he was Ribqah's son, and she ran and told her father. [13]When Laban heard the news of Yaʿaqob, his sister's son, he ran to meet him, hugged him and kissed him,[6] and brought him into his house. He told Laban all these things, [14]and Laban said to him, "You are indeed my own bone and flesh." He[7] stayed with him for a whole month.[8]

Interpretation

In its own right, scene 3 in the account of the time Jacob spends away from Canaan describes

how Jacob discovered where his extended family lived in Harran,
how he met Rachel, and
how he found acceptance into Laban's family.

The story comprises a reprise of the account of the journey undertaken by his grandfather's servant (Gen. 24). It is one of several stories about how someone comes to a well and there meets the girl whom he will marry (cf. Exod. 2:15–20; the meeting is vicarious in Gen. 24). While the story reaches its goal with Jacob's acceptance into Laban's household, the larger amount of space it gives to his meeting with Rachel hints at where scene 4 will take us. It is an idyllic picture, though the idyll will fairly soon be shattered.[9]

29:1–8. The story begins with a unique expression to describe Jacob resuming his journey; he "lifted up his feet," which perhaps suggests that there was a spring in his step after Yahweh appeared to him and gave him his promises (Tg. Ps.-J.; cf. Gen. Rab. 70.8). "His heart lifted his feet."[10] As usual, Genesis skips over the long journey, which would have taken two or three weeks, though mentioning the Easterners hints at how far he needs to go. They are

5. In the sense of relative; as the previous verse indicates, Jacob is actually Laban's nephew.

6. In the (intensive) piel; Jacob had delicately kissed Rachel only in the qal.

7. The Vg's "And after the days of one month were fulfilled . . ." takes v. 14b as subordinate to v. 15, but the lack of any explicit subject for the verb in v. 14b suggests that the MT is right to link v. 14b with what precedes; it is v. 15 that begins the next scene.

8. Literally, "a month of days."

9. Cf. Seebass, *Genesis*, 2:328.

10. Rashi, *Brʾšyt*, 321.

so mentioned only here in the Torah. The expression can apparently cover anyone living east of the Jordan; Harran is north-northeast of Beer Sheba. Here the term's connotation is that Jacob is in a distant, alien, and foreign territory; it "might reflect Jacob's perspective that he is going backwards."[11] And it could suggest that looking for his extended family might be like looking for a needle in a haystack.

But he has the same luck as his grandfather's servant (vv. 2–3). While Genesis does not refer to his praying, as the servant did, Jacob has made his implicit profession of trust in Yahweh on the basis of Yahweh's promises (28:20–22), and his trust has been vindicated. Yahweh has kept his promises. The circumstances are similar to those that applied to the servant, though Jacob does not come with camels needing watering. But arriving at a well in the open country where herds of sheep are gathered, ready to be watered, could make him feel quite at home. Apparently he is not afraid that the well may become a place of conflict as it was for his father (25:19–33), though the words and actions he is about to indulge in might imperil that assumption (KSG). But as happened then and there, it will become a place where Yahweh provides. Further, Jacob surely knows about the usefulness of a big rock to prevent the well from being filled with dirt accidentally or on purpose (26:15, 18) or to stop animals from falling in. He would also know the schedule shepherds would follow.

Like the servant (vv. 4–6), Jacob finds that "coincidence" works in his favor. The narrator does not tell us exactly where the well is, but through the shepherds we discover this. A well is usually somewhere outside of town. Towns are usually in an elevated place, and wells by their nature are on lower ground. Maybe this well is a little farther from the town than the one in 24:11. But the local town is still Harran. Not only so, but Laban still lives there. Strictly, he is Laban ben Bethuel, the son of Nahor, but Bethuel tended to get sidelined in Gen. 24, and later Laban's God is "the God of Nahor," as Jacob's God is "the God of Abraham" (31:53). Not only does Laban live in the nearby town, but the shepherds know him and know he is doing well; and lo and behold, here comes his daughter. Once again, the dynamics of the story in Gen. 24 recur. The way things turn out suggests that the reference to *šālôm* trades on the word's ambiguity, as was the case at 28:21, though in a different direction. Here Jacob will enter into friendly relationships with his extended family, but the harmony will not last.[12]

The shepherds apparently hang around the well for a good part of the day (vv. 7–8), though they should be pasturing the sheep and then watering them in the evening, or watering them and then pasturing them. Jacob knows about shepherding, and he is not afraid to share his expertise. Perhaps Rachel is

11. Assis, *Identity in Conflict*, 42.
12. Cf. Westermann, *Genesis 12–36*, 465.

doing the right thing: either she is watering the sheep before pasturing them, or she has been pasturing them and is only now bringing them to the well. Either way, she is not just hanging around the well like some people. Maybe the other shepherds' excuse is that rolling the rock off the mouth of the well takes the strength of several people, or maybe it's that no one is allowed to do it on their own lest there should be some kind of wrongdoing like that of Abimelek's shepherds, who put dirt in the well.

29:9–14. Meanwhile Rachel arrives. Like Reuel's daughters (Exod. 2:15–22), she is a shepherd. Once again the story makes clear how mythical is the idea that women did not mix with men and could not have responsible jobs. In each case one should perhaps see the girls as under-shepherds, looking after the family flocks on their father's behalf, though evidently they have real responsibility for them.

Anticipating Moses's action in Exod. 2:15–22, Jacob shows that he is a real man (v. 10), not like these other pathetic Harran shepherds; he reverses the roles in Gen. 24, where Rebekah shows herself to be a real woman in watering the servant's camels. Either he does what it would take several of them to do, or he ignores the local custom that all the shepherds draw from the well together.

And he kisses Rachel (v. 11). Although the listeners may know where this story is going, there is no suggestion at this point that Jacob fancies Rachel; kissing is an intrafamilial gesture with no sexual connotation (e.g., 27:26–27; 29:13; 31:28; 31:55 [32:1]; 33:4). His bursting into tears reflects how the focus in his heroic action has increased his excitement at finding his uncle Laban's family. Three times the narrator refers to Laban as "his mother's brother," an unnecessary repetition as a means of conveying information about Laban to the listeners, but it stresses the importance of this fact to Jacob and to the story.

Rachel deserves some explanation for his excitement and emotion (v. 12), though maybe Genesis again deviates from chronological order here—perhaps Jacob identifies himself first and kisses later.[13] Rachel's running then mirrors her aunt's running in 24:20, 28.

In turn Laban's running (29:13) repeats his own running in 24:29, notwithstanding his being now the family's patriarch. There is more kissing and hugging and welcoming, and Jacob tells Laban his story as the servant had told his, though here, in contrast to Gen. 24, the story is not repeated. Did he really tell him "all these things"? The story of how things have been with the family? And/or the story of his having the blessing of the firstborn, minus the way he obtained it? And/or the story of how his parents have commissioned him to find a wife from "back east"? And/or the story of the way Yahweh appeared to him and made commitments to him? Some aspects of his story would commend him as a potential son-in-law, like his father.

13. Cf. Calvin, *Genesis*, 2:128.

Laban indeed welcomes him as a member of the family (v. 14). He is the same bone and flesh, a similar expression to 2:23 and one that implies a commitment (Judg. 9:2; 2 Sam. 5:1; 19:12–13 [19:13–14]). The recognition might imply an acknowledgment that Laban's family is indeed a proper place for Jacob to find a wife. Events will also reveal that Jacob and Laban are "cut from the same cloth" in a more specific sense; they are both tricksters.[14] Laban's welcome is expressed in Jacob's being given a whole month's hospitality, though the next scene will suggest he has been earning his keep.

14. De La Torre, *Genesis*, 266.

30

Jacob Acquires a Wife or Two

(29:15–30)

Overview

In scene 4 of the account of Jacob's time in Harran, Jacob works for Laban to earn the right to marry his younger daughter, but Laban deceives him into marrying his older daughter first. Jacob does also marry Rachel, and he continues to be more fond of Rachel than of Leah.

Translation

15Laban said to Yaʿaqob, "Because you're my brother,[1] are you to serve
me for nothing? Tell me what your wages are to be." **16**Now Laban had
two daughters. The name of the elder was Leʾah and the name of the
younger Raḥel. **17**Leʾah's eyes were soft,[2] but Raḥel was attractive in
shape and attractive in appearance, **18**and Yaʿaqob liked Raḥel. So
he said, "I'll serve you seven years for Raḥel, your younger daughter."
19Laban said, "My giving her to you will be better than my giving her to
another man. Stay with me." **20**So Yaʿaqob served seven years for Raḥel,
but in his eyes they were like a short time because of his liking for her.
21Then Yaʿaqob said to Laban, "Give me my wife, since my time is com-
plete, so I can be with her."[3] **22**So Laban gathered all the people of the
place and made a banquet. **23**But in the evening he got Leʾah his

1. I.e., a member of my family.

2. *Rak* can mean soft in the sense of weak (so the LXX, Vg), but it need not carry this implication (cf. Deut. 28:54, 56), and in this context the positive connotation fits better (cf. Aq, Sym, Tg). Either way, Jacob's attraction for Rachel is based on her appearance.

3. Literally, "come into her"; so also in vv. 23, 30; 30:3, 4, 16.

daughter and brought her to him, and he was with her ([24]and Laban gave
to her Zilpah his maidservant—to Leʾah his daughter as maidservant).
[25]So in the morning: there, it was Leʾah! He said to Laban, "What's
this that you've done to me? It was for Raḥel that I served with you,
wasn't it? So why have you beguiled me?" [26]Laban said, "It's not done
like that in our place, giving the younger one before the firstborn. [27]Com-
plete the week for the one, and the other will be given you as well,[4]
for the service that you'll give with me for another seven years more."
[28]Yaʿaqob did so. He completed the week for the one, then he gave him
Raḥel his daughter as wife ([29]and Laban gave to Raḥel his daughter
Bilḥah his maidservant to her as maidservant). [30]So Yaʿaqob both was
with Raḥel and also liked Raḥel rather than Leʾah,[5] and served with him
another seven years more.

Interpretation

We know that Jacob had ambitions from birth and that he has learned trickery from his mother. He now discovers that trickery is built into the family's genes. Scene 4 answers the question "How did Jacob come to marry two sisters, with two maidservants?" (the significance of mentioning the maidservants will become apparent in scene 5). Or better, how did Jacob come to marry Leah as well as Rachel when it was Rachel that he really liked? The plot of the story thus works as follows:

1. Laban initiates a negotiation with Jacob (v. 15)
2. Jacob thinks he has made the negotiation work his way (vv. 16–22)
3. His plan is put on hold through Laban's deception (vv. 23–25)
4. Laban initiates another negotiation (vv. 26–27)
5. Jacob achieves his aim, though we wonder how the dynamics will work out in the future (vv. 28–30)

29:15. The implication is perhaps that Jacob has been earning his keep in an informal way over the first month; he has not just been sitting around while other people worked. But the arrangement needs regularizing. Wages will now be a key word through Gen. 29–31: related nouns and verbs come eleven times.[6] Jacob is in an ambiguous position. The members of a family do not receive wages; there is no such thing as money, and there is nothing

4. There being no other first-person plurals in the context, I take *wənitnâ* as third-person niphal, as in 38:14.

5. Verses 31–34 imply not just "more than"; cf. the use of *min* in Ps. 52:3 [52:5] (Fokkelman, *Narrative Art in Genesis*, 129); but see also Gen. 38:26 and the footnote, and GKC 133b.

6. Fokkelman, *Narrative Art in Genesis*, 126; he notes that *ʿbd* (serve) and related words also recur.

to spend it on. Ideally, a shepherding family (for instance) will grow some things as well as look after flocks (cf. 26:12) and will aim to be more or less self-sufficient but also in a position to barter with its wool to get whatever else it needs. The head of the family will no doubt control the disbursement of assets. But Jacob doesn't really belong to this family, and when he told his story after his arrival, he surely revealed that he isn't committed to it in the long term. He would also have made clear why he has come to Harran. So both parties know why Jacob is here, and it's quite appropriate for Laban to raise his question.

29:16–22. But Laban may be acting ingenuously or speaking euphemistically. He will have in the back (or the front) of his mind his two daughters, who will eventually need husbands. They are perhaps teenagers and rather younger than Jacob, though they are evidently old enough to be entrusted with the sheep. We don't know how many years older Leah was than Rachel.

Both girls have their alluring features (vv. 17–19), but Rachel has a broader attractiveness, and Jacob fancies her. Is the basis for his preference (not confirmed by God) to be questioned?[7] The context does not suggest that at this stage he "loves" her; for him as for his father (24:67), love would more likely follow marriage. However, Isaac did not have to work for years for Rebekah; instead, his father's servant came with those camels and their loads. Jacob is therefore more like the servant in a household who is envisaged later in the Torah, to whom the master of the house may give one of his daughters in marriage as part of the arrangement for his service (Exod. 21:2–11). While Laban would not know that marriage between cousins has slight genetic disadvantages, he will know that it has significant advantages in family and community relationships and thus in overall human well-being. On the other hand, there is no reference to Laban consulting (e.g.) Leah or her mother (let alone Rachel herself), and maybe he would be in a lot of trouble when he got home and told them about the deal (hence perhaps the ploy that follows; KSG).

The seven-year period (v. 20) also compares with conventions in Israel, where servitude (in theory) came to an end after six years. Possibly that difference between six and seven years in itself suggests the high price Jacob is prepared to pay for Rachel's hand. Rebekah had envisaged him staying in Harran for just a short time (lit., "a few days," 27:44); a short time is all it seems to Jacob.[8] The seven years would be a betrothal period, implying a quasi-legal marriage commitment: thus Rachel is already "my wife" in v. 21 even though the marriage has not been consummated. Genesis makes no reference to Rachel's having an opinion about the match, though her aunt's story (and common practice in societies where the family arranges a marriage) may imply that she would have the chance to say yes or no. Other women

7. Cf. T. J. Schneider in Eskenazi and Weiss, *Torah*, 176.
8. Cf. Rashi, *Br'šyt*, 327–28.

in the First Testament do get the chance to express an opinion about whom they marry, and there are no stories about women being married off against their expressed will.

Eventually the "time" is completed (vv. 21–22)—the word "days" recurs. It's easy to imagine that Jacob can't wait, for all his happiness with the seven years for which he's been killing time. So Laban organizes the first of the only two wedding banquets in the First Testament; the other comes in Judg. 14. Like most other banquets in the First Testament, both these wedding banquets are occasions when things go wrong.

29:23–25. Leah would be wearing a veil to cover her face (cf. 24:65) when she is given to Jacob, so even those soft eyes are invisible, as Tamar's face will be to his son Judah (38:13–16). Jacob has never set his own eyes on any other parts of either of these two women and has had no physical contact with them beyond a familial kiss; it's dark now, and Jacob is well-fed and well-drunk, like his great-uncle Lot (cf. 19:30–35).[9] So deception is not so hard. Just as we are not told whether Rachel has any opinion about the match, so we are not told whether Leah has any opinion about the deception or whether she even knows about it. Nor are we told how Laban keeps Rachel out of the way that night.

The note about Zilpah (v. 24) keeps the listeners on their toes as they wait to hear what happens next. A maidservant is another member of the household who has been put into servitude there by her father, perhaps because he was in debt to Laban. She would have been involved in household management for Laban (we hear nothing about Laban's wife or wives), but she will now be thus involved in the household of Jacob and Leah—though it will turn out not to be her only role. Genesis mentions no dowry that Laban gives Rachel or Leah,[10] another marker of the brevity of this story compared with Gen. 24. It focuses on matters that provide background to what follows.

What immediately follows (v. 25) is the First Testament scene that one would most like to have witnessed. The narrator draws us into that wish with the "there," inviting us to imagine that we look at the scene through Jacob's eyes. Jacob's first indignant question repeats the one in 3:13; 12:18; and 26:10. The verb "beguile" (*rāmâ* piel) comes eight times in the First Testament, and four of them ask Jacob's question (cf. Josh. 9:22; 1 Sam. 19:17; 28:12). Ironically, "guile" (*mirmâ*) is the word Isaac used of Jacob's trickery (27:35). Yes, Jacob has swallowed a dose of his own medicine, and without irony he asks why.

29:26–27. Did Jacob really think Laban would do something that is not done? With audacity Laban speaks of Jacob expecting to engage in an action that is equivalent to gross sexual impropriety (cf. 20:9; 34:7). With further irony, Laban is working with the principle that Jacob resisted in his own life and has ignored in connection with Leah and Rachel. Once again with irony,

9. Cf. Hamilton, *Genesis 18–50*, 262–63.

10. See the comment on 24:52–53.

Genesis takes up terms from Gen. 25–27, the references to Esau and Jacob as the "firstborn" and the "younger." It is strangely appropriate that Jacob would seek to displace Leah by her little sister, he being the younger brother who two or three times set about displacing his big brother. But what he succeeded in doing in relation to Esau and Isaac, he has failed to do with Leah. In Laban he has met his match. And anyway, Laban has said that Jacob can have Rachel, but he didn't say that she could come first ("Jacob, of all people, should know to be careful when negotiating for something of value").[11] How can Laban act in this way?!

Nor is Laban finished with his cunning (v. 27). He needed to find husbands for two daughters, and he has done so. A wedding takes a week to celebrate; Judg. 14 again provides a parallel. When the week is over, Jacob may also marry Rachel if he commits himself to work for Laban for another seven years. Laban has no unease about two sisters marrying the same man, and Jacob has no unease about the idea, though the Torah will later prohibit such a practice (Lev. 18:18). Perhaps it is no wonder that the Torah later prohibits such a practice; there are several stipulations in the Torah that one might see as intended to prevent a recurrence of events in Genesis. However, the entire story is not interested in passing ethical judgments on Laban, any more than it was on Jacob earlier, though it may rejoice in the way people such as Jacob and Laban get their comeuppance. It is implicitly more interested in the way these two marriages (not to say Jacob's having sex with the two maidservants) will bring about the fulfillment of God's promise to make Jacob exceedingly fruitful.[12]

29:28–30. Rachel becomes Jacob's second wife straightaway; there is no seven-year betrothal. She too brings a maidservant with her. Thus the scene comes to a close, though we won't be surprised if the inequality in Jacob's affections brings consequences; there will be no "and they lived happily ever after" here.[13] Nor will we be surprised if events have generated a tension in relations between Laban and Jacob that will not go away. But maybe Jacob would rather put up with that tension than go home and face the situation there (KSG).

11. Brayford, *Genesis*, 358.
12. See further J. Anderson, *Jacob*, 97–102.
13. Wenham, *Genesis 16–50*, 237.

31

Eleven Sons and a Daughter

(29:31–30:24)

Overview

In scene 5 of the account of Jacob's time in Harran, Leah gives birth to Reuben, Simeon, Levi, and Judah; Bilhah gives birth to Dan and Naphtali; Zilpah gives birth to Gad and Asher; Leah gives birth to Issakar, Zebulun, and Dinah; and at last Rachel gives birth to Joseph. Difficulty in conceiving issues in resentment and conflict; fruitfulness issues from a combination of God's activity, wifely initiative, and the cooperation of Jacob; and it results in gratefulness to God and a sense of honor.

Translation

29:31 Yahweh saw that Leʾah was rejected[1] and he opened her womb,
whereas Raḥel was infertile. **32**So Leʾah became pregnant and gave
birth to a son and named him Reʾuben, because (she said), "Yahweh
has seen my humbling—because now my husband will like me." **33**She
became pregnant again and gave birth to a son, and said, "Because Yah-
weh has heard that I was rejected[2] and has given me this one as well,"
so she named him Šimʿon. **34**She became pregnant again and gave birth

1. The Vg makes explicit that it is Jacob (not Rachel) who does the rejecting. Wells ("First Wives Club") argues that this rejection implies a demotion from the quasi-legal position of senior wife.

2. I infer the tense of the noun clause from the context, but no doubt it implies "and I *am* rejected still."

to a son, and said, "Now this time my husband will become attached to
me, because I've given birth to three sons for him." That's why he named
him[3] Lewi. **35**She became pregnant again and gave birth to a son and
said, "This time I will confess Yahweh." That's why she named him Yehu-
dah. Then she stopped giving birth.

30:1 Raḥel saw that she couldn't give birth for Yaʿaqob, and Raḥel was
jealous of her sister and said to Yaʿaqob, "Give me children![4] Otherwise,
I'm going to die!" **2**Yaʿaqob's anger raged[5] at Raḥel. He said, "Am I in
the place of God,[6] who has held back the fruit of the womb from you?"
3She said, "Here's my handmaid Bilhah. Be with her, so she can give
birth on my knees and I can also be built up through her."

4So she gave him Bilhah her maidservant[7] as wife, and Yaʿaqob was
with her. **5**Bilhah became pregnant and gave birth to a son for Yaʿaqob.
6Raḥel said, "God has given judgment for me; yes, he's listened to my
voice[8] and given me a son." That's why she named him Dan. **7**Bilhah,
Raḥel's maidservant, became pregnant again and gave birth to a second
son for Yaʿaqob. **8**Raḥel said, "An almighty[9] wrestling match I've fought[10]
with my sister; yes, I've won." So she named him Naptali.

9Leʾah saw that she had stopped giving birth, and she got Zilpah her
maidservant and gave her to Yaʿaqob as wife. **10**Zilpah, Leʾah's maidser-
vant, gave birth to a son for Yaʿaqob, **11**and Leʾah said, "What luck / luck
has come!"[11] So she named him Gad. **12**Zilpah, Leʾah's maidservant,
gave birth to a second son for Yaʿaqob, **13**and Leʾah said "What good
fortune I have, because daughters are calling me fortunate."[12] So she
named him Asher.

3. The LXX^{A}'s "it was called" takes the third-person verb as impersonal; it confirms the MT's unexpected masculine verb.

4. Targum Ps.-J. has Rachel urging Jacob to pray that Yahweh would enable her to become pregnant.

5. He did not merely "get angry" (LXX, Vg), nor does *ḥārâ* suggest kindling in the sense of starting a fire (so BDB, *HALOT*, *DCH*). His rage became overpowering (Tg).

6. Targums Onq. and Ps.-J. have Jacob suggesting that Rachel should be praying: "Is it from me that you are asking—isn't it from before Yahweh you should ask?" Even more neatly, Tg. Neof. has Jacob suggesting that they should both pray.

7. On the two words translated handmaid and maidservant in vv. 3–4, see the footnote to 21:10.

8. Targum Onq. has "He has accepted my prayer" (cf. Tg. Ps.-J.).

9. For this use of *ʾĕlōhîm*, cf. 23:6 and the translation note.

10. Literally, "Twistings of God I have twisted." The Tg takes this as another reference to prayer—in effect, "[In] twistings in relation to God, I have twisted with my sister"; the subsequent reference to "winning" encourages one to read the puzzling expression in light of 32:28.

11. The ketib *bgd* (what luck), implying *bəgād* (in pause; cf. the LXX, Vg), anticipates *bəʾošrî* in v. 13. Perhaps both are instances of *bə* as *b* of identity (*bet essentiae*; cf. Job 23:13; Ps. 54:6; Isa. 28:16), on which see GKC 119i; *HALOT* 104. Hartmann ("'Es gibt keine Kraft,'" 119) gains a similar meaning by seeing the *b* as a kind of copula, thus "It's luck / it's my good fortune" (cf. *HALOT* 105). The qere has *bāʾ gād*, "luck has come" (cf. Tg, Aq, Sym).

12. The qatal verb suggests something so certain that it can be described as having already happened (GKC 106n).

14At the time of the wheat harvest, Reʾuben went and found love-
plants in the open country and brought them to Leʾah his mother. Raḥel
said to Leʾah, "Please give me some of your son's love-plants." **15**She
said to her, "Was it a small thing, your getting my husband, and you're
also going to get[13] my son's love-plants?" Raḥel said, "Therefore he can
sleep with you tonight in return for your son's love-plants." **16**In the eve-
ning Yaʿaqob came from the open country, and Leʾah went out to meet
him and said, "I'm the one you're to be with, because I've definitely paid
wages[14] for you, with my son's love-plants." So he slept with her that
night, **17**and God listened to Leʾah.[15] She became pregnant and gave
birth to a fifth son for Yaʿaqob. **18**Leʾah said, "God gave me my wages,
in that I gave my maidservant to my husband." So she named him
Yiśśakar.[16]

19Leʾah became pregnant again and gave birth to a sixth son for
Yaʿaqob. **20**Leʾah said, "God has given me a good endowment—me; this
time my husband will elevate me[17] because I've given birth to six sons
for him." So she named him Zebulun. **21**Later she gave birth to a daugh-
ter and named her Dinah.

22But God was mindful of Raḥel. God listened to her[18] and opened her
womb, **23**and she became pregnant and gave birth to a son. She said,
"God has gathered up my reviling." **24**So she named him Yosep, saying,
"May Yahweh add another son to me!"

Interpretation

Scene 5 is the center and climax of the palistrophe relating Jacob's time in Harran. It concerns itself exclusively with the birth of eleven sons, who will give their names to the Israelite clans, and one daughter, who will feature in a later story in Genesis (the twelfth son will be born on the way back to Canaan).

To Leah: Reuben, Simeon, Levi, Judah (29:31–35)
To Rachel's maidservant Bilhah: Dan, Naphtali (30:1–8)

13. Literally, "and for taking" (cf. *TTH* 204). The SP suggests adding a shewa at the end of the verb, which then becomes second-person qatal, "and you will take" (cf. Tal, *Genesis*, 151–52*).

14. Leah uses the idiom that combines an infinitive and its cognate finite verb to indicate emphasis.

15. Again, the Tgs have God accepting Leah's prayer.

16. The qere has *yiśśśākār* (!), the ketib *ysskr*. The name might comprise two components (see Skinner, *Genesis*, 389) or might goes back to an archaic verb form meaning "He [God] rewards" (see Sarna, *Genesis*, 210): the qere spelling perhaps suggests that behind the meaning "hire" for the verb *śākar* is a more general meaning, "reward" (cf. BDB).

17. Targum Onq.'s "the dwelling of my husband will be with me" (cf. Tg. Ps.-J.; Aq) works with a different meaning of *zābal*, for which see *DCH*. The MT's verb having a direct object makes this understanding difficult, though Ibn Ezra (*Genesis*, 287) notes possible parallels.

18. Once again Tg. Onq. has "accepted her prayer."

To Leah's maidservant Zilpah: Gad, Asher (30:9–13)
To Leah with the aid of some love-plants: Issachar, Zebulun, also Dinah (30:14–21)
To Rachel when God is mindful of her: Joseph (30:22–24)

The section's focus on the birth of these offspring fits the way Genesis as a whole is "structured by genealogical tag lines tracing lineal descendants (the *tôlĕdôt*–structuring clauses)."[19] The birth of these offspring is what counts most in the Jacob story. As was the case with Jacob's parents and grandparents, the capacity to have children is key to the fulfillment of God's purpose with Jacob and of his promises to him, but it is also a great challenge for Jacob and his wives. Genesis 29:31–30:24 takes that fact for granted and relates how the challenge is met (the medieval chapter division oddly links Leah's first four pregnancies with what precedes rather than with the birth of the other eight children).

Although previous genealogies have explained the relationships between "our" family and other families (notably, "us" and the Ishmaelites, or "us" and the Edomites), genealogies from now on implicitly account for "our" relationships with one another—here specifically, for the interrelationships of the Israelite clans. Thus while previously "women have partaken in the promise of birthing nations"—as was the case with Sarah, Hagar, and Rebekah—now "women cease birthing nations" and become the means by which the house of Israel comes into being, "the means by which a nation is established."[20] Admittedly, the section does not directly refer to the Israelite clans, as Gen. 49 will; the focus lies on the development of the family, with the background it provides for the continuing Genesis story, and on the mothering of these women.[21] But the members of the clans will hear of their own origins as they listen to the account.

The offspring, then, especially count in this section. They are organized by mother: four for Leah, two for Bilhah, two for Zilpah, two more and a daughter for Leah, one for Rachel (thus we should not infer that the twelve births are related in chronological order). Jacob himself "is hardly present—in 30:2 he furiously explains why"; he appears only a couple of times to do his creative duty in silence"[22] (Jub. 28 makes explicit that he is the father each time). Yet he is omnipresent in the background of the story: "Leah struggles with her esteem in the eyes of Jacob (29:32, 33, 34; 30:15, 20), and Rachel with the reproach of her childlessness in the eyes of Jacob (30:1–2, 6, 23)."[23]

19. Arnold, *Genesis*, 267.
20. De La Torre, *Genesis*, 268–69.
21. Cf. W. Bailey, "Intimate Moments," 3.
22. Fokkelman, *Narrative Art in Genesis*, 131.
23. Fretheim, "Genesis," 554.

The focus of Leah's life, as the story tells it, is having children and gaining her husband's love.[24]

The section brings together material of varied forms and origins. One can extract a sequence of simple birth announcements that report a woman's pregnancy, her giving birth, her naming the child, and an explanation of the name's significance. There are commonly two explanations; neither indicates the etymological meaning of the name (of which we are ignorant in most cases), but both indicate what the name signifies for the mother. The announcements are collected into sets relating to each of the mothers: some sets have an introduction and/or conclusion, and/or have comments on how Yahweh was involved in the women getting pregnant and/or on actions the women took when they could not get pregnant. The form of the announcements again brings out how Jacob is a subordinate figure in the story's action, subject in varying ways to the maneuvering of his wives.

The names and their significance are different from the general run of First Testament names.[25] The comments on them bring into focus the complicating feature that runs through the account: a motif characterizing it is the rivalry between Leah and Rachel, the one who has a functioning womb, the other who has a husband's love. "The whole episode is governed by Leah's longing for Jacob's love and Rachel's craving for children."[26] The section thus combines genealogy with the exposition of a theme, the tortuous ups and downs of four women's fertility and their mutual relationships. It is not exactly a story; it does not go anywhere. It is more a series of episodic moments with this common theme. The vignettes about the women and their babies are significant in the context of Genesis's concern with marriage and family, but more specifically, the genealogy matters to the story line of the Genesis narrative, though the births' significance for this broader story line comes from the section's setting in Genesis rather than from any explicit references within the material. The section also pays special attention to Yahweh's involvement with Leah and Rachel and their relationship with Yahweh. God is invoked thirteen times, by Leah, Rachel, Jacob, and the narrator.[27]

29:31–35. "After all the penetrating worldliness of the previous story, God is again the subject of the event," though the section will go on to interweave references to God's activity and references to wholly human initiative and motivation in a "truly unedifying thicket of passions and naked human characteristics" without theological comment.[28]

It begins with Leah (v. 31). Since Jacob married Leah and Rachel at the same time, they might both have had children at about the same time, but

24. T. Schneider, *Mothers of Promise*, 75.
25. Cf. Fokkelman, *Narrative Art in Genesis*, 133.
26. Wenham, *Genesis 16–50*, 240.
27. Fretheim, "Genesis," 554.
28. Von Rad, *Genesis*, 289, 292.

it didn't work out that way, and the narrator has intuited why. Maybe Jacob simply liked or loved Rachel and didn't like or love Leah at all, or maybe he liked or loved Rachel more than Leah. It might not make much difference to Leah. Genesis doesn't just say Leah felt rejected; she was rejected. It is the converse of the fact stated in v. 30: Jacob did like or love Rachel more than or rather than Leah.[29] "Reject" (*śānēh*) and "like/love" (*ʾāhēb*) are antonyms. To say that Jacob "hated" Leah (LXX) is misleading. As well as implying an absoluteness when that antithesis can simply imply preference, it implies a strength of feeling when the antithesis denotes action (a useful illustration is Mal. 1:2–3, quoted in Rom. 9:13). The pattern of rejecting one while liking/loving the other recurs from the story of Jacob's grandparents. It occurs again in the rule in Deut. 21:15–17, where these verbs recur and constitute quasi-legal language: rejecting a wife is close to repudiating her as wife, and 30:14–15 implies that Jacob has broken off his marital relationship with Leah. By contrast, such parallels make the more noteworthy Elqanah's commitment to both Hannah and Peninnah in 1 Sam. 1. In describing Yahweh's response to the situation, Genesis does not say that Yahweh loves Leah and rejects Rachel, as it may imply that he loved Jacob and rejected Esau (the point Mal. 1:3 makes explicit)—indeed, the Torah never says that Yahweh rejected anyone. Genesis simply says that on this occasion Leah's having a baby is a sign that God is responding to her husband's having rejected her; and it simply observes that Rachel is infertile, as Sarah and Rebekah were initially (11:30; 25:21), not that Yahweh has closed her womb (cf. 20:18). Yahweh's opening Leah's womb might imply that she had been trying to have children for a while, though it need not mean this; using a different root (*pāṭar*), the Torah refers to any firstborn as one who opens the womb (e.g., Exod. 13:2, 12, 13, 15). It is the first reference to Yahweh's activity (the first time Yahweh has been the subject of a verb) since his speaking to Jacob at Beth El.

The mother is the one who names the child (v. 32), as will usually be the case and as is common in the First Testament (though Jub. 28 has Jacob doing much of the naming). Each time there is a relationship of sound rather than of meaning between the names and the mother's comments. *Rəʾûbēn* could be construed to mean "Look, a son," which would be apposite. But Leah also sees an overlap with the idea of Yahweh looking "at her humbling" (*bəʿonyî*), as he once listened to Hagar's (16:11). And she deludes herself with the thought that her son's birth will make a difference in Jacob's attitude toward her.

Leah herself (v. 33) then expresses what the narrator has told us about Yahweh's recognizing her rejection. We don't know the etymology of the name *šimʿôn*, but it makes Leah think of the verb *šāmaʿ* and thus she speaks not of Yahweh seeing her rejection but of Yahweh hearing of it (cf. the name Ishmael).

29. See the footnote to v. 30.

Her comments on the birth of her third son (v. 33) indicate that the yearning she expressed in naming Reuben has not been fulfilled; she is still holding on to her delusion about Jacob. Once again, we don't know the etymology of the name *lēwî*. Leah connects it with the verb *lāwâ* (attach).

Yet again the etymology of her fourth son's name (v. 34) is unknown, but *yəhûdâ* does overlap with the verb *hôdâ*, from the root *yādâ*, which appears in the yiqtol as *yəhôdeh*. Has Leah stopped focusing exclusively on Jacob's love and started focusing on Yahweh? Do the listeners notice that these third and fourth sons are the ancestors of the line of Moses and Aaron and of David, so that "priesthood and kingship . . . have their origin in an unwanted and unplanned marriage"?[30] Is it significant that in connection with her first two sons, she mentions both Yahweh's mercy and her yearning in relation to her husband, while in connection with the third she mentions only her husband, and in the fourth she mentions only Yahweh?

30:1–8. "Meanwhile, night after night Rachel hears the sons of Leah crying to be fed. Day after day she hears the babies cooing with joy. Occupying the adjacent tent, she most desires her own children."[31] Understandably, she can't cope with the way Leah gives birth to sons so easily. One wife has children but no love, the other has love but no children, and "they are competing with each other, one for love and the other for children."[32] It is the first reference to individual jealousy in the Scriptures; Jacob will eventually facilitate another reference (37:11). Indeed, it is the first reference to Rachel's feelings in the feelings-laden story of what has happened since Jacob arrived in Harran. Neither has she spoken, but now she does.[33] While Sarah and Rebekah chafed over their infertility, the contrast between Rachel's experience and Leah's in the context of their shared marriage underlies the heated immoderation of her protest to Jacob. Leah has not referred in so many words to bearing children "for Jacob," though her phraseology implies that it would be neat if he would look at her sons that way and that it would then make a difference in the way he looks at her. Rachel can talk in such terms because she is the woman he likes or loves. Yet that fact complicates things and imperils their relationship. "Give me," she says, using the same verb form that Jacob used about her to Laban a few verses earlier (29:21). With some illogic, she implies that her not having become pregnant is Jacob's fault; if he can beget sons with Leah, how can it be? She is consumed by her inability to conceive. Her whole life seems pointless. People listening to the story might recall the story of Hannah as well as those of Sarah and Rebekah and wonder if there should be some reference to Rachel praying as Hannah did.[34] Perhaps "Rachel's infertility is

30. Hamilton, *Genesis 18–30*, 268.

31. De La Torre, *Genesis*, 270.

32. M. Jacobs, *Gender, Power, and Persuasion*, 170.

33. Cf. Alter, *Art of Biblical Narrative*, 186–87.

34. Tg provides such references: see the translation notes on 30:2.

the Deity's way of challenging an otherwise privileged life," but she goes on to challenge Jacob instead of God, "to target what one can control in a situation that appears to be beyond one's control."[35]

Rachel's anguish ruins the relationship in both directions (v. 2). Jacob doesn't just get angry. His anger rages at Rachel. "The whole dialogue is a matter of a few lines, but it succeeds in amply suggesting the tangle of emotions—love, consideration, jealousy, frustration, resentment, rage—that constitutes the conjugal relationship."[36] Why should Rachel blame Jacob? Yet (perhaps with wisdom and even love) he doesn't blame her. Rather, he makes the affirmation from which the narrator held back: it's God who has closed Rachel's womb. His magnificent conviction of God's sovereignty is the kind of affirmation that leads to outrageous prayers in the Psalms. So why is there no reference to his praying either, as his father prayed?

Like Jacob's grandmother, Rachel has an alternative proposal (v. 3). Desperate times require desperate measures, and Rachel is desperate. Like Sarah, she speaks of building herself up[37] through her maidservant, in that Bilhah's child will count as Rachel's. The child that a woman receives onto her knees or lap immediately after its mother gives birth to it, or that a man subsequently dandles on his knees, is her or his child. Even if it is not their birth child, it is a child that they recognize or adopt or claim, like Joseph later (50:23).

So Bilhah becomes Jacob's third wife (vv. 4–6). Strictly or technically, we will later learn, her status is that of a secondary wife (35:22).[38] Although she is a wife, she remains a maidservant, but there is no indication that her sons have a lower status than Jacob's other sons. She duly gives birth to a son "for Jacob," but also for Rachel. The relationship between Rachel and Bilhah does not implode like the relationship of Sarah and Hagar, and Rachel accepts Bilhah's son as Sarah did not accept Hagar's. It is Rachel who names the child. The name *dān* is a participle from the verb *dîn*, which means exercise authority or make a decision, particularly by taking action on behalf of the needy and oppressed (cf. 15:14); Gen. 49:16 will pick up the significance of the name. Rachel speaks of Yahweh listening to her voice: is it simply the voice that has cried out in sadness at not being able to conceive, or do her words indicate that she has prayed after all?

When Bilhah bears a second son for Rachel and for Jacob (vv. 7–8), we again do not know the etymology of the name *naptālî*, but Rachel is able to make a link with the verb *pātal* (niphal), which means "twist." Her greeting in v. 6 focuses on what her son's arrival says about Yahweh; her second greeting focuses on what this son's arrival says about her rivalry with Leah. She has fought with her sister by having children through her maidservant, and she

35. M. Jacobs, *Gender, Power, and Persuasion*, 167, 168.
36. Alter, *Art of Biblical Narrative*, 188.
37. See the footnote to 16:2.
38. See the comment on 16:3.

has in some sense won. Although Rachel is apparently prettier than Leah, she doesn't seem to be nicer.[39] But Genesis makes no comment on the propriety or otherwise of these goings on. They are simply the family history. Perhaps it invites readers to be sympathetic rather than judgmental.

30:9–13. Leah evidently thinks that four sons is not enough. Is she afraid that Rachel will catch up with her? So Jacob receives a fourth wife. And "it seems that everybody except Rachel is able to conceive a child."[40]

Leah attributes similar meanings to the names of both Zilpah's sons (vv. 11–13). Elsewhere in the Middle East, Gad is the name of a deity who brings good luck, but in the First Testament it is simply a term for luck (except in Isa. 65:11). Words from the root *ʾāšar* are much more common, especially the exclamation *ʾašrê* . . . , "the good fortune of . . ."

30:14–18. A vignette illustrates the ongoing tension between the two original wives, and the ongoing yearning in Rachel's heart for children of her own and in Leah's heart for more children.

Once again, Genesis makes clear (v. 14) that being shepherds does not exclude some subsistence farming on the side (cf. 26:12). The wheat harvest happens in May, later than the barley harvest. Reuben is the eldest child, so it is not surprising that he should be the one who is out with the harvesters. He is perhaps seven or eight or nine. The love-plants are *dûdāʾîm*, a name that suggests a link with words such as *dôd* (beloved). The LXX and Vg take them as mandrakes, a plant often understood to have hallucinogenic and narcotic effects and used in traditional medicine and rituals. Love-plants are apparently a species similar in appearance: a thick root, no stem, large leaves, violet flowers, and yellow or orange berries that appear in spring. They were evidently believed to be able to encourage conception as well as sexual desire, like perfume (cf. Song 7:13 [7:14]),[41] though these qualities hardly fit with the smelly and soporific reputation of mandrakes.[42]

It is now some years since the great marriage deception (v. 15), but it is still a cause of hostility between the sisters. When and how has Rachel taken Jacob from Leah? Simply by being the one he likes? By having her shapely form? Apparently Rachel, as the woman Jacob has always wanted, can control who he goes to bed with. But does Leah stop getting pregnant because Jacob stopped having sex with her, or has he stopped having sex with her because she has stopped getting pregnant? Like the English expression "sleep with," *šākab* as a euphemism for having sex applies to irregular sexual liaisons rather than regular relations between husbands and wives (19:32–35; 26:10; 34:2, 7; 35:22; 39:7–14). So Rachel's use of this verb is neatly snide.

39. Cf. T. Schneider, *Mothers of Promise*, e.g., 87.
40. Hamilton, *Genesis 18–20*, 271.
41. See Keel, *Song of Songs*, 256–60.
42. See further Willet, *Hexapla in Genesin & Exodum*, 272.

Having made the bargain (v. 16), Leah needs to head off Jacob as he makes his way toward Rachel's tent.[43] Both Leah and Rachel believe in the potency of the love-plants, but Leah has surrendered some of them to the woman who needs them not in order to be sexually attractive but to overcome her infertility. "Jacob, apparently, has no say in the matter. He seems to sleep with anyone his wives demand of him."[44]

Once again, Genesis brings God in (v. 17). If Leah surrendered only some of the love-plants, is the implication that she made use of some of them? Whether she did or not, Genesis makes explicit that God is the one who is key to her regaining her fertility, with or without their help.

Leah recognizes it too (v. 18). God has listened to her, as she herself said in 29:33, though one would think that she was more interested in God hearing her yearning about Jacob's love. Issachar's name suggests a link with *śākār*, a key word in Gen. 29–31.[45] The name suggests how Jacob has moved from being paid wages by Laban to being himself the payment for wages paid by Leah. To put it the other way, Leah relates to Jacob the same way as her father had.[46] Jacob is a hired hand. It's hardly calculated to help with her real problem.

30:19–21. No love-plants are required for Leah to have a sixth son. Once again she sees him as God's gift, and once again she harbors her hope that her fecundity will make a difference to Jacob's attitude to her. Once again we see that "the first motif that runs through the narrative is the unhappiness of Leah";[47] she births more sons than the other three wives combined, but it doesn't make up for the missing love. So "Leah fails in her own lifetime," though she attains some measure of victory after her death: it is "she, after all, not Rachel, who lies forever beside Jacob in the Cave of Makhpelah" and who is looked back on as the mother of most of the clans, including Levi and Judah.[48] Zebulun's name can suggest a double way in which Leah articulates hope. The name overlaps with the root *zābad*, meaning "endow"—though that root more obviously links with names such as Zabdi (and eventually Zebedee). But it is closer to the root *zābal*, meaning "be on high" (cf. Beelzebul).

The brief mention of Dinah (v. 21), among the other daughters that the wives had (cf. 37:35; 46:7),[49] provides background to what will happen in Gen. 34.[50] The lack of reference to Leah becoming pregnant in connection with Dinah's birth prompts the inference that she and Zebulun are twins (see, e.g.,

43. Cf. Qimchi, *Genesis*, on v. 16.
44. Brayford, *Genesis*, 361.
45. See the comment on 29:15.
46. M. Jacobs, *Gender, Power, and Persuasion*, 173.
47. Sarna, *Genesis*, 206.
48. Frankel, *Five Books of Miriam*, 56.
49. Cf. Dillmann, *Genesis*, 2:244.
50. On the paucity of reference to daughters in Genesis, see Rashkow, "Daughters and Fathers in Genesis."

Jub. 28.23). Genesis makes no comment on the significance of Dinah's name, which looks as if it links with the same root as Dan.

30:22–24. While Rachel has the love-plants, they apparently haven't worked so far, and when she does eventually become pregnant, it is because at last God is mindful of her, as he was mindful of Noah and Abraham (8:1; 19:29). The account of Joseph's birth thus rounds off the section. God has listened to her as he listened to Leah and has opened her womb as he opened Leah's long ago (see 29:31; 30:17). For neither woman was it the love-plants that made the difference. There are four keys that God personally holds on to, so that only he can open the door: rain, food, tomb, and womb (Tg. Neof.). As was the case with Zebulun, there are two ideas that Joseph's name could suggest. *ʾĀsap* means "gather," and it can refer not least to gathering things up in order to get rid of them (e.g., Isa. 4:1; there too it refers to getting rid of reviling). *Yāsap* means "add"; Rachel hopes that this birth will not be the only one for her, and she puts her hope in the possibility that Yahweh could take action to that end. The "historical" Rachel would say "God" rather than Yahweh; the name *yôsipyâ* (May Yahweh add) comes in Ezra 8:10. Joseph will indeed not be Rachel's only son; the interpretation of the name is a placeholder for Benjamin.[51] While closing off this section, the account of Joseph's birth thus also looks forward to Benjamin's. But that second son will cost Rachel her life (Gen. 35:16–18), which is ironic when put alongside her opening statement about having children (30:1).

Implications

God, Leah, Rachel, Jacob, Laban, Life

The theological genius of narrative or story is that it can do justice to the complexity of who God is and the way life is in a manner that systematic analysis cannot. It may be impossible to know whether a narrator was conscious of making a statement that carried the implications one may see in it; one can only say that the statement does carry them or that it provides the raw materials for such a theological statement. Near the beginning of Genesis, the Noah story provides an example: it juxtaposes declarations concerning Noah's finding grace in Yahweh's eyes and concerning his faithfulness (6:8–9). Near the end, Genesis will provide another example: the dynamics of Joseph's brothers' actions and their consequences, summed up in Joseph's declaration that they intended something bad but God intended something good (50:19–20). There Joseph uses the same expression that Jacob uses here: "Am I in the place of God?" (they are the only occurrences of this phrase in the First Testament, though see also 2 Kings 5:7).[52]

51. Seebass, *Genesis*, 2.2:337.
52. Cf. Driver, *Genesis*, 273.

Here Genesis comments first on Yahweh's seeing. It is a theological commonplace that God is omniscient, that he sees everything, but the Scriptures show more interest in occasions when God looks at things, when he pays attention and then takes action in response to what he sees. He may always see; he does not always look. If one can get God to look, it is almost inevitable that he will take action (but only "almost": at the cross, he may look, but he takes no action, at least that day). God does not initiate things that happen in this section. He is always responding to concrete human situations,[53] to things he sees.

Second, Genesis comments on what God sees. He does not always look at someone who is rejected in such a way as to do something about it, but he sometimes does so. He sometimes exercises a preferential option for the poor. Leah is right that Yahweh has seen her humbling (and perhaps likewise that he has heard about her rejection) and has taken action about it, though she is sadly wrong in her inference regarding what his action will achieve. Could Yahweh make Jacob like or love Leah? Though Exodus will go on to talk about God making hearts hard, it's difficult to find in Scripture any reference to God's making hearts soft, though the two processes would presumably be similar, and perhaps circumcising the heart or giving people a soft heart (Deut. 30:6; Ezek. 36:26) are other ways of describing the same action. It looks as if Yahweh lets someone like Jacob love or like or dislike or reject as he wishes.

Third, Genesis comments on God's opening a womb. As with his seeing and his omniscience, his omnipotence is a theological commonplace. His creative power lies behind every birth. If God did not give life, there would be no life. In particular, his creative activity lies behind every first birth; there is something especially marvelous about the initial opening of a womb. Yet the process of creation at the beginning involved his bestowing generative power on the animate world. He does not need to take direct action every time an animal or a human being is to give birth. Conversely, the infertility of a human being or an animal need not imply that God has closed the womb in question, though Jacob speaks in virtually those terms. But there are some occasions when he does take direct action, and the Scriptures show at least as much interest in specific occasions when he opens or closes wombs. They may be significant because a woman is in special need, or because she has been unable to have children, or because this particular birth has a key place in his purpose, or because he is acting in chastisement. An unexpected birth or a closed womb properly makes one ask questions about what God is doing, though this does not make it appropriate to fret about obtaining answers. These experiences may be just one of those things.

So what can a human being do? Rachel and Leah make use of surrogacy, like Sarah and like some women in the West, and Genesis indicates no

53. Fretheim, "Genesis," 555.

disapproval. Genesis is generally sparing in ethical judgments.[54] Is surrogacy a way of resisting Yahweh's purpose that Rachel should not have children? Or is it a way of facilitating the fulfillment of Yahweh's purpose that Jacob should have many children? Or is it a theologically neutral action? Certainly Yahweh does not disapprove of surrogacy enough to decline to make use of it in bringing about the fulfillment of his promise to make Jacob the father of a numerous people. Is Rachel right that Bilhah is the means of Yahweh's acting on her behalf?

Rachel and Leah both believe in the efficacy of love-plants, a form of traditional medicine. And the First Testament does not always disapprove of medicine (Isa. 38:21), though it does disapprove of it when medicine replaces God (2 Chron. 16:12). Genesis leaves neatly ambiguous whether the love-plants worked. If they worked, Genesis does make clear that they did so because God made them work. They did not sideline God. "God listened to Leah."

Genesis offers no universalizable statements about the sense in which it is always God who opens wombs or closes wombs or about the significance of whether or not a woman can have children. Leah's fertility is a gift from Yahweh, a gift responding to her rejection by her husband (29:31); Rachel's infertility was just one of those things. How does the narrator know? He intuited it; God inspired this insight.

54. For ethical judgments with varying bases, see, e.g., Chrysostom, *Homilies on Genesis* 46–67, 125–32; Calvin, *Genesis*, 2:134–49; De La Torre, *Genesis*, 268–75.

32
Jacob Gains a Large Flock

(30:25–31:2)

Overview

In scene 6 of the account of Jacob's time at Harran, Jacob agrees to work for Laban for a further period so as to accumulate resources that will enable him to take his family back to Canaan. Earlier, Laban had pulled one over Jacob; now Jacob pulls one over Laban, and he does accumulate resources in clever and spectacular fashion, though his success arouses suspicion and ill-feeling on the part of Laban and his sons.

Translation

30:25 When Raḥel had given birth to Yosep, Ya'aqob said to Laban, "Send
me off, so I may go to my place, to my country. **26**Give me my wives and
my children for whom I've served you so I may go, because you yourself
know the service that I've given you." **27**But Laban said to him, "Please,
if I've found favor in your eyes: I've divined[1] that[2] Yahweh[3] has blessed
me because of you." **28**So he said, "Specify your wages with me, and I'll
give it to you." **29**He said to him, "You yourself have acknowledged how
I've served you and how your livestock have been with me, **30**because

1. For the verb *nāḥaš*, cf. 44:5, 15. Targums Onq. and Neof. have "I have tested," a less shocking thought than the idea that Yahweh responded to divination (Tg. Ps.-J. retains that idea). The Akkadian verb *naḫāšu* means "prosper" (cf. *DCH*), and a verb with this meaning would fit in the context and avoid that thought, but such a Hebrew cognate is not otherwise known.

2. Literally, "and."

3. The LXX, Vg have "God": Laban of course would not say "Yahweh," but the narrator knows that it was Yahweh who so acted.

the little that you had before me has exploded so as to become a large number. Yahweh has blessed you wherever I've gone.[4] But now, when am I myself also to do something for my household?" **31**So he said, "What am I to give you?"

Yaʿaqob said, "You aren't to give me anything, if you'll do this thing for me. I will again pasture your flock I keep. **32**I'll pass through your entire flock today, removing[5] from there every speckled and spotted sheep, and every dark sheep among the lambs, and the spotted and speckled among the goats. It will be my wages. **33**My faithfulness will aver[6] against me[7] on the future day when you come to look at my wages before you. Each one with me that's not speckled or spotted among the goats, or dark among the lambs: that one with me will have been stolen."

34Laban said, "There, yes, let it be in accordance with your word." **35**That day he removed the streaked and spotted he-goats and all the speckled and spotted she-goats, each one that had white on it, and each dark one among the lambs, put them into the charge of his sons, **36**and put three days' journey between him and Yaʿaqob, while Yaʿaqob was pasturing the rest of Laban's flock.

37Yaʿaqob got for himself fresh cane of poplar, and almond and plane tree, and peeled white stripes in them, exposing the white that was on the rods. **38**The canes that he had peeled he stationed in the troughs, in the water containers that the flock came to drink from, in front of the flock. They were in heat when they came to drink, **39**so the flock were in heat by the canes; and the flock gave birth to streaked, speckled, and spotted young. **40**The lambs Yaʿaqob divided off, and he put the flock's faces toward the streaked and the completely dark animals in Laban's flock. So he set herds for himself each on its own and didn't set them by Laban's flock. **41**Every time the flock was in heat (the ones who were clustered),[8] Yaʿaqob would put the canes in the troughs before the eyes of the flock so they would be in heat by the canes. **42**But with the feebler in the flock, he didn't put them there. So the feeble ones were Laban's, and the clustered ones were Yaʿaqob's.

4. Literally, "blessed you for my foot."

5. Following on the opening first-person verb, the ambiguous *hasēr* is more likely infinitive absolute than imperative (cf. Tg). The LXX, Vg have both verbs as imperative, assimilating to what actually happens in v. 35.

6. On this translation, see the footnote to 18:27.

7. We would expect Jacob to say "for," but this would be an unparalleled use of *ʿānâ b* (Skinner, *Genesis*, 392; cf. *DCH* 6:496). Jacob's usage involves a kind of catachresis.

8. *Qāšar* (pual passive here, qal passive participle in v. 42) usually means bind/bind together (cf. Aq), and then conspire. Whereas BDB takes this unique usage to denote ewes that are (individually) well-knit and thus vigorous, the idea of crowding together and pushing forward fits the more regular use better; the implication will not be so different. The Vg, Tg, and Sym have "early/first," which might also link with the idea that the stronger sheep conceive in the spring, the weaker in the autumn, and/or with the idea that the animals are having their firstborn (see, e.g., Pliny the Elder, *Natural History* 8.72; Jerome, *Hebrew Questions on Genesis*, 68, with Hayward's notes, 204; Driver, *Genesis*, 280).

[43]So the man exploded very greatly. He had a large flock, maidservants, servants, camels, and donkeys. [31:1]But he heard the words of Laban's sons: "Yaʿaqob has gotten everything that was our father's. It's from what was our father's that he's made all this substance." [2]And Yaʿaqob saw Laban's face: there, he wasn't[9] the same toward him as he had been in previous days.[10]

Interpretation

With scene 6, the palistrophe in 28:10–33:20 begins its return journey. This scene in the sequence corresponds to scene 4 (29:15–30), which recounts how Jacob agrees to work for Laban so as to earn the right to marry his daughter. Here Jacob agrees to renegotiate his contract with Laban.[11] This renegotiation initiates the process whereby Jacob and his family will return to Canaan, though the scene turns out to represent a false start. But the result is that Jacob gains much more to take back to Canaan than the human assets he initially refers to.

The question underlying this section, then, is whether and how Jacob will be able to return to Canaan with his new and extensive household. There are perhaps two obstacles that he must overcome. The overt implication of his opening request is that he needs Laban's permission to leave, but the question behind that question may be that he needs Laban's practical help. He has wives and children, but as far as we know he has no other resources. So how can he make the journey back to Canaan, which would take several weeks, and how can he survive back there without simply being a big burden on his family (and who knows what their state is?).

It is to those unstated questions that Laban responds in giving Jacob the chance to earn the wherewithal to make it on his own. Jacob will continue his work as a shepherd who is involved in breeding sheep, but he will now share in the profits. As it turns out, he finds a way of doing far better than anyone could have expected, which also provides him with the bartering resources to gain a wider range of assets.

The medieval chapter division closes this scene in 30.43 with a summary reference to those enhanced assets, which would make a satisfactory ending to a section. But the following verses continue without a break. Although the LXX and many modern translations add explicit reference to Jacob as the subject in 31:1, the MT continues straight onward. Though it then does make

9. The singular suffix on *ʾênennû* implies that the subject is Laban, not "his face," which is a plural noun and would make one expect a plural suffix (though Lam. 4:16 has *pānîm* governing a singular verb: see Ibn Ezra, *Genesis*, 297).

10. Literally, "as yesterday, the third."

11. Wauters notes ironies in the relationship of 30:25–43 to 29:15–30 (and in its relationship to 27:1–40): see "Un retournement" and "Ironie."

"Jacob" the subject in 31:2, this reference issues from the change of subject within 31:1, and in content 31:2 again continues from 31:1. This feature of the beginning of Gen. 31 subverts the inference that 30:43 constitutes closure. While one might then take 31:3 as also continuing the narrative sequence, the parallel with Gen. 12 suggests rather that Yahweh's instruction in 31:3 begins the account of the family's return. So it is 30:25–31:2 that constitutes scene 6, and the scene concludes with the note that Jacob has done considerably better than pleases his brothers-in-law or his father-in-law. Although Jacob has thus resolved the question behind the question at the beginning of the scene, he has not resolved the overt question, his need of Laban's permission if he is to leave. Indeed, his relationship with Laban has deteriorated. It doesn't seem likely that this permission will be forthcoming.

30:25–26. At least fourteen years have passed since Jacob arrived in Harran (seven years of service each for Leah and for Rachel). Although we need not assume that all the births have been listed in chronological order, the section does imply that Joseph came last. Rachel has finally been able to have a baby, and this event apparently signals that it is time to go home. Perhaps there is a quasi-legal rationale: there are several senses in which a woman's having a baby make the marriage a full marriage, in terms of her relationship with her husband and with her father.[12] And "from his birth, Joseph is the motor of Jacob's future, and therefore motor of the future of the covenant."[13] Anyway, Jacob thinks the time has come; he had hardly envisaged staying this long.

His reference to the service he has given Laban (v. 26) implies an allusion to the fourteen-year stint. He is perhaps aware of the possibility that Laban may assume a rule like the one in Exod. 21:2–11. Laban is responsible for the family of which he is head, and his offspring are both part of his responsibility and part of that family's resources. In some sense he is the owner of his daughters and of the children whom they have birthed (cf. 31:43). A servant such as Jacob can't simply assume the right to take them away. Yet Jacob has surely furnished Laban with the kind of service that gives him some rights in relation to them. Further, while Jacob might be okay about arriving back home with nothing to show for his fourteen years away but four wives and a large number of children, he might equally feel that he needs to be able to return with some further assets. Indeed, we have noted that it might be hardly practicable for him simply to set off with these dependents: what about their needs on the long journey? Possibly he is not really asking Laban for permission to leave; he might even be wondering whether the framework within which Laban could be expected to work would be an equivalent to Deut. 15:12–14. There the term for releasing a servant with the means to start a new life is "send off" (*šālaḥ* piel), and Jacob uses that verb here (see further 31:42),

12. Cf. Frankel, *Five Books of Miriam*, 60.
13. Reno, *Genesis*, 240.

though it was also the expression for Isaac "sending off" Jacob to Harran in 28:6 (cf. 24:54, 56, 59). Or (with similar implications) the subtext of his words to Laban might be "We need to renegotiate our work relationship now that I have served my fourteen years for your two daughters, so that I can accumulate enough resources to be self-sufficient and go home."

30:27–31a. This possibility links with the way the negotiations in this section recall the negotiations between Abraham and the Hittites (Gen. 23), in which statements may not need to be understood at their face value.

This comparison (v. 27) links with the fact that Laban is formally more courteous than he was in 29:26–27, and more courteous than Jacob in 30:25–26. Jacob does not say "please," though neither does Abraham in the opening rounds in Gen. 23. Laban's civility has the same rationale as his straightness in 29:26–27: he is concerned for himself and his family. By the blessing that Jacob has brought to him, Laban means the flourishing of his flocks, which has come about either because Jacob is an expert shepherd or because Yahweh has been gracious to Laban for Jacob's sake—or both. Either way, it is a fulfillment of the promise that people outside Abraham's immediate family will find blessing through that family. While Laban may speak metaphorically about divining, a literal reference fits with the subsequent allusion to effigies (31:19),[14] which appear in association with divination in Ezek. 21:21 [21:26]. While such divination is forbidden to Israelites, Ezekiel accepts it as appropriate to foreigners who don't have the same resources as Israelites and who may obtain guidance from Yahweh by means of the resources they have. Strictly, divination applies to discovering what one should do in the future, so the implication here may be that it is his divination that has revealed to Laban that he needs to find a way of holding on to Jacob.

So he needs to negotiate a new contract with Jacob (v. 28), because the original contract for seven years, and then for seven more, has expired. Laban speaks as if he is prepared to write Jacob a blank check, though his extravagant offer is likely the kind of overstatement that simply opens up a discussion (cf. Gen. 23).

Jacob consents to take part in a polite conversation (vv. 29–30) that discreetly avoids putting hard figures on the table. He does take up Laban's (perhaps unwise) admission of how he has done well through Jacob's work and makes it more concrete: "Blessing? Yes, look at how many sheep you have now compared with fourteen years ago." And he does imply that his statement in vv. 25–26 is simply an opening gambit in the negotiation he wants to have with Laban, like Laban's statement in vv. 27–28. He doesn't really mean he's itching to set off for Canaan next week, though sometime he will want to do so. In the short term, the question is crucial: how can he build up his family assets in the way he has enabled Laban to build up his? For his fourteen

14. Cf. Ibn Ezra, *Genesis*, 289.

years of service thus far, he has been compensated by the provision of food and shelter and by the granting of wives (and children). But that contractual time is over, and now he needs a different form of compensation, one that will establish his family for the future. And he needs Laban to make him an offer in this connection.

Laban's response is to invite Jacob to be more concrete (v. 31a). The negotiation is becoming real.

30:31b–33. Jacob continues to negotiate in the Gen. 23 manner. "You needn't give me anything" means "You need give me only what follows." For his part, he is willing to continue to pasture Laban's flocks in his expert fashion and to look after them and protect them.

He then defines what Laban is to give him (v. 32). Middle Eastern sheep are usually white, and goats are usually black or brown (cf. Song 4:1–2; 6:5–6),[15] but some sheep may be speckled, spotted, or dark, and some goats may be spotted or speckled. Jacob suggests that both now and in future the small minority of nonstandard sheep and goats among Laban's flocks will belong to Jacob. It is they and their future offspring that will be his wages. The proposal might seem modest but realistic for a man who has nothing at the moment.

This arrangement will apply (v. 33) for as long as Jacob continues to pasture and look after the flocks. On the "future day" when the arrangement comes to an end, Laban will be free to examine Jacob's flock, and what he finds will testify to Jacob's honesty—or as Jacob puts it, to the faithfulness that Jacob claims will testify against him (that is, for him). Laban won't find any stolen dark goats or white sheep there. In the event, 31:38 will imply that this arrangement holds for another five or six years.

30:34–36. Laban knows he is being offered a bargain, and he accepts it. But being a sharp operator himself, he deems it wise personally to separate out from his flock the sheep and goats that are to be Jacob's and put them in the care of his sons, rather than risk having Jacob cheat or having Jacob's animals mate with his and produce more animals like Jacob's. We have not heard of Laban's sons before; Laban's family is a bigger enterprise than we realized. These sons would be adults of similar age to Jacob, who perhaps live and work semi-independently of their father and look after flocks that Jacob has not been involved with and that are not covered by the agreement. It wouldn't be too complicated for Laban to slide off some of his sheep and goats and attach them to theirs while Jacob is looking the other way.

30:37–42. We wonder whether Laban is aware that Jacob has been known to be as deceptive and can be as clever as Laban himself. Even if he does, he is perhaps overcome by the apparent good terms of the employment contract that Jacob has offered him, and he fails to ask questions about how the expert

15. Cf. Skinner, *Genesis*, 391.

sheep breeder might make the contract work in his favor. There are three strands to his way of doing so and of encouraging Laban's flocks to produce offspring that will belong to Jacob. In part, his selective breeding operation was a shepherdly equivalent to the traditional medicinal procedures involved in the use of love-plants or mandrakes. As with traditional medicine, modern Western readers may now be less dismissive of such breeding methods than when we assumed that Western science had plumbed all truth about how nature works.[16] But the nonplussed reaction of Laban and his sons does not suggest that Jacob is simply doing what any knowledgeable sheep breeder would do, and at this point Genesis offers no hint regarding what gave Jacob his ideas about sheep breeding, so the story leaves us with a question. In 31:10–12 Jacob will give his own account of where the idea came from and why it worked (the SP adds those verses here). That explanation will parallel the narrator's implicit comments on the effectiveness of the love-plants: it wasn't the love-plants that were key but Yahweh's taking action. In 31:10–12 Jacob will imply that he hadn't originally known that he was going to go in for this stratagem; the idea came in connection with the mating. "God is the power, the force, behind Jacob's trick."[17]

First (vv. 37–39) there is a strategy for the goats. Jacob partially peeled off the bark of some canes from certain trees so that the canes resembled the mixed appearance of the animals he wanted to breed and placed them where the animals came to drink. We don't know why it was these particular trees, except that one of them was poplar (*libneh*), in which he peeled white (*ləbānôt*) stripes and thus exposed the white (*lābān*) inside them. To defeat his father-in-law (*lābān*), Jacob is engaging in some "white magic."[18] It is as if Laban ("Whitey") is harnessed to aid his son-in-law's project. Genesis does not say that the animals needed to see the canes; it may be that somehow the juxtaposition of the mixed canes and the monochrome animals leads to the birth of animals that are mixed in appearance. Perhaps it's an enacted prayer, like family members preparing a room for someone they hope will live to come home from the hospital, or like parents preparing a baby's room before the pregnancy (KSG).

For the sheep, there is a further element in Jacob's strategy (v. 40), though it presupposes the same logic. Jacob places the (white) sheep so that they face the streaked and dark goats. The result of the double strategy is that the mating process issues in the birth of speckled, spotted, and dark sheep as well as white ones, and spotted and speckled goats as well as black ones, and Jacob can divide the flocks into animals that will belong to Laban and ones that will belong to him.

16. But for ideas on how Jacob's ploy may have operated, see, e.g., Sarna, *Genesis*, 212; Hamilton, *Genesis 18–50*, 284.

17. Park, "Transformation," 676.

18. Fokkelman, *Narrative Art in Genesis*, 151.

Then, third (vv. 41–42), Jacob makes a point of putting the stronger animals to the front of his process while leaving the feebler ones among the white sheep and the black goats to their own devices. Other things being equal, the stronger offspring would then be in the category that belonged to Jacob, while the weaker ones would be straightforward white sheep and black goats and would belong to Laban.

30:43–31:2. As a result (v. 43), Jacob does very well over time. Indeed, the growth of his assets is explosive, as v. 30 said of the growth of Laban's assets through Jacob's work, but also as Yahweh had promised Jacob himself in 28:14. And it is not just a matter of sheep and goats but also of servants, camels, and donkeys—like Abraham on his Egyptian adventure (12:16).

Not surprisingly (31:1), Laban's sons are riled by this flourishing at the expense of their father (and in due course at their own expense, when they inherit his flocks). Equally unsurprising is that Laban himself is also not too pleased. The form of words invites us to look at things from Jacob's angle: "There . . ."

"A classical example of understatement" follows (31:2).[19] Jacob has engaged in no deception; he has simply been a shrewd operator. But it threatens to get him into trouble just as his deception did. "Laban is not going to readily accept the fact, that for seasons on end succeeding generations of flocks 'go over,' as it were, to Jacob."[20]

19. Coats, *Genesis*, 216.
20. Fokkelman, *Narrative Art in Genesis*, 152.

33

Jacob Makes a Run for It

(31:3–54)

Overview

In scene 7 of the story of Jacob's time in Harran, Yahweh bids Jacob leave Harran and go back to his homeland, and Yahweh promises his protective presence. Jacob persuades Rachel and Leah to make a run for it with him, but Laban gives chase and catches up with them. Once again, Yahweh appears and this time bids Laban "hands off." Laban and Jacob nevertheless confront each other but then agree on a mutual pact that protects their respective interests, and scene 7 ends happily.

Translation

> **3**Yahweh said to Yaʿaqob, "Go back to your forebears' country, to your homeland, and I will be with you."[1] **4**So Yaʿaqob sent and called Raḥel and Leʾah into the open country, to his flock, **5**and said to them, "I see your father's face, that he's not the same toward me as he was in previous days. But the God of my father—he has been with me. **6**You yourselves know that with all my energy I've served your father, **7**and your father[2]—he's played about with me and changed[3] my wages ten times.[4] But God didn't

1. Simple waw plus yiqtol, practically signifying "so I may be with you," as in 26:3.

2. Putting the subject before the verb juxtaposes the two references to "your father" and underscores the contrast between vv. 6 and 7.

3. The weqatal verb indicates that this verb does not denote an event that was consecutive on the playing about; it further defines the playing about.

4. Cf. Tg. Onq. and the Vg for this traditional understanding of the hapax *mōnîm* from *mānâ*, "count." Targum Ps.-J. has ten "portions" (the meaning of other more common nouns from *mānâ*), while the LXX has ten "lambs" (on the basis of what follows).

let him act badly with me. **8**If he would say, 'The speckled will be your wages,' the entire flock would give birth to speckled. If he would say, 'The streaked will be your wages,' the entire flock would give birth to streaked. **9**So God has rescued your father's livestock[5] and given them to me. **10**And at the time of the flock's being in heat, I lifted my eyes and looked in a dream: there, the rams that were mounting the flock were streaked, speckled, and mottled. **11**In the dream God's envoy said to me, 'Yaʿaqob!' I said, 'I'm here.' **12**He said, 'There, lift your eyes, please, and look. All the rams that are mounting the flock are streaked, speckled, and mottled, because I've seen everything that Laban has been doing to you. **13**I am God, of Bet-ʾel,[6] where you anointed a standing stone, where you made a pledge to me. Now, set off, get out of this country, go back to the country that is your homeland.'"

14Raḥel and Leʾah answered him, "Do we still have a share, a domain, in our father's household? **15**Aren't we deemed outsiders by him since he sold us and also totally consumed the silver paid for us? **16**Because all the wealth that God has rescued from our father: it belongs to us and to our children. So now: everything that God has said to you, do it."

17So Yaʿaqob set off. He put his children and his wives on camels **18**and drove all his livestock and all his property that he had gained, the livestock he had acquired, which he had gained in Paddan Aram, to come to Yiṣḥaq his father in the country of Kenaʿan.

19Now Laban had gone to shear his flock, and Raḥel stole the effigies that belonged to her father. **20**So Yaʿaqob stole away without Laban the Aramite knowing, by not telling him that he was taking flight. **21**He took flight, he and all that he had, set off, and crossed the River and set his face toward the highland of Gilʿad.

22It was told Laban on the third day that Yaʿaqob had fled. **23**He got his brothers with him and pursued after him a seven days' journey. He caught up with him in the highland of Gilʿad. **24**But God came to Laban the Aramite in a dream by night and said to him, "Keep watch over yourself so you don't speak anything with Yaʿaqob, either good or bad."

25So Laban reached Yaʿaqob when Yaʿaqob had pitched his tent in the highland, and Laban pitched, with his brothers, in the highland of Gilʿad.[7] **26**Laban said to Yaʿaqob, "What have you done? You stole away without

5. Targum Onq. reads "some of . . ." to make explicit that Jacob hasn't appropriated the entire flock. Targums Neof. and Ps.-J. read "emptied" and thus move in the opposite direction; the LXX likewise has "all."

6. *Hāʾēl bêt-ʾēl* with the article, and thus not the regular construct expression for "God of Beth El" (see GKC 127f and contrast Gen. 35:7). The Tgs gloss as "the God who revealed himself to you at Beth El" (cf. LXX); Ibn Ezra (*Genesis*, 299) presupposes an ellipsis, "God, the God of Beth El."

7. The Vg and Tg. Ps.-J. make explicit that Laban thus camps "in the same highland of Gilead."

me knowing[8] and you drove off[9] my daughters like captives of the sword.
27Why did you secretly take flight and steal away from me[10] and not tell
me? I would have sent you off with rejoicing and with singing, with tam-
bourine and with guitar. **28**You didn't give me leave to kiss my children
and my daughters. You've been idiotic just now in doing that. **29**It was[11]
in the almightiness of my hand[12] to act badly with you. But the God of
your father—last night he said to me: 'Keep watch over yourself to avoid
speaking anything with Yaʿaqob, either good or bad.' **30**So while just now
you surely went because you were longing so much[13] for your father's
household, why did you steal my gods?"

31Yaʿaqob answered Laban, "Because I was afraid, because I said,
'So that you don't seize your daughters from me.' **32**Given that the per-
son with whom you find your gods will not live, in front of our brothers
recognize for yourself what I have and get it for yourself." (Yaʿaqob didn't
know that Raḥel had stolen them.)

33Laban came into Yaʿaqob's tent, into Leʾah's tent, and into the two
handmaids' tent, but he didn't find them. He went out of Leʾah's tent and
came into Raḥel's tent. **34**Now Raḥel had gotten the effigies, put them
in the camel saddle, and sat on them. Laban felt through everything in
the tent and didn't find them. **35**She said to her father, "May it not cause
rage in my lord's eyes that I can't get up before you, because the way of
women applies to me." So he searched but didn't find the effigies.

36It enraged Yaʿaqob, and he got into an argument with Laban.
Yaʿaqob averred to Laban, "What was my offense, what was my wrong-
doing, that you chased after me, **37**that you felt through all my pos-
sessions? What did you find of all your household possessions? Put
it here in front of my brothers and your brothers, so they can decide
between the two of us. **38**Indeed,[14] twenty years I've been with you. Your
ewes and your goats, they haven't miscarried. Rams from your flock, I
haven't eaten. **39**Animals that had been killed, I haven't brought you; I

8. Literally, "you stole my mind."

9. The verb *nāhag*, which applied to cattle in v. 18 but here is piel rather than qal, further heightens the implied enormity of the action.

10. Literally, "steal me": cf. v. 26 and the footnote.

11. The context suggests a past-tense translation for the noun clause: he had this power, until God took it away.

12. Literally, "It was for the god [power] of my hand" or "My hand was for a god [power]." "The meaning is certain, but the expression is very obscure" (Skinner, *Genesis*, 398). "I cannot adduce anything certain to bring out the meaning of this idiom" (Luther, *Genesis 31–37*, 52).

13. Both "surely went" and "so keen" involve the combination of an infinitive and its finite verb, an idiom that recurs in v. 15 ("totally consumed," though there the word order is the reverse). In light of the asyndetic relationship between v. 30a and v. 30b, I have taken the first clause as circumstantial; the same logic applies in v. 32, though there the long subject preceding the verb ("the person with whom you find your gods") gives a clearer signal.

14. The LXX has "these twenty years," but singular *zeh* before the noun can hardly have this meaning; it is rather an instance of *zeh* used adverbially (cf. v. 42; 27:36; 43:10; 45:6; see Tal, *Genesis*, 157*).

myself would deal with the shortfall.[15] From my hand you would look for what was stolen by day and what was stolen by night. **40**I became—by day heat consumed me, and frost by night, and my sleep fled from my eyes. **41**Indeed,[16] I've had twenty years in your household; I served you fourteen years for your two daughters and six years for your flock, and you changed my wages ten times.[17] **42**If the God of my father, the God of Abraham and the Reverence of Yiṣḥaq, had not been mine, empty-handed you would now have sent me off. But my humbling and the weariness of the palms of my hands—God saw, and he decided last night."

43Laban answered Yaʿaqob, "The daughters: my daughters; the children: my children; the flock: my flock. All that you see is mine. But about my daughters: what can I do today about them or about their children to whom they have given birth? **44**So now, come, let's solemnize a pact, you and I, and it will be[18] a witness between you and me."

45So Yaʿaqob got a rock and set it up as a standing stone, **46**and Yaʿaqob said to his brothers, "Collect rocks." They got rocks and made a heap, and they ate there by the heap. **47**Laban called it Yegar Sahaduta, while Yaʿaqob called it Galʿed. **48**Laban said, "This heap is a witness between me and you today." That's why he named it Galʿed **49**and "The Watchtower," because (he said), "May Yahweh watch between me and you when one is hidden from the other. **50**If you humble my daughters or get wives on top of my daughters, there being no one with us, see, God will be a witness between me and you." **51**And Laban said to Yaʿaqob, "Here is this heap and here is the standing stone that I have thrown up between me and you. **52**This heap will be a witness and the standing stone will be a witness that I will not go past this heap to you and you will not go past this heap to me, or this standing stone, to act badly. **53**The God of Abraham and the God of Nahor—may he decide[19] between us (the God of their ancestor)." And Yaʿaqob swore by the Reverence of his father Isaac. **54**Yaʿaqob offered a sacrifice at the mountain and invited his brothers to eat bread, and they ate bread and stayed the night at the mountain.

Interpretation

In scene 7 Jacob sets off southwest to get away from Laban. It thus parallels scene 3 of the story of Jacob's time in Harran (29:1–14), where Jacob had

15. Piel privative from *ḥāṭāʾ*, related to the noun *ḥaṭṭʾāt* in v. 36. The LXX's "pay for" may take the verb (lacking the final root letter aleph) to be *ḥûṭ*, meaning "pay for" (see *DCH*; Hamilton, *Genesis 18–50*, 307).

16. See the footnote to v. 38.

17. Regarding the wages, see the third footnote to v. 7, above.

18. It's not clear what is the "it." "Pact" is feminine and the verb is masculine; see the comment.

19. For the MT's plural verb, the SP, LXX, and Vg have singular.

set off northeast to meet Laban. Scene 7 also continues the sequence whereby the narrative alternately speaks in purely human terms or brings God into events. In scene 1 people speak of God, but God stays silent and seemingly inactive; scene 2 involves God; scenes 3 and 4 speak only in terms of human action (and coincidence); scene 5 involves God; scene 6 speaks only in terms of human action; scene 7 involves God again. The narrator refers to Yahweh (v. 3); Jacob refers to his father's God (v. 5), as does Laban (v. 29); and Jacob later refers to "the God of my father, the God of Abraham and the Reverence of Isaac" (v. 42; cf. v. 53). Jacob also refers simply to God (vv. 7, 9, 11, 42), as do Rachel and Leah (v. 16) and Laban (v. 50) and the narrator (v. 24), and Jacob refers to the God of Beth El (v. 13). God appears to Laban (v. 24), and Laban refers to Yahweh (v. 49) and to "the God of Abraham and the God of Nahor," whom the narrator identifies as "the God of their ancestor" (v. 53).

Scene 6 left us in the middle of things. Jacob has solved the problem implicitly raised at the opening of the scene in that he has accumulated flocks and other assets and is thus in a position to sustain the journey home and to sustain his family's life back in Canaan. But solving that problem has raised another: the hostility of Laban and his sons. What is he to do? Should he wait to see whether the conflict can be resolved and he can leave with Laban's goodwill, or should he make a run for it? Yahweh bids him make a run for it, which threatens not to work too well, but Yahweh intervenes again and warns Laban off. After some straight talking, Jacob and Laban make a pact. Scene 7 thus ends happily, though listeners with long memories will remember that Jacob must now face Esau, so this scene by no means constitutes a resolution to the question with which the story of Jacob's journey to Harran began.

So two questions appear for this section: How is Jacob to handle the antagonism of Laban and his sons? How he is to get out of Harran so he can return to Canaan?

- The preliminary to the answer is the reassurance that comes from Yahweh (v. 3).
- In practical terms, the first stage of the answer is then to persuade Rachel and Leah to agree that they should make a move (vv. 4–13).
- It works (vv. 14–16).
- It thus makes departure possible (vv. 17–18).
- But a series of further notes indicate that this simple account of the departure can't be the end of the story (vv. 19–21).

- Laban's giving chase raises the question whether Jacob will make it to Canaan (vv. 22–23).
- Another preliminary answer is another intervention from Yahweh (v. 24).

- That intervention doesn't deal with all the issues raised by those footnotes: what about Laban's questions (vv. 25–30)?
- Jacob has two responses; the second sets up a further question because of what the listeners know but Jacob doesn't know (vv. 31–32).
- Laban takes up the second matter but doesn't find out what happened; Jacob thus gets the chance to vent his protests about Laban's treatment of him over the years (vv. 33–42).
- Laban reverts to the first matter and proposes a way of resolving it (vv. 43–44).
- Jacob and Laban implement the proposal (vv. 45–54).

The result is that relations between Laban's family and Jacob's family are mended, and Jacob's family is safe to continue its journey to Canaan, though the matter of the effigies is never tidied up.

After the making of the pact, the medieval chapter divisions in their English version make Laban's departure for Harran (31:55 [32:1]) the closing verse in this scene. But the immediately following account of Jacob's departure to continue his journey (32:1 [32:2]) pairs with that account of Laban's departure. I thus prefer the alternative version of the medieval chapter divisions that appears in printed Hebrew Bibles, and I see Laban's departure as the beginning of scene 8.

Jacob's accounts of preceding events in 31:6–13 and 38–42 offer new angles on the events related in Gen. 29–30, and they might come from a different, earlier version of the story. Yet in the context these unusually long speeches offer illuminating retrospective insights and climactic summary reflections on Jacob's time in Harran. The phenomenon whereby repetitions work in this way recurs in Genesis and adds to the drama. The account of the pact in vv. 43–53 is complicated: it incorporates the names of two places (Galʿed and The Watchtower), and it describes two monuments (a standing stone and a cairn), which has also raised the question whether the narrative combines two versions of the making of the pact.

31:3. One is perhaps to infer that despite what he has discerned, Jacob "dared not move a foot" until God speaks to him.[20] "In these straits the Lord speaks to him when he would have nothing else but faith and prayer left."[21] Yahweh's intervention once again plays a vital role in the story. The narrative's introduction uses the same phrase as 12:1; just the name is changed from Abram to Jacob. And Yahweh speaks in the same location, in Harran, where he spoke to Abram. But here Yahweh says "go back" instead of "go," and "to your forebears' country" instead of "from your country" or "from your ancestor's/father's household," and "to your homeland" instead of "from

20. Calvin, *Genesis*, 2:163.
21. Luther, *Genesis 31–37*, 8.

your homeland." Thus "your ancestors' country" has changed places: it is now Canaan, not Mesopotamia.[22] The verb "go back" also makes the point. Yahweh adds the promise "I will be with you," the promise first made to Jacob's father (26:3) and now renewed for Jacob. Although Laban is not the same "with him" as he was (31:2), over against that troublesome fact Yahweh makes the promise that he will be with Jacob (cf. Jacob's own version of the contrast in v. 5).[23]

31:4–13. Jacob is out in the open country, pasturing the flock that now belongs to him, and it seems to be there that Yahweh speaks to him. While shepherds in the Negev might need to travel long distances to find pasture and be away from home for a while, and 30:35–36 has located Laban's sons' flocks three days' journey away, the Harran area is more hospitable than the Negev, and 30:16 has also perhaps implied that Jacob comes home each evening. So he is not too far away and can send one of his boys to get Rachel and Leah (the order of their mention is noteworthy). Perhaps he wants to have a conversation that Laban and his sons can't overhear, or perhaps he simply can't abandon the flock. Whatever the case, he knows that he needs to talk to Rachel and Leah about what they are to do. Like other wives in Genesis, such as Sarah and Rebekah, they are not women you can take for granted or mess with.

Jacob's first words to them (v. 5) thus presuppose the developments related at the end of scene 6, including the change in the look on Laban's "face," which "is not the same" as in "previous days," noted in v. 2. On the other hand, Jacob knows that Yahweh's being with him is not simply a declaration of principle ("I am with you," a noun clause) or a promise for the future for when he is on his return journey or for when he gets back to Canaan ("I will be with you," v. 3). He can speak in past-tense terms of this reality ("He has been with me"). The promise Yahweh made to his father in 26:3 has already been true for Jacob. It is thus appropriate that Jacob's distinctive title for God is "the God of my father" (cf. 31:42; 32:9 [10], where it also applies to Abraham; otherwise it appears only in a special connection in Exod. 18:4). It is echoed in Laban's "the God of your father" in 31:29 and in Joseph's use of that phrase with regard to Jacob himself as the father in question, in 43:23.

The significance of Jacob's continuing words (vv. 6–7) is less clear. Jacob's complaint about Laban is entirely believable, but we have had no previous hint of such a charge. Since his escape from his mother's manipulation, Jacob has indeed become a man of initiative and energy, while the story has indicated that Laban knows how to manipulate situations in a less than straightforward way; "tactfully, Jacob does not mention the occasion on which Laban really

22. Cf. Brett, *Genesis*, 94.

23. Fokkelman, *Narrative Art in Genesis*, 152–53.

made a fool of him, at his wedding."[24] Maybe Jacob is being economical with the truth or elaborating it in the manner of his father and grandfather and thereby indicating that he is still operating in light of his mother's mentoring. Or maybe his statement gives us a picture of what has actually happened over the six years since he completed his fourteen years of service for Leah and Rachel. If so, 30:25–42 then gives us the short version of those six years, either focusing on the coup de grâce that brought things to a climax or focusing on Jacob's breeding ploy at the beginning, whose results Laban then tried to circumvent. On either of those understandings, Gen. 30–31 is another example of Genesis providing its listeners with a summary, then going back to give them more information, and sometimes incorporating two accounts of an event. Either way, the passage also complements scene 6's speaking only in terms of Jacob's initiative. Here he himself speaks of God's involvement in thwarting Laban's maneuvering.

Jacob goes on to make more concrete both his accusation and his testimony (vv. 8–9). The elaboration involves a third instantiation of a pattern: Jacob relates Laban's attitude or actions and follows it with a "but" to relate Yahweh's attitude or actions (vv. 5a and 5b, then vv. 6–7a and 7b, now vv. 8 and 9). Jacob spells out his earlier hyperbolic "ten times" in the specific accusations about the speckled and the striped. The accusation implies a different and earlier resolution of the initial negotiation about wages in 30:25–28, though it parallels the later resolution in granting Jacob small proportions of the animals that he manages to breed. The testimony is that Jacob managed to breed extraordinary numbers of speckled and then streaked—except that he doesn't claim the credit for this result but describes it as God's way of transferring Laban's assets to him.

Jacob's alternative account of the coup de grâce (v. 10) underscores the move from speaking purely in terms of human action to speaking in terms of God's activity. Jacob again dreamed, as in 28:12. In 30:34–39 the rams are white, but in the dream they are streaked, speckled, and mottled (the last word is an addition to the earlier description). Once again the narrative invites us to follow the scene as Jacob describes how God spoke and directed his gaze: "There, lift your eyes. . . ." We might say that the white rams are streaked, speckled, and mottled inside, that they have the capacity to generate streaked, speckled, and mottled offspring—as of course they do.

God's envoy interprets the dream to Jacob (vv. 11–12), as he spoke to Hagar in 21:17; compare the references to Yahweh's envoy in 16:7–13; 22:11, 15. The attention-getting exchange in which Jacob is addressed and says "I'm here" parallels that between the envoy and Abraham in 22:11, while the bidding "Lift your eyes, please, and look" parallels that given to Abraham in 13:14 (and cf. 22:13). The logic of the envoy's words follows that in

24. Wenham, *Genesis 16–50*, 271.

vv. 7 and 8–9, though here the divine action comes first and the rationale follows.

The envoy then moves from speaking for God to speaking as God (v. 13), as happened in 16:7–13; 22:11–12 and 15–18. And as Hagar then identifies God as El Roʾi and Abraham identifies the place of the envoy's appearing as Yahweh Yirʾeh, here God reminds Jacob that he is the God of Beth El, the one who appeared to Jacob there twenty years earlier. God now speaks explicitly of Jacob "anointing" the standing stone and of his "pledging" his tithe. The association of the oil with the pledge suggests a link with the use of oil in sealing pledges, treaties, and contracts;[25] making a pledge will be the significance of the stone to which 31:45–52 will refer. Finally, Jacob's summary jumps forward to share with Rachel and Leah the message related in v. 3, which prompted his sending for them. God told him to start going for home. He will get there, but it will not be the end of his wanderings or of his conflicts.[26]

31:14–18. Although Rachel and Leah are married to Jacob, his words to them have presupposed that nevertheless they are still members of Laban's family (cf. Laban's words in v. 43), especially in a situation where in effect Jacob has become part of Laban's family. Jacob cannot simply assume that they will choose him rather than their birth family.

But maybe there is nothing like a mean father to turn rival wives into friends (v. 14). "Share" and "domain" are technical terms from family life. Both refer to the same thing, but they have different meanings. "Share" (*ḥēleq*), as the word suggests, denotes the specific slice of something that belongs to a person; usually it signifies the portion of the clan's land that belongs to a particular family. "Domain" (*naḥălâ*) denotes something as a person's inalienable property: the Hebrew word is conventionally translated "inheritance," but it does not draw attention so much to the process whereby one gains something (that is, by its owner passing it on, probably on dying) but to one's secure ownership or possession of it. The sisters are saying that there is no allotment in their father's estate that belongs to them or is going to belong to them.

The reason (v. 15) is simple. Metaphorically speaking, their father sold them to Jacob, and as far as Laban is concerned, they don't belong to the family anymore. They belong to Jacob. He has paid for them. In a sense a father receives such a payment when he accepts a marriage gift from the man who marries his daughter. Speaking of this arrangement as selling is their unique and sharp-edged way to describe it. Given that there were various marriage customs in different parts of the Middle East at different times, there are various ways of interpreting the practices lying behind Rachel and Leah's

25. So Sarna, *Genesis*, 200.
26. Cf. Reno, *Genesis*, 242.

words.[27] But in Israel, as far as we know, "obtaining a wife is not a 'purchase.'"[28] Yet Jacob did (as it were) pay Laban for them with his fourteen years' labor, and Laban has (as it were) spent that marriage gift by having Jacob work for him and by thus accumulating flocks in which his daughters have no share. Laban has done nothing wrong, and they are not accusing him of wrongdoing, though they sound somewhat resentful. It's just the way things work. A man abandons his father and mother, joins his wife, and they become one new flesh, one new family; and the same applies to a woman.

With poetic justice, however (v. 16), God has "liberated" the wealth that Laban gained from Jacob, because Jacob's labor has resulted in his having substantial flocks that would have belonged to Laban if God had not liberated them. And therefore they also belong to the women and to their children through their being part of Jacob's family. Their future, their destiny, lies with Jacob. They are therefore happy to hightail it out of Harran, if that's what Jacob wants—or rather, what God proposes. There's nothing for them in Harran.

So Jacob gets going (vv. 17–18). The account of the process whereby he sets his household on the move (riding on camels, driving livestock) draws attention again (cf. 30:43) to the way Jacob has flourished over these last six years.

31:19–21. The story pauses for a moment to tell us three further things we need to know as background to what follows.

First (v. 19), Jacob could set his household on the move without entering into more negotiations with Laban because by chance Laban was away from home. Sheepshearing in the spring is a shepherdly equivalent to harvest, a time when the year's work comes to a climax but also a time that involves shepherds in intensely hard work for some days. The work's completion is marked by a festival, as happens at harvest (cf. 38:12–13). But apparently not all shepherds are shearing at the same time, and Jacob is still at home. So is the rest of the family, which gives Rachel the chance to steal Laban's effigies, his *tərāpîm*—this note forms the second piece of background to what follows. We do not know the origin of this word, but Ezek. 21:21 associates *tərāpîm* with divination (cf. Zech. 10:2), and elsewhere they appear along with the chasuble that was associated with divination (Judg. 17:5; 18:14–20). It thus is natural to link them with the practice of divination to which Laban referred in 30:27.[29] They might be figurines that represent family members who have passed, who can be honored and remembered by means of these likenesses, and can also be consulted for information (esp. about the future) to which they are privy now that they are beyond the confines of this world. We noted in connection with 30:27 that recourse to them on the part of non-Israelites could be viewed with condescension but with understanding and tolerance.

27. See, e.g., Van Seters, *Abraham*, 78–85.

28. Gunkel, *Genesis*, 333.

29. See T. J. Lewis, "Teraphim," in *DDD* 844–50.

Rachel might have wanted to keep hold of these effigies for both emotional and practical reasons. Maybe they were like a good-luck charm. Maybe she was simply glad for the chance to get back at Laban for deceiving Jacob when she was the girl he wanted. But the narrative doesn't show an interest in their inherent significance or in their significance to Rachel. The point that interests the narrative is that their theft and the way Rachel prevents Laban from finding them will make a fool of him.

Jacob's stealing away (vv. 20–21) neatly complements Rachel's stealing; it is arguably "a far more serious theft than Rachel's."[30] It will give Laban another reason for his protests about stealing in vv. 26–30. The verb "steal" (*gānab*) comes eight times in this section (vv. 19, 20, 26, 27, 30, 32, 39 [2×]), by far the densest concentration in the First Testament; in v. 31 Jacob also speaks of robbery (*gāzal*). Soon Jacob is across the Euphrates and making his way farther south on the several weeks' journey (three hundred miles) to Gilead, the mountain range east of the Jordan that will later be the home of some of Jacob's descendants. This reference constitutes the third piece of background to what follows. The narrator doesn't tell us why Jacob is aiming for Gilead. He made the first stage of his northward journey from Beer Sheba to Harran via the mountain range west of the Jordan, where God appeared to him at Beth El, but maybe from Beth El he crossed the Jordan into Gilead and continued toward Harran by the eastern route; and/or at least he intends to return that way. But eventually we discover that he needs to face Esau, and following the eastern route would link with that commitment. In more than one way, then, events have come full circle for him. Rebekah urged him to "set off, take flight" from his native land to Harran to her brother Laban (27:43). Now Jacob "takes flight" again and "sets off" from Harran and from Laban back to his native land.[31] Crossing the River (Euphrates) would imply that he was back in the promised land (cf. 15:18).[32]

31:22–24. Apparently someone goes from Laban's regular encampment to the site of the sheepshearing to bring him the news. While someone might also have discovered the theft of the effigies, Laban would perhaps anyway need to return home to prepare to chase Jacob and would then discover the theft, especially if he had recourse to them for guidance in the situation. How would Jacob expect Laban to react? Jacob doesn't know about the theft, and it might even have been this news that tipped Laban into chasing Jacob. The effigies would be really important to him as a means of gaining supernatural guidance. By now Jacob has several days' head start on Laban; "the third day" is a conventional expression like "two or three days" in English, but it is a plausible period to think in terms of.

30. Luther, *Genesis 31–37*, 35.
31. Cf. Sarna, *Genesis*, 217.
32. Cf. Calvin, *Genesis*, 2:171.

So Laban takes his "brothers" (v. 23), and they set off in pursuit; while these brothers or relatives will include his sons, the term suggests a broader extended-family group. Whether or not "third day" is a literal figure, "seven days' journey" is likely a figurative one, even though Laban's posse would be able to travel much faster than Jacob's entourage. But "the formulaic seven days actually serves to convey the terrific speed of the chase" (cf. Jacob's later comment about Laban racing after him, in v. 36).[33]

Once more (v. 24), Genesis backtracks. Had Laban and his company been intent on attacking Jacob, reappropriating the property and the people by force, and taking them back to Harran? After telling us that Laban has caught up with Jacob, the narrative relates how God meanwhile had appeared to Laban in a dream, as he had to Abimelek (as well as to Jacob himself). In both cases appearing and speaking in a dream to people outside the family of Israel's ancestors is God's way of protecting both the ancestors and the dreamers; dreams will feature in related connections in Gen. 40–41. Laban knows about speaking bad or good (see 24:50): he and his father recognized that they could not say anything about what should happen to Rebekah in light of what Abraham's servant told them about the process that brought him to Harran. God urges Laban to recognize that he is in the same position again. Jacob should be allowed to go home. The sudden note that Laban is of course an Aramaean forms another piece of background to what will follow in v. 47: the Aramaean would name things in Aramaic.[34] Strictly, Laban may have been Amorite rather than Aramaean, but he was living in Aram;[35] further, the audience would know about conflict between Israel or Judah and Aram, and the paragraphs that follow would have political resonances for them in terms of boundaries between Israel and Aram.[36]

31:25–32. After the summary announcement in v. 23 and the background information in v. 24, the listeners wonder what will happen next. The suspense is first heightened by another summary, which makes explicit that Laban makes camp in the same area as Jacob.

Then he confronts Jacob (vv. 26–28a). His words remind one of a plaintiff in a case brought before the elders at the town gate, or of a commander in chief expressing a grievance as the basis for threatening to make war.[37] Is his plaint serious? Laban is a deceiver; indeed, "What have you done?" was Jacob's question to Laban in 29:25. Yet he had implicitly claimed to undertake that act of deception for Leah's sake. And one can imagine that even the deceiver would want to bid farewell to his daughters and (grand)children.

33. Alter, *Genesis*, 170.
34. Cf. Brett, *Genesis*, 96.
35. See Speiser's comments, *Genesis*, 245–46.
36. See, e.g., Driver, *Genesis*, 290.
37. Cf. Hamilton, *Genesis 18–50*, 300.

Either way (vv. 28b–29), Laban moves from his ostensible sense of offense to the retaliatory possibilities that are open to him. Jacob has been stupid in the risk he has taken. How could he have thought he would get away with it? The answer is in v. 3, but Laban doesn't know about that encouragement and promise. Whereas Laban thought he had omnipotent capacity to do as he liked to Jacob, God has informed him that he is wrong. In v. 5 Jacob spoke of the way "the God of my father" has been with him, and Laban here gives conscious or unconscious testimony (even if he is being sarcastic; KSG) to the way "the God of your father" is continuing to protect Jacob.

Laban assumes (v. 30) that there is nevertheless no prohibition on speaking badly about the past. Although he recognizes that Jacob has the right to go home, he has no right to steal Laban's "gods"—Laban's own word for the *tərāpîm*. To call them *ʾĕlōhîm* is not to imply that he thinks of them as deities that should be worshiped: the word *ʾĕlōhîm* applies to a variety of entities other than simply ordinary human beings.

Jacob's answer (vv. 31–32) suggests that he didn't want to rely too much on what Yahweh said in v. 3. His response concerning the *ʾĕlōhîm* sets up further suspense, not least because the listeners know, as Jacob does not, who is the thief. The prescription of death seems extreme and looks like a hyperbole; Jacob's more literal point lies in his commitment to restoring the *ʾĕlōhîm*. But the narrative is beginning to anticipate both the story of Akan in Josh. 7 and the story about Jonathan in 1 Sam. 14, though it will issue in a outcome that is different from either.

31:33–35. Dramatically, we follow Laban through the different tents of the party. He comes to Rachel's tent last, giving her time to take action to avoid getting caught. One can evidently remove a camel saddle (which is presumably padded) and use it as a seat. Perhaps the saddle is actually a more substantial palanquin. Either way, the effigies are small enough to hide in it, apparently unlike the *tərāpîm* referred to in 1 Sam. 19:13–17. In that passage the word that looks plural refers to one object, and it would make sense if there was only one object here also, notwithstanding the plurals in vv. 30–34.[38] When Rachel says that the way of women applies to her and that she can't get up, she may mean that she is menstrual and unwell (and perhaps is therefore liable to convey impurity through contact with her or with what she has been sitting on); and Laban would then believe her, because she is after all his dear daughter, who loves him. Thus "she devises a very fine lie."[39] But her form of words doesn't elsewhere refer to menstruation, and she might be alluding to her inability as a woman to take her stand and take part in the kind of public disputation that Jacob and Laban have been engaging in.[40] Either way, her

38. Cf. Dillmann, *Genesis*, 2:256–57.
39. Luther, *Genesis 31–37*, 60.
40. See Lapsley, "Voice of Rachel."

deception of Laban is "a final act of retribution for the fraud he had perpetrated on her and Jacob on what was to have been their wedding day."[41] And as a result "the great loser" has simply made a fool of himself.[42]

31:36–42. One has sympathy for Jacob in his indignation as well as for Laban in his sense of affront. Some parallelism runs through Jacob's expression of his indignation; though parallelism is not confined to poetry and Jacob's words are prosaic in other ways, the parallelism does mark his words as heightened speech.

The language of "contention" (*rîb*) and "aver" (*ʿānâ*; v. 36) is the language of a quasi-legal confrontation at the town gate. Jacob has been accused, and he is responding to an accusation. The LXX likewise takes the word for "offense" (*pešaʿ*) to denote a "crime," but the word refers to an affront against a person rather than against a law; it commonly denotes rebellion against an authority (the Vg's "blame" is more appropriate). Likewise, "all perceived unscrupulous behavior by a subordinate" counts as "shortfall" in the eyes of the superior.[43] The word pair "offense" and "wrongdoing" (*ḥaṭṭʾāt*) recurs in words put on Jacob's lips by his sons in 50:17.

Either Jacob's "brothers" (v. 37) are the servants of whom 32:16 will speak, or Laban's brothers here become "my brothers and your brothers": that is, Jacob identifies himself with his broader adoptive family who will be the arbiters in this family conflict, like the elders at the town gate. But Jacob speaks rhetorically. He knows that Laban has found nothing of his household possessions in the tents—effigies or anything else.

Jacob now builds further on the opportunity to vent his sense of affront (vv. 38–41), which he assumes to be totally justified. It gives him an opportunity to pour out his feelings about the past twenty years of tending and breeding in a "tale of hardships" that is "an astringent corrective to romantic ideas of the biblical shepherd."[44] He has cared for the animals in a way that likely implies going well beyond the call of duty.[45] He has not made lamb stew. He has accepted responsibility for animals that were mauled by wild creatures or were stolen. He has put up with the heat of the desert day and the cold of the desert night. He has hardly slept. And he has put up with Laban's maneuvering his wages; ten times is again a hyperbole.

It is God who has made all the difference (v. 42). Jacob again testifies to the way the God of his father has been with him, as he did in v. 5 and as Laban did in v. 29. But here he glosses that title. The God of his father is also the God of Abraham, who set Jacob on this journey from Harran back to Canaan as he

41. Sarna, *Genesis*, 219.

42. Fokkelman, *Narrative Art in Genesis*, 170.

43. Hamilton, *Genesis 18–50*, 306 (but he uses "offense" to translate *ḥaṭṭʾāt*).

44. Kidner, *Genesis*, 166.

45. See, e.g., the rules about shepherds in Hammurabi's "Lawcode," §§261–67 (*ANET* 177); cf. Seebass, *Genesis*, 2.2:367.

set Abraham on his journey from Harran in the first place. And as the God of his father, he is also "the Reverence of Isaac." This title comes only here and in v. 53. The one before whom Isaac stands in awe and who invites awe from other people is the one who has been protecting his son. He is the one who has seen Jacob's low position and the exhausting nature of the work he has done for Laban over those twenty years. He is the one who has given Jacob the ideas about breeding that led to his not leaving Harran empty-handed. The reference to Laban sending him off harks back to 30:25, where we noted the connection with Deut. 15:12–15 and its reference to sending off a servant "empty-handed." And the previous night when he appeared to Laban, God had already made the decision for which Jacob has called (rhetorically) in v. 37. Jacob has been in the right and Laban in the wrong at every point, and God recognizes it.

31:43–54. Jacob cannot be held responsible for Rachel's thievery and deception, and his own story may seem convincing. But now we must look at the situation from Laban's angle. "The first person in a dispute seems in the right; then his neighbor comes and examines him" (Prov. 18:17). Everyone and everything that sits before Laban and Jacob was once Laban's, and Laban thinks that in a way they still are. In the back of his mind may be the assumption that a servant never becomes the actual possessor of the wife he receives from his master (cf. Exod. 21:4–6).[46] However, Laban knows that he must be realistic, not least because of God's appearing to him. Yet Jacob has taken away his daughters and his grandchildren. When daughters get married, it doesn't stop their parents from worrying about them—they may do so even more. What is going to happen to them and to their children at the hand of this son-in-law who takes them away so precipitously and so furtively?

Laban therefore proposes a pact or covenant between him and Jacob (v. 44). It is a sign that he admits defeat. He cannot overpower Jacob in any sense. He has failed to find the effigies, and he apparently cannot dispute Jacob's self-defense. Given that pacts or covenants are needed only between people who do not belong to the same family, it shows the sadness of the situation that Laban needs to propose a pact. To say that the pact will be a witness involves an ellipsis: it is the making of the pact combined with the erecting of the standing stone and the cairn that will generate a witness, as the subsequent verses will indicate. "Solemnizing" is literally "cutting"; it may be simply a metaphor derived from the kind of formal procedure described in 15:9–21, or the verses that follow may imply some kind of actual cutting. Either way, it will be an agreement entered into with gravity and earnestness, which will reassure Laban about the fate of his daughters and grandchildren.

Formal procedures follow (vv. 45–46). It is only Laban who feels the need of the pact; Jacob is done with Laban and with Harran. But the pact making

46. Cf. De La Torre, *Genesis*, 279–80; and the comment on v. 26.

must involve both parties, and Jacob doesn't object to the idea of setting up a standing stone as he did in 28:18. It will commemorate what the God who appeared to him at Beth El has now done,[47] though v. 51 will make clear that it implicates both Jacob and Laban. In addition, Jacob gets his "brothers" to collect rocks to make into a cairn. The unnecessarily double commemorative marker indicates the significance of the pact for Laban and for Jacob; there are two witnesses to it.[48] There follows a ceremonial meal as an aspect of sealing the mutual commitment (cf. 26:26–31). These two verses summarize what follows in vv. 47–54.

Laban and Jacob both call the cairn "Witness Heap" (vv. 47–48) in Aramaic and Hebrew. Strictly, then, Laban does not name the heap Galʿed: he gives it a name in Aramaic that can be understood to mean Witness Heap in Hebrew when it is split into two parts. So now we know one aspect of the significance of Jacob's journeying initially to Gilead (*gilʿād*; the different spelling indicates that it is a name in its own right, unrelated in meaning to the phrase *gal ʿed*).[49] Possibly the single rock or the cairn incorporated an inscription recording the pact.

There is also a place called Watchtower (*miṣpâ*) in Gilead (v. 49), possibly more than one,[50] which also makes for an apposite link with this pact. Both parties are to be prepared to take the risk of having Yahweh "watch over" what they are doing from there. To use the imagery of 28:10–22, this place is one where one could imagine divine envoys traveling up and down, reporting on events in the world and returning to take action in light of discussions in Yahweh's court about them. Laban asks that Yahweh may indeed keep a watch on Jacob and Laban when they cannot keep a watch on each other.

Specifically (v. 50), like many a father, he is indeed concerned for his daughters. There is some irony in his envisaging the possibility that Jacob might humble them (*ʿānâ* piel), since it was this word that Jacob used of Laban's treatment of him in v. 42. It is a serious potential accusation: the verb has referred to the way the Egyptians will treat the Israelites (15:13) and the way Sarah treated Hagar (16:6), and it will refer to the way Shechem treats Laban's granddaughter (34:2). Perhaps taking wives who effectively displace Leah and Rachel is one way Laban can envisage such humbling. If Jacob behaves in this way, Laban may not hear (there are no social media). But Yahweh will know.

Laban identifies with both the cairn and the standing stone (vv. 51–52), as if he himself has erected them. For him, too, both will be a witness. On his part, they will witness to a commitment to stay on his side of them, in effect to stay in Aram and leave Canaan to Jacob. He will not come south of this

47. Cf. Fokkelman, *Narrative Art in Genesis*, 188–92.

48. Wenham, *Genesis*, 279–80.

49. See *HALOT*.

50. Cf. BDB. There is also a better-known Miṣpah north of Jerusalem, and more than one place called Miṣpeh.

point, raiding or attacking. He will not thus deal badly with Jacob; it is what Yahweh has forbidden in vv. 24 and 29.

To be more local in the way he speaks of God (v. 53), this God is the God of Abraham (the God of the line from which Jacob comes) and the God of Nahor (the God of the line from which Laban comes). The collocation of these two expressions with the plural verb "decide" makes it sound as if Laban thinks in terms of two deities, though the idea of two gods trying to determine something that concerns their respective devotees seems like a recipe for problems. Laban (or the narrator) goes on to refer to *ʾĕlōhê ăbîhem*. Laban perhaps sees the plural deities of Abraham and Nahor as the plural deities of their father Terah, which in part fits Josh. 24:2. Or perhaps the God of Terah is the God of Abraham (and thus of Isaac) and also the God of Nahor (and thus of Laban), and the plural verb which follows issues from the juxtaposition of these two designations of that God. If there is some ambiguity about Laban's theology, however, there is none about Jacob's. He simply swears by his father's God—that is, he opens himself to that God's judgment if he fails to live by the pact. Here as elsewhere in the stories of the ancestors, they "deal always with but one God." While it's not philosophical monotheism, "there is yet no trace of polytheistic influence" in their stories. "What later became the first commandment and confession of the religion of Israel (Deut. 6:4) is present here without command or confessional formula. It is *one* God who deals with and speaks to Abraham, Isaac, and Jacob, their wives and children. It is *one* God whom they invoke and in whom they trust."[51]

The account of the sacrifice and sacrificial meal (v. 54) gives more detail on the meal mentioned in v. 46. A sacrifice (*zebaḥ*) as opposed to a burnt offering is shared by offerers and God, and by the offerers among themselves. Leviticus 7:11–18 associates such sacrifices with gratefulness to God for a blessing or an answer to prayer, and such connotations will be appropriate here. The sacrifice seals the mutual commitment they have made before God and further seals their nonaggression pact with one another.

51. Westermann, *Genesis 12–36*, 575, with his emphasis.

34

Envoys Divine and Human

(31:55–32:32 [32:1–33])

Overview

As Jacob draws near a reunion with Esau, scene 8 in the account of his journey to and from Harran relates further appearances of God's envoys to him. Interwoven with these two appearances (and with Jacob's prayer, which comes in between) are accounts of the parting of Laban and Jacob, of Jacob's sending envoys to Esau, and of Jacob's sending offerings to Esau to seek to mollify him before their meeting.

Translation

> **31:55**Laban started early in the morning, kissed his children and his
> daughters, and blessed them. Then Laban set off and went, back[1] to his
> place, **32:1**while Yaʿaqob went on his way. God's envoys came upon him,
> **2**and Yaʿaqob said when he saw them, "This is God's encampment." He
> named that place Maḥanayim.
>
> **3**Yaʿaqob sent envoys before him to Esaw his brother in the country of
> Seʿir (the land of Edom). **4**He ordered them: "You're to say this: 'To my lord,
> to Esaw. Your servant Yaʿaqob has said this: "As I have resided as an alien
> with Laban and have delayed until now, **5**ox, donkey, and flock, and servant
> and maidservant have come to belong to me. I've sent to tell my lord so
> as to find favor in your eyes."'" **6**The envoys came back to Yaʿaqob, saying,
> "We came to your brother, to Esaw, and actually he's coming to meet you,

1. Literally, "set off and went and returned."

and 400 men[2] with him." **7**Yaʿaqob was very fearful. It put him under pressure, and he divided the people that were with him, the flock, the herd, and the camels, into two camps, **8**and said "If Esaw comes to the one camp and strikes it down, the remaining camp may be an escape group."

9Yaʿaqob said, "God of my father Abraham, God of my father Yiṣḥaq, Yahweh, you who said to me, 'Go back to your country, to your homeland, and I will do good things with you,' **10**I'm too small for all the acts of commitment and all the truthfulness with which you've acted toward your servant. With my cane I crossed this Yarden, and now I've become two camps. **11**Rescue me from the hand of my brother, please, from the hand of Esaw, because I'm fearful of him, in case he comes and strikes me down, mother with children. **12**But you yourself said, 'I will definitely do good things[3] with you and make your offspring like the sand of the sea, which cannot be counted because of the large number.'" **13**He spent the night there that night.

Then he got an offering for Esaw his brother from what had come into his charge: **14**200 she-goats and twenty he-goats, 200 ewes and twenty rams, **15**thirty milch camels and their young, forty cows and ten bulls, and twenty she-donkeys and ten he-donkeys. **16**He put them into the charge of his servants, herd by herd on its own, and said to his servants, "Cross over before me, but put a space between herd and herd." **17**He ordered the first: "Esaw my brother will meet you and ask you, 'To whom do you belong? Where are you going? To whom do these belong, before you?' **18**You're to say, 'They're your servant Yaʿaqob's. They're an offering sent to my lord, to Esaw. Here, he himself is behind us as well.'" **19**He ordered both the second and the third and also all the ones who were going behind the herds: "You're to speak these very words to Esaw when you reach him. **20**You're also to say, 'Here, your servant Yaʿaqob is behind us,'" because (he said), "I'll cover his face with an offering that goes ahead of my face, then afterward when I see his face, maybe he'll lift my face." **21**Thus the offering crossed ahead of his face, while he was spending that night in the camp. **22**But he set off that night[4] and got his two wives, his two maidservants, and his eleven children and crossed the Yabboq crossing. **23**So he got them and took them across the wadi and took what belonged to him across.

24But Yaʿaqob was left on his own, and someone wrestled[5] with him until dawn rose. **25**He saw that he had not overcome him, so he

2. Targum Neofiti makes explicit that they are a military force.

3. Jacob uses the idiom that combines an infinitive and its cognate finite verb and thus makes the reminder more emphatic than it was in v. 9 [10].

4. The Vg has him getting up early, to solve the question of the relationship between the statements in vv. 21b and 22a [22b and 23a].

5. The verb *ʾābaq*, which etymologically perhaps implies "get dusty" (cf. BDB), comes only here. Did the narrator invent it to generate the assonance with the names in the context—"he wrestled [*wayyēʾābēq*] with *yaʿăqōb* at the *yabbōq*"? Tongue (*Between Biblical Criticism*, 3) notes that this story itself is a text that "raises dust, obscuring the scene, provoking many commentators to try and interpret what is going on before the dust settles again."

touched[6] the hollow of his thigh, and the hollow of Yaʿaqob's thigh re-
coiled[7] as he wrestled with him. 26He said, "Let me go away, because
the dawn has risen." He said, "I won't let you go away unless you bless
me." 27He said to him, "What is your name?" He said, "Yaʿaqob." 28He
said, "You will no longer be named Yaʿaqob, but Yiśraʾel, because you
have exerted yourself[8] with God and with human beings and you have
overcome."[9] 29Yaʿaqob asked, "Tell me your name, please." He said,
"Why is it that you ask my name?" But he blessed him there, 30and
Yaʿaqob named the place Peniʾel, "because I saw God face-to-face, and
my life was rescued." 31The sun rose on him as he crossed by Penuʾel;
he was limping because of his thigh. (32That's why the Israelites don't
eat the sciatic nerve, which is at the hollow of the thigh, until this day,
because he touched Yaʿaqob at the hollow of the thigh at the sciatic
nerve.)

Interpretation

We noted in the introduction to 31:3–54 that 31:55 in English Bibles is the beginning of a new section rather than being the close of 31:3–54. This understanding is suggested by the parallel between 31:55 (which relates the northward departure of Laban) and 32:1 (which relates the southward departure of Jacob). Printed Hebrew Bibles thus appropriately make Gen. 31:55 the first verse of Gen. 32. The MT itself makes 32:2 the close (at last) of its paragraph (and lection) that began at 28:10 and also the close of the immense unit (and the previous lection) that began at 25:19. But the rest of Gen. 32 continues to speak of envoys and camps, and in particular incorporates a further encounter between God and Jacob, which suggests that Gen. 32 as a whole comprises scene 8. God's encounter with Jacob parallels and balances the appearance when Jacob was on his way out of Canaan in scene 2 (28:10–22). Scene 8 then leads straight into scene 9 (the MT has no break at all at the end of Gen. 32); it prepares the way for the meeting between Jacob and Esau. In the comments that follow, I will give only the English verse references.

The chapter alternates movement and action (31:55; 32:3–8, 13–22) and meetings between supernatural figures and Jacob (32:1–2, 9–12, 22–32), each alternating pair longer than the previous one:

6. BDB notes that occasionally the verb *nāgaʿ* nearly equals "strike," but it does not cite this instance as an example.

7. Cf. the Vg for this translation of the rare verb *yāqaʿ*.

8. See BDB for the rare verb *śārâ*. Aq, Sym "ruled" derive the verb from *śārar*. The LXX, Vg "were strong" suggests the Aramaic verb *šārar*.

9. The LXX, Vg suggest "you have exerted yourself with God, and with human beings you will overcome," which makes good sense in the context but involves treating "and with human beings" as an extraposed object, and there is no direct pointer to that understanding.

1. Laban departs: Jacob's relations with Laban are finally resolved (31:55)
2. God's army appears to Jacob, with the implications unspecified (32:1–2)
3. Jacob sends envoys to Esau, with equivocal results (32:3–8)
4. Jacob prays for God's protection but gets no response (32:9–12)
5. Jacob prepares an offering for Esau, sends it across the Yabboq, and takes his family across (32:13–23)
6. A supernatural figure wrestles with Jacob and renames him (32:24–32)

The section thus speaks more explicitly of Jacob's actions and reactions than it does of the things that happen to him, though even in connection with Jacob the narrative leaves things unclear. Why do God's envoys come upon Jacob? Why is he going to see Esau, anyway (given his fear)? What is the effect of his prayer? Why does he stay north of the Yabboq after taking everyone else across? Who is the wrestler and why does he want to leave when dawn rises? There are further detailed puzzles, such as why there are the variant forms *maḥănayim*, *maḥăneh*, and *maḥănôt*, and the variant forms Peni'el and Penu'el. Ambiguity is pervasive; fear is explicit. Arguably, the chapter constitutes one great raising of suspense.

31:55–32:2. It's the morning after the meal that sealed the covenant relationship between Laban and Jacob. The two men will perhaps have eaten and drunk late into the night and then drifted off to sleep where they were. But early in the morning, Laban springs into action: the opening verb (*šākam*) suggests as usual a commitment to doing what needs to be done. What now needs to be done is the saying of goodbyes. Laban really is letting go of his (grand) children and their mothers, and he prays for God to bless them. Against the odds, Jacob's Harran adventure has come to a satisfactory ending.

Jacob now sets off in the opposite direction from Laban (32:1). But there is an elephant in the room, though it will not be named until v. 3. Jacob must now face Esau. The expression "God's envoys" comes otherwise only in the parallel scene in 28:12, while the verb and the construction (*pāgaʿ b*) are the ones that described Jacob's coming upon the site at Beth El in 28:11. There is no doubt here that the verb denotes a deliberate "coming upon." What is the significance of their coming to meet Jacob? They don't do anything or say anything. Are they a threat or an encouragement? Whereas one might wonder whether the account of the event at Mahanayim is truncated, its allusiveness will turn out to be just the first instance of an allusiveness that runs through the chapter. The parallel with 2 Kings 6:16–17 suggests that the event could remind Jacob and the listeners that there is more going on than meets the eye and that there are grounds for encouragement. The envoys' appearing suggests the promise of support;[10] they signify the reality of God's protection that Ps.

10. Cf. Josephus, *Ant.* 1.20.1.

91:9–11 describes.[11] To anticipate Elisha's comment to his servant in 2 Kings 6:16–17, "there were many more [angels] with Jacob than were with Esau."[12] Both passages are characterized by an allusive brevity; they hint at another reality without revealing all that we would like to know about it. They also thus compare with the appearance in Josh. 5:13–15,[13] where the response of the commander in chief of Yahweh's army to a question from Joshua is to decline to answer his question about whose side he is on.

The narrative tells us only of Jacob's reaction to seeing the envoys (v. 2). That reaction is to name the place, as he did in 28:19. The parallels with 28:10–22 embolden hope for the return to Canaan of which Jacob spoke in 28:21, "with things being well."[14] The parallel with 28:17–19 supports the idea that Jacob's declaration "This is God's encampment" refers not to the envoys but to Jacob's camp, which God's envoys are indeed protecting.[15] The subsequent First Testament narrative mentions Mahanayim a number of times as a place of some significance east of the Jordan, especially as an off-the-beaten-track place of refuge (e.g., 2 Sam. 2:8; 17:24). It is also mentioned as a marker of borders (Josh. 13:26, 30), which fits the context here as Jacob is about to cross the Yabboq, the border river.

32:3–8. It now becomes more explicit why Jacob was proceeding through Gilead down the east side of the Jordan rather than (for instance) crossing the Jordan north of Lake Kinneret at the site of the modern Bridge of the Daughters of Jacob. Even from where he now is, he could cross the Jordan to proceed to Beth El or Mamre or Beer Sheba. Yahweh told him to go back to his own land (31:13), he set off to go back to Canaan to his father (31:18), and Esau has evidently left the promised land (as 36:6–8 will relate).[16] But for reasons that are not stated, Jacob wants to get back on friendly relations with his brother, which involves continuing southward.

We are not done with envoys, but now they are Jacob's envoys (v. 3). Like Abraham's servant's entourage in Gen. 24, Jacob's party evidently includes people other than the ones who have been explicitly mentioned; only when

11. So Sarna, *Genesis*, 223.

12. Ephrem, *Genesis*, 180.

13. Cf. Westermann, *Genesis 12–36*, 505.

14. Cf. Fokkelman, *Narrative Art in Genesis*, 198.

15. Cf. Bunn, "'Return to the Land of Your Fathers,'" 104. While "encampment" is the regular singular *maḥănēh*, *maḥănayim* is an example of names that look dual but have singular meaning, such as *yərûšālayim*, *miṣrayim*, and perhaps *ʾărām nahărayim* (24:10: see the footnote). The quasi-dual ending is apparently an archaic locative. What is different about *maḥănayim* is that it also occurs here in the singular (cf. also vv. 8 and 21), whose plural is *maḥănôt* (which comes in vv. 7 [8] and 10 [11], where a genuine dual would be appropriate). The parallel with names such as *yərûšālayim* and *miṣrayim* suggests that (as often happens) *maḥănayim* was this place's longstanding name, which finds a new significance through the appearance to Jacob of a quasi-army.

16. Cf. Calvin's comments, *Genesis*, 2:187.

they have a part to play do they receive mention. Presumably these envoys are the servants mentioned in 30:43. Jacob sends them to where he evidently knows Esau is now located, the region that can be designated as Seʿir on the basis of the dominant presence of Mount Seʿir, in what will later be known as Edom (as the explanatory phrase notes).

The charge Jacob gives his envoys (v. 4) comprises a commission, an address, an introduction of the kind that comes in a prophetic message ("thus has said so-and-so"), and then the main content of the message for Esau. Messages structured in this way are more familiar from the Prophets, but the story offers a useful example from ordinary life, such as are also instanced in Middle Eastern letters.[17] Jacob notes that he has been away a long time. He has stayed all that time as a resident alien in Harran and has delayed coming back—Jacob uses the verb his grandfather's servant used in 24:56 when he told Laban that he could not delay returning to Canaan. So why did Jacob delay? Does the verb acknowledge that it was not merely because he needed to work seven years, then seven, then six, but because he hadn't wanted to deal with the implications of returning—and facing Esau?

At least he has done well there (v. 5). We knew about the donkeys, flock, and male and female servants; Jacob here adds mention of oxen. If we are to take that note as more than local color or hyperbole, they would have made the journey from Harran even slower. Jacob provides his list of assets in order to find favor or grace in Esau's eyes. Jacob neatly exemplifies the use of the word "favor" or "grace" (*ḥēn*) as implying something undeserved; it can only be a gift. Given the history of their relationship, Jacob can only throw himself on Esau's grace or mercy, though he offers no expression of contrition, and giving his list of assets introduces some ambiguity into the appeal for grace. His deference is also expressed in his extravagantly obsequious use of the terms servant and lord: only Abraham's servant in Gen. 24 (again) has used that language more than Jacob now does. Jacob may seem to be "nullifying" the prediction of their relationship in 25:23.[18] His action invites the audience to recall the formulation of that prediction and note the way it allowed for the possibility of the younger serving the greater after all. Whatever the significance of his having extracted from Esau the transfer of the firstborn's position and having swindled him out of the firstborn's blessing, Jacob is not behaving like someone who is the senior party in this relationship.

The response the envoys bring back is worryingly equivocal (vv. 6–8), or at least it seems so to Jacob, because a body of 400 men can suggest a fighting force (cf. 1 Sam. 22:2; 25:13; 30:10, 17).[19] Of course it need not do so; Esau might even be simply bringing his family group as a whole, so that the

17. See, e.g., *ANET* 623–26; cf. Speiser, *Genesis*, 254.
18. Brayford, *Genesis*, 371.
19. Cf. Sarna, *Genesis*, 224.

two family groups will meet.[20] Esau doesn't need to come as far as Laban did, but it would require several days to get to Jacob's encampment.[21] The envoys' return ahead of Esau implies a day or two's delay while he collects his entourage and gets it ready. Here is where camps reappear.[22] Although Jacob has a substantial entourage, it comprises women, children, servants, and animals—nothing like a fighting force of 400. "The shepherd, with all his success, is at the mercy of the fierce marauder who was to 'live by [his] sword'" (27:40).[23] If Esau is coming to attack them, as v. 11 will note, they are doomed, and dividing them into two groups seems a pathetic and hopeless gesture. But if these camps have supernatural support (cf. Exod. 17:8–13) . . . So we are not done with fear on Jacob's part: "once fear of Laban faded and was no more, then fear of his brother took hold of him."[24] Fortunately, Yahweh's envoy camps around those who fear other people as well as those who fear Yahweh (Ps. 34:7 [34:8]).

32:9–13a. Fear drives Jacob to prayer. The shape of the prayer overlaps with that of other First Testament prayers (e.g., Isa. 37:15–17). Like most of the psalms, it contains no expression of contrition; unlike most of the psalms, it is not dominated by protest. It is more specific and concrete in relation to Jacob's situation than a psalm; the psalms avoid concrete references in order to be more broadly useful. But like a psalm, Jacob's prayer incorporates address to God (v. 9a), recollection of God's words in the past that Jacob longs for God to fulfill (v. 9b), description of the petitioner as one who has seen God's faithfulness in the past (v. 10), an actual petition (v. 11), and another recollection of God's words in the past that relate to the present situation (v. 12). While the last element is the most direct suggestion of motivation for God to answer the prayer, the whole is an exercise in such persuasion. It is the first such prayer in the Scriptures.

Jacob addresses God (v. 9) in virtually the same terms as those God used toward him in 28:13 and summarizes commitments God made to him there and in 31:3, though he speaks of God doing good things with him rather than of being with him.

His saying "I am small" (v. 10) recalls the description of him as the "small son" of Isaac and Rebekah, Esau being their "big son" (27:15, 42). He didn't want to be small then, but he wants to be treated that way now. He's willing to be Esau's servant; he's also willing to see himself as Yahweh's servant.[25] The

20. Cf. Heard, *Dynamics of Diselection*, 129–30.

21. Cf. Seebass, *Genesis*, 2.2:382.

22. There is a hint of a further significance in the name Mahanayim, with its quasi-dual form (see the footnote above on v. 2), though v. 7 uses the plural *maḥănôt* rather than the quasi-dual *maḥănayim*.

23. Skinner, *Genesis*, 406.

24. Chrysostom, *Homilies on Genesis 46–67*, 155.

25. Cf. Frey, *Das Buch des Kampfes*, 131–32; cf. Fokkelman, *Narrative Art in Genesis*, 203.

expression "acts of commitment and truthfulness" (in other words, acts of steadfast commitment) is again the phraseology of his grandfather's servant (24:27, 49), though Jacob makes it concrete by using the plural of the word for commitment. The phraseology comes in Yahweh's own classic self-description in Exod. 34:6 (cf., e.g., Pss. 25:10; 26:3; 40:10–11 [40:11–12]; 57:3, 10 [57:4, 11]). Yahweh's acting with commitment has expressed itself in "doing good things" and has thus issued in Jacob's having so much by way of people and possessions that they now constitute two camps. The reference to the Jordan coheres with the idea that Jacob had come this way on his outbound journey to Harran.

But now he is scared (v. 11). It's all very well for God to have rescued property from Laban (31:9, 16). Now Jacob himself needs rescue from Esau; at least that's what Jacob thinks. His understandable but unfounded fear anticipates that of Joseph's brothers (50:15).[26] Esau will surely obliterate mothers and children alike: the bleak expression recurs in a similar context in Hosea 10:14 (cf. Deut. 22:6). Is Jacob even gloomier than v. 8 implies, or is he giving the bleakest possible portrait of his situation in order to move God to act? The verb "rescue" makes for another link with the Psalms, where it is a standard appeal, while the brevity of Jacob's petition in the prayer (just one word in Hebrew) also corresponds to the Psalms.

Finally, Jacob again reminds Yahweh of the nature of his promises (v. 12), as Israel does in its prayers (e.g., Pss. 89:19 [89:20]; 119:25, 28). They are the promises given to his grandfather and his grandmother and his father (16:10; 22:17; 26:4), and they again recall God's promise to do good things for Jacob. Actually, Jacob does well "in requesting nothing from the Lord other than fulfillment of his promises."[27]

Jacob spends the night there, where he prays (v. 13a). But the narrative tells of no response from God.

32:13b–23. How are the listeners to see Jacob's initiative in relation to his prayer? It more obviously follows from his understandable sense of anxiety at the report of the returning envoys, related in v. 6, and his sending this offering to Esau makes for a contrast with Esau's apparent military expedition.[28] The inventory of the offering boggles the mind and makes one laugh out loud, as do the instructions to the servants regarding the way they are to explain this monumental cavalcade. Convoy after convoy is to meet Esau, assuring him that there is more to follow, even as his eyes go wider and wider. Perhaps Jacob is seeking to forestall the military action by inviting Esau to see him as returning the blessing that he stole as well as restoring the senior position that Esau gave over to him (cf. 33:11).[29]

26. Cf. Hamilton, *Genesis 18–50*, 320.
27. Chrysostom, *Homilies on Genesis 46–67*, 156–57.
28. Cf. Seebass, *Genesis*, 2.2:388.
29. Cf. Westermann, *Genesis 12–36*, 511.

Having given instruction concerning his "offering," Jacob goes on to speak of being accepted by Esau (v. 20). In the First Testament an "offering" (*minḥâ*) is more often than not something presented to God (cf. 4:3–5). The related talk of being "accepted" can also belong to the context of sacrifice (e.g., Job 42:8–9). But behind those sacral references are everyday contexts such as are presupposed here. An offering is something a subordinate person gives to someone in a higher position in the hope of finding acceptance (cf. 43:11–26); it's different from a "gift" such as someone might give without there being an implication that the giver is in a subordinate position. Malachi 1:8–13 illuminates the usage as it brings into juxtaposition talk of "offerings" and of having one's "face lifted" and of thus being accepted, and it explicitly compares offerings to God and offerings to the governor. So in this respect, too, Jacob puts himself in a subordinate position in relation to his brother, hoping that Esau may "lift his face." The image is again of someone approaching a more powerful person with deference, not presuming to look them in the face, but hoping that the recipient of the offering will lift their face and encourage the offerer to look the recipient in the face (cf. 19:21; 1 Sam. 25:35). The expression "cover" the face (*kāpar* piel) comes only here and is thus trickier. Proverbs 16:14 does speak of covering the king's wrath, which would be expressed in his face, and in the present context the use of the word "face" coheres with the focus on the face (Jacob's, Esau's, God's): the chapters' references to face "crescendo" in this verse.[30] In its more common usage, the verb "cover" appears in connection with the covering over of offenses, while Mal. 1:9 speaks of mollifying (*ḥālâ* piel) God's face (Tg. Onq. here has "soothe his fury"). One might thus see the expression "cover his face" as a cross between "cover his anger" and "mollify his face," with similar meaning to both; "covering the face" points to Jacob's hope of mollifying Esau. Verse 20 is then "the key to everything" insofar as it shows that Jacob has a bad conscience (or at least that he is scared) and knows he needs to appease Esau.[31] "The gift shows Jacob to be concerned solely with Jacob; he merely wants to mollify Esau so as to save his own skin."[32]

The last thing Jacob wants is to "face" Esau (v. 21). He keeps pushing someone or something ahead of him to avoid coming face-to-face with him: the servants, the offering, the animals, and so on.[33] As the little brother had wanted to be the big brother but now wants to be treated as little, so the guy who had wanted to push to the front now wants to be at the back.[34] The references to his crossing the Yabboq and to his spending the night are then confusing. I take it that v. 21b refers to an original intention to stay north of the Yabboq after sending on the convoys. But he changes his mind.

30. B. A. Anderson, "Intersection," 38.
31. Gunkel, *Genesis*, 346.
32. J. Anderson, *Jacob*, 141.
33. Cf. Hamilton, *Genesis 18–50*, 325–26.
34. Cf. Fokkelman, *Narrative Art in Genesis*, 205–7.

In his anxiety, then (vv. 22–23), that evening he personally sees his wives, maidservants, and sons across. Once again, there is no mention of daughters since the narrative focuses on the ancestors who will give their names to eleven of the clans to which the listeners belong. Although v. 23 refers to the Yabboq as a wadi, it is one of the two perennial rivers that flows down from the eastern mountains into the Jordan. While it is quite fordable, it runs through a deep gorge so that the crossing as a whole could be tricky. Perhaps Jacob takes the family across group by group until they are all on the other side.

32:24–32. After the unexpected twist involving Jacob's making an approach to Esau rather than proceeding to Canaan, another unexpected twist follows.[35] "Jacob has been in tight situations—but the tightest is yet to come."[36]

Jacob himself apparently crosses back to where the camp had been (v. 24) since v. 31 indicates that in due course he needs to cross again from the north to the south. Although one can imagine him returning to make a final check that no one and nothing has been left behind,[37] going back would fit with a desire to put everyone and everything between him and Esau.[38] Whatever the reason, he is now on his own as he was at Beth El in 28:10–22. What happens at the Yabboq has some parallels with what happened at Beth El, though it has major differences. In some sense one could no doubt describe the event as a dream or a vision, but Genesis does not use those terms. Nor does the account compare closely with tales about river spirits that oppose travelers crossing their river or demons who must disappear before dawn[39] or accounts of the bad spirit that comes on Saul or the evil spirits that attack people in the Gospels. Nor can Jacob's experience be "spiritualized into wrestling in prayer: it does appear that a real fight was involved."[40] The narrative does not imply something happening simply within Jacob's spirit. Who, then, is the "someone"?[41] The word *ʾîš* indicates an individual person, and it would normally denote a human being. Is it Esau?[42] But 33:1 does not point in this direction, and v. 28 will refer to Jacob fighting with God. The story in Gen. 18–19 has Yahweh and his companions described as *ʾănāšîm*, the plural of *ʾîš*. In the nearest First Testament parallel to this passage, Exod. 4:24–26, the assailant is Yahweh, and in due course the story will suggest that Jacob's attacker is indeed God. As far as Jacob is concerned at this stage, he is attacked either by a human being or by a supernatural being who takes human form, like the

35. Cf. Bunn, "'Return to the Land of Your Fathers,'" 116.

36. Fokkelman, *Narrative Art in Genesis*, 197.

37. Cf Ibn Ezra, *Genesis*, 317.

38. On his cowardice and its implications, see Frolov, "Other Side."

39. See, e.g., Gunkel, *Genesis*, 352.

40. Cf. Wenham, *Genesis 16–50*, 295.

41. On the rereading and rewriting of this figure over the centuries, see Tongue, *Between Biblical Criticism*, esp. 169–78.

42. Cf. Bunn, "'Return to the Land of Your Fathers,'" 137–44.

ones who appear in Gen. 18–19. Hosea 12:4 [12:5] calls the attacker an envoy (*malʾāk*), and Jacob might wonder if he is one of the envoys that appeared in this very place in vv. 1–2.[43] Or his being an attacker might rather suggest that he could be Esau's guardian angel,[44] someone representing Esau's interests.

The identity of the subsequent he/him/his (v. 25) is also initially not explicit, and this momentary ambiguity will recur through vv. 25–28. Retrospectively, the identity of each he/him/his becomes clear, but initially it is not so, which adds to the allusiveness and mystery of the event. Is the assailant holding back from utilizing his supernatural capacities and fighting like a human being?[45] If so, it gets him nowhere in the fight, though it gets him somewhere in understanding Jacob; this "he saw" compares with the "now I know/acknowledge" of 22:12. Eventually the "man" resorts to a fighter's classic cheating maneuver: the "hollow of the thigh" is the groin (cf. 24:2, 9).[46] It is a painful place to be punched, and even a touch makes the body recoil. Once again the cheat is the victim of cheating.

Surely that touch or punch will make Jacob let go (v. 26)? It's an odd question, because it was the assailant who started the fight. But apparently he can't end it, though he doesn't want to continue the fight after morning has dawned. If the assailant is God, then Exod. 33:20 might suggest that it is because it will be too dangerous for Jacob to see him[47] (in Tg. Neof. and Tg. Ps.-J. it is because the angel has to get back for morning worship). Why does Jacob insist on continuing to fight? At the beginning of his story, he was concerned about the blessing, and he cheated Esau of it. One would think that subsequently he has had ample evidence of God's blessing. But apparently it is still his concern.[48] And by now he perhaps recognizes that there is something supernatural about this assailant and that it is therefore a good idea to seek a blessing from him. This plea suggests that Jacob is not thinking that his assailant is an evil angel,[49] though he might still think of him as Esau's guardian angel, whom he could urge to yield the blessing to him, Jacob.[50]

The assailant's question about Jacob's name (vv. 27–28) illustrates how such an inquiry need not be a request for information unavailable to the questioner. The question is the lead-in to giving Jacob a new name. Typically, the significance given to the new name is different from the name's inherent meaning, though there are several possibilities regarding that inherent meaning. *Yiśrāʾēl* in itself would likely imply "God will rule / May God rule" (cf. the name

43. Targum Neof. identifies him with the archangel Sariel.

44. See Rashi's comment, *Brʾšyt*, 374.

45. Cf. Howell, "God's White Flag?," 41.

46. See, e.g., S. Smith, "'Heel' and 'Thigh.'"

47. See Fretheim, "Genesis," 566.

48. Cf. Arnold, *Genesis*, 285.

49. Cf. Willet, *Hexapla in Genesin & Exodum*, 288.

50. Cf Rashi, *Brʾšyt*, 375.

Sarah) or perhaps "God will exert himself / May God exert himself." But the adversary's words make Jacob the subject of the verb. The fight between the adversary and Jacob has illustrated not only the relationship between Jacob and a supernatural adversary but also the relationship between Jacob and human adversaries such as Esau and Laban. For the audience, it encapsulates something of Israel's life and destiny. The LXX and Vg suggest taking the final verb as a promise; the giving of the name then constitutes the blessing that Jacob asked for.[51] The listeners would know that there is more to the promise than meets the ear in the immediate context. In the short term the name Israel does not replace the name Jacob, as the name Abraham replaced the name Abram (the name Jacob recurs another sixty-six times in Genesis). Neither is Jacob a changed person, any more than Abram was, though his fear of Esau evaporates. The promise that Jacob is destined to become Israel is in effect a reaffirmation that he is going to be the ancestor of a vast nation.

Why does Jacob ask after his assailant's name (v. 29)? Such a question recurs on two occasions. Moses asks about God's name so he can tell the Israelites (Exod. 3:13), and God gives him an answer. Manoah asks about the name of Yahweh's envoy in order to be able to honor him (Judg. 13:17), and the envoy refuses on the grounds that his name is extraordinary or supernatural or mysterious (*pilʾî* or *pelî*). Based on these parallels, one cannot be sure whether Jacob has yet come to a conclusion about his assailant's identity as God or as a divine envoy, though the second passage makes clear that this dichotomy may be false. Yahweh's envoy is an embodiment of Yahweh, and Genesis can also move between these two alternatives (see 16:7–14; 22:11–18; 31:11–13).[52] Whether Jacob thinks of his assailant as God or as God's envoy, it might be natural to ask his name, though the assailant doesn't think so. He gives no reason for sidestepping the question, though we might infer from the Judges story that there is something dangerous about it. There is no indication here or elsewhere that the name would be withheld because knowing someone's name conveys power in relation to them or enables people to misuse it. Yahweh seems not to worry about identity theft and is prepared to live with the consequences of revealing his name. The further reference to blessing might resumptively confirm that giving Jacob his new name *is* the blessing, or it might simply indicate that the assailant is now saying farewell (cf. 31:55). As it is an exaggeration to say that "all the profound theological consequences drawn from Jacob's supposed encounter with God . . . have no basis in the text,"[53] so it is worth asking the further question that the passage raises but does not answer: why does God or his envoy attack Jacob in the first place? There are some points of comparison with Yahweh's attack on Moses in Exod. 4:24–26,

51. Cf. Dillmann, *Genesis*, 2:279.
52. See further Wessner, "Toward a Literary Understanding."
53. Westermann, *Genesis 12–36*, 519.

which thus suggests insights. Both Moses and Jacob are going through liminal experiences; both are migrants on the way home.[54] Like Jacob, Moses is on the way back to his people after being in exile, where he had taken refuge because he was afraid of being killed on account of something he had done. Yahweh attacks Moses as he or his envoy attacked Jacob but holds back from utilizing all his firepower ("Yahweh sought to kill him"—but was unable to!).[55] The reason for the attack on Moses is apparently his failure to circumcise his son, which indicates his not taking seriously the covenant relationship between Yahweh and Israel of which Moses is supposed to be a servant. So perhaps there is a parallel reason for God's attack on Jacob: perhaps it is the fear that is a prominent feature of his portrait.

Once again there is an oblique relationship between a place's name (vv. 30–31) and the name's significance. Peniel/Penuel and Mahanayim are perhaps places on either side of the Yabboq at this crossing point. Both *pənî* and *pənû* have archaic case endings (genitive and nominative),[56] but both are close to the first element in the regular expression for "the face of God," *pənê ʾēl*. Insofar as the assailant is God's true representative, Jacob has seen God face-to-face and been "rescued" from the possible consequences of such an experience (the verb recurs from 31:9, 16; 32:11). Perhaps the implication is that the fight does not come to an end before daybreak (though it does before sunrise), so that Jacob does see God face-to-face (at least in the person of the envoy) without being struck blind or dead. The sun had set on him at Beth El; the sun rises on him at Peniel[57] as he crosses the Yabboq for the final time. At this point "Jacob was at one and the same time blessed and lame."[58] But there is no further mention of his lameness in the First Testament and no suggestion that he is permanently affected by the wrestler's touch; Gen. Rab. 78.5 argues that the point about the reference to the sun rising is that it brought Jacob healing (cf. Mal. 4:2 [3:20]).[59]

There is a footnote (or rather a thigh-note) to the story (v. 32). "You know we don't eat the sciatic nerve," it says to the audience? "Uh, no," most of them reply, because they haven't heard of such a rule. It doesn't appear in the Torah. But evidently there were Israelites who did observe this rule. And they can find its background here.[60]

54. See Gorospe, *Narrative and Identity*, 166–67.
55. On this theme, see Fretheim, "Jacob's Wrestling."
56. See GKC 90.
57. Cf. Sarna, *Genesis*, 228.
58. Augustine, *City of God* 16.39.
59. Gen. Rab. 79.5 also links the healing with the description of Jacob as *šālēm* in 33:18.
60. Ibn Ezra (*Genesis*, 318) reports the understanding that v. 32 refers to eating the penis.

35

The Reunion

(33:1–20)

Overview

In the closing scene of the palistrophe, Jacob and Esau meet again. Jacob is no longer afraid of Esau, but he bows down low to him as his lord. Esau is not very interested in his submission or in his offering, only in enjoying an enthusiastic reunion with his brother. After this reunion Esau goes back home to Seir while Jacob stays for a while near the Yabboq before crossing into Canaan proper and settling near Shechem.

Translation

> **1**Yaʿaqob lifted his eyes and looked: there, Esaw was coming, and with
> him 400 men. He divided the children among Leʾah, Raḥel, and the
> two maidservants, **2**and put the maidservants and their children first,
> Leʾah and her children after, and Raḥel and Yosep last, **3**while he himself
> passed on before them. He bowed low on the ground seven times until
> he came right up to his brother. **4**But Esaw ran to meet him, embraced
> him, threw his arms around his neck, and kissed him, and they cried.[1]
> **5**He lifted his eyes and saw the women and the children and said, "Who
> are these of yours?" He said, "The children with whom God has favored[2]
> your servant." **6**The maidservants came up, they and their children, and
> bowed low. **7**Leʾah also came up, she and her children, and bowed low.

1. The Vg has "he cried," assimilating to the context.
2. The LXX has "shown mercy"; but Aq's "graced" is a more appropriate rendering of *ḥānan*.

Last, Yosep came up,[3] he and Raḥel, and they bowed low. **8**He said,
"What did you mean by this entire camp[4] that I met?" Yaʿaqob said, "To
find favor in my lord's eyes." **9**Esaw said, "I have much, brother. What you
have should be yours." **10**Yaʿaqob said, "No, please. If I've found favor
in your eyes, please, get my offering from my hand, because of the fact
that I've seen your face, like seeing God's face,[5] and you accepted me.
11Please get my blessing that has been brought to you, because God has
favored me, and because I have everything." So he urged him, and he
took it.

12Then he said, "Let's move on, let's go, I'll go in front of you." **13**But
he said to him, "My lord knows that the children are frail and the flock
and herd are suckling with me. Were people to drive them hard for one
day, the entire flock will die. **14**My lord should please pass on before
his servant. I myself will lead on gently, at the pace[6] of the stock[7] that
are before me and at the pace of the children, until I come to my lord in
Seʿir." **15**Esaw said, "May I please place alongside you some of the com-
pany that's with me?" He said, "Why is this? I want to find favor in my
lord's eyes."

16So Esaw went back that day on his journey to Seʿir, **17**while Yaʿaqob[8]
moved on to Sukkot. He built a house for himself, and for his livestock
he made bivouacs; thus they named the place Sukkot.

18Yaʿaqob came to Šalem,[9] Šekem's town,[10] which was in the coun-
try of Kenaʿan, when he came from Paddan Aram, and camped facing
the town. **19**He acquired the division in the open country where he
spread his tent, from the sons of Hamor, Šekem's father, for a hundred
qesitahs. **20**He put up an altar there and called it "God is the God of
Yiśraʾel."[11]

3. This last occurrence of *nāgaš* is niphal rather than qal, but with no apparent difference in meaning.

4. Literally, "Who to you this entire camp?" The time reference is suggested by the past tense verbs in the context.

5. The Vg's "as if I might have seen" draws attention away from the actual seeing of God's face to which 32:30 [32:31] referred.

6. Literally, "the foot."

7. On this unique usage of *məlāʾkâ*, see Tal's comments, *Genesis*, 160*.

8. As happened in 32:1 [2], Genesis underscores the contrast over against the previous verse by placing Jacob as the subject before the verb.

9. I follow the LXX, Vg in taking *šālēm* as the name of a place, as in 14:18 (the phrase "Shechem's town" then makes clear that this is a different Shalem/Salem from there), rather than an adjective (cf. the Tg), which would then mean "safe" or more likely "peaceful" (cf. 34:21). The latter is also appropriate in the context, however, and the text may invite both readings (an invitation accepted by Jub. 30.1).

10. Not "the town of Shekem," with the genitive then being defining; *ʿîr* followed by a name is regularly possessive (cf. Nahor's town, 24:10).

11. The LXX, Vg, Tg have Jacob calling on "God the God of Israel" (cf. Dillmann, *Genesis*, 2:293), which makes good sense but is hard to fit with the use of *lô*. I rather read the name as a sentence (like the name Israel), not an asyndetic phrase (cf. Keil and Delitzsch, *Pentateuch*, 311).

Interpretation

Scene 9 in the story of Jacob's time in Harran continues straight on from scene 8. The advance parties that composed his offering have disappeared from the scene, though v. 8 will refer to them. There is no more reference to fear on Jacob's part, but he is obsequiously deferential to Esau as servant to lord. In contrast, Esau meets Jacob with enthusiasm as his long-lost brother. Scene 9 thus forms an extraordinary contrasting pair with scene 1 in the palistrophe. In the account of events leading up to the parting of the two brothers, Isaac and Esau were gullible, and eventually Esau was violently aggressive, while Rebekah and Jacob were deceptive and eventually fearful. Here, Esau gives the impression of having no memory of those events, and perhaps of having done fine over the past twenty years so that his theoretical loss of the blessing hasn't made much difference to him. But Jacob (or at least the narrator) hasn't forgotten, as is suggested by Jacob's reference to "my blessing" in v. 11; it is the expression Esau used in 27:36. There is a further irony about the use of that term "blessing." Although Jacob has continued to speak of his "offering" in v. 10, a term that suggests something presented by a person in a less powerful position to a more powerful person, the term "blessing" applies to gifts from one human being to another and usually denotes something given by a more powerful person to a less powerful one. Scene 9 closes with a brief and slightly disjointed account of Jacob's arrival west of the Jordan. The MT treats that brief account in vv. 18–20 as a paragraph of its own, whereas the medieval chapter division unequivocally links it with his meeting with Esau. It both brings the account of Jacob's time away from Canaan to a final end and also provides the background to the story in 34:1–31.

33:1–11. Esau's appearance on the horizon follows immediately on the account of Jacob's crossing the Yabboq. The listeners know that Jacob goes into this meeting in the safety and protection of things the assailant said on the other side of the Yabboq. What difference does that context make to Jacob's mind-set?

We stand with Jacob (vv. 1–3a) as he discerns Esau approaching. It will become clear that the 400 men are not a military force, though not clear what they are; they might be just a sign of how impressive and important a person Esau is. At first Jacob's "dividing" the family group in accordance with their preciousness to him recalls the "dividing" of the offering earlier, with the idea that Esau might get tired or satisfied with slaughter before he gets to the end. But it transpires that Jacob takes the lead in this procession; he does not maintain the principle of making as extensive as possible the distance between himself and Esau. Jacob's being "before them" now contrasts with the repeated "before me/behind us" of 32:16, 18, 20 [32:17, 19, 21]. Conversely, there are now no references to Jacob's fearfulness, like the ones in scenes 7 and 8. In this sense the event at the Yabboq did bring about a change in Jacob. The family advances in increasing order of their status for Jacob.

Release from fear does not mean release from deference and submissiveness (v. 3b), though in the language of the First Testament one could call it another kind of fear. But there is nothing wrong with such deferent submissiveness. While bowing prostrate need not imply abject self-humbling (see 23:7, 12), an Egyptian king's underlings in Canaan speak metaphorically in their letters of bowing prostrate before him seven times,[12] which suggests such deferent submission, like that of a once-rebellious underling appearing before his overlord.[13] Here Jacob does the sevenfold prostration literally; no one else in the First Testament does. It is an extreme and complete expression of self-lowering. As Jacob's servant-lord language in 32:4 [32:5] reversed the obvious implication of 25:23, his bowing low (to be followed by that of the rest of his family in vv. 6–8) forms an extreme inversion of Isaac's blessing in 27:29, "Your mother's sons are to bow low to you." The relationship between these two mother's sons is now opposite to the one spoken of there. While Jacob originally drew up his offering in the context of his fearfulness, its overt aim was to "cover Esau's face" in such a way as to lead him to "lift Jacob's face" (32:20 [32:21]). It constituted a recognition that Jacob had no basis for assuming Esau's goodwill and wanted to acquire it, which continues to be his aim. To "cover someone's face" likely implies having foregone that goodwill; the context of Jacob's relationship with Esau confirms that implication. In seeking Esau's goodwill, Jacob need not be implying contrition, but he is at least indicating remorse or shame. The gift and the self-lowering honor Esau and put right the exalting of himself above Esau. The verb for "came up" (*nāgaš*), which also recurs in vv. 6–7, likewise suggests an approach where some deference is felt to be needed; it often applies to approaching an altar.

Esau's approach to Jacob then makes for a startling incongruence (v. 4). It is hardly that Jacob's submissiveness has turned Esau from hostility to magnanimity.[14] "Jacob only breaks down open doors with all his preparations."[15] Esau does not behave like the overlord receiving the submission of the rebel; the running, the enthusiasm, and the expressiveness contrast sharply with the sevenfold bowing. Embracing (*ḥābaq*) is so similar to but so different from wrestling (*ʾābaq*).[16] The significance of a kiss (27:26) is also here reversed.[17] The crying, one can imagine, has different significance for each of the brothers, but it joins them together. "Our Lord could find no better model for the

12. See *ANET* 483–85 (the "Amarna Letters").
13. Cf. Westermann, *Genesis 12–36*, 524–25.
14. So Skinner, *Genesis*, 412.
15. Gunkel, *Genesis*, 354.
16. See further the footnote to 32:24 [25].
17. Cf. Sarna, *Genesis*, 229.

prodigal's father at this point than Esau" (Luke 15:20).[18] Like the account of Jacob's offering in 32:14–20 [32:15–21], the portrait of Esau invites a smile from the story's listeners. Jacob has been understandably so wrong in his expectations of his brother. Although God did not intervene to speak to Esau so as to restrain him as he did Laban, one way or another God has acted even more spectacularly in accordance with his words to Jacob in 32:26–29 [32:27–30].[19] He has proved that the mind of a king (or other superior) is a stream of water that he can channel in his direction (Prov. 21:1).[20] "When the Lord of all wishes to give evidence of his providence in our regard, he makes those hostile to us become gentler than lambs."[21] What is happening to Jacob is illustrating for the listeners that whatever happens to Jacob-Israel and whatever Jacob-Israel does, God will not only protect but also honor him/it.

Esau looks beyond Jacob, who is now at the front of the line (vv. 5–7) in the procession of wives, maidservants, and children joining in humbling themselves and thereby honoring him. Notwithstanding the implications of Jacob's ordering of the wives and children in v. 2 and again in vv. 6–7, the children as a group are equally the fruit of God's gracing Jacob, and this uniformity of status compares with the sense that the old tension between Leah and Rachel has eased (e.g., 31:14)—as the indications of differences of position and significance among the later clans do not relate to who their mothers were.

The "camp" (v. 8) is not this family grouping but the other of the two camps into which Jacob divided his entourage, the assemblage of animals and servants that Jacob sent on ahead (32:7–8 [32:8–9]). It is this camp that constitutes an offering by means of which Jacob is seeking grace with Esau. Tellingly, the only First Testament chapter that speaks more of grace and gracing is Exod. 33, which speaks systematically of the grace or favor that God shows because he decides to do so and not because we manage to gain access to it by some action or argument. Here Jacob starts from the common human expectation or reality that one finds grace with someone because one earns it, although seeking grace does not imply seeking forgiveness. Jacob shows no signs of seeking forgiveness; seeking to cover someone's face need not have that implication.

Esau disclaims Jacob's understanding of their relationship (v. 9), and the narrative subverts the general assumption about earning grace from someone. Jacob has spoken of Esau as his lord and of himself as Esau's servant, but as far as Esau is concerned, Jacob is his brother. In the context of a story such as Gen. 23, one might take Esau's declining the offering as a formal refusal that

18. Kidner, *Genesis*, 171.
19. Cf. Calvin, *Genesis*, 2:207–8.
20. Willet, *Hexapla in Genesin & Exodum*, 296.
21. Chrysostom, *Homilies on Genesis 46–67*, 162.

expects itself to be turned down, and it is turned down.[22] But the context of this transformation of the terminology and the expressions of Esau's emotional welcome of Jacob suggests that Esau means what he says. Evidently he has somehow not missed out through his loss of the firstborn's blessing. His declaration that he already has enough constitutes another subversion of regular human speech. Whoever thinks they have enough and does not like the idea of more?

But Jacob starts from having now had two potentially fatal face-seeing experiences (v. 10). To see someone's face is to be admitted into their presence, in particular into the presence of someone important and powerful, and thus to be accepted by them—as Jacob also puts it. Seeing God's face is life-threatening (32:31 [32:32]); Jacob assumed that seeing Esau's face would also be life-threatening. But Esau accepts him. Jacob's verb (*rāṣâ*) comes only here in Genesis, but elsewhere it can refer to God's accepting (or not accepting) someone bringing an offering, or accepting (or not accepting) the offering itself (e.g., Ezek. 20:40–41; and Mal. 1:8–13, which we noted in connection with 32:20 [32:21]). Esau's acceptance means that the relationship is restored.

Once again Jacob finds himself unintentionally subverting the logic of the imagery (v. 11). He thought he needed to bring an offering in order to be accepted. Actually, Esau has accepted him for reasons unrelated to his offering, and now the offering becomes Jacob's own means of sealing the relationship. Indeed, Jacob finds himself engaged in a neat illustration of the way any process of reconciliation cannot be captured in a formulation. On the way, discreetly or indiscreetly, Jacob turns his "offering" into a "blessing." Apart from the reference to Abraham's blessing in 28:4, it is the first occurrence of the word since it played its key role in Gen. 27. Jacob leaves undetermined whether he sees what he calls "my blessing" as equivalent to what Esau called "my blessing" in 27:36, the blessing Jacob appropriated. However, Jacob sees the link and has now brought the blessing to Esau.

33:12–15. Polite negotiation again becomes a factor at the close of the story. Ideally, the Jacob-Esau narrative needed to end with the two brothers reconciled and with their two groups settled in the respective future homelands with which the listeners would associate them. The first aim has been achieved; the second remains. Esau is a long way from home, and Jacob needs to turn west across the Jordan to get back into the promised land.

As an aspect of his generosity and a further sign of his acceptance of Jacob (vv. 12–14), Esau invites him back to Seir, but he may not expect Jacob to accept the invitation. Jacob's "diplomatic" response[23] in turn may be a plausible excuse (Chrysostom calls it "specious")[24] that enables him to decline a move

22. Cf. Seebass, *Genesis*, 2.2:407.

23. Alter, *Genesis*, 187. Cf. Bridge, "'Slave' Is the 'Master.'"

24. Chrysostom, *Homilies on Genesis 46–67*, 163. J. Anderson (*Jacob*, 165–66) sees Jacob as continuing to be deceptive.

that will not fit into the story in the long run, and Esau may know very well that he's not meant to take seriously Jacob's implicit undertaking to come to Seir in due course.[25] In Los Angeles people say, "We must have lunch one day," and in a sense they mean it, but they don't mean what the words literally say. In the real world, the lunch will never happen.

Esau's offer to leave behind some of his staff (v. 15) carries some irony: the apparent menace now becomes the potential protection squad. It is another expression of Esau's generosity and acceptance, though also perhaps not one to be taken literally. And Jacob's gracious request to be excused from accepting this favor also means he recognizes Esau's gesture but does not take Esau up on it. Perhaps the further implication is that God has been fulfilling his commitment to protect Jacob, and it can be assumed that he will continue to do so. The brothers do each other a favor in making and declining these offers (vv. 12–15).

33:16–17. There follows a parting of the ways that corresponds to the one in 31:55–32:1 [32:1–2]. The summaries are similarly expressed, comprising descriptions of Laban/Esau "going back" home, then contrasting descriptions of Jacob. "The narrative concludes in *reconciliation with separation and an open-ended future*."[26] Insofar as people listening to the story see Jacob and Esau as mirroring Israel and Edom, the story's vision would seem to be challenging.[27]

While Esau, like Laban, begins a long journey homeward, Jacob finds somewhere to settle not far away. *Sukkôt* are bivouacs such as the Israelites will make for themselves after the exodus (hence the Festival of Sukkot [Booths/Tabernacles]). The Jerusalem Talmud (y. Shev. 9.2)[28] identifies this Sukkot with Deir Alla, a couple of miles east of the Jordan but just north of the Yabboq, which implies that Jacob crossed back again over the Yabboq. For Israelite readers, Jacob is therefore actually home, since the Yabboq/Mahananim/Peniel/Sukkot area is part of the country allocated to the twelve clans by Moses. Following Esau would mean leaving the land that Jacob entered when he came into Gilead; it would result in "a disruption in the theological aim of the narrative."[29] At the same time, Judg. 7–8 suggests an awareness that Sukkot is on the way from the Peniel area to the Jordan and thus on the way to Shechem and to Canaan proper, so that Jacob's moving to Sukkot would imply a move toward Canaan proper.[30] While Jacob evidently settles in Sukkot for a while, one need not read too much into the word "house," though something a bit more solid than a tent is implied.[31]

25. Cf. Westermann, *Genesis 12–36*, 527.
26. Fretheim, "Genesis," 573, with his emphasis.
27. See Crüsemann, "Dominion."
28. Neusner, *Talmud of the Land of Israel*, 5:307.
29. Bunn, "'Return to the Land of Your Fathers,'" 152.
30. Cf. Sarna, *Genesis*, 231.
31. Speiser (*Genesis*, 260) has "quarters."

33:18–20. From Sukkot, Jacob would cross by the ford near the modern ed-Damiyeh Bridge, from which the road ascends to Shechem. He really is now within Canaan proper, even more unequivocally his own country. His return from Paddan Aram/Harran comes to a definitive end, though still not quite a complete one.

Presumably Shalem (v. 18) is the later village of Salem/Salim, just east of Shechem, mentioned in Jdt. 4:4 (cf. Jub. 30.1; John 3:23). But the name would also recall Jacob's first leaving on his sojourn with the conviction that God would bring him back to his father's household *bəšālôm* (28:21). Further, with some appropriateness Jacob arrives where Abraham first arrived when he reached Canaan from Harran. There the town is referred to as Shechem; here Shechem is the name of a person who lives there. The double usage corresponds to that of Mamre in Gen. 13–14 and 23.

Jacob's purchase of some land (v. 19) would no doubt be designed to ensure secure possession of it; his encampment is evidently intended to be a long-term one. But the account of his purchase also indicates that it gives the people of Abraham further actual ownership of land in Canaan. Jacob's action parallels his grandfather's when he bought a burial plot in Hebron. (Stephen apparently conflates the two stories in Acts 7, while John 4 presumably refers to this purchase while also presupposing further traditions.) The word "division" (*ḥelqâ*) would remind the listeners of the Israelites "dividing up" (*ḥālaq*) the land that Yahweh gave them (e.g., Josh. 14:5). Like Abraham and like Lot, who camped near Sodom, Jacob wants to maintain an encampment and not simply become part of the town, but he does want to settle near the town. And the sons of Hamor, the Hamorites, are the Shechem equivalent to the sons of Het, the Hittites, at Hebron. Since the name of the Hetites of Gen. 23 may have nothing to do with that of the Hittites who ruled a great northern empire, so the name of Hamor and the Hamorites may have nothing to do with the word *ḥămôr* meaning "donkey" (BDB lists four roots for *ḥāmar*), but the readers of Genesis will appreciate the paronomasia.[32] The qesitah is a measure of weight like the sheqel, but we don't know its value (the LXX, Vg, and Tg nicely take the qesitahs to denote sheep).

Like Abraham, too, Jacob builds an altar in the area (v. 20); while building an altar can commemorate God's appearing, it can also mark a broader sense of God's having acted and of one's settling in an area as a result. Genesis actually describes Jacob as "putting up" an altar, which corresponds to the way one "sets up" or "puts up" a standing stone to commemorate God's appearing (28:18, 22; 31:45; 35:14, 20). His setting up an altar marks the significance of this moment, though it need not imply that the story of his journey has come to an end—and it has not (see 35:1–20). Again, like Abraham when he plants the tamarisk at Beer Sheba (21:33), Jacob associates his action with giving

32. Cf. De La Torre, *Genesis*, 285.

God a new name. Like other such names for God in Genesis, it starts off with the word El, a standard way of speaking of God that Israel's ancestors shared with other peoples and that in both contexts can function both as a generic word for deity and as a name for God. It thus compares with the English word God/god. As happens with other names in Genesis—such as *ʾēl ʿôlām*, *ʾēl rŏʾî*, and *ʾēl šadday*—Jacob then modifies and further describes that word/name in a way that is allusive and suggestive, though Jacob's title is more allusive than most. First, it can be construed either as "El, the God of Israel" or as "El is the God of Israel,"[33] but the latter is more suggestive. Either way, it is the first occurrence of the expression "God of Israel." Though it is unusual for Genesis to take literally the idea that Jacob's own name is Israel, Jacob's here speaking of God (*ʾēl*) as the God of Israel (*yiśrāʾēl*) would carry those overtones. The name testifies to God's having shown himself to be the God of Israel (see 32:28 [29]). In the context of the story, the name could thus mean something for Jacob himself. "He named the altar thus in commemoration of the fact that God had saved him while he was en route, and had sent an angel to accomplish that, and had also changed his name to Israel."[34] It would also signify that he recognizes this God as his God.[35] But when Israelites read this story, it suggests an identity between Yahweh as the God of Israel and El and Jacob's God. Within sight of the location of Jacob's altar, Joshua later builds an altar for "Yahweh the God of Israel" (Josh. 8:30).

But has Jacob failed to keep his promise in 28:20–22?[36]

33. See the translation note on v. 20.

34. Qimchi, *Genesis*, on v. 20.

35. Cf. Geoghegan, "Jacob's Bargain with God," 29–30.

36. So Hankore, *Abduction of Dinah*; he sees the events in 34:1–31 as a consequence of his failing to return to change to Beth El to establish the stone as God's house.

36
Dinah and Shechem

(34:1–31)

Overview

Some time after Jacob's arrival at Shalem, a local Hivvite has sex with Jacob's daughter Dinah, and he and his father seek to negotiate her marriage and a wider coming together of the two groups. Jacob's sons insist first on the circumcision of the village's men. When they are incapacitated after their circumcision, the brothers kill all of them and take the women and the property. Jacob expresses his disapproval.

Translation

> **1**Dinah daughter of Le'ah, to whom she had given birth for Ya'aqob,
> went out to see[1] the daughters of the region, **2**and Šekem ben Ḥamor,
> the Hivvite,[2] leader in the region, saw her. He got her, slept with her,[3]
> and overwhelmed her. **3**With his whole being he was attached[4] to Dinah,

1. *Rā'â b*, more literally "look into"; "the active *qal* verb is highly unsuitable for the following prepositional indirect object" (Tal, *Genesis*, 162*). *DCH* 7:352 gives this occurrence alone the meaning "visit, meet." The translation "see" makes the link with *rā'â* in the next verse.

2. The LXX has Horite.

3. *Šākab* usually requires a preposition but it is occasionally transitive, especially when there is a question about the legitimacy of the sexual act (cf. English "he laid her" or "he bedded her"); in v. 7 the *'et* could be read either as the mark of the accusative or as the preposition meaning "with." Seebass (*Genesis* 2.2:420) compares 2 Sam. 13:14.

4. Literally, "his whole being attached"; similarly in v. 8.

Yaʿaqob's daughter. He liked the girl, and he sought to encourage[5] the
girl. **4**Šekem said to Ḥamor his father: "Get me this child as wife."

5When Yaʿaqob heard that he had defiled Dinah his daughter, but his
sons were with his livestock in the open country,[6] Yaʿaqob remained
silent[7] until they came. **6**Ḥamor, Šekem's father, went out to Yaʿaqob to
speak with him. **7**When Yaʿaqob's sons came from the open country, the
men were pained when they heard. It deeply enraged them, because
he had done something villainous in Yiśraʾel in sleeping with Yaʿaqob's
daughter. Such a thing is not done.

8But Ḥamor spoke with them: "Šekem my son—with his whole being
he has gotten attracted to your daughter. Please give her to him as wife.
9Make marriages with us:[8] your daughters you can give to us and our
daughters you can get for yourselves. **10**With us you can live, and the
region—it will be before you. Live and traverse it[9] and have holdings in
it." **11**And Šekem said to her father and to her brothers, "May I find favor
in your eyes: what you say to me, I will give. **12**Set a very large marriage
payment and gift[10] upon me, and I will give as you say to me. But give
me the girl as wife."

13Yaʿaqob's sons answered Šekem and Ḥamor his father with guile.[11]
They spoke (in that he'd defiled their sister Dinah) **14**and said to them,
"We can't do this thing, give our sister to a man who has a foreskin, be-
cause that would be a reviling to us. **15**Only on this basis could we con-
sent to you: if you become like us, by every male of yours being circum-
cised, **16**then we'll give our daughters to you and get your daughters for
ourselves and we'll live with you, and we'll become one people. **17**But if
you won't listen to us by being circumcised, we'll get our daughter[12] and
go." **18**Their words were good in the eyes of Ḥamor and in the eyes of
Ḥamor's son Šekem, **19**and the boy didn't delay doing the thing, because
he wanted Yaʿaqob's daughter.

Now he was the most honored person in his father's household.
20So Ḥamor and his son Šekem came to the gateway of their town and
spoke to the men of their town: **21**"These people are peaceable with
us. They should live in the region and traverse it. This region—here,
it's wide enough for them. Their daughters we will get for ourselves as
wives and our daughters we will give to them. **22**It's just on this basis

5. Literally, "he spoke upon the heart/mind of" (*lēb*). The expression often belongs in a context where a person has reason to be discouraged or worried.

6. The subject comes before the verb in the first two clauses, marking them as circumstantial (so also v. 7a).

7. The weqatal carries the past continuous meaning that can attach to a yiqtol (GKC 112ss; *TTH* 133, note).

8. "Us" is the direct object of the hitpael verb; the odd usage recurs in 37:18. See GKC 117w.

9. The LXX, Vg, Tg, "trade in" (cf. the participle in 23:16; 37:28) would make good sense, but the use with a direct object makes this understanding difficult (Speiser, *Genesis*, 264–65).

10. The LXX takes the two expressions as a hendiadys, but see the comment.

11. The Tg has "smartness," as at 27:35.

12. The LXX has plural, "daughters."

that the people will give their consent to us to live with us, to become one people—by every male of ours being circumcised as they are circumcised. **23**Their livestock and what they have acquired and all their animals: they'll become ours, won't they?[13] Let's just give our consent to them so they will live with us." **24**They listened to Ḥamor and to Šekem his son, all who went out to the gateway of his town; and every male, all who went out to the gateway of his town, were circumcised.

25On the third day, when they were hurting, two of Yaʿaqob's sons, Šimʿon and Lewi, Dinah's brothers, got each his sword, came on the town, confident of safety,[14] and killed every male. **26**Ḥamor and Šekem his son they killed with the mouth of the sword, and they got Dinah from Šekem's house and left **27**while Yaʿaqob's sons[15] came on the men who had been run through and plundered the town because they had defiled their sister. **28**Their flock, their herd, and their donkeys, what was in the town and what was in the open country, they got. **29**All their resources, all their little ones, and all their women, they captured and plundered, with[16] everything that was in the house.

30Yaʿaqob said to Šimʿon and Lewi, "You've brought disaster on me, making me stink to the people who live in the country, the Kenaʿanite (the Perizzite).[17] I'm few in number. They'll gather against me and strike me down and I'll be annihilated, I and my household." **31**But they said, "Like a whore should he treat our sister?"

Interpretation

The story of the conflict between Jacob and the Hivvites balances the story of the conflict between Isaac and the Philistines in 26:1–33. That earlier story bridged the opening of Genesis Part Three and the long account of Jacob's sojourn in Harran; this story bridges the end of that long account and the close of Genesis Part Three, which will follow in Gen. 35. Once again, a conflict issues from the ancestral family's living cheek-by-jowl with another settled local people, notwithstanding the family's living in the setting to which the God of the promise has brought them. Once again, trouble arises because of the local people's interest in one of the family's women. Once again,

13. But on the words in this verse see Mastin, "What Do *Miqneh* and *Bohema* Mean?"

14. I follow the LXX, Vg in taking *beṭaḥ* to denote the brothers' confidence rather than the villagers' sense of security (so Tg. Onq.): cf. the use of the verb *bāṭaḥ* in Prov. 14:16; Job 6:20; 40:23 (BDB).

15. The word order with the subject coming first in the sentence implies that "Jacob's sons" refers not to the two sons named in v. 25 (so that the entire action in vv. 25–31 is undertaken by the two) but rather to the rest of Jacob's sons, as the Vg makes explicit; the SP's *w* and the LXX's *de* point in the same direction.

16. The *wə* is explanatory; the closing phrase recapitulates "all their resources" (Tal, *Genesis*, 164*).

17. The *w* is presumably explanatory, as in 13:7 (see the footnote to 4:4).

the head or the men of the family respond with action that involves deception. Once again, the family eventually does very well out of the sequence of events. Once again, the story thus handles questions about the relationship between Israel's ancestors and other peoples that will be significant for an Israelite audience and raises questions about the position of women in the society. Once again, the story reports on conflicts and on other actions that may look reprehensible but makes no moral comment, though it also raises issues that later are the subject of rules within the Torah. More broadly, it shares with the rest of the Torah "concerns about the relationship of Israel to its neighbors; Israel's identity defined from intra- and intergroup perspectives; appropriate sexual behaviors; and the place of violence."[18] It is thus "a story about *issues*: through pondering . . . upon the (largely unsatisfactory) ways in which the characters handle their situation, the reader's own moral sensibilities are sharpened."[19] At the end of Gen. 34, no one wins, and the story leaves us with a plethora of ethical ambiguities, though its effect is thereby to demand a response from readers, so that Gen. 34 "has created the possibility for ethics."[20]

Although thematically the story has a different focus from Gen. 27–33, it links with it in detailed ways, picking up the reference to Simeon and Levi's position as Leah's sons and to Dinah as their full sister; Simeon and Levi's action will be taken up again in 49:5–7. In the MT, Gen. 34 forms the last section in 32:3 [32:4]–34:31. It is similar in length to 26:1–33, but it differs in comprising a single complex story (framed by narrative but dominated by dialogue), whereas 26:1–33 consisted of a more loosely linked sequence of stories about a series of conflicts. Further, whereas Gen. 26 reported a series of issues that get resolved, this conflict does not get resolved. As is the case with Gen. 26, it is hard to trace how Gen. 34 may have developed: "all modern expositors are agreed about the extraordinary difficulty of a literary analysis of this narrative, but there is no agreement on the means of arriving at a satisfying solution. Indeed, it seems that ultimate scientific clarification is no longer possible."[21] Consideration of the traditions that lie behind the chapter raises parallel difficulties. The story takes up a number of social, theological, and moral categories that reappear in the First Testament: defile (*ṭāmēʾ*, v. 5), villainy (*nəbālâ*, v. 7), something that is not done (v. 7), acquire a holding (*ʾāḥaz*, v. 10), marriage payment (*mōhār*, v. 12), reviling (*ḥerpâ*, v. 14). In addition,

18. M. Jacobs, "Love, Honor, and Violence," 11.

19. Noble, "'Balanced' Reading," 195, with original emphasis.

20. Yamada, "Dealing with Rape," 157, 163. Yamada includes a study of how Sternberg (*Poetics of Biblical Narrative*, 445–75) and Fewell and Gunn ("Tipping the Balance") seek to resolve the ambiguities. Cf. also Sternberg, "Biblical Poetics and Sexual Politics." See further Noble, "'Balanced' Reading"; Brenner, "Literary Approaches"; Lockwood, "Disentangled"; Earl, "Toward a Christian Hermeneutic"; R. Parry, *Old Testament Story*.

21. Von Rad, *Genesis*, 325.

an important part is played by questions about groups intermarrying and assimilating, about the importance of circumcision, and about conventions regarding looting. These features can link with a wide variety of contexts in the First Testament story—second millennium times, early Israelite times, the monarchic period, and the Persian period. And they can be linked with many strands of First Testament tradition.

The story contrasts with Gen. 26 in having no reference to God's involvement in events. In this respect it parallels several of the scenes within Gen. 27–33; further, a contrast will emerge between the absence of God from Gen. 34 and the presence of God speaking, terrorizing, appearing, and blessing in 35:1, 5, and 9. Theological or moral understanding of the story thus depends on reading it in the context of its broader narrative. The closing two verses do suggest two questions that underlie it. Among the Israelite clans, Judah has a prominent place as the clan from which David comes (cf. 49:8–12). One can imagine Israelites asking why Judah has this prominent position when Judah himself is only the fourth of the sons of Jacob, following Reuben, Simeon, and Levi. We will soon discover why Jacob declares that Reuben will lose his position (see 35:22; cf. 49:3–4), and one significance of Gen. 34 is that it explains why Jacob also declares that Simeon and Levi will lose theirs (cf. 49:5–7)—and fail to keep their place as regular clans. The other question underlying the story is: "Why are the local people so hostile to us and why are we so vulnerable to them?" And the answer it gives is: "Because we must be somewhat separatist in relation to them, and because getting involved with them tends to lead to them defiling our women, and because they want to take over our land, and because we may feel we have to take action against them." Paradoxically, the chapter affirms the principle that the descendants of Jacob must not let themselves be defiled through intermarriage with other local peoples, but tells a story about how the effort to avoid or counter that defilement can raise problems of its own. There is no concrete "lesson" to be drawn from that fact. A story does not work in that way, which accounts for the story's not offering theological or moral judgments. The story just tells of how things are or can be. But its theological setting in Genesis and specifically in Part Three of Genesis conveys to the audience the good news that God can be working out his purpose and fulfilling his promises notwithstanding the pressures, dilemmas, and mistakes that his people make. This consideration means that it matters less if it is hard to be sure about making moral judgments concerning where the mistakes lie.

34:1–4. The reason why Dinah is the one daughter whose birth Gen. 30 reports is presumably that it provides background to this chapter. She is specifically the daughter of Leah, who is not the wife that Jacob wanted, but Genesis also notes that Leah births Dinah "for Jacob," which works against the idea that there is something negative about the reference to Dinah's mother. Dinah is of marriageable age, perhaps in her middle teens, and her brothers are at least young adults, so some years have passed. The account of an ordinary girl or boy going out to see the young people in the area has no parallel in the First Testament, but there is no indication of whether the story hints that such an action is a bad idea[22] (there would be no doubt that a girl hanging out with local boys or vice versa would be a bad idea). Her venture does fit in the context of there being a relationship between tent-dwelling people who live near a town or village but who focus on tending sheep and goats and do some agriculture on the side, and village-based people who focus on agriculture and keep a few animals on the side. These groups could live in collaborative interaction but could find themselves in conflict, and this double possibility is part of the story's background. But the Torah recognizes that within Israel itself a girl out on her own is vulnerable, and it includes rules to cover the kind of event that follows here (see Exod. 22:16–17 [22:15–16]; Deut. 22:28–29). Thus, the implication is not that Dinah gets into trouble because she mixes with foreigners and they are inclined to act immorally in a way that members of her own people are not; the same issues arise within Israel. But the fact that it happens to be a foreigner who gets involved with her provides the premise for the story that follows.

The boy (v. 2) bears the name of the town Shechem, which as such is not mentioned in the story. Perhaps the implication is that his father Hamor is the "leader" (*nāśîʾ*) in the region named after Shechem, but that Hebrew term (like the English word "leader") does not suggest an office, like the word "king"; it comes in the singular elsewhere in Genesis only when the Hittites apply it to Abraham (Gen. 23:6). Further, Late Bronze Age Shechem was a major city-state, and it is hard to imagine the story that follows, with the slaughter of its entire male population by a couple of Jacob's sons, as an account about that actual town. We will get the picture better if we think in terms of something more like a village such as Shalem, which is "Shechem's town" (33:18). Genesis uses seven verbs in vv. 2–3 to describe Shechem's action—he saw, he got, he slept, he overwhelmed, he was attached, he loved, he encouraged. They are a sequence of waw-consecutives with no other indication of how they interrelate. They resemble "I came, I saw, I conquered," but they hardly make sense as descriptions of a chronological sequence of actions. I have assumed that the first "he saw" stands on its own, following on from the fact that Dinah went out "to see" the local girls. "He got, he slept, he overwhelmed" then form three more or less parallel descriptions of the action that ensued. He got her, laid her, ravished her: "three verbs describe the rapid-fire action of the rape" in a kind of hendiadys[23]—or hendiatris. "Got" (*lāqaḥ*) is the standard verb for marrying someone, in which connection it will come

22. So, e.g., Gen. Rab. 80.1–5; and for subsequent such readings, J. Thompson, *Reading the Bible with the Dead*, 188–93; R. Parry, *Old Testament Story*, 87–122; Blyth, *Narrative of Rape*, 152–93.

23. Scholz, "Through Whose Eyes?," 165, 167.

in v. 4, and it is not an inherently aggressive or forceful word, but it is also the verb Genesis uses for the four kings getting the resources of Sodom and getting Lot (14:11–12). Further, the sequence seeing-getting is a worrying one (cf. 3:6; 6:2; Josh. 7:21).[24] The verb "slept [with]" or "laid" (*šākab*) is applied chiefly to sex outside marriage (e.g., 19:32–35; 26:10; an exception that tests the rule is 30:15–16).[25] The third verb (*ʿānâ* piel) implies that their having sex was not consensual. It's the nearest to a Hebrew verb for rape, though it can also refer (e.g.) to a man having sex with a woman whom he has captured in war and married (Deut. 21:14). While it thus need not indicate that he has violent sex with Dinah, it does suggest that he is behaving like a man who assumes he can do as he likes with a woman and that he violates her. Shechem and his father "are influential men in the city and likely are accustomed to getting—and taking—what they want."[26] Maybe Shechem would be able to say that she agreed to their having sex, but he at least put pressure on her.[27]

Yet the boy is apparently not just interested in sex (v. 3). "Abductive marriage" is a well-known way of achieving marriage in some traditional cultures.[28] And from the beginning Shechem was interested in marriage, not a "casual liaison."[29] In the cultural context (indeed in most cultural contexts) it is just as well, because a girl who is known to have had sex has become "damaged goods."[30] She would likely have a hard time finding someone who wants to marry her; hence those rules in the Torah to deal with the situation when boys and girls have had sex. It seems psychologically implausible to imagine that Shechem's feelings of love emerge only after they have had sex that was not very consensual. More likely the feelings lay behind the action, as was the case with Amnon in relation to Tamar in 2 Sam. 13, whose deed Shechem anticipates. It is Shechem's whole being (his *nepeš*) that becomes attached to Dinah. While attachment is a physical thing (2:24), it is Shechem's whole person that becomes attached. He has fallen in love with her, as we say (again like Amnon), though admittedly his feelings may not deserve the word "love" and might rather be an obsession (like Amnon's). And he engages himself in seeking to encourage her about what happens now, to reassure her. He tells her that he loves her, and tells her that it is going to be okay, and tells her that his father will fix things with her father. No doubt that process starts before they have sex, and he hardly thinks of himself as raping her. It is not

24. Cf. R. Parry, *Old Testament Story*, 137.

25. See the footnote to v. 2.

26. Brayford, *Genesis*, 376.

27. See the arguments in, e.g., Bechtel, "What If Dinah Was Not Raped?"; Scholz, "Was It Really Rape?"; Shemesh, "Rape"; Joseph, "Understanding Genesis 34:2"; Blyth, *Narrative of Rape*, 40–92.

28. See Hankore, *Abduction of Dinah*, 185–86, 232–35.

29. Cf. Kidner, *Genesis*, 174.

30. Frankel, *Five Books of Miriam*, 68.

like the rape that takes place in war as an expression of violence—after all, she goes along with it, doesn't she? But Genesis doesn't tell us anything about her feelings or about whether she goes along with it or resists—here there is a contrast with the story of Amnon and Tamar. Tamar's angle is significant for the bigger story there. Dinah's angle is not significant for the bigger story here.[31] And if Shechem has raped Dinah, the monstrous nature of his action is not lessened by any feelings he may have or any commitment he may then be prepared to make.[32]

Shechem does set about getting his father to fix it (v. 4). In his cultural context, there is perhaps nothing odd about the process and the order of events. Indeed, we have noted that the presence of rules in the Torah to deal with the situation when boys and girls have had sex presupposes that life in an Israelite village might not be so different. Yet there is another factor that the story does not make explicit but maybe the listeners will not be surprised at. Shechem's family has held on to Dinah, with or without her willingness (see vv. 17, 26). She herself is now termed a "child" (*yaldâ*), etymologically a girl who has been birthed—maybe with the implication that she is someone who as a female is capable of birthing.[33] Dinah herself remains silent; "Shechem was not dumb . . . but he acts as if Dinah was deaf."[34]

34:5–7. Once again, Genesis tells its story in nonchronological order, putting in the forefront a key factor that it wishes to highlight.

This key factor (v. 5) is not Dinah's possible rape or seduction but her defilement. Whether she was pressured by Shechem or whether she was a willing participant, defilement is the framework that the narrative uses.[35] Although the First Testament will go on to see adultery as defiling a person, it will give no indication that premarital sex does so. In a First Testament context, the idea is that people and areas outside Israel are lacking in purity and that sex across these frontiers is defiling.[36] Purity is a quality of a place or of a people that God has set apart and made special to him. It's not a moral quality but a theological one, though various moral and religious actions can compromise it. Genesis does not otherwise speak in terms of defilement, which suggests that Jacob and his family would not think in terms of this category, but the story is using a category that would be familiar to the people listening to the story. Built into the wider Genesis story is the fact that God has set Abraham's family apart, as was presupposed by the need to find wives for his family from outside Canaan. The question whether to marry inside the clan (endogamy) or outside it (exogamy) is important in Genesis, though it's

31. See Blyth, "Terrible Silence."
32. See Blyth, "Redeemed by His Love?"
33. See Julie-Anne Kelso, "Reading the Silence of Women."
34. Havea, "Whoring Dinah," 178.
35. Cf. A. Wagner, "Considerations."
36. Cf. Rofé, "Defilement."

quite an exaggeration to say that "the essential problem with which Genesis is concerned is that of endogamy and land rights."[37] Endogamy can have a religious basis or an economic/political one.[38] No doubt Israel's ancestors would be concerned about the economic/political aspect, but Genesis puts any such concern in the framework of a charge from God that sets Israel's ancestors apart. The language of purity and defilement is then a way of conceptualizing that setting apart and its implications. The problem in this story, then, is that Shechem has spoiled Dinah by virtue of being a Canaanite. The talk of defilement would also hint at the later Israelite sense that the local peoples (the "Canaanites") had defiled the country by their sexual practices, that this defiling was one reason why Yahweh had the country vomit them up out of it, and that the Israelites needed to make sure they did not fall into the same defilement (Lev. 18:24–30). Although the statement about Jacob hearing of Dinah's "defilement" therefore need not imply that he himself would look at the event within this framework, the comment that "his daughter" has been treated in this way does suggest that as her father he is scandalized by what he has heard. But the unfolding story will associate more of the sense of scandal about defilement (and of a need to do something about it) with his sons than with Jacob. As we have noted, it is going to emerge that Hamor and Shechem have taken Dinah into their home, which would presumably also make Jacob realize the need to take action. But at the moment his sons are some distance away, pasturing the flocks; their absence apparently makes it difficult to do anything, and he says nothing.

The account of the visit from Hamor (v. 6) then explains how Jacob knows what has happened. Hamor has set about doing as his son requested, like a dutiful father, though we will discover that he has more in mind than fulfilling his son's desires. Hamor does not see anything defiling to have gone on, or even anything untoward. The boy and the girl becoming involved sexually just means that a marriage needs to be arranged. Maybe Jacob would feel the same if Dinah had become involved with someone within the clan. But anyway, he says nothing for the moment: "I'll talk about it with her brothers," he says to Hamor.

Their reaction is something else (v. 7). They have their own sequence of words: pained, enraged, villainous, not done. "Pained" is the word that describes Yahweh's reaction to the degenerate state of the world (6:6). "Rage" is Moses's reaction to Israel's apostasy at Sinai and Saul's response to the Ammonites' threat against the people of Yabesh in Gilead (Exod. 32:19; 1 Sam. 11:6). "Villainy" (*nəbālâ*) is the term in Judges for sexual assault and rape in Gibeah (Judg. 19:23–24; 20:6, 10) and the term Tamar uses to describe Amnon's rape, which she also calls something that is not done in

37. Pitt-Rivers, *Fate of Shechem*, 139.
38. Pitt-Rivers, *Fate of Shechem*, 164–65.

Israel (2 Sam. 13:12–13; cf. also Gen. 20:9). Villainy denotes "an obstinate insensibility to moral and religious relations, and repudiation of the claims which they impose."[39] Shechem's action is something villainous "in Israel." The expression is anachronistic in a different way from that in which the talk of defilement is anachronistic, but like the talk of defilement, it implies that the audience is expected to look at the event this way and that the brothers are quite right in their assessment of what Shechem has done.[40]

34:8–12. When they are back, Hamor returns to talk to them; all the second-person verbs and pronouns in vv. 8–12 are plural. Maybe adult brothers come to be party to decision making in the family (cf. 24:50)[41] and/or maybe it will be the brothers who will be interested in the marriages and eventually the land rights to which Hamor will refer.[42] Hamor's proposal assumes the key importance of endogamy/exogamy and land rights.

So, in a sense, Dinah becomes her brothers' daughter (v. 8). Hamor adds another verb to describe Shechem's love, the verb "be attracted to" (*ḥāšaq*), which further underscores the depth of the boy's feelings for the girl. On its basis Hamor makes a formal proposal for the two to be allowed to wed. In doing so, he indicates no sense that there has been anything improper about the boy's action, given that young people often got married this way, but his implicit perception is quite different from that of Dinah's brothers.

But he is not proposing a one-of-a-kind match (vv. 9–10). It is to be a first instance of a pattern that will follow; it will seal relationships between the two groups. They will intermarry and intermingle. Groups do come together by intermarriage, as famously happens at another level through Solomon's marriages. Jacob's family will then have even more freedom in the trade between sheep farmers and agriculturalists. Perhaps by way of the greatest temptation, Hamor points out that Jacob's family can thus gain holdings in the land, as the readers know they are destined to do (see esp. Lev. 25 for the noun from this verb). He is indeed making a proposal about exogamy/endogamy and about land rights. But unconsciously, he proposes exactly a relationship that will count as defilement. Deuteronomy 7:1–3 explicitly prohibits what Hamor proposes (it mentions the Hivvites), with the implication that it is indeed what happened as the Israelites settled in Canaan. And in the Persian period, Ezra 6:21 emphasizes the importance of avoiding defilement through accepting the practices of the community's neighbors. The story's preoccupation with endogamy is thus one aspect of its ongoing theological significance. For Christians and Jews, the continuing distinctive existence of the people of Abraham was integral to the fulfillment of God's purpose. Only if there was such a distinctive Jewish people could there be a Jewish Messiah

39. Driver, *Genesis*, 303.
40. Cf. Wenham, *Genesis 16–50*, 312.
41. Cf. Gunkel, *Genesis*, 363.
42. Cf. Frankel, *Five Books of Miriam*, 67.

in whom Christians could also come to believe; hence the positive theological significance of the action of Ezra and Nehemiah to safeguard the distinctive existence of that people. Further, in the early decades of the church's life, Paul warns about defilement that issues from being improperly yoked with unbelievers (2 Cor. 6:14–7:1).

Shechem, of course, is more focused on the girl he has fallen for (v. 11). While the arranging of a marriage is formally the concern of the two fathers, it will also involve the boy and the girl; in his enthusiasm Shechem cannot resist the temptation to take part in the negotiations by declaring that he will give whatever they ask for the girl he loves or wants. Shechem "is in effect showing willingness to abide by the terms of the Deuteronomic law"[43]—that is, the aspect of it that concerns marriage between two people who have already had a sexual relationship. But he is bound to fall foul of the broader and more fundamental aspect of the Deuteronomic law regarding intermarriage and to meet with "a rejection by her family which is much more impassioned than he can understand, and no one tells him the reason for the irritation, even though he is quite ready for any compensation which will enable him to marry Dinah."[44]

Specifically, Shechem recognizes the need for two sorts of marriage gifts (v. 12). They compare with the two forms of gift mentioned in 24:53 and overlap with the forms of conventional transaction traditionally involved in a Western marriage. In neither case is the term "bride price" illuminating; the groom is not buying the bride, and she does not become his property as a result of the transaction except in the sense that any bride or groom comes to belong to the other person (cf. Song 6:3; 1 Cor. 7:4). The "marriage payment" (*mōhar*; cf. Exod. 22:16–17 [15–16]; 1 Sam. 18:25) will go to Dinah's family and will seal the relationship between the two families; it is the equivalent to the payment Jacob himself made to Laban (by working for him all those years) by which he recompensed Laban for the "cost" of bringing up Leah and Rachel. The "gift" (*mattān*) will go to Dinah herself; it will belong to her and give her a degree of potential independence (not least if her husband dies or divorces her). It parallels the provision traditionally denoted as a dower in European law (there is no equivalent to any dowry that the bride brings with her into the marriage). As a leader in the region, Hamor surely is well-to-do, and since he has agreed to set up this marriage for his son, Shechem knows he can give better marriage gifts than anyone. He will pay any price.

34:13–19a. The narrative reaches its turning point.[45] Actually, the price will be other than he has imagined and will eventually be far greater than he dreams. The answer comes not from father or from father and brothers but

43. Brett, *Genesis*, 101.
44. Von Rad, *Genesis*, 326–27.
45. Cf. R. Parry, *Old Testament Story*, 160.

simply from the brothers. Jacob continues to say nothing. Again the story anticipates the Tamar and Amnon narrative, where David does nothing and Tamar's brother takes action. Here as there, too, the action involves trickery. "Guile" (*mirmah*) is the word Isaac used of Jacob (27:35; these are the only two occurrences of the word in the Torah). It is thus striking that the guile does not involve Jacob! Have the sons learned from their father, or have they inherited this trait? There needs be no implied criticism in the word "guile," any more than there is in (say) the lying of the Israelite midwives in Exod. 1:15–22.[46] "Misinformation in some cases may not have adverse effects, while accurate information may be used to violate others," and in the First Testament deception can be "a sanctioned way that the weaker party exercises power over more powerful people."[47] Hamor and his family have abducted the young men's sister, and her brothers need a stratagem to free her to return to her family. If vv. 1–12 see "the accumulation of maximal sympathy for Jacob's sons," vv. 13–19a only deepen that sympathy; it is, after all, "their sister" whom Shechem has "defiled" and for whom they surely must do something.[48]

The brothers then nuance the nature of the boy's defilement of Dinah (v. 14): Shechem and the rest of the men in his community are not circumcised. Strictly or historically, in one way or another, this lack might not suffice as a way of distinguishing Jacob's community from Hamor's community. The Hivvites (v. 2) are admittedly something of a puzzle, though Josh. 9:7 and 11:19 do speak of the people of Gibeon (not far away) as Hivvites. In the First Testament, Hivvites are in effect a subset of Canaanites, like the Perizzites, whom Jacob will mention in v. 30 (see, e.g., 10:15–18; Exod. 3:8; Judg. 3:5). As is the case with some of the groups mentioned in such passages, we know nothing about the Hivvites except what the First Testament tells us. Unlike many of these groups, they do not appear in the list of Ezra 9:1–2 as the kind of people with whom the Judahites intermarried in the Persian period. But further, such groups likely practiced circumcision. It was the Philistines who were the great uncircumcised people; Judg. 14:3 makes this point in connection with Samson's desire to marry a Philistine girl. Perhaps the Hivvites were another non-Semitic people.[49] But in any case, circumcision becomes a kind of synecdoche. Genesis 17 has presupposed that it distinguishes Abraham's clan from other peoples and that it is a mark of God's distinctive commitment to Abraham's clan and of their distinctive commitment to God. Isaiah 52:1 sets up an association between defilement and lack of circumcision on the part of people such as the Babylonians, who invaded Jerusalem and destroyed the temple, and it affirms that the restored Jerusalem will be protected from the uncircumcised and the defiled. It is a telling collocation for this story. Read

46. Cf. Rashi's comment, *Brʾšyt*, 389.
47. M. Jacobs, "Love, Honor, and Violence," 27, 29.
48. Sternberg, *Poetics of Biblical Narrative*, 446, 461.
49. See Arnold, *Genesis*, 294.

against such contexts, "whereas Hamor stressed the economic advantages of intermarriage, the brothers emphasize the religious impediments."[50] The link between lack of circumcision and defilement would make intermarrying with people who do not practice circumcision a cause of reviling (*ḥerpâ*) to Jacob's family. It would be a disgrace; it is another term that Tamar uses (2 Sam. 13:13). The brothers thus add another powerful notion to the list in v. 7. It is in a way a puzzling notion: who will be doing this reviling? Reviling is something other peoples do to Israel. On the other hand, the delayed circumcision of the Israelites on their arrival in Canaan from Egypt removed their reviling (Josh. 5:9). Perhaps God's insistence on circumcision as a sign of his relationship with them means it would be his reviling.

So circumcision would solve the problem (vv. 15–17), understood in that broader symbolic context. Intermarriage with peoples who maintain their own traditions with their religious implications is one thing (Ezra 9). But foreigners who come to live in Israel can take part in Passover if the men are circumcised (Exod. 12:48); intermarriage with people who are prepared to accept circumcision is another thing. So people listening to this story might be able to understand the theological theory behind (or in front of) the brothers' proposal. The Hivvites need to be prepared to look at the matter this way. If they are not, the brothers will take their daughter (!) and go (v. 17). Of course, we know the brothers are speaking with guile. Drawing the Hivvites into the Abrahamic covenant is not the perspective with which they are actually operating. Ironically, by broadening the negotiation with the brothers so that it concerns not just the question about Shechem and Dinah but also the interrelationship of the two entire communities, Hamor and Shechem have made their community horribly vulnerable.

Neither is Shechem interested in that broader significance of circumcision (vv. 18–19a). He's just a boy in love. He'll pay any price.

34:19b–24. So without delay, Shechem sets about implementing the brothers' requirement. Fortunately for him he is the favorite son of the big man in the community, "the most eligible man in the district."[51] So he and his father can easily take up the matter with the men of the town. The town gateway is as usual the informal and formal meeting place (cf. 19:1; 23:10, 18), and it is the townsmen as a group that father and son approach. They in effect count as the town's elders, though a town that is really more the size of a village might not need to distinguish between the grown-up men and the elders.

Hamor and Shechem put forward their proposal (vv. 21–22). On the assumption that this town is Shalem (33:18), which can mean "peaceable," saying that Jacob's clan are peaceable people especially commends them. Describing them in these terms will turn out to imply a massive irony, but neither they

50. Wenham, *Genesis 16–50*, 313.
51. Sternberg, *Poetics of Biblical Narrative*, 464.

nor the audience realizes it yet. There are no disadvantages about agreeing to form one community with Jacob's clan by intermarrying with them. Well, there is this slight physical price to pay.

Hamor and Shechem hasten on to the big advantage of making this commitment (vv. 23–24). Jacob's sons are not the only people operating with guile, and Shechem is not only operating as a boy who is in love. But the words of Hamor and Shechem will turn out to contain another massive irony: it will transpire that the transfer of livestock and other property will happen in the direction opposite to the one of which they speak. But the townsmen took little persuading.

34:25–29. For all the intimations that something is going to happen that involves trickery, action against the defilement, and the retrieval of Dinah, what now follows is jaw-dropping. The plot of the story turns out to focus less on the rape of Dinah by Shechem than on the rape of Shechem by Dinah's brothers,[52] on "the Sack of Shechem."[53] Simeon and Levi are perhaps operating on behalf of the brothers as a group, yet they are certainly acting on behalf of "their sister"—that is, their full sister, because Leah is both their mother and Dinah's mother. They are the second and third sons whose births are recorded in Gen. 29, following Reuben, who will lose his honor as senior son because of the event recorded in 35:22 (see 49:3–4)—though is Reuben's absence here something to be commended?[54] The listeners will not be surprised that Hamor and his community are in pain after their circumcision, like someone who has had surgery, and they are incapable of defending themselves against attack. Perhaps the brothers take the view that it is not Shechem alone who is responsible for what has happened, because the rest of the community did nothing about it, and/or that attacking everyone is the only way to retrieve Dinah. (On the basis of this verse, b. Shabb. 134b allows the washing of a baby on the third day after circumcision even if it is the Sabbath, because the pain and the danger of infection are then particularly high.)

At the same time, Shechem obviously bears special responsibility, as does his father (v. 26). One again imagines Israelites reading the Tamar story in light of this story, and vice versa. And again, the jaw drops: only at this point do we discover that Dinah has been in Hamor and Shechem's house all along. Has she been taken captive? Is this a rescue mission? Or has she been as committed to Shechem as he is to her? In effect, has the marriage already happened, so that the result of the brothers' action is to make Dinah a widow?[55]

Dinah is not the only one who is taken (vv. 27–28). Whereas Simeon and Levi focus on the slaughter of the menfolk and the retrieval of their sister, the

52. Coats, *Genesis*, 234.

53. See Geller, "Sack of Shechem." Like Coats, Geller assumes that the town is Shechem, though we have seen reason to doubt that idea.

54. See Goldin, "Reuben."

55. Cf. M. Jacobs, "Love, Honor, and Violence," 14.

rest of the brothers operate according to the conventions of war as Deut. 20 will later lay them out in respect of a town that insists on fighting rather than making peace.[56] The brothers have treated the Shalemites as if they were people who had declined terms for peace and have paid the price. The brothers' action also overlaps with the Israelite treatment of Midian in Num. 31.[57] The story may thereby further honor Simeon and Levi, because they are interested only in rescue and redress, not in looting, whereas the brothers' looting "reduces them to the moral level of the Hivites."[58] Further, having the Hivvites take one of their girls is one thing. Taking over the Hivvites' women is another.[59]

34:30–31. The narrative has not indicated whether Jacob has shared the outrage of Simeon and Levi, and his comment about their action is simply negative. But neither does he offer any moral or legal objection to their action as he will in 49:5–7, which will reduce their redress on the Hivvites to "an outbreak of blind fury"[60] and will envisage Simeon and Levi scattered in Israel (as their clans were) because of their violence (Levi's violence will have a different outworking in Exod. 32). Here, Jacob thinks Simeon and Levi have been stupid. His objection is only strategic or military; his mention of the Canaanites and specifically the Perizzites matches the association of the Canaanites and specifically the Perizzites with this area in Josh. 17:15.[61] Fortunately, Gen. 35:5 shows that his fears will not be realized.[62] Far from it: "nearly all the future violence will be within the family itself."[63]

Simeon and Levi's response (v. 31) is something like a moral one. The family has a responsibility to take action in connection with wrong done to one of its members. If Jacob embodies one possibility for Israel in relation to the Canaanites, that of fear, Simeon and Levi embody a different attitude whereby the clans will face the Canaanites with confidence, firmness, and solidarity.[64] "As with the Book of Jonah, the closing rhetorical question provides an irresistible argument."[65] The rhetorical question closing the chapter also parallels 27:45; there are further examples of dramatic statements closing sections of Genesis (29:14; 30:24; 37:35; 42:38; 45:28).[66] The trouble with a rhetorical question, however, is that it leaves an opening for the addressees to answer it in a way other than the questioner intends. Both Jacob's comment and the brothers' question raise issues that will be taken further in Genesis

56. Cf. Seebass, *Genesis*, 2.2:421.
57. Driver, *Genesis*, 306.
58. Sternberg, *Poetics of Biblical Narrative*, 471.
59. Cf. Pitt-Rivers, *Fate of Shechem*, 166.
60. Sternberg, *Poetics of Biblical Narrative*, 453.
61. Seebass, *Genesis*, 2.2:421.
62. Cf. Keil and Delitzsch, *Pentateuch*, 315.
63. Brayford, *Genesis*, 382.
64. Cf. Hyman, "Final Judgment."
65. Sarna, *Genesis*, 238.
66. Wenham, *Genesis 16–50*, 307.

and in the Torah more broadly. The broader context of the Torah suggests, on one hand, that it was appropriate for judgment to come upon the Hivvites for their defilement, and Judith is unambiguous in her approval of the brothers' action (Jdt. 9:1–4; cf. Jub. 30.5–6). But Gen. 49:5–7 suggests a negative judgment on Simeon and Levi for their violence.[67] And by no means does this chapter's story come to a complete end. At the end, the wrong done to Dinah is described not as defiling but as treating her like a whore, which might have several implications. Like the English word "whore," a *zônâ* can be someone involved in the sex trade (cf. 38:15), and the brothers may mean that Shechem had sex with Dinah and was then prepared to pay for it.[68] But calling someone a whore can also be a way of designating more broadly anyone whose sexual life does not fit in with society's norms. Yet further, the association of whoring with defilement suggests a link with the First Testament's use of whoring as a term for religious faithlessness or compromise, and the chapter's sense of offense at Shechem's action suggests such a connotation.

67. See further R. Parry, *Old Testament Story*, esp. 179–204.
68. Cf. Noble, "'Balanced' Reading," 194.

37

Jacob's Return to Beth El and the Passing of Rachel and Isaac

(35:1–29)

Overview

The chapter brings Part Three to an end by narrating the "journey's end for Jacob and Isaac."[1] It describes Jacob's move back to Beth El, where Rebekah's nanny is buried; summarizes God's renewing of his promises to Jacob there; relates Jacob's further move to Eprat, where Rachel dies in giving birth to Benjamin; recounts his onward move to Herd Tower, where Reuben sleeps with Bilhah; lists the now complete register of the twelve sons of Jacob; and finally narrates Jacob's arrival at Mamre and Isaac's death, along with his burial by Esau and Jacob.

Translation

1God said to Yaʿaqob, "Set off and go up to Bet-ʾel. Live there and make
an altar there for the God who appeared to you when you were taking
flight from your brother Esaw." **2**Yaʿaqob said to his household and to all
who were with him, "Remove the foreign gods[2] that are among you. Purify
yourselves. Change your clothes. **3**We are to set off and go up to Bet-ʾel
and make an altar there for the God who averred to me[3] in my time[4] of

1. Wenham, *Genesis 16–50*, 319.
2. The Tg nicely translates *ʾĕlōhîm* as "waywardnesses/deceptions/idols."
3. On this translation, see the footnote to 18:27.
4. Literally, "on my day."

pressure, and has been with me on the way that I've gone." **4**They gave
Yaʿaqob all the foreign gods that were in their hand and the rings that
were in their ears, and Yaʿaqob hid them under the oak that was near
Shekem.[5]

5So they moved on, and an almighty[6] terror came over the towns
that were around about them, and they didn't pursue after Yaʿaqob's
sons. **6**So Yaʿaqob came to Luz, which is in the country of Kenaʿan (i.e.,
Bet-ʾel), he and the entire company that was with him. **7**He built an altar
there and called the site "God of Bet-ʾel," because God had revealed
himself[7] to him there when he was taking flight from his brother. **8**Debo-
rah, Ribqah's nanny, died, and was buried beneath Bet-ʾel, beneath the
oak; people named[8] it Crying Oak.

9So God appeared to Yaʿaqob again when he came from Paddan
Aram and blessed him. **10**God said to him, "Your name is Yaʿaqob. You
will no longer be named Yaʿaqob; rather, Yiśraʾel will be your name." So
he named him Yiśraʾel. **11**God said to him, "I am El Šadday. Be fruitful
and numerous. A nation and a congregation of nations will come into
being from you. Kings will come out from your insides. **12**The country
that I gave to Abraham and to Yiṣḥaq I will give to you, and I will give the
country to your offspring after you." **13**Then God withdrew from him at the
site where he spoke with him, **14**and Yaʿaqob put up a standing stone at
the place where God had spoken with him, a standing stone of rock, and
poured out a libation on it and poured oil on it. **15**Yaʿaqob named the site
where God spoke with him Bet-ʾel.

16They moved on from Bet ʾEl. There was still a stretch[9] of country
in order to come to Eprat,[10] and Raḥel gave birth. She had a tough time
in giving birth. **17**When she was having a tough time in giving birth, the
midwife said to her, "Don't be afraid, because this one is a son for you,
too." **18**As her breath was leaving her, because she died,[11] she named
him Ben-ʾoni;[12] but his father called him Binyamin. **19**So Raḥel died and
was buried on the road to Eprat (i.e., Bet Leḥem). **20**Yaʿaqob put up a

5. The LXX reassuringly adds "and destroyed them until the present day."

6. For this use of *ʾĕlōhîm*, cf. 23:6 and the footnote, also 30:8, though this context with the references to God's involvement could also suggest the more literal connotation: "a terror from God" (so the Tg).

7. On the plural verb, see the translation note to 20:13. Qimchi (*Genesis*, on the verse) refers *hāʾĕlōhîm* to the *malʾăkê ʾĕlōhîm* of 28:12, which works better grammatically but less well contextually.

8. The verb is singular, and the LXX assumes it is Jacob who does the naming.

9. On the puzzling word *kibrâ*, see Tal, *Genesis*, 165–66*.

10. Comparison with 48:7 suggests that the *h* on *ʾeprātâ* is locative, though elsewhere the actual name seems to be *ʾeprātâ* (see BDB).

11. Following the MT, which marks *mētâ* as qatal rather than participle by putting the accent on the first syllable.

12. The LXX, Vg, Tg derive *ʾônî* from *ʾāwen* meaning "trouble," but the LXX and Tg recognize that in 49:3 it derives from *ʾôn*, meaning "vigor."

standing stone over her grave (it's the standing stone at Raḥel's Grave until today).

21Yiśra'el moved on and spread his tent beyond Herd Tower. 22While Yiśra'el was dwelling in that region, Re'uben went and slept with Bilhah, his father's secondary wife; and Yiśra'el heard.[13]

Ya'aqob's sons were twelve:

- 23The sons of Le'ah: Ya'aqob's firstborn, Re'uben; Šim'on; Lewi; Yehudah; Yiśśakar;[14] and Zebulun.
- 24The sons of Raḥel: Yosep and Binyamin.
- 25The sons of Bilhah, Raḥel's maidservant: Dan and Naptali.
- 26The sons of Zilpah, Le'ah's maidservant: Gad and Ašer.

These were Ya'aqob's sons who were born to him in Paddan Aram.

27Ya'aqob came to Yiṣḥaq his father at Mamre at Arba Township
(i.e., Hebron), where Abraham and Yiṣḥaq resided as aliens. 28Yiṣḥaq
was a man of 180 years. 29Yiṣḥaq breathed out and died, and joined
his kin,[15] old and full of time.[16] Esaw and Ya'aqob, his sons, buried
him.

Interpretation

Genesis 35 constitutes an episodic sequence of short units or "snapshots"[17] that close off Isaac's story:

How God bade Jacob return to Beth El, where Deborah died (35:1–8)

How God appeared to Jacob and renewed his promise of increase and land (35:9–15)

How the clan moved on from Beth El to Herd Tower and Rachel died in giving birth to Benjamin (35:16–20)

How Jacob moved on from Herd Tower and Reuben slept with Bilhah (35:21–22a)

A summary list of Jacob's sons (35:22b–26)

How Jacob came to Isaac at Mamre and Isaac died and was buried by Esau and Jacob (35:27–29)

13. One would expect a new verse to begin here; perhaps the actual verse division means that "the reader did not linger over such a doubtful passage, but hurried on" (Dillmann, *Genesis*, 2:310). Jubilees 33 offers a contrast with its expansion of this brief report to a whole chapter, incorporating an assurance that Bilhah was Reuben's unwilling victim (see Segal, *Book of Jubilees*, 73–82).

14. See the translation note to 30:18.

15. On this expression, see the comment on 25:8.

16. Literally, "days."

17. Fretheim, "Genesis," 586.

The MT treats the chapter as three units, vv. 1–8, 9–22a, and 22b–29. Although the chapter comprises these separate short sections, in a variety of ways they together close off the account of Isaac's line of descent, begun in 25:19. Following on Gen. 34, a striking feature is that the first two sections refer to God speaking, terrifying, appearing, blessing, and naming (vv. 1, 5, 9, 10, 11, 13). The second half of the chapter reverts to more theologically austere narration, much of it relating troublesome events (Rachel's death, Reuben's incest, Isaac's death). The chapter is thus typical of the Jacob narrative as a whole in moving between talk of events in which God's activity can be seen and of events in which that activity is invisible, behind the scenes—between the revealed God and the invisible God.[18] A further feature is that the chapter always refers to God as *ʾĕlōhîm* or *ʾēl*, not as Yahweh, which contrasts with (e.g.) 25:19–26; 26:1–33; 27:1–29 (the opening sections of Part Three); 28:10–22 (Yahweh's first appearing at Beth El); and 29:31–30:30 (the main sequence of births and namings). Various views are held regarding the extent to which the material has a background in the work of the Yahwist, the Elohist, the Priestly writer, or a redactor.

35:1–8. There is no indication of how long a time elapses before Jacob's company makes this move. Possibly the logic is the same as that in 31:1–3: Jacob is scared (34:30–31), and God responds by telling him to move.[19] But the ancestors' lifestyle as sheep farmers means that they do move around, so there might be nothing odd about relocating twenty miles or so south from the Shalem/Shechem area toward the Beth El area, notwithstanding their having acquired land at Shalem (33:19–20). Nor in the context of Genesis is there anything surprising about God commissioning such a move. God is taking Jacob one stage further toward the completion of a journey back to the family from whom he departed, farther south in Beer Sheba, though God does talk about "living" or settling (*yāšab*) there at Beth El; it's not just a staging post. God's explicit point is that the move to Beth El pairs with his having appeared to Jacob there on his way out of Canaan (28:10–22). God notes this fact in commissioning Jacob to return to Canaan (31:13), though neither the story of his appearance at Beth El nor the commission to return to Canaan specifically envisaged Jacob going back to Beth El in particular. There is again no explicit reference to Jacob's fulfilling the tithing commitment he made in 28:22 (Jub. 32 makes up for the lack). But Jacob made this commitment, and when he set up the standing stone at that point, he designated the worship site at Beth El as a house of God, so a return is natural. God's own directive is that Jacob is to build an altar there. It is the only time in Genesis when God commissions the building of an altar. Jacob is going to retrace Abraham's steps

18. Cf. von Rad, *Genesis*, 333 (he associates the first with P, the second with J and E).

19. Cf. Westermann, *Genesis 12–36*, 543 (though he associates this idea with the suggestion that 35:5 originally followed directly after 34:27–29).

and repeat the sequence of Abraham's altar making (12:6–8). But the divine commission follows on the defilement story and leads into Jacob's charge about renunciation and purifying in v. 2, which suggests that something else underlies the commission. Shechem was a major Canaanite town, and Beth El "had a long Canaanite prehistory" as a sanctuary, so here the building of an altar at Beth El points to the dedication of the worship site there to the true God.[20] Jacob would need to "go up" from Shechem to Beth El: Shechem stands at one of the lower points on the mountain ridge, at another crossing point between west and east, at about 1,800 feet, while Beth El stands near the highest point on the ridge, more like 3,000 feet. But the audience might also recall the idea of going up to Beth El or to Jerusalem for a pilgrimage festival (e.g., Hosea 4:15). In a sense God is inviting Jacob on such a pilgrimage, back to where God first met with him.

The requirement to dispose of foreign gods (v. 2) then raises eyebrows. But Rachel's theft of the teraphim opens a window on the possibility that people within Jacob's household have brought their images with them from Harran; the teraphim count as gods in the broad sense that can attach to that word (cf. 31:30, 32). Other people, such as his servants and shepherds, who are not members of his immediate family, would have done the same thing; Tg. Ps.-J. adds reference to idols that would have been among the plunder referred to in 34:29. Having images like the teraphim need not stand in conflict with the idea that Yahweh or the God of Abraham or El Shadday was the only real God. But one needs to be somewhat theologically sophisticated to live by that view, and Jacob apparently recognizes that with this pilgrimage the time has come when the gray area becomes black and white. And for some people listening to the story, it would contain a nudge (see Deut. 31:16; Josh. 24:20, 23—at Shechem; Judg. 10:16; 1 Sam. 7:3; 2 Chron. 33:15; Jer. 5:19), particularly people in Ephraim who were accustomed to going up from Shechem to the sanctuary at Beth El for festivals (again, cf. Hosea 4:15).[21] Read in light of the exhortation to repudiate their foreign gods, the exhortation to purification would suggest that this repudiation will be the action that has the purifying effect, which fits the motif of defilement in Gen. 34. Defilement and purity form a related pair of concepts, and these two chapters are the only ones in which either word group appears in Genesis except for the reference to clean animals in Gen. 9. Foreign people defile because they serve foreign gods, and people who serve foreign gods or worship in foreign ways need purifying (e.g., 2 Chron. 34:3; Jer. 13:27; Ezek. 36:17–20; 37:23). The requirement that people change their clothes points in a different, complementary direction. At Sinai the Israelites will need to safeguard their sacredness and wash their clothes when Yahweh is about to appear, and here the change of clothes along

20. Sarna, *Genesis*, 239.
21. Cf. von Rad, *Genesis*, 331.

with the purification links with the fact that the community (not just Jacob) is about to meet with God.

Jacob goes on (v. 3) to personalize further the reason for the journey and the altar making. It will be an act of thanksgiving and testimony. His "we" underscores the significance of God's actions for the entire group even though it was only Jacob who had the experience of God reaching out to him at Beth El and being with him over the twenty-plus years that have since passed. The time when he was under pressure was the time when Esau was threatening to kill him, and the time when God reached out to him and averred his protection was the time a few days later when he was on his way to Harran. Like the English word, "pressure" (*ṣārâ*) can suggest both something objective ("Esau is planning to kill me!") and something subjective (the sense of distress that naturally follows; v. 3). But God said, "I am with you: I will keep you wherever you go" (28:15), and he has kept the promise. The listeners might recognize the expression "my time of pressure" from the pleas that appear in the psalms (see Pss. 77:2 [77:3]; 86:7). Jacob is now in the position that the psalms also reflect, of being able—indeed under obligation—to testify that God "rescued me from every pressure" (Ps. 54:7 [54:9]).

The people do as they are told (v. 4). There is no other First Testament allusion to a link between earrings and foreign worship, though the reference could imply a kind of catachresis if it reminds listeners of the way earrings can be turned into a means of foreign worship (Exod. 32:2–3; Judg. 8:24–27). More likely "their ears" means the images' ears: the earrings are an adornment of the divine images and not of the people, and they have been appropriated as part of the plunder.[22] The allusion to the oak near Shechem (the only reference to Shechem the place in Gen. 33–35) suggests another link with Abraham, though here the word for the tree is *ʾēlâ*, not *ʾēlôn*,[23] but the reference to hiding might be slightly worrying: what is hidden can be dug up.[24]

The background to the possible need of protection from the towns around (v. 5) lies in 34:30. God makes sure that the action by Jacob's sons doesn't have the effect that Jacob feared. "Terror" parallels "pressure" in having both an objective and a subjective aspect (e.g., Ezek. 32:23–32). Here the communities between Shechem and Beth El are overwhelmed by subjective terror even when Jacob's company is not objectively terrifying, as Jacob has realistically commented. Although they could have attacked Jacob's group and treated them the same way as Jacob's sons had treated Shalem, they hold back from doing so.

Explaining that Luz is the same place as Beth El (v. 6) is unnecessary after 28:19, and it is even less necessary to tell us that the place is in Canaan, but

22. Cf. Hurowitz, "Who Lost an Earring?"
23. See the footnote to 12:6.
24. See the footnote to v. 4.

rhetorically this note functions to remind us once again that Jacob is back home in the promised land. God has fulfilled his pledge.

Jacob in turn fulfills God's commission (v. 7), designating God by the name of a place rather than by the name of a person (e.g., "God of Abraham") even more unequivocally than God himself did in 31:13. Such is the vital importance of God's having "revealed himself" (*gālâ* niphal) to Jacob at that place when he was under pressure and on the run. This verb comes elsewhere in Genesis only at 9:21 and only here in the niphal; indeed, the First Testament elsewhere uses it only in connection with Eli's line, with Samuel, and with Isaiah (1 Sam. 2:27; 3:21; Isa. 22:14).

What has been happening to Rebekah (v. 8) over the past twenty-plus years? We never get to hear that story or to hear when she died. Perhaps she has sent her nanny Deborah (24:59) to get Jacob in fulfillment of her promise in 27:45, and Deborah died on the way home.[25] Or perhaps Rebekah and Deborah have spent time at Beth El and Deborah has died there some while before, so that Jacob has found her tomb there, somewhere just below the height on which Beth El itself stood, under a tree (cf. 1 Sam. 31:13), where graves are often still located.[26] It might thus be a place well known to some of the audience. The account of Deborah's death and burial is just the first such account in this chapter, all part of closing off the story of Isaac's line of descent.

35:9–15. The account of God's appearing to Jacob constitutes an alternative summary account of much of the story in 28:10–35:8. Its opening implies reference to God's appearing to Jacob after he left Paddan Aram, recounted in 32:24–31. But the formulation of God's words of blessing takes up God's promise to Abraham in 17:1–22, whose wording already recurred in Isaac's blessing in 28:3–4, as the following table shows:

17:1–8, 22	28:3–4, 18–19	35:9–14
Yahweh appeared to Abram		God appeared to Jacob
and said to him, "I am El Shadday.	"May El Shadday himself bless you	and blessed him . . . "God said to him, I am El Shadday.
I will make you very, very numerous.	and enable you to be fruitful	Be fruitful
I will enable you to be very, very fruitful.	and numerous,	and numerous.
You will no longer be named Abram.		You will no longer be named Jacob.
Your name will be Abraham.		Israel will be your name.

25. Cf. Rashi, *Brʾšyt*, 396.
26. Cf. Gunkel, *Genesis*, 368.

17:1–8, 22	28:3–4, 18–19	35:9–14
You will become the ancestor	so you become	A nation and a congregation of nations
of a horde of nations.	a congregation of peoples.	will come into being from you.
From you kings will go out.		Kings will come out from your insides.
I will give to you,	May he give to you Abraham's blessing,	The country that I gave to Abraham . . . I will give to you,
and to your offspring after you,	to you and to your offspring with you,	and I will give the country to your offspring after you."
the country	so you take possession of the country	
where you are residing as aliens."	where you're residing as aliens,	
	which God gave Abraham."	
So he finished speaking with him.		Then God withdrew from him
And God withdrew from Abraham.		at the site where he spoke with him.
	Jacob got the rock . . . ,	Jacob put up . . .
	put it up as a standing stone	a standing stone,
		a standing stone of rock,
		and poured out a libation on it
	and poured oil on the top of it.	and poured oil on it.
	He named the site Beth El.	Jacob named the site where God spoke with him Beth El.

The only new note in vv. 9–15 is thus the comment on pouring a libation, which was a regular feature of daily, monthly, and annual offerings in Israel according to Num. 28–29. The emphasis in vv. 9–15 and the significance of the section is that God has affirmed for Jacob his commitment to Abraham (ironically, after Gen. 34, the great omission in Gen. 35's recollection of Gen. 17 is any reference to circumcision) and has confirmed Isaac's blessing prayer for him.

35:16–22a. Whereas God told Jacob to move from the Shechem area to Beth El, there is no such commission in connection with this move farther south. The end of the chapter will imply that the clan is on its way to Mamre, but there is no indication at this point that Jacob is deliberately working his way there. They have come about halfway, perhaps two or three days' journey from Beth El. Eprat (nothing to do with Ephraim, to the north) is apparently an area that includes Beth Lehem. Rachel gives birth a little further north of that area, not far from Jerusalem (other references make the location of Eprat a more complicated matter and raise the question of whether there were two places called Eprat, north and south of Jerusalem: see 1 Sam. 10:2; Jer. 31:15).[27] One wonders about the background to the clan's undertaking this move when Rachel is extremely pregnant, but maybe she went into labor early and they had been hoping to reach Eprat or Mamre before the baby came.

Rachel's midwife (v. 17) is "the functional counterpart of Rebekah's nurse."[28] Her words of encouragement recur in a similar context in 1 Sam. 4:20, reflecting the way death in childbirth is a recurrent event in a traditional society—and perhaps a woman is more or less as likely to die in childbirth if she stays put as if she is on the move (KSG). "There is scarcely a text in the patriarchal stories which shows so clearly the harshness of their life-style."[29] Yet the midwife's encouragement indicates that Rachel's own prayer in 30:24 is being answered.

Only for this son of Jacob does Genesis make no comment on his name(s) (v. 18).[30] Ben-ʾoni could mean "Son of my sorrow" or "Son of my vigor,"[31] and both meanings would be applicable. Like the change from Abram to Abraham, the change to Benjamin does not involve too drastic an alteration. The adjective *ben-yəmînî* could imply "My right-hand son," with which one might compare the English expression "right-hand man"; perhaps the name indicates that Jacob will keep his youngest son at his right hand, for his mother's sake.[32] Or the adjective might imply "Son of the south" (for people who orient on the east, the south is on their right-hand side); Benjamin is the only son not born in the north, in Harran. But the actual name is *binyamin* (as opposed to *benyamin*), and it corresponds to the name *binu jamina* known from Mari on the Euphrates, the area from which Jacob has returned, where it does mean "Son of the south."[33] So Jacob likely brought the name from Harran. Does he rename the baby because either of the possible meanings of Ben-ʾoni is too painful? But a modern midrash has Rachel commenting, "In choosing this name for my son, I wanted Jacob to know that this child was the fruit of our love and that I didn't regret dying to give him life. And Jacob respected my wishes . . . by repeating my meaning within his own act of naming. He knew precisely what I meant when I chose my baby's name."[34]

Rachel's death and burial (vv. 19–20) follow on the reference to Deborah's death and burial, but it is a more grievous death for Jacob than that of his

27. See, e.g., Sarna, *Genesis*, 407–8.

28. Hamilton, *Genesis 18–50*, 384.

29. Westermann, *Genesis 13–36*, 554.

30. Cf. Pirson, *Lord of the Dreams*, 26–28.

31. See the translation note on 35:18.

32. So Willet, *Hexapla in Genesin & Exodum*, 304.

33. See, e.g., Lemche, "Is It Still Possible to Write a History of Ancient Israel?," 175–79; his argument that the Benjaminites as a clan came from Mari is a different matter. See further D. Fleming, "Syrian Background."

34. Frankel, *Five Books of Miriam*, 70.

mother's nanny. Jacob marks it in the same way as Deborah's death had been marked, but he does so with a more solid and notable monument that reflects what Rachel means to him, a kind of gravestone to mark the place where they laid Rachel. Like Western people who may go to talk to a loved one at their grave, it would be a place where people could go and talk to Rachel. "The caravan then departs, leaving the grave of the mother behind it, and the newly born child, who has now no mother, is taken along."[35] The story thus continues to prepare the way for the final death in Gen. 35 to be related, at Mamre. And from her tomb Rachel continues to weep in Jeremiah's day, not just for this one child but for all her children trudging off into exile (Jer. 31:15–17), and she does so again for the babies who die as a result of Jesus's birth (Matt. 2:17–18). "Dying always happens in the midst of new life. Living always happens in the midst of death. There is, after all, a time to be born and a time to die (Eccles. 3:2). And this time . . . is both times."[36]

Herd Tower (v. 21) was presumably farther south on the road along the ridge. It must have been one of many towers that provided shelter and lookout posts for farmers and shepherds (cf. Isa. 5:2). If Jacob "spread his tent," he was settling down for a while again, not simply making an overnight stay (cf. 26:25; 33:19), which confirms that we are not reading about a simple relocation from Beth El to Mamre.

Reuben's bedding Bilhah (v. 22a) further prepares for the end of Part Three of Genesis. Reuben is Jacob's eldest son and as such has a natural claim to be the head of the family when Jacob dies. To start appropriating his father's women underscores his perception of himself and his presentation of himself to other people as the natural next head of the family (see, e.g., Deut. 22:30 [23:1]; 2 Sam. 3:7; 12:7–8; 1 Kings 2:13–25). Bilhah is regularly the object of things that people do: Laban gives her to Rachel, Rachel gives her to Jacob, Jacob takes her off from Harran and pushes her ahead to meet Esau with the rest of the family, and Reuben beds her. We will discover that he has miscalculated: see 49:3–4, where ironically (in light of Rachel's naming of Benjamin) Jacob calls Reuben *rēʾšît ʾônî* (the firstfruit of my vigor). Bilhah was Rachel's maidservant, and there may be a suggestion that after Rachel's death Bilhah might take her place as Jacob's favorite wife, so that bedding Bilhah in particular is significant in connection with Reuben's ambitions. Once again, Jacob hears about it, which (notwithstanding 34:5) hints that there may be action in due course (see 49:3–4); compare the sequence in Num. 12:2, 4.[37]

35:22b–26. Benjamin's birth has brought to completion the roster of Jacob's twelve sons, the ancestors of the twelve Israelite clans; Benjamin is, of course, the exception to the general statement that all the sons were born

35. Westermann, *Genesis 13–36*, 554.
36. Brueggemann, *Genesis*, 283.
37. Cf. Sarna, *Genesis*, 245.

in Paddan Aram. The list notes (pointedly in the context of v. 22a) that Reuben is Jacob's firstborn, another term that recurs in Jacob's description of him in 49:3–4. The sons come in a different order from the account in Gen. 29:31–30:24—there the order was Leah, then her handmaid, then Rachel's handmaid, and finally Rachel herself.

35:27–29. At last we arrive at the end of Genesis Part Three. Jacob has understood God to be promising that he would come back to his father's household with things being well (28:21), and he has done so. "The description of Jacob and Isaac's reunion is laconic and utterly devoid of all emotional detail, unlike the meeting between Jacob and Esau."[38] What matters is the objective fact. The cycle has reached completion.

We arrive also at the end of the Isaac story (v. 28). Apparently Rebekah has died, so she never experienced the reunion with her favorite son that she expected. And apparently Isaac has moved from Beer Sheba to Mamre and Rebekah has died there, and so she has been buried in the Double Cave (49:31).

So Isaac "breathed out and died, and was gathered to his kin" (v. 29), like his father and his brother (cf. 25:8, 17). He was "full of time," with the implication of being "satisfied" (*śābēaʿ*) with his span of life. While Abraham was "full" (25:8), elsewhere only Job is called "full of time" (42:17). In the Abraham story "Isaac and Ishmael, his sons, buried him" (25:9). Here, neatly, Isaac's two sons (named in the Esau-Jacob order) bury him.

Implications

Beth El

Beth El is a puzzle in more than one sense. There is a puzzle about its relationship to Luz. Whereas this story implies that Jacob here renames Luz as Beth El, the name Luz does not seem to die out (see 35:6; Josh. 16:2; 18:13; Judg. 1:22–26). Further, Josh. 16:2 implies that Luz and Beth El are distinguishable, although nearby, places (cf. Josh. 18:13). Possibly Beth El was originally the name of a sanctuary near Luz, but the fame of the sanctuary eventually led to its replacing the town's name.[39] Whereas Luz was just a "town," Beth El is a worship site, a place where God appeared.[40] There is a related question about Beth El's location. Archaeologists have assumed that it corresponds to the modern Beitin,[41] ten miles north of Jerusalem, but we have no direct evidence for the correctness of this assumption. Further, Beth El may also have been the name of a god,[42] and Jacob later calls this place El Beth El (35:7).

38. Assis, *Identity in Conflict*, 56.
39. Cf. Sarna, *Genesis*, 200.
40. Cf. Fokkelman, *Narrative Art in Genesis*, 68–69.
41. See James Kelso, *Excavation of Bethel.*
42. See Sarna, *Genesis*, 399–400.

The biggest puzzle concerns its status or reputation in different periods. In the First Testament narrative covering the time before David, it is a respected sanctuary (1 Sam. 7:16; 10:3), and the Jacob story would make sense against this context. After David's day it became one of the renegade Ephraimite sanctuaries (e.g., 1 Kings 12–13). It was a center of Elijah and Elisha's activity in their day (see 2 Kings 2), but soon afterward Hosea and Amos speak snidely about it as a "house of wickedness" rather than a "house of God" and declare judgment on it (e.g., Amos 3:14; 5:5; Hosea 4:15; 10:15); Josiah destroys it (2 Kings 23). But subsequently, people from Beth El feature among the people who return from Babylon (Ezra 2:28), and people send from Beth El to inquire of Yahweh in Jerusalem (Zech. 7:1–3).

It is not clear how the Jacob story relates to the long history of this town and sanctuary. On one hand, "the Old Testament tradition contains not the slightest hint that 28:10ff could have served as a later legitimation for the worship arrangements of Jeroboam I."[43] On the other, if the Jacob story existed in Jeroboam's day, Jacob would surely seem to have anticipatorily done a favor to Jeroboam as the first king of Ephraim, when Jeroboam made Beth El the location of one of his nation's sanctuaries. He would have been able to assert that Beth El had a great Israelite ancestry, unlike Johnny-come-lately Jerusalem.

43. Seebass, *Genesis*, 2.2:323

Part Four

Jacob's Lines of Descent, Focusing on Joseph

(36:1–50:26)

Like Part Three of Genesis, Part Four focuses on one long story, though a more interconnected one. First, a preamble in 36:1–43 summarizes the family line of Jacob's brother (paralleling the preamble summarizing the family line of Isaac's brother in 25:12–18 at the beginning of Part Three). Then 37:1–2a invites the listeners to see what follows as indeed the story of Jacob's family line as a whole (likewise 25:19 introduced the main story in Part Three as the story of Isaac's family line). Jacob's son Joseph is then the central figure in the account of Jacob's lines of descent (as Jacob himself was the central figure in the account of Isaac's lines of descent). So Gen. 37–50 is not merely a story about Joseph: it is also the story of Joseph's brothers and his family.[1] Like Part Two and Part Three, it is the story of a family with a father figure at its head, a story focusing on the family's destiny and thus on its children, a story about conflict in the family, and a story about people engaged in shepherding who find that famine imperils their lives.[2] Thus Abraham, Isaac, and Jacob all had a problem with whether their families would survive because they could not feed them, and Abraham and Isaac both had to handle the question of whether their families would die out because they could not have

1. Cf. Clifford, "Genesis 37–50."
2. Cf. Westermann, *Genesis 37–50*, 27.

children. The further problem for Jacob is whether his family can achieve enough harmony to survive as one clan.[3]

After the preamble, Part Four divides into three acts: one focuses on how Joseph came to be in Egypt and to be supplies master there, one focuses on how his brothers and his father came to join him (in this section the division into scenes is more hazardous), and one focuses on Jacob's last days. Part Four thus outlines as follows:

Esau's lines of descent (36:1–43)

How Joseph came to be in Egypt (37:1–36)
How Judah learned his lesson (38:1–30)
How Joseph came to be in jail (39:1–23)
How Joseph came to be a dream interpreter (40:1–23)
How Joseph came to be supplies master in Egypt (41:1–56)

How the ten brothers went to Egypt (41:57–42:38)
How the eleven brothers went to Egypt (43:1–45:28)
How Jacob and his family settled in Egypt (46:1–47:12)
How Joseph rescued the Egyptians (47:13–26)

How Jacob began to prepare for his death (47:27–48:22)
How Jacob addressed each of his sons before his death (49:1–27)
How Jacob died, the aftermath, and how Joseph died (49:28–50:26)

One big question lying behind Part Four is apparent: how did the Israelites come to be in Egypt (and therefore need to be rescued from there)? Part Four "opens the door for the exodus theme."[4] Targum Ps.-J. flags that point by describing Jacob's commission of Joseph in 37:13 as the beginning of the exile in Egypt, the moment when the deep design communicated to Abraham in 15:13 began to find fulfillment, though b. Shabb. 10b sees the link more negatively, claiming that this exile would never have happened if it had not been for Jacob's favoritism toward Joseph.[5] Either way, the story points out the strangeness of this element in the Israelites' story. They know that their ancestors have had a complicated origin that involves Mesopotamia, Canaan, and also (mysteriously) Egypt. Part Four of Genesis plays a key role in tying together the narrative threads of this story. In doing so, it also answers the

3. Cf. Reno, *Genesis*, 271.

4. Coats, *Genesis*, 259.

5. Cf. Qimchi, *Genesis* on 37:3 (though Qimchi notes the positive point in his comment on 37:13).

question of how Israel came to comprise the twelve clans with their sense of familial unity notwithstanding the tensions and strife between them. Handling that question in Part Four means that Genesis as a whole takes us all the way from creation to the existence of the twelve clans of Israel.

In answering that question, the story of Joseph plays a dominant role. Joseph has many marks of the hero in a traditional story. He is the son and grandson of someone important, his birth is unusual, he is ambitious and his older brothers try to kill him, he is saved by a stratagem, he grows up in a foreign country, he gets undeservedly trapped by a woman, he is a dreamer, he is the victor in a contest (in dream interpretation), he marries someone of high rank, he becomes a ruler, he is the lowly person who saves the community, he rules effectively, he prescribes laws, and he is not buried (in Genesis).[6] These marks of a traditional story are worked into a narrative of literary and theological sophistication.

As a literary work, and considered in isolation, the Joseph story parallels the stories of Ruth and Esther.

a. It is a short story or novelette[7] (4,000–5,000 Hebrew words)
b. about an individual who is an actual person,
c. but this ordinary individual ends up having extraordinary significance.
d. The story is focused on life in an exotic foreign land and/or relationships with foreigners who behave in surprising ways.
e. It is history-like in its provision of background information,
f. imaginative in its relating people's conversations and their inner thoughts,
g. and thus not giving the impression that it is simply factual.
h. The story is provocative in portraying characters in their ambiguity and making the listeners think and ask questions about them.
i. It is concerned to hold attention and entertain,
j. and it is skillful in raising suspense and resolving it.
k. Though using traditional motifs, it is more a creative work of art than the deposit of traditions.
l. The story is complete in its own right and plotted (unlike modern Western short stories),
m. yet it is integrated into Israel's story (more systematically than Ruth and much more than Esther).
n. It is a portrayal of events working out through human decision-making and coincidence
o. yet pointing to God's involvement in events (more explicitly than Ruth and much more than Esther).

6. Cf. Raglan, "Hero of Tradition," esp. 149.

7. So von Rad, *Genesis*, 428. It is common to use the Latin-looking word "novella" (e.g., Humphreys, *Joseph*).

Among the distinctive features of the account of Jacob's lines of descent is thus the way "belief in providence has taken the place of belief in theophanies."[8] Parts Two and Three of Genesis have portrayed the effectiveness of much human decision making, have related important conversations between characters, have described conflicts and reconciliations between them, and have sometimes left ambiguous the attitudes and motivations of key characters in a way that requires the listeners to enter into the narrative in order to interpret them. Such features become central markers in Gen. 36–50. Related to them are further distinguishing markers, "the pivot of irony upon which the entire plot turns,"[9] and the raising and resolving of suspense.

It's possible to disentangle the story centering on Joseph himself (roughly, Gen. 37; 39–47) from the broader account of Jacob's family line, and it may have existed as a separate short story or novelette that then came to be the dominant element within Part Four of Genesis. Yet the characteristics and motifs of Part Four as a whole—such as irony, deceit, sibling rivalry, the favoring of a younger son, and the focus on clothing and food—appear in Gen. 36–50 outside the Joseph story as well as inside it. As with the rest of Genesis, the scholarly world has worked hard to trace the history of the development of the chapters,[10] but it has reached no consensus on the nature of this development.

8. Gunkel, *Genesis*, 382.
9. Redford, *Study*, 73.
10. See, e.g., Golka, "Genesis 37–50"; Ede, *Die Josefsgeschichte*.

38

Esau's Family Line, Marginalized but Not Forgotten

(36:1–43)

Overview

As the story of Isaac's family line opens with a preamble giving an account of his elder brother's (Ishmael's) descendants, so the story of Jacob's family opens with a preamble giving an account of Jacob's elder brother's (Esau's) descendants before it moves on to its own focus.

Translation

1These are the lines of descent of Esaw (i.e., Edom). **2**Esaw got his wives
from the daughters of Kenaʿan: Adah daughter of Elon the Ḥetite, Ohol-
ibamah daughter of Anah, daughter of[1] Ṣibʿon the Hivvite, **3**and Basmat
daughter of Yišmaʿeʾl, sister of Nebayot. **4**Adah gave birth to Elipaz for
Esaw, Basmat gave birth to Reʿuʾel, **5**and Oholibamah gave birth to Yeʿuš,
Yalam, and Qorah. These are the sons of Esaw who were born to him in
the country of Kenaʿan. **6**Esaw got his wives, his sons, and his daugh-
ters, and all the persons in his household, his livestock, all his animals,[2]
and all his acquisitions that he had gained in the country of Kenaʿan,
and went to a country away from Yaʿaqob his brother, **7**because their
property was too much for them to live together and the country where

1. In vv. 24–25, at least, Anah must be a man; the SP and LXX thus have "son of." The MT implies that "daughter of" is a further description of Oholibamah and means more precisely "granddaughter of" (cf. Wenham, *Genesis 16–50*, 337).

2. See the translation note to 34:23.

they were residing as aliens couldn't support them because of their live-
stock. 8So Esaw lived in the highland of Seʿir (Esaw is Edom). 9These are
the lines of descent of Esaw, the ancestor of Edom, in the highland of
Seʿir.

10These are the names of Esaw's sons:

Elipaz, son of Esaw's wife Adah
Reʿuʾel, son of Esaw's wife Basmat.
11The sons of Elipaz were Teman, Omar, Ṣepo, Gaʿtam, and Qenaz.
12Timna was a secondary wife to Esaw's son Elipaz; she gave birth to Amaleq for Elipaz.
These were the descendants of Esaw's wife Adah.
13These were the sons of Reʿuʾel: Nahat, Zerah, Šammah, and Mizzah.
These were the descendants of Esaw's wife Basmat.
14These were the sons of Esaw's wife Oholibamah daughter of Anah, daughter of[3] Ṣibʿon: she gave birth to Yeʿuš, Yalam, and Qorah for Esaw.

15These are Esaw's descendants' clans.[4]
The descendants of Elipaz, Esaw's firstborn:
the Teman clan, the Omar clan, the Ṣepo clan, the Qenaz
clan, 16the Qorah clan, the Gaʿtam clan, the Amaleq clan;
these are the clans of Elipaz in the country of Edom; these are the descendants of Adah.
17These are the descendants of Reʿuʾel, Esaw's son:
the Nahat clan, the Zerah clan, the Šammah clan, the Mizzah clan;
these are the clans of Reʿuʾel in the country of Edom; these are the descendants of Basmat, Esaw's wife.
18These are the descendants of Oholibamah, Esaw's wife:
the Yeʿuš clan, the Yaʿlam clan, the Qorah clan;
these are the clans of Oholibamah daughter of Anah, Esaw's wife.
19These are the descendants of Esaw and these are their clans (i.e., Edom).

20These are the sons of Seʿir the Horite, the people living in the
country: Lotan, Šobal, Ṣibʿon, Anah, 21Dišon, Eṣer, and
Dišan.

3. The SP and LXX have "son of": see the footnote to v. 2.

4. *ʾAllûp* comes from *ʾelep*, the word for a thousand. In Exod. 15:15; Zech. 12:5–6 (and cf. Zech. 9:7) it means "chief," someone who was etymologically or nominally commander of a thousand, and the LXX, Vg, and Tg assume this meaning here, but it fits poorly in the context. I take it here and in 1 Chron. 1 (the vast majority of the occurrences) to mean (nominally or etymologically) "a group of a thousand" (so, e.g., Seebass, *Genesis*, 2.2:463).

These are the Horites' clans, Seʿir's descendants, in the country of Edom.

22The sons of Lotan were Hori and Hemam; Lotan's sister was Timna.

23These are the sons of Šobal: Alwan, Manaḥat, Ebal, Šepo, and Onam.

24These are the sons of Ṣibʿon: both Ayyah and Anah (he was the Anah who found the hot springs[5] in the wilderness when he was pasturing the donkeys of Ṣibʿon his father).

25These are the children of Anah: Dišon and Oholibamah, Anah's daughter.

26These are the sons of Dišan: Hemdan, Ešban, Itran, and Keran.

27These are the sons of Eṣer: Bilhan, Zaʿavan, and Aqan.

28These are the sons of Dišan: Uṣ and Aran.

29These are the Horites' clans: the clans Lotan, Šobal, Ṣibʿon, Anah, 30Dišon, Eṣer, and Dišan.

These are the Horites' clans by their clans in the country of Seʿir.

31These are the kings who reigned in the country of Edom before a king reigned among the Yiśraʾelites:

32Bela ben Beʿor reigned in Edom; his town's name was Dinhabah.

33Bela died and Yobab ben Zerah from Boṣrah reigned in his place.

34Yobab died and Hušam from the Temanites' country reigned in his place.

35Hušam died and Hadad ben Bedad, who struck down Midyan in Moʾab's region, reigned in his place; his town's name was Avit.

36Hadad died and Samlah from Masrekah reigned in his place.

37Samlah died and Šaʾul from Broads on the River reigned in his place.

38Šaʾul died and Baʿal ben Akbor reigned in his place.

39Baʿal Hanan ben Akbor died and Hadar[6] reigned in his place; his town's name was Paʿu, and his wife's name was Mehetabel daughter of Matred, daughter of Gold Water.

5. I follow the Vg for the translation of the hapax *yēmim*. According to Jerome (*Hebrew Questions on Genesis*, 74), the translation is based on the word's meaning in Carthaginian, which was a Semitic language; the idea that there were hot springs in the region (esp. near the Dead Sea) is entirely plausible (Driver, *Genesis*, 316), though Hayward is doubtful about Jerome's comment (*Hebrew Questions on Genesis*, 217–18).

6. The SP and 1 Chron. 1:50 have Hadad; the LXX has Arad by metathesis.

40These are the names of Esaw's clans by their kin groups, by their places, with their names: the Timna clan, the Alvah clan, the Yetet clan, 41the Oholibamah clan, the Elah clan, the Pinon clan, 42the Qenaz clan, the Teman clan, the Mibṣar clan, 43the Magdiʾel clan, the Iram clan. These are the clans of Edom, by their settlements in the country that is their holding (i.e., Esaw, Edom's ancestor).

Interpretation

In form, the account of Esau's lines of descent overlaps with the shorter account of Ishmael's lines of descent, which also appears in a similar location before the account of Isaac's lines of descent in 25:12–18; in these respects it also compares in part with the account of Terah's lines of descent in 11:27–32. But whereas 25:12–18 focused on listing Ishmael's sons and then moved on to his death, 36:1–43 is much longer and more discursive. Both accounts have an introduction parallel in form with the introduction to the subject's brother that follows (cf. 25:19a and 37:2a). And in each case this following introduction to the brother's family line (Isaac's and Jacob's) turns out to be but the preliminary to a long and sprawling story. The accounts of Ishmael and Esau are both preliminaries to the accounts of their younger brothers, on which Genesis needs to focus. So Genesis is dealing with Esau's line in a way that does not ignore it but positions it so as to clear the way for the treatment of Jacob's line. As the people in Ishmael's line are heirs to a promise to Abraham, so the people in Esau's line are heirs to a blessing by Isaac. "Esau and Ishmael lacked this promise, but they were not excluded from mercy. . . . Moses tells the story of Esau . . . that we may know that he became a partaker of the blessing that Jacob had."[7] They are part of the penumbra of the story that leads to Israel itself, even though Yahweh is doing something distinctive with that narrower story.

In any period, the relatively positive attitude to Esau and Edom reminds Israelite listeners that the subservience of Edom to Israel in the early monarchy, or the conflict between Edom and Israel in the later monarchy, or the bitterness of attitude toward Edom after its infiltration into Judahite territory in the Babylonian and Persian periods are not the only things to be said about Israel's relationship to Edom or about Yahweh's relationship with Edom. The chapter gives expression to the permanent "brotherhood of Edom" with Israel.[8] It constitutes a compilation of lists that overlap in content, which suggests that they are of separate origin. Possibly it was Edom's becoming part of the Davidic empire that led to Israel's having this information about Edomite history, geography, and administration. If so, "the origin and

7. Luther, *Genesis 31–37*, 284.

8. Bartlett, "Land of Seir"; cf. Westermann, *Genesis 12–36*, 562.

transmission of Gen. 36 . . . is to be understood from its 'setting in life,' the task of administering a conquered land."[9]

36:1–9. In giving its account of Esau's marriages, Genesis is again backtracking. Initially (vv. 2–5), "the elements forming the unit orient around the themes of marriage and birth," which also suggests a comparison with 29:31–30:24.[10] The opening quasi-formal listing of Esau's wives overlaps with the listing in 26:34–35; 28:6–9, but it is far from identical. Here Esau's wives are Adah daughter of Elon (Hittite), Oholibamah daughter of Anah (Hivvite), and Basmat sister of Nebayot (Ishmaelite), but in 26:34–35 and 28:6–9 they are Judith daughter of Be'eri (Hittite), Basmat daughter of Elon (Hittite), and Mahalat sister of Nebayot (Ishmaelite). The information has been passed down in varying forms, and we have no basis for knowing which (if either) is historically correct. As is often the case in the scriptural story, the narrator and the readers are not troubled by differences in the way the story is told. Perhaps they have an equivalent to the modern or postmodern recognition that the details of a story (even a historical story) are often designed to give a history-like impression rather than to be taken as factual, and therefore that the details do not need to be pressed and differences between them are not a problem. The detail affirms that Genesis is talking about real people and a real story; but it is not a story that one can turn into history, and to do so is to miss its point. "Attempts in modern research to 'decode' these stories like allegories in order to reconstruct ancient histories are projections which miss the semantics inherent to those traditions."[11] And what the different accounts have in common may be especially significant: "the nationalities of Esau's wives are more important than their names."[12] Marrying Canaanite women is by implication an inferior move compared with marrying within the clan of Terah, as Isaac and Jacob do. The account underscores the point by listing the two Canaanite wives first (though this order does correspond to the narrative in 26:34–35; 28:6–9), whereas in the next verse and later in the chapter Oholibamah comes second, not third.[13] Esau's marriages are a mark of his standing outside the main line of the Genesis story, the line that inherits the main Abrahamic promise. The Hittites and Hivvites, subsets of the Canaanites in the broad sense, are peoples we know from 23:1–20; 26:34–35; 27:46–47 and 34:1–31. Although the account of the Hittites in 23:1–20 was quite friendly, we already know from 26:34–35 and 27:46–47 that Esau's Hittite marriages were for some reason "a source of bitterness in spirit" to Isaac and Rebekah, and it was a Hivvite who defiled Dinah. Marrying a daughter of Ishmael could not be objectionable in the same way

9. Cf. Westermann, *Genesis 12–36*, 561.
10. Coats, *Genesis*, 246, 247.
11. Blum, "Jacob Tradition," 186.
12. Brayford, *Genesis*, 386.
13. Cf. Sarna, *Genesis*, 247.

(as 28:6–9 implies), but it is another mark of standing outside the main line of Yahweh's promise, which is working via Isaac. Paradoxically, the wives who by marriage do not come to belong to the line of promise seem to bear children without trouble.[14]

Genesis perhaps continues to backtrack (vv. 6–9) as it recalls how Esau relocated from Canaan, the area west of the Jordan, to the Seʿir highlands east of the Arabah, the area that will later be known as Edom. Presumably it was from the Beer Sheba area, where the story situated Isaac in Gen. 27–28, that he made this transition, and he thus simply moved some way to the southeast. But he thereby left the promised land, another appropriate indication that he does not belong to the main line of the Abrahamic promise. His move parallels Lot's move in Gen. 13. It simultaneously solves a problem and avoids conflict between Esau's growing clan and Jacob's growing clan, while also removing Esau from association with the main Abrahamic family. There seems again to be some slippage in connection with the passage's historical context and reference. Esau was already living there in Gen. 32–33, which implies that his relocation took place during Jacob's twenty-plus years in Harran. But in 35:29 he is in Canaan for Isaac's funeral, and these verses imply that his move took place when he and Jacob were both living in Canaan, so maybe the story in Gen. 32–33 locates Esau in Seʿir in light of his later move there. The narrative's taking up the motif from Gen. 13 perhaps makes it more likely that vv. 6–8 are a piece of creative writing,[15] but Esau might have been on the move between the region west and east of the Arabah, and vv. 6–8 may refer to a final move east.[16] Whatever is the right historical answer, the key point is that Esau has given up his place in the promised land. Genesis 36 keeps emphasizing that Esau is Edom.[17] Esau is not in Canaan. On the other hand, he is moving to a country that Yahweh is giving him as his assured possession, his *yərušâ* (Deut. 2:5; cf. Josh. 24:4). "The Esau (Edom) of the Old Testament is not one who is forsaken by God but the ancestor of a covenant people who is recognised in his way by God and the people of Jacob and provided with a genealogy of his own which both in Gen. 36 and 1 Chron. 1 is set forth in great detail alongside that of Israel. This should not be forgotten in arriving at the biblical interpretation of what is to be described as 'rejection' in contrast or rather in relation to election."[18]

36:10–14. There follows a more formal account of Esau's sons born by his different wives, and of his grandsons, though the list is not formulaic. Esau's line here works as follows:

14. Cf. T. Schneider, *Mothers of Promise*, 125.
15. Cf. Gunkel, *Genesis*, 377.
16. Cf. Qimchi, *Genesis*, on v. 6.
17. Cf. Assis, *Identity in Conflict*, 59–60.
18. Barth, *CD* 2.2:217.

Adah	Basmat	Oholibamah
|	|	|
Elipaz	Reʿuʾel	Yeʿuš, Yaʿlam, Qorah
|	|	
Teman, Omar, Sepo, Gaʿtam, Qenaz, Amaleq (also Qorah, v. 16)	Nahat, Zerah, Shammah, Mizzah	

As is the case with other lists in Genesis, some of the names (Teman, Qenaz, Amaleq) are more familiar as the names of clans or towns in the area south of Israel, so the list offers insight on the interrelationships of Israel with other peoples as well as providing snippets of family history. The account makes relatively friendly reference to Amaleq—relatively, in that he is the offspring of only a secondary wife, but so were many of Jacob's sons. It would have the same implication as the substantive treatment of Edom in this chapter: there is more to be said about Amaleq than is said in (say) Exod. 17:8–16.

36:15–19. The interest in clans becomes more overt; many of the names overlap with the names of individuals in vv. 10–14. The double mention of the Qorah clan might imply that it split and that the two parts linked up with different confederations. Verse 19 is the conclusion both to vv. 10–14 and to vv. 15–19.

36:20–30. It raises eyebrows that there now follows a list of people who were living in Seʿir before Esau arrived—people whom Esau's clan displaced, as Jacob's clan will displace the Canaanites (Deut. 2:12, 22). But the Horites' inclusion in the chapter implies that they were absorbed into Esau's clan and not simply driven out or slaughtered; absorption is regularly the pattern when one people group moves into the area of another (expulsion or slaughter is hard to effect; KSG). As Canaan was the eponymous ancestor of the Canaanites, so Seʿir gave his name to the area where his descendants lived. The Horites also featured in 14:6, but we know nothing else about them except what appears in these two biblical references. Possibly they were a local group related to the Hurrians, the Northern Mesopotamian people associated with the Hittites (as the Hittites of Gen. 23 were perhaps a local group related to the Hittites from the north).[19] They have names that look Semitic, but maybe they have assimilated to the local people's ways of speech.[20] If the inclusion in Genesis of the lines of Ishmael and Esau implies that in their way they are part of the outworking of Yahweh's promise to Abraham, then the inclusion of the Horites' clans implies a reaffirmation of a point implicit in Gen. 10–11, that people who are quite outside the Abrahamic line are not outside the story of God's work in the world.

36:31–39. The point is reaffirmed by the further inclusion of the list of Edomite kings, who represent the first stage of a fulfillment of the promise

19. Cf. von Rad, *Genesis*, 341.
20. Cf. Alter, *Genesis*, 205.

to Abraham in 17:16. When the Israelites wanted kings "like other nations" (1 Sam. 8:5), the Edomites were one nation they could have had in mind. We don't know when this sequence of kings begins or when it stops, though its reference to Israelite kingship indicates that it dates from Saul's time or later, which thus incidentally becomes the earliest time when Genesis could have been completed. The list indicates that Edomite kingship was non-dynastic, as was Israel's initially—that is, there was no necessary expectation that Saul should be succeeded by his son. Like Israel before David's time, Edom had no capital, and the king ruled from his hometown, like Saul.[21] We might guess that the process whereby successive Edomite kings came to the throne from a succession of different towns was analogous to the process whereby "judges" arose in Israel, and perhaps the authority of these kings was local rather than extending to the whole of Edom, like the authority of the "judges." Perhaps the last king in the list, Hadar, was the last king for a while because it was in his time that David took control of Edom (2 Sam. 8:13–14). In Solomon's day Edom asserted its independence and apparently had a hereditary monarchy (1 Kings 11:14). But in Jehoshaphat's day "there was no king in Edom" (1 Kings 22:47 [22:48]), though Edom later "set up its own king" and subsequently maintained its independence (2 Kings 8:20–22).

36:40–43. The chapter closes with another list of the clans of Esau/Edom. Speaking of the country as their holding (see the comment on 23:4) again suggests that they have secure possession of their land, as Israel has secure possession of its land.

21. Cf. Westermann, *Genesis 12–36*, 565.

39

How Joseph the Dreamer Comes to Be in Egypt

(37:1–36)

Overview

After the heading introducing these chapters as the story of Jacob's lines of descent, the chapter focuses on Jacob's son Joseph, who will be a key figure throughout Part Four of Genesis. The main part of the chapter is thus also the first scene in Act One of the account of Jacob's family line. It tells of Joseph's father's favoritism, his dreams of the family bowing down to him, his brothers' resentment, their selling of him into servitude in Egypt, and their reporting to his father that he is dead. It thus introduces motifs that will underlie interactions within the family through Gen. 37–50.

Translation

> 1So Yaʿaqob lived in the country where his father had resided as an alien, the country of Kenaʿan. 2These are Yaʿaqob's lines of descent.
>
> Yosep, as a seventeen-year-old, was pasturing the flock with his brothers; he was a boy with the sons of Bilhah and with the sons of Zilpah, his father's wives. But Yosep brought their father a report[1] about them that was bad.

1. While *dābâ* always has negative implications, to make this connotation explicit it can be qualified by *rāʿâ* (cf. Num. 14:37). There are no clear examples of its denoting a true report.

[3]Now Yiśraʾel loved Yosep most of all his sons, because he was the son of his old age,[2] and he made[3] an ornamented[4] coat for him. [4]His brothers saw that he was the one their father loved more than all his brothers, and they were hostile to him and couldn't speak of things being well for him.[5]

[5]Yosep had a dream and told his brothers, and they went on to be yet more hostile to him.[6] [6]He said to them, "Listen to this dream that I've had, please. [7]So there—we're binding sheaves in the middle of the open country. And there—my sheaf is getting up, yes, standing.[7] And there—your sheaves gather around, and they've bowed down to my sheaf." [8]His brothers said to him, "Are you really to reign over us? Are you really to rule over us?"[8] They went on to be yet more hostile to him because of his dreams[9] and because of his words.

[9]He had another dream and told it to his brothers. "There—the sun and the moon and eleven stars are bowing down to me." [10]He told his father and his brothers, and his father reprimanded him. He said to him, "What's this dream that you've had? Are we really to come, I and your mother and your brothers, to bow down to the ground to you?" [11]So his brothers were incensed at him, while his father kept the thing in mind.

[12]His brothers went to pasture their father's flocks at Šekem. [13]Yiśraʾel said to Yosep, "Your brothers are pasturing the flocks at Šekem, aren't they? Come on, I'll send you to them." He said to him, "I'm here." [14]So he said to him, "Go see if things are well with your brothers and if things are well with the flock, please, and bring back word to me." So he sent him from the vale of Hebron, and he came to

2. The Tg has varying versions arising from the fact that this description applies more naturally to Benjamin: see the comment.

3. I take the weqatal form to continue the circumstantial clause rather than as indicating that Jacob made these coats often (GKC 112h).

4. See Speiser, *Genesis*, 289–90. For *passîm* (which comes only in this chapter and in 2 Sam. 13:18, 19) the LXX and Vg have "multicolored," Aq "ankle-length," Sym "long-sleeved." *Pas* means "palm" or "sole," which might suggest either of the last two. See further Tal, *Genesis*, 168*.

5. Literally, "speak [of] him regarding *šālōm*." For *dabbərô*, the LXX, Vg have "speak to him," the Tg "with him," but this use of *dibber* with a direct object would be "strange" (GKC 115c) and unique or virtually unique (see BDB 181a). Following on their understanding of *dabbərô*, the LXX and Vg take *ləšālōm* to mean "peaceably," but even on that understanding of *dabbərô* it could as easily mean "regarding *šālōm*," and "regarding *šālōm*" is more likely if *dabbərô* means "speak of him."

6. The LXX omits the last clause, perhaps not recognizing that it is an anticipatory summary. Cf. Becking, "'They Hated Him.'"

7. The MT's accents make these two verbs qatal, but following the participle "binding" and the yiqtol "gather," I take them as participles, like the verb in v. 9.

8. Twice the verb is preceded by the infinitive of the same root, adding emphasis; vv. 11 and 33 have further occurrences of the idiom.

9. The plural might be anticipatory, as vv. 9–10 will tell of another dream; dreams come in twos in Gen. 37–50. And/or it might be pejorative ("him and his dreams!"). But the plural recurs in Dan. 2:2 as plural of extension, suggesting the parts of the one dream (cf. GKC 124), or abstract plural (Seebass, *Genesis*, 3:18).

Šekem. **15**A man found him: there, he was wandering about in the open country. The man asked him, "What are you looking for?" **16**He said, "It's my brothers I'm looking for. Do tell me, please, where they're pasturing." **17**The man said, "They've moved on from here, because I heard them saying, 'Let's go to Dotayn.'" So Yosep followed his brothers and found them at Dotan.[10] **18**They saw him from a distance, and before he got near them, they plotted against him[11] to put him to death. **19**They said one to another, "Here: that master of dreams is coming! **20**So now, come on, let's kill him and throw him into one of the cisterns. We'll say a wild[12] animal ate him. We'll see what will become of his dreams." **21**But Reʾuben heard them and rescued him from their hand and said, "We won't take his life."[13]

22So Reʾuben said to them, "Don't shed his blood. Throw him into this cistern that's in the wilderness. Don't lay a hand on him" (in order that he might rescue him from their hand and give him back to his father). **23**So when Yosep came to his brothers, they stripped Yosep of his coat, the ornamented coat that was on him, **24**got him, and threw him into the cistern (the cistern was empty; there was no water in it), **25**and sat down to eat.[14]

Then they lifted their eyes and saw: there, a caravan of Yišmaʿeʾlites coming from Gilʿad, their camels carrying spices, balm, and myrrh, going to take them down to Miṣrayim. **26**Yehudah said to his brothers, "What's the gain when we kill our brother and cover up his blood? **27**Come on, let's sell him to the Yišmaʿeʾlites. Our hands—they shouldn't be on him, because he's our brother, our flesh." His brothers listened. **28**So some Midyanite traders passed by, and they pulled Yosep out and got him up from the cistern. They sold Yosep to the Yišmaʿeʾlites for twenty silver pieces, and they brought Yosep to Miṣrayim.[15]

29So Reʾuben went back to the cistern, and there—Yosep wasn't in the cistern. He tore his clothes **30**and went back to his brothers and said, "The boy—he isn't there! And I—where am I going to go?"[16]

31They got Yosep's coat, slaughtered a goat, dipped the coat in the blood, **32**sent off the ornamented coat, had it come to their father, and said, "This, we found. Please recognize: is it your son's coat, or not?

10. Consonantally, the name is *dtyn* the first time (also with the locative ending), *dtn* the second time; the first is perhaps the original form, the latter a simplified Hebraized version (see Skinner, *Genesis*, 446).

11. For the hitpael with direct object, see 34:9 and the note.

12. Literally, "bad"; so also in v. 33.

13. Literally, "We will not strike him [as to] his life." The negative *lōʾ* (not *ʾal*) suggests that *nakkennû* is to be taken as yiqtol rather than cohortative; and see the footnote to 28:1.

14. Literally, "to eat bread."

15. What is the relationship of "Midyanites" and "Yišmaʿeʾlites," and who is the subject of the verbs in v. 28? I take "Midyanites" as a subset of "Yišmaʿeʾlites," and the brothers as the ones who pull up, get up, and sell Joseph; rather than the Midianites being a different group, and they being the ones who pull up, get up, and sell. See the comment.

16. Literally, "come."

[33]He recognized it. He said, "My son's coat! A wild animal has eaten him! Yosep has been mauled to pieces!"

[34]Yaʿaqob tore his clothes, put coarse cloth around him,[17] and mourned for his son for a long time. [35]All his sons and all his daughters[18] set about consoling him, but he refused to be consoled and said, "I will go down to Šeʾol to my son mourning." So his father cried for him.

[36]Meanwhile the Medanites[19] sold him to Miṣrayim, to Poṭipar, an official[20] of Parʿoh, the officer over the sentries.[21]

Interpretation

So Isaac has died (Gen. 35), and his elder son has done rather well for himself; his family has grown into a nation with kings, and they are well settled in their own land (Gen. 36). There now begins the account of the fortunes of Isaac's other son and his family, which are going to be much more complicated; Josh. 24:4 sums up the point in retrospect.[22]

In the MT Gen. 37 constitutes a complete unit, and it constitutes a complete chapter in modern Bibles, but it is only the beginning of a story; it sets the scene for Gen. 37–50 in a variety of ways. It begins to answer the question of how Jacob's clan came to be in Egypt despite the fact that Canaan was the country God promised them and the one in which they resided for three generations. It also begins to suggest part of the background to the recurrently tricky relationships between the Israelite clans (not least between the Joseph clans and Judah) and/or to encourage Israelites to reflect on those relationships. In beginning to open up such questions, it raises a series of questions of its own, which succeeding chapters will need to answer:

Will Joseph's dreams come true?
Can this divided family ever be united again?
Will Jacob ever discover that Joseph is alive?

17. Literally, "on his hips."

18. What daughters? Targum Ps.-J. assumes they are his daughters-in-law, and "daughters" could include "daughters-in-law," while Jub. 34.16 corrects to "daughter" (i.e., Dinah). But the odds are huge against Jacob having twelve sons but only one daughter, and 46:7 will refer to his daughters, of whom the plot has not required previous mention.

19. *Midyānîm* and *mədānîm* are variant ways of spelling a word for "arguments" (Prov. 6:19; 10:12; 18:18); the same is apparently true of the homonyms for this ethnic group.

20. Cf. the Tg; the LXX and Vg have "eunuch," which could provide background to his wife's fancying Joseph (Brayford, *Genesis*, 398), but this is likely a later meaning of *sārîs* (see *HALOT*; Redford, *Study*, 51).

21. The etymology of *ṭabāḥ* supports the LXX's "chief butcher," Tg. Onq.'s "head of the killers," but OT usage (e.g., Jer. 39:9) suggests that its meaning has become watered down (cf. the Vg).

22. Sarna, *Genesis*, 254.

What will happen to Joseph in Egypt, and specifically in the household of Pharaoh's officer over the sentries?

The chapter's alternating between reference to the Ishmaelites and the Midianites (and the Medanites) has been the starting point for seeing the chapter as combining J and E versions of the story.[23]

37:1–2aα. The account of Jacob's lines of descent begins with a reprise picking up Jacob's story after the long chapter about Esau. One might translate the opening of v. 1 as "but"; v. 1 functions as a footnote to Esau's story and also makes a link with what will now follow. It makes for a contrast between Esau's settling in Edom and Jacob's settling in Canaan (cf. v. 1 with 36:8), and it indicates that Jacob is free to live securely (cf. Tg. Ps.-J.) in Canaan because Esau is settled off to the east (cf. Gen. Rab. 84.1–5). The verb for "lived" (*yāšab*) is related to the word for "settlements" in 36:43 (*môšāb*), and "the country of Canaan" contrasts with "the country that is their [the Edomites'] holding" in 36:43. Verse 1 thus also notes a feature of the audience's life: whereas Esau's descendants have their proper home in Edom, Jacob's descendants have their proper home in Canaan. In addition, the reprise affirms a key point from the end of Part Three, that Jacob has come home to Canaan after his long absence in Harran, where he had "resided" as an alien; he is now "living" in Canaan, though he will not do so forever. So the verb "lived" suggests a comparison between Jacob and Esau and a contrast between Harran and Canaan. It also suggests a contrast with his father's relationship to the land, since he was often described as "living" in the Negev (e.g., 25:11) but not in Canaan proper; in 35:27 he was "residing" as an alien in Canaan. And the account thereby introduces the first great irony of Gen. 37–50, since the verse would make one think that Jacob's clan is now securely ensconced in Canaan. However, Gen. 37–50 tells another story, though one hinted at long ago by 15:13–16. The irony will emerge when the same formulation recurs in 47:27, at the beginning of Act Three in Gen. 37–50, which finds Jacob/Israel now "living" in Egypt.

The formal heading (v. 2aα) then corresponds to 25:19 in Part Three.

37:2aβb–4. As happened in Part Three, the account of Jacob's lines of descent now leaps forward to an event that introduces the entire narrative that will follow and will unfold over subsequent chapters. Jacob's clan is settled near Hebron (v. 14), where Isaac had been when Jacob arrived back from Harran (35:27).

If Joseph is seventeen (v. 2aβb) and he was born before Jacob's final stint in Harran (30:22–26), nearly a decade will have passed since the clan's return to Canaan. Whereas Benjamin would be barely ten and would be staying at

23. Schwartz ("How the Compiler of Genesis Worked") gives a detailed analysis, but see the critique in Watson, *Text, Church and World*, 46–59.

home, Joseph is old enough to be a junior shepherd, learning from his older brothers, though not old enough to go on a long trek with the flocks (vv. 12–14). He's still a "boy," a helper or servant, with some of Jacob's older sons. The sons of Jacob's secondary wives, Bilhah and Zilpah, were Dan, Naphtali, Gad, and Asher. As the youngest and as a mere teenager, he is "at the bottom of the heap in his family," just a lackey to Bilhah's and Zilpah's sons,[24] or (to put it more positively) a kind of apprentice.[25] The note about his being the junior of the family links the theme of Joseph's story with the story of Ishmael and Isaac and that of Esau and Jacob. Thus it is not surprising that the kid brother becomes the key figure in the story. His report about his brothers might refer to their shortcomings as shepherds, such as are implied in 29:7 or such as indicate that they fall short of the standards that Jacob expects and has claimed for himself in 31:38–41 (it might then relate only to the conduct of Dan, Naphtali, Gad, and Asher). But that understanding requires some inference. More likely v. 2b is one of Genesis's typical anticipatory summaries, and v. 4b will explain the bad report.[26] Either way, Joseph's reporting back to Jacob is the first piece of background to what will follow in this chapter.

The second piece of background (v. 3) is that Joseph's feeling free to pass on information to his father is matched or anticipated by Jacob's feeling free to be fonder of Joseph than of his brothers, and Jacob feels free to show it. Joseph's ornamented or long-sleeved or ankle-length coat, a "party-coloured coat,"[27] is the kind of garment worn by someone who does not need to work; Jacob treats Joseph like a prince (2 Sam. 13:18–19).[28] It is both surprising and not surprising that Jacob has not learned from the role that favoritism played in his parents' relationship with him and his brother and in his own relationship with Leah and Rachel. The explanation for the favoritism is doubly surprising. One would think that Joseph's significance lay in his being the long-anticipated son of Rachel, and one would infer that Jacob has transferred to him his feelings for the woman he really loved. The explanation would then not lie in his being the son of Jacob's old age; and as 44:20 recognizes, if anyone is the son of Jacob's old age it is Benjamin. But Joseph is also *a* son of Jacob's old age, and at this point the youngest of his working sons (in a traditional society, children may not "count" when they are very young because of the high rate of infant mortality). But this description of what Joseph means to Jacob may be an indication that again chronologically this note belongs earlier in Jacob's story, before Benjamin's birth, perhaps when the clan was still at Beth El. Indeed, perhaps the dream and its aftermath

24. So Frankel, *Five Books of Miriam*, 73.

25. So Pirson, "What Is Joseph Supposed to Be?"

26. Cf. Qimchi, *Genesis*, on v. 2.

27. Willet, *Hexapla in Genesin & Exodum*, 325: the expression means "variegated," but the resonances in modern English are noteworthy.

28. Gunkel, *Genesis*, 390.

happened back then, which would fit the reference to Joseph's mother in v. 10 and the geography of vv. 12–17.

What follows (v. 4) is illogical but not uncharacteristic of human instinct: Jacob's liking or love for Joseph generates the older brothers' dislike or hostility toward the object of Jacob's preference. And "hatred directed toward someone is like the strain in a bow: the resolution of the tension must issue in action."[29] Joseph's brothers simply can't speak about him in terms of *šālōm*. Already we know that something bad is going to happen to him. Ironically, in v. 14 Jacob will commission Joseph to investigate their *šālōm*, and in 43:27 Joseph will ask them about *šālōm* in connection with their father (cf. Exod. 18:7). Indeed, what will follow in this chapter suggests that not being able to speak of Joseph in connection with *šālōm* is a litotes; they could only speak of him in connection with putting him down. "Love unwittingly produces hate": it is the first instance of "the pivot of irony" upon which the entire plot of the Joseph story might be described as turning.[30] The Jacob family illustrates the dynamics of many a family, with someone loved too much, someone loving too much, and some people not feeling loved enough.[31]

37:5–11. There is yet a further piece of background and explanation for the story that will unfold. The narrative first summarizes what will follow in accordance with that common pattern in Genesis; it will go on to elaborate the point in the rest of the chapter. Again the story parallels the account of Isaac's lines of descent, which began with a revelation about the future and about the relationships of the subject's offspring. In 25:21–23 the revelation came because Rebekah had a pressing, possibly life-threatening question. Here, why does Joseph dream? But what else can you do when you are the youngest brother?[32] We might think of the dreams as "the notions of a vainglorious heart."[33] But people in a traditional society know that there is often more to dreams than wish fulfillment. If the audience has not heard the story before, it might not be sure whether to assume that Joseph's dreams are guides concerning what to expect in the chapters that will follow. So the dreams put in place the beginning of an arc of tension: will they find fulfillment? In 25:21–23 it is explicit that the revelation comes from Yahweh; here it is not (though Josephus in *Ant.* 2.2.3 makes it so). Neither there nor here is it said that the revelation concerns something Yahweh intends to make happen; in both passages it is simply something that will happen. In both stories Yahweh's will is put into effect through the fulfillment of the revelation, but both stories leave some wiggle room over whether the events that fulfill the revelation are directly Yahweh's will or issue from human actions that Yahweh has harnessed (see

29. Westermann, *Genesis 37–50*, 37. On the antonymous verbs, see the comment on 29:31.
30. Redford, *Study*, 73.
31. Brueggemann, *Genesis*, 300, referring to Laing, *Politics of the Family*.
32. Cf. Brueggemann, *Genesis*, 301.
33. Von Rad, *Genesis*, 346.

50:20). The dreams also parallel the revelations to Abimelek, to Jacob himself, and to Laban (20:3–7; 28:10–17; 31:10–13, 24), though those dreams were either the means of straightforward, literal communication or revelations of something supernatural lying behind earthly events; each of Joseph's dreams involves imagery that represents something else, something this-worldly and human, though it might not be difficult to work out at least part of what they represent. As well as leading into what happens in this particular chapter, Joseph's dreams introduce the motif of double dreams in Gen. 37–50. In sharing the dreams, Joseph shows a further incautious freedom of speech, with a result that is hardly surprising given the dream's content.

Joseph invites his brothers to imagine the dream as he relates it (vv. 6–7): "There . . . there . . . there." Three participles encourage them to see the scene unfolding before their eyes. "Joseph describes the dream in rhythmic, almost choreographic language. . . . He is full of his dream, which compels him to tell it to his brothers. In contrast, his brothers' reply is a cool, almost threatening question."[34] The story again presupposes that, as shepherds, the family is also involved in some sowing and reaping; the farming takes place in the open country since they do not own land. The narrative gives no direct hint of Joseph's understanding of the dream, though it may imply that he is either naive or full of himself in sharing it. But it does not directly suggest any disapproving of Joseph; in this chapter he becomes a victim who hardly deserves what happens.

In a broad sense the dream does not take much interpretation (v. 8), and the brothers assume that the answer to their rhetorical questions is "Yes, actually." They evidently and understandably find pejorative implications in the dream. It seems humiliating, though in the event its implications will be less so, and they may read too much into it: bowing down need not mean submission to someone's authority.[35] But ironically, it will be their pejorative reading of the dream that brings about its fulfillment in a way that saves their lives. The fulfillment will result from their speaking of Joseph in terms opposite to *šālōm*, but they will be grateful for the results. With hindsight, the listeners might see further significance in the imagery of grain harvest, because a grain harvest will be the cause of the brothers prostrating themselves before Joseph.[36] The more technical reference to Joseph's "reigning" might make an audience recall that a descendant of Joseph was the first person to reign over the northern kingdom of Israel (1 Kings 11:26), and the double reference to Jacob as Israel in vv. 3 and 13 (the only occurrences in Gen. 37–41) underscores that link.

Joseph recounts the second dream more briefly (vv. 9–11), but in the same listener-involving fashion: "there . . . bowing down." The meaning of the

34. Westermann, *Genesis 37–50*, 38; Westermann also describes the brothers as "testy."
35. Cf. Pirson, *Lord of the Dreams*, 47–50.
36. Cf. Qimchi, *Genesis*, on v. 7.

second dream is not as clear as that of the first, but in effect the brothers assume that it has a similar meaning. If the eleven stars stand for the brothers, then Benjamin is included. On the basis of the first dream, one could infer that Joseph "has internalized his most-favored status" among the brothers,[37] yet the second dream would go beyond that implication. With further incautious freedom of speech, Joseph tells his father about this dream. If Jacob's reference to Joseph's mother does not imply that this story belongs chronologically to an earlier stage in the Genesis narrative, perhaps Joseph's "mother" is Leah, as the female head of the family, or perhaps it is Rachel's handmaid Bilhah as his foster mother (cf. Gen. Rab. 84.11), or perhaps in Jacob's imagination (or metaphorically speaking) it is Rachel. In the event, neither does Jacob bow down to Joseph as his brothers do; it is Joseph who bows down to his father (48:12). There is often some slippage between revelations and their fulfillment, as b. Ber. 55 notes in connection with Joseph's dream.[38] Jacob treats the dream as if every element has a concrete meaning, but a dream need not be an allegory. As with stories "based on fact," one may not be able to press the details; yet with such stories the details may still be important, and the difference between the revelation and the event may be significant.

The response of Joseph's father and his brothers to the dream (v. 11) parallels their response in Gen. 34. There is no ambiguity about the brothers' reaction; there is some ambiguity about Jacob's. The reference to the brothers' fury (on top of the reference to their being unable to speak of *šālōm* in connection with Joseph) makes us expect them to take some action, as they do in Gen. 34. Our expectation will soon be fulfilled. Jacob's keeping the dream in mind suggests his wisdom in this connection and hints that the audience should join him in watching for the fulfillment. The rest of Gen. 37–50 indicates how Joseph's dreams do come true more or less in a way that they would not have if he had kept them to himself. If he is stupid and arrogant, this implication is not the angle on the story that interests Genesis.

37:12–20. So vv. 2aβ–11 have provided the background to the action that follows. As often happens, the shepherds must lead their flocks quite far from home to find pasture. Movements of some distance in connection with drought and/or from one season to another are a normal feature of shepherding, as earlier stories in Genesis have shown. With further irony, given that this story follows Gen. 34 (with two intervening chapters), the brothers first go to Shechem.

Jacob wants to check up on their *šālōm* (vv. 13–14; cf. v. 4); perhaps by implication Joseph recognizes the danger of venturing into the Shechem area. In what sense is he "keeping in mind" what we learned in vv. 5–11? Somewhat naively, neither Jacob nor Joseph realizes the potential danger of Joseph's

37. Brayford, *Genesis*, 391.
38. Cf. Qimchi, *Genesis*, on v. 10.

mission. Only here do we read of the "vale of Hebron," but there is undulating pastureland around Hebron, and Jacob's clan would be encamped in that pastureland, not living in the town. Shechem is several days' north of Hebron, a long way to go looking for pasturage, so this note may be another hint that the clan is actually still settled near Beth El.[39] Either way, Joseph walks or rides a donkey north; if he is starting from Hebron, he goes past his mother's tomb and past Beth El.

If Jacob knew that Joseph had gotten lost in the Shechem area (vv. 15–17), he would now have reason to worry about him. Why does God disregard both Jacob and Joseph, in letting the brothers treat Joseph as they do, so that Jacob grieves as he does? Joseph will later imply that God is looking the other way as an aspect of his implementing a plan to protect the entire family in due course.[40] The story raises suspense when things look as if they are going wrong, and we suspect that something nasty is going to happen when Joseph finds his brothers. It might be better if he doesn't find them and has to go back home. But the anonymous guide directs him to Dothan, another day's travel north along the mountain ridge, "where the pasturage is even finer than it is about Shechem."[41] There is hardly a basis in the chapter for identifying the "man" as another supernatural envoy (so Tg. Neof. and Tg. Ps.-J.); indeed, one might ask where now are the envoys, the camp, that protected Jacob earlier? The man's appearance is one of the coincidences on which the Joseph story depends.[42]

Now (vv. 18–19) "the point of view changes from that of Joseph, who is about to find them in Dothan, to that of his brothers, who see him coming before he sees them."[43] To judge from what we have already read, it is not the sight of Joseph that starts them thinking, for the first time, about giving vent to their fury toward him. But they are now miles away from his doting father, and they have the chance to take action. Surprisingly for someone on such a journey, but dramatically, Joseph is wearing the famous coat, as v. 23 will indicate. While the coat would help them recognize him from a distance, it is the dreams rather than the favoritism or the bad reports that have gotten to them.

A cistern (v. 20) is a large, deep, rock-hewn pit for collecting rainwater, which would be drawn by letting down a pitcher, as in a well. Throwing Joseph's body into one would mean no one would know what has happened to him. The idea that he has been killed by a lion or some other wild animal would be entirely plausible. Their own implicit answer to their rhetorical question concerning what will become of Joseph's dreams is that they will thereby avert

39. Cf. Skinner, *Genesis*, 446.
40. Cf. Luther, *Genesis 31–37*, 350, 351.
41. Driver, *Genesis*, 323.
42. Cf. Sarna, *Genesis*, 254.
43. Brayford, *Genesis*, 392.

their fulfillment. The First Testament (like other Middle Eastern writings) knows that a revelation about something to come is not an announcement of something inevitable but a warning or promise that requires a response from its recipients. But the brothers are stupid to think that killing the dreamer will kill the dream. As if you can hope to frustrate a dream in that way! Their response to it will actually facilitate its coming true, though eventually they will have reason to be glad.

37:21–24. Notwithstanding his action in 35:22, or perhaps in keeping with it, Reuben acts as the responsible eldest brother. Yet again Genesis first gives us a summary and then goes on to the particulars, beginning in v. 22. It is perhaps because Reuben is the eldest brother that he can say not "Let's not take his life" but "We won't take his life." He is making a strong negative declaration, like the ones in the Decalogue.

This cistern (v. 22) is empty. Perhaps Reuben just wants to give his little brother a nasty experience to teach him a lesson. Being thrown into a cistern is the opposite of having everyone bow down to him. And Reuben means to rescue him later. But perhaps Reuben invites the brothers to envisage Joseph dying of dehydration and starvation there—at least it will then mean that he died of natural causes; he was not directly murdered.

Reuben prevails (vv. 23–24). While it is indeed surprising that Joseph wears his princely coat while undertaking his errand, it would not be surprising if it does add to his brothers' bitterness,[44] and stripping him of it would give further expression to their resentment at their father's favoritism as well as aiding them in giving their alternative account of his fate. How terrifying that there should be such murderous hatred within God's family! But it is the way things have been within Israel, Judaism, Islam, and the church.[45]

37:25–28. Is there something callous about the apparent ease with which the brothers then sit down to eat? Are they solemnizing their mutual commitment (compare the meal in Gen. 31; KSG)? Either way, their dinner is interrupted. Ishmaelites and Midianites seem to be alternative names for the traders (cf. Judg. 8:24); another version of their name will feature in v. 36. Both groups are descended from Abraham (see 25:1–11 and the comment there). Here, perhaps Ishmaelites is a more general term for traders and Midianites a more specific ethnic term.[46] The Tg translates "Ishmaelites" as "Arabs,"[47] and an English writer could similarly move between referring to "Arabs" and (say) "Egyptians" or "Syrians." Like Jacob's clan some while ago, the traders are on the way from Gilead to Canaan; to be passing Dothan, they must have crossed from Gilead farther north than Jacob did when he had traveled on the east side of the Jordan as far as the Yabboq. And they are on their way further

44. Alter, *Genesis*, 213.
45. Seebass, *Genesis*, 3:28.
46. So Hamilton, *Genesis 18–50*, 423.
47. Cf. also Josephus, *Ant.* 2.3.3.

than Jacob's clan traveled. Their cargo would be of great value in connection with medicine, cosmetics, perfumery, and embalming.

Judah (v. 26) is perhaps assuming that one way or another Joseph is in danger of death, and like Reuben, he wants to rescue Joseph. But killing him will mean that his slain body cries out for redress. In theory, they can overcome that problem if they can cover over his blood so that it can no longer draw attention to itself (cf. Job 16:18; Isa. 26:21; Ezek. 24:7–8). But can they?

Further (vv. 27–28), Judah can think of a financial incentive for action that will still mean the brothers give expression to their resentment and also teach Joseph a lesson. So that's how Joseph ends up in Egypt, which for Joseph is preferable to being dead; it will also turn out to be preferable for Jacob's clan. The figure of twenty silver pieces fits ballpark figures for the sale of human beings in the Middle East and also fits the evaluation of a teenager such as Joseph if his parents dedicate him to Yahweh (Lev. 27:5)—on the assumption that a silver piece means a silver sheqel.

37:29–35. Reuben has apparently been away, perhaps scouting for pasture,[48] out with some of the sheep, or away bartering for food. He therefore cannot fulfill his plan to rescue Joseph and return him to Jacob. Tearing his clothes as a sign of grief perhaps implies that he assumes Joseph is dead. He doesn't know what to do now; more specifically, his words imply that he can't go home to tell Jacob. Presumably the other brothers tell him what has happened, though the narrative isn't interested in tying up such ends.

The important thing is how the news gets to Jacob (vv. 31–33), and what is the precise fake news that they are to send him. Once again the story is told in a brisk sequence of verbs: "got, slaughtered, dipped, sent off, had it come, said." Once again a role can be played by the hated coat, a symbol of Jacob's favoritism, Joseph's favored status, and their resentment.

Now it is Jacob who tears his clothes in grief (v. 34). He puts on the coarse clothing that one would normally wear only for work or in private; it is the sole reference in Genesis to this expression of grief. Jacob mourns thus for a long time.

It is not surprising that Jacob's daughters seek to comfort him (v. 35), though we have not heard of such daughters before; it is more noteworthy that Joseph's brothers—who could have revealed that the mourning was unnecessary—also do so. The consoling implies that they take part in mourning rites with Jacob. But he will not be comforted. The point is not that he refuses to cheer up; it is that he insists on carrying on living and dressing like someone in mourning (cf. the reference to mourning in 38:12).[49] The entire Joseph story is "rich in tears."[50] One can imagine that the brothers' resentment might increase the

48. So, e.g., Peter Comestor, *Scholastic History*, 82, as quoted by Schroeder, *Genesis*, 182.
49. Gunkel, *Genesis*, 394.
50. Gunkel, *Genesis*, 383.

more their action shows that they have solved nothing. Joseph is still the one who matters to their father. "I will mourn until I die," Jacob says. "He wants to go to Sheol with ashes still on his head and sackcloth on his loins."[51] It is the first reference to Sheol in Genesis; other references recur in connection with Jacob's grief in 42:38; 44:29, 31. While Sheol is not a place of suffering, it's a place of lifelessness, and the term lacks positive resonances. In connection with Abraham, Ishmael, and Isaac, Genesis has spoken of joining one's kin (25:8, 17; 35:29), an expression with more affirmative connotations. Jacob cannot look at death that way, though when he has discovered that Joseph is alive after all, he will do so (49:29). But "nothing further will now be said about Jacob for a long time. The timeless veil of sorrow sinks over his life for many years."[52] According to Genesis's figures, it will be over twenty years before he discovers that Joseph is alive (see Gen. 45). Perhaps the audience is invited to see an irony or an appropriateness in Jacob's having to live with the consequences of his sons' jealousy and deception.

37:36. Meanwhile, alongside Jacob's grim and mistaken belief, Genesis simply sets what looks like the not-much-less-grim actual facts, though they also make the listeners wonder what will happen next and wonder what Joseph is thinking and feeling. Genesis "speaks of him just as if he were dumb or a stone or a tree trunk." And what is God thinking, who "also kept silent"?[53] While Jacob's feelings are relevant to the plot, Joseph's are not so relevant,[54] and God's mind will be revealed in due course (50:20). That perspective indicates that in some sense the dream *did* come from God. Both Jacob and the brothers surely think that the dream is nullified. Only this single verse hints at another possibility.[55]

Medanites (v. 36a) come only here. Medan was another son of Abraham by Qeturah, like Midian (25:2). Ishmaelites, Midianites, Medanites: it's the coup de grâce of a confused and confusing story. The brothers want to kill Joseph and throw him into a cistern or just throw him into the cistern. Reuben wants to rescue Joseph but is missing at the vital moment. The brothers consider selling Joseph to some Ishmaelite traders, but they wait until after dinner, and some Midianites get to him first and sell him to the Ishmaelites, and they take him to Egypt—or was it the Medanites? The way the story is told conveys something of the bumbling nature of wrongdoers and the self-defeating nature of wrongdoing.[56] But switching from Ishmaelites to Midianites and then Medanites might catch the audience's attention in a suggestive way.[57] And

51. Gunkel, *Genesis*, 394.
52. Von Rad, *Genesis*, 350.
53. Luther, *Genesis 31–37*, 386.
54. Gunkel, *Genesis*, 394.
55. Brueggemann, *Genesis*, 298.
56. Cf. Reno, *Genesis*, 264–65.
57. Radday, "Humour in Names," 69–70.

Medanites and Midianites could simply be two ways of spelling the name of the same people; both words can also mean "arguments."[58]

Anyway, Joseph ends up being sold into a significant household in Egypt (v. 36b), and the story continues to provide the background for the story that will unfold through Gen. 37–50. The importance of Poṭiphar is that he has an important place on Pharaoh's staff. The story shows one way in which someone might become a bondservant. The brothers had no right to sell Joseph, and Middle Eastern law could view their action as so reprehensible that it would count it as a capital offense,[59] as will the Torah in due course (Exod. 21:16; Deut. 24:7). But once sold, a person has little chance of gaining their freedom, and there was a lively trade in the buying and selling of servants between Syria, Canaan, and Egypt.[60] The subsequent story (like Gen. 24) will show that a servant's position could be quite agreeable and be characterized by opportunity for achievement. In this sense, to speak of Joseph as a "slave" would be misleading.

Implications

What You Wear, How You Dream, What You Eat, How You Lie, How You Cry

Genesis 37 introduces five motifs that will run through Gen. 37–45 and beyond. All are themes that have been important already in Genesis; all are important human realities.[61]

In Gen. 37 Jacob's gift of clothing to Joseph is a sign of his special love and thus a provocation to Jacob's other sons. Removing it is therefore an expression of their resentment and a means of presenting it to Jacob to give the impression that Joseph has died. For Reuben and Jacob, tearing their clothes is a symbol of their grief, to which Jacob adds the wearing of coarse cloth as a sign of mourning. In Gen. 38 Tamar wears widow's clothes, abandons them for clothing that will give a misleading impression of her identity, then puts them back on. In Gen. 39 Potiphar's wife grabs at Joseph's garment, he abandons it, and it becomes a key piece of evidence in his indictment. In Gen. 44 the brothers tear their clothes in grief.

In Gen. 37 Joseph dreams twice, which establishes him as a dreamer. Revealing the dreams increases his brothers' antipathy toward him and makes them want to be rid of him, thinking they can thereby frustrate them. In Gen. 40 Joseph's fellow prisoners dream twice, and Joseph interprets their dreams,

58. See the translation note.

59. So Hammurabi's Code §14 (*ANET* 166).

60. See Sarna, *Genesis*, 261.

61. See further Matthews, "Anthropology of Clothing"; Huddlestun, "Divestiture"; Heffelfinger, "From Bane to Blessing"; Chapman, "Food."

which establishes him as a dream interpreter. His interpretations prove right, but it does not help him. In Gen. 41 Pharaoh dreams twice, which establishes the importance of the dreams' message. Joseph interprets it, which leads to his being put into a position of power. In Gen. 42 Joseph remembers his dreams and acts accordingly.

In Gen. 37 the brothers sit down to eat after they have sold Joseph into servitude. In Gen. 39 food is the only concern Potiphar retains. In Gen. 40 the dreams concern what Pharaoh drinks and eats, the dreamers are his butler and baker, and the climax of the story is a banquet. In Gen. 41 Pharaoh's dreams are all about food, and the key question is how Pharaoh can manage the sequence of there being more than enough and then not enough for people to eat. In Gen. 42–45 food is the reason why the brothers come to Egypt and thus the cause of their meetings with Joseph, and in Gen. 43 Joseph gives his brothers a spectacular meal.

In Gen. 37 the brothers plan to lie about Joseph's fate, which they themselves have engineered, and Reuben lies to them about his plan to rescue Joseph, though his deceit fails. In Gen. 38 Judah lives in a place called Deception, he deceives Tamar into thinking that his son will enable her to have children, and Tamar deceives him into thinking she is a prostitute. In Gen. 39 Potiphar's wife lies about Joseph and gets him put into prison. In Gen. 40 Pharaoh's butler makes Joseph a promise that he fails to keep. In Gen. 42–45 Joseph pretends not to be who he is, falsely accuses his brothers of being spies, and secretly puts their silver and later his chalice back in their bags.

In Gen. 37 Jacob cries as he grieves over the apparent death of Joseph. In Gen. 42 Joseph cries as Reuben tells his brothers that they are paying for the wrong done to Joseph. In Gen. 43 Joseph is overwhelmed when Benjamin arrives, and he needs to find somewhere private to cry. In Gen. 45 Joseph cries when he reveals himself to his brothers, and when the initial self-revelation and explanation is over, he cries again on Benjamin and on the rest of his brothers, and Benjamin cries on him.

40

Another Deceiver Is Deceived but Learns His Lesson

(38:1–30)

Overview

An inter-scene within this story in which Joseph is the prominent figure relates how Judah fails in his obligation to his daughter-in-law, Tamar. She had married his eldest son, and he had died. His next son had evaded his obligation to enable her to have children and had also died, so Judah had avoided marrying his youngest son to her lest he die too. But Tamar pretends to be a prostitute and tricks Judah into impregnating her. He acknowledges that he has done wrong and she has not, and she gives birth to twins (one of whom will be David's ancestor).

Translation

1At that time Yehudah went down from his brothers and turned aside
near a certain Adullamite; his name was Ḥirah. **2**Yehudah saw there the
daughter of a certain Kenaʿanite[1] (his name was Šuaʿ).[2] He got her and
slept with her.[3] **3**She became pregnant and gave birth to a son, and he

1. A number of versions of the Tgs take *kənaʿănî* to mean "merchant," as it sometimes does, which avoids attributing such a questionable marriage to the ancestor of the clan of Judah. Targum Ps.-J. doubly safeguards against the idea that Judah married a Canaanite by also telling us that Judah converted Shua's daughter, not that he married her.

2. The LXX takes *Šuaʿ* to be the woman's name.

3. Literally, "came into"; so also in vv. 8, 9, 16, 18.

named him[4] Er. **4**She became pregnant again and gave birth to a son and named him Onan. **5**Once more she became pregnant and gave birth to a son and called him Šelah. He was[5] at Kezib when she gave birth to him.

6Yehudah got a wife for his firstborn, Er; her name was Tamar. **7**But Er, Yehudah's firstborn, was bad in Yahweh's eyes, and Yahweh had him die. **8**Yehudah said to Onan, "Sleep with your brother's wife. Be a brother-in-law to her and raise up offspring for your brother." **9**Onan knew that the offspring would not be his, so if he slept with his brother's wife, he would waste it on the ground in order that he would not give offspring to his brother. **10**What he did was bad in Yahweh's eyes, and Yahweh also had him die. **11**So Yehudah said to Tamar his daughter-in-law, "Live as a widow in your father's household until Šelah my son grows up," because (he said), "So that he may also not die like his brothers." So Tamar went and lived in her father's household.

12Time went on, and Šua's daughter, Yehudah's wife, died. Yehudah found consolation and went up to the men who were shearing his flock, he and his friend[6] Ḥirah the Adullamite, to Timnah. **13**Tamar was told, "There, your father-in-law is going up to Timnah for the shearing of his flock." **14**Tamar put aside her widow's clothes from upon her, covered herself with a veil and wrapped herself up, and sat at the entrance to Enayim,[7] which is on the road to Timnah, because she saw that Šelah had grown up but she had not been given to him as wife.

15Yehudah saw her and thought she was a whore, because she had covered her face. **16**He turned aside to her by the road and said, "Come on, can I sleep with you?" because he didn't know that it was his daughter-in-law. She said, "What will you give me when you sleep with me?" **17**He said, "I myself will send a kid goat from the flock." She said, "If you give me a pledge until you send it." **18**He said, "What's the pledge I should give you?" She said, "Your seal and your cord, and the staff that's in your hand." He gave them to her and slept with her, and she became pregnant by him. **19**She set off and went and put aside her veil from upon her and put on her widow's clothes.

20Yehudah sent the kid goat by the hand of his friend the Adullamite, to get the pledge from the hand of the woman, but he couldn't find her.**21**He asked the people of her place, "Where's the hostess who was[8] at Enayim, by the road?" They said, "There's been no hostess here."

4. The SP, some medieval MSS, and Tg. Ps.-J. have "she named him," assimilating to v. 4.

5. The LXX's "She was" implies *wəhîʾ* for the MT's *wəhāyâ*.

6. The LXX and Vg's "his shepherd" presuppose *rōʿēhû* for the MT's *rēʿēhû* (so also v. 20).

7. To speak of a town's entrance is slightly odd (though cf. 1 Kings 17:10), and the Vg, Tg. Onq., and Tg. Ps.-J. take *petaḥ* to mean crossroads (in English one could say that Judah is indeed coming to a crossroads). In addition, the place name *ʿênayim* is otherwise unknown; it could mean "springs," which would be a plausible place name. But the description of the location makes for a double entendre (Hamilton, *Genesis 18–50*, 440, and his references) since "the entrance to Enayim" could also mean "the opening of eyes" (see the comment). It will also be for this reason that Enam (Josh. 15:34) is here called Enayim (cf. Bos, "Eyeopener").

8. I take the masculine *hûʾ* as predicative (see Tal, *Genesis*, 171*).

[22]He went back to Yehudah and said, "I couldn't find her. Moreover, the people of the place said, 'There's been no hostess here.'" [23]Yehudah said, "She can have it for herself, so that we don't become a laughing-stock. There, I sent her this kid goat, but you couldn't find her."

[24]About three months later, Yehudah was told, "Tamar your daughter-in-law has been whoring. Actually, there: she's pregnant through whoring." Yehudah said, "Get her out so she can be burned." [25]As she was being got out, she sent to her father-in-law, "It is by the man to whom these belong that I'm pregnant," and said, "Please recognize who is the one who owns the seal and the cord and the staff." [26]Yehudah recognized them. He said, "She is more faithful than me,[9] because of the fact that I didn't give her to my son Šelah." He didn't sleep with her[10] again.

[27]At the time of her giving birth, there—twins were in her womb. [28]When she was giving birth, one put out a hand, and the midwife got a red thread and tied it on his hand, saying "This one got out first." [29]But as he was taking back his hand, his brother got out, and she said, "How you've broken out for yourself!" So they named him[11] Pereṣ.[12] [30]Afterward his brother, who had the red thread on his hand, got out. They named him Zeraḥ.[13]

Interpretation

This story within a story is a self-contained narrative about Jacob's fourth son, who (the audience would likely know) will be the ancestor of the leading southern clan and of King David, and the places in the story (Adullam, Kezib/Akzib, Timnah, Enayim/Enam) are all in Judah. The story would thus have special interest for Judahite listeners. "Judah's lineage" is here "in jeopardy."[14] How did the sons of Tamar come to be the link between Judah and the clan descended from him? The answer is shocking. Judah's three older brothers have already disgraced themselves one way or another, and now Judah, the fourth, does so, having already emerged not very creditably from Gen. 37.[15] The story would make listeners in Judah and in Ephraim/Samaria smirk in

9. Such a confession might seem an understatement (cf. Jeremiah, "Reclaiming," 147), and the implication may be "she is the faithful one, not me" (cf. 1 Sam. 24:17 [24:18]; see *IBHS* 14.4e; and the translation note to 29:30). But usually *min* denotes comparison rather than absolute contrast (see *DCH*; GKC 133b).

10. Whereas vv. 1–9, 16, 18 use the expression *bôʾ ʾel* (come into) to signify having sex, v. 26 uses the verb *yādaʿ* (know/acknowledge).

11. While Judah might be the subject of the singular verb, it is several verses since he was mentioned, and elsewhere this verbal expression is impersonal (cf. 11:9; 16:14; 19:22; 25:30; 27:36; 33:17; 50:11). The SP and Tg. Ps.-J. have "she named," and the LXX implies this understanding.

12. "Breakout."

13. "Shining" (though Genesis does not note this name's meaning).

14. Kidner, *Genesis*, 187. See further Abasili, "Genesis 38."

15. Cf. Brett, *Genesis*, 113.

different ways. But Judah will play a key positive role in 43:3–10 and 44:14–34[16] and will share prominence with Joseph in Gen. 49, which anticipates the key position of Judah and Joseph in the southern and northern kingdoms. So how did it come about? Did he become a changed person?

At one level Gen. 38 is a placeholder that fulfills a parallel function to 26:1–33 in Part Three of Genesis. It suggests the lapse of time between the opening of Part Four's wider narrative in Gen. 37 and the next stage in its story, which will come in Gen. 39. It raises suspense as we wonder what will happen to Joseph now: the narrator "leaves the anxious reader to cool his heels for thirty verses."[17] Yet it has several links with its context. It is another story of deception,[18] though this time one of the brothers is the victim, and he deserves it. The connection between this story and the context finds more concrete expression in some verbal ties. Judah is told to "recognize" the seal, cord, and staff, and he indeed "recognized them," as Jacob was bidden to "recognize" Joseph's coat and "recognized" it (37:32–33; 38:25–26). Jacob could not be consoled over his bereavement; Judah was consoled over his bereavement (37:35; 38:12). Judah "went down" to Adullam; Joseph was "made to go down" to Egypt (38:1; 39:1). Er and Onan do what is bad in Yahweh's eyes, which in Onan's case involves sex; Joseph refuses to do what would be bad and would be an offense against God in the realm of sex (38:7–10; 39:9). The MT hints at these links by making Gen. 38 only a section within Gen. 38–40.[19] It is part of the story of Jacob's lines of descent (37:2); Jacob was prominent in Gen. 37, and we do not yet know that Joseph is going to be so prominent in the wider narrative as to make the chapter about Judah look out of place.

38:1–5. The note of time is vague; it might imply a moment soon after Joseph arrives in Egypt or a sequence of events that began some time before the events in Gen. 37. Either way, Gen. 38 covers more than a couple of decades, from Judah's marriage to a time when his youngest son is grown up, so it covers at least a similar period to the story of Joseph's down-and-up fortunes related in Gen. 37–41.

Likewise, the background to Judah's going to Adullam (v. 1) is unspecified; perhaps he was simply finding pasturage for some of the family flock (cf. v. 12, and the comment on 37:29). Adullam was a Canaanite town (Josh. 12:15; 15:35) a day's journey northwest of Hebron or several days southwest of Beth El or Shechem, within a more populated area of Canaan in the lowlands between the mountain ridge and the coastal plain. There need be no implication that Judah has gone to live there semi-permanently nor that he has no business associating with Hirah, though the precedent in Gen. 34 is

16. Cf. Fretheim, "Genesis," 592; Clifford, "Genesis 38."
17. Redford, *Study*, 75.
18. See Kruschwitz, "Type-Scene."
19. See, e.g., Fokkelman, "Genesis 37 and 38."

not promising, and neither is the aftermath in this chapter. The reason for mentioning Adullam and Hirah will emerge in vv. 12–23.

"Getting" a Canaanite girl (vv. 2–5) is a different matter. Genesis has assumed that Abraham's family should marry within the extended family. The verb "get/take" does imply marrying her; it is the regular expression for marriage (e.g., 11:29; 28:2, 6). But "seeing and getting" is a combination with unfortunate resonances (3:6; 6:2; 12:15; 34:2).[20] Kezib ("deception"!) looks like a variant on Akzib (Josh. 15:44); in a story such as this one, the name is significant.[21] It is a town an hour or two southwest of Adullam; presumably Judah is pasturing there too. Marrying the girl need not imply that he lived with her (cf. Judg. 15:1).

38:6–11. The story leaps forward fifteen or twenty years. Tamar is presumably another Canaanite from somewhere in the Adullam/Kezib area; Judah will later send her back to her father's household, which suggests that she is not a member of Jacob's clan. Judah's getting a wife for Er need not imply that the couple has no say in the matter; it means only that Judah takes the initiative as a father commonly would. But in this context, the idiom is telling: there is no reference to Tamar's having a say in this marriage or later in Onan's having sex with her, nor in his sexual practice or in her eventual return to her father's household until Shelah is of age.

The information that Er was bad in Yahweh's eyes (v. 7) might simply be an inference from his death at a young age. The narrator tells us nothing about how he died or how he was displeasing to Yahweh,[22] and he might have died of what Western thinking would call bad luck and/or natural causes. Yet the narrative sees it as Yahweh making him die or letting him die in a more direct or specific sense than this implies; narratives can make a distinction between a woman who simply gets pregnant or cannot get pregnant and a woman whose womb Yahweh opens or closes. But what Er did, and how Judah responded to his son's death, are irrelevant to the story's plot.

The convention behind Judah's expectations of Onan (vv. 8–10) is a variant on the one expounded in Deut. 25:5–10 and known in other traditional societies, though Judah does not require Onan actually to marry Tamar. Onan agrees to have sex on several occasions with Tamar and thus looks as if he is fulfilling the obligation expected of him, but he practices coitus interruptus and thus avoids impregnating her (the term onanism for masturbation rests on a misunderstanding of the passage). His thinking likely parallels that of Mr. So-and-so in Ruth 4, who declines to be Ruth's "restorer" because it will involve paying Naomi's debts and imperiling his own family. If Er remains childless, Onan inherits Er's share of the family estate. If Onan impregnates

20. Cf. Wenham, *Genesis 16–50*, 366.

21. Cf. Jerome, *Hebrew Questions on Genesis*, 76–77; cf. the footnote on Enayim in v. 14.

22. Jubilees 41.1–3 has Er refusing to have sex with Tamar because she was an Aramean, whereas Er's mother was a Canaanite.

Tamar, the child inherits Er's estate. His act is thus more cynical than that of Mr. So-and-so (who stood to lose from the estate he already possessed, not merely to forgo a prospective gain) and a less honest one, and he pays a more serious penalty than the public shaming that Mr. So-and-so has to accept.

So Tamar must wait until Judah's third son grows up (v. 11). It's odd that Judah sends Tamar back to her father's household; she is a member of Judah's family now. The explanation lies in what follows, but there is an ellipsis in the account of Judah's words and logic. Really, he is hoping that the problem will simply go away. Indeed, there is more than one ellipsis in his logic. He implies that his two sons' deaths are somehow Tamar's fault, whereas the narrator has made clear that it is theirs and God's.[23] "Judah is successful in protecting his son against contact with a 'dangerous' woman,"[24] but he is not fulfilling his duty as father-in-law to Tamar as a member of his family. As the story unfolds, he makes one decision after another that takes him further and further away from the faithful lifestyle that one would like to expect.

38:12–15. Again time passes. Shelah has grown up and has not married Tamar. Judah has lost his wife; we never discover her name, as we never discover the name of Mr. So-and-so in Ruth. As there may be a slur on him because he declines to fulfill his obligation, so there may be a slur on her because she is a Canaanite, but again the basis for including or omitting information in the chapter is how it relates to the plot. Whether or not the report implies that Judah's recourse to a whore is reprehensible, it does imply that it would have been reprehensible if his wife had still been alive.[25] But she has died, and Judah's time of mourning is over, and Judah is free to join in the sheepshearing celebration (cf. 31:19). The shearing is evidently done by experts, not by everyday shepherds, but a shepherd naturally shows up to watch and to join in the celebration. Timnah is another town in the lowlands, twenty miles north of Adullam and Kezib. It is lower in elevation (Samson goes "down" there: Judg. 14:1), so "going up" does not refer to a literal climb but to going "up-country" (cf. the translation note to 26:23).

Tamar needs to think about her future (vv. 13–14). She has seen Judah work out the implications of his fear for Shelah, reported in v. 11. His allegedly temporary sending of her back to her father's family is clearly not temporary at all. His neglect means that she and Er will never have children and will thus have no one to continue their line and no one to inherit from Judah. While v. 8 has indicated Judah's concern about Er, Tamar may also be concerned about herself and her own security. And she now moves from being someone who is acted upon to being someone who takes action, like Naomi and Ruth, to showing herself someone characterized by "resistance and resilience,"[26] who

23. Cf. Brett, *Genesis*, 114.
24. Van Dijk-Hemmes, *Double Voice*, 81.
25. Cf. Gunkel, *Genesis*, 399.
26. Siwila, "From a Father-in-Law," 148.

"reverses her position of powerlessness to one of power."[27] In the circumstances, what options does she have?[28] She will use her woman's body (which as such is liable to abuse) as a means of finding justice.[29] She will "stand on crooked and cut straight."[30] As is the case in some other traditional societies (including that of the other Tamar in 2 Sam. 13), in her culture women dress in a way that indicates their marital status, and Tamar removes her widow's garb. She then veils herself. The logic is not that a whore would veil herself; if anything, the opposite would be true.[31] But the veil would mean Judah cannot recognize her, and he can therefore think in terms of her being sexually available to him. Enayim ("Eyes") is likely the same place as Enam, in the same area (Josh. 15:34), somewhere between Adullam and Timnah. When Judah meets Tamar there, his eyes are closed in more than one sense, but Tamar will make the incident the means of opening them.[32]

38:16–19. Judah is perhaps ready for some further comfort after his wife's death, and the sheepshearing festival may be an occasion when people indulge themselves one way or another. Yet his not having brought his credit card with him suggests that his recourse to a "whore" was not premeditated. The First Testament has firm rules prohibiting adultery and implying disapproval of sex between two single people, but neither sort of rule quite forbids the action of Judah and Tamar.[33] It has no rule against a woman being in the sex trade or against a man paying for sex, and it can shrug its shoulders about it (e.g., Josh. 2:1; Judg. 16:1). While its predominant use of "whoring" as a metaphor for unfaithfulness to Yahweh does not indicate enthusiasm for it, Genesis is more concerned with Judah's likely unwillingness to have sex with Tamar because he is still uncaring about his family obligations to her. In the social context it might have been just as acceptable for a father-in-law to beget a son on his dead son's behalf as for a brother-in-law to do so.[34] One principle here, which the First Testament elsewhere accepts with its explicit brother-in-law obligation (Deut. 25:5–10), is that the protection of the family in the long term is at least as important as the protection of the individual; another may be that a family has an obligation to do what it can to enable a wife such as Tamar to become a mother (KSG). Tamar is manipulating Judah into doing what he should do.

27. See van Dijk-Hemmes, "Tamar," 150. On the positive picture of Tamar in Jewish interpretation, see Reif, "Early Rabbinic Exegesis," 231–32.

28. Cf. M. Jacobs, *Gender, Power, and Persuasion*, 189–92.

29. See García Alfonso, "El silencio del cuerpo."

30. Lewis, "'You Have to Stand.'"

31. See paragraph 40 in the Middle Assyrian Laws (from a little later than the setting of the Joseph story) in *ANET* 180–88, esp. 183; cf. Sarna, *Genesis*, 268.

32. See the translation note to v. 14.

33. But contrast the critique of Judah in Jub. 41.23–26 and the warning about following his example.

34. See paragraph 193 in the mid-second millennium Hittite laws, in *ANET* 188–97, esp. 196; cf. Sarna, *Genesis*, 266.

The fee (vv. 16–18) seems large, but the pledge seems larger; Judah's "cavalier" attitude[35] reminds one of Esau. Both surrender something vital to their identity for a momentary satisfaction (and both married Canaanites). No wonder Judah is embarrassed in due course. A person's seal, made of stone or metal, was a personal identifier worn on a cord around the neck and used for impressing on clay, in the manner of a signature. The staff is a less formal sign of a person's status. Herodotus reports that a Babylonian carried a seal and a carved staff with a distinctive image.[36] Taking his seal and staff would guarantee that Judah will return with the goat to collect the pledges. For Tamar, they are the items that will identify the man who had sex with her. The brisk sequence of verbs—"he gave, he had sex, she became pregnant," continued in "she set off, she went, she set aside"—recalls the brisk sequences in vv. 2–3 and in 34:2 in not-dissimilar contexts.

38:20–23. Events then mystify Judah, and the Judahite or Ephraimite audience grins some more. Does Judah get the Adullamite to do his work to avoid scandal? The narrator refers to Tamar simply as "the woman," as if he is using the expression Judah would have used. "She is simply a woman with whom he had a tryst."[37] He of course does not know she is Tamar, his daughter-in-law.

The Adullamite (v. 21) now describes her as a hostess, a *qədēšâ*. Etymologically this word suggests a holy woman, someone engaged in a ministry of some kind at a sanctuary. Applying the term to a woman engaged in the sex trade could imply someone with a role in a sanctuary involving sexual activity, such as an enacted prayer for fertility. So maybe there was a sanctuary at Enayim, and maybe the Adullamite is implying that the woman to whom Judah is in debt is such a person. The term might make his question more respectable in a Canaanite context but not in a Torah-abiding Israelite context, where a Canaanite hierodule is indeed simply a whore (see the parallelism in Deut. 23:17–18 [18–19]; Hosea 4:14) or something worse (cf. *zônâ* in Gen. 34:31 and the comment there). But it is hard to find evidence that "sacred prostitution" existed in Israel or elsewhere in the Middle East, and there is no hint in the context here that such a hierodule might be present and available to someone coming to the festival or that a regular whore might hang around at the sanctuary hoping for trade. More likely *qədēšâ* is a more polite term for a woman who is sexually available outside the framework of regular community and familial life.[38]

Either way (vv. 22–23), Judah doesn't want the Adullamite to make ongoing inquiries in the town and make it look as if somehow a whore has made a fool of him and robbed him of key possessions.

35. Frankel, *Five Books of Miriam*, 77.
36. Herodotus, *Histories* 1.195.2; cf. Skinner, *Genesis*, 454.
37. Hamilton, *Genesis 18–50*, 446.
38. See DeGrado, "*Qdesha*," and the references in the article.

38:24–26. The truth now starts to come out. The scene is back home, wherever that is—somewhere such as Adullam or Kezib.

Getting pregnant (v. 24) is a hazard of being engaged in the sex trade, and the First Testament can also shrug its shoulders about that fact (1 Kings 3:16–28), though some shame attaches to being the offspring of a prostitute (Judg. 11:1). But Tamar wanted to get pregnant. With some irony, once-off sex between her and Judah produces a pregnancy when regular sex with Er and Onan did not. At three months pregnancy starts being rather certain, and soon afterward it becomes hard to conceal (cf. the Vg, which has the reporters describing Tamar as having an enlarged belly). If anything, Tamar is interested in her pregnancy becoming public, not in hiding it. So someone takes the news to Judah from the town where she lives in her father's household, and Judah comes to the town. Is it his business because she has been betrothed to Shelah, or do her widow's clothes mean she is still reckoned to be bound to Onan (in either case, despite her having gone back to her father's household)? As well as not prohibiting prostitution, the Torah does not prescribe any punishment for it or describe any prostitute being punished. It does prescribe the burning of a man who has sex with a woman and also with her daughter, along with the burning of them, which is ironically close to what has happened in Gen. 38, and it also prescribes the burning of a priest's daughter who acts as a whore (Lev. 20:14; 21:9). Hammurabi's Code §157 prescribes burning for having sex with one's widowed mother.[39] But such rules in Hammurabi and in the Torah are more like statements about theological ethics and social standards (ways of saying how bad such actions are) than rules for the elders at the town gate simply to implement, and Judah's declaration with its "naked unreflective brutality"[40] may not be intended literally. Nevertheless, Judah is presupposing the common assumption that there is one standard for men and another for women.[41]

So Tamar is brought out (v. 25), as a girl who is found not to have been a virgin when she married is to be brought out to the entrance of her father's house for stoning and as a couple who have sex when the girl is betrothed to someone else are to be brought out to the town gate for stoning (Deut. 22:13–24). Tamar is brought out to be exposed and at least shamed, but dramatically, when all attention is on her and when Judah is there, the shaming turns out to work in another direction.

The account of Judah's reaction (v. 26a) is compressed; it parallels the ellipsis in v. 11. His initial words will be paralleled by David's simple acknowledgment "I have done wrong in relation to Yahweh" (2 Sam. 12:13). Tamar is the faithful one (*ṣādəqâ*).[42] Words related to this verb have earlier been translated

39. See *ANET* 172.
40. Alter, *Art of Biblical Narrative*, 9.
41. Cf. Kidner, *Genesis*, 189.
42. This declaration is the starting point for Blachman's study, *Transformation of Tamar*.

by the words "faithful" and "faithfulness" (e.g., 6:9; 15:6; 18:19), and that connotation continues to apply here. In being willing to have sex with Onan and in waiting for Shelah, Tamar has been faithful to God's expectations of a woman whose vocation is to build up her family and that of her husband, and she has thus been faithful to Er. But *ṣādēq* can have quasi-legal connotations, "to be acknowledged as faithful," "to be in the right" (e.g., Isa. 43:9, 26; Ps. 51:4 [51:6]), and these connotations fit the present quasi-legal context where Judah has declared a quasi-legal judgment on Tamar. He thought that he was in the right and she was in the wrong, and he demanded her execution, but he has been exposed and shamed. The exposure and shaming do not relate to having recourse to a prostitute. Nor do they relate to having had sex with his daughter-in-law, which social convention would generally prohibit in a way that the Torah will in due course ratify (Lev. 18:15). Having sex with Tamar was legitimate to the end that Tamar needs, and Judah now acknowledges it and leaps to the recognition of Tamar's being uniquely in the right. There is a further parallel in the David story as Nathan's parable, like Tamar's acted parable, will help David make the leap to acknowledging that he is in the wrong. The present story marks a stage in the development of Judah as a person "from someone who advocates for the sale of Joseph, to a man who later stands up as a substitute for his younger brother," a transformation in which Tamar plays a key role.[43]

The closing assurance that Judah did not sleep with Tamar again (v. 26b) might imply that sex with her is an element in his guilt: although he did the right thing, it was for the wrong reason and/or in the wrong way, and he recognizes his wrongdoing and does something about it. In this sense he repents (Jub. 41 makes his repentance more explicit), and here David's action will not match Judah's. But the reference to not sleeping with her again more directly presupposes that sex with his daughter-in-law was legitimate as a means of fulfilling a family obligation, even if it was irregular, and it should have been Shelah who took this action. But Tamar will not need to allow anyone else to have sex with her unless she agrees to undertake another regular marriage. Perhaps the note indicates that Tamar is then restored to her position in Judah's family. We do not learn what now happens to her or about her ongoing relationship with her two sons and with Judah and with Judah's family, though her son does appear in David's genealogy in Ruth 4:18–22.

38:27–30. One might have thought that Genesis was not interested in the fruit of this shady union. Actually, the theme of propagating a family is of key importance to the story.[44] Indeed, the birth of the children is perhaps the validation of Judah's declaration that Tamar is the faithful one.[45] The

43. Adelman, *Female Ruse*, 5; cf. 68–89.

44. See D. Kim, "Structure of Genesis 38," 554.

45. Cf. D. Lim, "Study on the Re-canonicity of Genesis Chapter 38," 14.

account of birthing that closes the chapter forms no anticlimax for Judahites listening to this story.

First (v. 27), Tamar turns out to be someone like Rebekah (v. 27). Whereas she apparently didn't have the troublesome pregnancy that Rebekah had, it transpires that she too is pregnant with twins. In her case this is discovered only at the birth.

And her babies turn out to be like Esau and Jacob (vv. 28–30). During this birth, in a way similar to the earlier one, one of the twins stretches out his hand as they are born. If a baby threatens to emerge hand or foot first, the situation is mortally dangerous for babies and mother,[46] but things turn out fine. The one who would have been designated the elder son puts out a hand, but then falls back and (as in the Rebekah story) the one who would have been the younger son pushes him out of the way. Yes, the breakout boy is rather like the heel-grabber.

Implications

The Right Thing for the Wrong Reason

"Why did God and the Holy Spirit want to have these shameful and abominable matters written and preserved to be recounted and read in the church? . . . Who would believe that the teaching of such matters can be useful for the salvation and edification of the church?" Yet "examples of this kind are recounted to us for the purpose of teaching and consolation, and for the strengthening of our faith, in order that we may consider the immeasurable mercy of God, who has saved not only the righteous . . . but also the unrighteous." The story gives background to the fact that "Christ, then, participates in the blood of the Canaanites . . . in order that He may bear witness at the very beginning that He does not reject the Gentiles, whom He has received and has deigned to assume into His person."[47] The breakout boy turns out to be an ancestor of David (see Ruth 4:18–22; 1 Chron. 2:1–17) and thus of Jesus (Matt. 1:1–17).

The inclusion in Genesis of this chapter about Judah thus has a paradoxical effect. Ruth and 1 Chronicles belong in the Second Temple period, so maybe anyone in the First Temple period listening to other stories that now appear in Genesis would be unaware of this juicy piece of information, but people listening in Second Temple times might know and might enjoy another grin.[48] And if they sneered at the Ammonites and Moabites as they listened to the story in 19:30–38, they would need to recognize that their sneers have come home to roost. The story reflects the importance of Judah's clan, yet it brings discredit

46. Cf. Luther, *Genesis 38–44*, 47–48.

47. Luther, *Genesis 38–44*, 10–11, 18.

48. But on actual Jewish interpretation of the story, see Reif, "Early Rabbinic Exegesis."

on Judah. And in a paradoxical way it also brings glory to Jesus as the descendant of Judah who was willing to be born of and associated with this clan.[49]

Perhaps it is Tamar's appearance in Jesus's genealogy that encourages Ephrem when he "reads Tamar as a heroine, perhaps even something of a holy fool, who eschews sexual mores in an effort to obtain the 'blessing' of Judah and thereby a role in the lineage of Christ."[50] The story is not explicit about her seeking to turn Judah around, but she does so. And thus the story also indicates that even someone like Judah, who behaves in a faithless way, can be turned around. "What seems the simple satisfaction of sexual hunger for Judah is, in fact, the redemption of his future."[51] And not just of his future, but of Tamar's and of ours, even if he does unwittingly illustrate the awareness expressed by Thomas Becket in T. S. Eliot's play *Murder in the Cathedral*:

> The last temptation is the greatest treason:
> To do the right deed for the wrong reason.

Judah does the right thing for the wrong reason, but God brings extraordinary fruit from his action, in Judah's life, in Tamar's, and in ours. Joseph's later judgment about the way human wrongdoing can be Yahweh's means of fulfilling his purpose (50:20) is already embodied in Yahweh's working through Judah's marriage to a Canaanite and his recourse to an apparent whore and through Tamar's deception.

49. Cf. Calvin, *Genesis*, 2:277–78.

50. Wickes, "Ephrem's Interpretation of Genesis," 60. Cf. also Chrysostom's comments, *Homilies on Genesis 46–67*, 199–200.

51. Reno, *Genesis*, 267.

41

How Joseph Is Put in Jail, but Yahweh Is with Him

(39:1–20a)

Overview

Scene 2 in the Joseph story relates how Yahweh enables Joseph to do well in Potiphar's household but how he then falls afoul of the attentions of Potiphar's wife and ends up in jail. Although Judah did the wrong thing and good came out of it, Joseph does the right thing and trouble comes out of it. Tamar used her sexuality one way; Potiphar's wife uses her sexuality another way.

Translation

1So Yosep had been taken down to Miṣrayim and Poṭipar, an official of Parʿoh, the officer over the sentries, a Miṣrayite, had acquired him from the hand of the Yišmaʿeʾlites who had taken him down there.

2But Yahweh was with Yosep, and he became a successful individual.
He came to be in the household of his Miṣrayite lord, **3**and his lord saw
that Yahweh was with him and that Yahweh was making succeed[1] in his
hand everything that he was doing. **4**So Yosep found favor in his eyes,
and he attended on him. He appointed him over his household and put
into his charge everything that belonged to him. **5**From the time that he
appointed him in his household and over everything that belonged to
him, Yahweh blessed the Miṣrayite's household on account of Yosep.
Yahweh's blessing was on everything that belonged to him, in the house
and in the fields. **6**He abandoned everything that he had into Yosep's

1. Verse 2 used the hiphil of *ṣālaḥ* in a declarative sense; vv. 3 and 23 use it in a causative sense.

charge, and with him he did not acknowledge anything except the bread that he was eating.

Yosep became handsome in body and handsome in look, **7**and subsequently[2] his lord's wife lifted her eyes to Yosep and said, "Do sleep with me."[3] **8**But he refused. He said to his lord's wife, "There, with me my lord doesn't acknowledge what's in the house, in that everything that belongs to him he has put in my charge. **9**There's no one bigger in this household than me. He hasn't kept back from me anything except you, because you're his wife. So how could I do this exceedingly bad thing and do wrong in relation to God?"[4] **10**When she spoke to Yosep day after day, he didn't listen to her by sleeping beside her, by being with her.

11But on this day[5] he came into the house to do his work, and none of the people of the household was there in the house. **12**She caught hold of him by his coat, saying "Do sleep with me." He abandoned his coat in her hand, fled, and went outside. **13**When she saw that he had abandoned his coat in her hand and fled outside, **14**she called the people of the household and said to them, "Look,[6] he brought us an Ibrite man to play around with us! He came in to me[7] in order to sleep with me, and I called out in a loud voice. **15**When he heard that I raised my voice and called out, he abandoned his coat with me and fled, and went outside."

16She put his coat down with her until his lord came home, **17**and she spoke to him in the same words: "The Ibrite servant that you brought to us came to me in order to play around with me. **18**When I raised my voice and called out, he abandoned his coat with me and fled outside." **19**When his lord heard[8] the words that his wife spoke to him, "These are the very things that your servant did to me," his anger blazed. **20a**Yosep's lord got him and put him in the roundhouse,[9] the place where the king's prisoners were confined.

Interpretation

The main story returns to Joseph and moves back chronologically. It takes up the question raised at the end of Gen. 37: what will happen to Joseph in

2. See the footnote to 22:1.
3. Potiphar's wife uses the lengthened form of the imperative here and in v. 12.
4. The Vg has "my God."
5. That is, this particular day that we are now to hear about. The construction at the beginning of v. 11 compares and contrasts with that in v. 10: both begin *wayəhî kə*. The construction recurs in vv. 13, 15, 18, 19. The unusual non-elision of the article in the expression *kəhayyôm* clarifies the significance of the *kə*.
6. Genesis uses the imperative verb rather than the particle *hinnēh*, suggesting that she is urging people actually to look at the garment.
7. In 38:8–9 and elsewhere the Hebrew expression is a term for having sex, and the context will hint at this connotation here and in v. 17.
8. The Vg makes explicit that he listened too well.
9. The LXX translates "fortification," which no doubt it was.

Egypt, and specifically in the household of Pharaoh's officer who is over the sentries? First he flourishes, but then disaster happens. The medieval chapter division follows the MT in taking Gen. 39:1–23 to compose the second of three sections comprising Gen. 38, 39, and 40, but actually 39:20b is the beginning of another narrative sequence that repeats the sequence in 39:1–20a, so I treat the units as 39:1–20a and 39:20b–40:23.[10]

39:1–20a	39:20b–40:23
so Joseph has been sold into servitude to Potiphar	so Joseph has been put in jail by Potiphar
but Yahweh is with him	but Yahweh is with him
making things succeed for him	making things succeed for him
thus he proves to be an able head of the household	thus he proves to be an able head of the jail
subsequently he impresses Potiphar's wife	subsequently he impresses Pharaoh's officer
but she betrays him	but he lets him down
and Joseph ends up in jail	and Joseph ends up stuck in jail

Genesis 37 had the shape of a tragedy: whereas there seemed to be no reason why the future should not work out well for Jacob and his line, through Joseph's sharing his dreams and his brothers' reaction, Jacob's story fell apart, the family came to be sullied by conflict and deceit, and Joseph ended up in exile and in servitude. At first it looks as if 39:1–20a will have more the shape of a comedy as it takes Joseph from servitude to success. But the comedic plot does not reach resolution; Joseph is successful but is still an exile in servitude. Even the impression that things have turned a corner is false; the movement of the story continues to be downward. But the key role played by the fact that Yahweh is with Joseph provides a basis for hoping that exile, servitude, and imprisonment may be reversed. For Judahites in exile or in dispersion, not least in Egypt, a story about the possibility of being faithful yet successful could be an inspiration.[11] Genesis 39:1–41:57 will in fact portray the varied possible experiences of someone who becomes hostage to the empire. One might become its victim (39:1–20a). One might be let down (39:20b–40:23). But one might eventually triumph (41:1–57).

39:1. The opening verse makes for a parallel with 38:1: Joseph goes down (*yārad*) as Judah did, though Joseph does so involuntarily—he is made to go down. It more systematically resumes from Gen. 37 after the inter-scene in Gen. 38. The double reference to Joseph's being "taken down" also picks up the use of that verb in 37:25 in connection with the Ishmaelites. To them, Joseph had been just another piece of cargo. The point is underlined by the

10. Cf. Coats, *Genesis*, 276–81.

11. See H. Kim, "Reading the Joseph Story."

reference to his becoming simply something that Potiphar "acquired." Conversely, there is a slight slur involved in referring to someone important like Potiphar as "a certain Egyptian" (*ʾîš miṣrî*).

39:2–6a. Little has prepared the audience for the turnaround in Joseph's fortunes that now follows, though it does parallel his father's experience when he took flight from Esau. It is a total turn around: "everything . . . , everything . . . , everything . . . , everything . . . , everything" (vv. 3–6a). First he comes to be working in the house rather than outside (v. 2), then he does well in his work in the house and comes to be working for Potiphar personally (vv. 3–4a), then he is appointed over the affairs of the entire household and Yahweh blesses the household and matters outside it (vv. 4b–5), so that the final result is that Potiphar leaves everything to Joseph (v. 6a).

Yahweh is "with" Joseph, and it is something Potiphar can see (vv. 2–3). It is an objective fact that makes a difference to a person's outward circumstances. The result is spelled out in terms of success. Four times Abraham's servant had referred to Yahweh making him successful in his commission to find a wife for Isaac (Gen. 24:21, 40, 42, 56); three times this chapter refers to Joseph's success on a broader front. It seems that originally Joseph works outside, but then Potiphar brings him in to work inside the house,[12] but it will be his undoing. Presumably his initial work involves menial chores, but he shows his potential in the way he accomplishes them.

Speedy promotion follows (v. 4). Though "found favor" can imply something inexplicable (as is suggested by the traditional translation "found grace"), Potiphar's favor is quite explicable, though the phrase nevertheless implies something astonishing, in the circumstances. So Joseph becomes personal assistant to Potiphar: "attend on" (*šārat*) will describe Joshua's position in relation to Moses and Elisha's in relation to Elijah (Exod. 24:13; 1 Kings 19:21). A man like Potiphar will possess quite an estate, and Joseph comes to be in charge of the estate as well as the house.

And Potiphar experiences the results of Yahweh's being with Joseph (vv. 5–6a). There is a contrast between saying that Yahweh is with Joseph and that Yahweh blesses Potiphar:[13] while the former implies a personal relationship, the latter implies things going well in the concrete realities of life. It is the first and only time in Genesis that Yahweh blesses people outside Abraham's family, if we count Laban as within the family (see 30:27, 30)—though there is a parallel between Jacob bringing blessing to Laban and Joseph bringing blessing to Potiphar,[14] and with things going wrong later. But Joseph's doing so is in keeping with the recurrent references in Genesis to blessing coming to the nations through Abraham and his family, so the idea that blessing comes

12. Cf. Skinner, *Genesis*, 457.
13. Cf. Westermann, *Genesis 37–50*, 63.
14. Cf. Ephrem, *Genesis*, 185.

to the Egyptians on account of Joseph is significant. "In every place in which the righteous go, a blessing goes along with them" (Gen. Rab. 86.6). Potiphar's abandoning (*ʿāzab*) concern with anything into Joseph's hand or charge, as opposed to merely putting this concern into Joseph's hand or charge (vv. 4, 8), testifies to the quality of Joseph's work, though in light of what follows in vv. 6b–10 it raises the question of whether he was being irresponsible and in particular should have paid as much attention to his wife's needs as he did to his stomach's needs. Perhaps he needed to keep an eye on the kitchen because "the Egyptians could not eat a meal with the Hebrews because this would be an offense to Egyptians" (43:32). Hands will continue to be a key motif in this story (vv. 1, 3, 4, 6, 8, 12, 13): Joseph's fate lies in his hand and in the hand of other people.[15]

39:6b–10. There now begins the long account of how things go wrong for Joseph, paralleling the account in Gen. 37, which 39:1 summarizes.

Joseph has inherited his mother's looks (vv. 6b–7; cf. 29:17). He is growing into a handsome young man, and Potiphar's wife (Zuleika, according to later tradition)[16] eventually notices and pays attention. Proverbs 1–9 frequently warns young men about the possibility of being seduced by another man's wife (e.g., 2:16–19; 5:1–23; 6:20–35; 7:1–27). It is a pressure that a young man with average hormones might find hard to resist.[17] Joseph (who is now nineteen or twenty or so) might have been expected to yield to the blandishments of Potiphar's wife, in which case the story might have worked out in a different way (or might not). In Proverbs and here, there may be other pieces of background to what happens. "Subsequently" presumably denotes Potiphar's abandoning all responsibility in the household to Joseph—including his wife. Perhaps she consequently has a sense of being neglected and of longing for a relationship with a man. If Joseph had not been handsome, or if Potiphar had been paying attention, or if his wife had not been lonely. . . . Perhaps all three conditions are fulfilled. Do "Potiphar's wife and Tamar provide two models of the feminine": one sensual and verbally aggressive and tempting, the other a marginal figure who turns the weakness of her position into a source of strength?[18] Yet Genesis makes no comment on the woman's attractiveness. Further, an audience knowing that the word for official (*sārîs*) also means "eunuch" might have allowed itself a sardonic grin: what would you expect of the poor woman (and how stupid was Potiphar leaving a handsome young man alone with her in the house)? In her situation and need, is his wife so different from Tamar?[19] Western readers would be inclined to assume that she is

15. Cf. Brueggemann, *Genesis*, 314–15.

16. See, e.g., the late medieval midrash *Sefer HaYashar* on the passage: Noah, *Book of Jasher*, 140.

17. Cf. Luther, *Genesis 38–44*, 75–86.

18. So S. Niditch in Eskenazi and Weiss, *Torah*, 226.

19. Cf. McKay, "Confronting Redundancy," 218.

interested in sex for sex's sake, but sex for sex's sake was a less realistic hope for a woman before the development of modern methods of birth control; sex was tied up with having a baby (KSG). Genesis itself rather draws attention to the power differential between her and Joseph.[20] It refers to her only as "his lord's wife"; it never names her. The incident presupposes the way sex and power get mixed up. Usually the dynamic involves a man possessing the power and being in a position to force himself on a woman, but on this occasion the woman possesses the power and thinks she can use it to her sexual advantage.

Though handsome in body, Joseph was even more handsome in character (vv. 8–9).[21] If he was an egotistical teenager in Gen. 37, he has come a long way.[22] His rationale for resistance is threefold (is he partly trying to bolster his own commitment?).[23] First, there is a relationship of trust between him and his master, which he cannot betray. Second, having sex with Potiphar's wife would be something very bad; it is a common evaluation of adultery in the Middle East. And third, it would involve doing wrong against God or offending God or falling short of God's expectations. The description of adultery as a terrible thing, especially when it involves betraying one's relationship with someone, recurs in the Egyptian Story of Two Brothers from about the time of Moses, where a young man resists the advances of his sister-in-law, who then accuses him of making advances toward her.[24]

Potiphar's wife perhaps moderates her pleas: won't he just sleep beside her? (v. 10).[25] Even that act of companionship would be a comfort. If he could just be with her. . . . But perhaps Joseph knows that neither he nor she could be expected to let things stop there.

39:11–15. But a day comes when the coast is clear. Grabbing him by his garment perhaps implies that she is trying to pull it off him. The garment might be more like a coat or more like a shirt, though either way it would likely mean that running out of the house would look odd if not incriminating. It is doubtless an instinctive and apparently wise reaction in a context of temptation, but with hindsight it might have seemed unwise in its own way. "Joseph's flight not only enrages but also compromises his mistress."[26]

And his continuing resistance issues (vv. 13–15) in another illustration of the volatility of one-sided sexual relationships (cf. Gen. 34; 2 Sam. 13). Potiphar's wife's introduction of reference to her husband without naming him and with the implication that he is to blame for what has (not) happened

20. Cf. Brett, *Genesis*, 115–16.

21. Cf. Chromatius of Aquileia, *Incipit de sancto patriarcha Ioseph* 2, in *Opera*, 108; cf. Sheridan, *Genesis 12–50*, 250.

22. Cf. Reno, *Genesis*, 268.

23. So Bakon, "Subtleties," 171–72.

24. See *ANET* 23–25, esp. 24.

25. Cf. Ibn Ezra, *Genesis*, 362.

26. Sternberg, *Poetics of Biblical Narrative*, 424.

reinforces the suspicion that he has been neglecting her. The term Ibrite/Hebrew recurs from 14:13 (see the comment there), more explicitly illustrating the way it commonly occurs on the lips of people outside Israel, often as something of a slur. It designates him as a foreigner, as the "other."[27] Her talk of Joseph's "playing around" also makes for a comparison with Sarah's pejorative comment about Ishmael (21:9) and with the narrator's description of Isaac and Rebekah (26:8), where the verb is a euphemism for sexual play; the occurrences of the verb here in vv. 14–17 are the last two of the eleven in Genesis (there are only two elsewhere in the First Testament: Exod. 32:6; Judg. 16:25). There is a lot of play in Genesis.

39:16–20a. The version of her accusation that Potiphar's wife gives her husband is the third account of her encounter with Joseph, following one by the narrator in vv. 10–12 and one by her to the servants in vv. 14–15. Such repetitions and recapitulations run through the Joseph story[28] as they have featured earlier in Genesis. The contrast between her accounts and the narrator's account underscores the blatancy of her lie.[29] She again says he left his garment "with" her, not "in her hand," which would be incriminating.[30] Her second account is more diplomatic than her first; she doesn't speak as if Potiphar deliberately brought Joseph to cause trouble. Her description of Joseph is more disparaging: in v. 14 he is a Hebrew, a foreigner, someone who is not one of us; now he is also a mere servant.

Joseph's punishment (v. 20a) is surprising. Jail is not a common form of punishment in traditional societies as it is in Western societies, though it may have been more common in Egypt than elsewhere in the Middle East.[31] In both contexts it is a punishment for offenses against the state (so it is the king's prisoners who are in the prison). Traditional societies, where the state is less important than it is in Western societies and there is less of a state structure, are less inclined to see wrongdoing as an offense against the state. When Joseph objects to committing adultery with Potiphar's wife, he does not portray it as an offense against the state. The Torah will later see rape and adultery as offenses for which someone should pay with his life, and Proverbs warns young men such as Joseph that they may pay for adultery with their lives. So one would not have been surprised if a powerful man such as Potiphar had imposed a severe punishment on Joseph. According to the first-century Greek historian Diodorus Siculus, Egyptian law prescribed that a man who violated a free married woman should be castrated,[32] though actual practice

27. See Sternberg, *Hebrews between Cultures*.

28. They are the first of the story's "narrative techniques" discussed in Humphreys, *Joseph*, 93–99.

29. Alter, *Art of Biblical Narrative*, 109.

30. Cf. Skinner, *Genesis*, 458–59.

31. So Sarna, *Genesis*, 275.

32. Diodorus Siculus, *Historical Library* 1.78.4; cf. Gunkel, *Genesis*, 409.

in Egypt was rather different and usually less drastic,[33] and likewise in Israel. Potiphar's failure to impose a severe punishment might raise the question whether he believes his wife's story[34] and raise the possibility that he is angry with her and/or with himself for whatever might have happened, while continuing to appreciate Joseph for what he has seen earlier. Maybe the lightness of his punishment is just another fruit of the fact that Yahweh is with Joseph.[35]

Implications

Yahweh Was with Joseph

Both Testaments show how God has various ways of relating to the world and to people and how he adopts different ways at different times and with different people. While Yahweh does not appear or speak to Joseph as he does to Abimelek, Jacob, and Laban (20:3–7; 28:13; 31:10–13, 24; 46:3–4), both Joseph himself and the narrator refer to Yahweh's being involved in Joseph's life. To describe this involvement, a distinctive motif in Gen. 39 is the declaration that Yahweh was "with" Joseph (vv. 2, 21, 23). The narrator reports it, and both Potiphar and the jailor can see it. So by implication can Pharaoh later, though he does not use the expression; instead, his distinctive observation is that God's spirit is in Joseph. God's being with Joseph is the key factor in his move from servitude and from imprisonment to freedom and success. God's spirit being in him is the key factor in his being able to interpret Pharaoh's dreams and to offer advice on action to take in light of them.

While the report that Yahweh is with Joseph recalls declarations Yahweh made to Isaac and Jacob and recalls testimonies given by them or by witnesses (26:3, 24, 28; 28:15, 20; 31:3, 5; 35:3), the two stories in 39:1–40:23 are the first where the narrator makes the comment. The declaration is the "theological entrance piece to the Joseph story."[36] Thus William Tyndale translated 39:2, "The Lord was with Joseph and he was a lucky fellow." As was the case with Isaac and Jacob, Yahweh being "with" him does not refer to an internal awareness of that presence. Nor does it refer to the sense in which Yahweh was objectively with Joseph when he was trapped in the cistern or in the midst of being transported to Egypt. Yahweh being with him means that Yahweh protects and blesses him (beyond Genesis, see Josh. 6:27; Judg. 1:19, 22; 2:18; 1 Sam. 3:19; 18:12, 14, 28; 2 Kings 18:7; 1 Chron. 9:20; 17:3; 2 Chron. 1:1; 15:9). "Nothing . . . was less probable than that the family of Jacob should be preserved by his means, when he was cut off from it, and

33. See Eyre, "Crime and Adultery."
34. Cf. Tg. Ps.-J.; Ibn Ezra, *Genesis*, 363.
35. Cf. von Rad, *Genesis*, 362.
36. Westermann, *Genesis 37–50*, 62.

carried far away, and not even reckoned among the living."[37] But Yahweh was with him to that end.

The expression in Genesis is "Yahweh was with him," not "God was with him" (this phrase comes only in 21:20—significantly, applied to Ishmael). Genesis 37 did not refer to Yahweh or God; explicit reference to Yahweh's presence and action did feature in Gen. 38, though not in an encouraging way. There are eight occurrences of the name Yahweh in Gen. 39; in the whole of Gen. 40–50 there will be only one more (49:18).[38] While the presence and activity of the God of Israel stands over Gen. 37–50 as a whole, after Gen. 39 the narrative has Joseph use the more general word for God in the way that would seem less odd to an Egyptian and on the lips of a quasi-Egyptian (e.g., 40:8, 41:16). It also retains that manner of speech for conversations within the family (e.g., 42:28; 45:5–9) and in due course for the narrator's own statements and for God's statements (46:2–3), and into Exod. 1–2. This way of speaking corresponds more closely to the way Abraham's descendants would actually speak, before Yahweh revealed his name to Moses. By default, it prepares the way for Yahweh's sharing of his name in Exod. 3.

Genesis does not offer any analysis of how Yahweh's being with someone makes things happen. It perhaps implies that things happen in large part by circumstances working together so that, for instance, Joseph has opportunity to show the kind of person that Yahweh made him (but how does Potiphar know it is because Yahweh was with him?). Yet that formulation only restates the question: how does Yahweh make things work together in that way? The chapters that follow will show how Yahweh also acts via the good and bad human decisions that people make, but they will not attempt to explain how that works.[39]

37. Calvin, *Genesis*, 2:260.

38. See further Keil and Delitzsch, *Pentateuch*, 330–31.

39. See further the section on "Whereas You Intended Something Bad for Me . . ." at the end of the comments on 49:28–50:26.

42

How Joseph Becomes a Dream Interpreter

(39:20b–40:23)

Overview

Scene 3 relates how Joseph again does well in a situation of adversity. When two victims of Pharaoh's wrath join him in prison, he is able to interpret dreams that they have, which are similar yet forecast reinstatement for one and execution for the other. But the man who is reinstated fails to put in a good word with Pharaoh on Joseph's behalf. Thus the pattern of the story parallels that of scene 2 (and scene 1). Will things ever go right for Joseph?

Translation

39:20b So he was there in the roundhouse. **21**But Yahweh was with Yosep,
and he extended commitment to him and gave favor toward him[1] in the
eyes of the roundhouse officer. **22**The roundhouse officer gave into Yo-
sep's charge all the prisoners who were in the roundhouse. Everything
that they were doing there, he was the one doing it. **23**The roundhouse
officer didn't look at any matter in his charge, because Yahweh was with
him, and whatever he was doing, Yahweh was making succeed.

40:1 Subsequently,[2] the king of Miṣrayim's butler and the baker did
wrong in relation to their lord, the king of Miṣrayim. **2**Parʿoh was irate with

1. Literally, "gave his favor," a genitive of advantage.
2. See the footnote to 22:1.

his two officials, the officer over the butlers and the officer over the bakers, **3**and he put them under guard in the house of the officer over the sentries, in the roundhouse, the place where Yosep was confined. **4**The officer over the sentries appointed Yosep with them, and he attended on them.

They were some time under guard, **5**and the two of them had a dream, each his own dream, in one night, each according to the interpretation of his dream—the king of Miṣrayim's butler and baker who were confined in the roundhouse. **6**Yosep came to them in the morning and saw that they were vexed. **7**He asked Parʿoh's officials who were with him under guard in his lord's house, "Why are your faces grim today?" **8**They said to him, "We've had a dream, and there's no one to interpret it." Yosep said to them, "Interpretations belong to God, don't they? Tell me, please."

9So the officer over the butlers told Yosep his dream. He said to him, "In my dream: there, a vine before me. **10**On the vine, three branches. As it was budding, its blossom grew and its clusters ripened as grapes. **11**Parʿoh's cup was in my hand, and I got the grapes, pressed them into Parʿoh's cup, and put the cup into Parʿoh's grasp." **12**Yosep said to him, "This is its interpretation. The three branches are three days. **13**In yet three days, Parʿoh will lift up your head and put you back in your position. You'll put Parʿoh's cup in his hand in accordance with the former rule when you were his butler. **14**Only[3] you will have been mindful of me with you when things are good for you and you will act in commitment with me, please, and have Parʿoh be mindful of me,[4] and get me out of this house. **15**Because I was actually stolen[5] from the country of the Ibrites, and also I've done nothing here that they should have put me in the cistern."

16The officer over the bakers saw that the interpretation was good. He said to Yosep, "In my dream, also: there, three baskets of white pastry[6] on my head. **17**In the top basket, all kinds of food for Parʿoh, a baker's work. But the birds were eating it from the basket, from on my head." **18**Yosep answered, "This is the interpretation. The three baskets are three days. **19**In yet three days, Parʿoh will lift up your head from on you and impale you on a tree, and the birds will eat your flesh from on you."

20On the third day, Parʿoh's birthday, he made a banquet for all his servants, and lifted up the head of the officer over the butlers and the head of the officer over the bakers, among his servants. **21**He put the officer over the butlers back into his butler's position, and he put the cup

3. On the unusual use of *kî ʾim*, see GKC 163cd, which also notes that *kî ʾim* commonly leads into a qatal, as in 32:27.

4. Conventionally, one would translate as "Make mention of me to Pharaoh," but Joseph is repeating the verb *zākar*, which he earlier used in the qal and here uses in the hiphil.

5. The verb is preceded by the infinitive of the same root, adding emphasis.

6. For the hapax *ḥōrî*, the root *ḥûr* suggests something white, but "white bread" (BDB, *DCH*) seems misleading since v. 17 refers to all kinds of baked goods, though the LXX, Vg imply ordinary bread.

in Parʿoh's grasp, [22]and the officer over the bakers he impaled, as Yosep had interpreted to them. [23]But the officer over the butlers was not mindful of Yosep. He disregarded him.

Interpretation

Scene 3 follows the pattern of scene 2, so that throughout Gen. 38–40 the account of Jacob's lines of descent stands still—at best. Once again Yahweh makes it possible for Joseph to flourish in a situation of adversity, and the arrival of two of Pharaoh's staff in the prison and their having dreams give further opportunity for it to be shown that Yahweh is with Joseph, though he expresses it in terms of God being with him or, more precisely, of God enabling him to interpret the dreams. So Joseph is successful, but he is still an exile in prison; indeed, it's worse to be in Pharaoh's prison than to be in Potiphar's service. But one of the men is released in fulfillment of his dream as interpreted by Joseph, which ought to have opened up the way for Joseph's release. However, it doesn't. "The turning-point of Joseph's fortunes begins,"[7] though one would not have guessed so at the end of the chapter as things seem to be miscarrying again. Thus once again Genesis sets alongside each other the wonder of Yahweh's presence with the flourishing that follows, and the letdown when things miscarry. It honors both realities.

39:20b–23. Joseph moves from one confinement (a hole in the ground, Gen. 37) to another confinement and from one house (Potiphar's) to another house.[8] The narrative thus summarizes the situation in a way that parallels 39:1.

It then goes on (v. 21) to the vital second statement that corresponds to 39:2: Yahweh was with Joseph. So the answer to the question "Where is Joseph's God now, to liberate and rescue him?"[9] is that he's watching keenly as Joseph goes through one of the experiences that Joseph will later describe as meant by human beings to do something bad but meant by God to do something good (50:20–21) and/or to help shape one's character.[10] "God, before he opened the door for his servant's deliverance, entered into the very prison to sustain him with his strength."[11] But the practical implications of Yahweh's being with him are spelled out in the reference to Yahweh's commitment and then in the further reference to Joseph finding favor, but in the parallelism of the two narratives in 39:1–20a and 39:20b–40:23, the second version heightens the first. Yahweh "extends" commitment to him (like someone extending a hand or extending a tent; it is a rare expression), and Yahweh gives the favor

7. Dillmann, *Genesis*, 2:359.
8. Hamilton, *Genesis 18–50*, 471.
9. Luther, *Genesis 38–44*, 98.
10. Cf. Seebass, *Genesis*, 3:52.
11. Calvin, *Genesis*, 2:305.

with the "roundhouse officer," the prison guard. In the LXX and Vg the replacement of the name Yahweh by the word for "Lord" makes for a nice contrast: "the lord [i.e., Potiphar] . . . threw him into prison" but "the Lord was with Joseph" there.[12]

In a further heightened parallel (vv. 22–23), as Potiphar put into Joseph's hand *everything* in his household, the prison guard puts into Joseph's hand *everyone* in the prison as well as all the tasks that needed to be undertaken there. Potiphar had not felt the need to look into anything that Joseph was doing; so it is with the prison guard. As happened earlier, the narrative repeats the declaration that Yahweh was with Joseph. "Christ comes and lights up hell with gracious eyes."[13] Then Genesis likewise makes another reference to Yahweh granting success to everything that Joseph was doing, which completes the parallelism with the opening statement of this point in v. 2. So where will we go from here? The MT paragraph division and the medieval chapter division which associate vv. 20b–23 with what precedes make for an interim happy ending, but alas, the parallelism continues in 40:1–23.

40:1–4a. Its continuation is signaled by the "subsequently" (cf. 39:7).[14] Again there is no indication of how much time has elapsed. The terms that etymologically signify "butler" (more literally, one who gives someone a drink) and "baker" suggest more exalted roles than those words imply, the reverse of the situation with the word for sentries in 37:36[15] that recurs here in vv. 3–4. Nehemiah was the emperor's butler (Neh. 1:11), and his promotion to governor suggests that he was more than a wine waiter. The linguistic usage compares with the use in English of terms such as chamberlain, purser, or bursar—words with meanings that are unrelated to their etymology. It seems likely that butler and baker are responsible members of Pharaoh's staff, which would mean positions of power, temptation, and danger. There's no indication of the nature of the two men's (alleged) wrongdoing, though the use of the verb *ḥāṭāʾ* (the verb Joseph used in 39:9) suggests that we are not to think of something trivial to which the king is overreacting. Targum Ps.-J. explains that they were suspected of seeking to poison Pharaoh (the butler was then vindicated). It is perhaps because they are more than butler and baker that they get a trustee to serve them. Apparently the roundhouse under its guard is attached to the house of the officer over the sentries and responsible to him,[16] and the imprisonment might be more like house arrest, though in v. 15 Joseph still calls it a cistern or dungeon. It would make sense if the two men were put under guard while Pharaoh decided what to do next.[17] The omission of

12. Cf. Brayford, *Genesis*, 403.
13. Luther, *Genesis 38–44*, 100.
14. Literally each time, "and it happened after these things."
15. See the footnote there.
16. Cf. Alter, *Genesis*, 229.
17. Cf. Gunkel, *Genesis*, 412.

the name of the officer over the sentries might indicate that the person has changed and that it is no longer Potiphar, which would fit with his apparently treating Joseph as a trustee.

40:4b–8. Again there is no indication how much time has elapsed until one night the two men both have dreams that are evidently significant but not of self-evident meaning. They need interpreting. The narrative keeps us in suspense about the content of the dreams and builds suspense by the way it characterizes them: one night, two important people, two significant dreams, but two dreams with different meanings, "each according to the interpretation of his dream." Within the First Testament, the Hebrew terms for "interpretation" and "interpret" (*pitrôn*, *pātar*) come only in Gen. 40–41, though related terms are frequent in Daniel and elsewhere, especially in Qumran writings.[18] Genesis and Daniel both testify to special revelations from God and to the capacity of individuals to perceive things about the future. Although English is more inclined to distinguish between the ascertaining of meaning and the meaning that is ascertained, the Hebrew expressions cover both the process of interpretation and the interpretation that results, and the use of the expressions can move between these significances. The point in v. 5 is thus that each of the dreams has a different meaning.

The prisoners themselves then refer to the process of interpretation (v. 8), though Joseph's response concerns the fact that the meaning of significant dreams belongs to God, as the one who sends them—not that the process of interpretation belongs to God, though that would also follow. Egyptians were accustomed to the idea of revelations coming in the form of dreams that might need interpretation;[19] if they were not in confinement, the two officers might know where to go for interpretation. It is thus perhaps at least as much the lack of an interpreter as the occurrence of the dreams that troubles the men. While Genesis has referred to a number of significant dreams (20:3–7; 28:12–17; 31:10–11, 24; 37:5–9), their meaning was clear; none required much interpretation. The dreams in Gen. 40–42 and in Daniel do require interpretation. Joseph himself having his symbolic dreams has hardly prepared us for the idea that he can interpret dreams or has special access to God that would enable him to do so. The boldness of his invitation to the two dreamers thus compares with Daniel's boldness in Dan. 1–2 (the setting of Daniel is centuries later than that of Joseph, so an obvious inference is that the Daniel stories have taken up motifs from the Joseph story; uncertainty about dating Genesis complicates that subject, but comparing the two without making any assumptions about relative dating is still illuminating).[20] There Daniel, without any divine guidance, asks the Babylonian official to test them to show whether they will

18. See, e.g., *DCH* on *pātar* and *pešer* and related words.
19. See, e.g., Szpakowska, *Behind Closed Eyes*.
20. See further Goldingay, *Daniel*.

flourish on a non-defiling diet; then he undertakes to provide Nebuchadnezzar with the interpretation of his dream and only afterward thinks to pray about the matter. As the Daniel story has a significant background in Daniel and his friends' location in Babylon, so the Joseph story has a significant background in Joseph's being in Egypt. There, as in Babylon and as in the Western world, the interpretation of dreams is a scientific procedure in the sense that it works on the basis of an accumulated corpus of data possessed by the culture. Like Daniel, Joseph dismisses this approach to interpretation. The key to interpretation is not professional expertise but contact with God. Interpretation involves divine revelation, not scientific reasoning. It is admittedly "a pious disclaimer but not exactly a modest one."[21] Like Daniel, Joseph implicitly claims to be in touch with the God who grants such revelation. This ridiculous claim would arouse scorn from the two royal ministers if they were outside with their usual access to resources, but here they have no alternative to taking a chance on their lowly Hebrew duty officer.[22]

40:9–15. The dream indicates that "butler" is not merely a theoretical or honorary title, as it was not for Nehemiah. As will again be the case in Gen. 41, Joseph "chooses" which elements in the dream to comment on. He does not treat the dream as an allegory. His interpretation does not issue from the application of a method but from intuitive discernment or divine gift. "Lifting up the head" is not very different from the more common expression "lifting up the face" (e.g., 32:20 [32:21]), whether one lifts one's own or someone else lifts it: it suggests holding one's head high or having someone else enable one to do so.[23] Here the less common expression (for which cf. 2 Kings 25:27) opens up the possibility of the horrifying double entendre that will follow in v. 19.

Asking for a favor in return for the act of interpretation (vv. 14–15) would hardly surprise or offend the butler; priests, pastors, interpreters, diviners, and prophets get paid. We didn't hear anything of Joseph's feelings or protests in Gen. 37, but now we do; and it transpires that even though Joseph is gifted as a dreamer and interpreter, he will need the initiative of other people in order to find freedom and see his own dreams come true.[24] His request makes more explicit that the butler was indeed not merely a wine waiter, again like Nehemiah. He could speak to Pharaoh on Joseph's behalf. While Joseph's capacity to interpret dreams will be of ongoing significance in Gen. 37–50, this possibility is the immediate reason why Joseph's capacity is of significance. There is a "pathos" about Joseph here. He's a Hebrew. He was "stolen," an expression that was not used before and another example of the way the retelling of an event can incorporate a different way of describing it. His reference to a cistern draws attention to the similarity between his experience in Egypt

21. Fox, "Joseph and Wisdom," 245.
22. Cf. von Rad, *Genesis*, 366.
23. See *DCH* 5:760.
24. Cf. Fretheim, "Genesis," 616.

and the experience that brought him there. "The man who seems to be quite in control is here needful." He uses some key First Testament words in his plea. He asks for the butler to remember and be mindful (*zākar*) and asks for commitment on his part (*ḥesed*), which Daniel experienced from a royal official (Dan. 1:9). He thus asks for mindfulness and for *ḥesed* not from God but from a fellow prisoner (contrast 30:22; 39:21).[25]

40:16–19. Again the dream fits the fact that the dreamer is a baker; the Egyptian dictionary lists thirty-eight varieties of cake and fifty-seven varieties of bread.[26] But "any normal man would have interpreted these very similar dreams similarly. Joseph, however, shows his great skill by discerning their quite opposite meanings."[27] "Lifting up the head" now becomes a negative action. Joseph describes the head baker's fate in a way designed to bring home its gruesomeness to people listening to the story. The interpretation implies not merely punishment but execution and not merely regular execution but beheading and not merely beheading but also impaling, which facilitates the birds' work. While impaling shames a person and dissuades others from imitating the victim's offense, the comment about the birds suggests that it is also designed to ensure that the punishment continues after death. It means that there will not be enough of the victim to bury, and he will not be able to rest with his ancestors in the family tomb; hence the limit on the period of impaling in Deut. 21:22–23 and Josh. 10:26–27 and the merciful action of the Yabeshites in 1 Sam. 31:8–13. The dream's meaning is thus horrifying, though the narrator makes no comment on Joseph's reaction or on the baker's reaction. The story's interest lies in what follows.

40:20–23. It was Pharaoh who put the two officers into the roundhouse, and it is Pharaoh who can take them out. He operates a little like a president with power to pardon anyone. The narrator reports what happens with a repetition of Joseph's sardonic conceit. Pharaoh lifts the head of both of his officers, in different ways but in fulfillment of Joseph's different interpretations of the dreams. Has Pharaoh made inquiries and concluded that one man is guilty and the other innocent? Again the narrator reports things briskly without comment in order to move on to what matters from the point of view of the story. Instead of remembering, there was forgetting. And to forget injustices is "to participate in the sin of the chief cupbearer," and it is "the most injurious that a people can commit."[28] Like 39:1–20a, this section has gotten Joseph nowhere. But fortunately, it is not the end of the story. "You may have forgotten him, but I have not forgotten him" (Gen. Rab. 88.7).

25. Brueggemann, *Genesis*, 324–25.
26. So Vergote, *Joseph en Égypte*, 37; cf. Wenham, *Genesis 16–50*, 384.
27. Gunkel, *Genesis*, 413.
28. De La Torre, *Genesis*, 326.

43

How Joseph Becomes Supplies Master in Egypt

(41:1–56)

Overview

Once again there is a pair of dreams that need interpreting, and once again Joseph can interpret them. This time Pharaoh is the dreamer and the dreams relate to national affairs—they lay out the prospect of flourishing but then of famine, and Joseph also suggests the action needed to manage this sequence. His ability to interpret the dreams leads to the lifting up of his head in the positive sense. It takes him from being a prisoner to being Pharaoh's agent in implementing the action he has suggested. Pharaoh provides him with a wife, and they have children who will be the ancestors of two of the Israelite clans, Manasseh and Ephraim.

Translation

1At the end of two full years,[1] Parʿoh himself was dreaming, and there,
he was standing by the Yeʾor.[2] **2**There, from the Yeʾor seven cows going
up, lovely in appearance and sturdy in body, and they grazed among the
reeds.[3] **3**And there: seven more cows going up from the Yeʾor after them,

1. Literally, "two years days."

2. A Hebrew adaptation of the Egyptian term for the Nile; the latter name is an adaptation of a Greek term of unknown origin.

3. *ʾĀḥû* is one of several Egyptian words in Gen. 41: *ḥarṭumîm*, "diviners"; *šēš*, "linen"; the possibly puzzling word *ʾabrēk* in v. 43; and several names. All of these give local color to the story (Alter, *Genesis*, 234).

bad in appearance and thin in body, and they stood beside the cows on
the bank of the Yeʾor. **4**The cows that were bad in appearance and thin in
body ate the seven cows that were lovely in appearance and sturdy.
Parʿoh woke up, **5**but went to sleep, and dreamed a second time.
There: seven ears of wheat going up on a single stalk, sturdy and good.
6And there: seven ears that were thin and scorched by the east wind
springing up after them. **7**The thin ears swallowed the seven sturdy, full
ears.
Parʿoh woke up. There: it was a dream. **8**In the morning his spirit was
agitated, and he sent and called for all Miṣrayim's diviners,[4] all its experts.[5] Parʿoh told them his dream, but no one could interpret them for Parʿoh.
9Then the officer over the butlers spoke with Parʿoh: "My wrongdoings I am going to be mindful[6] of today. **10**When Parʿoh was irate with his
servants, he put me under guard in the house of the officer over the sentries, me and the officer over the bakers. **11**We had a dream, I and he, in
one night. Each in accordance with the interpretation of his dream, we
dreamed. **12**With us there was an Ibrite boy, a servant of the officer over
the sentries. We told him and he interpreted our dreams to us. Each in
accordance with his dream, he interpreted. **13**As he interpreted it to us,
so it came about. Me, he put back into my position; him, he impaled."[7]
14So Parʿoh sent and called for Yosep, they hurried him from the
cistern, he shaved and changed his clothes, and he came to Parʿoh.
15Parʿoh said to Yosep, "I had a dream and there is no one to interpret it.
I myself have heard about you, that you can listen to a dream so as to interpret it." **16**Yosep answered Parʿoh, "Not me at all.[8] God is the one who
will aver[9] Parʿoh's well-being."
17So Parʿoh spoke with Yosep. "In my dream: there am I, standing
by the bank of the Yeʾor. **18**There, from the Yeʾor seven cows going up,
sturdy in body and lovely in appearance, and they grazed among the
reeds. **19**And there, seven more cows going up after them, lean and very
bad in appearance, skinny[10] in body. I haven't seen the like of them in
the entire country of Miṣrayim for how bad they were. **20**And the skinny,
bad cows ate the first seven sturdy cows **21**and they came inside them.

4. The Vg nicely calls them conjecturers (*coniectores*).

5. The familiar Hebrew word *ḥākām* explains the Egyptian word *ḥarṭōm*.

6. Conventionally, the hiphil of *zākar* translates as "make mention of," and the verb can denote the giving of evidence in court—so that the butler implies that he is testifying against himself (von Rad, *Genesis*, 370–71). But he is picking up the verb from Joseph's words to him in 40:14 (see the footnote).

7. The head butler continues to speak deferentially to Pharaoh in the third person; Pharaoh himself is the "he."

8. On this rare emphatic expression, see the footnote to 14:24.

9. On this translation of *ʿānâ*, see the footnote to 18:27.

10. Pharaoh switches from *daq* (thin) to *raq* (skinny); the two words, similar in meaning, are even more similar in appearance in Hebrew than in English because the Hebrew letters for *d* and *r* look similar. Thus, e.g., the SP has *raq* in v. 3.

But it wouldn't have been acknowledged that they had come inside them; their appearance was as bad as it was at the beginning. I woke up, **22**then I saw in my dream, and there—seven ears of wheat going up on one stalk, full and good quality; **23**and there—seven withered ears, thin, scorched by the east wind, springing up after them. **24**The thin ears swallowed the seven good ears. I said it to the diviners, but no one could tell me."

25Yosep said to Parʿoh, "Parʿoh's dream is one. What God[11] is going to do, he has told Parʿoh. **26**The seven good cows are seven years and the seven good ears are seven years. It's one dream. **27**The seven skinny, bad cows that were going up after them are seven years, as are the seven empty[12] ears, scorched by the east wind. There will be seven years of famine. **28**That's the thing that I am stating[13] to Parʿoh. What God is going to do, he has shown Parʿoh. **29**There: seven years are coming, great abundance in the entire country of Miṣrayim, **30**but seven years of famine will arise after them, and the entire abundance in the country of Miṣrayim will be forgotten. The famine will consume the country, **31**and the abundance in the country won't be acknowledged in the face of that famine afterward, because it will be very severe. **32**Concerning the repeating of the dream to Parʿoh, twice: the thing is fixed by God. God is going to do it quickly.

33"So now, Parʿoh should look for an insightful, expert individual, and set him over the country of Miṣrayim. **34**Parʿoh should act and appoint appointees over the country and acquire a fifth of[14] the country of Miṣrayim in the seven years of abundance. **35**They should collect all the food in these good years that are coming, lay up grain under Parʿoh's charge in the towns as food, and keep it. **36**The food will be something appointed[15] for the country for the seven years of famine that are going to happen in the country of Miṣrayim so the country is not cut off by the famine."

37The thing was good in the eyes of Parʿoh and in the eyes of all his servants, **38**and Parʿoh said to his servants, "Shall we find a man like this, in whom is the spirit of God?" **39**So Parʿoh said to Yosep, "Since God has made all this known to you, there is no one insightful and expert like you. **40**You yourself will be over my household, and to your bidding all my people will submit.[16] Only with respect to the throne will I be greater than you."

11. The four occurrences of *ʾĕlōhîm* on Joseph's lips in vv. 25–32 have the article, perhaps implying "the real God" (cf. Arnold, *Genesis*, 341).

12. To make the linguistic links even more subtle (see the translation note at v. 19), "empty" is *rēq*; in meaning it also contrasts with "full" in v. 22.

13. The declarative/performative qatal suggests a speech act: "I hereby state."

14. For "acquire a fifth of," Tg. Onq. has "equip" (BDB's *ḥmš* IV).

15. A third expression from the root *pāqad* (see v. 34), "one of the most elegant words in the Hebrew language" (Luther, *Genesis*, 38–44, 157); cf. the varied occurrences in 21:1; 39:5; 40:4; 50:24, 25.

16. Cf. the LXX and Vg for the translation of this verb, which I take as *DCH*'s *nāšaq* III, as in Ps. 2:12.

41So Parʿoh said to Yosep, "See, I'm putting[17] you over the entire country of Miṣrayim." **42**Parʿoh removed his signet ring from on his hand and put it on Yosep's hand, had him clothed in linen robes, and put a gold collar[18] on his neck. **43**He had him ride in the chariot of his second-in-command, and people called out before him, "Kneel down!"[19] He put[20] him over the entire country of Miṣrayim. **44**Parʿoh said to Yosep, "Whereas I am Parʿoh, without you no one will raise his hand or his foot in the entire country of Miṣrayim." **45**Parʿoh named Yosep Ṣapenat Paʿneah and gave him Asenat daughter of Poṭi Pera, the priest[21] in On, as wife. And Yosep went out[22] over the country of Miṣrayim. **46**Yosep was a man of thirty years when he took his stand before Parʿoh, the king of Miṣrayim.

So Yosep went out from before Parʿoh and passed through the whole country of Miṣrayim. **47**In the seven years of abundance, the country produced by fistfuls,[23] **48**and he collected all the food of the seven years that passed in the country of Miṣrayim and put food in the towns (the food of a town's open country that was around it, he put inside it). **49**Yosep laid up grain like the sand of the sea in huge amounts until he stopped accounting, because accounting was impossible.

50To Yosep two sons were born before the famine year came, sons to whom Asenat daughter of Poṭi Pera, the priest in On, gave birth for him. **51**Yosep named the firstborn Menaššeh, because "God has made me forget all my trouble and my father's entire household." **52**The second he named Eprayim, because "God has made me fruitful in the country of my affliction."

53The seven years of abundance that passed in the country of Miṣrayim came to an end **54**and the seven years of famine began to come, as Yosep had said. The famine happened in all the countries, but in the entire country of Miṣrayim, there was bread. **55**So the entire country of Miṣrayim was hungry and the people cried out to Parʿoh for bread, and Parʿoh said to all Miṣrayim, "Go to Yosep; do what he says to you." **56**When the famine was over the entire face of the country, Yosep opened all that was in them and traded grain supplies[24] to Miṣrayim. So the famine prevailed in the country of Miṣrayim.

17. The declarative/performative qatal suggests another speech act, "I hereby put."

18. Alter (*Genesis*, 240) notes that Egyptian bas-reliefs portray people wearing a collar incorporating gold wire.

19. The meaning of *ʾabrēk* has to be guessed from the context, but a Hebrew speaker would plausibly link it with *bārak*, "kneel" (cf. Aq, Vg), and might not be mistaken (see Redford, *Study*, 224–26). The LXX has "herald": see Stadel, "Septuagint Translation."

20. The infinitive absolute takes the place of a finite verb.

21. The Tg makes Joseph's father-in-law ruler rather than priest.

22. In light of what precedes, one might translate *yāṣāʾ* as "arose" (cf. the literal use in 19:23); but with the recurrence of the verb in v. 46, it more likely has the literal meaning "went out."

23. "They stored up fist over fist, hand over hand" (Rashi, *Brʾšyt*, 465).

24. Genesis introduces its third word for wheat or grain. In vv. 5–7, 22–27 it uses the word *šibbōlet*, which refers to ears of wheat as they grow. In vv. 35, 49 it has the word *bar*, which

Interpretation

This closing scene brings the story in Gen. 37–41 to an interim climax; to put it the other way, Gen. 37–40 has provided the background to Gen. 41. Genesis 41 would have been impossible without Gen. 39:20b–40:23, which in turn would have been impossible without the events of Gen. 39:1–20a, which ultimately would have been impossible without Gen. 37. The wheel has turned full circle: "Joseph's misfortunes began with dreams and now end through dreams."[25] Not that all the questions raised by Gen. 37–40 are answered here, though the close of the chapter points toward them. Indeed, one could say that vv. 50–52 form a false conclusion to the story begun in Gen. 37—Joseph hasn't really forgotten his family. Further, Gen. 42 and the continuing unfolding story would be impossible without Gen. 37–41. While the chapter thus relates to what precedes, it also brings us to "the main action" in the story.[26] The MT thus marks it as the beginning of a new unit comprising 41:1–44:17, but the English chapter division rightly recognizes that Gen. 41 comprises a complete scene (though I associate v. 57 with what follows).[27] It constitutes a turning point in the account of Jacob's lines of descent, and in particular, a turning point in what happens to Joseph in Egypt. It marks a transition from Act One to Act Two in his story; for convenience I treat it as the closing scene within Act One of the account of Jacob's lines of descent. It takes up the theme of famine, which is not only a central motif in Part Four of Genesis but also a theme that has featured through Part Two and Part Three.

A pair of dreams again need interpreting, but there is some heightening of the parallelism in relation to the preceding chapter. Pharaoh is now the dreamer, not (disgraced) members of his staff. And after the disappointment of Gen. 40, the chapter relates a reversal. We could fear that the sequence that occurred twice in Gen. 39–40 would recur, but it doesn't. The previous two units began hopefully but then disappointed; Gen. 41 begins perhaps despondently but then encourages.

Pharaoh dreams but can't get his dreams interpreted (41:1–8)
The officer over the butlers remembers about Joseph (41:9–13)
Pharaoh summons Joseph (41:14–16)
Pharaoh recounts the dreams to Joseph (41:17–24)
Joseph interprets the dreams (41:25–32)

strictly denotes grains of wheat when they have been harvested. In vv. 56–57 it uses the verb *šābar*, a denominative verb from *šeber*, which denotes trading in grain. Elsewhere the qal denotes buying and the hiphil selling, but here in vv. 56–57 the MT uses the qal with both meanings.

25. Sarna, *Genesis*, 280.

26. Gunkel, *Genesis*, 415.

27. See the translation note at 41:57, below.

Joseph advises Pharaoh about what to do (41:33–36)
Pharaoh appoints Joseph as controller and marries him to Asenat (41:37–46a)
Joseph implements his proposal about collecting surplus grain (41:46b–49)
Joseph has two sons (41:50–52)
The famine comes and Joseph distributes the accumulated surplus (41:53–56)

41:1–8. "Two full years" passed for Joseph; Yahweh "took all human grounds of hope away from him."[28] But then (Tg. Ps.-J. nicely adds), God was mindful of Joseph.

Genesis narrates Pharaoh's dreams (vv. 1b–4a)—"or better yet, nightmares"[29] —in the regular way. The pointer "there" introduces different stages in the dreams, drawing the listener into the dreams. The cows would be among the reeds and in the water in order to cool off. Cows do so in temperate countries, but they might be expected especially to do so in a country as hot as Egypt. In Gen. 37 we learn the content of the dreams only in the course of their being reported, and then their interpretation is related only by the family and is not confirmed. Then in Gen. 40 we again learn the contents of the dreams only in the course of their being reported, but it is repeated in the course of their interpretation by Joseph. Now in Gen. 41 the narrator relates the content of the dreams as Pharaoh has them, then we hear it again as Pharaoh reports them to Joseph, then we hear it again as Joseph interprets them. Their importance is thus underlined, and suspense keeps rising.

The motif of the dreamer waking up then going back to sleep (vv. 4b–7a) and having another dream is partly paralleled in Dan. 2, where the king then cannot remember his dream, as well as in the Gilgamesh story and elsewhere in Middle Eastern writings.[30] While the symbolism of the dreams in Gen. 40 was odd (as is the way with dreams), the symbolism in Pharaoh's dreams is more bizarre. They combine the everyday (the Nile, the khamsin—strictly, in Egypt it would be a south wind)[31] and the fantastic. Whereas the dream gives no explanation of the cows' thinness, it explains the thinness of the ears of grain, which perhaps retrospectively raises the question of whether the Nile was somehow responsible for the fate of the second set of cows.

Pharaoh realizes it was a dream (vv. 7b–8), which means it is important and needs to be taken note of. But what does it signify? It doesn't look positive in its implications. Like Nebuchadnezzar in Dan. 2:1, Pharaoh becomes agitated and has his experts in dream interpretation summoned. Unlike Nebuchadnezzar, Pharaoh relates the dream to the diviners rather than expecting them also to know what the dream was. The dreams of Joseph's fellow prisoners in

28. Calvin, *Genesis*, 2:318.
29. De La Torre, *Genesis*, 326.
30. See *ANET* 76–77; cf. Hamilton, *Genesis 18–50*, 487–88.
31. Cf. Wenham, *Genesis 16–50*, 391.

Gen. 40 were of vital personal importance; but like Nebuchadnezzar, Pharaoh has dreams that relate to national affairs. "Does not everybody dream? But when a king dreams, it serves the whole world" (Gen. Rab. 89.4). Dream divination is thus a key expertise in Egypt as also in Babylon.[32]

Like Nebuchadnezzar, however, Pharaoh finds his resources not up to the task. Genesis Rabbah 89.6 reports the nice hypothesis that they plausibly interpret the dream as revealing that the king will have seven daughters but will also bury them. "They all sweat in vain."[33] Yet the symbolism of the dreams ought to have made them fairly easy to interpret.[34] Perhaps God arranged for the interpreters to be unable to do so (so Tg. Ps.-J.); it can be the fate of this world's wisdom to fail even when the question might not look so difficult, because God can cut off the speech of the people one trusts and take away the wisdom of elders (Job 12:20),[35] making nonsense of the insight of the experts (Isa. 44:25).[36] Or was it evident to the interpreters that the dreams conveyed bad news, and were they afraid to say so? The narrator literally says, "There was no one interpreting them for Pharaoh"; it leaves open whether they couldn't or wouldn't. Either way, it now turns out that "the problem of Pharaoh is more acute than the problem of Joseph."[37]

41:9–13. At this point Gen. 41 differs from Dan. 2 as it makes a link with the previous chapter (in the manner of the link between Dan. 4 and 5). The butler makes the connection explicit in his reference to being mindful—which is what Joseph had asked for. Again Tg. Ps.-J. makes a neat observation as it has the head butler attributing Pharaoh's anger to God; it will be God's means of exalting Joseph and providing for Jacob and his family. Joseph could be called a boy, as he was in 37:2, when he was seventeen, but the intervening chapters imply that he has grown up somewhat (see v. 46). So "boy" may more explicitly have the pejorative implications that can attach to the word in American English, especially when applied to servants, just as in 37:2.[38]

41:14–16. Joseph is summoned like the experts and rushed to the king like Daniel in Dan. 2:25–27. Unlike Daniel, he needs to be cleaned up, either because he is coming from the prison or because Egyptian men are clean-shaven, or both—the need is underscored by the prison again being called a cistern. As the head butler has implied, Pharaoh understands that Joseph needs only to hear a report of a dream, and then he can interpret it; he is not

32. See the comment on 40:4b–8.

33. Luther, *Genesis 38–44*, 149.

34. Cf. Driver, *Genesis*, 339.

35. Baumgarten, *Theologischer Commentar zum Pentateuch*, 1:325; cf. Keil and Delitzsch, *Pentateuch*, 349.

36. Qimchi, *Genesis*, on 41:1.

37. Brueggemann, *Genesis*, 326.

38. Cf. Rashi, *Brʾšyt*, 455.

like the experts with their dream books (which had apparently turned out to be useless anyway).

Like Daniel, and like himself in 40:8, Joseph sets the king right about how someone can interpret a dream (41:16). It is not because he has the ability or because he has expertise superior to that of Pharaoh's staff but because God is prepared to reveal something about the future to the king. Like Daniel, he speaks with outrageous confidence about how God will reveal it. Unlike Daniel, Joseph has something to convey that promises well-being and not just trouble, though presumably he doesn't yet know what the dreams are and in that sense has no basis for thinking he can put a positive spin on them in a way that the Egyptian interpreters perhaps could not. But these dreams refer to wide-ranging events, involving more than simply looking after Jacob's family. Pharaoh's dreams imply that God cares about Egypt itself and the other peoples who will benefit from Egypt's being able to supply them during the famine.

41:17–24. Genesis sometimes moves quickly, sometimes slowly. Here it recounts how Pharaoh relates the dreams we already know about, as Abraham's servant recounts the story we already know in 24:34–49. In both contexts the repetition underscores the importance of what is repeated. "In the Holy Scriptures a tautology is not an idle matter."[39] Further, in both contexts the effect is to heighten suspense. Here we wait to discover what interpretation Joseph will offer. Further, here Pharaoh elaborates on what Genesis reported earlier, as Daniel's interpretation of Nebuchadnezzar's vision adds to the vision itself. The cows in the dream were the most emaciated that Pharaoh had ever seen, and eating the sturdy cows made them look no better.

41:25–32. Whereas Gen. 37 and 40 had not explicitly taken their dreams to refer to something God would do, Joseph speaks in terms of God's acting and not only in terms of God's interpretation.

Joseph does not explain every element in the dream (vv. 26–31), as is the case with the dreams in Daniel; he does not comment on the scrawny cows being just as scrawny after eating as they were before. He puts the emphasis on God's involvement—on what God is going to do, on God's speaking to Pharaoh, on God's showing, on what God has fixed. He puts more emphasis on the bad news than on the good news, as Pharaoh has done. It might therefore seem odd that in v. 16 Joseph spoke of Pharaoh's well-being. But there are indeed seven years of abundance to come, even if they are to be followed by seven years of famine. While there is not a self-evident meaning to the symbolism of seven, of cows coming up from the Nile, and of ears of grain, Joseph's interpretation makes one say, "Ah, yes."[40] The Nile is the source of Egypt's flourishing and grain is key to it; more broadly, the country of Egypt

39. Luther, *Genesis 38–44*, 156.
40. Cf. Luther, *Genesis 38–44*, 148–49.

is "the gift of the Nile."[41] The downside is that when the rains fail to the south, in Sudan, the level of the Nile falls, the land loses its irrigation, grain does not grow, and famine follows. There are other references to a seven-year food shortage in Egypt because the Nile failed to flood.[42] The seven-years-plus-seven-years motif thus schematizes a familiar pattern. And seven holy cows feature briefly in the Egyptian *Book of the Dead*.[43]

The thing is indeed fixed by God (v. 32). God will take action to effect his decision and will do so quickly. The dreams have once again come in twos (cf. 37:5–11; 40:4–15), but here the implication is different: the doubling evidences the fact that God has decided on something and that it will happen. Joseph offers no insight on why God will act as he will; both flourishing and famine seem to be just one of those things. But it will be the means of reuniting Jacob's family.

41:33–36. A second reason why the word "well-being" was not inappropriate is that God's revelation offers the prospect of life continuing through the seven years of famine. But this prospect requires human action. The sovereign power of God and the reality of God's revelation about the future do not issue in human quietude. Not only was Egypt accustomed to the periodic failure of the Nile and to the consequent food shortages, but Egyptian texts also refer to occasions when local administrators took responsibility for supplying resources during famine years, or claimed to have done so.[44] Egyptian texts also refer to the Pharaoh's acceptance of responsibility for seeing that people did not starve during a famine.[45] But to safeguard against the famine's issuing in the death of the country, Joseph suggests that the coming situation requires a new, double layer of comprehensive administration—a supplies master and a countrywide body of administrators. The responsibility of royal advisers is first to make predictions about likely events and then to propose action that should be taken in light of their predictions, and Joseph thus moves from the first to the second.[46] In this connection too Joseph shows himself to be more expert than Pharaoh's regular advisers.[47]

41:37–45a. So Joseph leaps from being a royal prisoner to being the second most important person in the kingdom. Pharaoh's talk of God's spirit being key to Joseph's gift of interpretation recurs in Nebuchadnezzar's acknowledgment in Dan. 4:8, 9, 18 [4:5, 6, 15]; 5:11, 14, though it contrasts with Joseph's own prescription of an insightful, expert individual. While it might

41. Herodotus, *Histories* 2.5; cf. Seebass, *Genesis*, 3:66.

42. See the inscription quoted in *ANET* 31–32, with the heading "The Tradition of Seven Lean Years in Egypt"; and further, Hamilton, *Genesis 18–50*, 497.

43. See, e.g., T. Allen, *Book of the Dead*, 139.

44. See Sarna, *Genesis*, 290.

45. Cf. Driver, *Genesis*, 346–47.

46. Cf. Arnold, *Genesis*, 342.

47. Cf. Hamilton, *Genesis 18–50*, 499.

not seem logical to infer that the capacity to interpret a dream qualifies a person for the job Joseph has described, being indwelt by God's spirit might be a qualification (cf. Isa. 11:2); if Pharaoh is correct in his observation, it hints at the implication that God's spirit cares about the Egyptians. If God has given Joseph not only the interpretation of the dreams but also the suggestion about the action that needs to be taken, then God can enable Joseph to do the job he has described.

Pharaoh's "household" in the present context (vv. 40–41) will be the "country" itself, to which Pharaoh goes on to refer, the "family" of which he is head. As his senior minister, Joseph will be its "father" in his stead (cf. the description of Eliakim in Isa. 22:20–21). Genesis does not give Joseph a formal title such as something equivalent to prime minister. His responsibility relates to the particular focus of the issue raised by Pharaoh's dream.[48] He apparently holds "the well-known Egyptian office of 'Overseer of the Granaries of Upper and Lower Egypt'"; Egypt was quite accustomed to elevating people of foreign origin to important positions.[49] Did Joseph envisage himself as the supplies master? It would fit with the estimate of himself that was implied by his own dreams. But even if we do not assume that his dreams have implications regarding his self-estimate nor that he just now envisaged Pharaoh's deciding to appoint him to the post he prescribes, Pharaoh's decision does actually open up the way for the fulfillment of those dreams.

Pharaoh immediately seals Joseph's appointment ceremonially and substantially (vv. 42–44), speaking as someone with the authority to do so ("I am Pharaoh").[50] His signet ring would be his seal (see, e.g., Esther 3:10, 12).[51]

As a senior Egyptian official, Joseph will need an Egyptian name (v. 45). Pharaoh's naming of Joseph is a further sign of his exercising authority over him, as is the case with another Pharaoh in 2 Kings 23:34.[52] So is his arranging Joseph's marriage; the particular match that Pharaoh prescribes would be another mark of giving him proper status in the country. The apparently relaxed attitude of Joseph and of Genesis to this marriage compares with its attitude to Melchizedek and Genesis's general attitude of "ecumenical bonhomie,"[53] as well as with Moses's later marriage to a Sudanese woman (Num. 12:1; however, the Hellenistic story of Joseph and Aseneth has Aseneth converting to Judaism). Marrying an Egyptian is apparently not subject to the critique that applies to marrying a Canaanite. Joseph's new name and his wife's name are plausible Egyptian ones, when one allows for changes that would come about when they are transliterated into Hebrew. Genesis

48. Cf. Ward, "Egyptian Office."
49. See, e.g., Sarna, *Genesis*, 288.
50. Cf. Alter, *Genesis*, 240.
51. Cf. Skinner, *Genesis*, 469.
52. Seebass, *Genesis*, 3:71.
53. Cf. Wenham, "Religion of the Patriarchs," 184.

does not comment on their meaning as it does with other names (including those of Joseph's sons in vv. 51–52), and early translations and modern commentators differ on their possible meanings. Situated on the northeast side of Cairo, On was a center of the worship of the sun-god and was thus also known as Sun City (Jer. 43:13; hence its Greek name Heliopolis). Its (high) priest would therefore be a significant person. His name is a variant on the name of Joseph's original master (see BDB). "By these new connections Joseph has become completely Egyptian."[54]

41:45b–49. Beginning his work involves going around the entire country to discover the dimensions of the task and to set about appointing the staff who will be involved in implementing his proposal. It's not explicit whether Pharaoh will buy the annual surpluses from people for the first seven years or whether he is imposing a 20 percent tax rate, though it does seem that a 20 percent tax rate became a permanent feature of Egyptian life (47:24–26). Grain was a regular medium for the payment of taxes, and the towns would be set up for its storage.[55] Ironically, the descendants of Joseph and his brothers will find themselves laboring on the building of store cities for what the government levies (Exod. 1:11). Thus "Joseph's counsel to Pharaoh is troublesome for all who have ever lived under the shadow of empire."[56] On the other hand, the alternative might be self-indulgence or waste followed by starvation, and action such as Joseph recommends could ensure that life would continue and guard against profiteering.[57]

41:50–52. If we wonder whether Joseph's marriage indicates that he is out of touch with his God (or whether grain like the sand of the sea indicates that he has forgotten the promise about offspring as numerous as the sand of the sea), the names he gives to his sons indicate that it is not so. God has a twofold gift for Joseph: the possibility of forgetting and the possibility of being fruitful.[58] At one level and in a good sense, Joseph has forgotten the family that sold him into servitude in Egypt many years before, in his teenage years. An audience that puts out of mind its knowledge of how the story will unfold could imagine that there will be no more talk of Joseph's relationship with his birth family—or at least that Joseph thinks this way. Yet the names he gives his sons suggest that he has forgotten yet not forgotten.[59] The name *mənaššeh* suggests a link with the verb *našâ* and the meaning "he [God or the child] makes [me/us] forget," in a good sense—forget suffering and affliction. But Genesis adds reference to forgetting the family. The name *ʾeprayim* could remind one of the verb *pārâ*, "be fruitful"; but the explanation again

54. Von Rad, *Genesis*, 372.
55. Cf. Driver, *Genesis*, 343.
56. De La Torre, *Genesis*, 327; cf. Brett, *Genesis*, 119.
57. Cf. Qimchi, *Genesis*, on vv. 35–36.
58. Fretheim, "Genesis," 624.
59. Cf. Wenham, *Genesis 16–50*, 397–98.

indicates that Joseph has not actually forgotten the tough experiences he has been through.

41:53–56. Pharaoh's dream comes true and Joseph's plan works. "Famine . . . famine . . . famine . . . famine . . . famine," Genesis keeps repeating. The closing verses incidentally refer to other countries also being affected by famine, which key observation leads into the next chapter.

44
How the Ten Brothers Come to Egypt

(41:57–42:38)

Overview

In light of the famine in Canaan, Joseph's brothers (less Benjamin) go to Egypt to buy grain; they do not recognize Joseph, but he recognizes them. He accuses them of being spies and sends them (holding on to Simeon) to get Benjamin, to prove their integrity, and he has their silver put back in their bags when they leave. Jacob refuses to let Benjamin go in order to make it possible for Simeon to return.

Translation

41:57 Now the entire world came to Miṣrayim to trade grain supplies with
Yosep, because the famine prevailed in the entire world.[1] **42:1**So Yaʿaqob
looked:[2] there were supplies in Miṣrayim. Yaʿaqob said to his sons,
"Why do you look at each other?"[3] **2**and said, "There: I've heard that
there are supplies in Miṣrayim. Go down there and get supplies for us
from there so we can live and not die." **3**So ten of Yosep's brothers went
down to get supplies of grain from Miṣrayim; **4**Binyamin, Yosep's brother,

1. The subject rather than the verb comes first in v. 57, which is thus a similar circumstantial clause to 43:1; both give background information to what follows. I thus associate 41:57 (which changes the subject over against what precedes) with 42:1–38, against the medieval chapter division.

2. Literally, "saw that"; the translation reflects the link with the recurrence of the verb in v. 1b.

3. Targum Ps.-J. has "Why are you afraid?" implying a form from *yārēʾ* rather than *rāʾâ*; cf. Jerome, *Hebrew Questions on Genesis*, 188–89. The LXX's "Why are you taking things easy?" and the Vg's "Why are you neglectful?" convey the implication, as indeed may Tg. Ps.-J.

Yaʿaqob did not send with his brothers, because (he said), "so that harm doesn't befall him." **5**So Yiśraʾel's sons came to get supplies among the people who were coming because there was the famine in the country of Kenaʿan.

6Now Yosep being the person with power over the country was the one who was trading supplies to the entire people of the country.[4] So Yosep's brothers came and bowed down to him, their faces to the ground. **7**Yosep saw his brothers and recognized them, but he acted without recognition to them[5] and spoke toughly with them. He said to them, "Where have you come from?" They said, "From the country of Kenaʿan, to get food supplies."

8So Yosep recognized his brothers, but they didn't recognize him, **9**and Yosep was mindful of the dreams that he had about them. He said to them, "You're investigating things.[6] It's to see the country's bareness[7] that you've come." **10**They said to him, "No, my lord, in that your servants have come to get grain supplies. **11**We're all of us sons of one man. We're upright[8] men. Your servants have not been investigating things." **12**He said to them, "No, you've come to see the country's bareness." **13**They said to him, "Your servants were twelve, we were brothers, the sons of one man in the country of Kenaʿan. But there: the littlest is with our father at the moment, and one[9] is no more."[10] **14**But Yosep said to them, "It's as I stated to you: you're investigating things. **15**By this you'll be tested. Parʿoh's life,[11] you won't leave here unless the littlest of your brothers comes here. **16**Send off one of you so he can get your brother, and you yourselves be confined, so your words may be tested, whether there is truth with you. Otherwise, Parʿoh's life, you're investigating things." **17**And he confined them under guard for three days.

18But Yosep said to them on the third day, "Do this and live; I revere God. **19**If you're upright, one of your brothers must be confined in your guardhouse, and you—go, and bring grain supplies for the famine in your

4. For the translation of the circumstantial clause, see Geller, "Cleft Sentences," 26–27.

5. BDB, *DCH*, and B. Lang (*TDOT* 9:423–31) derive the two forms of *nākar* from separate roots, one meaning "recognize" and one meaning "be foreign." *HALOT* takes them as antithetical meanings from the same root. Either way, the juxtaposition has the effect of paronomasia: he recognizes, but he acts so as not to be recognized, or he knows they are not foreigners but acts as if they are. The point is underscored by the double recurrence of the verb in v. 8. It also makes a link with 37:32–33 (and 38:25–26).

6. Etymologically, people "going about on foot."

7. Targum Onq. has "defects/breaches," the Vg "weaknesses," the LXX "tracks," Sym "secrets," Tg. Neof. "entrances," Tg. Ps.-J. "the bareness of the whores." The word order highlights the nature of the accusation (Bandstra, "Word Order and Emphasis," 121).

8. The LXX's "peaceable" sacrifices the irony in their claim.

9. The LXX, Vg "another" implies *ʾaḥēr* for *ʾaḥad*.

10. Targums Neof.'s and Ps.-J.'s "one left us, and we do not know what became of him in the end" perhaps lets them off the hook.

11. The Vg has "by Pharaoh's life," which makes good sense of the asyndetic expression, on which see JM 165e; *IBHS* 40.2.2b.

households, [20]and the littlest of your brothers you are to bring to me so your words may be shown to be true and you may not die." They did so, [21]but they said to each other, "Really, we're paying the penalty for our brother. We saw the distress of his spirit[12] when he pleaded for favor with us and we didn't listen. That's why this distress has come upon us." [22]And Reʾuben averred[13] to them, "I said to you, 'Don't do wrong against the child,' didn't I? And you didn't listen. Yes, his blood—there, it's being required."

[23]Now they didn't know that Yosep was listening, because there was an interpreter between them. [24]He turned away from them and cried, but came back to them and spoke to them, and got Šimʿon from among them and confined him before their eyes. [25]But Yosep gave orders and people filled their bags with grain—and to put back their silver, each man, into his sack, and give them provisions for the journey.

So he did this for them, [26]they loaded their grain supplies onto their donkeys, and they went from there. [27]One of them opened his sack to give feed to his donkey at the lodging, and he saw his silver. There it was, in the mouth of his bag. [28]He said to his brothers, "My silver has been put back! Yes, here it is, in my bag!" Their understanding failed,[14] and they turned trembling to one another, saying, "What is this that God has done to us?"

[29]They came to Yaʿaqob their father in the country of Kenaʿan and told him all that had happened to them: [30]"The man who is lord of the country spoke toughly with us and treated us as people who were investigating the country. [31]We said to him, 'We're upright. We haven't been investigating things. [32]We were twelve, brothers, the sons of our father; one is no more and the littlest is with our father in the country of Kenaʿan at the moment.' [33]But the man who is lord of the country said to us, 'By this I shall know that you're upright. Your brothers: leave one with me, and in respect of the famine in your households: get something and go, [34]and bring the littlest of your brothers to me, so I may know that you're not investigating things but are upright. I'll give your brother to you, and you can move about in the country.'" [35]Then as they were emptying their sacks, there—each man's silver pouch was in his sack. They and their father saw the silver pouches, and they were afraid.

[36]Yaʿaqob their father said to them, "Me: you have bereaved me of children. Yosep is no more and Šimʿon is no more and Binyamin you will get. On me it has all fallen." [37]But Reʾuben said to his father, "You may put my two sons to death if I don't bring him back to you. Put him into my charge, and I myself will bring him back to you." [38]But he said, "My son is not to go down with you, because his brother is dead and he

12. The LXX sees the *ʾăšer* at the beginning of this clause as a rare causal use of the conjunction; the Vg sees it as referring back to the suffix on "our brother"; I take it as referring forward to the suffix on *napšô*—literally, "brother, the distress of whose spirit we saw."

13. On this translation of *ʿānâ*, see 18:27 and the note.

14. Cf. the Tg; lit., "their heart went out," the heart being the locus of understanding.

alone is left. Should harm come to him on the journey that you would go on, you will send my gray hair down with grief to Še'ol."

Interpretation

Act One in the story of Jacob's lines of descent took Joseph from dissension within the family to having a key role in Egypt. But the story is not interested in events in Egypt, or even in Joseph's success, for their own sake. Its real interest always lies in Jacob's family, and how they end up in Egypt, on which it now focuses. Act Two in the story (41:57–47:26) focuses on a series of movements between Canaan and Egypt on the part of the brothers and eventually of Jacob, initially to get food during the famine. There are two visits by the brothers as there were two dreams in Gen. 37, two imprisonments in Gen. 39–40, two dreams in Gen. 40, and two more dreams in Gen. 41. On each visit Joseph avoids revealing to his brothers who he is, until he can hold back no longer. As the story unfolds, "the writers tax their inventiveness to the utmost in retarding the *dénouement* of the plot," with these repeated journeys to Egypt, interviews with Joseph, and expedients by Joseph "to excite the compunction of his brethren,"[15] who "go from one fear and distress to another."[16]

In one sense, then, nothing happens in Gen. 42–44, as nothing happened in Gen. 39–41. In another sense something vital happens as the brothers are driven to articulate some truths and to relate to themselves, to one another, and to Jacob in a more wholesome human way than they did in Gen. 37. During the second visit, Judah in particular is a different person from the man he was at the beginning of Gen. 38 and even at the end of Gen. 38. And as Joseph moves from harshness to the tears that indicate he has not forgotten his trouble and his family although he claimed to forget in 41:51, he implicitly confirms their recognition that in the events related in Gen. 37, he knew a distress of spirit that was there unexpressed.

Scene 1 within Act Two covers the first visit. It comprises four main subscenes, the first pair and the last pair being linked by a briefer account of a journey, the whole being arranged abcc′b′a′:

Jacob and the brothers: a conflict and a commission (41:57–42:4)
  The brothers arrive in Egypt (42:5)
    Joseph and the brothers: an accusation and an arrest (42:6–17)
    Joseph and the brothers: a condition and a ploy (42:18–25)
  The brothers leave Egypt (42:26–28)
Jacob and the brothers: a report and an offer (42:29–38)

15. Skinner, *Genesis*, 473.
16. Gunkel, *Genesis*, 422.

As commonly happens with parallelism and palistrophes, the second half represents an enhanced version of the first half. So the brothers and Joseph are more self-revealing in vv. 18–25, the journey is more complicated in vv. 26–28, and Jacob's emotions and focus on Benjamin and the conversation between Jacob and his sons are more deeply felt in vv. 29–38.

Although Egypt and Joseph have been the focus in Gen. 39–41, this chapter starts and ends in Canaan with Jacob.[17] In this sense the audience looks at events through Jacob's eyes, though it is aware that Jacob and the brothers only half-know what is going on. They don't know what Joseph knows, and they don't know that Joseph is manipulating them. Indeed, through scene 3 until Joseph reveals himself, Joseph knows what he is doing, but the brothers and their father have no clue. But Joseph too doesn't know how upright they really are or whether they are telling the truth about Benjamin, and his own experience of them must make it an open question. The audience also only three-quarters knows what is going on. It doesn't know for sure how to evaluate the brothers' admission of guilt and their conversations with one another and their question about God in v. 28. Both Joseph and the audience know that the brothers are only half-telling the truth in v. 11 ("We are upright men") and v. 13 ("One is no more"). And the audience has to try to work out why Joseph is behaving the way he is. Is he simply testing the brothers, as he says? Or getting his own back? Or trying to teach them a lesson, and if so, what lesson? Or seeking to bring about a more complete fulfillment of his dream than that implied by v. 6? Or seeking to draw them to proper repentance? Or what? Why does he insist on Benjamin coming? Why doesn't he respond to their admission of guilt? Does he really revere God, as he says in v. 18? And what is the significance of his crying? The audience must listen carefully until many of these questions are at least clarified by the end of the chapter.

41:57–42:4. The new scene goes straight on from what precedes but it also picks up from Gen. 37: thus "the two main lines of the Joseph story come together."[18]

That the famine would extend beyond Egypt (41:57) was suggested neither by Pharaoh's dream nor by Joseph's interpretation, but it did so, as 41:54 has incidentally noted. Actually, the widespread famine would really mean different famines. While Egypt's problem would be the Nile's failure to irrigate the fields on either side because of a fall in its level caused by a failure of the rains to the south, the problem in Canaan would be caused by a failure of the rains on the land itself, which would have a different explanation and would be more frequent. So it will be a nasty coincidence when famine strikes in both regions in the same year.

17. Cf. von Rad, *Genesis*, 376.
18. Westermann, *Genesis 37–50*, 103.

Jacob is looking at what is happening in Egypt (42:1–3) and perhaps looking at groups of people from Canaan returning with supplies from there, whereas the brothers are just looking at each other. They are frozen in inactivity. Jacob, who hasn't been very active in this story for quite a while, comes back to life. The narrative's following up his question with the further "he said," which introduces his statement, implies that the brothers have had nothing to say in response to the question, and his "almost excessive spelling out" of things ("so we can live and not die") further reflects his impatience with his sons, "who are acting as though they did not grasp the gravity of the situation."[19]

His concern about harm coming to Benjamin (42:4) through the trek to a foreign land may derive partly from harm having come to Joseph on his trek (Jacob thinks). It may also derive from Benjamin's being still relatively young; he was born when his brothers were almost grown up. He really was the son of Jacob's old age (see 37:2–3 and the comment there): Joseph was once his favorite son, and now Benjamin has taken his place. Further, Benjamin alone was the full brother of the lost Joseph, the two of them being the only two sons of Rachel. Since Benjamin was only a tiny clan (even before the events in Judg. 19–21), though it did produce Israel's first king, Benjaminites might hear of his status with some ruefulness (though in 46:21 Benjamin has ten sons).

42:5. Without Benjamin, then, the brothers arrive in Egypt, as just one company of foreigners among many such companies coming to buy grain. Referring to them as "Israel's sons" means using the regular expression for "Israelites" and could suggest to the audience that their journey down to and back up from Egypt anticipates how "the Israelites" will eventually go down to Egypt and come back up from there.

42:6–17. Thus these ten brothers are by no means the only people appearing before Joseph and doing obeisance; other people like them are doing so every week.

But Joseph recognizes them (v. 7), notwithstanding his recent declaration in 41:51 that God had enabled him to forget them. It's not surprising that they don't recognize him, given that he is now an adult and looks like an Egyptian. "Disparity of knowledge" is now key to the unfolding of the Joseph story.[20] Initially it's more surprising that Joseph acts like a stranger or foreigner, that he acts tough, toward them. Does he treat all foreign grain-seekers this way? Is he simply acting in a way consistent with the earlier portrait of the "spoiled favorite"?[21] Might we be asking the wrong question of the narrative if we focus on his possible motivation for acting in the tough way he does?[22] Is the deceit that he practices excusable as it aims at the restoration of *šālôm*? Part

19. So Alter, *Genesis*, 244, 245.
20. Humphreys, *Joseph*, 108.
21. Sternberg, *Poetics of Biblical Narrative*, 289.
22. Cf. M. Williams, "Lies."

of the point, at least, is what is going to be achieved by his tough stance.[23] He needs to get through to the brothers (see vv. 21–22, 28). But at this point in the story the answers to these questions are not clear. The audience must wait for them to be clarified.

His remembering his dreams (vv. 8–9a) begins to provide an explanation for his behavior. This memory relates to their now bowing down to him; the verb recurs from 37:7, 9, and 10. They have bowed "to the ground"; ironically, it was they who had added this phrase in 37:10. Though they had tried to put Joseph down to stop his dream becoming reality, by selling him to Egypt they have enabled it to become so.[24] With further irony, it was sheaves that stood for Joseph and his brothers in his first dream, and now grain is the reason for their bowing down. In the terms of the second dream, ten "stars" have bowed down to him, though only ten,[25] and not the sun and moon. Yet even without the dream, Jacob's favoritism and the brothers' resentment would have taken Joseph into Egypt. Realizing that their arrival and their necessary bowing down to the supplies master fulfills the dream means realizing that the events that have taken place were not mere chance. The narrative does not explicitly bring God in at this point, but Joseph's words in 50:20 will spell out the implications that are left unstated here.

Joseph goes on to express or invent a suspicion (vv. 9b–10) that might be both plausible and ludicrous. Egypt would need to be wary of espionage on the part of foreign agents working for some big power such as the Hittites or Hyksos[26] or for Canaanite coalitions interested in throwing off Egyptian authority. So why are there so many men in this group? Yet are these raggedy shepherd-types people who are investigating the country with hostile intent, looking into the bareness or emptiness or nakedness (the most common meaning of *ʿerwâ*) of the one country in the region that is neither bare nor empty nor naked? Is Egypt really vulnerable to them? And what is the connection between Joseph's remembering his dreams and his accusing the brothers of espionage: is it resentment, or mistrust, or what?[27] Is it that he needs to bring the rest of the family there? Or is it that the story is about Joseph's journey from trauma to resolution,[28] and the memory is traumatic? Again we must wait for such questions to be clarified.

But no, they are a family group, not an espionage team (v. 11), "sons of one man . . . upright men," not spies, they add asyndetically and anxiously. The first statement is unexceptionable but significant: spies wouldn't be family. The audience knows that the second is questionable in light of what the story

23. Cf. Seebass, *Genesis*, 3:92.
24. Fretheim, "Genesis," 599.
25. Cf. Jerome, *Hebrew Questions on Genesis*, 189.
26. See, e.g., Brayford, *Genesis*, 425–26.
27. Alter, *Art of Biblical Narrative*, 163.
28. Polliack, "Joseph's Journey."

has narrated about them, and Joseph knows it too. The third is true but is the one Joseph pretends not to swallow. One of the brothers is no more, they have to acknowledge, again with irony; Joseph doesn't press them about this laconic admission.

Instead (vv. 12–15), he persists with the accusation that they have denied, no matter what they say, like an actual anti-espionage interrogator. Three times he repeats the declaration, but his reason is different from that of a CIA or FBI cross-examiner. His talk of testing involves a double entendre.[29] He is not really thinking that they are spies. He is entitled to wonder what kind of men they now are, whether they are the same men they once were. One reason for the repeated questioning might be the suspicion that they could have treated Benjamin the same way as they treated him.[30] Their reference to Benjamin may also give him his chance to exercise an initiative that works toward the more complete fulfillment of the dreams. He underscores his avowal by the expression "Pharaoh's life," which implies "as sure as the fact that Pharaoh is alive and well, what follows will happen."

In putting them under confinement in the first instance (vv. 16–17), he subjects them to the same experience as he had (cf. 40:3, 4, and 7). As an alternative to testing them, he could have simply thrown them in prison permanently to rot and thereby get revenge or have sent them off without the grain they sought. Alternatively, he could have told them who he was and thrown his arms around them in the way he eventually does. One can imagine that after they had recovered from the shock, they would say how wrongly they had behaved toward him in selling him into servitude in Egypt. But would their expression of sorrow be genuine?

42:18–25. He keeps the brothers under arrest for less time than he experienced it and then indicates that he will be more merciful than he threatened earlier. Earlier he backed up his statement by saying that it was as sure as the fact that Pharaoh was alive; now he backs it up with his declaration that he is someone who lives in awe and submission to God and who therefore keeps his word. Instead of one of them going to get Benjamin while the others stay under guard, one of them must stay under guard while the rest take supplies back to Canaan and get Benjamin. Holding on to one won't help to establish whether they are spies, but it will help to establish whether they (now) care about each other.[31] The brothers might wonder why revering God does not issue in a more merciful plan the first time around. The audience might wonder whether he does change his mind or whether he always intended to make the arrangement less tough; vv. 25–28 will support the idea that he always knew what he intended.

29. Cf. von Rad, *Genesis*, 378.
30. Cf. Chrysostom, *Homilies on Genesis 46–67*, 226–28.
31. Cf. Brayford, *Genesis*, 421.

The realization they now express (vv. 21–22) suggests part of the answer to the audience's possible question; the time in custody has functioned as a successful test.[32] Over the years that have passed, have they not thought about their action? "But now they are compelled (so to speak) to enter into their own consciences."[33] They are starting to change. It's only a start. Their statement is impersonal, suggesting an outworking of fate or karma. But it's a start. Joseph is enabling his brothers to achieve a new relationship with their past.[34] Although Gen. 37 says nothing about distress, their treatment of Joseph could hardly have failed to have the effect they describe; as they had caused Joseph distress, they can hardly complain that they are now experiencing distress. Reuben's "I told you so" with its reference to blood being required (see 9:5 and the comment there) also suggests an impersonal process. It too indicates how their rethinking is only a start, but it is a start.

Joseph's crying (vv. 23–25) suggests that his chastisement is intended to draw them toward repentance rather than merely being a way to get back at them. "As Joseph hears his brothers' expression of remorse, the first strong impulse of reconciliation takes place in his own feelings, though he cannot yet trust them and so must go on with the test."[35] His specifying Simeon as the hostage perhaps reflects his being the next senior brother after Reuben. Following on the tears of v. 24, the return of the money might be a gesture of generosity rather than a trap, but it might be another form of test or part of a strategy for gradually getting them to the point where they will face what they have done.

42:26–28. Perhaps only this one man's silver was in the mouth of the sack rather than pushed farther down.[36] "What is this that God has done to us?" In one sense, the rhetorical question will find its answer in 50:19–20. But elsewhere, "What is this that you have done?" is an accusatory question (3:13; 12:18; 26:10; 29:25; cf. also 4:10; 20:9). The brothers are protesting about God doing something bad.[37] They think of it as a trap. It will lead to their being falsely accused.[38] They are asking, "What does God have in mind? . . . Why is God doing this?" They have not yet gotten as far as confession and repentance.[39] But they do ask what God is doing; they don't wonder whether some human hand is responsible.[40] Thus they refer to God, as they did not in vv. 21–22, but their question seems rhetorical.

32. Westermann, *Genesis 37–50*, 110.
33. Calvin, *Genesis*, 2:343.
34. S. Singer in Eskenazi and Weiss, *Torah*, 254.
35. Alter, *Art of Biblical Narrative*, 167.
36. So Qimchi, *Genesis*, on the verse.
37. Cf. Hamilton, *Genesis 18–50*, 532.
38. Cf. Rashi, *Br'šyt*, 478.
39. Luther, *Genesis 38–44*, 275, 277.
40. Cf. Calvin, *Genesis*, 2:347.

42:29–35. As usual, the report of events about which we already know contains telling variants on the narrator's version. They tell Jacob everything, the narrator says, but they don't. They don't tell him about being held in custody for three days. "Leave" is a nice word: it's the word for God putting Adam in the garden in 2:15. It doesn't suggest imprisonment. As a whole, the brothers' report is blander than the reality was.[41] The repetition of the story also incorporates a promise of permission to move about in the country of Egypt, the same offer Hamor made in 34:10 and 21 for his land. They don't tell Jacob about the money in the sack either, but then money pours out everywhere;[42] everyone finds their money in their sacks, not just the one person mentioned in vv. 27–28.

42:36–38. "Jacob their father" repeats the unnecessary description from the previous section (v. 29) and leads poignantly and accusingly into the indictment that follows.[43] Jacob's words are understandable. Reuben once again speaks as the eldest of the brothers. He will have four sons by the time of 46:9; maybe he has only two by now, or maybe he speaks in terms of two to double the loss that Jacob fears. If his "I told you so" (v. 22) was unfortunate, he now redeems himself, though "Jacob does not dignify the suggestion with a reply."[44] Instead, he almost repeats the words he had uttered about Joseph. Again there is irony. He alone is left? He alone is left of the love between Jacob and Rachel. Jacob has learned nothing about favoritism. Whether or not God has enabled Joseph to forget, he has not enabled Jacob to forget. "The promises of God seem powerless and empty. The covenant seems to have come to a dead end."[45]

41. Cf. Wenham, *Genesis 16–50*, 410.
42. Sternberg, *Poetics of Biblical Narrative*, 297.
43. Cf. Westermann, *Genesis 37–50*, 113.
44. Brett, *Genesis*, 121; Gen. Rab. 90.9 imagines Jacob's dismissive reply, "Are your sons not my sons too"?
45. Reno, *Genesis*, 277.

45

How the Eleven Brothers Come to Egypt

(43:1–44:13)

Overview

Jacob sees that he has no alternative to letting the brothers return to Egypt to buy more grain, taking Benjamin with them. Joseph gives them a bemusingly generous welcome but then orders his staff to put more silver into their sacks along with his personal chalice. They set off to get back to Canaan, but Joseph has them chased, the chalice is found in Benjamin's bag, and they return to the town.

Translation

43:1 Now the famine in the world[1] was severe. **2**So when they had finished
eating the supplies that they had brought from Miṣrayim, their father said
to them, "Go back, get us a little by way of food supplies."[2] **3**But Yehudah
said to him, "The man solemnly affirmed[3] to us, 'You will not see my
face unless your brother is with you.' **4**If you actually are going to send

1. The parallel with 41:57 suggests that *ʾereṣ* refers to the world and not just the country of Canaan.

2. More literally, "Go again, get us supplies, a little food." The asyndetic sequence of verbs suggests that *šub* functions as a semi-auxiliary verb (cf. JM 177bcd) meaning "repeat," as in 30:31 (cf. Tal, *Genesis*, 181–82*), though as part of a commission to the brothers to go back to Egypt, it likely also suggests the connotation "go back" (as the Vg assumes; the LXX has a double translation). Contrast v. 13 and the note.

3. The infinitive precedes the finite verb for emphasis: "in affirming he affirmed." The idiom (infinitive + finite verb) recurs twice in 43:7, in 43:20, and in 44:5.

our brother with us, we'll go down and get supplies for you.[4] **5**But if you actually aren't going to send him, we won't go down, because the man himself said to us, 'You will not see my face unless your brother is with you.'"

6Yiśraʾel[5] said, "Why did you act badly with me by telling the man whether you had another brother?" **7**They said, "The man specifically asked about us and about our family, saying 'Is your father still alive? Do you have a brother?' and we told him in accordance with these words. Could we possibly know that he would say, 'Bring your brother down here?'"

8Then Yehudah said to Yiśraʾel his father, "Send the boy with me so we can set off and go, and live and not die, both we and also you and also our little ones. **9**I myself guarantee him: from my hand you can require him. If I don't bring him back to you and set him before you, I will be in the wrong in relation to you for all time. **10**Because had we not delayed, we could by now have gotten back here twice."

11Yiśraʾel their father said to them, "If so, then, this is what you must do. Get some of the country's treats[6] in your bags and carry them down to the man as a gift: a little balm and a little syrup,[7] spices and myrrh, pistachios and almonds. **12**And silver, a double amount, get in your hand. And the silver that was put back in the mouth of your bags: carry it back in your hand. Perhaps it was a mistake. **13**And your brother: get him and set off, go back to the man.[8] **14**May El Šadday himself[9] give you compassion before the man so he will send off your other brother to you, and Binyamin. Me—when I am bereaved, I am bereaved."[10]

15So the men got this gift, and a double amount of silver they got in their hand, and Binyamin, and they set off and went down to Miṣrayim. They stood before Yosep, **16**and Yosep saw Binyamin with them and said to the person over his household, "Bring the men to the house and slaughter an animal and get it ready, because with me the men will eat at noon." **17**So the man did as Yosep said. The man brought the men to Yosep's house, **18**but the men were afraid because they were brought to Yosep's house. They said, "It's because of the silver that came back in our bags the first time that we've been brought, to overwhelm us[11] and fall upon us and get us as servants, and our donkeys."

4. The two verbs are cohortative, indicating willingness.

5. It's not clear why Jacob is called Israel in vv. 6, 8, and 11.

6. The hapax *zimrâ* might derive from *zāmar* II, "prune" (the LXX has "fruits"), or from *zāmar* I, "make music" (the Tg has "what is praised"; the Vg "the best of the fruits," perhaps a double translation), or from *HALOT*'s *zāmar* III, suggesting "strength."

7. The *dəbaš* that flows in Canaan along with milk commonly denotes the sweet sauce made from fruits such as dates, rather than bee honey.

8. Here *šûb* is a full verb and is helped by a semi-auxiliary (contrast v. 2 and the note).

9. The name of God comes before the verb, as it regularly does, suggesting emphasis.

10. Targums Neof. and Ps.-J. nicely take Jacob to mean "as I have been bereaved of Joseph, so I will have been bereaved of Simeon and Benjamin."

11. Literally, "roll on us."

19So they went up to the man who was over Yosep's household and spoke to him at the entrance of the house. **20**They said, "Excuse me, my lord, we did come down the first time to get food supplies. **21**But when we came to the lodging, we opened our bags and there: each man's silver was in the mouth of his bag, our silver by its weight. We've brought it back in our hand **22**(we've brought down other silver in our hand to get food supplies).[12] We don't know who put our silver in our bags." **23**He said, "Things are well regarding you. Don't be afraid, in that your God, yes,[13] the God of your father, gave you the treasure in your bags, given that your silver came to me." And he brought Šimʿon out to them. **24**So the man brought the men to Yosep's house, gave them water, and they washed their feet, and he gave them feed for their donkeys. **25**They got the gift ready for Yosep's coming at noon, because they'd heard that they were to eat a meal there.

26Yosep came to the house, and they brought him the gift that was in their hand, to the house, and bowed down to him to the ground. **27**He asked them about whether things were well: "Is it well with your elderly father of whom you spoke? Is he still alive?" **28**They said, "It's well with your servant our father. He's still alive," and they did obeisance and bowed down. **29**He lifted his eyes and looked at Binyamin his brother, his mother's son, and said, "This is the littlest of your brothers, of whom you spoke to me, isn't it?" and said, "God himself show favor to you, son."

30But Yosep hurried, because his feelings were strong toward his brother and he needed to cry, and he came to a room and cried there. **31**Then he washed his face and went out. So he got control of himself and said, "Set out the meal." **32**They set it out for him by himself and for them by themselves and for the Miṣrites who ate with him by themselves, because the Miṣrites could not eat a meal with the Ibrites because this would be an offense to Miṣrayim.[14] **33**But they sat before him, the firstborn according to his position as firstborn and the youngest according to his youth. The men looked in astonishment at one another: **34**someone carried servings from before him to them, and Binyamin's serving was bigger than the servings of all of them, by four or five times.[15] They drank and got tipsy with him.

44:1 But he ordered the person over his household, "Fill the men's bags with food, as much as they can carry, and put each man's silver in the mouth of his bag. **2**And my chalice, the silver chalice, put in the mouth of

12. The word order shows v. 22a to be a circumstantial clause.

13. A waw prefixes "the God of your father."

14. Only in 12:12, 14; 43:32 does Genesis use the gentilic *miṣrîm*, apparently referring to some Egyptians as opposed to Egyptians generally, for which it uses *miṣrayim* (as one uses "America" to denote Americans in general).

15. Literally, "five times," but five is a round figure to suggest "several" and not to be pressed, like "two or three" or "a dozen" in English (cf. 45:22; 47:2; Lev. 26:8; Judg. 18:2; 1 Sam. 17:40; 21:3 [4]).

the bag of the youngest, with his silver for his grain supplies." He acted
in accordance with the word that Yosep said.
3When morning dawned and the men had been sent off, they and
their donkeys,**4**though they had left the town they had not gone far when
Yosep said to the person over his household, "Set off, chase after the
men and catch up with them, and say to them, 'Why have you repaid
bad for good? **5**This is the one that my lord drinks with and actually
practices divination with, isn't it? You've acted badly in what you've
done.'" **6**So he caught up with them and spoke these words to them.
7They said to him, "Why does my lord speak words such as these? A
desecration[16] for your servants to do such a thing as this. **8**There: silver
that we found in the mouth of our sacks we brought back to you from
the country of Kenaʿan. So how would we steal silver or gold from your
lord's house? **9**Whoever of your servants it is found with, he will die, and
also we will become servants to my lord." **10**He said, "While now it will
indeed be in accordance with your words, whoever it is found with,[17] he
will become a servant to me, but you will be free of guilt." **11**They hur-
ried, each man, and lowered his bag to the ground, and opened, each
man, his bag. **12**He searched, beginning with the biggest and ending
with the littlest, and the chalice was found in Binyamin's bag. **13**They
tore their clothes, and they loaded, each man his donkey, and went back
to the town.

Interpretation

Within Act Two of the Joseph story, scene 2 (Gen. 43–45) begins in a way that parallels scene 1: some time has passed, and 43:1 begins with a circumstantial clause relating to this passage of time and the worldwide prevalence of the famine. Scene 2 then unfolds in a way that develops the parallel. There is another confrontation between Jacob and the brothers, another journey to Egypt, another initial meeting with Joseph, another second meeting, and another departure. The repetition of the sequence thus corresponds to the way earlier scenes or events come in pairs and to the way the second iteration of a scene or event may go beyond the first. Here the initial confrontation between Jacob and the brothers is more substantial. The account of the long journey is again brief. The first meeting with Joseph and then with his aide is of similar length to the one in Gen. 42 but diametrically opposed in what happens, though once again there are differences between what the brothers know, what Joseph knows, and what the audience knows; the same is true of the second meeting. Once again there then follows the setting out for home,

16. On *ḥālîlâ*, see the translation note to 18:25.

17. The LXX translates "But he said, 'And now, as you say, so it will be: the man with whom the chalice is found . . .'" But this makes the second half of the verse contradict the first half. Rather, the man begins with a concessive clause (cf. Qimchi, *Genesis*, on the verse).

but here the correspondence seems to collapse since the brothers do not make it home but instead go back to Egypt. The second half of the sequence will in due course repeat: further meetings with Joseph, another departure, then at last an arrival home, and a report to Jacob.

The MT makes 44:17 the end of its unit (which began at 41:1), but neither here nor elsewhere are there markers within Gen. 43–45 suggesting the end of one scene and the beginning of another. The medieval chapter divisions in printed Hebrew and English Bibles separate off Gen. 43 and then Gen. 44, but 44:1 needs to be read in continuity with what precedes since it gives no indication of the speaker, and 45:1 simply continues the narrative flow. "Chapters 43–44 do not have their aim in themselves. They point beyond themselves."[18] It is Gen. 43–45 as a whole that composes scene 2, balancing 41:57–42:38, but for convenience I divide it into scene 2A, comprising 43:1–44:13 (where the sequence follows the earlier pattern); and scene 2B, comprising 44:14–45:28 (where the sequence deviates but eventually comes to its conclusion). Thus set alongside the sequence in scene 1, scene 2A unfolds:

Jacob and the brothers: a conflict and a commission (41:57–42:4)	Jacob and the brothers: a commission and a conflict (43:1–14)
The brothers arrive in Egypt (42:5)	The brothers arrive in Egypt (43:15)
Joseph and the brothers: an accusation and an arrest (42:6–17)	Joseph and the brothers: a welcome and an explanation (43:16–25)
Joseph and the brothers: a condition and a ploy (42:18–25)	Joseph and the brothers: a meal and a ploy (43:26–44:2)
The brothers leave Egypt (42:26–28)	The brothers leave Egypt (44:3–13)
Jacob and the brothers: a report and an offer (42:29–38)	[see 45:25–28]

43:1–10. Genesis 43 thus begins in a parallel way to 41:57–42:38, with a report of an exchange between Jacob and the brothers that sets them going on a journey to Egypt. The confrontation between Jacob and his brothers is more substantial than the earlier one because the brothers initially resist Jacob's bidding and because the narrative relates the actual conversations. The detail slows down the story and raises suspense.

Specifically (v. 1), the chapter begins with a parallel circumstantial clause explaining the background to what follows in terms of the severity of the worldwide famine. The implication of the previous chapter is that the brothers come back with quite a lot of grain (at least ten donkey loads), but the reference to continuing famine perhaps implies the assumption that in Canaan the rains failed again the following winter, so that the next year's harvest failed. Thus maybe a year has passed.

18. Seebass, *Genesis*, 3:105.

Perhaps Jacob remembers (v. 2) that the Egyptian supplies master said that the brothers must bring Benjamin if they want more grain, and it is for this reason that he does not set his hopes too high—maybe the supplies master will sell them just a little grain. He makes no reference to the fate of Simeon, which Josephus (*Ant.* 2.6.5) has Judah referring to. If the famine had not continued, would Jacob have accepted the loss of Simeon?[19] But v. 14 will make explicit the need to gain release for him.

Judah insists that Jacob face the facts (vv. 3–5). The brothers did not argue with Jacob the first time around, but Judah does so now. Jacob must make his choice: do nothing and starve or risk Benjamin and maybe live. Judah knows which choice he would make. Judah's prominence here continues the pattern from Gen. 37, 38, and 42; the audience continues to anticipate the importance of Judah alongside Joseph in the relationships of the Israelite clans. In (twice) speaking of not being able to see the face of the supplies master, he sharpens his account of what happened the previous time (see 42:14–20), in another example of the way the reprise of an account may vary from the first account and thus fill things out for the audience and maintain interest. Judah's referring to Joseph simply as "the man" (cf. 43:5, 6, 7, 11, 13, 14) draws attention to their ignorance of who he actually is.[20]

"Jacob was under pressure from all sides" (vv. 6–7).[21] One can sympathize with his frustration. In speaking of Joseph's questioning, the brothers' account continues to tell us more than Gen. 42 did; when Judah addresses Joseph in 44:19, he puts it yet another way. But the audience knows that one might also sympathize with the brothers. The supplies master would hardly be asking his questions if he hadn't actually known the answers.

Neither can one complain at Judah's frustration (v. 8). He knows there is only one realistic thing to do. Otherwise all three generations of the family will die. He thus takes up Jacob's comment about living and not dying (42:2) and "throws it back in his face."[22] Benjamin is still "the boy" (as in 44:22, 30–34), he will still be "the littlest" in 43:29 (as also in 42:13, 15, 20; 44:23, 26), and Joseph can call him "son" (43:29). Benjamin must be twenty or so, but he is still the kid brother and the son of Jacob's old age (44:20).

Judah is not just exasperated (43:9–10). He is prepared to accept responsibility for his little half brother, who means so much to his father. He knows that if things go wrong, he will "bear the blame forever."[23] Jacob will be able to treat Judah as responsible for Benjamin's death and therefore as himself liable to death. "No sacrifice could ever remove the particular 'sin' of failing

19. Cf. Arnold, *Genesis*, 355.
20. Cf. Alter, *Genesis*, 252.
21. Chrysostom, *Homilies on Genesis 46–67*, 232.
22. Alter, *Genesis*, 253.
23. Ephrem, *Genesis*, 191.

to restore Benjamin to his father."[24] He speaks ironically in view of the treatment of Joseph in which he is implicated. And he speaks rhetorically; Judah knows that it would not help Jacob to have him put to death for causing Benjamin's death. But he speaks seriously and as someone on the move morally and personally.

43:11–14. Jacob eventually accepts Judah's argument. There is no alternative but to take the risk, though he is no more helped by Judah's words in v. 9 than he was by Reuben's offer in 42:37. But he formulates a plan to encourage a friendly stance on the part of the supplies master, and he prays.

In fostering relationships, one brings gifts (vv. 11–13), and this assumption applies especially to less powerful parties seeking to encourage relationships with more powerful parties; Jacob has already operated on this assumption with Esau (see Gen. 32–33; also 1 Sam. 10:27; 1 Kings 4:21 [5:1]; 10:1–10).[25] The gifts need not be of great intrinsic value, though Jacob's list does overlap with the cargo of the camels in 37:25; the symbolism counts. The brothers are to take some choice produce from Canaan, things apparently unaffected by the drought. "Long before Aleppo became a bombed-out ruin, it was famous for pistachios. And Ghouta, now a place of horror and chlorine gas, meant orchards of peaches, apricots, pears and almonds that supplied Damascus with sweetness."[26] The brothers are further instructed to "get" two other things to take with them. There is the silver that had been returned, along with another equivalent amount to buy more grain (cf. vv. 21–22). And there is Benjamin himself.

Accompanying the human action is a prayer (v. 14), with the recurrent implication that the two need to accompany each other; neither alone will do. El Shadday will then look after things: Isaac prayed for El Shadday's blessing on Jacob when he would need protection, and El Shadday appeared to Jacob himself with a promise of fruitfulness when he returned to Canaan (28:3; 35:11). One prays with the knowledge that God can do as one pleads, though one cannot know whether God will do so. If the journey results in his losing Benjamin, Jacob will need to accept it. Ironically, Jacob echoes his mother's fear or resignation about him (27:45)—which accompanied the action she successfully took. "When I [will] have perished, I [will] have perished," Esther declares, in a similar formulation (Esther 4:16).[27] It signifies not resignation but acceptance. Jacob is a little like his grandfather, Abraham, taking Jacob's father, Isaac, to kill him. He sends off all his sons. But perhaps "in the solitude of his tent, the promise to Abraham seems to have reached a bitter, empty end.[28]"

24. Brett, *Genesis*, 122.
25. Cf. Gunkel, *Genesis*, 428–29.
26. "Obituary Bassam Ghraoui," *The Economist*, 12 May 2018, 82.
27. Cf. Willet, *Hexapla in Genesin & Exodum*, 358.
28. Reno, *Genesis*, 278.

43:15. So Jacob sends off the gift and the silver—and the boy, attached at the end of the list without a verb, almost as if unwillingly on Jacob's part or as if he doesn't want to say that Benjamin has gone. The form of expression communicates something of the way Benjamin is a "pawn" in the story.[29]

43:16–25. On their arrival in Egypt, there is again a first meeting with Joseph, which is overtly more friendly than the previous time. Previously they had no reason to fear a grilling, but they got one, and baseless and nonsensical charges were made against them. This time they have reason to fear a grilling, and instead they get an invitation to lunch. A formal meal of the kind that Joseph announces would look like an event to honor and celebrate the visitors, but they have no idea what is going on, and the event functions more like the return of their silver: it leaves them scared and bemused. Maybe "the man" has a prison attached to his house (cf. 39:20)?[30] The audience might wonder whether Joseph is aiming at that effect, as part of seeking to work a change in them. But again the audience cannot guess what he is thinking.

In their anxiety (vv. 19–22) the brothers begin to defend themselves as soon as they enter the courtyard of Joseph's house and before they have been accused of anything.[31] Once again there is variation in the way the story is told; they speak of everyone finding their silver at the lodging place, which is a simpler version than the one in 42:26–35.

One would have thought that the steward (43:23a) would have been involved in the return of the silver to them in 42:25, in which case he speaks here as someone who is part of the plot, whatever the plot is; perhaps he assumed that his master was being inexplicably generous. He speaks to the brothers in terms strangely reminiscent of ones that someone in Jacob's family might use: he refers to "your God, the God of your father," in words most like those of Laban in 31:29. Ironically, when the first silver fell out of one of the bags, in 42:28, they had spoken in terms of what God had done, and now the steward confirms God's involvement. His language invites the audience to see his words as more than a random or conventional comment. "God did not personally insert the money in their sacks (cf. 42:25), but because this human action was in tune with the divine purposes, one could claim God as the subject of the action."[32]

To their astonishment, out comes Simeon (vv. 23b–25), and in they go to get ready for this festive lunch, treated in the way appropriate to house guests.

43:26–34. As happened in Gen. 42, a second meeting with Joseph follows. Once more there is bowing down, now in complete fulfillment of Joseph's first dream and of the first part of his second dream with its eleven stars (37:5–9).

29. Brueggemann, *Genesis*, 342.
30. Cf. Sarna, *Genesis*, 300.
31. Cf. Gunkel, *Genesis*, 430.
32. Fretheim, "Genesis," 636.

That second dream has also spoken of the sun, and here Joseph goes on to ask about Jacob.

Then he lifts his eyes and looks at Benjamin (v. 29), which implies a deliberate permitting of himself to settle his eyes on his younger brother (compare this expression in 13:10, 14). Benjamin is the one who is not only his brother like the other ten but also "his mother's son." We know from v. 16 that he saw him when they all arrived, so that whereas he "asked" about how things were with Jacob, and the brothers told him, he has no need to "ask" about Benjamin; his rhetorical question about him needs no reply and gets none.

Once more the story does make clear one element in Joseph's feelings (vv. 30–31)—his affection for Benjamin. Once more Joseph cries, and the narrator uses the word *raḥămîm*, which Jacob used in v. 14 (they are the only two occurrences in Genesis). It is the plural of the word for a womb in 20:18; 29:31; 30:22, which can thus point to a mother's compassion for her children, but here it suggests the fellow feeling of two people born from the same womb. The paradox is that Joseph could at any point have assuaged his painful feelings by revealing his identity, but it seems that he needs to wait until the work is done in the brothers—just as God needs to wait and live with his own pain on the way to the fulfillment of his purpose. "Joseph's own anguished weeping provides an occasion to contemplate the mystery of God's sovereign participation in time. God himself endures the delay necessary for the fulfillment of the plan initiated in Abraham, an anguishing delay fraught with enmity and unbelief."[33]

We do not know wherein lay the offensiveness of the Hebrews (v. 32). Classical literature sometimes refers to the Egyptians' chauvinism, and Herodotus (*Histories* 2.41) notes that their regarding the cow as sacred meant (among other things) being unwilling to kiss Greeks,[34] while the Tg includes the explanation that the Hebrews ate the cattle that the Egyptians worshiped. But we have no evidence of an Egyptian discipline against eating with foreigners. Herodotus (*Histories* 2.47) also notes that the Egyptians agreed with the Israelites that the pig was defiling,[35] and people listening to this story might be amused at the apparent Egyptian reciprocation of common Israelite attitudes.

It is easy to imagine that the brothers are "stunned" by the entire event (vv. 33–34).[36] Usually the verb (*tāmah*) denotes a negative astonishment. The experience continues to be too positive not to be worrying. If there is a particular reason for their astonishment, it might be their sitting in order of age, or it might be that they sit "before" Joseph in a way that imperils the assumption about Egyptian convention that was presupposed by Joseph's staff in v. 32, or

33. Reno, *Genesis*, 279.
34. Cf. Seebass, *Genesis*, 3:100.
35. Cf. Redford, *Study*, 235.
36. Cf. Wenham, *Genesis 16–50*, 424.

it might be the favoring of the youngest guest that follows. But no worrying possibility seems to have "disturbed the party atmosphere."[37]

44:1–2. Notwithstanding the medieval chapter division, the story continues without a break with a further action on Joseph's part that corresponds to 42:25. The action in 42 seemed an act of generosity. The one here is more spectacular, but adding the chalice seems odd. The silver plays no further role in events (Tg. Ps.-J. has Judah referring to it, to tidy the matter up), though one may guess at reasons for its appearing here but not later. Perhaps it anticipates the gifts that Joseph will send with the brothers in due course (see esp. 45:21–23). It also recalls the twenty silver pieces for which the brothers sold Joseph (37:28). Silver is a key motif in Gen. 42–45;[38] it almost qualifies for addition to the list of motifs that run through Gen. 37–45.[39] But the point about the eventual investigation is to isolate Benjamin, not to convict everyone.[40]

44:3–13. The account of the departure from Egypt and the journey back toward Canaan corresponds to 42:26–28 but takes a more elaborate form and has a contrasting outcome. Whereas Joseph gave the brothers a welcome that contrasted with their reception on the previous occasion, his action in sending them off contrasts with his action on the previous occasion in the opposite way. What is he seeking to achieve? But "Joseph's strategy . . . now produces its master-stroke," comparable to the judgment of Solomon.[41]

After the unexpected banquet, the day begins for the brothers (vv. 3–4) with a sense that everything is going far better than they could have hoped and with anticipation of reaching home. For them and for the audience, the reversal that follows is then devastating.[42] Here the steward is explicitly part of the plot as Joseph continues to act in a way that would bemuse the audience and might give his brothers the impression that they are living in some Kafkaesque nightmare.

The chalice (vv. 5–6) was evidently used in the kind of divination that involves, for instance, mixing oil and water or pouring flour on liquid, looking for the patterns that emerge and then asking after the significance of the patterns in light of the way such patterns had appeared on other occasions. Such examination could then reveal whether someone might recover from illness or offer other insight on coming events.[43] It might surprise the audience that Joseph practiced divination, which the Torah later bans (Lev. 19:26), though it would be another example of people in Genesis being free to act in ways

37. Cf. Wenham, *Genesis 16–50*, 424.
38. Cf. Sarna, *Genesis*, 303.
39. See "What You Wear, How You Dream, What You Eat, How You Lie, How You Cry" at the end of the comments on Gen. 37.
40. Cf. Willet, *Hexapla in Genesin & Exodum*, 362.
41. Kidner, *Genesis*, 204.
42. Cf. von Rad, *Genesis*, 384.
43. See, e.g., Annus, *Divination*.

that the Torah will later forbid. But the Torah's concern would be divination by means of processes that did not involve Yahweh; the Urim and Tummim were a form of divination, and the selection of Matthias eventually involved a not dissimilar process (Acts 1:26). But maybe it's an open question whether Joseph actually practices divination or whether that idea is just part of the deceptive tale that he spins. In 44:15 he implies that it was by divination that he knew about the chalice's theft, which was not true though it would be a plausible claim for an Egyptian.[44] The Tg protects Joseph's honor by describing him as "testing" rather than divining.

In their response (vv. 7–10) the brothers sidestep the point about divination and refer only to the chalice's value. Declaring that any thief among them should be executed makes for an ironic parallel with 31:32. On that occasion there was a real thief, the mother of Joseph and Benjamin, but no exposure; here there is exposure but no real thief. Here as there, the reference to execution is not a literal judicial declaration (we know of no Egyptian law that makes theft a capital offense) but a serious figurative affirmation of innocence. This declaration, along with the further affirmation that the rest of them should become servants to Joseph's chief of staff (maybe here the word "slaves" would be appropriate), involves a hyperbole; it is a strong way of denying that there is such a person. The chief of staff (who is party to what has really happened) takes it that way but is more literal in his prescription of what will actually happen, and he accepts the principle that the individual who stole the chalice should be treated differently from the rest of the brothers. Both he and they assume the reality of individual responsibility while also recognizing that each individual lives in the context of the family. But he prescribes that the guilty person should become a servant to Joseph rather than being executed, and that the other brothers should be treated as innocent.

Dramatically (vv. 11–12), the narrator invites us to imagine the scene whereby the inevitable discovery happens and to imagine the brothers' horror. The steward knows where the chalice is because he put it there, and so does the audience. But in the drama the investigation proceeds one by one toward the final denouement, in another parallel with the story of Laban and Rachel (see 31:25–35). "We are to imagine how the brothers exhale in relief ten times and are already sure of their sacks when the cup is found after all—in Benjamin's sack."[45]

One might expect the brothers to react (v. 13) by turning on Benjamin and saying, "You thief, son of a woman-thief" (Gen. Rab. 92.8). But they don't. Notwithstanding the steward's modification of their declaration about sharing in responsibility and punishment, they treat themselves as corporately implicated. Even if they are sure that they didn't steal the chalice, the case against

44. Cf. Alter, *Genesis*, 260.
45. Cf. Gunkel, *Genesis*, 433.

them would seem irrefutable. It is one reason why they tear their clothes, as they had once caused Jacob to tear his (37:34). Perhaps the impossibility of returning to Jacob without Benjamin is also one reason why they go back to the town. But their corporate grief, their accepting corporate responsibility, and their sticking with Benjamin hints at a change in their character.[46]

46. Cf. Driver, *Genesis*, 364.

46

How Joseph Makes Himself Known

(44:14–45:28)

Overview

Joseph confronts the brothers and declares that as a penalty Benjamin must stay as his servant, but Judah pleads to be allowed to take his place because of the hurt Benjamin's loss will cause to Jacob. Overwhelmed, Joseph reveals his identity, affirms how God's purpose lay behind the brothers' wrongdoing, and suggests that they come and live near him with his provision. Pharaoh backs the proposal, and they go back to take the news to Jacob, who initially cannot believe it but eventually resolves to make the journey.

Translation

44:14 Yehudah and his brothers came to Yosep's house. He was still there.
They fell to the ground before him, **15**and Yosep said to them, "What is
this deed that you people have done? You know that a man like me does
practice divination,[1] don't you?" **16**Yehudah said, "What could we say to
my lord? What could we speak? How could we show we are in the right?
God has found out your servants' waywardness. Here we are, servants
to my lord, both we and the one in whose hand the chalice was found."
17But he said, "A desecration[2] for me to do this. The man in whose hand
the chalice was found, he will become a servant to me. You people: go
up with things being well, to your father."

1. The infinitive before the finite verb adds emphasis.
2. See the translation note to 18:25.

18Yehudah went up to him and said, "Excuse me, my lord, may your
servant please speak a word in my lord's ears, and may your anger not
flame up at your servant, because you are the same as Parʿoh. **19**My lord
asked his servants, 'Do you have a father or brother?' **20**and we said to
my lord, 'We have an elderly father and the child of his elderly years, lit-
tle. In that his brother is dead, he alone remains of his mother's, and his
father loves him.' **21**You said to your servants, 'Bring him down to me so
I can set my eye on him.'[3] **22**We said to my lord, 'The boy can't abandon
his father. Were he to abandon his father, he would die.' **23**But you said
to your servants, 'If the littlest of your brothers doesn't come down with
you, you will not see my face again.' **24**When we went up to your servant
my father, we told him my lord's words. **25**Our father said, 'Go back, get
us a little by way of food supplies,' **26**and we said, 'We can't go down. If
the littlest of our brothers is with us, we can go down, because we won't
be able to see the man's face with the littlest of our brothers not being
with us.' **27**Your servant my father said to us, 'You yourselves know that
my wife[4] gave birth to two sons for me. **28**One went away from me, and
I said, "Yes, he has been mauled to pieces."[5] I haven't seen him until
now. **29**If you get this one from my presence as well and harm comes,
you'll send my gray hair down to Šeʾol with things being bad.'

30"When I now come to your servant my father and the boy is not with
us, given that his life is bound up with his life, **31**when he sees the boy
is not there, he will die. Your servants will send your servant our father's
gray hair down to Šeʾol with grief. **32**Because your servant guaranteed
the boy with my father, saying 'If I don't bring him back to you, I will be in
the wrong in relation to my father for all time.' **33**So may your servant now
please live as a servant to my lord instead of the boy, and the boy—may
he go up with his brothers. **34**Because how can I go up to my father with
the boy not with me?—so that I do not see the bad fate that will come
upon my father."

45:1 Yosep couldn't control himself in front of all the people who were
stationed with him. He called, "Get everyone out from being with me!"
So no one stood with him when Yosep made himself known to his broth-
ers. **2**But he raised his voice as he cried, and the Miṣrayites heard, and
Parʿoh's household heard.

3So Yosep said to his brothers, "I'm Yosep! Is my father still alive?"
His brothers couldn't answer him because they were petrified at his
presence. **4**But Yosep said to his brothers, "Come up to me, please."
They came up and he said, "I'm Yosep your brother, whom you sold into
Miṣrayim, **5**but now, don't be distressed; it's not to cause rage in your
eyes that you sold me here, because it was for the maintaining of life
that God sent me before you, **6**because this has been two years of fam-
ine within the country, and there'll be five more years when there is no

3. For good, Tg. Ps.-J. clarifies.
4. The LXX omits "my"; Rachel was not Jacob's only wife (Tal, *Genesis*, 184*).
5. The idiomatic expression recurs from 37:33; see the first translation note to 37:8.

plowing and reaping. **7**And God sent me before you to put in place for you
a group remaining in the country[6] and to make you live as a big escape
group.[7] **8**So now, it was not you who sent me here but God. He has put
me in place as a father to Parʿoh and as lord of his entire household,
ruler over the entire country of Miṣrayim.
9"Hurry and go up to my father and say to him:

> Your son Yosep has said this: God has put me in place as lord of all Miṣrayim.
> Come down to me, don't stand about. **10**You'll live in the Gošen region and be
> near me, you and your children and your grandchildren, your flock, your herd,
> and all that's yours. **11**I'll provide for you there, because there will be five more
> years of famine, so that you and your household and all that are yours aren't
> in want.[8]

12"Here: your eyes can see and my brother Binyamin's eyes can see
that it's my mouth that's speaking to you. **13**You're to tell my father about
all my honor in Miṣrayim and all that you have seen, and hurry and bring
my father down here." **14**He fell on his brother Binyamin's neck and cried,
and Binyamin cried on his neck, **15**and he kissed all his brothers and
cried on them. And after that his brothers spoke with him.
16When the sound made itself heard in Parʿoh's household, "Yosep's
brothers have come,"[9] it was good in Parʿoh's eyes and in his servants'
eyes. **17**Parʿoh said to Yosep, "Say to your brothers, 'Do this: load your
animals and go, come to the country of Kenaʿan, **18**get your father and
your households, and come to me so I can give you the best of the coun-
try of Miṣrayim, and you can eat the fat of the country. **19**You yourself
are ordered, this is what to do: get for yourselves from the country of
Miṣrayim wagons for your little ones and your wives, and carry your father
and come. **20**Your eye—it is not to look with sadness at your belongings,
because the best of the entire country of Miṣrayim will be yours.'"
21Yiśraʾel's sons did so. Yosep gave them wagons in accordance with
Parʿoh's bidding and gave them provisions for the journey. **22**To them
all he gave changes of clothes for each person, and to Binyamin he
gave three hundred pieces of silver and four or five[10] changes of dress
clothes.[11] **23**To his father he sent as follows: ten donkeys carrying some
of the best things of Miṣrayim and ten she-donkeys carrying grain, bread,

6. Rather than "the earth," in the context.

7. More literally, "to make live for you for a big escape group": the expression mixes two possible forms of expression, the syntactical equivalent of a composite morphological form. Instead of repeating *l*, it would have been more regular to make either "you" or "a big escape group" the direct object, as in v. 7a.

8. For the translation of *tiwwārēš* from *yāraš*, cf. Tg. Ps.-J.; "perish" (the LXX, Aq, Vg, Tg. Onq.) seems to be simply a loose translation. With this meaning, the verb might be read as a by-form of, or as having the resonances of, *rûš* (be in want).

9. The sentence involves an ellipsis: the sound (*qôl*) was the sound of Joseph's voice (v. 2) that made itself heard, and the explanation of the noise is that Joseph's brothers have come.

10. See the translation note to 43:34.

11. The Vg "five best robes" conveys the sense.

and provisions for his father for the journey. **24**So he sent his brothers
off, and as they went, he said to them, "Don't be agitated[12] on the way."
25So they went up from Miṣrayim and came to the country of Kenaʿan
to Yaʿaqob their father **26**and told him, "Yosep is still alive, and actually
he's ruler over the entire country of Miṣrayim." His heart went numb, be-
cause he didn't believe them. **27**But they spoke to him all Yosep's words
that he had spoken to them, and he saw the wagons that Yosep sent to
carry him, and the spirit of Yaʿaqob their father came to life. **28**Yiśraʾel
said, "Great,[13] my son Yosep is still alive! I must go and see him before
I die!"

Interpretation

The main part of scene 2B deviates from the pattern of scene 1.[14] Instead of the brothers reaching home, initially they go back to the town to be confronted by Joseph. Judah makes an impassioned appeal to Joseph to be allowed to stay in Egypt in Benjamin's place, and his appeal overwhelms Joseph. Genesis 45 opens with a summary description of his revelation of himself, at which one could imagine the audience sitting dumbfounded. It has a moment to draw breath before the narrative gives a more detailed account and relates Pharaoh's commission to go fetch Jacob. The brothers depart for Canaan, and the pattern disturbed at 44:3–13 comes to completion.

44:14–17. Judah comes first in the account of the brothers' return because he is the one who gave the final word to Jacob about Benjamin, a promise that will now become important. If Joseph would commonly go off to do his work, he has stayed home, waiting for the brothers to come back with their tails between their legs. Once again they fulfill his dream as they fall to the ground (cf. 37:5–10), though "fell" was not the verb there; it suggests a desperate prostration.

Joseph addresses them corporately (v. 15) rather than focusing on the individual apparent thief. He apparently implies that the theft of his chalice has not stopped his divining what has happened by some other means. He is of course lying again, all in the cause of the fulfillment of his dreams, the family's survival, and his brothers' transformation as they come to a new view of themselves.

That point is hinted at by Judah's declaration (v. 16) that "God has found out your servants' waywardness." On the brothers' behalf, in his one statement about God he accepts that they share in some corporate responsibility for the wrongdoing. But there was actually no waywardness, and anyway

12. Cf. Aq. The LXX and Vg have "don't be angry," but this is not the usual meaning of *rāgaz*, nor does it fit the context.

13. The Vg's "it is enough" understates the significance of *rab*.

14. See the introduction to the comments on 43:1–44:13.

God would hardly need to find it out (as if he were ignorant of it); is Judah assuming that Benjamin really did steal the chalice? The narrative sidesteps the question and the assumption that the discovery would surely have led to a protest by Benjamin (who as usual says nothing and does nothing) in favor of letting the statement suggest a kind of ironic displacement. What is really happening is that the brothers are finding out their own waywardness, expressed in the way they treated Joseph (and Jacob) long ago. So Judah's statement compares with the statements and questions in 42:21–22 and 28, which express more truth than the speakers realize.

Joseph will not agree that they all pay the penalty (v. 17). Like the brothers and like his steward, Joseph assumes that the individual who stole the chalice has to suffer distinctive consequences, even if the brothers share in responsibility. The narrative tempts the audience to suspect that Joseph simply wants to keep his little brother in Egypt and get rid of the rest of the brothers.[15] But his speaking as he does constitutes a further test for them. Are they willing to abandon Benjamin—who looks guilty but whom Joseph knows to be innocent?[16] It is more than a test that reveals who they are; it is a temptation that gives them a chance to grow.

44:18. The MT begins a new unit here, which marks the pivotal nature of the address to Joseph that Judah now gives.[17] Judah "goes up" to Joseph (the verb *nāgaš* suggests some deference).[18] He begins with an appeal for a hearing, which presupposes the recognition that he is taking a risk; he acknowledges that Joseph has the same absolute power as Pharaoh, to act against people in anger as Pharaoh did in 40:2–3, or to be merciful.[19] In vv. 19–29 he will go on to review the events covered in scene 2A, then in vv. 30–32 he will point out the inevitable results of Joseph's proposed action, and in vv. 33–34 he will make an alternative proposal.

44:19–29. So the bulk of Judah's poignant appeal summarizes the story so far. It is framed as an address designed to convince the supplies master, and it is fashioned to achieve this end, though one of its subtleties is that it is shaped to appeal to his compassion without ever explicitly doing so.[20] It takes up phrase after phrase from conversations that have been reported earlier, with the recapitulation as usual noteworthy for what it repeats, for what it adds or for points at which it nuances and thus maintains interest, and for what it omits. It keeps referring to the servant status of the brothers and of Jacob in relation to Joseph; "servant" comes twenty times in the chapter.[21] It

15. Cf. Coats, *Genesis*, 292.
16. Cf. von Rad, *Genesis*, 388.
17. Cf. Skinner, *Genesis*, 485.
18. See the comment on 33:3b.
19. Cf. Keil and Delitzsch, *Pentateuch*, 364.
20. Joosten, "Biblical Rhetoric," 23–25.
21. Cf. Hamilton, *Genesis*, 569.

thus again suggests a fulfillment of Joseph's dreams: they are servants; he reigns or rules (37:8). On the other hand, it makes no mention of Joseph's tough and unjustified treatment of the brothers on their first visit or of the detaining of Simeon. The address is mostly unnecessary in terms of conveying information about the events, but it conveys an impression of Judah's state of mind and of his understanding of Jacob's. "This remarkable speech is a point-for-point undoing, morally and psychologically, of the brothers' earlier violation of fraternal and filial bonds." As well as accepting Jacob's arbitrary favoritism, Judah demonstrates the deepest empathy for his father. He doesn't want him to suffer the way he made him suffer before.[22] Genesis makes no reference to repentance, but the First Testament often talks about or describes or presupposes repentance without using the word, and Judah's address manifests the reality of repentance. It manifests *metanoia*. The time for a change of heart had to come. When it comes, there is no need for a call to repentance or a profession of repentance.[23]

Resentment at Jacob's favoritism thus gives way (vv. 20–24) to acceptance of what the two sons of Rachel mean to Jacob and what Benjamin means to him now. Judah ironically makes explicit that Joseph is dead, even though he has less grounds for saying so than Jacob has. The idea that they can leave Benjamin behind and go back to Jacob "with things being well," as Joseph said in v. 17, makes no sense. It would fulfill Jacob's worst fear. Whereas Joseph reasonably describes Benjamin as a man in 44:17, Judah speaks of him as the "little" son who is just a "boy."[24] Yes, he's still just the kid brother. It's odd that Judah speaks of Joseph wanting to set his eye on Benjamin (v. 21), because this expression implies paying him special attention, for good or ill (e.g., Jer. 24:6; Amos 9:4). Perhaps it's a clever formulation.[25] But it is just what Joseph wants to do.

In due course Judah comes back again (vv. 25–29) to Joseph's question about the brothers' father and mother and once again makes explicit that Benjamin is the only surviving son of his mother, the one whom Jacob calls "my wife," as if she were the only one; Judah "thereby in effect delegitimizes himself."[26] He notes that Jacob is especially fond of Benjamin because his brother was torn to pieces (!). Does Jacob's comment about not having seen him since imply "some lingering doubt"?[27] Anyway, Jacob said he would die if he lost Benjamin. His life is bound up with Benjamin's life, and Judah has guaranteed to bring him back. "The shadow of Joseph, who no longer lives but is present, lies across the speech and is revealed more and more as the

22. Alter, *Art of Biblical Narrative*, 174, 175.
23. Cf. Westermann, *Genesis 37–50*, 137.
24. Alter, *Genesis*, 263, 264.
25. So Driver, *Genesis*, 360.
26. Wenham, *Genesis 16–50*, 427.
27. Cf. Sarna, *Genesis*, 307.

really troubling factor. . . . Because Joseph is gone, the loss of the second favorite son would inevitably destroy the father."[28]

44:30–34. The review is over, and Judah comes to its implications. He can't face seeing how Jacob would react if he returned without Benjamin. Finally he comes to his concrete request, that he rather than Benjamin may stay as Joseph's servant—the position into which he had once proposed they sell Joseph. Events have had the effect they needed to have on Judah, who goes much further than he did in 37:26–27.

45:1–2. "Now, finally, after such a long climb, the narrative has reached the climax."[29] The pathos of Judah's appeal finally overcomes Joseph, though he knows it would be indiscreet to lose control of himself before everyone. Whether or not Joseph could have forgiven his brothers irrespective of whether they repented, the change of mind and heart implied by Judah's words means that mutual reconciliation and the restoring of the family relationship are now possible. Once again, Genesis gives us a summary in vv. 1–2, which vv. 3–15 and vv. 16–20 respectively will elaborate.

45:3–8. The elaboration of the brief account goes back first to relate Joseph's actual announcement. He had previously asked about "your father," but now his incredulous question concerns "my father."[30] Joseph knows the answer to his opening question, and it receives no reply, like his rhetorical question about Benjamin in 43:29. Judah has referred to their father fourteen times, which may be one element in his address that "shook Joseph and brought his self-restraint to an end."[31] Not surprisingly nor unreasonably, his brothers assume that they are being flung into another stage of their Kafkaesque drama.

Joseph picks up the verb "come up" (vv. 4–5a), which described Judah's deferential approach in 44:18. While Judah there ventured to approach Joseph, the main body of the brothers would be standing at a respectful distance from the Egyptian official. He urges them to come nearer to this man who is now going to tell them who he really is. They are not to be caused pain by facing what they have done—Joseph uses the word for the pain involved in motherhood and in farming (3:16–17). And they are not to be furious with themselves over it.

The reason (vv. 5b–6) is that they were fulfilling God's purpose, even if unwittingly. God was behind their actions. The reality of this dynamic is a further consideration in enabling Joseph to be so forgiving toward his brothers and to refer to their action without being resentful about it.[32] "In this speech of Joseph, the power of the conspiracy of chapter 37 is broken."[33]

28. Von Rad, *Genesis*, 389.
29. Gunkel, *Genesis*, 436.
30. Brett, *Genesis*, 124–25.
31. Sarna, *Genesis*, 308.
32. Cf. Luther, *Genesis 45–50*, 24–37.
33. Brueggemann, *Genesis*, 345.

When he refers to what they did to him, he does so in order to rob it of this power. God sent Joseph, and they were the means of the sending. God so acted for the sake of maintaining life, given that for five more years there'll be plowing but not reaping ("plowing and reaping" is a hendiadys).[34] Perhaps Joseph only now becomes aware of this dynamic whereby God has been at work through the brothers' action. But his recalling his dream when the brothers first showed up (42:9) rather suggests that his maneuvering of them was designed to relate to that dynamic and to bring them to the point when it can be articulated. Retrospectively, one can thus see that this insight into God's purpose and way of operating underlies the story of his testing his brothers. It is now apparent that the dreams in Gen. 37 pointed in this direction and that for a long time God has been working to that end, as an aspect of his commitment to maintain life. But Genesis itself is more interested in how the grim sequence of events that it relates contributed to the fulfillment of that aim than in who knew what when and what their motivation was.

God's purpose (v. 7) was to make sure that a group from Jacob's family remained in Egypt, in the context of the widespread famine in the region. Joseph introduces the expression *šəʾērît*, commonly translated "remnant," which would ring bells for people listening to the story (e.g., Jer. 23:3; Amos 5:15). When they were reduced to a remnant of their former selves, it would be tempting for them to wonder whether they would survive; Joseph reassures them that God's purpose for them to survive goes way back to the vulnerability of their beginning. "As often in the Old Testament, 'remnant' is a word of hope."[35] To underscore the point, he adds the term *pəlîṭâ*, which appears elsewhere in parallelism with *šəʾērît* (Ezra 9:14; Isa. 37:32). Joseph sets the two words against each other by talking in terms of "a big escape group." While God's plan was to preserve the relatively small group comprising the family of Jacob, it was also to turn them into a huge people. That promise will be reformulated in even more spectacular terms in 46:3 and realized in between Genesis and Exodus (see Exod. 1:1–7). The "maintaining of life" (*miḥyâ*) of which he speaks in v. 5, which will mean that he will "make them live" (*ḥāyâ* hiphil), will not mean merely keeping them (barely) alive or saving them from losing their life. At one level that project would not require the brothers to come to recognize what they have done, to own it, and to become reconciled with Joseph. "What God has done stands *independent of the brothers' repentance*,"[36] but at another level making them live and enabling them to fulfill the destiny of the remnant requires that development. The future of the family requires it.

34. Speiser, *Genesis*, 338.
35. Von Rad, *Genesis*, 394.
36. Fretheim, "Genesis," 646, emphasis original.

Joseph can be the means of maintaining life (v. 8) because he has become a kind of father to Pharaoh—that is, a counselor who can give him wise advice (cf. 2 Kings 6:21; 13:14), like the father who instructs his "sons" in Proverbs. As the brothers know (42:30, 33), he has been put in control of the country's economy and has thus become the most powerful figure in the country. So he is in a position to see that his family is looked after there. He is ruler not merely over them (see 37:8) but over all Egypt.

45:9–15. Now that the testing of his brothers is over, Joseph can urge them to get back to Jacob quickly and give him the news, which he does by dictating a message in the manner of the administrator that he is.

If Goshen (vv. 10–11) is a Hebrew equivalent to Kesem or Gesem (the LXX has Gesem) in Wadi Tumilat in the eastern delta of the Nile,[37] it is a region with several advantages. It is good pastureland, near Canaan and therefore easy to leave if and when leaving should become desirable (as it will!), and near the centers of Egyptian administration where Joseph would be based. The entire family of Jacob is to come—by now Joseph's brothers would have children, like Joseph himself—and its herds and flocks. They will be there at least five years. "Living" (*yāšab*) need not imply being there permanently; Jacob's mother used this verb to denote the short-term stay that she ironically envisaged for him (27:44). As it turns out, the family's stay is much longer. Jacob and Joseph will always envisage the family's return to Canaan, but they will never attempt it and will talk only of God taking them back, as God is taking them to Egypt. For people listening to the story, Joseph's reference to being in want would imply a paronomasia and a link with the talk of a remnant and a big escape group, since the verb for being in want (*yāraš*) is a homonym for a much more common verb that denotes possession and dispossession, and possessing land (in Goshen) is another important aspect of God's dealings with Jacob's descendants and a theme that has already been important in Genesis (15:1–8; 21:10; 22:17; 28:4).

The brothers have been standing there openmouthed (vv. 12–15), hardly able to believe their ears. They have been unable to speak since v. 3, with its hint at a reasonable suspicion that they are the victims of another trick. But by now Joseph's words have convinced them that they can take him at face value. As the Tg makes explicit, he would now presumably be speaking in their own language rather than communicating via an interpreter as he had previously. So now there can be mutual embracing; for Joseph, the reunion with his full brother, Benjamin, is of particular significance. And now their mouths can open.

45:16–20. The summary account of the reunion in vv. 1–2 has already reported that the noise in Joseph's office reached the palace. The narrative now elaborates on that report and on Pharaoh's reaction. The plural "households" again recognizes that each brother has his own family, except perhaps "little"

37. See Skinner, *Genesis*, 488; more recently, Van Seters, "Geography of the Exodus," 267–69.

Benjamin. The overlap between vv. 3–15 and 16–20 suggests that we need not see the two as simply sequential. Verses 3–15 must summarize conversations over a little while that will have interwoven with the conversations reported now.

45:21–24. Likewise, Pharaoh's instructions are implemented with features unmentioned in vv. 16–20 that might or might not have been added by Joseph. The new sets of robes are likely not merely changes of clothes but garments of the kind that one would wear on festive occasions (cf. 2 Kings 5:5).[38] Now everyone has one, not just Joseph as at the beginning of the story (KSG). Given the way Joseph has been playing games with his brothers and the mind-blowing nature of what has now happened, one can imagine that they might get twitchy on the way home. And later events will make clear that they do indeed still have some "residual doubt about the extent to which they have been forgiven" (see 50:15–18).[39]

45:25–28. At last the narrator can bring an end to the sequence that occupies Gen. 43–45 and parallels the one in 41:57–42:38, though again the report both matches and sharply contrasts with the equivalent one in 42:29–38.

And one can imagine that Jacob finds the report too much to believe (v. 26). The brothers' report has a paralyzing effect on him. It is inviting him to think of a possibility that he would love to be real but cannot contemplate, so that he is more disturbed after the brothers flaunt this impossible possibility before him than he was when he had been assuming for years that Joseph was dead. "What other word does a father ever want to hear except, 'My son is alive'?"[40] But whereas he believed his sons when they were lying (37:31–35), he can't believe them when they are telling the truth.[41] "Look at what happens to a liar. Even when he tells the truth, people do not believe him" (Gen. Rab. 94.3).

Repetition and visual evidence bring Jacob back to life (vv. 27–28). He has more than once spoken of going down to Sheol with sorrow (37:35; 42:38; twice further as quoted by Judah, 44:29, 31). Now he can talk about Joseph and about death in a more positive way. His life has been dominated by grief for years, but as he gets nearer the end of his life, he finds relief, not because he grows out of grief but because God has mercy.

Implications

Joseph and Judah

Although Gen. 36–50 is the account of Jacob's lines of descent, this account focuses on Joseph and Judah. The story of each of these brothers is told in a dynamic way, but not the same dynamic way.

38. Cf. Dillmann, *Genesis*, 2:409.
39. Brett, *Genesis*, 125.
40. Brueggemann, *Genesis*, 350.
41. Hamilton, *Genesis 18–50*, 587.

The dynamic of Joseph's story lies in the manner of its telling. There is no clear indication of change in Joseph during the story. The dynamic lies in the gradual process whereby the audience is able to discover the truth about him. It is the kind of story that gives the audience clues as it goes along but also leaves questions open so that it leaves itself susceptible to different interpretations until the story comes to an end. From the end one can then look back and make sense of all the clues. They now make a picture. The questions are answered. In isolation, the initial account of Joseph does not indicate whether the dreams are wish-fulfillment on the part of a bumptious teenager. And the middle of the story, with its account of the tough experience he puts his brothers through, does not indicate whether he is simply getting revenge. And neither bumptiousness nor vengefulness can be totally ruled out. But the end of the story suggests that the dream relates to God's having an intention to do something good. It is God who sent Joseph to Egypt ahead of his brothers. And Joseph's recurrent crying suggests that he was not merely engaged in getting back at the brothers. He was working toward their coming to own what they had done. It's been said that at the other end of Genesis from Adam, Joseph succeeds in many ways where Adam failed.[42] Or perhaps Joseph succeeds where Cain failed, if a key question in Gen. 37–50 is "Who is your brother?" (KSG).

The dynamic of Judah's story lies not in the telling, which is more straightforward. His story does not raise questions that it declines to answer as it goes along, as Joseph's story does. The dynamic of Judah's story lies in what happens to him. He appears four times. In Gen. 37 he is keen to avoid killing Joseph, but chiefly because he is afraid of the consequences and prefers the idea of making some money through selling him. In Gen. 38 he engages in a questionable marriage, lets down his daughter-in-law, and gets into a mess with a whore, but she opens him up to a revelatory insight about himself. In Gen. 43 he is prepared to accept responsibility for seeing that Benjamin visits Egypt safely. And in Gen. 44 he makes the fervent appeal to Joseph in which he offers to take Benjamin's place in servitude, whose evidence of being a changed man stirs Joseph into revealing who he really is.

In view of the dynamic of the story, it is apposite that Judah and Joseph should be prominent in Jacob's testament (Gen. 49). Although the imagery used of them is different, its implications are similar. For the victories he will win, Judah is now promised the recognition by his brothers that had been Joseph's destiny in his dreams; Joseph's courage and vigor are likewise affirmed. Both Judah and Joseph are promised that they will flourish. Both will need to keep his own story in mind. The great Judahite, David, will need to do so, but so will the Judah that declines and eventually finds itself a shadow of its former self in the Babylonian and Persian periods. The northern Israelite

42. See Stone, "Joseph in the Likeness of Adam."

nation will need to do so when it is flourishing and then when it is reduced to almost nothing in the Assyrian, Babylonian, and Persian periods.

What is the significance of God not appearing to Joseph and not speaking to him? Joseph is not the head of the ancestral clan, nor is he a prophet. He is closer to being an ordinary guy. He lives in between Abraham, Isaac, and Jacob on one hand, and Moses on the other. He embodies the way God can be involved with an ordinary guy.

47

How Joseph Settles His Family and Rescues the Egyptians

(46:1–47:26)

Overview

The last part of the story about Jacob's lines of descent covers the time spent by Jacob and his family in Egypt. Jacob stops at Beer Sheba, where God appears to him, but he eventually reaches Egypt. A list of the people who make the journey follows. The section goes on to recount the family's arrival in Goshen, Jacob's reunion with Joseph, a meeting of some of the brothers with Pharaoh, and his confirmation of where they can settle. It then recounts how Joseph rescues the Egyptian people through implementing a system whereby the state administers grain and controls land.

Translation

46:1 So Yiśra'el moved with all that was his and came to Be'er Šeba and
offered sacrifices to the God of his father Yiṣḥāq.
2God said to Yiśra'el in visions[1] at night, "Ya'aqob, Ya'aqob!" He said,
"I'm here." **3**He said, "I am God, the God of your father. Don't be afraid
of going down to Miṣrayim, because I will establish you as a big nation
there. **4**I myself will go down with you to Miṣrayim, and I myself will also

1. For the plural, cf. Ezek 1:1; 8:3; 40:2; 43:3. In Ezekiel, at least, the plural may suggest the various things that appeared in the vision.

definitely bring you up[2] from there, when Yosep puts his hand on your eyes."

5So Yaʿaqob set off from Beʾer Šeba. Yiśraʾel's sons carried their father Yaʿaqob, their little ones, and their wives in the wagons that Parʿoh had sent to carry him. **6**They got their livestock and their property that they had acquired in the country of Kenaʿan, and Yaʿaqob and all his offspring with him came to Miṣrayim. **7**His sons and his grandsons with him, his daughters and his granddaughters—all his offspring he brought with him to Miṣrayim.

8These are the names of the descendants of Yiśraʾel who came to Miṣrayim, Yaʿaqob and his descendants:

- Yaʿaqob's firstborn: Reʾuben; **9**Reʾuben's sons: Ḥanok, Pallu, Heṣron, and Karmi.
- **10**Šimʿon's sons: Yemuʾel,[3] Yamin, Ohad, Yakin, Ṣohar,[4] and Šaʾul, the son of a Kenaʿanite woman.
- **11**Lewi's sons: Geršon, Qehat, and Merari.
- **12**Yehudah's sons: Er, Onan, Šelah, Pereṣ, and Zerah (but Er and Onan had died in the country of Kenaʿan); Pereṣ's sons were Ḥeṣron and Ḥamul.
- **13**Yiśśakar's sons: Tola, Puwwah, Yob,[5] and Šimron.
- **14**Zebulun's sons: Sered, Elon, and Yaḥleʾel.
- **15**These are the sons of Leʾah, to whom she gave birth for Yaʿaqob in Paddan Aram, with his daughter Dinah. Every person, his sons and his daughters:[6] thirty-three.
- **16**Gad's sons: Ṣipyon,[7] Ḥaggi, Šuni, Eṣbon,[8] Arodi, and Arʾeli.
- **17**Ašer's sons: Yimnah, Yišwah,[9] Yišwi, and Beriʿah; Seraḥ their sister; and Beriʿah's sons: Ḥeber and Malkiʾel.
- **18**These are the sons of Zilpah, whom Laban gave to his daughter Leʾah. She gave birth to these for Yaʿaqob, sixteen persons.
- **19**The sons of Yaʿaqob's wife Raḥel: Yosep and Binyamin.
- **20**To Yosep were born in the country of Miṣrayim, to whom Asenat the daughter of Poti Pera, the priest of On, gave birth for him: Menaššeh and Eprayim.
- **21**Binyamin's sons: Bela, Beker, Ašbel, Gera, Naʿaman, Eḥi, Roʾš, Muppim, Ḥuppim, and Ard.[10]

2. The infinitive absolute (here qal following hiphil and following the finite verb) makes it emphatic.
3. Nemuʾel in Num. 26:12.
4. Ṣeraḥ in Num. 26:13.
5. Yašûb in Num. 26:24.
6. The plural is conventional—there was only one (cf. v. 23).
7. In Num. 26:15 Ṣepon.
8. In Num. 26:16 Ozni.
9. He does not appear in Num. 26:44.
10. The list of names in v. 21 is particularly different from that in Num. 26:38–39.

- **22**These are the sons of Raḥel who were born to Yaʿaqob. Every person: fourteen.
- **23**Dan's sons:[11] Ḥušim.[12]
- **24**Naptali's sons: Yaḥzeʾel, Guni, Yeṣer, and Šillem.
- **25**These are the sons of Bilhah, whom Laban gave to his daughter Raḥel. She gave birth to these for Yaʿaqob. Every person: seven.

26Every person belonging to Yaʿaqob who came to Miṣrayim, the people who went out of his loins, apart from the wives of Yaʿaqob's sons, every person: sixty-six; **27**Yosep's sons, a person who was born to him in Miṣrayim: two; every person belonging to Yaʿaqob's household who came to Miṣrayim: seventy.

28Yehudah he sent before him to Yosep, to give instructions[13] before him to Gošen. So they came to the Gošen region, **29**and Yosep harnessed his chariot and went up to meet Yiśraʾel his father, to Gošen. He appeared to him, fell on his neck, and cried on his neck again and again.[14] **30**Yiśraʾel said to Yosep, "I can die[15] now, after I've seen your face, that you're still alive."

31Yosep said to his brothers and to his father's household, "I'll go up[16] and tell Parʿoh: I'll say to him, 'My brothers and my father's household, who were in the country of Kenaʿan—they've come to me. **32**The men are shepherds of a flock, because they've been livestock men, and their flock and their herd and all that's theirs, they've brought.' **33**When Parʿoh calls you and says, 'What's your work,' **34**you're to say, 'Your servants have been livestock men from our youth until now, both we and our forebears'[17]—so you may live in the Gošen region, because every shepherd of a flock is an offense to Miṣrayites."

47:1 So Yosep came and told Parʿoh, "My father and my brothers, and their flock and their herd and all that's theirs—they've come from the country of Kenaʿan. There, they're in the Gošen region." **2**From the total number[18] of his brothers he got four or five,[19] and presented them before Parʿoh. **3**Parʿoh said to his brothers, "What is your work?" They

11. The plural follows the regular formula even though there is only one son to name.

12. In Num. 26:42 Šuḥam.

13. *Yārâ* hiphil without an object is unusual; the LXX's "appear" takes *hôrōt* as niphal from *rāʾâ*.

14. While both Joseph and Jacob have done a fair amount of crying in Genesis so far, and an unannounced change to Jacob as subject in the middle of v. 29 would be possible, the change to Jacob as subject in v. 30 supports the more obvious assumption that Joseph is the subject through v. 29.

15. The verb is cohortative.

16. Whereas Joseph "went up" to Goshen (v. 29), which was higher in altitude than the Nile and was on the way to Canaan (to which Israelites "went up"), here "go up" will mean "go upriver" or "go uptown" (cf. the translation note to 26:23).

17. The phraseology implies an ellipsis—it has been their occupation from their youth and also their ancestors' occupation.

18. For this meaning of *qāṣeh*, cf. BDB 892a; *DCH* 280b.

19. See the translation note to 43:34.

said to Parʿoh, "Your servants are shepherd of a flock, both we and our forebears." **4**They said to Parʿoh, "It's to reside as aliens[20] in the country that we've come, because there's no pasture for your servants' flock, because the famine is severe in the country of Kenaʿan, so now may your servants please live in the Gošen region." **5**Parʿoh said to Yosep, "As your father and your brothers have come to you, **6**the country of Miṣrayim is before you. Have your father and your brothers live in the best part of the country. They should live in the Gošen region, and if you know that there are capable men among them, make them livestock officials over all that's mine."[21]

7Yosep brought his father Yaʿaqob and got him to stand before Parʿoh, and Yaʿaqob blessed Parʿoh. **8**Parʿoh said to Yaʿaqob, "What is the span of[22] the years of your life?" **9**Yaʿaqob said to Parʿoh, "The span of the years of my residing as an alien is one hundred and thirty. Little and bad has been the span of the years of my life; it has not reached the span of the years of my forebears' lives during the span of their residing." **10**Yaʿaqob blessed Parʿoh and went out from Parʿoh's presence.

11Yosep had his father and his brothers live, and gave them a holding, in the country of Miṣrayim, in the best part of the country, in the Raʿmeses region, as Parʿoh ordered. **12**Yosep provided his father, his brothers, and his father's entire household with bread, for the mouth of each little one.

13There being no bread in the entire world[23] because the famine was very severe, the country of Miṣrayim and the country of Kenaʿan suffered[24] in the face of the famine. **14**Yosep collected[25] all the silver to be found in the country of Miṣrayim and in the country of Kenaʿan in payment for the grain supplies that they were buying. Yosep brought the silver to Parʿoh's house. **15**So the silver from the country of Miṣrayim and from the country of Kenaʿan came to an end, and all Miṣrayim came to Yosep saying, "Hand over bread to us: why should we die in front of you because silver is gone?" **16**Yosep said, "Hand over[26] your livestock,

20. On this verb, see the comment on 12:10.

21. The LXX has an unusually different version of vv. 5–6 (see, e.g., Speiser, *Genesis*, 350–51), possibly to tidy up the jerky sequence of questions and answers; Pharaoh's addressing his response to the brother's question by speaking to Joseph might reflect courtly protocol (cf. Wenham, *Genesis 16–50*, 446).

22. Literally, "the days of"; so also in v. 9.

23. Prefixing *hāʾāreṣ* with the word "entire" implies that the verse refers to more than the country of Egypt, which then gets an explicit reference later in the verse; the expression refers to the entire "world" that concerns Genesis at this point (cf. 41:57; 43:1).

24. Cf. the LXX and Vg for the meaning of *lāhâ*, which comes only here and looks like a by-form of *lāʾâ*; the use of the noun *təlāʾâ* (Exod. 18:8; Num. 20:14; Neh. 9:32; Lam. 3:5) helps to clarify the verb's meaning. But the MT's mappiq in the *h* of *wattēlah* suggests *lāhâ*, meaning "be confused/crazy" (cf. Qimchi, *Genesis*, on the verse).

25. Ironically, *lāqaṭ* most often means "gather" in the sense of "glean."

26. The LXX, Vg have "bring," the verb that will come in v. 17, but the verb is *hābû* (picking up the Egyptians' *hābâ*) from *yāhab*, not *hābîʾû* from *bôʾ*.

and I will give to you in exchange for your livestock, if there's no silver." **17**So they brought their livestock to Yosep, and Yosep gave them bread in exchange for the horses, for the livestock in the flock, for the livestock in the herd, and for the donkeys. He nurtured[27] them with bread in exchange for all their livestock that year.

18That year came to an end, and they came to him the second year and said to him, "We won't hide from my lord, but the silver has come to an end, and the animal stock belong to my lord: there's nothing left before my lord except our corpses[28] and our land. **19**Why should we die before your eyes, both we and our land?[29] Acquire us and our land in exchange for bread. We ourselves and our land will become serfs to Parʿoh. Give seed, so we may live and not die, and the land not become desolate."

20So Yosep acquired all the land in Miṣrayim for Parʿoh, because Miṣrayim, each person, sold their fields because the famine prevailed over them, and the country came to belong to Parʿoh. **21**And the people: he caused them to move into the towns[30] from one end of Miṣrayim's border to its other end. **22**However, he didn't acquire the priests' land, because the priests had something prescribed by Parʿoh, and they ate their prescription that Parʿoh gave them. Thus they didn't sell their land.

23Yosep said to the people, "There, today I have acquired you and your land for Parʿoh. Here is seed for you. You'll sow the land, **24**and with the ingatherings you will give a fifth to Parʿoh, but four-fifths—it will be yours, as seed for the fields and as food for you and for those in your households, and for eating by your little ones." **25**They said, "You've kept us alive—should we find[31] favor in the eyes of my lord, we will become serfs to Parʿoh." **26**Yosep made it a statute, until this day, for the land in Miṣrayim: a fifth is Parʿoh's. However, the priests' land alone did not become Parʿoh's.

Interpretation

Within the story of Jacob's line in Gen. 37–50 as a whole, we noted that Gen. 41 faces both ways as it marks the transition from Act One to Act Two.

27. *Nāhal* etymologically means "lead to a watering-place (or station), and cause to rest there" (BDB 625a); cf. Isa. 51:18; Ps. 23:2 (cf. Rashi, *Brʾšyt*, 523).

28. The LXX has *sōmata*, which could cover live bodies as well as dead ones, but *gəwiyyâ* more often means a dead body (Judg. 14:8–9; 1 Sam. 31:10, 12; Ps. 110:6; Nah 3:3).

29. The LXX and Vg manipulate the text to avoid speaking of people and land both dying, which involves a zeugma (Skinner, *Genesis*, 500); more literally, the land will become a waste (v. 19b).

30. The Tg takes *leʿārîm* to mean "by towns" (cf. *DCH* 6:238a, though not noting this passage). For *heʿĕbîr . . . leʿārîm* ("he moved to towns") the SP and LXX suggest *heʿĕbîd . . . laʿăbādîm* ("he made them into serfs") which assimilates to v. 19 and makes easier sense.

31. For the yiqtol *nimṣāʾ* it is hard to justify the LXX's "we have found" (but cf. *HALOT* 352b, which sees it as an instance of this phrase being an expression of gratitude). The Vg seems to take the verb as cohortative; final aleph verbs generally lack a special cohortative form (see JM 114b). The subsequent waw-consecutive suggests an unmarked conditional clause (GKC 159c).

Genesis 46:1–47:26 likewise faces both ways as it marks the transition from Act Two to Act Three. It forms the conclusion to the main Joseph story, though viewed purely in this connection it may seem to be an "anticlimax" after Gen. 43–45.[32] It also constitutes the beginning of Act Three, which takes Jacob and his family to Egypt and relates his blessing of them and his death there. It thus reasserts the fact that Genesis Part Four is the story of Jacob's lines of descent. Genesis 46:1–47:26 constitutes a set of separate pieces juxtaposed without many connecting markers, rather than a continuous story like Gen. 37–45; seeing it as a unit is a less objective conclusion than is the case with many other units. The MT has a paragraph break after 46:7, then begins a new unit after 46:27 and another after 47:31. A new synagogue parashah (lection) begins after 47:27.

Genesis 46:1–7 begins the process of reestablishing the fact that Gen. 36–50 is the story of Jacob's lines of descent, with its opening account of God appearing to Jacob, giving a commission to him, and making a promise to him. In form and significance the commission and promise parallel the ones to his grandfather (12:1–3), and they thus mark this passage as part of the story of Israel's ancestors and not part of the Joseph story.[33] They look beyond the horizon of Jacob's own life yet do so in a way that speaks of what God will do for Jacob himself, because his story leads into the transition from the story of the ancestors to the story in Exodus: "The twilight of Israel the man coincides with the dawn of Israel the nation."[34] The beginning of Act Three is then also marked by a list of who the family comprises, in 46:8–27.

Narrative then resumes in 46:28–47:26. It describes in more detail the family's arrival in Goshen and the reunion of Jacob and Joseph, thus taking up the retrospective aspect to 46:1–47:12. It relates Joseph's plan for the family's settlement (46:28–34) and then goes on to Joseph's presenting some of his brothers and his father to Pharaoh and Jacob's blessing of Pharaoh (47:1–12).

By now we might have forgotten the crisis that brought about the reunion between Joseph and his family and brought Jacob's family to Egypt. It was a crisis that spelled disaster for every family in Egypt and Canaan, which was effectively part of Egypt's empire. Genesis 47:13–26 presupposes that Joseph has already acquired the surplus grain over the seven years of good harvests. He now sells it to the people and thus acquires all the silver (the financial resources) in Egypt and Canaan. When the people have no silver to buy grain, he barters them grain for their livestock. When they have no more livestock, he barters them grain for the ownership of their land, so that they become state sharecroppers. The story thus raises logistical questions, among others. Joseph collected all the silver in Egypt and Canaan? People brought all

32. Coats, *Genesis*, 294.

33. Cf. Westermann, *Genesis 37–50*, 154.

34. De La Torre, *Exodus*, 338.

the livestock in Egypt to Joseph? Joseph moved all the people into the towns?[35] It seems unlikely that the audience would be interested in the origin of the Egyptian tax system or the system of land tenure. They would more likely be interested in this account as a further example of Joseph's smartness, and they would either rejoice in his rescuing the Egyptians from starvation and/or grin at the way he was able to turn them into state serfs. They might have asked "Well, how did Joseph's advice to Pharaoh turn out, then?" In other words, the wider story needs this last episode to tie it off. Joseph by his wisdom saves the people from a giant catastrophe.[36] As Jacob blessed Pharaoh, Joseph makes it possible for the people of Egypt to survive the famine. As Joseph made it possible for his family to live and not die (42:2; 43:8), so he did for the people of Egypt (47:19). As God took action to ensure that Jacob's family stayed alive and even flourished for the future (45:7; 50:20), Joseph took action to ensure that the people of Egypt stayed alive and even flourished for the future (47:25). The story would also provide background to the deplorable account of the Pharaoh who didn't acknowledge Joseph (Exod. 1:8).

Is it possible to locate the arrival of a group such as Jacob's family and/or action such as Joseph's in Egyptian history? Through much of the second millennium, there was interplay between Egypt and Canaan, which could involve the exercise of Canaanite power in Egypt (particularly in the Nile Delta area, nearer Canaan) as well as the exercise of Egyptian power in Canaan. One might hypothesize that in some of these periods the Egyptians might well allow a Canaanite group to enter Egypt in the way Genesis describes, and the system of state-controlled land tenure and the special treatment of priests fits evidence from Egypt in some periods. In this context the scenario in Gen. 37–50 is thus plausible in general terms, though we do not have a basis for linking it with a specific period.[37]

46:1–7. Yet again Genesis summarizes an event, in v. 1, before narrating the details in vv. 2–7. Genesis 37–45 has referred to Jacob as Israel a few times (37:3, 13; 42:5; 43:6, 8, 11; 45:21, 28), apparently randomly. Here in vv. 1–2 the double reference looks deliberate, especially given the contrast with God's own double use of the name Jacob. It is the family that will become the nation of Israel in Egypt that is making the move to Egypt at this point.

Jacob was presumably in Hebron (v. 1) (see 35:27; 37:14). He is not setting out on a short-term sojourn in Egypt of the kind that Abraham made but taking everything that he has. Moving south off the mountain ridge, he first comes to Beer Sheba, a day or two's journey, and the traditional southernmost point of the promised land ("from Dan to Beer Sheba"). Continuing west from there implies a commitment to moving into foreign territory. Further,

35. See further Westermann, *Genesis 37–50*, 173–76.

36. Von Rad, *Genesis*, 405.

37. See, e.g., Redmount, "Bitter Lives."

Beer Sheba had been a significant center for Abraham, and even more so for Isaac, and it had been the starting point for Jacob's move to Harran (28:10). His "sacrifices" (*zəbāḥîm*), the only ones in Gen. 12–50 apart from 31:54, are offerings shared between God and the offerers, unlike whole burnt offerings (see Gen. 22). Such sacrifices link more with answers to prayer than with petitions.[38] These sacrifices will thus be responses to the revelation that Genesis is about to report, rather than vice versa. The description of them is part of the way v. 1 comprises a summary of what vv. 2–7 will elaborate.

Perhaps it's not surprising that God appears to him at Beer Sheba (v. 2), given the various significances of that place. God's appearing also recalls his appearing to Abraham when he arrived in Canaan and subsequently built an altar there (12:7); his appearing to Isaac, who subsequently built this altar in response to God's appearing to him (26:24–25); and his appearing to Jacob when he was on his way out of the land northward and subsequently set up a standing stone (28:18). Yet this "vision" (*mar'â*) is the only one mentioned in Genesis, though 15:1 used another word with this meaning (*maḥăzeh*) in connection with a night vision, and Yahweh did "appear" here (*rā'â* niphal) at night in 26:24 (cf. 12:7; 17:1; 18:1; 26:2; 35:1, 9). Since it is a vision and it's at night, the implications are not very different from Jacob dreaming (28:12); Genesis more often refers to dreams than to visions. Paradoxically, especially as "visions" is plural here, Genesis will speak only of what Jacob heard; the event again parallels Yahweh's appearing to Isaac when he built this altar (26:24). The implications of "vision" thus parallel those of the English word "revelation"; Tg. Ps.-J. says that God "spoke to Israel in a prophecy of the night." God speaks with the double address, "Jacob, Jacob," that Yahweh's envoy used to Abraham (22:11). It is not a moment with the same urgency as obtained there, but the doubling implies some insistence and the importance of what God is about to say. Jacob replies in the proper fashion of a servant or a son, "I'm here," like Abraham in 22:11 (see also, e.g., 22:1; 31:11). If the language is "stylized," it's because the emphasis lies on the commission and the promise that follow.[39]

On this occasion Genesis has God saying "I am God [*hā'ēl*]" (v. 3a), not "I am Yahweh," thus in accordance with proper historical theology (contrast 28:13). This passage and Jacob's report in 31:13 are the only occasions where Genesis uses the expression *hā'ēl*. In 31:13 God qualifies the self-description by referring to himself as the Beth El God (which thus makes a link as well as a contrast with 28:13). This time he qualifies it by reminding Jacob that he is "the God of your father" who built the altar at Beer Sheba. It's the title for God that Jacob himself had used as he recalled how God had been with him (31:5; cf. 31:42, 53) and the title that is his distinctive way of referring to God.

38. See the comment on 31:54; and cf. Chrysostom, *Homilies on Genesis 46–67*, 245–46.
39. So Westermann, *Genesis 37–50*, 155.

"Don't be afraid," God says again (v. 3b), as he had said to Isaac there at Beer Sheba when he built the altar (26:24) and as he had earlier said to Abraham (15:1; see the comment there). In light of the way Jacob experienced the God of his father proving himself to him on that long journey northeast, he has reason to trust in this God for his journey southwest. The exhortation to trust addressed to Abraham and Isaac was associated with a promise that the addressee would be the father of many descendants, and so it is here, but in the context of Jacob's leaving the land (again)—though there has been no indication that Jacob was afraid. Was he wondering whether it is really okay to be leaving Canaan?[40] God declares that he will establish Jacob as a big nation there in Egypt, which picks up not only God's declaration concerning Abraham (12:2; 18:18) but also more recently Joseph's talk of God establishing this family as a great escape group (45:7). It will happen *there*, in Egypt! That word "there" is a key variant on Yahweh's promise to Abraham. It seems an implausible notion, but the beginning of Exodus will indicate that God has done what he says.

The promise to be with Jacob (v. 4) is familiar (e.g., 26:2–3 [in connection with not going down to Egypt], 24; 28:15; 31:3). Here, too, there is a needed modification of the familiar formulation: the familiar language about being "with you" is nuanced with a reference to going down to Egypt. Although Canaan is the country that God intends to give to Jacob's family, Jacob hardly needs any reminder that God is not confined to Canaan. He has proved it many times over, and this fact about God is deeply embedded in his family's story. In a nice ambiguity the promise about going down and bringing back sounds in English like a promise referring to Jacob and his family, with the implication that the "exodus" will coincide with his return.[41] The promise understood thus will then find paradoxical fulfillment since it will transpire that Jacob's return and the family's return happen so differently and so separately. But the "you" is singular; it refers solely to Jacob. Again it will find paradoxical fulfillment as Jacob will indeed come back but only as a dead man, as the last clause in the verse implies. The outworking of the promise is nevertheless the assurance that Jacob will not be stuck in Egypt forever. The promise presupposes that Jacob will be okay about returning only after his death. He will have seen Joseph again, and Joseph will be there to close Jacob's eyes when he dies. And returning as a dead man counts as returning. Jacob will rest in the promised land forever. God's promise to Jacob again compares and contrasts with his promise to Abraham in 15:13–16. Abraham knew that his family would be resident aliens and serfs somewhere but would eventually return to the promised land, while he himself would die in Canaan. Yahweh's promise to Jacob speaks of the family's becoming a big nation in the

40. Cf. Luther, *Genesis 45–50*, 76–77.

41. Cf. Dillmann, *Genesis*, 2:412. Targum Ps.-J. takes the promise to refer simply to the exodus.

foreign land that is now specified, but of only Jacob's returning. If leaving the land that he knows and leaving the land of promise is a frightening venture that makes him fear he will never come back and will be buried in a foreign land, he is reassured.[42] Thus he has reason to offer a sacrifice of thanksgiving.

The entire family and all its possessions therefore move into Egypt (vv. 5–7). Once again, Genesis gives a summary account in its reporting of the journey; both the list and the further narrative in 46:8–47:12 will elaborate on this summary. The names Jacob and Israel again interweave, and the reference to daughters and grandchildren also suggests a change of focus, from the immediate family to the people into which it will grow. The word "offspring," which commonly refers to more than merely someone's immediate family, makes the same point; it occurs for the first time since the promise in 35:12 (cf. also, e.g., 12:7; 13:15–16; 15:5, 13; 22:17–18; 26:3–4).[43]

46:8–27. The alternating of the names Israel and Jacob continues; Jacob is moving to Egypt, but he does so as the ancestor of the people of Israel. The list of sons is the same as that in 29:31–30:24 (Dinah also again gets a mention), but the order has a different rationale. There it interweaves the chronological and the systematic; here it is more consistently systematic.

1. The six sons of Leah, plus Dinah (46:8–15)
2. The two sons of Leah's maidservant Zilpah (46:16–18)
3. The two sons of Rachel (46:19–22)
4. The two sons of Rachel's maidservant Bilhah (46:23–25)

The basic shape of the presentation is systematic in some other ways, as is suggested by the arrangement of the translation as printed above. Ten lines begin with the name of one of Jacob's sons and then give a list of this son's sons; the formulation is slightly different for Rachel's sons. After the lists of sons comes the mother's name, along with the sum total of the descendants born through that mother. Qualifying this systematic arrangement are some nuances, a number of which make clear that only in a broad sense is it a list of the family that came down to Egypt.

In v. 8, the first line notes that Reuben is Jacob's firstborn.

In v. 9, Reuben now has four sons (contrast 42:37).

In v. 10, Simeon's son Saul is noted as having a Canaanite mother, which does not make Saul unique (see 38:2) but is presumably a slur (cf. 24:3, 37; 28:1, 6, 8; 36:2).[44] Perhaps it provides an implicit explanation for

42. Cf. Nicolas of Lyra, *Postilla super totam Bibliam*, on the passage; cf. Schroeder, *Genesis*, 216.

43. Cf. Westermann, *Genesis 37–50*, 158.

44. So, e.g., Ibn Ezra, *Genesis*, 403.

the effective disappearance of Simeon's clan later; the clan's descent is traced entirely through Saul in 1 Chron. 4:24–43. As is generally the case with references to Jacob's sons, there is otherwise no indication that the ordering reflects aspects of the later position and interrelationships of the twelve Israelite clans.

In v. 12 there is a note of the death of Er and Onan, and of Perez's two sons, who must have been born later.

In v. 15 Dinah as a sister appears.

In v. 17 Beriah's sister Serah appears (presumably because she was the author of Genesis),[45] along with his two sons.

In v. 19 Rachel is distinguished as Jacob's wife as if Leah were not (cf. 44:27).

In v. 20 Asenat, the mother of Joseph's sons, the daughter of the priest from On, is mentioned.

In v. 21 Benjamin has ten sons, which fits uneasily with his status as kid brother in Gen. 44 and is another indication that the list does not simply comprise people who went down to Egypt. Most of these ten were perhaps born there; further, Num. 26:36–40 makes five of them his grandsons.[46]

In v. 27 it is noted that Joseph's two sons were born in Egypt.

Most of these nuances introduce women into the list (and Tamar is standing in the shadows in v. 12),[47] which anticipates the presence of four women in Jesus's genealogy. A further distinctive feature of this list over against 29:31–30:24 is that it is now in a position to include the names of Jacob's grandsons. This process of development continues in the elaborated alternative versions of the list incorporated into the account of the Israelite clans after the exodus from Egypt in Num. 26:5–50 and into the material in 1 Chron. 1–8. The many detailed differences in the names when they recur, there and, say, in the Septuagint,[48] presumably reflect the way the lists were preserved before making their way into the text of the Torah and of Chronicles and also the subsequent process of textual transmission; sometimes one may guess which version is older, sometimes not. The general parallels between the three lists suggest the significance of the list in its latter narrative contexts. The people that came out of Egypt is indeed the family that went down into Egypt (Num. 26); so is the people that formed the First Temple community and the Second Temple community (1 Chron. 1–8).

45. This playful observation develops comments in Frankel, *Five Books of Miriam*, xx.

46. The LXX has only three of the ten as Benjamin's sons; six are grandsons and one a great-grandson. First Chronicles 7:6 also has just three sons, though the names vary slightly.

47. Cf. Brett, *Genesis*, 127.

48. The more notable differences are listed in the translation notes.

The pattern of the fulfillment of God's promise so far has included a narrowing of the family: Isaac but not Ishmael, Jacob but not Esau. One might have expected this pattern to continue, and there is no theological or ethical reason why it shouldn't—but it doesn't.[49] The sum total of the figures for Leah (thirty-three including Dinah), Zilpah (sixteen), Rachel (fourteen), and Bilhah (seven) comes to seventy, and that figure appears in v. 27 (cf. Exod. 1:5; Deut. 10:22), while v. 26 mentions sixty-six. Seventy suggests a complete company (cf. Exod. 15:27; 24:1, 9; Num. 11:16, 24, 25; Isa. 23:15, 17; Jer. 25:11–12), though not a vast company (see Deut. 10:22). There are various ways of making the lists come to seventy or sixty-six: for example, by omitting Er and Onan, who died earlier, and Manasseh and Ephraim, who were born in Egypt, seventy becomes sixty-six. The LXX has seventy-five (cf. Acts 7:14) as a result of attributing nine sons to Joseph.[50] If "the computation of those who went down to Egypt . . . is so confused that no interpreter has been able to unravel it," what's the point of including it? From it "we may learn that God exercises such anxious care for His saints that He does not want to omit counting even one person with the greatest faithfulness and diligence."[51]

46:28–34. The narrative backtracks to say more about the process whereby Jacob found his way to the family's destination in Egypt, but with a focus on his reunion with Joseph. It was Judah who suggested selling Joseph into servitude in Egypt (37:26–27); now Jacob sends Judah to meet Joseph. "The wolf and the lamb shall feed together" (Isa. 65:25; cf. Gen. Rab. 95.1); the commission suggests the possibility of reconciliation.[52] Judah's being the brother Jacob sends on ahead also reflects the leadership role he has been fulfilling (43:3, 8; 44:14, 16, 18) and anticipates the leadership role that will focus on him in the future (49:8–12). Perhaps it presupposes that Reuben, Simeon, and Levi have disqualified themselves; if Judah had done so (Gen. 38), he has redeemed himself. And for the audience, Judah and Joseph being the key figures anticipates the domination of their clans in Israel's life. Genesis 37–50 is not about Judah as much as about Joseph, but it is nearly so.[53]

Joseph indicates his eagerness to see Jacob by harnessing his own chariot (vv. 29–30), like Abraham saddling his donkey in 22:3; albeit it is an eagerness he must have restrained for several years. Thus he "appears" (*rā'â* niphal) before Jacob; apart from references to God appearing, the verb commonly

49. Cf. Hamilton, *Genesis 18–50*, 592–93.

50. On these numbers, see further Hamilton, *Genesis 18–50*, 597–99. Jerome (*Hebrew Questions on Genesis*, 80–81) has a nice discussion of the theological implications of Acts's quoting the Septuagint's version of the numbers.

51. Luther, *Genesis 45–50*, 87, 89.

52. Cf. Neusner, *Genesis Rabbah* 3:327.

53. Cf. B. Smith, "Central Role."

suggests someone presenting himself (KJV) with due humility before God (e.g., Exod. 23:15, 17; 34:20, 23, 24). Jacob's tears of sorrow (37:35) give way to Joseph's tears of joy. From one perspective the crying in 45:1–2 marks the climax of Joseph's story; the crying that follows here marks another necessary aspect to the climax, as this reunion happens. Joseph cries and cries; Jacob's response comes in words that are at least as telling.

The account of negotiations with Pharaoh (vv. 31–34) again overlaps with the account in 45:1–20, which might suggest that at a literary level the stories are allowed to overlap or might imply that Joseph will need to take up the earlier conversation he had with Pharaoh. One point about the negotiation may be that Joseph has no expectation that his brothers would work with Joseph in the administration and heighten the possibility of a foreign takeover of power in Egypt—not an unknown issue there. The offensiveness of shepherds may link with the ideas noted in connection with 43:32. Given that we don't know otherwise of negative Egyptian attitudes to shepherding or a tension between farmers and shepherds, "shepherds" likely suggests Bedouin, the kind of people who belong out in Sinai, not in Egypt proper, people of whom Egyptians might be suspicious in the way that urban Westerners are suspicious of gypsies. Placing them on the Sinai side of Egypt would suit the Egyptians as well as suiting them.[54] Shepherds would be a subset of "livestock men" (that phrase comes only here) and an alternative and possibly more acceptable self-description.

47:1–9. They describe themselves to Pharaoh as shepherds, which would perhaps reassure Pharaoh that they had no needs except for some grazing land.[55] The good land of Goshen is a logical place for them to have that role. Being in charge of Pharaoh's livestock would be a more exalted position.

The story reaches a further climax (v. 7) with the account of Jacob blessing Pharaoh; it is an appropriate response to Pharaoh's welcoming and generous endowment (cf. Job 29:13; 31:20). The blessing would include not only thanksgiving (as when people bless God) but also a prayer for God's blessing (cf. Tg. Ps.-J.). While in other contexts *bārak* can simply mean "greet" (e.g., 2 Kings 4:29), in this context and in the context of the importance of blessing in Genesis, the audience would be invited to pick up the overlap with the theme of Abraham, Isaac, and Jacob being a means of blessing. Members of the chosen family "include within the circle of blessing even *those who seem least in need of it*" and who are going to be problems in the future.[56] The older man who is bearer of Yahweh's promise blesses the younger man who is the foreign ruler (in Exod. 12:32 Pharaoh asks for Moses's blessing). "The lesser is blessed by the greater" (Heb. 7:7).[57]

54. Cf. Redford, *Study*, 235.
55. Cf. Skinner, *Genesis*, 497.
56. Fretheim, "Genesis," 655, emphasis original.
57. Cf. Skinner, *Genesis*, 498.

For Pharaoh to ask about Jacob's age (vv. 8–9) suggests the same framework of thinking. It is to ask how God's blessing has worked out for Jacob. Jacob's reply maintains the gloomy stance he has taken before (37:35; 42:38). Although the final span of his life will be shorter than that of his father and grandfather (147 years over against 180 and 175), it doesn't look short and neither does it look very bad compared with theirs, even though he had that long exile in Harran and the long years of grieving for Joseph. But he characterizes his life as a temporary residing, "a precarious landless existence (cf. Deut. 26:5)."[58] There is indeed a sense in which one spends one's whole life residing as an alien on earth ("This world is not my home, I'm just a passing thru");[59] one's life is "borrowed time."[60] Yet there is little indication that the First Testament itself thinks this way,[61] and "residing as an alien" in one country or another is a common theme in Genesis, most recently in v. 4. Jacob has been a resident alien in Harran (32:4 [32:5]) as well as sharing the position of his father and grandfather in Canaan (35:27). Such residing was "the characteristic of the entire road of life which God had pointed out to the patriarchs." It meant "renunciation of settlement and land ownership" and thus "a life which was oriented toward future fulfillment, namely, toward the promise of land which was often renewed to the patriarchs. Thus the patriarchs had lived in Canaan in a curiously ambiguous relationship to promise and fulfillment in the 'land of their sojourning.'" But as Jacob apparently sees it, "the circumstances of this life of sojourning became much more unfavorable in [Jacob's] generation. In comparison with his father's life his life has been briefer and more difficult."[62] Genesis is reminding the audience that the end of the story of Jacob's life is drawing near.

47:10–12. Genesis summarizes the significance of that meeting between Jacob and Pharaoh as one of blessing, then moves on to the implementing of Pharaoh's generosity. In v. 4 the brothers spoke of "residing as aliens" in Egypt but then of "living" in Goshen, and in v. 6 it was that second verb that Pharaoh picked up. Now, surprisingly, Joseph gives them a "holding" (*ʾăḥuzzâ*), which implies a tract of land possessed on a permanent basis (cf. 17:8; 23:4; 36:43; 47:27; 48:4; 49:30; 50:13). Actually, the stay of Jacob's descendants in Egypt is going to be longer than the term resident aliens would suggest. The name Raʿmeses strictly belongs in a later context (see Exod. 1:11); the city was named after Raʿmeses II, a long-lived Pharaoh of the thirteenth century. That city indeed lay in the northeast of Egypt and thus helps to make clear the location of Goshen in a later context.

58. Brueggemann, *Genesis*, 355.
59. First line of the hymn, "I Can't Feel at Home Any More," by Albert E. Brumley.
60. Speiser, *Genesis*, 351.
61. See *HALOT*, against BDB on *māgôr*.
62. Von Rad, *Genesis*, 402–3.

47:13–19. Once again Genesis backtracks[63] as it returns to the beginning of the famine years;[64] the chapters in between have focused on the story of Jacob and his sons. These verses revert to the wider picture.

There is a broader food problem that needs solving (v. 13), beyond the fact noted in v. 12 that Joseph is in a position to ensure that even the children in his family have food. It's not just a food problem. The famine has such a devastating effect that it threatens the life or morale or existence of both Egypt and Canaan.

But a result of the action Joseph took during the seven good years (v. 14) is that he can now take action to ensure the people's survival. First, the people bring all their silver (that is, their cash) to buy from Joseph's grain mountain that they presumably sold to him during the good years. Bringing the silver to Pharaoh's house means bringing it to the treasury that is in his palace,[65] which might imply that Joseph is not stashing any away for himself and/or that Pharaoh benefits from Joseph's course of action and/or that this course of action facilitates development in Egypt.

Then the people have no alternative (vv. 15–17) to bartering their animals. If the passage as a whole covers the entire seven years of famine, then "that year" will likely not imply that purchasing with their silver simply takes them through year 1 of the famine and that bartering their animals takes them through year 2; by the end of vv. 13–19, we are near the end of the famine.[66] Presumably they do not physically deposit the animals with Joseph and thereby make work on the farm impossible while he would have nothing to do with them; rather, the ownership passed to Pharaoh, as will happen with the land.

In due course (vv. 18–19) they have nothing left but their land and the corpses they will soon become. Indeed, in the absence of irrigation their land is as dead as they are. They need food for themselves, and they need seed for their land for the time when the Nile floods once more, so they may eventually grow grain again. Their plea depends on an offer for Pharaoh to take over the ownership of their land and of themselves. The independence of a family depends on its possessing land, so parting with land means, in a sense, surrendering freedom.[67] For the land, on the other hand, losing its inhabitants means losing the people who are supposed to "serve" it and look after it (2:15). It would become just a waste and be unable to reach the purpose for which God created it.

47:20–26. In effect Pharaoh thus becomes the lord of the estates that comprise the country as a whole, and the people become his laborers.

63. Cf. Rashi, *Brʾšyt*, 521.
64. Gunkel (*Genesis*, 442) notes how this passage fits the earlier context.
65. Cf. Driver, *Genesis*, 372.
66. Cf. Luther's comments, *Genesis 45–50*, 122–23.
67. Cf. Skinner, *Genesis*, 500.

Moving the population from the country to the towns (vv. 21–22) is a surprising idea, though it compares with a motif in the First Testament prophets who imply that many ordinary people were forced off their land and found themselves living in towns and commuting to their former farms in order to labor for the land's new owners; this development reinforces the reality that the land no longer belongs to them.[68] The lucky exceptions are the priests, who receive a regular allocation from the government and therefore are not vulnerable to the vagaries of the Nile like ordinary people.

Joseph's declaration (vv. 23–26) presupposes that irrigation is now no longer a problem and they can farm successfully again. The farmers become sharecroppers who give the owner of the land a portion of the harvest as rent. And they can be positive about the arrangement.

Implications

Joseph's Economic Policy

Genesis 47:13–26 has been described as "the showpiece in the arsenal of anti-Semitic polemic against the Old Testament."[69] Modern Western interpreters live in liberal democracies with liberal/capitalist economic policies that in theory can work well for ordinary people but frequently do not do so, and the people who write commentaries and read them are usually people whom liberal democracy and liberal capitalism serve. Thus Joseph's economic policy may meet with our disapproval.[70]

The story assumes that there is such a thing as benevolent autocracy. Whereas governments in the West as elsewhere routinely work for their own benefit at least as much as for the benefit of those they govern, the story portrays an occasion when the central government worked for the benefit of people—indeed, for their salvation from starvation. Perhaps Pharaoh personally profited from Joseph's policies, though Genesis does not claim this. It focuses on the way ordinary people benefited from it. The governed do become state serfs, though modern translations mislead if they call them "slaves" (e.g., NRSV). The arrangement is not "total slavery."[71] It is some distance from the limited-term bond service approved by Exodus and Deuteronomy, but a long way from the serfdom described in Exodus, where serfdom indeed becomes oppressive, and nothing like Roman or African-American slavery. The government is not described as having control over people's lives or as

68. Rashi, *Brʾšyt*, 524.

69. Von Rad, *Genesis*, 405.

70. A striking instance is the puzzled dismay expressed by Chrysostom's translator, R. C. Hill (*Homilies on Genesis 46–67*, 251), that the commentator ("usually sensitive to social injustice") fails to critique Joseph on this point.

71. Coats, *Genesis*, 299.

limiting their freedom or as behaving oppressively. Pharaoh cannot do as he likes with them, as if they were his property.[72] His control is economic. Whereas elsewhere "servant" is a useful translation of *ʿebed*, English does also have the useful word "serf" from the context of the feudal system, which denotes a laborer working on his lord's estate.

The story in 47:13–26 was told in contexts where Israel was ruled by monarchs or by empires, and it makes for telling reading against the background of Samuel's warning about monarchy in 1 Sam. 8, which also talks in terms of the king making his people serfs and refers to a 10% rate of taxation though also of other costs to people (the audience would also recall that they were supposed to pay a 10% tithe). A 20% taxation rate was below average for the Middle East.[73] First Maccabees 10:30 refers to a one-third tax on grain and one-half on fruit.[74] The warning in 1 Sam. 8 contrasts with the vision for benevolent autocracy laid out in a passage such as Ps. 72, with which Joseph's policy might compare. As a "tax etiology,"[75] then, Gen. 47:13–26 implicitly sets a standard for the operation of a taxation system. Genesis, Ps. 72, and much of the rest of the First Testament presupposes government by monarchs and presents the important question: how ought monarchy to operate? In Egypt people were "suffering" and Joseph "nurtured" them (vv. 13, 17).[76] If Israelite monarchy operates as benevolently as this Egyptian monarchy with Joseph as its administrator, one may imagine that Israelites would be as appreciative as the Egyptians in this story. The same is true of millions of people governed by democratically elected leaders in Britain or the United States.

When this system Joseph devises becomes a permanency[77] rather than just a way of coping with a once-off crisis, it favors the central administration. It would presumably help to pay for the army and for monumental buildings and no doubt for Pharaoh to be living better than his people—again, just as is the case in a liberal democracy. But Joseph's system had the capacity to mitigate the effects of the ups and downs of the Nile's flooding in some years and not in others and to provide a kind of equivalent of a social security system for the people—again, in a way not so different from that which is possible in a liberal democracy, though not always actual there.

72. Cf. Fretheim, "Genesis," 654.
73. See, e.g., Sarna, *Genesis*, 322.
74. Dillmann, *Genesis*, 2:429, gives other examples.
75. Coats, *Genesis*, 298.
76. See the translation notes to these two verses.
77. Josephus (*Ant.* 2.7.7), however, has Joseph giving it back again after the famine is over.

48

How Jacob Begins to Prepare for His Death

(47:27–48:22)

Overview

The account of Jacob's death opens with his appeal to Joseph to bury him in Canaan, not in Egypt. When Jacob begins to ail, Joseph brings his sons to see Jacob, and Jacob blesses them, reversing their birth order by blessing Ephraim with his right hand and Manasseh with his left.

Translation

> **47:27**So Yiśraʾel lived in the country of Miṣrayim in the Gošen region.
> They acquired a holding in it, they were fruitful, and they became very
> numerous. **28**Yaʿaqob lived seventeen years in the country of Miṣrayim,
> and Yaʿaqob's span, the years of his life, came to a hundred and forty-
> seven years. **29**But the days drew near for Yiśraʾel to die. He called his
> son Yosep and said to him, "Please, if I have found favor in your eyes,
> please put your hand under my thigh and act in commitment and stead-
> fastness to me: please don't bury me in Miṣrayim. **30**I will lie down with
> my forebears,[1] and you're to carry me from Miṣrayim and bury me in their
> burial place." He said, "I myself will act in accordance with your word."
> **31**He said, "Swear to me," and he swore to him, and Yiśraʾel bowed low
> at the head of the bed.[2]

1. The asyndeton suggests that the first clause is circumstantial.

2. The LXX's "on the top of his staff" implies *hammaṭṭeh* for *hammaṭṭâ*, but Aq, Sym imply *hammaṭṭâ*.

48:1 Subsequently,[3] someone told Yosep, "Here, your father is ailing."[4] He got his two sons with him, Menašše̱h and Eprayim, **2**and someone told Yaʿaqob, "Here, your son Yosep has come to you." Yiśraʾel summoned his strength and sat on the bed. **3**Yaʿaqob said to Yosep, "El Shadday himself[5] appeared to me at Luz in the country of Kenaʿan and blessed me **4**and said to me, 'Here, I am going to make you fruitful and numerous and make you a congregation of peoples, and give this country to your offspring after you as an agelong holding.'

5"And now, your two sons who were born to you in the country of Miṣrayim before my coming to you in Miṣrayim: they are mine. Eprayim and Menaššeh will be mine like Reʾuben and Šimʿon. **6**Given that your family that you will have fathered after them will be yours,[6] by the name of their brothers they will be named, in their domain. **7**I—during my coming from Paddan,[7] Raḥel died on me,[8] in the country of Kenaʿan, on the way, when there was still a stretch of country before coming to Eprat,[9] and I buried her there on the way to Eprat" (i.e., Bet Lehem).

8So Yiśraʾel looked at Yosep's sons and said, "Who are these?" **9**Yosep said to his father, "They are my sons, whom God has given me here." He said, "Please get them to me so I may bless them." **10**As Yiśraʾel's eyes were heavy because of age, he couldn't see. So he brought them up to him, and he kissed them and hugged them. **11**Yiśraʾel said to Yosep, "To see your face! I didn't pray for[10] it. And here—God has let me see your offspring as well." **12**Then Yosep got them away from his knees and bowed low,[11] with his face to the ground.

13Yosep got the two of them, Eprayim with his right to Yiśraʾel's left, and Menaššeh with his left to Yiśraʾel's right, and brought them up to him. **14**But Yiśraʾel put out his right hand and placed it on Eprayim's head, though he was the younger, and his left hand on Menaššeh's head, crossing his hands, when Menaššeh was the firstborn, **15**and he blessed Yosep:[12] "May the God before whom my fathers Abraham and Yiṣḥaq walked, the God who has been shepherding me from whenever until this

3. See the translation note to 22:1.

4. *Ḥālâ* suggests weakness such that one might associate with the approach of death more than simply an illness from which one might expect to recover (cf. Aq).

5. The name of God comes before the verb, as it regularly does, suggesting emphasis.

6. The word order with the subject before the verb suggests that this clause is circumstantial; so also v. 10.

7. The LXX has Paddan Aram, as elsewhere.

8. *ʿAlay*, an expression suggesting one is overwhelmed: see BDB 753b, also the occurrence in 42:36 (Alter, *Genesis*, 288).

9. See the footnote to 35:16.

10. The usual meaning of the hitpael of *pālal* fits this occurrence of the rare piel, though in postbiblical Hebrew the verb can mean thought or expected (cf. Tg; Ibn Ezra, *Genesis*, 414). The LXX, Vg have "I was not deprived."

11. The LXX takes *wayyištaḥû* as plural, but it has been singular elsewhere (e.g., 47:31), and for the plural Genesis has used *wayyištaḥăwû* (e.g., 43:26).

12. The LXX has "blessed them," conforming the text to what seems to happen.

day, **16**the envoy who has been restoring me from everything bad, bless the boys. Through them may my name be named, and the name of my fathers Abraham and Yiṣḥaq. May they teem[13] numerously in the middle of the earth."

17Yosep saw that his father was putting his right hand on Eprayim's head, and it was bad in his eyes. He grasped his father's hand so as to move it from on Eprayim's head onto Menaššeh's head. **18**Yosep said to his father, "Not like that, father, because this one is the firstborn. Place your right hand on his head." **19**But his father refused and said, "I know, son, I know. He will become a people as well, he will become big as well, but nevertheless his little brother—he will be bigger than him, and his offspring—it will become a full number of nations." **20**So that day he blessed them: "By you Yiśra'el will bless,[14] saying, 'God make you like Eprayim and Menaššeh.'" But he put Eprayim before Menaššeh.

21Yiśra'el said to Yosep: "There, I'm going to die, but God will be with you [all] and will take you back to the country of your forebears. **22**And I myself am giving[15] to you[16] a shoulder,[17] one above your brothers, which I am getting[18] from the hand of the Amorites with my sword and with my bow."

Interpretation

In Abraham's story, Gen. 23 announced that its last part would focus on his preparations for his passing, which are then the focus of 23:1–25:10. In a whimsical way, Isaac's story was even more dominated by such preparations; they begin in 27:1–2, though he passes only in 35:28–29. Then "the whole Joseph narrative presupposes that Jacob is near death (37:35; 42:39; 43:27–28; 44:22–29, 31; 45:9, 13, 28; 46:30). In order to see Joseph once more before he dies, he came to Egypt (45:28). Now that he has seen him, he is ready to die (46:30). Inherent in the account, then, is the notion that Jacob's journey to Egypt will be followed immediately by his death." So what follows in the final chapters of Genesis is not an independent narrative but "an extended conclusion" to the entire story.[19] But the last verses of Gen. 47 mark the shift

13. *Dāgâ* looks like a denominative from *dāg* (fish), as the Tg implies.

14. The LXX's "will be blessed" implies *yəbōrak* for the MT's *yəbārēk*, an easier reading.

15. The declarative/performative qatal suggests a speech act: "I hereby give" (Seebass, *Genesis*, 3:157).

16. "You" in v. 21 is plural; in v. 22 it is singular.

17. The Vg and Tg have "share," but *šəkem* does not have that meaning elsewhere; the LXX has "Shechem," but "one" is then masculine, and names of towns are usually feminine; Aq has "shoulder," the usual meaning of the common noun.

18. I take the qatal as another declarative/performative (see the translation note to v. 22a), but it might rather have future perfect reference, "which I will have got" (cf. Ibn Ezra, *Genesis*, 417); see the comment.

19. Gunkel, *Genesis*, 445.

to a more explicit focus on Jacob's preparations for his death and on the aftermath of his passing, which will occupy those closing chapters.

Whereas the MT has a unit running from 46:28 to 47:31, and the medieval chapter division makes the same break as the MT at 47:31, this understanding does not take account of the shift of focus that already comes in the closing verses of Gen. 47. Indeed, the MT also notes that 47:27 marks the end of the lection that began at 45:18. But 47:27 does not directly link back to what precedes in 47:13–26, which does not talk about Israel the man or Israel the people. Genesis 47:27–28 is rather a resumptive summary leading into what follows. The "subsequently" of 48:1 is then not a marker of a new unit (as it is in 22:1, 20) but a marker of a transition within this new unit (as it is in 39:7; 40:1).

This unit has been seen as a particularly clear example of the interweaving of J, E, and P.[20] As a unit it provides answers to a series of possible questions about Manasseh and Ephraim. They are Jacob's grandsons, and Manasseh is the elder. But the Torah will later make clear that in effect they count as Jacob's sons. How did that situation come about? Israelites listening to this story would know that the clans of Manasseh and Ephraim ended up as two of the most significant clans: Manasseh had the biggest territory, and Ephraim occupied the most central position. Ephraim was thus politically more important than Manasseh, and it gave the northern kingdom its distinctive name. Shechem was in Ephraim, Samaria was there, Tirzah was there. How did all that come about? The story will provide answers to such questions.

47:27–28. Genesis brings us back to the main story and effects a transition to a focus on Jacob's passing.

The opening sentence (v. 27) thus compares and contrasts with the opening sentence of the story of Jacob's line as a whole (37:1). As that sentence functioned resumptively after the account of Esau's lines of descent, this sentence does so after the account of Joseph's rescue of the Egyptian people. But this sentence contrasts with that earlier one in noting that Jacob is "living" in a settled fashion in Egypt, specifically in Goshen, as opposed to "living" in the country of his father's residence, specifically in Canaan. In a further contrast, the verse speaks of Israel rather than Jacob, picking up the use of that name in 46:28–30, which will recur in 47:29. But then with a jolt 47:27 goes on to speak of Israel as "they," suggesting a "merging of Israel the individual and Israel the people."[21] And Israel's settling is a serious settling. It includes having holdings in Egypt; here Genesis picks up from v. 11 (see the comment there). The Israelites were fruitful and became numerous in fulfillment of the commission or promise in 35:11 and the blessing in 28:3—and of God's original commission or promise to the first human beings and to the people

20. But see the discussion in Wenham, *Genesis 16–50*, 461.
21. Hamilton, *Genesis 18–50*, 621.

who survived the great deluge (1:22, 28; 8:17; 9:1, 7). It is the first time that being fruitful and becoming numerous has been a fact rather than a promise.

Genesis then reverts (47:28) to speaking of Jacob, as it jumps through the next seventeen years, which recall the seventeen years of 37:2. Further, Abraham had lived to 175, which is 5 × 5 × 7, and Isaac had lived to 180, which is 6 × 6 × 5; Jacob's 147 will be 7 × 7 × 3.[22] This "rhetorical device" gives expression to these lives being "not a concatenation of haphazard incidents."[23] The arrangement compares with the 3 × 14 sequence of the genealogy in Matt. 1:1–17.

47:29–31. "After all his talk of dying, Jacob is finally near death."[24] Genesis goes on to announce its focus on his passing. Reference to the time drawing near could mean it has actually arrived (cf. 27:41), but in Gen. 47–49 there is a lot still to happen—or a lot to be said. First, Jacob wants to make sure of the fulfillment of God's promise in 46:4 that he will return to Canaan. The desire to be buried in one's own country among one's own people is common, but Canaan's being *the* promised land gives extra background to this desire. Joseph is still evidently a favorite if not the favorite among Jacob's sons; he is also the son in a position to see that his father's wishes are met. Jacob's concern, even anxiety, about his burial is underlined by his talk of finding favor: it is the phrase he used in the context of his relationship with Esau (32:5 [32:6]; 33:8, 10, 15)—and the phrase that Shechem and the starving Egyptians used (34:11; 47:25). It is a term that the lesser party uses in relation to the senior party. He repeats the request that Abraham used to his servant in a different connection in 24:2, but also in the part of Abraham's story where he is doing what needs to be done before he dies and where he is also taking action in relation to his son and the future of the family. Jacob further underlines the importance of the matter to him by using the hendiadys "commitment and steadfastness," which also recurred in that story in 24:27, 49 and on Jacob's lips in the Esau story in 32:10 [32:11]. It would be natural to bury Jacob in Egypt where he dies, which will be the destiny of his many descendants over the coming years. Jacob doesn't want it to be his destiny.

The terms in which Jacob then speaks of his death (47:30) are a little paradoxical. Lying down with one's ancestors is a euphemism for dying, and it precedes burial (cf. e.g., 1 Kings 2:10).[25] Jacob wants it to be a literal reality.

It is not enough (v. 31) for Joseph simply to reassure Jacob. Jacob wants a formal, sworn promise. When he gets it, he bows low. Presumably he does so on his bed because of being of advanced age and near death, like David in 1 Kings 1:47. Bowing low can be a gesture of respect to God (e.g., Gen. 22:5), as it was in David's case; the Vg and Tg. Neof. take it as an expression of worship here. But it can also be a gesture of respect to a human being (e.g.,

22. Gevirtz, "Life Spans."
23. Sarna, *Genesis*, 324.
24. Brayford, *Genesis*, 440.
25. Rashi, *Br'šyt*, 528–29.

23:7). Joseph's brothers have already bowed low in 42:6; 43:26, 28, fulfilling the dream about them in 37:7. Now it is Jacob's turn, fulfilling the dream about him in 37:10.

48:1–7. The theme of the story that follows is Jacob's changing the status of Joseph's two sons so that they become his own. It suggests background to some later realities in Israel.

The time reference (vv. 1–2) is vague, but when a man of Jacob's age gets weak and sickly, it opens up the possibility that this illness might be the last one (cf. v. 21). Is Joseph thinking that he should take his sons to see Joseph before he dies, and is Jacob thinking the same way as he summons up his strength to sit up in bed? For the audience, the story that follows helps to explain the puzzling facts that Ephraim and Manasseh are two of the twelve clans even though their ancestors were not among Jacob's twelve sons and that Joseph does not have a clan bearing his name.

Jacob's testimony (vv. 3–4) is a "pastiche"[26] of phrases from several accounts of God's dealings with him. It was God who spoke of his "appearing" to Jacob. It was El Shadday whose blessing Isaac had declared on Jacob in 28:3–4, a blessing that would issue in his being fruitful and numerous and becoming a congregation of peoples and being given the country where he was residing as an alien. It was then as Yahweh and as the God of Abraham and Isaac that God had spoken to Jacob at Luz in 28:13 and had affirmed these promises. Behind those passages, the declaration that the country would be an agelong holding goes back to God's promise to Abraham in 17:8. So Jacob speaks as heir to Abraham's promises, as beneficiary of Isaac's blessing, and as himself recipient of God's revelation and God's promises.

He intends to treat Joseph's two sons as his own (v. 5), with parallel status to his own eldest sons. The declaration links with the one in vv. 3–4: God had said that Jacob was to have numerous descendants, and Ephraim and Manasseh will be the means of that promise coming true. But as his grandchildren they would have that role anyway. Jacob's action has different implications. It compares with Middle Eastern conventions for making someone an heir.[27] As Reuben and Simeon will be two clans called by their names, Ephraim and Manasseh will be two clans called by their names.[28] It will be as if they are Jacob's sons—which is in effect what he is making them. Indeed, perhaps Jacob is implying that Ephraim and Manasseh will be more than the equal of Reuben and Simeon—as indeed the clans of Ephraim and Manasseh were. Jacob hints at the first reason for this action: their having been born in Egypt before his arrival. This looks like a euphemistic way of alluding to their mother being Egyptian, which means there is some ambiguity about whether they are

26. Brett, *Genesis*, 132.
27. Cf. Sarna, *Genesis*, 325.
28. Cf. Jerome, *Hebrew Questions on Genesis*, 82.

really Israelites. In this connection one might speak of their "legitimation"[29] rather than their adoption.

Any more offspring Joseph has will continue to count as his (v. 6). We do not hear of any, so in effect Jacob's words refer to descendants Joseph will have via his two sons. Since the descendants of people such as Reuben and Simeon will share in the nation's land through their father, those other offspring of Joseph will share in the nation's land through their father, either Ephraim or Manasseh, according to who was their ancestor. It means that the arrangement whereby some of Jacob's grandsons become heads of clans happens just this once. Later, a big clan like Manasseh will have powerful subgroups such as Makir and Gilead (see 50:23; and, e.g., Judg. 5); they might fancy the idea of becoming clans in their own right. It's not going to happen. For the audience there is thus another question that Jacob's action answers. The prevalence of the name Israel in this chapter fits with this focus on possible implications for the later clans.

A third possible implication in Jacob's action (v. 7) is apparently something to do with Rachel's passing: if only she had had the chance to bear Jacob other children as well as Joseph (the father of these two) and Benjamin (whose birth was the occasion of her passing). "Jacob's whole life is filled with love for Rachel, a love that has caused him so much distress and pain. First, he had to serve many years for her, then she bore him no sons for a long period, and she died giving birth to the second child. Then he transferred his love for her to her sons."[30] Now Jacob is making a further gesture to Joseph's two children and thereby increases (posthumously) Rachel's offspring to four.[31] Will the flourishing of these two clans to descend from him and Rachel take the edge off his imminent burial without her at his side?[32] "My poor beloved Jacob! So many years had passed since my death—but he still couldn't let go of his grief. Here at the end of his life he tried to compensate by adopting our grandsons, Ephraim and Manasseh, as his own, and so gave our firstborn, Joseph, a double portion of the inheritance." And at the end of his life "he suddenly realized that he would lie forever separate from me. . . . So just as my sister Leah was his first bride instead of me, she remained his eternal companion in death."[33]

48:8–20. Yet again, Genesis goes back on its account of an event to tell us more. The theme is now the elevation of Ephraim over Manasseh.

Jacob's question (v. 8) might indicate that the event recorded here happened on his original arrival in Egypt. Or it might indicate that Jacob cannot see well (cf. v. 10). Or it might parallel questions traditionally asked in a marriage

29. Cf. Westermann, *Genesis 37–50*, 185.

30. Gunkel, *Genesis*, 447.

31. Hamilton, *Genesis 18–50*, 630.

32. Cf. Wolowelsky, "Rachel's Burial."

33. Frankel, *Five Books of Miriam*, 87, 88.

service such as "Who gives this woman to be married to this man?" or "Do you take this man as your lawful wedded husband?"[34] The purpose of the question is then not to establish otherwise unknown facts but to articulate known facts as part of a legal or quasi-legal process. The story does not simply concern a touching meeting between grandfather and grandchildren.

Jacob wishes to bless Joseph's sons (vv. 9–11). The theme of blessing, of key importance in Genesis, will be of key importance in these closing chapters: verb and noun come fifteen times in Gen. 48–50. Although in English "blessing" can suggest especially an inner sense of well-being, expressed in an awareness of God's presence and favor, Hebrew *bərākâ* suggests especially an outward experience of that favor and of well-being expressed in experiences such as having a flourishing family and having plenty to eat (the First Testament does value that inner sense of well-being and of God's presence and favor—it just doesn't link it with *bərākâ*). Such gifts need to come from God, but in some respects God delegates to humanity the capacity to convey them. The head of a family is especially significant in having control of them and deciding who receives them. When Jacob talks about blessing his grandsons, he refers to that power, and his words of blessing will be the means of conveying them, as (say) the words of a dean are the means of admitting someone to a program or of graduating them, or as the words of the head of a Western family can still transfer the ownership of the family's possessions to different offspring upon the death of its head. It is as he nears death that Jacob will especially do some blessing, as his father did.

Joseph's bowing (v. 12) nicely reverses the bowing of 47:31. It is perhaps an expression of his submission to his father as he seeks his blessing for the two young men—or boys, if Genesis implies that they are sitting on Jacob's knee, but they may be kneeling in front of him.

Once again Genesis goes back to give us more detail (v. 13).[35] Cultures will commonly have conventions about questions such as how blessing should work—for instance, that the eldest son has more responsibility and receives a more substantial share of the family's estate. Joseph assumes that convention. Because the right hand is the more effective hand for most people, it is often the hand that counts in legal procedures ("Raise your right hand and repeat after me"). So because Manasseh is Joseph's elder son (41:51–52), Joseph puts him in a position to receive the blessing that comes from Jacob's right hand, which one might expect to be more powerful or effective.

But Jacob insists (v. 14) on frustrating Joseph's expectations by crossing his hands so that his right hand rests on Ephraim. People with the power of blessing may indeed not be bound by the cultural conventions. Though in this case, Manasseh and Ephraim need not have the same rights within the

34. Cf. Hamilton, *Genesis 18–50*, 634.
35. Cf. Ibn Ezra, *Genesis*, 415.

family because of their hybrid nationality, and as Jacob's grandchildren they do not have the same rights as his children, Jacob has already bypassed these considerations. He now intends to bypass the principle that the eldest son has a privileged position, as he and Rebekah had circumvented it for him and as his grandfather had bypassed it for his father. He has already hinted as much in v. 5 when he speaks of "Ephraim and Manasseh."

A blessing is a prayer (v. 15a) and an act of faith; in Heb. 11:21 this blessing is Jacob's "outstanding act of faith."[36] It is God who blesses, even though God can delegate to human beings the power to bestow his blessing and bind himself to the way they do so, and fathers thus have the power to bless.[37] And consciously or unconsciously, they may do so in a way that embodies the way God's blessing may be arbitrary in the sense that it may not work by rules. The divine landowner feels free to pay people the same amount no matter how long they have labored (Matt. 20:1–16; KSG). On this occasion, in blessing Joseph's sons, Jacob is blessing Joseph. Blessing the young men counts as blessing their father. Of course it does! Further, when he gives the boys two shares within the family inheritance, it would not be a big jump to see him as making Joseph his firstborn (cf. Deut. 21:17). It is the jump that 1 Chron. 5:1–3 may presuppose.[38] Jacob also noted in v. 5 that Reuben and Simeon are his two oldest sons, but he is here implicitly treating his favorite, Joseph, as his eldest son, explicitly treating Ephraim as Joseph's eldest son, and implicitly explaining the later dominance of the Joseph clans and of Ephraim. The distinction between the individual and the community indeed becomes hazy here, and the story's importance links with the importance of that development. It would boggle Judahite minds in the monarchic period or in the Persian period.

The form of Jacob's blessing (v. 15b) recalls that of a hymn of praise such as Ps. 103.[39] The blessing is "completely focused on God."[40] Jacob has three descriptions of God. He is the God before whom Abraham and Isaac walked (see 17:1; 24:40). Jacob thus makes a link with the past and with his past family and with the long saga of God's promise and covenant. He is the God who has been shepherding Jacob himself. In contrast to that first description, this one is original and unique to Jacob in the Torah. It will recur in 49:24 and famously reappear in Ps. 23:1; also 80:1 [80:2]. Jacob of course knows all about shepherding. It is a remarkable description, because a shepherd normally looks after a flock, not a single sheep.[41]

Third (v. 16a), Jacob in effect identifies God with the envoy who represents God and thus draws attention to God's having been present with him spatially

36. Kidner, *Genesis*, 212.
37. Cf. von Rad, *Genesis*, 410–11.
38. Cf. Willet, *Hexapla in Genesin & Exodum*, 380.
39. Cf. von Rad, *Genesis*, 412.
40. Brueggemann, *Genesis*, 361.
41. Cf. Gunkel, *Genesis*, 449.

and visibly. The envoy who rescues from trouble compares with the earlier envoy of 21:17–19. But with further originality, Jacob describes him as the one who has "restored" him (*gā'al*) from all the bad experiences he has had. God has acted in relation to Jacob like the member of a person's extended family who has the resources to get someone out of trouble and uses those resources to that end. The verb comes only here in Genesis, but Jacob's use of it nicely anticipates Exod. 6:6; 15:13. His words would ring bells with Judahites in exile to whom Yahweh spoke especially as "restorer" (e.g., Isa. 44:6, 22, 23, 24) even while also being the one who made bad things happen (Isa. 45:7). The blessing of a God capable of being described in these three ways in vv. 15b–16a is a powerful reality whether one is the younger son or the older. It reminds Israel itself (e.g., in the context of the exile) that its hope lies not in the promise of the land or in being the people of promise but in the God of the ancestors.[42] And as this blessing is effective, and as the two clans are known as belonging among the descendants of Abraham, Isaac, and Jacob, so will the names of these ancestors be known and honored.

As a footnote (v. 16b), Jacob articulates the usual promise about becoming numerous to make sure that it explicitly applies to them, but he expresses it again in an innovative way by using a verb for multiply (*dāgâ*) that comes only here and suggests that they will teem like the fish in Lake Kinneret, on either side of which Manasseh strides.

Yet once more Genesis backtracks (vv. 17–20) to tell us further about the process that has just been summarized. As Isaac's father could bless him as the younger son even though Jacob was acting deceptively, so Jacob can bless Joseph's younger son even though Joseph wants to avoid it. Once again, the fact that one is blessed or chosen does not mean that the other is cursed or rejected.[43] The difference between the two blessings is not great; more noteworthy is the magnitude of the blessing both receive. Thus the Israelites will pronounce a blessing by each of them: "you" at the beginning of v. 20 is singular, as is the later "you." Both Ephraim and Manasseh will embody the promise about Abraham and thus about all Jacob's descendants. They are just as much descendants of Jacob as (say) Reuben and Simeon.

48:21–22. Jacob's closing words to Joseph first take up God's promise to be "with you," made earlier to Jacob himself, but here reformulated so that for the first time it takes the plural form and thus applies to the entire family. "Though Iacob died, yet the promise of God died not."[44]

Jacob then (v. 22) incorporates a promise that is more distinctly a blessing of Joseph: the "you" is now singular. Shoulder is *šəkem*, and Shechem is in the heart of the area that will belong to the Joseph clans; it is also the

42. Seebass, *Genesis*, 3:162.
43. Cf. Barth, *CD* 2.2:355–56.
44. Willet, *Hexapla in Genesin & Exodum*, 383.

place where Joseph will be buried (Josh. 24:32). What does Jacob mean by taking the town with his sword and his bow? He hardly refers to the event related in Gen. 34; and the First Testament records no subsequent taking of Shechem by Jacob or by Israel itself. Indeed, Yahweh proclaims at Shechem that the Israelites did not take Canaan by the use of sword and bow (Josh. 24:12). Actually they did do so; the point about Yahweh's denial is that it was not merely by their sword and bow. They would not have succeeded without Yahweh's involvement.[45] Jacob's point here is the promise that he (through his descendants) will take the mountain ridge at whose center Shechem sits, and Joseph (through his descendants) will possess it. The story provides another bit of background to and explanation of later realities in Israel. In making this promise, Jacob "continues to favor Joseph over all his brothers, even on his deathbed."[46] And his promise finds fulfillment.

45. Cf. Qimchi, *Genesis*, on the verse.
46. Brayford, *Genesis*, 443.

49

How Jacob Addresses Each of His Sons before Dying

(49:1–27)

Overview

The peak of Gen. 36–50 and perhaps of the whole book of Genesis comes in a picture of the "embryonic nation" incorporating the Judah and Joseph clans in their preeminent positions in the north and south.[1] To each of his sons, Jacob reveals aspects of their future destiny as it will unfold in the lives of the clans that will descend from them.

Translation

1Ya'aqob called his sons; he said, "Gather together so I may tell you[2] what is to befall[3] you in days to come.[4]

> **2**Assemble and listen, sons of Ya'aqob,
> listen to Yiśra'el your father.
> **3**Re'uben: you, my firstborn,
> my strength and the initiation of my vigor,

1. Wenham, *Genesis 16–50*, 345, following Longacre, *Joseph*, 54.

2. The cohortative makes explicit that a final clause follows the imperative.

3. While the form *yiqrā'* is the same as that of "and he called" earlier in the verse, one should presumably derive this word from BDB's *qārā'* II, a by-form of *qārâ*, though perhaps the expression invites the brothers to think in terms of their destiny "summoning" them.

4. Literally, "in the latter part of the days." The LXX has "the last of the days," the Vg "the last/newest days."

Excellence in high position
  and excellence in strength.
4Turbulence[5] like water: you are not to excel,
  because you climbed your father's big bed.[6]
Thereby[7] you polluted—[8]
  one who climbed my couch![9]

5Šimʿon and Lewi, brothers,
  their blades[10] tools of violence:
6In their council my person is not to come,
  in their congregation my soul[11] is not to join.
Because in their anger they killed someone,
  in their pleasure they hamstrung[12] an ox.[13]
7Cursed their anger because it was strong,
  their outburst because it was tough!
I will divide them in Yaʿaqob,
  disperse them in Yiśraʾel.

8Yehudah: you,[14]
  your brothers will confess you.
Your hand on your enemies' neck,
  your father's sons will bow down to you.
9A lion cub, Yehudah
  (from prey, son, you've gone up):

5. The LXX takes the hapax *paḥaz* to denote Reuben's willful turbulence, but v. 4 is making a transition to talk of his fate (Vg, Tg).

6. "Bed" is plural, perhaps pejorative (cf. Lev. 18:22; 20:13); cf. Sarna, *Genesis*, 331.

7. For this meaning of *ʾāz* here, see BDB.

8. "My couch" in the parallel colon does double duty as also the object of the first verb; cf. Sarna, *Genesis*, 331.

9. The final colon is an unmarked relative clause (Ehrlich, *Randglossen*, 1:243) in which the verb can therefore be third person (see JM 158n, GKC 144p), like an English sentence such as "you are one who climbs," not "you are one who climb."

10. *Məkērōt* comes only here, but a derivation from *karat* seems plausible and makes a good link with 34:13–29. See *DCH*, which also notes the possible meanings of counsel, weapon, staff, and beguilement: and if the word could be understood as having any of these meanings, they would not be inappropriate.

11. While *kābōd* usually means "honor," sometimes (e.g., Ps. 30:12 [13]) it seems to be an alternative form to *kābēd* and to refer anatomically to the liver but metaphorically to the inner person, like words such as heart in English; *nepeš* in the parallel colon helps clarify the meaning of *kābōd*. The masculine noun is preceded by a feminine verb from *yāḥad* whose gender may be assimilated to that of the verb in the previous colon.

12. *ʿĀqar* (piel) recalls *ʿākar* in 34:30; Carmichael, "Some Sayings in Genesis 49," 435–36.

13. Given that Gen. 34 does not refer to hamstringing oxen, Vg, Sym, and Tg take *šûr* to be the other *šûr*, meaning "wall," which comes in v. 22.

14. The extraposed pronoun anticipatorily emphasizes the subsequent verbal suffix (GKC 135d) and also draws attention to a paronomasia: "You, as Judah [*yəhûdâ*], are one whom people confess [*yôdûkā*]." "You are what your name means" (Westermann, *Genesis 37–50*, 227). Indeed, the "Jews" are etymologically the Judahites: Judah gave them their name (cf. the Tg).

He has bent down, lain, like a lion,
like a cougar[15]—who would rouse him?
10The staff will not leave from Yehudah,
the scepter from between his feet,
Until[16] there comes tribute to him[17]
and the obedience of the peoples to him.
11Tying[18] his donkey to a vine,
the offspring of his she-donkey to a choice vine,
He has washed his clothing in wine,
his garment in grape-blood:
12Darker of eyes than wine,
whiter of teeth than milk.[19]

13Zebulun: toward the shore of the seas he will dwell,
toward the shore for ships, him,
his flank at Sidon.

14Yiśśakar: a donkey, sturdy,
lying among the sheepfolds.[20]
15He has seen a resting place, how good it was,
and the region, how beautiful.
But he has bent his shoulder to the burden,
become a conscript servant.

15. We do not really know how to distinguish the different Hebrew words for lion.

16. Or "ever": Steiner ("Four Inner-Biblical Interpretations") sees this ambiguity subsequently picked up by Nathan, Ahijah, Ezekiel, and Zechariah.

17. The obvious translations of this colon are "until Shiloh comes" or "until he comes to Shiloh" (cf. Frolov, "Judah Comes to Shiloh"), but it is not obvious what they might refer to. I follow what Rashi (*Br'šyt*, 546) calls the midrashic interpretation that *šîlô* (K *šhlh*) needs redividing and repointing as *šay lô* ("[until there comes] tribute to him"); cf. the discussion in de Hoop, *Genesis 49*, 122–39; and see Steiner ("Poetic Forms," 219–24), who thinks the repointing is unnecessary. It would not be surprising if the rare word *šay* had gotten lost from the colon, and the change generates good parallelism with the next colon. The LXX implies *šellô* "[until there comes] what belongs to him," which also provides good parallelism with the next colon and has similar implications. Rashi himself follows the Tg in assuming that the literal interpretation is "until the Messiah comes"; Ibn Ezra (*Genesis*, 430) assumes that it refers to David himself—Judah will be in the lead until then (e.g., Num. 10:14). The NT does not refer to v. 10, though v. 11 is significant in Mark 11 in connection with the story of Jesus's messiah-style entry to Jerusalem; see, e.g., Krause, "One Who Comes"; Ahearne-Kroll, "Genesis in Mark's Gospel," 34–37.

18. *'Ōsərî* is an anomalous but not unparalleled construct of the participle (see Hamilton, *Genesis 18–50*, 655–56).

19. The LXX's "dark from . . . white from" makes poorer sense.

20. Or among the saddlebags or campfires: *mišpətayim* comes only here and in Judg. 5:16. Whereas etymology supports "campfires" (see BDB), the parallelism in Judg. 5:16 supports "sheepfolds"; de Hoop (*Genesis 49*, 151–56) argues for "saddlebags." As in v. 5, if the word could be understood as having any of these meanings, they would not be inappropriate.

16Dan: his people will govern[21]
as one of the clans of Yiśraʾel.
17May Dan be[22] a snake by the road,
a viper by the path,
One that bites the horse's heels
so its rider falls backward:
18for your deliverance I have waited,[23] Yahweh.

19Gad: an attacker[24] will attack him,
but he himself will attack their heel.

20From[25] Ašer: rich his bread,
and he, one who will give a king's delicacies.

21Naptali: a hind[26] set free;
it gives[27] fawns[28] of the fold.[29]

22A son,[30] a wild donkey,[31] Yosep,
a son, a wild donkey:

21. The LXX and Vg translate "his people" as the object rather than the subject, but this understanding makes poor sense and eliminates the parallel with other verses that begin with an extraposed noun. Further, they translate the verb *dîn* with words meaning "judge," which gives a misleadingly judiciary meaning to the verb.

22. GKC 109k sees this *yəhî* as an example of a jussive form that is really yiqtol in significance, but jussive meaning fits in the context of a number of wishes and prayers in the testament.

23. On such quasi-stative verbs, see GKC 106g.

24. More precisely, a gang of attackers. *Gədûd* comes from the root *gādad*, whereas the two succeeding verbs come from the by-form *gûd*.

25. The LXX and Vg lack the odd "from," and the LXX may attach the *m* to the end of the previous line, making explicit that the heel is "their heel."

26. For *ʾêlâ* the LXX implies *ʾēlâ*, "oak' (cf. 35:4), but Aq has "deer."

27. The masculine participle takes its gender from the word for the clan rather than from the word for "hind."

28. I take *ʾimrê* as not from *ʾōmer* ("saying") but from the hapax *ʾimmēr*, denoting a baby animal such as a lamb (*HALOT*, 67b), though the audience might be reminded of the "sayings" of Baraq and Deborah in Judg. 4–5. Baraq was a Naphtalite and maybe Deborah was too, even though she was working in Ephraim, and Midrash Tehillim on Ps. 22 (whose introduction refers to a hind) puts two and two together and infers that she is the hind set free; see Braude, *Midrash on Psalms*, 1:297.

29. The LXX and Vg take *šeper* as an Aramaism meaning "beauty"; I take it as an Ugariticism or Akkadianism meaning "fold" (see Gevirtz, "Naphtali"). But the existence of the Aramaic word would add to the possibilities of paronomasia suggested by the previous note.

30. BDB takes *bēn* as an anomalous construct; JM 96Eb would provide a rationale, though it does not treat this word as an example; and the LXX, Vg, and Tg take it as absolute.

31. The LXX, Vg, and Tg then take *pōrāt* as a participle from *pārâ*, qualifying *bēn* and meaning fruitful, but the form is anomalous, and the feminine is odd. More likely *pōrāt* is a noun. If it denotes a fruitful tree, its "daughters" would be its branches, but *bānôt* never elsewhere refers to plants, only to human beings and animals (cf. de Hoop, *Genesis 49*, 184). See further the comment.

Its daughters by a spring,[32]
it has stridden[33] by a terrace.[34]
23People made things bitter for him[35] and fought,[36]
archers were hostile toward him.
24But his bow stayed firm,
his arms and hands[37] were agile,
From the hands of the Strongman of Yaʿaqob,
from there, the Shepherd, the Stone of Yiśraʾel,
25From God, your Father,[38] so he will help you,
and Šadday,[39] so he will bless you,
With blessings of the heavens above,
blessings of the deep lying below.
Blessings of the breasts and the womb,
26your father's blessings—
They have been stronger than the blessings of those who conceived me,[40]
beyond the desirable things on the agelong hills.
They will come on Yosep's head,
on the brow of one set apart[41] among his brothers.

27Binyamin: a wolf who will maul,
in the morning will eat prey,[42]
and toward the evening will divide spoil."

32. The translation reverses the Hebrew word order ("by a spring its daughters"; this colon and the one that follows thus work abca′ rather than abcb′), which in English generates an even more elliptical impression. The MT's accents associate "by its spring" with the preceding words; the line is then a neat 3-3-3 tricolon, but one even harder to construe.

33. The Vg takes the daughters as the subject of the apparently singular verb (see the comments in GKC 44m; JM 42f). But if *pōrāt* is a feminine noun (see the earlier note), it can be the subject, which fits regular grammar and makes sense in the context. The SP has *ṣʿry* ("little") for *ṣʿdh*, and the LXX implies something similar (cf. Tal, *Genesis*, 203*).

34. *Šûr* can mean a wall and *šûrâ* a row of fruit trees (see BDB, *DTT*), which together suggests a terrace.

35. They "embittered him," not in the sense that they made him feel bitter but that they made his life bitter; cf. *mārar* piel in Exod. 1:14 (Rashi, *Brʾšyt*, 557).

36. The LXX implies taking *wārōbû* as from a by-form of *rîb* (the SP reads a form from that verb) or as trading on the similarity between *rîb* and *rābab* (shoot), which is much rarer but is signaled by the parallel colon and by v. 24.

37. Literally, "the arms of his hands."

38. The LXX, Vg have "God of your father," but "God" is *ʾēl* not *ʾĕlōhê*, and there are no parallels for *ʾēl ʾābîkā* as a construct phrase (none at all for *ʾēl* as a construct in Genesis, and not many elsewhere). See comment.

39. "From" carries over from the previous colon (cf. Ibn Ezra, *Genesis*, on the passage), though the *ʾet* is odd.

40. The LXX's "of the steadfast mountains" suggests reading *hārê* for *hôray* and linking it with *ʿad* in the next colon (cf. *harărê* in Deut. 33:15); either way, it draws attention to a paronomasia between *hôray ʿad* and *gibʿōt ʿôlām*.

41. A *nāzîr*: "there is no need to invent the meaning 'prince'" for the word (G. Meyer, "*nzr*," in *TDOT* 9:306–11 [308]).

42. For the rare *ʿēd*, LXX presupposes *ʿôd*, "still."

Interpretation

The term "testament" describes a number of Jewish works from late Second Temple times that characteristically present themselves as addresses by an important scriptural figure who is about to die. While they are not testaments in the sense that they convey bequests, they may testify to events in the life of the figure and/or challenge the hearers to live holy lives and/or make promises and issue warnings about the future. A testament is not exactly a prophecy or a prediction; it is more like a blessing, the term that comes in v. 28 (cf. Deut. 33). It announces good news, but also possibly bad news, and it incorporates compliments and critique. Given the variety in the form and nature of testaments, their single distinctive, defining feature is their setting on the lips of someone who is about to die and who speaks about the future as it will affect the rhetorical and actual addressees. Both their variety and the nature of this defining feature make "the Testament of Jacob" a convenient description of Gen. 49:1–27.[43] Each end of this testament shows its character: v. 1 announces it as a prophecy, v. 2 pictures it as fatherly instruction, and v. 28 describes it retrospectively as a blessing. It informs, warns, promises, wishes, and (by virtue of the power of the words of the one who speaks) ensures and effects its own fulfillment.

The sayings about the individual people and about the clans that trace their ancestry back to these individuals all take poetic form, but beyond that feature they vary. They differ in how far they focus on the individual and how far they focus on the clan. They differ in length from two or three cola to eighteen or nineteen. The length of the Judah and Joseph sections reflects the prominence of these individuals in Gen. 37–50 and the prominence of these clans in Israel, but otherwise there is no evident explanation for the variation. The variety among the sayings may suggest that they are of separate origin, perhaps as sayings formulated within each clan,[44] but we do not have evidence of the development of clan sayings in this way, and it seems just as plausible that the testament was composed in its varied form rather than compiled and allowed to stand in its varied form.[45]

The testament is "the first sustained piece of Hebrew poetry in the Torah,"[46] and its poetry follows common Hebrew poetic form. Most lines comprise two parts in which the second complements the first, usually by restating it or completing it. In many lines the two parts comprise three words, though in some lines one part may comprise two or four words. I refer to a single part of a line as a colon; thus one line is usually a bicolon, while occasional lines are tricola—they comprise three parts. Poetry in the Hebrew Scriptures switches

43. Cf. Dillmann, *Genesis* 2:444.

44. See de Moor, "Genesis 49."

45. See further de Hoop, *Genesis 49*, 252–308.

46. Sarna, *Genesis*, 331.

easily between the second person and the third person; the switch happens in the Judah and Joseph declarations (the Reuben declaration is entirely second person, the others are entirely third person). Poetry uses the second person because rhetorically it directly addresses the people named. It uses the third person since it speaks about these people to others who are listening because the declaration has significance for them and/or since it puts the addressees into the position of people overhearing statements that are actually about them. For related reasons Jacob himself can switch between speaking as "I" and referring to himself as "he." Whereas in general the Hebrew of the Joseph story may seem "unsophisticated,"[47] the Hebrew of Gen. 49 can be allusive and elliptical, and sophisticated in its use of paronomasia; it parallels the poetry of a prophet such as Hosea. It makes use of repetition or anaphora, a feature of Hebrew poetry elsewhere (cf. vv. 3, 4, 13, 22, 25, 26). But it also follows the form of a list as lists commonly appear in the Hebrew Bible, beginning with a name and continuing asyndetically.

In more detail, the poetry works as follows.

Verse 2: Jacob's bidding comprises two parallel cola. Rhythmically, the MT punctuates them as 4-3; one could repunctuate them as 3-3 by hyphenating "sons of Jacob" (cf. e.g., 36:20, 22). In substance they work aba′c. Thus both cola contain a bidding, which is doubled in the first colon, heightening the effect; the second verb then recurs in the second colon in the first occurrence of anaphora in the poem. Only the first colon contains a vocative (which thus also applies to the second) and only the second contains an (indirect) object (which thus also applies to the first). Tightening the two cola further, however, the indirect object (Israel your father) refers to the person named in the vocative (sons of Jacob). In other words, formally there is an aba′b′ parallelism in the line, between the two verbal expressions and the two noun expressions.

Verses 3–4: the declaration begins with two parallel cola (3-3); the second works out the implications of the first. Then v. 3b comprises two briefer cola (2-2) whose parallelism is more precise; they include the poem's second example of anaphora as it repeats the word for excellence. The line prepares the way for v. 4a. The MT here punctuates the line as 3-4, and one might imagine that here the *kî* does not count metrically; sometimes in a poetic line *kî* is hyphenated into the next word (e.g., Deut. 32:22, 32, 36, 40). The four lines would then be a neat 3-3, 2-2, 3-3, 2-2. Verse 4a follows on v. 3b in several contrasting ways. "Turbulence like water" continues the sequence of asyndetic noun phrases that leave the audience to provide the syntactical links in

47. Redford, *Study*, 45; though the comments on language and syntax at the end of the introduction to this commentary imply a qualification to this judgment.

order to make sense of the lines, though its noun phrase has a different significance: it constitutes a threat, not a description like the phrases in v. 3b. Then the verb "excel" takes up the root of that repeated noun. The internal relationship between the two cola within v. 4a involves not parallelism but clarification; the second explains the reasoning behind the first and thus explains the need for a change in the talk of "excelling." Finally, both cola in v. 4b expand on that explanation and thus have a tighter relationship with it than with each other. The first colon extends that explanation, answering the question "What was so wrong about climbing into his father's bed?" The second colon parallels and restates that earlier explanation, with a further repeat of forms of the verb *ʿālâ*.

Verses 5–7: the five lines exploit several potentials of parallelism. In v. 5, the first colon raises a question ("What do you mean by saying that they are brothers, in some special sense?"), which the second colon answers. Verse 6a is an especially neat 3-3 line in which the second colon expresses the point in a less everyday way. Something similar applies to v. 6b (4-2), except that the opening "because" is resumed by a *w* at the beginning of the second colon, and again it applies to v. 7a (4-3), which also has a word in one colon ("cursed") carrying over into the other. Further, vv. 6–7a work aba′b′: two cola in v. 6a referring to the brothers' planning, one in v. 6bα to their anger, then one more in v. 6bβ referring to their planning, and two more in v. 7a to their anger. The punchy 2-2 final line (v. 7b) again has the second colon expressing the point in a less everyday way.

Verses 8–12: in both lines of the opening declaration (2-2, 3-4), the second colon completes and clarifies the first, and the two lines are also themselves parallel. In the opening further brisk, no-nonsense 2-2 bicolon, the point about the initial "you" is that "you" will be the person with his hand on his enemies' neck; the second line begins by answering the question raised by the first ("Why will they confess him?") then goes on to restate "Your brothers will confess you" in the words "Your father's sons will bow down to you."

In v. 9, the 3-3, 3-3 starts again, though it has some partial parallels with v. 8. In its opening colon it makes another reference to Judah, but it starts with the poem's first animal metaphor. The opening colon thus raises a question ("How is Judah like a lion cub?"), which the rest of the verse answers. Momentarily, the second colon begins that answer with a switch back to second person, but the third-person form of v. 9b probably confirms that the opening colon was third person rather than vocative address to Judah, like v. 8. Verse 9b works roughly abb′a′. In beginning with a double verb that underlines its point, it follows the precedent of v. 2. At the center the two words for a lion parallel each other. The closing question in substance parallels the doubled verb.

Verses 10–12 comprise five straightforwardly parallel lines, 3-3, 3-3, 3-3, 3-2, 3-2 (again one could easily punctuate the two odd lines so they were 3-3). Hypothesizing that v. 10b composes two parallel cola like the others in this sequence helps to make sense of a line that has been a puzzle, as "obedience to him" provides a plausible parallel and clarifier for the rare expression "tribute to him," though the word for "obedience" is almost as rare. Three further internally parallel lines describe Judah's flourishing in other ways. The two lines comprising v. 11 again each have a verb that governs the second colon as well as the first, with the second otherwise restating the first in slightly less straightforward, more vivid fashion. The Judah sequence closes with an enjambment in two parallel cola that take up the wine image but then move in another direction.

Verse 13: Zebulun is the subject of Jacob's first tricolon (4-3-2), with the three cola parallel in their geographical references governed by Zebulun's own verb (*zābal*) in between the first two, which are more tightly tied by the anaphora "toward the shore."

Verses 14–15: the three lines on Issachar work 3-3, 4-3, 3-2. In the first line, the double description of the donkey raises the question of what lies behind it. Verse 15 provides a poignant answer. One verb governs the two parallel cola in the v. 15a line developing the idyllic implications of "lying among the sheepfolds." But then two more parallel cola reveal the downside to being a sturdy donkey. Its strength gets harnessed.

Verses 16–18: the three lines on Dan (3-3, 3-2, 3-3-3) overlap in their working with the three lines on Issachar, though they start from literal statement and segue into imagery, whereas vv. 14–15 had started with an animal image and worked toward the literal. Verse 16 starts with another paronomasia, then the second colon simply completes the line. Yet poetically it leaves the audience asking, "So what does that mean, what's the point of that comment?"—though an Israelite audience might be able to guess that it relates to Dan not looking as if that clan can live up to its name. In parallel cola v. 17a expresses a wish that it may be able to find its way into a position where it can do so. Verse 17b then develops the point; the second colon completes the first. The unexpected third colon (v. 18) expresses in a prayer the wish that dominates the three verses.

Verse 19: the characterization of Gad depends on paronomasia:

gād gədûd yəgûdennû
wəhû' yāgud 'āqēb

In Jacob's testament it is the only example of antithetic parallelism: the second colon in the 3-3 line contrasts with the first.

Verse 20: in the parallelism of the 3-3 line, the verbal clause in the second colon complements the noun clause in the first, and "a king's delicacies" vividly reexpresses the nature of "rich food."

Verse 21: in the animal imagery relating to Naphtali (3-2), the second colon spells out the implications of the first.

Verses 22–26: the first line in v. 22 (3-2) repeats itself in an anaphora paralleling the Reuben verses, which gives the audience the chance to absorb the intriguing description of Joseph as a son who is *pōrāt*. The third and fourth cola (v. 22b; 2-2) make the audience work harder. The parallel clauses begin and end with similar prepositional phrases, but the audience has to wait until the second colon for the verb, which is indeed the entire verse's main verb. In vv. 23–26 (2-3, 3-3, 3-4, 3-3, 3-4, 3-2, 3-3, 3-3) the prosody is more straightforward. In each line the cola are parallel, and each time the second colon restates the first. In v. 23 the second clarifies the first, answering the possible question "How did they fight?" (they were archers). In v. 24a, the second colon complements the first. The further line of description (v. 25a) comprises two further "from" phrases, but the parallelism between vv. 24b and 25a is complemented by a change, as each colon continues with a verbal clause. Jacob's sentence continues to run on in another rather unusual and unrestrained enjambment. I take the six cola (vv. 25b–26a) as three bicola rather than the two tricola implied by the MT, with the enjambment continuing into the first colon of v. 26. In the parallelism of the first pair of blessings, "above" and "below" complement each other. The middle cola refer to blessings that Jacob especially knows about in his family as well as in his work as a shepherd; thus "your father's blessings" restates "blessings of the breasts and the womb."

Verse 27: The testament closes with a tricolon full of drama and energy, its imagery a little reminiscent of the lion imagery applied to Benjamin's brother. In the parallelism, the subject in the first colon applies also to the second and third cola. There's no "who" in the Hebrew (that is, it's an unmarked relative clause), so the three verbs are parallel, with the second and third spelling out the implications of the first (which is the verb used four times of the assumed fate of Benjamin's brother). The second and third are word-for-word parallel, with "in the morning" and "toward the evening" balancing each other as a merism (they imply "all day"). "Prey" and "spoil" balance each other, with the more common word coming second and clarifying the uncommon first word.

Genesis 49 "is somewhat obscure and difficult, especially because it has many teachers and interpreters with completely divergent views. Therefore we must make the crooked and curved road we are following smooth and straight. But we shall do what we can."[48] The testament communicates in an allusive and enigmatic fashion and uses a number of unusual or unique Hebrew words. Many suggestions have been made for the clarifications of its distinctive words by comparing them with Ugaritic expressions,[49] but it is hard to evaluate these suggestions, and I have focused on the way the poem would communicate to people who were used to ordinary classical Hebrew. The poem's language is not characterized by manifest archaisms or by clearly late Hebrew expressions,[50] so it does not point to a date any different from that of the rest of Genesis—whatever that date might be. It has been dated in the pre-monarchic period, the Davidic/Solomonic era, the period of the two monarchies, the Babylonian period, and the Persian period.[51] The poem itself invites the audience to keep in mind two chronological contexts, the time of Jacob himself and the pre-monarchic/Davidic period. In other words, Jacob's own viewpoint is that of Israel in the time of the judges, though it presupposes the dominance of Judah and the Joseph clans.[52] It makes no reference to the big events of the times of Moses and Joshua or to the separating of Levi as the ministerial clan; there is no hint of the division of the monarchy[53] or of the exile or the circumstances of the Second Temple period. To say that the poem draws attention to the period of the judges and of David is to say nothing about when it was composed; it is simply to say that these are the periods the poem invites the audience to focus on.

The testament covers Jacob's twelve original sons, in another distinctive order compared with previous listings:

Genesis 29–30		Genesis 46		Genesis 49
Leah	Reuben	Leah	Reuben	Reuben
	Simeon		Simeon	Simeon
	Levi		Levi	Levi
	Judah		Judah	Judah
Bilhah	Dan		Issachar	Zebulun
	Naphtali		Zebulun	Issachar
Zilpah	Gad	Zilpah	Gad	Dan
	Asher		Asher	Gad

48. Luther, *Genesis 45–50*, 199.

49. See, e.g., Hamilton, *Genesis 18–50*, 644–87.

50. For the contrary view and references, see Hendel, "Historical Context," 52–54.

51. See de Hoop, *Genesis 49*, 594–621; Macchi (*Israël et ses tribus selon Genèse 49*) argues systematically for a Persian origin of the Testament of Jacob.

52. Cf. Westermann, *Genesis 37–50*, 221.

53. Cf. Skinner, *Genesis*, 508, 533.

Genesis 29–30		Genesis 46		Genesis 49
Leah	Issachar	Rachel	Joseph	Asher
	Zebulun		Benjamin	Naphtali
Rachel	Joseph	Bilhah	Dan	Joseph
	Benjamin		Naphtali	Benjamin

It's not clear why Zebulun precedes Issachar here only. Deuteronomy 33 has yet another order for its blessings, an approximate geographical order that again starts with Reuben and works clockwise.

The question underlying the testament is how should Israel think of the situation and experience of the twelve clans? It serves to mediate between the persons of the twelve sons and the destiny of the clans that will grow from them (vv. 1–2 focus on the sons, but v. 28 retrospectively links the pronouncements with the clans). Genesis has referred to the actions or experiences of five of the brothers as individuals—Reuben, Simeon, Levi, Joseph, and Judah—and their actions or experiences are the main background to Jacob's declarations about the first three and part of the background in connection with Judah and Joseph. For the six brothers who come between Judah and Joseph, Jacob's declarations relate to the geographical positions of the clans that will issue from them; it is also the other consideration that applies to Joseph. For Benjamin the declaration relates to his clan's later action, though this consideration also applies to Judah. Jacob sometimes expresses his own commitment or hopes. One way or another, the testament thus provides some account of these later realities.

Reuben fails to have the prominence that one would expect.
Simeon and Levi disappear geographically from the number of the clans.
Judah provides Israel with its leadership.
Zebulun's territory lies between the two seas.
Issachar has fine territory in Jezreel but must submit to the Canaanites there.
Dan must fight for territory in the southwest and then in the north.
Gad must defend itself from its rivals for territory east of the Jordan.
Asher has rich country on the northwest coast.
Naphtali has broad rolling pastures to the north.
Joseph thrives in a way that manifests the persistence its ancestor showed.
Benjamin is especially violent.

The declarations include a variety of verb forms, with some possible ambiguity in their significance. I have translated them as deriving their significance from the fact that they feature on the lips of Jacob at his stage in the First Testament story and have rendered them as follows.

There are some modal forms: verbs preceded by *ʾal* in vv. 4 and 6, and a jussive in v. 17. These forms are related in substance to the curse in v. 7 and the declaration of trust, which suggests the context of prayer in v. 18.

There are many other yiqtols (including yiqtols preceded by *lōʾ*) which all make sense as having future reference from Jacob's perspective.

Some qatal verbs refer to the past from Jacob's perspective (e.g., vv. 4, 23–24); I translate them as aorists.

Many qatal verbs refer to what is future from Jacob's perspective, but they are uttered as if something has already happened because it is so certain, being set in the context of Jacob's vision (e.g., vv. 9, 11, 15); I translate these as perfects.

49:1–2. The father of the twelve male ancestors of the twelve Israelite clans speaks, the father whose original name was Jacob but who is also himself Israel. He is able to tell the twelve ancestors and thus the twelve clans themselves something about the clans' destiny. So he speaks like a prophet and also like the father instructing his son in Proverbs. In referring to "days to come" (*ʾaḥărît hayyāmîm*), he is not alluding to "the end of the days" in the sense of the end of time. His expression does suggest a period that can be distinguished from the present time, and one that will probably not arrive next week. It will be a time that is not merely a continuation of this time, one that does introduce a new situation—virtually the beginning of a new age. The other occasions when the Torah uses this expression, it is looking forward from the position of Israel outside the promised land to what will happen after it enters the land, to the reign of David, to the exile, and to God's restoring the people from exile (Num. 24:14; Deut. 4:30; 31:29). Here it similarly looks beyond the present life of Jacob and his sons to the life of the clans when they have left Egypt and settled properly in Canaan. But a phrase that literally denotes "the end of the days" could come to suggest the end of the age, the end of our time. For the later Jewish community, it could come to suggest "the end of the exile";[54] in light of the fact that the end of the ages has come in Jesus (1 Cor. 10:11), it could be natural to take Jacob to be speaking of the "last days."[55]

49:3–4. For the background, see 29:31–32; 35:22. Reuben has inherited an abundance of energy and forcefulness because he is Jacob's firstborn; he is thus the firstfruit of his father's manly strength (cf. Deut. 21:17; Ps. 78:51). One might half expect a first child to be full of such dynamism and vitality. But there are also temptations attaching to the position of number one, and Reuben fell to them. In light of what follows, one can imagine that Jacob is

54. Rashi, *Brʾšyt*, 539.

55. Denis the Carthusian (15th cent.), "Enarratio in Genesim," 437; cf. Schroeder, *Genesis*, 242.

also aware of the other possible meaning of *rēʾšît ʿônî*, "the initiation of my trouble."[56]

Despite the excellence of his position and his energy (v. 4), Reuben will therefore not excel in the future. Typically, poetry sucks us into one direction, then discomforts us (KSG). Because of his "grab for power," he "will cease to be foremost."[57] "You would have been worthy of the birthright, the dignity of the priesthood and the kingship. But because you sinned, my son, the birthright was given to Joseph, the kingship to Judah, and the priesthood to Levi" (Tg. Ps.-J.). Reuben will be overcome by tumult like that of the rushing water in a wadi after a storm.[58] Jacob is speaking of Reuben the individual, but he implies that his descendants will be affected by his demotion from primacy among the brothers. Deborah critiques their lack of energy (Judg. 5:15–16).[59] And the clan of Reuben does subsequently fade into relative insignificance. But in Deut. 33:6 Moses prays that Reuben may not actually die out, later parts of the First Testament occasionally refer to the Reubenites, and Ezek. 48 and Rev. 7 make sure they have a place in the future. Jacob's reference to Reuben polluting his bed (the verb *ḥālal* piel) compares and contrasts with the reference to Shechem defiling Dinah (*ṭāmēʾ* piel). The curt condemnation comprising v. 4b closes the declaration. Following on the plural word for "bed," the repetition of the verb "climbed" draws further attention to the impressive nature of that bed; normally one lies "down" on a mat on the floor.

49:5–7. For the background, see 34:25–30. Simeon and Levi are full brothers, but they also have four other full brothers. The further special brotherhood between Simeon and Levi is a brotherhood in violence. They were experts with blades: indirectly they used blades to get Shechem's townsmen to accept circumcision, and then directly they used blades to kill them.

Jacob abhorred the plan they formulated and implemented (v. 6a) and does not wish to be associated with any group that makes plans their way. His act of dissociation from their council/congregation will be matched by the blessing in Ps. 1:1, where the words recur; the parallelism of "person" and "soul" also suggests the Psalms.[60]

The "someone" and the "ox" (v. 6b) are collectives: one does not need to ask about a single individual who is their victim. There need not be anything wrong with killing someone in anger—at least, God does so, and Moses in his anger commissions people to do so at Sinai, and (oddly enough) the Levites especially respond (Exod. 32:26–29). Literal hamstringing also might not be wrong (Yahweh commissions it in Josh. 11:6). Here the parallelism signals that hamstringing oxen is a metaphor for killing people. And alongside the

56. So the Vg, Aq, Sym; see 35:18 and the comments.
57. De La Torre, *Genesis*, 344.
58. Seebass, *Genesis*, 3:167.
59. Cf. Willet, *Hexapla in Genesin & Exodum*, 389.
60. Cf. Westermann, *Genesis 37–50*, 226.

parallelism of men and oxen and of killing and hamstringing is the parallelism of anger and pleasure. This parallel finally indicates one aspect of what was wrong in the brothers' action: in Dan. 8:4; 11:3, 16, 36 "pleasure" (*rāṣôn*) suggests doing what you like, fulfilling your own self-driven plans.

Jacob then comments further (v. 7a) on their anger and suggests another aspect of what was wrong about it. It was so strong; ironically, it is the adjective from the quality of "strength" associated with Reuben in v. 3. The overflowing of their rage was tough (*qāšâ*)—the root used of Rachel's labor pains and of the way Joseph first spoke to his brothers (35:16–17; 42:7, 30). Jacob gives no concrete reason for cursing Simeon and Levi's ruthless anger as opposed to that of Moses or Saul. He just knows it was wrong and feels free to declare a curse on the brothers (like Noah in 9:25)—or rather, on their anger and their outburst.

The consequence will be their dispersion (v. 7b). In this closing abrupt and solemn line of judgment, Jacob speaks as if he were God (who is addressed in the second person in v. 18 and referred to in the third person in vv. 24–25). Perhaps speaking in this way links with a sense that cursing is God's business more than that of human beings—or that when someone curses, they are taking the risk of being godlike. Being divided (*ḥālaq*) would not be unequivocally a threat (see 14:15). Nor would being dispersed (*pûṣ*; see 10:18), but the connotations of dispersal are more often negative (see 11:4, 8, 9): what the nations feared but experienced will come to Simeon and Levi.[61] The reference to the two clans and not just the brothers themselves is more overt than was the case with Reuben. Does Jacob imply that there can be no forgiveness for Simeon and Levi?[62] There is no reference to such a possibility, any more than there had been for Reuben, though this omission does not deter Tg. Neof. from affirming that there was the possibility of forgiveness for him. But prophecies, blessings, and curses are always implicit challenges to a response, and the response plays a part in whether the words find fulfillment. Regarding Simeon and Levi, division and dispersal is as much preemptive as judgmental—it is designed to stop them from indulging further in their angry violence. In the event, Levi as the ministerial clan will have towns spread around the promised land; Simeon will be enclosed within Judah (Num. 35; Josh. 19:1–9). Jacob says nothing about the harnessing of Levi's violence (Exod. 32) or of Levi becoming the ministerial clan. Deuteronomy 33:8–11 not surprisingly sees this development as a blessing; Simeon does not appear at all in Deut. 33.

49:8–12. The critique of Reuben, Simeon, and Levi opens the way for positive comments on Judah. Although Leah had associated Judah's name

61. And to Reuben, if v. 7 also applies to Reuben (so Macchi, *Israël et ses tribus selon Genèse 49*, 66–69).

62. De La Torre, *Genesis*, 344.

with confessing or praising or acknowledging Yahweh (the verb *yādâ*), Jacob associates it with Judah's brothers confessing or praising or acknowledging Judah, as they will when David becomes king. In David, Judah will put down people such as the Philistines and the Moabites, and Judah's brothers will bow down in recognition of him. The declaration compares and contrasts with Joseph's dream, which Jacob dismissed in 37:10. Israelites will sing of the way David has killed his ten thousands (1 Sam. 18:7). God will give him his enemies' necks (2 Sam. 22:41) as they turn tail before him. They will run for their lives, but David will catch up with them and his hand will grasp them.

So Jacob imagines Judah having the energy and spirit of a lion's whelp (v. 9). Jacob can see Judah going (say) to fight the Philistines or Moabites and coming back up into the Judahite mountains with the plunder gained in the battle. He can see Judah then crouching and relaxed, like a lion or a cougar; no one can make him get up again if he doesn't feel like it.

And Judah is destined to be the longtime repository of rule in Israel (v. 10). A staff or scepter is a symbol of authority. While the feet are commonly a euphemism for the genitals and the vision could suggest that descendants of Judah will always rule, a ruler might simply hold his scepter between his feet as he sits. The second line declares that this rule will continue until it is acknowledged by all the peoples around. The word for tribute (*šay*) comes only here,[63] and the word for obedience (*yiqhâ*) only here and in Prov. 30:17. If anyone was on the way to having a descendant be king, one would have thought it was Joseph, but it will turn out to be otherwise.[64] If in some respects the viewpoint or background of Gen. 49 is the judges period, Jacob's blessing here "binds two chapters in history together; in the time of the judges, when the tribes became sedentary, the period of the kings is promised."[65] The perspective in Deut. 33:7 is different. There Moses envisions the diminishing of Judahite power that came soon after David's day. That vision implies an assumption regarding Judah that complements one about Reuben, Simeon, and Levi: as the fulfillment of threats to them depends on their response, so the fulfillment of promises to Judah depends on Judah's response.

There is more to Judah's destiny than power (vv. 11–12). If Judah rides a donkey, it suggests another sign of being in a significant position—he does not need to walk. But the point here is that he tethers his donkey to a vine. It would be risky, but he evidently possesses plentiful vineyards about which he can be a little cavalier and from which he gathers a plentiful grape harvest.[66] The harvest is so abundant that treading the grapes results in a splashing about in them that makes him resemble someone bathing in wine. There will be so much wine to drink, v. 12 goes on to comment, that he will seem

63. See the translation note.

64. See T. Alexander, "Regal Dimension."

65. Cf. Westermann, *Genesis 37–50*, 232.

66. Cf. Ibn Ezra, *Genesis*, 433.

to have wine-colored eyes. This third line pairs wine with another image for the flourishing of nature. His country will flow with milk, as passages such as Exod. 3:8 and 17 will soon be describing it: its pasturage will be so good that there are countless sheep and thus rivers of milk.

49:13. According to Josh. 19:10–16, Zebulun's land does not in fact lie either on the Mediterranean or on Kinneret. Indeed, the verses about Zebulun and the subsequent clans stand out for their lack of points of connection with other parts of the First Testament.[67] The term "aphorism," which has been applied to the sayings in Gen. 49 in general,[68] is also more applicable to those clans, though they are not universalizable in the manner of aphorisms in Proverbs. Zebulun does lie between the two seas (cf. Deut. 33:18–19), in the center of the Jezreel plain, with Issachar to its east and Asher to its west. Sidon to the northwest perhaps stands for the Phoenicians as a whole, with whom Zebulun could have come into contact in the area of the Akko Plain,[69] and perhaps Zebulunites worked in the Phoenician coastal towns.[70]

49:14–15. Issachar (who shares Deut. 33:18–19 with Zebulun) will then have the eastern part of the Jezreel plain, land between Zebulun and the Jordan. It is also between the Samarian highlands and the highland of northern Galilee and thus between the sheepfolds. Issachar's allocation is beautiful country, a great place to rest. But that expression turns out to be ironic. The problem with Issachar's area is that it will be long dominated by the Canaanites, who will hold on to the plains while the Israelites are able to occupy the mountain areas. So Issachar will need to function as a conscript workhorse for the Canaanites, the reverse of the way Josh. 16–17 and Judg. 1 picture things. The final colon brings the poetry down to earth with a bump. Being a sturdy donkey is not so good after all.

49:16–18. The comment on Dan starts off from the name, which brings to mind a verb meaning "govern." But the comment presupposes Dan's inability to come into possession of the land allocated to it, in the southwest, the area around modern Tel Aviv (Josh. 19:47). In this sense Dan failed to have a part in the government of the land. Jacob promises that Dan will. It will not lose its place as one of the clans. And it did gain its permanent home by migrating to the far northeast (Josh. 19:47b; Judg. 18).

The image of the snake or viper (v. 17) might suggest Danite involvement in "guerilla warfare" against the Canaanites with their chariots, in the area originally allocated to it,[71] or to the activity of the great Danite adventurer

67. Thus Macchi (*Israël et ses tribus selon Genèse 49*, 141–84) sees these verses as of more separate, distinctive, northern, and earlier origin than the rest of the material.

68. E.g., von Rad, *Genesis*, 416; Coats (*Genesis*, 310) uses the term in a more defined way.

69. Cf. Hamilton, *Genesis 18–50*, 664.

70. Cf. Sarna, *Genesis*, 338.

71. Cf. Sarna, *Genesis*, 341.

in Judg. 13–16 (so the Tg). The Bashan lion provides an alternative image in Deut. 33:22. The snake image is not accusatory.[72]

The subsequent confession (v. 18) corresponds to lines in the Psalms; the verb and the word order are different from 119:166, but the substance is the same.[73] In the Psalms such a confession occurs as a statement of faith concerning a deliverance not yet experienced, which fits the context here. There is nothing to suggest that it is Dan's own confession rather than Jacob's prayer for Dan, which compares with Jacob's other personal comments in vv. 6–7.

49:19. Gad's territory will be across the Jordan and bordering Ammon, so it will be vulnerable to attack in a way many clans were not. The First Testament refers specifically to trouble coming to Gad (2 Kings 10:33; Jer. 49:1), but Gad shared with Reuben and Manasseh the broader area referred to as Gilead, and references to trouble in Gilead (e.g., Judg. 10–12; 1 Sam. 11; 1 Kings 22; Amos 1:3, 13) may well be references to trouble in Gad. Other clans thus will share Gad's vulnerability. There is some irony in Jacob speaking of a clan attacking someone else's heel (cf. Gen. 25:26; 27:36). Presumably his comment implies that Gad too is snakelike (cf. 3:15), though not in a bad way; Gad, like Dan, is compared to a lion in Deut. 33:20–21.

49:20. Asher will occupy fertile land and the seacoast from Mount Carmel north to the border of the promised land. It will thus produce food fit for a king. The audience might recall that Asher's name would make one think of blessing (cf. 30:13). "Rich" is etymologically "oily," which might imply a reference to the richness of Asher's olive production (cf. Deut. 33:24).

49:21. Naphtali's land stretches north-south next to Asher's but is thus inland. It extends to include the western shore of Lake Kinneret and the Jordan Valley running north to the border of the land (though the northernmost part was appropriated by Dan when it moved from the southwest). Whereas Deut. 33:23 speaks of its richness in more literal terms that compare with the ones Jacob uses of Asher, Jacob confines himself to a single animal image for Naphtali, but the image also rejoices in Naphtali's liveliness and fruitfulness.

49:22–26. Not surprisingly, Joseph gets extensive space, about the same as Judah. Though Judah is the ancestor of the clan that produces David, Joseph is the son who in the person of his own sons inherits the position of firstborn (1 Chron. 5:1–3).[74] The portrait of Joseph combines fruitfulness and activism, and the same combination appears in Deut. 33:13–17, with the description of fruitfulness being at points verbally identical; opinions vary on whether one of the passages is dependent on the other or whether both depend on some traditional formulation.

72. Cf. von Rad, *Genesis*, 422.

73. Cf. Westermann, *Genesis 37–50*, 235.

74. Cf. the comment on 48:15.

Though Joseph must surely come next (v. 22a) because only he and Benjamin remain for mention, Jacob does not immediately name him, as he names the son at the beginning of each other saying. Knowing the treatment of Joseph's sons in Gen. 48 and the combined mention of Simeon and Levi in vv. 5–7, we might expect Jacob to be concerned with Joseph's two sons in the paragraph about Joseph. While eventually Jacob does name Joseph, lo and behold, the first word in this verse is "son." Then the second is *pōrāt*, a word that comes only here but could suggest a fruitful tree (cf. the Tg, LXX, Vg), and the Joseph clans will indeed flourish spectacularly within Israel. But the word also makes one think of the name of Ephraim, the son blessed as if he were Joseph's firstborn, whose name was linked with the verb lying behind *pōrāt* when he was born (see 41:52). Directly or overtly, Jacob speaks only of Joseph, but Ephraim is hiding between the formulation of his words.[75]

Its subject is Joseph the *pōrāt* and by implication his or its daughters—though they do not have a proper syntactical place in the verse. These cola also require the audience to think again about the meaning of *pōrāt*,[76] which also resembles the word for a wild donkey (*pereʾ*; cf. 16:12), of which *pōrāt* could be the feminine;[77] *ʾEprātî* can mean Ephraimite, so the feminine-looking word could facilitate the paronomasia. That understanding leads well into the reference to striding: the verb is feminine and suggests something animate. So the Joseph clan is a female donkey (evidently not an insult), an understanding that fits the animal imagery used to characterize other brothers in vv. 9, 14, 17, 21, and 27. Joseph's daughters are equivalent to Judah's daughters (e.g., Pss. 48:11 [48:12]; 97:8), the villages in Joseph's territory. The line then suggests that Joseph (esp. in the person of Ephraim) has the energy and agility that ranges free by springs and by the walled terraces that stretch along mountain slopes.

Jacob goes on to speak of Joseph himself rather than the clan (vv. 23–24a). Joseph is now a warrior whose arms and hands manipulate his taut bow, which fits the image of a wild donkey back in v. 22 better than the image of a tree. If he is a warrior under attack, who are the attackers? The Tg sees Joseph as defeating the Egyptian diviners, which he did, but the only attack on Joseph that Genesis has mentioned is the one in Gen. 37, when the brothers were furious with him because of his dreams. Even in taking aim at him verbally, they were like archers shooting arrows at him.[78]

But he was someone who could stand firm under attack (v. 24b) because of the supernatural support he received. Jacob offers another version of the interwoven nature of the human will and the divine will. Not only was God involved in Joseph's destiny in order to achieve something for the entire family, so that his will and the brothers' will worked together in a paradoxical

75. Cf. Luther, *Genesis 45–50*, 295.
76. Cf. Speiser, *Genesis*, 368, though he develops the point in a different direction.
77. Cf. *DCH*.
78. Cf. Hamilton, *Genesis 18–50*, 680.

fashion, God's involvement also means that his energy and Joseph's energy mysteriously worked together. Jacob describes God in a sequence of parallel cola incorporating a series of images that speak of Jacob's God as also Joseph's God. He is Jacob's strongman (*ʾābîr*), one with the strength of a bull or a warrior (*ʾabbîr*), someone who fights for you and cannot be defeated. He is (Jacob's) shepherd, who guides and protects the sheep as Jacob has his sheep. He is Israel's stone, a unique title contrasting with the idea of God as Israel's crag or rock (*ṣûr*). The parallelism of the cola suggests that "Israel" refers to Jacob himself, and the significance of stones for Jacob might suggest that God is a protection and a lasting witness (28:10–18; 31:45–46; 35:14).

Whereas the context in Genesis suggests reading the verbs in vv. 23–24a in light of the way Joseph's brothers once treated him, so that v. 24b speaks of God's defense of him in light of their hostility, these new verbal clauses speak of the future. The way God has protected him is the way God will protect him. The first colon couples "God" (*ʾēl*) and "your Father" as the previous one coupled "Shepherd" and "Stone." God is "your Father," as Moses will say to Israel (Deut. 32:6), the one to whom Israel can say "my Father" (Jer. 3:4, 19), the one to whom David can say "my Father" (Ps. 89:26 [89:27]. For God to be his Father has implications similar to God's being the Shepherd: he is the faithful one who is committed to and protective of him. His being helper restates the point again; helping (*ʿāzar*) characteristically suggests not a mere bit of assistance in a task that someone couldn't quite do alone but a decisive act of deliverance in a predicament that someone could never escape. The verb follows on the description of God as "stone of Israel," which suggests a comparison with Samuel's talk of a "help stone" (1 Sam. 7:12). To follow "God" (*ʾēl*) one might have expected *Shadday*; and in the parallelism of the cola, *Shadday* duly appears (the two halves of the title are divided between two cola in other passages such as Job 8:3, 5). Jacob's reference to God as Shadday reopens questions about the ambiguous imagery in v. 22, supporting reference both to activity and to fertility there. The verb *šādad* can suggest taking violent action against someone; it is the link made between this root and the name Shadday in Isa. 13:6. But Jacob takes the name's significance in a different direction in speaking of Shadday who blesses you; six forms of the words "bless/blessing" come in six successive cola. The stress on blessing takes one back to the possibility in v. 22 of Joseph being a fruitful tree by a spring or by a terrace, which would fit the idea of blessings from above—the blessing that comes from the gift of rain. "Blessing" and "help" complement each other.

Further, "breasts" is *šādayim*; in this context the name Shadday could make the listeners think of such happy human fruitfulness on the part of Joseph's clan(s). In upbeat terms such as we are not used to hearing from his lips, Jacob acknowledges that the blessings he has received have been extraordinary. These twelve sons are a spectacular embodiment of his blessing. They surely exceed the blessing of his parents with their two children and his grandparents with their one or two. The application to a male of the verb "conceive" recurs in Num. 11:12; Ps. 7:14 [7:15]; Isa. 59:4. The parallel colon again returns to the theme of fruitfulness in the world of nature as it refers to "the desirable things on the agelong hills."[79]

The theme continues in Jacob's final blessing on Joseph (v. 26b); the positive acknowledgment of God's blessing serves this concern. Jacob wants the same blessing for his favorite son. In the 3-3 line's parallelism, the head is where one who is set apart, a *nāzîr*, has his distinction (see Num. 6).[80] The implications of being "set apart" (*nāzîr*) vary: the word can apply to someone who is especially dedicated, but here the context suggests that Jacob calls down special treatment for Joseph because he is, after all, his own favorite son, and because God is indeed going to give his clan(s) a position of leadership.

49:27. There is one more son to be blessed. But eating and dividing seem logically back-to-front (one would divide and then eat), but this oddity points to a move from the metaphorical to the literal: Benjamin will be literally a fighting force that takes plunder. Nothing in what we know of Benjamin as an individual explains the terms that Jacob uses (Deut. 33:12 fits it better), but the story of the Benjamin clan fits his description (see Judg. 20–21), as do the exploits of the great Benjaminites Saul and Jonathan (1 Sam. 10–14).

Implications

Testament, Poetry, Theology

Genesis 49 invites listeners to see the outworking of events in the life of the ancestors and of the clans as part of a big picture and as having a meaning within that context. They are not random or chance. They are not "the product of causes which had no prevision of the end they were achieving," so that a member of each clan would infer that "his origin, his growth, his hopes and fears, his loves and his beliefs, are but the outcome of accidental collocations of atoms."[81]

Here "Father Jacob" lays out the fruit of his insight to his sons, as "Father Solomon" will later lay out his insight to his sons in Prov. 1–9. Both teachers speak in poetry, which makes for some denseness and memorability and allows the average line to look at its subject from two angles and sustain interest. But Solomon's poetry in Proverbs works by being univocal. There may be double meanings (the strange woman may be an allegorical figure), but the surface meaning is clear and important. Jacob's poetry is denser and thrives on being equivocal.

79. See the footnote for the LXX's extension of the parallelism.
80. Hamilton, *Genesis 18–50*, 685–86.
81. B. Russell, "Free Man's Worship," 47.

The actual authors of Gen. 49 and of Prov. 1–9 hide discreetly away behind Jacob and Solomon; they draw attention away from themselves and enhance the impact of their teaching by inviting their audiences to collude with them in imagining it on the lips of these key figures. In neither case do we know the author's identity. But there is no great scholarly heart-searching about the background of Prov. 1–9, whereas the background of Gen. 49 is a mystery, and scholarly study of it is in disarray. More than one commentator ruefully observes that there is nothing like a scholarly consensus on the interpretation of aspects of Jacob's words (with no sense of irony over the fact that one generation's scholarly consensus is the next generation's out-of-date misconception).

While "Jacob" does introduce himself as a teacher instructing his sons (v. 2), he precedes that introduction by speaking of himself as more like a prophet who will declare what is to happen in days to come (v. 1), and prophets speak in dense and puzzling ways. Jacob is as much like Hosea as like Solomon. Hosea makes for an apposite comparison because he is a northerner, and there are hints of northern forms of speech in Gen. 49[82] (thus unusual forms of speech and unusual expressions are no indication of an early date). Hosea is also more puzzling than, say, Amos; he likes paronomasia as Jacob does, and he likes animal imagery as Jacob does. Some of the impasse over Jacob's poetry (as over aspects of Hosea) derives from the assumption that "Jacob" surely spoke univocally. There are advantages to being easy to understand, but it is also possible to make things too easy for people, with the result that they understand it at one level but at another level fail to catch the meaning, and sometimes needing to work hard to understand ultimately helps one understand. When Jacob is difficult to understand, the answer may be to work with the puzzles and the ambiguities rather than to seek to eliminate them.

In terms of substance, a key characteristic of poetry that features in the testament is its use of imagery, in metaphor and simile. "In elevation, power, and richness of imagery, [Jacob's] words surpass other similar poetic utterances" such as those in Gen. 27,[83] or (we might add) Deut. 33. Such imagery both adds to the content, power, and effectiveness of the lines and occasionally adds to the difficulty of understanding. "Normal words are not involved here, but those that are miraculous, effective, and productive."[84] They are designed to communicate even when they are allusive and elliptical. They are a challenge to interpretation, like Jesus's parables and some First Testament prophecies.

If we seek to express the implications of Jacob's words in prosaic terms, what results? The question underlying the testament is apparent: how should Israel think of the situation and experience of the twelve clans? Part of the

82. See Rendsburg, "Israelian Hebrew Features."

83. Dillmann, *Genesis*, 2:445.

84. Gunkel, *Genesis*, 450.

perspective it suggests is that the clans' destiny sometimes relates to the action of their ancestors, sometimes to aspects of their political situation, sometimes to factors in their geographical position: "All the sayings—with or without blessing—show a deft attention to the role that each environmental micro-system has played in shaping tribal identity."[85] Always their experience forms part of the outworking of Jacob's words. Further, Jacob's words imply the assumption that there can be something revelatory about words themselves (e.g., v. 19), as well as something revelatory about animals, who feature so prominently in the sayings.

Traditional interpretation assumes that the declarations report Jacob's actual words near the end of his life. Modern interpretation assumes that they are a collection of sayings resulting from reflection on events from Israel's history. God can inspire both forms of declaration—Daniel's visions incorporate both. Genesis as a whole does not simply transcribe events but tells stories that have varying relationships to actual events. One might compare Gen. 49 with Gen. 1, which gives us no information on the literal, concrete process whereby God brought the world into being but does give us information on what God was doing in bringing the world into being. Or one might compare Gen. 49 with Dan. 11, which expresses itself as talk about the future but is nearly all talk about the past; expressing an account of the past as prophecy makes clear that the sequence of events was under God's control. Much of Gen. 49 reflects the actual experience of the twelve clans, which is projected back into Jacob's awareness to express how it was not chance but part of a coherent, broader story going back to the ancestor who gave Israel its name. Whereas 25:23 tells the audience that Rebekah's revelation came from Yahweh, Gen. 37 does not make the same comment about Joseph's dreams, and neither does Gen. 49 about Jacob's revelations; the same mixed pattern appears in Daniel. In Genesis, it was no ordinary human being who passed on what seem to be revelations from God, but Israel's original father figure. Further, while some of Jacob's words are statements, some are prayers, and prophecy regularly presupposes the assumption that what actually happens will depend on an interaction between God's declarations of intent and people's response to them.

What Jacob had to say to each clan was significant for all the clans. And the inclusion of his testament in the Scriptures implies that it continues to be significant for the people of God.

1. Reuben needed to learn that one act whereby he grossly flouted society's proper values in the realm of family and sex could have disastrous results for his clan. The same applied to Simeon and Levi in the realm of violence. (Outside the framework of this testament, Levi found that God could use its violence and make Levi his servant.)

85. Fontaine, "Forgotten Voices of Earth," 203.

2. The clans as a whole would properly acknowledge Judah for the achievements that stemmed from its violence, and for its marvelous flourishing, and so would the peoples who submitted to him. (As they did, outside the framework of this testament, in David's day, though Judah's hegemony and flourishing did not last, so that for a later audience Jacob's words would raise the question whether that hegemony and flourishing would return—as prophets said they would.)
3. Zebulun, Issachar, Dan, Asher, Naphtali, and Benjamin would have futures that involved an interaction between their geographical position with its blessings, their political position with its threats, and their personal qualities with their potentials.
4. Joseph has already had to deal with hostility but has survived and triumphed through his own firmness and agility and the support and blessing of God, which will also issue in blessing in the future that parallels Judah's. (This they did outside the framework of this testament in the flourishing of the northern kingdom, though this blessing too did not last, but prophets again said they would return.)

50

How Jacob Dies, and the Aftermath

(49:28–50:26)

Overview

Jacob speaks of his imminent death and of how they should ensure that he is buried in Canaan, and his family does as he says. Joseph's brothers are then afraid that his passing will leave Joseph free to avenge their treatment of him, and he explains why it is not an issue for him. Joseph, too, then speaks of his imminent death and of how they should ensure that he eventually gets buried in Canaan, and his family does as he says.

Translation

49:28 All these are the twelve clans of Yiśra'el,[1] and this is what their fa-
ther spoke to them. So he blessed them, each of whom he blessed in
accordance with his blessing. **29**Then he ordered them and said to them,
"I am joining my people. Bury me with my forebears in the cave that's
in the field of Epron the Ḥetite, **30**the cave that's in the field at Double
which is east of Mamre, in the country of Kenaʿan, the field that Abra-
ham acquired from Epron the Ḥetite as a burial holding. **31**There they bur-
ied Abraham and Sarah his wife, there they buried Yiṣḥaq and Ribqah his
wife, there I buried Le'ah— **32**an acquisition (the field and the cave that's
in it) from the Ḥetites." **33**Yaʿaqob finished giving orders to his sons and

1. The LXX has "sons of Jacob," which fits what follows; see the comment.

drew his feet into the bed, breathed out, and joined his kin. **50:1**Yosep fell on his father's face[2] and cried over him and kissed him.

2Yosep ordered the physicians who were his servants to embalm his father. So the physicians embalmed Yiśraʾel **3**and completed forty days for him, because that is how they would complete the days for embalmings.[3] Miṣrayim cried for him seventy days. **4**The days of crying for him passed, and Yosep spoke to Parʿoh's household: "If I find favor in your eyes, please speak in Parʿoh's ears and say, **5**'My father himself got me to swear, "Here, given that I am going to die: in the tomb that I dug[4] for myself in the country of Kenaʿan, there you're to bury me." So I will please now go up and bury my father, and come back.'" **6**Parʿoh said, "Go up and bury your father as he made you swear."

7So Yosep went up to bury his father. All Parʿoh's servants went up with him, the senior people in his household, all the senior people in the country of Miṣrayim,[5] **8**Yosep's entire household, his brothers, and his father's household. Only the little ones, and their flock and their herd, did they abandon in the Gošen region. **9**Both chariotry and cavalry went up with him. It was a very substantial camp. **10**They came to the Thorn Threshing Floor, which is across the Jordan, and held a very big and solemn lamentation there. He made seven days of mourning for his father. **11**The Kenaʿanite inhabitants of the country saw the mourning at the Thorn Threshing Floor and said, "This is a serious mourning on the part of Miṣrayim." Hence it was called Miṣrayim's Mourning Meadow,[6] which is across the Jordan.

12So his sons did for him as he had ordered them. **13**His sons carried him to the country of Kenaʿan and buried him in the cave in the field at Double, the field that Abraham acquired as a burial holding from Epron the Ḥetite, east of Mamre. **14**Then Yosep went back to Miṣrayim, he and his brothers and all the people who had gone up with him to bury his father, after he had buried his father.

15Yosep's brothers saw[7] that their father was dead and said, "If Yosep feels hostile to us and turns right back[8] on us all the bad dealing

2. LXX^{A} has "neck" (cf. 33:4; 45:14; 46:29), as one does when someone is alive (cf. Brayford, *Genesis*, 448).

3. The plural suggests the complex nature of the process.

4. Rashi (*Brʾšyt*, 566) notes the possibility of taking this verb as *kārâ* II (purchase), while Tg. Onq. has "prepared."

5. These three phrases might denote one or two or three groups.

6. *ʾĀbēl miṣrayim.* In place names (e.g., Num. 33:49; Judg. 7:22; 11:33), *ʾābēl* means meadow (BDB) or brook (*HALOT*), though in other contexts it can be an adjective meaning "mourning" (37:35); the noun for mourning is *ʾēbel*. So this comment on the name parallels comments on names in, e.g., 11:9; 16:14; 19:22, which suggests paronomasia rather than etymology and notes a new significance that a name gains rather than recording the name's origin.

7. In the sense of "learned" or "realized." The Vg's "were afraid" implies *wayyārəʾû* for the MT's *wayyirʾû*.

8. The verb is preceded by the infinitive of the same root, adding emphasis; the usage recurs in vv. 24 and 25.

that we did to him. . . ."[9] **16**So they gave orders[10] to Yosep: "Your father gave orders before his death: **17**'Say this to Yosep: Oh, please carry your brothers' offense and their wrongdoing, in that they acted badly with you.' So now please carry the offense of the servants of your father's God." Yosep cried when they spoke to him.

18His brothers indeed came and fell before him and said, "Here are we as servants to you," **19**but Yosep said to them, "Don't be afraid, because am I in the place of God? **20**Whereas you yourselves intended something bad for me, God intended it for good, in order to act today so as to keep alive a numerous people. **21**So now, don't be afraid. I myself will provide for you and your little ones." Thus he consoled them and encouraged[11] them.

22So Yosep lived in Miṣrayim, he and his father's household. Yosep lived a hundred and ten years **23**and saw the third generation[12] of Eprayim; the children of Makir, son of Menaššeh, were also born on Yosep's knees. **24**Then Yosep said to his brothers, "I'm going to die, but God—he will definitely attend to you and take you up from this country to the country that he swore to Abraham, to Yiṣḥaq, and to Yaʿaqob." **25**Yosep got the sons of Yiśraʾel to swear, "God will definitely attend to you, and you're to take up my bones from here." **26**Yosep died as a man of a hundred and ten years. They embalmed him and he was put[13] in a chest in Miṣrayim.

Interpretation

The account of Jacob's testament leads straight into the account of his death and of Joseph's death. But it is convenient to make a break somewhere in 49:1–50:26, and the resumptive conclusion/introduction at 49:28 provides a suitable place to do so; the medieval chapter division between Gen. 49 and 50 divides the testament and the dying from its aftermath. The MT's closing unit is 49:27–50:26; the break before rather than after the Benjamin blessing looks whimsical, but it does correspond to the MT's break at 49:12—that is, these two breaks draw attention to the Judah and Joseph blessings. In principle it does seem appropriate to link the last verses of Gen. 49 with what follows; it marks how Genesis's double ending relates the double deaths and embalmings of Jacob and Joseph, both being preceded by an appeal for their remains to return to Canaan.[14] I thus

9. A conditional sentence with "suppressed apodosis" (Skinner, *Genesis*, 539).

10. The verb is odd, but see the comment; the LXX has "they approached," which would seem a more plausible verb, but it hardly indicates that the LXX had a different text.

11. See the second translation note to 34:3.

12. Literally, "the children of thirds"—which might mean the fourth generation (cf. Tal, *Genesis*, 205*).

13. Literally, "he [someone] put."

14. Cf. Westermann, *Genesis 37–50*, 197.

treat 49:28–50:26 as one unit, closing Genesis as a whole. It is surprising that Genesis closes with the account of Joseph's passing, almost as if Gen. 37–50 turns out to be the Joseph story after all.[15] But Joseph has been central in the story of "Jacob's lines of descent" since Gen. 37. Further, the closing reference to Joseph is an aspect of the way Gen. 50 and Exod. 1 interrelate (see esp. Exod. 1:8), and the account of Joseph's death does make explicit that it looks forward to what follows.

49:28–50:1. The opening verse is both a conclusion and an introduction. It summarizes where we have been and in itself is simply a conclusion to what precedes. But v. 29 will begin simply "and he," so that it needs v. 28 as an introduction. The verse does stand in slight tension with vv. 1–27. First, it speaks explicitly of the "twelve clans" rather than the "twelve sons," in the first mention of the "twelve clans" in the Scriptures. Either term would have been appropriate here: 49:1–27 related both to the individuals and to the clans to which they gave their names, with the sons sometimes in more focus and the clans sometimes in more focus. Second, the conclusion/introduction three times speaks of blessing, whereas the contents of vv. 3–27 have been more equivocal than this word implies. The testament began with something more like curses—indeed, that word came in v. 7. Perhaps the implication is that each clan to whom a blessing was appropriate received the appropriate blessing.

Jacob's instructions about his burial follow (vv. 29–32); the common verb "order" (*ṣāwâ* piel) can be used in particular to denote someone's dying "will" (e.g., Deut. 3:28; 2 Kings 20:1).[16] Whereas Genesis has elsewhere spoken of people joining their kin (the plural of the word *ʿam*; 25:8, 17; 35:29; the expression will recur here in v. 33),[17] Jacob himself speaks of joining "my people" (*ʿam* singular—the distinction is purely one of pointing, since consonantally either first-person expression would be *ʿmy*). "My people" can suggest the broader "people of Israel" who are coming more into focus as the Genesis scroll nears its end, though Jacob's succeeding words draw more attention to his own family. He makes a general point about burial, that it is natural to want to be buried with them. As the gospel folk song puts it, "I'm going there to see my father, I'm going there no more to roam, I'm just a going over Jordan, I'm just a going over home."[18] Yet the way he expresses that desire links with the broader point, in that Jacob wants to be buried in the promised land. In the short term, he won't be joining his family or his people in body, only in spirit, and in speaking of joining them, he uses a conventional expression for death.[19] But the conventional expression reminds the audience of something

15. Cf. Coats, *Genesis*, 301.
16. Cf. Sarna, *Genesis*, 346.
17. See the comment on 25:8.
18. From "The Wayfaring Stranger" (early nineteenth century).
19. Cf. von Rad, *Genesis*, 425.

important. "No matter how long his children remain in Egypt, Jacob knows that Canaan is his home."[20]

The continuing lack of the verb "die" (49:33) and the repetition of the idea of joining one's kin or people (in 25:8, 17 and 35:29 the verb "died" does come)[21] again puts the emphasis on the positive side to "breathing out." Here the place of "died" is taken by the unique expression "drew his feet into the bed." Jacob is getting ready to pass away; "drew" (*ʾāsap* qal) is a form of the verb for "join" (*ʾāsap* niphal), which follows. He is settling down to die.[22] Genesis speaks of it "as though accepting the event with enjoyment."[23] Yet "there is something very sober about the dying of the father of Israel. With respect to his own lot the dying man is neither especially sorrowful nor especially hopeful. There is no stirring gesture in the face of death. . . . But precisely in this, these narratives about the deaths of the patriarchs show obedience to the reality of death."[24]

Presumably the other brothers were grieved too (50:1), but the story is told from Joseph's angle because of his central place in Genesis's story at this stage.

50:2–6. Although it may seem odd to associate physicians (lit., "healers") with embalming, embalming and mummification involves considerable surgery, including the removal of the brains and internal organs.

The account of Jacob's embalming (v. 3)—the first stage of mummification—and of the mourning for him expresses how important a person Jacob was. It was especially kings who were mummified, and forty days is a long time to spend doing the embalming.[25] Diodorus Siculus 1.72 and 1.91 talks in terms of thirty days for embalming and of seventy-two days' mourning for a king in Egypt, while Herodotus (*Histories* 1.86–88) speaks of a seventy-day period following the embalming.[26] Israel will mourn Aaron and Moses for thirty days (Num. 20:29; Deut. 34:8), so perhaps Jacob's seventy days of mourning covers forty days of embalming followed by a thirty-day mourning. Though in Egypt mummification was an act of preparation for resurrection life, Israelites did not expect bodily resurrection but only a continuing semi-life in Sheol (the irony is that the Egyptians were right for the wrong reasons and the Israelites were wrong for the right reasons: there would be resurrection but only on the basis of Jesus's resurrection). To put it another way, the basis of Israel's hope was God's promise of ongoing life in Canaan, and for Jacob and Joseph, mummification could make that possible. But both for Egyptians and for Israelites, mummification was an option only for really important people.

20. Arnold, *Genesis*, 372.
21. Cf. Hamilton, *Genesis 18–50*, 689.
22. Cf. Sarna, *Genesis*, 347.
23. Cf. Chrysostom, *Homilies on Genesis 46–67*, 273.
24. Von Rad, *Genesis*, 425.
25. Cf. Fretheim, "Genesis," 669.
26. See further Redford, *Study*, 240–41.

Joseph's sending word to Pharaoh (vv. 4–5) might issue from his own involvement in the mourning, which would make him unpresentable and/or defiling, or it might just mean he is being deferential. His request to go up to Canaan to bury Jacob carries subtle undertones as it anticipates Moses's plea for the Israelites to take a trip out of Egypt, along with the awareness that Joseph might therefore be planning not to come back. Joseph has Jacob speaking loosely about his burial place, which actually his grandfather metaphorically dug (Nicolas of Lyra suggests that Jacob had dug his own place in the cave);[27] once again, Genesis has one of its characters speaking in a way that differs from the previous account. Here, Joseph speaks in terms that would make sense to an Egyptian.[28] While the account of Jacob's passing has given another expression of Joseph's deep embedding in Egypt, it also expresses how deep is the two-way nature of his position. In a sense Jacob dies an Egyptian, but his dying an Egyptian is framed by an insistence and a report such as make clear that he does nothing of the sort.[29] The story is an exercise in "identity politics," about the way the members of a marginalized community assert ways of understanding themselves with their distinctive reality of self and community, which has been an issue through the Joseph story.[30]

The undertones in Joseph's request to "go up" become louder (v. 6) as Pharaoh says, "Go up!" The verb recurs in vv. 7, 9, 14, 24, 25, and the audience recalls God's promise to Jacob in 46:4, which made an emphatic double use of that verb.

50:7–14. The account of the funeral journey with military escort continues to underline the two-way embedding. Leaving the little ones and the herds behind would provide evidence that they intend to return (cf. Exod. 10:7–11). The next Egyptian camp will be a hostile one, pursuing Jacob's people (Exod. 14:19–24).

The funeral party's journey (vv. 10–11) also continues to anticipate the future. The obvious route to Mamre would take it up the Mediterranean coast, so that the Thorn Threshing Floor and Miṣrayim's Mourning Meadow would be in that area, in the region where the Philistines later had their towns. But the narrative twice describes these places as "across the Jordan," or perhaps "at the side of the Jordan."[31] Though people on the east of the Jordan can speak of the west side as "across the Jordan" (e.g., Num. 32:19; Deut. 3:20; Josh. 5:1—the "West Bank" was once part of "Transjordan"), it is hard to picture these verses as taking that perspective, especially to refer to places on

27. Nicolas of Lyra, *Postilla super totam Bibliam*, on the passage; cf. Schroeder, *Genesis*, 276.

28. Cf. Westermann, *Genesis 37–50*, 200.

29. Cf. Brueggemann, *Genesis*, 368.

30. Cf. Berman, "Identity Politics."

31. Cf. Dillmann, *Genesis*, 2:487. Taking the expression to mean "at the side of the Jordan" (Gemser, "*Beʿēber hajjardēn*") hardly reduces the puzzle of why the cortege was in the vicinity of the Jordan. Demsky ("Route") suggests that Jordan is a place near the Mediterranean.

the Mediterranean. More likely the funeral party is pictured as taking the route the later Israelites would take and halting by the Jordan before entering the promised land from the east, on the way up to Mamre. From there Canaanites could be pictured as aware of what was going on from their side of the Jordan. Either way, the entire party holds its further lamentation there. Joseph does a son's proper seven days of mourning (cf. 1 Sam. 31:13; Job 2:13) at the Thorn Threshing Floor; it will be so called because it was enclosed by a thorn hedge and/or because the thorn hedge provided the means of winnowing.

The brothers (vv. 12–14)—in other words, the family, not the Egyptians—then transport Jacob into the promised land, onto the mountain ridge of Canaan proper, to Mamre, where they inter him.

50:15–21. We might have thought that at 47:26 or 27 we had reached the end of the story of Joseph and his brothers and thus of Joseph himself, except for a note about his death that might eventually come. And we might not have noticed that Gen. 45 told us nothing about the brothers' response to Joseph's revelation of himself except that they talked with him.[32] Perhaps one cannot blame them, given the ambiguity of Joseph's actions.[33] But "what an almost incurable wound sin and an evil conscience are." How easily the brothers sinned, "but with what difficulty they are healed."[34]

The narrator and the brothers (vv. 16–17a) pick up from 49:29 the verb "order," where it has the sense of the charge that someone may give while dying; the odd repetition of the verb in v. 16 is thus ironic. Genesis has not made any previous reference to Jacob giving a charge of this kind (in *Ant.* 2.8.1 Josephus writes it back into Jacob's earlier words). When they appeal to what they say Jacob said, then, are they lying in their fearful attempt to forestall any subsequent revenge from Joseph? Do "they still rely on deception as a way of life"?[35] More likely their words comprise yet another instance of Genesis amplifying or putting things differently when recapitulating earlier words or events and thus giving the audience something to think about and reason to keep reviewing the story they already know. The brothers do go on to acknowledge (indirectly!) their bad dealing, their offense, and their wrongdoing. And they have Jacob urging Joseph to be like God in carrying their wrongdoing, which is one of God's characteristic practices (e.g., Exod. 32:32; 34:7; Pss. 25:18; 32:5). The basis of their appeal is their position as the servants of the God who is their God and Joseph's God.

Is Joseph then distressed (v. 17b) because their words bring the past back to him, or because he's sorry that they still think he might act in the way they describe, or because they speak of "your father" and of themselves as his servants, or because he's moved that at last they now acknowledge

32. Cf. Pirson, *Lord of the Dreams*, 112.
33. Brett, *Genesis*, 135.
34. Luther, *Genesis 45–50*, 323, 325.
35. Coats, *Genesis*, 312.

their wrongdoing? His tears repeat a motif from 42:24; 43:30; 45:14, 15; 46:29; 50:1 and build up further the impression that Joseph has no interest in taking revenge on his brothers. While God expects human authorities to take action against wrongdoing, Joseph knows that it is the job of the individual (even the individual who is a person in authority) to turn the other cheek. Ancient Near Eastern wisdom urged people not to pay other people back for their wrongdoing,[36] and the Torah, the Prophets, and the Writings agree (e.g., Lev. 19:18; Isa. 53:1–9; Prov. 24:29).[37] Joseph accepts and lives by that principle.

The further reference to the brothers coming to Joseph (v. 18) might mean that they originally sent the charge in vv. 16–17 via a third party. Jacob did something similar in Gen. 32, but there the point was explicit. Here Genesis is more likely again giving a resumptive further report of the preceding event. Separating the giving of the charge from the going to bow down draws attention to the bowing down as a further fulfillment of Joseph's dream. And the commitment to being Joseph's servants underscores the fulfillment.

How is Joseph to respond (v. 19)? If he simply says, "Of course I will carry it," would that help? In effect, his words presuppose an ellipsis. It is more important to make certain other things explicit. First, the brothers are not to be afraid. It is a regular First Testament way of urging people to believe that they have nothing to worry about (if the word *šālôm* were used to mean inner peace, it could feature in an equivalent exhortation). Here Joseph will indicate the significance of the exhortation when he repeats it in v. 21. But before doing so, he protests that they are treating him as if he were God. He asks the accusatory rhetorical question that his father had once asked of his mother (30:2). Here as there, the background to the question lies in what has just preceded. They said they were the servants of their father's God. They then said they would be Joseph's servants. He himself has pointed out that he is lord and ruler over all Egypt (45:8). And for a long time they have been addressing him as "lord" and speaking of themselves as his "servants" (e.g., 42:10; 44:16–24). They are willing to continue in that subservient relationship. But they said it because they were scared. If they are God's servants (especially the servants of the one who is the God of their father and his father) and if God is thus their master, how can they talk in terms of Joseph as their master? He is not God! They are taking the implications of the dream too far. The Torah will later outlaw the idea of treating your brother as your servant, precisely because your brothers are Yahweh's servants (Lev. 25:39–42). Joseph makes that assumption. It's easy for persons in power to think that they are God. They can do what they like, and everyone should treat them as God.

36. See, e.g., the Akkadian "Counsels of Wisdom," *ANET* 426–27.
37. Cf. von Rad, *Genesis*, 432.

Joseph would be under unequaled temptation to think that way, but he does not. It's said that the difference between God and us is that he doesn't think he is us. Joseph's rhetorical question implies a key principle in his theology and spirituality.

Paradoxically, one might say (v. 20), they have actually been unconsciously acting as God's servants in the way they have treated Joseph. Joseph reformulates the point he made to them in 45:5–8 in a way that makes the antithesis of "good" and "bad" almost close Genesis as it almost began it.[38] Once more Joseph's point is not that "you intended what was bad, but God turned it to what was good" (so the Vg), though that declaration may sometimes be applicable. If anything, God's intention preceded theirs. Nor is his contrast the one that appears in Psalms between human beings intending to do wrong to people and God intending to deliver them (Pss. 40:5, 17; 14:1, 4),[39] though that contrast does also describe how God acts with Joseph. His point is that they have been the unwitting executors of an intention that God had, as he said in 45:5–8. And that intention was to bring good fortune to them. How can Joseph try to frustrate God's plan?[40] How can he refuse the will of God (the Vg's rendering of v. 19b)? As he earlier spoke of a big escape group, so he speaks here of a numerous people. And here as there, the brothers can think in terms of keeping alive the relatively big family that they are, but the audience will also think of making alive the really numerous people that they are soon (narratively) to become (see Exod. 1:1–7)—the verb *ḥāyâ* (piel) can mean keep alive or make alive.

Thus the renewed exhortation not to be afraid (v. 21), like most occurrences in Genesis (15:1; 21:17; 26:24; 35:17; 46:3), suggests that they need not worry about the future. Joseph is going to take care of it. He has been "providing for" them and their little ones while Jacob was alive (45:11; 47:12), and he will continue to do so. Is he in the place of God? Well, in a sense, yes, given that God is the great provider (Neh. 9:21; Ps. 55:22 [55:23]). But with that commitment Joseph can be their consoler and encourager, the first two verbal expressions in Isa. 40:1–2, where they too are God's initiatives. "Since God has deposited your life with me, I should be engaged in war against him, if I were not to be the faithful dispenser of the grace which he had committed to my hands."[41]

50:22–26. It was with Joseph that the account of Jacob's lines of descent started, and it is with Joseph that it ends.

He is apparently head of Jacob's household (v. 22). It fits his promise to provide for the family, though perhaps his older brothers have now passed. While a number of Egyptian texts indicate that 110 years is "the ideal lifetime

38. Cf. Arnold, *Genesis*, 388.
39. Cf. Brueggemann, *Genesis*, 373–74.
40. Cf. Gunkel, *Genesis*, 464.
41. Calvin, *Genesis*, 2:487.

of the Egyptians,"[42] the number also follows on the sequence expressed in the ages of Abraham, Isaac, and Jacob, since 110 is $5^2 + 6^2 + 7^2$.[43]

To say that his grandchildren are born on his knees (v. 23) is to say that he can treat them as his own, as his mother treated Bilhah's children (cf. 30:3). Perhaps the idea is that they take the place of Ephraim and Manasseh, whom Jacob has adopted.

The account of Jacob's line of descent ends with Joseph's death (v. 24), as it started with Joseph as a youngster. In a brief alternative version of the kind of account that Genesis has given of Jacob, Genesis first tells us that Joseph knows he is about to die. But there the similarity ends. Jacob goes on to express his longing to be buried back in Canaan. Joseph goes on to bring back to life God's promise to the family as a whole, that God will come to take the family back from Egypt to the country he swore to give them. Here too the close of Genesis anticipates the future, looking beyond the exodus and claiming the promise that runs through Gen. 12–50. Joseph's talk of God "definitely attending" to the family[44] will be vindicated by Exod. 3:16 and taken up by Exod. 13:19 (see also Exod. 4:31); it is a fine statement of faith (Heb. 11:22). This verbal expression and the one that follows, "take you up," indicate how the verse functions to "throw a bridge across to the exodus event."[45] The bridging is underscored by the Scriptures' first reference to "Abraham, Isaac, and Jacob." It is also the first allusion in Part Four to God's promise of the country of Canaan to Abraham and his descendants (48:4, 15, 16, 21 are the nearest to such references). It's another way in which Gen. 50 is preparing the way for Exodus and a return to the focus of Parts Two and Three of Genesis. The entire description of the relationship between Joseph and the Egyptians will underscore the contrast when a Pharaoh arises who does not acknowledge Joseph.[46]

Joseph himself does want to end up in the promised land (v. 25), like his father. And he does so (see Exod. 13:19; Josh. 24:32; Stephen seems to get a bit confused in this connection in Acts 7:9–16). The account of Joseph's death is a briefer and simpler account than that of Jacob's. Joseph and the narrator talk straightforwardly about him dying, not about him joining his ancestors and drawing in his feet, and Joseph will settle for an oath that just his bones will find their way to Canaan. He doesn't go on about his burial, and he is given a simpler interim funeral, though bones might not need to be taken too literally if Joseph was mummified. The sons of Israel whom Joseph binds by an oath will need to be not the immediate sons of Israel but

42. Janssen, "Egyptological Remarks," 71. See, e.g., the closing paragraph of the Teachings of Ptah-hotep (*ANET* 414).

43. See the comment on 47:28.

44. On this verb, see the comment on 21:1.

45. Westermann, *Genesis 37–50*, 209.

46. Cf. Seebass, *Genesis*, 3:191–92, 196–97.

the descendants of Israel in general, who represent the people who will fulfill the promise sometime later. Given that (Benjamin apart) Joseph's actual siblings are all older than him, it is hard to imagine that they are all still alive when Joseph is dying, though Denis the Carthusian speculates that Joseph died before his brothers as a result of the spicy food and strong drink of his well-to-do Egyptian lifestyle.[47] Thus more likely, "brothers" and "sons of Israel" in vv. 24–25 have broader reference, as back in Gen. 31 "brothers" means members of the family in a broader sense than siblings. They will be the "brothers" of Exod. 2:11.

Implications

Whereas You Intended Something Bad for Me . . .

The Joseph story has been called "a story of divine providence,"[48] and etymologically it is indeed a story about God's pro-vidence, his seeing ahead of time and his providing ahead of time—though Gen. 22:14 (see the comment there) is where God is more explicitly described as the one who sees to things. If God's providence implies that God is leading history to a set goal in accordance with a plan that he formulated at the beginning, this belief is hardly justified by the story.[49] On the other hand, Joseph does not simply mean that God saw ahead of time the decisions people would make and harnessed those decisions to his purpose, or makes even bad things work together for good (Rom. 8:28), true though those formulations are in other connections. Such understandings underestimate the implications of Joseph's statement that God, not his brothers, "sent" him (45:8). Nor does Joseph declare that God decides on things and human beings cannot frustrate their fulfillment or speak of "the overriding power of God's rule."[50] Genesis does not talk about God overruling human decision making. God did not merely permit the brothers' action but then frustrate it. God ordained it.[51] But nor can such formulations imply that God was like a puppet master manipulating his brothers or like a hypnotist causing them to do things they would not otherwise have envisaged. Nor is God using human beings in the way that I use my coffee machine, which has no will of its own and makes no decisions of its own. Such understandings would underestimate the implications of his talking of what they themselves "intended." Indeed, "ultimately it was not the brothers' hate but God who brought Joseph to Egypt and moreover 'to

47. Denis the Carthusian, "Enarratio in Genesim," 469; cf. Schroeder, *Genesis*, 281.

48. The subtitle of Longacre, *Joseph*.

49. I take it that it is this understanding of providence that Westermann (*Genesis 37–50*, 143) disputes.

50. Brueggemann, *Genesis*, 294.

51. Calvin, *Genesis*, 2:378.

preserve life'"; thus it's half true that "in the entire Joseph story" what is of paramount importance is "God's hand which in all the confusion of human guilt directs everything to a gracious goal." For all the focus on human actions in this story, "God is the real subject of the whole occurrence; God, not the brothers, 'sent' Joseph here."[52] But they "intended" it, too.

The taking of Joseph to Egypt was brought about by God and by his brothers. How is one event brought about by two agents? Genesis has given many examples of how the decision making and action of God and of human beings interact. In one sense there may be nothing mysterious about it.[53]

Sometimes human beings make decisions and take initiatives to which God responds:

a. Human beings may do things to which God responds by doing something that he seems not to have originally intended (Gen. 16–17).
b. God may formulate an intention, then check out what human beings are doing before implementing it (Gen. 18–19).
c. Human beings may do something on their own initiative that conforms to God's general purpose, to which God responds by making sure that it works out well (Gen. 24).
d. Human beings may do something that has different results from the ones the actors had in mind. Pharaoh was concerned to see that his people got fed; he accidentally made it possible for Joseph and his brothers to reconcile.
e. Human beings may make plans that fail because God wants something else to happen (Gen. 14:1–16; cf. Prov. 19:21; 20:24).[54]

In Genesis such events are set in the framework of God's taking initiatives, though those initiatives do require a human response:

a. God commissions human beings to rule the earth on his behalf (Gen. 1), but their response is at best mixed and the result is a situation in which things don't work out as God would have wished.
b. God gives Noah and Abraham commissions (Gen. 6:13–7:16; 12:1–4). If they had declined to do as God said, perhaps God would have commissioned someone else. But the Scriptures give a number of examples of God refusing to take no for an answer (Moses, Jonah, Jeremiah).
c. God's envoy appears to Hagar to send her back to Abraham and Sarah and to save her life (Gen. 16; 21).

52. Von Rad, *Genesis*, 393

53. In the examples that follow, I have assumed that Genesis itself affirms the convictions expressed by Joseph (and Pharaoh).

54. Cf. Westermann, *Genesis 37–50*, 248; with Fox's comments in *Proverbs 10–31*, 658, 674–75.

d. God appears to Abimelek to warn him away from a relationship with Sarah (Gen. 21).
e. God sends Pharaoh dreams to reveal what is to happen by way of flourishing and famine (Gen. 41:25, 28).

But there are yet other events where God does something that involves human beings without their being aware of it or that involves working through natural processes:

a. God was with Joseph, and what he did succeeded (Gen. 39:21, 23).
b. God inspired favor toward Joseph in the eyes of his jailer (Gen. 39:21).
c. God caused the flourishing and the famine in Egypt (Gen. 41:25, 28, 32).
d. God enabled Joseph to forget the past and to be fruitful in Egypt (Gen. 41:51–52).
e. God made Joseph a "father" to Pharaoh and someone with power in Egypt (Gen. 45:8).

So it wasn't they who sent him there but God (Gen. 45:8), even though they did the selling (45:5).

Genesis does not always comment on how God's acts and human acts work together. What was the status and interrelationship of Joseph's bringing bad reports to his father, Jacob's favoritism, and his brothers' jealousy? What was the relationship between Joseph's dreams and the events that follow? The dreams hang over the story in Gen. 37–44. Perhaps Joseph knows how things need to work out, though he apparently doesn't know how they will do so. It is possible to affirm the conviction expressed in 45:8, but it is likely impossible to know how God's purpose and human purposes will interrelate. Joseph perhaps knew that God had sent him to Egypt, though this awareness does not surface for a while. Indeed, his naming of his sons (41:51–52) rather implies that he has given up on the dreams until his brothers arrive and he thinks about them again (42:9). He then doesn't leave it to God to make things work out, yet he perhaps recognizes that things cannot work out without God. The brothers' attempts to frustrate the dreams bring about their fulfillment. Joseph's attempts to bring about their fulfillment (in a way that also brings about transformation in the brothers) succeed.

Genesis assumes that it is possible for human beings to make their own decisions about doing things and to do them and for these acts to be also God's acts with a different and even prior aim; it does not seek to explain how this works. God inspires the human decision. Though it was the brothers' decision to sell him, Joseph is more interested in the fact that before it was their decision, it was God's decision. God sent Joseph. He gave Joseph the dream that revealed what was going to happen and thereby caused it to happen. Joseph's reporting it to his brothers understandably antagonized them and stimulated their (freely) deciding to take action designed to frustrate its fulfillment, but what they did actually facilitated the dream's fulfillment, to their great advantage. This instance of the way God sometimes works finds its ultimate parallel in what God does through Jesus as he formulates his plan beforehand, but it is put into effect through human wrongdoing.[55] It was "by the defined plan and foreknowledge of God" that Jesus was handed over, crucified, and killed "by the hands of lawless people" (Acts 2:23). Judas and the religious and political authorities were the means of God's purpose being put into effect. God knew what he wanted to achieve; they took action that they wanted to take for their own reasons, which contrasted with what God wanted, and unwittingly they brought about what God wanted, for their own benefit.

While Exod. 4–14 will talk about Yahweh hardening hearts and about Pharaoh hardening his own heart, Ezek. 18:31 and 36:26 will talk about making for oneself a new heart and about Yahweh giving people a new, soft heart. There is no transforming of a person such as Judah without God being involved and without Judah being involved.

Christian theology has traditionally affirmed that God is one, is omnipresent, is hidden, is invisible, is omnipotent, is omniscient, and expresses these characteristics in love.[56] The story in Gen. 37–50 embodies these convictions.

55. Cf. Seebass, *Genesis*, 3:113–14.

56. Sonderegger expounds them in her *Doctrine of God*.

Bibliography

Aageson, J. W. "Genesis in the Deutero-Pauline Epistles." Pages 117–29 in Moyise and Menken, *Genesis in the New Testament*.

Aaron, D. H. "Early Rabbinic Exegesis on Noah's Son Ham and the So-Called 'Hamitic Myth.'" *JAAR* 63 (1994–95): 721–59.

Abasili, A. I. "Genesis 38." *SJOT* 25 (2011): 276–88.

Abela, A. "The Inversion of Genesis 18:7a." *Bible Translator* 60 (2009): 1–4.

Aberbach, M., and B. Grossfeld, trans. and eds. *Targum Onkelos to Genesis*. New York: Ktav, 1982.

Abraham, J. "Feminist Hermeneutics and Pentecostal Spirituality." *AJPS* 6 (2003): 3–21.

Achenbach, R., and M. Arneth, eds. *"Gerechtigkeit und Recht zu üben" (Gen 18,19): Studien zur altorientalischen und biblischen Rechtsgeschichte, zur Religionsgeschichte Israels und zur Religionssoziologie; Festschrift für Eckart Otto zum 65. Geburtstag*. BZABR 13. Wiesbaden: Harrassowitz, 2009.

Achenbach, R., M. Arneth, and E. Otto. *Tora in der Hebräischen Bibel: Studien zur Redaktionsgeschichte und synchronen Logik diachroner Transformationen*. BZABR 7. Wiesbaden: Harrassowitz, 2007.

Adamo, D. T., and E. F. Eghwubare. "The African Wife of Abraham: An African Reading of Genesis 16:1–16 and 21:8–21." Pages 275–92 in Brenner, Lee, and Yee, *Genesis*.

Adelman, R. E. *The Female Ruse*. Sheffield, UK: Sheffield Phoenix, 2015.

Ahearne-Kroll, S. P. "Genesis in Mark's Gospel." Pages 27–41 in Moyise and Menken, *Genesis in the New Testament*.

Ahn, J. J., and S. L. Cook, eds. *Thus Says the Lord: Essays on the Former and Latter Prophets in Honor of Robert R. Wilson*. LHBOTS 502. New York: T&T Clark, 2009.

Aitken, J. K., et al., eds. *On Stone and Scroll: Essays in Honour of Graham Ivor Davies*. BZAW 420. Berlin: de Gruyter, 2011.

Alexander, P. S. "In the Beginning." Pages 1–29 in Grypeou and Spurling, *Exegetical Encounter*.

———. "The Targumim and Early Exegesis of 'Sons of God' in Genesis 6." *JJS* 23 (1972): 60–71.

Alexander, T. D. "The Regal Dimension of the *twldwt-y*ʿ*qb*." Pages 196–212 in McConville and Möller, *Reading the Law*.

Allen, D. M. "Genesis in James, 1 and 2 Peter and Jude." Pages 147–65 in Moyise and Menken, *Genesis in the New Testament*.

Allen, J. J. "The Mixed Economies of Cain and Abel." *Conversations with the Biblical World* 31 (2011): 33–52.

Allen, T. G., trans. *The Book of the Dead*. Chicago: University of Chicago Press, 1974.

Alston, W. M., and M. Welker, eds. *Reformed Theology: Identity and Ecumenicity II; Biblical Interpretation in the Reformed Tradition*. Grand Rapids: Eerdmans, 2007.

Alter, R. *The Art of Biblical Narrative*. New York: Basic Books, 1981.

———. *Genesis*. New York: Norton, 1986.

———. "Literature." Pages 13–27 in Hendel, *Reading Genesis*.

Althann, R. "*mwl*, 'Circumcise,' with the *lamedh* of Agency." *Biblica* 62 (1981): 239–40.

Ambrose of Milan. *Hexameron, Paradise, and Cain and Abel*. Washington, DC: Catholic University of America, 1961.

Ames, F. R., and C. W. Miller, eds. *Foster Biblical Scholarship: Essays in Honor of Kent Harold Richards*. Atlanta: Society of Biblical Literature, 2010.

Anderson, B. A. "The Intersection of the Human and the Divine in Genesis 32–33." *ZAW* 128 (2016): 30–41.

Anderson, B. W. "From Analysis to Synthesis: The Interpretation of Genesis 1–11." *JBL* 97 (1978): 23–39.

Anderson, J. E. *Jacob and the Divine Trickster*. Siphrut 5. Winona Lake, IN: Eisenbrauns, 2011.

Andrews, S. R. "Genesis 16:1–16." *Int* 68 (2014): 305–7.

Angel, H. "Sarah's Treatment of Hagar." *JBQ* 41 (2013): 211–18.

Angelats, J. "Elements per a una lectura de Gn 4,1–16." *Scripta biblica* 9 (2009): 11–32.

Angélico, J. P. "Agonia, Cristianismo e Saudade." *Humanística e Teologia* 33 (2012): 407–19.

Annus, A., ed. *Divination and Interpretation of Signs in the Ancient World*. Chicago: University of Chicago Press, 2010.

Anthonioz, S. *Babel la tête dans le ciel*. Paris: Gabalda, 2015.

———. "Le sang est la vie." *RB* 116 (2009): 5–14.

Arnold, B. T. *Genesis*. New Cambridge Bible Commentary. Cambridge: Cambridge University Press, 2009.

———. "Genesis as Holiness Preamble." Pages 331–43 in Provain and Boda, *Let Us Go Up to Zion*.

Assel, H., et al., eds. *Beyond Biblical Theologies*. WUNT 295. Tübingen: Mohr Siebeck, 2012.

Assis, E. *Identity in Conflict: The Struggle between Esau and Jacob*. Siphrut 19. Winona Lake, IN: Eisenbrauns, 2016.

Atwell, J. E. "An Egyptian Source for Genesis 1." *JTS* 51 (2000): 441–77.

Auerbach, E. *Mimesis*. Berne: Franke, 1946. English translation: *Mimesis*. Repr., Princeton: Princeton University Press, 2003.

Auffarth, C., and L. Stuckenbruck, eds. *The Fall of the Angels*. TBN 6. Leiden: Brill, 2004.

Augustin, M., and H. M. Niemann, eds. *Thinking Towards New Horizons: Collected Communications to the XIXth Congress of the International Organization for the Study of the Old Testament, Ljubljana 2007*. Frankfurt am Main: Lang, 2008.

Augustine of Hippo. *The Literal Meaning of Genesis*. Translated and annotated by John Hammond Taylor. 2 vols. Ancient Christian Writers 41. New York: Newman, 1982.

———. *On Genesis: Two Books on Genesis against the Manichees; and, On the Literal Interpretation of Genesis: An Unfinished Book*. Washington, DC: Catholic University of America Press, 1990.

———. *On the Literal Interpretation of Genesis*. Pages 143–90 in *On Genesis*.

———. *Two Books on Genesis against the Manichees*. Pages 45–142 in *On Genesis*.

Ausloos, H., and B. Lemmelijn, eds. *A Pillar of Cloud to Guide: Text-Critical, Redactional, and Linguistic Perspectives on the Old Testament in Honour of Marc Vervenne*. BETL 269. Louvain: Peeters, 2014.

Awabdy, M. A. "Babel, Suspense, and the Introduction to the Terah-Abram Narrative." *JSOT* 34 (2010): 3–29.

Azize, J., and N. Weeks, eds. *Gilgameš and the World of Assyria: Proceedings of the Conference Held at the Mandelbaum House, the University of Sydney, 21–23 July, 2004*. Ancient Near Eastern Studies Supplement 21. Louvain: Peeters, 2007.

Baden, J. S. "The Tower of Babel." *JBL* 128 (2009): 209–24.

Baer, D. A., and R. P. Gordon, eds. *Leshon Limmudim: Essays on the Language and Literature of the Hebrew Bible in Honour of A. A. Macintosh*. LHBOTS 593. London: Bloomsbury T&T Clark, 2013.

Bailey, R. C., et al., eds. *They Were All Together in One Place: Toward Minority Biblical Criticism*. SemeiaSt 57. Atlanta: Society of Biblical Literature, 2009.

———. "Why Do Readers Believe Lot?" *OTE* 23 (2010): 519–48.

Bailey, W. A. "Intimate Moments." *Proceedings: Eastern Great Lakes and Midwest Biblical Societies* 29 (2009): 1–14.

Bakon, S. "And He Called by the Name of the Lord." *JBQ* 42 (2014): 8–10.

———. "Subtleties in the Story of Joseph and Potiphar's Wife." *JBQ* 41 (2013): 171–74.

Bal, M., ed. *Anti-covenant: Counter-Reading Women's Lives in the Hebrew Bible*. JSOTSup 81. Sheffield, UK: Almond, 1989.

Ballenger, I. "Missiological Thoughts Prompted by Genesis 10." *RevExp* 103 (2006): 391–401.

Bandstra, B. L. "Word Order and Emphasis in Biblical Hebrew Narrative." Pages 109–23 in Bodine, *Linguistics and Biblical Hebrew*.

Bar, S. "Abraham's Trees." *Irish Biblical Studies* 28 (2010): 2–20.

———. "What Did the Servant Give to Rebecca's Brother and Mother?" *Biblica* 94 (2013): 565–72.

Barr, J. "Is God a Liar?" *JTS* 57 (2006): 1–22.

Bartlett, J. R. "The Land of Seir and the Brotherhood of Edom." *JTS* 20 (1969): 1–20.

Barton, S. C., and D. Wilkinson, eds. *Reading Genesis after Darwin*. Oxford: Oxford University Press, 2009.

Bascom, W. R. "Four Functions of Folklore." Pages 279–98 in Dundes, *Study of Folklore*.

Basil the Great. "De Spiritu Sancto." In *Letters and Select Works*, *NPNF*[2] 8:1–50.

———."On the Hexaemeron." In *Exegetic Homilies*. Washington, DC: Catholic University of America Press, 1963.

Batto, B. F. "The Institution of Marriage in Genesis 2 and in *Atrahasis*." *CBQ* 62 (2000): 621–31.

Batto, B. F., and K. L. Roberts, eds. *David and Zion: Biblical Studies in Honor of J. J. M. Roberts*. Winona Lake, IN: Eisenbrauns, 2004.

Bauckham, R. *The Bible in Politics: How to Read the Bible Politically*. London: SPCK, 1989.

———. "Humans, Animals, and the Environment in Genesis 1–3." Pages 175–89 in MacDonald, *Genesis and Christian Theology*.

Bauks, M. "Sacred Trees in the Garden of Eden and Their Ancient Near Eastern Precursors." *Journal of Ancient Judaism* 3 (2012): 267–301.

———. "Text- and Reception-Historical Reflections on Transmissional and Hermeneutical Techniques in Genesis 2–3." Pages 139–68 in Dozeman, *Pentateuch*.

Baumgarten, M. *Theologischer Commentar zum Pentateuch*. Kiel: Universitäts, 1843.

Bechtel, L. M. "Boundary Issues in Genesis 19.1–38." Pages 22–40 in Washington, *Escaping Eden*.

———. "A Feminist Reading of Genesis 19.1–11." Pages 108–28 in Brenner, *Genesis*.

———. "Rethinking the Interpretation of Genesis 2:4b–3:24." Pages 77–117 in Brenner, *Feminist Companion to Genesis*.

———. "What If Dinah Was Not Raped?" *JSOT* 62 (1994): 19–36.

Beck, M., and U. Schorn, eds. *Auf dem Weg zur Endgestalt von Genesis bis II Regum: Festschrift Hans-Christoph Schmitt zum 65. Geburtstag*. BZAW 370. Berlin: de Gruyter, 2006.

Becking, B. "Signs from the Garden." Pages 22–36 in Eidevall and Scheuer, *Enigmas and Images*.

———. "'They Hated Him Even More.'" *BN* 60 (1991): 40–47.

Becking, B., and D. Human, eds. *Exile and Suffering: A Selection of Papers Read at the 50th Anniversary Meeting of the Old Testament Society of South Africa OTWSA/OTSSA, Pretoria, August 2007*. OtSt 50. Leiden: Brill, 2009.

Ben Zvi, E. "The Dialogue between Abraham and Yhwh." *JSOT* 53 (1992): 27–46.

Bergen, W. J., and A. Siedlecki, eds. *Voyages in Uncharted Waters: Essays on the Theory and Practice of Biblical Interpretation in Honor of David Jobling*. Sheffield, UK: Sheffield Phoenix, 2006.

Bergey, R. “Pathologie et guérison spirituelle: La “douleur” et le remède en Genèse 3.” *Revue réformée* 62 (2011): 7–22.

Bergsma, J. S., and S. W. Hahn. “Noah’s Nakedness and the Curse on Canaan.” *JBL* 124 (2005): 25–40.

Berman, J. “Identity Politics and the Burial of Jacob.” *CBQ* 68 (2006): 11–31.

Beyerle, S., et al., eds. *Viele Wege zu dem Einen historische Bibelkritik: Die Vitalität der Glaubensüberlieferung in der Moderne*. Biblisch-theologische Studien 121. Neukirchen: Neukirchener Verlag, 2012.

Biddle, M. E. “Genesis 3.” *RevExp* 103 (2006): 359–70.

Biden, J. S. “The Morpho-Syntax of Genesis 12:1–3.” *CBQ* 72 (2010): 223–37.

Blachman, E. *The Transformation of Tamar (Genesis 38) in the History of Jewish Interpretation*. Contributions to Biblical Theology and Exegesis 71. Louvain: Peeters, 2013.

Bledstein, A. J. “Binder, Trickster, Heel and Hairy-Man: Re-reading Genesis 27 as a Trickster Tale Told by a Woman.” Pages 282–95 in Brenner, *Feminist Companion to Genesis*.

Blenkinsopp, J. *Abraham: The Story of a Life*. Grand Rapids: Eerdmans, 2015.

———.“Abraham and the Righteous of Sodom.” *JJS* 33 (1982): 119–32.

———. “The Judge of All the Earth.” *JJS* 41 (1990): 1–12.

Blum, E. “The Jacob Tradition.” Pages 181–211 in Evans, *Book of Genesis*.

Blyth, C. *The Narrative of Rape in Genesis 34*. Oxford: Oxford University Press, 2010.

———. “Redeemed by His Love?” *JSOT* 33 (2008): 3–18.

———. “Terrible Silence, Eternal Silence.” *BibInt* 17 (2009): 483–506.

Boase, E. “Life in the Shadows.” *VT* 51 (2001): 312–35.

Bodine, W. R., ed. *Linguistics and Biblical Hebrew*. Winona Lake, IN: Eisenbrauns, 1992.

Boer, R., et al., eds. *The One Who Reads May Run: Essays in Honour of Edgar W. Conrad*. LHBOTS 521. New York: T&T Clark, 2012.

Bokovoy, D. E. “Did Eve Acquire, Create, or Procreate with Yahweh?” *VT* 63 (2013): 19–35.

Bolin, T. M. “The Role of Exchange in Ancient Mediterranean Religion and Its Implications for Reading Genesis 18–19.” *JSOT* 29 (2004): 37–56.

Bonhoeffer, D. *Creation and Fall; Temptation*. Repr., New York: Simon & Schuster, 1997.

Booij, T. “Hagar’s Words in Genesis xvi 13b.” *VT* 30 (1980): 1–7.

Bornapé, A. “El motive de un ‘nombre’ en la historia de la Torre de Babel.” *Davar-Logos* 9 (2010): 127–133.

Bos, J. W. H. “An Eyeopener at the Gate.” *LTQ* 27 (1992): 119–23.

Bouteneff, P. C. *Beginnings: Ancient Christian Readings of the Biblical Creation Narratives*. Grand Rapids: Baker Academic, 2008.

Boyd, R. T. *Tells, Tombs, and Treasure: A Pictorial Guide to Biblical Archaeology*. Grand Rapids: Baker, 1969.

Brams, S. J. *Biblical Games: Game Theory and the Hebrew Bible*. Cambridge, MA: MIT Press, 2003.

Branch, R. G. "Genesis 20." *In die Skriflig* 38 (2004): 217–34.

Braude, W. G. *The Midrash on Psalms*. New Haven: Yale University Press, 1959.

Brayford, S. A. *Genesis*. Septuagint Commentary Series. Leiden: Brill, 2007.

Bream, H. N., et al., eds. *A Light unto My Path: Old Testament Studies in Honor of Jacob M. Myers*. Gettysburg Theological Studies 4. Philadelphia: Temple University Press, 1974.

Brenner, A., ed. *Exodus to Deuteronomy*. A Feminist Companion to the Bible. 1st series. Sheffield, UK: Sheffield Academic, 1994.

———, ed. *A Feminist Companion to Genesis*. Sheffield, UK: Sheffield Academic, 1993.

———, ed. *Genesis*. A Feminist Companion to the Bible. 2nd series. Sheffield, UK: Sheffield Academic, 1998.

———. "Literary Approaches to Biblical Literature." Pages 45–75 in Greenspahn, *Hebrew Bible*.

Brenner, A., A. C. C. Lee, and G. A. Yee, eds. *Genesis*. Minneapolis: Fortress, 2010.

Brenner, A., and J. W. van Henten, eds. *Recycling Biblical Figures: Papers Read at NOSTER Colloquium in Amsterdam 12–13 May 1997*. Studies in Theology and Religion 1. Leiden: Deo, 1999.

Breslauer, S. D., ed. *The Seductiveness of Jewish Myth: Challenge or Response?* Albany: SUNY Press, 1997.

Brett, M. G. "Abraham's 'Heretical' Imperative." Pages 166–78 in Cosgrove, *The Meanings We Choose*.

———. *Genesis*. London: Routledge, 2000.

Brettler, M. Z., and M. A. Fishbane, eds. *Minḥah le-Naḥum: Biblical and Other Studies Presented to Nahum M. Sarna in Honour of His 70th Birthday*. JSOTSup 154. Sheffield, UK: JSOT Press, 1983.

Brichto, H. C. *The Names of God: Poetic Readings in Biblical Beginnings*. New York: Oxford University Press, 1998.

Bridge, E. J. "An Audacious Request." *JSOT* 40 (2016): 281–96.

———. "The 'Slave' Is the 'Master.'" *JSOT* 38 (2014): 263–78.

Briggs, R. S. "Humans in the Image of God and Other Things Genesis Does Not Make Clear." *JTI* 4 (2010): 111–26.

Brock, S. P. "Creating Women's Voices." Pages 125–42 in Grypeou and Spurling, *Exegetical Encounter*.

Brown, W. P. "Manifest Diversity." Pages 3–25 in MacDonald, Elliott, and Macaskill, *Genesis and Christian Theology*.

———. *Structure, Role, and Ideology in the Hebrew and Greek Texts of Genesis 1:1–2:3*. Atlanta: Scholars Press, 1993.

Brown, W. P., and S. D. McBride, eds. *God Who Creates: Essays in Honor of W. Sibley Towner*. Grand Rapids: Eerdmans, 2000.

Browne, J. K. "Genesis in Matthew's Gospel." Pages 42–59 in Moyise and Menken, *Genesis in the New Testament*.

Brueggemann, W. *Genesis*. Interpretation: A Commentary for Teaching and Preaching. Louisville: Westminster John Knox, 1982.

———. “Genesis 17:1–22.” *Int* 45 (1991): 55–59.

Buck, M. “God as Tempter.” *Logia* 24 (2015): 23–27.

Bührer, W. “Göttersöhne und Menschentöchter.” *ZAW* 123 (2011): 495–515.

Bunge, M. J., et al., eds. *The Child in the Bible*. Grand Rapids: Eerdmans, 2008.

Bunn, D. D., Jr. “‘Return to the Land of Your Fathers’: A Narrative Reading of Genesis 31–33, the Return of Jacob to the Land of Canaan.’” PhD diss., Fuller Theological Seminary, 2015.

Byron, J. *Cain and Abel in Text and Tradition: Jewish and Christian Interpretations of the First Sibling Rivalry*. TBN 14. Leiden: Brill, 2011.

Cadwallader, A. H., with P. L. Trudinger, eds. *Where the Wild Ox Roams: Biblical Essays in Honour of Norman C. Habel*. Hebrew Bible Monographs 59. Sheffield, UK: Sheffield Phoenix, 2013.

Cairus, A. “Grain and Rain in Genesis 2:5, 6.” *Journal of Asia Adventist Seminary* 13 (2010): 93–101.

Callender, D. E., Jr., ed. *Myth and Scripture: Contemporary Perspectives on Religion, Language, and Imagination*. Resources for Biblical Study. Atlanta: SBL Press, 2014.

Calvin, J. *Commentaries on the First Book of Moses Called Genesis*. 2 vols. Repr., Grand Rapids: Eerdmans, 1949.

Campbell, G. Van Pelt. “Refusing God’s Blessing: An Exposition of Genesis 11:27–32.” *BSac* 165 (2008): 268–82.

Carlson, R. “The Open God of the Sodom and Gomorrah Cycle.” *JPT* 21 (2012): 185–200.

Carmichael, C. M. “Legal and Ethical Reflections on Genesis 18 and 19.” Pages 101–11 in Lipton, *Universalism and Particularism*.

———. “Some Sayings in Genesis 49.” *JBL* 88 (1969): 435–44.

Carr, D. “*Biblos Geneseōs* Revisited.” *ZAW* 110 (1998): 159–72, 327–47.

Carroll R., M. D., et al., eds. *The Bible in Human Society: Essays in Honour of John Rogerson*. JSOTSup 200. Sheffield, UK: Sheffield Academic, 1995.

Cavanaugh, W. T., and J. K. A Smith, eds. *Evolution and the Fall*. Grand Rapids: Eerdmans, 2017.

Chalmers, A. “The Importance of the Noahic Covenant to Biblical Theology.” *TynB* 60 (2009): 207–16.

Chan, H. “‘The Distance of a Bowshot.’” *Journal of Song-Yuan Studies* 25 (1995): 29–46.

Chapman, S. B. “Food, Famine, and the Nations.” Pages 323–33 in MacDonald, Elliott, and Macaskill, *Genesis and Christian Theology*.

Charles, J. D., ed. *Reading Genesis 1–2*. Peabody, MA: Hendrickson, 2013.

Cheon, S. “Filling the Gap in the Story of Lot’s Wife.” *AsJT* 15 (2001): 13–23.

Childs, B. S. *Biblical Theology of the Old and New Testaments*. London: SCM, 1992.

———. *Myth and Reality in the Old Testament*. 2nd ed. London: SCM, 1962.

Chilton, B. "Genesis in Aramaic." Pages 495–518 in Evans, *Book of Genesis*.

Chromatius of Aquileia. *Opera*. Corpus Christianorum: Series Latina 9A. Turnhout: Brepols, 1974.

Chrysostom, J. *Homilies on Genesis*. 3 vols. Washington, DC: Catholic University of America Press, 1986, 1990, 1992.

Chung, Y. "Conflicting Readings in the Narrative of Cain and Abel." *AJPS* 14 (2011): 241–54.

Clifford, R. J. "Genesis 37–50." Pages 213–29 in Evans, *Book of Genesis*.

———. "Genesis 38." *CBQ* 66 (2004): 519–32.

Climacus, J. *The Ladder of Divine Ascent*. Rev. ed. Boston: Holy Transfiguration Monastery, 1991.

Clines, D. J. A., S. E. Fowl, and S. E. Porter, eds. *The Bible in Three Dimensions: Essays in Celebration of Forty Years of Biblical Studies in the University of Sheffield*. JSOTSup 87. Sheffield, UK: Sheffield Academic, 1990.

Coats, G. W. *Genesis: An Introduction to Narrative Literature*. FOTL 1. Grand Rapids: Eerdmans, 1983.

Cogan, M., B. L. Eichler, and J. H. Tigay, eds. *Tehillah le-Moshe: Biblical and Judaic Studies in Honor of Moshe Greenberg*. Winona Lake, IN: Eisenbrauns, 1997.

Cohen, A. "Hagar and Ishmael." *Int* 68 (2014): 247–56.

Cohen, C., et al., eds. *Birkat Shalom: Studies in the Bible, Ancient Near Eastern Literature, and Postbiblical Judaism Presented to Shalom M. Paul on the Occasion of His Seventieth Birthday*. Winona Lake, IN: Eisenbrauns, 2008.

Cohen, C., A. Hurvitz, and S. M. Paul, eds. *Sefer Moshe: The Moshe Weinfeld Jubilee Volume; Studies in the Bible and the Ancient Near East, Qumran, and Post-Biblical Judaism*. Winona Lake, IN: Eisenbrauns, 2004.

Cohen, Jeffrey M. "*Be-Dorotav*: Noah's 'Generations' in Light of Antediluvian Longevity." *JBQ* 21 (2013): 187–90.

Cohen, Jeremy. *"Be Fertile and Increase, Fill the Earth and Master It": The Ancient and Medieval Career of a Biblical Text*. Ithaca, NY: Cornell University Press, 1989.

Cohn, R. L. "Negotiating (with) the Natives: Ancestors and Identity in Genesis." *HTR* 96 (2003): 147–66.

Cole, H. R. "The Sabbath and Genesis 2:1–3." *AUSS* 41 (2003): 5–12.

Conrad, E. W., and R. Boer, eds. *Redirected Travel: Alternative Journeys and Places in Biblical Studies*. LHBOTS 382. London: T&T Clark, 2003.

Coogan, M. D., ed. *The Oxford History of the Biblical World*. Oxford: Oxford University Press, 1998.

Cook, J. E. "Mothers and Wives." *Proceedings of the Great Lakes and Midwest Bible Societies* 27 (2007): 1–17.

Cook, Johann. "The Septuagint of Genesis." Pages 315–29 in Wénin, *Genesis*.

Cosgrove, C. H., ed. *The Meanings We Choose: Hermeneutical Ethics, Indeterminacy and the Conflict of Interpretations*. LHBOTS 411. London: T&T Clark, 2004.

Counet, P. C., and U. Berges, eds. *One Text, a Thousand Methods: Studies in Memory of Sjef van Tilborg*. BibInt 71. Boston: Brill, 2005.

Craig, K. M. "Questions outside Eden." *JSOT* 86 (1999): 107–28.

Croatto, J. S. "A Reading of the Story of the Tower of Babel." Pages 203–23 in Segovia and Tolbert, *Teaching the Bible*.

Crotty, R. "The Near Sacrifice of Isaac." Pages 192–209 in Cadwallader and Trudiger, *Where the Wild Ox Roams*.

Crouch, C. L. "*ḥṭṭʾt* as Interpolative Gloss." *ZAW* 123 (2011): 250–58.

Crüsemann, F. "Dominion, Guilt, and Reconciliation." *Semeia* 66 (1994): 67–77.

Dafni, E. G. "*ʾšh ky mʾiš—gunē oti ek tou andros autēs*." Pages 569–84 in Wénin, *Genesis*.

Daly, M. F. *Beyond God the Father: Toward a Philosophy of Women's Liberation*. Repr., Boston: Beacon, 1985.

Darshan, G. "The Biblical Account of the Post-Diluvian Generation (Gen. 9:20–10:32) in the Light of Greek Genealogical Literature." *VT* 63 (2013): 515–35.

Davidson, J. A. "Genesis Matriarchs Engage Feminism." *AUSS* 40 (2002): 169–78.

Davies, P. R. "And Enoch Was Not, for Genesis Took Him." Pages 97–107 in Hempel and Lieu, *Biblical Traditions in Transmission*.

———. "Making It: Creation and Contradiction in Genesis." Pages 249–56 in Carroll, *Bible in Human Society*.

Davies, P. R., and D. J. A. Clines, eds. *The World of Genesis*. Sheffield, UK: Sheffield Academic, 1998.

Davis, A. R. "Eden Revisited." *CBQ* 78 (2016): 611–31.

Davis, E. F. "Self-Consciousness and Conversation." *BBR* 1 (1991): 27–40.

Day, J. *From Creation to Babel: Studies in Genesis 1–11*. London: Bloomsbury, 2013.

———. "Where Was Tarshish?" Pages 359–69 in Provain and Boda, *Let Us Go Up to Zion*.

Day, L., and C. Pressler, eds. *Engaging the Bible in a Gendered World: An Introduction to Feminist Biblical Interpretation in Honor of Katharine Doob Sakenfeld*. Louisville: Westminster John Knox, 2006.

Dearman, J. A., and M. P. Graham, eds. *The Land That I Will Show You: Essays on the History and Archaeology of the Ancient Near East in Honor of J. Maxwell Miller*. JSOTSup 343. Sheffield, UK: Sheffield Academic, 2001.

DeClaissé-Walford, N. L. "Genesis 2." *RevExp* 103 (2006): 324–58.

DeGrado, J. "The *qdesha* in Hosea 4:14." *VT* 68 (2018): 8–40.

De Hoop, R. *Genesis 49 in Its Literary and Historical Context*. OtSt 39. Leiden: Brill, 1999.

De la Lama, S. G.-J. "Reiteraciones." *Scripta Theologica* 32 (2000): 719–55.

De La Torre, M. A. *Genesis*. Louisville: Westminster John Knox, 2011.

Dell, K. J., ed. *Ethical and Unethical in the Old Testament: God and Humans in Dialogue*. LHBOTS 528. New York: T&T Clark, 2010.

Dell, K. J., G. Davies, and Y. V. Koh, eds. *Genesis, Isaiah, and Psalms: A Festschrift to Honour Professor John Emerton for His Eightieth Birthday*. VTSup 135. Leiden: Brill, 2010.

De Moor, J. C. "The Duality in God and Man." Pages 112–25 in de Moor, *Intertextuality in Ugarit and Israel.*

———. "Genesis 49 and the Early History of Israel." Pages 176–98 in de Moor and van Rooy, *Past, Present, Future.*

———, ed. *Intertextuality in Ugarit and Israel.* OtSt 40. Leiden: Brill, 1998.

———, ed. *Synchronic or Diachronic? A Debate on Method in Old Testament Exegesis: Papers Read at the Ninth Joint Meeting of Het Oudtestamentisch Werkgezelschap in Nederland en Belgie and the Society for Old Testament Study Held at Kampen, 1994.* OtSt 34. Leiden: Brill, 1995.

De Moor, J. C., and H. E. van Rooy, eds. *Past, Present, Future: The Deuteronomistic History and the Prophets.* OtSt 44. Leiden: Brill, 2000.

Demsky, A. "The Route of Jacob's Funeral Cortege." Pages 54–64 in Brettler and Fishbane, *Minḥah le-Naḥum.*

Denis/Denys the Carthusian. *See* Dionysius Cartusianus.

Dennison, J. T. "The Eschatological Reversal of the Protological Reversal." *Kerux* 23.2 (2008): 3–13.

De Regt, L. J., et al., eds. *Literary Structure and Rhetorical Strategies in the Hebrew Bible.* Assen: Van Gorcum, 1996.

Derouchie, J. S. "The Blessing-Commission, the Promised Offspring, and the *Toledot* Structure of Genesis." *JETS* 56 (2013): 219–47.

Derrida, J. *The Gift of Death.* Chicago: University of Chicago Press, 1995.

Dershowitz, A. M. *The Genesis of Justice.* New York: Warner, 2000.

De Silentio, J. [Søren Kierkegaard]. *Fear and Trembling.* Princeton: Princeton University Press, 1983.

De Villiers, G. "Sin, Suffering, Sagacity." Pages 3–17 in Becking and Human, *Exile and Suffering.*

Didymus the Blind. *Commentary on Genesis.* Washington, DC: Catholic University of America Press, 2016.

Diepstra, G. R., and G. J. Laughery. "Exploring the Possible Worlds of Genesis 2–3." *EvQ* 85 (2013): 309–27.

———. "Interpreting Science and Scripture." *EuroJTh* 18 (2009): 5–16.

———. "Sculpting in Time." *EvQ* 83 (2011): 291–307.

Diesel, A. A., ed. *"Jedes Ding hat seine Zeit": Studien zur israelitischen und altorientalischen Weisheit; Diethelm Michel zum 65. Geburtstag.* BZAW 241. Berlin: de Gruyter, 1996.

Diffey, D. S. "The Royal Promise in Genesis." *TynBul* 62 (2011): 313–16.

Dillmann, A. *Genesis.* 2 vols. Edinburgh: T&T Clark, 1897.

Dionysius Cartusianus [Denis/Denys the Carthusian]. "Enarratio in Genesim." In *Omnia Opera* 1–469. Montreuil: Cartusiae, 1896.

Dishi, G. "Saving Zoar." *JBQ* 38 (2010): 211–18.

Docherty, S. "Genesis in Hebrews." Pages 130–46 in Moyise and Menken, *Genesis in the New Testament.*

Doerfler, M. E. "Entertaining the Trinity Unawares." *JEH* 65 (2014): 485–503.

Dolansky, S., ed. *Sacred History, Sacred Literature: Essays on Ancient Israel, the Bible, and Religion in Honor of R. E. Friedman on His Sixtieth Birthday*. Winona Lake, IN: Eisenbrauns, 2008.

Doyle, B. "'Knock, Knock, Knockin' on Sodom's Door.'" *JSOT* 28 (2004): 431–48.

———. "The Sin of Sodom." *Theology and Sexuality* 9 (1998): 84–100.

Dozeman, T. B., et al., eds. *The Pentateuch: International Perspectives on Current Research*. FAT 78. Tübingen: Mohr Siebeck, 2011.

Drey, P. R. "The Role of Hagar in Genesis 16." *AUSS* 40 (2002): 179–95.

Driver, S. R. *The Book of Genesis*. 4th ed. London: Methuen, 1905.

Dundes, A., ed. *The Study of Folklore*. Englewood Cliffs, NJ: Prentice-Hall, 1965.

Durant, E. "It's Complicated." *Conversations with the Biblical World* 35 (2015): 78–93.

Earl, D. S. "Toward a Christian Hermeneutic of Old Testament Narrative." *CBQ* 73 (2011): 30–49.

Eberhart, C. A. "The Term 'Sacrifice' and the Problem of Theological Abstraction." Pages 47–66 in Helmer and Higbe, *Multivalence of Biblical Texts*.

Ede, F. *Die Josefsgeschichte Literarkritische und redaktionsgeschichtliche Untersuchungen zur Entstehung von Gen 37–50*. BZAW 485. Berlin: de Gruyter, 2016.

Efthimiadis-Keith, H. "Genesis 2:18–25 from a Jungian and Feminist-Deconstructionist Point of View." *OTE* 23 (2010): 44–65.

Egger, M. *"Hagar, woher kommst du? und wohin gehst du?" (Gen 16,8*): Darstellung und Funktion der Figur Hagar im Sara(i)-Abra(ha)m-Zyklus (Gen 11,27–25,18)*. Herders biblische Studien 67. Freiburg: Herder, 2011.

Ehrlich, A. B. *Randglossen zur hebräischen Bibel*. Leipzig: Hinrichs, 1908.

Eichler, B. L. "On Reading Genesis 12:10–20." Pages 23–38 in Cogan, Eichler, and Tigay, *Tehillah le-Moshe*.

Eichler, R. "When God Abandoned the Garden of Eden: A Forgotten Reading of Genesis 3:24." *VT* 65.1 (2015): 20–32.

Eidevall, G., and B. Scheuer, eds. *Enigmas and Images: Studies in Honor of Tryggve Mettinger*. Coniectanea Biblica: Old Testament Series 58. Winona Lake, IN: Eisenbrauns, 2011.

Eilberg-Schwartz, H. *The Savage in Judaism: An Anthropology of Israelite Religion and Ancient Judaism*. Bloomington: Indiana University Press, 1990.

Ekblad, B. *Reading the Bible with the Damned*. Louisville: Westminster John Knox, 2005.

Elgavish, D. "The Encounter of Abram and Melchizedek." Pages 495–508 in Wénin, *Genesis*.

Ellul, J. *The Meaning of the City*. Grand Rapids: Eerdmans, 1970.

Embry, B. "The 'Naked Narrative' from Noah to Leviticus." *JSOT* 35 (2011): 417–33.

Engar, A. W. "Old Testament Women as Tricksters." Pages 143–57 in Toller and Maier, *Mappings*.

Ephrem the Syrian. *Commentary on Genesis*. In *Selected Prose Works*. Washington, DC: Catholic University of America Press, 1994.

Erasmus, D. *Collected Works of Erasmus*. Toronto: University of Toronto Press, 1999.

Eskenazi, T. C., and A. L. Weiss, eds. *The Torah: A Women's Commentary*. New York: URJ, 2008.

Eslinger, L. "The Enigmatic Plurals Like 'One of Us.'" *VT* 56 (2006): 171–84.

Evans, C. A., et al., eds. *The Book of Genesis: Composition, Reception, and Interpretation*. VTSup 152. Leiden: Brill, 2012.

Exum, J. C. "Who's Afraid of 'The Endangered Ancestress'?" Pages 90–113 in Exum and Clines, *New Literary Criticism*.

Exum, J. C., and D. J. A. Clines, eds. *The New Literary Criticism*. Sheffield, UK: Sheffield Academic, 1993.

Eynde, S. van den. "The Missing Link—"Berit" in the Flood Narrative." Pages 467–78 in Wénin, *Genesis*.

Eyre, C. J. "Crime and Adultery in Ancient Egypt." *Journal of Egyptian Archaeology* 70 (1984): 92–105.

Falk, D. K. "Divergence from Genesis in the *Genesis Apocryphon*." Pages 193–203 in Parry, *Qumran Cave 1 Revisited*.

Fenton, T. "Nimrod's Cities." Pages 23–31 in Dell, Davies, and Koh, *Genesis, Isaiah, and Psalms*.

Fewell, D. N., ed. *Reading between Texts: Intertextuality and the Hebrew Bible*. Louisville: Westminster John Knox, 1992.

Fewell, D. N., and D. M. Gunn. "Tipping the Balance." *JBL* 110 (1991): 193–211.

Fidler, R. "Genesis xv." *VT* 57 (2007): 162–80.

Fieger, M. "Die Erschaffung der Schöpfung." Pages 65–88 in Fieger and Lanckau, *Erschaffung und Zerstörung der Schöpfung*.

Fieger, M., and J. Lanckau, *Erschaffung und Zerstörung der Schöpfung: Ein Beitrag zum Thema Mythos*. Alte Testament im Dialog 4. Bern: Lang, 2011.

Field, F. F. *Origenis Hexaplorum quae supersunt*. Vol. 1. Oxford: Clarendon, 1871.

Fields, W. W. *Sodom and Gomorrah: History and Motif in Biblical Narrative*. LHBOTS 231. Sheffield, UK: Sheffield Academic, 1997.

Firmage, E. "Genesis 1 and the Priestly Agenda." *JSOT* 82 (1999): 97–114.

Fishbane, M. A. "Composition and Structure in the Jacob Cycle." *JJS* 26 (1975): 15–38.

———. *Text and Texture*. New York: Schocken, 1979.

Fitzgerald, J. T., F. J. van Rensburg, and H. F. van Rooy, eds. *Animosity, the Bible, and Us: Some European, North American, and South African Perspectives*. Society of Biblical Literature Global Perspectives on Biblical Scholarship 12. Atlanta: Society of Biblical Literature, 2009.

Fleishman, J. "On the Significance of a Name Change and Circumcision in Genesis 17." *JANESCU* 28 (2001): 19–32.

Fleming, D. E. "The Syrian Background of Israel's Ancestors, Reprise." Pages 193–232 in Hoffmeier and Millard, *Future of Biblical Archaeology*.

Fleming, E. E. "'She Went to Inquire of the Lord': Independent Divination in Genesis 25:22." *Union Seminary Quarterly Review* 60 (2007): 1–10.

Fockner, S. "Reopening the Discussion: Another Contextual Look at the Sons of God." *JSOT* 32 (2008): 435–56.

Fokkelman, J. P. "Genesis 37 and 38." Pages 152–87 in de Regt, *Literary Structure*.

———. *Narrative Art in Genesis*. Assen: Van Gorcum, 1975.

Fontaine, C. R. "Forgotten Voices of Earth." Pages 200–210 in Habel and Wurst, *Earth Story in Genesis*.

Forti, T. "The Polarity of Wisdom and Fear of God in the Eden Narrative and in the Book of Proverbs." *BN* 149 (2011): 45–57.

Fouts, D. M. "Selected Lexical and Grammatical Studies in Genesis 1." *AUSS* 42 (2004): 79–90.

Fox, M. V. "Joseph and Wisdom." Pages 231–62 in Evans, *Book of Genesis*.

———. *Proverbs 10–31*. New Haven: Yale University Press, 2009.

Frankel, E. *The Five Books of Miriam*. Repr., San Francisco: Harper, 1996.

Freedman, T. "*rwḥ ʾlhym*." *JBQ* 24 (1996): 9–13.

Fretheim, T. E. *Abraham*. Columbia: University of South Carolina Press, 2007.

———. "The Book of Genesis." In L. E. Keck et al., eds., *The New Interpreter's Bible* 1:319–674. Nashville: Abingdon, 1994.

———. "God, Abraham, and the Abuse of Isaac." *WW* 15 (1995): 49–57.

———. *God and the World*. Nashville: Abingdon, 2005.

———. "The God of the Flood Story and Natural Disasters." *CTJ* 48 (2008): 21–34.

———. "'God Was with the Boy.'" Pages 3–23 in Bunge, *Child in the Bible*.

———. "Jacob's Wrestling and Issues of Divine Power." Pages 181–91 in Cadwallader and Trudinger, *Where the Wild Ox Roams*.

———. "The Self-Limiting God of the Old Testament." Pages 179–91 in Noll and Schramm, *Raising Up a Faithful Exegete*.

———. "Violence and the God of the Old Testament." Pages 108–27 in Zehnder and Hagelia, *Encountering Violence in the Bible*.

Frey, H. *Das Buch der Anfänge*. Repr., Stuttgart: Calwer, 1964.

———. *Das Buch der Führung*. Repr., Stuttgart: Calwer, 1964.

———. *Das Buch des Glaubens*. Repr., Stuttgart: Calwer, 1964.

———. *Das Buch des Kampfes*. Repr., Stuttgart: Calwer, 1964.

Frolov, S. "Judah Comes to Shiloh." *JBL* 131 (2012): 417–22.

———. "The Other Side of the Jabbok." *JSOT* 91 (2000): 41–59.

García Alfonso, C. "El silencio del cuerpo." *Apuntes* 19.3 (1999): 80–83.

García Martínez, F. "Hagar in Targum Pseudo-Jonathan." Pages 263–74 in Goodman, *Abraham, the Nations, and the Hagarites*.

García Martínez, F., and G. P. Luttikhuizen, eds. *Interpretations of the Flood*. Leiden: Brill, 1998.

Gardner, A. "Ecojustice: A Study of Genesis 6.11–13." Pages 117–30 in Habel and Wurst, *Earth Story in Genesis*.

Geller, S. A. "Cleft Sentences with Pleonastic Pronoun." *JANESCU* 20 (1991): 15–33.

———. "The Sack of Shechem: The Use of Typology in Biblical Covenant Religion." *Prooftexts* 10 (1990): 1–15.

Gemser, B. "*Beʿēber hajjardēn*." *VT* 2 (1952): 349–55.

General Synod of the Dutch Reformed Church. *Human Relations and the South African Scene in the Light of Scripture*. Cape Town: Dutch Reformed Church, 1976.

Geoghegan, J. C. "Jacob's Bargain with God." Pages 23–36 in Malena and Miano, *Milk and Honey*.

Gericke, J. "A Philosophical Clarification of the Axiological Assumptions behind the Concept of Goodness in Genesis 1." *JSem* 22 (2013): 201–25.

Gertz, J. C. "Antibabylonische Polemik im priesterlichen Schöpfungsbericht?" *Zeitschrift für Theologie und Kirche* 106 (2009): 137–55.

———. "The Formation of the Primeval History." Pages 107–35 in Evans, *Book of Genesis*.

———. "Hams Sündenfall und Kanaans Erbfluch." Pages 81–95 in Achenbach and Arneth, *"Gerechtigkeit und Recht zu üben."*

———. "Variations autour du récit de Caïn et Abel." *Revue d'histoire et de philosophie religieuses* 94 (2014): 27–50.

Getui, M., et al., eds. *Interpreting the Old Testament in Africa*. Biblical Studies in African Scholarship. New York: Lang, 2001.

Gevirtz, S. "The Life Spans of Joseph and Enoch." *JBL* 96 (1977): 570–71.

———. "Naphtali in 'The Blessing of Jacob.'" *JBL* 103 (1984): 513–21.

Gibson, J. C. L. *Genesis*. 2 vols. Philadelphia: Westminster, 1981–82.

Gillmayr-Bucher, S. "The Woman of Their Dreams." Pages 90–101 in Davies and Clines, *World of Genesis*.

Giorgetti, A. "The 'Mock Building Account' of Genesis 11:1–9." *VT* 64 (2014): 1–20.

Gitay, Y. "The Promise: The Winding Road." *OTE* 32 (2007): 352–64.

Goldin, J. "Reuben." Pages 133–41 in Brettler and Fishbane, *Minḥah le-Naḥum*.

Goldingay, J. *After Eating the Apricot*. Carlisle, UK: Paternoster, 1996.

———. *Daniel*. Rev. ed. Grand Rapids: Zondervan, 2019.

———. *The First Testament: A New Translation*. Downers Grove, IL: InterVarsity, 2018.

———. *Israel's Gospel*. Vol. 1 of *Old Testament Theology*. Downers Grove, IL: InterVarsity, 2003.

———. "The Place of Ishmael." Pages 146–49 in Davies and Clines, *World of Genesis*.

———. "Postmodernizing Eve and Adam." Pages 50–59 in Davies and Clines, *World of Genesis*.

———. *Psalms 42–89*. BCOT: Wisdom and Psalms. Grand Rapids: Baker Academic, 2007.

———. "The Significance of Circumcision." *JSOT* 88 (2000): 3–18.

Goldingay, J., and T. Wright. *The Bible for Everyone: A New Translation*. London: SPCK, 2018.

Goldstein, R. "Looking Back at Lot's Wife." *Commentary* 34.3 (1992): 37–41.

Golka, F. W. "Genesis 37–50." *CurBR* 2 (2004): 153–77.

Goodman, M., et al., eds. *Abraham, the Nations, and the Hagarites: Jewish, Christian, and Islamic Perspectives on Kinship with Abraham*. TBN 13. Leiden: Brill, 2010.

Gordon, R. P. "'Couch' or 'Crouch'?" Pages 195–209 in Aitken, *On Stone and Scroll*.

———. "The Ethics of Eden." Pages 11–33 in Dell, *Ethical and Unethical in the Old Testament*.

———. "Evensong in Eden." Pages 17–30 in Baer and Gordon, *Leshon Limmudim*.

———. "Who 'Began to Call on the Name of the Lord' in Genesis 4:26b?" Pages 57–68 in Provain and Boda, *Let Us Go Up to Zion*.

Görg, M. "Beobachtungen zu den biblischen Bildern vom 'Garten (in) Eden.'" *Münchener Theologische Zeitschrift* 63 (2012): 98–108.

Gorospe, A. *Narrative and Identity: An Ethical Reading of Exodus 1*. BibInt 86. Leiden: Brill, 2007.

Granerød, G. *Abraham and Melchizedek: Scribal Activity of Second Temple Times in Genesis 14 and Psalm 110*. BZAW 406. Berlin: de Gruyter, 2010.

Grant, J. A., et al., eds. *A God of Faithfulness: Essays in Honour of J. Gordon McConville on His 60th Birthday*. LHBOTS 538. New York: T&T Clark, 2011.

Greengus, S. "The Anachronism in Abraham's Observance of the Laws." *HUCA* 86 (2015): 1–35.

Greenspahn, F. E., ed. *The Hebrew Bible: New Insights and Scholarship*. New York: New York University Press, 2008.

Greenstein, E. L. "Presenting Genesis 1, Constructively and Deconstructively." *Prooftexts* 21 (2001): 1–22.

Gregory, D. S, and W. W. Evert. "The Book of Genesis Unfolded." *Christian Faith and Life* 6 (1907): 65–77.

Gregory of Nyssa. "On the Making of Man." In *Select Writings and Letters*, *NPNF*[2] 5:387–427.

Grossman, J. "'Associative Meanings' in the Character Evaluation of Lot's Daughters." *CBQ* 76 (2014): 40–57.

———. "The Double Etymology of Babel in Genesis 11." *ZAW* 129 (2017): 362–75.

Gruen, E. S., ed. *Cultural Borrowings and Ethnic Appropriations in Antiquity*. Stuttgart: Steiner, 2005.

Grundke, C. L. K. "A Tempest in a Teapot?" *VT* 51 (2001): 549–51.

Grüneberg, K. N. *Abraham, Blessing and the Nations: A Philological and Exegetical Study of Genesis 12:3 in Its Context*. BZAW 332. Berlin: de Gruyter, 2003.

Grünwaldt, K. *Exil und Identität*. Frankfurt: Hain, 1992.

———. "Wenn Gott nur einer ist." *KD* 60 (2014): 95–110.

Grypeou, E., and H. Spurling, eds. *The Exegetical Encounter between Jews and Christians in Late Antiquity*. Jewish and Christian Perspectives 18. Leiden: Brill, 2009.

Gudbergsen, T. "God Consists of Both the Male and the Female Genders." *VT* 62 (2012): 450–53.

Guillaume, P. "The Demise of Lady Wisdom and of *Homo Sapiens*." *Theological Review* 25.2 (2004): 20–38.

Gunkel, H. *Genesis*. Macon, GA: Mercer University Press, 1997.

Gzella, H. "Zum periphrastischen Infinitiv in Genesis viii 5." *VT* 58 (2008): 469–79.

Ha, J. *Genesis 15: A Theological Compendium of Pentateuchal History*. BZAW 181. Berlin: de Gruyter, 1989.

Habel, N. C. "Canaan, Land of Promise." Pages 269–78 in Ames and Miller, *Foster Biblical Scholarship*.

Habel, N. C., and P. Trudinger, eds. *Exploring Ecological Hermeneutics*. SymS 46. Atlanta: Society of Biblical Literature, 2008.

Habel, N. C., and S. Wurst, eds. *The Earth Story in Genesis*. Sheffield, UK: Sheffield Academic, 2000.

Hamilton, V. P. *The Book of Genesis: Chapters 1–17*. Grand Rapids: Eerdmans, 1990.

———. *The Book of Genesis: Chapters 18–50*. Grand Rapids: Eerdmans, 1995.

Hamori, E. "Divine Embodiment in the Hebrew Bible." Pages 161–83 in Kamionkowski and Kim, *Bodies*.

Han, J. H. "The Role of 'an Audience' in Isaac's Blessing in Genesis 27." *PRSt* 42 (2015): 5–10.

Hankore, D. *The Abduction of Dinah: Genesis 28:10–35:15 as a Votive Narrative*. Cambridge: Clarke, 2013.

Hanna, W., and J. P. Norris. *The Patriarchs*. London: Cassell, 1879.

Harland, P. J. *The Value of Human Life: A Study of the Story of the Flood (Genesis 6–9)*. VTSup 64. Leiden: Brill, 1996.

———. "Vertical or Horizontal: The Sin of Babel." *VT* 48 (1998): 515–33.

Harrison, P. "Subduing the Earth." *JR* 76 (1999): 86–109.

Hart, I. "Genesis 1:1–2:3 as a Prologue to the Book of Genesis." *TynBul* 46 (1995): 315–36.

Hartmann, B. "'Es gibt keine Kraft und keine Macht ausser bei Gott.'" *Oudtestamentische Studiën* 14 (1965): 115–21.

Havea, J. "Whoring Dinah." Pages 172–84 in Bergen and Siedlecki, *Voyages in Uncharted Waters*.

Hawking, S. *A Brief History of Time*. New York: Bantam, 1988.

Hayes, E. R., and K. Vermeulen, eds. *Doubling and Duplicating in the Book of Genesis: Literary and Stylistic Approaches to the Text*. Winona Lake, IN: Eisenbrauns, 2016.

Haynes, S. R. *Noah's Curse: The Biblical Justification of American Slavery*. Oxford: Oxford University Press, 2002.

Hays, C. B. *Hidden Riches*. Louisville: Westminster John Knox, 2014.

Hayward, C. T. R. *See* Jerome.

Heard, R. C. *Dynamics of Diselection: Ambiguity in Genesis 12–36 and Ethnic Boundaries in Post-Exilic Judah*. SemeiaSt 39. Atlanta: Society of Biblical Literature, 2001.

———. "On the Road to Paran." *Int* 68 (2014): 270–85.

———. "What Does the Mob Want Lot to Do in Genesis 19:9?" *HebS* 51 (2010): 95–105.

Heffelfinger, K. M. "From Bane to Blessing." *JSOT* 40 (2016): 297–321.

Helmer, C., and C. T. Higbe, eds. *The Multivalence of Biblical Texts and Theological Meanings*. SymS 37. Atlanta: Society of Biblical Literature, 2006.

Helyer, L. R. "The Separation of Abraham and Lot." *JSOT* 26 (1983): 77–88.

Hempel, C., and J. M. Lieu, eds. *Biblical Traditions in Transmission: Essays in Honour of Michael A. Knibb*. JSJSup 111. Leiden: Brill, 2006.

Hendel, R. S. "Cultural Memory." Pages 28–46 in Hendel, *Reading Genesis*.

———. "Genesis 1–11 and Its Mesopotamian Problem." Pages 23–36 in Gruen, *Cultural Borrowings*.

———. "A Hasmonean Edition of MT Genesis?" *Hebrew Bible and Ancient Israel* 1 (2012): 448–64.

———. "Historical Context." Pages 49–81 in Evans, *Book of Genesis*.

———. "Leitwort Style and Literary Structure in the J Primeval Narrative." Pages 93–109 in Dolansky, *Sacred History, Sacred Literature*.

———. "The Nephilim Were on the Earth." Pages 11–34 in Auffarth and Stuckenbruck, *Fall of the Angels*.

———. "Other Edens." Pages 185–89 in Schloen, *Exploring the Long Durée*.

———. "The Poetics of Myth in Genesis." Pages 157–70 in Breslauer, *Seductiveness of Jewish Myth*.

———, ed. *Reading Genesis: Ten Methods*. Cambridge: Cambridge University Press, 2010.

———. *The Text of Genesis 1–11: Textual Studies and Critical Edition*. New York: Oxford University Press, 1998.

Hendel, R. S., C. Kronfeld, and I. Pardes. "Gender and Sexuality." Pages 71–91 in Hendel, *Reading Genesis*.

Hepner, G. "Abraham's Incestuous Marriage with Sarah." *VT* 53 (2003): 143–55.

Hermanns, W. *Einstein and the Poet*. Brookline Village, MA: Branden, 1983.

Herring, S. I. "A 'Transubstantiated' Humanity." *VT* 58 (2008): 480–94.

Heschel, A. *The Sabbath*. Repr., New York: Farrar, 1984.

Hessel, D., and L. Rasmussen, eds. *Earth Habitat: Eco-Justice and the Church's Response*. Minneapolis: Fortress, 2001.

Hick, J. *Evil and the God of Love*. London: Macmillan, 1966.

Hiebert, T. "Babel: Babble or Blueprint?" Pages 127–45 in Alston and Welker, *Reformed Theology*.

———. "The Tower of Babel and the Origin of the World's Cultures." *JBL* 126 (2007): 29–58.

Hieke, T. *Die Genealogien der Genesis*. Freiburg: Herder, 2003.

———. "Die Völkertafel von Genesis 10." Pages 23–40 in Renger and Toral-Niehoff, *Genealogie und Migrationsmythen*.

Hilbrands, W. "Die Länge der Schöpfungstage." *BN* 149 (2011): 3–12.

Hilhorst, T. "Abel's Speaking in Hebrews 11:4 and 12:24." Pages 119–27 in Luttikhuizen, *Eve's Children*.

Hock, A. "From Babel to the New Jerusalem." *Biblica* 89 (2008): 109–18.

Hoffman, Y. "The First Creation Story." Pages 32–53 in Reventlow and Hoffman, *Creation*.

Hoffmann, H. W. "Die Afformativkonjugation mit präfigiertem waw in der Genesis." Pages 75–78 in Beck and Schorn, *Auf dem Weg zur Endgestalt*.

Hoffmeier, J. K., and A. R. Millard, eds. *The Future of Biblical Archaeology: Reassessing Methodologies and Assumptions*. Grand Rapids: Eerdmans, 2004.

Holloway, S. W. "What Ship Goes There?" *ZAW* 103 (1991): 328–55.

Holmgren, F. C. "Looking Back on Abraham's Encounter with a Canaanite King." *CurTM* 37 (2010): 366–77.

Holmstedt, R. "The Restrictive Syntax of Genesis i 1." *VT* 68 (2008): 56–67.

Hom, M. K. Y. H. ". . . A Mighty Hunter before YHWH." *VT* 60 (2010): 63–68.

Horn, C. "Genesis 21:8–21." *Int* 68 (2014): 308–11.

Houston, W. J. "Sex or Violence." Pages 140–51 in MacDonald, *Genesis and Christian Theology*.

Howard, C. B. R. "Animal Speech as Revelation in Genesis 3 and Numbers 22." Pages 21–29 in Habel and Trudinger, *Exploring Ecological Hermeneutics*.

Howell, B. "God's White Flag?" *Southeastern Theological Review* 1 (2010): 29–46.

Huddlestun, J. R. "Divestiture, Deception, and Demotion." *JSOT* 98 (2002): 47–62.

Hudson, D. M. "From Chaos to Cosmos." *ZAW* 108 (1996): 87–97.

Huffmon, H. B. "The Treaty Background of Hebrew *Yādaʿ*." *BASOR* 181 (1966): 31–37.

Humphreys, W. L. *Joseph and His Family: A Literary Study*. Studies on Personalities of the Old Testament. Columbia: University of South Carolina Press, 1988.

Hunt, M. "The Two Daughters of Lot." *Lutheran Theological Journal* 47 (2013): 173–86.

Hurowitz, V. A. "The Genesis of Genesis." *BRev* 21.1 (2005): 36–48, 52–54.

———. "In Search of Resen." Pages 511–24 in C. Cohen, *Birkat Shalom*.

———. "*kæsæp ʿober lassoḇer*." *ZAW* 108 (1996): 12–19.

———. "Who Lost an Earring?" *CBQ* 62 (2000): 28–32.

Hutzli, J. "Interventions présumées des scribes concernant le motif de l'arbre sacré dans le Pentateuque." *Sem* 26 (2014): 313–31.

———. "The Procreation of Seth by Adam." *Sem* 54 (2012): 147–62.

Hwang, Y. "Eschatology in Genesis 15:6." *HS* 55 (2014): 19–41.

Hyman, R. T. "Final Judgment." *JBQ* 28 (2000): 93–101.

Ibn Ezra, A. ben Meir. *Commentary on the Pentateuch: Genesis (Bereshit)*. Translated and annotated by H. N. Strickman and A. M. Silver. New York: Menorah, 1988.

Isaak, J. M., ed. *The Old Testament in the Life of God's People: Essays in Honor of Elmer A. Martens*. Winona Lake, IN: Eisenbrauns, 2009.

Jacobs, A. *A Theology of Reading: The Hermeneutics of Love*. Boulder: Westview, 2001.

Jacobs, J. "Willing Obedience with Doubts." *VT* 60 (2010): 546–59.

Jacobs, M. *Gender, Power, and Persuasion: The Genesis Narratives and Contemporary Portraits*. Grand Rapids: Baker Academic, 2007.

———. "Love, Honor, and Violence." Pages 11–35 in Kirk-Duggan, *Pregnant Passion*.

Jacobsen, T. *The Harps That Once . . . : Sumerian Poetry in Translation*. New Haven: Yale University Press, 1987.

———. *The Sumerian King List*. Chicago: University of Chicago Press, 1939.

Janssen, J. M. A. "Egyptological Remarks on *The Story of Joseph in Genesis*." *Jaarbericht van het Vooraziatisch-Egyptisch Genootchap* 14 (1955–56): 63–72.

Jeremiah, A. "Reclaiming 'Her' Right." *Bangalore Theological Forum* 38 (2006): 145–56.

Jeremias, J. "Gen. 20–22 als theologisches Programm." Pages 59–73 in Beck and Schorn, *Auf dem Weg zur Endgestalt*.

Jericke, D. *Die Ortsangaben im Buch Genesis: Ein historisch-typographischer und literarisch-topographischer Kommentar*. Göttingen: Vandenhoeck & Ruprecht, 2013.

Jerome. *Hebrew Questions on Genesis*. Edited by C. T. R. Hayward. Oxford: Clarendon, 1995.

Johnson, J. "Genesis 1:26–28." *Int* 59 (2005): 176–78.

Jónsson, G. A. *The Image of God: Genesis 1:26-28 in a Century of Old Testament Research*. Lund: Almqvist, 1988.

Joosten, J. "Biblical Rhetoric as Illustrated by Judah's Speech in Genesis 44:18–34." *JSOT* 41 (2016): 15–30.

———. "Que s'est-il passé au jardin d'Eden?" *RevScRel* 86 (2012): 493–501.

Jørstad, M. "The Ground That Opened Its Mouth." *JBL* 135 (2016): 705–15.

Joseph, A. L. "Understanding Genesis 34:2." *VT* 66 (2016): 663–68.

Kahl, B. "Fratricide and Ecocide." Pages 53–68 in Hessel and Rasmussen, *Earth Habitat*.

Kalimi, I. "'Go, I Beg You, Take Your Beloved Son and Slay Him.'" *Review of Rabbinic Judaism* 13 (2010): 1–29.

———. "The Land of Moriah." *HTR* 83 (1990): 345–62.

Kaminski, C. M. "Beautiful Women or 'False Judgment'?" *JSOT* 32 (2008): 457–73.

———. *From Noah to Israel: Realization of the Primaeval Blessing after the Flood*. JSOTSup 413. London: T&T Clark, 2004.

Kaminsky, J. S. *Yet I Loved Jacob: Reclaiming the Biblical Concept of Election*. Nashville: Abingdon, 2007.

Kamionkowski, S. T., and W. Kim, eds. *Bodies, Embodiment, and Theology of the Hebrew Bible*. LHBOTS 465. New York: T&T Clark, 2010.

Kant, I. "The Conflict of the Faculties." Pages 233–327 in Kant, *Religion and Rational Theology.*

———. *Religion and Rational Theology*. Translated and edited by A. W. Wood and G. di Giovanni. Cambridge: Cambridge University Press, 1996.

Kant, L. H. "Arguing with God and *Tiqqun Olam*." *LTQ* 40 (2005): 203–19.

———. "Some Restorative Thoughts on an Agonizing Text." *LTQ* 38 (2003): 77–109, 161–94.

Karrer-Grube, C., et al., eds. *Sprachen-Bilder-Klänge: Dimensionen der Theologie im Alten Testament und in seinem Umfeld; Festschrift für Rüdiger Bartelmus zu seinem 65. Geburtstag*. Alter Orient und Altes Testament 3590. Münster: Ugarit-Verlag, 2009.

Kawashima, R. S. "Sources and Redaction." Pages 47–70 in Hendel, *Reading Genesis*.

Keel, O. *The Song of Songs*. CC. Minneapolis: Fortress, 1994.

Keel, O., and S. Schroer. *Creation: Biblical Theologies in the Context of the Ancient Near East*. Winona Lake, IN: Eisenbrauns, 2015.

Keil, C. F., and F. Delitzsch. *The Pentateuch*. Biblical Commentary on the Old Testament. Edinburgh: T&T Clark, 1885.

Keiser, T. A. "The Divine Plural." *JSOT* 34 (2009): 131–46.

Keiter, S. T. "Noah and the Dove." *JBQ* 40 (2012): 261–64.

Kelso, James L. *The Excavation of Bethel (1934–1960): Joint Expedition of the Pittsburgh Theological Seminary and the American School of Oriental Research in Jerusalem*. AASOR 39. Cambridge, MA: ASOR, 1968.

Kelso, Julie-Anne. "Reading the Silence of Women in Genesis 34." Pages 85–109 in Conrad and Boer, *Redirected Travel*.

Kidner, Derek. *Genesis: An Introduction and Commentary*. TOTC. Leicester, UK: Inter-Varsity; Downers Grove, IL: InterVarsity, 1967.

Kierkegaard, Søren. *See* De Silentio.

Kim, D. "The Structure of Genesis 38." *VT* 62 (2012): 550–60.

Kim, H. C. P. "Reading the Joseph Story (Genesis 37–50) as a Diaspora Narrative." *CBQ* 75 (2013): 219–38.

Kimchi. *See* Qimchi.

Kirk-Duggan, C. A. "Characterizations, Comedy, and Catastrophe: Divine/Human Relations, Emotions, and Rules of Law." Pages 221–46 in Brenner, Lee, and Yee, *Genesis*.

———, ed. *Pregnant Passion: Gender, Sex, and Violence in the Bible*. SemeiaSt 44. Atlanta: Society of Biblical Literature, 2003.

Kissling, P. J. "The Rainbow in Genesis 9:12–17." *Stone-Campbell Journal* 4 (2001): 249–61.

Klein, D. A. "Who Counted Righteousness to Whom?" *JBQ* 36 (2008): 28–32.

Klopfenstein, M. A. "'Und siehe, es war sehr gut!'" Pages 56–74 in Mathys, *Ebenbild Gottes*.

Knafl, A. K. *Forming God: Divine Anthropomorphism in the Pentateuch*. Siphrut 12. Winona Lake, IN: Eisenbrauns, 2014.

Knohl, I. "Nimrod, Son of Cush." Pages 45–52 in C. Cohen, *Birkat Shalom*.

Knust, J. "Who's Afraid of Canaan's Curse?" *BibInt* 22 (2014): 388–413.

Koenen, K. "Wer sieht wen?" *VT* 38 (1988): 468–74.

Köhler, L. *Theologie des Alten Testaments*. 2nd ed. Tübingen: Mohr, 1947.

Konkel, M. "'Und siehe, es war sehr gut.'" *TGl* 99 (2009): 588–604.

Kotzé, Z. "An Interpretation of *kswt ʿynym* in Genesis 20:16." *JSem* 20 (2011): 487–96.

Kozlova, E. E. "Abraham's Burial." *JSOT* 42 (2017): 177–97.

Kraus, W., et al., eds. *Die Septuaginta—Text, Wirkung, Rezeption. 4. Internationale Fachtagung veranstaltet von Septuaginta Deutsch (LXX.D), Wuppertal 19.-22. Juli 2012*. WUNT 325. Tübingen: Mohr Siebeck, 2014.

Krause, D. "The One Who Comes Unbinding the Blessing of Judah." Pages 141–53 in J. Sanders and Evans, *Early Christian Interpretation of the Scriptures of Israel*.

Kreider, G. R. "The Flood Is as Bad as It Gets." *BSac* 171 (2014): 418–39.

Krueger, P. "Etiology or Obligation: Genesis 2:24 Reconsidered in the Light of Text Linguistics." Pages 35–47 in Augustin and Niemann, *Thinking Towards New Horizons*.

Krüger, T. "Genesis 1:1–2:3 and the Development of the Pentateuch." Pages 125–38 in Dozeman, *Pentateuch*.

———. "Schöpfung und Sabbat in Genesis 2,1–3." Pages 155–69 in Karrer-Grube, *Sprachen–Bilder–Klänge*.

———. "Sündenfall?" Pages 95–109 in Riedweg and Schmid, *Beyond Eden*.

Kruschwitz, J. "The Type-Scene Connection between Genesis 38 and the Joseph Story." *JSOT* 36 (2012): 383–410.

Kundert, L. *Die Opferung/Bindung Isaaks*. 2 vols. Neukirchen: Neukirchener Verlag, 1998.

Kuruvilla, A. "The *Akedah* (Genesis 22)." *JETS* 55 (2012): 489–508.

LaCocque, A. "About the 'Aqedah' in Genesis 22: A Response to Laurence A. Kant." *LTQ* 40 (2005): 191–201.

———. "Whatever Happened in the Valley of Shinar?" *JBL* 128 (2009): 29–41.

Ladoceur, P. "Evolution and Genesis 2–3." *St. Vladimir's Theological Quarterly* 57 (2013): 135–76.

Laing, R. D. *The Politics of the Family and Other Essays*. Repr., New York: Pantheon, 1971.

Lambden, S. N. "From Fig Leaves to Fingernails." Pages 74–90 in Morris and Sawyer, *Walk in the Garden*.

Lambert, W. G., and A. R. Millard. *Atra-ḫasīs: The Babylonian Story of the Flood*. Oxford: Clarendon, 1969.

Lanckau, J. "Gottliche Reue und menschlicher Trost." Pages 89–130 in Fieger and Lanckau, *Erschaffung und Zerstörung der Schöpfung*.

Landes, G. M. "Creation Tradition in Proverbs 8:22–31 and Genesis 1." Pages 279–93 in Bream, *A Light unto My Path*.

Lanfer, P. T. *Remembering Eden: The Reception History of Genesis 3:22–24*. Oxford: Oxford University Press, 2012.

Lang, B. "Three Philosophers in Paradise." *SJOT* 28 (2014): 298–314.

Lapsley, J. E. "The Voice of Rachel." Pages 233–48 in Brenner, *Genesis*.

Lawrence, L. L., and M. I. Aguilar, eds. *Anthropology and Biblical Studies: Avenues of Approach*. Leiden: Deo, 2004.

Leder, A. C. "Bound to the Altar: The Isaac of Genesis 22:1–19." *CTJ* 51 (2016): 283–96.

Lemaire, A., ed. *Congress Volume Leiden 2004*. VTSup 109. Leiden: Brill, 2006.

———, ed. *Congress Volume Ljubljana 2007: Nineteenth Congress of the International Organization for the Study of the Old Testament, 2007, Ljubljana, Slovenia*. VTSup 133. Leiden: Brill, 2010.

Lemche, N. P. "Is It Still Possible to Write a History of Ancient Israel?" *SJOT* 8 (1994): 165–90.

LeMon, J. M., and K. H. Richards, eds. *Method Matters: Essays on the Interpretation of the Hebrew Bible in Honor of David L. Petersen*. Sources for Biblical Study 56. Atlanta: Society of Biblical Literature, 2009.

Letellier, R. I. *Day in Mamre, Night in Sodom: Abraham and Lot in Genesis 18 and 19*. BibInt 10. Leiden: Brill, 1995.

Levenson, J. D. *The Death and Resurrection of the Beloved Son: The Transformation of Child Sacrifice in Judaism and Christianity*. New Haven: Yale University Press, 1993.

———. *Inheriting Abraham: The Legacy of the Patriarch in Judaism, Christianity, and Islam*. Princeton: Princeton University Press, 2012.

Levin, C. "Jahwe und Abraham im Dialog." Pages 237–57 in Witte, *Gott und Mensch im Dialog*.

Levin, Y. "Nimrod the Mighty, King of Kish, King of Sumer and Akkad." *VT* 52 (2002): 350–66.

———. "Understanding Biblical Genealogies." *CurBS* 9 (2001): 11–46.

Levison, J. R., and P. Pope-Levison, eds. *Return to Babel: Global Perspectives on the Bible*. Louisville: Westminster John Knox, 1999.

Lewis, M. "'You Have to Stand on Crooked and Cut Straight.'" Pages 13–18 in Sheerattan-Bisnauth, *Righting Her Story*.

L'Hour, J. "*Ré'shît* et *beré'shît* encore et toujours." *Biblica* 92 (2010): 50–65.

Lichtenstein, M. "The Fearsome Sword of Genesis 3:24." *JBL* 134 (2015): 53–57.

Lim, D. W. "A Study of the Repetition Found in Genesis 21:8–21 and 22:1–19." *Korea Journal of Christian Studies* 25 (2002): 47–58.

———. "A Study on the Re-canonicity of Genesis Chapter 38." *Korea Journal of Christian Studies* 36 (2004): 5–20.

Lim, J. T. K. "Did the Scholar(s) Get It Right?" Pages 69–79 in Boer, *One Who Reads May Run*.

———. "Explication of an Exegetical Enigma in Genesis 1:1–3." *AsJT* 16 (2002): 301–14.

Lipton, D. “The Limits of Intercession.” Pages 25–41 in Lipton, *Universalism and Particularism.*

———. *Revisions of the Night: Politics and Promise in the Patriarchal Dramas of Genesis.* JSOTSup 288. Sheffield, UK: Sheffield Academic, 1999.

———, ed. *Universalism and Particularism at Sodom and Gomorrah: Essays in Memory of Ron Pirson.* Ancient Israel and Its Literature 11. Atlanta: Society of Biblical Literature, 2012.

Loader, W. “Genesis 3:16–19 LXX in Reception.” Pages 381–91 in Kraus, *Die Septuaginta.*

Lockwood, P. F. “Disentangled from the Web of Deceit: Sin and Salvation in the Story of Shechem and Dinah (Genesis 34).” Pages 20–40 in Reid and Worthing, *Sin and Salvation.*

Lohr, J. N. “Righteous Abel, Wicked Cain.” *CBQ* 71 (2009): 485–96.

———. “Sexual Desire?” *JBL* 130 (2011): 227–46.

Loiseau, A.-F. “Gen. 4,7.” *ZAW* 125 (2013): 479–82.

Longacre, R. E. *Joseph: A Story of Divine Providence; A Text Theoretical and Textlinguistic Analysis of Genesis 37 and 39–48.* Winona Lake, IN: Eisenbrauns, 1989.

Louth, A., ed. *Genesis 1–11.* ACCS 1. Downers Grove, IL: InterVarsity, 2001.

Lowery, D. D. *Toward a Poetics of Genesis 1–11: Reading Genesis 4:17–22 in Its Ancient Near Eastern Context.* Winona Lake, IN: Eisenbrauns, 2013.

Luc, A. “Like One of Us?” *JAB* 1 (1999): 219–23.

Luciani, D. “Gn 4,17 (la première ville) et ses commentaires.” *Nouvelle revue théologique* 137 (2015): 21–31.

Luger, S. “Flood, Salt and Sacrifice.” *JBQ* 38 (2010): 124–26.

Lundbom, J. R. “Parataxis, Rhetorical Structure, and the Dialogue over Sodom in Genesis 18.” Pages 136–45 in Davies and Clines, *World of Genesis.*

Luther, M. *Lectures on Genesis.* 8 vols. St. Louis: Concordia, 1958–66.

Luttikhuizen, G. P., ed. *The Creation of Man and Woman: Interpretations of the Biblical Narratives in Jewish and Christian Traditions.* TBN 3. Leiden: Brill, 2000.

———. *Eve’s Children: The Biblical Stories Retold and Interpreted in Jewish and Christian Traditions.* TBN 5. Leiden: Brill, 2003.

Luzzatto, S. D. *Genesis.* Northvale, NJ: Aronson, 1998.

Lyke, L. L. “Where Does ‘the Boy’ Belong?” *CBQ* 56 (1994): 637–48.

Lyons, W. J. *Canon and Exegesis: Canonical Praxis and the Sodom Narrative.* JSOT Sup 352. London: Sheffield Academic, 2002.

———. “The Eternal Liminality of Lot.” Pages 3–23 in Lipton, *Universalism and Particularism.*

Macchi, J.-D. *Israël et ses tribus selon Genèse 49.* Orbis Biblicus et Orientalis 171. Göttingen: Vandenhoeck & Ruprecht, 1999.

MacDonald, N. “Did God Choose the Patriarchs? Reading for Election in the Book of Genesis.” Pages 245–66 in MacDonald, Elliott, and Macaskill, *Genesis and Christian Theology.*

———. "Driving a Hard Bargain." Pages 79–96 in Lawrence and Aguilar, *Anthropology and Biblical Studies.*

———. "Hospitality and Hostility." Pages 179–89 in Lipton, *Universalism and Particularism.*

———. "The *Imago Dei* and Election." *International Journal of Systematic Theology* 10 (2008): 303–27.

———. "Listening to Abraham—Listening to Yhwh: Divine Justice and Mercy in Genesis 18:16–33." *CBQ* 66 (2004): 25–43.

———. "A Text in Search of Context." Pages 3–16 in Baer and Gordon, *Leshon Limmudim.*

MacDonald, N., M. W. Elliott, and G. Macaskill, eds. *Genesis and Christian Theology.* Grand Rapids: Eerdmans, 2012.

Madueme, H., and M. Reeves, eds. *Adam, the Fall, and Original Sin: Theological, Biblical, and Scientific Perspectives.* Grand Rapids: Baker Academic, 2014.

Magonet, J. *Bible Lives.* London: SCM, 1992.

———. "The Themes of Genesis 2–3." Pages 39–46 in Morris and Sawyer, *Walk in the Garden.*

Maher, M., trans. and ed. *Targum Pseudo-Jonathan: Genesis.* Vol. 1B of *The Aramaic Bible.* Collegeville, MN: Liturgical Press, 1992.

Malena, S., and D. Miano, eds. *Milk and Honey: Essays on Ancient Israel and the Bible in Appreciation of the Judaic Studies Program at the University of California, San Diego.* Winona Lake, IN: Eisenbrauns, 2007.

Mallen, P. "Genesis in Luke-Acts." Pages 60–82 in Moyise and Menken, *Genesis in the New Testament.*

Marin i Tourné, J. R. "'Demanaré comptes de la vostra sang': La sang i la vida humana en Gn 9,1–7." Pages 33–65 in Puig i Tàrrech, *La violència en la Bíblia.*

Marlowe, W. C. "The Sin of Shinar." *EuroJTh* 20 (2011): 29–39.

Marsden, R. "Cain's Face, and Other Problems: The Legacy of the Earliest English Bible Translations." *Reformation* 1 (1996): 29–51.

Martin, T. W. "The Covenant of Circumcision." *JBL* 122 (2003): 111–25.

Marwil, D. J. "A Soothing Savor." *JBQ* 42 (2014): 169–72.

Masenya, M. "A Bosadi (Womanhood) Reading of Genesis 16." *OTE* 11 (1998): 271–87.

Mason, S. D. "Another Flood?" *JSOT* 32 (2007): 177–98.

Mastin, B. A. "What Do *Miqneh* and *Bohema* Mean in Genesis xxxiv 23, xxxvi 6; Numbers xxxi 9, xxxii 26?" *VT* 45 (1995): 491–515.

Mathews, J. G. *Melchizedek's Alternative Priestly Order: A Compositional Analysis of Genesis 14:18–20 and Its Echoes throughout the Tanak.* BBRSup 8. Winona Lake, IN: Eisenbrauns, 2013.

Mathys, H.-P., ed. *Ebenbild Gottes—Herrscher über die Welt: Studien zur Würde und Auftrag des Menschen.* Biblical-Theologische Studien 33. Neukirchen: Neukirchener Verlag, 1998.

Matthews, V. H. "The Anthropology of Clothing in the Joseph Narrative." *JSOT* 65 (1995): 25–36.

Matthews, V. H., and D. C. Benjamin. *Old Testament Parallels: Laws and Stories from the Ancient Near East*. Mahwah, NJ: Paulist Press, 1991.

Mays, J. L. "Now I Know." Pages 172–89 in Alston and Welker, *Reformed Theology*.

Mbuvi, A. B. *Belonging in Genesis: Biblical Israel and the Politics of Identity Formation*. Waco: Baylor University Press, 2016.

Mbuwayesango, D. R. "Childlessness and Woman-to-Woman Relationships in Genesis and in African Patriarcal [*sic*] Society." *Semeia* 78 (1997): 27–36.

McBride, S. D. "Divine Protocol." Pages 3–41 in Brown and McBride, *God Who Creates*.

McCarthy, C. *The Tiqqune Sopherim and Other Theological Corrections in the Masoretic Text of the Old Testament*. Orbis Biblicus et Orientalis 36. Göttingen: Vandenhoeck & Ruprecht, 1981.

McConville, J. G., and K. Möller, eds. *Reading the Law: Studies in Honour of Gordon J. Wenham*. LHBOTS 461. New York: T&T Clark, 2007.

McDowell, C. L. *The Image of God in the Garden of Eden: The Creation of Humankind in Genesis 2:5–3:24 in Light of the Mīs Pî Pīt Pî and Wpt-r Rituals of Mesopotamia and Ancient Egypt*. Siphrut 15. Winona Lake, IN: Eisenbrauns, 2015.

McKay, H. A. "Confronting Redundancy as Middle Manager and Wife." *Semeia* 37 (1999): 215–31.

McKinlay, J. E. "Who's/Whose Sarah?" Pages 131–43 in Conrad and Boer, *Redirected Travel*.

McLaughlin, R. P. "A Meatless Dominion." *Biblical Theology Bulletin* 47 (2017): 144–54.

McNamara, M., trans. and ed. *Targum Neofiti: Genesis*. Vol. 1A of *The Aramaic Bible*. Collegeville, MN: Liturgical Press, 1991.

Menken, M. J. J. "Genesis in John's Gospel and 1 John." Pages 83–98 in Moyise and Menken, *Genesis in the New Testament*.

Mettinger, T. N. D. *The Eden Narrative: A Literary and Religio-Historical Study of Genesis 2–3*. Winona Lake, IN: Eisenbrauns, 2007.

Meyers, C. L. *Discovering Eve: Ancient Israelite Women in Context*. New York: Oxford University Press, 1988.

———. "Food and the First Family." Pages 137–57 in Evans, *Book of Genesis*.

———. "Gender Roles and Genesis 3.16 Revisited." Pages 118–41 in Brenner, *Feminist Companion to Genesis*.

———. *Rediscovering Eve: Ancient Israelite Women in Context*. New York: Oxford University Press, 2013.

Middleton, J. R. "The Liberating Image." *Christian Scholars Review* 24 (1994): 8–25.

———. *The Liberating Image: The Imago Dei in Genesis 1*. Grand Rapids: Brazos, 2005.

Míguez-Bonino, J. "Genesis 11:1–9." Pages 13–16 in Levison and Pope-Levison, *Return to Babel*.

Millard, A. R., and D. J. Wiseman, eds. *Essays on the Patriarchal Narratives*. Leicester, UK: Inter-Varsity, 1980.

Miller, A. *The Untouched Key*. Repr., New York: Anchor, 1991.

Miller, J. M. "In the 'Image' and 'Likeness' of God." *JBL* 91 (1972): 289–304.

Miller, K. B. *Perspectives on an Evolving Creation*. Grand Rapids: Eerdmans, 2003.

Miller, P. D. "Syntax and Theology in Genesis xii 3a." *VT* 34 (1984): 472–76.

Miller, T. "Relationships, Haggling, and Injustice in Genesis 18." *Journal of Theta Alpha Kappa* 36.2 (2012): 29–38.

Mincato, R. "A Questão Do 'Subjugai a Terra' em *Gn* 1,28." *Teocomunicação* 39 (2009): 366–77.

Moberly, R. W. L. "Did the Interpreters Get It Right?" *JTS* 59 (2008): 22–40.

———. "How Should One Read the Early Chapters of Genesis?" Pages 5–21 in Barton and Wilkinson, *Reading Genesis after Darwin*.

———. "The Mark of Cain." *HTR* 100 (2007): 11–28.

———. "On Interpreting the Mind of God." Pages 44–66 in J. Wagner, *Word Leaps the Gap*.

———. "Why Did Noah Send Out a Raven?" *VT* 50 (2000): 345–56.

Möller, K. "Images of God and Creation in Genesis 1–2." Pages 3–29 in Grant, *God of Faithfulness*.

Moltmann, J. *God in Creation: A New Theology of Creation and the Spirit*. London: SCM, 1985.

Montgomery, J. A. *Arabia and the Bible*. Repr., New York: Ktav, 1969.

Morales, L. M. "Crouching Demon, Hidden Lamb." *BT* 63 (2012): 185–91.

Morris, P., and D. Sawyer, eds. *A Walk in the Garden: Biblical, Iconographical and Literary Images of Eden*. JSOTSup 136. Sheffield, UK: Sheffield Academic, 1992.

Morschauser, S. "Campaigning on Less Than a Shoe-String." *JSOT* 38 (2013): 127–44.

———. "'Hospitality,' Hostiles and Hostages." *JSOT* 27 (2003): 461–85.

Moskala, J. "Interpretation of *Bereʾšît* in the Context of Genesis 1:1–3." *AUSS* 49 (2011): 33–44.

Moyaert, M. "A 'Babelish' World." *Horizons* 36 (2009): 215–34.

Moyise, S., and M. J. J. Menken, eds. *Genesis in the New Testament*. Library of New Testament Studies 466. London: Bloomsbury, 2012.

Mozeson, I. E. "Could Pre-Hebrew Be the *Safa Ahat* of Genesis 11:1?" *JBQ* 38 (2010): 55–61.

Mulzac, K. D. "Genesis 9:1–7." *JATS* 12 (2001): 65–77.

Musculus, W. *In Mosis Genesim plenissimi commentarii*. Basel: Johannes Herwagen, 1565.

Neusner, J., trans. and ed. *Genesis Rabbah*. 3 vols. Atlanta: Scholars Press, 1985.

———, ed. *The Talmud of the Land of Israel*. Chicago: University of Chicago Press, 1991.

Neville, R. "Differentiation in Genesis 1." *JBL* 130 (2011): 209–26.

Newman, R. C. "The Ancient Exegesis of Genesis 6:2, 4." *Grace Theological Journal* 5 (1984): 18–36.

Newsom, C. A. "Common Ground." Pages 60–72 in Habel and Wurst, *Earth Story in Genesis*.

Ng, A. H. S. "Death and the Double." Pages 107–13 in Sabbath, *Sacred Tropes*.

Nicholson, E. W. *The Pentateuch in the Twentieth Century: The Legacy of Julius Wellhausen*. Oxford: Oxford University Press, 1998.

Nicol, G. G. "The Chronology of Genesis." *VT* 46 (1996): 330–38.

———. "The Narrative Structure and Interpretation of Genesis xxvi 1–33." *VT* 46 (1996): 339–60.

Nicolas of Lyra. *Postilla super totam Bibliam*. Vol. 1. Repr., Venice: Ottaviano Scoto, 1488.

Niehaus, J. J. "God's Covenant with Abraham." *JETS* 56 (2013): 249–71.

———. "In the Wind of the Storm." *VT* 44 (1994): 263–67.

Nielsen, K. "To See and to Be Seen." *SJOT* 27 (2013): 22–31.

Niskanen, P. "The Poetics of Adam." *JBL* 128 (2009): 417–36.

Nissinen, M. *Homoeroticism in the Biblical World: A Historical Perspective*. Minneapolis: Fortress, 1998.

Noah, M. M., trans. *The Book of Jasher Referred to in Joshua and Second Samuel*. New York: Noah & Gould, 1840.

Noble, P. R. "A 'Balanced' Reading of the Rape of Dinah: Some Exegetical and Methodological Observations." *BibInt* 4 (1996): 173–204.

Noegel, S. B. "A Crux and a Taunt." Pages 128–35 in Davies and Clines, *World of Genesis*.

Noll, K. L., and B. Schramm, eds. *Raising Up a Faithful Exegete: Essays in Honor of Richard D. Nelson*. Winona Lake, IN: Eisenbrauns, 2010.

Noort, E. "Abraham and the Nations." Pages 3–31 in Goodman, *Abraham, the Nations, and the Hagarites*.

———. "Created in the Image of the Son." Pages 33–44 in Goodman, *Abraham, the Nations, and the Hagarites*.

———. "The Creation of Light in Genesis 1:1–5." Pages 3–20 in van Kooten, *Creation of Heaven and Earth*.

———. "The Creation of Man and Woman in Biblical and Ancient Near Eastern Traditions." Pages 1–18 in Luttikhuizen, *Creation of Man and Woman*.

———. "Genesis 4:1–16." Pages 93–106 in Luttikhuizen, *Eve's Children*.

———. "The Stories of the Great Flood." Pages 1–38 in García Martínez and Luttikhuizen, *Interpretations of the Flood*.

———. "'Was ist der Mensch?'" Pages 1–22 in Beyerle, *Viele Wege zu dem Einen*.

Noort, E., and E. Tigchelaar, eds. *Sodom's Sin: Genesis 18-19 and Its Interpretations*. TBN 7. Leiden: Brill, 2004.

Novick, T. "'Almost, at Times, the Fool.'" *Prooftexts* 24 (2004): 277–90.

———. "Pain and Production in Eden." *VT* 58 (2008): 235–44.

Nwaoru, E. O. "Genesis 1,28." *BN* 153 (2012): 3–17.

Oberhänsli-Widmer, G. *Bilder vom Bösen im Judentum: Von der Hebräischen Bibel inspiriert in jüdischer Literatur weitergedacht*. Neukirchen: Neukirchener Verlag, 2013.

Oblath, M. "'To Sleep, Perchance to Dream . . . .'" *JSOT* 95 (2001): 117–26.

Oduyọye, M. *The Sons of God and the Daughters of Men: An Afro-Asiatic Interpretation of Genesis 1–11*. Maryknoll, NY: Orbis Books, 1984.

Oecolampadius, J. *An Exposition of Genesis* [chapters 1–3]. Milwaukee: Marquette University Press, 2013.

Ojo, J. O. "Is Globalization a Re-enactment of One World Language in Genesis 11:1–9?" *Practical Theology* 6 (2013): 101–15.

Okoye, J. C. "Sarah and Hagar." *JSOT* 32 (2007): 163–75.

Okyere, K. "Bible, Ecology and Sustainable Development." *Ilorin Journal of Religious Studies* 1.2 (2011): 81–96.

Ollenburger, B. C. "Creation and Peace." Pages 143–58 in Isaak, *Old Testament in the Life of God's People*.

Olley, J. "Mixed Blessings for Animals." Pages 130–39 in Habel and Wurst, *Earth Story in Genesis*.

Olrik, A. "Epic Laws of Folk Narrative." Pages 129–41 in Dundes, *Study of Folklore*.

Olson, D. "Untying the Knot?" Pages 72–86 in L. Day and Pressler, *Engaging the Bible in a Gendered World*.

Origen. *Homilies on Genesis and Exodus*. Washington, DC: Catholic University of America Press, 1982.

Ortlund, G. "Image of Adam, Son of God: Genesis 5:3 and Luke 3:38 in Intercanonical Dialogue." *JETS* 57 (2014): 673–88.

Osborne, J. *Luther*. Repr., New York: New American Library, 1963.

Osborne, W. R. "Anteriority and Justification." *OTE* 25 (2012): 369–82.

Oswald, W. "Das Erstlingswerk Gottes." *ZAW* 120 (2008): 417–21.

Otto, E. "Die Paradieserzählung Genesis 2–3." Pages 167–92 in Diesel, "*Jedes Ding hat seine Zeit.*"

———. "Die Urmenschen im Paradies: Vom Ursprung des Bösen und der Freiheit." Pages 122–33 in Achenbach, *Tora in der Hebräischen Bibel*.

Ouro, R. "The Earth of Genesis 1:2." *AUSS* 35 (1998): 259–76; 37 (1999): 39–53; 38 (2000): 59–67.

———. "Linguistic and Thematic Parallels between Genesis 1 and 3." *JATS* 13 (2002): 44–54.

Palmquist, S. R., and P. M. Rudisill. "Three Perspectives on Abraham's Defense against Kant's Charge of Immoral Conduct." *JR* 89 (2009): 467–97.

Pardes, I. "Modern Literature." Pages 176–95 in Hendel, *Reading Genesis*.

Park, S. S. "Transformation and Demarcation of Jacob's 'Flocks' in Genesis 30:25–43." *CBQ* 72 (2010): 667–77.

Parker, J. F. "Blaming Eve Alone." *JBL* 132 (2013): 729–47.

Parry, D. W., et al., eds. *Qumran Cave 1 Revisited: Texts from Cave 1 Sixty Years after Their Discovery; Proceedings of the Sixth Meeting of the IOQS in Ljubljana*. STDJ 91. Leiden: Brill, 2010.

Parry, R. A. *Old Testament Story and Christian Ethics: The Rape of Dinah as a Case Study*. Milton Keynes, UK: Paternoster, 2004.

Paul, M. J. "Genesis 4:17–24." *TynBul* 47 (1996): 143–62.

Peels, E. "The World's First Murder: Violence and Justice in Genesis 4:1–16." Pages 19–39 in Fitzgerald, van Rensburg, and van Rooy, *Animosity, the Bible, and Us*.

Peels, H. G. L. "In het teken van Kaïn." *Verbum et ecclesia* 29 (2008): 172–93.

Peerbolte, L. J. L. "Man, Woman, and the Angels in 1 Cor. 11:2–16." Pages 76–92 in Luttikhuizen, *Creation of Man and Woman*.

Peery, P. "Genesis 1:1–2:3." *Int* 65 (2011): 392–94.

Peleg, Y. *Going Up and Going Down: A Key to Interpreting Jacob's Dream (Genesis 28:10–22)*. LHBOTS 609. London: Bloomsbury, 2015.

———. "Was Lot a Good Host?" Pages 129–56 in Lipton, *Universalism and Particularism*.

Pellikan, K. *Commentaria Bibliorum*. Zurich: Froschov/Froschauer, 1532–39.

Penchansky, D. "Staying the Night." Pages 77–88 in Fewell, *Reading between Texts*.

Penley, P. T. "A Historical Reading of Genesis 11:1–9." *JETS* 50 (2007): 693–714.

Pentiuc, E. "Holding Sway in Companionship." *GOTR* 56 (2011): 221–38.

Perkins, W. "An Exposition of the Creed." In vol. 1 of *The Works of That Famous and Worthy Minister of Christ in the Universitie of Cambridge, M. William Perkins*. London: Legatt, 1631.

Peter Martyr. *See* Vermigli.

Petersen, D. L. "The Genesis of Genesis." Pages 27–40 in Lemaire, *Congress Volume Ljubljana 2007*.

———. "Polities in Genesis 12–36." Pages 75–88 in Strong and Tuell, *Constituting the Community*.

Peterson, B. N. "The Sin of Sodom Revisited." *JETS* 59 (2016): 17–31.

Petit, F., ed. *La chaîne sur la Genèse*. 4 vols. Louvain: Peeters, 1991–96.

Petrovich, D. "Identifying Nimrod." *JETS* 56 (2013): 273–305.

Pfoh, E. "Genesis 4 Revisited." *SJOT* 23 (2009): 38–45.

Pfost, J. "A Literary Analysis of the Flood Story as a Semitic Type-Scene." *Studia Antiqua* 13.1 (2014): 1–22.

Phillips, T. O. "Creation, Sin and Its Curse, and the People of God." *HBT* 25 (2003): 146–60.

Pickering, J. "Divine Silence." *Scriptura* 113 (2014): 1–13.

Pirson, R. "Does Lot Know about *Yada*ʿ?" Pages 203–13 in Lipton, *Universalism and Particularism*.

———. *The Lord of the Dreams: A Semantic and Literary Analysis of Genesis 37–50*. JSOTSup 355. London: Sheffield Academic, 2002.

———. “What Is Joseph Supposed to Be?” Pages 81–92 in Brenner and van Henten, *Recycling Biblical Figures*.

Pitt-Rivers, J. *The Fate of Shechem: Or, the Politics of Sex; Essays in the Anthropology of the Mediterranean*. Cambridge: Cambridge University Press, 1977.

Pleins, J. D. *When the Great Abyss Opened: Classic and Contemporary Readings of Noah’s Flood*. Oxford: Oxford University Press, 2009.

Pobee, J. S., and B. von Wartenberg-Potter, eds. *New Eyes for Reading: Biblical and Theological Reflections by Women from the Third World*. Quezon City, Philippines: Claretian Publications, 1986.

Polak, G. G. “Poetic Style and Parallelism in the Creation Account.” Pages 2–31 in Reventlow and Hoffman, *Creation*.

Polliack, M. “Joseph’s Journey: From Trauma to Resolution.” Pages 147–74 in Brenner, Lee, and Yee, *Genesis*.

Provain, I., and M. J. Boda, eds. *Let Us Go Up to Zion: Essays in Honour of H. G. M. Williamson on the Occasion of His Sixty-Fifth Birthday*. VTSup 153. Leiden: Brill, 2012.

Puig i Tàrrech, A., ed. *La violència en la Bíblia*. Scripta biblica 9. Barcelona: Publicacions de l’Abadia de Montserrat, 2009.

Qimchi, D. [Rabbi David Kimchi = RaDaK]. *Radak on Genesis*. https://www.sefaria.org/texts.

Rabanus Maurus. “Commentariorum in Genesim Libri Quattuor.” In *PL* 107:439–670.

Radday, Y. T. “Humour in Names.” Pages 59–97 in Radday and Brenner, *On Humour*.

Radday, Y. T., and A. Brenner, eds. *On Humour and the Comic in the Hebrew Bible*. Bible and Literature 23. Sheffield, UK: Almond, 1990.

Raglan, Lord. [F. R. Somerset]. “The Hero of Tradition.” Pages 142–57 in Dundes, *Study of Folklore*.

Ramantswana, H. “Conflicts at Creation.” *OTE* 27 (2014): 553–78.

———. “Day Two of Creation.” *JSem* 22 (2013): 101–23.

———. “Humanity Not Pronounced Good.” *OTE* 26 (2013): 425–44, 804–18.

Rashi [Rabbi Shlomo Yitzḥaqi]. *Brʾšyt = Bereishis*. Rev. ed. Hoboken: Ktav, 1993.

Rashkow, I. N. “Daughters and Fathers in Genesis.” Pages 22–36 in Brenner, *Exodus to Deuteronomy*.

———. “Intertextuality, Transference, and the Reader in/of Genesis 12 and 20.” Pages 57–73 in Fewell, *Reading between Texts*.

Rathbone, M. “Unity and Scattering: Toward a Holistic Reading of Genesis 11:1-9 in the South African Context.” Pages 99–106 in Brenner, Lee, and Yee, *Genesis*.

Redford, D. B. *A Study of the Biblical Story of Joseph (Genesis 37–50)*. VTSup 20. Leiden: Brill, 1970.

Redmount, C. A. “Bitter Lives.” Pages 78–121 in Coogan, *Oxford History of the Biblical World*.

Reid, D., and M. Worthing, eds. *Sin and Salvation*. Task of Theology Today 3. Hindmarsh, Australia: ATF, 2003.

Reif, S. C. "Early Rabbinic Exegesis of Genesis 38." Pages 221–43 in Grypeou and Spurling, *Exegetical Encounter*.

Reimer, S. "The Tower of Babel." *Direction* 25 (1996): 64–72.

Reis, P. T. "What Cain Said." *JSOT* 27 (2002): 107–13.

Reiss, M. "The Melchizedek Traditions." *SJOT* 28 (2012): 259–65.

Rendsburg, G. A. "The Biblical Flood Story in Light of the Gilgameš Flood Account." Pages 115–27 in Azize and Weeks, *Gilgameš and the World of Assyria*.

———. "Israelian Hebrew Features in Genesis 49." *Maarav* 8 (1992): 161–70.

———. "Some False Leads in the Identification of Late Biblical Texts." *JBL* 121 (2002): 23–46.

Renger, A.-B., and I. Toral-Niehoff, eds. *Genealogie und Migrationsmythen im antiken Mittelmeerraum und auf der Arabischen Halbinsel*. Berlin Studies of the Ancient World 29. Berlin: Topoi, 2014.

Reno, R. R. *Genesis*. Brazos Theological Commentary on the Bible. Grand Rapids: Brazos, 2010.

Retief, C. W. "When Interpretation Traditions Speak Too Loud for Ethical Dilemmas to Be Heard." *OTE* 23 (2010): 788–803.

Reuling, H. "The Christian and the Rabbinic Adam." Pages 63–75 in Grypeou and Spurling, *Exegetical Encounter*.

Reventlow, H., and Y. Hoffman, eds. *Creation in Jewish and Christian Tradition*. JSOTSup 319. London: Sheffield Academic, 2002.

Richelle, M. "La structure littéraire de l'Histoire Primitive." *BN* 151 (2011): 3–22.

Rickett, D. "Creating an Unrighteous Outsider." *CBQ* 76 (2014): 610–33.

———. "Rethinking the Place and Purpose of Genesis 13." *JSOT* 36 (2011): 31–53.

Riecker, S. "Ein theologischer Ansatz zum Verständnis der Altarbaunotizen der Genesis." *Biblica* 87 (2006): 526–30.

Riedweg, C., and K. Schmid, eds. *Beyond Eden: The Biblical Story of Paradise (Genesis 2–3) and Its Reception History*. FAT 34. Tübingen: Mohr Siebeck, 2008.

Rindge, M. S. "Reconfiguring the Akedah and Recasting God." *JBL* 130 (2011): 755–74.

Robertson, O. P. "Current Critical Questions concerning the 'Curse of Ham.'" *JETS* 41 (1998): 177–88.

Robinson, E., and E. Smith. *Biblical Researches in Palestine and in the Adjacent Regions: Journal of Travels in the Year 1938*. 2nd ed. 3 vols. London: Murray, 1856.

Robinson, G. L. "The Wells of Beersheba." *The Biblical World* 17 (1901): 247–55.

Robinson, R. B. "The Poetry of Creation." Pages 114–24 in Ahn and S. Cook, *Thus Says the* Lord.

Rofé, A. "Defilement of Virgins in Biblical Law and the Case of Dinah." *Biblica* 86 (2005): 369–75.

Rogland, M. "Interpreting *ʾd* in Genesis 2.5–6." *JSOT* 34 (2010): 379–93.

Romanska, M. "Sarah's Gift." Pages 393–408 in Sabbath, *Sacred Tropes*.

Römer, T. "Abraham's Righteousness and Sacrifice." *Communio Viatorum* 54 (2012): 3–15.

———. "La création des hommes et leur multiplication." *Sem* 55 (2013): 147–56.

Ron, Z. "The Book of Jubilees and the Midrash on the Early Chapters of Genesis." *JBQ* 41 (2013): 143–55.

———. "The Book of Jubilees and the Midrash Part 3." *JBQ* 42 (2014): 165–68.

———. "Isaac's Personality." *JBQ* 43 (2015): 29–34.

———. "Wordplay in Genesis 2:25–3:1." *JBQ* 42 (2014): 1–7.

Rose, M. *The Evolution-Creation Struggle*. Cambridge, MA: Harvard University Press, 2015.

Rosenblatt, J. P., and J. C. Sitterson, eds. *"Not in Heaven": Coherence and Complexity in Biblical Narrative*. Bloomington: Indiana University Press, 1991.

Routledge, R. "'My Spirit' in Genesis 6.1–4." *JPT* 20 (2011): 232–51.

Rudman, D. "A Little Knowledge Is a Dangerous Thing." Pages 461–66 in Wénin, *Genesis*.

Rudolph, D. J. "Festivals in Genesis 1:14." *TynBul* 54 (2003): 23–40.

Rulon-Miller, N. "Hagar." Pages 60–89 in Davies and Clines, *World of Genesis*.

Russell, B. "A Free Man's Worship." Pages 46–57 in Russell, *Mysticism and Logic*.

———. *Mysticism and Logic and Other Essays*. Repr., London: George Allen, 1959.

Russell, S. C. "Abraham's Purchase of Ephron's Land in Anthropological Perspective." *BibInt* 21 (2013): 153–70.

Rüterswörden, U. Dominium terrae*: Studien zur Genese einer alttestamentlichen Vorstellung*. BZAW 215. Berlin: de Gruyter, 1993.

Sabbath, R. S. "Sacred Tropes." Pages 349–60 in Sabbath, *Sacred Tropes*.

———, ed. *Sacred Tropes: Tanakh, New Testament, and Qur'an as Literature and Culture*. BibInt 98. Leiden: Brill, 2009.

Sabo, P. J. "Blurred Boundaries in the Lot Story." Pages 433–44 in I. Wilson and Gersoni-Edelman, *History, Memory, Hebrew Scriptures*.

Safren, J. D. "Hospitality Compared." Pages 157–78 in Lipton, *Universalism and Particularism*.

Sakenfeld, K. D. *Just Wives? Stories of Power and Survival in the Old Testament and Today*. Louisville: Westminster John Knox, 2003.

Sanders, E. P. *Paul and Palestinian Judaism*. Philadelphia: Fortress, 1977.

Sanders, J. A., and C. A. Evans, eds. *Early Christian Interpretation of the Scriptures of Israel: Investigations and Proposals*. JSNTSup 148. Sheffield, UK: Sheffield Academic, 1997.

Sarna, N. M. *Genesis*. Philadelphia: Jewish Publication Society, 1989.

Sasson, J. M. "The Servant's Tale." *JNES* 65 (2006): 241–65.

Sawyer, J. F. A. "The Image of God, the Wisdom of Serpents and the Knowledge of Good and Evil." Pages 64–73 in Morris and Sawyer, *Walk in the Garden*.

Scarlata, M. W. *Outside of Eden: Cain in the Ancient Versions of Genesis 4:1–16*. LHBOTS 573. London: T&T Clark, 2012.

Schachter, L. "The Garden of Eden as God's First Sanctuary." *JBQ* 41 (2013): 73–77.

Scheetz, J. M. "Canon-Conscious Interpretation." *OTE* 27 (2014): 263–84.

Schellenberg, A. "Humankind as the 'Image of God.'" *TZ* 65 (2009): 97–115.

Schlimm, M. R. *From Fratricide to Forgiveness: The Language and Ethics of Anger in Genesis*. Siphrut 7. Winona Lake, IN: Eisenbrauns, 2011.

Schloen, J. D., ed. *Exploring the Long Durée: Essays in Honor of Lawrence E. Stager*. Winona Lake, IN: Eisenbrauns, 2008.

Schmid, K. "Genesis in the Pentateuch." Pages 27–50 in Evans, *Book of Genesis*.

———. "Loss of Immortality?" Pages 58–78 in Riedweg and Schmid, *Beyond Eden*.

Schmutzer, A. J. "Did the Gods Cause Abraham's Wandering?" *JSOT* 35 (2010): 149–66.

Schneider, S., and M. Seelenfreund. "Kotnot Or." *JBQ* 40 (2012): 116–24.

Schneider, T. J. *Mothers of Promise: Women in the Book of Genesis*. Grand Rapids: Baker Academic, 2008.

Scholz, S. "Through Whose Eyes? A 'Right' Reading of Genesis 34." Pages 150–71 in Brenner, *Genesis*.

———. "Was It Really Rape in Genesis 34?" Pages 182–98 in Washington, *Escaping Eden*.

Schöpflin, K. "Genesis 4,7—ausgelegt von John Steinbeck." *BN* 154 (2012): 3–28.

Schroeder, J. A. *The Book of Genesis*. Grand Rapids: Eerdmans, 2015.

Schüle, A. "'Und siehe, es war sehr gut . . . und siehe, die Erde war verdorben' (Gen. 1,31; 6,12)." *Jahrbuch für Biblische Theologie* 26 (2011): 3–28.

Schwager, R. *Must There Be Scapegoats? Violence and Redemption in the Bible*. 2nd ed. New York: Crossroad, 2000.

Schwantes, M. "'Do Not Extend Your Hand against the Child.'" Pages 101–23 in Vaage, *Subversive Scriptures*.

Schwartz, B. J. "How the Compiler of Genesis Worked." Pages 263–78 in Evans, *Book of Genesis*.

Scofield, C. J. *The Scofield Reference Bible*. New York: Oxford University Press, 1909.

Scotchmer, P. F. "Lessons from Paradise." *Evangelical Review of Theology* 28 (2004): 80–85.

Seebass, H. "Gen. 15 2b." *ZAW* 75 (1963): 317–19.

———. *Genesis*. 2 vols. Neukirchen: Neukirchener Verlag, 1996–97.

Segal, M. *The Book of Jubilees*. Leiden: Brill, 2007.

Segovia, F. F., and M. A. Tolbert, eds. *Teaching the Bible: The Discourses and Politics of Biblical Pedagogy*. Eugene, OR: Wipf & Stock, 2004.

Selnecker, N. *In Genesin*. Leipzig: Johannes Rhamba, 1569.

Sexton, J. S. "The *Imago Dei* Once Again." *JTI* 4 (2010): 187–206.

Sharon, D. M. "The Doom of Paradise: Literary Patterns in Accounts of Paradise and Mortality in the Hebrew Bible and the Ancient Near East." Pages 53–80 in Brenner, *Genesis*.

Sheerattan-Bisnauth, P., ed. *Righting Her Story: Caribbean Women Encounter the Bible Story*. Geneva: WCRC, 2011.

Shemesh, Y. "Rape Is Rape Is Rape: The Story of Dinah and Shechem (Genesis 34)." *ZAW* 119 (2007): 2–21.

———. "Vegetarian Ideology in Talmudic Literature and Traditional Biblical Exegesis." Pages 107–27 in Brenner, Lee, and Yee, *Genesis*.

Shepherd, D. "Translating and Supplementing." *JAB* 1 (1999): 125–46.

Sheridan, M., ed. *Genesis 12–50*. Ancient Christian Commentary on Scripture 2. Downers Grove, IL: InterVarsity, 2002.

Sherman, P. M. *Babel's Tower Translated: Genesis 11 and Ancient Jewish Interpretation*. BibInt 117. Leiden: Brill, 2013.

Sherwood, Y. "Hagar and Ishmael." *Int* 68 (2014): 286–304.

Shisanya, C. "A Reflection on the Hagar Narratives in Genesis through the Eyes of a Kenyan Woman." Pages 147–51 in Getui, *Interpreting the Old Testament in Africa*.

Simango, D. "The Imago Dei (Gen 1:26–27): A History of Interpretation from Philo to the Present." *Studia historiae ecclesiasticae* 42.1 (2016): 172–90.

———. "The Meaning of the *Imago Dei* (Gen. 1:26–27) in Genesis 1–11." *OTE* 25 (2012): 638–56.

Simopoulos, N. M. "Who Was Hagar?" Pages 63–72 in West, *Reading Other-Wise*.

Sipilä, S., and R. van der Spuy. "'To Lift Up,' but by Whom and What?" *BT* 63 (2012): 192–96.

Siwila, L. C. "From a Father-in-Law to a Client." *JTSA* 154 (2016): 141–55.

Ska, J. L. "Gen 12,6." Pages 449–54 in Ausloos and Lemmelijn, *Pillar of Cloud*.

———. "Genesis 22." *Biblica* 94 (2013): 257–67.

Skillen, J. W. "The Seven Days of Creation." *CTJ* 46 (2011): 111–39.

Skinner, J. *A Critical and Exegetical Commentary on Genesis*. 2nd ed. Edinburgh: T&T Clark, 1930.

Smith, B. "The Central Role of Judah in Genesis 37–50." *BSac* 162 (2005): 158–74.

Smith, D. E. "The Divining Snake." *JBL* 134 (2015): 31–49.

Smith, M. S. "Is Genesis 1 a Creation Myth?" Pages 71–102 in Callender, *Myth and Scripture*.

———. "Light in Genesis 1:3." Pages 125–34 in C. Cohen, *Birkat Shalom*.

———. *The Priestly Vision of Genesis 1*. Minneapolis: Fortress, 2010.

Smith, S. H. "'Heel' and 'Thigh.'" *VT* 40 (1990): 464–73.

Snoeberger, M. A. "Nakedness and Coverings in Genesis 3." *Detroit Baptist Theological Seminary Journal* 22 (2017): 21–33.

Soden, J. M. "From the Dust." *BSac* 172 (1915): 45–66.

Soggin, J. A. "'And You Will Be like God and Know What Is Good and What Is Bad.'" Pages 191–93 in C. Cohen, *Sefer Moshe*.

Somerset, F. R. *See* Raglan.

Sonderegger, K. *The Doctrine of God*. Vol. 1 of *Systematic Theology*. Minneapolis: Fortress, 2015.

Sonek, K. *Truth, Beauty, and Goodness in Biblical Narratives: A Hermeneutical Study of Genesis 21:1–21*. BZAW 395. Berlin: de Gruyter, 2009.

Sonnet, J.-P. "God's Repentance and 'False Starts' in Biblical History." Pages 469–94 in Lemaire, *Congress Volume Ljubljana 2007*.

Sparks, K. L. "*Enūma Elish* and Priestly Mimesis." *JBL* 126 (2007): 625–48.

Speiser, E. A. *Genesis*. AB 1. Garden City, NY: Doubleday, 1964.

Spiegel, S. *The Last Trial: On the Legends and Lore of the Command to Abraham to Offer Isaac as a Sacrifice; The Akedah*. Philadelphia: Jewish Publication Society, 1967.

Splawn, J. "Reckless Eyeballing." *Feminist Theology* 21 (2012): 173–79.

Stadel, C. "A Septuagint Translation Tradition and the *Samaritan Targum* to Genesis 41:43." *JBL* 131 (2012): 705–13.

Stager, L. E. "Jerusalem as Eden." *BAR* 20.3 (2000): 37–47, 66.

Stancil, D. C. "Genesis 16:1–16; 21:8–21." *RevExp* 91 (1994): 393–400.

Stanton, R. T. "Asking Questions of the Divine Announcement in the Flood Stories from Ancient Mesopotamia and Israel." Pages 147–72 in Azize and Weeks, *Gilgameš and the World of Assyria*.

Staubli, T. "Is There an Iconographic Pattern of the Binding of Isaac?" *Journal of Asia Adventist Seminary* 12 (2009): 111–31.

Steinbeck, J. *East of Eden*. Repr., Harmondsworth, UK: Penguin, 1979.

Steinberg, N. A. "The Genealogical Framework of the Family Stories in Genesis." *Semeia* 46 (1989): 41–50.

———. "The World of the Family in Genesis." Pages 279–300 in Evans, *Book of Genesis*.

Steiner, R. C. "Four Inner-Biblical Interpretations of Genesis 49:10." *JBL* 132 (2013): 33–60.

———. "Poetic Forms in the Masoretic Vocalization and Three Difficult Phrases in Jacob's Blessing." *JBL* 129 (2010): 209–35.

Sternberg, M. "Biblical Poetics and Sexual Politics." *JBL* 111 (1992): 463–88.

———. *Hebrews between Cultures: Group Portraits and National Literature*. ISBL. Bloomington: Indiana University Press, 1998.

———. *The Poetics of Biblical Narrative*. Bloomington: Indiana University Press, 1987.

Stone, T. J. "Joseph in the Likeness of Adam." Pages 62–73 in MacDonald, Elliott, and Macaskill, *Genesis and Christian Theology*.

Stordalen, T. "Genesis 2,4." *ZAW* 104 (1992): 163–77.

———. "The God of the Eden Narrative." Pages 3–21 in Eidevall and Scheuer, *Enigmas and Images*.

———. "Heaven on Earth—or Not?" Pages 28–57 in Riedweg and Schmid, *Beyond Eden*.

Strawn, B. A. "Comparative Approaches." Pages 117–42 in LeMon and Richards, *Method Matters*.

Stroes, H. R. "Does the Day Begin in the Evening or Morning? Some Biblical Observations." *VT* 16 (1966): 460–75.

Strong, J. T. "Shattering the Image of God." *JBL* 127 (2008): 625–34.

Strong, J. T., and S. S. Tuell, eds. *Constituting the Community: Studies on the Polity of Ancient Israel in Honor of S. Dean McBride, Jr.* Winona Lake, IN: Eisenbrauns, 2005.

Stuart, D. K. "'The Cool of the Day.'" *BSac* 171 (2014): 259–73.

Swenson, K. M. "Earth Tells the Lessons of Cain." Pages 32–39 in Habel and Trudinger, *Exploring Ecological Hermeneutics*.

Sylva, D. "The Blessing of a Wounded Patriarch." *JSOT* 32 (2008): 267–86.

Szpakowska, K. M. *Behind Closed Eyes: Dreams and Nightmares in Ancient Egypt*. Swansea: Classical Press of Wales, 2003.

Tadiello, R. "La dispersione occasione positiva di crescita." *BeO* 249–250 (2011): 129–48.

Tal, A. *Genesis. Biblia Hebraica Quinta*. Stuttgart: Deutsche Bibelgesellschaft, 2015.

Tamez, E. "The Woman Who Complicated the History of Salvation." Pages 5–17 in Pobee and von Wartenberg-Potter, *New Eyes for Reading*.

Tanner, B. L. "My Sister Sarah." Pages 60–72 in L. Day and Pressler, *Engaging the Bible*.

Tanner, J. P. "Old Testament Chronology and Its Implications for the Creation and Flood Accounts." *BSac* 172 (2015): 24–44.

Tarkovsky, A. *Sculpting in Time: Reflections on the Cinema*. Austin: University of Texas Press, 1986.

Tatu, S. "Making Sense of Melchizedek." *JESOT* 3 (2014): 49–76.

Teugels, L. M. *Bible and Midrash: The Story of "the Wooing of Rebekah" (Gen. 24)*. CBET 35. Louvain: Peeters, 2004.

Thiessen, M. "The Text of Genesis 17:14." *JBL* 128 (2009): 625–42.

Thomas, M. A. *These Are the Generations: Identity, Covenant, and the "Toledot" Formula*. LHBOTS 551. New York: T&T Clark, 2011.

Thompson, J. L., ed. *Genesis 1–11*. Reformation Commentary on Scripture 1. Downers Grove, IL: InterVarsity, 2012.

———. "Hagar, Victim or Villain?" *CBQ* 59 (1997): 213–33.

———. *Reading the Bible with the Dead: What You Can Learn from the History of Exegesis That You Can't Learn from Exegesis Alone*. Grand Rapids: Eerdmans, 2007.

Thompson, T. L. "Genesis 4 and the Pentateuch's Reiterative Discourse: Some Samaritan Themes." Pages 9–22 in Zsengellér, *Samaria, Samarians, Samaritans*.

Tigay, J. H. *Deuteronomy*. JPS Torah Commentary. Philadelphia: Jewish Publication Society, 1996.

Todd, J. "Patriarch and Prophet." *JESOT* 3 (2014): 185–202.

Toensing, H. J. "Women of Sodom and Gomorrah." *JFSR* 21 (2005): 61–74.

Tollers, V. L., and J. Maier, eds. *Mappings of the Biblical Terrain: The Bible as Text*. Bucknell Review 33. Lewisburg, PA: Bucknell University Press, 1990.

Tongue, S. *Between Biblical Criticism and Poetic Rewriting: Interpretive Struggles over Genesis 32:22–32*. BibInt 129. Leiden: Brill, 2014.

Tonson, P. "Mercy without Covenant." *JSOT* 95 (2001): 95–116.

Tonstad, S. K. "The Message of the Trees in the Midst of the Garden." *JATS* 19 (2008): 82–97.

Tov, E. "The Genealogical Lists in Genesis 5 and 11." Pages 37–52 in Werman, *From Author to Copyist*.

———. "The Harmonizing Character of the Septuagint of Genesis 1–11." Pages 315–32 in Kraus, *Die Septuaginta*.

———. "Searching for the 'Original' Bible." *BAR* 40.4 (2014): 48–53, 68.

Towner, W. S. "Clones of God." *Int* 59 (2005): 341–56.

———. "Genesis 9:8–17." *Int* 63 (2009): 168–71.

Trible, P. "Genesis 22." Pages 170–91 in Rosenblatt and Sitterson, *"Not in Heaven."*

———. *Texts of Terror: Literary-Feminist Readings of Biblical Narratives*. Philadelphia: Fortress, 1984.

Tsumura, D. T. *Creation and Destruction: A Reappraisal of the Chaoskampf Theory in the Old Testament*. Winona Lake, IN: Eisenbrauns, 2005.

Turner, L. A. "Lot as Jekyll and Hyde." Pages 85–101 in Clines, Fowl, and Porter, *Bible in Three Dimensions*.

Uehlinger, C. *Weltreich und "eine Rede": Eine neue Deutung der sogenannten Turmbauerzähung (Gen 11,1–9)*. Orbis Biblicus et Orientalis 101. Göttingen: Vandenhoeck & Ruprecht, 1990.

Ulrich, E., et al. *Qumran Cave 4.IX: Deuteronomy, Joshua, Judges, Kings*. DJD 14. Oxford: Clarendon, 1995.

Umbarger, M. "Abraham's Tamarisk." *JESOT* 1 (2012): 189–99.

Vaage, L. E., ed. and trans. *Subversive Scriptures: Revolutionary Christian Readings of the Bible in Latin America*. Valley Forge, PA: Trinity Press International, 1997.

Vall, G. "What Was Isaac Doing in the Field?" *VT* 44 (1994): 513–23.

Van der Kooij, A. "The City of Babel and Assyrian Imperialism." Pages 1–17 in Lemaire, *Congress Volume Leiden 2004*.

———. "The Story of Paradise in the Light of Mesopotamian Culture and Literature." Pages 3–22 in Dell, *Genesis, Isaiah, and Psalms*.

Vandermeersch, P. "Sodomites, Gays and Biblical Scholars." Pages 151–71 in Noort and Tigchelaar, *Sodom's Sin*.

van Dijk-Hemmes, F. *The Double Voice of Her Desire: Texts by Fokkelien van Dijk-Hemmes*. Edited by J. Bekkenkamp and F. Dröes. Translated by David E. Orton. Tools for Biblical Study 6. Leiden: Deo, 2002.

———. "Tamar and the Limits of Patriarchy." Pages 135–56 in Bal, *Anti-Covenant*.

van Dyk, P. J. "In Search of Eden." *OTE* 27 (2014): 651–65.

Vanier, J. *Man and Woman He Made Them*. London: DLT, 1985.

van Kooten, G. H., ed. *The Creation of Heaven and Earth: Re-interpretations of Genesis I in the Context of Judaism, Ancient Philosophy, Christianity, and Modern Physics*. TBN 8. Leiden: Brill, 2005.

van Ruiten, J. T. A. G. M. *Abraham in the Book of Jubilees: The Rewriting of Genesis 11:26–25:10 in Jubilees 11:14–23:8*. JSJSup 161. Leiden: Brill, 2012.

———. "Back to Chaos." Pages 21–30 in van Kooten, *Creation of Heaven and Earth.*

———. "The Book of Jubilees and the Genesis Apocryphon." Pages 545–75 in Assel, *Beyond Biblical Theologies.*

———. "Eve's Pain in Childbearing?" Pages 3–26 in Luttikhuizen, *Eve's Children.*

———. "Nomadic Angels." Pages 247–76 in Ausloos and Lemmelijn, *Pillar of Cloud.*

———. *Primaeval History Interpreted: The Rewriting of Genesis 1–11 in the Book of Jubilees.* JSJSup 66. Leiden: Brill, 2000.

Van Seters, J. *Abraham in History and Tradition.* New Haven: Yale University Press, 1975.

———. "The Geography of the Exodus." Pages 255–76 in Dearman and Graham, *The Land That I Will Show You.*

van Wolde, E. "Cognitive Linguistics and Its Application to Genesis 28:10–22." Pages 125–48 in Counet and Berges, *One Text.*

———. "Facing the Earth." Pages 22–47 in Davies and Clines, *World of Genesis.*

———. "One Bow or Another? A Study of the Bow in Genesis 9:8–17." *VT* 63 (2013): 124–49.

———. "Outcry, Knowledge, and Judgment in Genesis 18–19." Pages 71–100 in Lipton, *Universalism and Particularism.*

———. "Separation and Creation in Genesis 1 and Psalm 104." *VT* 67 (2017): 611–47.

———. "Telling and Retelling." Pages 227–44 in de Moor, *Synchronic or Diachronic?*

———. "Why the Verb *br'* Does Not Mean 'to Create' in Genesis 1.1–2.4a." *JSOT* 34 (2009): 3–23.

Vaughn, A. G. "'And Lot Went with Him.'" Pages 111–23 in Batto and Roberts, *David and Zion.*

Vergote, J. *Joseph en Égypte.* Louvain: Publications Universitaires, 1959.

Vermeulen, K. "Verbal Creation." *SJOT* 31 (2017): 294–313.

Vermigli, P. [Peter Martyr]. *In Primum Librum Mosis.* 2nd ed. Zurich: Froschouerus, 1579.

Verster, P. "Respek vir die lewe en die doodstraf." *AcT* 24 (2004): 168–77.

Vervenne, M. "Genesis 1,1–2,4." Pages 35–79 in Wénin, *Genesis.*

Visotzky, B. L. *The Genesis of Ethics: How the Tormented Family of Genesis Leads Us to Moral Development.* New York: Crown, 1996.

———. "Will and Grace." Pages 43–62 in Grypeou and Spurling, *Exegetical Encounter.*

Vogels, W. "'And God Created the Great *Tanninim.*'" *ScEs* 63 (2011): 349–65.

———. "'The Guardian of My Brother, Me?'" Pages 297–313 in Ausloos and Lemmelijn, *Pillar of Cloud.*

von Rad, G. *Genesis.* Rev. ed., London: SCM, 1963.

Wagner, A. B. "Considerations on the Politico-Juridical Proceedings of Genesis 34." *JSOT* 38 (2013): 145–61.

Wagner, J. R., et al., eds. *The Word Leaps the Gap: Essays on Scripture and Theology in Honor of Richard B. Hays.* Grand Rapids: Eerdmans, 2008.

Wagner-Tsukamoto, S. "The Paradise Story." *JSOT* 34 (2009): 147–70.

Walker, G. B. "Noah and the Season of Violence." *RevExp* 103 (2006): 371–90.

Wallace, H. N. "Rest for the Earth?" Pages 49–59 in Habel and Wurst, *Earth Story in Genesis*.

Walton, J. H. "Creation in Genesis 1:1–2:3 and the Ancient Near East." *CTJ* 43 (2008): 48–63.

———. *Genesis 1 as Ancient Cosmology*. Winona Lake, IN: Eisenbrauns, 2011.

———. *The Lost World of Adam and Eve: Genesis 2–3 and the Human Origins Debate*. Downers Grove, IL: InterVarsity, 2015.

———. *The Lost World of Genesis One: Ancient Cosmology and the Origins Debate*. Downers Grove, IL: InterVarsity, 2009.

Ward, W. A. "The Egyptian Office of Joseph." *JSS* 5 (1960): 144–50.

Wardlaw, T. R. "The Meaning of *brʾ* in Genesis 1:1–2:3." *VT* 64 (2014): 502–13.

Warner, M. "Keeping the Way of Yhwh." Pages 113–26 in Lipton, *Universalism and Particularism*.

———. "'Therefore a Man Leaves His Father and His Mother and Clings to His Wife.'" *JBL* 136 (2017): 269–88.

Waschke, E. J. "Zum Verhältnis von Ruhe und Arbeit in den biblischen Schöpfungsgeschichten Gen. 1–3." Pages 69–80 in Achenbach and Arneth, *"Gerechtigkeit und Recht zu üben."*

Washington, H. C., et al., eds. *Escaping Eden: New Feminist Perspectives on the Bible*. Sheffield, UK: Sheffield Academic, 1999.

Waters, S. E. "Reading Sodom through Sexual Violence against Women." *Int* 71 (2017): 274–83.

Watson, F. *Text and Truth: Redefining Biblical Theology*. Grand Rapids: Eerdmans, 1997.

———. *Text, Church and World: Biblical Interpretation in Theological Perspective*. Edinburgh: T&T Clark, 1994.

Wauters, A. "Ironie et jeux de mots sur les noms propres." *ETL* 90 (2014): 515–24.

———. "Un retournement de situation aussi amusant qu'insoupçonné." *RB* 121 (2014): 321–37.

Weiss, S. "The Ethics of Price Gouging." *JRE* 45 (2017): 142–63.

Welker, M. "What Is Creation?" *ThTo* 48 (1991): 56–71.

Wells, B. "First Wives Club." *Maarav* 18 (2011): 101–29.

Wenham, G. J. *Genesis 1–15*. WBC. Nashville: Nelson, 1987.

———. *Genesis 16–50*. WBC. Nashville: Nelson, 2000.

———. "The Religion of the Patriarchs." Pages 157–88 in Millard and D. Wiseman, *Essays on the Patriarchal Narratives*.

Wénin, A. "Le précepte d'Adonaï Dieu en Genèse 2,16–17." *RevScRel* 82 (2008): 303–18.

———, ed. *Studies in the Book of Genesis: Literature, Redaction and History*. BETL 155. Louvain: Peeters, 2001.

———. "'Une chair unique' ou 'une seule chair'?" *RSR* 102 (2014): 277–80.

Werman, C., ed. *From Author to Copyist: Essays on the Composition, Redaction, and Transmission of the Hebrew Bible in Honor of Zipi Talsh*. Winona Lake, IN: Eisenbrauns, 2015.

Wessner, M. D. "Toward a Literary Understanding of 'Face to Face.'" *ResQ* 44 (2002): 169–77.

West, G. O., ed. *Reading Other-Wise: Socially Engaged Biblical Scholars Reading with Their Local Communities*. Atlanta: Society of Biblical Literature, 2007.

Westermann, Claus. *Genesis 1–11*. CC. Minneapolis: Fortress, 1994.

———. *Genesis 12–36*. CC. Minneapolis: Fortress, 1995.

———. *Genesis 37–50*. CC. Minneapolis: Augsburg Fortress, 1986.

White, H. C. "The Initiation Legend of Isaac." *ZAW* 91 (1979): 1–30.

Whitekettle, R. "Oxen Can Plow, but Women Can Ruminate." *SJOT* 23 (2009): 243–56.

Wickes, J. "Ephrem's Interpretation of Genesis." *St. Vladimir's Theological Quarterly* 52 (2008): 45–65.

Wilder, W. N. "Illumination and Investiture." *WTJ* 68 (2006): 51–69.

Willet, A. *Hexapla in Genesin & Exodum*. Repr., London: Man, 1932.

Williams, D. S. *Sisters in the Wilderness: The Challenge of Womanist God-Talk*. Maryknoll, NY: Orbis Books, 1993.

Williams, J. G., ed. *The Girard Reader*. New York: Crossroad, 1996.

Williams, M. J. "Lies, Lies, I Tell You!" *CTJ* 43 (2008): 9–20.

Wilson, I. D., and D. Gersoni-Edelman, eds. *History, Memory, Hebrew Scriptures: A Festschrift for Ehud Ben Zvi*. Winona Lake, IN: Eisenbrauns, 2015.

Wilson, S. M. "Blood Vengeance and the *Imago Dei* in the Flood Narrative." *Int* 71 (2017): 263–73.

Winitzer, A. "Etana in Eden." *JAOS* 133 (2013): 441–65.

Wiseman, P. J. *Creation Revealed in Six Days: The Evidence of Scripture Confirmed by Archaeology*. London: Marshall, 1948.

Witte, M., ed. *Gott und Mensch im Dialog: Festschrift für Otto Kaiser zum 80. Geburtstag*. BZAW 345. Berlin: de Gruyter, 2004.

Wittenberg, G. "Alienation and 'Emancipation' from the Earth." Pages 105–16 in Habel and Wurst, *Earth Story in Genesis*.

Wöhrle, J. "Dominium terrae: Exegetische und religionsgeschichtliche Überlegungen zum Herrschaftsauftrag in Gen 1,26–28." *ZAW* 121 (2009): 171–88.

Wolowelsky, J. B. "Rachel's Burial." *JBQ* 45 (2017): 111–14.

Woods, C. "At the Edge of the World." *JANER* 9 (2009): 183–238.

Wright, G. E. *Shechem*. New York: McGraw, 1965.

Wurst, S. "'Beloved, Come Back to Me.'" Pages 87–104 in Habel and Wurst, *Earth Story in Genesis*.

Wyatt, N. "A Royal Garden: The Ideology of Eden." *JSOT* 28 (2014): 1–35.

Yamada, F. M. "Dealing with Rape (in) Narrative." Pages 149–65 in Cosgrove, *Meanings We Choose*.

———. "What Does Manzanar Have to Do with Eden?" Pages 97–117 in R. Bailey, *They Were All Together in One Place*.

Yayward, R. "What Did Cain Do Wrong?" Pages 101–23 in Grypeou and Spurling, *Exegetical Encounter*.

Yoo, P. Y. "Hagar the Egyptian." *CBQ* 78 (2016): 215–35.

Younker, R. W., and R. M. Davidson. "The Myth of the Solid Heavenly Dome." *AUSS* 49 (2011): 125–47.

Yovel, J. "The Creation of Language and Language without Time." *BibInt* 20 (2012): 205–25.

Zakovitch, Y. "Inner-Biblical Interpretation." Pages 92–118 in Hendel, *Reading Genesis*.

Zehnder, M., and H. Hagelia, eds. *Encountering Violence in the Bible*. Sheffield, UK: Sheffield Phoenix, 2013.

Zimmerli, W. *1. Mose 1–11*. 3rd ed. Zurich: TVZ, 1967.

———. *1. Mose 12–25*. Zurich: TVZ, 1976.

Zsengellér, J., ed. *Samaria, Samarians, Samaritans: Studies on Bible, History and Linguistics*. SJ 66. Berlin: de Gruyter, 2011.

Zucker, D. J. "The Deceiver Deceived." *JBQ* 39 (2011): 46–58.

———. "What Sarah Saw." *JBQ* 36 (2008): 54–62.

Subject Index

Author Index

Index of Scripture and Other Ancient Writings

Old Testament

Genesis

2 Samuel

1 Kings

2 Kings

1 Chronicles

2 Chronicles

Jeremiah

Lamentations

Ezekiel